The ABA Guide to International Business Negotiations

A Comparison of Cross-Cultural Issues and Successful Approaches, 3rd Edition

James R. Silkenat, Jeffrey M. Aresty,
Jacqueline Klosek—Editors

ABA Section of
International Law
Your Gateway to International Practice

**Defending Liberty
Pursuing Justice**

Library of Congress Cataloging-in-Publication Data

ABA guide to international business negotiations : a comparison of cross-cultural issues and successful approaches / [editors] James R. Silkenat, Jeffrey M. Aresty, Jacqueline Klosek.—3rd ed.
   p. cm.
  Includes index.
  ISBN 978–1–60442–369–3 (pbk. : alk. paper)
  ISBN 978–1–60442–370–9 (pdf)
  1. Commercial law. 2. Negotiation in business. I. Silkenat, James R. II. Aresty, Jeffrey M., 1951–III. Klosek, Jacqueline, 1972–IV. American Bar Association. V. Title: Guide to International Business Negotiations.

K1005.A22 2009
346.07—dc22
                                 2009009983

CONTENTS

FOREWORD TO THE THIRD EDITION

Corporate Social Responsibility in the Global Economy

> We are experiencing a fundamental transformation in society's understanding of the role of business. Business leaders and entrepreneurs themselves are increasingly redefining the purpose of enterprise. While the profit motive is key to the functioning of the market economy, there is a growing consensus that the creation of value for society is what will drive profit and shareholder value in the long term. The acceleration of globalization has brought a radical change, highlighting the potential influence of business on society and also providing more opportunities for the media, NGOs and others who want more information about the behaviour and impacts of companies.
>
> —Gunther Verheugen, "Interview: A question of values and diversity," *European Agenda*, March 2008.

Over the past decades, business, governments, academics, the media, and the remaining part of civil society alike have displayed inconceivable levels of interest and enthusiasm for a still vague and undefined concept of corporate social responsibility (CSR)—so much so that the economic activity of the twenty-first century cannot be understood without such a concept and CSR has become a buzzword in the business world. Just try Google and you will get five million "hits" and you will find over one million Web pages.

The reason for the CSR explosion is to be found in the role corporations play in the new economic order and the tremendous power and influence that they exercise around the world. Out of the one hundred largest economies of the world today, fifty-one are corporations and only forty-nine are nation states. These levels of power and influence are exacerbated by the economic globalization, privatization, and deregulation, communications revolution, increased access to information, and the prevailing of material over spiritual values, not to forget the myriad of corporate scandals that emerged at the outset of the twenty-first century. The new corporate role is at the same time the cause and the consequence of such power and influence.

For many centuries, corporations had been seen just as human enterprises to produce goods and services needed by any given society. Today this conception is obsolete, since corporations' activities go beyond the production of goods and services in the exclusive interest of their owners, and it is expected that they will help address the major global issues in society. Winston Churchill used to say that with more power came more responsibility.

It is not the first time that businessmen are called to fix the problems of the world in modern times. In Europe, in the middle of the last century, when the world became crazy and tried to annihilate itself in the two world wars, it was not the politicians nor the military who found the formula to eradicate wars and build a new peaceful Europe. It had to be the businessmen, who, through treaties like those for coal and steel, found a modus vivendi, inviting the human race to survive through using the plow and not the sword.

However, in this flat and globalized world, many people do not trust the traditional role of corporations, especially after the scandals in the United States and in the EU at the turn of the century. This requires rethinking the role of corporations in our knowledge society.

In his 2008 book *Common Wealth: Economics for a Crowded Planet*, Jeffrey Sachs has denounced the most basic economic reckonings that the world is facing: poverty, climate change, and environmental destruction. The world has discovered that there needs to be new ways of handling its future and these new ways rely precisely on the importance and influence of corporations.

As the World Business Council on Sustainable Development[1] said, CSR is the continuing commitment by business to behave ethically and contribute to economic development while improving the quality of life of the workforce and their families, as well as of the local community and society at large. Today, CSR has moved from the periphery of business to central stage and is an honest movement that has produced millions of proselytes within business, governments, and civil society.

As with many things in this world, CSR activities may be genuine or twisted and distorted. While some CSR activities are probably just window dressing or a public relations exercise, many companies are convinced that economics, society, and the environment are not invariably in conflict and are genuinely committing to addressing labor, environment, health, and economic justice issues and the promotion and protection of human rights. On the other hand, the movement

---

[1] Lord Holme & Richard Watts, *Making Good Business Sense* 3 (The World Business Council for Sustainable Development, 2000) (1988).

has been so successful that it has pervaded all sorts of activities of all types of entities, economic as well as noneconomic. So pervasive and expansive is it that one of the problems affecting the current CSR is the difficulty of defining the concept and setting boundaries to its scope.

I would like to make a call from these paragraphs. We individual mortal beings have become accustomed to impassively watch and sometimes feebly criticize the constant abuses that are being made on human rights or on the planet's rights. And we accuse "them" for such intolerable abuses without even realizing our indirect participation in such wrongdoings. Each one of us, with our choices, consumption, actions and often inaction, and silence are cooperating in such abuses. In a meeting organized by Resources for the Future Forum (RFF) in October 2003, Paul V. Tebo remarked how our consumers' interest in the environment was ironic because for one thing we "drive huge cars with 'save the polar bear' bumper stickers."[2]

Our goal must be that the CSR movement may not remain the stringent romantic ideal of a few charitable-sensitive businessmen, but it may soon become a natural and indissoluble element in all corporations and on the top of their managers' agendas, and make it the role of each individual person, corporation, and organization to help in transforming the present new economy for the benefit of real world progress.

One of the main drivers of CSR is the intensive activity of transnational corporations in a globalized market. International law and lawyers are essential for this global activity. That is the reason why the *ABA Guide to International Business Negotiations,* edited by James Silkenat, Jeffrey Aresty, and Jacqueline Klosek and published by the Section of International Law of the ABA, which third edition I have the honor to introduce, is most opportune and commendable for all international lawyers and enterprises.

Ramón Mullerat OBE
Former President of the Council of the Bars and
Law Societies of the European Union (CCBE)
Barcelona, Spain, September 2008

---

[2] Paul V. Tebo, Vice President, Safety, Health and Environment of E.I. du Pont de Nemours, Overview, Resources for the Future (RFF) Council Meeting: Forum on CSR (October 16, 2003).

ACKNOWLEDGMENTS

International business negotiation is not a new topic, but the cross-cultural problems and misperceptions it engenders have only rarely been the subject of in-depth analysis. An initial discussion of this topic was included in the first edition of this book. We expanded those ideas and concepts in the second edition, five years later. This new third edition is intended to further expand on that discussion and is the outgrowth of continuing research within the ABA Section of International Law, not only on these issues, but also on the substantive legal differences that surround them.

The variations in personal and national style that are present in the range of chapters presented in this volume are considerable. Such chapters, however, also are an indication of the wealth of legal talent that exists across cultures in today's global village. The one common denominator of the contributors to this volume has been their willingness to work to a tight deadline and to produce high-quality work. The editors have benefited greatly from a generosity of effort and patience by our contributors.

Within the ABA Section of International Law there has been significant support and substantive contribution for this book from a number of sources: Bill Hannay, Tim Dickinson, Lucinda Low, Jay Vogelson, Jim Carter, Josh Markus, Jeff Golden, Deborah Enix-Ross, Mike Byowitz, Gerry Libby, and Homer Moyer as former Chairs of the Section; Aaron Schildhaus as the current Section Chair; and numerous current and future leaders of the Section, including Salli Swartz, Mike Burke, Mark Wojik, and Glenn Hendrix.

From my son, David, and my daughter, Katherine, have come the continuing support and encouragement (and frequent constructive criticism) of my writing and research that have resulted in this volume. From my grandchildren, Chamberlain, Dawson, and Thessaly, have come big smiles (and many questions) when I have returned to the United States from negotiating trips abroad.

James R. Silkenat
New York, New York

I am privileged to join Jim Silkenat and Jackie Klosek in the creation of the third edition of *The ABA Guide to International Business Negotiations*. Without Jim and Jackie, the third edition would have remained a vision. It is fortunate both for me and for all who have written a chapter or who will, hopefully, read many of the chapters, that these two hardworking and brilliant minds took so much of their time to bring this new edition to publication.

I want to thank Alina Huiu, my former law clerk and now my associate, for her tremendous effort in reading, editing, formatting, and offering insights on all of the chapters in Part One of the book. Alina understands the multidisciplinary approaches that Internet technology requires its users to master, and she was able to help me gather and organize the new Part One for this edition. As we reviewed each chapter together, her skill in weaving the thoughts of different writers from different cultures and perspectives into a coherent whole made Part One an important contribution to the field of building online trust. In addition, she took the laboring oar and wrote the chapter on the lessons learned in e-commerce regulation in the European Union.

I also want to thank Gillian Neer, my former student and now my colleague and the vice-president of InternetBar.org, the online community the mission of which is to bring the rule of law to cyberspace. There is a close connection between subjects written about in this book and InternetBar.org's mission. As online communities become the place where global business is conducted in the twenty-first century, building trust through our communications with each other and our institutions is the foundation for a global culture of collaboration. When she found out about the third edition of this book, in the middle of working on many other tasks, she immediately jumped in to lend a helping hand.

A special thanks goes to Demetrios Eleftheriou, an ABA International Law Section leader and great friend, who helped get this third edition under way, and who has always watched the work of InternetBar.org and kept us in the good graces of both young lawyers and senior lawyers wherever he travels. Also, professors Gerald Ferrera and Stephen Lichtenstein of Bentley University have made it their mission to bring the rule of law to virtual communities through the Bentley Global Cyberlaw Center, and have opened new vistas both for me and for InternetBar.org. Thank you!

Sherman Teichman, director of the Institute for Global Leadership at Tufts University, has made it his personal mission to change the world for the better. His inspirational leadership is a beacon to young people everywhere. It was my good fortune to meet Sherman in the midst of creating these new chapters. Described to me by his friends as a "force of nature," Sherman has afforded InternetBar.org and me great opportunities to do the work of poverty alleviation. You are the best!

I would also like to thank the following people who have spent a great deal of their time to point me, they hope, in the right direction: Ordélio Sette, Frank Fowlie, Dan Rainey, Ramon Mullerat, Vince Polley, Amelia "Mel" Maguire, Ken Vacovec, Mohamed Wahab, Colin Rule, Sanjana Hattotuwa, Ayo Kusamotu, Alan Gaitenby, Susan Waters, Hongxia Liu, Don DeAmicis, Joe Vrabel, Rob Perlman, Christopher To, Tamar Frankel, Ethan Katsh, Leah Wing, Daewon Choi, and Mark Mason.

I want to especially thank my brother, Neil Aresty. He has been there every step of the way, caring and sharing no matter how many times I have fallen down. Thank you from the bottom of my heart.

The spirit and endurance to realize this book comes to me directly from my family: my late father, Victor, and my mom, Pola; my dearest partner in life, Ellen; and our now "flown the coop" children, Josh, Abby, and JoJo, who always stay in touch and show what it truly means to build trusting relationships.

And, finally, to all of our authors who contributed their collective wisdom, time, effort, and patience, many thanks.

Jeffrey M. Aresty
Sudbury, Massachusetts

I am so pleased to have been invited by Jim and Jeff to participate in this third edition of *The ABA Guide to International Business Negotiations*. So, first of all, I must thank them for involving me in this interesting project. I've learned so much from working with these intelligent and accomplished attorneys and have had a great time in the process.

I wish to extend my heartfelt thanks to the authors who graced us with their time and expertise and never lost their patience with me, despite my incessant reminders about deadlines. Your dedication, hard work, and enthusiasm is most appreciated.

I am also most grateful to my dear colleague, Davina Reid, who spent countless hours editing and reformatting numerous chapters. It is remarkable that Davina took on this task while facing her first year in a major U.S. law firm and navigating all of the challenges that that entails. It is even more remarkable that she has kept her trademark smile and superb good humor firmly in place throughout the whole process.

On a personal side, I wish to thank Tom Lozinski, who was an endless source of support for me throughout this process, sacrificing free time and our scheduled surf sessions to hang out with me while I edited and reviewed chapter after chapter, lending his support, insight, and valuable advice. In addition, I am grateful to my little brother, Jason Klosek, who always inspires and encourages me to keep going to see this book though. Acknowledgments are also due to my parents, my

Aunt Mary, Brian, and my nieces and nephews, Mathew, Meredith, and William.

Jacqueline Klosek
New York, NY

ABOUT THE EDITORS

**James R. Silkenat** is a partner in the firm of Arent Fox LLP in New York City. He is a former Chair of the ABA Section of International Law and helps coordinate Arent Fox's international practice in New York, where he specializes in international finance, securities, and corporate law. He is also a former Chair of the ABA's Section Officers Conference and a member of the Executive Committee of the ABA Board of Governors. He has served for almost twenty years as a member of the American Bar Association House of Delegates, the past nine as Chair of the New York Delegation in the ABA House of Delegates.

From 1980 to 1986 Mr. Silkenat was Legal Counsel for the International Finance Corporation, the private-sector-oriented affiliate of the World Bank in Washington, D.C., where he concentrated on privatization issues (including projects in China, Pakistan, Indonesia, Zimbabwe, and other countries). He has also handled significant privatization efforts in Australia, Peru, and Turkey, and is the founder and former Chair of the ABA's Privatization Committee.

Mr. Silkenat received his J.D. from the University of Chicago Law School, where he was an Editor of the *University of Chicago Law Review*. He also received an LL.M. in International Law from New York University School of Law.

Mr. Silkenat was formerly Chair of the ABA Committee on the People's Republic of China and was the founder of the *China Law Reporter*. He has led delegations to China for both the ABA and the Association of the Bar of the City of New York, to the Common Market and Mexico for the ABA, and to China and Russia for People-to-People. He has served as a Fellow of the National Endowment for the Humanities and as a Fellow in the U.S. State Department Scholar/Diplomat Program.

Mr. Silkenat is the editor of *The Law of International Insolvencies and Debt Restructurings*, *The Imperial Presidency and the Consequences of 9/11*, *The Moscow Conference on Law and Bilateral Economic Relations*, *The ABA Guide to Foreign Law Firms* (1988, 1993, 1999 and 2004 editions), and *The ABA Guide to International Business Negotiations* (1994 and 2000 editions). He is also the author of more than 100 articles on international law, finance, and public policy and has published articles in the *Harvard Law Review, Business Week, The New York Times,* and the *Stanford*

Law Review, among other publications. He served as Adjunct Professor of Law at Georgetown University Law Center from 1982 to 1986, where he taught a graduate seminar on international project financing.

Mr. Silkenat previously served as Chair of both The Lawyers Committee for International Human Rights (now Human Rights First) and The Council of New York Law Associates (now The Lawyers Alliance for New York). He is a Life Fellow of the American Bar Foundation, having served as national Chair of the Fellows, and a member of the Council on Foreign Relations. Mr. Silkenat is also a former Chair of the International Human Rights Committee of the Association of the Bar of the City of New York and the City Bar's Task Force on International Legal Services and its Council on International Affairs. In 2000, he received the Distinguished Alumni Award for Career Achievement from Drury University and in 2007 the Lifetime Achievement Award of the ABA Section of International Law.

Mr. Silkenat has particular expertise in the negotiation and drafting of international investment funds and international joint-venture agreements, Eurodollar and other international loan agreements, and related documentation, and has worked on international mergers and acquisitions (including privatizations) in both developing and developed countries.

Currently, Mr. Silkenat is Chair of the ABA's World Justice Project, a multinational and multidisciplinary effort to strengthen the Rule of Law around the world.

 **Jeffrey M. Aresty** is the senior partner of Aresty International Law Offices, P.C., where he develops and manages the firm's cyberlaw, mediation, and international law practice. Aresty International concentrates its practice on e-commerce, mediation, and dispute resolution. The firm is a leader in the emerging area of cyberspace law and the use of online tools for negotiation, mediation, and the resolution of disputes.

Mr. Aresty has been involved in international business law and the role of technology in the transformation of the practice of law for almost three decades. Mr. Aresty is co-founder and the first president of InternetBar.org, a global effort to shape the online justice system, build a global culture of collaboration, and alleviate poverty.

Mr. Aresty is a Fellow at the National Center for Technology and Dispute Resolution at the University of Massachusetts. His activities with the Center focus on promoting the use of online dispute resolution technology as an alternative to traditional methods. His ongoing law-technology activities concern e-lawyering training, including ODR, and initiating global law reform in online communities, focusing on the harmonization of private international law for any activity occurring in cyberspace.

Mr. Aresty is also an Inspire Fellow at the Institute for Global Leadership at Tufts University, where he works on the development of legal principles for connecting e-commerce projects to microfinance borrowers in developing countries.

Mr. Aresty teaches global cyberlaw at Bentley University and works closely with the Bentley Global Cyberlaw Center, the Bentley Service Learning Center, and the Center for Business Ethics to initiate both poverty alleviation programs and training for online mediators.

Mr. Aresty has served the Massachusetts Bar Association on the Executive Committee and Board of Delegates, the Tax Council, and the Law Practice Section Council, where he served as both Vice-Chair and Chair. While on the Tax Council, he was the Editor of the Massachusetts Corporate Tax Manual. As Chair of the Law Practice Section in 1983, he envisioned and cofounded the Computer College Program with a $25,000 grant from Digital Equipment Corporation. In 1997, Mr. Aresty was the developer of the Massachusetts Bar Association's first Web site. He is a Life Fellow of the Massachusetts Bar Foundation.

Mr. Aresty has served two terms on the American Bar Association Standing Committee on Technology and Information Systems. He served the ABA's Law Practice Management Section on its Council and as membership Chair and Vice-Chair and as the Computer Division Vice-Chair. He also served as ABA Techshow Co-Chair for two terms. In 1992, he cofounded a multisection International Commercial Negotiations Task Force, which he Chaired from 1993 through 1995. During that time, the Task Force produced numerous publications and programs with the purpose of teaching cross-cultural skills to lawyers involved in international business negotiations.

Mr. Aresty has previously served the ABA General Practice Solo and Small Firm Division as a member of its Publications Board and was a member of the Editorial Board of its *Technology and Practice Guide,* for which he wrote two articles: "Practicing Law in Cyberspace" and "Your Virtual Law Office."

He is the past Chair of the American Bar Association Section of International Law's Information Services, Technology, and Data Protection Committee and has volunteered in other capacities for the ABA and the Massachusetts Bar Association.

Mr. Aresty is a Fellow of the American Bar Foundation.

 **Jacqueline Klosek** is Senior Counsel with Goodwin Procter LLP in New York. She is a member of the firm's Intellectual Property Transactions and Practice Area and is a founding member of the firm's Privacy and Data Security Task Force.

Her practice focuses on transactions involving technology and intellectual property. Ms. Klosek drafts and negotiates various technology agreements and advises on different aspects of the law related to intellectual property and technology. She also advises clients on various issues related to privacy and data security.

As a Certified Information Privacy Professional, Ms. Klosek is on the advisory board for The Privacy Advisor of the International Association of Privacy Professionals, and is the Co-Chair of the International Working Group of that organization.

Ms. Klosek is a member of the American Bar Association and the Co-Chair of the Information Services, Technology & Data Protection Committee of the ABA's Section of International Law. She is a Fellow of the American Bar Foundation.

Ms. Klosek is the author of four books: *The Right to Know: Your Guide to Using and Defending Freedom of Information Law in the United States* (2009), *The War on Privacy* (2006), *The Legal Guide to e-Business* (2003), and *Data Privacy in the Information Age* (2000). She also contributed to *Corporate Legal Departments* and *International Corporate Practice*, both by Carole Basri, and *The New Virtual Money* by Olivier Hance and Suzanne Dionne-Baltz.

Ms. Klosek has an LL.M. in International, European and Comparative Law from the Vrije Universiteit in Brussels, a J.D. from the Benjamin N. Cardozo School of Law, and a B.A. in Psychology from New York University. While attending law school, Ms. Klosek was the senior articles editor of the Cardozo Journal of International and Comparative Law. She also was the recipient of the Telford-Taylor Fellowship in Public International Law.

Ms. Klosek received *NJBiz* magazine's "40 Under 40" Award, given annually to the top forty achievers in New Jersey with an established record of leadership who have taken on key decision-making roles at an earlier-than-usual stage in their lives.

Prior to joining Goodwin Procter, Ms. Klosek was employed as a legal adviser with the IT, E-Commerce and Electronic Financial Services Group in the Brussels office of Deloitte & Touche. She also completed internships with a number of international organizations, including the International Commission of Jurists in Geneva and the International Atomic Energy Agency.

Ms. Klosek has also lectured on international intellectual property law and the law of e-commerce as an adjunct professor at New York University.

Ms. Klosek is on the Board of Directors of the Internet Bar Organization.

ABOUT THE CONTRIBUTORS

Alina Bica-Huiu is a graduate of the New England School of Law, with an interdisciplinary bachelor of arts from Reed College in Political Science and Economics. Her academic research addresses global comparative questions regarding the study of public spending, regulatory policy, emerging technology, and economic strength. She has, in particular, studied contrasts in governance between nations belonging to the Organisation for Economic Co-operation and Development, with a focus on the United States and the European Union. Additionally, she has provided assistance to the Reed College Public Policy Lecture Series, and contributed to course design in describing the recent trends regarding the relationship between information technology and the law for Boston University. She has been admitted to practice in California, New York, Massachusetts, and the District of Columbia, and speaks French, Spanish, Romanian, and Hungarian. She currently works as an associate with Aresty International Law Offices, P.C. in Sudbury, Massachusetts.

Leonardo Bonadies is an Associate of Pardini & Associates. He regularly advises foreign corporations on commercial law, litigation, and arbitration law matters. He holds a law degree from Universidad Santa María La Antigua (1995), Master's Degree in procedural Law from Latin University of Panama (2006). He also completed a post-graduate course in Civil Law, Contracts, and Consumer Right Law (2006) from University of Salamanca in Spain. He was previously an assistant judge in civil courts in Panama City.

Caroline Brennan is an associate with the law firm of Arthur Cox in Dublin, Ireland.

Leigh Brown is a senior corporate partner of Minter Ellison's Sydney office and is recognized as a leading Australian corporate and commercial lawyer both in Australia and internationally. Mr. Brown's expertise is in the areas of mergers and acquisitions (including schemes of arrangement), capital raisings, major projects, private equity, and advice to ASX-listed companies. He regularly leads Minter Ellison teams on major transactions for leading Australian and international companies in diverse industries, including financial services, resources, gaming, biotechnology, property development, wine, and technology.

Daniel Burnstein is a graduate of New England School of Law and took additional study at Harvard Law School, where he directed the Interactive Videodisk project and was an associate of the Program on Negotiation. He coauthored a number of videodisks on mediation and negotiation, which are published by Harvard Law School. He has also coauthored a guide and video for managers for the American Management Association. He has authored several book chapters contained in the *Electronic Classroom* (Boschmann ed., 1995), and *Sexual Exploitation of Patients by Health Professionals* (Burgess and Hartman eds., 1986). Mr. Burnstein has been active in the ABA Law Practice Management Section as well as the National Lawyers Guild. With Professor Robert Burdick, he has created over fifty negotiation simulation/games that are available at www.negotiatorpro.com for use by high school teachers, trainers, and law and business professors. Mr. Burnstein has practiced law for over twenty-five years and lives in Clearwater, Florida.

Carlos de Cárdenas Smith is based in the Madrid office of Uría Menéndez. He joined the firm in 1989 and became a partner in 1998. He was resident partner in the firm's New York office between 1997 and 2000. Mr. de Cárdenas Smith focuses his practice on mergers and acquisitions, banking, and finance. He has worked on many of the most significant financial transactions in Spain. International legal directories (Chambers & Partners, *IFLR 1000*, PLC's *Which Lawyer? Yearbook*, etc.) name Mr. de Cárdenas Smith a leading lawyer in Spain in Project Finance, Banking and Finance, and PFI/PPP. According to the *Who's Who Legal* edition of 2007, he is considered by his peers as one of the world's leading banking lawyers. *Chambers Global 2007* has nominated him as a Tier 1 leading individual for Projects and Energy: Latin America, Banking and Finance, and Project Finance. He was a commercial law lecturer at the Universidad Pontificia de Comillas (ICADE) and at the Centro de Estudios Universitarios (CEU), both in Madrid. He is a regular speaker and commentator at law seminars and conferences pertaining to his field of expertise. Mr. de Cárdenas Smith has written, among others, a book on tender offers and contributes articles to both Spanish and foreign law reviews.

Eva Das is an associate at Stibbe. She has worked in the firm's Amsterdam office and is currently based in the New York office. Her practice areas include general corporate, mergers and acquisitions, private equity, equity capital markets, and finance.

Megan Denos joined the Appleby firm in October 2007 as a Professional Support Lawyer (PSL) in Appleby's global Knowledge Management team. Ms. Denos's role involves drafting precedents and guidance materials; monitoring and summarizing legislative developments; providing legal research support for several Appleby offices; preparing legal guides and contributing to comparative materials for all practice areas. She also works closely with PSLs in other Appleby offices, and with the Director of Knowledge Management, on several joint projects and initiatives that develop Appleby's knowledge management services. Prior to joining Appleby, Ms. Denos worked in the area of securities law at the Ontario Teachers' Pension Plan and TD Bank. She has an Honours B.Sc. Zoology degree from the University of Western Ontario. In 2000, she graduated from the University of Toronto with a Bachelor of Laws degree. Ms. Denos was called to the Ontario Bar in February 2002, after articling at a major Bay Street law firm in Toronto, Ontario.

Paul Fitzgerald is the director of the Stamford Law Corporation in Singapore and has had over fifteen years' experience in corporate law, with an emphasis on mergers and acquisitions, corporate insolvency, and competition law. Mr. Fitzgerald has practiced law in both New Zealand and Singapore and seeks to develop commercial sense and wide-ranging legal knowledge to provide effective common-sense solutions to complex problems. He was named as a Leading Lawyer in the Mergers & Acquisitions and Competition & Anti-Trust categories of the 2007 and 2008 editions of *Asialaw Leading Lawyers*. He has recently been actively advising on the restructuring of the debts of Asia Pulp & Paper in China (winner of the 2008 ALB Insolvency and Restructuring Deal of the Year Award) and the establishment of a private jet aviation business in Southeast Asia.

Jay G Foonberg was sworn in as a lawyer in January 1964 and immediately opened his own practice. Today he is a senior partner of Jay G Foonberg & Associates, a Beverly Hills law firm with affiliate offices in South America and Europe. His firm specializes in business law, international law, corporate law, and disputes involving attorney's fees and legal ethics. Mr. Foonberg has been awarded the Harrison Tweed Special Merit Award by the American Law Institute–American Bar Association (ALI-ABA) Committee on Continuing Professional Education for his long-term efforts in continuing legal education. He has also been honored nine times by the ABA, including receiving the Gold Key and Highest Honors awards of the ABA Law Student Division and the Award of Merit from the ABA Young Lawyers Division. He was a founder and member of the Executive Council of the ABA Section of Law Practice Management and was the first chair of the Law Office Economics Section of the Inter-American Bar Association. Mr. Foonberg has been decorated by the governments of Brazil and Argentina and honored by the State of California for his work to stimulate and increase trade between the United States and these countries. He has been knighted by the Knights of Malta (Order of St. John) for his international efforts with hospitals and has been granted a Papal Audience at the Vatican in recognition of his international charitable work. He is author of the best-selling *How to Start and Build a Law Practice,* now in its third edition, and *How to Get and Keep Good Clients,* currently in its second edition. He is a prolific author and lecturer and has lectured on international trade in several foreign countries in English, Spanish, and Portuguese.

Tamar Frankel is a professor of law at Boston University. She is an expert in the areas of mutual funds, securitization, fiduciary law, and corporate governance. She has authored *The Regulation of Money Managers* (2d ed. 2001), *Investment Management Regulation* (3d ed. 2005), *Fiduciary Law* (2008), *Trust and Honesty in the Real World* (2007), *Trust and Honesty, America's Business Culture at a Crossroad* (2006), and *Securitization* (2d ed. 2006), and approximately sixty articles on related subjects. She was a visiting scholar at the Securities and Exchange Commission (1995–1997) and at the Brookings Institution (1987). Professor Frankel has taught and lectured in Japan, India, Malaysia, Oxford UK, and Switzerland. A native of Israel, she served in the Israeli Air Force. She is a member of the Massachusetts Bar, a life member of the American Law Institute, and a member of the board of editors of *Regulation and Governance* (Blackwell, Inc). Professor Frankel holds law degrees from the Jerusalem Classes, and LL.M. and S.J.D. degrees from Harvard Law School.

Soichiro Fujiwara is a partner with Nagashima Ohno & Tsunematsu, one of the largest law firms in Japan. His primary practice focus is on mergers and acquisitions and technology transactions. He received his LL.B. from the University of Tokyo, Department of Law in 1996, and was admitted to practice law in Japan in 1998. Upon pursuing postgraduate legal studies, he obtained an LL.M. from Columbia Law School in 2003. Subsequently, from 2003 to 2004, he worked in the San Francisco office of Morrison & Foerster LLP as a visiting international attorney.

Sara Galletly is an associate with the law firm of Maples and Calder in the Cayman Islands.

Samuel García-Cuéllar is a senior partner with Creel, García-Cuéllar, Aiza y Enríquez, S.C., in Mexico City, where he heads the merger and acquisitions practice group. He also practices in the areas of private equity, dispute resolution, and insurance. He obtained his J.D. from Escuela Libre de Derecho in 1968. He is founder and president of the Mexican Mediation Institute, and member of the Regulations Committee of the Board of Directors of the Mexican Stock Exchange and the Arbitration Committee of the Arbitration Center of Mexico. For decades, Mr. García-Cuéllar has worked on the major privatizations of companies owned by the Mexican government such as the privatization of Teléfonos de México, as counsel for France Telecomm and Mexicana de Aviación, and as counsel for the Mexican and foreign investors. He has been actively involved in major acquisitions by foreign multinationals such as the acquisition of Cigarrera La Moderna by BAT Industries, the acquisition of GEMEX by the Pepsi Bottling Group through a tender offer, and the acquisition of Grupo Iusacell by

Vodafone Group. He acted as counsel for Anheuser-Busch Companies in the acquisition of an investment in Grupo Modelo. He regularly advises large multinational and private equity funds in their investments in Mexico. Since its inception, he has acted as Mexican counsel of The Mexico Fund, Inc. Mr. García-Cuéllar is a member of the Mexican Bar Association and the Ilustre y Nacional Colegio de Abogados. His native language is Spanish and he is fluent in English.

Johan Gernandt is a senior partner and founder of Gernandt & Danielsson in Stockholm. His areas of practice include corporate law, mergers and acquisitions, and litigation and arbitration. Among other things, he has been counsel and arbitrator in a large number of international arbitrations. Further, he is chair of the governing board of the Central Bank of Sweden, advisor to the Swedish Company Law Committee, Vice-Chair of the Arbitration Institute of the Stockholm Chamber of Commerce, a member of the Board of the Stockholm Chamber of Commerce, and a member of the ICC Commission on International Arbitration.

Georgi T. Gouginski is a partner in Djingov, Gouginski, Kyutchukov & Velichkov in Sofia, Bulgaria.

Wendy Guo is a partner of Beijing Kang Da Law Firm, People's Republic of China. She was admitted to be an attorney in 1994. She obtained her bachelor's degree in law and master's degree in economics from Renmin University, China. She works in the areas of general corporate law, corporate finance, and securities law, and specializes in public and private domestic and cross-border mergers and acquisitions, joint ventures, equity offerings, and private equity investments.

Gayle E. Hanlon is affiliated with the law firm of Hadef Legal Consultants & Advocates in Abu Dhabi, United Arab Emirates.

Ashleigh Hammond is a candidate attorney at the Webber Wentzel firm in South Africa. Her areas of expertise include corporate, commercial, and aviation law. She has acted for major corporations over a broad spectrum of commercial transactions, with a particular emphasis on mergers and acquisitions. She recently joined the firm's insurance litigation practice group, representing major insurance companies in defending medical malpractice claims and claims against organs of state.

W. Michael Hoffman is the founding executive director of the Center for Business Ethics at Bentley University in Waltham, Massachusetts, a thirty-two-year-old research and consulting institute and an educational forum for the exchange of ideas and information in business ethics. He is also senior partner of the business ethics consulting firm Hoffman Rowe, and the managing partner of the consulting collaborative The Ethics Trust. Dr. Hoffman received his Ph.D. in Philosophy in 1972 at the University of Massachusetts in conjunction with Amherst, Hampshire, Mount Holyoke, and Smith Colleges. He is the Hieken Professor of Business and Professional Ethics at Bentley

University and was chair of the Department of Philosophy for seventeen years. He has authored or edited sixteen books, including *Business Ethics: Readings and Cases in Corporate Morality* (now in its fourth edition), *Ethics Matters: How to Implement Values-Driven Management* (2000), and *The Ethical Edge: Tales of Organizations That Have Faced Moral Crises* (1995). He has also published over ninety articles. Dr. Hoffman has consulted on business ethics for numerous corporations, universities, and government agencies. Clients have included Baker Hughes, Blue Shield of California, Cablevision, CBS, Coopers & Lybrand (now PwC), El Paso Corporation, Exelon Corporation, Fidelity Investments, GTE, General Electric, GlaxoSmithKline, Johnson & Johnson, KPMG, NYNEX (now Verizon), PeopleSoft, Textron, TRW Systems, and Tyson Foods. He has been a National Endowment for the Humanities fellow and consultant, a lecturer at universities and conferences around the world, and an expert witness on business ethics in numerous legal cases. He is on the Board of Editors of many business ethics journals, was a founding member and president of the Society for Business Ethics, and served on the Advisory Board of the U.S. Sentencing Commission. He was the founding executive director of the Ethics Officer Association (now the Ethics & Compliance Officer Association) from 1992 to 1995, a member of its board of directors until 1997, and then advisor to the board until 2005. He was named the 2007 Humanist of the Year by The Ethical Society of Boston. He has been quoted extensively on business ethics in newspapers and magazines, including the *Boston Globe, BusinessWeek, Chicago Tribune, Christian Science Monitor, Financial Times, Industry Standard, Los Angeles Times, New York Times, Newsweek, Philadelphia Inquirer, San Francisco Chronicle, USA Today, U.S. News and World Report, Wall Street Journal,* and *Washington Post* and is interviewed frequently for television and radio programs around the country. Dr. Hoffman resides in West Newton, Massachusetts, with his wife, Bliss Read Hoffman.

Bob Johanson is a partner at the law firm Gernandt & Danielsson in Stockholm, Sweden. He has a broad transaction-based practice and vast experience from leading and coordinating large and complicated domestic and international transactions. His main practice areas are mergers and acquisitions, real estate, and capital markets law. He is a member of the Swedish Bar Association and IBA.

Kairas N. Kabraji is a partner in Kabraji & Talibuddin in Karachi, Pakistan. He is an Advocate of the High Court of Sindh and was educated at the University of Cambridge (Trinity College). He has acted generally in numerous commercial transactions of all kinds in Pakistan, contentious and noncontentious, both domestic and transborder, including joint ventures; inward foreign investment; mergers and acquisitions; domestic and global capital markets transactions; foreign and domestic debt and equity financings; admiralty, maritime, and aviation law; and environmental law. Among his publications are

"Damages and forum and jurisdiction considerations—multiple jurisdictions, forum shopping and widely diverse damage awards complicate the speedy resolution of aviation claims—in an Islamic Jurisdiction" (*Air Law,* Vol. IX, No. 4, 1984), and a chapter on Pakistan in
Enforcement of Foreign Judgments Worldwide (Platto ed., 1989).

Satoko Kametaka is an associate with Nagashima Ohno & Tsunematsu, one of the largest law firms in Japan. She received her LL.B.
from Keio University, Department of Law in 2003, and was admitted to
practice law in Japan in 2004.

Ethan Katsh is a graduate of the Yale Law School and was one
of the first legal scholars to recognize the impact that new information technologies would have on law. He has authored three books on
law and technology, *Law in a Digital World* (1995), *The Electronic Media
and the Transformation of Law* (1989), and, with Professor Janet Rifkin,
Online Dispute Resolution: Resolving Conflicts in Cyberspace (2001). His
articles have appeared in the *Yale Law Journal,* the *University of Chicago
Legal Forum,* and other law reviews and legal periodicals. His scholarly
contribution has been the subject of a review essay in *Law and Social
Inquiry* (Summer 2002). Since 1996, Professor Katsh has been involved
in a series of activities related to online dispute resolution. He participated in the Virtual Magistrate project and was founder and codirector
of the Online Ombuds Office. In 1997, with support from the Hewlett Foundation, he and Professor Rifkin founded the National Center
for Technology and Dispute Resolution at the University of Massachusetts. His work has been supported by the Hewlett Foundation, Markle
Foundation, eBay Foundation, and the National Science Foundation.
He has provided advice on online dispute resolution to eBay, Square-
Trade, Cybersettle, eResolution, the National Mediation Board, and
the Wounded Warriors Program of the U.S. Army. Professor Katsh has
chaired the UN International Forums on Online Dispute Resolution,
held in Geneva in 2002 and 2003, Melbourne in 2004, Cairo in 2006,
Liverpool in 2007, Hong Kong in December 2007, Victoria (Canada)
in June 2008, and scheduled to be held in Israel in June 2009. He has
been Visiting Professor of Law and Cyberspace at Brandeis University;
is on the board of advisors of the Democracy Design Workshop, the
legal advisory board of the InSites E-governance and Civic Engagement Project, and the board of editors of *Conflict Resolution Quarterly;*
and is a Fellow of the American Bar Foundation.

Henry T. King, Jr. is a graduate of Yale College and Yale Law
School. A former U.S. prosecutor at the Nuremberg trials, a former
general counsel of the U.S. Foreign Economic Aid Program, as well as
a former chair of the Section of International Law and Practice of the
ABA, Mr. King is U.S. Chair of the Joint ABA–Canadian Bar Association–Barra Mexicana Working Group on the Settlement of International Disputes, which made recommendations for the settlement of
disputes under the North American Free Trade Agreement (NAFTA),

many of which became part of NAFTA. He is now U.S. Director of the Canada–United States Law Institute and professor of law at Case Western Reserve University School of Law, where he teaches international arbitration and has taught international business transactions. He is also of counsel to the law firm of Squire, Sanders & Dempsey. He is program chairman of the Greater Cleveland International Lawyers Group, of which he was a cofounder.

Lilia Kisseva is an associate with the law firm of Djingov, Gouginski, Kyutchukov & Velichkov in Sofia, Bulgaria.

James M. Klotz is a partner and co-chair of the International Business Transactions Group of the Canadian law firm Miller Thomson LLP. He has been recognized as a leading international lawyer by *Canada's Best Lawyers* and *Lexpert,* in the fields of international finance and international trade. He is the author of *Power Tools for Negotiating International Deals* (2d ed. 2008) and *International Sales Agreements: A Drafting and Negotiating Guide* (2d ed. 2008). Mr. Klotz is currently vice-chair of the Bar Issues Commission of the International Bar Association (IBA), and was previously co-chair of the IBA's International Sales Committee. He has served as a divisional chair of the American Bar Association's International Law Section, and chair of its Canada Law Committee. He has also served as chair of the International Law Section of the Canadian Bar Association and of the Ontario Bar Association. He is currently vice-chair of Transparency International (Canada). He has taught international business law as an adjunct professor of international law at Osgoode Hall Law School, where he received his LL.B. in 1982. He is admitted to practice in Ontario, England, and Wales, and speaks both French and Mandarin.

Matthias Kühn is admitted to the Berlin Bar and is an associate at the Berlin office of Heuking Kühn Lüer Wojtek. He has been with the firm since 2006, specializing in the fields of international contract law, corporate law, and antitrust and regulatory law. He received a doctoral degree from Saarland University (2006) and an LL.M. in International Business Law from the University of Exeter, UK (2002).

William C. F. Kurz is an attorney in New York City. He received his A.B. from Harvard College and his LL.B. from Harvard Law School. Mr. Kurz's practice consists principally of banking, securities, derivatives, and other international financial transactions, including loan syndications and trading, and equity, debt, and commodity derivatives. He works extensively with American, Asian, and European banks, investment banks, and financial services, energy and industrial companies. He has served as resident partner in his firm's London and Hong Kong offices and from 1987 to 1992 was a lecturer in law at Columbia Law School.

Ayodele Musibau Kusamotu was born in Lagos. He was called to the Nigerian Bar in 1998. He graduated from the University of Lagos in 1997 and has been in private legal practice since then. He was an associate at Abdulai, Taiwo & Co., a leading intellectual property and corporate law firm in Nigeria. In 2001 he joined Kusamotu & Kusamotu to focus on intellectual property, innovation, technology, and commercial law. Kusamotu & Kusamotu is the legal project lead for Creative Commons Nigeria and provides pro bono legal services to One Laptop per Child Association Inc. Mr. Kusamotu is a Fellow of the National Centre for Technology and Dispute Resolution at the University of Massachusetts, and chair of the Africa Committee of InternetBar.org.

Kyu Wha Lee is a partner at Lee & Ko in Seoul, Korea. He holds an LL.B. from the College of Law, Seoul National University; is a graduate of the Judicial Training and Research Institute, Korea Supreme Court; and holds an M.C.L. from George Washington University Law School and a J.D. from Tulane Law School. He served as a judge advocate officer in the Korean Army from 1983 to 1986 and as a foreign associate with Morrison & Foerster, New York, in 1990 to 1991. He is a member of the Korean, Seoul, and New York Bar Associations.

Robert Leigh is a corporate partner in the Dubai office of Simmons & Simmons. Recognized by Chambers and Legal 500 as a "Leader in Transport," Mr. Leigh specializes in projects, commercial, corporate, and corporate finance work, public and private company takeovers and mergers, outsourcing, joint ventures, and privatizations (particularly in the water and rail industries). He is a member of the Law Society of England and Wales, and he took up residency in Dubai in May 2005.

Stewart L. Levine is the founder of ResolutionWorks, a consulting and training organization dedicated to providing skills and ways of thinking needed to build strong organizational cultures. He spent ten years practicing law before becoming an award-winning marketing executive serving the legal profession at AT&T, where he was recognized as a pioneer "intrapreneur." He uses his approach to form teams and joint ventures in a variety of situations. Organizations he has worked for in the United States and abroad include American Express, Chevron, ConAgra, Deloitte Consulting, Kaiser, EDS, Honda, NASA, Oracle, Safeco, University of San Francisco, Washington DC Corporate Counsel, and the U.S. Departments of Agriculture, EPA, Navy, and Treasury. Mr. Levine serves on the Council of the American Bar Association Law Practice Management Section where he was chair of the Education Board from 2000 to 2003. He was featured in an article about trendsetters in the legal profession in *Law Practice* magazine. His book *Getting to Resolution: Turning Conflict into Collaboration* (1998) was called "a must read" by *Law Practice Management* magazine. It was an Executive Book Club Selection; featured by Executive Book Summaries; named one of the Thirty Best Business Books of 1998; endorsed by Dr. Stephen Covey, author of *Seven Habits of Highly Effective People*; and featured in *The Futurist* magazine. *The Book of Agreement* (2003) has been called more practical than the classic *Getting to Yes*, and named among the best books of 2003 by CEO Refresher (www.Refresher .com). Along with David Coleman he wrote *Collaborate 2.0*, released in February 2008. He teaches communication, relationship management, and conflict management skills for The American Management Association and The International Partnering Institute. He is a frequent contributor to legal publications. He currently has a monthly column, "Managing by Agreement" in the monthly e-zine of the ABA Law Practice Management Section. Mr. Levine is an honors graduate of Rutgers Law School, where he was the student writing editor of the Law Review. He served as a deputy attorney general for the State of New Jersey and was a Law and Humanities Fellow at Temple Law School, where he was a law teacher.

Barbara G. Madonik is a communication strategist who is recognized internationally as an authority on nonverbal communication. She is a University of Toronto graduate, backed by years of solid domestic and international experience as a communication consultant and hands-on trainer. She has received two Order-in-Council appointments and has been invited to the United Nations by the Office of Internal Oversight. In the 1980s Ms. Madonik pioneered using nonverbal communication practically in Canadian business and legal venues. She is founder and President of Unicom Communication Consultants Inc., a company specializing in communication consulting and training and dispute investigation and resolution. The company provides customized services for individuals, businesses, governments, universities, law schools, law firms, mediation organizations, and the judiciary. Ms. Madonik consults, investigates, mediates, negotiates, coaches, lectures, and writes. She also keynotes conferences and conducts strategic verbal and nonverbal communication workshops and seminars that are CLE and CEU accredited. She has been guest faculty for the RCMP's Canadian Police College; University of Toronto; University of Alberta; University of Massachusetts; California State University; Osgoode Hall Law School; Vrije Universiteit (Law School/Amsterdam); Center for Alternative Dispute Resolution (USA); Risoluzione Alternativa Controversie (Rome); York University's Faculty of Graduate Studies; Cornell University School of Industrial and Labor Relations; and Atlanta, Connecticut, Ontario and American Bar Associations. Clients include Ministries of the Attorney-General, Environment, and Natural Resources; The Advocates' Society Institute and National Institute of Justice; and the Australian and U.S. federal governments. Ms. Madonik has been a board member of York University Dispute Resolution Advisory Committee, director of the ADR Institute of Ontario, appointee to the Health Professions Appeal and Review Board, member of the Society of Ontario Adjudicators and Regulators, and associate member of the American Bar Association. She sits on international advisory boards that include People & Solutions (Rome) and Center for Electronic Dispute Resolution (Netherlands). Well-known for pushing the communication envelope and creatively resolving conflict, Ms. Madonik's landmark book *I Hear What You Say, But What Are You Telling Me? The Strategic Use of Nonverbal Communication in Mediation* (2001) quickly became required reading in undergraduate and graduate programs. Her book for mediating parties, *Ready, Set, Go to Mediation*, will be released shortly.

Robert E. McNulty is Director of Programs, Center for Business Ethics, at Bentley University. He joined CBE after many years in both business and academia. The focus of his Ph.D., which he received from Columbia University, Teachers College, was in the philosophy and psychology of ethics. Earlier, he received his bachelor's degree magna cum laude from the University of Massachusetts, Amherst, and a Master of International Affairs degree from Columbia University's School of International and Public Affairs. He has taught at several universities and has had a lengthy career in international business, specializing in the application of strategic communications to assist countries in their economic development efforts. He has also served as a consultant to many Fortune 500 and foreign-based firms. For the last decade and a half, the focus of his work has been ethics, both in its theoretical and applied forms. Dr. McNulty heads Applied Ethics, Inc., a nonprofit organization with the mission of seeking ethical solutions to significant social issues through projects, education, counseling, and advocacy. An internationalist by disposition, he has traveled extensively and has lived overseas in France, Taiwan, Indonesia, and Singapore.

Vlad Movshovich is a senior associate in the Webber Wentzel firm in South Africa. He is an Attorney of the High Court of South Africa. Mr. Movshovich's areas of expertise include administrative, regulatory, constitutional, and international law; commercial dispute resolution, expropriation, and mineral and petroleum law. Notably, he is co-counsel for the plaintiffs in the bilateral investment treaty arbitration *Piero Foresti, Laura de Carli et al. v. Republic of South Africa*, conducted under the auspices of the International Centre for Settlement of Investment Disputes (ICSID case no. ARB(AF)/07/1). He also represents various South African and multinational companies, in both commercial negotiations and litigious matters. He has made submissions to various parliamentary committees, on behalf of companies and public interest groups, on topics that include administration of justice, foreign military assistance legislation, and mineral and petroleum regulatory and expropriation regimes. Mr. Movshovich is also a sessional lecturer in law in the University of the Witwatersrand, Johannesburg. He is a former Commonwealth Scholar, having read law at St. John's College, University of Oxford.

Ramón Mullerat, OBE, is a lawyer in Barcelona and Madrid, Spain, and Avocat à la Cour de Paris, France; Honorary Member of the Bar of England and Wales (UK); Honorary Member of the Law Society of England and Wales (UK); and Honorary Member of the Florida

Bar (U.S.). He has also served as adjunct professor at the Faculty of Law of Barcelona University; adjunct professor of the John Marshall Law School, Chicago; member of the EMEA Board of Emory University, Atlanta; president of the Council of the Bars and Law Societies of the European Union (CCBE); member of the American Law Institute (ALI); member of the American Bar Foundation (ABF); co-chair of the Human Rights Institute (HRI) of the International Bar Association; co-chair of the Commission of Corporate Social Responsibility of the IBA; member of the LCIA; member of the Board of the Club Español del Arbitraje; member of the Board of the North American Studies Institute; member of the Council of Justice of Catalonia; chairman of the board of *The European Lawyer*; member of the editorial board of *Iberian Lawyer*; and KPMG Abogados, S.L. Mr. Mullerat has written numerous books and other publications on different legal fields, including commercial arbitration and legal ethics. He was educated at the University of Barcelona. He speaks English, French, Spanish, and Catalan.

Giovanni Nardulli is managing partner of Legance, resident in the Rome office. He graduated in law from La Sapienza University in Rome, Italy (1983) and was admitted to the Italian Bar in 1987. He provides legal advice to U.S. clients on their investments in Italy focusing on joint ventures, mergers and acquisitions, private equity, and real estate. Mr. Nardulli has written several articles on corporate and commercial law and is a regular speaker and commentator at law seminars and conferences. In 1987 he obtained the English Law Certificate from the City of London Polytechnic in London; in 1988 he attended the Parker School of Foreign and Comparative Law of the Columbia University in New York; and in 1989 was a visiting attorney at Morrison & Foerster. Mr. Nardulli is licensed as Foreign Legal Consultant in New York State and is former vice-chair of the International Securities Committee of the ABA-ILS.

Matthew N. Nolan is a partner in the international trade group in the Washington, D.C., office of Arent Fox LLP. His international trade and business regulation practice encompasses customs regulations and disputes, import investigations, U.S. export controls and trade sanctions, trade and investment disputes, trade policy, and the Foreign Corrupt Practices Act. With over twenty years of experience, he has worked extensively on issues pertaining to trade and investment in the Americas, Europe, South Africa, Turkey, and other countries. Mr. Nolan also has experience in international commercial transactions, disputes, and arbitrations. He has worked extensively in Canada and Mexico on issues related to the North American Free Trade Agreement, and has worked for major U.S. and foreign corporations on export control and sanctions matters; antidumping, countervailing duty, safeguards, and section 301 investigations; customs audits and focused assessments; NAFTA verification audits by U.S., Mexican, and Canadian authorities; civil and criminal investigations on export, import, and FLPA issues; development, implementation, and audits of internal compliance programs; and trade policy initiatives. He has also worked with companies in a range of industries, including softwood lumber, steel, oil exploration and production, chemical products, beverage and snack foods, biotechnology, computer electronics, defense, airlines, textiles, tobacco, banking telecommunications, and insurance. Mr. Nolan is a member of the board of directors of the Canadian American Business Council and the Gulf States Partnership, and a member of the International Council for the Elliott School of International Affairs at George Washington University. He is a frequent author and speaker on issues pertaining to the World Trade Organization, NAFTA, trade litigation issues, and U.S. trade embargoes.

Pádraig Ó Ríordáin is based in Dublin and is a partner in Arthur Cox, one of the most prominent Irish law firms. He is a graduate of the National University of Ireland and of Harvard Law School and has been both an Irish barrister and solicitor. He is also admitted as an attorney in the state of New York. Mr. Ó Ríordáin practiced with a Wall Street law firm before moving to Arthur Cox, initially as head of its New York office. He is a member of the Arthur Cox International Business Group and specializes in mergers and acquisitions and securities law.

Victoria Page (M.A., Oxon) is a senior associate at the Webber Wentzel firm in South Africa. She has experience in litigation and arbitration, both domestic and international. Qualified as a solicitor of the Supreme Court of England and Wales, she has acted for major corporates, state-owned enterprises, educational institutions, and civil society groups in the United Kingdom and South Africa. Her work covers a broad range of commercial disputes, including claims arising out of sale and purchase agreements, as well as disputes relating to prospecting and mining rights. She advises clients operating in a variety of sectors, including mineral and petroleum resources, manufacturing and engineering, entertainment, and education. Ms. Page has made submissions to parliamentary portfolio committees and specializes in opinion work on complex legal issues. She has also completed postgraduate studies in international economic law.

Juan F. Pardini is senior partner in the firm of Pardini & Associates in Panama City, Panama.

Ángel Pérez López is an associate practicing in the corporate law department (banking and finance) of the Madrid office of Uría Menéndez. Mr. López joined the firm in 2000. He had previously worked as financial advisor in Alpha Corporate, a corporate finance company that belonged, at that time, to the Arthur Andersen Worldwide group. Mr. López focuses his practice on structured finance, acquisition finance, and project finance, and he has taken part in some of the most significant finance transactions closed in Spain during the last several years.

He has advised lenders and borrowers in deals in the energy, biofuel, waste treatment, and media sectors. From September 2007 to March 2008, Mr. López worked in the New York headquarters of the U.S. firm of Debevoise & Plimpton, joining its Acquisition Finance group as an International Associate. *Chambers Global 2008* has nominated him as an "Up and Coming" individual for banking and finance and project finance. Mr. López has written several articles for Spanish and Galician reviews, among other publications. He has codrafted the Spanish chapter of the Oxford University Press book *International Acquisition Finance,* (Griffiths ed., 2006). He is also coauthor of the chapter dedicated to Spain in the book *International Acquisition Finance: Global Jurisdictional Comparisons* (Haag and Mueller eds., 2008).

Henry H. Perritt, Jr. is professor of law at Chicago-Kent College of Law, where he served as dean from 1997 to 2002. He is the author of more than seventy law review articles and fifteen books on technology and law and employment law, including the 730-page *Law and the Information Superhighway.* He served on President Clinton's transition team, working on telecommunications issues, and drafted principles for electronic dissemination of public information that formed the core of the Electronic Freedom of Information Act Amendments adopted by Congress in 1996. During the Ford administration, he served on the White House staff and as deputy undersecretary of labor. Mr. Perritt served on the National Research Council's Computer Science and Telecommunications Board and on NTSB's Committee on Global Networks and Local Values. He led the interprofessional team that evaluated the FBI's Carnivore system for Attorney General Janet Reno. He serves as a neutral in hearing Internet domain-name disputes. Mr. Perritt has made it possible for groups of law and engineering students to work together in using the Internet to build a rule of law, promote the free press, assist in economic development, and provide refugee aid in the former Yugoslavia through Project Bosnia and Operation Kosovo. Mr. Perritt was the Democratic candidate for the U.S. House of Representatives in the 2002 general election in the 10th Congressional District of Illinois. He is a member of the Bars of Virginia, Pennsylvania, the District of Columbia, Maryland, Illinois, and the United States Supreme Court. He is a member of the Council of Foreign Relations, serves on the board of directors of the Chicago Council on Foreign Relations, and was secretary of the Section of Labor and Employment Law of the American Bar Association. He earned his B.S. degree in engineering from the Massachusetts Institute of Technology (MIT) in 1966, a master's degree in management from MIT's Sloan School in 1970, and a J.D. from Georgetown University Law Center in 1975.

Daniel Rainey has spent his career in the fields of communication and dispute resolution both in the academic arena and as a practitioner. Currently, he is the Director of Alternative Dispute Resolution Services for the National Mediation Board, a Fellow of the National

Center for Technology and Dispute Resolution, and a member of the Board of InternetBar.org. He is the immediate past chair of the Online Dispute Resolution Section of the Association for Conflict Resolution. From 1978 to 1990 he taught at George Mason University, and, immediately before coming to the National Mediation Board, he had a consulting practice focused on dispute resolution, training, and organizational development. He is an adjunct faculty member at Southern Methodist University, where he teaches courses in online dispute resolution, international dispute resolution, and intercultural influences on dispute resolution for the SMU graduate dispute resolution program, and he is working to develop an online ODR course for the Creighton University online graduate program in dispute resolution. For the past five years Mr. Rainey has been involved with the University of Massachusetts and the National Center for Technology and Dispute Resolution in a research project funded by the National Science Foundation to study the impact of technology on dispute resolution.

Nigel Read is a partner in the London office of Lovells, specializing in corporate finance, mergers and acquisitions, and company and securities law. Mr. Read focuses on the real estate, retail, and leisure sector. He has acted for a number of major corporations and investment banks, including J.P. Morgan and Goldman Sachs, on a broad range of transactions.

Alasdair Robertson is a partner in the Cayman Islands office of Maples and Calder. He is vice president, secretary, and treasurer of the Cayman Islands Law Society.

Jeswald W. Salacuse is Henry J. Braker Professor of Law at the Fletcher School of Law and Diplomacy, Tufts University, the senior graduate professional school of international relations in the United States. Professor Salacuse served as the Fletcher School's dean for nine years and was dean of the School of Law of Southern Methodist University for six. Professor Salacuse holds a J.D. from Harvard Law School, an A.B. from Hamilton College, and a diploma from the University of Paris. He has been a lecturer in law at Ahmadu Bello University in Nigeria, a lawyer with a Wall Street law firm, a professor of law and director of research at the National School of Administration in the Congo, the Ford Foundation's Middle East advisor on law and development based in Beirut, Lebanon, and later the Foundation's representative in the Sudan. Professor Salacuse has traveled and lectured widely. He has been a visiting professor at the University of London, the University of Bristol, the École Nationale des Ponts et Chaussées, Paris, and the Instituto de Empresa, Madrid. In 2000, he held the Fulbright Distinguished Chair in Comparative Law in Italy. Professor Salacuse has written twelve books and numerous articles, including *Seven Secrets for Negotiating with Government* (2008); *Leading Leaders: How to Manage Smart, Talented, Rich, and Powerful People* (2006, selected by *The Globe and Mail* as one of the ten best business books of the year); *The Global*

Negotiator: Making, Managing, and Mending Deals Around the World in the Twenty-First Century (2003, selected as one of the best business books of the year by *Library Journal*); *The Wise Advisor: What Every Professional Should Know About Consulting and Counseling* (2000, Chinese edition 2004); *Making Global Deals* (1991 ten foreign language editions); with W.P. Streng, *International Business Planning: Law and Taxation* (six vols.); *An Introduction to Law in French-speaking Africa* (two vols.); and, with Alfred B. Kasunmu, *Nigerian Family Law* (1966). Professor Salacuse has served as the chairman of the Institute of Transnational Arbitration, chairman of the board of the Council for International Exchange of Scholars, president of the International Third World Legal Studies Association, and the founding president of the Association of Professional Schools of International Affairs (APSIA). An international arbitrator and consultant to multinational companies, government agencies, international organizations, universities, foundations, and foreign governments, he is a member of the Council on Foreign Relations, the American Law Institute, and the executive committee and faculty of the Program on Negotiation at Harvard Law School. He is the lead independent director of several mutual funds managed by Legg Mason, Chairman of the India Fund and Asia Tigers Fund, and president of an ICSID international arbitration tribunal.

Philippe Sarrailhé is a partner in the Paris office of White & Case. His main areas of practice are mergers and acquisitions, LBOs, securities, and international commercial arbitration. He has considerable experience in commercial and financial matters generally. Mr. Sarrailhé has represented top French and foreign clients in major cross-border private and public mergers and acquisitions transactions involving banking institutions and automotive, space, aeronautical, chemical, pharmaceutical, food, and other industrial companies. He has advised on leveraged buyout transactions, acting for leading U.S., UK, and Dutch private equity houses, as well as venture capital transactions. He also has advised on the issuance of various types of equity and debt instruments, and on the offering, listing, and placement thereof. Mr. Sarrailhé has experience in IPOs as well as structured finance, having advised several banks in relation to statutory and offshore securitization schemes. He is also active on the dispute resolution side; particularly, he is regularly involved as counsel on behalf of substantial French, European, and North American parties in international arbitrations governed by French law or other laws based on the French legal system. He has lectured on European commercial law and international business transactions at the University of Paris Law School. Prior to joining White & Case, Mr. Sarrailhé was a partner with a leading French law firm and was the managing partner in the New York office of that firm from 1991 to 1994.

Ramón M. Segura holds a J.D. from the University of Buenos Aires in Buenos Aires, Argentina. Since July 2002, he has been with Marval,

O'Farrell & Mairal; in September 2005, he was appointed legal manager of the New York office of the firm, a position he still holds. Prior to his employment with Marval, O'Farrell & Mairal, Mr. Segura was an associate with Baker & McKenzie in Buenos Aires, Argentina, a position he began in November 1997. His primary area of practice is in transactional and corporate law and involves banking and finance; mergers and acquisitions; capital markets; and general corporate counseling.

Ordélio Azevedo Sette belongs to a family with three generations of lawyers in practice. Mr. Sette specializes in international joint ventures in Brazil, Africa, and Asia, and international contract negotiation and privatization. He is a partner with Azevedo Sette Advogados, a firm engaged in Brazilian and international law practice, with offices in Belo Horizonte, São Paulo, and Brasilia (DF), Brazil. Mr. Sette is a graduate in law from the University of Brasilia Law School and did postgraduate work in constitutional law there. He also did postgraduate work at the Inter-American Center of Qualification in National and International Commercialization of the Organization of American States in Washington, D.C. Mr. Sette was a Professor of International Law at the OAB-MG School of Lawyers in 1986. He has been a board member of the Brazilian Bar Association, Minas Gerais Section; a member of the Council of Taxpayers of Minas Gerais State; president of the International Chamber of Commerce of Brazil; and a member of the International Fiscal Association (IFA) and the ABA. Mr. Sette is the author of the book *Economic and Tax Aspects of Mercosur Integration* (1992), and approximately seventy other works on legal issues published in legal magazines and specialized national and international publications.

Cyril Shroff is managing partner of Amarchand & Mangaldas & Suresh A. Shroff & Co., in Mumbai, India (India's largest law firm). With twenty-five years of experience in a range of corporate areas, including banking, infrastructure, and others, Mr. Shroff has been consistently rated as India's top corporate, banking, and project finance lawyer by several international surveys, including those conducted by *International Financial Law Review, Euromoney*, Chambers Global, Asia Legal 500, Asia Law Magazine, and others. He has also been voted regularly by the *Economic Times* as one of India's top 100 CEOs in the country. Mr. Shroff has authored several publications on legal topics. He is a part-time lecturer on securities law at the Government Law College. He is a member of the Centre for Study of the Legal Profession established by the Harvard Law School and a member of the Advisory Board of National Institute of Securities Markets. Mr. Shroff has participated in several Technical Assistance (TA) projects of the Asian Development Bank in relation to the reform of laws relating to secured lending, bankruptcy, and other related topics. Mr. Shroff was admitted to the Bar in 1982 after receiving his B.A. LL.B. degree from the Government Law College in Mumbai. He has been a solicitor of the High Court of Bombay since 1983.

Jane E. Smith, Esq. is the founder and president of LiSimba Consulting Services, Inc. LiSimba's work centers on "Building Relationships for International Business Success." She is a graduate of William Mitchell College of Law, St. Paul, Minnesota; she also earned an M.Ed. at the University of Texas at Denton, Texas; studied at Macalester College in St. Paul, including study at the Facultad de Filosofiá Y Letras, University of Madrid, Madrid, Spain; and completed two years reading ancient history and theology at Wycliffe Hall, Oxford University, Oxford, England, through the WEST Course. Some of her writings and presentations include "The Maquiladora System as a Bridge Between the United States and Mexico," *International Business Law News*, Minnesota State Bar Association; the online simulation "Managing Cross Cultural Concerns in Global Contracting," in collaboration with the IACCM; "The International Aspect of Post Merger/Acquisition Integration: Setting Strategic and Tactical Priorities to Capture the Value of the Deal," written and presented for Executive Enterprises; "The Global Civil Law System: Its History and Function as Compared with the Common Law System, Its History and Function," written and presented for the American Corporate Counsel Association; "The Civil Law Systems of the World," written and presented for the Section of International Law and Practice, American Bar Association; "Managing Interpersonal Relationships Between Middle and Upper Management," facilitated with Wilson Learning in Buckinghamshire, England.

Sasha Štěpánová is an attorney with Kocián Šolc Balaštík in Prague, Czech Republic (*Who's Who Legal* Firm of the Year, Czech Republic, 2006, 2007, and 2008), and her practice is focused on advising incoming international investors in the Czech Republic, particularly in the fields of new business establishment, corporate acquisitions, joint ventures, and real estate. Educated and also legally qualified in Australia and the UK, she is registered as an EU advocate with the Czech Bar Association and has been based in Prague since 1994, experiencing firsthand the legal and commercial evolution of the Czech business environment.

Charles M. Taylor is an attorney in private practice in Philadelphia, emphasizing corporate law in an international setting, with related financial, immigration, and antitrust aspects. Often, this has been with start-up corporations or mergers and acquisitions for growing firms, which seek out and acquire other businesses and must comply with an ever-increasing list of local and federal regulatory requirements. His extensive immigration experience has ranged from assisting corporations in hiring qualified foreign workers to counseling individuals wishing to come to this country for employment and permanent residency. Mr. Taylor has served as Honorary Consul General of the Federal Republic of Germany in Philadelphia and was president of the Philadelphia Consular Corps. He was a founding director of both the French-American Chamber of Commerce and the German-

American Chamber of Commerce in Philadelphia and remains active in these organizations. He serves on the board of directors of the Friends of the Free University of Berlin and of the German Society of Pennsylvania. He is the founder and managing director of the European-American General Counsels Association. Mr. Taylor is an honors graduate of Harvard University and a recipient of a graduate German Dankstipendium fellowship. He studied law at the Free University of Berlin and then worked with a German law firm. Thereafter, he graduated from Columbia Law School and is admitted to the bar in New York and Pennsylvania. He is also licensed as a Rechtsberater (Legal Advisor) in Germany, where he maintains a law office.

Nils Unckel is an associate with the law firm of Gernandt & Danielsson in Stockholm, Sweden.

David A. Victor is associate professor of management at the Gary Owen College of Business at Eastern Michigan University, as well as president of the Human Resources Advisory Council, a management and business-communication consulting firm based in Bloomfield Hills, Michigan. Dr. Victor has led workshops, conferences, and seminars worldwide. He designed the first course in international business communication taught in an Association to Advance Collegiate Schools of Business (AACSB) accredited U.S. college of business and authored a groundbreaking book on the subject, *International Business Communication* (1992). He was the first recipient of the Distinguished Visiting Foreign Professorship of the Instituto Tecnológico y de Estudios Superiores de Monterrey, Mexico.

Katrien Vorlat is a partner at the Brussels office of Stibbe. She is a Belgian corporate mergers and acquisitions lawyer. She has negotiated and structured a wide variety of M&A transactions, joint ventures, investment schemes, and syndicated loans. She has also assisted several Belgian companies during fund-raising through private placements and/or public offerings. Ms. Vorlat is a 1990 graduate of the law faculty of Katholieke Universiteit Leuven (lic. jur., K.U. Leuven). She also obtained an LL.M. from Yale Law School in 1992. In 1993 she obtained a comparative law degree from the Faculty of Comparative Law of Strasbourg. She was admitted to the Brussels Bar in 1993.

Tomasz Wardynski is a Polish *adwokat* and founding partner of Wardynski & Partners, one of the first and largest independent Polish law firms, which has been successfully operating since the early 1990s. In 2001, as one of the very first law firms in a country in line to become an EU member, Wardynski & Partners opened an office in Brussels. Since 1986 Mr. Wardynski has been an honorary legal advisor to Her Britannic Majesty's Ambassador to Poland and is an Honorary Commander of the Civil Division of the Most Excellent Order of the British Empire. Mr. Wardynski is a graduate of the law faculty at Warsaw University (1970), the College of Europe, Bruges, Belgium (1973), and the Institute of European Studies and Law Faculty, University of

Strasbourg, France (1974–75). He is a member of the Polish Bar Association and the International Bar Association (IBA Legal Practice Division Councillor). He is an arbitrator in the Court of Arbitration at the Polish Chamber of Commerce in Warsaw and in the Vienna International Arbitral Centre (VIAC).

Richard Warner is professor of law at the Chicago-Kent College of Law, where he is a Norman & Edna Freehling Scholar, and faculty director of the Center for Law and Computers. He is director of Chicago-Kent's Project Poland. He is a graduate of the University of California, Berkeley (Ph.D., philosophy) and the University of Southern California (J.D.). He teaches contracts, remedies, jurisprudence, Internet law, and e-commerce law and has published several articles and books on philosophical and legal topics. His research concerns the regulation of business competition on the Internet and Internet security as well as the nature of human rights and their grounding in personal freedom.

Jaap Willeumier is a partner in the Amsterdam office of Stibbe. He is the head of the firm's banking and finance practice. His areas of expertise include banking, securities, corporate and structured finance, asset finance, securitization, and debt and equity capital market transactions. His work encompasses complex securitizations, syndicated loans, bond issues, and other debt capital market transactions, big-ticket cross-border asset finance, debt restructuring, and regulatory and securities advisory work. He was the resident partner in Stibbe's New York office from 1989 to 1994.

Andrew Wingfield is the partner responsible for the Qatar office of Simmons & Simmons and is the group head for their Middle East Corporate Practice provided out of his firm's Qatar, Dubai, and Abu Dhabi offices. Mr. Wingfield joined Simmons & Simmons in London in 1983, then moved to the Hong Kong office in 1985, New York in 1999, and Qatar in 2005. He has been a partner since 1992. Prior to joining the Doha office in 2005, Mr. Wingfield was the managing partner of his firm's New York office for seven years and before that was head of his firm's Corporate and Finance Department in Hong Kong.

Ralf Wojtek is a partner of Heuking Kühn Lüer Wojtek, a law firm with offices in seven major cities throughout Germany as well as in Brussels and Zurich. He is a practicing attorney in the Hamburg office and a registered lawyer at the Brussels (EU) office. He advises in corporate law, mergers and acquisitions, and regulatory and antitrust law, as well as in EU competition law matters. Before entering into private practice, he was general counsel of Dow Chemical in Germany. He was awarded an LL.M. at the University of California (Berkeley) and a doctorate for his thesis on insider trading from Hamburg University. Mr. Wojtek has testified at various occasions before the German legislative bodies during proceedings on the change of postal and transportation laws and regulations. He has published a number of legal articles and books in his field. He has been appointed as chairman of industry associations of the transportation and logistics industry in Germany.

Alison J. Youngman passed away in March 2009. She was a senior partner in the Toronto office of Stikeman Elliott. She has wide-ranging corporate and commercial experience in a variety of industries, advising both public and private corporations, and was co-chair of the firm's Negotiated Acquisitions Group. She dealt primarily with mergers and acquisitions, commercial matters, joint ventures, outsourcing, licensing and distribution, and cross-border investments. She chaired the firm's Marketing Committee and served as co-chair of the American Bar Association Negotiated Acquisitions Committee Task Force on Joint Ventures. She was also a member of the Canadian Bar Association Corporate Laws Committee and the Finance and Economic Affairs Committee of the Toronto Board of Trade. She participated as a speaker and panelist at various conferences, and was the author or coauthor of a number of publications, including *Mergers and Acquisitions in Canada,* to be published by Kluwer International. Ms. Youngman attended Concordia University and the University of Toronto (Arts), Osgoode Hall Law School (LL.B., 1984 and LL.M., 1999). In 1986, she was called to the Ontario Bar and in 1994 was admitted as a solicitor in England.

INTRODUCTION

James R. Silkenat
ARENT FOX LLP
NEW YORK, NEW YORK

Jeffrey M. Aresty
ARESTY INTERNATIONAL LAW OFFICES, P.C.
SUDBURY, MASSACHUSETTS

Jacqueline Klosek
GOODWIN PROCTER LLP
NEW YORK, NEW YORK

In the new era of e-commerce at the beginning of the twenty-first century, the opportunity exists to establish a less hostile social and cultural environment for ourselves and for future generations. This can be accomplished if we collectively use Internet technologies to negotiate a social contract for the emerging global society. This environment can be achieved, in part, through continued contributions to the creation of economic opportunity across national boundaries. The international order that will be necessary to support global economic growth presupposes, to a considerable extent, that global relationships are governed by the rule of law. A vision of international cooperation is one that almost all lawyers can share and help implement by bringing the rule of law to all parts of the world.

As the trend toward globalization and internationalization of business becomes even more evident, lawyers will be called upon to become more familiar with the laws, customs, and cultures of other nations and groups within nations. This was the premise underlying the creation of the ABA Section of International Law more than seventy-five years ago. Today, almost all parts of the organized bar are participating in this effort. The Futurist Committee of the ABA's Section of Law Practice Management, for example, has pointed out that "international law, international law firms, and universal principles will be developed in order to facilitate the development of global business activities. A universal business and legal ethic will develop to deal with the expectations of parties and their advisors in international dealings." The Committee's observations continued:

> Lawyers will have to become more sensitive to different modalities of communication, style, and custom to be used in dealing

with others. In order to understand and effectively communicate, more than language and custom differences need to be addressed. There may well be an increase in the use of conventions in order to facilitate communication and establish reasonable expectations by those who meet from different cultures. Common language, ethical behavior, and custom will also develop in order to facilitate expectations and communications.

This book and its two predecessor editions were written to address the concerns noted above. When international business negotiations succeed, it is largely because all sides have clearly articulated their objectives and confirmed that the parties understand the context of the negotiated agreement. When international business negotiations do not succeed, it is frequently because there is a lack of communication and understanding among the negotiators. Differences between cultures, languages, value systems, and legal systems can all serve to cloud communication and create obstacles that can potentially bring negotiations to a halt. This situation is exacerbated by digital communication. Information technology has the potential to bring together the world's communities, but does so with the risk of greater misunderstanding. These differences in perspective are not merely cultural: no global consensus has emerged regarding the rule of law that governs the electronic marketplace, despite the legal contributions of involved nation-states.

A group of distinguished international lawyers with many years of practical business law background have contributed to this volume by sharing their experiences on both the legal and cultural aspects of doing business in various countries around the world. *The ABA Guide to International Business Negotiations* is intended to be helpful to business people who engage in cross-border negotiations, to lawyers who represent parties in international business transactions and who want to avoid the obstacles that still exist to successfully negotiating international business deals, and to people interested in bringing a just and ethical rule of law to cyberspace.

The international negotiator must be aware of various constraints inherent in international negotiations and be prepared to deal with them in order to achieve successful business agreement for his or her clients. This book is a collection of practical papers that highlight the obstacles faced by the international negotiator, and how to overcome them in a constructive way.

In the first section of this volume, we focus on national, legal, and cultural issues that are generally present when negotiators must bridge the international gap, including a special focus on the impact of using the Internet to conduct negotiations. Additionally, we examine the rapidly evolving challenges of electronic commerce (regarding both regulation and negotiation), and compare the different approaches that are emerging internationally to cope with them.

The second section of this volume comprises a series of individual country chapters focusing on the specifics of negotiations involving each country, including a look at the impact of e-commerce in each country. The authors for each chapter were selected on the basis of their expertise in international commercial negotiations and their wide familiarity with international business law issues concerning a particular country.

We hope this volume will be of help both to the private practitioner and to corporate counsel who work in the international arena. We also hope that our readers will share with us their own experiences in this complex area of international business negotiations.

—The Editors (January 2009)

James R. Silkenat
Arent Fox LLP
1675 Broadway
New York, NY 10019
Phone: (212) 492-3318
Fax: (212) 484-3990
E-mail: silkenat.james@arentfox.com

Jeffrey M. Aresty
Aresty International Law Offices. P.C.
365 Boston Post Road #135
Sudbury, MA 01776
Phone: (508) 314-0916
E-mail: jaresty@cyberspaceattorney.com

Jacqueline Klosek
Goodwin Procter LLP
620 Eighth Avenue
New York, NY 10018-1405
Phone: (212) 459-7464
Fax: (212) 355-3333
E-mail: jklosek@goodwinprocter.com

PART 1:

Building Trust in Online Negotiations: A Cross-Cultural Approach to International Business in the Twenty-First Century

and is strengthened by proof.[6] Gullibility, hope, and faith are relatives of trusting,[7] but reflect different degrees of the parties' requirements for verification.[8] Reasonable belief should depend on the context of the relationship. Reliability in love does not necessarily mean reliability in business relationships, and vice versa. The scope of deeper trust, such as trust in a doctor, lawyer, or priest, is usually limited to particular areas of knowledge or brands of honesty. Reasonable belief can be established by verifying the trustworthiness of the other party or, as an alternative to trust, by resorting to other sources of information, usually depending on the relative costs.

Cultural norms shape the parameters of reasonableness of the belief. Reasonableness may differ depending on whether the social norm is lying, frankness, or vagueness of the other parties' statements and promises as well as the acceptable social norms.[9] The law both affects and is affected by these norms. Moreover, trusting is a reflexive and reciprocal relationship.[10] Trusting often creates pressure on trusted persons to meet the expectations of the trusting parties. Signals of mistrust may breed mistrust.[11] Dirty tricks invite reciprocal dirty tricks. As compared to verification cost in real space, verification cost on the Internet is higher.[12]

---

[6] *See* GOVIER, *supra* note 4, at 153. *See also* Ann Marie Zak et al., *Assessments of Trust in Intimate Relationships and Self-Perception Process*, 138 J. SOC. PSYCHOL. 217, 225 (1998) (finding that the trusting behavior of the participants in the experiments is often self-fulfilling and explaining that blind trust is usually a product of one's self-perception). Trustworthy people are more likely to blindly trust others. *See id.*

[7] Trusting does not mean believing all unverified representations; rather, it means believing unverified representations when it is not unreasonable to do so. "[B]elieving when most people of the same social group would consider belief naive and foolish" qualifies as gullibility. *See* Julian B. Rotter, *Interpersonal Trust, Trustworthiness, and Gullibility*, 35 AM. PSYCHOLOGIST 1, 4 (1980).

[8] Gullibility is an unreasonable belief, while hope involves a strong component of wishing for a future event. See GOVIER, *supra* note 4, at 14, for an elaboration on the distinctions and similarities between faith and trust.

[9] "Do it yourself" verification is not always less costly and more reliable than verification by others. Cost depends on the time spent and lost opportunities, as compared to the compensation of experts and agency costs of delegation. Thus, one's own judgment may be decisive because one bears the consequences of the decision, but one's level of wisdom, knowledge, and expertise may be lower, drawing a distinction between "verification" and "judgment." *See* GOVIER, *supra* note 4, at 230, citing SISSELA BOK, A STRATEGY FOR PEACE (1989).

[10] *See* GOVIER, *supra* note 4, at 27.

[11] An attempt by teachers in a Canadian law school to control students through minutely detailed rules of examinations led to a culture of mistrust; the attitude of mistrust bred more mistrust. *See id.* at 87–88.

[12] *See generally* D. Scott Anderson, Comment, *What Trust Is in These Times? Examining the Foundation of Online Trust*, 54 EMORY L.J. 1441 (2006).

However, there are persons and organizations that feed on such traits. Discovering their tendencies and signs of behavior is often difficult, especially when verification is costly. Thus, "[b]usinesses [should] learn how to establish trust in the new [environment and] communication medium."[13]

Some believe that the Internet is a free space that should not, and cannot, be regulated, and that markets can resolve the trusting problem. I argue that trusting on the Internet will not develop without law. Law punishes breach of trust and compensates those who reasonably trust. It also provides trusted persons with a good reputation, which is very valuable for them.[14]

2. Trusting and Non-Trusting

2.1 Relative Costs, Benefits, and Risks

"Trusting involves costs, benefits, and risks to both the trusted and the trusting parties."[15] When trust is absent, parties must resort to verification. If the cost of verification is too high, people will not interact. On the Internet, verification can be very costly. Unless there is a way to reduce the verification costs or raise the level of trust, the Internet will not reach its potential.

There are indications that social trusting is crucial to economic prosperity, and perhaps the very existence of individuals and society.[16] Specialization is a necessary component of a prosperous economy. Specialization requires interdependence, which cannot exist without a measure of trusting.[17] In an entirely non-trusting relationship, interaction

---

[13] *See* JOHN O. WHITNEY, THE ECONOMICS OF TRUST LIBERATING PROFITS AND RESTORING CORPORATE VITALITY (1996). *See also* RODERICK M. KRAMER & TOM R. TYLER, TRUST IN ORGANIZATIONS: FRONTIERS OF THEORY AND RESEARCH 232 (1996).

[14] Frankel, *supra* note 1, at 459.

[15] *Id.* at 460.

[16] Social capital is defined as a moral resource and a public good that is self-perpetuating and lubricates the growth of trust in society: *See* GOVIER, *supra* note 4, at 153 ("For politics, economics, and personal well-being, social trust is a valuable resource."). Lack of trust is costly in psychological terms. The unknown is risky; it breeds fear and anxiety, which can be debilitating. *See* NIKLAS LUHMANN, TRUST AND POWER (1980), *quoted in* BERNARD BARBER, THE LOGIC AND LIMITS OF TRUST 10 (1983): "But a complete absence of trust would prevent him even from getting up in the morning. He would be prey to a vague sense of dread, to paralyzing fears. He would not even be capable of formulating distrust and making that a basis for precautionary measures, since this would presuppose trust in other directions. Anything and everything would be possible. Such abrupt confrontation with the complexity of the world at its most extreme is beyond human endurance." *See also* Lawrence E. Mitchell, *Fairness and Trust in Corporate Law*, 43 DUKE L.J. 425 (1993).

[17] In complex societies we need to trust many people, including experts on information that we would not understand even if it were disclosed to us. *See* GOVIER, *supra* note 4, at 26. *See also* Tamar Frankel, *Fiduciary Law*, 71 CAL. L. REV. 795 (1983).

would be too expensive and too risky to maintain. There is a correlation between the level of trusting relationships on which members of a society operate and the level of that society's trade and economic prosperity.[18]

Benefits on the Internet are no different. The cost to businesses and people who seek to be trusted is also higher on the Internet because many of the signs that signal trustworthiness do not appear on the Internet.

One effective mechanism that reduces the cost and risks of personal trusting is the utilization of trusted legitimate institutions and intermediaries, both private and public. Institutions reduce trusting costs regardless of consumers' culture and regardless of whether personal trust is mixed with skepticism.

"The benefits of institutional or impersonal trusting are very great. People can trade with strangers through trusted intermediaries and institutions based on impersonal trust.[19] ...[T]he number of institutions is smaller than the number of people with whom business can be conducted, a factor that reduces the investment in verifying the trustworthiness of the institutions. In addition, buyers, investors, borrowers, and depositors can move from one institution to another with little cost. [Further,] institutions have relative longevity, and can build impressive reputations. . . .

[In addition,] institutions reduce lost opportunities of interacting with strangers,[20] allowing people to deal with strangers and benefit from services of capable strangers who function under the umbrella of the institutions.[21]. . .

[Finally,] and most importantly, risks from trusting commercial and financial institutions are reduced by law."[22]

---

[18] *See* FRANCIS FUKUYAMA, TRUST: THE SOCIAL VIRTUES AND THE CREATION OF PROSPERITY 7 (1995); FRANCIS FUKUYAMA, GREAT DISRUPTION: HUMAN NATURE AND THE RECONSTRUCTION OF SOCIAL ORDER 256 (1999); WHITNEY, *supra* note 13; and Bruce Chapman, *Trust, Economic Rationality, and the Corporate Fiduciary Obligation*, 43 U. TORONTO L.J. 547 (1993).

[19] In comparing American impersonal trusting with Japanese personal trusting, one can see the weakness of the Japanese system. The focal point of this weakness is with regard to financial institutions, which Japan is now remodeling. In an international economy, impersonal trusting has become crucial to national economic prosperity.

[20] Modern "urban" trust is strikingly different from trust in, for example, Swedish village life where consumers only transact with known merchants. "Modern trust" is more tied "to people's sense of how institutions operate than to their attitudes towards unknown individuals." *See* GOVIER, *supra* note 4, at 24–25.

[21] *See id.* at 29: "To live in a complex society without going mad, we must have trust in systems too."; and Grabner-Kraeuter, *supra* note 2, at 45. Institutional trust is especially important on the Internet because it does not depend on past interactions or personal characteristics.

[22] Frankel, *supra* note 1, at 466-67 (footnote omitted). Regarding the ability of parties to move among institutions, many state laws prohibit banks from penalizing borrowers who wish to refinance mortgages (that is, pay off their mortgage loans and take loans at lower interest).

As mentioned, situations that do not require trusting and involve low or no verification costs involve higher costs on the Internet. In real space, the purchaser of a newspaper bears little or no cost in verifying the newspaper and its price, and no promise is involved because the exchange is simultaneous. Transactions on the Internet are usually not simultaneous.

However, in 2008 consumers can buy software that is downloaded immediately upon purchase or subscriptions to Web sites that are activated immediately. A good example of an instantaneous transaction on the Internet would be the purchase of music from Apple's iTunes service.

> Risks from third parties [that acquire the consumers' personal identities and credit card numbers] undermine consumers' trust in the Internet.... Under United States law, if stolen credit cards are used for unauthorized purchases, banks or sellers must indemnify consumers for losses above $50. But on the Internet, consumers may not know that their card numbers have been stolen because they still hold their cards.... Third parties harm consumers by malicious hyperlinks, spyware, and "spamming"—an avalanche of advertising causing bottlenecks on consumers' computers.[23]

The problem of spyware is not limited to malicious and obscure third parties. Sony BMG Music Entertainment was subject to a lawsuit under California's antispyware legislation for the use of embedded "rootkit" software on their music CDs that monitored users' computer usage, and made itself difficult to find and remove.[24] In its monthly "State of Spam" report for July 2008, Symantec Messaging and Web Security reported that spam levels had climbed from 56 percent in 2006 to over 80 percent of all e-mails today.[25] Malicious third parties can also injure online reputations of businesses. These include, for example, third parties known as "phishers." Phishers send e-mails and create Web sites disguised as legitimate businesses in order to trick victims into sending personal or financial information. The practice of phishing is a significant obstacle for businesses seeking to gain trust on the Internet because the practice uses the good reputation of legitimate businesses as a ploy to trick consumers. Recipients of fake e-mails and victims of phishing have been reported to become less trusting of e-mails and less likely to transact business online.[26] Technology

---

[23] *See* Laura L. Edwards, *Oh What a Tangled World Wide Web We Weave: An Analysis of Washington's Computer Spyware Act in a National Context*, 31 SEATTLE U. L. REV. 645 (2008).

[24] *Id.*

[25] *See* SYMANTEC, THE STATE OF SPAM, http://www.symantec.com/business/theme .jsp?themeid=state_of_spam (last visited Sept. 6, 2008).

[26] *See* Jasmine E. McNealy, *Angling for Phishers: Legislative Responses to Deceptive E-Mail*, 13 COMM. L. & POL'Y 275 (2008).

provides some redress from these harms, at a cost, and only temporarily, until spammers design software to circumvent the protections.

There has been legislation over the last decade in response to the ever-increasing flood of spam and spyware. Congress attempted to address the spam issue in 2003, by enacting the CAN-SPAM Act.[27] The CAN-SPAM Act does not grant a private remedy for victims of spam but rather authorizes the FTC to bring actions against individuals who violate the provisions of the CAN-SPAM Act. A single violation can result in a fine of $10,000 and spammers could face prison sentences of up to five years. However, few individuals have been prosecuted under the CAN-SPAM Act to date. The Act was widely criticized as ineffective.[28] The CAN-SPAM Act does not aim at outlawing spam altogether as much as regulating it.[29] More importantly, though, spam is a global problem and spam e-mails can come from anywhere in the world. A law enacted in the United States that subjects citizens to fines for failing to include an opt-out clause in their e-mails will not realistically stop a spammer in eastern Europe from sending spam to American inboxes. Because of the global nature of spam, no single nation or state can draft laws that would eliminate or drastically lower spam.[30] The best that can be hoped for in unilateral antispam legislation would be to lower the creation and dissemination of spam within the borders of the countries or states that enact it.

Various forms of spyware legislation have been proposed in Congress, but none have yet been enacted.[31] While no spyware laws have been passed on the national level, the FTC has targeted and punished multiple spyware distributors under existing laws regulating deceptive business practices.[32] Also, some states, such as Washington and California, have tried to tackle the spyware problem with various forms of antispyware legislation.[33] However, because the distribution

---

[27] *See* Controlling the Assault of Non-Solicited Pornography and Marketing Act of 2003, Pub. L. No. 108-187, 117 Stat. 2699 (codified at 15 U.S.C. §§ 7701–7713, 18 U.S.C. § 1037 (Supp. IV 2004)).

[28] *See* Edwards, *supra* note 23, at 657–58.

[29] *See* Samuel Boone-Lutz, *Just Say Yes: Drug Trafficking Treaties as a Model for an Anti-Spam Convention*, 39 Geo. Wash. Int'l. L. Rev. 367 (2007).

[30] *See id.*

[31] For example, in 2005, four pieces of federal spyware legislation were introduced into the House and Senate, none of which have yet been made into law: Securely Protect Yourself Against Cyber Trespass Act (SPY ACT), H.R. 29, 109th Cong. (2005); Internet Spyware (I-SPY) Prevention Act, H.R. 744, 109th Cong. (2005); Software Principles Yielding Better Levels of Consumer Knowledge (SPY BLOCK) Act, S. 687, 109th Cong. (2005); and Enhanced Consumer Protection Against Spyware Act, S. 1004, 109th Cong. (2005).

[32] *See* Megan M. Engle, *Anti-Spyware Enforcement: Recent Developments*, 3 ISJLP 581 (2008).

[33] For a discussion on Washington's antispyware legislation, *see* Edwards, *supra* note 23.

of spyware invariably crosses state and national lines, state legislation can do little to solve the spyware problem.[34] Spyware is arguably more damaging to consumer trust online than spam and viruses because whereas spam and viruses are created by hackers for their own benefit or for the benefit of criminal organizations, spyware is more commonly created by large corporations that bundle spyware with legitimate software.[35] Furthermore, while spyware is by definition a subversive program, the existence of spyware in software is frequently included in the end-user license agreements of the software. It is bundled in to protect the distributors from legal action based on a contract theory of liability or based on trespass to chattels.[36] To make matters worse for consumers, spyware manufacturers utilize the current state of the law not just to protect themselves but also to attack the manufacturers of antispyware programs for creating the programs that remove their malicious software from consumers' computers.[37] The proliferation and acceptance of spyware in the e-commerce marketplace led one commentator to remark that "the spyware wars are over—and spyware has won."[38]

The rise of online social networking sites adds a new aspect into the discussion of online trust. With millions of users sharing their personal information on sites such as MySpace[39] and Facebook,[40] opportunities for online fraud, deception, and exploitation have increased dramatically. The two most troubling uses of online social networking sites have been as "one-stop shopping catalogues" for child predators who look for victims[41] and as "virtual bathroom walls" for "cyberbullies" to harass peers.[42] Recognizing the problems that have accompanied

---

[34] *See* Erica Pines, Note, *Spyware Regulation: National Regulation Should Prompt Industry Self-Policing*, 38 Loy. L.A. L. Rev. 2219, 2239 (2005) ("A state law only affects one state, while spyware is truly a global problem").

[35] *See* Jacob Kreutzer, *Somebody Has to Pay: Products Liability for Spyware*, 45 Am. Bus. L.J. 61 (2008). For examples of successful spyware manufacturers, see Stefanie Olsen, *Gator Sinks Teeth into New Image*, CNET News, Oct. 30, 2003, http://news.cnet.com/Gator-sinks-teeth-into-new-image/2100-1024_3-5099601.html, and Annalee Newitz, *Don't Call It Spyware*, WIRED Magazine, Dec. 2005, *available at* http://www.wired.com/wired/archive/13.12/spyware.html.

[36] *See* Kreutzer, *supra* note 35, at 62–63.

[37] *See* Paul Festa, *See You Later, Anti-Gators?* CNET News, Oct. 22, 2003, http://news.cnet.com/See-you-later%2C-anti-Gators/2100-1032_3-5095051.html.

[38] *See* Newitz, *supra* note 35.

[39] http://www.myspace.com.

[40] http://www.facebook.com.

[41] *See* Jessica S. Groppe, *A Child's Playground or a Predator's Hunting Ground? How to Protect Children on Internet Social Networking Sites*, 16 CommLaw Conspectus 215 (2007).

[42] Cyberbullies, also known as "trolls," typically post degrading and cruel messages and pictures on social networking sites' "walls." Cyberbullying (or "trolling") causes more than hurt feelings and has led to death threats, suicide, and murder. *See id.* at 227–28.

online social networking sites, various safeguards have been suggested and put into action. There has been a significant push in the legislature to address the issue,[43] most notably in the Keeping the Internet Devoid of Predators Act of 2008,[44] and the Internet Stopping Adults Facilitating the Exploitation of Today's Youth (SAFETY) Act of 2007.[45] Those who oppose regulation of online social networking sites argue that permissible speech will be "chilled" and would possibly force sites overseas in order to escape regulations.[46] In addition to state and national legislation, various self-help and educational programs have been put into action. Three educational campaigns that have been launched are (1) Help Delete Online Predators (HDOP), which is designed to educate parents about online child predators, (2) Don't Believe the Type, which is designed to educate teens about predators, and (3) Think Before You Post, which is designed to educate teens about posting personal information online.[47]

The rising pressure has caused some social networking sites to change their user policies to protect children. Most notably, MySpace has made serious efforts in order to render its site safer for children and teenagers. (MySpace hired a former Department of Justice prosecutor as its security officer, developed parental notification software, and banned sex offenders from its site using a program called Sentinel Safe.)[48] Self-help and education may be the most effective remedy for the problems on social networking sites because so much of the damage is self-inflicted and easily preventable if better judgment is used. Teaching children and teenagers the consequences of posting harmful personal information and pictures would nip much of the social networking problems in the bud. However, it is unrealistic to believe that children will be able to consistently protect themselves. Therefore, for online social networking sites to be safe and trustworthy environments, there is a need for legislation, regulation, and tougher self-policing by the sites.

In addition, traditional policing and enforcement against illegal actions is weaker on the Internet, although the Internet does offer

---

[43] For an extensive discussion on the legislative response to the problem of child predators on online social networking sites, see Susan Hanley Duncan, *Myspace Is Also Their Space: Ideas for Keeping Children Safe from Sexual Predators on Social Networking Sites,* 96 Ky. L.J. 527 (2008).

[44] Keeping the Internet Devoid of Sexual Predators Act of 2008, S. 431, 110th Cong. (as passed by Senate, May 20, 2008).

[45] Internet Stopping Adults Facilitating the Exploitation of Today's Youth (SAFETY) Act of 2007, H.R. 837, 110th Cong. (2007).

[46] *See* Michael D. Marin & Christopher V. Popov, *Doe v. MySpace, Inc.: Liability for Third Party Content on Social Networking Sites,* 25 COMM. LAW. Spring 2007, at 3, 8 (2007).

[47] *See* Duncan, *supra* note 43.

[48] *See* Groppe, *supra* note 41, at 238–39.

added enforcement tools, including publication and automated monitoring. Thus, both costs and risks for buyers (and some for sellers) on the Internet are higher than in real space. Sooner or later, consumers recognize the danger.[49]

3. Risk Reduction

In general, common interests can reduce the risks associated with trusting, as can similarity of character.[50] Similar incentives operate on the Internet. Information about persons on the other side of an e-mail message is costly to verify, making personal trust-building on the Internet better achieved by sharing, as in real space. Proof of one party's trustworthiness, through consistent behavior, can reduce the risks associated with trusting. A similar approach works on the Internet. Self-help can also reduce the risks associated with trusting.

On the Internet, some of the verification costs and burdens have shifted from buyers to sellers. The shift is efficient. First, commercial and financial institutions can reap enormous benefits from Internet communications. Presumably, that gives them incentives to expend more efforts to gain customers' trust. New market entrants, or sellers of new products, recognize the need to capture customers' trust even in real space.

Second, as compared to real space, the level of customers' commitment to cyberspace is not as high. While buyers are exposed to more costs and risks in Internet transactions, buyers also have alternatives to buy in real space, even though these alternatives lack the convenience and choices of Internet shopping. As their risks and costs rise, many customers are inclined to expend little effort in reducing their risks. Thus, in relation to verification, the bargaining power between these two groups has changed and shifted from buyers to sellers.

Third, the cost of proof and risk reduction may be lower for the sellers than for the consumers. Although sellers can shift the added costs to consumers, competition limits such increases. Therefore, even if sellers transfer some of the costs, buyers' increased costs will still be lower than if the buyers had to verify the facts and promises themselves. Fourth, the more sellers succeed in convincing customers of

---

[49] Consumers who are not familiar with communicating on the Internet seem to be more gullible than they would be in real space. They view experts in Internet communications as more trustworthy. Thus there is something like a reverse order: expertise produces dependency and dependency produces trust.

[50] Russell Hardin defines trust mostly in terms of encapsulated interest. *See* RUSSELL HARDIN, DISTRUST (2004). I argue that encapsulated interest is a risk-reducing situation that contributes to trusting but is not trusting per se.

their facts and promises, the lower their burden becomes as they build a trusting relationship with their customers.

Finally, many sellers have begun to recognize that they are better off uniting rather than competing on the issue of trustworthiness. A race to the bottom will bring Internet use to the bottom as well. Therefore, there should be (and hopefully there is) a growing tendency to monitor others, at least within the same industry, to maintain a minimal level of trustworthiness.

Market actors can reduce the risks associated with trusting. Sellers can offer self-binding obligations, such as warranties and "no questions asked" return policies. Lower information and verification costs can reduce the risks associated with trusting. A reputation for being trustworthy is one such mechanism that businesses can also acquire in the market.[51] Reputation serves the dual role of being a source of information for consumers and a source of possible sanctions for businesses.[52] Hence, people rely on reputation, good or bad, as a form of verification, as an added comfort, or as the least expensive alternative when direct sources of information are too costly.

On the Internet, information tools can develop for individuals. For example, direct traders can create a personal business reputation on the Internet, as the eBay[53] experience has shown. Traders on the Internet eBay site are likely to rely on their own experiences, and on those of others regarding other individuals' behavior, and choose their trading partners according to the reputation they developed for telling the truth and keeping their word.[54] The low publication costs and eBay's services provide powerful information that helps make or break a reputation fairly quickly. The reputation of traders on eBay's site affects the prices traders can obtain or are willing to pay. A trader with a good reputation will attract more bidders, who will bid the price

---

[51] Market reputation has a different weight than personal observation, yet can carry weight of the aggregate opinion of others. It is more like price, a "black box," unless others have similar concerns. Reputation is a marketing device, distinguishing competitors in the markets. Trustworthy people offer reduced information costs to other parties, and can therefore charge more for their services and products. When transactions are trust-dependent to the extent that most people would not engage in a business relationship without trusting, the assurance of trusting becomes crucial to the transaction. In such a case, the interference of the law as a guarantor of trustworthiness may be cost reducing and even necessary.

[52] *See* Grabner-Kraeuter, *supra* note 2, at 48.

[53] *See* eBay, Keeping You Safe on eBay, http://pages.ebay.com/help/account/safety.html (last visited Dec. 10, 2008).

[54] "Feedback is the foundation of security and trust in the eBay community. If a user is untrustworthy or unreliable, the user's feedback score will reflect this reality. This creates a system of normative behavior, which allows users to self-regulate within the eBay community." *See* Jeffrey Aresty, *Digital Identity and the Lawyer's Role in Furthering Trusted Online Communities*, 38 U. Tol. L. Rev. 137, 137, 157 (2006).

up. A trader with a poor reputation will attract fewer bidders, who will not bid as much for the same item.[55]

Recognizing the importance of reputation, some sellers on eBay have created a "market for feedback" where they buy and sell items of nominal value among themselves in order to artificially boost their feedback ratings.[56] This practice degrades the effectiveness of the feedback system and thereby makes eBay reputations suspect and achieving trust on eBay more difficult.

A reputation-forming device, such as membership in professional and other groups, can also reduce the risks associated with trusting. Internet businesses have followed the real space model and formed societies whose main function is to gain the customers' trust. Internet businesses recognize that their competitors, who may act unwisely, can adversely affect their own reputation. For example, Financial Services Technology Consortium is composed of competitors who combine to create a "public good," that is, trustworthiness for all, and monitor their members to maintain this public good.[57]

Markets are populated by private sector professionals and organizations with significant reputations that can act as reliable verifiers of others' assertions of facts and promises. They can verify the information or actually lend their credit and name to back the sellers' obligations. That involvement offers parties both an additional trusted obligor and an indirect assurance of verified information, which the obligor will gather to protect its interests. Accountants and lawyers act as market verifiers of information. They command trust by membership in self-regulating organizations, and by strict government regulation. They verify information about the trustworthiness of strangers.

There are organizations that check businesses for trustworthiness in terms of expertise and proof.[58] Rating agencies perform a similar function. They evaluate bonds after gathering information about issuers including an evaluation of the creditworthiness (trustworthiness) of the issuers. The rating agency Moody's Investors Service[59] offers, for a fee, "trust packages" to parties who wish to reduce their risk of business

---

[55] *See* Susan Block-Lieb, *E-Reputation: Building Trust in Electronic Commerce*, 62 LA. L. REV. 1199 (2002).

[56] *See* Jennifer Brown & John Morgan, *Reputation in Online Auctions: The Market for Trust*, 49 CAL. MGMT. REV. 61 (2006).

[57] *See* Financial Services Technology Consortium, http://www.fstc.org/about/index.php (last visited July 15, 2008) (comprising over 100 organizations working in collaboration to "solve shared problems and challenges, as well as pioneer next generation technology that benefits us all").

[58] It is suggested that the value of board directorship for busy corporate leaders is in "networking" and current information, including information about other actors in their field.

[59] http://www.moodys.com.

relationships with unknown parties abroad. It ascertains whether the unknown party abroad is trustworthy by verifying information, offering the same kind of fact-finding that people engage in to develop a trusting relationship. Moody's has developed a list of factors that demonstrate trustworthiness, and collects information about the unknown party's consistency in performing its promises, paying its debts, making true statements, and conducting long-term relationships.[60] In fact, Moody's has commodified, and is selling, trustworthiness.[61]

Internet businesses have followed the same model. The Internet markets have additional third-party fact verifiers, especially when information can be manipulated on the Internet. For example, pictures shown on the Internet can be digitally changed. Third parties can provide verification of products, such as the true color of women's clothes. This verification was adopted as a selling point to consumers who otherwise mistrust the online display. Unauthorized persons can alter and sign documents transferred through the Internet. Technology is developing to ensure the integrity of documents and signatures. Third-party intermediaries offer trust services for Internet businesses, such as iEscrow escrow services, to ensure that buyers pay money in advance but the money reaches the sellers only upon delivery.[62]

Like reputation-building in real space, businesses build their reputation through associations. The U.S. government offers verification, in the negative sense, about those who are not trustworthy. The Federal Trade Commission issues "Consumer Alerts!" on its Web site.[63] Other associations issue positive recommendations about businesses that act on the Internet, similar to the Better Business Bureau's, such as the Center for Democracy and Technology.[64]

---

[60] Banks have offered a similar service in the form of letters of credit since the seventeenth century. The letters of credit, however, provide a guarantee to parties abroad, who do not know the domestic parties and therefore do not trust their promises. The bank undertakes, unconditionally, the obligation to pay upon presentation of the bills of lending, providing evidence that the goods have arrived.

[61] *See* Bernard S. Black & Ronald J. Gilson, *Venture Capital and the Structure of Capital Markets: Banks Versus Stock Markets*, 47 J. FIN. ECON. 243 (1998); *see also* Donald C. Langevoort, *Angels on the Internet: The Elusive Promise of "Technological Disintermediation" for Unregistered Offerings of Securities*, 2 J. SMALL & EMERGING BUS. L. 91 (1998); Stephen J. Choi, *Gatekeepers on the Internet: Rethinking the Regulations of Small Business Capital Formation*, 2 J. SMALL & EMERGING BUS. L. 27 (1998).

[62] According to the Craigslist's About Scams page, most online escrow services are fraudulent and should be avoided. *See* About Scams, http://www.craigslist.org/about/scams (last visited Dec. 10, 2008).

[63] e.g., Office of Consumer & Bus. Educ., Fed. Trade Comm'n, *How Not to Get Hooked by a 'Phishing' Scam* (2006), http://www.ftc.gov/bcp/edu/pubs/consumer/alerts/alt127.pdf."The FTC works for the consumer to prevent fraudulent, deceptive, and unfair business practices in the marketplace and to provide information to help consumers spot, stop, and avoid them."

[64] http://www.cdt.org.

In order to maintain a good reputation, online businesses often pay for inspections and certification of their Web sites by trusted third parties.[65] The display of "seals" by such trusted third parties is a strategy used by Web sites to enhance consumer trust.[66] The use of seals is an especially valuable tool for Web sites without brand recognition, as the seal itself can act as a "surrogate brand name."[67] The display of trusted third-party seals has become so much a part of the culture of online business that even individual sellers on eBay have begun to utilize them through the warranty service SquareTrade.[68] Studies have shown that while these seals do increase consumer confidence in the Web sites that bear them, they are not always reliable indicators of the privacy policies of the sites, and sites that bear these seals on average actually collect more personal data from the consumers that visit them.[69]

"Both on the Internet and in real space, trustworthiness can evaporate on disappointing evidence. But it seems that on the Internet, it can disappear even faster. One organization, created on the Internet, offered to attach its mark 'TRUSTe' to businesses as a sign of trustworthiness."[70] It is of questionable success because some businesses that carried the sign did not live up to the reasonable expectations of the consumers. Once TRUSTe allows its seal to be displayed by a Web site, it will rarely cancel the relationship to demand that its seal to be taken down. In 2005, TRUSTe ended its relationship with Gratis Internet because of privacy violations and demanded its seals be taken off the company's Web site. This was the first time in two years that TRUSTe had revoked the use of its seal for privacy violations.[71] Many consumers reached the conclusion that TRUSTe did not sufficiently monitor, enforce, or inform about the promises of its sign.[72] Although many

---

[65] *See* Bruce L. Benson, *The Spontaneous Evolution of Cyber Law: Norms, Property Rights, Contracting, Dispute Resolution and Enforcement Without the State*, 1 J.L. Econ. & Pol'y 269 (2005).

[66] *See* Wang & Emurian, *supra* note 2, at 118.

[67] *See* Daryl Koehn, *The Nature of and Conditions for Online Trust*, 43 J. Bus. Ethics 3 (2003).

[68] *See* Gillian K. Hadfield, *Delivering Legality on the Internet: Developing Principles for the Private Provision of Commercial Law*, 6 Am. L. & Econ. Rev. 154 (2004). For details on SquareTrade's seal program, see SquareTrade, http://www.squaretrade.com (last visited Sept. 6, 2008).

[69] *See* Nora J. Rifon et al., *Your Privacy Is Sealed: Effects of Web Privacy Seals on Trust and Personal Disclosures*, 39 J. Consumer Affs. 339 (2005).

[70] Frankel, *supra* note 1, at 473. http://www.truste.org.

[71] *See* Ted Bridis, *Privacy-Assurance Seal Yanked Off Web Sites*, USA Today, Feb. 10, 2005, *available at* http://www.usatoday.com/tech/news/internetprivacy/2005-02-10-truste-seal_x.htm.

[72] For criticism of TRUSTe, see Paul Boutin, *Just How Trusty Is TRUSTe?* WIRED Magazine, Apr. 9, 2002, *available at* http://www.wired.com/techbiz/media/news/2002/04/51624.

consumers have identified TRUSTe as unreliable and untrustworthy, there are many more consumers who are unaware of its shortcomings and continue to trust in its label. Because of this, many big-name Web sites such as Microsoft, Disney, and AOL continue to use the TRUSTe seal.[73]

Internet businesses have piggybacked on trusted real space businesses because customers seem to trust businesses in real space more than they do businesses in cyberspace.[74] For example, community banks with a loyal customer base can establish similar relationships on the Internet, and far larger financial institutions may desire to link their products to such banks. Sometimes brick-and-mortar enterprises that have the loyalty and trust of their customers become aligned with Internet enterprises to bestow on those Internet enterprises the trust of the retailers' customers.

This arrangement is similar to franchising—franchising not of expertise or quality of goods, but of trust. For a similar reason, the value of real space brand names has risen on the Internet.[75] Perhaps this may be one reason why trademark owners are so concerned about their trademarks and well-known brand names have acquired special protection by Congress.

For trust purposes, presentation on the Internet is as important as, if not more important than, presentation in the physical world. Online businesses must display a presentable virtual storefront if they wish to garner the trust of consumers. Attributes that have been found to have a positive impact on trust include ease of navigation, good use of visual design, lack of grammatical errors, and an overall professional look to the site.[76] The inverse is true as well. Studies have found that poor visual designs, mixing advertisements with content, and broken links act as cues that a Web site is untrustworthy.[77]

Collection and dissemination of personally identifying information (PII) such as names, addresses, social security numbers, and credit card numbers by Web sites pose serious privacy risks to Internet users that can often lead to spam and even identity theft. Many Web

---

[73] Groups with similar interests undertake to enforce the members' obligations to be trustworthy, thereby maintaining the trustworthiness of the group. *See* Tamar Frankel, *Should Funds and Investment Advisers Establish a Self-Regulatory Organization? in* THE FINANCIAL SERVICES REVOLUTION: UNDERSTANDING THE CHANGING ROLES OF BANKS, MUTUAL FUNDS, AND INSURANCE COMPANIES 451 (Clifford E. Kirsch ed., 1997).

[74] *See* Grabner-Kraeuter, *supra* note 2, at 48.

[75] Different variables that may enhance an online business's reputation include the presence of a physical store, and the size and age of the business. *See* Miriam J. Metzger, *Effects of Site, Vendor, and Consumer Characteristics on Web Site Trust and Disclosure*, 33 COMM. RES. 155 (2006).

[76] *See* Cynthia L. Corritore, Beverly Kracher & Susan Wiedenbeck, *Online Trust: Concepts, Evolving Themes, a Model*, 58 J. HUM.-COMPUTER STUD. 737 (2003).

[77] *See id.* at 747.

sites collect PII. The most common way this is done is by simple surveys that visitors must fill out in order to utilize the Web site's services or complete orders. While most users do not mind, and are aware to some extent, that sites are collecting their personal information, the danger and loss of trust come from the sharing and sale of this personal information by the reputable sites to unknown and untrustworthy third parties. The sharing of personal information with third parties is not limited to shady and disreputable Web sites. Of the top twenty-five Web sites, only one (Apple Computer) states in its privacy policy that it will not share collected personal information with unrelated third parties.[78]

Once personal information has been disseminated to third parties, it is impossible to know who will eventually get it. Unfortunately, consumers have little choice but to submit their personal information in order to utilize the services of these Web sites. Compounding this problem is the fact that many Internet businesses often make their privacy policies esoteric and hard to find on the Web sites, so that even curious consumers have difficulty finding out if they are at risk. The combination of Web sites that force consumers to submit PII, sharing the consumers' PII with third parties, and making it difficult, if not impossible, for consumers to find out to what extent their PII is being spread around the Internet is a toxic mix of practices that can only hurt and certainly not foster the growth of trust on the Internet.

The United States offers very limited protection against Internet users' PII collection and distribution to third parties. That is not to say that Congress has provided no protections concerning the collection of Internet users' PII. For example, children under the age of 13 are protected under the federal Children's Online Privacy Protection Act (COPPA)[79] and the Gramm-Leach-Bliley Act (GLBA)[80] requires financial institutions to provide comprehensible privacy policies and an opt-out clause before disseminating PII.[81] However, most consumer PII is not adequately protected by the law. Web sites are free to use PII without providing clear privacy policies.[82] Since online businesses are primarily concerned with turning a profit and not with protecting the best interests of consumers, they use visitors' PII in the most profitable ways they can. If businesses are allowed by law to make their privacy policies vague and to sell visitors' PII to third parties, there is no reason to expect that the industry would rein in the practice as long as it proved profitable. Because the practice is so meshed within the fabric

---

[78] *See* Corey Ciocchetti, *Just Click Submit: The Collection, Dissemination, and Tagging of Personally Identifying Information*, 10 VAND. J. ENT. & TECH. L. 553 (2008).

[79] *See* Children's Online Privacy Protection Act of 1998, 15 U.S.C. §§ 6501–6506 (2000).

[80] *See* Gramm-Leach-Bliley Act of 1999, 15 U.S.C. § 6802(a)–(b) (2000).

[81] *See* Ciocchetti, *supra* note 78, at 609–10.

[82] *See id.* at 609–11.

of e-commerce, it is up to the legislature to put limits on this practice or at least to force online businesses to inform consumers in a clear manner about how their PII will be used. The lack of regulations concerning how our personal information is used by Web sites is a serious barrier to online trust.[83]

The online classified ads company Craigslist[84] demonstrates the best and worst examples of Internet trust. Craigslist was started by Craig Newmark in 1995 as a nonprofit e-mail list designed to notify San Francisco residents of local events.[85] Craigslist evolved into a virtual personal ad service spanning 500 cities in 50 countries, where people can post everything from job openings to tickets for sale to romantic want ads.[86] Craigslist became a for-profit corporation in 1999, and in 2004 eBay acquired 25 percent equity in Craigslist.[87] Craigslist derives its profits by charging fees for job ads in ten cities and for apartment listings in New York City.[88] Craigslist is a powerful and useful tool that relies on the communities that use it. However, even though Craigslist is a very useful tool, some people abuse it, and it has some significant dangers that users have to be aware of. In addition to run-of-the-mill fraud,[89] Craigslist has been used to facilitate many types of illegal and morally reprehensible activities. These activities include the solicitation of underage prostitutes[90] and soliciting the services of a hit man,[91] and in one case a couple may have attempted to use the site to sell their newborn baby.[92] Verification is another major problem on Craigslist.

---

[83] Studies show that Americans resent the freedom of companies to do whatever they want with their personal information and that people are becoming more unwilling to spend money and submit personal information online due to lack of trust. *See id.* at 557.

[84] http://www.craigslist.org.

[85] *See* Craigslist Factsheet, http://www.craigslist.org/about/factsheet.html (last visited Sept. 6, 2008).

[86] *Id.*

[87] *Id.*

[88] Craigslist charges $25 for job ads in cities including Boston and Chicago, and $75 for job ads in San Francisco. *See id.*

[89] *See* Craigslist—About Scams, *supra* note 62.

[90] *See* Ethan Baron, *Five Girls in Care Have Been Selling Sex on Craigslist, Police Say,* Province, May 9, 2008, *available at* http://www.canada.com/theprovince/news/story.html?id=c1e6d15c-21d9-4619-ada5-f954a0367129.

[91] A Michigan woman placed an ad on Craigslist offering $5,000 for the murder of the wife of a man she met online. *See* Matthew Philips, *I Need a Hit Man. Now.,* Newsweek, Feb. 11, 2008, *available at* http://www.newsweek.com/id/107602.

[92] The couple who put an ad up for the sale of their newborn later claimed it was only a hoax and were arrested on charges of mischief, which were dropped. *See* Bob Heye, *Man in Trouble over Craigslist Ad with Baby for Sale,* KATU.com, Mar. 27, 2008, http://www.katu.com/news/local/17036956.html.

Users can pose as other persons and place malicious ads that can cause embarrassment and worse to others.[93]

4. The Role of Law in Support of Trusting

Under certain circumstances, the reliability of trusted persons, institutions, and other intermediaries cannot be fully supported by the trusted parties themselves. There comes a point when the parties will not interact because their costs of verification and proof of trustworthiness will exceed their joint benefits from the transaction. In these circumstances, legal backing is necessary.[94] Law offers benefits to both parties. It offers trusting people reduced risks by preventive regulation of institutions and intermediaries, before the fact, and compensation as well as punishing violators, after the fact. Law offers trusted persons a "brand name" guarantee of their trustworthiness, which may be too costly for trusted persons to create or buy in the markets. These supports for trusting are financed not by private sector interested persons, but by all taxpayers. Hence, the cost of maintaining a trusting system as a whole, in addition to the users of trust relationships, is subsidized and distributed among a large group through government intermediation. Further, law strengthens norms of behavior, and reduces the cost of enforcement. People become trustworthy through habit, with a lower threat of punishment.

Trust verification, especially verification by third parties, is layered. The first layer is composed of direct trusting relationships. The second layer, in lieu of or in addition to personal trust, consists of market verifiers. The third layer is composed of verifying the verifiers: the law. Law regulates trusted persons and intermediaries as well as market verifiers, who establish the trustworthiness of others.[95]

Ultimately, third-party regulatory institutions, such as BBB*OnLine* and TRUSTe, require the backing of law in order to effectively serve their purpose.[96]

---

[93] One couple placed an ad on Craigslist posing as a man they had previously burgled, offering to give away everything in his house, in order to cover the tracks of their burglary. *See* Teresa Blackman, *Cruel Craigslist Hoax Was Elaborate Burglary Coverup, Police Say*, KGW.COM, Apr. 1, 2008, http://www.kgw.com/news-local/stories/kgw_040108_news_craigslist_hoax_arrest.1fa31526.html.

[94] Market verifiers can offer verification at a reduced rate relative to personal time, and the law, through a requirement for insurance, examinations, and other preventive measures, can ensure either that the money will not be converted or that (for example) a bank manager is competent. Trusted private sector qualifiers, however, must also prove their trustworthiness. The law regulates the most trusted private sector qualifiers, such as lawyers and accountants.

[95] *See* Hadfield, *supra* note 68, at 175–76.

[96] BBB*OnLine* and TRUSTe rely on the government and the courts as a last resort if firms do not accept their proposed solutions. *See* Jay P. Kesan, *Private Internet Governance*, 35 LOY. U. CHI. L.J. 87 (2003).

The law can regulate intermediaries more effectively than individuals. Intermediaries are often less mobile than individuals and their number is smaller.[97] As the size of private sector actors and intermediaries increases, they are likely to be the first-tier gatekeepers and enforcers of the law within their operational territories, including international enforcement.[98] Mergers of banks and businesses are usually accompanied by stricter requirements for self-regulation, control of illegal acts within the organizations, and trustworthiness towards customers. Professional private sector gatekeepers, such as accountants, are subject to increasingly strict regulation as they testify to the trustworthiness of businesses in real space and on the Internet. In contrast, individuals' costs of establishing the trustworthiness of institutions and other specialized intermediaries are very high. Even though the number of intermediaries is small, they are composed of many individuals and their internal activities are not open to individual customers. More importantly, individuals cannot adopt preventive measures to ensure the intermediaries' trustworthiness even though the risks that individuals take, in entrusting their property to institutions, may be very high.

As the importance of the role of intermediaries increases on the Internet, the importance of law in reducing the customers' risks and increasing the trustworthiness of the intermediaries increases. In reaction to consumers' concerns and Congressional prodding, industries began to establish best practices with respect to privacy issues. While customers may rely on some industries' best practices, for financial intermediaries best practices were held insufficient. The danger of losing public trust is too great and the consequences too grave. Further, the law is most important when the public voices its concern on particular issues.

After recognizing the importance of intermediary regulation on the Internet, the next question is: what form will this regulation take, and how best should it be implemented? Ronald Mann proposes three different types of potential remedies: a tort remedy, a takedown regime, and a hotlist regime, which could be imposed against online intermediaries under different circumstances.[99] The utilization of traditional tort remedy would give intermediaries the most incentive to act carefully.

The recent case of *Tiffany v. eBay*[100] highlights many of the problems facing e-commerce as well as important issues of online trust and

---

[97] *See* Ronald J. Mann, *Emerging Frameworks for Policing Internet Intermediaries*, J. Internet L., Dec. 2006, at 1.

[98] *See id.* at 5–6.

[99] *See id.* at 6 .

[100] Tiffany (NJ) Inc. v. eBay, Inc., No. 04 Civ. 4607, 2008 WL 2755787 (S.D.N.Y. July 14, 2008).

responsibility. Tiffany was justifiably upset about the large amount of counterfeit Tiffany goods that were being sold on auctions hosted on eBay's Web site, and did not find eBay's reaction to the problem to be sufficiently effective. In response to the problem Tiffany made demands to eBay, which eBay refused to meet.[101] In 2004, Tiffany sued eBay for "direct and contributory infringement of Tiffany's trademarks by virtue of the assistance that it provides to, and the profits it derives from, individuals who sell counterfeit Tiffany goods on eBay."[102] At its core, this case was about who should bear the burden of policing the sale of trademarked goods: the intermediary that hosts the transactions or the holder of the trademark?[103] The court found that the holder of a trademark (Tiffany) should bear the burden of policing the transactions, even if it is more cost effective for the intermediary (eBay) to do so.[104] This is not to say that Internet intermediaries cannot be held responsible for the infringement of trademarks by third parties on their Web sites.[105] EBay could have been held liable for contributory trademark infringement if it continued to supply its services to a seller that it knew or had reason to know was infringing on Tiffany.[106] EBay was not found to be liable for contributory trademark infringement because it neither facilitated nor turned a blind eye to the sale of counterfeit Tiffany goods. EBay used its own antifraud engine and worked with Tiffany through its verified rights owner (VeRO) program[107] to take down postings of sellers believed to be selling counterfeit Tiffany goods.[108]

On the Internet, financial intermediaries need a higher degree of public trust, as they are eager to cut their costs by establishing Internet communications with customers. Hence, Congress directed regulators to impose rules of confidentiality on financial intermediaries.[109] On November 13, 2000, the Securities and Exchange Commission put into effect a rule that restricts broker-dealers', investment companies', and

---

[101] These demands included the institution of a "five-or-more rule" in which eBay would ban any seller who was selling five or more pieces of Tiffany jewelry, *see id.* at *14 .

[102] *See id.* at *2.

[103] *See id.* at *1.

[104] *See id.* at *47.

[105] "One who distributes a device with the object of promoting its use to infringe copyright, as shown by clear expression or other affirmative steps taken to foster infringement, is liable for the resulting acts of infringement by third parties." *See* Metro-Goldwyn-Mayer Studios Inc. v. Grokster Ltd., 545 U.S. 913, 919 (2005).

[106] *See* Tiffany (NJ) Inc. v. eBay, Inc., No. 04 Civ. 4607, 2008 WL 2755787 at *1 (S.D.N.Y. July 14, 2008) (citing Inwood Labs., Inc. v. Ives Labs., Inc., 456 U.S. 844, 854 (1982)).

[107] *See* eBay, How eBay Protects Intellectual Property (VeRO), http://pages.ebay.com/help/tp/programs-vero-ov.html (last visited Dec. 10, 2008).

[108] *Tiffany*, 2008 WL 2755787 at *9.

[109] *See* Gramm-Leach-Bliley Act § 504, 15 U.S.C. § 6804 (2000) (requiring specified federal agencies to adopt rules restricting the ability of certain financial institutions to "disclose nonpublic personal information about consumers").

registered investment advisers' ability to utilize customers' personal nonpublic information.[110] Bank regulators enacted similar rules.[111]

The Internet has both increased and decreased the cost of law enforcement. It is unclear what the net costs are. The increased costs are caused by the global impact of the Internet beyond state boundaries. The decrease is based mainly on ease of communication, such as consumers' complaints, information from other agencies and other countries, and technical innovations, such as surfing the Internet for fraudulent advertising.[112]

The FTC operates a program called "Surf Days" in which employees of various agencies surf the Internet looking for Web sites containing solicitations, which likely violate the law.[113] The FTC also operates the "Consumer Sentinel Network," which allows participating law enforcement access to a database of complaints given to the FTC from consumers and participating organizations including the BBB.[114] These programs utilize the benefits of the Internet, such as ease of searching and instantaneous communication, to help law enforcement.

The Internet and the law affect each other. For example, the contract rule of caveat emptor is sufficient to create trusting among buyers and sellers in face-to-face relationships, but not in e-mail communications. Hence, contract doctrine may change and become more "fiduciary-like" and customer friendly. The requirement to tell the truth and be reliable will not be linked to the parties' explicit agreements, but to the default rules that underlie fiduciary law or to stronger fairness concepts in contract law. These may creep into, and create, the "contract law of the Internet." Not only will these rules reflect best practices of industries doing business on the Internet, but they also will be recognized as crucial to the development of e-business, and as such, acquire the power and weight sufficient to change legal doctrine.

---

[110] Privacy of Consumer Financial Information (Regulation S-P), Exchange Act Release No. 42,974 (June 22, 2000), 65 Fed. Reg. 40,334 (June 29, 2000) (codified as amended at 17 C.F.R. pt. 248 (2008)).

[111] Surf Days are days when staff members from certain governmental and private agencies band together and surf the Internet for suspicious Web sites. The suspicious sites are downloaded as evidence and an e-mail warning is sent to the Web sites that explains the law and links them to the FTC's Web site. After a short period of time has passed law enforcement teams visit the sites to see if the suspicious behavior has been suspended. Between 20 and 70 percent of sites that receive the e-mails end up complying with the warnings. *See* Privacy of Consumer Financial Information, 65 Fed. Reg. 35,162 (June 1, 2000) (codified at 12 C.F.R. pt. 332 (2008)).

[112] For a discussion on various cost reduction methods in prosecuting Internet fraud cases, see Patrick E. Corbett, *Prosecuting the Internet Fraud Case Without Going Broke*, 76 MISS. L.J. 841 (2008).

[113] *See* Eric Carlson, *Phishing for Elderly Victims: As the Elderly Migrate to the Internet Fraudulent Schemes Targeting Them Follow*, 14 ELDER L.J. 423 (2006).

[114] http://www.ftc.gov/sentinel.

5. The Role of Technology in Support of Trusting

Technology has helped reduce customers' risks by eliminating the need to send card account information over the Internet directly to sellers. While the solution is not yet certain, it seems clear that the issue must be resolved if consumers are to consider the Internet as their main form of communication with businesses.

In some situations, enforcing the law against violations on the Internet may be as easy as, or even easier than, enforcing the law in real space. In recognition that "code is law," as Professor Lawrence Lessig argues, government may regulate certain aspects of Internet operations through code—the means of Internet communication.[115] It is likely that the government will use this method to fight against serious crimes, which the Internet greatly facilitates. This method raises issues of government accountability that are beyond the scope of this paper. But technology and government protection can prompt distrust and eliminate some trusting behavior, as Professors Lessig and Helen Nissenbaum note.[116]

The solutions devised to date are operational, technological, and organizational. On the operational and organizational side, experts suggest that consumers avoid some forms of payment on the Internet, such as debit cards. These cards resemble cash and are too risky. Processes, such as the process by which credit cards are settled, may have to change. Credit card transactions that follow real world processes, from the merchant to a merchant processor and then to a credit card processing association, expose the parties to risks from thieves. Among others, a safer approach is to let the merchant directly query the credit-card-issuing bank for payment authorization. Non-face-to-face merchants are required to take an additional step when they authorize a purchase. Businesses are using different payment systems for online shopping, such as digital certificates. There are digital identity services and technical forms of authentication that help reduce consumers' risk. Non-technical solutions are also recommended, such as the use of employees for internal controls, response to possible threats and risks, and the hiring of experts.

On the technological side, businesses are adopting technical solutions to protect against third-party attacks on the Internet business. These include antispamming software and filters against "denial of service attacks." Most companies have installed secure sockets layer (SSL) mechanisms to protect Web transactions.[117] Unfortunately, phishers

---

[115] *See* Lawrence Lessig, Code and Other Laws of Cyberspace (1999); Lawrence Lessig, *Preface to a Conference on Trust*, B.U. L. Rev. 329 (2001).

[116] *See* Lessig, *supra* note 115, and Helen Nissenbaum, *Securing Trust Online: Wisdom or Oxymoron?* 81 B.U. L. Rev. 635 (2001).

[117] *See* Peter P. Swire, *Trustwrap: The Importance of Legal Rules to Electronic Commerce and Internet Privacy*, 54 Hastings L.J. 847 (2003).

have discovered ways to acquire SSL certificates and thereby create a false sense of security by displaying the padlock icon, which appears on the browser bar when a Web site has an SSL certificate, on their fraudulent Web sites.[118] Businesses injured by harmful misinformation that frightens customers away use trusted sources to combat these harmful effects. In addition to having SSL certifications, Internet businesses often utilize trusted third parties, such as VeriSign, to serve as another source of authentication for consumers. So rather than just relying on the padlock on their browser bars, careful consumers can click on the VeriSign seal and receive real time updates on the status of the Web site's SSL certification, and confirmation that the site is what it claims to be and not a fake designed by a phisher to steal their personal information.[119] The important point is that corrections come from a trusted source. And, of course, some businesses choose not to disclose the problems they have, but to simply correct them.

Online dispute resolution (ODR) is a growing field with a plethora of tools and services that can be used to foster online trust. ODR can best be described as any method of alternative dispute resolution, such as mediation or arbitration, that utilizes the Internet.[120] While traditional legal remedies are important tools in the upholding of online trust, some problems are best solved through alternative means. Recent numbers show that the average transaction on the Internet is approximately $146.00; considering the costs and effort of pursuing legal remedies for disputes regarding Internet transactions, it is simply not worth it for most people to seek legal recourse in online transaction situations.[121] This knowledge combined with the frequency of online scams makes the use and evolution of different forms of ODR critical to the maintenance of an online culture that can sustain trust. EBay's online mediation service SquareTrade illustrates the impact an ODR system can have in maintaining a trusting online environment. From February 2000 to June 2004, SquareTrade resolved over 1,500,000 disputes.[122] A large number of these disputes would not have been settled without SquareTrade or some other form of ODR, and thousands of

---

[118] The problem of fake SSL certificates is being combated by the introduction of a new form of SSL certification called Extended Validation Secure Socket Layer certification (EV SSL), which adds a green bar in addition to the familiar padlock to verify the safety of a Web site. *See* Byron Achohido, *Don't Do Business Online Without the Green Bar,* USA Today, June 6, 2008, http://blogs.usatoday.com/technologylive/2008/06/dont-do-busines.html.

[119] *See* VeriSign UK Ltd., Establish Trust to Protect and Grow Your Online Business, http://www.verisign.co.uk/static/029631.pdf (last visited Dec. 10, 2008).

[120] *See* Philippe Gilliéron, *From Face-to-Face to Screen-to-Screen: Real Hope or True Fallacy?* 23 Ohio St. J. on Disp. Resol. 301 (2008).

[121] *See id.*

[122] *See id.*

consumers presumably would have been left even more dissatisfied with their online auction experiences.

Digital identities (DIDs) also play an important role in the cultivation and maintenance of Internet trust going forward. Identification and verification are difficult to achieve on the Internet, which in turn makes the development of trust difficult to achieve as well. When interacting with others in the physical world, we use our real names, look at each other's faces, and can show government-issued identification. On the Internet we are primarily identified through various pseudonyms, which are usually only verified through the use of single passwords. The relative anonymity and lack of security with respect to this system seriously hinder trust relations on the Internet because people have virtually no way of verifying who the person behind the pseudonym is. However, there has been progress in the realm of verification and DIDs that should prove conducive to trust building on the Internet. One advance that has been gaining steam in certain areas is the use of biometrics in identification.[123] By requiring a fingerprint or retinal scan in addition to a password, a physical connection is made with the user that provides a very solid form of verification in that it cannot be easily replicated or stolen by a third party or given away by the user. Another method to improve the authenticity of DIDs that has been proposed is to make a "second layer" of identification on the Internet referred to as "Identity 2.0."[124] Instead of carrying multiple usernames and passwords, users under Identity 2.0 would have a single online identification that they would use for banking, shopping, e-mailing, and other online activities. Under this model, DIDs would be closely tied to the individual user and would produce an accurate online reputation to reflect the user's dealings on the Internet.

With every passing year the Internet becomes further integrated into our lives. Trust on the Internet becomes increasingly important. This is especially true in the case of Internet voting, which may play a very important role in the future of democracy. Internet voting has already been used widely by corporations for the purpose of shareholder voting,[125] and millions use the Internet for extremely important activities such as banking and paying taxes. However, it must be recognized that the use of Internet voting for democratic elections would bring certain problems with it. While current voting methods are not 100 percent fraud-proof, they have earned the trust of the voters. The Internet opens up whole new possibilities of fraud, verification problems, and exclusivity, which could have potentially devastating

---

[123] *See* Aresty, *supra* note 54 at 154–55.

[124] *See id.* at 153–54.

[125] *See* Joshua F. Clowers, *I E-Vote, U I-Vote, Why Can't We All Just Vote?!: A Survey of the Changing Face of the American Election*, 42 GONZ. L. REV. 61 (2006).

effects on an election. One hurdle that Internet voting would have to overcome is the current "digital divide."[126] That is, while in theory Internet balloting would make voting more accessible for the masses, it would really only serve to further widen the gap between the rich and the poor voters, as the rich are far more likely to have Internet access. Beyond this problem are the various new security issues that would crop up. A recurring theme in the discussion of Internet trust is the problem of verification, which would be especially problematic in the context of Internet voting. Since the voting would be taking place away from a polling station, there would also be greater opportunity for voter bribery or coercion, as a third party could be present while the voter cast his votes.[127] Lastly, there is the ever-present danger of hackers manipulating voter data or otherwise disrupting the system.[128] Even if these problems can be dealt with, as long as there is the public perception that Internet voting is less trustworthy than the current voting forms, Internet voting should be refined to put to rest the public's doubts.[129] If trust cannot be established in Internet voting to the extent that it is already established in current voting procedures, then it should not be adopted.[130]

6. Conclusion

In real space and on the Internet, trust and non-trust pose the same issues. The ways people come to trust in real space and cyberspace differ, however. That is mainly because the benefits, costs, and risks in Internet interaction have changed and have been reallocated among

---

[126] The "digital divide" is "an invisible chasm sitting between those in society who have the means to own—or at least have access to—a computer, BlackBerry, or mobile phone with Internet connectivity and those who do not." See David M. Thompson, *Is the Internet a Viable Threat to Representative Democracy?* 2008 DUKE L. & TECH. REV. 10, 26.

[127] See Clowers, *supra* note 125, at 83.

[128] Security patches are implemented in response to threats, and Internet security is in a constant state of catch-up with the latest dangers. Since there is an inevitable lag between the aggressors and the defenders of Internet security, some feel that Internet voting will never be a safe or viable alternative to traditional methods. See id. at 86–87.

[129] Absentee ballots have a lot of the same security issues as Internet voting, such as coercion and fraud, yet they are for the most part trusted and have been widely accepted and used by the populace. See Bryan Mercurio, *Democracy in Decline: Can Internet Voting Save the Electoral Process?* 22 J. MARSHALL J. COMPUTER & INFO. L. 409 (2004).

[130] "If voting technology mediates the relation between people and democracy in such a way that the experience of trust and stability is reduced, for whatever reason, the actions that are invited are political passivity on the one hand, and protest and obstruction on the other." See W. Pieters & M. J. Becker, *Ethics of E-Voting: An Essay on Requirements and Values in Internet Elections, in* ETHICS OF NEW INFORMATION TECHNOLOGY: PROCEEDINGS OF THE SIXTH INTERNATIONAL CONFERENCE OF COMPUTER ETHICS: PHILOSOPHICAL ENQUIRY (Philip Bray, Frances Grodzinsky & Lucas Introna eds., 2005).

sellers and buyers. The costs have shifted to sellers in order to achieve the same goal—establishing trusting relationships on which economic activity depends.

The model that emerges is that of "layered trusting supports." No one layer can create a culture of trust. Reputable institutions and intermediaries, verifiers, and providers of trust services contribute to public trusting. But more of them are needed on the Internet, and the law must continue to provide the backbone of legitimacy for their trustworthiness. Perhaps stronger support is needed on certain issues. For example, the Internet offers grand-scale opportunities to destroy software in which communications and ideas are stored. To prevent such destruction we may need a worldwide meta-norm. Today, destructive hackers are not just the "smart kids" who playfully show off their genius.

Hackers have become vital centerpieces in organized crime and terrorist groups, both as weapons and sources of funding through frauds such as identity theft.[131] As hacking has been increasingly integrated into larger criminal schemes, focus has intensified on finding ways not only to provide greater security on the Internet but also to change the culture that nurtures and develops these hackers.

Against such damaging games, there is no strong norm that brings a general revulsion. If children were told, with their first computer, that computers are for creating, not for destroying, and develop this attitude as they develop the inhibition about playing with matches to avoid destruction—while recognizing that fire is good, as the parents show by lighting candles and the fireplace—then over time a meta-norm can rise to be enforced not only by governments but also by the public. As the meta-norm becomes stronger, law's interference can become weaker. But this is a goal for the future. We can begin by using the tools, based on the elements of benefits, costs, and risks, and adjusting them to the new Internet environment.

Tamar Frankel, Professor of Law
Boston University School of Law
765 Commonwealth Ave., Room 1144
Boston, MA 02115
Phone: (617) 353-3773
Fax: (617) 353-2444
E-mail: Tfrankel@bu.edu

---

[131] *See* Michael Ena, *Securing Online Transactions: Crime Prevention Is the Key*, 35 FORDHAM URB. L. J. 147 (2008).

CHAPTER 2

Business Ethics Perspectives on International Negotiations

Robert E. McNulty
CENTER FOR BUSINESS ETHICS, BENTLEY UNIVERSITY
WALTHAM, MASSACHUSETTS

W. Michael Hoffman
CENTER FOR BUSINESS ETHICS, BENTLEY UNIVERSITY
WALTHAM, MASSACHUSETTS

1. Introduction

1.1 Negotiation from the Perspective of Business Ethics

The purpose of business ethics has been to help in the positive transformation of business. Negotiation is crucial to this process because negotiators have a critical role as engineers of business change. In this paper we will suggest that business ethics has been crucial in the reconceptualization of the practice of business, and that as part of this rethinking of the nature of business, we also need to think anew about the process of negotiation. In this regard, we see negotiation not as a form of hostile struggle, but as a process of guided transformation, the power of which can be greatly enhanced when conducted according to sound principles of business ethics.

The practice of business and negotiation is rendered more problematic when we move into the international realm. Our judgment becomes less certain when we are dealing with people whose customs are foreign to us. Whenever our understanding is clouded, we open the door to potential problems. To minimize the risks associated with transcultural negotiation, skillful negotiators will seek to learn as much as they can about the culture and values of their co-negotiator and work from a space of shared aspiration so as to arrive at a mutually beneficial outcome. The possibility of arriving at such an outcome is greatly enhanced when the negotiators recognize that there is a common ethical ground that they share with people from around the world. It is this shared ethical common ground that is central to business ethics and that greatly improves the chances for successful international negotiations.

2. On the Ethics of Business

The contribution of business ethics has not been (as some might think) to stand with moral imperiousness and scold business for its transgressions. To the contrary, the great value of business ethics has been to help business leaders see that their job is not to be perpetuators of the tried-and-true business practices, but to guide businesses to flourish as responsive and responsible social/economic actors.

2.1 Learning the Lessons of Business Ethics

Because social change is often imperceptible, many valuable lessons can be overlooked. A striking example of this "proximity blindness" pertains to business ethics. Business ethics began to take shape as a formal discipline in the United States in the mid-1970s and in the intervening years the field has exploded and spread around the world. Today, virtually every major corporation has a code of ethics and an officer responsible for advising the company on matters of ethics and legal compliance.

It is important because we often tend to assume that the way business is conducted today is essentially the same as it was in the past. However, business has changed drastically from its meager roots in bartering on the margins of subsistence to its current form as the engine of a multitrillion-dollar global economy. In this long history, however, the most dramatic and rapid change has occurred over the last few decades since the advent of the discipline of business ethics. A vivid example of this change is illustrated in an article published in 1968 entitled *Is Business Bluffing Ethical?* In this article, which appeared in the prestigious *Harvard Business Review*, the author, Albert Carr, claimed quite brazenly that businesses were perfectly justified in lying, cheating, and bribing, all in the name of achieving business objectives. According to Carr, the ethics of ordinary life were inapplicable to business because the latter was governed by its own "gaming" morality that required the businessman to leave at home the Golden Rule and his commitment to principles such as honesty and fairness. To make his point, Carr quotes a Midwestern executive who had "given a good deal of thought to the question." According to this person, "If the law as written gives a man a wide-open chance to make a killing, he'd be a fool not to take advantage of it. If he doesn't someone else will. There is no obligation on him to stop and consider who is going to get hurt. If the law says he can do it, that's all the justification he needs. There's nothing unethical about that. It's just plain business sense."[1]

---

[1] Albert Z. Carr, *Is Business Bluffing Ethical?* Harv. Bus. Rev., Jan.–Feb. 1968, at 143, 146.

In the same article, Carr goes on to assert the legitimacy of lying on one's résumé, engaging in industrial espionage, and deceptively adulterating the contents of consumer goods in order to increase profits. Carr's view is a clear example of the problem that arises when one attempts to reduce ethics to compliance with the law. He may claim that if an action is not illegal, it is fair game. However, by providing these examples, Carr demonstrates that he himself recognizes that these actions are unethical. He tries to deflect culpability by claiming that personal morality does not apply to business, but the error of this position is evidenced in at least two ways: First, since the publication of this article, people in all sectors of society have squarely turned against such scurrilous behavior. The idea that business operates in a morality-free zone is universally recognized as a self-serving fallacy. Secondly, Carr's position depends on the view that when a person enters an office he abandons his human identity. Not only is this impossible, but this view attributes an autonomy to business that it simply does not have. It is not businesses that make decisions, but people. And, like it or not, because our moral status as human beings is neither suspended nor absolved when we engage in business, the conduct of business occurs always within a moral domain that is integral to our human nature.

2.2 Seeking Normative Standards for Business: The Protocols of Business Ethics

Some have suggested that the idea of "morality" is simply a function of what we like or desire as individuals or as communities. Yet we know that what is good or right to do is often not what we want to do, and that we get in trouble when we give free rein to our wants at the expense of what we know to be right. It is this idea that is behind not only business ethics but also human rights. Indeed, before the field of business ethics was established, it was germinating and taking root in the ideas of universal human rights. Once the concepts of human rights and business ethics took root, they grew in strength and sophistication as they were given new expression in a series of protocols pertaining to the ethical rights and duties of persons and organizations. The following is a list of some prominent codes on the ethical duties of organizations:

2.2.1 The Universal Declaration of Human Rights

The Universal Declaration of Human Rights[2] (UDHR) was adopted by the UN General Assembly in 1948. Although it was not intended specifically to be a guide for the ethical conduct of business or negotiations, it is the most important international expression of the rights that are deemed to apply to all human beings. As such it provides guidance

---

[2] *Available at* http://www.unhchr.ch/udhr.

that can be of direct applicability on what is and is not permissible business activity. For example, the UDHR states that all human beings have the right to freedom, to property, to education, and to work, and that elementary education for all children not only is a right but should be universally compulsory. What is profoundly significant about the UDHR is that it was an expression of moral claims on individuals, organizations, and even countries irrespective of their consent. The Declaration expresses a view in which morality is coextensive with humanity and moral duties apply not only to individuals but also to human institutions including governments and businesses.

2.2.2 The Sullivan Principles

The Sullivan Principles[3] were first published in 1977 by Rev. Leon Sullivan as a way of providing guidance on how international businesses could conduct business in South Africa without supporting the apartheid regime of that time. Then in 1999, with the support of the UN Secretary General Kofi Annan, Sullivan published the Global Sullivan Principles of Social Responsibility. These eight essential principles are as follows:[4]

1. Support universal human rights and, particularly, those of employees, the communities within which businesses operate, and those with whom a business does business.
2. Promote equal opportunity for all employees, and operate without unacceptable worker treatment such as the exploitation of children, physical punishment, female abuse, involuntary servitude, or other forms of abuse.
3. Respect employees' voluntary freedom of association.
4. Compensate employees to enable them to meet at least their basic needs and provide the opportunity to improve their skill and capability in order to raise their social and economic opportunities.
5. Provide a safe and healthy workplace and promote sustainable development.
6. Promote fair competition including respect for intellectual and other property rights, and not offer, pay, or accept bribes.
7. Work to improve the quality of life in the communities in which a business operates and seek to provide training and opportunities for workers from disadvantaged backgrounds.
8. Promote the application of these Principles by those with whom we do business.

---

[3] *Available at* http://muweb.marshall.edu/revleonsullivan/principled/principles.htm.
[4] *See* THE GLOBAL SULLIVAN PRINCIPLES (1999), *available at* http://www.thesullivanfoundation.org/gsp/principles/gsp/default.asp.

2.2.3 The Caux Round Table Principles of Business

The Caux Round Table (CRT) was founded in 1986 as an international network of business leaders working to promote a moral capitalism for a fair, free, and transparent global society. Central to the CRT are seven philosophical propositions,[5] followed by six stakeholder principles. The essence of the propositions is as follows:

1. Beyond Shareholders toward Stakeholders
2. Economic and Social Responsibility
3. Beyond the Letter of the Law toward Trust
4. Beyond Trade Friction toward Cooperation
5. Beyond Isolation toward World Community
6. Beyond Environmental Protection toward Enhancement
7. Beyond Profit toward Peace

The central business "stakeholders" are defined by the CRT as:

1. Customers
2. Employees
3. Owners/Investors
4. Suppliers
5. Competitors
6. Communities

The principles are general and aspirational, and include tools for self-assessment.[6]

2.2.4 The United Nations Global Compact

The United Nations Global Compact was announced in 1999 by then United Nations Secretary General Kofi Annan, in order to encourage businesses to align their operations and strategies with ten universally accepted principles in the areas of human rights, labor, the environment, and anti-corruption. These principles are as follows:[7]

Human Rights
Principle 1: Businesses should support and respect the protection of internationally proclaimed human rights; and
Principle 2: make sure that they are not complicit in human rights abuses.

---

[5] *See* CAUX ROUND TABLE, PRINCIPLES FOR BUSINESS (1994), *available at* http://www.cauxroundtable.org/principles.html.

[6] Kenneth E. Goodpaster, *The Caux Round Table Principles: Corporate Moral Reflection in a Global Business Environment, in* GLOBAL CODES OF ETHICS: AN IDEA WHOSE TIME HAS COME (Oliver F. Williams ed., 2000).

[7] See THE TEN PRINCIPLES, *available at* http://www.unglobalcompact.org/AboutTheGC/TheTenPrinciples/index.html (last visited Sept. 7, 2008).

Labor Standards	
Principle 3:	Businesses should uphold the freedom of association and the effective recognition of the right to collective bargaining;
Principle 4:	the elimination of all forms of forced and compulsory labor;
Principle 5:	the effective abolition of child labor; and
Principle 6:	the elimination of discrimination in respect of employment and occupation.
Environment	
Principle 7:	Businesses should support a precautionary approach to environmental challenges;
Principle 8:	undertake initiatives to promote greater environmental responsibility; and
Principle 9:	encourage the development and diffusion of environmentally friendly technologies.
Anti-Corruption	
Principle 10:	Businesses should work against corruption in all its forms, including extortion and bribery.

2.2.5 ISO 26000

The International Organization for Standardization (ISO) is currently developing an international standard on social responsibility (SR), which is to be known as ISO 26000. The final form of the ISO SR is not expected to be published until 2010. It is noteworthy that an organization as influential as ISO has included social responsibility among the areas that it is attempting to define. In so doing, ISO is taking a stand that social responsibility is a subject that is neither subjective nor discretionary, but rather something with sufficient definition that international standards can be identified and promulgated.[8]

Two things that all of the proposed standards mentioned above have in common are that they are all voluntary and none of them involve outside certification.

---

[8] See International Organization for Standardization, Social Responsibility, http://isotc.iso.org/livelink/livelink/fetch/2000/2122/830949/3934883/3935096/home.html (last visited Sept. 7, 2008). For an informative discussion of this emerging standard, see Han-Kyun Rho, Assistant Professor, Coll. Bus. Admin., Kookmin Univ., Korea, Understanding the Nature of ISO 26000, Paper prepared for an international conference on Combining Sustainability Management and Governance Structure at Nankai University, China (Dec.7–9, 2007), *available at* http://ssrn.com/abstract=1275586.

3. Universal Dignity: The Foundational Principle of Business Ethics

Since none of the above-listed protocols have the binding force of law and each of them consists in a different set of principles, one might argue that this is evidence that business ethics lacks substance. That view is incorrect for at least two reasons. First of all, the lack of formal certification has no bearing on the ethical validity of these protocols any more than a lack of certification would somehow render gravity less a force of nature. Secondly, an essential characteristic of ethics is that it is a function of our nature as human beings and its validity does not depend on legislation. Murder, slavery, and deception are wrong regardless of what any individual or group says, does, or legislates.

Most importantly, despite the lack of perfect uniformity, what these various protocols demonstrate is that across a broad spectrum of regions, societies, and institutions, a clear and definitive ethical consensus is emerging. We would suggest that these protocols all follow from a foundational principle, which we would express as follows:

> All human beings, irrespective of the ethnicity, gender, economic or social status, or any other factor, have intrinsic worth or dignity by virtue of their being a person, i.e., their humanity, and no individual or group has the authority or capacity to deny them of their inherent dignity.

Ethics in business as expressed through the various protocols, as well as other branches of professional ethics such as medical ethics or legal ethics, gives expression in a variety of ways to this foundational principle.

Inasmuch as negotiation can be considered an integral business practice, the following principles should also be seen as applicable to the ethical conduct of negotiation.

3.1 Some Essential Ramifications of the Ethics of Universal Dignity

Let us look at some important ideas that follow from the principle of universal dignity. As we will see later in this paper, all of these ideas are relevant in the rethinking of negotiation from the perspective of ethics.

3.1.1 From a Shareholder to Stakeholder Model: Reconceptualizing Business

As we have stated, in recent decades the general understanding of the nature of business has changed significantly, and the gist of this change is captured in the shift from the shareholder to stakeholder model of business. Let us take a quick look at this.

It was only a few decades ago that the Nobel Prize–winning econo-mist Milton Friedman infamously gave voice to the prevailing business misconception of that time, which was that the sole responsibility of a business is to maximize profits for its shareholders.[9] This view is based on an incomplete understanding of business that fails to recognize that businesses depend on and are responsible to a collection of groups, all of whom have a stake in it. Responding to this view, R. Edward Free-man articulated the "stakeholder" model of the corporation, in which the corporation was recognized as a social organization in which a variety of groups have significant and authentic stakes in a business, to some extent necessitating businesses to conduct their affairs in such a way as to respect its community of stakeholders.[10]

The beauty and strength of stakeholder theory is that it recognizes businesses as entities embedded in a complex web of social dependen-cies. Moreover, in the idea of "stakeholder" we recognize a worth or dignity that applies to the various members of the business ecology who are affected by the business's actions. With the globalization of business, we can see in the stakeholder theory an implied affirmation of the dignity of all people, be they customers, employees, sharehold-ers, or even competitors, not only at home but also around the world.

3.1.2 Injustice and "the Other"

The idea of the universal dignity that follows from our shared human-ity is an ancient and universal insight. However, one of the predom-inant characteristics of moral transgressions is that they often arise from regarding "the other" as wholly different from oneself or one's group and as such lacking in the characteristics of humanity. When one strips another of his or her status as a fellow person, the "other" is deemed unworthy of moral reciprocity. The universal dignity of per-sonhood is thereby proscribed and selectively applied to oneself or one's own community, nation, ethnic group, etc. This unwillingness to acknowledge the shared worth of others is one of the primary sources of injustice and often follows from a collective resentment associated with past conflicts or the desire to justify accruing to oneself or one's group unfair access to resources.

The business ethics outlook firmly rejects this perspective and never loses sight of the fact that no matter how intense the competi-tion, our counterpart in business is no less of a human being than ourselves, and, as such, is worthy of our respect.

---

[9] Milton Friedman, *The Social Responsibility of Business Is to Increase Its Profits*, N.Y. TIMES, Sept. 13, 1970, Magazine, at 32.

[10] *See* R. EDWARD FREEMAN, STRATEGIC MANAGEMENT: A STAKEHOLDER APPROACH (1984).

3.1.3 Aiming at Human Flourishing

Our moral awareness is often expressed in negative terms as prohibitions on deception and unfair action. But ethics is equally concerned with the positive manifestations of morality, or that which is deemed "good." The term "good" is used in a variety of ways, but in this context, given the shared dignity and worth of all, we understand good to be that which constitutes an optimal outcome for all. This may seem to be an overly idealistic aspiration, but we would suggest that, to the contrary, it is a simple and practical idea, the essence of which is this: In seeking our own best interests we should never lose sight of the validity of the interests of other. To put it otherwise, we see "the good" as a commitment to our own personal flourishing in the context of the shared interest we have with others in their own personal and community flourishing. Applied to business, this implies that our work should not be solely in our own interest but be respectful of the interests of others as well.

3.1.4 Transparency

The development of civilization has been possible in large part because of the remarkable capacity human beings have for communication. Our communicative capacities are an essential aspect of our human experience. Therefore, when one communicates in a way that deliberately misrepresents what one understands to be the truth, that is a violation of the dignity of another because it undermines our ability to rely on the communicative process that is essential for all human cooperation. Applied to commerce, this implies that business should be conducted as transparently as possible. While there are legitimate trade secrets, most information about corporate dealings, especially as pertains to finances, must be publicly disclosed in order to safeguard against corruption. Without transparency, businesses run the risk of showing unjust favoritism or discrimination, or at least the appearance of such unjust actions. Transparency is needed to maintain much-needed trust necessary for healthy and strong business-stakeholder relations, without which businesses cannot flourish.

4. Applying Business Ethics Perspectives to Negotiations

Negotiation is one of life's crucial skills: from birth, children negotiate with their parents; on a macro level, human civilization has been shaped in large part through the negotiations of our civic leaders; and when faced with the seeming inevitabilities of fate, man has sought to negotiate with God. It is in business, however, where negotiation has taken on a particularly important and institutionalized role—negotiation is one of the vital organs of business. Good negotiation skills are central to business, and without them, business will fail. This simple idea, however, is complicated by the fact that business has changed significantly in recent decades and these changes are relevant to the practice of negotiation. Why? Because just as business was earlier misrepresented as a kind of economic warfare that was somehow situated outside the moral domain, so too negotiation has been described as an essentially amoral activity.

We will argue that just as business is unable to escape from the moral domain, the same holds true for negotiation. Let us provide a provisional definition of ethical negotiation:

> Ethical negotiation is a process of guided transformation that occurs through dialogical exchange aiming at an optimal agreement that responds fairly to the co-negotiators' aspirations as persons of equivalent moral worth.

This is a view consistent with the understanding of business ethics. We will explicate and defend this view on negotiation in the section after the next.

In this section, we will first consider some well-established views on negotiation and suggest that these views suffer from attributing to the process of negotiation characteristics that are not essential to it. We will then identify what we see as the essential characteristics of negotiation, and consider how the potential of negotiation as a process of guided transformation is greatly enhanced when it is conducted in light of ethics.

4.1 Standard Views on Negotiation

There are many definitions of negotiation, but the interpretations provided in a well-known article by Roy Lewicki and Robert J. Robinson is representative of a standard interpretation.

> Lex and Sebenius define negotiation as "a process of potentially opportunistic interaction by which two or more parties, with some apparent conflict, seek to do better through jointly decided action than they could otherwise." Lewicki, Litterer, Minton and Saunders state that a negotiation situation has the following parameters: (a) two or more parties who are interdependent; (b) a conflict of interest; (c) the parties are attempting to use one or more form of influence to obtain a "better" set of outcomes; and (d) the parties expect that there will be some "give and take," or concession making, to resolve their conflict.[11]

In this article, Lewicki and Robinson state that "those who have written about effective negotiation strategies have often suggested that some types of dishonest behavior may be appropriate or even necessary

---

[11] Roy J. Lewicki and Robert J. Robinson, *Ethical and Unethical Bargaining Tactics: An Empirical Study*, 17 J. Bus. Ethics 665, 665–66 (1998).

to be an effective negotiator."[12] They then state, "Information is one of the most dominant sources of power, particularly in negotiation. Information control enhances power. Since negotiation is primarily a process of exchanging and communicating this information in a persuasive manner, the opportunities for unethical conduct are ones of dishonest communication."[13] They go on to identify the various forms of lying that negotiators use that they affirm constitute a continuum ranging from "ethically appropriate" to "ethically inappropriate." The tactics they identify are:

1. Misrepresentation of one's position to an opponent
2. Bluffing
3. Falsification
4. Deception
5. Selective disclosure or misrepresentation to constituencies.[14]

Besides the various forms of lying, another group of tactics negotiators may draw on is "inappropriate information collection," which includes such activities as bribery, seduction, and threats. Although these tactics were recognized as representing a range of available tactics, most were deemed morally unacceptable to the participants in the study.

This article and its five-point analysis are both widely referred to in the negotiation literature. Here and in many other pieces we find scholars attributing to negotiation characteristics that are not essential to it. Let us review some common associations:

1. **Hostility:** Negotiation is frequently described as a hostile struggle. However, although negotiation may involve a struggle, it need not be hostile. To the contrary, it could be an amicable exchange.
2. **Opponents:** Many scholars describe the negotiators as "opponents." This implies hostility, but as we just asserted, hostility is not an essential attribute of negotiation.
3. **Deception:** To some degree, all of the negotiating techniques described involve either some form of deception or coercion (see below). Although deception is seen as pervasive to the negotiation process, it is inimical to negotiation because it destroys trust, and in so doing imposes extra costs on the negotiators, as they will have to expend extra effort trying to discern the veracity of their co-negotiators.
4. **Coercion:** Negotiation is described as frequently involving coercion. Coercion is a strong form of hostility that involves threatening the security of one's counterpart. However, rather than being essential to negotiation, coercion is antithetical

---

[12] *Id.* at 665.
[13] *Id.* at 666.
[14] *Id.* at 666–67.

to it, as coercion transforms the encounter between the two negotiators into an exercise in domination.

4.2 Essential Characteristics of Negotiation

When reflecting on negotiation as ethicists, we need to begin by trying to be as clear as possible on the essential constituents of our subject matter. After stripping away common preconceptions, we would suggest that the following are essential characteristics of negotiation.

4.2.1 Dialogical Exchange

Negotiation is a process that involves an exchange. That exchange need not be hostile, but it does necessarily involve the give and take that we associate with "dialog"; thus we say that negotiation is a process that involves a "dialogical exchange."

4.2.2 Exploration and Discovery

In order for the process of negotiation to be a true dialogical exchange, each side should come to understand something new, such as what would constitute an acceptable outcome. Although this exploration might imply a lack of perfect transparency, it need not denote deception, because often the optimal outcome may not be fully understood in advance by either party and instead is something that is discovered in the exploratory process of negotiation.

4.2.3 Co-negotiators

To have a dialogical exchange, there must be two or more parties (individuals or groups of people joined together as corporate entities, such as businesses or governments). Because the relationship between these parties may range from the amicable to the hostile, the emotional quality of the relationship is not essential. What can be said with certainty, however, is that no one can negotiate alone. Negotiation requires at least two parties. The most neutral term to describe these parties, we would suggest, is "co-negotiators."

4.2.4 Aimed at an Agreement

The purpose of negotiation is to achieve some kind of agreement. If one of the co-negotiators does not share in the aim of reaching an agreement, then the exchange may be interesting and informative, but it cannot be considered a negotiation.[15]

---

[15] We should note that if the outcome is not one that is mutually agreed upon, but one that is forced, then the activity should not be considered negotiation but coercion. From this perspective, therefore, there may be various exchanges, which are conducted as if they were negotiations but which in fact are forms of coercion. Ury et al. (*infra* note 16) describe "power" as one approach to negotiation, and while we agree that power is a factor in negotiation, if the use of power does not leave open the possibility of respectful exchange leading to an agreement, the exchange is a negotiation in form only and would more accurately be viewed as structured domination.

4.2.5 Guided Transformation

Bringing these various characteristics together, it can be seen that in the exploratory process of dialogical exchange, the co-negotiators are not simply participating in a conversation, but are directed toward a concrete agreement that will affect both sides. As such, negotiation is a process of "guided transformation."

According to this interpretation of negotiation, we can see it as a kind of "due diligence" in which co-negotiators explore the mutually determined limits of the possible and permissible in order to arrive at a mutual agreement. This view holds true even if negotiations break down. In such a case, what the parties discover is that the expected value of the outcome is deemed insufficient to justify the cost.

In this regard, we can see in negotiation the essence of communication in which the give and take of the dialogical exchange leads the negotiators from a position of relative ignorance to one of greater knowledge and understanding. As such, we see negotiation as a process that provides optimal circumstances for ethical or unethical communication.

4.3 Ethics and the Guiding Parameters of Negotiation

Quite a number of scholars have adopted the heuristic framework proposed by Ury, Brett, and Goldberg (hereinafter, "Ury et al."), according to which negotiations are understood to be carried out along one or more of three parameters, namely, "interests," "rights," and "power."[16] This framework can be very helpful in analyzing the parameters that are at play in motivating negotiators. However, we also would suggest that this analysis does not adequately appreciate the place of ethics in negotiation.

To illustrate their theory Ury et al. give an example of a miner whose boots were stolen. The miner demands that he be reimbursed. The shift boss, however, citing company regulations, refuses. Infuriated, the miner rallies his fellow miners to strike. The mine's superintendent says that under similar circumstances he had replaced the boots and the shift boss should have done the same. According to Ury, the superintendent was negotiating based on "interests," the shift boss relied on "rights," and the disgruntled miner relied on "power." According to Ury et al., the job of the negotiator is to decide on which parameter to choose in trying to negotiate a settlement. To choose among these options, Ury et al. suggest that there are four criteria:

- **Transaction costs**, according to which what is optimal is that which minimizes the cost of disputes

---

[16] William Ury, Jeanne Brett & Stephen Goldberg, Getting Disputes Resolved 3–19 (1988).

- **Satisfaction with outcomes**, which is the mutual satisfaction the parties have with the result
- **Effect on relationship**, which refers to the long-term effect of the negotiation on the relationship
- **Recurrence**, by which is meant the durability of the resolution

By defining "better" in terms of these four characteristics, Ury's criteria are practical, and yet we find them insufficiently sensitive to ethics. Let us take another look at the three guiding parameters he identifies.

4.3.1 Interests

Ury et al. state, "A focus on interests can resolve the problem underlying the dispute more effectively than a focus on rights and power."[17] However, while negotiating competing interests might be cost effective, that does not make it the right position to take.

Let us take an example of a drug dealer and a narcotics officer. The dealer's interest may be in selling as much heroin as possible. The officer's interest is to get heroin entirely off the street. An interests-based negotiation might lead to a compromise of allowing the dealer to sell a portion of his supply. The officer would have succeeded in reducing the sale of heroin, the drug dealer would end up selling much less than he would have, but according to the compromise he might avoid jail time and still earn an adequate amount. However, from the perspective of business ethics, we would see any sale of heroin (outside of its use in legitimate pharmaceutical applications) to be unethical and therefore non-negotiable. One might ethically negotiate various issues with a drug dealer, such as the terms for his exiting the market, rewards for information about his drug network, etc., but such proposals would follow from an understanding not of what was cost-effective but of what was morally good for the various stakeholders, including the drug dealer himself. Given the devastating effects of drug addiction, we would see the officer's compromise as a violation of the worth or dignity of both the buyers and dealers and therefore impermissible.

4.3.2 Rights

Although it may generally seem pragmatic to try to resolve disputes by addressing interests, Ury et al. state that "resolving all disputes by reconciling interests alone is neither possible nor desirable."[18] They state, "Although reconciling interests is generally less costly than determining rights, only adjudication can authoritatively resolve questions of public importance."[19] To illustrate this point, they refer to the 1954

---

[17] *Id.* at 13.
[18] *Id.* at 15.
[19] *Id.* at 17.

Supreme Court case *Brown v. Board of Education*, outlawing racial segregation in public schools. Ury et al. are right that this was a landmark case, but as we see it, what made this case so important was not that it was backed by a particular court, but that it was the morally correct position that overturned previous unjust Jim Crow laws. Both the Jim Crow laws and *Brown v. Board of Education* were examples of adjudication but only the latter had the weight of moral rectitude, and it was the moral strength of this decision and not the fact of adjudication in itself that ensured that this ruling achieved its landmark status.

This case is also illustrative of the fact that when forced to choose between adherence to solid ethical principles and compliance with the law, ethics trumps compliance because it is the job of ethics to serve as the touchstone against which laws are judged to be just or unjust.

4.3.3 Power

Ury et al. recognize that costs associated with settling a dispute by power can be high. A typical example of negotiation by power would be when negotiations break down and the labor union calls for a strike. Ultimately, the outcome of the negotiation is likely to be determined by whichever group has more power: if the determination and financial reserves of labor are sufficient, they may be able to outlast management; otherwise, the advantage would be management's. But here again, while power may determine who will win a particular instance of negotiation, it does not determine whether the negotiations are good or just.

A vivid example of this can be found by contrasting the treaties that ended the First and Second World Wars. After the Allies won the First World War, their power was such that they could virtually dictate the terms of the treaty, which is what they did. These terms were so onerous that they all but ensured that Germany would be humiliated and embittered and primed to seek vengeance. In these negotiations, the seeds for the next world war were sown. By contrast, in the wake of the Second World War, Germany was again defeated. However, in the negotiations that followed, instead of wielding power with impunity, the United States launched the Marshall Plan that aimed at rebuilding Europe, including Germany. In the treaties that followed both wars, the victors negotiated from positions of power. However, in the treaty that ended the First World War, power was used in a way that violated the dignity of the Germans and showed a lack of the compassion that would follow from a spirit of reciprocity. As for the treaty that ended the Second World War, power was wielded in a way that followed from ethical principles of respect and reciprocity. Not only were the economic and political outcomes much better following the Second World War, but the generally respectful manner in which the United States exercised its power in the negotiation and execution of this treaty laid the foundation for a strong and lasting friendship between Germany and the United States.

All three of the parameters identified by Ury, Brett, and Goldberg represent legitimate modes for analyzing negotiations, but we would suggest that interests, rights, and power are all ethically neutral and are in need of ethical criteria in order to be heuristically useful as parameters of negotiation.

4.4 Ethical Negotiation

Bringing these ideas together, we can see that the standard view of negotiation has much in common with the shareholder view of business, according to which the negotiator seeks to serve the interests of his or her side only. And like Albert Carr's view of business as an activity conducted in a morality-free zone, negotiation is often depicted as if it were an essentially amoral activity. By contrast, negotiation from the perspective of business ethics is comparable to the stakeholder view of business. Rather than being amoral, the dialogical exchange that is at the heart of negotiation is a quintessentially moral activity because in it we are engaged in an encounter with the other in which we are faced with either affirming or denying the intrinsic shared worth or dignity of the other. We affirm the dignity of our "co-negotiators" by seeing them as such, rather than as "opponents" to be defeated. And from this perspective, we aim for an agreement that is optimal for all parties—or to use the popular negotiation term, an agreement that is "win-win." Finally, rather than seeing deception and coercion as legitimate negotiation tactics, we see these as violating the dignity of our co-negotiators because they vitiate the entire communicative process that permits negotiation to serve as a valid form of communication. Rather than seeing deception as a standard negotiation tactic, we can view it as a perversion of negotiation that robs it of its capacity to achieve its intended function.

5. Negotiating in the International Sphere

An additional level of complexity is added to negotiation when it involves people from different cultures. In Thomas Donaldson's words, "When we leave home and cross our nation's boundaries, moral clarity often blurs."[20] Why? To begin with, people of different cultures generally speak different languages. If a person were to say to us in Urdu something as simple as "The cat is on the mat," we would have no idea what was being expressed. If he continued to speak in his language,

---

[20] Thomas Donaldson, *Values in Tension: Ethics Away from Home*, HARV. BUS. REV., Sept.–Oct. 1996, at 29, 48.

our bewilderment would grow. Add to that variations in physical appearance including attire, culturally influenced mannerisms such as etiquette, and differences in religion, and the "foreignness" of the other can appear quite pronounced. As we discussed earlier, a source of moral trouble occurs when one fails to recognize the humanity of the other and, as a result, denies them the moral reciprocity that one would want to see accorded to oneself were one in a similar situation. It has been our observation that this is a human problem that occurs without regard for geography or income level. Consequently, the ethical risks associated with negotiation escalate when our co-negotiators are perceived as "foreign." Alex C. Michalos quite clearly made this point, noting that several studies show that "most people think most people are not as nice as they are themselves and, therefore, cannot be trusted to behave as well."[21]

Over the last decade there have been a number of studies that tried to identify the cultural characteristics that could serve as impediments to international negotiations. These studies make claims that cultures can be categorized according to various dimensions and that these analyses will contribute to the creation of culturally specific sets of values, each of which can influence the way in which the negotiators will respond.[22]

These studies shed light on the complexity of negotiation in the international sphere, but as we see it, they are of limited value. While they may alert us to a general predisposition to be found in one group or another, it is hard to see how any such study could paint a picture that was adequately complex and subtle to be of much practical value. Moreover, as we see it, such studies may indirectly show how prone we are to see cultural stereotypes in others. One of the contributions of business ethics in this regard is that it challenges us not to be misled by what may be superficial differences among people of different cultures. Yes, perhaps there is some truth to the idea that the Chinese tend to be more collectivistic in their negotiating style than Americans, but from an ethical perspective they are of identical moral worth. Therefore,

---

[21] Alex C. Michalos, *The Impact of Trust on Business, International Security and the Quality of Life*, 9 J. Bus. Ethics 627 (1990).

[22] *See, e.g.*: Geert H. Hofstede, Culture's Consequences : Comparing Values, Behaviors, Institutions, and Organizations Across Nations (2001); Roger Volkema, *Demographic, Cultural, and Economic Predictors of Perceived Ethicality of Negotiation Behavior: A Nine-Country Analysis*, 57 J. Bus. Res. 69 (2004); Anna Zarkada-Fraser & Campbell Fraser, *Moral Decision Making in International Sales Negotiations*, 16 J. Bus. & Indus. Mktg. 274 (2001); John B. Ford, Michael S. LaTour, Scott J. Vitell & Warren A. French, *Moral Judgment and Market Negotiations: A Comparison of Chinese and American Managers*, 5 J. Int'l Mktg. 57 (1997); Mohammad N. Elahee, Susan L. Kirby, & Ercan Nasif, *National Culture, Trust, and Perceptions About Ethical Behavior in Intra- and Cross-Cultural Negotiations: An Analysis of Nafta Countries*, 44 Thunderbird Int'l Bus. Rev. 799 (2002).

when engaging in transcultural negotiations our goal should be to exert our best efforts so as to minimize the risk that cultural differences will detract from the outcome.

An important job of business ethics is to help keep business leaders from falling into the trap of mistaking differences in form (such as attire or conventions of etiquette) with matters of substance. On the negative side, the ethical outlook calls on us to eschew positions that in any way deny the essential humanity of the other. This does not mean that we should presume our counterpart is guided by high standards of virtue. However, even if the negotiating tactics of the other are unacceptable, bad behavior is not grounds for denying the essential humanity of one's co-negotiator.

In this way, the contribution of business ethics to the process of international negotiation is to challenge us to find the ethical common ground with our co-negotiator when our first reaction might be to adopt a combative position with someone we may be inclined to see as failing to belong to the group we consider essentially human. Ultimately, by seeking to guide international negotiations with ethical principles, negotiators create a context of trust that not only will be conducive to win-win exchanges, but will also lay the foundation for a long-term relationship. We cannot control whether our co-negotiator will reciprocate. What we can do, though, is to undercut the basis for their assuming the worst in our behavior.

6. Ethical Universalism in a Culturally Pluralistic World: An Emerging Consensus

From the business ethics perspective, negotiation is a process whereby we are navigating in unknown territory, but guided by the belief that we can conduct our international exchanges in a context of shared ethical principles. In this regard, business ethics, as we understand it, is founded on a universalist view of ethics that has important implications for our understanding of the nature of negotiation. Ethical universalism does not mean that people will universally follow a particular ethical norm. Rather, it means that regardless of a person's geographic location or period in history, all people are endowed with certain basic moral dispositions that they may or may not choose to respect. This is crucial, because if we cannot trust that fundamental principles of morality hold up across cultures, then negotiation will have no substantive value and we will be left simply with power as the only substantive factor.

Despite its widespread appeal, moral relativism is false. The credibility that is unjustifiably accorded to this view reflects a shallowness in understanding the natures of culture and morality. Ethical universalism may be best illustrated through an example. Irrespective of culture, it is recognized that automobile driving can be dangerous. As a result, in every country, drivers are expected to respect the principle of safe driving. However, conformity to this principle leads drivers in North America to drive on the right side of the road, whereas drivers guided by the identical principle will drive on the left in Indonesia, the U.K., and various other countries. While drivers in all these countries are governed by the same principle of safe driving, local conventions will lead to variations in behavior. Moreover, the universality of the principle of safe driving in no way precludes the fact that some people will choose to drive recklessly regardless of their ethical obligation.

Let us turn to a somewhat more challenging example from the world of business: bribery. It was not long ago that bribery was commonly justified as a "pragmatic cost of doing business," and because bribery has been so widespread, that fact has been used to justify the practice. Such rationalizations are ethical mistakes. Bribery is a form of deception used to gain unfair advantage over those who act according to the norms governing transactions. If bribery were simply a cost of doing business, then the cost of the bribe ought to be stated clearly and openly in the contract, and if that were done, it would no longer be a bribe. Bribery is not disclosed in this way because this would deprive it of the unfairness that leads people to engage in it. It is for this reason that bribery brought to light, irrespective of the country, is a scandal and source of shame. To combat this form of unethical practice, the government of the United States promulgated the Foreign Corrupt Practices Act in 1977. However, because this is not simply a concern of American businesses, the Organisation for Economic Co-operation and Development (OECD) member countries adopted a similar antibribery measure in 1997.[23] The important point here is that bribery is not unethical because it is illegal, but the illegality of bribery is legitimate because it is unethical. Business ethics has not eliminated bribery, but it has cast a bright light on the unacceptability of this practice and revealed the hollowness of arguments that seek to justify it.

7. On the Power of Ethical Negotiation

We have all heard the hackneyed saws that the successful negotiators are wily and unwilling to be bound by any rules, least of all the niceties of ethics. Such have been the myths associated with the "captains of business." We read, for example, of John D. Rockefeller that "[t]o ensure that he won, he submitted to games only where he could dictate the rules."[24] Such an approach to business is inherently unfair and is sustainable only so long as one group can take advantage of others. We now are aware of much better models of leadership.

---

[23] Gerald F. Cavanagh, *Global Business Ethics: Regulation, Code, or Self-Restraint*, 14 Bus. Ethics Q. 629 (2004).
[24] Ron Chernow, Titan: The Life of John D. Rockefeller, Sr. 18.

To provide a brief illustration of the power of ethical negotiation, we would like to take a look at two people who are paramount examples: Mohandas Gandhi and Nelson Mandela. The work of these men is highly relevant to our discussion because it was by virtue of their power as ethical negotiators that they were able to shepherd change of historic proportions. In this regard, we want to emphasize two points: First, the principles that guided their work were consistent with the ideas we associate with business ethics described in this piece: namely, upholding a commitment to universal dignity, reciprocity, transparency, and social flourishing. Secondly, both of these men confronted powers that categorically outweighed their own and yet they succeeded in engineering colossal societal transformations, above all because of the ethical strength of their positions.

When Mohandas Gandhi challenged the British Crown, it was the world's undisputed imperial power. Gandhi, by contrast, lacked a formal political power base, had no army, and had no wealth. The challenge to the United Kingdom was monumental because if Gandhi succeeded, the entire empire would be at risk. The significance of his accomplishment is that he did not lead India to independence through armed struggle, but based on the power of principled negotiation. The essence of Gandhi's approach to negotiation was *satyagraha*, variously translated as "passive resistance," "nonviolent resistance," "nonviolent direct action," and even "militant nonviolence."[25] The following list, drawn from the analysis of Thomas Weber, represents some of the key principles at play in satyagraha as an approach to negotiation:[26]

- To "convert" the opponent[27] so that you both end up on the same side;
- To avoid humiliating and provoking the other;
- To seek clarity on the purpose of the negotiation;
- To discern what are the common interests of both parties;
- To judge one's opponent in a way that is not more harsh than how one would judge oneself;
- To not exploit the position of weakness of one's opponent.

Let us now consider Mandela, whose approach to negotiation bears great similarity to that of Gandhi. Although Mandela was confined to prison for some twenty-seven years, he succeeded in negotiating the end of the apartheid regime by virtue of the unquestioned integrity with which he comported himself, the respect he showed to his nego-

---

[25] Thomas Weber, *Gandhian Philosophy, Conflict Resolution Theory and Practical Approaches to Negotiation*, 38 J. PEACE RES. 494 (2001).

[26] *Id.* at 505–06.

[27] We retain Weber's language in which he refers to the two sides in the negotiation as "opponents."

tiation partners, and his unwavering commitment to social justice for all. As Mark Young put it:

> [Mandela] had no particular political power. . . . He certainly commanded no significant military forces. . . . Financially, he was no match either for the South African government. . . . What Mandela did have and used brilliantly to his advantage was a power source often overlooked by the analysts: the power of ethics. Rightly or wrongly, he was perceived through it all—not just by his negotiation partners but by much of the outside world—as a man of unquestioned integrity. In the face of much unfairness and indignity, he stood by his principles and refused to play tit-for-tat. And so his mighty opponents, humbled by the strength Mandela gained by standing on "the high ground," found themselves offering concession after concession, and finally ceding power completely to the new president of South Africa.[28]

According to Anthony Sampson not only did Mandela negotiate with his captors, but against the advice of many comrades

> Mandela himself studied Afrikaans systematically, reading many Afrikaans books, and spoke it quite well. . . . He acquired an understanding of the Afrikaner which colleagues in exile would later envy.[29]

In short, he sought to understand them from the inside, and in so doing he was able to show his respect for them, and they in turn could not help but respect him.[30]

Both Gandhi and Mandela were able to achieve historic changes by negotiating in a way that always respected the dignity of others, by acting with transparency, and by fighting for justice based on Golden Rule reciprocity. Their negotiating strength flowed from moral strength. This same strength is available to negotiators operating across all spheres, from the economic to the political, social, and personal. Gandhi and Mandela are both illustrative of the power of ethical negotiation.

8. Concluding Thoughts on the Power of Ethical Negotiation

Business is the ingenious way we humans have learned to survive and build our societies. This is an evolving process, and in recent decades,

---

[28] Mark Young, *Sharks, Saints, and Samurai: The Power of Ethics in Negotiations*, 24 Nego-tiation J. 146 (2008).

[29] Anthony Sampson, Mandela: The Authorized Biography 26 (1999).

[30] *See* Nelson Mandela, Long Walk to Freedom: The Autobiography of Nelson Mandela (1994).

business has taken an enormous leap forward after the awareness grew among business leaders that the strength of business increases dramatically when it is conducted ethically. The lessons of business ethics need to be embraced by negotiators. In a period of rapid globalization such as our own, business and social leaders have a duty to evaluate business with a critical eye so as to ensure that business benefits all stakeholders. This is to say that business must be conducted in a manner sincerely respectful of the shared humanity, dignity, and worth of all people. The path of business development will be formed largely through the process of negotiation. By embracing ethics, negotiators will gain access to the capacity of guided transformation that empowered not only giants such as Gandhi and Mandela but also leaders everywhere whose work is informed by a commitment to the universal goodness of our common dignity.

Robert E. McNulty, Ph.D.
Director of Programs
Center for Business Ethics, Bentley University
112 Adamian Academic Center
175 Forest Street
Waltham, MA 02452
Phone: (781) 891-2501
Fax: (781) 891-2988
E-mail: rmcnulty@bentley.edu

W. Michael Hoffman, Ph.D.
Executive Director, Center for Business Ethics, and
Hieken Professor of Business and Professional Ethics
Bentley University
175 Forest Street
Waltham, MA 02452
Phone: (781) 891-3434
Fax: (781) 891-2988
E-mail: mhoffman@bentley.edu

CHAPTER 3

Reinventing Law in Cyberspace: A Social Contract for the Digital Age and International Business Negotiations

Jeffrey M. Aresty
ARESTY INTERNATIONAL LAW OFFICES, P.C.
SUDBURY, MASSACHUSETTS

Richard Warner
CHICAGO-KENT COLLEGE OF LAW
CHICAGO, ILLINOIS

While on a safari across the Saudi Arabian desert in early 1995, my oldest son and I came across some Bedouin camel herders with an encampment of tents, miles from the nearest roads and electrical lines, but with a satellite dish pointed at the heavens and an electrical generator to power it. They were watching on TV what you and I watch on TV.

—Lester C. Thurow[1]

Today the five hundred richest people on the planet control more wealth than the bottom three billion, half of the human population. Is it possible even to grasp the process that led to this most extraordinary imbalance? More important, how do we even begin to redress it?

—Paul Rogat Loeb[2]

1. Introduction

Ready or not, we are all creating a new society in cyberspace. Rapid and far-reaching advancements in digital technology over the past twenty years have laid the foundation for the development and the globalization of the world's economy, as well as the formation of new, never-thought-of-before communities across the globe. Understanding the challenges of the digital age and the shifts of economic and political

---

[1] Lester C. Thurow, *An Era of Man-Made Brainpower Industries, in* THE KNOWLEDGE ECONOMY 199 (Neef ed., 1998).
[2] PAUL ROGAT LOEB, SOUL OF A CITIZEN LIVING WITH CONVICTION IN A CYNICAL TIME (1999).

power inherent in this structure is of critical importance to the international legal profession, which has the opportunity to bring the rule of law to the electronic frontier in cyberspace. Others have already taken initial steps on the global plane. Many researchers, including the American Bar Foundation, report that there are many new international participants from civil society who are acting globally. They are working to effectively transform which groups will have geopolitical power and which values will be transcendent in our new society. As in every society that has preceded this one, the new one needs order for it to be just. As guardians of the rule of law, the legal profession has the responsibility to reinvent law in cyberspace. To that end, this chapter proposes a new model for global rulemaking and standards-setting. A virtual law-related community better suited for the global needs of the emerging knowledge-based civilization can, hopefully, emerge from these changes. Some readers may question why this chapter is in a book on international business negotiations. It has been placed here to provide a context for the chapters that follow.

As many have noted, the technological era and the rise of the Internet change everything. The cost of doing business, the meaning of privacy, the barriers to communication, the definition of community, and even the act of governing are being transformed by the information age. Since so many of us have begun to use the Internet, we have found ourselves coming into contact almost daily with people from all over the world. This increased global contact has led to a rise in international opportunities and thus business negotiations. To understand the implications of the trends resulting from this flattening world, we need to start by understanding the distinct culture of the Internet.

First, the Internet must be viewed as a living system that is enveloping our world. For those who are involved in international business, understanding the culture of the Internet as well as its technology is essential in order to continue practicing law in the digital era. To do so we need to look at two levels: learning the culture of the Internet (which means understanding how cyberspace relates to the real world) and understanding that technology is shaping new societal roles and creating new civil institutions. At a higher level, the legal profession can play a significant role in society's great transformation by helping to define the social contract for the new civilization.

Professor Gary Munneke, in his Foreword to the first edition of this book, explained that "in order to practice competently and compete effectively, American lawyers need to master the skill of negotiation in the context of clients, adversaries, and business partners whose cultural experiences and mores are different from those of Americans." That was penned in 1994 when cyberspace was something only thought about by scientists, researchers, and visionary business leaders. Today, we are living in the middle of a global negotiation about the future of society. A global ethic is beginning to emerge out of the battle between money and human rights. In many cases, facilitated by Internet technology in cyberspace, civil society is galvanizing human consciousness to agree upon minimally acceptable standards for living cooperatively on the planet.

Lawyers can play a unique role in this process, but first we each have to discover the Internet for ourselves. As ABA Techshow keynote speaker Sam Guiberson noted in 1999, "discovering the Internet is for each of us a meeting with the electronic frontier. Some of us walk away and return to the comfort of doing what we know how to do. Others recognize that the Internet is a collective human consciousness, which is a teaching and learning tool for the entire planet. We are building a new civilization by creating a new economy utilizing Internet technology to spawn it." He added a warning. He predicted, "Fiercely competitive battles for the electronic frontier's wealth could prevent a digital renaissance from taking hold and bringing prosperity around the globe. We don't know what great advances in civilization have been squandered. The question before us is—which future does the Internet define?" Finally, Sam challenged all lawyers to "do our part to sustain the digital revolution by promoting its ethical and ecological use by establishing social projects that are worthy of the Internet itself, and capture the world's imagination in the process." That is where we begin.

1.1 Vision

> In the networked world, you cannot—and cannot expect to—control your company's image; the best you can do is influence it. Anything and everything about a company can be known—every slipup, every policy, every practice. You can't control what people say about your company. On the Internet, they'll say anything they like, which may be a mixture of fact, fiction, and opinion. Living with this transparency requires executives to change their thinking fundamentally: they have to learn that their company is what people see it to be and that they must figure out how to turn that visibility to their advantage.
>
> —Esther Dyson[3]

Esther Dyson's observations about transparency extend well beyond business. Give Internet access to Thurow's Bedouins, and they can talk to the world as well as watch it. They can convey information about, and express their views on, desert ecology, government policies, the accuracy of CNN coverage, the frequency of *I Love Lucy* reruns, or whatever they may wish. It is the world, not just business, that the Internet makes more transparent. Imagine a future—one that may not be so distant—where

---

[3] Esther Dyson, *Mirror, Mirror on the Wall*, HARV. BUS. REV., Sept.–Oct. 1997.

the world is networked into a virtual community in which *all* have both access to information and an outlet for their political and cultural views; disputes (even deep rifts and vehement disruptions) occur, but are resolved without large-scale violence, in part because of a pervasive belief in a "world community": a virtual community consisting of members from all sectors of society who approach the Internet with the same sense of civic duty they might bring to a Town Hall meeting, and learn how to live and work side by side, despite disagreements.

This world is not at hand, but the power and the possibility to work toward it are. Obstacles to that world are tremendous divisions of wealth and values among the nations and peoples of the world. There is also a global struggle for equity and justice because of the so-called "digital divide" between those having access to the Internet and those without. Even among those who are digitally connected, a vast divide exists between the "Internet savvy" and the average digital consumer. Meanwhile, new alliances are quickly taking shape in the New Economy as it replaces the Industrial Economy. The New Economy's power lies in its potential as a universal knowledge resource for all. As a result, the New Society that is taking shape must figure out a way to share this resource from the outset. Technology now gives us the means to conceive of a new social contract on a global scale that has thus far been unimaginable, but achieving that goal requires helping to spread both the connectivity and capability of society.

Joe Jaworski, in the preface to his 1996 book *Synchronicity: The Inner Path of Leadership,* addresses the need for leaders from all areas of society to explore these "frontiers of human knowledge" and create a just future by "understanding . . . how human beings, both individually and collectively, might develop the capacity to see what wants to emerge in the world and thus have the opportunity to shape the future instead of simply responding to the forces at large." One of the most exciting opportunities in this wired world is the opportunity to create a social contract among the connected people of the world (netizens), a new understanding of and process for the development of international governance.

2. Two Ideals

The globalization of the economy and the phenomenally rapid growth of the Internet and e-commerce raise a number of critical issues. Accordingly, investors, nations, multinational corporations, and supranational bodies (both governmental and nongovernmental) now vie for power and play a crucial role in determining policy issues.[4] This power struggle often slights the following two key democratic ideals:

---

[4] For a discussion of this situation, see THOMAS FRIEDMAN, THE LEXUS AND THE OLIVE TREE (1999).

- *The ideal of representation*: **Those affected by a policy should have a say in its adoption and application.** Virtually all individuals, most groups and organizations, and even some nations are effectively excluded from the international policymaking arena. The 1999 protests in Seattle against the World Trade Organization (WTO) illustrate the point. As *Reuters* noted,

> The WTO's meteoric rise from obscurity to villainy is partly its own fault. It operates largely behind closed doors in rooms filled largely with corporate executives, trade bureaucrats and politicians. No wonder the Geneva-based organization is perceived in the United States and elsewhere as an agent of big business.[5]

- *The ideal of explanation*: **A decision-maker "accepts the responsibility . . . to explain, particularly to those adversely affected, why different treatment of others in other circumstances is not capricious or arbitrary or discriminatory."**[6] A decision-maker shows that a policy is not "capricious or arbitrary or discriminatory" by articulating the reasons for the policy. This is a requirement of political legitimacy. The ideal of legitimacy is the ideal of a government that commands compliance, not through force, but by reason, where citizens comply because they see themselves as having adequate reason to do so. The WTO illustrates this point as well. Third World nations often perceive WTO policy as being formed in the European Union and United States, which the Third World is then bullied into accepting.

2.1 The Question

Our question is: how do we best approximate these two democratic ideals in the context of globalization, the Internet, and e-commerce? The question is highly relevant to business negotiation (particularly international business negotiation). There is little doubt that society's sociopolitical organization stands to change considerably as a result of these technologies. New players will emerge and change the types of alliances a business should make and the partners with whom it should make them. Consider Alvin Toffler's well-known analysis:

> The shrinkage of the nation-state reflects the appearance of a new-style global economy . . . Nation-states were the necessary political containers for nation-sized economies. Today the

---

[5] Christopher Wilson, *Chaos at WTO Talks Reflects Public Mistrust*, Reuters, Mar. 12, 1999, http://www.planetark.com/dailynewsstory.cfm/newsid/4906/newsDate/3-Dec-1999/story.htm.

[6] Ronald Dworkin, *Pragmatism, Right Answers, and True Banality*, in PRAGMATISM IN AMERICAN LAW AND SOCIETY 359, 373–74 (Michael Brint & William Weaver eds., 1991).

containers have not only sprung leaks, they have been made obsolete by their own success. . . . [Their success] gives rise to groups with larger than national interests. These form the base of an emerging globalist ideology . . . [At] every level, from economics to politics to organization and ideology, we are witnessing a devastating attack, from within and without, on . . . the nation-state . . . We can expect next decades to be torn by struggle over the creation of new global institutions capable of fairly representing the prenational as well as postnational peoples of the world.[7]

Toffler's claims capture the sense that we are at a defining moment in history. According to Toffler, "a growing body of reputable opinion asserts that the present moment represents nothing less than the second great divide in human history, comparable in magnitude only with that first great break in historic continuity, the shift from barbarism to civilization."[8] One might well complain that "the shift from barbarism to civilization" was quite gradual, hardly a matter of a sudden, discontinuous change. One might contend that the same is true for the changes arising out of globalization and the Internet. But our point is that the Internet facilitates the proliferation of new international players, such as nongovernmental organizations (NGOs) or political "infomediaries" (discussed below), and that fundamental change is happening, whether it be continuous or discontinuous, and whether or not it is as momentous as the change from barbarism to civilization. An initial consideration of globalization shows what is at stake.

2.2 Globalization

Globalization is an effect (as well as a cause) of dramatic changes in transportation, capital availability, and communication. As Lester Thurow notes, "[m]odern transportation costs have created a world where resources can be cheaply moved to wherever they are needed. Capital availability has also fallen out of the competitive equation. With the development of a world capital market, everyone essentially borrows in New York, London, or Tokyo."[9] Further,

[t]ransportation and communication technologies mean that skilled workers in the first world can effectively work together with the unskilled in the third world. Skilled components can be made in the first world and then shipped to the third world to be assembled with low-skilled components that have been made there . . . Research and design skills can be electronically

---

[7] Alvin Toffler, THE THIRD WAVE 324–25 (1981).

[8] Alvin Toffler, FUTURE SHOCK 14 (1970).

[9] Thurow, *supra* note 1, at 200–01.

brought in from the first world. What sells can be quickly communicated to the third-world factory and retailers know that the speed of delivery won't be significantly affected by where production occurs. Instant communication and rapid transportation mean that markets can be effectively served from production points on the other side of the globe.[10]

As Thurow points out, corporations will locate their high-wage, skilled, leadership workers in countries with the lowest costs for the development and support of such workers. Furthermore, in the decade since the above was written, the developing world has become home to more and more highly skilled labor.

The countries best positioned to take up those roles will have well-developed information and communication infrastructures (as well as adequate research, development, and educational infrastructures). Relevant infrastructures become a key to predicting and explaining the distribution of workers and production facilities. Consequently, if

a firm or country wants to stay at the leading edge of technology so that it can continue to generate high-disequilibrium wages and profits, it must be a participant in the evolutionary process of man-made brainpower industries so that it is in the right position to take advantage of the technical and economic revolutions that occasionally arise. The costs of being forced out of such industries are not just the costs of having to move people from one industry or geographic location to another, or of the lower wages that laid-off workers will receive upon reemployment . . . In the long run, the costs are those of getting shut out of future developments and not being a player in the new high-wage, high-profit opportunities that will arise.[11]

Communication is the common thread that links globalization and the Internet together. The development of adequate communication infrastructures is a key factor in globalization, and the Internet not only greatly facilitates but also profoundly changes communication. Globalization and the Internet are locked in a lasting cycle, feeding one another.

There is a great deal at stake in this cycle. Regions that fail to develop the necessary infrastructures allowing interference-free communications among their communities will be greatly disadvantaged. In building these infrastructures, it is essential that they rely on the two ideals with which we began: the ideal of representation (that those affected by a policy should have a voice in that policy's adoption and application) and the ideal of explanation (decision-makers should give

---

[10] *Id.* at 206.
[11] *Id.* at 205.

reasons for their decisions that explain and justify the way a policy distributes burdens and benefits). A distribution consistent with these ideals should be a distribution under a democratic rule of law; the virtues of a rule of law help ensure that the ideals be respected and fulfilled. The Internet offers possibilities for political organization that aid in the approximation of these ideals; however, these same possibilities, misused, work counter to the goals of world peace and world justice. We begin with a look at these goals and then turn to an outline of the potential perils.

3. Conflict and Justice

A first and essential point is that individuals often disagree profoundly on fundamental moral and political issues. As John Rawls notes,

> Long historical experience suggests, and many plausible reflections confirm, that reasoned and uncoerced agreement are not to be expected ... Our individual and associative points of view, intellectual affinities and affective attachments, are too diverse, especially in a free democratic society, to allow of lasting and reasoned agreement. Many conceptions of the world can plausibly be constructed from different standpoints. Diversity naturally arises from our limited powers and distinct perspectives; it is unrealistic to suppose that all our differences are rooted solely in ignorance and perversity, or else in the rivalries that result from scarcity. [The appropriate view of social organization] takes deep and unresolvable differences on matters of fundamental significance as a permanent condition of human life.[12]

To offer just one example, suppose Party A believes that we should incur the costs of very high unemployment and greatly reduced social benefits to reap the long-run benefits of free global trade. Party B, however, thinks the costs are too high and that globalization should proceed more slowly. This disagreement is an example of a moral and political disagreement about the proper response to human suffering. Some are willing to trade a large amount of present suffering for possible future gains; others are not. It is, of course, possible that we may resolve our disagreement on our own, but it is unlikely unless we can find common ethical grounds to work from. To the extent we cannot find a common ground, we should, as Stuart Hampshire says,

> look in society not for consensus, but for ineliminable and acceptable conflicts, and for rationally controlled hostilities as the normal condition of mankind; not only normal, but also the

---

[12] John Rawls, *Kantian Constructivism in Moral Theory*, 77 J. PHIL. 515, 534 (1980).

best condition of mankind from the moral point of view, both between states and within states. This was Heraclitus's vision: that life consists in perpetual conflicts between rival impulses and ideals, and that justice presides over the hostilities and finds sufficient compromises to prevent madness in the soul, and civil war or war between peoples. Harmony and inner consensus come with death, when human faces no longer express conflicts but are immobile, and at rest.[13]

How in the emerging world of a global economy, e-commerce, and the Internet do we ensure that "justice presides over the hostilities and finds sufficient compromises to prevent madness in the soul, and civil war or war between peoples"? To answer, let us first see what forms "the hostilities" may take in a networked world.

The Internet makes it possible for all those affected by social, political, and economic developments to communicate with each other. Prior to the Internet, it was, for example, difficult for relatively low-wage, nonunion employees in a Mercedes plant in Alabama to communicate with high-wage Mercedes employees in Germany, employees of the union IG Metall. Telephoning, mailing, or advertising involves time, effort, and monetary investment. The Internet reduces the investment, and can somewhat diminish the language barrier. Efficient communication is possible, however, through e-mail, Web sites, and bulletin boards. The Internet allows allies and competitors all to communicate with each other. What are the social and political implications of such communication? There are serious implications for national governments. Internet communication adds a very significant, unpredictable variable to a problem that governments already face.

3.1 The Problem

To see the problem, consider the ideal of explanation, the ideal that a decision-maker should offer reasons that explain and justify its decision. This would seem to verge on the impossible where we face—as we do—rationally unresolvable disagreement on fundamental moral and political matters. Contemporary democracies confront the challenge of finding a reasoned way to govern in the face of disagreements that reason cannot resolve. This is the problem that confronts the massive nation-states and the supranational governmental bodies of our day. The Internet adds a novel variable to this problem by allowing the expression and discussion of a vast number of diverse ideas and ideologies. What will happen if—or, more accurately, when—there is a worldwide discussion of fundamental moral and political matters? What will happen when a broad spectrum of the American middle

---

[13] Stuart Hampshire, Innocence and Experience 189 (1989).

class engages in discussions with Europeans and Asians whose political and economic perspectives are markedly different than those that most Americans tend to hold? Is it possible for fringe groups, considered too small or weak to matter in national politics, to link up with and build alliances with similar groups in other countries? Will they become sufficiently powerful to suddenly play a significant role? More generally, what will happen when citizens discover that the Internet allows groups—small, large, fringe, or central—to organize and mobilize quickly, effectively, and at low cost? What power will these groups wield nationally and internationally?

Interest groups have, of course, demonstrated growing importance in politics. What the Internet does is make it much easier to organize a group. People who would never even know they shared the same interests and goals can—and will—discover this on the Internet, and they will realize that the Internet provides the means for easy and effective coordinated action. Just look at the following dispatch from the online version of the *Washington Post* from April 14, 2000:

> The Internet emerged in Thursday's South Korean parliamentary elections as a powerful political tool that will affect how future elections are run here and perhaps elsewhere in Asia, according to politicians and analysts today.
>
> If there is any doubt, they say, just ask 58 of the losing candidates. The Internet played an instrumental role in their defeat.
>
> "The Internet has proven itself to be a medium to be reckoned with," said Auh Taik Sup, a professor of mass communications at Korea University and president of the Korean Cyber-Communications Society.
>
> In the South Korean election campaign, the Internet was used to bypass a timid mainstream media and publish what proved to be damning and crucial information about the unsavory records of some parliamentary candidates.
>
> The Web also became a virtual Speakers' Corner for free political expression, usually exercised warily in South Korea by a populace that was under dictatorial control for more than three decades. And it was the catalyst for organizing hundreds of grass-roots citizens groups into a powerful national force.
>
> "We helped create a culture where people could debate," said Lee Kyoung Suk, 29, who ran the umbrella citizens group's Web operation. "Our site was the only marketplace where people could express their opinion."

Some foresee the weakening of regional cultures and the rise of a world culture, while others anticipate the growth of "buffer cultures" on the Internet that act as strange hybrids of traditional cultural models. Still others point to the emergence of cultures that are Internet-specific, adapted to the peculiar properties of digital communication.

While such predictions may exaggerate the effects of the Internet, the explosive growth of Internet communication will undoubtedly affect the integrity of cultures. A culture consists in part of shared norms, ideals, and forms of social action and understanding. Typically, these shared attitudes play (and are seen by members of the culture as playing) a significant formative role in the historical development of the culture: we are the way we are now because our culture has evolved from what it was in the past. Cultures are self-sustaining systems of thought and action. Geographical boundaries (such as the Swiss Alps or the English Channel), a shared language, social class, and racial identification (of self and of others) all contribute to the self-sustaining nature of cultures. Geographical boundaries can partially isolate the culture from developmental influences extrinsic to the culture. The same is true for a shared language and racial identification. Some cultures minimize extrinsic influences to the extent that members of the culture prefer to communicate with each other in their native tongue, rather than with foreigners in some other language or in translation; others enthusiastically explore and embrace "the Other." Racial identification and class status can have the same effect to the extent that members of a culture identify themselves and are predisposed to communicating and associating with those perceived as most similar.

3.2 The Cultural Impact of the Internet

The Internet has the potential to reduce the geographical, linguistic, socioeconomic, and racial contributors to cultural identity. The geography of the Internet is very different from that of the terrestrial world, defined in terms of download speeds rather than distances, making it much "smaller" and far more accessible. It strengthens the so-called major languages (particularly English, the lingua franca of the Information Age) and reduces the importance of the approximately 7,000 "minor" living languages still spoken today.[14] To a great extent, the Internet conceals race and nationality, at least when users use written communication rather than voice or video.

Of course, these same points hold to some extent for telephones, TV, radio, magazines, books, and movies. The Internet differs, however, in two crucial ways. First, it has the potential to be much cheaper. Even taking into consideration the infrastructure and equipment costs, the Internet gives users worldwide the ability to address a global audience as easily as a local one: they can publish digitally on Web sites, correspond with e-mail, converse with real-time audio and video feeds, and even organize like-minded groups using social networks. Second,

---

[14] ETHNOLOGUE: LANGUAGES OF THE WORLD (Raymond G. Gordon Jr. ed., 2005).

the underlying protocol of the Internet is open to all: provided they can access the Net, any user has the ability to publish whatever content he or she chooses. These features alleviate an important constraint on group action: the costs of communication and organization. It takes time, effort, and money for a group to meet, for its members to communicate with one another, and for them to plan and carry out actions. Prior to the Internet, people organized group action by face-to-face communication, telephoning, mailing, or advertising. Depending on the size of the group, the cost and effort required can be considerable. The Internet reduces the necessary investment by reducing the time, effort, and monetary costs of communication. E-mail, Web sites, and bulletin boards are cheap, efficient means of communication with a worldwide reach. These features explain the impact of e-mail on the politics of organizations.

3.3 Opportunities and Dangers

There is much to be gained (and that has already been gained) from the Internet's lowering the costs of group action. Researchers around the world can, and do, readily pool their knowledge; culture can flourish as information, art, and literature are readily shared and discussed; friends separated by the vagaries of their careers can easily stay in touch. But there is also an obvious danger. Group discussion always has the potential to degenerate into demagoguery: any like-minded community may become a cult of personality. Individuals who are reasonable on their own may feel compelled, as a group, to commit irrational, destructive, or even morally heinous actions at the behest of a clever speaker (or even a poor speaker in the right place at the right time) who exploits the group's ignorance, fears, desires, and prejudices. Lowering the costs of group organization and coordination may increase the frequency and efficacy of irrational and destructive group action.

The Internet newsgroup alt.fan.unabomber is one such group. Devoted to the discussion of "Unabomber" Ted Kaczynski and his views, the group is frequented by some who feel the Unabomber's violent radicalism was justified and laudable. Kaczynski's manifesto calls for violent protest against technology and, as one commentator notes, the "Internet—with its varied cast of characters and its penchant for political discussion—is in some ways very reminiscent of that turbulent era [of the 1960s] when manifestos were a dime a dozen, were widely debated and were, in some cases, the basis for violence."[15] In an irony that should not go without comment, this discussion of Kaczynski appears in the issue of *Scientific American* devoted to wireless communication, the issue containing the prediction quoted earlier that

---

[15] Anne Eisenberg, *The Unabomber and the Bland Decade*, Sci. Am., Apr. 1998, at 35.

the "world will soon be a place where not just communications but also torrents of information will be available just about everywhere."[16]

Many may react with a call for regulation. But the only adequate antidote to destructive attitudes that fail to properly respect the dignity, concerns, and lives of others is a culture that inculcates self-restraint, toleration, and an appreciation of the limits inherent in any individual's or group's point of view. Legal regulation, especially in a free, democratic society, has only a limited power to control behavior. People will violate laws when they are driven by sufficiently powerful incentives. Both ideology and self-interest can easily supply such incentives. As we build the information infrastructure, it is essential that we also build the culture that should go with it. As William Ury points out in the introduction to his 1999 book, *Getting to Peace,*

> Never before in human evolution have people faced the challenge of living in a single community with billions of other human beings. Anthropologists have identified more than fifteen thousand distinct ethnic groups on the planet. Far from bringing a lessening of conflict, the ingathering means, in the short run at least, a heightening of hostilities as people are forced to confront their differences, as jealousies and resentments over inequities flare up, and as identities are threatened by different customs and beliefs. Coming together can produce more heat than light, more conflict than understanding. Family reunions are often far from peaceful and this one is no exception.

These reflections suggest two extreme visions. One is the "nightmare of mobocracy," also known as the "tyranny of the majority," an idea put forward by both John Stuart Mill and Alexis de Tocqueville in the nineteenth century. As recently as 2005 Rawls observed, "Our individual and associative points of view, intellectual affinities and affective attachments, are too diverse, especially in a free democratic society, to allow of lasting and reasoned agreement."[17] In the modern world, it is no longer merely the mob, however, that can disrupt the civic dialog. A worldwide discussion, facilitated by the Internet, may produce irreconcilable opposition among groups both large and small that organize themselves locally, nationally, and internationally for political and social action.

The May 1992 uprising in Thailand—the "mobile telephone revolution"—illustrates both the possibilities and the concerns. After a military coup deposed the government, students, businesspeople, intellectuals, labor, and social activists occupied the national freedom

---

[16] John V. Evans, *New Satellites for Personal Communication*, Sci. Am., Apr. 1998, at 77.
[17] John Rawls, Political Liberalism (2005).

shrine. They "united spontaneously, armed with cell phones, cameras and radios ... they faxed their daily bulletins to the international news."[18] The army crushed the rebellion, killing fifty-two people, but the ensuing scandal toppled the regime. The communication and multimedia possibilities of the Internet make such collective action, and the collective awareness that grew out of it, possible on a worldwide scale. National governments may not be able to negotiate with such groups (as was the case for the Thai military regime), and national and international orders may destabilize as a result.

Of course, it would be wrong to think of anyone who resists governmental control as simply irrational. The uprising in Thailand, for example, is considered a victory of democracy over tyranny by many. People can rationally refuse to obey their government if they feel it is unjust or illegitimate, and governments at odds with their citizens on fundamental moral and political matters rarely survive for very long through any means short of brutal repression. But it is not enough for a population to have a revolutionary spirit and a sense of conviction: they must also support the idea of civic discourse. Reasoned government may be toppled by radical sentiments, just as radical government may be toppled by a reasoned populace. The Internet creates a stronger possibility that some governments will fail to govern in a reasonable way precisely because of disagreements that reason cannot resolve.

The second vision is as optimistic as the first is pessimistic. In this vision, governments not only find a reasoned way to govern, but Internet activity actually promotes this process by encouraging a cooperative (rather than adversarial) approach to policy. As game theory emphasizes, provided all players have equal information, many competitive situations can achieve a happy medium in which everyone received an equitable share. It is not naive to hope that shared interests in national and international stability, economic prosperity, and human welfare may be sufficient to promote transparency, cooperative regulation, and self-restraint.

Reality, known to stray from the ideal, will undoubtedly present a middle ground between. Our question is: What can we do to move developments toward the second vision? The nineteenth century "tyranny of the majority" thrived on a sense of disempowerment that can divide the disempowered into embittered groups disinclined to compromise. It thrived, in other words, on the belief that dialog was impossible, and that discussion cannot test, refine, and improve ideas. Today's Internet still exhibits that difficulty, but also presents a second problem: a "tyranny of the minority" in which isolated groups can consolidate their political clout and destabilize an otherwise reasonable system. We empower the people affected by policy when we give them a

---

[18] WILLIAM GREIDER, ONE WORLD, READY OR NOT 350 (1997).

voice in policymaking, but at the same time we must promote reasoned discussion by offering reasons that explain and justify. The Internet is a source of both new possibilities and new threats to public discourse. The key to understanding both lies in a deeper understanding of how the Internet has altered the nature of communication.

3.4 Competing Norms in Digital Society

The power of the Internet to consolidate like-minded groups is now well-established, and one need look no further than the war of ideas being waged over what constitutes the "normative practices" of Internet behavior. This debate, which ranges from lively to litigious, is unique precisely because the possibilities inherent in digital communications and transaction are new, and thus it is unclear what traditions digital society should draw upon.

The most-discussed area of disagreement relates to ideas of copyright and intellectual property (or "IP"). The technology now exists to share virtually any "information product," including software, movies, music, and even books. The distribution of these products, particularly without authorization, now constitutes the overwhelming majority of Internet traffic volume.

At one extreme, the entertainment industry has historically enjoyed considerable control over the mediums used to sell its products. Consequently, its reactions toward unauthorized duplication and distribution have been firm, to say the least. Comfortable with the theory that unauthorized duplication is a form of theft (a legal reality they have lobbied hard to see enacted),[19] it has pursued infringement zealously, while at the same time trying to re-establish control over its content with strict mechanisms. With close corporate connections to telecommunications, the entertainment industry remains the giant of the IP wars. Its hard-line positions may have the support of the law, but have helped promulgate a great deal of legal confusion in the public sphere, where new urban copyrights myths[20] seem to be appearing almost daily.

At the opposite extreme, an international community of self-described pirates has thumbed its nose at traditional views of intellectual property and taken the radical (and, for the most part, legally unfounded) position that private ownership of intellectual property is a fundamentally unreasonable proposition. Despite limited technological and legal resources, the ringleaders of this digital underground

---

[19] Daniel J. Cohen & Roy Rosenzweig, *A Brief History of Copyright, in* DIGITAL HISTORY: A GUIDE TO GATHERING, PRESERVING, AND PRESENTING THE PAST ON THE WEB (2005).

[20] RICHARD KEYT, TOP 10 URBAN COPYRIGHT MYTHS (2007), http://www.keytlaw.com/Copyrights/top10myths.htm (last visited Dec. 10, 2008).

have largely been winning, at least in terms of succeeding in distributing unauthorized copies of copyrighted works. Although these pirates take a position that is not supported by most interpretations of copyright law, their successes (a product in no small part of the Internet's characteristics) have helped make their philosophy a fairly widespread view, akin to speeding on the freeway ("It's not a crime if everyone does it").

Treading a cautious line between these two extremes is the "copyleft" movement, which in many ways represents the role model that the legal community should emulate. The copyleft position is that copyright law itself is flawed, but can be reformed within the confines of the law through the development of new tools and licenses that reflect the Internet's distinctive qualities. Examples of such agreements are the GNU General Public License[21] (used mainly to distribute open-source software) and the Creative Commons[22] family of licenses. There is also an emphasis in the copyleft community to revive and refine the legal interpretation of "fair use," so that copyright holders cannot use copyright claims as a means of quashing legitimate scholarly or journalistic activities.

What makes the copyleft movement admirable is the desire to find a practical compromise on these difficult issues by applying the law, rather than by abusing it (as industry officials have sometimes done) or breaking it (as pirates enthusiastically do). Their solutions are part of a push to shift the normative view in a healthy direction, and other legally oriented movements should take their cues from this example.

The debate over copyright is just one of several disagreements about Internet norms. Similar disagreements exist about such topics as censorship, privacy, libel, and commercial jurisdiction. What all of these debates have in common is that the letter of the law routinely lags behind the state of the technology. Thus, to promote the rule of law, the legal community cannot merely wait for new legislation or judicial interpretation: instead, it is the responsibility of legal professionals to promote the norms we wish to see propagated.

3.5 Old and New Economics of Information

Until the Internet, communicating information involved a trade-off between *richness* and *reach*.[23] Richness is both a quantitative and qualitative matter, a function of the quantity, relevance, and clarity of information. This balancing act forces those who produce the information

---

[21] The GNU General Public License, Version 3 (June 29, 2007), *available at* http://www.gnu.org/copyleft/gpl.html.

[22] http://creativecommons.org/.

[23] Remarks adapted from Philip Evans & Thomas Wurster, BLOWN TO BITS (1999).

to find the correct balance between presenting as much information as possible and keeping the information relevant and packaging the whole in a way that is clear to those consuming the information.

Reach is also both quantitative and qualitative. On the surface, quantity is everything; reach mainly refers to the number of people receiving the communication. More people means more reach. But reach also means getting information to the *right* people. Advertising has long struggled with the balancing act between broadly spreading awareness of their product and narrowly targeting the people most likely to buy it. The cost of a purely quantitative approach to reach has classically restricted advertising to a far more qualitative gamble.

The interaction between richness and reach has also generally been a trade-off. Increasing the richness of information generally constrains the reach: not only are space limitations a factor, but so too is the technical expertise of the reader. As a result, information has generally approached this trade-off as a zero-sum game. Billboards have broad reach but generally have very little richness. Small-group discussions, by contrast, have very narrow reach but enrich their information considerably by presenting highly relevant information as it addresses the questions the participants raise. The richness is diminished (and reach expanded) in a lecture to three hundred people, but such a lecture still has far narrower reach and far greater richness than a billboard.

This inverse relationship has historically stemmed from the cost of replicating information. Buying up every billboard in town is very expensive. Printing a thousand copies of a book requires payment for each copy. A live presentation must be redone for each audience. The Internet, combined with storing information digitally, dramatically alters this relationship, for three fundamental reasons.

First, the Internet provides a universal, low-cost medium that has tremendous reach. Only one person at a time can read a particular copy of a book, but a Web page can be viewed by thousands of people simultaneously. The reach of a Web site can potentially encompass everyone connected to the Internet regardless of geography. Businesses no longer rely on brick-and-mortar storefronts because they can display their goods on the Internet, and a political manifesto can now be read by anyone who knows the Web address without any printing costs.

Second, the Internet's digital nature presents information on a sliding scale, with the potential for tremendous amounts of information, hugely enhancing richness. A lengthy Wikipedia article may not only present a comprehensive description of a subject, but may have dozens or hundreds of links to related topics. We can look at a picture of the globe, and then zoom in all the way down to a picture of our house using Google Maps. This enhanced, dynamic richness has few physical constraints, and ensures that accessing relevant information is practically effortless.

Third, the Internet can make effectively any information interactive. Just as the interactivity of a conversation enhances richness, so too does the give-and-take of the Internet. Unlike traditional mediums, which tend to be linear (such as books or lectures), users can explore the Internet in any direction they wish, later returning to explore a different branch. Social networks are perhaps the most important manifestation of this interactivity: they enable vast, decentralized conversation and collaboration by groups of effectively any size.

It is tempting to conclude that the Internet has eliminated the inverse relationship between richness and reach, but it has not. The Internet has changed many of the costs, but has not eliminated the need for compromise between the two. The most fundamental constraints on the Internet are time and cognition: with only twenty-four hours in a day, users have no choice but to ignore all but a tiny slice of the Internet. The limits of human cognition also place a serious limit on how much information we can digest. This has led to the development of various tools that can distill the staggering volumes of information being exchanged into meaningful images. These "aggregators" are built on algorithms that attempt to convert a superhuman volume of rich information down to a level that is comprehensible. In one sense, this impoverishes the information, making it noisy and distorted. In another view, however, this amounts to compression. As one commentator points out:

> The remarkable thing is that, because many of us are participating in the creation of information, we understand the amount of noise that comes with it. The very knowledge that details are missing allows us to consume lower quality information. If a particular detail that's important to us is missing, we know there's a way to find it.
>
> Many publishers make money off of taking time to provide high quality information with little noise. But nowadays, we want our information quickly and that comes with noise. We're willing to sacrifice the trees for the forest because we know what's what we're doing.[24]

Amazon.com is an excellent example of this "compression" tradeoff between richness and reach. Its customer base is literally worldwide, and it combines this worldwide reach with rich information. It offers customers a list of 2.5 million books, a list ten times the size of the largest chain stores. Visitors to the site can search this list using almost any set of criteria they find relevant. This interactivity makes locating a specific volume in that vast catalog effortless. In addition

---

[24] *The Show with Ze Frank* (episode of Aug. 28, 2006), http://www.zefrank.com/theshow/archives/2006/08/082806.html.

to this catalog, Amazon tracks the purchasing habits of its customers and encourages users to rate products and write reviews. It then makes recommendations based on sophisticated algorithms comparing the tastes of customers. Because Amazon is able to provide this service to all of its customers at once, it derives the benefits of a low-reach, high-richness conversation with the customers while simultaneously presenting all customers with high-reach, low-richness ratings of products based on their cumulative popularity.

The possibility now exists to burn the candle at both ends and provide both customized and generalized information simultaneously. This allows new interactions of richness and reach that benefit consumers of any form of information. How this new dynamic will be exploited may prove vital not only for Internet business but for both national and international politics as well.

4. The Infomediary Solution

An "infomediary" is any service that permits large groups of people to express their views in a collaborative fashion in order to aggregate and distill that information. This could be something as simple as providing a common meeting place (such as an online forum) for discussion, or could be something as abstract as a sophisticated "preference-judging algorithm." Amazon is an example of the latter, operating on the principle that the voice a customer is most likely to trust is that of many other customers (rather than, for example, ad agencies). The objective is to overcome the powerlessness that individuals often experience when faced with problems that are bigger than themselves.

The benefits to consumers in a commercial setting are immediately obvious, because consumers have historically been unable to have a say in the nature of the marketplace:

> No consumer has the power (or the time) to challenge vendors alone. A particular vendor represents a small slice of consumer spending and warrants a correspondingly small share of customer attention and emotional engagement . . . As a result, vendors make the rules about products, price, services, and company policy on any variety of topics . . . Customers can basically take it or leave it—and they do, with firms frequently failing to understand just why consumers have made the choices they have made.[25]

When vendors such as Amazon give consumers the opportunity to work together, both groups win. Not only do consumers receive far more fine-grained (and arguably more honest) information about the

---

[25] JOHN HAGEL III & MARC SINGER, NET WORTH 247 (1999).

products they are buying, but so too are vendors better able to gauge popularity and demand. The distilled wisdom of the crowd is effectively public, even if the underlying algorithms are trade secrets, and this wealth of information helps the marketplace run more smoothly at every level.

The principles by which infomediaries operate are by no means limited to commerce, however. In many ways, there are parallels between consumer decisions and voter decisions, and infomediaries can provide a way to overcome the disenfranchisement many voters feel when they cannot influence the political process as individuals. To overcome this, participants in a sociopolitical infomediary could aggregate individuals with similar interests and ideologies. Such political groups have only recently begun to emerge on the Internet, and are likely to become much more common in coming years.

4.1 Two Approaches to Infomediaries

From a logistic point of view, infomediaries can generally be divided into two varieties: profit-motivated and interest-motivated. Each tends to take a different form, a result of the resources available to the service's designers and the degree of control participants have over the process.

Most profit-motivated infomediaries are owned by corporations and are structured to create a more perfect marketplace. These online businesses are interactive and take into consideration the opinions of users, but are ultimately controlled by private entities that are not accountable to users. This is not to say that all for-profit infomediaries are strictly commercial—some political infomediaries are profit-driven as well. The Web site Newsvine,[26] for example, allows users to comment on current events, "vote up" stories they like, and even write their own news pieces, but is owned by MSNBC and thus is beholden to MSNBC's stockholders, with a revenue stream primarily derived from advertising. Profit-motivated infomediaries rely on a business model in which collaboration with users is encouraged, but operates within fixed confines. Such infomediaries very rarely solicit donations from users, as their revenue streams are sufficient to cover the upkeep of running the site.

Interest-motivated infomediaries function very differently from those that are profit-motivated. Many are nonprofit organizations that have no business model beyond charitable contribution; others derive some profits but are nevertheless primarily motivated by a particular ideology, philosophy, or topic. Interest-motivated infomediaries are not necessarily political: Wikipedia, the highly successful online

---

[26] http://www.newsvine.com/.

encyclopedia, and its parent company, the Wikimedia Foundation, are both nonprofit and support the idea of freely available, collaborative information without any particular partisan agenda.[27] And, as a result, they rely heavily on charitable grants and user donations.

Most interest-motivated infomediaries, however, are organized around some central concern. They depend on the passions of their users for a specific cause to sustain their operations, and have become the rallying points of the Internet. One such example is the organization "A SEED." Formed in 1991, A SEED is a network of volunteers dedicated to taking action "against ecological destruction and social injustice."[28] In its modern form, it links like-minded organizations together around the globe and promotes activism such as "initiating and coordinating actions and campaigns on environment, development, and social justice issues" and "promoting discussion and disseminating information about critical emerging issues among youth groups."[29] Among A SEED's accomplishments is its role in helping to mobilize the protesters who would achieve international notoriety for the 1999 "WTO riots" in Seattle.

The Seattle WTO riots have been the subject of considerable scrutiny and have been identified by many as a watershed moment in Internet-facilitated activism, as well as an example of activism out of control. Some have argued that the WTO riots were an unusual exception and that activists are still learning how to maximize their impact using digital mediums,[30] but it is nevertheless the case that online organizations are having a growing influence not only on fringe activism but on mainstream politics as well. As more politically active people look to the Internet for information, the tenor of American politics appears to be changing, and many suggest it is for the worse. As Gene Weingarten comments:

> It is possible to know too much. It is possible to care too much. Hunger for information can become gluttony.
>
> This has always been true, but it is more so now because the opportunities for abuse are greater. There are too many voices, competing too hard, fighting for attention, ranting, redundant, random. The dissemination of fact and opinion is no longer the sole province of people and institutions with the money to buy network monopolies or ink by the ton, as it was a half-century ago when information was delivered to us, for better or

---

[27] Wikimedia Foundation home page, http://wikimediafoundation.org/wiki/Home.
[28] A SEED Europe home page, www.aseed.net.
[29] *Id.*
[30] Katja Cronauner, Activism and the Internet (April 2004) (unpublished PhD thesis, University of British Columbia) (www.cs.ubc.ca/grads/resources/thesis/May04/Katja_Cronauer.pdf).

worse, like the latest 1950s-era cigarette: filtered, for an illusion of safety. Now, all is out of control. Everyone with a computer is a potential pundit; anyone with a video camera can be on a screen.

And so it has come to this: a Web site called Memeorandum .com, which brags, in its mission statement, that it "auto-generates a news summary every 5 minutes, drawing on experts and pundits, insiders and outsiders, media professionals and amateur bloggers." Driven by algorithm, largely unimpeded by the human mind, this information-aggregating Web site offers an obsessively updated menu of hyperlinks to hundreds of morsels of political news and commentary, many of which lead to dozens more of the same, creating a bottomless pyramid of punditry, a tessellated spider work of interconnected news and opinion that canvasses virtually everything that is being publicly written or uttered minute by minute on every subject everywhere by everyone.[31]

Weingarten's sobering examination of what he calls the "pundus-try" recalls the warnings about the tyranny of the majority, and reminds us once again that unfiltered information is essentially too widespread today to be able to process it all. While opportunities exist for political infomediaries to generate informed discussion and collaboration, they can just as easily contribute to a growing political shouting match.

In this increasingly unregulated digital medium, how can we strengthen the positive and minimize the negative? Can infomediaries help ensure that "justice presides over the hostilities and finds suffi-cient compromises to prevent madness in the soul, and civil war or war between peoples"?[32] There is promise here. Where we disagree on fun-damental moral and political matters, compromise is the order of the day if we are to find just, productive, and peaceable resolutions to our disagreements. This requires effective dispute resolution procedures, and such procedures work best if no one party has any greater power (financial, political, or social) than the rest. Infomediaries promise better dispute resolution by empowering individuals, groups, and orga-nizations that might otherwise go unheard. Ideally, we can ensure that the new infomediaries resolve disputes in productive ways as opposed to violence (e.g., the WTO riots) or shouting (e.g., the pundustry).

4.2 A Problem with the Political Role of Infomediaries

There is a problem. Consider that the state, or some statelike entity such as the United Nations, has been, and still is, a key player in dispute

---

[31] Gene Weingarten, *Cruel and Usual Punishment*, Wash. Post, Mar. 23, 2008 (Magazine), at W.12.
[32] Hampshire, *supra* note 13.

resolution through the promulgation and application of laws, rules, regulations, treaties, and the like. This is not to deny the obvious: that informal, nonlegal forms of dispute resolution abound. There are, however, two good reasons the state plays a formal, law-governed dispute resolution role, and these considerations argue *against* giving infomediaries an extensive role in dispute resolution.

The first reason the state plays a critical dispute resolution role is legitimacy. Recall the ideals of legitimacy with which we began: the ideal of *representation* (those affected by a policy should have a say in its adoption and application) and *explanation/justification* (those making policy must make a persuasive case to those the policy affects, especially those it affects adversely). The state, in the tradition of democracy, is the organization that has ensured representation for all citizens in the promulgation and application of laws, rules, regulations, and policies. Further, it is the state that plays a central role in ensuring that decision-makers give reasons for their policies. It would, of course, be extremely unrealistic to insist that every public decision-maker respond to demands for explanations from every person adversely affected by a decision. In principle, however, a reasonable, informed, and intelligent citizen should possess or be able to construct an adequate explanation for policies. Political leaders, political parties, and general political discourse *should* play leading roles in ensuring that citizens adequately approximate such an ideally rational, informed, and intelligent citizen (even if most democracies fall lamentably short of this ideal). The state, in the extended sense of political parties, leaders, and the like, should be the catalyst for the explanatory and justificatory political discourse.

The second reason the state plays a crucial role in dispute resolution is *enforcement*. To avert chaos and to curb the abuse of power, the right to use violence to enforce laws, rules, and decisions lies in the hands of the state. Giving the state the authority to maintain public order and enforce policy flows from the ideal that those who enforce policy should be accountable to the people through political processes: in a democracy, citizens rely on the state to enforce policy because, ultimately, the state is accountable to the voters.

These points suggest that is unlikely that infomediaries will be allowed to play a law-promulgating and law-enforcement role. Infomediaries need not be accountable to the populace as a whole, and this casts considerable doubt on the idea that the issues raised by globalization and the Internet can be resolved by these kinds of collaborative independent entities.

The emerging role of infomediaries does much to resolve these doubts by suggesting that participants in infomediary processes be willing to acknowledge a degree of legitimacy to them, as well as permit them a degree of enforcement power. Esther Dyson, among others, has articulated this vision; she contends that "the Net has created a new division between 'legitimate' terrestrial governments (which own/control physical territory and the people thereon) and 'legitimate' Net governments (which control Net territory by consent and indeed request of the governed) ... Over time, tension will grow, pitting the global world of digital commerce and online society against the more local worlds of traditional government and of people who aren't part of the 'brave new world.' Call it the disintermediation of government."[33] Dyson claims that "self-organizing bottoms-up government is now emerging on the Net."[34] While such "Internet government" cannot replace the role of the state, it can mitigate the state's influence in digital domains.

4.3 The ICANN Example

The Internet Corporation for Assigned Names and Numbers (ICANN) is often cited as an example of an "Internet governmental body." Some have gone so far as to suggest that ICANN clearly demonstrates that law-promulgating and law-enforcement roles can exist outside of traditional governmental hands. ICANN describes itself as a "non-profit corporation that was formed to assume responsibility for the IP address space allocation, protocol parameter assignment, domain name system management, and root server system functions performed under U.S. government contract by IANA and other entities."[35]

There is much at stake, as noted in the following:

> Imagine for the moment that you had control over operation of the root server. You alone get to decide which machines are "authoritative" domain servers for the COM, NET, ORG, EDU, and the other top-level domains, the machines to which all Internet users worldwide will be directed when they try to send any message to any address in those domains. You have the power, therefore, to determine who gets an address in those domains—who gets a passport without which passage across the border into cyberspace is impossible. You can say "From now on, we will use the data in machine X as the authoritative list of COM names and addresses, but only so long as the operator of that machine complies with the following conditions," and then you can list—well, just about anything you'd like, I suppose. It's your root server, after all.[36]

---

[33] ESTHER DYSON, RELEASE 2.0 106 (1999).

[34] *Id.* at 112.

[35] ICANN home page, www.icann.org.

[36] DAVID POST, GOVERNING CYBERSPACE (Jun. 6, 1999), http://www.icannwatch.org/archive/governing_cyberspace.htm.

The first point to note about ICANN is that it is *not* an infomediary. Its structure is highly centralized, and it does not qualify as a "self-organizing bottoms-up government" that it is often taken to be. As Milton Mueller notes:

> Self-regulation of Internet names and numbers is not at all comparable to the other areas where the concept has been applied. Content labeling standards and privacy codes of conduct, for example, both involve collective action by well-established industries around narrowly circumscribed areas of conduct. The basic institutional regime under which these businesses operate pre-date the "self-regulation" process and are fairly clear and stable. Internet governance, on the other hand, involved creating an entirely new institutional and property rights framework. At its centre was the problem of who owned critically important, valuable assets: the name and address spaces. Control of these assets had to be transferred from an informal set of relationships loosely centred in the U.S. government and its private contractors to a formal, internationally representative, legally incorporated entity. A host of related and very complicated property rights issues flowed from that. How could domain name registration, which provided globally exclusive control of a character string, be reconciled with trademark protection, which provided jurisdiction-, industry-, and product-specific forms of protection to certain names? What rules or procedures governed access to the root of the domain name space? How much control did a domain name registry have over the zone files containing the authoritative list of second-level names? These and many other difficult questions were fundamentally legal in nature; that is, the way in which they were decided assigned property rights to specific actors and strengthened or diminished various individuals' freedom of action. The legal questions were greatly complicated by the global, trans-jurisdictional scope of the system. The Commerce Department basically devolved global state power to ICANN. To call such a policy a form of "self-regulation" comparable to the voluntary adoption of a code of conduct by an established group of businesses is not just mistaken, but dangerously obtuse.[37]

In summary, ICANN is not an infomediary aggregating, protecting, and pursuing the interests of a group of like-minded individuals. It is a quasi-governmental entity, organized as much from the top down as the bottom up, an entity to which the American Department of Commerce effectively granted the powers to dictate global policy.

---

[37] Milton Mueller, *ICANN and Internet Governance: Sorting Through the Debris of "Self-Regulation,"* 1 J. Pol'y, Reg. & Strategy Telecomm., Info. & Media 477 (1999).

This is not to criticize ICANN. Such a hybrid of private and public power promises to be an effective way to provide international regulation of the Internet and e-commerce. Nevertheless, a crucial concern about ICANN (and indeed any similar entity) is that it lacks fundamental legitimacy despite its prodigious enforcement powers:

> Whoever controls the DNS will be subject to immense pressure to stray far beyond any limited technical functions because, for all the talk over the past few years about how difficult it will be for anyone to regulate the Internet, the domain name system looks like the Holy Grail, the one place where enforceable global Internet policy can be promulgated without any of the messy enforcement and jurisdictional problems that bedevil ordinary law-making exercises on the Net. Businesses, which now realize the huge economic stake they have in this medium, and governments, which have spent the last few years worrying about how they would ever get back their taxing and regulatory authority over Internet transactions, will view ICANN as the means to impose their particular vision on Internet users worldwide. Power corrupts, and absolute power corrupts absolutely—on the Internet as elsewhere. Governance means nothing more— and nothing less—than the search for mechanisms to ensure that absolute power is not exercised in an unjust or oppressive manner. How can we be assured that ICANN will be able to resist the pressure that will be brought to bear upon it? Where are the checks on the new corporation's exercise of its powers? How can all of those with a stake in the Internet's future, i.e., all of us, be assured that ICANN will exercise its powers in the best interests of the Internet community as a whole, rather than on behalf of one particular faction or another?[38]

Much as infomediaries have arisen to influence and safeguard democracy in government, so too have infomediaries arisen to play a watchdog role over entities such as ICANN. The group ICANNwatch .org is one such example. By applying the model of citizen oversight used for government bodies, infomediaries can also help to ensure that ICANN's enforcement powers are paired with an adequate degree of legitimacy. Despite ICANN existing outside the traditional confines of democracy, infomediaries can help police its actions and ensure that its power is not abused.

We predict that this hybrid public/private regulatory regime for the Internet will persist and become more common. The interplay between quasi-governmental entities such as ICANN and infomediaries playing a variety of watchdog, representative, or communicative roles can help to sustain democratic values in areas of policy that are not directly beholden to voters.

---

[38] *Id.*

5. Convening the Global "Virtual Community"

Practicing lawyers, judges and law schools are in the early stages of a revolution driven by the forces of information technology. The quality of justice in the 21st Century will be determined by the clarity of our vision in understanding these revolutionary forces and our entrepreneurial creativity in adapting to them.[39]

It is not enough to say, as we have thus far, that we have a vision of the future. Empowering voters also requires "entrepreneurial creativity" to bring the benefits of the infomediary approach to specific issues. How can we create an infomediary that promotes an international rule of law, for example? As Henry H. Perritt notes,

> There are many engines of international law. While there is no universally accepted international legislature, there are many international legislatures with overlapping memberships ... There is a wide variety of rulemaking, adjudication, and enforcement arenas in the international context.[40]

Perritt provides a masterful review of the complex array of international bodies involved in generating and enforcing an international rule of law, and he notes that

> the Internet improves the effectiveness of international regimes by making it easier to negotiate treaties and treaty modifications, by increasing the range of procedural options for adjudication, and by improving the flow of enforcement information generated by NGOs and others.[41]

What contribution do we propose in this already complex and well-occupied area? The question is especially relevant given the abstract theoretical discussion in which we have engaged. Even if we assume that we can use the Internet to get people around the world to communicate with one another, how do we get from there to giving them an effective political voice? How can we promote the rule of law through technology without appeals to naive optimism?

5.1 Beginning with a Clear Need

We hope to achieve these goals in an area where there is a clear need for such an effort. We believe that the New Economy needs a just rule of law to be developed in cyberspace. The American Bar Association

---

[39] Henry H. Perritt, Jr., and Ronald W. Staudt, *The 1% Solution: American Judges Must Enter the Internet Age*, ARK. B.J. (forthcoming.

[40] Henry H. Perritt, Jr., *The Internet is Changing International Law*, 73 CHI.-KENT L. REV. 997 (1998).

[41] *Id.* at 1035.

House of Delegates has already adopted recommendations in this area, namely to:

1. Support electronic commerce as an important means of commerce among nations.
2. Support commerce through electronic networks that are global in nature and require international communication and cooperation among all nations, including developing nations.
3. Encourage discussion in open international forums to remove unnecessary legal and functional obstacles to electronic commerce.
4. Encourage the private sector, governments, and international organizations to cooperate to establish a legal framework within which global electronic commerce can flourish in an environment that provides appropriate legal protection to the participants, while eliminating unnecessary legal and functional barriers to electronic commerce.
5. Encourage the private sector to develop self-regulating practices that protect the rights of individuals and promote the public welfare.

Our project builds on an early example of how the rule of law is being reinvented in cyberspace: the pioneering effort by Chicago-Kent College of Law in the emerging democracies of Central and Eastern Europe. In Chicago-Kent's *Global Law and Policy Initiative Summary* of March 2000, the underpinnings of the rule of law through technology are defined by three quotes:

> The Rule of Law is a body of principles, institutions and procedures based upon "some fundamental ideas of human natures, about the individual, and about the relationship of the individual to the State."
> —International Commission of Jurist, New Delhi, 1959

> (I)t is essential if man is not compelled to have recourse as a last resort, to rebellion against tyranny and oppression, that human rights should be protected by the Rule of Law.
> —Universal Declaration of Human Rights, 1948

> If there are three prime requisites for the rule of law, they are a strong bar, an independent judiciary, and an enlightened public opinion.
> —Justice Khanna of the Supreme Court of India

The emerging democracies, in Eastern Europe and elsewhere, need to have an effective voice in international rulemaking. These democracies not only need to develop the technological infrastructure for widespread access to the Internet. They must also develop the culture and practice of using the Internet as a mechanism for cultural and political expression. Chicago-Kent has already taken many steps in this direction. We focus on just two of these initiatives to make the point that concrete progress has already been made.

5.2 Two Polish Initiatives

Poland is rapidly emerging as a model of a successful transition from communist government and planned economy to a democratic government and a market economy. Poland still faces a number of political and economic problems, however; these problems include much-needed judicial reforms.[42] Chicago-Kent's Project Poland is, with the cooperation of Iustitia (Poland's only national association of judges), building a private intranet linking the twenty-one regional offices of Iustitia. Iustitia was formed to promote the independence of judges, due process, and human rights. Iustitia promotes the independence of the judiciary through training of judges, public relations on behalf of judges, lobbying governmental organizations on behalf of the judiciary, and working toward the continued improvement of the administration of justice in Poland. The association also provides a forum for judges to keep pace with the rapid development of Polish law and to prepare for issues resulting from European integration. Iustitia has branches in twenty-one Polish cities representing over 1,200 Polish judges.

The Iustitia intranet has grown to become a full-fledged infomediary. It now not only comprises judges but also members of the public in a way that gives their combined voice greater influence over issues critical to the development of the judiciary. The service now provides four functions:

1. It provides a place for judges to communicate with each other, both by participating in online discussions and by posting written commentary. Communication among judges is vital to the rule of law.
2. It offers the general public information about the Polish legal system, educating citizens about legal rights and the operation of the court system.
3. It gives Iustitia a more powerful political voice in its efforts to develop an effective, efficient, and independent judiciary in Poland.
4. It provides a locus for a potential link to similar sites throughout the world, such as Chicago-Kent's Justice Web Collaboratory site, a network for all the federal courts in the United States.

---

[42] *See* MARCUS B. ZIMMER, STRUCTURAL AND ADMINISTRATIVE REFORM IN THE POLISH JUDICIARY (1998), a report prepared for ABA/CEELI. A copy is on file with the authors. See http://pbosnia.kentlaw.edu for a summary and links to the various projects.

Technical support and in-kind funding for the Iustitia effort come from the Polish legal publisher, ABC Publishing House. We offer the Iustitia Intranet project as an example of how academia, political organizations, and business can cooperate in the construction of infomediaries. Because it not only strengthens the consistency of judicial interpretation but also informs the public, the Iustitia's infomediary strengthens the rule of law by avoiding idiosyncratic and unfair decision-making. To benefit from such a decision-making regime, the public must be adequately educated about legal rights and the court system, which the service also provides.

Chicago-Kent has also recently addressed the training of Polish lawyers. In cooperation with the University of Gdańsk, it founded a School of American Law at that university. Students receive instruction in English from Chicago-Kent professors. The program is highly valued by Polish law firms because it trains students in the pragmatic American style of legal reasoning. The Internet plays a crucial role in enabling long-distance, interactive instruction to supplement onsite visits. Chicago-Kent will open another School of American Law at the University of Wrocław, Poland, in October 2008, and will open a third such program in February 2009 at the Polytechnic University of Łódź, Poland.

5.3 Kosovo Economic Development

Chicago-Kent is also playing an active role in the economic redevelopment of Kosovo.[43] As the Web site devoted to this task explains, "Chicago-Kent, in collaboration with Kosova Foundation for Economic Reconstruction and Development, ASG Group and TAMS, is providing technical assistance to the Ministry of Reconstruction and Development of the Interim Government of Kosova."[44] The site includes a discussion forum in which all interested parties can participate. The Web site illustrates another concrete step toward developing a virtual international community devoted to international business issues and the emergence of an international rule of law.

6. Conclusion: A Call to Action

As Chicago-Kent's efforts show, we can take practical steps to create the "new global institutions" predicted by Toffler. Though the state clearly remains the de facto "political container" for voter actions, the now-global economy will inevitably necessitate a growing role for international cooperation in nongovernmental or pseudo-governmental forums. But still one may rightly ask, how do you get from discrete efforts in Eastern Europe to a global political discussion?

---

[43] Nationbuilding in the Balkans: Operation Kosovo, http://pbosnia.kentlaw.edu/projects/ (last visited May 29, 2008).
[44] Id.

To begin with, consider that globalization and e-commerce, as realized in international business transactions, have driven and will continue to drive the development of an international rule of law. This means the Eastern European projects described above need to be linked to Web sites that will allow them to have a voice in this development. The Internet gives us the technological means to link more people than any international physical conference could, on a single platform where each can have a say and a chance for explanation. The emergence of this networked world offers a whole range of new opportunities for people from all countries and cultures to communicate and interact. There is finally a place for people to talk and discuss how best to create a just society. We need to take this opportunity to conclude a new social contract among the Internet users, so that we recognize cyberspace as a world community governed by the rule of law. It would be wrong to ask for a detailed blueprint here, for a detailed explanation of how everyone has a "voice," a "say" in policy matters. The fact that we cannot see clearly where a road ends does not mean we should not begin a journey of exploration. In this spirit, we propose to actively promote the emergence of such an international rule of law through the creation of a virtual community that builds new rules for the new economy that are fair to all.[45] The new community is the Internet Bar Organization (www.internetbar.org) whose mission is to promote fairness and equity in shaping the emerging online justice system.

We should ensure that any effort toward global rulemaking avoids the mistakes of the past. The numerous top-down international treaties failed to get the world to agree on even some basic sets of rules. If we are to create a new kind of institution for the Third Wave civilization predicted by Toffler, we need to overcome the disabilities of world lawmaking from the Industrial Age and create a virtual learning community where the learning, as the Chicago-Kent efforts show, occurs among all the participants. The creation of a virtual global community dedicated to the rule of law in cyberspace is an important step toward developing a process that will lead the world in a cross-cultural negotiation to establish the guiding principles that will shape our New Economy and ensure a smooth transition to the digital age.

Jeffrey M. Aresty
Aresty International Law Offices. P.C.
365 Boston Post Road #135
Sudbury, MA 01776
Phone: (508) 314-0916
E-mail: jaresty@cyberspaceattorney.com

---

[45] The virtual community has been in existence since 2005. You can join the community at www.internetbar.org.

Richard Warner
Professor of Law
Chicago-Kent College of Law
Chicago, IL 60661
Phone: (312) 906-5340
Fax: (312) 906-5280
E-mail: rwarner@kentlaw.edu

CHAPTER 4

Negotiating Globally and Virtually

Henry H. Perritt, Jr.[1]

Chicago-Kent College of Law
Chicago, Illinois

1. Introduction

Globalization and the Internet are two realities of modern life for a lawyer. No longer can American lawyers expect that their practices will be purely domestic. A growing proportion of business transactions involve foreign customers, suppliers, or joint venturers. As labor markets extend across national boundaries, employment agreements must cover foreign workers. International human rights norms are gradually intruding into criminal law litigation. Even in domestic relations practices, marital partners often take children across international borders. As securities markets go virtual, they also become inherently global. International business negotiations implicate public policy and success requires an appreciation of international politics. In this world of blurring borders, it is easy to take the Internet's role in this global space for granted. It is the world's library, its cable office, and—from time to time—the scene of its gold rush.

In the past, many American lawyers were ill prepared to deal with accelerating globalization—or accelerating technology. Until relatively recently, law schools treated international law as a specialized compartment, mostly disconnected from the doctrine and procedural knowledge that make up the mainstream of law school curricula. Even courses in conflict of laws, a subject that lawyers in other countries call "private international law," focused on U.S. cases, mostly to the exclusion of transactional or foreign cases. Now, it is hard to find a law school that does not trumpet its emphasis on international subjects or to find a casebook without some reference to transnational issues in

---

[1] Professor Perritt has been involved in a wide range of negotiations over collective bargaining agreements, political candidacies, legislation, administrative agency regulation, business deals, and international disputes. He also was a pioneer in analyzing the effects of small computers and the Internet on law and lawyers, with his 1985 *How to Practice Law with Computers*, from PLI, and his 1996 *Law and the Information Superhighway*, now available in its second edition from Aspen. He served on the National Research Council's Computer Science and Telecommunications Board.

the doctrines it covers. At the same time that law students are showing increasing proficiency with portable computing, wireless Internet connections, and virtual communication, however, some professors are trying to ban this new technology from the classroom.

Many practitioners are scrambling to catch up. They encounter problems involving the application of foreign substantive law; they must deal with treaty frameworks that channel trade and define intellectual property rights; and they must struggle to participate effectively in discussions of Internet regulation involving European privacy principles, Japanese concepts of personal jurisdiction, German hate speech law, and Russian cybercrime.

But learning the principles of private international law, human rights, the outline of the World Trade Organization, and the terms of new copyright treaties is not enough; most representation involves negotiation. Negotiation is a quintessentially human process, requiring careful analysis of the interests on all sides, an appreciation of behavioral norms for negotiators, and creativity in finding "win-win" solutions that improve the position of all sides on underlying interests, while permitting those wishing to compromise to save face.

Experienced negotiators in domestic U.S. business deals, labor management negotiations, and lawsuit settlement negotiations know how to assess party positions in terms of "Best Alternatives to Negotiated Agreement," how to use initial offers to infer reservation prices, and how to act so as to ensure a problem-solving approach rather than a personally antagonistic one.

But how can these modes of thinking—this art of negotiation—be applied across cultural and national boundaries? How should one deal with an opponent who comes from a culture where internal consensus is a paramount value? With a situation where the culture encourages bribery? With an opponent who has been taught to say what another party wants to hear, regardless of whether the message is likely to translate into an agreement?

This chapter provides an introduction to some of these issues, while later chapters probe other topics more deeply. This chapter reviews foundational material on negotiations, beginning with the BATNA concept, and then assesses how technology can be used to facilitate negotiations across national borders. Some experienced international negotiators will find many of the points made in this chapter obvious. Others will find the framework beneficial for thinking about negotiation and the use of technology to facilitate it.

2. Negotiation Basics

2.1 BATNA: Best Alternative to Negotiated Agreement

Most basic to any conceptual framework for understanding negotiations is the concept of BATNA. A party's BATNA is that party's reservation price in the negotiations. BATNA is an acronym for Best Alternative to Negotiated Agreement.[2] A rational party to a negotiation will not agree to a negotiated outcome that is less favorable to that party than the party believes he could obtain in the absence of a negotiated agreement. The "settlement" range is the area of overlap between the BATNAs of two parties.

Suppose Alice is negotiating with Bob about the sale of Alice's automobile to Bob. Alice has a standing offer from Carol to buy the automobile for $21,000. Carol's offer sets Alice's BATNA to $21,000, because Alice will not agree to sell it to Bob for less than $21,000. If Bob believes that he can obtain an equivalent automobile for $23,000 from Dirk, he will not agree to pay any more than $23,000 to Alice. His BATNA is therefore $23,000. In this example there is a settlement range between $21,000 and $23,000, with each party's BATNA as the outer limit of that range.

In some cases, there is no settlement range because the BATNAs do not overlap. Suppose that Bob believes that he can get an equivalent automobile for $19,000. He will not agree to pay any more to Alice than his BATNA of $19,000. Alice's BATNA is $21,000, and there is no settlement range.

Cases where no settlement range exists can deadlock a negotiation. For example, in the internationally mediated negotiations over Kosovo's final status, no settlement range emerged. The Serbian government apparently believed it could prevent the international community from making Kosovo independent and thus, in the absence of an agreement, Kosovo would remain a part of its sovereign territory. The Kosovo Albanian side believed that the United States and major European nations would recognize it if it declared independence, and thus would not agree to anything less than independence. Despite considerable effort to forge an agreement on less controversial issues related to the protection of minority Kosovo Serbs within an independent Kosovo, negotiations proved fruitless in the end because both parties knew they would never be able to agree on the main issue of Kosovo's legal status. (Kosovo declared independence on February 17, 2008 and has so far been recognized by forty-seven countries, including the United States and most of Western Europe.)

BATNAs are usually produced by a mix of subjective perceptions and objective facts. Therefore, it is important for all parties to find common ground in some set of facts, and then to evaluate everyone's subjective views. Understanding the BATNA concept and focusing on the evaluation of BATNAs in a negotiation helps everything else fall into place for a coherent approach.

---

[2] The phrase and the acronym were popularized by Roger Fisher and William Ury's 1981 book GETTING TO YES, the current edition of which is ROGER FISHER, BRUCE M. PATTON & WILLIAM L. URY, GETTING TO YES (2d ed. 1992).

2.2 The Functions of Negotiation

One negotiates more effectively if he is clear about the goals of communications with the opposing party during the negotiation. Four goals can be identified as being present in any negotiation: changing the opposing party's BATNA, refining one's understanding of the opposing party's interests, revising one's own BATNA, and building trust between the parties.

2.2.1 Persuade Opponents to Revise Their BATNAs

Because the opposing party's position in the negotiation is determined by that party's BATNA, a negotiator can change her opponent's position by persuading the opponent to revise his BATNA. In the simple hypothetical of negotiations over sale of an automobile, Alice surely will try to persuade Bob that he cannot get an equivalent car for less than, say, $25,000, and that Alice has a ready buyer for almost that much. If Bob's opening BATNA is determined by the belief that Dirk will sell for $19,000, Alice would try to persuade Bob that Dirk will demand a higher price, such as $28,000. In the same negotiation, Bob will try to persuade Alice that Carol will be unwilling to pay Alice more than $18,000 or that Carol is not willing to buy the automobile at all.

In order for this process to work, each party must know the opponent's BATNA and have an understanding of how that BATNA was determined.

While parties have an incentive to exaggerate, it is in their interest to communicate about their own BATNAs. For example, in the automobile-sale negotiation, Alice should tell Bob that she has another buyer for the car at $21,000 and thus will not consider any offer less than that. Bob, likewise, should disclose to Alice that he believes he can get the same car or an equivalent car for $19,000. There is no reason to conceal this information; mutual knowledge of such basic facts helps the parties know whether negotiations can be fruitful and what to talk about if they negotiate.

2.2.2 Determine the Other Party's Interests

Real negotiations are more complicated than the examples offered. Even in a simple negotiation about the sale of an automobile, it is likely that the parties have interests other than simple zero-sum[3] monetary ones. For example, if Alice has an emotional attachment to the automobile, she may be interested in selling it to someone who will take good care of it. If Bob knows that, he can seek to influence Alice's position by persuading her that he will take better care of the car than Carol would. This is an example both of Bob's seeking to change

---

[3] "Zero-sum" signifies that one party's gain comes at the other party's expense, dollar for dollar. A win-win negotiation is the opposite of a zero-sum negotiation.

Alice's BATNA with respect to the care that Carol will give the car and of his seeking to increase the value of his offer to Alice. If Bob doesn't know that this is one of Alice's interests, he will not be motivated to communicate on the subject.

With this kind of consequence in mind, one of the essentials for any negotiation session is that each party inquire about what the other party wants out of the negotiation. This can be done through open-ended questions or, especially as negotiations proceed, through more specific questions, such as, "Don't you care about what happens to the car?"

In almost any real negotiation, each party seeks to maximize the value of an array of interests. In a real-world negotiation about purchase of an automobile, each side cares about price, the delivery date, driving qualities, warranties, insurability, status of the title, and so on. Often, specific interests get added to the array as the result of communications that occur during negotiation. For example, consider settlement negotiations over a lawsuit for defamation. In such a negotiation, the plaintiff is concerned with the monetary amount of a settlement offer but may be more concerned about other, nonmonetary interests, such as the psychic value of an apology, the reputational value of a public retraction of the allegedly defamatory statement, and the possible retributive value of inflicting costs or other pain on a defendant. The plaintiff also should be concerned about the further costs to the plaintiff's reputation and mental well-being by having a public airing of the validity of the allegedly defamatory statements. Even if the matter is resolved short of a public trial, participating in depositions and other discovery may be painful for the plaintiff.

An effective negotiator for the defendant will make sure that these related reputational and psychic-comfort interests are part of the array against which the plaintiff calculates his BATNA. The plaintiff's BATNA with respect to these interests can be worsened if the defendant describes concrete plans with respect to the content of discovery or evidence to be presented by the defendant at any trial.

2.2.3 Reassessing One's Own BATNA

A good negotiator seeks not only to influence his opponent's BATNA but also to improve the accuracy of his own BATNA. BATNA calculation is always a guessing game, at least to some extent. To the extent a negotiator can get better data pertinent to his own BATNA calculations, he can negotiate more rationally.

There is no reason not to be fairly candid in seeking such additional negotiation by asking questions such as "Why do you think you can get a car this good for less than $21,000?" Or "What evidence do you have to support the damaging statements the defendant made about me?" Or, in a labor management negotiation, "What makes you think that your low-wage constituents will be able to stay out on strike for more than one weekly pay period?"

It is not uncommon for a negotiator to learn that the other side has stronger support for its position than could be anticipated before the negotiation began, and it would be irrational to fail to revise one's position as information about such support becomes available.

2.2.4 Building Trust

All of the above discussion of how to approach a negotiation relies on each side being able to rely on the validity of information obtained from the other side, especially if such information is to influence the recipient's negotiating position. If one believes that one's opponent is an unreliable source of information, little that the opponent can say in a negotiation will have any effect on the recipient's position. Conversely, if a negotiator trusts his opponent and believes that the opponent never lies, then what the opponent says can have significant effect on the recipient's position.

This creates a conundrum. If the negotiator is too transparent, too readily revealing the most important weaknesses in her position, the outcome obtainable by that negotiator will be worse than if she is less forthcoming. To return to the simple auto sale negotiation, suppose Alice is selling the car because she desperately needs the money to pay arrearages on her mortgage before foreclosure proceedings start. It is not necessarily helpful to disclose this to Bob: if Bob is invested in the negotiation, Alice may gain more if Bob is unaware of Alice's financial hardship; on the other hand, if Bob is about to walk away from the negotiations altogether, Alice may be motivated to share this information to keep Bob negotiating.

A good negotiator never lies overtly but also does not disclose everything that she knows. Any objective facts are subject to "spin." A good negotiator spins the facts supporting her position in the most optimistic way, but must be careful not to undermine her own credibility. A good negotiator also is attentive to the dynamics of the negotiation. What is important to keep secret at one point may be important to disclose at another point.

2.3 Setting the Agenda

The agenda for negotiations should be set by the parties from the beginning. Sometimes they explicitly talk about an agenda, the number of negotiating sessions, the issues to be negotiated, and the order in which the issues will be addressed. Other times, the agenda is set implicitly by the parties making their respective proposals. In very simple negotiations, of course, an agenda is hardly necessary. Alice knows she wants to sell her car. Bob is interested in buying it, and the parties know that they have to agree on price, delivery terms, and any warranties as to the car's condition.

In formulating proposals in more complex negotiations, especially when there are considerable zero-sum aspects to the negotiation, parties must be aware that some proposals they might make will cause significantly negative emotional responses by the other side. For example, in a labor-management negotiation, if the management negotiator begins with a proposal to decertify the union, he can expect a hostile reaction. Good negotiators are tactful but pragmatic. A negotiation is not a cocktail party conversation or a courtship. An effective negotiator must be willing to make proposals that are likely to prove unpopular to the other side. Sometimes a negotiator is surprised by the reaction, however. The negotiator may anticipate strong opposition by the other side and instead be greeted by indifference or a mild "We'll consider it." As the aphorism goes, "You have to ask for what you want," and productive negotiation relies on the ability both to present and to confront unpopular proposals with a cool head.

Almost any experienced negotiator considers it bad faith for new proposals to be introduced in the middle of a negotiation. A professional and well-prepared negotiator puts everything on the table at the beginning.

Once an agenda is understood and all parties have presented proposals, the parties must decide on the order in which issues should be addressed. One approach is to start with the issues on which agreement is likely and resolve those tentatively as a way of building mutual confidence that the negotiation can be successful. This can be useful if the negotiators do not know each other and need to build mutual trust. On the other hand, it can be a waste of time if more difficult issues are likely to produce an impasse.

The alternative is to start with the hard issues. If they can be resolved, then the less contentious issues can be wrapped up at the end, with party positions on those issues influenced by how much each party had to give up to resolve the difficult issues. This approach is best suited to scenarios where negotiators have basic trust for one another, whether from reputation or from personal experience.

Making proposals is important not just in terms of an agenda, but also in terms of gathering information. If one is uncertain about the opposing side's BATNA, one can learn something about the BATNA by making an ambitious proposal and evaluating the counterproposal for other reactions. Because of this, most skilled negotiators believe it is a bad idea to begin with one's most generous offer. If the opposite side agrees to it immediately, the proposer is left wondering whether the opponent's BATNA was such that he would have been willing to agree to a more favorable proposal than the one actually made.

2.4 Developing a Text

A number of theorists of negotiations emphasize the advantage of focusing a negotiation on one's own proposed text of an agreement. It generally is true that if only one side brings a proposed text to the negotiation, then that draft frames the agenda for the negotiation according to the drafter's preferences. It also may induce the other side to focus on relatively minor changes to the text rather than a diametrically different approach that might be less favorable to the drafter.

On the other hand, the advantage of negotiating from one's own draft may be lost when both sides are sophisticated and the agreement (if any) is likely to be memorialized in a complex text such as a treaty, a settlement agreement, a financing agreement, a shareholder agreement, or a collective bargaining agreement. Beginning the negotiation with detailed texts presented by both sides is likely to be counterproductive. Each side will insist on negotiating from its text, and if the texts are dissimilar in structure it may be hard to figure out where to begin. In such situations, it would be more fruitful to begin with a basic assessment of issues and interests. Then it can be useful for one side or the other (or perhaps both) to bring a statement of principles or a simple statement of areas of agreement and disagreement to a subsequent negotiating session. Drafting such statements can be done in one or two pages, and is an important test of the trustworthiness and professionalism of the party that drafts it. Such a document should be short, simply stated, and written so as to reflect the positions of all parties fairly. Trying to sneak something by at this stage can produce significant setbacks in trust and negotiation progress. From there, the negotiation can proceed to exchanges of language on particular sections of an ultimate agreement.

3. Negotiation at a Distance

Personal computer and Internet technologies have revolutionized the methods of negotiation while leaving the fundamental strategies and tactics of negotiation intact. In any negotiation today, technology facilitates the exchange of documents and messages between the parties, even when face-to-face meetings are more appropriate to the work of assessing interests and BATNAs and persuading the other side to change them. And in simple, less contentious negotiations, face-to-face meetings are altogether unnecessary.

3.1 What Is Gained

Exchanging documents electronically is more efficient than exchanging them as paper. An electronic document may be transmitted to the other side as soon as it is complete rather than waiting for delivery by hand. Different versions of the same document can easily be compared electronically with changes highlighted. Regular e-mail exchanges automatically create a record of the negotiations. Properly constructed spreadsheets permit the parties to do sensitivity analysis, evaluating the effect of specific changes in assumptions or values of key variables. Presentation software such as Microsoft's PowerPoint permits the parties to make structured presentations to each other (although this technique is overused and many PowerPoint presentations could be replaced by simpler forms of direct informal oral communication).

All of these advantages can be realized regardless of whether face-to-face meetings occur. Experience with computer-facilitated communication among members of groups suggests that these technologies are most effective when the members of the group have already had some personal interaction to form impressions of each other and to begin the process of establishing some kind of basic social bond. In contrast, purely electronic communications among strangers can more easily go awry because of the possibility that nuances may be missed or misconstrued.

3.2 What Is Lost

Negotiations involve both pure communication and persuasion. As long as the participants write clearly, electronic communication is just as effective as, and sometimes more effective than, communicating face to face. Written efforts to persuade, however, are often less effective than face-to-face encounters. When the persuader and his target are face to face, the persuader can adapt his persuasive arguments and their expression in real time, based on the instantaneous reactions of the target. Many of these reactions are communicated nonverbally. A persuader can see confusion or resistance in facial expression or body language of the target before the target makes any kind of verbal response.

Accordingly, a good negotiator will select the methods of interaction carefully depending on the type of negotiation and with respect to particular issues within a single negotiation. Purely electronic communication is sufficient and may be superior for relatively noncontroversial issues and for those particularly dependent on textual expression. Face-to-face meetings should be scheduled if practicable for more contentious issues in which persuasion is important and maximizing communication channels is key.

4. Technologies for Negotiation

While personal computer and Internet technologies expand the tools available to negotiators, negotiation remains a deeply human process. Only the simplest and most structured deals can be negotiated mainly through computer-to-computer interaction. Specifying the features of a new computer system to be purchased or selecting the details of an airline flight or a hotel reservation are examples in which offers and acceptances can easily be expressed by clicking options on a computer screen.

In contrast, trying to negotiate a collective bargaining agreement, arranging a financing agreement for a major loan, or working out a status of forces agreement for military assistance by clicking boxes on a form or by programming one's computer to search the Web for offers would be ludicrous. The subject matter of such negotiations is too varied and subtle to be captured by computer software written in advance.

Accordingly, a good negotiator thinks carefully about the technologies that will be most helpful, beginning with more sophisticated tools for tracking interests and the value of proposals against those interests and ranging down to the sampling exchange of e-mail.

4.1 E-mail

Any negotiation can be facilitated by the use of e-mail, and since almost everyone in the world now has access to e-mail, negotiators are likely to take its use for granted. The interesting question relates to what tools beyond e-mail and word processing attachments to e-mail may be helpful as well.

Everyone has a story, of course, about an internal e-mail falling into an opponent's hands. Everyone close to a negotiation should be careful to take a moment before clicking Send, especially when a message has sensitive contents, as well as double-checking who is in the recipients list. Some matters of strategy should not be discussed by e-mail at all, or even reduced to any kind of writing. They should be handled face to face. That is the best way to maintain confidentiality.

4.2 Voice over Internet Protocol (VoIP) Software

Telephonic communication was a mainstay auxiliary to face-to-face negotiations long before e-mail use was widespread. When the parties are a considerable distance from each other, however, the cost of long telephone conversations and of telephone conferencing can be a problem. The widespread availability of IP-based telephony through services such as Google Talk and Skype now mitigate the cost of telephonic communication and also facilitate arranging conference calls. Both services are free for communication between personal computers, provided a microphone and speakers/headphones are attached. Both services permit users to quickly download the necessary software and then to establish communication simply by knowing each other's screen name. It also is possible to add a video link to these IP-based telephonic communications, although it is questionable how much value a relatively low quality headshot of another party adds to the communication.

With or without video, Google Talk and Skype add the possibility of cheap, real-time verbal communication to the basic platform of asynchronous e-mail communication.

4.3 Chat and Texting

A multitude of software platforms permit chat communications, in which the parties exchange textual messages in real time. Texting now is available for most cell phone plans in the United States and elsewhere. Chat communication and texting can be useful supplements to Internet-based telephony when microphones or headphones are unavailable or when the parties simply want to schedule a telephonic communication or a meeting, to confirm receipt of a document, or to exchange small amounts of data such as telephone numbers or e-mail addresses. It is also an efficient way to exchange information poorly suited to speech (such as Web addresses) in real time.

4.4 Spreadsheets

Spreadsheets are an effective way to organize and display numerical data and to embed basic calculations, such as those involved in computing the total value of a multiyear agreement, the impact of assumptions about the value of basic variables, and the like.

Any negotiation with a significant monetary or other quantitative component can be facilitated by the exchange of well-constructed spreadsheets that opposing parties can modify and send back. Spreadsheets, like word processing documents, can easily be attached to e-mail messages. The use of spreadsheets in the business world, however, still outpaces proficiency, which can lead to misunderstandings. When sharing spreadsheets that contain extensive embedded calculations, it is often best to "lock" those cells doing the calculation to minimize the chances of accidental changes made by the receiving party.

4.5 Negotiation Software Frameworks

A number of vendors offer products that promise to facilitate negotiations and improve negotiated outcomes. Some of these products can be useful in helping a party to a negotiation calculate BATNAs and set priorities. For example, one can input assumptions about the value to one's own side of a particular element in a negotiated agreement and the cost or value to the other side. Because the specific elements of most agreements are asymmetrical in their effect on the parties (i.e., more valuable to one side than the other) and because many negotiations involve a significant number of such asymmetric effects, computer programs can be useful in evaluating the combined effect of various outcomes on multiple issues.

On the other hand, human communication cannot be replaced effectively by computers in any but the simplest negotiations. Parties should beware of products that promise a completely different approach to negotiations and should, before purchasing or using such products, be clear about exactly what value they can add given the context of a particular negotiation. Often the designers and programmers behind such products know much more about software and systems analysis than they do about how negotiations occur in the real world.

The author has considerable experience in the labor-management negotiation and international negotiation contexts. He has never seen an international negotiation that could benefit particularly from computerized assessment of interests and outcomes. On the other hand, some years ago the author participated in formulating a strategy for a major round of negotiations between a railroad and the unions representing its operating employees. Railroad collective bargaining agreements are notoriously complex, addressing a wide variety of compensation elements and work rules. In one such strategy session, the author recalls considerable benefits being realized from the railroad's negotiating team spending a couple of days at a conference center equipped with video displays and well-designed software that permitted users to input various assumptions about the value of outcomes on particular work rules and compensation elements to the parties and then to see a graphical portrayal of the "pareto optimal"[4] frontier of possibilities. It is reasonable to credit these strategy sessions with the negotiation approach that led first to the reduction in train crew size and eventually to the elimination of collectively bargained rules that required cabooses on most freight trains.

The difference between the two contexts was that the railroad negotiations, while complicated in terms of the number of potential issues, involved relatively easily quantifiable outcomes on each issue. The international negotiations, on the other hand, involve more uncertain and less quantifiable results.

5. Conclusion

Even though the subjects will vary widely and the cultural contexts can be diverse, international negotiators can benefit from appreciating the underlying purposes of their negotiation efforts and the ways in which small-computer and Internet technology can facilitate the negotiations.

Henry H. Perritt, Jr.
Professor of Law
Chicago-Kent College of Law
565 West Adams Street
Chicago, IL 60661
Phone: (312) 906-5098
Fax: (312) 906-5280
E-mail: hperritt@kentlaw.edu

---

[4] Pareto-optimality is the condition under which no party can get more without making another party worse off. The objective of win-win negotiations is to approach the condition of pareto-optimality.

CHAPTER 5

Cross-Cultural Skills in International Negotiations: Technology as a Catalyst and Barrier in the Internet Age

Daniel Rainey
DIRECTOR, ALTERNATIVE DISPUTE RESOLUTION SERVICES
THE NATIONAL MEDIATION BOARD
WASHINGTON, D.C.

1. Introduction

In 1803, James Monroe and Robert Livingston began negotiations with the government of France on a deal that would literally change the face of the United States: the Louisiana Purchase. Assuming they were going to Paris to negotiate for the "Isle of Orleans" (now New Orleans) and West Florida, the U.S. negotiators were sent with instructions to expend as much as $2 million to make the purchase. As is common in negotiations, they were presented with several surprises.

The first surprise was that West Florida was off the table. The second surprise was that Napoleon I's chief negotiator, Charles Maurice de Talleyrand, offered an "all or nothing" deal for the Louisiana Territory. In what must be one of the all-time great exhibitions of negotiator *chutzpah*, Monroe and Livingston negotiated a deal that settled the purchase price ($15 million), payment terms, interest rate, and transfer of liability for outstanding claims, all in the space of less than a month. For good measure, they also negotiated a twelve-year tariff agreement. Then they got on a sailing ship and headed back to tell the "home office" what they had done.[1]

Although this example of international/intercultural negotiation is more than two hundred years old, there are a number of elements

---

[1] There are many good histories of the Louisiana Purchase, including Thomas Fleming's THE LOUISIANA PURCHASE (2003) and The History Channel's 2005 publication THE LOUISIANA PURCHASE. For quick reference, see Francis Coughlin's nomination of Monroe and Livingston in the NEGOTIATOR MAGAZINE (http://www.negotiatormagazine .com/outstanding.shtml), or the Questia entry at http://www.questia.com/library /encyclopedia/louisiana_purchase.jsp (last visited Dec. 12, 2008).

faced by Monroe and Livingston that have remained constant over the centuries, and that are affected by the development and application of technology:

- There were developments at the table unanticipated by the negotiators or the parties giving instructions to the negotiators.
- There were opportunities presented at the table that were not consistent with the limits set for the negotiators.
- There were multiple languages used in the negotiations and in drawing up the final agreement.
- There was a communication lag between the negotiators and their clients back in Washington.
- There were multiple influences and interested parties away from the table, spread across a wide geographical area, all of whom had to be taken into consideration and brought in to agree on the final deal.

It goes without saying that Monroe and Livingston would face a much different negotiating environment if they were working today. Information and communication technology (ICT) has changed the way people around the world communicate generally, and it has radically changed the environment in which international/intercultural negotiations take place.[2]

In the early 1960s, J.C.R. Licklider, an MIT professor and the first director of the Information Processing Techniques Office (IPTO) at the Advanced Research Projects Agency (ARPA), conceived of what he called the "Galactic Network."[3] Today, Licklider's name for his idea is a bit reminiscent of Star Trek, but a series of articles by Licklider and work by scientists across the United States eventually led to the creation of the Internet. Today the idea of "the Internet in space" is being pursued by a number of researchers, so we may soon have Licklider's Galactic Network after all.[4]

What matters to negotiators, however, are the concrete changes that ICT has wrought here on this planet. Negotiations are ultimately exercises in communication, and, generally speaking, ICT has changed

---

[2] Throughout this chapter I will use ICT to refer to a wide range of communication technologies, including telephonic and mobile telephonic communication, as well as e-mail, text messaging, and other Internet-based communication platforms.

[3] BARRY M. LEINER ET AL., A BRIEF HISTORY OF THE INTERNET (version 3.32, last rev. Dec. 10, 2003), http://www.isoc.org/internet/history/brief.shtml; also see FREE ENCYCLOPEDIA OF ECOMMERCE, MIT AND THE GALACTIC NETWORK, http://ecommerce.hostip.info/pages/741/Mit-Galactic-Network.html (last visited July 7, 2008).

[4] Joanna Glasner, *Pushing the Internet into Space*, WIRED MAGAZINE, March 14, 2006, *available at* www.wired.com/science/discoveries/news/2006/03/70377; also see BBC News Online, *Net Reaches Out to Final Frontier*, April 13, 2007, http://news.bbc.co.uk/2/hi/technology/6551807.stm.

the way we communicate (including the way we communicate across cultural boundaries) in some significant ways.

As a rule, it is fair to say that all of the intercultural barriers and problems associated with international/intercultural negotiations remain when technology becomes part of the negotiation environment. There are some direct intercultural effects of the use of technology (some enhancing intercultural communication and others impeding it), but for the most part technology serves as a channel for communication, not as a substitute for the communication that must occur in order for negotiations to be successful. The technology tools discussed in this chapter should be seen as elements of the *process* of negotiation, not as elements of the *substance* of negotiation, and as such may amplify or diminish intercultural aspects of negotiation, but not eliminate them.[5]

The goal for this chapter, as given by the editors, is not to focus solely on culture and technology, but also to present a snapshot of some of the ICT platforms available to negotiators and to discuss possible uses of that technology.

How has ICT radically changed the way we communicate? The most obvious radical change is that communication is now near-instantaneous. Even fast clipper ships in the mid-nineteenth century took two weeks or more to cross the Atlantic, so Monroe and Livingston could have expected it to take, at the very best, more than a month to get a reply to any message. ICT makes it possible to talk in real time, to conference multiple parties into the conversation, and to share documents and images so that the discussion is not limited to oral summaries of proposals or related material. Further, ICT makes it possible to have the conversations with full audio and video, synchronously, or with text, audio, and/or video asynchronously.

ICT is being used around the world for a variety of dispute resolution and negotiation efforts that suggest how flexible and rapid communication has become since Monroe and Livingston's day.

Through its Ombudsman, the Internet Corporation for Assigned Names and Numbers (ICANN) uses e-mail to resolve disputes about assigned Internet addresses arising from all over the world.[6] The U.S. National Mediation Board (NMB) uses Web video to conduct arbitration hearings and uses online asynchronous workspaces to manage

---

[5] For an extended discussion of the impact of technology on culture, see Daniel Rainey, Dir., Alternative Disp. Resol. Servs., Nat'l Mediation Bd. & Alma Abdul-Hadi Jadallah, Doctoral Candidate, Geo. Mason U., The Culture in the Code, Presentation at the Fourth International Forum on Online Dispute Resolution, Cairo, Egypt (March 22–23, 2006), *available at* http://sites.google.com/site/danielraineyorg/Home/recent-activity.

[6] ICANN home page, http://www.icann.org.

ongoing labor-management negotiations in the airline and railroad industries.[7] The American Arbitration Association (AAA) has teamed with CyberSettle to use blind bidding "smart" software to manage arbitration cases around the world.[8] The Camera Arbitrale Nazionale e Internazionale di Milano has created an online dispute resolution service for commercial disputes in Italy and the E.U.[9] The ICT for Peace Foundation has created a network of Web-based platforms to further the cause of peace and stability in Sri Lanka and other nations in strife.[10] In all of these cases, ICT facilitates communication between and among parties with diverse cultural, national, and linguistic backgrounds.

2. What Tools Have Been Developed for Negotiation?

Until comparatively recently the technology used by international negotiators had changed little from the technology used by Monroe and Livingston: oral briefings, written instructions, handwritten and/ or edited agreement drafts, and written communication with the clients very much out of sync with the actual pace of negotiations. The advent of basic telecommunications technology added telegraph, telex, telephone, and fax to the technology arsenal, but still the pace of negotiations routinely outstripped the ability of the negotiators to communicate in a reasonable time frame with clients or interested parties in other geographic locations. Developments in global communications, particularly in digital media, have recently produced a host of new tools[11] to tackle this problem.

For purposes of this discussion, consider information and communication technology (ICT) grouped into five categories: basic communication technology, synchronous video and audio, virtual table platforms, function-related applications, and "smart" software.

Everyone currently involved in negotiations is familiar with the options offered by basic communication technology, and it is highly unlikely that any successful negotiator today can avoid using mobile phones, e-mail, scanned documents, and fax machines. Monroe and Livingston had to rely on the prescience of the Congress when they

---

[7] National Mediation Board home page, http://www.nmb.gov.

[8] American Arbitration Association home page, http://www.adr.org.

[9] Camera Arbitrale di Milano home page, http://www.camera-arbitrale.com.

[10] ICT for Peace Foundation home page, http://www.ict4peace.org.

[11] There are literally hundreds, perhaps thousands, of ICT applications and platforms available for use in negotiation. In this chapter I will mention a number of them, but the nature of technology development suggests that by the time this goes to press, some will have disappeared and new ones will have become available. The applications and platforms cited here are given purely for the purpose of reference and example; mention in this chapter does not guarantee that the specific applications and platforms will be available, nor does it suggest endorsement or recommendation.

were instructed to negotiate with Talleyrand. If the Congress had foreseen every opportunity and every twist in the negotiations, and if the negotiators had adequately understood and accepted their instructions, there would have been no surprises. Faced with changes, Monroe and Livingston were left to react in what they thought was a reasonable manner, hoping that they could sell their reasonable actions to the President and the Congress well after the fact.

In a modern negotiating environment it is possible to wake the client in the middle of his or her night's sleep with a mobile phone call, or to send an e-mail with the expectation of a rapid response, or to send a text message with the expectation of an immediate response. Fax and e-mail allow for transmission of documents and make multiple rounds of editing possible in very little time. For contemporary negotiators working at a table far removed from the client, crying "Help, give me some guidance" is now possible, and even easy. Basic communication technology has opened the process of negotiation and made it possible for far-flung parties to have a "presence" at the table in a way that was not possible when there was a pronounced time lag in communications.

Still, the use of basic communication technology does not change the fundamental nature of the negotiation process. Input is obtained more quickly, and it is possible to use phone teleconferencing to engage in synchronous negotiations with parties in remote geographic locations, but the give-and-take of the process remains essentially the same as in Monroe and Livingston's time. More advanced communication technology and Internet-based applications have the ability to subtly change the nature of the negotiation process.

Perhaps the first step beyond basic communication technology to affect the negotiating environment was the development of synchronous video and audio meeting technology. At its inception, video teleconferencing technology was expensive, tied to fixed locations, and of dubious quality. Current Web video teleconferencing technology is inexpensive, is not tied to a fixed location, and has increasingly high fidelity. In addition, much of the currently available video teleconferencing technology incorporates document sharing and single text editing capabilities.

The accessibility and quality of Web video systems notwithstanding, the best systems in terms of picture quality are those using IP and ISDN (Internet Protocol and Integrated System Digital Network) technology. These systems are not cheap to install, they demand equal installations on both the sending and receiving ends, and they are tied to fixed locations, but the picture and sound quality rivals digital cable television. Some are even arranged to exactly duplicate the size and location of meeting rooms at distant locations so that all those involved in the meeting from multiple sites appear to be in the same room, at the same table.

Web-based video and audio systems offer a cheaper and much more flexible online environment. Systems such as WebEx[12] are very inexpensive, and they make up for a loss of picture quality with other significant advantages. First, they are accessible from any Internet-capable computer anywhere in the world. Second, they generally offer a choice of VoIP (Voice over Internet Protocol), commercial teleconference, or telephone-to-telephone audio. Third, they generally incorporate easy-to-use document sharing and editing capabilities as part of their basic service. This author has, on many occasions, been able to hold meetings online with participants on different continents, using a "laser pointer" or highlighter to discuss documents, and single text editing to allow all participants to edit final draft documents.

Finally, there are a number of free services, such as Skype,[13] that offer good quality audio and video conferencing without the document sharing and single text editing features. Most laptops now come with built-in wireless connections and built-in cameras and microphones that automatically operate with Skype and other services, making a high level of computer skills for the negotiator unnecessary.

If Monroe and Livingston were negotiating in Paris in 2008, they would have some interesting choices. When Talleyrand completely changed the terms of the negotiation with no warning, they would have been able to promise a response based on input from the principals by the following morning.

In Monroe's Paris hotel room (equipped, naturally, with wireless Internet access), or in an Internet café where they could work while having an espresso, Monroe and Livingston could log on to an easily accessible Web-based video conferencing application with VoIP, through which they could have a real-time meeting with President Jefferson. In a secure online environment they could present the new negotiation terms, share the opening document from the French, and work out a new negotiation strategy with new instructions in time for the next morning's meeting. If they were particularly well equipped with technology, they would be able to receive instructions even faster by using a mobile device, such as the iPhone, to conduct the conference and share documents with President Jefferson while caucusing in the hallway as Talleyrand waited inside the meeting room.

The Internet has not yet been able to eliminate the influence of time zones, but it has made it possible to negotiate in real time with participants spread across vast geographical distances, with costs that range from free to nominal, sometimes with no travel involved at all. Still, this type of technology does not necessarily change the essential

---

[12] Cisco's WebEx is one of many Web-based video conferencing systems available commercially. See http://www.webex.com.

[13] Skype is a free service, owned by eBay, that provides high quality VOIP and video from any Internet-capable computer. See http://www.skype.com.

nature of negotiations; it just makes it possible to share information faster and bring more people to the table.

The term *virtual table* refers to programs that attempt to offer all of the functions that are basic to the negotiation process in an online, generally asynchronous, environment. Telephone, text messaging, and video and audio conferencing technology are based on synchronous communication, with the parties engaged simultaneously. Virtual table platforms, such as The Mediation Room[14] or Juripax,[15] offer the possibility of conducting negotiations asynchronously, using text-based communication, without ever meeting face to face or synchronously.[16] Because these platforms are designed around a standard negotiating process, they offer the option of a soup-to-nuts approach online. It is possible to convene the session, establish the parties who will have access to the system, set rights and security parameters, develop positions, discuss and adjust positions, develop draft agreements, and finalize agreements, using asynchronous text-based communication throughout.

Even though virtual table platforms have the capability to replace face-to-face interaction in negotiations, they rarely do so. More often, virtual table platforms are used to accomplish tasks associated with various phases of negotiation. Another way to augment face-to-face negotiations with technology is to use any of the myriad function-related applications available free or for very low cost on the Web. Function-related applications offer the ability to perform one or more essential functions of the negotiation process, such as scheduling, generating agendas, information sharing, brainstorming, or document preparation. Applications such as GoogleDocs,[17] MindMeister,[18] and Central Desktop[19] allow negotiators to share information easily and

---

[14] The Mediation Room servers are based in the U.K. The platform is in use around the world in a variety of contexts and offers the basic ability to convene, set agendas, conduct discussions, offer options, and develop agreements in a secure asynchronous environment. See http://www.themediationroom.com.

[15] Juripax servers are based in the Netherlands and Germany and offer basically the same services as The Mediation Room. See http://www.juripax.com.

[16] Many participants use the virtual table platforms to conduct part, but not all, of the negotiation process. For example, it is possible to use the asynchronous platform to set agendas and/or share information before a face-to-face meeting, or to use the document-sharing capabilities to hammer out final agreements after face-to-face sessions.

[17] GoogleDocs is a free application available through Google that allows posting of documents for review or editing by invited participants. See http://docs.google.com.

[18] MindMeister is a free mind-mapping application that allows invited participants to brainstorm, categorize information, and develop options asynchronously online. See http://www.mindmeister.com.

[19] Central Desktop is an inexpensive group workspace with full encryption and password protection that allows invited participants to share documents, engage in discussions, and jointly edit documents online. See http://www.centraldesktop.com.

engage in discussions from any Internet-capable computer anywhere in the world, either as a substitute for face-to-face negotiations or as an adjunct to face-to-face discussions.

The University of Massachusetts at Amherst, in conjunction with NMB, has been awarded two National Science Foundation research grants to investigate the impact of technology on dispute resolution and negotiation. Part of the research process necessitated the development of a function-related application called STORM, which is being used to study ways in which online technology can actually change the negotiation process. For example, it is possible to use the Internet to conduct anonymous brainstorming and discuss option generation. Having anonymous input in multiparty negotiations obviously changes the dynamic of the discussion, and allows for a type of information-sharing discussion that is not possible in face-to-face discussions. One of the things that the research team learned early in the research process was that it is not possible to simply recreate a face-to-face negotiation environment online. Putting the process online actually changes the process by adding elements that did not exist, such as the ability to get anonymous input, and by adding dimensions to elements of the face-to-face process.

Even more radical changes to the negotiating environment are created by "smart" software, such as SmartSettle[20] or CyberSettle.[21] The essence of smart software is that the negotiation process can be broken into identifiable units, and behavior among participants can, to some degree, be predicted. Using algorithms incorporated into a blind bidding process, smart software can guide participants to a negotiated settlement without any of the time-consuming steps involved in face-to-face negotiation.

3. What Is the Impact of Technology as a Catalyst for and a Barrier to International Negotiations?

Negotiators Monroe and Livingston would have a wide range of options available if they were negotiating today. In addition to the ability to conduct the rapid conferencing that has already been discussed, they could craft a number of strategies to change the negotiating dynamic.

---

[20] SmartSettle is an algorithm-driven application that uses blind bidding and other techniques to encourage settlement, and that claims to result in better outcomes than either party could achieve in traditional face-to-face negotiations. See http://www.smartsettle.com.

[21] CyberSettle is a very successful platform that has operated in the insurance industry for several years. It is currently the platform being used by the American Arbitration Association (AAA) to augment online arbitration and case handling for cases in a wide variety of venues. CyberSettle uses a patented blind bidding process to encourage settlement with no human intervention. See http://www.cybersettle.com.

To prepare for the negotiation, they could have set up an online workspace that would let them get input from the President and Congress. The worksite could have stayed up for the entire negotiation, updated constantly to make all the information available to the team in Paris available to the clients, no matter where they were or when they wanted to check on progress. They could have used document sharing and single text editing to present the draft agreement for comment, and to prepare the final offer. They could have used e-signatures to ratify the contract and enact the agreement before leaving the bargaining room.

It is easy to fall into the trap of thinking of technology as a catalyst and as a positive influence on the negotiation process, but there are some cautionary notes to sound. For example, technology could have made the negotiation process easier for Monroe and Livingston, but it's just as likely that an immediate conference with the interested parties in the United States would have resulted in this kind of instruction: "Are you nuts? Fifteen million? That's more than seven times what we told you to spend, and anyway who wants all that empty space out west? Get on a boat and come home today!"

There are, however, some advantages to using technology in a broad range of dispute resolution efforts, including contract negotiations.

4. Technology as a Catalyst

Some of the catalytic effects of ICT have already been mentioned, but for review, here are a few of the most obvious:

- Technology provides for instant communication and sharing of information. Whether by voice, text, or video, negotiators can get up-to-the-minute information and instructions, or bring remote parties into the discussion with no time lag.
- With the use of technology, geographic barriers are minimized. In a negotiation session in the United States, one party was reviewing documents on a handheld mobile device in a parking lot in Florida while using his cell phone to conference and discuss the documents with parties in San Francisco and Chicago. Given the parties' willingness to be up late or early, depending on time zones, participants in negotiations can be anywhere in the world.
- With the use of technology, information processing is faster. This is not the same as making it easy and quick to talk to remote parties. Keeping electronic notes for all to see via a computer projector, ideas can be recorded, edited, approved, and sent to writing committees or counsel in text form, with little work other than the formatting needed to turn the notes into agreements. In a round of contract negotiations over several months in which a text program was used to compile notes and agreements, the

parties indicated that they had saved approximately one work-day per week over the course of the negotiations due solely to the use of e-notes.

- One of the most discussed aspects of online technology, the loss of nonverbal cues, turns out to not always be a bad thing. Particularly in the opening stages of proposal-based negotiations, it is common for parties to "posture" and engage in confrontational behavior to establish boundaries. This is not always negative, but it can set a combative tone for the negotiations. Using either synchronous or asynchronous technology seems, by experience and research, to produce less confrontational environments.[22]

5. Technology as a Barrier

Obviously, not all of the influences of technology are positive. As ICT becomes more and more an integral part of international negotiations, there are a number of points that negotiators should be aware of:

- With technology, control is an illusion. When negotiations are held face to face, and when basic ICT, such as mobile phones, is involved, it is possible, within limits, to keep information at the table and in the control of relatively few directly involved individuals. While it is possible for parties to share information and bring in outside influences using oral reports and paper copies, technology makes the process much easier. Three examples will demonstrate how technology changes the negotiating environment and how it makes control of the negotiating environment more tentative.
    - At a labor-management negotiation session the parties broke for lunch almost, but not quite, at a tentative agreement on a contract clause. The parties had agreed to keep all discussion private until agreements were announced, so the mediator was surprised when he was informed, before he had time to order his lunch, that the not-yet-agreed-to language had already been posted on one of the parties' Web sites.
    - In another case, parties were asked to use an online asynchronous brainstorm tool to generate options related to a certain issue. The parties, after generating over two hundred options, were then asked to use an online polling tool to rate and rank the options. At a subsequent face-to-

---

[22] *See* Jaime Tan, Int'l Conflict Resol. Ctr., Diane Bretherton, Int'l Conflict Resol. Ctr. & Gregor Kennedy, U. Melbourne, Negotiating Online, Presentation at the Third Annual Forum on Online Dispute Resolution, The University of Melbourne, 2005, *available at* http://www.odr.info/unforum2004/tan.htm.

face session, one of the parties at the table revealed that she had used a telephone conference to involve more than a dozen other people, not directly involved in the issue, to guide her judgments regarding which options were acceptable or desirable.

- At a recent meeting of the Association of Labor Relations Agencies (ALRA), an FMCS mediator reported that when he first entered the room in a labor negotiation, he saw five members of one of the negotiating teams, all of whom had identical laptop computers, all of which were streaming live video and audio from the bargaining table.

- Security concerns take on new importance with the use of technology. Keeping tentative agreements and information related to the negotiations secure from theft and out of the hands of potential competitors is a primary consideration. Introducing laptop computers, online communication tools, and Web sites offers a wide range of ways for information to be compromised. Again, information can be compromised orally or by the distribution of paper copies, but security in an ICT environment takes on much more significance. With risks ranging from misplaced jump drives or laptops to invasion of Web sites by hackers, electronic data is inherently somewhat insecure. Ironically, the ICT that most negotiators use and are comfortable with (e-mail and mobile phones) are probably the *least* inherently secure of all technologies. The use of hosted software with SSL encryption and password protection is much safer, and in the end just as flexible as basic ICT.

- When negotiators are sitting across a real table in a room together, there may be some questions of identity or authority, but there is a real person with whom one interacts. Online, identity concerns are legitimate concerns. How do I know you are who you say you are? How do I know who is being allowed to see the information I'm sending or posting? Even the use of passwords does not remove this concern. One of the participants on a very sensitive online discussion site thought it was perfectly safe to save his password and user name on a yellow sticky note on his computer monitor. Anyone passing by could have written down the information and posed as him online.

- Questions of venue or authority exist in any international negotiation, but can be exacerbated by the use of technology. EBay is the classic example of this problem: a buyer in Calcutta and a seller in San Diego may not meet, in fact may not be able to meet, and yet they engage in a transaction that can cause a dispute. Which venue rules—Calcutta or San Diego? EBay solved the problem by creating a user agreement that makes eBay's dispute resolution program the controlling venue, no matter where the parties are physically located, but this is a solution that is not available to most international negotiators. InternetBar.org (IBO)[23] is one of the leading bodies attempting to address the issues of venue, trust, and enforceability in cyberlaw.

- Using technology, it is possible to suffer from the "too many cooks" syndrome. It is easy to bring participants into the discussions, and to make the principals an active part of the negotiations, but that brings along the possibility that the judgment of the negotiator and the natural ebb and flow of negotiations can be disrupted, making agreements harder to reach. Just remember the possibility that Monroe and Livingston could have been told to take a boat home instead of pursuing an interesting possibility.

All of the barriers to the use of technology can be mitigated or overcome, but they serve to demonstrate that injecting technology into negotiations does change the nature of the process, eliminating some issues and creating others unique to the ICT environment.

6. Technology as an Intercultural Element in Negotiations

All of the positive and negative aspects of ICT-assisted negotiations are at play in intercultural situations. In fact, it may be the case that, depending on one's definition of culture, any negotiation is an intercultural negotiation, with some merely presenting more extreme cultural differences than others.

It would be a mistake to assume that all interactions are fraught with cultural problems, just as it would be a mistake to assume that cultural differences never cause problems. Kevin Avruch has labeled these assumptions Type I and Type II errors.[24] So, how does ICT impact cultural differences in negotiation?

On the most basic level, Rainey and Jadallah argue that ICT applications that are created by programmers and developers from one culture reflect the creators' cultural biases in the software.[25] For most applications developed in Europe and North America, this means that a tendency toward linear discussions, naming the issue or problem first, creating a level playing field, giving equal weight to input from all parties, and other typical aspects of the "North American Model" are built into the applications. Obviously, not every culture accepts or values this model, and it is incumbent on the negotiator to make adjustments that consider cultural differences.

---

[23] http://www.ibo.org.
[24] Kevin Avruch, *Type I and Type II Errors in Culturally Sensitive Conflict Resolution Practice*, 20 CONFLICT RESOL. Q. 351.
[25] Rainey & Jadallah, *supra* note 5.

On the positive side, in cultures where consensus is necessary, and where negotiations are a "social" enterprise, online technology can actually enhance the comfort of the participants. Instead of putting a participant on the spot and forcing discussion, negotiators from cultures where group consensus is important can take online asynchronous information, distill it, discuss it among their social contacts, and then respond with more comfort. Language differences can be addressed by the ability of participants to take more time understanding information, or by the use of translators who can help post in multiple languages.

7. ICT-Assisted Negotiation

Using online video conferencing is a synchronous activity that should be familiar to most, and it is the use of technology that changes the negotiation process the least. The NMB uses Web video conferencing for arbitration hearings and discussion sessions with less than an hour's training for the participants and with no changes at all to the processes they use face to face.

The following case review reflects the actual use of asynchronous ICT for a contract negotiation process where the parties who meet at the table are scattered across multiple geographic locations and time zones. The case is a merging of several cases in which ICT was used for part of the negotiation process, but all of the uses cited in the example are real and have been used many times. In this example there was a mediator serving as a third party to guide the negotiations, but any of the actions described could be undertaken by one or more of the negotiating team members.

Before the first face-to-face meeting, the mediator created an online workspace for the negotiating team members, allowing them to establish their own passwords and user names. The inexpensive software used to create the workspace is fully SSL encrypted and password protected, and is easy enough to learn to use in an hour or less. Once the workspace was created, the parties had a place to share documents and engage in asynchronous online discussions. During the course of the subsequent negotiation, each member of the negotiating teams was informed by e-mail whenever there was an addition to the workspace or a change in any document in the workspace.

Using an online calendar program that is built into the workspace application, the negotiating teams were able to establish a schedule of meetings over a period of several months. The parties were able to access the calendar program, put in their meeting parameters, and establish a list of common dates without ever having to arrange even a telephone call.

Once the meeting dates were set, the mediator used a discussion forum that is built into the workspace to get input about what issues were on the table for discussion and in what order they should be addressed. The result, done asynchronously whenever any member of one of the teams had time to go online, was an agenda for the first meeting and a list of issues to be discussed at subsequent meetings.

Using the agenda for the first face-to-face meeting as a guide, the mediator established what information was needed for the first meeting and what documents needed to be reviewed in order to start the discussions. Those documents were posted on the workspace, in a read-only status, for all to review before coming to the face-to-face meeting.

All of the preparation for the first face-to-face meeting was done online, asynchronously, without the need for conference calls or side meetings. When the negotiating teams arrived for the first meeting, almost all of the preliminary work had been done, so they were free to start immediately discussing the opening issues.

During the face-to-face meeting the mediator took notes for the group on a computer with a projection screen so that all members of the teams could see the notes and verify their accuracy. Over the course of three days the group established bullet points for agreements on two issues and identified a third issue for which they wanted to brainstorm options. At the end of the first meeting, the mediator immediately posted the notes to the workspace and one member of each team was assigned the task of using the document-editing feature of the workspace to turn the bullet points into an agreement for signing at the next face-to-face meeting.

Between face-to-face sessions the mediator posted a triggering question based on the issue the groups wanted to brainstorm, and opened a discussion forum where the parties could, on their own time, post ideas and read ideas posted by others. Just before the next meeting, the mediator took the full list of ideas generated by the brainstorm and put them into an online polling program that allowed the parties to engage in an anonymous multivote process to see which ideas rose to the top as workable. This information and the edited agreements from the first session were presented at the beginning of the second face-to-face meeting.

The groups continued to use the online workspace and other online applications in this way throughout the course of the negotiations, until they had a final deal. They were able to use mobile phones and teleconferences between sessions in addition to the online workspace, but they never had to send their work via e-mail, and they were able to do much of the between-session work asynchronously without having to arrange synchronous meetings in person or by phone.

8. Conclusion

The twenty-first century brings with it some exciting possibilities for human communication, enhanced by an ever-expanding array of ICT that makes communication faster and easier around the world, and perhaps even evolving into the Galactic Network that was envisioned almost half a century ago.

There does exist what some have labeled the "digital divide," but the degree to which even "developing" countries have access to mobile phone and Internet technology is somewhat astounding. According to InternetWorldStats.com, at the end of 2007 there were over 1.3 billion users of the Internet. Europe, North America, and Australia are all at or over the 50 percent penetration mark for Internet users, and some sources suggest that China will have the largest number of Internet users within the next 3 to 5 years. Developing nations have lower penetration rates, but both Africa and the Middle East showed over a 1000 percent increase in penetration from 2000 to 2008, and Latin America showed over a 650 percent increase in penetration in the same time period.[26] With the rapid growth of Internet-capable mobile phone technology in the developing world, it will increasingly be the case that ICT tools can be applied, at some level, to negotiations anywhere.

Ultimately, ICT simply offers communication channels that can be exploited poorly or well by parties engaged in negotiations and conflict resolution efforts of all kinds. Many researchers think that using ICT does change us. Decades ago, Marshall McLuhan declared that "the medium is the message,"[27] and a number of researchers are currently suggesting that using the Internet as most of us now do actually changes the way we think and process information.[28] Even so, people are still people. It is up to the negotiator to survey the available ICT tools and to determine how best to use ICT in negotiations. After all, ICT is a channel for communication; the parties, the ideas, and the cultures are much the same as they were for Monroe, Livingston, and Talleyrand.

Daniel Rainey, Director
Office of Alternative Dispute Resolution Services
The National Mediation Board
1301 K Street, NW, Suite 250-E
Washington, DC 20005
Phone: (202) 692-5000
E-mail: rainey@nmb.gov

---

[26] *See* Internet World Stats, World Internet Users and Population Stats, http://www.internetworldstats.com/stats.htm (last visited July 8, 2008).

[27] MARSHALL MCLUHAN & QUENTIN FIORE, THE MEDIUM IS THE MESSAGE (1967).

[28] Nicholas Carr, *Is Google Making Us Stupid?* ATLANTIC, *available at* http://www.theatlantic.com/doc/200807/google.

CHAPTER 6

Current Issues in Negotiating International Sales Over the Internet

James M. Klotz[1]
MILLER THOMSON LLP
TORONTO, CANADA

1. Introduction

The Internet has collapsed territorial borders and created a borderless international business environment that was only a dream two decades ago. This change reaches into every country and affects almost all modes of commerce. However, the collapse of territorial borders has occurred more quickly than the legal framework to go with it has grown. As a result, the issues created are swirling in a melting pot of conflicting and often irreconcilable legal systems.

While every government is currently struggling with basic issues of how to regulate business activity over the Internet, the velocity of business change vastly outpaces the regulatory efforts to date. As a result, business is forced to adapt to the new Internet economy and compete in a new international business environment. While opportunities abound for international business, non–North American competitors feel freed of their territorial restrictions and are able to penetrate Canadian and U.S. markets with greater ease. When the goods sold are in the form of information transferred over the Internet, traditional legal controls, such as antitrust laws, dumping, and impermissible business practices, seem beyond the easy reach of the law. For example, Internet gambling companies located in the Caribbean are thriving as a result of the patronage of customers in the North American market, although such businesses are in most cases illegal to operate in either Canada or the United States without a license.

Non-North-American-based businesses are also able to compete against domestic North American businesses without the burden of

[1] The author acknowledges the assistance of Adria Leung, summer student, Miller Thomson LLP, for her research assistance, and his colleague David Buchanan, Miller Thomson LLP, for his editorial comments.

taxation, allowing competitive advantage. In the past, these competitive advantages were usually outweighed by lack of market access.

For manufacturers, traditional forms of international distribution of goods are being replaced by direct sales over the Internet. Distributors with territorial restrictions find themselves competing against each other in the borderless environment of the Internet. Cross-marketing techniques through hyperlinking and framing are becoming the new mode of advertising. Businesses that previously would not consider direct sales are now embracing the e-commerce model as the new paradigm. Instead of negotiating distribution and agency agreements, they are posting their wares to the Web, and entering into direct sales agreements with customers in countries they never would have imagined doing business with a decade ago.

For those businesses, their terms of sale are now negotiated by themselves internally and posted to the Web, for visitation and execution by faceless customers. This chapter will outline generally the principal international issues affecting the fundamental aspects of the sale of goods over the Internet and will provide some basic tips on drafting, planning, and negotiating contracts related to these issues.

2. Contracts Are Different

When a seller sells goods to a customer located in the same city, both are able to rely on the long history of legal practice in their jurisdiction and have a fairly good idea of the risks associated with the transaction. However, when the contract is entered into over the Internet—known as a "click-wrap," "Web-wrap," "browse-wrap" or "online agreement" (these include licenses and terms of service, or terms of sale, accessed from a vendor's Web site)—those risks multiply dramatically.

The principal risks that commonly arise from Internet contracts are information risk, technology risk, and business risk. Information risk includes copyright infringement and invasion of privacy issues, electronic bulletin boards containing defamatory statements, and intercepted credit card information disclosed or used for fraudulent purposes. Technology risk includes negligent errors or omissions in software design, unauthorized access to Web sites, Internet service provider server crashes, and risk of improperly integrating e-commerce systems with internal databases. Business risk includes contract formation issues created by the technology to ensure that a contract has been entered. However, many Internet contracts are between parties in different countries. Thus business risk also includes worldwide legal exposure resulting from breach of contract or violation of local or foreign laws. Even before a sale is made, the seller may trigger consequences in intellectual property laws, advertising laws, privacy laws, and even criminal laws in an innumerable number of legal jurisdictions. All of these risks can lead to events that cause loss.

3. Techniques for Making Binding Contracts on the Internet

What is a contract for? There are a limited number of terms that vendors require for the purpose of selling their goods or licensing their software. While license and sales agreements can contain many terms and conditions beyond the commercial issues of price, payment, and delivery, there are only a handful of terms that a vendor or supplier needs to significantly reduce its risk exposure in the license or sale, regardless of where the transaction takes place. These terms are

- a choice of law;
- a choice of exclusive jurisdiction;
- an exclusive remedy (return for refund or replacement);
- a disclaimer of all implied warranties;
- a limitation of damages, including indirect, special, or consequential damages;
- a shortening of the statute of limitations; and
- an export control compliance obligation.

In addition, software suppliers need

- a limitation of use to a specific computer or location;
- an "as is" warranty; and
- a ban on resale, reproduction, reverse engineering, or modification of the product.

These terms permit the vendor to limit its business risk by contract. Without them, the vendor takes an enormous and likely unquantifiable risk, unless the vendor has taken the effort to satisfy itself as to the application of each buyer's legal regime to the business transaction.

Since the customer does not sign a contract, is a contract formed over the Internet valid? For a framework, we can turn to "shrink-wrap" contracts. A shrink-wrap contract is one in which the license agreement is accepted upon the opening of the packaging or the installation of the software program. The law confirming the validity of shrink-wrap contracts has been fairly well settled (at least in the United States) since 1996. Given the nature of online agreements, in that the parties enter into the contract before goods are delivered (rather than after as in a shrink-wrap contract), there is more certainty with their validity than with shrink-wrap licenses. However, if shrink-wrap agreements are valid, then surely online agreements will also be valid.

Web-wrap cases in the United States generally indicate that the Internet itself will not stand in the way of contract formation, particularly if an Accept button is used. The requirement of a signature signed on a piece of a paper in traditional contracts cannot be implemented for online contracts.

In the United States, the *Electronic Signatures Act* (2000) provides uniform legislation to give legal status to electronic signatures. This

Act provides that all electronic contracts are valid unless they are illegal, unconscionable, or contain some other fatal flaw. An electronic signature can constitute a binding signature so long as the signature can be traced to a particular individual who took an affirmative act such as entering a password or clicking an I Agree button.

In addition, the *Uniform Commercial Code* (UCC) has recently adopted statute of frauds provisions, which require that contracts for the sale of goods over $500 must be in writing. Writing is defined as "printing, typewriting, or any other intentional reduction to tangible form." Parties that trade together frequently may eliminate the ambiguity that surrounds the writing issue by entering into a trading agreement that specifies that certain criteria are deemed by the parties to constitute a signed writing. Ultimately, however, these concerns are material only when the size of the individual transaction is significant, when payment is not obtained prior to delivery of the goods, or where there is no other ongoing relationship between the parties.

With international transactions, there are a number of additional issues to consider that differ from the approach taken by the United States. Many vendors have developed sophisticated contractual language to try to bind all those who click Accept. However, this language notwithstanding, some countries, such as China or Estonia, do not recognize contracts that are not in writing. Further, if the United Nations Convention on Contracts for the International Sale of Goods (CISG) applies to the contract (that is, a sale of goods over the Internet, together with several other requirements), some countries (Argentina, Belarus, Chile, Estonia, Hungary, and the Russian Federation), in their ascension to the CISG, specifically opted out of the ability to enter into a contract without writing. Thus, notwithstanding the wording of the online agreement, a party in, say, China will not be bound by the terms of the Webwrap agreement, even after clicking I Agree. If that party downloads software, she will not be bound by the vendor's restrictive terms, nor will she be bound by the limitations of liability contained in the online agreement. Indeed, it is often precisely for these limitations that the vendor requires an I Agree click on its contract in the first place.

When the CISG was drafted, e-mail communication did not exist. CISG Article 13 provides that "a writing" includes telegram and telex. However, CISG experts are of the opinion that the term "writing" includes any electronic communication retrievable in perceivable form. The parties are free to agree upon whatever form of communication they wish, and if they wish to include e-mail as a method of communication, they may do so.

Although there is no clear solution to this problem, some Web vendors who have recognized this issue use the following language:

> This product is not available to and may not be accessed by parties located in any jurisdiction that does not recognize the licensor's copyright, or does not recognize and enforce contracts

not made in writing. Any download made by any party located in such country is improper and is not permitted.

Although offers that may be accessed by the entire world may be illegal when made to persons in certain jurisdictions, regulators generally give weight to disclaimers in determining whether Web pages accessible in their jurisdiction constitute violations of local law.

Finally, an offer must be distinguished from a mere advertisement in which inquiries of interest are invited. Ambiguities are generally easy to avoid given the formalities that are necessary to enter into a contract. For example, identity information and credit card information are usually required for contracts.

3.1 The Contract Is Valid, But Is It Enforceable?

To determine if an online agreement will be enforceable, its nature must be examined. Standard form agreements are generally binding in commercial transactions provided that the customer assents to it and provided that it does not contain surprising terms. The terms do not have to be negotiated or even read by the customer. Most online agreements, however, are contracts of adhesion in that they are standard form contracts intended to bind a powerful seller and an insignificant customer. The terms are most often nonnegotiable, and the customer has only a Yes or No option for answering. For terms to be binding in an adhesion contract, they must be those that the consumer could foresee, although a rigorous standard may be imposed upon a party seeking to rely on terms that the court considers unreasonable.

In both the United States and Canada, the doctrine of unconscionability has been used successfully to void unfair contractual terms where one party has little meaningful choice. If terms and conditions are offered on a take-it-or-leave-it basis, an inherently disadvantaged bargaining position has been created. If there is an inequality between the parties, a taking advantage of the weaker party by the stronger party, and a resulting one-sided agreement created, courts will usually declare that the agreement is not enforceable. Generally, online agreements will meet the first requirement of this test. However, some measure of commercial reasonableness is required when deciding whether or not the agreement is enforceable.

4. Recent Issues and Developments in Online Contracting

Businesses are held to a higher standard than private sellers when it comes to ensuring that consumers are not confused or misled by electronic contract terms. Unless notice is given, contract terms that are outrageous, surprising, or unfair are unlikely to be upheld by courts, even if the consumer assented to them. However, this also depends on which country of the world the parties are in, as some countries are more proactive in protecting consumers who choose not to read. For example, a German consumer will have greater success in avoiding onerous but unread contract terms than will a U.S. consumer.

A fairly recent and rare development is the "negotiated release." A company can sell a product with no warranties or limitations on liability, but for a higher price. Alternatively, the same product can be sold for a lower price if the consumer agrees to sign a waiver and release for the seller, limiting the liability the seller may face. These provisions are generally upheld in court.

Finally, whether or not a vendor may change the terms of its contract by posting revised terms on its Web site is a topic that is currently heavily debated. An "illusionary contract" is one in which one of the parties can unilaterally change the terms without consent of the other party. In the United States, this type of contract is generally acceptable if the original contract contains a provision permitting the unilateral amendment of terms. However, this provision needs to be clearly brought to the attention of the consumer and assented to. Whether or not the consumer normally checks the Web site is the crucial factor in this scenario. For example, the services provided to a consumer by an Internet provider are not the same as those provided by, say, an energy provider. A fair approach in dealing with these types of provisions is usually to implement the changes to the contract at a renewal or subsequent purchase. The consumer then has the choice to reject the changed terms and not renew or repurchase.

4.1 Consumer Warranties

One of the difficulties in contracting with consumers over the Internet is the application of the consumer warranties found in most countries. Most consumer laws, including those in Canada, imply a warranty of merchantability and a warranty of fitness for purpose to retail consumer goods. These warranties may only be disclaimed if the goods are sold "as is." Most often, these warranties cannot be contracted out of, despite warranty negation language. For example, in the United States, the *Magnuson-Moss Warranty Act* requires certain labeling and notice requirements where standard contracts disclaim written warranties with respect to sales of most consumer products. A written warranty must disclose who is covered, which products or parts are warranted, how long the warranty lasts, and what remedy the consumer has under the warranty.

Failure to comply with the *Magnuson-Moss Warranty Act* will, at a minimum, void the limitations on the warranty. The limitation of liability clause, however, is arguably the most important clause of any sale. In this clause, the vendor protects itself against claims by the customer for all of its damages, whether they are direct damages caused by the vendor or whether they cause a consequential damage. Consequential damages can be extremely high. For example, if a product fails to arrive and the customer loses a business contract as a result, the vendor could be liable for the loss of that contract. The vendor obviously has no interest in having this level of immeasurable risk exposure. The purpose of the limitation of liability clause is to bind the customer contractually to an agreement as to the seller's maximum exposure for breach of the contract, including in the event of breach of the seller's warranty. Most western countries have their own consumer protection laws that must be investigated prior to selling goods into those countries.

Most limitation of liability clauses will provide that the seller is not liable for any damages, direct, consequential, or otherwise. Since the limitation of liability clause is the most onerous clause to a consumer, it should be presented in bold print and accompanied by a separate Accept button. Some U.S. states specifically require capital block letters for these clauses. Other states require a note made prominently on the first page that the contract has a limitation of liability in it. Even without these requirements, an argument exists that in all contracts, including commercial contracts, onerous clauses such as these should be specifically drawn to the customer's attention. Many countries, such as Italy, have specific obligations imposed upon the seller as a precondition to ensuring the validity of the limitation of liability clause. This aspect of the agreement should specifically be reviewed by foreign counsel.

In fact, many sellers now include in their standard clause liability for direct damages to a maximum cap. The purpose of doing this is to attempt to avoid the total invalidation of the limitation of liability clause, particularly if the attempt would be void in a foreign jurisdiction (such as some U.S. states). If used, what is the correct cap? Most sellers try to use the cost of the goods as the cap. However, where the cost of the goods is insignificant, this may subsequently be found to be unconscionable. In one standard international contract provided to the author, where services were being provided, the U.S. cap was $150,000, the German cap was $750,000, and the Malaysian cap was $40,000 (all in Canadian dollars).

Many countries also have consumer cooling-off periods during which a consumer may void a consumer sale. These cooling-off periods apply generally to door-to-door sales (for example, Ontario has a forty-eight-hour cooling-off period) and also to mail-order sales (for example, Taiwan has a seven-day cooling-off period). More recently, however, they have begun to apply to Internet sales as well. In Canada, the Internet Sales Contract Harmonization Template was approved by Industry Canada to harmonize consumer standards with respect to Internet sales contracts. The template sets out circumstances under which a consumer may cancel an Internet sales contract and provides the possibility of relief in the event that the cancellation of an Internet sales contract would be inequitable. However, each jurisdiction has its own circumstances defining what is inequitable.

In addition to cooling-off periods, many countries have laws that limit the ability of vendors to enforce certain of the typical clauses found in shrink-wrap and online agreements. For example, enforcement of a reverse-engineering prohibition would not likely be possible in France, and restrictions on the customer's right to use the product are limited in Germany. Careful investigation should be undertaken whenever selling consumer goods into any foreign country, whether by Internet or otherwise.

4.2 Exclusive Jurisdiction and Choice of Law

Canadian and U.S. vendors should choose to govern their online contracts by their home jurisdiction law. This, too, is quite insufficient to protect the vendor. Few vendors recognize that by simply choosing Canadian or U.S. law when they sell to persons in other countries, they may be also unwittingly allowing the sale to be governed by the CISG unless the CISG has been specifically excluded using specific wording. Most North American legal scholars currently recommend that the CISG should be excluded from all contracts, unless the contracts are revised to harmonize with the CISG provisions.

Note that if the customer in an online agreement is able to send an e-mail message to the vendor contemporaneously with its online assent, a "battle of the forms" may be on. Ordinarily, when a customer submits an order with its own terms of contract, that response is a counteroffer. If the seller does not accept it, there is no contract. Unfortunately, if the seller accepts the counteroffer, or if the seller performs the contract (performance thus indicating acceptance), the vendor may be deemed to have accepted the customer's terms. In recent Canadian cases, the battle is usually won by the party taking the last shot—for example, the manufacturer if the goods are shipped after it sent its own form of purchase order acknowledgement. Unfortunately, if the CISG applies and e-mail is used as a form of communication, then there are potential complications for determining when an offer "reaches" the offeree. CISG experts are of the opinion that an offer (or a withdrawal of an offer or a rejection of an offer) "reaches" the offeree when the e-mail enters the offeree's server. However, there are a myriad of complex situations within the realm of offer and acceptance that can arise when one party uses e-mail and the other uses another form of communication. Accordingly, it is advisable to clearly state those modes of communication that are acceptable only, and to avoid the potential for differing forms of communication.

Online vendors may wish to reconsider whether there should be any room for a customer to respond with comments as part of the online ordering process. For example, if the customer types "I will not be bound by your limitation of liability" in the response box and the vendor does not have a system in place to ensure that the sale does not get processed without a countering response, the limitation on liability provision may be invalid.

In addition to the governing law clause, vendors have the option of selecting the court and jurisdiction for disputes. This gives the vendor a substantially greater amount of control over the manner in which a dispute is resolved. However, the choice of setting their own jurisdiction as the place of exclusive jurisdiction is one that many vendors may subsequently regret.

For example, in the case of a license being breached by a Canadian company, the ability of an American company to enforce a U.S. judgment in Canada may be limited. In some export sales, it may ultimately be more advantageous for an American seller to sue the customer in its home jurisdiction, particularly if the customer has no assets in the United States. If so, then inserting a U.S. venue provision may actually be more limiting to the seller. In such circumstances, a nonexclusive clause may be more useful than an exclusive clause. The seller can pursue the customer or its assets, or both, in any jurisdiction that is appropriate, rather than just the one stated in the contract. Conversely, the purpose of choosing an exclusive jurisdiction clause is to avoid the enforcement of wild foreign court decisions in the vendor's home jurisdiction. An attornment to the jurisdiction of a U.S. or Canadian court is not the same as conferring exclusive jurisdiction upon a U.S. or Canadian court. One solution is to provide that any claim commenced by the customer against the vendor is subject to the exclusive jurisdiction of the vendor's home court, although this may run into enforcement problems.

Before agreeing to jurisdiction by court, the experience of the Loewen Group, Inc., a Canadian funeral home company, is instructive. In 1990, Loewen began expansion into the United States and quickly became America's second largest funeral home owner. In 1991, Loewen was accused of breach of contract in a routine $8 million acquisition in Mississippi. It was sued for $26 million, and turned down a $7 million offer. In 1995, a Mississippi jury awarded the plaintiff US$500 million. The Mississippi judge agreed that the award was reasonable. Loewen thought that it could appeal, but under Mississippi law it was obliged to post a bond equal to 125 percent of the jury award, which it was unable to raise. Ultimately, Loewen settled the case for US$175 million.

In addition to losing a substantial sum in the Mississippi case, Loewen learned a powerful lesson. In the company's annual report for 1995, in response to the question "What will the company do differently as a result of the Mississippi experience?" the company wrote: "One change we've already implemented is to follow the example of companies that include arbitration clauses in many of their contracts. We will have a heightened caution about the potential for abuse in a legal system which let us down."

All efforts should be taken to avoid being dragged into a foreign court system. This is best done by requiring disputes to be resolved in arbitration. There are many choices for arbitration, and the drafting of an arbitration clause in a contract requires some degree of skill.

4.3 Export Controls

Few Internet vendors realize that their goods may require an export permit or are subject to reporting requirements. In particular, this affects exports of software that may be downloaded over the Internet from a Web site. This likely represents the greatest potential source of contravention of export control laws.

In Canada, pursuant to the *Export and Import Permits Act*, an export permit is necessary only for exports of certain types of strategic goods and technologies that are defined on the Export Control List (ECL), or for exports to certain "unfriendly" nations listed on the Area Control List (ACL), or for goods found on the Automatic Firearms Country Control List.

The United States uses a dual system of export licensing administered by the U.S. Department of Commerce and the U.S. Department of State. Pursuant to the *Export Administration Act (EAA)*, which provides the statutory authority for export controls, a Department of Commerce export license is necessary for only certain types of goods depending upon their destination. However, any goods listed on the U.S. Munitions List require an export license from the Department of State under the Arms Export Control Act and the International Traffic in Arms Regulations.

The U.S. Department of the Treasury is also able to impose economic sanctions against an entire country (including a boycott), thereby prohibiting any economic dealings with that country unless one first obtains a license. For example, the United States has maintained fairly comprehensive economic sanctions on North Korea since the end of the Korean War. These include sanctions on trade, aid, arms sales and transfers, and access to assets under U.S. jurisdiction. Such sanctions are administered by the Office of Foreign Assets Control of the Department of the Treasury (OFAC). It is important to note that these sanctions are not product specific. Exporting goods to a boycotted country requires a license from the OFAC, which is difficult to obtain.

Additionally, these boycotts extend to certain "Specially Designated Nationals" (SDN) of the boycotted country. SDNs are front companies or persons acting on behalf of the boycotted government in other nations. There are also lists of certain individuals and organizations that are prohibited from receiving U.S. exports, and others that may only receive goods if they have been licensed. The seller must verify that it is not selling to any of these organizations or persons, which can be found on lists maintained by OFAC, the U.S. Treasury Department, and the U.S. Department of Commerce, such as the Entity List, the Specially Designated Nationals and Blocked Persons List, the Unverified List, and the Denied Persons List.

Under no circumstances should goods be sold outside of Canada or the United States without the vendor being absolutely sure that the export does not require a permit. Failure to ensure compliance with U.S. or Canadian export control legislation, as appropriate, is perhaps the single most dangerous error that a vendor can make, as it may result in a jail term, among other penalties. For example, in 2007, ITT Corp. was fined US$100 million for illegally exporting night-vision technology.

It is up to the online vendor to determine if the goods require an export license and, in so doing, to indisputably ascertain the identity of the customer. Without doing so and ensuring compliance with export control laws, the vendor takes a significant risk. To avoid exporting to restricted countries, there are a few steps that a software vendor can take with respect to downloads over the Internet. These include listing those countries to which sales are prohibited on the Web site and policing sales using geo-filtering software to ensure that downloads are not made by customers in those jurisdictions. A contract term should provide that the customer will comply with all export control laws. However, note that the laws of Canada and the United States are different. The U.S. version of an export control clause restricts exports to a number of countries, including Cuba. However, Cuba is not a restricted country for purposes of Canada's export controls. In fact, under Canada's *Foreign Extra Territorial Measures Act*, the directors of the Canadian vendor can be charged (by Canada) for agreeing to another country's export bans.

5. Internet Issues Still to Be Resolved

There are many Internet-related contract issues that remain confused and unresolved. These include jurisdiction, taxation, capacity, and language.

5.1 Jurisdiction

The primary issue is whether governments can impose their regulatory and criminal laws upon foreign businesses penetrating their markets over the Internet. For vendors the main concern is whether, regardless of the contractual terms and conditions of the online agreement, a customer can commence legal action in a foreign jurisdiction and obtain a judgment against the vendor. Many countries have laws, particularly laws affecting consumers, that permit legal action to be commenced notwithstanding the vendor's attempt to avoid liability contractually.

Often, the liability arises even before a contract is signed. Various attempts have been made to impose liability upon a company by virtue of the fact that its Web site may be accessed in the plaintiff's jurisdiction, irrespective of the location of the defendant or the server.

Several recent cases have dealt with jurisdictional issues. For example, Yahoo! U.S. was sued in a French court for violating French law prohibiting the display of Nazi memorabilia; Sato Slippers, a small family-owned shop in Japan, was sued in a court in California for infringing U.S. copyright; Harrod's department store sued the *Wall Street Journal* in the U.K. in response to critical statements written in the newspaper; and a former employee of the United Nations sued the *Washington Post* in Ontario in response to allegations of a scandal about him.

To minimize these difficulties, a Web site could include the following:

- A disclaimer stating that content available on the site is not intended to be accessed by users outside the country or who are not authorized to view the content on the site.
- A login screen used to permit access to only those who specify their country of residence as being within the local jurisdiction. Geo-filtering software can be employed to identify the region of the accessing user and block residents of certain countries.
- A notice that payment may be made by specified currencies only.
- A prohibition on shipment to specified countries for which jurisdiction is a concern.

Although these methods are not foolproof ways to avoid foreign lawsuits, they significantly decrease the likelihood of one arising.

This issue is becoming more defined in the United States, where a line of cases has developed to give some form to these otherwise murky issues. In several cases, courts have clearly rejected the notion that mere access to a Web site in the plaintiff's jurisdiction is sufficient to give rise to jurisdiction in the United States. However, courts have been more willing to seize jurisdiction where, rather than mere passive advertising, the vendor is doing business over the Internet. While the U.S. courts struggle to define what level of Web site/Internet activity gives rise to liability in the United States, foreign courts may still take a different view. Typically, the Canadian regulatory system looks at advertising that is directed at Canadian residents. Thus, if the advertising is directed at customers throughout the world, the potential for broad regulatory scrutiny is much higher. For example, comparative advertising, which may be permissible in Canada and the United States, is defamatory (and hence a tort giving rise to foreign jurisdiction) in some European countries, such as Germany. Even if the advertising is not specifically directed to particular jurisdictions, publication may still give rise to risk. For example, advertising may be found to be blasphemous in some ultrareligious countries.

Other than using a good contract, one solution is to avoid selling goods to persons in countries where the vendor does not have the benefit of legal advice. Realistically speaking, this would render the Internet impractical outside of roughly 20 countries. The Internet makes it possible to sell in markets ordinarily beyond the reach (or desire) of Canadian and American businesses, although the risk associated with sales to additional countries is exponentially greater. In fact, however, few North American vendors sell goods to more than 20 of the approximately 190 countries in the world.

However, even if no sale is made, jurisdictional issues arise instantaneously with respect to intellectual property issues. Copyright protection that otherwise attributes automatically to posted material on the Internet may not be protected in other countries. For example, to take advantage of international copyright conventions, at the minimum reference must be made to copyright ownership, including the year of copyright and that all rights are reserved to the copyright owner whose name is stated. Unless trademark or copyright registrations are obtained broadly, it is almost impossible to stop rogue metataggers, framers, and hyperlinkers unless these rights are protected in the country in which the offender is located.

5.2 Legal Structures and Taxation

Businesses have always had the option to relocate to low-tax jurisdictions. However, prior to the advent of the Internet, business activities in low-tax jurisdictions that could be carried on as easily as in high-tax jurisdictions were traditionally fairly limited. The Internet, though, has no boundaries. E-commerce business is portable. Thus, it is much easier for vendors to relocate their server and all business activity to an offshore locality and avoid the application of Canadian or U.S. taxation. The Organisation for Economic Co-operation and Development (OECD) and every government concerned about the loss of tax base are currently struggling with this issue. Nevertheless, e-commerce can give rise to unexpected taxation obligations. For example, Canada's Goods and Services Tax applies to goods purchased from a nonresident for importation. Where those goods are downloaded over the Internet and paid for by credit card, the tax still accrues, and the buyer is still technically obligated to withhold and remit the tax.

5.3 Capacity to Contract

With the advent of Internet access by adolescents, the ability of clever minors to enter into contractual relations over the Internet is worrisome. In the past, a minor had to make a telephone call or send a letter or fax to get a response from a vendor or customer. Now, with easy access to the Internet, a minor can become enmeshed in serious contractual obligations, to the detriment of the other contracting party.

There is no voice contact and no location visit when using the Internet, so how does one ascertain if a person is a minor or otherwise without any capacity? Unfortunately, there is currently no simple effective means over the Internet, other than for parents to supervise their child's use of it. Further, the age of majority varies in different countries. For example, the age of capacity to contract in Taiwan is twenty, whereas it is eighteen in Ontario. Generally, the rule is that if the contract is for necessities, it will be enforceable. Otherwise, the contract is voidable at the option of the minor. Although minors are not allowed to take advantage of infancy to support a fraud, it is only a matter of time before there will be a reported case in Canada of a seller suffering a serious loss caused by a minor.

A representation that the contracting party is over the age of majority in his or her jurisdiction might at least identify that the vendor is aware of this issue. However, a fifteen-year-old clicking I Acknowledge leaves the vendor no better off.

Some sales absolutely require the vendor to confirm the identity and age of the customer. For example, the United States recently proposed legislation to require Internet sellers of tobacco products to verify the age and identity of purchasers to cut down on sales to minors.

5.4 Language

One of the common attributes of an international sale is the fact that at least one party may not speak English as his or her mother tongue. With regard to contracts formed by e-mail correspondence, the language issue, while important, can be dealt with contractually. Good international contracts specify that one language, such as English, will be the governing language; one version of the contract, such as the English version, will govern; and all disputes will be heard in one language, such as English.

With online agreements, however, the issue of language becomes more problematic. It is possible, even likely, that non-English-speaking Web surfers will click through online agreements without the slightest idea of what they are doing. They may have no idea that by clicking they have agreed to purchase, license, or otherwise contract with the Web provider. Are contracts formed under these circumstances valid? The answer may in fact be negative, particularly if the agreement contains unusual terms.

6. Conclusion

The legal issues surrounding e-commerce and the Internet are already significant. Adding an international component to this causes an exponential increase in risk. Reduction of risk ultimately leads to an increase in the ability of a vendor to hold on to its profits.

7. Supplement #1: Tips for Drafting Contracts of International Sales over the Internet

7.1 Tips for Increasing the Likelihood of Validity

- Structure the Web site so that access to the site or to downloads that require a contractual obligation is restricted until the customer has reviewed the terms of the agreement and clicked an Accept button.
- Accept buttons should have a subsequent accept verification so as to ensure against accidental acceptance.
- Consider permitting the customer to review his or her entire order on the screen before one final acceptance.
- Restrict the countries from which you will accept customers.
- Monitor sales to ensure that sales do not get made with customers in jurisdictions you are unfamiliar with.

7.2 Tips to Ensure Enforceability

- Accept buttons should be attached to specific key clauses of the online agreement, such as negation clauses ("The vendor shall not be liable for any loss or damage . . ."), export controls, and taxes, to ensure that the customer recognizes their importance.
- To avoid the argument of unconscionability, interactive agreements that give the consumer choice as to contract provisions might be a reasonable solution (for example, choice of arbitration or litigation).
- Contract terms that are not typical to the vendor's industry, or that might be a surprise to the customer, should be specifically brought to the customer's attention before the transaction is completed—for example, by using bold capital letters.
- Agreements must be clearly readable on the screen, and should be written in very plain English. Many Web sites merely offer the customer the opportunity to click the license agreement or terms of sale. This is insufficient.
- Consider having the customer click a separate Accept button that states, "I acknowledge that these terms limit my rights and remedies."
- Consider making contract terms more concise so as to avoid having an unreasonably lengthy contract that a reasonable consumer would not read in its entirety.

7.3 Tips for Avoiding Consumer Warranty and Liability Issues

- Have an Accept button for the warranty terms.
- The vendor should keep a log of acceptances and copies of each Web site version to ensure availability of evidence in the event required.

- Users should be able to quit the process at any time without becoming contractually bound.
- E-mail communication with the customer as part of the process should be avoided unless the vendor can ensure that the communications are monitored for modifying changes to terms.
- Where telephone sales are produced from the Web site advertising, the seller should also ensure that the telephone operator verifies that the customer has read the terms and conditions. This can be done by faxing or e-mailing the terms and conditions to the customer in advance.
- Use a limitation of liability clause with a maximum dollar amount "cap" on direct damages.
- Make sure that the vendor's name and address as well as the refund and return policy can be easily found on the Web site.
- Adopt a broad policy for accepting cancellations and returns, particularly from foreign countries, so as to reduce the risk of foreign consumer complaints.

7.4 Tips for Selecting the Governing Law and Choice of Forum

- Use a choice of law clause that reads like the following: "This Agreement is made, executed, and delivered in Toronto, Canada, and any controversy arising hereunder or in relation to this Agreement shall be governed by and construed in accordance with the domestic laws of the Province of Ontario, Canada. The parties hereto hereby agree that the United Nations Convention on Contracts for the International Sale of Goods does not apply to this Agreement and is strictly excluded."
- Consider whether to select the vendor's home jurisdiction as the exclusive jurisdiction for disputes. If so, use a choice of forum clause that contains language like the following: "All disputes . . . arising out of . . . the contract . . . shall be submitted to and be subject to the jurisdiction of the courts of [home jurisdiction] which . . . shall have exclusive jurisdiction in the event of any dispute hereunder. The parties hereby irrevocably submit and attorn to the jurisdiction of such courts to finally adjudicate . . . any action . . . arising out of . . . this Agreement."
- Ensure that disputes are resolved by arbitration if there may be a need to pursue the customer in its home jurisdiction.

7.5 Tips for Handling Export-Related Issues

- List prohibited countries on the Web site (and update the list regularly).

- Have customers click a declaration box to confirm that they are not residents of a prohibited country, nor are the goods destined for such country.
- Monitor downloads by examining the domain suffix to determine in which country the downloader is located.
- Specify the limited jurisdictions that you are prepared to accept customers from, and monitor sales to ensure that sales are not made to customers in other countries. Note that many online travel agencies state that their packages are available only to those persons in their country.
- Include a contract term that prohibits the customer from contravening the vendor's export control laws. In itself, this will not protect the vendor from "willful blindness," and thus a criminal charge. If aware that the goods are being made for transshipment or re-export to a restricted country, the vendor could be charged with conspiracy.
- Ensure that customers are not listed on any of the published lists of prohibited persons and organizations.

7.6 Tips for Handling Jurisdiction-Related Issues

- List countries where the Web site may be freely perused. Use a significant disclaimer to clarify legal rights.
- Research business and consumer protection laws in key markets.
- Review the Web site with respect to foreign law issues, including intellectual property and illegal advertising.
- Confirm compliance with the advertising laws of the jurisdictions in which the Web site is intended to be accessed.
- Do not use personal information gathered over the Internet without ensuring that all applicable privacy laws are complied with.

7.7 Tips for Dealing with Structures and Taxation

- Consider locating the e-commerce activity offshore.

7.8 Tips for Dealing with Capacity and Language

- Customers should be required to confirm that they are over the age of majority in their own jurisdiction and in the jurisdiction of the Web site, and that they have the legal authorization to enter the agreement on their own behalf or on behalf of their employer, if appropriate.
- Customers should have to type some words in English to confirm their ability to read the terms of the agreement, and clearly

manifest their intent to be bound. At a minimum, the customer should have to type in the words "I understand English and accept the terms of this contract."

8. Supplement #2: Additional Resources

8.1 Shrink-Wrap Cases

ProCD, Inc. v. Zeidenberg, 86 F.3d 1447 (7th Cir. 1996). ProCD is the producer of a program that lists the white pages of phone books both in Canada and the United States. The defendant purchased the disk, and using his computer skills, he was able to extract the database. He placed the database on the Web, although he did not clearly use the search engine created by ProCD. The consequences were perhaps the worst nightmare of a software company—mass free distribution. The license agreement inside the packaging strictly prohibited this use of the program. The U.S. Seventh Circuit found that the terms inside a box of software bind consumers who use the software after they have been given an opportunity to read the terms and reject them by returning the product (although query the success of a consumer who tries to return an opened software box to the retailer). The incorporation of the separate license terms occurs only after the purchaser opens the package and has a reasonable opportunity to inspect the license terms. The Court recognized that although vendors can put the entire terms of a contract on the outside of a box, a microscope would be required to read those terms, at the expense of losing the more useful information that consumers require in order to make a purchase decision. The Court also recognized that most software sales occur through distribution channels, such as telephone and Internet orders, that do not allow the purchaser to review the terms of the license agreement prior to sale.

The Court noted the important fact that the license agreement popped up in front of the customer when loading the software, and would not allow him to proceed without first indicating acceptance. *Id.* at 1451:

> A vendor, as master of the offer, may invite acceptance by conduct, and may propose limitations on the kind of conduct that constitutes acceptance. A buyer may accept by performing the acts the vendor proposes to treat as acceptance. And that is what happened. ProCD proposed a contract that a buyer would accept by using the software after having an opportunity to read the license at leisure. This Zeidenberg did. He had no choice, because the software splashed the license on the screen and would not let him proceed without indicating acceptance.

Thus, vendors must ensure that their customers are aware of a license or other terms prior to acceptance.

Despite this case being distinguished and criticized a few times, it has been followed in thirty-nine subsequent cases since 1996. The decision is still good law and used as a starting point with many cases dealing with shrink-wrap agreements.

M.A. Mortenson Co. v. Timberline Software Corp., 970 P.2d 803 (Wash. Ct. App. 1999). This Washington case dealt with the issue of whether a limitation on consequential damages enclosed in a shrink-wrap license accompanying computer software was enforceable against the purchaser of the licensed software. The plaintiff was a general construction contractor and purchased the licensed computer software from the defendant. The plaintiff used the program to prepare a construction bid and later sued for breach of warranties alleging that the software was defective. The Court found that the purchase order between the parties was not an integrated contract, the licensing agreement contained in the software packaging and instruction manuals being part of the contract between the two parties.

Hill v. Gateway 2000, Inc., 105 F.3d 1147 (7th Cir. 1997). This case decided that shrink-wrap license provisions requiring that disputes be submitted to arbitration were enforceable. The Court in this case stated three principles: the practice of putting a license in a box was preferable to having it provided to the purchaser by the salesclerk at the time of purchase; the practice of enclosing a shrink-wrap license was consistent with consumer expectations and industry practices; and, by allowing a customer to return the product if he did not agree to the license, the rights of the consumer were balanced against the commercial convenience of enforcing the license. In addition to these factors, software vendors can include two additional provisions to ensure that the shrink-wrap licenses are enforceable: the purchaser must indicate acceptance of the shrink-wrap license terms by performing some positive, unambiguous act; and the purchaser and vendor must not have reached an agreement that would exclude any further conditions forming part of the license contract.

Klocek v. Gateway, Inc., et al., 104 F. Supp. 3d 1332 2000 U.S. Dist. LEXIS 9896 (D. Kan. June 16, 2000). The plaintiff purchased a computer from the defendant that had standard terms included stating that "by keeping your Gateway 2000 computer system beyond five (5) days after the date of delivery, you accept these terms and conditions." The issue was whether those terms created a binding contract with the consumer under the law of either Missouri or Kansas. The Court held that it did not create a binding contract despite the fact that the consumer retained the computer beyond the five-day period. The Court held that the transaction was governed by the *Uniform Commercial Code* under 2-207 and thus, the standard terms did not come into play because the plaintiff never accepted them. The conditional nature of the acceptance had to be clearly expressed in a manner sufficient to notify the offeror that the offeree is unwilling to proceed with the transaction unless additional or different terms are included in the contract. Note that this was one of the first cases that declined to follow the line of decisions that upheld the validity of shrink-wrap licenses delivered along with a product.

8.2 Web-Wrap Agreements

In *CompuServe Inc. v. Patterson*, 89 F.3d 1257 (6th Cir. 1996), the defendant entered into a Shareware Registration Agreement with CompuServe by typing "I agree" at various key points in the agreement. The online agreement contained a clause providing for exclusive jurisdiction in Ohio, and the court held that Ohio courts had jurisdiction over the contract. The jurisdiction was founded both on the fact that the online agreement had been entered and that the defendant had put its wares into stream of commerce in Ohio.

The case of *Hotmail Corp. v. Van$ Money Pie, Inc.*, No. C98-20064, 1998 WL 388389 (N.D. Cal. April 20, 1998), went further than *Patterson*. In *Hotmail*, the defendant had signed on to Hotmail's free Web-based e-mail by entering into a Web-wrap agreement. The agreement required the defendant to click a button marked I Agree. The Web-wrap agreement banned the use of Hotmail accounts for spamming and for pornography. The defendant spammers (of pornography) were found to be in violation of this agreement and an injunction was granted, although the Court did not pay great attention to the issue of the mode of entering the agreement.

Rudder v. Microsoft Corp., 1999 CarswellOnt 3570. This is the leading decision on Web-wrap licenses and forum selection clauses in Canada. The plaintiff brought an action against the defendant for improperly charging MSN subscribers' credit cards, violating the terms of the contract. The defendant argued that the contract between them and the subscribers contained a forum selection clause that gave them exclusive jurisdiction to Washington state to resolve any disputes. The plaintiff claimed that the clause was not valid because it was inadequately brought to the attention of the user. The provision was sufficiently important to require special notice. The Court found in favor of the defendant and held that the clause was enforceable. The Court observed that users were required to click the I Agree button to accept the terms and that the impugned clause was no harder to read than any of the others. The sign-up procedure required users to click I Agree twice, and the second time told the users that they would still be bound by the terms even if they did not read them at all. Thus, it was not reasonable for the plaintiff to argue for the enforcement of all other terms of the contract except for the forum clause. Web-wrap agreements in general should be "afforded the sanctity that must be given to any agreement in writing."

8.3 Browse-Wrap Agreements

Specht v. Netscape Communications Corp., 150 F. Supp. 2d 585 (S.D.N.Y. 2001). The plaintiffs claimed that the defendant's Smart Download software monitored their Internet usage, violating the *Electronic Communication Privacy Act* and the *Computer Fraud and Abuse Act*. The defendant moved to stay proceedings and compel arbitration, arguing that the disputes were subject to a binding arbitration clause in the Smart Download Software End User Agreement. The Court ruled that the license agreement was not binding because a binding contract means that both parties know the terms and agree to them. Firstly, the user did not have to click an icon or link to indicate assent before downloading and using the software. Secondly, the text near where the user could download the application was merely an invitation to view the license agreement and not a strong condition that the user must agree to the agreement terms before using the software. Finally, the full text of the license agreement was only visible if the user clicked a text next to the download button. Thus, the Court declined to compel arbitration for the plaintiff's breach of the license agreement.

Register.com, Inc. v. Verio, Inc., 356 F.3d 393 (2d Cir. 2004). The defendant was a competitor to the plaintiff in the Web-hosting business and used the plaintiff's database so that it could solicit business from new domain name registrants. This act was clearly prohibited according to the terms of the contract posted on the Web site. However, the defendant claimed that it was not bound by the terms and conditions because it never assented to them. The defendant never had to click an icon to signal agreement. The Court ruled in favor of the plaintiff and stated that the terms were presented with the results of the query and on the plaintiff's Web site. In order to be bound by terms, one must have notice of those terms at the time the contract is formed. The Court noted that the defendant had been to the site several times and sent daily queries to the site. Thus, it was deemed to have noticed the terms. This factor distinguished this decision from *Specht v. Netscape Communications Corp.*

Cairo, Inc. v. Crossmedia Services, Inc., No. C. 04-04825 JW, 2005 WL 756610 (N.D. Cal. Apr. 1, 2005). This case involved repeated and automated visits to a Web site as well. Each page had a notice that stated that by continuing past the current page, the user agreed to abide by the Terms of Use for the site. The Terms of Use could be clicked and viewed. The Court noted that such a format was a common and sufficient way to notify customers to the existence of terms and conditions to be followed. Repeated use of the Web site formed the basis of imputing knowledge to the visitor of the terms on which the Web site's services were offered.

Defontes v. Dell Computers Corp., No. Civ. A. PC 03-2636, 2004 WL 253560 (R.I. Jan. 29, 2004). The plaintiffs in this case argued that they were not bound by an arbitration clause contained in the defendant's Terms and Conditions, even though the Terms and Conditions were available to them in both shrink-wrap and browse-wrap format. The Court held that browse-wrap presentation in this case could not bind the plaintiffs because the terms could be viewed only by a hyperlink that was "inconspicuously located at the bottom of the webpage." This presentation was not sufficient to put the plaintiffs on notice. It was not enough that the terms could be found somewhere. Rather, they have to be presented in such a way that they can be found by a reasonable user.

8.4 Click-Wrap Agreements

Novak v. Overture Services, Inc., 309 F. Supp. 2d 446 (E.D.N.Y. 2004). This case involved a challenge to a forum selection clause in Google's Terms and Conditions of Use for Google Groups. The plaintiff had to click a button to signify his agreement with the terms during the registration process. Next to this button was a scroll box in which ten terms were visible. The plaintiff claimed that the forum selection clause was not part of these visible terms and thus, was not enforceable. The Court rejected the plaintiff's contention and stated that he had an adequate opportunity to read the whole contract because it was relatively short and in easy-to-read font, and unlimited time was given to allow the plaintiff to read these terms.

Mortgage Plus, Inc. v. DocMagic, Inc., No. 03-2582-GTV-DJW, 2004 WL 2331918 (D. Kan. Aug. 23, 2004). This case held that a click-wrap software license is enforceable where the licensee is required to click a Yes button to signify her assent to the license agreement as a prerequisite to installing the software. This case was distinguished from *Klocek v. Gateway* by making clear that the buyer in that earlier case had not been made aware that the acceptance of the licensing agreement was a condition to acceptance of the ordered computer.

Scarcella v. America Online, 798 N.Y.S.2d 348, 2004 WL 2093429 (N.Y. Civ. Ct. 2004). The plaintiff in this case claimed that it was unreasonable to enforce the forum selection clause found in the Agreement because the sign-up process required viewing ninety-one computer screens, two of which asked for consent to the Member Agreement. The Court said that the plaintiff did assent to the terms, since a person who signs a contract is deemed to know the contents of the contract and to have assented to the terms; to rule otherwise would "threaten the viability of the Internet as a medium of commerce." However, despite finding assent, the clause was not enforceable due to public policy in the statutory small claims court scheme.

Motise v. America Online, Inc., 346 F. Supp. 2d 563 (S.D.N.Y. 2004). This case found that a Web site's notice of terms was ineffective (but without negative consequences). The plaintiff was an AOL subscriber and argued that he was not bound by AOL's terms because he was not presented with the terms of use nor asked to agree to them when he signed on. AOL stated that all members were bound by the terms of use. The Court found that generally Web site users must be given notice of terms of use in order to be bound by them. However, the plaintiff was using his stepfather's computer and his stepfather had read the terms. Thus, derivative notice was received and the plaintiff was bound by them.

8.5 Offer and Acceptance

Corinthian Pharmaceutical Systems, Inc. v. Lederle Laboratories, 724 F. Supp. 605 (S.D. Ind. 1989). The plaintiff ordered a large quantity of drugs the day before a material price increase was to take effect. The wholesaler used the manufacturer's automated telephone order system and the "tracking number" was issued by the manufacturer's computer system. No human representative participated in taking the order. Subsequently, the manufacturer did not want to supply the large quantity of drugs at the lower price and therefore alleged that the tracking number issued by the computer was not an acceptance of the order, but merely an acknowledgment of the order. The Court agreed and concluded that no contract had been created, thus leaving the wholesaler with no choice but to pay the higher price for that product from the manufacturer.

Je Ho Lim v. The.TV Corp. International, No. B151987, 2002 Cal. App. LEXIS 4315 (2d Dist., June 24, 2002). Generally, American law regarding auctions states that an auctioneer can withdraw goods if he pleases. The plaintiff in this case offered the highest bid and was confirmed as the winner by e-mail. Shortly thereafter, however, the registrar had second thoughts and tried to rescind the deal by arguing that the reserve bid had not been met and that the confirmatory e-mail was sent in error. The Court sided with the plaintiff, finding that the advertisement for the bid was the offer and the plaintiff's highest bid was the acceptance. Alternatively, the Court stated that it was possible that the plaintiff's bid was an offer and it was accepted by the defendant's e-mail.

8.6 Applicable Law

For an example, see Dell's section on Governing Law, available from www.dell.com (Terms of Sale).

The CISG, often referred to in the past as the Vienna Sales Convention, is an international set of rules designed to provide clarity to most international sales transactions. It was adopted by Canada on May 1, 1992, and most western countries, including the United States, are signatories to it. The CISG can be both a discretionary and mandatory set of rules. It is discretionary when both parties agree to be bound by its rules; it has mandatory application when the parties do not choose to use it but become bound to it by virtue of its automatic application. As a result, most international sale of goods contracts between parties in western countries will be subject to the CISG, unless specifically excluded in accordance with the CISG's terms. Although there are many circumstances in which the CISG will not apply, it is best to assume that it will apply to every international sale of goods from Canada, unless it is specifically excluded.

8.7 Unconscionability

Craven v. Strand Holidays (Canada) Ltd., [1982] 142 D.L.R. (3d) 31 (Ont. C.A.).

Lord Denning in *J. Spurling Ltd. v. Bradshaw*, [1956] 1 W.L.R. 461 (C.A.): "Some clauses which I have seen would need to be printed in red ink on the face of the document with a red hand pointing to it before the notice could be held to be sufficient." However, see also the Quebec Civil Code, which permits a contract to be voided if one party has a superior bargaining power and the weaker party does not have a reasonable opportunity to negotiate the terms.

Brower v. Gateway 2000, Inc., 676 N.Y.S.2d 569, 1998 N.Y. App. Div. LEXIS 8872 (1st Dept. Aug. 13, 1998). In this case, the plaintiff bought a PC from Gateway through direct sales. The PC box had a shrink-wrap agreement that included an arbitration clause requiring arbitration under the rules of the International Chamber of Commerce (ICC). The French-based ICC's costs of arbitration were prohibitively high. The Court referred to the Uniform Commercial Code 2-302, which allows courts to flexibly police against clauses they find unconscionable as a matter of law, that is, a combination of grossly unequal bargaining power plus terms that are unreasonably favorable to the more powerful party. The Court thus found that the particular arbitral institution chosen was not fair and was designed to deter individual customers from using the arbitration process. The case was remanded to substitute a different arbitrator due to this unconscionability.

Comb v. PayPal, Inc., No. C-02-1227, 2002 U.S. Dist. LEXIS 16364 (N.D. Cal. Aug. 30, 2002). The Court concluded that the terms and conditions of a contract are not binding on the user if insufficient efforts are taken to bring the terms, or even the existence of the terms, to the attention of the user. Thus, if the words are too small to be noticed, they will not be binding on the user. While the Court was willing to assume that the user agreement was effective, the Court went on to find that the agreement was unconscionable and therefore its submission to arbitration provision was unenforceable.

8.8 Magnuson-Moss Warranty Act

Under the *Magnuson-Moss Warranty Act*, products sold to U.S. consumers must contain the following disclosures:

- Any written warranty must designate on the title that it is a "full" or "limited" warranty.
- Any limitation on the duration of implied warranties must include the statement "Some States do not allow limitations on how long an implied warranty lasts, so the above limitation may not apply to you."
- An exclusion or limitation on relief must include the statement "Some States do not allow the exclusion or limitation of incidental or consequential damages, so that above may not apply to you."
- All warranties must include the statement "This warranty gives you specific legal rights, and you may also have other rights which vary from State to State."

8.9 Convention on the Use of Electronic Communications in International Contracts (CUECIC), Uniform Electronic Transactions Act (UETA), Uniform Computer Information Transactions Act (UCITA)

Adopted by the United Nations Commission on International Trade Law (UNCITRAL) in 2005 and signed by eighteen countries by the end of 2007, this convention applies to electronic communications in connection with the formation or performance of a contract between parties whose places of business are in different states.

UETA broadly applies to electronic records and signatures in commercial or government transactions. UETA explicitly deems electronic signatures and documents to be in satisfaction of laws requiring signed or written contracts.

A proposed state law, UCITA applies to computer information transactions and has been adopted by several states. It recognizes authentication in electronic form and provides that electronic contracts are valid if the party against which enforcement is sought has a record sufficient to indicate that a contract has been formed and that reasonably identifies the copy or subject matter to which the contract refers. UCITA liberalizes contract validity even further by supporting electronic agents to make binding contracts. If the medium is reasonable in the circumstances, acceptance and validity are satisfied in the formation process. At the same time as UCITA was formed, UETA was also formed.

8.10 Jurisdiction Issues

For further detail on the "battle of the forms," see an earlier paper, James M. Klotz, Antonin Pribetic, and Peter Mazzacano, "Case Comment: All Quiet on the CISG Front—*Guiliani v. Invar Manufacturing*, the Battle of the Forms, and the Elusive Concept of Terminus Fixus," *Canadian Business Law Journal*, Fall 2008.

M/S Bremen v. Zapata Off-Shore Co., 407 U.S. 1, 92 S. Ct. 1907, 32 L. Ed.2d 513 (1972). A choice of forum clause in an international contract is presumed valid in the United States (although it is not dispositive). A nonexclusive jurisdiction clause looks like the following:

> All disputes, controversies or claims arising out of or in connection with or relation to the contract, including any question regarding the existence of the contract, its validity or termination, may be submitted to and be subject to the jurisdiction of the courts of the [home jurisdiction] which shall have nonexclusive jurisdiction in the event of any dispute hereunder. The parties hereby irrevocably submit and attorn to the nonexclusive jurisdiction of such courts to finally adjudicate or determine any suit, action or proceedings arising out of or in connection with this Agreement.[2]

8.11 Export Control

An example of such language is found on Netscape's Web site, as follows:

> Software available on the Netscape website is subject to United States export controls. No software from this site may be downloaded or otherwise exported or re-exported (1) into (or to a national or resident of) Cuba, Iraq, Libya, Sudan, North Korea, Iran, Syria, or any other country to which the United States has embargoed goods; or (2) to anyone on the U.S. Treasury Department's list of Specially Designated Nationals or the U.S. Commerce Department's Table of Denial Orders. By downloading or using the software, you are agreeing to the foregoing and you are warranting that you are not located in, under the control of, or a national or resident of any such country or on any such list.

8.12 Current Issues

Internet Jurisdiction: *See, e.g.,* in the United States, *Bensusan Restaurant Corp. v. Richard King,* 937 F. Supp. 295 (S.D.N.Y. 1996), *aff'd* 126 F.3d 25 (2d Cir. 1997); *Weber v. Jolly Hotels,* 977 F. Supp. 327 (D.N.J. 1997); in Canada, *Braintech, Inc. v. Kostiuk,* [1999] B.C.J. No. 622 (C.A.). *See also Zippo Mfg. Co. v. Zippo Dot Com, Inc.,* 952 F. Supp. 1119 (W.D. Pa. 1997); *CompuServe, Inc. v. Patterson,* 89 F.3d 1257 (6th Cir. 1996).

---

[2] James M. Klotz, International Sales Agreements: A drafting and negotiating guide, 2d. ed (New York: Kluwer Law International, 2008).

Metatagging: This is the practice of piggybacking on the goodwill of other Web sites by embedding the key identifiers, usually the trademarks, into the metatag of the site. Search engines locate and categorize Web pages on the basis of metatags. *See, e.g., Playboy Enterprises, Inc. v. Calvin Designer Label,* Civ. No. 97-3204 (N.D. Cal., Sept. 8, 1997).

Framing: This is the capturing of a Web page into the framer's Web page as a window. A less sophisticated tool is the simple hyperlink, which permits a user to go to another Web site by clicking a word or symbol. *See, e.g., Washington Post Co. v. Total News Inc.,* 97 Civ. 1190 (S.D.N.Y., filed Feb. 20, 1997).

Capacity to Contract: As reported in the *Toronto Star* newspaper, April 27, 1999, in "Net Plug Pulled After Big Bed Bid," a thirteen-year-old New Jersey boy bid US$900,000 on the Internet for Canada's first prime minister's bed. Likely, no real loss was suffered by the boy's actions, except that the bed had to be relisted for sale.

Web Site Service Contracts: Posting on a corporate Web site is sufficient notice to bind customers to changes in their user licenses. Providers do not have to e-mail each individual customer to properly notify them of periodic changes. Customers are obliged to check the Web site from time to time. *Kanitz v. Rogers Cable Inc.,* [2002] O.J. No. 665.

Contracts over Mass E-mail: A mass e-mail message fails to constitute the minimal level of notice required enabling the person receiving the e-mail to learn critical information required for a contract. The e-mail must be enough to put a reasonable person on inquiry notice of an alteration to the contractual aspects of the relationship. *Campbell v. General Dynamics Government Systems Corp.,* 407 F. 3d 546 (1st Cir. 2005).

Choice of Common Law or UCC: Following the UCC may be appealing in that it has a number of helpful terms and assistance for difficult issues such as the battle of the forms. It is also as "uniform" as the law in this area can get. However, some cases have ruled that if the crux of an agreement lies in preparing a service, not in preparing goods, it should be examined under the common law of contracts, not the UCC. *Mortgage Plus, Inc. v. DocMagic, Inc.,* No. 03-2582-GTV-DJW, 2004 WL 2331918 (D. Kan. Aug. 23, 2004).

Ratification: Even if an employee is not authorized to accept contracts on the company's behalf by monitoring communications to automated queries, the company may be bound by these contracts since a party "cannot sit back and wait to see if it will benefit or suffer from [its] agent's acts." The defense of ignorance is thus not always valid. *Mortgage Plus, Inc. v. DocMagic, Inc.*, No. 03-2582-GTV-DJW, 2004 WL 2331918 (D. Kan. Aug. 23, 2004).

James M. Klotz
Miller Thomson LLP
Scotia Plaza, Suite 5800
40 King Street West
Toronto, Canada M5H 3S1
Phone: (416) 597-4373
Fax: (416) 595-8695
E-mail: jmklotz@millerthomson.com

CHAPTER 7

Cross-Cultural Awareness

David A. Victor
DEPARTMENT OF MANAGEMENT
COLLEGE OF BUSINESS
EASTERN MICHIGAN UNIVERSITY
YPSILANTI, MICHIGAN

1. Introduction

Few areas of international negotiations are as important as cross-cultural awareness to understanding and developing appropriate responses. Yet, for the most part, U.S. lawyers have received very little in the way of formal training in those areas of behavior most likely to be affected by cultural difference. How each culture differs is highly variable. That they differ in specific ways is a constant.

This chapter lays out the behavioral factors and communication processes most likely to vary in the setting of international legal negotiations. The framework presented in this chapter for assessing cross-cultural variables affecting international legal negotiations and transactions is intended to benefit newcomers to the field by providing them with a system for asking the right questions before and during their international encounters.

The chapter may also prove valuable to those well acquainted with the field. While experience in an international setting is unquestionably the best means for acquiring cross-cultural skills, even those well versed in international transactions often find it difficult to pass on what they know in an organized way to those new to the culture in question. In short, some of the best international negotiators know when something feels right or wrong but would not be able to specifically explain why. The model described here is intended to help those lawyers organize their experiences in a useful way.

Moreover, a lawyer's experience in one culture is rarely valid when dealing with another. Negotiations in Tokyo, Frankfurt, and Mexico City are as conceptually different as they are geographically so. Yet in an increasingly integrated world economy, the lawyer expert in only one other culture is often called on to interact with those from cultures far removed from his or her area of experience. Still, no international lawyer is able to know every negotiation approach common in every nation. The sheer number of possible cultures the international lawyer may face at a given time thus presents a dilemma: to practice international law effectively, the lawyer must know the specifics of a vast array of cultures. This chapter attempts to provide a partial solution to this dilemma through describing a culture-general framework within which lawyers can recognize the right questions to ask about specific cultures.

2. The LESCANT Model

Lawyers can anticipate the sorts of experiences they will probably encounter when conducting legal negotiations in another country if they train themselves to identify those variables that often shift across cultures in international settings. The key here is to know what variables to look for in international negotiations and transactions. Lawyers trained to ask the right questions and observe the right behaviors are better prepared than any list of cultural truisms could make them.

These variables have been identified in an earlier book, *International Business Communication*,[1] under the acronym of LESCANT. The seven variables of **LESCANT** are: **L**anguage; **E**nvironment and technology; **S**ocial organization; **C**ontexting; **A**uthority conception; **N**onverbal behavior; and **T**emporal conception. This chapter applies each of these variables to the setting of international legal negotiations.

2.1 Language

U.S. lawyers are among the most monolingual in the world. Oddly, this ignorance of other languages often leads the typical U.S. lawyer to overestimate the importance of language as a cultural barrier.

Unquestionably, language is a factor. It is rarely, however, a hidden factor. If you speak English and your counterpart speaks only Spanish, the communication gap is much more readily apparent than in most of the other cross-cultural variables you are likely to encounter. Whether or not you need a translator or interpreter is, in most cases, obvious. Yet language as a factor in negotiations does pose several more subtle questions that the international lawyer should consider.

First, language structure affects common points of understanding. No language can ever be translated exactly into another language. There are two reasons for this. First, many words and phrases have no counterparts. The French *savoir-faire*, for instance, does not mean precisely its English counterpart "know-how." The Japanese word *wa*

---

[1] DAVID A. VICTOR, INTERNATIONAL BUSINESS COMMUNICATION (1992).

means "harmony" in English, but in Japanese the word has a sense of concreteness that makes it tangible and specific where its English counterpart is vague and abstract.

A second reason translation is generally inexact is that every word carries with it associations unique to its own language. The English phrase "to touch base with someone" has no associative meaning in a culture in which baseball is not played. Much more subtle and far more common are the overtones of associations. In English, for example, the verb *to procure* carries an awkward and even morally questionable shade of meaning. By contrast, its Italian equivalent *procurare* is the most common translation for the English verb *to get*. Thus, the Italian phrase "Mi sono procurato" is literally translated as something akin to "I have procured something for myself" when its closest equivalence should be "I have got hold of something." But that phrase in English carries other associations not present in Italian that change its connotative meaning (for example, "get hold of yourself"). In short, despite their common usage, the Italian verb *procurare* can never be exactly rendered in English, nor can the English verb "to get" fully carry the same message in Italian. And this is repeated again and again in any effort to translate.

At best, then, translation provides a rough equivalence of meaning. But in the law, where words constitute the most accurate rendering of meaning, a rough equivalence of translated meaning can add a whole new dimension to legal interpretation: understanding a foreign partner using a second language is subject to interpretive cloudiness.

Finally, the basic structure of a language affects negotiation strategies. In English, for instance, the verb usually comes in or near to the second position in a sentence. In German, by contrast, one has the choice of placing the main verb at the end of the sentence if an earlier helping verb is used. This simple grammatical difference creates an enormous difference for the lawyer in face-to-face negotiations. In English negotiations, your counterpart already knows your main position well before you have completed your sentence. To negotiate a transaction in English, therefore, it is not even necessary to listen to the entire sentence of one's counterpart. As a result, the negotiation style of native English speakers is often anticipatory and even interruptive. Because German allows for constructions in which the main verb comes at the end of the sentence, negotiators can change the verb before they have completed the sentence to accommodate the reaction they see in the face of their counterpart.

These issues are obvious when using the language itself. The more subtle point is that the negotiating pattern usually continues even when a different language is used. Negotiators whose first language is German, in other words, do not expect to be interrupted when they use English because they are accustomed to German patterns of negotiations.

An additional factor is the cultural attachment to language. Language creates an in-group and an out-group, dividing those who speak it from those who do not. The degree to which this dichotomy affects the negotiator is cross-culturally variable. The international lawyer needs to consider to what degree this issue affects his or her ability to negotiate an international transaction successfully.

Some cultures attach a social significance to the language chosen. The ability to use Korean in Korea carries considerable social meaning since Korean is only spoken in Korea. Thus the negotiator who speaks Korean by very virtue of knowing the language shows an interest in Korea and a respect for the culture, even if the language of negotiation turns out to be English.

In some cases, the social significance carries a political overtone with it as well. For example, for countries that were formerly part of the U.S.S.R., the use of the local language not only reflects the same social ramifications as Korean in Korea but also reflects the full recognition of these now independent states and the importance of their languages that were once officially limited or even suppressed. Thus, the use of Latvian in Latvia or Kazakh in Kazakhstan carries both a social and a political overtone.

In countries with a former colonial heritage, language choice can also be significant. Thus, while many Arabs speak excellent English, the use of Arabic is likely to be viewed very favorably, especially when used by an English speaker. The use of Arabic shows respect for Arabic culture that does much to erase the imperialist legacy of English speakers vis-à-vis their former Arabic colonies. By contrast, the speaker of Flemish—while assuredly receptive to the English speaker using Flemish—feels little of this political or social overlay of meaning in the choice of language. The Flemish speaker, however, might have a more gratified response to a French speaker using Flemish.

This brings us to the issue of language use in officially multilingual countries. Here too language choice can carry a similar political and social significance. The use of French in Flemish-speaking Flanders or of English in French-speaking Quebec becomes a political statement. For example, using English in Quebec City goes far beyond the Quebec legal requirement for the use of French. To a Quebecois counterpart, the inability of an Anglophone Canadian lawyer to speak French can be viewed as (and indeed may actually be) a *refusal* to speak French. Monolingual English-speaking U.S. lawyers in Quebec can find themselves in the same situation unless they clarify the situation. By contrast, the ability of a U.S. lawyer to speak French with his or her Quebecois counterpart also goes far beyond the legal requirement for using French. In essence, the U.S. lawyer who uses French in Quebec can be seen as validating the position held by Francophone camp. This can in many instances accrue credit to the U.S. lawyer as sympathetic to (or at the least culturally sensitive to) the Francophone position in the Francophone-Anglophone divide in Canada.

2.2 Environment and Technology

Our physical environment communicates key points within our own culture that may not be readily understood outside it. This is especially true in the arena of international legal transactions, where subtle differences may imply differences in status or power. For example, in Japan, where open-system offices are common, it is not possible to determine rank by office size. In contrast, office size is a major status symbol in Europe and the Americas.

Similarly, the concept of formal and informal negotiations may be affected by the place in which the discussion takes place. In the United States, open give-and-take in negotiations goes on in the boardroom and does not go on outside the boardroom. By contrast, in many other cultures, the negotiating table in a formal boardroom is *not* a place for an open discussion. This formal setting is only where the predetermined positions are officially stated. True negotiations take place elsewhere—in the hallway, over meals, in hotel lobbies, or in private homes. The U.S. lawyer must determine where the *actual* negotiation takes place (versus the formal negotiation) to be effective in foreign transactions.

Access to communication technology also affects international transactions. In the United States, the European Union, Canada, Japan, Singapore, New Zealand, or Australia, most lawyers can safely presume that at least a basic communication infrastructure exists. Elsewhere, such assumptions are dangerous. Access to telephones in the developed and rapidly developing nations may differ radically from access in underdeveloped countries. Thus the U.S. ratio is just over 53 land telephones per 100 people and that of Canada just under 65 per 100, with many nations even higher (reaching to a high of over 89 land telephones for every 100 people in Bermuda).[2]

At the opposite spectrum, dozens of countries have essentially no land telephone access at all, with 10 nations at a rate of less than 1 per every 100 people: Afghanistan, Angola, Bangladesh, Cambodia, Chad, East Timor, Myanmar, Niger, Rwanda, and Papua New Guinea.[3]

While the U.S. rate of cell phones exceeds that of landlines, the ratio is still somewhat comparable with 83.5 cell phones per 100 users

---

[2] INTERNATIONAL TELECOMMUNICATION UNION, MAIN TELEPHONE LINES, SUBSCRIBERS PER 100 PERSONS, 2007, http://www.itu.int/ITU-D/icteye/Reporting/ShowReportFrame .aspx?ReportName=/WTI/InformationTechnologyPublic&RP_intYear=2007&RP_ intLanguageID=1 (last visited Sept. 16, 2008).

[3] *Id.*

and 53 landlines per 100. In Canada, more people still have landlines than mobile phones but again the ratio is still fairly comparable with 65.5 landlines per 100 people versus 58.5 cell phones. By comparison, the United Arab Emirates averages 173.37 mobile phones per 100 people contrasted to only 31.6 landlines per 100 people.[4] While the UAE may have the highest number of cell phones per 100 people, it is joined in having an average of more than 1 mobile phone per person by 11 other nations (Antigua and Barbuda, Argentina, Aruba, the Bahamas, Bahrain, Israel, the Maldives, Qatar, Saudi Arabia, Singapore, and Taiwan). That said, in several nations large areas have very limited cell phone coverage, and 20 countries have fewer than 5 mobile phones per 100 people (Burundi, Central African Republic, Comoros, Cuba, Djibouti, East Timor, Eritrea, Ethiopia, Guinea, Kiribati, Malawi, Myanmar, Papua New Guinea, Niger, the Solomon Islands, Somalia, Tajikistan, Turkmenistan, Uzbekistan, and Zimbabwe).[5]

A particularly striking contrast exists between land telephones and mobile phones in much of the developing world. For example, while South Africa's landline infrastructure is very poor (only 100 mainline phones per 1,000 people), its cellular penetration exceeds that of the United States (870 mobile phones per 1,000 people, compared to 835 in the United States).[6] Indeed, mobile phones outnumber mainline phones by a ratio of five to one or more in many developing countries. This provides a marked difference in expectation in countries such as Canada, which actually has *fewer* mobile phones than mainline phones. Consequently, international negotiators need to have an understanding of what kind of phone services are available to their foreign counterparts.

All of these data to this point represent a mere "head count" of phones, however, and do not reflect the reliability of service. For example, even with just over 10 land telephones per 100 people in Papua New Guinea, the phone systems are so unreliable that on a bad day, phone communication may simply not be possible. A delay in responding by phone in such cases is understandable, provided that the technological context is understood by all parties. The U.S. lawyer waiting for an "immediate" phone response for two hours could easily draw an incorrect conclusion regarding a Papuan counterpart.

Another important communications capability is Internet access. Despite its name, the World Wide Web is not quite worldwide: in some

---

[4] INTERNATIONAL TELECOMMUNICATION UNION, MOBILE, CELLULAR SUBSCRIBERS PER 100 PERSONS, 2007, http://www.itu.int/ITU-D/icteye/Reporting/ShowReportFrame.aspx? ReportName=/WTI/CellularSubscribersPublic&RP_intYear=2007&RP_intLan guageID=1 (last visited Sept. 16, 2008).
[5] *Id.*
[6] *Id.*

regions, the Internet is a scarce luxury. Where access to telephones is impossible, so is access to the Internet. In 21 countries, less than 1 person in 100 has subscriber access to the Internet (Bangladesh, Burkina Faso, Burundi, Cambodia, Central African Republic, Chad, Democratic Republic of Congo, East Timor, Ethiopia, Guinea, Iraq, Liberia, Madagascar, Mali, Mauritania, Mozambique, Myanmar, Niger, North Korea, Sierra Leone, and Tanzania).[7] This does not mean that the Internet is entirely unavailable to visiting business people; in all of these countries except North Korea, some Internet access exists.

Nevertheless, there is tremendous contrast between the developing world and countries like the United States (719 users per 1,000), South Korea (738 per 1000), Canada (852 per 1,000), and the world leader, the Netherlands (over 913 per 1,000). Internet access is not necessarily linked to a highly developed economy. The Danish autonomous country (until 2009 a province) of Greenland has an Internet access rate of 90.75 percent (compared to the 64.3 percent in Denmark itself). The availability of Internet access, in turn, determines whether or not e-mail is available. More than that, Internet inaccessibility limits the ability to reach electronically stored files and records as well as research sources. All of these, then, affect the ability to conduct negotiations in a manner customary in one's own nation.

Similar situations may also exist regarding access to overnight package delivery or even mail delivery itself. Similarly, considerable disparity exists, depending on one's locale, regarding what lawyers in countries such as the United States would consider basics, including wire transfers, fax machines, copiers, or other office communication devices.

Indeed, the mere availability of technological devices can have a variety of meanings in different cultures. For example, the presence of a word processor may suggest increased status in a culture in which such technological devices are rare. By contrast, the same word processor in a culture in which these devices are commonplace may not even be noticed. In yet a third culture, the word processor may suggest that the owner has no secretary or must do his or her own clerical work.

2.3 Social Organization

Social organization refers to the common institutions and collective activities shared by members of a culture. These institutions and collective activities affect the behavior of people in all aspects of life,

---

[7] INTERNATIONAL TELECOMMUNICATION UNION, INTERNET INDICATORS: SUBSCRIBERS, USERS AND BROADBAND SUBSCRIBERS, 2007, http://www.itu.int/ITU-D/icteye/Reporting/Show ReportFrame.aspx?ReportName=/WTI/InformationTechnologyPublic&RP_int Year=2007&RP_intLanguageID=1 (last visited Sept. 16, 2008).

including business. Only experience can provide lawyers in a foreign setting with an adequate background to comfortably recognize the large array of social organizational factors they will encounter. Still, by looking for the most cross-culturally variable points of social organization, international lawyers can go a long way toward preparing themselves.

The six variables most likely to affect legal transactions and negotiations across cultures are:

- Kinship and family ties
- Friendship ties
- Education
- Class and social stratification
- Perception of work and the law
- Gender differences

Kinship and family ties are an important aspect of social organization affecting business. In many societies, kinship and business ties are relatively weak. This is the case in the United States, where nepotism is frowned upon. In many other societies, kinship and business ties are strong. Nepotism in such societies is viewed favorably. Having no kinship ties affects the foreign negotiator in such situations because he or she can never fully be trusted by the opposing side. No amount of paper, in short, can match a blood tie.

Short of blood ties, in many countries business is conducted only with friends. This difference in viewpoint presents the international negotiator with a difficulty in establishing trust. In the United States, trust is centered on contracts and written documentation. In a large number of other cultures, written documents are not trusted. Friendship and personal ties replace contracts as the main vehicle for reassurance.

As a result, a great gap exists between U.S. and foreign negotiators. For U.S. lawyers, the negotiated document is the purpose of the negotiation. For many negotiators from other cultures, the process of negotiating is itself the end goal of the negotiation. The written documents are secondary to the personal relationships formed through the process of negotiating.

Educational ties are often strongly set from one country to another. Where you were educated greatly affects your opportunities and how you are perceived, as well as your network of business contacts. This is generally not the case in the United States. While ties to key universities are recognized in the United States, they do not carry the weight of an Oxford or Cambridge education in Britain or of a University of Tokyo tie in Japan.

In other countries, a similar bond exists among those with a foreign education in particular countries. For example, in many nations that were once colonies of France, people may hold a higher view of a French university degree than one from their own country.

The nature of education among businesspeople is also cross-culturally variant. In some societies, such as France and Singapore, most lawyers—as well as business leaders and executives—are likely to have highly technical training. In other societies (Britain, for example), most business leaders have a generalist's background; specialists, including lawyers, may be seen as having too narrow a view to be effective negotiators when acting alone.

The United States has no formal class or caste system. Other countries have formalized class systems that help determine the perceived abilities of people as well as their likely interest or lack of interest in business matters. The U.S. lawyer unaware of these distinctions not only misses important insights into the expected behavior of those with whom he or she negotiates, but may risk insulting them. Additionally, as a member of a formally classless society, the U.S. negotiator may be scrutinized for behavioral clues to help place him or her in the appropriate foreign class.

Economic stratification takes the place of a formal class system in many societies. One's income level, for example, affects income and class in many other societies (as in the United Kingdom, for example) are often independent variables.

How the law and work in general are viewed shifts according to a culture's social organization. The pursuit of business as well as the role of lawyers in conducting that business are given a high degree of regard in the United States. This regard is often not shared in other cultures that may value government service, literature, or the arts more.

The nature of the work organization is also often different across cultures. Thus, in the United States, most people identify themselves by their profession; the organization is secondary to what one does. U.S. lawyers often feel their closest ties to other lawyers regardless of the firm or organization. In Japan, most people identify themselves by the company they work for: what you do is secondary to where you work. In Mexico, most people identify themselves primarily by the family to which they belong.

Gender issues often affect negotiations, too. Several social scientists have indicated that regardless of culture, we have formulated our views of the proper roles of each gender by the time we are toddlers. Considerable research indicates that much of the gender-linked preconceptions we hold have their foundations in place even before we are old enough to speak. As a result, gender-linked behavior is among the most deeply modeled of behavioral differences. Since each culture holds a different set of rules regarding appropriate and inappropriate behavior for each gender, views of how the genders should behave represent standards that are extremely difficult to remain flexible toward.

Some have argued that men and women each represent a separate culture within a culture. Psychologist Lillian Breslow Rubin most notably has demonstrated that men and women are raised differently to develop different aspects of their personality and to prefer certain activities over others.[8] This holds true for all cultures. In no society are men and women acculturated to behave identically.

That said, although all cultures make distinctions between the genders resulting in sex-type stereotyping, considerable similarity exists regarding the nature of stereotypes regardless of culture. For example, John Williams and Deborah Best in a study of thirty countries found that people in each country attached the same traits to the same gender.[9] For men, regardless of culture, these included adventurous, dominant, forceful, independent, and strong-willed. For women, regardless of culture, these included emotional, sentimental, submissive, and superstitious.

Despite widespread similarities of sex-trait stereotyping across cultures, how strongly members of each culture allow these differences to affect workplace behavior does vary markedly among cultures. There are three main ways that cultures manifest sex-trait stereotyping in the workplace: collegial interaction attempting to ignore gender stereotypes; collegial interaction attempting to cultivate gender stereotypes; and noncollegial or absent interaction.

Collegial interaction attempting to ignore gender stereotypes is representative of the U.S. view. It is not widely shared, but includes such countries as Canada, the United Kingdom, Russia, Australia, and New Zealand. In these cultures, both sexes have attempted to redefine their relationships by ignoring culturally learned stereotypes. It is a societal ideal, for example, in the United States to treat men and women as equal in the workplace. This ideal has been reinforced by legal requirements as well. Admittedly, in the United States such efforts have not fully eliminated differences in pay for equivalent jobs or proportionate distribution in key corporate positions between the sexes. Still, the premise of gender equality affects the way Americans communicate about sexual differences as well as the nature of ideal expected behavior.

Collegial interaction attempting to cultivate gender stereotypes is representative of cultures in which both genders work but are deliberately steered toward careers in which their jobs reinforce culturally held stereotypes. Thus, more women than men may be called on to use

---

[8] Lillian Breslow Rubin, Worlds of Pain: Life in the Working-Class Family (1976).

[9] John E. Williams & Deborah L. Best, Measuring Sex Stereotypes: A Multinational Study (1990).

interpersonal skills that they are perceived (through culturally learned sex-stereotyping) to have in greater abundance than men. Conversely, more men may be assigned to jobs using analytical skills for which they are perceived to have an innate affinity.

In recent years, considerable research has focused on the degree to which gender attributes actually represent the actual sex of the individual in question. In this view, gender behavior as a socially learned construct may be tied only partially (if at all) to one's sex. This affects the view of differences in sexual orientation as well as the views held within a given culture toward homosexuality or multiple versions of what constitutes male or female behavior. As Fred Jandt and Heather Hundley point out, "Typically, while any one culture endorses its own version of masculinity, several cultures constitute a myriad of masculinities."[10] As Jandt and Hundley explain, the earlier attempts to divide gender differences into either masculine or feminine result themselves from culturally learned views of gender: "While we find that earlier research attempts to explain masculinity as either a social phenomenon or biologically bound, both arguments leave little room for a non-Western perspective."[11]

Noncollegial or absence of interaction between the genders in the workplace represents a final cultural configuration of the relationship between men and women. In these cultures, women and men are divided along two possible approaches. In the first, women and men are strictly segregated at work, although both genders may work and rise to high levels within their fields. In many Islamic cultures, for example, women often achieve considerable reputation as physicians and often have larger practices than women in other cultures since women go only to female physicians. By contrast, virtually no women would be expected to be lawyers. The second formulation of this approach is one in which women may not work or may have very little opportunity to advance due to a perceived inferiority or closed system.

2.4 Contexting and Face-Saving

Directness in legal negotiations shifts drastically across cultures. Arguably, no two cultures negotiate in exactly the same manner. International negotiations in legal matters are particularly tied up with two key issues: contexting and face-saving.

Contexting is a term coined by Edward T. Hall to describe the way people read into what is communicated in words based on the surrounding circumstances.[12] Contexting deals with the amount one pays

---

[10] Fred Jandt & Heather Hundley, (2007) *Intercultural Dimensions of Communicating Masculinities*, 15 J. MEN'S STUD. 216.

[11] *Id.*

[12] EDWARD T. HALL, THE SILENT LANGUAGE (1959).

Figure 7.1
Cultures Ranked by Level of Contexting

High Contexting Cultures	Japanese	Information Implicitly Contained
	Arabic	
	Latin American	
SENDER	Italian	RECEIVER
	English	
	French	
	North American	
Low Contexting Cultures	Scandinavian*	Information Explicitly Conveyed
	German	
	Swiss-German	

* Scandinavian category excludes Finland (Tirkkonen-Conduit, 1987)

attention to how something is said over what is actually put into words. No two cultures share the same level of contexting. All cultures can be seen as either higher contexted or lower contexted than others.

High contexting refers to the practice of relying heavily on how something is said or written and on the circumstances surrounding that communication. In a high-context culture, negotiations are based more on what is understood than on what is explicitly stated. **Low contexting** refers to the practice of relying heavily on what is said. In a low-context culture, negotiations are based on hammering out specifics and on establishing the exact wording of an agreement. Relatively little importance is given to implied arrangements.

All cultures can be placed on a contexting scale from low to high. Figure 7.1 shows the relative level of contexting of several major groups. Note that the United States is generally considered a very low-context culture. High- and low-context cultures have predictable reactions relative to one another. Figure 7.2 contrasts high- and low-context negotiation style.

Face-saving may be defined as the act of preserving one's prestige or outward dignity. Face-saving—like contexting—varies drastically from culture to culture. In cultures with a strong face-saving element, negotiations may end if one party or the other is caused to lose face. In such cultures, face is more important than most business dealings. In cultures with a weak face-saving element, negotiations may continue if one or the other party is caused to lose face. In such cultures (including the United States), business dealings are generally considered

Figure 7.2
Variation in the Reliance on Verbal Communication
Between Extreme High- and Low-Context Cultures

	High Context	Low Context
Reliance on Verbal Communication	Low	High
Reliance on Non-Verbal Communication	High	Low
View of Silence	Respected Communicative	Anxiety-Producing Non-Communicative
Attention to Detail	Low	High
Attention to Intention	High	Low
Communication Approach	Indirect Inferential	Direct Explicit
Literalness	Low Literalness Interpretive	High Literalness Non-Interpretive

Figure 7.3
Characteristics of High and Low Face-Saving Cultures

	High Face-Saving	Low Face-Saving
Contexting	High	Low
Favored Business Communication Approach	Politeness Strategy Indirect Plan	Confrontation Strategy Direct Plan
View of Directness	Uncivil, Inconsiderate Offensive	Honest Inoffensive
View of Indirectness	Civil, Considerate Honest	Dishonest Offensive
Amount of Verbal Self-Disclosure	Low	High
Vagueness	Tolerated	Not Tolerated

more important than face. High and low face-saving cultures have predictable characteristics, described in Figure 7.3.

The most significant of these differences is how the law is viewed. In high face-saving cultures, shame and fear of losing face keep people in line. The courts serve as a resolution method of last resort. In low face-saving cultures such as the United States, the law is often the option of first recourse. The law—not face—keeps people in line.

2.5 Authority Conception

Authority conception varies from culture to culture. The degree to which people favor an authoritarian, egalitarian, paternalistic, or participative management varies from culture to culture and often from organization to organization within a given culture.

Of particular importance to the legal negotiator is the role of symbolic rank. In societies characterized by strict vertical hierarchies, it is inappropriate to conduct negotiations with someone of a notably different stature or rank. In the United States, where the negotiating lawyer—particularly outside counsel—may hold appropriate authority from the organization but not hold the same rank as the foreign negotiator, this may pose a serious problem.

An additional factor that often comes into play regarding authority conception rests in the symbolic or token appearance of high-ranking officials during negotiations. For example, in Japan, the chairman of the organization may enter the room where negotiations are under way. He is unlikely to add anything specific to the discussion and is indeed likely to leave after initial introductions, but his presence symbolically imbues the negotiator with greater authority. His token appearance symbolizes the level of importance the Japanese organization gives to the matter being negotiated. Not only does such an appearance of a high-ranking official give the U.S. counterpart an important clue to the direction of the negotiations at hand, but the U.S. side might risk being misread without some appropriate symbolic appearance from a high-ranking official on their side.

2.6 Nonverbal Communication and Face-to-Face Negotiations

People communicate with more than words in all cultures. The way we move, look in someone's eyes, and many other factors all contribute to what we mean to communicate. This method of communication is called nonverbal communication. No two cultures share the same nonverbal communication style.

Nonverbal communication in most legal settings varies across cultures in six major ways. The lawyer who wants to succeed in face-to-face international negotiations should observe those from the target culture to see how these nonverbal communication variations differ from his or her own culture. These six areas are **kinesics** (body movement and facial gestures); **proxemics** (distance); **oculesics** (eye movements and eye contact); **haptics** (touching behavior); **paralanguage** (tone of voice and nonlanguage sounds); and **appearance** (dress and grooming).

Nonverbal communication is learned well before language is acquired. As a result, it may be the most deeply ingrained of all cultural variables. Even as infants, we already have a strong sense of proper and improper nonverbal communication and of the unspoken messages that go along with it.

Because nonverbal communication is so deeply ingrained, it is hard to adjust to the differences that occur in cross-cultural interactions. For example, if someone were to stand closer to you than is customary in your own culture, you would have an extremely difficult time not moving away. Similarly, if someone were to stand farther from you than is customary in your own culture, you would have a very strong urge to move closer as you talked. In face-to-face, cross-cultural negotiations, it is necessary to overcome these strong feelings and adjust your own nonverbal communication to that of your counterpart.

When an error in translation of a language occurs, most people will ask what is actually meant because the lack of communication is obvious. Misunderstandings arising from nonverbal communication are less obvious, however. Moreover, most people are assumed to understand nonverbal messages without asking; indeed, asking may be considered rude. Few people, for example, ask a group of negotiators across the table why they are making intense eye contact.

2.7 Conceptions of Time

There are two major ways that cultures understand time. **Monochronic time** conceives of time as inflexible. In monochronic cultures, time can be divided easily, and schedules are adhered to closely. **Polychronic time** conceives of time as flexible. In polychronic cultures, time cannot easily be divided, and schedules are not closely adhered to.

The United States is a monochronic culture in most business settings. Relatively few other countries have cultures that are monochronic. These include Germany, Austria, Norway, Sweden, Iceland, Denmark, Great Britain, Luxembourg, the Netherlands, Australia, New Zealand, English-speaking Canada, the British and Afrikaner cultures of South Africa, the Flemish portion of Belgium, and the German-speaking portion of Switzerland. Most doctors' offices in the United States run on polychronic time because of the nature of the profession. Most of the world's cultures are polychronic.

The trade-off between the monochronic and polychronic conceptions is not limited to time only. The balance is between schedules and personal relationships. In polychronic cultures, personal relationships take precedence over preset schedules. In monochronic cultures, preset schedules take precedence over personal relationships.

Among the most difficult cultural chasms U.S. lawyers must hurdle in international transactions is the recognition that scheduling is not universal. Rather, scheduling is a culturally determined concept. U.S. lawyers often take great pains to negotiate a contract regarding specific dates. The schedules set, however, have a different reality in the United States and other monochronic cultures than they do in much of the world. While a negotiated schedule may in fact be agreed upon by all parties, it is not a given that such schedules will be honored. In a polychronic society, the schedule to which all parties agree—even in the form of a signed contract—remains approximate. Time in polychronic societies is determined by personal relationships and events. These in turn can never fully be predicted. From their perspective, scheduling specific times is akin to agreeing not to be sick on a given day; in short, one can plan but one can never fully guarantee it. As a result, schedules are seen as approximate goals, not as absolutes.

3. Conclusion

To even the experienced international lawyer, cross-cultural negotiations present a host of ever-changing challenges. To those less experienced, the challenges may seem very intimidating.

The LESCANT model gives the negotiators a toolkit for analyzing cultural differences in general. With this model, the international lawyer can learn to ask the right questions. Other chapters in this book provide for individual countries some of the specific answers the LESCANT model raises. Aimed with the right questions, U.S. lawyers who keep their powers of observation keen will find a means for bringing order to the cross-cultural differences they experience.

David A. Victor
Director of International Business Programs
College of Business
Eastern Michigan University
Ypsilanti, MI 48197
Phone: (734) 487-3240
E-mail: david.victor@emich.edu

CHAPTER 8

Minimizing Risk: Best Practices in Managing Cross-Cultural Concerns in Global Contracting

Jane E. Smith, Esq.
LISIMBA CONSULTING SERVICES, INC.
MINNEAPOLIS, MINNESOTA

1. Introduction

"Globalization is here to stay," as the Honorable Madeline Albright said in a speech on March 3, 2008.[1] Globalization is defined in many ways, including "the increase of working relationships among national entities and international entities."[2] Additionally, globalization implies the continually increasing mobility of capital across the globe with a powerful impact on the national economies affected.[3] As globalization is a part of the normal life of each person on this planet, work opportunities frequently bring global connections that impact our lives on a regular basis.

Whether you are a lawyer acting as outside counsel to a major global corporation (or nonprofit), a lawyer inside of a major global corporation, an individual with legal training tasked with managing global operations, an executive who manages those who are responsible for global operations, or are in any other professional scenario that can be imagined, this chapter outlines five "Best Practices" to empower the entire global operation and to maximize the opportunities both to the parent organization and to the hosting global setting.

In applying these five Best Practices, the intent is that the information and the Practices be used to support an informed, nonjudgmental approach to each global contracting scenario. Each culture has its own integrity, and in respecting each other's cultures we maximize the potential of each global business setting.

Before moving into the Best Practices, it is helpful to understand the risk issues that they address as a context for application.

---

[1] Madeline Albright, former U.S. Sec'y of State, Speech at the annual convention of the Mechanical Contractors Association of America, Palm Springs, California (March 3, 2008).

[2] RICHARD MEAD, INTERNATIONAL MANAGEMENT, CROSS-CULTURAL DIMENSIONS 244 (3d ed. 2007).

[3] *Id.* at 247.

2. Risk

When a major corporation wishes to invest outside of its national economy, whether through a joint venture or some other vehicle, it exposes itself to risk.[4] There are many forms of risk that affect global investments. Some examples include:

1. **Competitive risk:** A comprehensive competitive risk assessment includes thorough knowledge of what the local and international competitors are doing regarding product development and new technologies, as well as changes that may affect the supply and demand for the specified product or service.[5]

2. **Economic risk:** Managing for this form of risk means answering the following questions[6] using up-to-date research (such as the Index of Economic Freedom):

   a. How are public resources managed/mismanaged in a foreign setting?

   b. Are the economic and financial conditions of the foreign setting able to sustain reasonable day-to-day operations?

   c. How accessible are the potential markets?

   d. Are the local resources (including labor) available and affordable?

   e. Are existing inducements palatable to foreign investors?

   f. Is the local taxation favorable or discriminatory?

3. **Political risk:** Political risk can change especially rapidly, so it is essential to have up-to-date answers to the following questions:[7]

   a. Are the industrial and legal disputes of the region supported by strong local official policy?

   b. Is the local political situation stable? Is there war or terrorism? What other factors may have powerful effects in the foreign location?

   c. Is there a possibility that the foreign investments could be confiscated or expropriated?

4. **Technology risk:** Having experts provide up-to-date answers on a continuing basis to the following questions is key:[8]

   a. Is there a risk to the product technology being exported (including patents held on the product technology)?

---

[4] *Id.* at 314.
[5] *Id.* at 315.
[6] *Id.* at 315–16.
[7] *Id.* at 316.
[8] *Id.* at 318.

    b. Are the processes and the technical knowledge necessary to operate and produce a product abroad underdeveloped or at risk?

    c. How much local help can be hired, as opposed to expatriates sent to work in the foreign location?

5. **Cultural risk:** All of the above risks interact in ways that can lower or raise any particular risk being addressed. Beyond these is a higher-order concern that impacts all other risks: **cultural risk.** Its impact profoundly affects all other aspects of any foreign-based investment, particularly when movement of capital (especially labor capital) from one national culture to another is fundamental to the corporate entity's chosen foreign investment.

For an initial understanding of **cultural risk**, the following definition is helpful:

> When the national culture of the global headquarters or of the global purchaser, when global purchasing is the chosen corporate activity, is perceived to have a wide distance from the national culture of the foreign corporate locations, there is cultural risk which can maximize risk in all other areas, undermining the financial opportunity and the present and future work opportunity of the foreign based operation.[9]

Culture itself can be seen as "the unwritten book with the rules of the social game that is passed on to newcomers by its members, nesting itself in their minds."[10] Thus, not all cultures play by the same "rules." When cultural differences exist side by side, cross-cultural concerns arise that can powerfully impact each global contracting opportunity. How the cross-cultural concerns are addressed can lessen or increase **cultural risk.** The following set of Best Practices can help smooth international business transactions and reduce culture clash.

3. Best Practice Number One

The First Best Practice for successfully managing cross-cultural concerns in global contracting locations is *acquiring a critical awareness of what a "cross-cultural concern" is in a global contracting setting.* This Best Practice must come first in order for the other four to follow. Learning how to identify cross-cultural concerns within ourselves is the first

---

[9] *Id.* at 318–19.

[10] Geert Hofstede & Gert Jan Hofstede, Cultures and Organizations: Software of the Mind 36 (2005).

step toward any attempt to maximize the potential in each global contracting setting.

There has been extensive research on understanding foreign culture in the context of business investment. Cultural research, when integrated with other Best Practices, works to minimize risk and to maximize business opportunities. The cultural research can come in the form of theoretical applications and models such as the LESCANT model described in David Victor's chapter, or it can come in the form of specific detailed information relating to exact interactions between two identified cultures. Cultural research when integrated with the other Best Practices helps to minimize risk and maximize opportunity/success in the global setting. It does so by aiding in the identification of "clash" areas relating to culture, and allowing parties to begin the process of identifying solutions and pathways for circumventing potential culture-related business barriers.

Following is a brief review of some of the research that has been published in the past fifty years, addressing cross-cultural settings where individuals from different cultures live and work side by side. The natural result is that "conflicting expectations of their environment takes place."[11] The models described here have had a substantial impact on understanding cross-cultural concerns in global contracting settings. Using these models as lenses through which to understand cross-cultural concerns embodies the First Best Practice of achieving cross-cultural awareness.

3.1 Model Number One

In the early 1960s, Kluckholm and Stodtbeck published a model for understanding the cross-cultural concerns in global business. They stated, "Members of a culture group exhibited constant 'orientations' toward the world and other people. Different cultures could be compared on the basis of their different orientations."[12] Their model suggests that how a group answers the following six questions[13] can provide an understanding of the cultural orientation for that group.

1. What is the nature of people?

    a. **Good:** Optimistic about people's motivations and capacities.

    b. **Evil:** Pessimistic and suspicious of peers, negotiation partners; secretive.

---

[11] MEAD, *supra* note 2, at 27.

[12] *Id.* at 28.

[13] *Id.* at 29–32.

c. **Both/Mixed:** Uses middlemen and consultants; has discrepancy between optimistic attitudes and secretive or socially cautious behavior.

2. What is the person's relationship to nature?

    a. **Dominance:** Controls and plans; imposes one's will on the surrounding environment; seeks to change organizational culture.

    b. **Harmony:** Seeks coexistence; searches for common ground, averse to open conflict within the workplace; has respect for different others.

    c. **Subjugation:** Is fatalistic; readily accepts external control; averse to independent planning; pessimistic about changing the organizational culture.

3. What is the person's relationship to other people?

    a. **Lineal/Hierarchical:** Has respect for authority and seniority as determined by age, family, gender.

    b. **Collateral:** Relationships within the group influence attitudes towards work, superiors, other groups; outsiders are treated with suspicion; structures and systems that break down group boundaries or promote independence are disliked.

    c. **Individualist:** Primarily perceive themselves as individuals rather than as members of a group; need systems that maximize opportunities for personal achievement and status; more likely to value interesting work; encourage competition and informality; are egalitarian.

4. What is the modality of human activity?

    a. **Doing:** Performance (both financially and by accomplishment) is valued; work is central in life; orientation is practical; any ambiguity that frustrates performance causes anxiety.

    b. **Being:** Status is derived from birth, age, sex, family, and connections more than through achievement; feelings are valued; planning is often short-term; spontaneity is valued.

    c. **Containing:** Focus is on self-control; there is striving for balance between feeling and doing; self-inquiring.

5. What is the temporal focus of human activity?

    a. **Future:** Future planning is prioritized; past performance is less important; the concept of change is valued; career planning and training are valued.

    b. **Present:** Immediate realities are prioritized and used as the basis of planning; long-term plans are liable to modification; contemporary impact and style are emphasized.

    c. **Past:** The past is used as the model when planning for the future: there is a respect for precedence, a need for continuity; respect is paid to age.

6. What is the conception of space?

    a. **Private:** Personal ownership is respected; what is private is valued; private meetings are valued; strangers are kept at a distance.

    b. **Public:** Activities conducted in secret are held in suspicion; social proximity is taken for granted; public meetings are valued.

    c. **Mixed:** Private and public activities are distinguished.

This model is still used somewhat today with the full understanding that the answers to the above six questions are subjective. Clearly, the model and the answers an individual gives are not reliable as a basis from which to make business choices in which an entire culture must be considered. This is simply being offered as a springboard to explain the evolutionary process of cultural exploration.

3.2 Model Number Two

Another lens through which we can understand how cultures function is the Context Model. Edward Hall published research in 1976 that demonstrated the influences of context in effective interactions across cultural divides. He used the terms "high context" and "low context," which are commonly applied today when attempting to better understand a culture that is not well known. For our purposes, Hall's definition of high- and low-context communication (and the factors that Hall suggests for identifying a culture as high- or low-context) provide us with more daily, usable tools that are somewhat more objective for achieving the necessary critical awareness of what is a cross-cultural concern in a global business setting.

Hall defines the "high-level context" as:

> A [communication or message] in which most of the information is already in the person, while very little is in the coded, explicitly transmitted part of the message.[14]

Hall then lays out a series of identifying characteristics of a high-context culture, among which are the following:

---

[14] *Id.* at 33.

- Relationships are relatively long lasting, and the individuals feel deep personal involvement with each other.
- A shared code defines communication and so communications, both written and spoken, are "economical, fast and efficient." It is said that the individuals in a high-context culture exploit the communicative context.
- Communication is both verbal and non-verbal, using signaling and nonlanguage utterances.[15]
- People in authority feel personally responsible for the actions of their subordinates. Loyalty between the superiors and subordinates is reciprocal.[16]
- Agreements between members of the high-context culture are often spoken and not written. A contract is seen only as a "best guess."
- The difference between "insiders" and "outsiders" is clearly delineated. "Outsiders" include nonmembers of the family, clan, or organization, and those who are foreign to their culture.
- The cultural patterns of a high-context culture are deeply ingrained in its members, and as a result are very slow to change.[17]

In contrast, Hall stated that a culture with low-context communication is the opposite of a high-context culture, as the mass of the communication is "vested in the explicit code." This means that there is very little need to guess what is meant in a low-context culture communication.[18]

To further understand what Hall meant by a low-context culture, he suggests looking for the following descriptive characteristics[19] in the foreign culture where one works in a global contracting setting:

- Relationships between individuals are "relatively shorter in duration." Deep personal involvement with others is not valued as highly.
- Communicated messages must be explicit, with the sender depending very little on the receiver "inferring" the message from the context. There is much less use of nonverbal communication. Members of these cultures often feel that "explicit logical structures are best for presenting ideas."
- Authority is diffused throughout the bureaucratic system and personal responsibility is difficult to pin down.
- Agreements are generally written rather than spoken. Contracts are seen as final expressions of the relationship and are legally

---

[15] *Id.* at 33–34.
[16] *Id.* at 34.
[17] *Id.* at 35.
[18] *Id.* at 35.
[19] *Id.* at 33, 35.

binding to a degree that can be seen as an "obsession" by members of a high-context culture.

- The differences between "outsiders" and "insiders" are less absolute. One result is that "foreigners" fit into a low-context culture fairly easily, experiencing an easy acceptance by the general population of the culture.
- Cultural patterns are easily changed and change rapidly on their own.

3.3 Model Number Three

A third model or lens through which one can see a foreign culture is the cross-cultural research led by Andre Laurent in 1983. Laurent examined the attitude toward power and relationships and analyzed the values held by managers, native to the country in which they were working, in nine European nations (Switzerland, Germany, Denmark, Sweden, United Kingdom, Netherlands, Belgium, Italy, and France) and the United States. Six years later, Campbell and Adler along with Laurent added data on the People's Republic of China, Indonesia, and Japan.[20] The researchers focused on three questions:

1. How far the manager carries his or her status beyond the workplace
2. The manager's capacity to bypass levels in the hierarchy
3. Whether the manager is more judge and "contract-maker" or facilitator[21]

Survey responders were presented with the following statement: "Through their professional activity, managers play an important role in society." The answers in percentages of those agreeing with the statement were:[22]

Through their professional activity, managers play an important role in society.	
Country	Percent Agreed
Denmark	32%
United Kingdom	40%
Netherlands	45%
Germany	46%
United States	52%

---

[20] *Id.* at 36.
[21] *Id.* at 36.
[22] *Id.* at 36.

Sweden	54%
Switzerland	65%
Italy	74%
France	75%

One of the essential lessons of these data is that the managers in Denmark and the United Kingdom are not able to carry their work status over into their social status in their communities. On the other hand, managers in France and in Italy can (and are almost expected to) carry their work status into the communities, enhancing their social status in the process.

The second statement was "In order to have efficient work relationships, it is often necessary to bypass the hierarchical line." Those responding were asked if they disagreed with this statement.[23]

In order to have efficient work relationships, it is often necessary to bypass the hierarchical line.	
Country	Percent Agreed
United Kingdom	22%
United States	31%
Denmark	32%
Netherlands	37%
Switzerland	39%
Belgium	41%
France	42%
Germany	46%
People's Republic of China	66%
Italy	75%

If one is working in a global contracting setting where Danes and Italians are working side by side, the data from this question imply very different attitudes toward the chain of command. The Italians highly value a hierarchical setting but the Danes bypass hierarchy easily. Also, the Danish employees will be more likely to function well in an open, flexible hierarchy, while their Italian counterparts quite likely value the more rigid hierarchical structure.

The third statement judged by responders was: "It is important for a manager to have at hand precise answers to most of the questions that his subordinates may raise about their work." The data below, again,

---

[23] *Id.* at 37.

represents the percentages of the respondents who were in agreement with this statement.[24]

It is important for a manager to have at hand precise answers to most of the questions that his subordinates may raise about their work.	
Country	Percent Agreed
Sweden	10%
Netherlands	17%
United States	18%
Denmark	23%
United Kingdom	27%
Switzerland	38%
Belgium	44%
Germany	46%
France	53%
Italy	66%
Indonesia	73%
People's Republic of China	74%
Japan	78%

From these data, we can guess that Swedish organizations (where hierarchy is not as important as finding the right answer and that right answer does not have to come from a direct superior) contrast strikingly with Chinese or Japanese organizations. Also, a Swede may find it easy to get a needed answer from any relevant expert (no matter where that expert may work). As a result, if that Swedish individual is working in China, Japan, or Indonesia, the local workforce may not appreciate the Swede's approach to problem solving.

3.4 Model Number Four

The fourth model grows from the research completed by Geert Hofstede since 1984. His work has set a fair standard for understanding how national culture affects the values of the workplace. He examined the attitudes held by over 116,000 IBM employees working in branches or affiliates in fifty countries and three regions. While Hofstede has been criticized for drawing conclusions from statistical averages in a single industry, the strength of the work has been widely applauded for its practical workplace solutions.[25] His general findings[26] show that:

---

[24] *Id.* at 38.
[25] *Id.* at 39, 50–51.
[26] *Id.* at 39.

1. Work-related values are not universal.
2. When a multinational headquarters tries to impose the same norms on all its foreign interests, the local values are likely to persist.
3. Local values determine how headquarters regulations are interpreted.
4. By implication, a multinational that insists on organizational uniformity across its foreign investments is in danger of creating morale problems and inefficiencies.

The understanding that Hofstede brings to cross-cultural work continues to facilitate a greater in-depth understanding of foreign culture. Initially, Hofstede compared different cultures along four independent dimensions, which were assessed for twenty-three countries (a fifth dimension was later added). These dimensions reflect some of the previous work on cultural understanding as already briefly discussed. Hofstede's data acquisition and analysis produced highly reliable findings that correlate with other models. His five dimensions are as follow:

1. **Power Distance:** The distance between individuals at different levels of a hierarchy. Each culture teaches people how to manage themselves when they encounter the many forms that inequality may have when it enters their lives, and how that experience of inequality affects the individual's work experience. For example, a Swedish individual feels comfortable with power sources and shows little value for keeping sources of power at a great distance. In contrast, a Japanese individual may likely feel that it is valuable and comfortable to keep great distances between himself or herself and the source of power.
2. **Uncertainty Avoidance:** Greater or lesser need to avoid uncertainty about the future. A culture directs how each member of that culture adapts to uncertainty. Each individual is socialized into tolerating a high or a low level of uncertainty, according to how that particular culture functions.
   In the cultures with high uncertainty avoidance:[27]

   - Individuals have high levels of anxiety about workplace uncertainty.
   - There is a low level of willingness to take risks in the workplace.
   - Risk is broadly defined as any work experience that was not expected, or had not been the way of doing business in the past.

---

[27] *Id.* at 39–42.

- Expert managers are valued over those who facilitate the work of those that they manage.
- Clear work rules are valued.
- Precise job descriptions are essential.
- Entrepreneurial behavior is not valued.
- Job security is fundamental to maximizing job performance.
- Career planning is part of the education of each member of the society.
- A clear and detailed retirement plan is expected for each worker.

For those cultures with a low level of uncertainty avoidance:

- Individuals experience lower levels of anxiety/stress in the workplace.
- There is a willingness to take risks in the workplace.
- Entrepreneurial activity is encouraged and valued.
- Change in the workplace that constitutes "rational" reform is valued.
- Managers who are facilitators are most valued.
- There is little value of loyalty to the "boss."
- Foreigners can be effective as managers and are fairly easily accepted by the workforce.

3. **Individualism vs. Collectivism:** The relations between the individual and her fellows. The culture guides the individual's understanding of her identity either toward herself or toward the group as a whole.

Following are factors that describe what individualism expects:[28]

- A person will achieve for him/herself to meet his/her needs.
- Managers are expected to work hard for their rewards.
- Competition is expected.
- Individual decisions are valued over group decisions, and the individual has a right to hold views differing from the majority.
- Managers will aim for variety rather than conformity in the workplace.
- Loyalty to the corporation is not absolute and exists only until the loyalty does not suit the individual.
- Rebellion against conformity is clearly accepted, within bounds.

---

[28] *Id.* at 42–43.

- There is a great capacity for altruism, which is seen through extensive volunteer activity.

On the other hand, following are factors that describe collectivism:[29]

- Group interests prevail over the individual's interests in all cases.
- Each individual finds her identity through the group of which she is a member.
- Individual loyalty to the group is often valued over what is efficient.
- Competition between groups may exist, and is seen as between groups and not between individuals.

4. **Masculinity vs. Femininity:** The division of roles and values in society. The culture guides the individual to understand that certain roles and values in that culture are specific—or not—to one sex or to the other.
   Following are factors that describe masculinity in a culture:[30]

- Sex roles in the workplace are clearly differentiated.
- The social ideal is performance of your work duty.
- The top priority is given to the maintenance of economic growth.
- Men are to be competitive and assertive.
- Women are to be tender and able to take care of relationships.

On the other hand, following are factors that describe femininity:

- Sex roles are less sharply defined as reflected in the wide range of work available to members of the culture, regardless of sex.
- The spouse who is better paid is the one who works, regardless of sex.
- The corporation must not interfere with employee family lives.
- Achievement is measured in terms of human contacts rather than in terms of power and property.
- Relating to one another is valued over competition.
- Individual brilliance is suspect.
- An outsider and an "anti-hero" are regarded sympathetically.

---

[29] *Id.* at 44–46.
[30] *Id.* at 46.

5. **Long-Term vs. Short-Term Orientation:** Temporal orientation toward life. This dimension reflects the need to address the Pacific Asian value of "virtue" as defined by Confucius. In general, the long-term orientation fosters the "virtues oriented toward future rewards, in particular, perseverance and thrift."[31]

Cultures with a long-term orientation demonstrate:

- Persistence
- Relationships ranked according to status
- Thrift
- A sense of shame

The short-term orientation fosters the virtues related to the past and present. Cultures with a short-term orientation demonstrate:

- Personal steadiness and stability
- Protecting one's face
- Respect for tradition
- Reciprocation of greetings, favors, and gifts

Hofstede has produced a number of charts in his studies, reproduced below. The following is the key for identifying countries/regions on the charts.

Key To Countries/Regions[32]					
Abbr.	Country	Abbr.	Country	Abbr.	Region
ARG	Argentina	IRA	Iran	ARA	Arab-speaking countries (Egypt, Iraq, Kuwait, Lebanon, Libya, Saudi Arabia)
AUL	Australia	IRE	Ireland (Republic of)		
AUT	Austria	ISR	Israel		
BEL	Belgium	ITA	Italy		
BRA	Brazil	JAM	Jamaica	EAF	East Africa (Ethiopia, Kenya, Tanzania, Zambia)
CAN	Canada	JPN	Japan		
CHL	Chile	KOR	South Korea		
COL	Colombia	MAL	Malaysia	WAF	West Africa (Ghana, Nigeria, Sierra Leone)
COS	Costa Rica	MEX	Mexico		
DEN	Denmark	NET	Netherlands	SPA	Spain
EQA	Ecuador	NOR	Norway	SWE	Sweden

---

[31] *Id.* at 46–47.

[32] HOFSTEDE, *supra* note 10, at 35.

Abbr.	Country	Abbr.	Country	Abbr.	Country
FIN	Finland	NZL	New Zealand	SWI	Switzerland
FRA	France	PAK	Pakistan	TAI	Taiwan
GBR	Great Britain	PAN	Panama	THA	Thailand
GER	Germany, F. R.	PER	Peru	TUR	Turkey
GRE	Greece	PHI	Philippines	URU	Uruguay
GUA	Guatemala	POR	Portugal	USA	United States
HOK	Hong Kong	SAF	South Africa	VEN	Venezuela
IDO	Indonesia	SAL	Salvador	YUG	Yugoslavia
IND	India	SIN	Singapore		

The following chart[33] (Figure 8.1) is a description of the relationship between uncertainty avoidance and power distance for each noted country and its culture. The groupings that are shown in this chart are

Figure 8.1

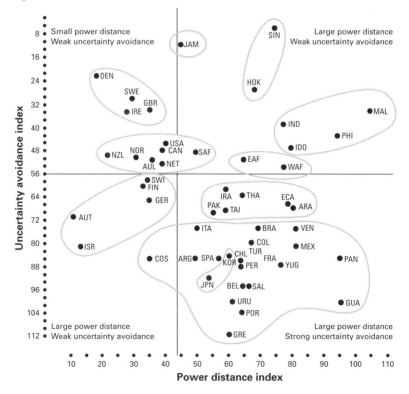

---

[33] MEAD, *supra* note 2, at 41.

suggested indications of potential similarities and differences among nations in regard to these two dimensions of work-related values.

What follows next is a chart[34] that Hofstede created to show the relationships between the "masculinity vs. femininity" dimension and the "individualism vs. collectivism" dimension. Again, the groupings that are shown infer perhaps some similarities as well as some differences in how these nations and their cultures function around these two dimensions.

Figure 8.2

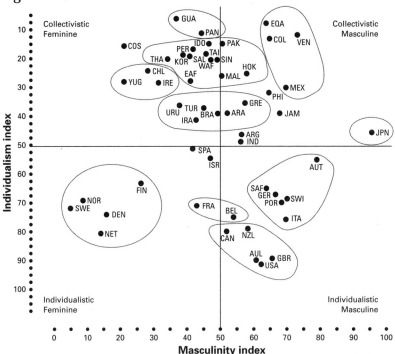

There is no nation in the world that does not have some form of hierarchy, but some nations encourage particular ways that a hierarchy manifests itself, while other nations discourage rigid hierarchy in general. The implications of this basic understanding are fundamental to managing a contracting opportunity in another culture.

3.5 Model Number Five

A final model or lens for acquiring a critical awareness of what is a cross-cultural concern in global contracting settings is the work of

---

[34] *Id.* at 45.

Trompenaars and Hampden-Turner. They offer two ways of further understanding a culture. The first term that they introduce is "Universalist" culture. They describe a Universalist as one that tends to rely on what is legal rather than following social mores. The opposite, according to these cultural researchers, is a "Particularist" culture. In this culture, the nature of a relationship supersedes the value of the legal consideration in determining how an individual will act. These two terms work as additional guides, offering perhaps greater understanding of how an employee may choose to function in a cross-cultural global contracting setting.[35]

With these models or lenses, one can work toward maximizing one's opportunities in cross-cultural work settings with a critical awareness of what is a cross-cultural concern in a cross-cultural global setting.

4. Best Practice Number Two

The Second Best Practice, which follows on the acquired skill in the first, is *acquiring a critical awareness of the impact of cross-cultural concerns on the financial outcome of the present scenario.* For example, imagine that you are a Swedish individual whose American employer has relocated you to manage a manufacturing site in southern China. You carry your Swedish style of management with you, as well as the American management style used by your employer, and you are now living and working in the middle of the cultural management and working style of the native Chinese who will be working for you. This is a *heavily* cross-cultural situation. Applying the First Best Practice, you can weigh each management decision you must make and can anticipate how your actions will be viewed.

This best practice, however, must also extend past the inner workings of a company and address the cultural environment of the intended consumer of a particular business venture. An example of the cultural impacts of the external environment (external to the company) could be the struggle Wal-Mart has faced opening locations in China where consumers are used to a much different shopping environment. Another would be the failure of the Nova model of car in Spanish cultures where the name "Nova" translates to "no go." In that example it is easy to see how cross-cultural misperceptions can cause revenue losses, and how a change as simple as a new product name can significantly impact sales.

By making cross-culturally informed decisions that are focused on minimizing the cultural risk, you will maximize financial gains.

---

[35] Nancy J. Adler & Allen Gundersen, International Dimensions of Organizational Behavior 60–61 (5th ed. 2008).

5. Best Practice Number Three

The Third Best Practice is *acquiring a critical awareness of the impact on present and future work opportunities of a cross-cultural concern in global contracting.* This Practice also relies on a sound foundation in the First Best Practice, as cross-cultural awareness is needed to forecast any amount of time into the future. Awareness of the present scenario, in turn, can equip you to make decisions that will maximize future work opportunities. Strictly speaking, the only difference between the Second and Third Best Practice is the difference between research and speculation: knowing what is, today, as opposed to guessing what will be, tomorrow. Saying these are similar is easy enough, but these Practices require very different processes to achieve successfully.

Consider the scenario where you imagine that you are the Swedish employee, working for an American corporation. You have been relocated to southern China to manage a manufacturing facility there for a minimum of three years, and with the opportunity to renew the expatriate contract every three years. The manufacturing operation is part of a joint venture that your American employer, who has been manufacturing these widgets in the United States for about eight years, has with a Chinese corporation that has been manufacturing these widgets for ten years; the latter now wants to join with your employer to access a more global market and to better saturate the Chinese market. Your employer is aware of the strong market potential for the widgets that are being manufactured at the southern China location.

Your employer has asked you to manage the operation there with a vision of doubling the size of the operation—both the physical plant and the number of employees—and maximizing the productivity of the location in three years. If you are successful in achieving these goals, you have been told, the market for the widgets in Asia and the rest of the world will support doubling the entire operation again in five additional years. There is a local Chinese workforce that has been part of the Chinese government's effort to modernize the location in southern China. The workforce that is available includes individuals who are age thirty or younger and have been taught English as a second language, and have achieved high levels of education in a manner that can support growing manufacturing operations. There is also an older component of the local workforce that has been experiencing a reeducation, learning English and other work-related skills, so that this segment of the local workforce can join in the modernization of this part of China.

Within this example, which is based on a composite of actual circumstances, it is clear that the first three Best Practices are fundamental to the Swedish plant manager's experiencing success in this setting, as concerns ranging from language to management styles to public perceptions and cultural trends are involved.

6. Best Practice Number Four

The Fourth Best Practice, which relies on the previous three for successful implementation, is *a critical awareness of the impact of one's communication skills across cultural gaps, through which trust is built.*

"Trust is the new currency in the new global economy," Stephen M.R. Covey said in a speech that he gave March 5, 2008.[36] The new world of the twenty-first century and the new global economy are founded on a collaborative work environment. This is especially true as globalization is driving business to further rely on technological collaborative cross-cultural environments to maintain a competitive edge. The establishment of trust in global, cross-cultural work settings is the foundation of collaboration globally. Understanding and applying Best Practices One through Three, along with the culturally appropriate communication skills, can establish and further the necessary trust relationships for successful business operations.

Trust is understood and established differently in each culture; it also manifests itself differently. Trust and the accompanying communication skills that are culturally respectful and appropriate are required for sealing any cross-cultural deal. Both trust and collaboration are necessary in order to achieve financial success in global business both today and in the future.

In his book *The Speed of Trust: The One Thing That Changes Everything*, Covey says:

> Financial success comes from success in the marketplace, and success in the marketplace comes from success in the workplace. The heart and soul of all of this is trust.[37]

For each person in global contract management:

> The ability to establish, grow, extend, and restore trust with all stakeholders—customers, business partners, investors, and co-workers—is the key leadership competency.[38]

Covey shares data[39] that demonstrates that trust is at a global low. He quotes data on "societal trust," i.e., how much trust an average citizen has in his or her society. Following is a sample of the societal trust measured in some countries:

- 34% of the citizens of the USA trust in their society.

---

[36] Stephen M.R. Covey, The Speed of Trust, Speech at the annual convention of the Mechanical Contractors Association of America, Palm Springs, California (March 5, 2008).

[37] STEPHEN M.R. COVEY, THE SPEED OF TRUST: THE ONE THING THAT CHANGES EVERYTHING xxiv (2006).

[38] *Id.* at 21.

[39] Covey, *supra* note 36.

- 29% of the citizens of Great Britain trust in their society.
- 20% of the citizens of Latin American countries trust in their society.
- 18% of the citizens of Asian countries trust in their society.
- 68% of the citizens of the Scandinavian countries trust in their society.

Another measure that Covey quotes to demonstrate a low level of global trust is drawn from the Global Survey of Organizational Trust, conducted by the World Economic Conference[40]:

- 49% of the employees surveyed said that they trust their organizational leadership.
- 36% of the employees surveyed believe that the top management of their organizations act with integrity and honesty.

Covey created two terms for describing trust and its effects on an organization. If there is a high level of trust in an organization, Covey says that there is

> [a] trust dividend . . . which is like a performance multiplier, elevating and improving every dimension of your organization.[41]

In short, "trust produces speed." Trust in an organization works like an aquifer does to a large body of water. As an aquifer feeds the body of water, trust feeds business innovation, complementary teams, collaboration, empowerment, and other key leadership initiatives.[42]

On the other hand, if there is a low level of trust in an organization, there is a "trust tax," which is a hidden tax on all organizational operations. A low level of trust is a burden that is carried by all employees, making speedy results impossible because low trust slows everything.[43] Low trust creates friction between individuals and departments, hidden agendas, defensive thinking and behavior, a win-lose way of thinking, and protective communication among individuals and departments.[44]

As a warning, Mr. Covey is an American author and as such his model of trust cannot be directly transplanted into other cultures. Covey's work has great cross-cultural value, but an application of cross-cultural awareness is important in trying to interpret his work through a foreign lens. With the critical awareness of the cross-cultural setting in which one is working, one can then adapt Covey's work to the global

---

[40] COVEY, *supra* note 37, at 21.

[41] *Id.* at 19.

[42] *Id.* at xxv–xxvi.

[43] *Id.* at 21.

[44] *Id.* at xxv.

contracting setting and, using culturally appropriate communication skills, work toward the establishment of trust among the cultures that are working together.

With that understanding, here is a brief introduction to Stephen M.R. Covey's approach to establishing trust within an organization.

6.1 Level One Trust: Self-Trust

The establishment of trust always begins with *you*. Self-Trust is the first level of trust necessary. Ask yourself this question: "Do I present to others a person whom they can trust?" With this question, I must then look at my own credibility, by looking at what Covey calls the Four Cores of Credibility:[45]

1. Integrity, being congruent inside and out
2. Intent, our motives
3. Capability, the means we use to produce results
4. Results, our performance[46]

Self-Trust depends on a strong, honest communication with ourselves so that we communicate, through our words and actions, a trusting and trustworthy person to our community.

6.2 Level Two Trust: Relationship Trust

The next level of trust is Relationship Trust. This aspect of trust is "all about behavior . . . consistent behavior."[47] When we behave in a consistent manner with other individuals, we create a "trust account." When you choose to behave in ways that build trust, you make deposits into your trust account with others. You are communicating trust in your relationships. When you behave in ways that do not build trust (e.g., behave inconsistently), you make withdrawals from the trust account. In other words, you are communicating that you are a nontrustworthy person to your community. The balance in the trust account demonstrates the amount of trust that exists in the relationship.[48] Covey lists thirteen behaviors that build Relationship Trust.[49] The use of these behaviors communicates that you are a trustworthy person within a relationship, as understood within American culture. These behaviors are:

1. Talk straight.
2. Demonstrate respect.
3. Create transparency.

---

[45] *Id.* at 45.
[46] *Id.* at 54–55.
[47] *Id.* at 125.
[48] *Id.* at 130.
[49] *Id.* at 136–229.

4.   Right wrongs.
5.   Show loyalty.
6.   Deliver results.
7.   Get better.
8.   Confront reality.
9.   Clarify expectations.
10. Practice accountability.
11. Listen first.
12. Keep commitments.
13. Extend trust.

These behaviors define how a trustworthy person who is a citizen of American culture would choose to demonstrate being trustworthy in a relationship.

When applying the models or lenses in Best Practice Number One, you can choose whether a behavior is applicable for building trust in a specific culture. For example, building trust in what Hall describes as a high-context culture (such as China) would perhaps benefit from behaviors 1, 3, 4, 6, 8, and 9. It is crucial to continually apply your awareness of what a cross-cultural concern is in any given culture.

6.3 Level Three Trust: Organizational Trust

The next level of trust, Organizational Trust, is one of the forms that must be built with the key stakeholders in any global work setting.[50] This trust is based upon the concept of alignment. An organization, as seen in a cross-cultural setting anywhere in the world, must walk the talk. If an organization says that it is built on trust, then it must function in a cross-cultural setting in a manner that clearly aligns with what trust looks like in the culture where the organization is doing business. With other cultures present, the leaders in the cross-cultural setting must be informed on how to create trust with each culture that is part of the global setting. This need brings the leadership back to Best Practice Number One.

Covey offers some signs of what low trust in an organization looks like.[51] Here are some of the signs of low trust. Each one of these signs may manifest in a culturally specific manner, especially in countries and cultures where there is little freedom to move from one work-place to another, where people can't speak openly, or where there are other cultural experiences not normally understood by a citizen of the United States.

---

[50] *Id.* at 232.
[51] *Id.* at 250–53.

1. **Redundancy:** Excessive organizational hierarchy
2. **Bureaucracy:** Complex rules, policies, procedures, and processes
3. **Politics:** The antonym of trust
4. **Disengagement:** Employees mentally distant and tending to daydream
5. **Turnover:** Loss of performers who have become disengaged
6. **Churn:** Loss or turnover among customers, suppliers, distributors, investors
7. **Fraud:** Dishonesty, sabotage, obstruction, deception, disruption

In turn, following are some signs of high organizational trust.[52]

1. **Increased value:** Greater pride among employees and with customers
2. **Accelerated growth:** Growth due to an ability to "outperform with less cost"
3. **Enhanced innovation:** A culture of innovation resulting in creative applications for product development and service
4. **Improved collaboration:** Fundamental for global business
5. **Stronger partnering:** Effective outsourcing, for example
6. **Better execution:** The goal of all strategies
7. **Heightened loyalty:** From employees to customers and distributors

Each sign of high organizational trust is reflecting an American cultural outlook and can be translated to a specific culture for use in cross-cultural global settings through application of the First Three Best Practices. For example, number 7, "heightened loyalty," with the application of Hofstede's work, may be highly visible in Sweden (where there is a small distance between the power source and the individual) but far less so in Thailand (where there is a larger distance from a power source), with America somewhere between the two. Through application of each model to each sign of high or low trust, you gain a more applicable cultural understanding of the sign.

6.4 Level Four Trust: Market Trust

The next level of trust, Market Trust, is another form of stakeholder trust. Reputation is integral to Market Trust. An excellent question to ask to better understand this form of trust is: "How do you establish, maintain, and build company brand and personal brand trust?"[53] Covey discusses the fact that a product's country of origin in our global

---

[52] *Id.* at 254–58.
[53] *Id.* at 35.

economy can result in a "country tax or dividend." For example, Covey says that U.S. brands that hold high trust in the United States and in Asia are "being taxed heavily in parts of Europe and in other markets."[54] The tax or dividend is the amount of trust placed in the country of origin. This is a clear cross-cultural concern affecting the financial success of a product or service and the present and future work opportunities available in a global market setting.

When working to create a Market Trust for any product, understanding the culture into which you are introducing the product, through Best Practice Number One, can alleviate the market tax that a product may experience in another culture. The creation of Market Trust also requires the application of Best Practices Two and Three, to keep both the present and the future in mind. For example, introducing a product made in the United States (or by an American corporation) into a foreign location must be aligned with branding and advertising that speaks to the values of the culture in the target market. Trust is then conveyed across the culture. In turn, with the movement of human, material, and financial capital around the world, conveying trust across each cultural gap builds functioning bridges across those gaps.

6.5 Level Five Trust: Societal Trust

The final level of trust that Covey discusses is Societal Trust, the final type of stakeholder trust. The value of societal contribution is the foundation of this aspect of trust.[55] In other words, the focus is on bringing something of value to society in general.

As globalization is now a major part of doing business, corporations must create value for each culture in which they are doing business. More importantly, as global citizens,[56] corporations and the individuals that work for the corporation in various cultures around the world must create value aligned to each local market. To achieve this end, the corporation must apply the First, Second, and Third Best Practices in that order. As always, the First Best Practice informs the Second and the Third. These all lead to the opportunity to establish a culturally valuable societal contribution in the global work setting.

For example, if you manufacture a product in Mexico, you must become familiar with the many lenses that clarify the Mexican culture and its work values, as well as any other cultures that will be in play at the job site. Next, you must understand the potential financial impact, and also consider how the cross-cultural concerns may affect

---

[54] *Id.* at 267.
[55] *Id.* at 275.
[56] *Id.* at 279.

the financial outcome of the product's manufacture and sale in the Mexican market. Finally, you must be aware of the impact on the present work opportunity and then on future work opportunities. In assuring a culturally respectful approach to the global work setting, you are honoring the individuals who are working in the manufacturing site where you are making the product on a daily basis.

You are working through your cross-culturally aware communications, to build trust with all stakeholders in the cross-cultural work setting. In this way you are contributing a positively functioning work location on a daily basis to the members of the society where you are manufacturing the product in a cross-culturally appropriate and cross-culturally valued manner.

7. Best Practice Number Five

Best Practice Number Five is *acquiring a critical awareness of one's skills in conflict resolution in a cross-cultural global contracting setting.* This practice builds on the previous four for successful implementation. To successfully resolve the cross-cultural conflicts that grow and exist on a global contracting site, it is important to be aware of each culture that is working at the site, and how they all interact. All of these Best Practices are made stronger by the organizational ability to resolve conflict and to bring resolution without going to outside sources. By engaging those in conflict on site and resolving their concerns, trust that may have been lost will be built again and trust in the work site overall will grow. True resolution, with all concerned parties working through the process, works to build a stronger form of working trust on a daily basis.

For this discussion I am suggesting the work of Stewart Levine, Esquire, resolutionary, and author of *Getting to Resolution: Turning Conflict into Collaboration.*[57] I have had the honor of studying conflict resolution with Mr. Levine. As he is an American author, I suggest applying the previous Best Practices One through Four, in order to appropriately translate the resolutionary process to the cross-cultural settings involved.

Why resolution? As Levine says, "Resolution provides relief and completeness. The situation no longer gnaws at your gut." Levine uses a dictionary definition of resolution, part of which states: "1. the act of unraveling a perplexing question or problem."[58] It is not possible "to be fully productive when you are angry."[59] Levine lists the following[60] among the costs of conflict:

---

[57] Stewart Levine, Getting to Resolution: Turning Conflict into Collaboration (1998).
[58] *Id.* at 3.
[59] *Id.* at 5.
[60] *Id.* at 16.

1. **Direct costs:** Lawyers and other professionals
2. **Productivity:** The value of time lost, and the value of what could have been accomplished had the time not been lost
3. **Continuity costs:** The loss of ongoing working relationships and perhaps the community that supports each individual
4. **Emotional costs:** The time spent on the pain and the pain itself, which allows for individuals to be "held hostage by our emotions"

In the global settings where corporations have invested their human, financial, material, and temporal capital, the ability to collaborate while cutting costs to maximize the profit is more highly valued than ever. Collaboration is more difficult to achieve when the business setting is a global one with the potential for cross-cultural concerns.[61] When individuals of differing cultures work side by side in a global setting, finding a resolutionary solution to a conflict that exists can return the entire workforce, management included, to what is a more highly productive, peaceful, and efficient job site. With this as a possibility, resolution is worth its weight in gold.

Following is a brief description of "Stewart Levine's Resolution Model," which can lead to true, functioning resolution. Best Practice Number One must be applied to each step to better assure that each of the seven steps is culturally adapted and thus appropriate for the cross-cultural setting where the conflict is taking place.

1. "The Attitude of Resolution," an intentionally adopted outlook, developed by listening, sharing concerns in a situation, and believing that "there is an agreement waiting to be discovered."[62]
2. "Telling Your Story," an information-gathering vehicle for all parties concerned in the conflict. Listening is fundamental to this step, and listen with the intent to hear all that is said by each party.[63]
3. "Listening for a Preliminary Vision of Resolution." The content of each side's story is the crucible that holds the potential for a solution honoring the concerns of all parties.[64]
4. "Getting Current and Complete," brings out greater disclosure, allows for the past events to be made current, brings out shared emotions, allows for a new understanding of others in the conflict, brought about by "saying what comes to mind."[65]
5. "New Vision: Reaching Agreement in Principle," a fairly broad understanding of a new agreement, after the full disclosure of

---

[61] *Id.* at 7.
[62] *Id.* at 97–107.
[63] *Id.* at 109–15.
[64] *Id.* at 117–23.
[65] *Id.* at 125–35.

the previous step, with a look at the real feasibility of the new vision.[66]

6. "Crafting the New Agreement," articulating the creative solutions that each participant in the process has brought for resolution of the conflict. Writing the new agreement will define how those disagreeing will coordinate their activities to work toward the desired collaboration, for greater synergy and high quality results.[67]

7. "Resolution," the last step that is an "outcome," allows the concerns of each party to be "put to rest," and each person involved in the initial conflict and now resolution can return to being a productive individual.[68]

When applying the lenses or models in Best Practice Number One to the seven steps, you may choose to begin by applying how each culture stands with Hofstede's four original dimensions:[69]

1. Power Distance
2. Uncertainty Avoidance
3. Individualism vs. Collectivism
4. Masculinity vs. Femininity

If a member of the resolutionary team is from Indonesia, that person will be comfortable with a large distance between herself and the source of power in the resolutionary process. The Indonesian will likely be a collectivist, meaning that she will go with what the group values and will tend to discard her personal concerns, even though those personal concerns have been part of the force leading to the resolutionary process taking place. On the uncertainty vs. avoidance scale, the Indonesian will tolerate with comfort a fair amount of uncertainty going into the resolutionary process. On the masculinity vs. femininity scale, the Indonesian will function with more of the feminine cultural traits than the masculine cultural traits.

Laurent's work on attitudes to power will help to better understand the same Indonesian employee who is participating in the resolutionary process.[70] She will rarely value bypassing the source of power, even the one directly above her. This attitude will make a special task for the leader of the resolutionary process to assure that the Indonesian participant does not feel threatened when looking at various ways to resolve the conflict at hand. The Indonesian individual may well see a manager as an expert who has all of the answers. Again this presents a challenging task for the resolutionary leader to assure that the

---

[66] *Id.* at 137–41.
[67] *Id.* at 143–50.
[68] *Id.* at 151–55.
[69] Hofstede, *supra* note 10, at 39.
[70] *Id.* at 37.

Indonesian employee feels that she can make a contribution to the resolutionary process by sharing what she may know of the conflict. Always remember that each participant in the resolutionary process has a participation in the conflict that is seeking resolution, which is why the Indonesian individual is in the resolutionary process.

Another lens that is very informative is Hall's model of either high- or low-context culture. It is likely that the Indonesian individual is from a high-context culture, which sees written agreements only as best guesses.[71] The same individual may well value agreements that are reached through a process that allows her to participate. Mediated agreements, rather than ones reached through an adversarial process, are an experience that the Indonesian may have experienced in her native culture. Her participation will depend on allowing her to feel empowered, an integral part of the process and not dominated by an authority figure. Loyalty in a high-context culture to one's superior is strong and often reciprocal.[72]

Each lens or model that is applied to each individual in the resolutionary process allows the leaders of the resolutionary process to be aware of the cultural values everyone brings to the process.

The seven steps of Levine's resolutionary process can be applied to any culture provided it is done mindfully. The critical awareness of the First Best Practice allows the facilitator of the resolutionary process to more assuredly engage each participant in the process, by working to honor the cultural work values that each participant brings to the group seeking resolution.

Application of Best Practices Number Two and Number Three will allow the facilitator to better understand the potential impact of the resolution on the financial outcome of the entire global work setting and on maximizing the present and future work opportunities of the global work setting where there are cross-cultural concerns.

Best Practice Number Four, an awareness of one's communication skills, is crucial before beginning to work toward conflict resolution on a daily basis. Conflict resolution in a global work setting, through the seven-step resolutionary process, relies on every level of trust. Continual communication with all employees in a trustworthy manner, and the skills as discussed in Best Practice Number Four, allow for the regular use of conflict resolution methodologies. The regular use of the resolutionary process, with the ongoing understandings provided by the various models for cultural awareness, assuredly works to increase the level of trust. The resolutionary model empowers those seeking resolution to a conflict to participate in the resolution and then, with the resolution that is culturally appropriate, to put the conflict behind

---

[71] MEAD, *supra* note 2, at 34.
[72] *Id.*

them and to work in a manner that reflects the agreement reached through the resolutionary process.[73]

8. Conclusion

In summary, in order to minimize risk in a cross-cultural global work setting, apply the Five Best Practices for Managing Cross-Cultural Concerns in a Global Contracting Setting.

1. Acquire a critical awareness of the cross-cultural concerns in a global contracting setting.
2. Acquire a critical awareness of the impact of cross-cultural concerns on the financial outcome of a global contracting setting.
3. Acquire a critical awareness of the impact of cross-cultural concerns on present and future work opportunities.
4. Acquire a critical awareness of the impact of one's communication skills through which trust is built in cross-cultural global business venture settings.
5. Acquire a critical awareness of one's skills in conflict resolution in cross-cultural global contracting settings.

Jane E. Smith, Esq.
LiSimba Consulting Services Inc.
3305 Eagle Bluff Road
Minneapolis, MN 55364
Phone: (612) 802-1240
Fax: (952) 472-2681

---

[73] LEVINE, *supra* note 57, at 95–96.

CHAPTER 9

The Role of a Lawyer: A Checklist

Jay G Foonberg
FOONBERGLAW
BEVERLY HILLS, CALIFORNIA

I originally developed this checklist for a program presented at the State Bar of California's International Law Section on the role of the attorney in international business transactions. In my professional career spanning 40 years, I have assisted U.S. companies with their overseas problems and foreign companies with their U.S. problems. This list is intended to highlight the most often repeated questions and problems.

By considering each of the points raised, you and your client will be better prepared for the job ahead. The checklist raises common questions and suggests where to get answers.

Any lawyer who is assisting a client in an international business transaction should consider the points raised by the checklist. As with any general list, different parts of it will be more or less important depending on the particular country or transaction involved. Accordingly, the order of listing does not indicate the order of importance in a given case.

Topics

1. How important is understanding the legal system of the foreign country?
2. How important is understanding the legal system of the foreign country as applied to the special problem (especially with respect to lack of attorney client privilege in many negotiations)?
3. How important is being fluent or literate in the foreign language of the country or having someone in your office who is?
4. How important is knowing the social and cultural customs of the foreign country?
5. Do you use the Internet in your international negotiations or representations?
    a. Take advantage of the fact that companies with an international presence will have an English version of their Web site.
    b. English is the main language for international business.

6. To what extent do you use the Internet in preparing for international negotiations?
    a. Learn about your client, the other parties, and the general political, social, economic, and legal climate.
    b. Search for individuals and companies by their foreign names as well as the English translations of their name. For example, try different combinations when searching for Jay von Berg (my original name) under V and B.
    c. Browse foreign newspapers. They often have an English language edition.
    d. Use foreign-language versions of search engines (for example, Google and Yahoo!) and foreign online directories.
    e. Visit foreign law firms, institutions, and governmental agencies Web sites. They often maintain legal databases, but do not rely on these versions as exact translations.
    f. Check out your own client (key employees and representatives). Often the foreign client may have preconceived opinions based on its Internet research about your client.
7. Do you prefer to use interpreters or to deal with bilingual people?
8. To what extent do you depend on the foreign lawyer or client understanding English?
9. While Americans might label payments as a bribe, other cultures consider the payments as being in the nature of user fees or simply as an accepted part of the system. What do you advise your client? (See also question 36.)
    a. Make the payments to avoid losing the business.
    b. Don't make the payments at the risk of losing the business.
    c. Tell a foreign lawyer to bill you for legal fees and to keep you ignorant of any such payments.
    d. Get a foreign partner or representative for the client and tell them you want to stay ignorant.
    e. Other advice given.
10. What do you tell a foreign client who wants to pay a bribe to speed along the administrative or legislative process in the United States?
    a. Introduce them to a public relations firm.
    b. Introduce them to a lobbyist.
    c. Introduce them to the appropriate PAC.
    d. Tell the foreigner that bribes are not necessary or helpful.
    e. Introduce them to an appropriate political fund-raiser who will tell them what they can and cannot do and how to do it.
    f. Other advice given.
11. What advice do you give your U.S. client concerning strict observance of foreign currency control laws and use of parallel

market or black market currency sources to make international payments for spare parts, equipment purchases, remittances, and so forth?

    a. Tell them it's all right as long as they do not violate U.S. laws.

    b. Tell them that it is the way business must operate to stay in business.

    c. Tell them to stay out of black market and parallel markets.

    d. Other advice given.

12. To what extent do you use or ignore these foreign and international entities?

    a. Foreign consulates and trade missions in your community.

    b. Foreign embassies and trade missions in New York and Washington.

    c. Other foreign and governmental agencies.

    d. Foreign bar associations or specialty bar associations or law firm marketing networks.

    e. Other international organizations (United Nations, World Health Organization, and so forth).

13. To what extent do you use or ignore these U.S. government and local agencies?

    a. United States embassies overseas.

    b. United States consulates and trade centers overseas.

    c. United States Department of Commerce offices in your community.

    d. United States Department of State in Washington.

    e. United States Department of Commerce in Washington.

    f. Your state's overseas offices.

    g. Your state's offices in your community.

    h. City and country trade promotional departments.

14. To what extent do you use the services of U.S.-Foreign Chambers of Commerce overseas?

15. To what extent do you utilize the services of Foreign-U.S. Chambers of Commerce in:

    a. Your community?

    b. Washington?

    c. New York or Miami?

    d. Other?

16. To what extent do you use the services of U.S. banks with representatives in the foreign country?

17. To what extent do you use the services of foreign banks with local offices in your community?

18. To what extent do you use the services of foreign banks with offices in U.S. cities, other than in your community?

19. To what extent do you use the services of international CPA firms with offices in your community?

20. Do you use the "Doing business in . . ." publications of:
    a. U.S. Department of Commerce?
    b. International CPA firms?
    c. Banks?
    d. Others?
21. To what extent do you feel it's appropriate to be involved in:
    a. Finding and/or evaluating potential foreign or U.S. business partners?
    b. Helping the client do market studies for the client's products or services?
    c. Helping the client access the foreign governmental legal and administrative process?
22. How do you find a foreign law firm to work with?
    a. Search engines and the Internet.
    b. Look in Martindale-Hubbell Law Directory for foreign firms that list themselves.
    c. Look for U.S. law firms with foreign offices.
    d. Get recommendations from:
        i.   Local lawyers
        ii.   Banks
        iii. U.S. government offices
        iv.   Foreign government offices
        v.   CPA firms
        vi.   Chambers of commerce
        vii. Law lists
        viii. Others
    e. Contact international bar associations or foreign bar associations.
    f. Other methods.
23. What methods do you find most useful for foreign communications?
    a. Mail
    b. Fax
    c. Telephone
    d. E-mail
    e. Face-to-face
    f. Other
24. How are your foreign clients most willing to pay your fees?
    a. Hourly
    b. Flat fee
    c. In advance
    d. Other
25. To what degree does your office accept or decline responsibility for translations of agreements and documents?
26. Do you offer to help your client access the entire system (banks, accountants, potential customers, potential suppliers, appoint-

ments with governmental officials, and so forth) or do you confine your activities to purely legal advice?

27. Do you offer to act as a communications and secretarial center for the foreign client? If so, do you charge the client?

28. Do you expect the foreign lawyer to be your communications and secretarial center? If so, do you offer to pay the cost?

29. Do you have difficulty or ease explaining any of the following to the foreign lawyer or the foreign client?

   a. The fact that each of the 50 states and 6 territories has independent laws and that an agreement may be valid in one state and invalid and possibly criminal in another state.

   b. The fact that deliberately underpaying taxes is criminal and can result in a jail sentence.

   c. The concept of the trust.

   d. The concept of the deed of trust when the client asks for a mortgage.

   e. The difference between paying a bribe and paying a campaign contribution or speaker's honorarium or consultant's fee to a legislator or governmental official or connected entity whose approval or vote the client needs.

   f. The fact that in some countries lawyers often take an active role in negotiating agreements rather than acting as typists after a deal is agreed to.

   g. How to distinguish in advance those countries where bringing or sending a lawyer will kill the deal as a sign of distrust and those countries where it will help make the deal as a sign of seriousness.

   h. The fact that multiple levels of governmental applications and approvals may be required for something as simple as building and operating a restaurant (for example, local health department, local fire department, local police department, state permits and licenses, federal registration for payroll taxes, and many other levels of permits and approvals).

   i. The fact that American English and British English often differ, both in commercial and in legal effect, and that one should not depend on a United Kingdom or Commonwealth lawyer to read and understand U.S. law or vice versa. (Example: words such as attorney, scheme, rubber, revenue, stock, turnover, and other words that have totally different meanings in U.S. and English legal systems.)

   j. The fact that there is no such thing as a national law license in the United States and that each state has its own system of allowing lawyers to practice law.

   k. Admission to practice before a Federal Court in one state is not a license to practice in either a State or a Federal Court in another state and it may be necessary to engage local counsel.

30. Do you explain to a client or a foreign lawyer that in some situations the law as written and the law as practiced have nothing in common?

31. Do you choose foreign lawyers who are flexible in giving written comfort for your client, or do you seek out foreign lawyers who are "reputable" in the eyes of the foreign government, but who are rigid in insisting on technical compliance with local law for foreigners even though local companies do not comply?

32. When a local government official strongly suggests that you hire a particular local law firm (in which the official may be a partner), or hire a particular local consultant (to whom the official is related) to represent or assist you in the matter before the official, what advice do you give your client?

33. Do you ask if the laws and administrative rulings of the foreign countries are honored or ignored?

34. Do you explain to foreign clients that enforcement of legal rights in some U.S. jurisdictions can take five years to get a trial and even longer for multiple appeals and post-trial procedures?

35. Do you ask if U.S. citizens or companies can get a fair trial in the foreign countries?

36. What guidelines do you give to advise a client to distinguish between permissible and nonpermissible payments under the Foreign Corrupt Practices Act?

37. Do you have the office capacity to drop everything on short notice and travel to a foreign country to represent a client in those cultures where face-to-face relationships determine the successful company?

38. Are you willing (and able) to spend evenings and weekends entertaining foreign lawyers and clients when they are in your city, and vice versa when you are in theirs?

Jay G Foonberg
FoonbergLaw
9461 Charleville Blvd., #416
Beverly Hills, CA 90212
Phone: (310) 652-5010
Fax: (310) 652-5019
E-mail: Jay@foonberglaw.com

CHAPTER 10

Selecting and Dealing with Foreign Lawyers

Henry T. King, Jr.
CASE WESTERN RESERVE UNIVERSITY SCHOOL OF LAW
SQUIRE, SANDERS & DEMPSEY
CLEVELAND, OHIO

James R. Silkenat
ARENT FOX LLP
NEW YORK, NEW YORK

1. Introduction

Like all businesses in this age of increasing globalization, continuing on an accelerated basis, the move toward truly global, transnational business continues to expand daily. Like any business, large law firms are becoming transnational in their structure. At the same time, new technology is helping smaller law firms form alliances and transact business regardless of national boundaries. A remarkable sensitivity to discrete cultures and legal systems is required of international lawyers and businesspeople. This, in turn, requires both small and large law firms to bring the best of both worlds to bear on the needs of their international and foreign clientele: local law firm savvy matched with twenty-first-century resources.

The world has changed greatly in its handling of international transactions, and the number of countries participating in the global market has grown rapidly. This makes life interesting, but also makes it more complex, because the approaches for dealing with this diversity have to be.

2. Selecting a Foreign Lawyer

Foreign lawyers are a primary means for bridging the gulf between U.S. negotiators and foreign parties. The selection of a foreign lawyer may well influence the success or failure of the negotiation. In light of this potential impact on transactions, a foreign lawyer must be selected with great care, and the differences between negotiating domestic transactions and international transactions must be recognized. Frequently, these differences are based on culture, religion, and historical background. The foreign lawyer is helpful by virtue of being a product of his national culture, but at the same time he must meet certain requirements.

In selecting foreign lawyers or law firms, keep in mind the need for technical skills and knowledge. Experience gained from other transactions is also important because almost inevitably it will be useful in your transaction. Particularly when government clearances are involved, a foreign lawyer doing multiple transactions needs to have a good feel for what will be approved and not approved. Furthermore, the lawyer may have the governmental contacts that will facilitate these approvals.

The foreign lawyer's objectivity in telling you what you need to know is important. He should have an understanding of what is doable and what is not doable, both in terms of the local context and in terms of your relationship with your client's preferred partner or any other party involved in the transaction.

American business operates with a sense of urgency. But this is not necessarily the way business is done in other countries. You need to find a lawyer with the same sense of the need for getting things done within a defined time frame as you have.

In some countries, particularly in the Far East, negotiations take significant amounts of time, almost by definition. Progress seems glacial, and your lawyer (wisely selected) can advise you on the time frame with which you are dealing. He can tell you when delaying tactics are being used and when time delays are simply par for the course and may actually be ways for the parties involved to get to know one another better. Bear in mind that business is, in general, more personal outside the United States, and that once a personal relationship has been established, it may well stand the test of time and indeed be more lasting than in countries where quick rapport is firmed up almost immediately.

An excellent working knowledge of both English and the host-country language is mandatory for an effective foreign counsel. This enables your local counsel to brief you on the slang, innuendos, and double meanings of the foreign language, and helps ensure that both parties fully understand the contractual relationship into which they are entering. The depth of understanding achieved will be insurance toward making the contract work for both parties.

It is also important that a foreign lawyer have as good an awareness of the U.S. context as possible. He needs to have an appreciation of our legislative ethics in dealing with foreign government officials. Our Foreign Corrupt Practices Act, for example, is different from the laws of many other countries that have such statutes, in that it is rigidly enforced. Indeed, both Germany and Japan have enacted similar legislation, but we do not know whether it will be followed by U.S.-style enforcement. The foreign lawyer needs to know what will and what will not fly under the law and be prepared to apprise you immediately of any unacceptable activities.

A sense of empathy can be an important glue in the relationship between the U.S. negotiator and a foreign counsel. There has to be a free exchange of ideas between you and your foreign counterpart. Any fears you have should be conveyed to your foreign counsel with complete candor and without holding anything back.

If possible, select a lawyer with good business sense. After all, the success of your negotiation will be determined by the bottom-line results of what you have negotiated. Some appreciation of the host-country tax context and how it relates to the U.S. tax context is, for example, a strong plus. A foreign lawyer's feel for the cost of any contract concessions you may have to consider is also important.

In negotiating a foreign contract you may have to sell the terms of the contract both to the foreign party and also to your own principal. Your foreign counsel's persuasiveness and credibility may go a long way in helping you establish the credibility of the results of the negotiation with your client.

Normally, your relationship with the foreign lawyer will not end with signing the contract. The foreign lawyer may well have to help you make the contract work. This means that his continuing relationship with the other parties to the contract will be critical. He must be loyal to you, yet maintain some working relationship with the other parties to the contract. He will probably be there as the results of the contract unfold and needs to keep you posted on how matters are progressing in the operation of the contract.

In the last analysis, your relationship with a foreign lawyer is a matter of trust and confidence. This will not come quickly but must develop over a period of time. When it has developed, it can be very fulfilling for both sides. But it takes time, and you always have to be aware of the context in which the foreign lawyer is operating when judging performance.

Thus, many highly specialized legal markets can only be served by establishing relationships with foreign firms as local counsel. This practice has resulted in an interesting hybrid: the large international firm staffed by that region's local legal elite. In some cases, this might offer the best of all worlds: sensitivity to and expertise in complex local cultural and legal issues, matched with the resources and expertise of a large "mega" firm.

Meanwhile, no assumptions should be made. The name and logo of a world-renowned firm do not in any way guarantee that this optimal fusion exists. One must carefully study the level of integration between the local office and the rest of the firm. Are the firm's offices technologically linked, so that information, including conflict checks, is shared across offices? Is the management structure of the firm such that local autonomy is grounded in the best practices of the larger firm as a whole? Further, is the staff of the local office a collection of home-office transplants, or has the firm invested in cultivating high-quality local lawyers?

3. Region and Country-Specific Observations

Following are some brief characterizations of foreign lawyers and their approach to the law on a country-specific basis, grouped under the various regions of the world. These observations, while necessarily simplifications, are designed to highlight some of the differences and similarities between foreign and U.S. lawyers that we have observed over a considerable period of time. Keep in mind that in a number of countries, particularly in Europe, American law firms have offices and their own way of doing things that may affect the style of local lawyers and the way they handle international transactions. Where available, they may well be a valuable resource.

3.1 Latin America

Argentina.   There has not been much economic or political certainty in Argentina in recent years, and the lawyers there have had to adjust to it. Given the context, there is a high degree of professionalism and integrity, but it is incumbent at times to include a sense of urgency so that matters get done within a preplanned time frame. Just as you make demands for performance, see that your foreign counsel is paid in a timely manner. There are a number of excellent firms with which to work here.

Brazil.   In Brazil, the caliber of lawyers varies widely, and the step down from top-flight to the next level is frequently significant. This means that a close check of possible Brazilian counsel before retaining them is essential.

Mexico.   Mexican lawyers are technically and ethically sound, but delays are frequently the order of the day. It is sometimes very difficult to secure a prompt response to questions posed. The day starts later in Mexico, which means that Mexican working hours parallel ours to only a limited extent. On the other hand, some Mexican lawyers work very late. If you want to get the job done, you may have to adjust your working hours to those of your Mexican colleagues.

3.2 Europe

United Kingdom.   In the United Kingdom, the caliber of lawyers is impressive, but they sometimes have a different business orientation than lawyers in the United States. At times they seem very legalistic, perhaps overly so. It is important, therefore, to make sure that U.K. counsel is aware of the business objectives behind the transaction on which you are seeking assistance, as well as the proposed time frame. Ethical standards are quite high.

Germany. German lawyers are generally very business-oriented and direct. In the international sector, they have a very good command of English. You can easily communicate what you want to accomplish in a few words, and can count on them to be very responsive. It is best to have German counsel who is tax-oriented. In the tax area, the line of demarcation between law firms and accounting firms is not clearly defined, and there are growing tendencies in companies to rely on accounting firms rather than law firms for tax advice.

Eastern Europe. Business lawyers, in the broad U.S. sense, did not exist under the previous communist regimes in the region. Lawyers familiar with international trade, finance, licensing, or joint ventures were few in number and employees of the communist governments. Currently, the legal profession in Central and Eastern Europe, like the legal system, is undergoing significant changes. The active study of western legal systems, associations with western law firms, and the emergence of new laws are all positive forces, as lawyers in these areas become familiar with a market economy system. Consequently, when selecting a local lawyer in Central or Eastern Europe, you should, with diligence, find numerous lawyers familiar with local laws and regulations, knowledgeable about required governmental approvals, and helpful with the language, culture, and local customs.

France. The French legal system seems in certain respects to be very conceptualistic and formalistic. There are ways of dealing with such matters, and French lawyers have learned how to utilize these approaches. French lawyers tend to be responsive and business-oriented. Documentation is almost always in French, but language is rarely a problem in negotiations. On the major questions of structuring transactions to limit tax exposure, French lawyers are quite knowledgeable. On tax matters involved in the operation of French companies, however, there is a tendency to refer such matters to firms of tax advisors (consisting of former French government officials) or to accounting firms.

Italy. In Italy, because of the nature of the Italian legal context, exchanges with Italian counsel may well be complex and extended. When exchanging legal views with Italian counsel, it is always important to keep your eye on the target and to make sure that the answer received responds to the question asked.

Spain. Spanish international lawyers are busy people. Additionally, significant legal work in Spain has until quite recently been concentrated in just a few firms, with the result that there has not always been an adequate supply of competent Spanish legal talent available to meet the foreign investor's needs. It is necessary to define priorities clearly so that your Spanish counsel has a good grasp of what is most important from your standpoint.

Switzerland.   There are some fine Swiss corporate lawyers, but they often lack the tax sophistication that is necessary for U.S. client purposes. It can be awkward to get knee-deep in a transaction and then find that your Swiss lawyer is not tax-oriented. If your reasons for being in Switzerland are tax-related, you can save yourself a lot of pain and suffering if you thoroughly check out your prospective Swiss lawyer's tax experience. This may take time, but it is well worth the effort.

Turkey.   There is not as much transactional experience historically in Turkey as in other European countries, and the role of your counsel, therefore, assumes special importance. As for location, you have two choices: Istanbul and Ankara. If it means an hour's flight to Ankara to get the right counsel, you should not be reluctant to make the trip. It may well save you much grief later on.

3.3 The Middle East

Iraq.   The situation here is sufficiently complex that any summary would be outdated before this volume reaches print. The position of local counsel is likely to remain unsettled for some time.

Egypt.   When selecting counsel in Egypt, a review of their capacity and competence should relate to their responsiveness and ability to serve you on a timely basis. One of the fine inheritances of Egypt from its colonial days is a very good legal system, but you need strong Egyptian legal assistance to make it work for you, and you need to be selective in locating such help because of the time pressures that will be on you.

Saudi Arabia.   It is always good to have a counsel who knows what the government will and will not allow you to do. Frequently, lawyers with this qualification have worked at some time in their careers in a government capacity. Governmental experience gives a prospective counsel an excellent feel for how things work in Saudi Arabia and is invaluable in problem solving.

3.4 The Far East

Indonesia.   There are a limited number of law firms in Indonesia that can adequately service international clients. To get the services you need, you may have to commit to a retainer arrangement. Get your arrangements with Indonesian counsel worked out prior to using the firm. If you have to go ahead on a retainer basis, by all means do so, but there should be a clear understanding between the parties as to just what legal areas the retainer arrangements cover.

Taiwan. Good legal services are available in Taiwan, but they do not come cheap. Internationally oriented law firms in Taiwan frequently have lawyers on board who have studied in the United States, so they are generally aware of U.S. requirements. Because of the distance from the United States, you will want an on-the-spot counsel who can promptly field many of the legal questions raised by the operating people who will be running your client's production facilities. It will be of particular importance to retain readily available counsel with whom your operating people feel compatible and with whom they can discuss proposed actions freely and candidly. Your Taiwan counsel should always be aware that it is his or her obligation to bring you into the loop on sensitive and important issues.

Former British Connections in Asia. Fortunately, Australia, New Zealand, Singapore, and Hong Kong have a common legal tradition. Lawyers from all these areas speak a common language, thereby avoiding the problems caused by translations. U.S. lawyers can generally expect prompt, courteous, and efficient service from their foreign counterparts in these jurisdictions.

Japan. In Japan, the situation has changed recently because of steps taken to open up to foreign lawyers the right to render legal services in that country. Previously, the few firms with western partners admitted to practice in Japan were at a premium and could pick and choose among the clients they served. The door has begun to open for U.S. lawyers who wish to practice in Japan, and the pressure is on the Japanese to widen that opening. This is a continuing process.

China. Chinese law firms of considerable talent and depth have emerged in the last decade. Several of them have offices in the U.S. and in multiple cities in China. English-language capacity can still be an issue, as can review of relevant conflict situations. The growth in sophistication of this market has been quite dramatic.

4. Conclusion

The capacity and status of foreign lawyers varies widely from country to country. In some instances, the pace of living is much different than that in the United States, and there can be less of a sense of urgency to finish a job. In other countries, the coverage of legal areas is not as well defined or complete as it is in this country, and there are gaps that foreign lawyers must try to fill with sound reasoning and good judgment. Finally, the ethical climate for business in many countries can vary greatly from that in the United States.

The role of the foreign lawyer in these countries assumes special importance because the lawyer may need to deal with both legal and ethical questions. What is more, he must have the confidence of the local management so that these questions are raised ahead of time, not after the fact. The role of counsel overseas in the greater business context is subject to wide variations. Our impression is that in the Middle East, it is best to have your documents prepared by U.S. counsel to the maximum extent possible. In Germany and certain other European countries, on the other hand, this is not as necessary. In fact, in Germany, lawyers prepare major transactions in their own desired form and frequently with great clarity and an economy of words.

In the tax area, which always has bottom-line impact, lawyers play a role that varies from country to country. We have always found tax competence to be a plus. But on matters such as reorganizations and mergers, as well as on operating problems, accounting firms are playing a more important role than in the past. There is often a good mesh between legal and accounting firms, but this is by no means always the case. The U.S. counsel's role is to see that matters requiring attention do not fall between the cracks.

Legal services overseas do not come cheap. You are sometimes charged the senior partner's rates (which will be quite high and may exceed U.S. rates) even though associates may actually be doing the legwork on a legal problem. It is, therefore, important that you think through problems prior to contacting foreign counsel. Often you will need to look into the foreign attorney's mind and see how he will view the question in his own context. By being precise with your questions, you can save time and money. For good order's sake and for the record, your questions to foreign counsel should always be by e-mail, fax, or letter. Telephone service in many areas of the world is still not good; moreover, recollections of an oral exchange may vary widely when the going gets rough.

The selection of foreign local counsel by U.S. companies needs to be done with a good sense of the legal context in which the foreign lawyer will operate. Some factors to be considered in your search include:

- Legal experience, including the handling of U.S. clients.
- Independence of judgment, particularly where the ethical context of business in the country is clouded.
- Business orientation or, specifically, an understanding of the bottom-line effects of particular legal approaches.
- Responsiveness: whether the proposed foreign counsel's track record and staffing equip the firm to handle your needs.
- Costs: These may, in some instances, be hard to establish beforehand, but must be considered in light of bottom-line requirements.

Henry T. King Jr.
Case Western Reserve University Law School
11075 East Boulevard
Cleveland, OH 44106
Phone: (216) 368-2096
Fax: (216) 368-2086
E-mail: hk@cwru.edu

James R. Silkenat
Arent Fox LLP
1675 Broadway
New York, NY 10019
Phone: (212) 492-3318
Fax: (212) 484-3990
E-mail: silkenat.james@arentfox.com

CHAPTER 11

Interest-Based International Business Negotiations

Daniel Burnstein
NEGOTIATOR PRO, INC.
CLEARWATER, FLORIDA

1. Introduction

As recently as January 2000, *Fortune* magazine was predicting international sales to hit a record $650 million, without counting international sales of services. But by June 2008 the U.S. export economy was roaring along at an annualized rate of $1,972.8 billion—roughly a 300 percent increase. Without these exports the current U.S. economy would have been negative, according to Bernard Baumohl, chairman of the Economic Outlook Group. This internationalization trend has pushed medium and large industries to seek 30 to 50 percent of their revenues from overseas sales—forcing even the most heartland-focused companies to look overseas or lose important revenue opportunities.

So what is a smart international company and its lawyers to do? According to Ghauri and Usunier in *International Business Negotiations*,[1] the answer is to offer good products and service but also to improve its approach to negotiations. Negotiation is all about the voluntary process in which the parties can quit the process at any time and the goal is to have a give-and-take where both parties modify their offers and expectations to come to agreement.

For Ghauri and Usunier, bargaining is a win-lose proposition, but negotiation is better thought of as a way to problem-solve. This new approach to negotiation requires that there be a far greater degree of information exchange between the parties of their objectives, a willingness to emphasize the common objectives of the parties, a willingness to attempt to understand each other's needs, and a joint search for a solution that solves the underlying needs of all parties. Note that it is impossible to efficiently carry out this process without understanding one's own interests as well as the interests of the other side(s).

This new approach focuses on the powerful "interests" tool. While new, it is not an overnight phenomenon. For the past thirty years a

---

[1] P.N. GHAURI & J.C. USUNIER, INTERNATIONAL BUSINESS NEGOTIATIONS (2001).

conscious research effort by practitioners and business and law professors centered at Harvard, MIT, Northwestern, Ohio, Pennsylvania, Princeton, Simmons, Stanford, Tufts, Utah, and elsewhere has yielded a new approach to negotiations loosely called "interest-based negotiation"—allowing negotiators to rise above immediate impulses—flight (yielding, giving in, or walking) or fight (such as win-lose jujitsu). Instead, a more efficient way of doing business is emerging. Over the last thirty years interest-based bargaining has begun to move into the mainstream of commercial and diplomatic negotiations in such venues as the United Nations, the Asian Development Bank, the Bank of America, and the U.S. Federal Board of Mediation and Conciliation. Most experts agree that interest-based bargaining is more efficient in terms of the time and resources needed to reach agreement, because if there is buy-in to this approach by both sides, then:

- less is left on the table;
- more is achieved in each trip, letter, and call;
- there are better long-range relations;
- parties are less defensive and there is less stress;
- fewer deals crumble needlessly;
- overhead costs go down; and
- there is less wasted travel and less disruptive behavior.

What if both sides don't buy in and only one side does or there is some pretense? It then might happen that old school competitive negotiators will 'game' the negotiation and pretend to be seeking win-win options that they are secretly working behind the scenes to sabotage. How would they sabotage the negotiation? They might do this by hiding their real interests or by seeking to reduce the value of the other side's alternatives. For instance, if you are trying to rent an anchor store in a mall and your open strategy is to go to other malls if one particular negotiation doesn't work out, the landlord could informally speak with other mall owners and let them know that you have a bizarre way of negotiating and you come up with endless ideas that seem not to pan out. They are not actually saying that you don't have the financing to complete a deal, but they are hinting at something akin to you being unable to carry through.

Since 1975, there has been a quiet revolution as law and business schools have recognized the concepts of interest-based bargaining and begun offering it in new courses. The texts used typically include *Getting to Yes*,[2] *The Art of Negotiation*,[3] *Negotiation*,[4] *The Manager as Negotiator*,[5] *Getting Past No*,[6] and *Legal Negotiation and Settlement*.[7]

---

[2] Roger Fisher, Bruce M. Patton & William L. Ury (1992).
[3] Howard Raiffa (2005).
[4] Roy Litterer & Joseph A. Lewicki (1985).
[5] David A. Lax & James K. Sebenius (1987).
[6] William Ury (1993).
[7] Gerald R. Williams (1983).

1.1 Computers to the Rescue?

Often negotiators are not as rigorous as they might be about listing all of their interests and assigning values to them. Perhaps they are too close to understand their real needs (interests) or perhaps they are not up to the task due to lack of time, energy, or support. Smartsettle, a new computer program from Canada created by Dr. Ernest Thiessen, helps them to do this with both the quantitative and qualitative (soft) values in their negotiation in a private way, and then the program looks for what are usually hidden ways to maximize the outcome. These ways are hidden because it is rare that the parties will feel safe enough to identify all of their strong and weak preferences and find ways to swap values in a "smart" fashion. Smartsettle is an online negotiation system that facilitates the process of identifying one's own preference priorities—what you care about and how much you care about it. It steps you through a "preference" elicitation and uncovers hidden value for all the parties in fair and efficient solutions to their negotiation. Negotiators may be located at geographically dispersed locations around the world as they take advantage of the asynchronous features of the system and move-by-move tracking made possible by the Smartsettle Server.[8]

Modeling of private interests on quantitative and qualitative issues enables parties to negotiate with packages of issues as opposed to the issue-by-issue bargaining that is typical in ordinary negotiations. Private preferences are kept hidden at a neutral site and are invisible to opposing parties. The system uses these private preferences to calculate ratings for packages, which enable each party to quickly evaluate incoming proposals and suggestions generated by the system.

Often the international aspects of a deal create special impetus for negotiation, given the difficulty and expense of international litigation and enforcement of judgments. Unfortunately, with international negotiations it is not always possible to have access to the courts due to choice of law obstacles, local bias, clogged dockets, and so forth.

In the United States, a movement to bring this approach to alternative dispute resolution (ADR) programs in corporate and court settings is gaining momentum. Most large corporations have a formal dispute resolution program designed to give the participants a chance to express their interests and attempt to find common ground. More and more state and federal courts are implementing ADR programs. Professor Frank Sander of Harvard Law School pioneered this concept,

---

[8] By means of sophisticated algorithms, Smartsettle is able to offer suggestions to negotiators and provide various means to solve impasses. If hidden value remains when a tentative agreement is reached, the system is able to generate an improvement that fairly divides gains among all sides. More information is available at www.smartsettle. com.

called the multi-door courthouse program. Sander explicitly links ADR to interest-based mediation and negotiation.

Internationally, a growing, parallel private dispute resolution movement influenced by the interest-based bargaining trend—often using retired judges and law professors as adjudicators and mediators—is replacing litigation with arbitration and mediation, thus avoiding expensive multiyear, multiparty commercial litigation. More and more contracts are incorporating "good faith" negotiation clauses that require senior-level executives to attempt to resolve a dispute before it is referred to arbitration, mediation, or court.

This chapter briefly describes the theory of interest-based negotiation and applies this theory to international commercial negotiations.

2. A Theoretical Overview of Interest-Based Negotiation

According to Fisher, Patton, and Ury there are three basic strategies in all negotiations. The cooperative strategy generally involves interest-based bargaining with the sharing of interest (underlying needs) and background information and the display of mutual concern. The competitive strategy is characterized by the withholding of interests, important data, and the true settlement range, as well as the use of coercion. The principled strategy, a term coined in *Getting to Yes* to refer to having a principle or reason, is a superset of the elements of the cooperative strategy. "Principled" negotiators adopt interest-based bargaining and come up with fair principles upon which to resolve a negotiation that satisfies their side well and the other side acceptably. A central component of the book's thesis of interest-based bargaining is described as follows:

> Behind opposed positions lie shared and compatible interests, as well as conflicting ones. We tend to assume that because the other side's positions are opposed to ours, their interests must also be opposed. If we have an interest in defending ourselves, then they must want to attack us. If we have an interest in minimizing the rent, then their interest must be to maximize it. In many negotiations, however, a close examination of the underlying interest will reveal the existence of many more interests that are shared or compatible than ones that are opposed.[9]

Principled negotiation suggests the following goals and strategies:

- Separate the people from the problem. Negotiators should see themselves as joint problem solvers rather than as adversaries.
- Focus on interests, not positions. Positions are what we say we want, while interests are our underlying needs. Focusing on

---

[9] Fisher et al., *supra* note 2, at 43.

interests brings out shared concerns that suggest efficient and stable, if not elegant, solutions.

- Invent options for mutual gains. Find solutions that will satisfy the needs of both parties.
- Use objective criteria. After you find the joint gains, and both parties want the same scarce resources, objective criteria lessen the chance of a failed negotiation or inefficient haggling. Use recent sales, a respected guidebook, or other objective standards.
- Learn everyone's best alternatives to the agreement—their BATNA (best alternative to a negotiated agreement)—if there is no deal.

If the other side doesn't play along:

- Develop your alternatives. Strengthen your BATNA and lessen their attachment to their alternatives to reaching agreement with you.
- Use negotiation "jujitsu." Welcome the thrusts of the other side, explore their complaints, and ask them what would result if you were to adopt their proposal.
- Tame the hard bargainer who uses dirty tricks by recognizing the tactic, raising it explicitly, and questioning the tactic's legitimacy and desirability.
- Prepare "yesable" propositions that contain action items that can be responded to with a yes or no.

This approach to negotiation has been criticized for suggesting that one side simply reveal all of its vital interests (needs) up front. However, Fisher, Ury, and Patton state explicitly that good-faith negotiation does not require total disclosure. Critics have also argued that the approach is only for nice people, that both sides have to agree to use principled negotiation, and that it is therefore inherently unrealistic in a world of competitive bargainers. However, *Getting Together: Building a Relationship That Gets to Yes*[10] and *Getting Past No: Negotiating with Difficult People*[11] answer the critics and elaborate on the issue of dealing with difficult people within the interest-based bargaining model.

3. Dealing with Difficult People

An estimated 10 to 30 percent of potential deals fall apart because of personality conflicts. These are deals in which there were solid reasons to reach agreement. Frequently in these failed deals, one or all of the principal negotiators is perceived as difficult. To deal with this

---

[10] Roger Fisher & Scott Brown (1989).
[11] William Ury (1991).

problem, Ury proposes a five-step process that he calls the strategy of breakthrough negotiation:[12]

1.   Control your emotional responses and behavior. Instead of overreacting, focus on obtaining your goals. In other words, do not give in to the basic responses of flight or fight. If you do, you lose control of the situation.

2.   Help your opponent hold back his or her negative emotions of defensiveness, fear, suspicion, and hostility. You have to get past the opposition's resistance.

3.   After creating a more positive climate, attempt to get the opponent to stop bargaining over positions and to try exploring options that will satisfy the other party's needs.

4.   Bridge the gap between the interests of the parties; help your opponent save face; make the outcome a victory for your opponent; and generally make it easy to agree.

5.   If the other side thinks it can prevail without satisfying your interests, you have to improve the perception of the value of your alternatives and other sources of power. In part, this means identifying all your sources of power. Be aware that overdoing this show of power sources may make the other side feel like an enemy. A delicate touch is important. Put things in a positive, nonjudgmental way to indicate that you have other options that the other side should be aware of, although you would really like to see this negotiation succeed.

Ury notes that his prescription for a breakthrough strategy is counterintuitive in that it has the negotiators do the opposite of what their natural feelings would suggest. When an opponent is aggressive, one tends either to be equally tough or to leave. Ury suggests going around the resistance:

> Rather than pounding in a new idea from the outside, you encourage him to reach for it from within. Rather than telling him what to do, you let him figure it out. Rather than trying to break down his resistance, you make it easier for him to break through it himself. In short, breakthrough negotiation is the art of letting the other person have your way.

For instance, one reported negotiation consisted of a developer (interested in a property held by a nonprofit) and the nonprofit (willing to move if the price was right). After a typical negotiation dance, the final offer of $300,000 from the developer was within the zone of agreement (that is, between the buyer's and seller's reservation price). However, the nonprofit seller suspected there may be more money to be had. The nonprofit's negotiator reported a divided opinion of the

---

[12] *Id.*

board on the last and best offer and suggested there were two ways the deal could happen: As a side agreement, the developer either could do $50,000 work on the nonprofit's new location, or the developer could make an equal cash contribution to the nonprofit. The developer was thus moved to make a new offer, namely a contribution of $25,000, and the deal went forward. Ultimately, for legal reasons, the offer of $300,000 plus a donation was converted into a straight $325,000 sale. In this case, the seller mentioned several possible ways around an impasse and the buyer picked a palatable solution from several offered, letting the buyer have it the seller's way.

4. Cooperative Behavior and Firm Bargaining

Many writers on the topic of negotiation support the interest-based bargaining model but offer more explicit comments about the role of power and bargaining in the negotiation process. There is general agreement that negotiation is a mixture of contending and claiming. Jeffrey Rubin calls this the pull of the negotiation "tightropes," noting that negotiators are pulled in extreme directions among which they must try to walk a tightrope. First, he says, negotiators are pulled between cooperation and competition. There is a strong desire to be tough in order to achieve the most favorable agreement possible, but that could drive the other party from the table. It is also tempting to be cooperative in order to reach a fair agreement, but that could lead to settling for less than might have been achieved. Negotiators also walk a tightrope between complete honesty and total misrepresentation. If you are completely honest, you run the risk of being exploited. Finally, effective negotiators must walk the tightrope between short- and long-term gain. A quick short-term gain at the other's expense may be achieved at the sacrifice of long-term mutual gain.

In a typical negotiation, there are efforts to form a partnership and efforts to maximize the value of the final deal to each negotiator. Effective negotiation typically creates a larger pie, allowing each negotiator to claim a bigger piece of the pie. There are three stages to good negotiating: (1) planning, (2) exploring the interests, and (3) bargaining to a close. Effective negotiators tend not to disclose interests that will injure their bargaining position during the sharing stage because of the logically inherent competitive aspects of the bargaining stage.

5. Sources of Power

Roger Fisher has commented on the issue of power.[13] He wrote that power flows from:

---

[13] Roger Fisher, *Negotiating Power: Getting and Using Influence*, in NEGOTIATION THEORY AND PRACTICE 127–40 (J. William Breslin & Jeffrey Rubin eds., 1991).

- Skill and knowledge
- Good relationships
- A good alternative to negotiating
- The power of an elegant solution
- Legitimacy
- Commitment.

Determination, resources, momentum, and powerful friends are also typical sources of power. Considerable data show that persistently high aspiration consistently results in better outcomes. In their American Management Association curriculum, this author and Robert Burdick suggest starting by building a nondefensive relationship and using an opening offer that is the strongest position that can be fairly justified by objective data. As such, the effective negotiator recognizes the propensity of humans to bargain, and to gain leverage or power from the use of objective data, other sources of power, and the power of high aspirations.

6. Obstacles to Interest-Based Bargaining

Interest-based bargaining takes a lot of preparation, but saves time in the long run. One must be a careful and active listener and watch for cultural and communication problems. Frustration with the negotiation process is exacerbated by cultural chasms, fear of the unknown, business paranoia, justifiable caution, language, technology, transportation, storage, housing, staffing, weather, health, and infrastructure support, and political obstacles. Other problems include inexperience with negotiation processes or refusal of the other side to bargain. Despite years of experience, the other side's representative may not be skilled at dispute resolution. The other party may know too little about the new negotiation science and instead use competitive techniques that substitute tricks, ploys, and bluster for stable, creative, and lasting win-win solutions.

One problem may be "knowing too much," i.e., believing one knows everything about bargaining. Many lawyers do not listen creatively to the needs or interests of the other side(s) or understand the difference between positions and interests. There is a great lack of negotiation training in the United States compared to the United Kingdom, Australia, China, and Japan. Surprisingly few lawyers and businesspeople over the age of thirty have had any exposure to formal negotiation training in general or to interest-based bargaining in particular. Even younger lawyers and executives may receive only minimal training despite all the law and business programs adopting negotiation or ADR courses since 1975 because students often cannot gain admission before graduation or they decide other courses are more relevant to their careers.

The obstacles to more effective negotiation behavior include prejudice based on emotion, class, gender, age, or national origin—feelings that make it harder to achieve win-win outcomes. There may also be other problems: paranoia, ego, anger, xenophobia, cultural and religious bias, jockeying for position, playing to the crowd, constituencies needing to be heard and to have an effect, and the power of traditional behavior. While a negotiator does not have to be a trained therapist, skills at "reading people" are vital—it is the social lubricant that helps people get past the inevitable sticking points.

7. How Useful Is Interest-Based Bargaining Internationally?

Is this interest-based bargaining approach useful in Mexico, or Japan, or Indonesia, or Ghana? The answer is a qualified yes, if you keep in mind that these cultures hold different values than your own. For example, Americans and Australians generally are more likely to be willing to engage in extensive trading of positions and counterpositions, while the Japanese and French are less flexible. With these sorts of cultural differences in mind, there is evidence that interest-based bargaining works in a variety of settings.

The clarity and power offered by interest-based bargaining and mediation are useful as a foundation from which participants can analyze all problems and proposed solutions. As the Israeli-PLO agreement of 1993 shows, although participants may not like each other, there are often more benefits to coming to an agreement than the alternative of not reaching agreement.

International negotiating is not identical to domestic negotiating. There are additional layers of analysis that add to the challenge. When confronting an international negotiation, ask yourself whether the following factors, identified in *Negotiating Across Cultures*,[14] are at play in your particular negotiation:

- Is this an individualistic culture or an interdependent culture, where family and patrimony are the dominant forces?
- Are roles prescribed in a hierarchy? Does truth repose in an individual's search for self-expression, or does it reside in the collective traditions of the group? Is there a strong collective sense? Are local affiliations more important than national affiliations?
- Is saving face (avoiding dishonor) more important than carrying out personal desires? Do people feel guilt or shame for not carrying out a given task? Are there still feuds and mechanisms to protect oneself from feuds?
- Are decisions made on a personal basis or because of group desires?

---

[14] RAYMOND COHEN (1997).

The answer to these questions will help shape your analysis of the interests, personalities, and impact of culture on the parties. In addition, the LESCANT model provides an analytical framework to assess the parties in a negotiation.

8. The Process of Cross-Cultural Negotiation

Negotiation is a personal relationship challenge as well as an analytical and financial challenge. People, like notes in a musical composition, do not exist outside of time, the context of other notes, progression, timbre, resonance, timing, and crescendo. These process dimensions are the dynamics of the negotiation as it unfolds over time. To really understand and plan a negotiation, one must understand the factual context, the cultural context, the people context, the financial context (to name a few parameters), and then see them as a process over time. A good offer is not good until its time has come and the negotiation process has "ripened" to the point where the other side is ready.

Further complications come about in cross-cultural interactions. Since communication is at the heart of negotiation, obstacles to communication will be obstacles to negotiation. Negotiation of issues is not merely a simple exchange of data and a decision about it. There are sensitivities over turf, status, and the like. These factors provide a complicating background noise and result in different views of how, when, where, timing, content, actors, and so forth. In intercultural negotiations especially, the background noise can drown out the foreground.

In his book, Raymond Cohen[15] helps the international lawyer to see the cultural differences in the use of language. He refers to Japan, Mexico, Indonesia, and the Philippines as "high-context" societies. "Low-context" societies include the United States and its North Atlantic allies such as Germany, Canada, England, and France. Here are some differences in these societies' use of language:

- Low-context societies use language to share facts and rights and to persuade, while high-context societies use language to allude, to avoid saying no, to connect with other people, and to make them feel at ease. Language is a social lubricant and has social implications.
- In low-context societies, language is used to share information about individual concerns, efforts, opinions, and rights. In high-context societies, individual concerns and efforts are not very important in themselves; social role and connections are the most important facts anyone can communicate.

---

[15] *Id.*

- In low-context societies, what you are doing is more important than your social role; the focus is on written and verbal communication, and the use of flowery phrases is believed to be distracting. In high-context societies, the focus is on verbal communication; the use of flowery phrases is a way to honor others; efforts are made to communicate a relationship, not the meaning of specific words.
- In low-context societies, family is very important except during business hours; while avoiding guilt is important, it is always possible to move and start over in a different part of the country. In high-context societies, family connections are a twenty-four-hour, seven-day-a-week matter of concern; avoiding shame is more important than life itself.
- In low-context societies, there is less attention and respect for the very old and the very young. In high-context societies, communal leaders are more authoritarian; the young and old are more revered than in low-context societies.

Cohen lists the following other cultural insensitivities of professionals from the so-called developed countries:

- Using too much pressure when the other side feels it is vulnerable
- Pressing any issue too hard
- Appearing to rush to an agreement, even if the agreement is mutually useful
- Haggling, where the cultural norm of the leadership of a country makes it a point of pride to present (and view) prices as inflexible
- Failing to personalize a proposal and presenting it as a strictly commercial deal

9. Stages of International Negotiation

Donald and Rebecca Hendon[16] have identified six stages of international corporate negotiations. These stages are presented in modified form here.

9.1 Stage One: Prenegotiation

This is a time to assess personal contacts and relationships and determine objectives in light of opportunities and obstacles. Listen

---

[16] WORLD-CLASS NEGOTIATING: DEALMAKING IN THE GLOBAL MARKETPLACE (1990).

to high-quality business tapes and read books on the country and industry you are dealing with. Use a written workbook template or one contained in software to prepare the important issues. Use a checklist to cover all-important variables. Double-check with other experienced hands. Ask if there have been changes since the last negotiation in political, financial, personnel, and technical variables. Who is at the bargaining table? Who is not, but is nevertheless concerned about the outcome? Who has authority to deal? Do you have your constituencies in agreement? Does the other side? What are everyone's alternatives in case the deal does not happen? How can you strengthen your alternatives? Have you brainstormed possible creative and new win-win options? Who will be on your negotiation team, and what are their roles? Brainstorm with others on your side. Here you can raise lots of creative ideas, without judging the ideas at first. Most importantly, ask where the other side is coming from and why. Plumb their thinking, and why they might not like your proposal. This will lead you to a picture of how they perceive their choices. To effect change in the long run, you must change how they perceive their choices.

9.2 Stage Two: Entry

This is the phase of meeting and making a formal presentation to the other side. At this early stage of the negotiation, most deal-makers avoid specifics. They should take this time to work on the relationship and try to sketch out the broad framework of a possible agreement that indicates their interest in doing a deal with the other parties. Acknowledge that they may have some other options, and leave all sides a lot of leeway to craft a fair and equitable agreement.

9.3 Stage Three: Establishing and Building Relationships

This is the time for founding trust and respect, if not rapport. What do you have in common—family, hobby, sports, travel, work matters, or something else? If you do disagree, you must find a way to leave the other side a face-saving means to change their position and get their constituencies to move also.

9.4 Stage Four: Reformulating Assumptions

This enables you to arrive at better proposals to meet the needs of the other side and your side. Use active listening and restate the other side's positions to ensure you are hearing them accurately. Roger Fisher suggests trying to meet the needs of the other side acceptably and your side well. Stuart Nagel suggests trying to find "super-optimal" solutions that are better than what both sides entered the agreement looking to achieve.

9.5 Stage Five: Bargaining

This is the give-and-take dynamic of the negotiation. Note that in some cultures, particularly France and some Arab countries, the give and take of U.S. negotiators is deemed to be haggling and demeaning. In other cultures, such as Japan, it has taken the other side a long time to reach a position and it is awkward for them to reach consensus on a new set of demands. In the cases of France and Japan, any sounding out of the other side needs to be done after a relationship is forged over drinks or in another informal setting. Where a give-and-take dialogue is possible, seek trade-offs based on asymmetries of interests. Here you look for things you value less than the other side and vice versa. Then each side goes for what it wants.

There are many sources of power available to achieve your goals, including:

- Your ability to satisfy the essential needs of the other side
- Objective standards (standards and data that support your position)
- Referent power (for example, powerful allies you can reference)
- Alternative power (the power of being able to walk away)
- Financial power
- Issue power
- Technology power
- Expert power
- Reward power
- Legitimate power
- Coercive power
- Moving power
- Relationship power

9.6 Stage Six: Reaching Agreement

At this stage, negotiators use "yesable" proposals to sound out the other side's willingness to undertake various action steps. This refers to creating proposals that are simple and can be agreed to by a yes. The more that emotions, theoretical concepts, organizational pride, resentment, and higher principles come into play, the harder it is to formulate actions that can be implemented by a yes.

10. Conclusion

Despite some obstacles, international negotiations should be interest-based to benefit both parties over the long term. The emphasis on thorough preparation, refraining from competitive fight-or-flight behavior reactions, listening to all parties to the negotiation, and increasing one's awareness of each side's interests and needs should produce a more meaningful and reliable international commercial relationship.

Daniel Burnstein
President
Negotiator Pro, Inc.
2427 Rhodesian Drive, #5
Clearwater, FL 33763
Phone: (727) 657-5501
Fax: (509) 757-4497

CHAPTER 12

Building Trust: Keeping the Heart and Mind in Online Negotiation

Barbara G. Madonik
UNICOM COMMUNICATION CONSULTANTS INC.
TORONTO, CANADA

1. Introduction

In one of Albert Einstein's last interviews, he reportedly commented on the most important question he would like answered. Interestingly, his response had nothing to do with physics. It had everything to do with people:

> I think the most important question facing humanity is, "Is the universe a friendly place?" This is the first and most basic question all people must answer for themselves.[1]

In addition to his legacy as a scientist, Einstein was keenly interested in "the human condition." This should not be surprising: whenever two or more people are about to interact for the first time, they generally seek to gain a sense about "those other people" before they move forward comfortably in the interaction. In this effort to establish a sense of understanding there is an inherent, existential drive to find trust—that is, to believe that a friendly universe exists. Indeed, trust is the glue that binds the hearts and minds of people. It allows for the free exchange of ideas. It allows people to dare to agree or disagree. Trust is the factor that allows any negotiation to move forward and, more importantly, to last.

2. Laying the Foundation

2.1 Creating Trust

Creating trust, therefore, is the key to making progress in human interactions. In the past, people often believed that personal interaction

---

[1] While this quote is fairly well-known, it is considered somewhat of an "urban legend" attributed to Einstein. One reputable source, however, citing this quotation is Robert Dilts of the Neuro-Linguistic Programming University, in his *Reflections on September 11* (Sept. 12, 2001), http://www.nlpu.com/Articles/Sept_11.html.

was the only reliable way to size up someone and build that trust. Often, however, distance intervened and prevented this face-to-face approach. Enter technology: far-off drum signals, Marconi's odd tapping noises, and Bell's newfangled telephonic machine—any one of these could bridge the gap enough for some trust to be created (or, for that matter, broken). Today, we face an explosion of communication technology. And, while the distances we can bridge have telescoped somewhat as a result of technology, opportunities to build trust are still missed because the medium itself often creates barriers instead of building bridges.

What can you do to develop this all-important trust that binds parties and seals settlements in online negotiation? That is what this chapter is about. In it, you will read how people strive to make sense of the ways that they connect and communicate. You will see that connection is the driving force that builds trust, bringing about successful negotiation. You will learn how certain dynamics outside of conscious awareness tend to facilitate compelling synergies that result in settlement. Consequently you will discover how to become clear about recognizing signals that tap into factors that establish trust.

2.2 The Two-Way Street

Building trust is not a spectator sport. You grow trust by behaving in a respectful way, and by acknowledging trust as a two-way street. In every interaction, no matter how small, you encourage trust to flow back and forth, to and from the people with whom you interact.

To create this flow you must become a positive link in communication chains, and you will encounter many communication chains during a negotiation. For example, you will want to build trust with members of your own corporate or legal team. If you are facilitating an international negotiation, you will want to forge links with one or more members of multiple teams. If you are one of only two people in a two-party negotiation, you will want to form a chain with your counterpart (often called an "adversary"). In every case, use the same approach to net the best results: building trust. When you succeed, everyone will feel as content as possible when he or she leaves the table. Simply put: respectful negotiation leads to successful negotiation.

2.3 Defining Success

How exactly should success be defined? Successful negotiation cannot just mean managing to get a signature . . . or there would never be "buyer's remorse," and no one would ever seek to nullify a contract or settlement. Practical success involves your using thoughtful, organized techniques that take into account how long-distance communication and negotiation have changed the business and legal worlds. Success means your ability to overcome obstacles such as time zones and cultural differences. Success requires your finding similarities and honoring differences, regardless of culture.

This raises another question: how do you define a culture? Generally, a "culture" denotes any group of people who share a common framework of rules and standards. An individual may belong to many cultures, depending on the context: examples include religious, ethnic, geographic, corporate, chronometric, spatial, relational, linguistic, and social contexts. In negotiation, you can most easily build trust by thinking in terms of a "metacultural" context: the negotiation itself. In this framework, the negotiation is the metaculture that cuts across all other contexts. You can use this inclusive context because all parties agree to the same rules.

Finally, appreciate that when building trust, your communication finesse may matter as much as (or more than) knowing the facts relevant to your negotiation. This chapter will give you tools and tips to achieve this skill.

2.4 Levels of Awareness

Einstein did not raise the issue of the friendly universe idly: he believed that all humanity sought the answer. So, consider the question from your own perspective within the environment of your international negotiations. You and everyone with whom you communicate will be wondering about the same questions: "Is this person friendly or not? And how can I find out?"

You can help others here by looking for clues and communicating positive messages on two levels of awareness: the conscious and the other-than-conscious.[2]

First, observe how people take in information at the more superficial conscious, surface level. You will notice, for example, that most people can hold approximately seven (plus or minus two) pieces of information in their minds at the same time.[3]

Next, look to a deeper level that affects people more profoundly. When you deal with this other-than-conscious level, you deal with the part of the brain that reportedly absorbs an estimated 20,000 to 200

---

[2] "Other-than-consciousness" is a term that describes a level of awareness that works in tandem with conscious awareness even though people do not realize that they are influenced by it. The term was coined by Dave Dobson, Ph.D., creator of "Other-Than-Conscious Communication™." An overview of Dobson's work is available from the Excellence Quest Training Institute, http://www.excelquest.com/funshop (last visited July 21, 2008).

[3] George Miller, *The Magical Number Seven, Plus or Minus Two: Some Limits on Our Capacity for Processing Information*, 63 PSYCHOL. REV. 81–97 (1956), *available at* http://www.musanim.com/miller1956/.

million bits of information per second and that resides outside of conscious awareness.[4] The brain not only takes in this monstrous amount of information concurrently, but also keeps vast amounts of information in storage, and available, almost on demand. You can prove this right now by finishing the lyric "Happy Birthday to . . ." or the rest of "I pledge allegiance to . . ." This information is always waiting to be summoned. You just have to call on it.

2.5 Respect

From a practical perspective, appreciating and learning to work with the other-than-conscious level of communication is not just handy for recalling lyrics—it is the leverage that can efficiently plant the seeds of trust. This is the level where trust takes root and grows. So, this is the place you begin when you negotiate.

Building trust in virtual worlds is the same as in any other communication environment. Your success still depends on your communicating on the other-than-conscious level. As a result, you benefit by learning to build trust on a solid foundation of respect because this, although not visible, is profound.

Building trust in any environment—in the same room or in the virtual world of cyberspace—always comes down to the perception and the conveyance of respect.

3. Crafting the Communication Map

3.1 Communication Preferences

One way to convey respect is to approach others in a way that they prefer. You can build trust most solidly by working with the communication patterns people reveal to you and using those patterns to communicate with them.

Begin by recognizing that each person filters information in his or her own unique ways. Fortunately, these unique ways follow patterns[5] and the patterns people display when they communicate tend to be the patterns they will most prefer in your messages to them. As a result, efficient communication grows from "mirroring" each person's unique patterns.

By reflecting someone's communication patterns, you convey that you "get them." That willingness to be flexible is a cornerstone of trust.

---

[4] BARBARA MADONIK, I HEAR WHAT YOU SAY, BUT WHAT ARE YOU TELLING ME? THE STRATEGIC USE OF NONVERBAL COMMUNICATION IN MEDIATION (2001).

[5] *See* RICHARD BANDLER & JOHN GRINDER, FROGS INTO PRINCES (1979); *see also* NOAM CHOMSKY, SYNTACTIC STRUCTURES (1957).

On an other-than-conscious level, the actual information or "content" you want to share becomes a secondary (albeit important) issue. A person's perception that you are prepared to communicate in a way that makes sense to him or her becomes the pivotal factor that influences acceptance or resistance.

3.2 Communication Channels

By the time children are seven years old, they have involuntarily developed a preference for giving and getting information through one of three communication systems or "channels": visual (sight), auditory (sound), or kinesthetic (touch, taste, smell, feelings). People are generally not aware of their bias because their favorite "flavor" of communication exists outside of their awareness.

The Three Communication Channels

Visual	➡	Sight
Auditory	➡	Sound
Kinesthetic	➡	Touch, Taste, Smell, Feelings

Accordingly, when you send your information (that is, your "content") to them via their favored communication channel, they understand it easily. They don't need to waste time or energy having to unwittingly "translate" it from a less-preferred channel into the one they understand and use most frequently. Thus, there are many advantages to matching another's style of communicating. You eliminate "translation fatigue" and allow the person to understand your message quickly. This rapid processing is vital because the brain must first understand a message before considering the value of an idea. Communicating this way also demonstrates that you see eye-to-eye, talk the same talk, and walk the same walk.

Words are one major way you can convey your information in a manner that builds trust virtually as well as in face-to-face communication. Therefore use terms that relate to each person's respective favorite communication channel. In the case of virtual communication, send information using technology that ties into each person's intuitive preference. You create a powerful link.

3.2.1 Visual Examples

For people with a visual preference, seeing is believing. To build trust virtually, some ways to show respect might be to:

- Use sight-related terms such as a "sight for sore eyes," "new horizons," and "great perspectives."
- Send pictures or e-mail attachments with a lot of white space, color, pictures, diagrams, and schematics.

- Take advantage of DVDs, videotape, or live pictures via technology.
- Videoconference in facilities that project a professional and inviting image.

3.2.2 Auditory Examples

For people with an auditory preference, build trust by using words, numbers, and sounds:

- Use sound-related terms such as "Tell me about it," "in twenty-five words or less," and "You don't say."
- Use fax, e-mail, testimonials, and numerically-based financial reports, and have references call to speak with them.
- Let them read Web sites with well-organized lists, outlines, and menu choices.
- Ensure live communication (that is, teleconference, videoconference) that provides clear sound.

3.2.3 Kinesthetic Examples

For people with a kinesthetic preference, build trust by creating an environment that is inviting:

- Use language peppered with terms such as "feels good," "bite the bullet," and "bend over backwards."
- Send samples or models, or send e-mail with attachments that can be held in their hands.
- Give them interactive tasks that include touch or work on interactive Web sites.
- Ensure that their surroundings are comfortable if you are interacting with them in a virtual environment.

All of these techniques are examples of ways you can honor people's preferences outside of their awareness. By giving a little thought to your approach, you make big differences. You change from a disembodied voice or collection of words on paper to a flesh-and-blood person. You are real. You make communication human. Your methods are respectful and establish trust online. Moreover, you do away with the myth that "boys with the best toys" always win. As a matter of fact, when you tap into other people's preferred communication channels online, you start to cement trust to the degree that many times you excel at negotiations in the virtual world even when using the most rudimentary equipment.

3.3 Filters

Without a doubt, communicating via people's preferred communication channels is powerful. Used in isolation, it lays a strong foundation for building trust. If you combine this technique with other patterns that people use outside of their awareness, you create an even stronger sense of trust and even better results both in person and online.

Earlier you read that people make sense of information on both conscious and other-than-conscious levels. To best understand just how significant this is in building trust, begin by appreciating that people believe they are in control. They think they act on the information they receive and analyze consciously and make their choices as a result of it. This, however, is not generally the case. The constraints of the brain prevent people from being consciously aware of exactly what information is influencing them.

A good metaphor for this process of cognition is a system of filters. People absorb millions of pieces of raw data (facts, tone, facial expressions, smells, pain, etc.) concurrently. However, they are only consciously aware of seven (plus or minus two) items at a time.

The other-than-conscious part of their brain absorbs, sifts through, and processes the other millions of bits of data. Processing is automatic and constant. Only after this is complete can the information pass through personal and sensory filters to ultimately "reach the surface" (that is, pop into people's conscious awareness). At that point, people communicate believing they have made their choices based on their conscious awareness and analysis. However, their sense of how they make decisions cannot, in the end, be totally conscious because so many of their choices have been influenced by other-than-conscious information.

Critical to your success is the realization of how people use these filters to understand your communication and how they make decisions as a result of this understanding. Because they are unaware of the filters that bias their decisions and behavior, how you work with these filters largely determines your success.

Figure 12.1: Filtering Information

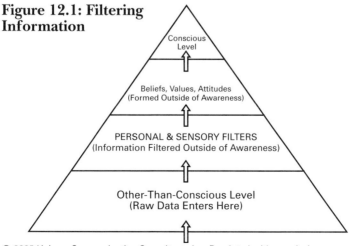

3.4 Patterns

Now that you are aware of how people unwittingly rely on filters to understand their world, it is important to see how the filters build patterns. If people had to consciously process each piece of information individually and then store it in a unique way, every task would be new and overwhelming. For that reason, the brain uses filters to generalize the information that it receives so it can turn the raw data into various models (or patterns). The brain then limits the number of patterns so that each pattern can be retrieved as easily as possible.

Thus, when people decide to send a message, the brain then extracts the needed information (that is, the content of the message) and conveys it by using a fairly limited number of "communication patterns." These patterns act like envelopes that carry their packages of information (that is, the content). Because each person's patterns are fairly consistent, you can easily identify them. As a result, all you need do to build trust is take note of people's patterns and send your message to them in envelopes that match their favorite envelopes. This makes your messages inviting on a level outside of their conscious awareness, and compels them to consider your ideas.

Communicating this way offers you a distinct advantage. Conversely, if you send a message by using a pattern unlike the recipient's preferred style, you run a high risk of neutralizing your chances at success.

3.4.1 Summary

- At the start of negotiation, set aside the "what" (that is, the information) people are communicating and pay close attention to "how" they are communicating. Notice the communication patterns that emerge.
- These patterns are the result of the channels and filters people use to understand their world, and will jump out at you.
- Establish trust online by selecting the appropriate patterns people demonstrate and then send your information to them using the patterns that match theirs.
- At this point people with whom you are communicating will pay closer attention to you and concurrently develop a sense of trust because you are sending messages respectfully on a level outside their conscious awareness. Consciously, they may not be sure why they feel comfortable about your communication and trust it . . . they just do.

3.5 Blueprints

Patterns blueprint ways to trigger action and develop comfortable virtual working frameworks. Replicating one pattern creates a sense of trust. Stacking multiple patterns on top of each other grows trust exponentially and creates compelling communication.

Look for the following patterns drawn from the Profile Element Grid (PEG).[6] They pinpoint different patterns and suggest techniques for crafting your negotiations to specifically suit people's preferences. This kind of personalized attention lets others know that you are interested in them. Focusing on detail is construed as respectful, both within and outside of conscious awareness.

Touchstones: People use specific words and phrases that have profound significance beyond their conscious meaning. When communicating with someone, play back those terms *exactly* as he or she uses them. (For example, if people say "retire debt" the term "debt retirement" does not have the same resonance for them.)

Initiation: People are either proactive (and initiate activity) or reactive (and wait for you to do something so they can respond). In the first case, respond to what they initiate; in the second, do something so they can respond.

Mental Movement: People either move toward a goal or away from a problem. In the first case, frame your communication in terms of achieving a goal; in the second, suggest resolving an issue to avoid dealing with it again.

Rationale: People think either in terms of opportunities/options or in terms of necessity/need. In the first case, offer them choices; in the second, advise them that there is only one way to go.

Thinking: Some people think in terms of details ("micro") and others in terms of the big picture ("macro"). With the first, give them micro-details or you risk being considered uncaring; with the second, provide as little detail as possible or you risk boring them and losing them mentally if not physically.

Focus: Some people are so inwardly-focused that they do not notice others. Rather than being vain or conceited, they are just spending their energy processing information by looking inward. Others look outward and focus on other people to ensure that everyone is included. In the first case, recognize that these people do not "check in" with others and you may need to compensate so that others are not offended or left out. In the second case, be aware that those people are continually checking to ensure everyone is considered (including team members and adversaries), and then operate accordingly.

Affiliation: Some people want to be treated as "loners" and are happiest with as little personal contact as possible; others like to operate as a "group"; still others, "collaborators," like to be in charge. With loners, connect minimally or you risk being seen as an intruder; with group people, talk in terms of "we" and "team" because they like people to become part of an ensemble; with collaborators, talk in terms such as

---

[6] Profile Element Grid, © 1986, 1993, 2001. Unicom Communication Consultants Inc. For details, see MADONIK, *supra* note 4.

"you and I" (and never "we" or "team") because, although they need people present so they can perform (like negotiators or presenters), they do not see themselves as part of a team.

Preference: Some of your contacts want to work with people; others prefer to work with objects; and the third group prefers to work with systems (which could be technological or interpersonal in nature). When you communicate online with these different groups, adjust your communication accordingly to develop trust.

Operating Code: Some people intuitively have a sense of rules for themselves and others; others are flexible about the operating parameters; a third group does not care about rules. When you plan your online interactions, craft your communication around each specific group. That way you can prepare your negotiations according to each relevant rule structure and anticipate in advance how to get and keep trust (especially if you can anticipate that some people will abandon rules and start freewheeling).

Pressure Reaction: Some people remember experiences by reliving them without disengaging from them; others are dissociated from past experiences; a third group relives experiences briefly and then disconnects from them. If you intend to use a negotiation strategy that invites people to remember past experiences, first identify the experience as positive or negative, look at potential pressure reactions of the people involved, and evaluate whether the invitation is productive.

Perception: Some people see the world as a series of similar, related things; others see the world as many totally distinct and unrelated things or events. When you broach your subjects online, craft your language to accommodate each person's respective perception of the world.

Target: Some people are perfectionists who obsessively believe that anything other than perfection is failure; others are optimizers content with "good enough." Both types of patterns generally need facilitation to help to foster trust. For example, two perfectionists can be helped by a facilitator who can craft a settlement that integrates ideas from both to form a "perfect" plan that satisfies both parties. A perfectionist and optimizer can be assisted by a facilitator who can prevent buyer's remorse by tempering the perfectionist's wishes even when the optimizer agrees to everything. Even optimizer-only negotiations can be helped by a facilitator who has the foresight to craft a durable settlement by preventing the optimizers from haphazardly slapping down terms that momentarily seem "good enough" but won't stand up to the test of time.

Placement: Some people are very strong "starters" and then lose steam; others are consistent "maintainers" and are superb at keeping relationships going, but cannot start them or shut them down; still others, "completers," have no patience to brainstorm or continue relationships, but they love to finish things. Use the first group to brainstorm solutions, the second group to keep equilibrium during the process, and the third to close the deal.

3.5.1 Summary

In each of the above sets of patterns, you can find unique ways to build trust. Just keep in mind the following:

- Identify each party's specific patterns.
- Establish whether it's the patterns or the information that is causing disagreement.
- Craft your communication (or reframe their communication) into each party's respective patterns if patterns are clashing.
- Send information in communication "envelopes" that are most productive for people and easiest for them to understand.
- Stack (that is, combine) as many patterns as possible to create the most powerful communication.

Remember always that these patterns exist outside people's awareness. While you have a powerful tool and hold an advantage when you carefully collect details of people's preferences, you also have an obligation to be respectful because the patterns are not consciously available to these people. As a result, you can use this reliable blueprint wisely to select any number of approaches to productively create trust online.

4. Decision Factor

The final and most powerful preference is the "decision factor." The decision factor is made up of two components: who the decision-maker is and how that decision-maker makes the decision. Armed with this knowledge you have an extraordinarily strong strategic advantage and ability to create trust online.

Once you know about these elements, you must also be aware of a caveat. During negotiation you may only be communicating with a "recommender" rather than the ultimate decision-maker. As a result, be flexible and prepare to craft your communication in multiple ways so you can accommodate all channels and patterns. That way, even if the offer must go up the negotiation "food chain" you will have satisfied the most highly valued criteria of the ultimate decision-makers so they can say yes.

4.1 Validation

Validation is about who decides. To develop online trust you need to reliably establish who makes the decisions. This is vital and goes a long way in increasing trust online. You risk eroding trust by investing confidence in people appearing to be decision-makers should you discover they are not.

Inside Validators: People who make the actual decisions themselves tell you that they make the decisions. And, even if they say that they check with others and then *they* decide, they are still the real decision-makers.

Outside Validators: People who absolutely need to seek out others for help or opinions are rarely the real decision-makers. In fact, no matter how much information you or others give them, they intuitively need other people to tell them what to do.

Knowing how to differentiate between actual decision-makers and recommenders is critical and the onus to do so rests with you if you want to build and maintain trust online. You must ascertain at the outset of negotiation who the actual decision-makers are and avoid eleventh-hour surprises such as the legal signatories being unavailable to finalize settlement. Establish facts up front in order to keep online trust. Otherwise you risk creating feelings of mistrust when other parties feel misled, duped, or even embarrassed when ostensible decision-makers flounder at the time when others are ready to sign.

4.2 Decision Framework

The decision framework indicates how decisions are made. You will notice that the framework contains two different components. You must satisfy each element before people can say yes. Accordingly, build your strategies around fulfilling both elements.

Activity: This is the first element for making a decision. Before people make any decision, they must see, hear, experience, or read something to satisfy this element. Thus, you must find out just what activity each person needs before the activity threshold is met.

Timeframe: The second element for making a decision relies on people's need to be convinced by a number of examples or over a period of time. There are people who experience what is known as a "reflex" timeframe wherein they accept ideas automatically. Others need either a specific number of examples or passage of a specific length of time before they are convinced. A final group needs repeated reassurance to be convinced. (In this last case you can deal most productively by talking in terms "as if" their needs had been satisfied and then ask them to move on from there.)

5. Technology and Environment

5.1 Einstein Revisited

As mentioned earlier, you can perform the most successful negotiation without using the latest technological "toys." In fact, the most effective technology varies with each negotiation. So, first pay attention to people's communication preferences and patterns, then look for technology that accommodates them best.

Avoid frustration. Evaluate what exists and implement mutually agreeable and compatible technology. Be aware that the highest common denominator usually produces the most effective results. Using advanced equipment at one end and antiquated apparatus at the other generally frustrates all parties. Get creative.

Start building trust by setting up technologically equal environments. That means bringing everyone's expectations and interactions into line. You must do this if you want to set up the most fluid communication when one negotiating side's technology far outstrips that of the other negotiating party (for example, in a case of real-time satellite abilities versus fax). This does not mean everyone sinks to the most primitive technology available. But it may mean you get creative by finding a mutually agreeable location that lends a viable platform that the parties can share.

Resourcefulness is the key. To quote Einstein once again, "Imagination is more important than knowledge."[7] If you approach communication without imagination, you risk setting up an environment that simultaneously frustrates one party with slow turnaround and embarrasses the other because of awkwardness, humiliation, or perhaps pressure resulting from feeling limited to an inferior or more basic technology.

There are two elements to creating trust in online negotiation:

- Learn about and arrange for technology that is generally available in everyone's respective location.
- Accommodate people's communication preferences by arranging for optimum technology and environments.

5.2 Available Technology

In regard to technological awareness you may need to do some homework. You risk much if you only consider simple elements such as synchronous versus asynchronous communication (due to time zones) and believe you have covered all bases.

You will benefit greatly by gaining as much detail as possible about the range and availability of technology in each person's locale. Unless you are so technologically savvy that you can teach a course on technology, you will also profit by finding a reliable consultant who can brief you on technology available in each party's area and can make recommendations, in advance, about reliable equipment. Moreover, keep that consultant's number handy for the times when things don't work as they were intended.

Finally, if you are conducting high-level negotiations, engage a consultant with reliable associates available in the locations of all

---

[7] Quoted by George Viereck, *What Life Means to Einstein*, Saturday Evening Post, Oct. 26, 1929, at 117.

negotiating parties. These associates can assist the parties when technological complications arise. By doing this you demonstrate not only efficiency but also professionalism and consideration that go a long way toward developing trust even before you exchange the first piece of negotiation-specific information.

5.3 Accommodating Preferences

When you arrange technology and environment around communication preferences, you wield considerable influence. Pay attention to communication patterns. In so doing you can choose technology that best fits communication preferences. That choice should override any current technological fads. Adapting to each negotiation is where the real power lies.

For example, consider a negotiation in which a developer is the decision-maker. Suppose she needs to see three examples before she can make a decision. For her, this might be as simple as your sending low-tech blueprints, renderings (i.e., drawings) of the intended elevations, and photos of a similar project already built by the company you represent. With this, you have satisfied her (other-than-conscious) decision-making criteria. This builds trust.

Now look at another example using mental movement (that is, moving toward a goal or avoiding a problem). Consider a vice president of finance who wants to avoid a financial penalty if a project comes in late and who is convinced by reading something once. Here you would do well to arrange to send him a fax or e-mail he could read that contains a contract clause that includes a penalty waiver. In this case, you will have satisfied the vice president's preferences in tandem with building trust online.

In both examples, you can see how technology takes a backseat to satisfying people's respective other-than-conscious preferences when it comes to making decisions.

Despite the preeminence of these decision factors, technology still can assist you when you are looking to create productive environments that build trust when people are connecting. For example, consider doing the following:

For people with visual preferences: Create a clean-looking and bright environment. If you are teleconferencing, consider, for example, placing photos of one party's children in view. This might perhaps personalize the situation and communicate a human side that tends to invite trust.

For people with auditory preferences: Create an environment that is free of distracting conversations and noises. If you negotiate on the telephone or by videoconference, for example, eliminate noisy backgrounds such as faxes, telephones, pagers, mobile telephones, and ambient conversations. When sending reading material make the font very legible. This attention to their preferences leads to trust.

For people with kinesthetic preferences: Ensure that their environment is comfortable and they have a place to put their "stuff." Fill the environment with inviting smells (such as coffee) or tastes (such as snacks). This way you set up a human versus technological environment that creates an inviting mind-set open to trust.

6. Steps to Create Online Trust

6.1 The Plan

It should be clear by now that there is no technological "magic bullet" to building trust. The real magic lies in your resourcefulness and taking your lead from those two-legged critters across the table (virtual or otherwise). And this is actually very good news. In looking back at Einstein's query about the universe, you now know you have the tools—and the ability—to create that friendly universe.

The steps are simple:

- Track people's patterns.
- Communicate using those patterns.
- Communicate respectfully.

Creating trust has always been a challenge, even when people beat drums and hollered over hills before finally seeing each other face-to-face. Today it is no more or less challenging: it is merely different. Technology does not change this. It simply brings greater numbers of people into contact. If you thought that technology has created bigger challenges, relax. And if you still think of technology as overwhelming, then perhaps you have not yet discovered the power in its opportunities.

Technology provides many more choices along with more challenges. As long as you act respectfully and remember that communication is about living, feeling people, you will excel. In doing this, you put the heart and mind in online negotiation. That simple act is how you build trust.

Barbara G. Madonik
President
Unicom Communication Consultants Inc.
379 Winnett Avenue
Toronto, ON M6C 3M2 Canada
Phone: (416) 652-1867
E-mail: barbara.madonik@utoronto.ca

CHAPTER 13

Online Dispute Resolution: Moving Beyond Convenience and Communication

Ethan Katsh[1]

NATIONAL CENTER FOR TECHNOLOGY AND DISPUTE RESOLUTION
AMHERST, MASSACHUSETTS

> If your customer is in Uzbekistan, and the deal goes sour, you better have a better plan than to sue him in the state of Delaware.
> —Peter Phillips[2]

Online dispute resolution (ODR) has recently celebrated a decade of development.[3] Ten years ago, the number of disputes publicly acknowledged to have been resolved through the use of online means was fewer than ten. A year later, in 1999, the National Center for Technology and Dispute Resolution did a pilot project for eBay in which over two hundred disputes were mediated.[4] This was considered a very large number until an Internet start-up called SquareTrade resolved several million disputes during the first few years of the twenty-first century. In 2008, eBay announced that the disputes addressed by its systems numbered over thirty million. All of eBay's disputes were being resolved online. As a result, it is not unfair to say that eBay is the proprietor of the largest small claims court in the world, and that the location of this court is in cyberspace.

In spite of increasing use of ODR, there is still some confusion about what it is. The most common question from people who

---

[1] This article is a product of research supported by National Science Foundation award #0429297: Process Families and Their Application to Online Dispute Resolution, http://www.fastlane.nsf.gov/servlet/showaward?award=0705772 (last visited Aug. 14, 2008).

[2] Attributed to Office.com, When Global B2B Deals Go Bad (Oct. 24, 2000) (article no longer available online).

[3] Ethan Katsh & Leah Wing, *Ten Years of Online Dispute Resolution (ODR): Looking at the Past and Constructing the Future*, U. TOL. L. REV. (2006).

[4] Ethan Katsh, Janet Rifkin, & Alan Gaitenby, *E-commerce, E-disputes, and E-dispute Resolution: In the Shadow of "eBay Law,"* 15 OHIO ST. J. ON DISP. RESOL. 705–34 (2000).

encounter the phrase "online dispute resolution" for the first time is the following:

> Is ODR focused on the resolution of online disputes, e.g. disputes arising out of online activities, or is it focused on the use of online tools and resources to help resolve any and all disputes?

In other words, does the use of the word "online" refer to the nature of the disputes being addressed or does it refer to the medium employed to resolve them?

The simple answer to these questions is that the history of ODR began with a concern over disputes arising out of online activities, such as buyer-seller disputes on eBay, and that success in that arena encouraged the use of ODR more generally. Currently, using the Internet to supplement or support the resolution of both offline and online disputes in some way is quite common. Perhaps more significantly, the value of using the Internet in lieu of (or along with) face-to-face interactions is increasingly recognized.

Interest in ODR during its fairly short history has largely focused on the efficiencies of communicating over a network. The earliest ODR experiments involved the use of e-mail and of people sending and receiving information over the network. Designating the field as *online* dispute resolution seemed appropriate because it was the network element that was novel and that seemed to be replacing the traditional medium of face-to-face communication. It was what the Internet could do (namely, communicate information almost instantly and over great distances) that was new and attractive. Potential savings in time and travel, in convenience and efficiency, were easily understood.

The Internet is a means of communication among humans but it is also more than that. It is a means of linking computers as well as humans and thus can take advantage of the combined information-processing power of both machines and humans. We are moving far beyond the early days of ODR when individuals connected to the network simply exchanged messages with each other. What we are in the midst of is the development of new methods for shaping and processing communication so that computers connected to the network work alongside humans in managing the flow of information. Until now, new opportunities for communication have been the center of attention. The network will always be an indispensable element but it will be joined by more and more powerful capabilities for exploiting the network and adding value to it.

Communication is at the heart of dispute resolution, but managing communication is at the heart of effective dispute resolution. The use of e-mail in early ODR experiments was understandable since it was widely available and easy to use. On the other hand, e-mail software provides relatively little in terms of organizing communications and managing the flow of information. Large numbers of e-mails are difficult to manage and it is not surprising that e-mail is among the least effective online tools available to online dispute resolvers.

The systems used by eBay and SquareTrade are most accurately characterized as technology-assisted negotiation. Communication takes place via password-protected Web sites. Most of this communication is controlled and shaped through forms in which parties select among choices. These are relatively simple disputes and the choices presented to users reflect the experience of the companies as to what the parties' interests might be. In most of these disputes, the parties have already used e-mail to try to resolve the problem and have been unsuccessful. Use of a Web site and forms in lieu of e-mail provides fewer opportunities for uncontrolled communication and, as a result, focuses attention (generally successfully) on options for settlement.

Dispute resolution is an informational process in which parties negotiate (selectively exchange information), mediate (selectively exchange information in a manner that is organized by a mediator),[5] or arbitrate (interpret and apply information that has been agreed upon as authoritative).[6] These informational processes have typically included one or more face-to-face sessions on the assumption that such settings are a rich and efficient means of accomplishing the necessary informational tasks. In mediation, for example, the face-to-face model is believed to be highly effective in generating solutions that are not simply compromises but that meet the interests of parties in creative ways.[7]

The value of the early ODR was questioned by many, who compared it to the richness of face-to-face interactions. The usual response to such challenges was to admit that while this manner of ODR might not match the quality of face-to-face alternative dispute resolution (ADR), it was adequate for many disputes in which the parties were located at a distance and where there were no opportunities for face-to-face meetings. As ODR began to employ the Web and rely less and less on e-mail, however, it became clear that more robust and novel forms of technology-assisted ODR were possible. One of the earliest forms of ODR, blind bidding, is a simple process but a very efficient use of technology that allows an online process to be employed in lieu of a cumbersome and inefficient offline process with the same goal.[8]

---

[5] John D. Feerick, *The Peace-Making Role of a Mediator*, 19 Ohio St. J. on Disp. Resol. 229–48 (2003).

[6] David Dickinson, *A Comparison of Conventional, Final-Offer, and "Combined" Arbitration for Dispute Resolution*, 57 Indus. & Lab. Rel. Rev. 288–301 (2004).

[7] Roger Fisher, Bruce M. Patton & William L. Ury, Getting to Yes: Negotiating Agreement Without Giving In (1992).

[8] Blind bidding involves each party privately submitting its offer or demand to a computer. If the parties are within a certain percentage, they agree ahead of time to split the difference. If there is no agreement, the offers and demands are not revealed to the other side.

Another prominent ODR application, Smartsettle,[9] is indeed smart, at least in the sense of employing a sophisticated algorithm to evaluate how parties value their interests and goals.

In *Online Dispute Resolution: Resolving Conflicts in Cyberspace*,[10] my colleague Janet Rifkin and I argued that technology can be looked at as a "fourth party," an element in the dispute resolution process that can play various roles in consensus building, in decision making and decision support, and in the interaction between the parties in dispute and a third-party neutral. The metaphor suggests that ODR should not strive to create online models that simply copy offline approaches. Rather, computers linked to the network can provide capabilities that were not available before and that were not employed in face-to-face meetings. We have only just begun to see the power of the fourth party. Over time, software will be developed that takes advantage of machines to compute as well as communicate, to model and monitor, to lay out options and also evaluate options, to provide data necessary for decisions and also to represent data visually so that it can be understood and employed in new ways.

The value of the fourth-party metaphor is that it focuses attention on capabilities that machines have that humans might not have or that cannot occur in a physical face-to-face setting. Processes relying on face-to-face interaction, for example, are framed by laws of physics that are accepted as inevitable. There are limits in how information can be exchanged and how meetings can take place. Face-to-face meetings are extraordinarily useful but the need to travel limits the amount and kind of interaction that might take place in between physical meetings. Networks open up the potential for lifting such constraints not only by making communication possible, but also by providing access to software that can assist in identifying and evaluating interests, options, and solutions.

As an example, consider a piece of software under development at the National Center for Technology and Dispute Resolution at the University of Massachusetts. The purpose of this software is to allow brainstorming at a distance. This is clearly a tool that can make the process of brainstorming more efficient, as the software removes the need for the large sheets of paper that are often taped to the walls of a room used for mediation or negotiation. There can be efficiencies, in other words, even when the parties use the tool when they meet face to face. More interesting, however, is when the software is used when the parties are at a distance. In such a context, brainstorming can occur anonymously. Whether this is desirable or not is something the mediator will need to determine, but it is an option that is not available in the traditional face-to-face setting.

---

[9] http://www.smartsettle.com.
[10] Ethan Katsh & Janet Rifkin, Online Dispute Resolution: Conflict Resolution in Cyberspace (2001).

ODR began as a means to deliver human expertise over the network. As ODR matures, the fourth-party metaphor suggests that the expertise and capabilities of machines will also be delivered over the network. Most users are already aware that the network can make it possible to do many things faster online, to do them at great distances, and often to do them more cheaply than was previously possible. On the other hand, it is not yet widely understood how computers connected to a network might supplement the expertise of a human third party or add quality and value to the dispute resolution process in ways that are not possible in traditional face-to-face processes.

How can we understand what this emerging relationship between human and machine will be like? How might, for example, interaction with distant computers be different from the manner in which many online tools are already being used? This is a challenging question because computers can have capabilities that range from the highly simple to exceedingly complex. They can appear to be discrete tools, such as a calculator or whiteboard, or a much more complex and sophisticated presence. Quite understandably, most of what we currently employ technology for in the dispute resolution process falls on the simple side of the spectrum. The computer is, in general, used as a tool that is invoked when needed. The growing array of available tools, such as calendars or mechanisms for prioritizing issues and concerns, already provide considerable conveniences and help the third party perform his or her role. Yet, the role of such tools is largely to bring more convenience and efficiency, a goal not all that different from many informational tools of the past, such as pencils, magic markers, or telephones. Processes that employ such tools may fall in the broad category of online dispute resolution but what the machine is doing might not be considered an altogether new role or process.

Dispute resolution is not the only field attempting to understand how growth in information processing capabilities can change the inherent nature of some process or concept. Professor Neal Katyal of the Georgetown University School of Law has explored the impact of computers on conspiracy law, an area of law that would seem to have almost no connection with processes of dispute resolution. Katyal's position about what computers are, about what they are capable of, and about how we should think of them is nevertheless quite relevant. Katyal suggests that a computer is not simply a tool but something that can substitute for a human co-conspirator. He writes:

> If the law treats an agreement between Jones and Smith to engage in illegal activity as a crime, why should it not equally treat Jones' use of a computer as a species of crime? By substituting a computer for co-conspirators, a culprit is in a sense simply choosing to conspire with his computer. And this fact might justify treating a computer as a living entity, the way

we see a corporation as a living entity, and suggest that Jones should be punished for engaging in a quasi-conspiracy with his computer. Federal law already punishes the use of the mails and wires to facilitate a criminal offense; these technologies are ones that permit co-conspirators to act in concert and magnify their power. . . . A computer can conduct many of the tasks co-conspirators used to undertake, from breaking and entering to asset management and inventory, to keeping accounting records . . . computers and co-conspirators are substitutes for each other. The solution proposed would not necessarily require treating computers as full co-conspirators, but it would require eliminating the law's current conceptualization of a computer as simply a method of crime, not a type of (or substitute for) a participant in crime.[11]

Katyal recognizes that there are qualitative differences between technical applications and tools that are at the simple end of the spectrum and that assist a person planning to commit a crime, and other more complex devices that can displace or even substitute for a co-conspirator. He points out, for example, that guns are tools that may be used as "force multipliers," reducing the number of conspirators needed to commit a crime. Yet, he adds, computers are different in that a computer "will generally have a multifaceted relationship with a criminal that more closely approximates the relationship to a co-conspirator than a one-dimensional item like a gun."[12]

There is a fine (and currently not very clear) line distinguishing the computer used as a tool from the computer playing a larger role. We are in an impressive but early stage of trying to both use and understand machines that are connected to the Internet. It is not surprising that tools that substitute for familiar tasks are understood better than machines that are doing something no tool has historically been capable of. Nor is it surprising that efficiency of simple tools is being perfected more quickly than that of more advanced applications. This is also a period, however, when we should be wary of treating computers as having only simple applications, or even of trying to infer future capabilities from current capabilities.

A Supreme Court opinion a few years ago referred to the Internet as being "another method for making information available in a school or library . . . [and is] no more than a technological extension of the book stack."[13] This is an unfortunate and highly incomplete characterization of what the Internet is, even today, and a thoroughly

---

[11] Neal Kumar Katyal, *Criminal Law in Cyberspace*, 149 U. Pa. L. Rev. 1003–14 (2001).
[12] *Id.*
[13] United States v. Am. Library Ass'n, 123 S. Ct. 2297 (2002), quoting S. Rep. No. 106-141, at 7 (1999).

incorrect analogy to what it will be like in the future. Ever since the beginning of the Internet, attempts to understand the new technology using metaphors have not met with much success. These have included libraries, the Wild West, information superhighway, and others. They have all proved to be inadequate because the Internet and World Wide Web can take many shapes and engage in many functions. For our purposes, a more suitable frame of reference might be the growing power of machines that play chess where, it has been written, "we are sharing our world with another species, one that gets smarter and more independent every year."[14]

For ODR to be successful, it is necessary to have software applications that use the information-processing powers of machines and that not only enable interactions among the parties but also enhance them. We would like software development in this field to be proceeding more quickly than it is. Perhaps as important as the software, however, is the development of a wider understanding of what computers are capable of.

The earliest Web pages only displayed information and many, if not most, users of the Web still think of the Web as primarily a vehicle for accessing information at a distance. Over time, however, the Web has morphed into a space with many familiar kinds of processes and activities. Shopping, investing, gambling, and learning are all informational activities in which accessing information combined with processing information leads to a new range of possible activities. Dispute resolution is a process that may not develop at the same speed as something like e-commerce, but growth of the field requires some understanding that the Web has moved beyond simpler informational processes such as publishing.

How shall we envision the future? Traditional alternative dispute resolution processes are generally not very *efficient* but they are *effective*. ODR, in its short history, has emphasized efficiencies but some of these efficiencies (e.g., reducing face-to-face meetings) have been assumed to be less effective than what is being replaced. Dispute resolution needs attention and even investment not merely because numbers of disputes are increasing. We also need intelligent "fourth parties" because the nature of disputing is changing as well. Disputes reflect the environment, and the environment in which we live and work is one that is growing more interactive and complex. In an increasingly global environment, negotiations and disputes frequently involve more parties, more issues, more diversity, more jurisdictions, and, as a result, more potential complications.

The technology of the future that probably intrigues the dispute resolution field the most concerns video. At high cost today, it

---

[14] Steven Levy, *Machine vs. Man: Checkmate*, NEWSWEEK, July 21, 2003, at 51.

is possible to create spaces where parties at a distance feel as if they are in the same room. It is reasonable to expect that costs will decline and high-resolution videoconferencing will be widely available. Yet, it is a mistake to think of such a development as the Holy Grail of ODR. Such capabilities will certainly be valuable, but face-to-face interaction, whether in a physical or virtual space, will still be labor intensive and, as a result, not necessarily the choice for many of the conflicts that will need to be addressed.

Another competitor for the ODR technology of the future is the cell phone. Cell phones, particularly "smartphones," are devices that combine communication with information processing. They are computers and are the computers with which most of us interact in a very varied manner, using voice and video in addition to text. As a ubiquitous wireless device with communications and computing power, it is the cell phone that has most of the elements that need to be programmed in order for us to have not a PDA that is a "personal digital assistant" but a PDA that is a "personal dispute assistant."

The original ideas for ODR came from an understanding that new kinds and very large numbers of transactions and relationships would inevitably lead to disputes. It was also clear that traditional legal institutions would be unable to meet the demand for adequate and appropriate dispute resolution. What was (and remains) more difficult to understand were the deep-rooted changes in many of our institutions that would be occurring and that would bring attention to the need for powerful new tools and resources. Consider, for example, the following framework for trying to understand how we should view the impact of digital information technologies on law. Writing in 1995 at a time when Amazon and eBay did not exist and predictions of an Internet bubble growing and then bursting would not have been believable, UCLA law school professor Eugene Volokh suggested the following:

> There are, in my view, four basic stories about technology that color much of how people speculate about the future. The first is the story of printing. In the mid-1400s, Gutenberg invented the printing press (or, to be precise, movable type). In the centuries that followed, printing helped bring about the Reformation, the Industrial Revolution, and modern liberal democracy. Gutenberg wasn't trying to change the world: He was just making a faster, cheaper way to produce a particular commodity. But, of course, the consequence wasn't simply that book buyers saved money; the technological change dramatically altered the social and political landscape. Likewise, three hundred and fifty years after Gutenberg, Eli Whitney patented the cotton gin. It certainly wasn't intended to extend slavery by decades and kill hundreds of thousands people in a civil war, but it may have had a big hand in doing both.

The second is the story of the slide rule. The slide rule was a marvelously elegant mathematical device, and it earned its manufacturers millions. In 1967, one such manufacturer, Keuffel & Esser Co., commissioned a study on what life would be like in a hundred years. The study predicted 3-D television and domed cities, but it didn't predict that within five years the electronic calculator would be the slide rule's death. Beware, the slide rule story says—if you don't foresee technological changes, you're in trouble.

The third is the story of videophones. Of course, there aren't any mass-market videophones, and that is the story. Thirty years ago, people were predicting them, and for thirty years they've been nowhere to be seen. Futurists also predicted "bedmaking machines, home dry-cleaning, showers that clean people with sound waves, robots that cut lawns and fight wars, steam- and electric-driven cars, foam-filled tires, plastic teeth and tooth-decay vaccine." We're still waiting.

Finally, the fourth story—one that's less exciting and therefore less often told—is the story of the ATM. ATMs have made banking more convenient and saved people countless hours of standing in bank lines—a really useful invention, but nothing earth-shattering. Technology solved a problem, made our lives easier, maybe changed the economics of an industry or two, but that was that.[15]

As we consider the future of dispute resolution, which is basically an informational activity, should we expect the appearance only of more conveniences or should we look forward to new models, approaches, and systems? We certainly do not envision that human third-party neutrals will go the way of slide rules. Given what has occurred in the past fifteen years, however, it is not unrealistic to expect that the tools and resources available to those involved in disputes will be greatly expanded. Today, a little more than a decade after Volokh was writing, we do have phones with video capabilities and, interestingly, these cameras are most common on cellular phones, devices that might have been considered more fanciful in 1995 than phones with cameras.

We also still have ATMs that are called ATMs and they are still a convenience. Yet ATMs are not simply a device to extract cash but are part of the revolution in banking and financial services. The ATM itself may not be "earth-shattering," but the changes in institutions dealing with money might very well fit in this category. For dispute resolution, the impact of the new technologies is slower but it is ongoing and will inevitably be of increasing interest and value to us. As Tom

---

[15] Eugene Volokh, *Technology and the Future of Law*, 47 STAN. L. REV. 1375–1403 (1995).

Stipanowich, a leading figure in the dispute resolution field, perceptively observed when asked about the future of dispute resolution, "the overarching factors are globalization and information technology."[16]

Ethan Katsh, Professor of Legal Studies
Director
National Center for Information
Technology and Dispute Resolution
107 Gordon Hall
University of Massachusetts
Amherst, MA 01002
Phone: (413) 545-5879
Fax: (603) 676-5752
E-mail: katsh@legal.umass.edu

---

[16] Q & A with Tom Stipanowich, http://law.pepperdine.edu/straus/news_events/news/032008_stipanowich.html (last visited Aug. 14, 2008).

CHAPTER 14

Communication Toolbox for a 2.0 World: Essential Actions for Effective Virtual Collaboration

Stewart L. Levine
RESOLUTIONWORKS[1]

Collaboration is a key driver of overall performance of companies around the world. Its impact is twice as significant as a company's aggressiveness in pursuing new market opportunities (strategic) and five times as significant as the external market environment (market turbulence). Collaboration can positively impact each of the gold standards of performance: profitability, growth and sales growth to determine a company's overall performance in the marketplace.

> —Impact of Collaboration on Business Performance, Frost and Sullivan (2007), sponsored by Verizon and Microsoft

Becoming a good communicator is hard and demands detailed, analytical work; however, communication skills are also the most important muscles you can develop for being more effective in your professional life. Communication skills help to effectively coordinate the work of many, develop teamship, and foster collaboration—deeds of effective leadership and management. The best part is that communication is a skill you can learn. In a globalizing world, communication is no longer limited by distance, time, culture, or even language. Technology facilitates international communications often in the form of written correspondences. Furthermore, communication in a virtual environment requires even more diligence in paying attention to the details and nuances than regular communication, and it is becoming increasingly more essential to the working environment.

---

[1] Note: Parts of this chapter were specially adapted from DAVID COLEMAN & STEWART LEVINE, COLLABORATION 2.0: TOOLS AND BEST PRACTICES FOR SUCCESSFUL COLLABORATION IN A WEB 2.0 WORLD.

1. Special Challenges and Opportunities for a 2.0 World

We are all navigating in uncharted territory. Computers and the Internet are a relatively new phenomenon, and genuinely virtual collaboration in a world of distributed work is even newer. Most people working in this area have little, if any, experience working in this way. Thus, we are presented with an environment in which people sink or swim according to their instincts, as well as to their ability to pay attention to the continuously available feedback loop as they "Braille" their way along. I believe that integrating the following seven considerations into your work ethic will make your virtual communications more effective:

1. Become a conscious communicator.
2. Recognize cultural differences.
3. Choose the communication channel.
4. Emphasize invitation, focus engagement, and build trust.
5. Honor formality and process design.
6. Use the 3 V's: visual, vocal, and verbal.
7. Leadership demands creativity.

1.1 Become a Conscious Communicator

It is always important to be a conscious communicator. Every time we communicate (verbally and nonverbally), we project a sense of who we are. How we are perceived by others is a reflection of how we communicate, and good leaders are attentive and considered in their communication styles. This is the most essential aspect of forming and/ or managing successful virtual teams, and it is the first thing that one needs to master for the virtual environment. The key things you need to stay conscious of include:

- **Trust-building and expectation-setting.** As a team leader it falls to you to create an environment in which people give trust to and receive trust from the other parties with which they are working. Before any work can be accomplished, trust must be established between parties. One of the key ways to do this is to ensure that clear expectations are set at the beginning of every project.
- **Technology and communication training.** Because the participants are working at a distance, people may find both their technological and communication skills challenged. It is important for everyone to have the resources for the education and learning they need. A little training before work is started can go a long way.
  - **Formality of process and communication.** When we work virtually, it is important to develop, agree on, and use more formal communication processes. This allows all parties equal

involvement in project planning and formation. If communication channels are not formalized, things can get out of hand very quickly as you lose immediate access to a receiver's unfiltered responses that in a face-to-face world you would be able to adjust to or push back against. In tense situations noninstant communication channels can be a double-edged sword as the buffer of time enables both sober reflection and growing anger. Checking in more regularly with parties on your team further opens up communication channels and can help to avoid the festering of emotions.

- **Checking in as a way of being.** When people work at a distance, it becomes essential for them to reach out and connect with each other to make sure they remain engaged, committed, connected, motivated, and inspired. The manner of reaching out is your choice, but staying connected is essential to building a high-performance team.

- **Metrics for both process and productivity.** After everyone is prepared for virtual communication and the pathways for communication have been established, metrics should be put in place because "that which cannot be measured cannot be managed." Every project needs objective metrics for determining success in terms of desired outcome and in terms of the process used. The objective is to have measurable criteria to which you can say "yes or no" in terms of results achieved and efficacy of the process.

- **Doable tasks.** Begin with small tasks that provide the empowering experience of accomplishment. It is important to acknowledge those triumphs.

- **100 percent responsibility.** Everyone on the team is responsible for results and everyone needs to take total responsibility for the project and its execution. It's all too easy to blame challenges on others when you are at a distance.

- **The reign of creativity.** Given that the territory is new, there is no off-the-shelf manual that will tell people exactly what to do and what will work. We are only limited by our own creativity and thoughtfulness.

1.2 Recognize Cultural Differences

Each cultural group (whether defined by race, religion, national origin, gender, age, values, work habits, or communication pattern) is distinctive and deserves the effort of a leader to appreciate what makes it unique. Although cultural characteristics appear to produce vast differences between people, which are very real, they are not the entire story. It is critical to remember that beneath these surface differences we still have more in common than not. A leader who becomes "multilingual" with respect to culture can bridge the gaps and draw on those deeper commonalities by maintaining awareness of cultural differences. Understanding these cultural differences and inclinations can then help you to pick the most effective communication channel(s) for your team.

1.3 Choose the Communication Channel

Text message, e-mail, voicemail, telephone, and videoconference are all available options. You must make deliberate choices about the channel you use, which often depends on what's available and at what cost. It is important to think about the nature of the interaction, importance, participants, objectives, and user sophistication. In general, more personal and more intimate mediums have a broader "bandwidth" for sharing information. However, when things become so hot between people that communication cannot be achieved without excessive emotion, the buffer of a narrower channel is useful.

1.4 Emphasize Invitation, Focus Engagement, and Build Trust

Once communication channels have been formalized, people need to be graciously invited into the project, welcomed by the leader, and introduced to the rest of the team. A virtual team space (such as Facebook) can be most helpful for introductions. The special skills and natural genius each person has should be communicated to the entire group. Part of forming the team involves articulating mission, vision, and values as an element of setting team norms. A team also needs a detailed agreement that will serve as a charter for their activity. If you find yourself on the edges of a group, it is important to be accountable for teaching others *how* to include you.

1.5 Honor Formality and Process Design

It is important to pay attention to formality and detail when building trust and setting expectations. This includes such things as clear agreements for action and results, maintaining "beginner's mind," and reframing rough patches as being learning experiences. Remember that function drives form and that the establishment of an ongoing feedback loop is essential for stewarding results in this new territory.

1.6 Use the 3 Vs: Visual, Vocal, and Verbal

Although it is sometimes hard to believe, our face-to-face interactions convey far more than the words we say. Face-to-face delivery is composed of 55 percent visual appearance, 38 percent tone or mood, and 7 percent word content. In other words, more than 90 percent of what we "say" is communicated nonverbally, allowing us to detect tone, humor, and irony. In the often-text-based world of virtual communication, we must choose our words carefully to fully describe our meaning, and in the case of multicultural communications it helps to avoid colloquial phrases that may not translate across languages. Written communication thus needs to become more like writing a novel, adding descriptions and specifying tone in our writings. Editing becomes crucial, as we can add layers of visual and auditory cues through revisions to our written communications. Equally important is the need to quickly switch communication channels depending on the kind of conversation we want to have. It becomes critical to "listen" very carefully to what is written. For example, emoticons (funny faces :-)) are a tool that adds nonverbal information (in this case, a lighter, playful tone) if used mindfully.

1.7 Leadership Demands Creativity

A guiding principle for collaborating in the virtual world is to use your creativity to interpolate and approximate the best practices that parallel what works in the physical, face-to-face (or "f2f") world. Team activities such as happy hours, lunches, walks, outings, celebrations, games, and contests will continue to work in virtual spaces, provided we can adapt them inventively to this new medium. This takes expansive vision and a willingness on everyone's part to play along, but this also keeps everyone in the same context.

2. Key Principles in Both Real-World and Virtual Communication

The following principles seem to be universal, applying in both in virtual worlds and face to face. Applying these principles virtually, however, takes some thought and intention.

1. Positive team-formation considerations
   a. Developing emotional intelligence
   b. Object/subject
   c. Nonverbal communications
   d. Listening skills
   e. S.O.F.T.E.N.
   f. Instruments demonstrate differences
   g. Goal "agreements for results"
   h. Delegating effectively
   i. Providing effective feedback
2. Working through conflict
   a. Moving through roadblocks
   b. Responding and reacting
   c. Automatic writing

    d. Don't bark back at barking dogs
    e. Anger and aggression
    f. No difficult people—only different people
    g. "I" statements
    h. Mirroring/identifying
    i. Know/do/feel

2.1 Positive Team Formations

2.1.1 Developing Emotional Intelligence

When dealing with virtual teams it helps to first develop your emotional intelligence. Traditionally, intelligence has been measured in terms of IQs or "intelligence quotients." Though this measure of cognitive ability is valuable, it is not the only critical factor. More-recent research suggests that many different kinds of intelligence are valuable when working with others. One of the most important ones for working collaboratively is "emotional intelligence" because communication involves the many nuances of human interaction. This serves us well for a few reasons that track the five basic tenets of emotional intelligence as conceived by Daniel Goleman and expressed in his 1995 book, *Emotional Intelligence*, that popularized the field:

- **Self-awareness:** This is the foundational skill that enables us to separate self from behavior through observation and reflection. It enables you to make more discerning assessments about yourself and your verbal and nonverbal communication.
- **Self-regulation:** The ability to control what you do or say and how you react in the face of communication coming at you.
- **Empathy:** Your ability to stand in someone else's shoes and understand his or her perspective. The following quote sums up empathy and compassion: "If you knew the secret history of those you would like to punish, you would see a sorrow and suffering enough to disarm all your hostility."
- **Self-motivation:** The ability to be proactive and not wait for things to come at you.
- **Social skills:** Your capacity for navigating in groups of people and recognizing the impacts of your words and deeds on others.

2.1.2 Object/Subject

In that vein, Martin Buber makes the very important distinction of "I-It" relationships and "I-Thou" relationships. I-It relationships are object oriented: we think of others as objects to be used and manipulated for our own purposes. I-Thou relationships, on the other hand, are subjective: you care about the person. When you are operating in a virtual environment, the use of language is essential, and object/

subject statements can add an element of the tone and flavor of communications lost without face-to-face interaction.

I believe that one of the tragedies of the global corporate culture that we have become part of is that we reduce others to objects, tools to be used for our own advancement. People stop being "instrumental" and are instead reduced to being "instruments." This is not merely a moral plea: our work often suffers from this failure to know about people as individuals. If you can step beyond the people-as-object mentality and relate to others as compassionate human beings, your connection and communication will be much more effective. The I-Thou context will generate a much deeper level of concern and respect, and others will listen more attentively to your messages.

2.1.3 Nonverbal Communications

Another skill that can aid in team building is a mastery of nonverbal communications. Communication is composed of three parts:

- **Visual:** appearance of the deliverer
- **Vocal:** tone or mood of our message
- **Verbal:** content of the words

About 90 percent of what we "say" is nonverbal, as mentioned previously. We communicate by the way we look and the tone, mood, and effect of what we say. This is critical to remember. You can deliver any kind of news and minimize the push-back depending on your appearance and the tone of your message. Mastering these "nonverbal communications" is difficult in the text-heavy world of virtual communication, but it is also critical for delivering bad news electronically. It is essential to use words or other symbolic visual and tonality representations when dealing in a verbal medium. The art of narrative becomes a critical skill as you do your best to add visual and tonal components to verbal communication.

2.1.4 Listening Skills

Effective communication is a two-way, give-and-take, interactive, iterative process. It is essential to spend as much time hearing their message as composing yours. The best way I know to fully understand and appreciate the value of listening is to spend some time only listening. I often suggest to people that they wear a sign throughout a normal day saying:

I'm not speaking today, only listening

People are often amazed at how much they miss because they are focused on their own voice. Even more important is the realization that most people never fully give themselves to the listening process because they are so focused on mentally preparing their response before the speaker has finished. Even a written message can take on a different meaning when you become an observer and read it for the second time. Here are some tips that will help:

- **Actively listen:** This means whole-being listening. Realizing what is behind the words, observing with your eyes, ears, and heart and thinking about what is not being said. It requires using your thinking speed wisely to interpret and fill in the blank spaces that the speaker's words do not fill because your mind processes information much more quickly than the speaker can speak.
- **Paraphrase:** This is the best way to make sure the bridge is connected—feed the message back in your own words and see if you are connected by the shared meaning that is established.
- **Engage fully:** Give all of your *attention* and *presence*.
- **Remove environmental distractions:** Make sure nothing gets in the way of you and the other speakers. Sorry: multitasking may be great in theory, but when your attention is diluted you miss critical parts of the message and you distance the speaker.
- **Do not interrupt:** One of our biggest mistakes is cutting people off after they deliver part of their message. We begin asking questions based on what we think is important and their complete message gets lost.
- **Hold judgments:** Our minds function like judgment machines making relative comparisons about what we see, hear, and think. Our minds have a constant chatter informing us that "his hair is too long" or "that will never work." We can mindfully observe our own internal judgments, hold them in abeyance, and not treat them as "truths" that must immediately be shared or acted upon. That way you can listen all the way through and make a more considered response.
- **Ask questions:** This demonstrates that you are interested and provides a more complete explication and understanding of what is said.
- **Take notes:** Rather than interrupt, save your questions by taking notes.
- **Do not anticipate what they are saying or focus on your response:** Wait until they are done; digest and then respond to the message.

Remember: Listening builds relationships!

2.1.5 S.O.F.T.E.N.

S.O.F.T.E.N. is an acronym describing how to be effective in face-to-face communication, but its advice can be adapted to have great value for any kind of exchange. Here's the acronym and my translation for the world of virtual communication:

Smile—Be pleasant in what you have to say. Communicate with diplomacy and tact even when delivering bad news. Be mindful of word choice.

Open—Do not hold back. Share the feelings behind your words when appropriate. Be available for the response.

Forward lean—Engage with them and show that you are interested.

Territory—Be alert to the other's response indicating that you are pushing too hard.

Eye contact—Meet them and engage, for five to seven seconds.

Nod—Always acknowledge what they say to show you are listening.

2.1.6 Instruments Demonstrate Differences

There are many different "instruments" that reveal style differences in different aspects of communication. They include:

- PSI—Personal Styles Inventory
- DISC—Dominance, Influence, Steadiness, Conscientiousness
- MBTI—Myers-Briggs Type Indicator
- Influence Inventory
- Relationship Strategies
- Thomas Killian Conflict Style

These instruments serve a few specific purposes in the workplace: they make us aware of the different ways people receive and deliver information. These differences usually explain why we are challenged communicating with particular individuals. They also enable us to use what we learn about our audiences so we can communicate more effectively.

Using an instrument for a team or work group and making people aware of the styles of others is a very useful tool for developing effectiveness in communicating to particular individuals. The instruments reveal preferences along a continuum of opposite styles. They shed light on why you may be having difficulty communicating with some individuals. They provide information and strategies on the best way to communicate with people of the opposite or the same styles. They deliver the message that although we tend to have preferences because of our experience, how we developed, or our genetic inclination, we have the capacity to consciously choose to "flex" our style so we can be more effective in dealing with people who have different preferences. "Flexing" is the way we develop our communication muscles!

2.1.7 Goal "Agreements for Results"

The best and most effective communication has a purpose in mind: action. Otherwise our talk is mere banter. What can we agree to actually *do* together? The goal is joint action; everything else is often frustrating idle chitchat. The purpose of collaborative communication is to construct a shared vision in terms of desired accomplishment and a road map to reaching that goal. You can think of your virtual teammates as family: since you can't spend your life in agonizing rebellion against it, you can instead chose to love it.

2.1.8 Delegating Effectively

When giving someone something to do, it is critical to provide clear directions that are:

- Specific
- Measurable
- Time-sensitive (as a "by when" requirement)
- Part of an ongoing conversation
- Negotiable

These help to ensure that responsibility is correctly allocated as task completion deadlines come and go.

2.1.9 Providing Effective Feedback

When you are providing feedback, you are usually responding to another person's product or service or opinions. In doing so, especially when it's negative feedback, you must take care of the person and provide actionable information. The tips for doing it well include:

- Comment on the behavior, not the person.
- Know that timeliness is essential.
- For negative feedback, consider telephone as a better channel.
- Treat the communication like in a long-term relationship.
- Be constructive, not judgmental—tell them what they can do and by when.
- Be specific.
- Ask if it would be valuable for them.
- Remember, it's about growth and learning.

2.2 Working Through Conflict

2.2.1 Moving Through Roadblocks

The context in which we communicate is filled with the potential for miscommunication. Let's say you want to get a message to your colleague in Germany (fluent in English, but as a second language) about a new person who will join your team on a very large consulting project. You both have known this person for many years and have your own perceptions of her. Although she has the reputation of "technical genius," she has some quirky personal characteristics.

When you are about to share your perceptions of this person, you begin by coding the message through your own filters. When your colleague receives the message, he decodes it through his perceptual filters. Add to this the use of asynchronous e-mail and you begin to understand how the filters and the medium present natural roadblocks to creating shared meaning, the goal of effective communication. All of these vectors make us realize how artful communication is, and how difficulties are usually more structural than intentional.

The most effective communicators work at it. They have the ability and persistence to both anticipate and move through roadblocks until shared meaning is created.

2.2.2 Responding and Reacting

How you engage with others is a critical part of the communication process. Whether you *respond* or *react* goes a long way in determining the outcome of the interaction. A reaction is a reply or behavior prompted by external influences. Reactions are automatic and immediate, and often have undesirable complications. The critical factor is remembering what my mentor told me many years ago:

You cannot unpunch someone!

A response, in contrast, is a reply or behavior stemming from internal knowledge based on values, ethics, and standards that have been personally developed. The response is based on a choice after reflection about the specific outcome you want. Self-control and self-reflection are both critical to responding instead of merely reacting.

2.2.3 Automatic Writing

If, while in the grip of emotion, you want to dash off a letter of rage, composing it can be a good idea. Let the rage rip through the page. Do not send it. **Always address it to yourself or put it in a word file**; saving the letter as a draft still risks the letter being sent even accidentally. Come back to it in twenty-four hours and think about the *response* (instead of the reaction) you really want to send in terms of the end result you are looking for. You can also use this technique if you are unsure of *how* you want to respond. Write for ten minutes to discover the response inside you.

2.2.4 Don't Bark Back at Barking Dogs

The worst mistake you can make with people who are speaking louder to make their point is to try and "out-loud" them. All that does is add fuel to the fire and generate an even louder response. When they are gripped with this kind of emotion, the best thing to do is to de-escalate the situation by speaking about the facts that have made them so emotional. This return to reason will usually calm people down. This applies particularly to purely verbal communication. In an e-mail, no one can tell if you are calm or shouting, so if you can, pick up the phone!

2.2.5 Anger and Aggression

Anger is the emotion engendered by an expectation of or unacceptable behavior on the part of others. Aggression is the behavior to which you are driven by unpleasant negative emotions, including anger. These emotions will always get in the way. It's not unusual to feel anger as a result of someone's words or actions. The skill is to manage what you do in response.

One way of looking at what we do after someone communicates to us is to choose how we tend to respond. The choice might be characterized by one of the following modes: Passive, Assertive, or Aggressive.

PASSIVE	ASSERTIVE	AGGRESSIVE
Failure to care for self	Courage	Failure to care for other
Violation of own rights	Connection	Violation of other's rights
	Caring	

Assertive behavior respects everyone's needs!

The chart sums it up beautifully. Following it is guaranteed to improve your effectiveness.

2.2.6 No Difficult People—Only Different People

Many of us have the tendency to give up too quickly and abandon our goal of building bridges to communicating with others. We make the assessment that others will not (or cannot) understand the message we are trying to deliver because they are too "difficult." A critical distinction is the difference between "difficult behavior" and "being a difficult person." One is about character, the other about action. I always assume that the trouble is behavioral, and that the behavior can be improved through learning and feedback that is given in the spirit of generating improved effectiveness and delivered without revealing personal judgments. See "Providing Effective Feedback" earlier in this chapter for more on how to make this distinction.

2.2.7 "I" Statements

Taking ownership of your message is one of the most critical and most underutilized techniques for effective communication. In my experience, the great mistake we make is to criticize the words or deeds of another by judging them. A classic example is:

"You make me so angry when you are late."

That is a double whammy, blaming someone for your negative emotion and judging his behavior as "late." This type of communication is guaranteed to generate the push-back of a defensive response. A much more effective message would be:

"I was very angry when you arrived at nine after you promised to be here at eight."

Let him assess his behavior and you will likely get an apology and a promise to do better. The formula is:

"I was (your emotion) when you (describe their behavior)."

2.2.8 Mirroring/Identifying

Communicating is about building a bridge between you and the other. It is always a give-and-take process, so it is critical to establish rapport before delivering your message. One of the best techniques for doing so is to mirror and identify. You want to send a message back with a similar mood or tone to establish connection. You can demonstrate your connection by showing that you understand what they are saying by using an example from your own life. Once you are synchronized, then you can deliver your message.

This technique takes a page from neurolinguistic programming (NLP). This powerful body of communication tools from the 1980s was so popular in the world of sales and influencing others that some people were concerned it was unethical because of the inherent power of manipulation. The premise was that once you mirrored and established rapport you could then lead the conversation where you wanted it to go and others would follow at an unconscious level. Essentially, it puts people at ease, which fosters open communication.

2.2.9 Know/Do/Feel

One of the key failures of the communication process is the failure to think carefully about the message you want to deliver before composing and delivering your words. I frame this kind of communicating as "thinking out loud." It is the antithesis of the way author Ernest Hemingway described his process: "I think a lot and write very little." For me, a simple formula for avoiding this pitfall is the mantra of "Know/Do/Feel." Before you deliver any communication it is imperative to ask yourself:

"What do you want them to know?"
"What do you want them to do?"
"How do you want them to feel?"

If you do not have a clear answer to at least one of the questions, then you have nothing to say and you might refrain from speaking.

3. Summary and Conclusion

Thoughtfulness, emotional intelligence, consciousness: if we can communicate in a manner consistent with those principles, we will navigate the virtual world in a more effective manner.
Remember:

Show Up
Pay Attention
Tell Your Truth
Don't Be Attached to the Outcome
—Angelis Arrien, Ph.D., *The Four-Fold Way*

Here is my translation:

Presence is essential.
Listen.
Be cautious when thinking you have THE truth.
Hold communication as a teaching and learning process.

Stewart L. Levine
9015 Golf Links Rd.
Oakland, CA 94605
Phone: (510) 777-1166
Fax: (510) 291-9697
E-mail: resolutionworks@msn.com

CHAPTER 15

Understanding the Game and the Playing Field

Charles M. Taylor
CHARLES M. TAYLOR, PC
PHILADELPHIA, PENNSYLVANIA

1. Introduction

An international business negotiation presents many more variables than a domestic transaction, and it is useful to draw on the experience of competitive games in preparing a checklist and strategy for the negotiation. The analogy cannot be pursued too far, but it is helpful to use the experience of preparing for athletic competition as one prepares for the unexpected and the unknown aspects of a negotiation. The issues are similar: one tries to estimate a relatively unknown opponent and then devise a strategy for successful action.

Americans often use sports analogies to explain or clarify business situations. Such analogies are readily understood, and the American business press has adopted this approach in describing domestic and international problems. Commentators refer to the "rounds" in the World Trade Organization (WTO) negotiations and the need for a "level playing field" (equality). Seeing a business negotiation in terms of athletic competition may be somewhat adversarial, but in most business relationships there is a distinct competitive aspect that cannot be ignored. Considering a business negotiation as a game builds on the experience of the participant and may prompt a more thorough understanding and analysis of a transaction.

Think of an international business negotiation as a team game on a playing field. Almost any game, from tennis to capture the flag, can be used as an example, but it is probably more realistic to think in terms of games such as soccer or hockey, where there are significant numbers of players with differing functions and there are some general expectations concerning the nature of the game and the playing field. The "game" is the negotiation for the buying or selling of a product or service to or from a foreign entity. The other party is the "opponent," even though—if the negotiation succeeds—the parties may combine as partners, colleagues, or perhaps even co-conspirators.

2. Preparing for the Game: Evaluating the Teams

In preparing for an international business negotiation, it is important to understand not only your specific economic strengths and weaknesses but also your place in the particular industry and the significance of the industry in the nation's economy. These same factors will also be measured and evaluated by your opponent in preparation for the negotiation.

To the extent possible, you must undertake exactly the same measurement and evaluation of your opponent. A prime concern is determining whether appearance is reality. Does the opponent have, in fact, the economic and political capabilities ascribed to it in the local business community? Does its general business reputation hold up to scrutiny? Be imaginative and resourceful to obtain accurate and insightful information about the opponent, and then carefully analyze your findings as part of planning for the negotiation. The ever-increasing amount of information on the Internet means that details are often available, but one must ascertain the accuracy of the data obtained. Additionally, it is useful to know the value of the contract for both sides because the level of commercial interest will influence the corporate response to actions or threats by either party.

In an international transaction, there may be foreign governmental involvement or influence on the other party. If this is discovered, you must then evaluate the political situation to understand the potential impact. Government involvement brings with it the likelihood of government review over all aspects of the transaction, and of pressure to achieve governmental objectives.

Even when the government is not involved directly, there may be a significant level of governmental interest because of the negotiation's political implications. Facilitation of a highly visible humanitarian effort to benefit the general population is a situation where the government may have great interest in the project without having any direct control over it. In such a case, the positive attitude of the government probably contributes to the resolution of potential bureaucratic difficulties.

It is important to focus on when and where performance and payment will be made, both in terms of geography and in the chronology of the transaction. Issues relating to payment and performance alone can fill books; some examples include matters such as prepayment, performance payments, payment upon completion, avoidance of the currency risk, and so forth. Once all the available information about both sides has been assembled and evaluated, a game strategy must then be developed.

3. The "Game"—Negotiation and Performance of an International Contract

As a tactical matter, it is preferable to have made a policy decision to be open, candid, and fair, even though one may not be totally convinced that the opponent is motivated by the same concerns of "fair play." Once prepared for the possibility of dishonesty, however remote, it is far better to have been open and sincere, rather than have some intended unfairness or deceit come out in the negotiations or during public proceedings.

3.1 Teammates and Opponents

Before starting a negotiation, you must assemble the best possible team to handle the technical problems and the proposals expected from the other side. In selecting teammates, evaluate the skills and abilities of each player in terms of contribution to the effort and what is expected from the other side. This is no different from picking a starting squad.

The selection of a local lawyer may be the single most important step because that outsider's assistance will be crucial to those technicians already on staff. In some societies and business situations, the lawyer functions not only as legal expert but as counselor and facilitator as well. The challenge is to find appropriate counsel, especially when it is possible that the local opponent may well have connections to the best, most qualified lawyers in the area. Web pages of law firms can provide a start in the search for counsel, as can local banks and accounting firms. The Foreign Commercial Service and the local American consul are also resources to be consulted.

In any negotiation, you must ascertain quickly whether the parties are "speaking the same language and playing the same game" to determine the level of trust or suspicion. If you do not have the time to determine the level of openness and communication, you must rely on the advice of others who claim to understand foreign businesspeople. Internet contact means there are fewer elements of evaluation available. All signals conveyed by body language are concealed in an e-mail. As a general rule, you should be cautious about the local agent's descriptions since his or her skill is as a "salesperson" rather than as an evaluator of a situation for American eyes and ears. The risk is that he or she may simply report what is already assumed, which can result in misunderstanding the opponent.

At the start of face-to-face negotiation, clarify whether the parties have full negotiating authority to make binding commitments. If they do not, they will be transmitting the essence of the discussions or contractual drafts back to the head office and awaiting responses. This will enable the invisible negotiators to veto or change matters that had been agreed to in the face-to-face meeting. Depending on how this proceeds, the victimized party can either require the presence of a fully authorized negotiating representative or can accept the arrangement as presented. It is most desirable for the decision-makers to be in direct contact. E-mail can facilitate contact, but it is difficult to determine if there is real substance behind the e-mail address.

3.2 Language for the Game

Who does the traveling and what language has been used in the preliminary discussions will probably determine the choice of language used in the contract, without anyone actually realizing that there was a language issue and that a decision has already been made. In addition, it is possible that the parties will have already succumbed to a choice through the recognition that one party cannot speak the other language.

The choice of language will automatically influence the "comfort level" of the transaction from the beginning. In many cases, sellers are in a position to urge the utilization of their native language on the theory that they know what their product is intended to do and are best able to describe these capabilities in their native language. The counterargument for buyers is that they are entitled to understand what it is that they are buying and it is unfair to give them the translation risk of not understanding what the sellers are saying.

The choice of language may also significantly influence both the legal remedies available and the jurisdiction of enforcement. Because of the difficulties of translation and explaining a second judicial system, a contract in any particular language will be most easily understood and enforced in countries having that language as their native language. Between the two contracting parties, if the native language of either one is selected, this immediately creates a "home-court advantage" for that party. In examining that situation, the opponent will have had to consider whether there is a disadvantage in speaking the language of the opponent or whether there is a power-politics posture in asserting one language over another.

In general, there should be consistency in the choice of language, law, and jurisdiction. If not, there will be difficulties of translation as well as problems of finding people able to make a decision under the stipulated law, which is then to be enforced in the particular jurisdiction. In certain situations, the language and negotiations of the contract will not be the native language of either party. In such circumstances, both sides have to undertake appropriate research to be sure that they are able to understand the obligations of the contract and what they are to supply or receive.

Use of a third language, such as English, is often offered when neither party speaks the other's language but both sides believe they are competently able to negotiate in English. In such a situation, the risk of language misunderstanding is considerably greater. One side may not know the appropriate terminology in the third language, and the understanding of that terminology by the other side may be entirely different from what is intended. E-mail enables the author to use correction technology before a message is sent, which means the reader cannot necessarily determine if the author really means what has been written or if there has been a technological mistranslation. Usually the suggestion to use a third language is made at the beginning of a negotiation, when the parties are not addressing the communication needs of performance or the implicit selection of a legal system and venue for enforcement.

3.3 The Draftsperson

Once the parties have reached a generalized oral agreement, the next step is to draft an agreement for review by all parties. In many cases, the party whose language is being used will be in a position to suggest that it be the draftsperson of the contract. There is already a degree of trust in permitting one party to draft the agreement. The working assumption is that the draftsperson will be careful to reflect all agreements, and this is not easily checked unless the opponent establishes detailed review and revision procedures to assure that nothing is overlooked.

The presentation of the draft contract brings with it diplomatic worries as well as the requirement of being able to understand the working assumptions of the opponent. For example, the American-drafted contract seeks to omit nothing, whereas contracts based on many other legal systems will often rely upon statutory provisions that include elements such as representations and warranties without further reference. For the recipient of a contract draft, the length or brevity of an agreement is, in itself, a potential cause for suspicion.

The parties may have had similar transactions in third countries and may offer textual examples for the proposed agreement. Such a suggestion becomes a mixed blessing, since it requires an understanding of the other transaction and an awareness of the legal and commercial practices of the third country and how these apply to the proposed transaction. Another potential complication exists when the drafting party uses a third language, but selects a contractual format that comes from his or her own country. An example would be reference in a French contract to "disclaimers in accordance with the Uniform Commercial Code," which can only refer to United States law. The contracting parties must be careful that the resulting document is clear not only in its language but also in its selection of applicable law and the place of enforcement.

In many cases, the draftsperson exercises a degree of dominance in the control of both the negotiation and the structuring of the transaction. The draftsperson is responsible for including topics raised by the opponent as well as phrasing the issues and objectives of both parties. In such a role, the draftsperson imparts his or her own perceptions and tone to the agreement.

Having the other party act as draftsperson is generally a mixture of positive and negative aspects. Clearly it is more work for the draftsperson, who is responsible for paying attention to all discussions and being sure that topics are reflected in the document, as well as being assured that the document, at a minimum, reflects objectives of the particular party. The non-drafting party is spared the burden of additional work (or the expense of counsel drafting the document), but it must follow very carefully to be sure that the document is clear and adequately reflects its agreements and concerns.

The course of the negotiations and the drafting of the agreement will demonstrate whether there has been recognition of various legal issues and, perhaps, some assumptions as to how they will be resolved. For example, reference to specific statutory provisions of a particular country or verbal compliance with statutory requirements as to disclosure or waiver should raise the question of whether one party is assuming the possibility of a dispute or the utilization of a particular legal system in resolution.

3.4 Referees and Rules

The "game" may well include jurisdictional expectations of the parties, whether or not they ever discuss this topic directly. The domiciles of both parties are clearly potential jurisdictional bases as well as the location of performance. Should payment be made in yet another jurisdiction, there are potentially four different places that may have jurisdiction over the transaction and disputes concerning it.

Generally, at the end of the negotiation, brief reference will be made to "boilerplate terms," which often include choice of language, choice of law, jurisdiction, and possibly a provision for arbitration in a neutral country. These boilerplate terms have to be understood and correlated because it is possible to agree to contradictory terms that later require extremely difficult or expensive resolution. As an example, if two non-English-speaking parties have accepted an agreement in English that provides for arbitration in Paris without a choice of law, any dispute resolution will be complicated and expensive, since it is unclear what law should apply and what language should be used in the arbitration. In such a situation, the arbitrators may simply apply their own sense of fairness instead of any particular body of law.

The issue of whether to arbitrate and where to arbitrate has serious ramifications requiring careful analytical review, especially when considering the likelihood of being respondent rather than claimant. The usual arbitration agreement provides that the decision of the tribunal will be enforceable against the offending party, but there is no automatic assurance that the decision of a panel of arbitrators can be enforced against a company in the courts of the domicile of that company.

Depending on the business culture and legal system, the parties may be assisted by the laws and business practices of the particular jurisdiction. As already noted, in the European "Napoleonic Code" countries, representations and warranties are provided by law and are not required to be set forth specifically. In such a situation, it is important to ascertain whether such terms are being assumed by operation of law or whether the omission of them creates a gap in the otherwise expected representations, warranties, and covenants of the agreement.

An American-drafted agreement normally will spell out all the terms, conditions, representations, warranties, exclusions, limitations, and potential variations from statutory law provisions (for example, exclusion of the measures of damages provided by the Uniform Commercial Code). Faced with such a document, the reaction of the foreign opponent may be to say that the contract is surely twice as long as it should be and, perhaps, because it is so long, there is some scheme or deception. Many pages of fine print certainly create a suspicious atmosphere for the foreign party well aware that "what the large print gives, the small print takes away."

In such a situation, the proposing party should recognize the necessity of "education to a mutual understanding" and take steps that will establish an acceptable level of comfort between the parties. Often the best approach is to take nothing for granted and provide other similar contracts as examples, so that the opponent can understand the other deals and, at the same time, realize that the documentation of the present proposal is consistent with what was done in the past.

4. The Playing Field (Place of Performance)

Depending on the type of contract and the contract terms, there are at least two potential locations for performance: FOB at the supplier's facility or delivered to the buyer's site. The nature of the contract may determine the place of performance. If the contract is to build a plant in the buyer's country, the contract cannot be completely performed FOB the dock or airport in the seller's country.

Similarly, if the seller is providing a packaged commodity, delivery can equally well be FOB the seller's country or after delivery in the buyer's country. In most cases, there will be a commercial expectation because of prior experience with that product that will tend to direct the parties' agreement as to the place of performance. When one of the parties has greater economic strength or there is a significant imbalance between supply and demand, the "stronger" party can often achieve a variance in payment terms and the otherwise expected place of performance.

4.1 The Tilt of the Commercial System

Assume that the playing field (the place of performance) will be designated or controlled by the opponent and that the American company is the "visitor" or foreigner. Were the situation reversed, it would not have to be analyzed so carefully since without being able to identify the distinctions, the American company is experienced and able to "play" in the American "home field." The first question in such analysis is whether a foreign company has any chance at all of doing successful business in the country. Then one must ascertain the requisite style and commercial behavior.

Background issues are present in almost every international negotiation, but only several basic ones are mentioned here. The foreigner must ascertain whether there is an "old boy network" and whether it is receptive to the proposed business. There can be situations in which the old boy network does its best to hamper or prevent the performance of a contract. An example would be the arrest of sales and service personnel for alleged violations of local law. Such activity sends a clear message to the contracting parties, especially when it may not be totally clear that the government is not involved in these activities.

In agreeing to an "away game," one is dependent upon the local commercial system as well as the domestic infrastructure and all that it involves. At a minimum, this includes problems of lodging, the electrical system, communications capabilities, and the potential difficulties of travel and banking. Understanding the communications constraints should be an immediate concern. Cell phones will permit communication where there are no other telephones, but they may not be secure. Encrypted e-mail may still be intercepted. The availability and confidentiality of the postal and telephone systems will automatically determine how and where you negotiate and how you communicate with "teammates." If neither the postal nor the telecommunications system is secure, they can still be used for purposes of misdirection. It is equally important to know if the postal and telecommunications systems are well-meaning but inept. In such situations, it may be appropriate to utilize alternatives, such as having the entire team on site so telecommunications are not needed.

Depending on the transaction, it may be useful to have local accountants available. They may be needed in the evaluation of the financial statements and of the entire proposed transaction, as well as being able to suggest payment procedures. Arrangements for the calculation or confirmation of royalties also should be coordinated with local accountants. In many countries, accounting and tax advocacy are often combined in a way that would be unusual in the United States, so you must determine the scope of an accounting firm. You must also learn to what extent the accountants are proactive as opposed to being simply reactive. Your findings will clarify the extent to which you can rely on them as teammates.

A related concern is the currency and banking system. Is it possible to get money into and out of the country? The laws might appear to permit repatriation of funds, but the exchange rate or governmental pressure may require reinvestment of earnings. The strength of the banking system and the central bank will have a major role in determining the economic stability of the country during the life of the contract. These concerns are included in the general concept of currency risk.

The commercial system may simply expect an obligatory "old boy" local partner, whether desired or not. Such a situation will not be legally required, but it would be made quite clear that without such a partner, you could anticipate significant operational difficulties at every stage.

A similar but somewhat easier situation is found in those countries that require, by law, a local partner. Having such a situation out in the open makes it easier to handle and there is a greater degree of predictability. However, a potential problem is the risk that the obligatory partner, in doing business as usual, will violate laws such as the Foreign Corrupt Practices Act on your behalf. Payment of a "facilitation fee" to a government official would be an example of an illegal payment under that act. Such a situation can clearly pose a dilemma because you are anxious to have the business, but not in violation of the law here or there.

The sophistication of the players and the audience (the general public) has to be determined as early as possible. It is cause for concern if one party is worrying about problems that the opponent has neither considered nor experienced. Such a situation presents a double risk: unreadiness or inability to consider it in the negotiation stage and unwillingness to be particularly sympathetic if and when the unexpected occurs. The inexperience of the opponent, rather than making things easier, may make performance significantly more difficult because it will not have prepared for or anticipated the requirements that would normally be expected. An example would be not recognizing that the equipment being purchased would require stable and consistent electrical power.

The attitude and experience of the "audience" can become important, especially if you seek local support and understanding in resolution of a possible dispute. If the general public is not aware of the infrastructure requirements of capital-intense investments, they will not be particularly sympathetic to a request for renegotiation based on such inadequacies.

A final concern is the effectiveness of the media. Will the local or international press be receptive to the proposed transaction, and does it make any difference? Even with an unreceptive press corps, is there a bureaucratic or administrative barrier that precludes meaningful assistance either from the home office or the American embassy? If the answer to that question is yes, you should probably refuse to have the foreign country be the place of performance and payment.

4.2 The Tilt of the Justice System

As part of investigating the "playing field," you must evaluate the entire justice system, which includes not only the legal structure itself but also how justice is sought and obtained. In such an effort, the first step is to determine whether the concepts of the transaction and desired remedies are available under local law. Topics of concern would include the availability of interest following late payment, the possibility of seizure, injunctive relief, and possible specific performance. In the enthusiasm of the deal, you may be tempted to overlook these concerns, but since checking these factors is relatively simple, they should not be disregarded. Direct inquiry of local law firms or of the Foreign Commercial Service of the U.S. Department of Commerce can often provide answers.

The legal system and the system of justice are intertwined. You have to know whether there is an available remedy for the alleged wrong. To some extent, this may require prowling around in the business community to ascertain whether the proposed transaction is considered possible, including finding out the availability of potential remedies in case of dispute. As an example, patents and copyrights are not universally recognized and it might not be possible to prosecute infringers, thus defeating a royalty arrangement.

After determining that there is law in support of a proposition, there is the question of enforceability. Surely the first concern is whether enforceability is available to all parties, including foreign companies. The practicalities and costs of bringing a complaint or seeking enforcement of a judgment are factors in the utility of the justice system. In many countries, both court costs and attorneys' fees are set as a percentage of the amount of the claim or the controversy. While this structure is seen as preventing frivolous litigation and exaggerated claims, it may also have the effect of preventing the presentation of a significant claim by a small (cash poor) claimant. In *ex parte* seizures and arrests, a substantial bond may be required in advance, usually set by the judge or magistrate who has been asked to permit the seizure. There may be some guidelines concerning the size of the bond (for example, "two or three times the amount of the claim"), but often the amount is at the discretion of the judge. In such a situation, the otherwise unexpressed prejudices of the judge may come into play. Where there is already discretion, it is practically impossible to prevent abuse, should the judge be so inclined. The lesson for the claimant or commercial party is to consider at the beginning the available legal remedies and the practicalities of using them.

Additionally, there are potential anti-foreigner prejudices that can occur in seeking enforcement of a legal claim. While the law may be clear, supportive people are needed to make it happen. Having access to knowledgeable people with good connections in the justice system is essential when evaluating the utility of potential legal remedies.

In considering any legal claim, the time required to obtain a judicial determination should be ascertained. If the procedures are slow and the court backlog large, the practical effect is that there are no readily available judicial remedies. The opponent may be well aware of the difficulties with the domestic legal system, which becomes part of its home-court advantage. When faced with such a situation, the standard response is to seek arbitration in a forum that will proceed promptly and fairly.

5. Changing the Game

In the situation in which one of the parties has the ability to alter some aspect of the basic arrangement and has done so, the parties may choose to continue to "play the same game." An example would be when a licensee unilaterally reduces the royalty payment from 4 percent to 3 percent. Even at a reduced rate, the business may still be attractive, but there should be a careful investigation to determine why the change occurred and whether it indicates further trouble to come.

If the changes are so significant as to constitute a totally new game, the situation must be reevaluated, since it was unexpected that the opponent had either the desire or the ability to change the relationship completely. Perhaps the signs and signals were misinterpreted and the party should now consider getting out rather than finding some way to accommodate the changes. The message is clear that if the opponent has the ability to change the game, presumably that ability will continue throughout the transaction and, as a practical matter, there is no commercial assurance for the transaction. In such a situation, the best course of action is to consider how to get out as quickly and cheaply as possible.

Events beyond the control of the parties may change the game as well. A change in the government or the nationalization of certain companies or industries can threaten or change the original transaction. This possibility should be considered in the initial planning and alternative strategies should be developed.

6. Completing the Game (Delivery and Payment)

In the ideal arrangement, delivery and payment occur at the same time. In any other situation, there is a risk for one or both parties concerning the performance or activities of the other party. If the timing cannot be concurrent, the parties will have to agree on a different performance schedule acceptable to them.

The nature of the contract may influence the parties in their selection or acceptance of partial payment or partial performance. Examples include situations in which it would be difficult for the seller to withdraw its performance if there is a failure of payment by the buyer (for example, the painting of a house). Perhaps more often than not, the buyer must make a down payment, which may represent the seller's profit should the transaction then not go forward, or which may simply be the funds necessary to purchase materials and equipment needed for performance of the contract (for example, the purchase of the paint for the house to be painted).

The economic strength of one party may be such that it may be unwilling to comply with the normal payment timing expected in the industry. Faced with such a situation, the other party must decide whether to accept an increased risk of nonpayment or risk the possibility of losing the order completely. In making that evaluation, the parties will rely on the analysis made in the beginning, evaluating the proposed transaction and deciding, in advance, where to be flexible.

In the partial performance situation, the parties must address the issue of creating security for the unfulfilled performance. The challenge is to ascertain whether the desired protective measure can be obtained and enforced. For instance, requiring retention of ownership until full payment is made would probably not be effective if the government of the buyer nationalized all American property in that country.

7. Problems After Performance

Whether the game is over "when it's over" or not is also a concern. The order of payment and performance will probably determine when a transaction is completed. In negotiating this chronology, the parties may specifically avoid establishment of a structure that would permit the assertion of claims. Examples include refusing to consent to jurisdiction in the other party's courts, requiring cash on delivery, or refusing to permit retention of a fraction of the purchase price until after delivery. The strategic implications of such demands are generally obvious, so that the parties will know whether they have achieved closure in the performance of the negotiated agreement. The dynamics of a relationship may effectively prevent the assertion of claims. An example might be the futility of asserting a shortage claim against a foreign agrarian collective. The procedural difficulties would be so great that one simply wouldn't start.

8. Conclusion

The use of the analogy of preparing for a team game can help in planning to negotiate with an unknown foreign business. The value of this approach is that it can clarify potential risks and prompt further analysis as you seek to understand the other party. The analogy cannot be stretched too far, but there is value in thinking about a pending negotiation in something other than strictly commercial terms.

Charles M. Taylor, PC
Honorary Consul General of Germany a.D.
248 Kent Road
Wynnewood, PA 19096
Phone: (610) 620-3149
E-mail: cmtaylor@post.harvard.edu

CHAPTER 16

Negotiating with Foreign Governments

Jeswald W. Salacuse
HENRY J. BRAKER PROFESSOR OF LAW
THE FLETCHER SCHOOL OF LAW AND DIPLOMACY
TUFTS UNIVERSITY
MEDFORD, MASSACHUSETTS

1. Foreign Governments in International Business

Despite the powerful forces of privatization, deregulation, and globalization that have swept the world since the 1980s,[1] foreign governments are still important players in international business. Indeed, with the rise of sovereign wealth funds potentially holding trillions of dollars in assets and the renationalization of key industries in certain countries, their role has heightened in recent years. As a result, governments are an actual or potential presence in the negotiation of any significant international business deal. Therefore, whenever lawyers and executives undertake international business negotiations anywhere in the world, they must be prepared to negotiate with a foreign government.

Foreign governments may play many different roles in the negotiation of an international deal. They may be parties to the transaction as buyers, suppliers, financiers, or partners whose representatives are active participants at the bargaining table. In other transactions, their role is that of regulator whose permission or authorization is necessary if a deal is to go forward, necessitating negotiations with one or more government departments or agencies to obtain the authorizations needed. In still other cases, even when a government entity is not physically present at the negotiating table and has no specific authority to regulate the deal, it may be lurking in the wings as a "ghost negotiator" exerting a powerful influence on local parties to assure that governmental interests are protected. So even if you are not negotiating directly with a government in those situations, you may still eventually have to deal indirectly with one or more governmental units to make

---

[1] *See* Jeswald W. Salacuse, *From Developing Countries to Emerging Markets: A New Role for Law in the Third World*, 33 INT'L LAW. 875 (1999).

the transaction you want. And finally, if the public becomes concerned about a deal that you are trying to negotiate, be prepared for the government to make its presence felt at the negotiating table.

As you approach any significant international business negotiation, you should always ask three important questions:

1. To what extent does a government have an actual or potential interest in this deal?
2. How and to what extent will that government be involved in the negotiation?
3. If a government is not directly involved, how might it nonetheless intervene in the negotiation or the resulting transaction to protect its interests?

The purpose of this chapter is to provide some general guidance on negotiating with foreign governments. The reader should bear in mind that no two governments are alike and that effective negotiation with any government requires a thorough knowledge of its particular political history, culture, and bureaucratic traditions. As part of their preparation, international business negotiators should therefore do the necessary research and secure appropriate advice on these subjects.

2. Government Attitudes Toward Negotiation

At the outset, it is important to recognize that government officials often have a different attitude toward the process of negotiation with private parties than do individuals and companies. Whereas corporate executives usually consider business negotiation as a freewheeling process to make deals and solve problems, many government officials in their dealings with private parties often view themselves as merely carrying out the laws and regulations they are obligated to apply. They are dispensers of the transactions that the law allows, not negotiators. As one official from the Mexican Central Bank told me, "For government officials, negotiation is not proper. Law is a not a negotiable thing when you are in charge of applying it."

Despite the Mexican official's protestations, few governmental systems in reality make automatic, mechanical decisions. Because legislators do not have perfect foresight, they cannot make laws or regulations that provide for all possible eventualities that may happen in the future. As a result, all governmental systems require in varying degrees that their operators exercise some discretion in making their decisions, whether it is granting a concession to operate a public service, issuing a building permit, or purchasing a weapons system. Discretion in this context means the ability to make a decision involving a choice among various options. The existence of discretion is the opening to negotiation, and the goal of a business negotiator is to persuade the government official across the table to exercise that discretion in a desired way. It is therefore important for business negotiators to determine precisely how much discretion the officials with whom they are dealing have.

Despite the widespread prevalence of negotiations between government departments on the one hand and foreign companies and individuals on the other, many government officials, like the one from the Mexican Central Bank, strongly resist the idea that when they do their jobs they are engaged in "negotiation." An understanding of the reason for this attitude provides some useful insights into government officials as negotiators, and indeed into the whole process of negotiating with governments.

First, many officials take comfort in the fiction that their decisions are made according to rules, automatically applied. Thus, their decisions are not their responsibility, but that of the institution that made the rules. If you or your competitors don't like that decision, you should blame the institution—the legislature or the ministry—that made the rule, not the public official who merely applied it. This rationalization protects officials from complaints and criticism by various interest groups and individuals. For an official to acknowledge that the issuance of a contract or permit resulted from a negotiation, which implies a back-and-forth exchange of proposals and counterproposals, is to admit that the decision did not result from an automatic application of the rules, thus opening government officials to questions, challenges, and even threats that might undermine their positions and injure their careers.

Second, for many people, compromise is implicit in the notion of negotiation. Although the public accepts compromise in certain contexts, it considers compromise inappropriate in others. For example, while it is one thing for a business executive to acknowledge engaging in compromise when negotiating a merger with another private company, it is quite another thing for a public official to admit compromising in granting a permit or making a contract. In the public's view, the application of public policy, law, and regulations should not be subject to compromise. Rather, the public expects governments to apply law, regulations, and policies uniformly to all persons. It is this attitude, for example, that has caused public opposition in certain countries to negotiated infrastructure and public service contracts as opposed to those arrived at by a strict competitive bidding process.

To accept the notion that the application of laws and regulations is the product of negotiation and that therefore some persons benefit from them and others don't is seen as an affront to basic notions of democracy and equality before the law. For most officials and regulators, a model government decision with respect to a company or individual is objective, impersonal, and uniform. A negotiated decision, on the other hand, implies just the opposite. A negotiated decision is subjective, personal, and special to the party concerned.

These considerations have certain important implications for conducting business negotiations with governments. First, it is important to find a justification for the deal in the law, regulations, or objective standards that are defensible to the public, civic groups, and the government's political opponents. Second, the process by which the deal was negotiated must also be defensible, and this may require business negotiators to abandon certain cherished precepts of business deal making. For example, openness and transparency may be more important than confidentiality. And third, in many of your interactions with governments, it is often best to avoid the word "negotiation" in referring to the process in which you are engaged. To respect governmental sensitivities, refer to your negotiations with government officials by other names: "discussions," "conversations," "requests," or "interactions."

3. Governments Feel Different

"Governments feel different," an experienced corporate deal-maker once told me in reflecting on his years of negotiating international business deals. What he meant was that governments as negotiators are not like private parties. They approach, prepare for, conduct, and conclude negotiations in ways that are different from those used by individuals and corporations. In order to deal with governments effectively, private persons and companies must understand these differences and develop strategies to cope with them.

If governments as negotiating counterparts feel different from private organizations, it is particularly because of two factors: the special powers that governments wield and the special constraints to which they are subject at the bargaining table. The nature and extent of government powers and constraints will of course vary from country to country and from government department to government department. But in preparing to negotiate with any foreign government, you should seek to understand their special powers, as well as the special constraints affecting their ability to use those powers.

4. Governments' Special Negotiating Powers

Within the context of any negotiation, "power" means the ability to influence the decisions of another party in a desired way.[2] In addition

---

[2] *See generally* POWER AND NEGOTIATION (I. William Zartman & Jeffrey Z. Rubin eds., 2000) and Jeswald W. Salacuse, *How Should the Lamb Negotiate with the Lion: Power in International Negotiations, in* NEGOTIATION ECLECTICS (Deborah Kolb ed., 1999).

to the negotiating power gained as a result of such natural attributes as wealth, resources, and physical location, all governments derive special powers in business negotiations from (1) their monopoly position; (2) their special governmental privileges and immunities; (3) their role as defenders of the public interest and welfare; and (4) their special protocols and forms. Let's examine each one.

4.1 Power No. 1: The Power of Monopoly

Most of the time, when you are negotiating with other individuals and companies, you have alternative courses of action if the negotiations fail. If you are trying to make a deal with a particular distributor to handle your products, you know that you have the option of seeking other possible distributors if you can't reach agreement. If you are negotiating to acquire another company as part of your strategy of corporate growth, you usually have yet another company as a possible target for acquisition. These alternatives may be good or bad, but other options do exist.

The nature and extent of your other options affect your bargaining power in a negotiation. If you have other good options, you have a position of strength in negotiation. If your alternatives are poor, you have less power. So if there is heavy market demand for your product or service, you have many options and will therefore be able to play a strong hand at the negotiating table. If market demand is weak, your negotiating power will be proportionately reduced.

Most of the time when we negotiate with governments, we are negotiating with an entity that has a monopoly over what we are seeking. As a result, we often feel that we have few other options, if any, to satisfy our interests. That realization has the effect of giving us a sense that we are in a weak bargaining position when we negotiate with a government department because our alternatives for making a deal are usually not very good. For instance, if you want to sell a drug in the United States, you have to obtain approval from the Food and Drug Administration (FDA), and the Food and Drug Administration alone. You can't go to the SEC, the IRS, or OSHA to get it. The FDA's monopoly position gives it a position of power in its negotiations with pharmaceutical companies.

Sometimes you may have to negotiate with another company that has a dominant position in the market, such as Microsoft or Wal-Mart, a position that seems close to a monopoly. The difference between negotiating with a Microsoft or a Wal-Mart on the one hand and a government on the other is that a government usually has a legal monopoly over what you are seeking. That legal monopoly makes it impervious to various market factors, such as share price or technological change, that strongly influence a Wal-Mart or Microsoft, no matter how dominant it is for the time being.

Governments' legal monopoly makes them impervious to market forces and gives them a sense of permanence that few companies in the private sector enjoy. Also, unlike a company that has a dominant market position, a government department has the ability to use force to maintain its legal monopoly. So if you try to sell that drug without FDA approval, federal authorities will close down your plant and charge you with a crime.

On the other hand, a government's monopoly rarely extends beyond its territory. One way of countering the power of a governmental monopoly is to develop other options in other territories beyond its reach and to make the government aware of your efforts. Thus, for example, Japanese auto manufacturers seeking to establish car plants in the United States engaged in a process of simultaneously negotiating benefits from several different state and local governments before making a decision on the precise locality in which to build a plant.

4.2 Power No. 2: The Power of Privilege and Immunity

Governments also feel different from other negotiators because they enjoy many legal privileges and immunities that private companies and persons do not. Not only do they have the power to regulate how businesses operate, they also have the ability to seize property, cancel contracts, threaten force, and, if need be, actually use force against you to obtain their objectives. Moreover, in many countries, you can't sue the government in a court of law no matter how arbitrary its actions, nor can you force it to respect the contracts it has signed, no matter how detailed. Even if a suit is legally possible, governments nonetheless often benefit from judicial bias in their favor. National legal systems give governments an array of privileges and immunities in order to allow them to perform their basic task of governing.

These extensive privileges and immunities also give governments special power at the negotiating table. The implicit or explicit threat by a government to exercise its special powers against a counterpart has influenced the results of many negotiations between government units and private corporations. Multinational corporations, while having a vast pool of capital and technology at their command, don't have these kinds of powers. The result, as a senior executive at a giant global pharmaceutical company once told me, is that even "the smallest governments can jerk you around."

Many times, a government's explicit or implicit threat to use this power causes private negotiators to make concessions that they would not normally make in a negotiation with another private company. It is the exercise of this power that often forces companies with advantageous government contracts to renegotiate them and thereby give a government more favorable terms.

One way to reduce this power differential is for a private party to enlist the assistance of another government or organization as an equalizer. For example, to avoid the problems of judicial partiality toward the government, your transaction might provide for all disputes to be settled by international arbitration in a neutral country. And if you are having a problem with a local government in a foreign country, you might seek help from the national authorities. If you are stymied by the national foreign government, you can seek help from your own government. The risk inherent in such an approach is that other governments and organizations have their own interests and you may not be able to control their actions once you involve them in your negotiation.

4.3 Power No. 3: The Power of Representing the Public Interest

Governments cloak all of their actions, legal or not, on grounds that they are acting in the public interest rather than for private gain. They normally justify their actions as being for "national security," "public welfare," or "the good of the people." In many negotiations, government officials often take the moral high ground in order to justify their demands and obtain concessions from the other side. After all, they are altruistically seeking to achieve the public good in the negotiation, while you, as the representative of a private company, are merely looking to make a selfish profit. Thus in one negotiation with an African tax official in which I was asserting that the country's "development tax" did not apply to the organization I represented, the official responded with a pained look: "Don't you want to help us develop our country?" He ultimately agreed to grant the exemption, but not before he had made me feel as if I were selfishly putting in jeopardy his country's future through my self-seeking and unreasonable demands.

Away from the bargaining table, the government's role as representative of the public interest also gives it the ability to mobilize popular support for its negotiating positions and to use political influence to gain advantages that no private corporation ever could. For example, during its financial crisis in 2001, the Argentine government refused to pay its international debts, declaring that to do so would threaten the basic welfare of the Argentine people. It portrayed foreign creditors and investors as imperiling the very survival of the country, a tactic that gained the government great popular support and foreign banks widespread hostility. African governments have used a similar tactic in their negotiations with international pharmaceutical companies to obtain low prices on HIV drugs and other medicines essential to public health.

As a result of the power of governments to represent the public interest, companies engaged in negotiations with governments often find that they must conduct two related but separate negotiations to achieve their objectives: one inside the negotiating room with government representatives and the other outside in the media and in public relations. You therefore should keep in mind that almost any negotiation with a government has the potential to become a public issue in which civic organizations, nongovernmental organizations, and the public in general take an active, vocal part, thus turning what you thought was a bilateral negotiation into a multilateral negotiation. Plan for this eventuality in shaping your negotiating strategy with any government.

4.4 Power No. 4: The Power of Protocol and Form

Governments and their representatives are usually acutely sensitive to matters concerning their status, prestige, and dignity, since these elements are essential to carrying out their primary task: governing. All other things being equal, a government that is respected by its people and by other nations will find it easier to govern than a government that is not.

One of the ways in which governments seek to preserve and enhance their status and power is through their use of various forms and protocols, particularly those that relate to how private persons and companies are to communicate and interact with the government and its officials. Governments usually have express or implicit rules about the way private persons are to approach them, what form of address they are to use, and where they are to sit or stand in relation to government representatives. Officials consider the failure to respect these forms as a sign of disrespect or, worse, a challenge to their authority.

Governments also use these forms in order to enhance their power in a negotiation, and their officials therefore frequently bring to the negotiating table attitudes and approaches that seem to introduce rigidity into the deal-making process. By virtue of their governmental status, negotiators for government departments, ministries, and state corporations often behave differently in negotiations from the way private company executives and lawyers would. For one thing, government officials resist being considered equals to the private businesspeople on the other side of the table. Indeed, any suggestion that the two sides are equals may be considered an insult. Government officials represent the "the state," "the nation," and "the people," and a sovereign country, no matter how small, is not the equal of a private business firm, no matter how large. Any slight to a government official may be considered an affront to the dignity of the nation.

In one instance, an African minister asked for a meeting with the head of a foreign mining company that had operations in his country. The meeting took place in the office of the minister of mines and was attended by nine other government ministers. The minister of mines said that the government wanted to renegotiate its concession agreement with the company to obtain a greater share of mineral revenues, and he listed the points that needed to be discussed. In response, the chairman of the mining company reviewed each item, but at one point he flatly said, "We cannot entertain that." To emphasize his position, he struck the table with his hand. The minister immediately adjourned the meeting and refused to continue the discussions.

While the response of the mining company chairman might have been acceptable in a negotiation between two private companies, it was inappropriate in a discussion with what amounted to nearly the entire government of a sovereign state. Instead of an outright rebuff, the chairman should have shown a willingness to listen and to discuss all of the government's concerns. Such flexibility, of course, does not mean that a company has to give in on every point. In this case, it took nearly nine months to get the negotiations going again, and during that time the government made operations difficult for the company. Ultimately, the two sides did renegotiate the mining concession.

African government officials are by no means the only ones to look unkindly upon challenges to their authority. U.S. bureaucrats can be equally sensitive and reactive.[3] Indeed, one can find similar examples of such sensitivities throughout all governments. The lesson they teach is very clear. In your negotiations with government officials, avoid challenging their authority. As one experienced government affairs professional told me, "You need to give people the respect due their office." A government department's basic capital is its authority, and it is authority that enables it to function. If you challenge its authority, either directly or indirectly, you are in effect challenging the ability of that department to perform its basic tasks. When their authority is challenged, the instinct of government officials, like the African ministers, is to show you in the clearest possible and most forceful terms that you are wrong. Moreover, having been challenged once by your organization, they will remember that challenge in future dealings for a long

---

[3] For example, in 2001, the FDA was dissatisfied with certain aspects of Schering-Plough's manufacturing operations for its asthma inhalers and threatened to withhold approval of the company's new blockbuster allergy medicine Clarinex until the manufacturing problems were solved. A tense meeting between Schering-Plough's top management and FDA officials was held to discuss the matter. When the meeting seemed to have the two sides deadlocked, Schering-Plough's president, Raul Cesan, a hard-driving executive with an assertive style who had become frustrated with developments in the talks, asked his subordinates to leave the room so that he could talk to the FDA regulators alone. Cesan apparently thought that he could override them with the strength of his personality and strong words. It didn't work. As one of his associates would report later, "Raul is an extremely aggressive guy, but that kind of behavior doesn't go over well with regulators. I don't know what he said, but next week we had inspectors crawling all over every one of our plants." *See* Gardiner Harris, *A Hard-Learned Lesson on Dealing with U.S. Regulators*, N.Y. Times, Feb. 3, 2006, at C4.

time to come. In the theology of government, challenging a government official's authority is a bureaucratic mortal sin. You should bear in mind the wisdom of Admiral Hyman Rickover, the developer of the U.S. nuclear submarine and a redoubtable bureaucratic infighter in his own right: "If you must sin, sin against God, not against the bureaucracy. God may forgive you, but the bureaucracy never will."[4]

Wise negotiators learn the established protocols and forms for dealing with a particular government, and they respect them scrupulously. They also avoid actions that might be considered a challenge to them and thereby to the government itself. By virtue of their culture, American negotiators in particular tend to disregard formalities and seek to develop informal relationships with their counterparts on the other side of the table. For example, in a survey that I conducted among 310 negotiators from twelve different cultures, Americans showed the greatest tendency to value and use an informal negotiating style in business dealings.[5] Unfortunately, that tendency may in some cases be interpreted as a lack of respect. General Electric's inability to secure approval of its acquisition of Honeywell from the European Union competition authorities in 2001 is one example. Considering approval a "done deal," GE executives showed little deference to European officials. Early in the discussions, Jack Welch, GE's legendary CEO, said to Mario Monti, EU Competition Commissioner, as if they were in a private business negotiation, "Call me Jack." Monti, keenly aware that he represented the European public interest, replied: "I'll only call you Jack when this deal is over."[6] The talks went downhill from there.

5. Governments' Special Negotiating Constraints

A government's monopoly position, its array of privileges and immunities, its role as defender of the public interest, and its forms and protocols give it a clear position of power in its negotiations with private parties. A government in a negotiation with a private company would therefore seem to be an eight-hundred-pound gorilla sitting across the table. On the other hand, few governments are free to use that power in any way they wish. In one respect or another, they all are subject to constraints on its use. An understanding of those constraints may allow you to mobilize them to your advantage and thereby reduce the

---

[4] Quoted by A. Ernest Fitzgerald in a prepared statement before the Subcommittee on Retirement and Employee Benefits of the Committee on Post Office and Civil Service of the House of Representatives, April 24th, 1974.

[5] Jeswald W. Salacuse, *Ten Ways That Culture Affects Negotiating Style: Some Survey Results*, 14 Negotiation J. 221–40 (1998). *See also* Jeswald W. Salacuse, The Global Negotiator: Making, Managing, and Mending Deals Around the World in the Twenty-first Century 99 (2003).

[6] Jack Welch & John A. Byrne, Jack: Straight from the Gut 366 (2001).

power differential between you and government officials with whom you are negotiating.

5.1 Constraint No. 1: Negotiating Rules

Government bureaucracies exist to apply laws, regulations, and rules. Rules govern all their operations, including their negotiations with private persons and companies. As a result, negotiating with governments is very much a rule-driven process, not the freewheeling interaction that usually characterizes deal-making between purely private parties. Rules and regulations affect not only the kinds of deals governments make but the way they make them.

The rules incorporated in these laws and regulations will tell you how you are to engage the concerned government office, what kind of documentation you must present to it, the precise terms that will need to appear in your contract, and much, much more. Their effect is to limit the freedom of contract of governmental departments, agencies, and state corporations and your own interactions with them. Government officials may be required to use standard form contracts that include mandatory clauses on payment terms, insurance, and guarantees, to mention just a few. They may also be required to favor certain kinds of business over others—for example, by giving preference to national companies over foreign companies.

Like an elaborate ballet, the entire negotiation process may follow a strict choreography to its completion. Thus, making a deal to sell your products to the government often requires you to engage in distinct, intricate phases—tendering, evaluation, selection, and challenge—each of which is governed by detailed rules. The first phase is tendering, whereby the government announces its needs and requests interested and qualified persons to make an offer of the services or goods to be procured. Often, the tendering phase provides for a sealed bidding process. Next, the bids are subjected to evaluation, using criteria that have been decided upon and made public. Once the evaluation is completed, the government agency makes a selection and proceeds to enter into a formal agreement. But before such agreement is finalized, a process of challenge is possible, whereby disappointed bidders are given an opportunity to contest the selection decision. The whole process is time-consuming, costly, and complicated, often requiring the services of specialists in this domain.

Few companies in the private sector would conduct negotiations in this fashion, for the simple reason that it would not be "efficient" in the sense of achieving the maximum output for a given input. Here then is a further major difference between negotiations with governments and negotiations between purely private parties. Whereas ostensible "efficiency" is the highest goal sought by private negotiators, ostensible "fairness" is the goal sought by government negotiations. One of the reasons that purely private negotiations value efficiency so highly is that the participants' organizations will directly benefit from any savings or gains achieved in the negotiations. A win-win solution that allows both companies to save money or create new wealth in a particular transaction will have the result that both companies have increased earnings for investment in other projects and for possible distribution to shareholders.

A gain secured for a government in a negotiation, on the other hand, does not benefit the department concerned but passes directly to the state budget, without having a positive impact on the department's own resources. The inability of a government department to capture gains may influence the government negotiator's reluctance to try innovative solutions to problems, particularly if those innovative solutions are not specifically authorized by the rules and might be challenged by third parties as "unfair."

To say that the purpose of such rules and regulations is to assure that negotiations are "fair" does not just mean that they are fair to the government or fair to the private party that gets the contract; rather, they must also be "fair" to those who did not succeed in making a contract with the government—and to the public as well. In order to protect itself from accusations of unfairness, arbitrariness, or corruption, the government department must show that it has followed the rules in all respects, not by demonstrating that the deal is economically efficient. As a result, the process of conducting a negotiation according to the rules often becomes an end in itself. Because the rules on negotiations have such a central place in negotiations with governments, it is important for negotiators representing private individuals and companies to understand them. In any negotiation with a government, the power to convince an official will almost always depend on your ability to find a rule to justify your position.

The fact that no rule prohibits what you are asking may not be enough to convince the officials sitting across the table. If a government department is presented with two possible courses of action, one that is clearly authorized by the prevailing law or regulation and the other only vaguely permitted, that department will almost always favor the first and look dubiously on the second. For example, during the late 1970s, when Egypt began to open its doors to foreign investment after they had been closed for over twenty-years, President Sadat gave glowing speeches about Egypt's openness to and need for foreign investment and warmly urged investors to establish their operations in the country. Drawn by this rhetoric, investors were disappointed to find that the Egyptian bureaucracy was slow to approve their investment proposals. When investors pointed to the speeches that Sadat had been giving as justification for expediting approvals in their negotiations with the Egyptian Investment Authority, Egyptian bureaucrats replied that their job was to apply the law and rules governing investment, not the speeches of the president. The Egyptian laws and regulations on foreign investment were clear about the approval process for investment projects, and so the Egyptian bureaucracy applied them strictly, as it felt bound to do. The process of approving foreign investment proposals would become easier for investors only with the adoption of new regulations that abolished the old requirements and enabled the Egyptian bureaucracy to facilitate approvals.

5.2 Constraint No. 2: Constituents

Just because a particular government department or agency has a monopoly over what you are seeking in your negotiation does not mean that department or agency is omnipotent. Inevitably, any governmental unit relies on some constituency for resources and support, and that constituency can therefore influence the way that particular unit behaves. Depending on the country, state, or locality, government departments and officials rely on a wide variety of constituents and supporters—political parties, labor unions, the military, the media, and civic organizations—from which they derive power and authority. So, in negotiating with any government department, you need to try to understand its particular constituents and the levers they command to influence government action.

The key constituents of a government department are not always readily apparent. Like cultures, each of the world's governmental systems is distinct and different. The French government does not make policy the way the German government does. And an American lawyer or executive cannot assume that governments abroad work the way the U.S. government does at home. As a result, we are tempted to think that government and bureaucratic decision-making is some kind of a mysterious black box, whose workings are impossible for an outsider to fathom. One way of beginning to understand government decision-making is to look to the influence of constituents and opponents of the unit making the decision.

Raytheon, a major U.S. defense contractor, learned this lesson several years ago when it tried to put together a consortium of European companies to produce a weapons system for NATO that it had already built successfully for the U.S. military. Knowing the capabilities of various European firms, Raytheon selected those it thought would do the best job and began negotiating with them. These conversations were abruptly cut short when individual NATO governments told Raytheon that they, not the American manufacturer, would choose the European participants in the consortium. Recognizing political realities, Raytheon ended discussions with the firms it had selected, began negotiations with those chosen by individual governments, and ultimately put together a consortium that successfully produced the weapons systems for NATO.

A few years later, at the urging of the American government, Raytheon sought to produce a version of the same weapons system for Japan. Having learned what it thought was a useful lesson from its earlier experience in Europe, it opened talks directly with the Japanese government, expecting the government to indicate the Japanese companies with which the U.S. manufacturer was to work. No such indication was forthcoming. Japanese officials studiously avoided suggesting appropriate Japanese partners. Finally, in a private conversation with a Raytheon senior executive, the Japanese deputy minister of defense made it clear that Raytheon, not the Japanese government, should decide on the Japanese companies to participate in producing the weapons system. The reason was that two very powerful Japanese electronics firms were the primary contenders for participation, and the Japanese government did not want to incur the wrath and political antagonism of either one by choosing the other.[7] The Japanese Ministry of Defense needed the continuing support of both of these constituents if it was to preserve its influence, budget, and status.

In both the European and Japanese cases, the black box of government processed a political decision, but each came out with a different result. In Europe, in matters of national defense and the allocation of contracts among companies in different countries, there was a dominant supplier, often a government or government-financed entity itself, in each country, that had significant influence over the government departments concerned with the production of weapons systems. In Japan, the government, when faced with two competing Japanese electronics giants, recognized that if it favored one over the other, the losing company could make life difficult for the government through its political and financial clout.

Chrysler also used its knowledge of government constituents to good advantage several years ago in negotiations to sell its money-losing plants in the United Kingdom to the British government. It reacted to the government's low initial offer by threatening to liquidate its factories one by one, beginning with a plant located in an important electoral district in Scotland. The British Labour government at the time had a very slim majority and depended on Scotland to maintain its hold on power. In response to Chrysler's threat, Labour leaders in Scotland put strong pressure on the government to keep the plant open. In the end, the government increased its offer significantly and made a deal with Chrysler.[8]

---

[7] Author's interview with the late Charles Francis Adams, former chairman of Raytheon.

[8] DAVID LAX & JAMES SEBENIUS, THE MANAGER AS NEGOTIATOR: BARGAINING FOR COOPERATION AND COMPETITIVE GAIN 354–55 (1986).

5.3 Constraint No. 3: The Political Imperative

An understanding of interests, both yours and the other side's, is fundamental to success in any negotiation.[9] All negotiators, governmental or private, are driven by their interests. Those interests are often multiple and complex; consequently, you cannot assume that the interests of the persons across the table are the same as yours or those of other persons you have negotiated with in the past. You have to dig deeply to uncover them if you hope to succeed.

Because of their special interests, government officials and politicians perceive and act on negotiating issues and problems in ways that are often different from the way private parties would in similar situations. Part of the reason for this is that whereas corporate deal-makers usually respond to economic incentives—the need to make a profit, to increase share price, or to assure a fat bonus for the year—government officials respond to "political imperatives"—the need to protect departmental budgets, to preserve areas of authority, to defend themselves against political opponents, to support the interests of constituents, to enhance departmental prestige, and to ward off competition from other governmental agencies.

All government negotiators are agents; in other words, they are negotiating on behalf of the state or its subdivisions, not for themselves.[10] In practice, as agents they also have their own personal and bureaucratic interests to advance and they will certainly do so in their dealings and negotiations. An understanding of these undeclared interests is vital in dealing with any government department. Remember, a constant question in the mind of any government negotiator with whom you are negotiating is: How will this negotiation affect my career?

Concerned about "career-enhancing activities" and "career-destroying activities," bureaucrats eagerly seek the former and assiduously try to avoid the latter. The question weighs more heavily on some officials than on others, but it is always there. For example, in one negotiation over mineral rights in a Middle Eastern developing country, the representative of the American company and the deputy minister of mineral resources developed a strong, friendly relationship but the negotiations seemed to be going nowhere. After dinner one evening, the American executive asked what the problem was, and the deputy minister replied: "I have to be frank with you. If I make a deal with your competitor who is well known to the government ministers,

---

[9] For examples of the importance of interests in negotiation, see ROGER W. FISHER, WILLIAM URY & BRUCE PATTON, GETTING TO YES: NEGOTIATING AGREEMENT WITHOUT GIVING IN (2d ed. 1991).

[10] *See generally* NEGOTIATING ON BEHALF OF OTHERS (Robert Mnookin & Lawrence Susskind eds., 1999).

the deal will be approved with no problems. If I make a deal with your company that has never operated in our country before, any deal that I make will be questioned. Even though your company will probably do a better job for us because your technology is more effective, I just can't take the chance. I have two years to go before retirement and I need to protect my position in government and my pension. Also, my wife and son both work for the government, so I can't do anything that will put them in danger, either." Then he added, apparently sensitive to the American negotiator's own bureaucratic interests, "But if it will help you with your company, we can continue to negotiate, if you want to."

Generally speaking, the power of political imperatives in a given negotiation will vary inversely to the sense of security that government negotiators feel in their bureaucratic position. Politically insecure officials are usually more influenced by political imperatives than are politically secure officials.

One strategy that officials often use to defend their career interests is to follow the rules assiduously. The rules, which have usually been set down by some higher authority, function to protect that official from career-damaging criticism and censure. If in your negotiation you are seeking to achieve an innovative transaction that is not specifically authorized by the rule, you are likely to encounter an attitude characterized by the old bureaucratic maxim: "Never do anything for the first time." You will therefore need to find a tactic to blunt bureaucratic aversion to innovation.

Several years ago in Khartoum, I negotiated an agreement to allow the Ford Foundation to operate in Sudan with a bright and polished diplomat who was extremely cordial and seemed eager for the Foundation expand its activities in the country. As a result, our discussions went smoothly as we discussed the various issues to be included in the country agreement. However, when I asked for a complete tax and customs exemption for the Foundation and its personnel, the agreeable smile on his face was replaced with a look of consternation. A tax and customs exemption for a purely private organization? The Foreign Ministry had never done that before. The Sudanese diplomat wasn't sure whether the Ministry even had the power to grant such an exemption. Even if it did, he didn't know whether the government would be prepared to grant those exemptions to a wealthy foreign organization. The Sudanese government had no definite rules on this topic, and that presented a problem to my counterpart and, by extension, to his superiors in the ministry. We found a solution to the problem when I mentioned that the Ford Foundation country agreement with Egypt did provide for such a complete tax exemption. At the Sudanese diplomat's request, I eventually produced a copy of the Egyptian agreement, and within a week we had agreed on a complete text of a country agreement whose provisions on tax and customs exemptions followed the Egyptian country agreement word for word.

In any negotiation with a government official it is important to understand the political and bureaucratic interests at work and to find ways to satisfy them. It is also important to make deals that are politically defensible for the government making them. The use of an appropriate precedent, as happened in my Sudan negotiation, is one way of doing that.

5.4 Constraint No. 4: Operational Norms

Government departments normally operate according to norms that one rarely finds in private business.[11] In particular, these norms affect a government department's revenues, resources, and objectives. They not only influence how government departments act but also affect how they negotiate.

> **Revenue Norms:** A first important norm concerns departmental revenues. Part of the reason that governments are not influenced by commercial incentives to the same extent as private sector companies is that the government departments negotiating the deal usually cannot retain the commercial and financial benefits of the deals they make. Whereas a company in negotiating with a supplier will increase its earnings by a dollar for every dollar it saves at the negotiating table, a government department that saves a dollar in negotiating with a supplier will not increase its budget by an equal amount. Rather, that dollar goes to the general state budget. In fact, the government department may be penalized next year, when its budget is reduced because of the savings it made the preceding year in its negotiations with you. This may have some perverse effects. For one thing, it often leads to a flurry of negotiating activity as the end of a particular fiscal year approaches when government departments seeks to spend all of their annual budget, a factor sometimes used by private negotiators to their advantage in order to close a deal. Understanding the budgetary cycle of bureaucracies can work to the advantage of private negotiators as deadlines approach.
>
> **Resource Allocation Norms:** The second important operational norm is that most governments are not free to allocate the various factors of production, such as capital, labor, and technology, the way that the managers and negotiators in that department

---

[11] *See* James Q. Wilson, Bureaucracy: What Governments Do and Why They Do It 197 (2000).

judge best. Whereas private companies will decide whom to hire and whom to fire, and what equipment to buy or not to buy according to their view of that decision's impact on the profitability of their company, government departments often have to make similar decisions according to politically imposed rules. Since government entities in business are usually subsidized by the state treasury and are controlled by government officials, their principal goal may not be the maximization of profit, as is the case with private firms, but the advancement of social and political ends. For example, if a manufacturing joint venture between a U.S. company and a foreign state-owned corporation were to be faced with a decline in product demand, the reaction of the U.S. partner might be to lay off workers. However, the state corporation under government control, despite reduced profitability, might reject that solution to prevent an increase in unemployment in the country. In negotiating a transaction, it is often important to recognize and discuss at the table divergences in goals, rather than be surprised by them later on.

Objectives Norms: The third normative constraint is that government agencies and departments must pursue the objectives that the legislator has specified for them. They may not seek the goals that they themselves judge important. Companies change products and strategies in accordance with market demands. Government departments and agencies cannot change objectives as easily. When Ford Motor Company realized that the Edsel automobile, which it introduced in 1957, was a loser in the marketplace, it stopped making it in 1959. Had Ford been a government department, it would probably still be manufacturing Edsels today.[12]

6. A Government Deal Is Never Done

One of the risks of government negotiations is that governments tend to see any deal they make as always being open to reconsideration and renegotiation, even after the contract has been signed, when it suits that government's interests. In this regard, it is well to remember the British Prime Minister Benjamin Disraeli's remark to the House of Commons: "Finality is not the language of politics."

Despite lengthy negotiations, skilled drafting, and strict enforcement mechanisms, parties who solemnly signed and sealed agreements with governments often find themselves returning to the bargaining

---

[12] *Id.* at 115 et seq.

table later on to renegotiate their agreements. So a key challenge in negotiating with foreign governments is not just getting to yes, but also staying there. Thus, we have witnessed the renegotiation of state mineral and petroleum agreements in the 1960s and 1970s, often in the face of threatened host country nationalizations and expropriations; the loan reschedulings of the 1980s following the debt crisis in developing countries; the restructuring of government infrastructure projects as a result of the Asian financial crisis of the late 1990s; and the renegotiation of a host of deals as a result of the Argentine collapse at the beginning of the current century.

The risk of renegotiation of apparently definitive agreements is particularly present in dealings with governments for a variety of reasons. Governments often reserve to themselves the right to unilaterally change contracts on grounds of protecting national sovereignty, national security, or the public welfare. Moreover, the usual remedies in court for breach of contract may be unavailable or ineffectual against governments that take such actions. As we have seen, governments are particularly susceptible to political forces in their negotiations with private persons and companies. The changing nature of the political imperatives under which governments labor can cause them to change their position on agreements that they have previously made. Throughout the world, from Albania to Zambia, when political opposition develops toward agreements that governments have made, at some point, when the pressure becomes too great to resist, those governments will look for ways to cancel or redo those agreements in order to satisfy their political constituents. As a result, it is important to incorporate into your strategy tactics and mechanisms to deal with this risk. Because of its prevalence in dealings with governments, negotiators need to understand the forces that give rise to renegotiation, the nature of the renegotiation process, and the best ways to renegotiate deals that they thought were done.

7. Coping with Corruption

Although many public officials throughout the world work diligently for their governments, corruption is a particular risk in negotiations with governments. While corruption has many legal definitions, it is basically the abuse of a public office for private gain. Corruption arises in negotiations with governments when government negotiators employ their discretion to advance their own personal interests, instead of the interests of the government and the public they are supposed to represent. It can take many forms: cash payments to an official to secure a government contract, gifts to a politician's spouse to gain that politician's endorsement of a permit, or an interest-free "loan" to the brother of an official reviewing your company's tax returns.

The subject of government corruption is complex, and a full treatment is beyond the scope of this chapter. Its potential to affect a negotiation is influenced by a variety of intricate factors, including the legal or business traditions of the country or industry concerned, the strength of the bureaucracy with which you are dealing, the nature of the persons sitting across the table from you, and your company's own internal policies, culture, and controls, to mention just a few. In nearly all countries, the payment of a bribe to government officials to secure a favorable contract or action in a negotiation is a crime by law; however, the readiness of a particular legal system to enforce those laws varies from country to country, from state to state, and even town to town. From an institutional point of view, corruption, as Robert Klitgaard has pointed out, is a function of three factors: discretion, monopoly, and accountability.[13] The likelihood of corruption by government officials rises when that official has great discretion, when the official has monopoly power of what you are seeking, and when mechanisms to hold that official accountable for his or her decisions are weak.

Even if you are negotiating in a country with weak enforcement of antibribery laws, it is well to remember that the U.S. Foreign Corrupt Practices Act imposes severe penalties on U.S. companies and persons who pay bribes to foreign officials. Moreover, indulging in bribery has a corrosive effect on your own company and employees, damages your reputation with business associates and the public, and can lead to other types of financial losses.

The presence of a corrupt official on the other side of the bargaining table can obstruct your negotiation in two ways. First, it may confront you with the choice of walking away from the deal or making an illegal payment. Second, if you are in competition for a deal with another company that has made a corrupt payment, it may cause you to lose the deal.

How then should you protect yourself against the demands of corrupt officials in your negotiations with government? Although no foolproof protection exists, the following suggestions may help you cope with corruption in your government negotiations.

- Work to understand the nature of the laws and institutions affecting corrupt payments in the country or area in which you are negotiating and discuss them with your negotiating team as part of your preparation.
- If your company has prepared a code of business ethics or similar document, provide it to the other side as part of the introductory material you ordinarily furnish before or at the beginning of

---

[13] Robert Klitgaard, Controlling Corruption 75 (1988).

negotiations. When introducing your company to a governmental unit, you might review that statement in some detail.

- Develop a strong relationship with a reputable and honest local individual or organization in the area, preferably one that is politically influential. Often that person or organization has learned how to resist corruption and can advise you on whom to contact in order to counter the corrupt demands of local officials.

- If you are approached for a bribe, explain that while you have great respect for your counterpart, you risk prosecution under the Foreign Corrupt Practices Act if you make corrupt payments. When a West African minister during a break in a negotiating session poetically told an American executive that the minister was "the first tree in the forest and needed water," the American replied in friendly but blunt terms: "If I pay you, I'll go to jail. And since you are my friend, I know you don't want that to happen."

- Try to deflect a demand for a bribe by offering to make a legitimate charitable donation or providing a service that benefits the country or the local community. Your company might build a playground for a school or a dispensary for a village, allowing the officials with whom you have been negotiating to take full credit for persuading you to make this gift. Your company might also sponsor free cultural events such as an art exhibit, a play, or a rock concert. If you choose to go this route, you must be absolutely sure that the payments you make do indeed go to finance these charitable and social activities, not to line the pockets of local officials.

- If corruption is pervasive within an organization with which you are negotiating, you may have no other option than to walk away from the deal. If corruption is not pervasive, you might attempt to involve in the negotiation process persons or departments that are not corrupt with the hope that their presence will serve to control the behavior of negotiators seeking a bribe. Another approach is to build another channel of communication, hopefully at a higher level, then use that channel to persuade the government of the benefits of dealing with you.

- Recognize that in many cultures gifts are an essential part of building relationships between persons and groups. Not all such gifts are necessarily corrupt or equivalent to bribes. To reject abruptly and moralistically any suggested request for a gift may be interpreted as a rejection of the relationship. Try to set a policy as to the kind of gifts you are prepared to give that are consistent with the law and with your own company's business ethics.

- Finally, remember that efforts to satisfy the personal interests of your counterparts across the negotiating table are not always illegal or unethical. Their desire for your respect, for favorable standing in the eyes of their superiors, and for positive recognition from colleagues in their organizations are personal interests that you should recognize and in appropriate ways help to satisfy as a means to pursue your company's interests in the negotiation. For example, if the lead negotiator on the other side is having difficulty understanding the financial technicalities of the deal you are proposing, it may be better to explain them in a private conversation than to lecture him in detail in front of the whole team on the other side.

8. Conclusion

Governments "feel" different in international business negotiations because they are different. As this chapter has shown, governments require a different approach in negotiation. The following seven guidelines may be helpful:

Guideline No. 1: As you approach negotiations with any government, recognize that it possesses powers and is subject to constraints different from those to be found in negotiating with private persons and organizations. Then seek to understand how you may incorporate these factors into your negotiating strategies and tactics. As a result of these powers and constraints, government negotiators will often behave differently from their private sector counterparts at the negotiating table.

Guideline No. 2: All governments and their officials jealously guard their authority because authority is what allows them to govern. Never challenge the authority of a government department or agency and avoid any action that might be interpreted as a challenge. Respect and deference should guide all your negotiations with any government.

Guideline No. 3: Learn the rules governing the negotiation process and the protocols and forms expected of you as a nongovernmental negotiator. To gain that knowledge, seek the advice of consultants, people in the particular community concerned, and those persons who have had experience in negotiating with a particular governmental unit.

Guideline No. 4: All governments enjoy to a greater or lesser extent certain privileges and immunities. Learn what they are in the case of the particular government with which you are negotiating.

Guideline No. 5: The "public interest" is always an actual or potential factor in any negotiation with any government. It can turn any seemingly bilateral negotiation between you and a government department into a multilateral negotiation involving uninvited members of the public, civic groups, and the media. You should always plan your negotiations accordingly.

Guideline No. 6: Nearly three hundred years ago, François de Callières, a distinguished French diplomat who wrote one of the first practical manuals[14] on negotiating with governments, stressed "the necessity of continual negotiation" between states through their permanent representatives as the basis of modern diplomacy—a novel idea in its time but one that modern diplomats take for granted today. Twenty-first-century negotiators must also recognize that a productive relationship with a government is a constant process of negotiation. Just as negotiations do not stop when two countries seal a treaty, negotiations do not end when your company signs a contract with a government department or agency. Develop your business strategies and deploy your resources with that principle constantly in mind.

Guideline No. 7: Always search for the political imperatives driving your governmental counterparts in a negotiation and find ways to satisfy them while attaining your interests. Remember: a good deal to a government official is a deal that is defensible to his or her superiors, political opponents, and the public.

Jeswald W. Salacuse
Henry J. Braker Professor of Law
The Fletcher School of Law and Diplomacy
Tufts University
160 Packard Avenue
Medford, MA 02155
Phone: (617) 627-3633
Fax: (617) 627-3871
E-mail: Jeswald.Salacuse@Tufts.edu

---

[14] François de Callières, De La Manière de négocier avec les souverains. De l'utilité des négociations, du choix des ambassadeurs et des envoyés et des qualitiés nécessaires pour réussir dans ces emplois (1716). The book has been published in many languages since it was written. The most recent English-language edition is On the Manner of Negotiating with Princes (A.F. Whyte trans., Houghton Mifflin 2000) (1919), with an introduction by Charles Handy.

CHAPTER 17

The European Union's Regulation of E-Commerce: Lessons and Theory

Alina Bica-Huiu[1]

ARESTY INTERNATIONAL LAW OFFICES, P.C.

SUDBURY, MASSACHUSETTS

The twentieth century saw the human thirst for knowledge develop the Internet as a global information market and library. As the twenty-first century began, the Internet was experiencing explosive growth, transforming into a multifaceted medium for trade, in the form of e-commerce. At a dizzying pace, the Internet became the ubiquitous, global, and borderless marketplace for goods and services of any kind. Increasingly, consumers are pushing past the traditional confines of distance, expecting more of cyberspace and using it as a new, rapidly developing means of communication as well as a vital business tool.[2] Offering lower prices, greater choice, and better information, e-commerce has not only exponentially expanded variety and availability, but has also radically diminished the traditionally prohibitive costs of entry onto the international market. Indeed, e-commerce has helped make personal contact between sellers, distributors, and buyers increasingly unnecessary and, in some cases, even obsolete.

The emergence of e-commerce has also challenged conventional legal thinking, however, making notions of jurisdiction and consumer protection problematic at best, and often incompatible with existing laws. Courts in the United States have struggled to extend the principles of territoriality from previous legislation to Internet interactions, while consumers face continuing uncertainty in a largely unregulated environment.[3] The lack of a uniform legal framework for jurisdiction regarding Internet transactions, coupled with the application of traditional jurisdiction norms, leaves companies facing the possibility of

---

[1] The author would like to thank Mark Hoenike and Joachim Lehnhardt of Allen & Overy LLP, Germany, for their research and assistance regarding legislation in the European Union.

[2] Ljiljana Biukovic, *International Commercial Arbitration in Cyberspace: Recent Developments*, 22 NW. J. INT'L L. & BUS. 319 (2002).

[3] Marco Berliri, *Jurisdiction and Choice of Law in Cyberspace in Europe*, 16 SPG INT'L L. PRACTICUM 48 (2003).

being subject to any foreign legal judgments in any country in which their Web sites can be accessed. Yet, despite the challenges posed by this new-medium marketplace, e-commerce has become widely popular in the developed world.

By most available measures, the United States represents the original market for e-commerce, and since becoming a global phenomenon in the 1990s, e-commerce has grown into a substantial economic force. The U.S. Department of Commerce reports that the total value of U.S. shipments, sales, and revenue in 2006 was $20.9 trillion, fully 14 percent of which was designated as e-commerce.[4] There is little doubt that e-commerce is a vital part of the U.S. economy, contributing $2.7 trillion in business-to-business value and $0.2 trillion in business-to-customer value. European e-commerce in 2006 was still catching up to the American trendsetters, but nevertheless clocked in at a robust $1.4 trillion in just the combined markets of France, Germany, the United Kingdom, Spain, and Italy.[5]

With e-commerce growing rapidly, the United States and the European Union (EU) have both attempted to create adequate regulations and consumer protection norms. Albeit similar, the two approaches to e-commerce regulation reflect two diverging legal philosophies. The U.S. approach attempts to extend its laissez-faire business philosophy into the area of e-commerce regulations.[6] As such, the general goal of e-commerce regulation is believed to be to encourage industries to self-regulate and to support private sector organizations.[7] The U.S. Framework for Global Electronic Commerce lists five principles to be adhered to in any e-commerce regulation: (1) "The private sector should lead"; (2) "Governments should avoid undue restrictions on electronic commerce"; (3) "Where governmental involvement is needed, its aim should be to support and enforce a predictable, minimalist, consistent, and simple legal environment for commerce"; (4) "Governments should recognize the unique qualities of the Internet"; and (5) "Electronic Commerce over the Internet should be facilitated on a global basis."[8]

---

[4] U.S. Census Bureau, Econ. & Stats. Admin., U.S. Dept. of Commerce, E-Stats (May 16, 2008), available at http://www.census.gov/eos/www/2006/2006reportfinal.pdf.

[5] Anke Müller, Bradford Francis, Irina Saal & Mathias Koeckeritz, U.S. Dept. of Commerce, Germany: E-Commerce: Executive Summary, (Sept. 2007), available at www.buyusa.gov/arkansas/ecommgerm1007.pdf.

[6] See Joel R. Reidenberg, E-Commerce and Trans-Atlantic Privacy, 38 Hous. L. Rev. 717, 718 (2001).

[7] See The White House, A Framework for Global Electronic Commerce, Executive Summary (July 1, 1997), http://www.ibiblio.org/pub/academic/political-science/internet-related/technology-initiative-summary/report.txt [hereinafter "White House Framework"].

[8] Id.

The EU presents a stark contrast to the basic principles behind the U.S. approach. In 2000, the EU attempted to construct a basic framework for the future regulation of e-commerce, focusing principally on growing the internal marketplace while protecting member state sovereignty and the rights of consumers.[9] Because most barriers to trade in the e-commerce area are fading, it is one of the least-complicated facets of the EU Framework, where market cohesion can be achieved with relative ease. Moreover, the fundamental principle behind e-commerce regulation in the EU does not stem from the laissez-faire doctrine and principle of freedom of contract as in the United States, but rather from the fundamental human right to consumer protection.

However different these approaches are, both U.S. and EU regulations aim to support and enforce a predictable, minimalist, consistent, and simple legal environment for e-commerce.[10] Many consumer protection elements from the Universal Commercial Code (U.C.C.), one of the most relevant U.S. regulations applicable to e-commerce, parallel elements set forth by the EU directives. Yet proponents of the U.S. regulation scheme believe the European model to be overly protective of consumer rights and encroaching into the free market, while supporters of the EU regulation model consider the American regulation to be too lax with regard to consumer protection.[11]

Despite all flaws and contrary to the expectations of the proponents of the U.S. model, the EU regulatory system has yielded successful results, increasing consumer confidence and even surpassing the e-commerce growth rate of the United States. While traditional laissez-faire theories would suggest that government interference in the marketplace would yield poorer results, the European e-commerce regulation model, while not perfect, offers a viable and perhaps more successful alternative.[12]

1. The European Framework

As early as 1976, the European Council had expressed concerns about consumers being offered goods and services in an unequal fashion, or in environments with high litigation costs for businesses from other member states. Thus, it is unsurprising that access to the Internet as an essential element of economic growth, investment, and the stimulation

---

[9] *See* Council Directive 2000/31/EC, "Directive on electronic commerce," 2000 O.J. (L 178) 1, *available at* http://eur-lex.europa.eu/LexUriServ/LexUriServ.do?uri=CELEX: 32000L0031:EN:NOT [hereinafter the "e-Commerce Directive"].

[10] *Id.*

[11] James R. Maxeiner, *Standard-terms Contracting in the Global Electronic Age: European Alternatives*, 28 YALE J. INT'L L. 109 (2003).

[12] JOHN DICKIE, PRODUCERS AND CONSUMERS IN EU E-COMMERCE LAW (2005).

of e-commerce came to the forefront of the legislative agenda.[13] In attempting to create new uniform e-commerce regulation and harmonize state laws, the EU set forth a series of directives addressing jurisdiction, contracts, and choice of law and consumer protection.

Similar in concept to the American federal system, the EU legal system is unique and follows a complex formula, operating alongside the laws of the member states of the European Community. The EU currently consists of 27 independent and sovereign countries[14] that have their own independent legal system. Although the EU has the power to impose legal restrictions and regulations on the member states, in particular with regard to the harmonization of the internal market, each country tries to maintain autonomy of its judicial and government branches, while insuring what it believes to be the adequate protection of its population, a notion that varies widely from country to country.[15] EU directives are binding on the member states; however, they must be transposed into national law by the member states in order to take effect. The member states, in turn, retain some discretion as to how the directives are implemented. Moreover, directives only set out minimum standards, allowing the member states to impose higher standards, which in turn creates different rules that electronic traders have to comply with. When the time limit for implementing directives passes, directives may, under certain conditions, have direct effect on national law of the member states, even if they were not implemented by the member states. The EU e-commerce directives leave criminal laws and safety standards, including liability and labeling obligations, up to individual nations.[16]

2. Jurisdiction

In the matter of ensuring consumer protection, jurisdiction over e-commerce transactions is essential to establish an accessible justice system and proper enforcement.[17] Application of traditional notions of jurisdiction, anchored in geographical delineations, are insufficient to

---

[13] Comm. of Ministers, Council of Eur., Unfair Terms in Consumer Contracts and an Appropriate Method of Control, 262d Meet., Resolution (76) 47 (1977).

[14] Austria, Belgium, Bulgaria, Cyprus, the Czech Republic, Denmark, Estonia, Finland, France, Germany, Greece, Hungary, Ireland, Italy, Latvia, Lithuania, Luxembourg, Malta, the Netherlands, Poland, Portugal, Romania, Slovakia, Slovenia, Spain, Sweden, and the United Kingdom.

[15] Christopher W. Papas, *Comparative U.S. and EU Approaches to E-commerce Regulation: Jurisdiction, Electronic Contracts, Electronic Signatures and Taxation*, 31 DENV. J. INT'L L. & POL'Y 325 (2002).

[16] *See* e-Commerce Directive, *supra* note 9, at 1, 21.

[17] *See* Michael Geist, *Is There a There There? Toward Greater Certainty for Internet Jurisdiction*, 661 PLI/PAT 561, 575 (2001).

deal with e-commerce in general, and they become even more problematic in the EU, given the differences in the legal systems of the member states. One of the most important directives in the field of e-commerce is Directive 2000/31/EC (the "**e-Commerce Directive**"),[18] relating to certain legal aspects of information society services, in particular electronic commerce in the Internal Market. This directive provides the principle of the country of origin, which means that the law of the country where the offered item or service comes from is applicable. It consists of the principle of home country control and the principle of mutual recognition. This approach is clearly preferred by businesses, as it gives them control and certainty about which laws apply. Nevertheless, it is possible for the parties of a contract to derogate from this rule, as parties are allowed to choose the law applicable to their contract. In this case, the applicable law has to be determined, and the process is subject to the Rome Convention on the law applicable on contractual obligations.[19]

In a clear move toward consumer protection, the EU amended the 1968 Brussels Convention, through Brussels I or the Brussels Regulation, which mandates that "online sellers be subject to suit in all fifteen EU states when they sell over the Internet."[20] Thus, contracts concluded with consumers are always governed by the law of the country in which the consumer resides, where the contract in the consumer's country was preceded by an invitation or advertisement, where he took all the necessary steps for concluding the contract, and where the contract was concluded with the use of an interactive Web site that is accessible in the state where the consumer is domiciled. Consumer accessibility to the judicial system is further underlined by granting the courts jurisdiction over a merchant where he "pursues commercial or professional activities in the Member State of the consumer's domicile or, by any means, directs such activities to that Member State . . . [21]" As such, e-commerce companies must comply with the laws of all EU member states, or otherwise lose business in those states whose laws they are incompliant with.

Moreover, the European consumer protection philosophy is evident in that, while parties are (under certain conditions) allowed to choose a forum in any member state, the protection of the weaker party limits this freedom. Proceedings resulting from a consumer

---

[18] E-Commerce Directive, *supra* note 9.

[19] Council Regulation No. 44/2001/EC on jurisdiction and the recognition and enforcement of judgments in civil and commercial matters, art. 15(1)(c), 2001 O.J. (L 12) 1, *available at* http://eur-lex.europa.eu/LexUriServ/LexUriServ.do?uri=CELEX:32001R0044:EN:HTML [hereinafter "Enforcement Regulation"].

[20] Nicole Goldstein, *Brussels I: A Race to the Top*, 2 CHI. J. INT'L L. 521, 521–23 (2001).

[21] Enforcement Regulation, *supra* note 19, at 1, 6.

contract are only allowed in the country where the consumer resides. The consumer, on the other hand, has the choice where he wants to bring an action against his opponent.

Perhaps the most notorious representation of the universal jurisdiction of member states granted through Brussels I is the Yahoo! case, where the Paris Tribunal de Grande Instance exercised jurisdiction over Yahoo!, a U.S. company, and required that the company remove memorabilia from its auction Web site because the public display of Nazi-related materials violated French criminal law.[22] Although the French court ruled that it had jurisdiction, contrary to Yahoo!'s claims, the Northern District of California ruled, in a summary judgment, that the French judgment was unenforceable, as its compliance would violate the fundamental right to free speech guaranteed by the First Amendment of the U.S. Constitution.[23] Although the French court's judgment was based in part on expert testimony relating to blocking technologies available at the time, and although France had legal jurisdiction under the Brussels amendment, enforcement of the judgment was clearly not practical or likely.

In contrast to the European approach to jurisdiction, the U.S. courts have tried to adapt traditional jurisdiction approaches to e-commerce transactions, applying the minimum contacts test set forth by the Supreme Court in *International Shoe*, whereby a defendant, not present in the forum, must "have certain minimum contacts with it such that the maintenance of the suit does not offend traditional notions of fair play and substantial justice."[24] The U.S. courts further revised this approach to more accurately apply to e-commerce and held that a court's jurisdiction is dictated by a sliding scale between highly interactive contact and passive contact between the defendant company's Web site and the plaintiff,[25] or alternatively used a broader, effects-based approach that determines jurisdiction based on an analysis of where the actual effects of a Web site occurred. While somewhat different, and although the EU approach grants wider jurisdiction to the member states, favoring consumer protection, the U.S. effects-based approach is virtually equivalent and merely restricted by the due process requirements of the U.S. Constitution.

3. Electronic Contracts

E-commerce has not only raised issues of jurisdiction and enforceability of laws, but also created a new set of issues arising from contract

---

[22] Yahoo! Inc. v. La Ligue Contre le Racisme et l'Antisémitisme, 169 F. Supp. 2d 1181 (N.D. Cal. 2001).

[23] *Id.*

[24] *See* Int'l Shoe Co. v. State of Wash., 326 U.S. 310 (1945).

[25] *See* Zippo Mfg. Co. v. Zippo Dot Com, Inc., 952 F. Supp. 1119 (W.D. Pa. 1997).

formation and validity, unfair terms, and authentication. In trying to "bring some basic legal clarity and harmony to EU e-commerce laws,"[26] the EU has enacted regulations attempting to address all of the aforementioned issues. The e-Commerce Directive (2000/31/EC), applicable to all consumer contracts, was to be implemented by all EU members provisions by January 17, 2002, and required that consumers be given the ability to view and check all information prior to completing their order, and furthermore that an acknowledgment of the order details be transmitted to the consumer by electronic means, and without undue delay, upon their acceptance of the contract.[27]

3.1 Contract Formation and Validity

The e-Commerce Directive seeks to contribute to the proper functioning of the Internal Market by ensuring the free movement of information society services (including e-commerce) between member states (Article 1 (1)). It specifically provides that the member states must ensure that their legal system allows contracts to be concluded by electronic means. Moreover, the directive requires all service providers to grant easy, direct, and permanent access to essential information to the recipients of the service (e.g., the name, address, and further details of the service provider) and disclose certain information to the consumer before an order is placed, such as, for instance, the technical steps that are to be followed in the process of concluding a contract.[28]

Another important directive used to regulate electronic contracts is Directive 97/7/EC of May 20, 1997 on the protection of consumers in respect of distance contracts[29] (the "**Distance Selling Directive**"). The Distance Selling Directive applies to most contracts where a consumer and a supplier do not meet face to face at any stage until after the contract has been concluded. This directive provides an important instrument to ensure a high level of consumer protection. It tries to put consumers who purchase goods or services by electronic means in a position similar to consumers who buy goods or services in shops. To ensure this, the Distance Selling Directive grants consumers a right to withdraw within a period of at least seven days, with some exceptions for services, perishable goods, and custom-made goods. The consumer does not have to give any reasons or justifications for the withdrawal. The only charge that may be imposed on the consumer because of the

---

[26] E-Commerce Directive, *supra* note 9, at 1, art. 22.

[27] Papas, *supra* note 15. *See also* e-Commerce Directive, *supra* note 9.

[28] For further details see e-Commerce Directive, *supra* note 9, at art. 6.

[29] Council Directive 97/7/EC on the protection of consumers in respect of distance contracts, 1997 O.J. (L 144) 19, *available at* http://eur-lex.europa.eu/LexUriServ/Lex UriServ.do?uri=CELEX:31997L0007:EN:NOT.

exercise of his right of withdrawal is the direct cost of returning the goods.

Consumer protection is not only advanced by the Distance Selling Directive through the right of withdrawal, but also through the information requirements set forth in the directive. The directive mandates that consumers be given information concerning the details about the supplier and its business; the characteristics of the goods or services offered; the arrangements for payments, delivery, and performance; the right to withdraw and the procedures for exercising this right; the after-sale services and guarantees; and the conditions of the contract. This wide range of information is often not completely provided to the consumer. This can result in the cancellation of the contract or have effects on the right to withdraw. Moreover, all information required must be provided in a "clear and comprehensible manner . . . with due regard . . . to the principles of good faith . . . ."[30]

Vastly pro-consumer, the e-Commerce Directive and the Distance Selling Directive further mandate that if the information requirements are fulfilled, the period for exercising the right of withdrawal starts from the day the consumer receives the goods or services. If the information requirements are not met, the right of withdrawal should not expire before the lapse of three months. Member states also have the flexibility to go beyond the standards set up by directives. Thus, while under EU regulation the period for exercising the right of withdrawal has to add up to at least seven days, member states may grant a longer period to the consumer. In practice, in most member states this period is fourteen or fifteen days. In cases of inaccurate information, the minimum period required under the EU directives is three months. However, in Germany, for instance, this period does not even start before the information has been fully disclosed to the consumer; consequently, if a supplier does not provide a consumer in Germany with this information, the consumer will have an unlimited right to withdraw from the contract.

E-commerce information requirements for consumer protection are further outlined in Directive 1998/6/EC of February 16, 1998 on the indication of the prices of products offered to consumers (the "**Unit Pricing Directive**").[31] The directive improves consumer information and facilitates comparison of prices by stipulating the indication of the selling price and the price per unit of measurement (unit price) of products offered to consumers. As a general rule, the selling price and the unit price must be indicated in an unambiguous, easily identifiable

---

[30] *Id.* at art. 4(2).

[31] Council Directive 98/6/EC on consumer protection in the indication of the prices of products offered to consumers, 1998 O.J. (L 80) 27, art. 4, *available at* http://eur-lex .europa.eu/LexUriServ/LexUriServ.do?uri=CELEX:31998L0006:EN:NOT.

and clearly legible way. Member states are free to adopt provisions that are more favorable with regards to consumer protection. However, the member states may also waive the obligation to indicate the unit price of products for which such indication would not be useful or could lead to confusion. Furthermore, they may decide not to apply this rule to products supplied in the course of the provision of a service and to sales by auction and sales of works of art and antiques.

According to the e-Commerce Directive, the member states have to ensure that the national legislation allows for the binding conclusion of contracts by electronic means. The basic principles of how to enter into a contract are the same in all member states: contracts are binding if one party makes a binding offer that is accepted by the other party, where both the offer as well as the acceptance can be declared without any formal requirements. However, e-commerce raised the question of how to differentiate between a binding offer and an invitation to trade. Whether a declaration is qualified as a binding offer or as an invitation to trade is a question of shifting risks. In general, the qualification of the declaration depends on the case's special circumstances (e.g., how the Web page is designed, what payment devices are used, and if a will for a binding offer is expressed).

It is up to the member states' national courts to interpret and decide whether the offeror intended to be bound by its declaration, and thus whether an offer or merely an invitation arose. In some member states (for instance France, Italy, Portugal, and Spain), an advertisement on a Web page may be held to constitute a binding offer if all the relevant information is made available. However, in most of the member states such advertisements are considered as nonbinding invitations where by clicking on an "I agree" button the customer merely makes a binding offer that the supplier has to accept before a binding contract is concluded. Other member states even require that the customer has to be advised several times that a binding contract is going to be concluded. The Market Court in Sweden[32] established a "three clicks" requirement for a valid Internet order to become a binding contract: expressing an interest in buying, acknowledging having read the details of the order and the contractual conditions, and placing the order itself and accepting the contractual conditions. Most of the member states require similar proceedings.

In order to ensure that they are not bound to contract with persons they do not want to deal with, the sellers often use general terms and conditions in order to clarify that their initial "declaration" constitutes a mere invitation to trade. The purchaser's offer will then be accepted by the seller via electronically generated confirmation e-mails. These e-mails may lead to the conclusion of the contract even though automatically generated.

---

[32] The Swedish Market Court, MD 2004:18 (July 2004).

In comparison, the U.S. attempt to create a standard statutory system specifically designed to suit virtual transactions is the Uniform Computer Information Transactions Act (or UCITA). UCITA fell short of its expectations, being adopted by only two states, Maryland and Virginia.[33] Designed to provide "default rules, interpretations, and guidelines for transactions involving 'computer information,' including many, if not all, e-commerce transactions,"[34] UCITA was originally a proposal for a new U.C.C. Article 2 with a scope limited to "computer information" transactions, which are defined as agreements involving "information in electronic form which [are] obtained from or through the use of a computer or . . . capable of being processed by a computer."[35] Although UCITA arguably addresses most, if not all, issues raised by virtual transactions, e-commerce is currently regulated by the U.C.C. and state common law. As such, although the U.C.C. provides for consumer protection, while at the same is designed to promote business development under a uniform regulation, it does not take into account the special characteristics of e-commerce and thus is often inappropriate.

3.2 Unfair Terms

The European Council has long acknowledged the need for consumer protection against unfair terms that prejudice their interests but that they had no power to amend. The Council recommended that member states take steps to protect consumers against unfair terms in contracts, in particular "where the consumer has little, if any, possibility of negotiating or influencing their content."[36]

The Directive 1993/13/EC of April 5, 1993 on unfair terms in consumer contract (the "**Unfair Terms Directive**") sets out minimum standards, explicitly authorizing member states to maintain or adopt "more stringent provisions" in order to ensure "a maximum degree of protection for the consumer."[37] The Unfair Terms Directive aims at the approximation of laws concerning unfair terms limited to contracts with consumers, natural persons acting for purposes outside their trade, business, or profession.[38] In particular, it pertains to general

---

[33] Uniform Computer Information Transactions Act, (1999), final 2002 draft, available at http://www.law.uh.edu/ucc2b/UCITA_final_02.pdf.

[34] Dennis M. Kennedy, *Key Legal Concerns in E-Commerce: The Law Comes to the New Frontier*, 18 T.M. Cooley L. Rev. 17, 18–19 (2001).

[35] UCITA final draft, *supra* note 33, § 102(a)(10).

[36] Maxeiner, *supra* note 11, at 122.

[37] Council Directive 93/13/EEC on unfair terms in consumer contracts, 1993 O.J. (L. 95) 29, art. 8, *available at* http://eur-lex.europa.eu/LexUriServ/LexUriServ .do?uri=CELEX:31993L0013:EN:NOT.

[38] *Id.* at art. 2.

terms and conditions. The directive requires the invalidation of unfair terms used in a contract concluded with a consumer by a seller or supplier, as provided for under their national law, and that the contract continue to bind the parties upon those terms if it is capable of continuing in existence without the unfair terms.[39] According to the directive, a term is unfair if it causes a significant imbalance in the parties' rights and obligations arising under the contract, to the detriment of the consumer. The annex to this directive sets out certain examples of terms that have to be regarded as unfair.

Because of opposition from member states, the directive extends to pre-formulated standard contracts, which are not considered to be individually negotiated, but does not apply to terms that have been "individually negotiated," excluding from content review the "main subject matter of the contract" and the "adequacy of the price and remuneration."[40] However, in accordance with the consumer protection philosophy, the Unfair Terms Directive requires contract terms to be drafted in plain and intelligible language and states that ambiguities will be interpreted in favor of consumers. Moreover, the presence of either significant imbalance or action contrary to good faith is sufficient to constitute unfairness. Member states must make sure that effective means exist under national law to enforce these rights and to prevent the continued use of unfair terms. The Unfair Terms Directive introduces a notion of "good faith" in order to prevent significant imbalances in the rights and obligations of consumers on the one hand and sellers and suppliers on the other.

Unfairness may be found in clauses "irrevocably binding the consumer to terms with which he had no real opportunity of becoming acquainted before the conclusion of the contract," a concept that was in direct opposition to UCITA, which authorized this type of term. Terms "excluding or hindering the consumer's right to take legal action or exercise any other legal remedy, particularly by requiring the consumer to take disputes exclusively to arbitration not covered by legal provisions" have been held by the European Court of Justice to render invalid forum selection clauses with consumers.[41] Going even further, the Unfair Terms Directive also requires member states to take affirmative steps towards ensuring that such unfair terms cease to be used. Additionally, in furthering consumer protection, national courts shall, of their own motion, determine whether a term is unfair, and action to prevent the use of unfair terms may be brought by consumer groups so long as the actions are directed against sellers collectively and not just against a single seller.[42]

---

[39] *Id.* at art. 6.
[40] *Id.* at art. 3.
[41] *Id.*
[42] *Id.* at art. 7.

EU regulation applicable to e-commerce further protects consumers through the Directive 1999/44/EC of May 25, 1999 on certain aspects of the sale of consumer goods and associated guarantees (the "**Guarantees Directive**"), which makes certain guarantees mandatory, thus requiring no review to find such terms unfair, where the law makes the terms mandatory.[43] In order to ensure a uniform minimum level of consumer protection in the context of the Internal Market, this directive aims at the approximation of the laws, regulations, and administrative provisions of the member states on certain aspects of the sale of consumer goods and associated guarantees. The directive gives consumers a right to have defective goods repaired or replaced or to accordingly receive a price reduction. Under the directive, sellers are liable to consumers for any lack of conformity that exists when the goods are delivered to the consumer and where the lack of conformity becomes apparent within a period of two years. Any guarantees offered by the manufacturer or retailer are legally binding and must be presented with details of how to make a claim. If the defect is present within the first six months of ownership, it will be assumed that faulty goods have been sold with the fault unless disputed and proven otherwise by the manufacturer.

Similarly, the relevant U.S. legislation applicable to e-commerce (the U.C.C.) contains several provisions regarding consumer protection against unconscionable terms, and warranties. Under the American system, adhesion contracts (contracts between two parties that do not allow for any negotiation) are often considered unconscionable, and thus unenforceable under the U.C.C. provisions. While the American system is clearly less ambitious than its European counterparts, limited to striking down terms that "shock the conscience," the original intent of U.C.C. was to create a system that would "allow American courts to develop machinery for policing contract terms."[44] Such machinery has been developed from largely the same starting point by the German Supreme Court, thus confirming the vision of the drafters of the U.C.C. and proving "that efforts to delineate principles of general contract law able to take into account the realities of modern contracting are not radical efforts to be feared; rather, they are organic developments that hold true to the conceptual structure of contract law."[45]

---

[43] Council Directive 1999/44/EC on certain aspects of the sale of consumer goods and associated guarantees, 1999 O.J. (L 171) 12, *available at* http://eur-lex.europa.eu/Lex UriServ/LexUriServ.do?uri=CELEX:31999L0044:EN:NOT.

[44] Francis J. Mootz III, *After the Battle of the Forms: Commercial Contracting in the Electronic Age*, 4 I/S: J. L. & Pol'y for Info. Soc'y 271 (2008).

[45] Maxeiner, *supra* note 11, at .

3.3 Contract Authentication

E-commerce further raises the issue of the legal value of an electronic document, since documents produced by electronic means do not have a handwritten signature and their legal relevance is uncertain. The Directive 1999/93/EC on an EC framework for electronic signature (the "**e-Signature Directive**") attempts to "create a harmonized and appropriate legal framework for the use and legal recognition of electronic signatures within the EU."[46] The main objective of this directive is to create a framework for the use of electronic signatures, allowing the free flow of electronic signature products and services across borders and ensuring a basic legal recognition of electronic signatures. Through the Directive, member states are required to enact legislation recognizing "electronic signatures that are based on a 'qualified certificate' so long as they were created by a 'secure-signature-creation device . . .'"[47] The e-Signature Directive distinguishes between simple, advanced, and qualified electronic signatures. The simple electronic signature is defined as data in electronic form that serve as a method of authentication, while an advanced electronic signature is an electronic signature that meets additional requirements.[48] The qualified signature is defined as an electronic signature that is uniquely linked to the signatory, capable of identifying the signatory, created by using means that the signatory can maintain under his sole control and that is linked to the data to which it relates in such a manner that any subsequent change of the data is detectable written on a qualified document. For this purpose special software is needed, which has the effect that qualified signatures are not yet often used in electronic trading.

The directive does not affect national provisions such as a requirement for the use of paper for certain types of contracts, and it allows for parties in a closed system to negotiate their own terms for the use of electronic signatures within their system. Following the consumer protection theory, the EU Directive states no specific technology requirement, allowing for technological innovation, and dictates that authentication be provided by Certification Service Providers (CSPs) who are to be held liable to anyone who relies upon an issued certificate.[49]

The U.S. approach consists mainly of two broadly adopted federal regulations: ESIGN, which covers electronic signatures, and the federal Uniform Electronic Transactions Act (UETA), which governs

---

[46] Mark Owen, *International Ramifications of Doing Business On-line: Europe*, 661 PLI/Pat 627, 654 (2001).

[47] Papas, *supra* note 15.

[48] Council Directive 1999/93/EC on a Community framework for electronic signatures, 2000 O.J. (L 13) 12, *available at* http://eur-lex.europa.eu/LexUriServ/LexUriServ .do?uri=CELEX:31999L0093:EN:NOT.

[49] *Id.* at art. 2.

electronic signatures as well as other e-commerce transactions. ESIGN, an example of the application of Commerce's powers under the Commerce Clause of the U.S. Constitution, mandates that for all electronic contracts relating to interstate or foreign commerce a "signature, contract, or other record may not be denied effect, validity or enforceability solely because it is in electronic form."[50] However, despite being federal law (and unlike UCITA or UETA), it does not preempt state laws on the topic. UETA, by contrast, mandates more stringent requirements, considering a contract valid where an electronic signature can be attributed to a party, "if it can be shown in any manner, including use of a reliable security procedure, that it was the act of that person."[51] However, UETA applies strictly if the parties agree to use electronic commerce with regard to the transaction in question, while UCITA automatically applies unless the parties expressly opt out.

4. Data Protection

With the expansion of e-commerce, noncash means of payment have also become more prevalent. It is in the best interest of e-commerce, the credit industry, and companies to bolster consumer confidence in noncash means of payment, especially as identity theft (also called identity fraud) has steadily increased in recent years. In endeavoring to protect consumers from identity fraud, legislatures have either followed a *prevention* philosophy or a *restitution* philosophy. The EU has approached the issue of data protection and identity fraud from a prevention standpoint, aiming to prevent the theft or wrongful use of a consumer's identity before any damage is done.

Intended to prevent identity fraud, the EU approach regulates information databases created by financial institutions and government entities, providing substantial protection of personal data at its initial creation and storage points. While there are criminal statutes aimed at punishing identity thieves, the European attitude towards this issue favors international cooperation as well as private business and law-enforcement cooperation to protect consumers, rather than only legislating and punishing. The European legislature's focus on consumer protection is transparent from this approach, viewing "privacy with the utmost sanctity, putting commercial concerns at a distant second to consumer privacy concerns."[52]

---

[50] Electronic Signatures in Global and National Commerce Act, 15 U.S.C. §§ 7001 et seq., 7001(a)(1) (2000).

[51] Papas, *supra* note 15.

[52] Erin Suzanne Davis, *A World Wide Problem on the World Wide Web: International Responses to Transnational Identity Theft Via the Internet*, 12 WASH. U. J.L. & POL'Y 201, 207 (2003).

Directive 95/46/EC of October 24, 1995 on the protection of individuals with regard to the processing of personal data and on the free movement of such data (the "**Data Protection Directive**") embodies the EU approach, and has been viewed as "the culmination of over fifty years of devotion to recognizing, maintaining, restoring, and ensuring personal privacy."[53] The directive aims to protect the right to privacy with respect to the processing of personal data, directing the member states to "protect the fundamental rights and freedoms of natural persons, and in particular their right to privacy with respect to the processing of personal data."[54] It provides that the processing of personal data must be performed with appropriate security in the interest of protecting the rights and privacy of targeted persons, setting forth minimum standards of care in processing, handling, and storing personal data.[55]

Anchored in a fundamental human right to privacy, the Data Protection Directive is very ambitious, with a broad scope striving to maximize consumer protection of personal data held by any data controller in any sector of the economy. It applies "to the processing of personal data wholly or partly by automatic means, and to the processing otherwise than by automatic means of personal data which form part of a filing system or are intended to form part of a filing system."[56] The key elements of the directive, personal data and processing, are purposefully defined broadly to encompass as many scenarios of the use of personal data as possible. Thus, the directive applies to "any information relating to an identified or identifiable natural person," and any operation performed on personal data, such as "collection, recording, organization, storage, adaptation or alteration, retrieval, consultation, use, disclosure by transmission, dissemination, or otherwise making available . . . ."[57]

While adoption and actual implementation of the directive differ from state to state, member states are charged with ensuring that personal data is processed fairly and lawfully, and that the controller adheres to the EU criteria and implements appropriate technical and organizational measures to protect personal data against all unlawful forms of processing (e.g., accidental or unlawful destruction or

---

[53] Marsha Cope Huie, Stephen F. Laribee & Stephen D. Hogan, *The Right to Privacy in Personal Data: The EU Prods the U.S. and Controversy Continues*, 9 TULSA J. COMP. & INT'L L. 391, 441 (2002). *See also* Council Directive 95/46/EC on the protection of individuals with regard to the processing of personal data and on the free movement of such data, 1995 O.J. (L 281) 31, *available at* http://eur-lex.europa.eu/LexUriServ/LexUriServ .do?uri=CELEX:31995L0046:EN:NOT [hereinafter "Personal Data Directive"].

[54] *Id.*

[55] Andrea M. Matwyshyn, *Of Nodes and Power Laws: A Network Theory Approach to Internet Jurisdiction Through Data Privacy*, 98 Nw. U. L. REV. 493, 500 n.43 (2004).

[56] Personal Data Directive, *supra* note 53, at art. 3.

[57] *Id.* at art. 3.

accidental loss, alteration, unauthorized disclosure or access). More-over, the directive extends liability to controllers, granting standing to any person who "has suffered damage as a result of an unlawful processing or of any act incompatible with the national provisions adopted pursuant to [the] Directive."[58] Before processing of personal data may commence, at least one of six criteria must be met: overall, these criteria require that the processing must be consented to or must be necessary for the purposes of the legitimate interests pursued by the controller or a third party.[59]

The directive further grants the unique "Subject's Right of Access to Data," whereby consumers are allowed, without excessive delay or expense, to obtain confirmation from the controller as to whether or not their personal data is being processed; the purpose, the logic, and the recipients of the processing; categories of data concerned; and the recipients of such data.[60] Another critical right, not present in the U.S. legislation but granted by the EU under this directive, is the "Right to Object" where data is being processed for some public interest.[61] Although discrepancy exists between member states' legislation, the Data Protection Directive is vital to protecting consumers, as it recog-nizes consumers' rights to some control over personal data and is an important step in regional international cooperation.

An example of privacy rights espoused by the directive and applied by the member states is CIFAS (Credit Industry Fraud Avoid-ance System), the United Kingdom's fraud prevention service, which is equivalent to a not-for-profit corporation "dedicated to the preven-tion of financial crime."[62] With the cooperation of the public and pri-vate sector comprising telecommunications, insurance, commercial, and banking institutions, CIFAS has had large success in the United Kingdom. Not only were CIFAS members able to detect and prevent 64.7 percent of identity fraud before an account was ever opened, but also reportedly prevented £1,400 (US$2,715) in financial fraud every minute of every day, and was able to discover over 85,000 fraud cases during the months of January to June in 2006.[63]

Building upon the principles expressed in the Data Protection Directive, the Council of the European Union adopted a framework decision on Combating Fraud and Counterfeiting Means of Non-cash Means of Payment on May 28, 2001, directing the member states to criminalize theft or unlawful appropriation of a payment instrument,

---

[58] *Id.* at art. 23.
[59] *Id.* at art. 7.
[60] *Id.* at art. 12.
[61] *Id.*
[62] CIFAS, "What Is CIFAS?" http://www.cifas.org.uk/what_is_cifas.asp (last visited Aug. 21, 2008).
[63] Samuel H. Johnson, *Who We Really Are: On the Need for the United States to Adopt the Euro-pean Paradigm for Identity Fraud Protection*, CURRENTS: INT'L TRADE L.J. 123 (2006).

or its fraudulent use, as well as acts in which an individual "perform[s] or cause[s] a transfer of money or monetary value . . . causing an unauthorized loss of property for another person."[64] Additionally, the decision establishes the liability of legal persons and entities for the conduct it prohibits, when committed for the benefit of the entity by a person with a leading position in the entity, based on authority within the entity or power of representation of the entity.[65] The EU decision goes even further in establishing liability on the part of the entity where lack of supervision or control by a person in a leading position was present. In stark contrast to the U.S. approach, the decision gives incentive to entities to prevent such behavior from occurring, as companies as well as their officers who knowingly or negligently allow theft of personal data are personally liable, which "encourages companies with opportunities to benefit from misappropriation of personal data to refrain from taking advantage of such opportunities, and to prevent their employees from doing so as well."[66]

Another major divergence between the European and U.S. approaches has been America following the restitution philosophy, redressing a victim's injustice only after the consumer has become a victim of identity fraud and discovered the damage. This approach relies on deterrence, assuming that laws and fear of punishment will deter thieves from committing identity fraud, and consumer rights, which grant consumer access to credit reports. This approach provides no preventative protection, merely a criminal framework to punish those who have already committed identity fraud, and gives consumers a way to check whether or not they have already become a victim. One of the centerpieces of legislation criminalizing identity fraud is the Identity Theft Act, which makes it a crime to misuse both public and nonpublic information. The broad statutory language used in the statute mirrors the ambitious attempt of the EU Data Protection Directive by envisioning application not only in contemporary Identity Fraud, but also in unforeseeable methods and schemes. However, the Act is only deterrent in scope, and does not provide for its use against a foreign criminal in United States courts.

Complementing the Identity Theft Act, the Gramm-Leach-Bliley Act was signed into law in order to modernize the financial services industry and increase consumer information privacy. Unsurprisingly, the U.S. regulation is far less focused on consumer protection and does not provide any remedies for an individual harmed by an institution's failure to comply with the act. The act not only does not prevent

---

[64] Council Framework Decision 2001/413/JHA combating fraud and counterfeiting of non-cash means of payment, 2001 O.J. (L 149) 2, art. 3, *available at* http://eur-lex.europa.eu/LexUriServ/LexUriServ.do?uri=CELEX:32001F0413:EN:NOT.
[65] *Id.*
[66] Johnson, *supra* note 63, at 136.

the sharing of personal data between affiliates, but it also provides minimal incentives for compliance, as the "only enforcement is implementation by the institution, and a consumer has no standing to file suit against an institution that fails to implement the standards."[67] Later attempts to prevent identity theft and improve the accuracy of consumer records through the passage of the Fair and Accurate Credit Transactions Act left consumers with even more very serious concerns over the bill's preemption of state laws providing more protection of consumer personal data.[68]

Moreover, not only is identity fraud legislation relatively weak in the United States but also, despite a conclusion of the Safe Harbor Agreement between the United States Department of Commerce and the European Union that allows American companies to continue to do business with Europe in response to the Data Protection Directive, consumer protection within the United States remains unchanged, as the agreement does not contemplate providing greater protection of personal data for United States citizens, but merely applies to companies wishing to transact business in the EU.[69]

5. Other E-commerce Legislation

In addition to the aforementioned legislation, the EU has enacted several other provisions aimed at streamlining e-commerce throughout Europe and strengthening the internal market. With a view to simplifying, modernizing, and harmonizing the conditions laid down for invoicing with respect to value added tax, Directive 2001/115/EC of December 20, 2001 amending Directive 77/388/EEC (the "e-Invoicing Directive") facilitates adaptation to electronic trade improving the quality of invoice data and streamlining business processes for both seller and buyer. Because member states have different tax laws and VAT tax rates, the e-Invoicing Directive simplifies transactions by regulating the electronic transmission and electronic storage of invoices across the EC.

Consumer protection is also further evident from Directive 2005/29/EC of May 11, 2005 concerning unfair business-to-consumer commercial practices in the Internal Market and amending Directives 84/450/EEC, 97/7/EC, 98/27/EC, and 2002/65/EC (the "Unfair Commercial Practices Directive"). The directive outlines unfair commercial practices that will be prohibited throughout the EC, such as pressure selling, misleading marketing, and unfair advertising, and sets out certain rules on advertising to children, with the intent to give EU consumers the same protection against aggressive or misleading

---

[67] *Id.*

[68] Kathy M. Kristof, *Credit Reporting Act Would Null Tough State Laws*, L.A. TIMES, Nov. 30, 2003, at C3.

[69] Davis, *supra* note 52, at 214.

marketing regardless of whether they buy locally or from other member states' markets. The EU Distance Selling Directive and Directive 2002/65/EC concerning the distance marketing of consumer financial services (the "**Financial Service Directive**") also protects the consumer from unsolicited selling and fraudulent use of payment cards, providing for a right to cancellation of payment. The Distance Selling Directive has been amended by the Financial Service Directive, establishing common rules to govern the conditions under which distance contracts for financial services are concluded. The directive gives a certain right to withdraw from the contract and grants the consumer an opportunity to reflect before concluding a contract with a supplier.[70]

6. Drawbacks and Weaknesses

Although the EU e-commerce framework provides ample consumer protection and generally addresses all major legal concerns, the EU's inherent design poses the threat of inconsistency. EU directives are unable to enforce uniform legal standards throughout the EU, and given that application and enforcement of the EU directives by the member states varies substantially, so does the effectiveness of the EU regulations.

Moreover, a major problem in passing the directives is the difficulty in reaching a political consensus between the member states, which often leads to a ratified legislation that is broader, weaker, and includes much more politically neutral language. To reach consensus on the e-Commerce Directive, the final language had likely been watered down to vaguely calling for "cooperation" in the drive for a universal standard on electronic commerce.[71]

Political and cultural disagreement among the member states, in particular Germany's opposition to the adoption of complete consumer protection by the Unfair Terms Directive to the detriment of freedom of contract, was resolved by limiting the application of the directive. Although not necessarily a bad decision, the directive as finally adopted is a compromise between the two, reasoning that the principle of freedom of contract counsels not the free application of standard terms but rather their close scrutiny, whereas for actually negotiated terms, the principle of private autonomy should apply.[72]

One difficulty with e-commerce legislation in general is that the legislative process is so slow that many laws have lost some technological relevance by the time they are adopted. One such instance is the

---

[70] For further details see Article 6 of Directive 2000/65/EC, 2000 O.J. (L 269) 44, *available at* http://eur-lex.europa.eu/LexUriServ/LexUriServ.do?uri=CELEX:32000L0065: EN:NOT.

[71] Arno Lodder & Henrik Kaspersen, EDirectives: Guide to European Union Law on E-Commerce 92 (2002).

[72] Maxeiner, *supra* note 11, at 139.

Distance Selling Directive (1991), which was written before the Internet came into prominence as a tool of commerce. As a result, the language of that directive has been difficult to adapt to the high-tech environs of Internet commerce.[73]

7. European E-commerce: Present and Projection

At a glance, one might say that the United States has enjoyed more success in e-commerce. After all, our earlier comparisons of Internet transactions between the United States and Europe's five largest markets combined still gives the United States a two-to-one advantage in sheer business-to-consumer commercial volume. The real test of which regulatory model is succeeding, however, is not in describing Europe or the United States today, but rather in anticipating where both digital economies will be in the future.

One projection, put forth by JupiterResearch[74] in 2005, anticipated that Western Europe's online retail market would be roughly analogous to the growth of online retail in the United States:

> Although European markets will develop with distinctive characteristics, there is no doubt many of the same growth patterns that have been seen in the US will also apply. Consequently, historical adoption rates and expected adoption in the US were inputs into JupiterResearch's forecasts for the European markets.

Thus, we can consider JupiterResearch to be predicting an "American Model" for e-commerce growth. According to the American Model, JupiterResearch projected that the size of the European online retail market (business-to-customer, goods only) would grow to approximately €117.1 billion by 2010.

A different analysis, published by eMarketer in the same year,[75] projected a very different pattern of growth for Western Europe. According to their projections, e-commerce sales of retail goods in Western Europe would grow to €187.6 billion by 2010, over 60 percent higher than JupiterResearch's projection. The reasons for this difference lie in the methodology: unlike JupiterResearch, the analysis undertaken by eMarketer made the projections based on current European patterns of growth without using American data to calibrate the predic-

---

[73] Id.

[74] JupiterResearch, European Online Retail Forecast, 2005 to 2010 (Dec. 9, 2005), available for purchase at http://www.jupiterresearch.com/bin/item.pl/research:concept/91/id=96907/.

[75] EMarketer, Western Europe E-Commerce: Spotlight on the UK, Germany, and France (Aug. 2005), available for purchase at http://www.mindbranch.com/Western-Europe-Commerce-R203-345/.

tion. Thus, we can describe the eMarketer projection to operate on the "European Model."

With two models available to us, our task is to determine which will more accurately come to fruition. Embedded in that comparison is an examination of any available evidence that the "American Model" really is substantively different from the "European Model" on more than a legal level. To get a sense of the difference, it helps to examine the differences between the United States and Europe.

One simple comparison we can make is to examine rates of broadband Internet subscription. Broadband is a better indicator of access to the digital economy than "general Internet access" because e-commerce has generally relied on users with high-speed connections that enable them to browse image-rich Web sites or download large files. Consequently, measuring per-capita rates of broadband subscription creates a snapshot of the "power users" in a particular country's digital marketplace.

Figure 17.1 shows the rate of broadband subscription (per million people) for the United States (in black), the "EU 15"[76] overall (in gray), and those fifteen EU countries individually (gray dotted lines). What is striking about Figure 17.1 is that despite its growth beginning two years earlier than Europe overall, broadband penetration in the EU 15 now runs neck and neck with the United States. Furthermore, Europe's three largest markets (France, Germany, and the United Kingdom) all now surpass the United States. Still more interestingly, even countries with much higher subscription rates (such as Denmark and the Netherlands) are continuing to grow at approximately the same speed as the United States. Only a handful of European countries (Austria, Spain, Italy, and Portugal) are currently growing more slowly than the United States.

Europe's faster rate of adopting broadband and the higher levels of penetration in many markets strongly suggests that the American Model isn't going to effectively capture the growth of e-commerce in Europe. It also suggests a degree of hesitancy on the part of American consumers. This hesitancy can be easily captured by comparing broadband subscription to consumer confidence, as presented in Figure 17.2.

The consumer confidence index (average for 2007, from the *OECD Key Economic Indicators*) in Figure 17.2 is clearly related to degree of broadband subscription. Austria is the only really unusual exception, showing high consumer confidence despite low subscription (and low historical growth in subscription). Greece is also an outlier, but this is unsurprising given that its subscription growth lags about three years

---

[76] The "EU 15" refers to the fifteen countries making up the European Union from 1995 to 2004. They are Austria, Belgium, Denmark, Finland, France, Germany, Greece, Ireland, Italy, Luxembourg, The Netherlands, Portugal, Spain, Sweden, and the United Kingdom.

Figure 17.1

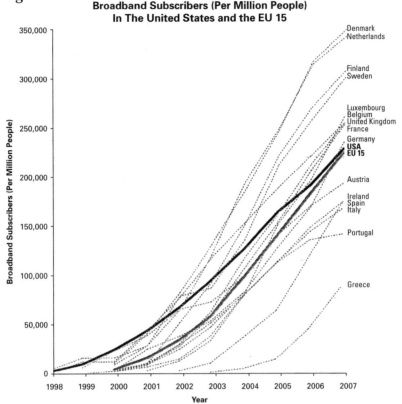

**Broadband Subscribers (Per Million People)
In The United States and the EU 15**

Shows the growth in broadband Internet subscription (per million people) for 16 countries: the United States and the 15 countries in the European Union in 1998. The solid black line shows subscriptions for the United States, while the solid gray line shows subscriptions for the EU 15 overall. Gray dotted lines show the growth for the 15 individual European countries. Data are drawn from *World Development Indicators Online* (1998 through 2005) and the *OECD Directorate for Science, Technology, and Industry* (2006 and 2007).

behind overall EU 15 growth, as we can see in Figure 17.1. Setting aside those two nations, however, we can see a clear relationship between consumer confidence and broadband penetration, suggesting that the accelerated growth and high per-capita broadband subscription of the EU 15 are related values.

We can already see manifestations of this growth in existing economic indicators. France and Germany, for example, continue to meet the 30-percent-or-more growth in business-to-consumer transactions per year projected through 2010 by eMarketer, while U.S. business-to-consumer transactions are only growing at around 19 percent per year. From this we can conclude that Europe is having more success in drawing new consumers into the marketplace.

Figure 17.2

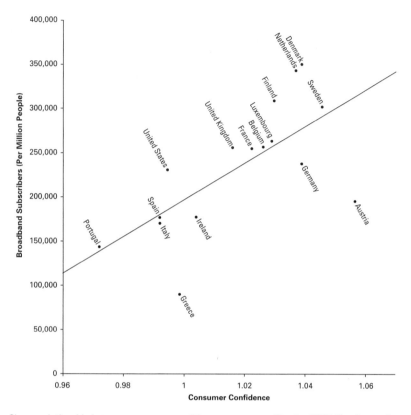

Broadband Subscription vs. Consumer Confidence in 2007

Shows relationship between consumer confidence as measured by the *OECD Key Economic Indicators* (2007) and broadband Internet subscription (per million people) for the United States and the EU 15.

Given these indicators, it seems likely that the European Model for projecting e-commerce growth is a better indicator for growth in Western Europe than the American model. As such, it is reasonable to assume that e-commerce in Europe will continue to grow at a faster rate than in the United States for some time, particularly in business-to-customer volume. The strengths and flexibility of the European Framework play a vital role in protecting consumers, as well as raising consumer confidence in a way that appears to have palpable economic benefits.

8. Conclusion

The European Commission has considered e-commerce to be of the utmost importance to the integration of the European market, and has attempted to regulate the field thoroughly while simultaneously leaving the member states discretionary room for interpretation and implementation. Although this often leads to the different application and interpretation of the directives, and business must in practice comply with national law, the EU has enacted a consumer-friendly legislation bolstering consumer confidence and thus e-commerce.

The impending implementation of the Single Euro Payments Area (SEPA) offers an unprecedented opportunity to further bolster consumer confidence in e-commerce and the Internal Market.[77] SEPA creates a unique opportunity for the development of a uniform dispute resolution system, based on the general EU principles and directives, which could in turn further boost consumer confidence in cross-border e-commerce. Although the EU system developed based on the philosophy of consumer protection, it is arguably still weak, because of the lack of transparency and uniformity of application and enforcement by the member states.

While the European model has its advantages, focusing mainly on consumer protection, it is important to note that not all legislation passed is necessarily effective. Furthermore, traditional free market approaches to legislation are also validly supported by economic arguments and data, and the U.S. economy remains one of the largest and strongest economies in the world. However, data shows that while business-to-business e-commerce levels in the United States are extremely high, business-to-consumer e-commerce still shows considerable room for growth. It is quite clear that America has low levels of consumer confidence relative to much of Europe, and that consumer confidence is correlated with the size of the digital marketplace (both displayed in Figure 17.2). As statistics suggest that consumer confidence is an important catalyst to business-to-consumer e-commerce development, the United States may be able to adapt some of the aspects of the European model and significantly boost the growth of its already-sizable share of business-to-consumer e-commerce by enacting legislation that boosts consumer confidence.

Alina Bica-Huiu, Associate
Aresty International Law Offices, P.C.
365 Boston Post Road #135
Sudbury, MA 01776
Phone: (508) 314-0916
E-mail: Alina.Bica.Huiu@gmail.com

---

[77] Press Release, Eur. Comm'n & Eur. Cent. Bank, Single Euro Payments Area, Joint Statement from the European Commission and the European Central Bank (May 4, 2006), http://www.ecb.int/press/pr/date/2006/html/pr060504_1.en.html.

PART 2:

Country-by-Country Guide to International Business Negotiations

CHAPTER 18

International Business Negotiations in Argentina

Ramón M. Segura
MARVAL, O'FARRELL & MAIRAL
BUENOS AIRES, ARGENTINA

1. Introduction

1.1 Broad Demographic Information

The Republic of Argentina comprises twenty-three provinces and the federal capital, the Autonomous City of Buenos Aires. Located at the extreme southeast of the South American continent, Argentina is the eighth-largest country in the world and the second largest in Latin America, covering some 3.8 million square kilometers (1.5 million square miles). Argentina has a population of approximately 37 million people, of which 12 million live in the city of Buenos Aires and the greater Buenos Aires area.

1.2 Historical and Cultural Background

Argentina has been heavily influenced by the Europeans, who arrived in the region back in 1502. Spain established a permanent colony on the site of Buenos Aires in 1580, and further integrated Argentina into its empire by establishing the Vice Royalty of Rio de la Plata in 1776. However, following Napoleon's invasion of Spain and Britain's unsuccessful attempts to seize control of the Spanish colonies located around the La Plata Basin in South America (*Invaciones Inlgesas del Río de la Plata*) in 1806 and 1807, Buenos Aires formally declared independence from Spain on July 9, 1816. Two forces combined to create the modern Argentine nation in the late nineteenth century: the introduction of modern agricultural techniques and the integration of Argentina into the world economy. Foreign investment and immigration from Europe aided this economic revolution. Investment, primarily British, went into such fields as railroads and ports.

    The culture of Argentina is as varied as the country's geography and mix of ethnic groups. Modern Argentine culture has been largely influenced by European immigration. Buenos Aires and other cities show a mixture of architectural styles imported from Europe. In the case of older settlements (and of older preserved neighborhoods within cities), modern styles are mixed with colonial features, relics from the Spanish-ruled past. Museums, cinemas, and galleries are abundant in all the large urban centers, as well as traditional establishments such as literary bars and bars offering live music of a variety of genres.

1.3 Business Organization and Culture

Argentina benefits from rich natural resources, a highly literate population, an export-oriented agricultural sector, and a diversified industrial base. As mentioned in 1.2 above, foreign investment played a central role in Argentina's economic development. Prior to World War I, it could be said that Argentina's capital investment was foreign capital investment. By far, Britain contributed the most funds of any foreign state to the Argentine economy, as it did for many other Latin American countries. However, foreign investment disappeared during World War I to finance the European war effort, and failed to return after peace was reinstated. The period between 1914 and 1945 devastated the Argentine economy, and after World War II, a new model of economic growth began to emerge. Import substitution industrialization was adopted into Argentina's economic policy. In an effort to limit the country's dependence on the international market, government-imposed economic measures such as the nationalization of domestic industry were aimed at encouraging a more internal, self-sustaining development. While Argentina was able to harness a modest level of growth through import substitution, the level of economic development was not sufficient enough to bring Argentina to developed-level status. In 1955, spurred by economic difficulties, a military coup overthrew the government. This led to three decades of military dictatorships.

In order to attract foreign investment to the country again, in 1989 Argentina implemented the 1958 treaty signed with the United States regarding the Overseas Private Investment Corporation, which is an agency of the U.S. government that provides insurance to U.S. investments in developing countries. In addition, in recent years Argentina has signed treaties for the promotion and protection of foreign investments with a number of countries, including the United States, Germany, Switzerland, Italy, the United Kingdom, Belgium, Japan, Canada, France, Chile, Spain, Sweden, Austria, Holland, Denmark, Australia, New Zealand, and China. During the 1990s President Carlos Menem launched a major overhaul of Argentine domestic policy. Large-scale structural reforms dramatically reversed the role of the state in Argentine economic life. Ironically, the Peronist Carlos Menem oversaw the privatization of many of the industries Juan Domingo Perón, the father of the Peronist party, had nationalized. Privatization and a massive influx of foreign direct investment funds helped to improve the economy. Carlos Menem's successful turnaround of the economy made the country one of the top performers among the developing countries of the world (Argentina's GDP increased 35 percent from 1990 to 1994).

During year 2000–2001, international conditions changed; an increase in the volatility of emerging markets, the fall in U.S. stock markets, and the stricter monetary policy that followed affected the demand for securities issued in emerging markets, which resulted in higher financial costs. These factors, coupled with the Argentine local crisis that had been faced since the second half of 1998, adversely impacted on economic activity performance, and in December 2001, Argentina defaulted on its foreign debt to private creditors. People fearing the worst began withdrawing large sums of money from their bank accounts, turning Argentine pesos into U.S. dollars and sending them abroad. The government then enacted a set of measures (informally known as the *corralito*) that effectively froze all bank accounts, allowing for only minor sums of cash to be withdrawn. On December 21, President Fernando de la Rua left the Casa Rosada by helicopter. After a few days of chaos and uncertainty, and interim presidents who were appointed one day and fired the following day, Eduardo Dualde, an old-school Peronist, was appointed by the Legislative Assembly to stay for as long as needed to reinstate peace and order in the country.

In January 2002 the fixed 1-to-1 parity between the Argentine peso and the U.S. dollar that had been in place for more than ten years was abandoned. In a matter of days, the Argentine peso lost a large part of its value in the unregulated market. In addition to the *corralito*, the Argentine government established the *pesificación*, by which all bank accounts denominated in U.S. dollars would be converted into Argentine pesos at an exchange rate of AR$1.40 per US$1. The economic situation became steadily worse with regards to inflation and unemployment during 2002. Interim President Eduardo Duhalde finally managed to stabilize the situation to a certain extent, and called for elections.

On May 25, 2003, President Néstor Kirchner took office. President Kirchner kept Duhalde's Minister of Economy, Roberto Lavagna, in his position. Lavagna, a respected economist with centrist views, showed a considerable aptitude at managing the crisis. The economic outlook was completely different from that of the 1990s; the high exchange rate made Argentine exports cheap and competitive abroad. In addition, the high price of soybean and other commodities in the international market produced an injection of massive amounts of foreign currency (with China becoming a major buyer of Argentina's agro commodities). The Argentine government encouraged import substitution and accessible credit for businesses, set out an aggressive plan to improve tax collection, and set aside large amounts of money for social welfare, while controlling expenditure in other fields. As a result of the administration's productive model and controlling measures, the Argentine peso slowly revalued, reaching an exchange rate of AR$3 per US$1. Agricultural exports grew and tourism returned. The huge trade surplus ultimately caused such an inflow of U.S. dollars that the Argentine government was forced to begin intervening in order to keep the peso from revaluing further. Argentina managed to return to growth with surprising strength (approximately 8 percent average rate for the last five years). In addition, unemployment has been considerably reduced.

1.4 Overview of Legal System

Argentina is a civil law country. Their laws are stated in detailed Codes (Civil, Commercial, Criminal, and Procedural). The Argentine Constitution, like that of most Latin American countries, is very long and explicit. There is an executive, legislative, and judicial branch of government. As previously mentioned, there are twenty-three provinces and the federal capital, the Autonomous City of Buenos Aires. The twenty-three provinces are autonomous, but not as autonomous as the states in the U.S. system of government. There are two court systems, the federal court system and the provincial court system. There are no jury trials in Argentina. The judge plays an important and active role in the Argentine legal system. The role of the Argentinean lawyer in negotiations is very similar to that of a U.S. lawyer.

2. Substantive Laws and Regulations Impacting Negotiations

As a general principle, Argentine law generally permits parties to a contract to select the laws that will govern their agreements as long as there is some connection to the system of law that is chosen. Further, the choice of foreign law will only be valid to the extent that it does not contravene Argentine public policies (*orden público* or *ordre public*). Typical public policy laws include criminal, tax, labor, and bankruptcy laws. Further, matters concerning religion, tolerance, and morality are considered as forming part of Argentine public policies. Where Argentine public policies are deemed applicable, an Argentine court will substitute the applicable rule of Argentine law for a foreign rule. Furthermore, if an act is invalid under foreign law, an Argentine court may apply Argentine law if it is more favourable to the validity of such act.

For doing business in Argentina the main laws to take into consideration are the following:

2.1 Corporate Laws

Corporations in Argentina are mainly governed by the provisions of Law No. 19,550, as amended (the "ACL"), in all aspects related to registration, capital requirements, information requirements, rights and obligations of directors, syndics, and shareholders. Some specific activities, such as insurance and banking, are governed by special laws, though the provisions of the ACL would still apply in certain cases.

In order to conduct business in Argentina on a permanent basis, a foreign company may either (i) appoint a representative or set up a branch, or (ii) set up a domestic company (subsidiary). The main types of investment vehicles used by nonresident individuals and foreign companies are the corporation with limited liability (*sociedad anónima*), the limited liability company (*sociedad de responsabilidad limitada*), and the branch.

The basic characteristics of each type of business structure are detailed below.

2.1.1 Branch of a Foreign Entity

In principle, any company duly organized and existing in accordance with the laws of its country of origin can set up a branch in Argentina. While an amount of capital may be allocated to the branch, in principle, no minimum capital is required. The branch must keep separate accounting records in Argentina and file annual financial statements with the Public Registry of Commerce (PRC), which is the agency that supervises companies. The parent corporation is liable for all the liabilities of the branch, as they are not considered to be separate entities. The manager of the branch is subject to the same liabilities as a director of an SA (as defined below) under the ACL.

2.1.2 Corporation with Limited Liability (Sociedad Anónima) (SA)

An SA requires at least two shareholders to be set up, which can be either corporate entities or individuals. The minimum capital required by the PRC is AR$12,000, though the activities included within the scope of the corporate purpose must bear a reasonable relation to the company's capital. The capital is divided into shares that must be issued as registered nonendorsable shares or book-entry shares, and must also be denominated in Argentine currency. Foreign individuals (whether residents in Argentina or not) or foreign companies may hold up to 100 percent of the share capital. Transfers of shares are generally unrestricted, but restrictions may be included in the bylaws provided that they do not effectively prevent the transfer of shares.

2.1.3 Limited Liability Company (Sociedad de Responsabilidad Limitada) (SRL)

An SRL requires a minimum of two and a maximum of fifty partners to be set up; they may be individuals or corporate entities (except for SAs and Argentine limited liability partnerships with share capital (*Sociedades en Comandita por Acciones*)). Foreign corporate entities have been admitted as partners of SRLs provided that they are empowered to participate in such partnerships according to the laws of their jurisdiction of incorporation. Capital must be fully subscribed, denominated in Argentine currency, and divided into quotas. There is no minimum capital required to set up an SRL. Transfers of quotas between the partners are not restricted by law, but may be restricted under the bylaws.

2.2 Securities Law

The Argentine securities market is regulated by Law No. 17,811, as amended (the "Securities Law"), and subject to the supervision and control of the Argentine Securities Commission (*Comisión Nacional de Valores*) (the CNV). The CNV is an autonomous government agency empowered to enact regulations in the form of mandatory resolutions. In May 1997, the CNV issued Resolution No. 290, which adopted all outstanding resolutions and compiled them in a single book. This resolution has been amended by other resolutions issued since then. The Securities Law imposes, *inter alia*, the following duties on the CNV: (i) authorize the public offering of securities; (ii) maintain records of the individuals and companies authorized to publicly offer securities; (iii) act as the controlling authority on all matters concerning the applicability of the Securities Law; and (iv) maintain an index of the stockholders registered at stock exchanges.

A securities transaction falls under the scope of the Securities Law if the relevant securities are publicly offered in Argentina. In this case, both the issuer and the security are subject to registration with and approval from the CNV. In addition, the Securities Law requires that over-the-counter (OTC) brokers who conduct business in Argentina must register with the CNV and are subject to its control and supervision. Furthermore, only banks, OTC brokers, and stockbrokers can act as underwriters in Argentina on a regular basis.

Since the Securities Law has not been construed as having extraterritorial effect, it would only apply to transactions and brokerage activities that take place within Argentina. A transaction would normally be deemed to be performed outside Argentina if all obligations thereunder (payments of amounts due) are to be performed outside of Argentina. Further, it is customary for foreign brokers and dealers to enter into brokerage agreements with local brokers or dealers.

The CNV may penalize breaches of the Securities Law with sanctions that include warnings, fines, and suspension for up to two years or prohibition of the right to make public offerings of securities.

2.3 Tax Laws

The main tax laws in Argentina applicable to business activities in general are the following:

2.3.1 Income Tax
The Income Tax Law No. 20,628, as amended (the "Income Tax Law"), has adopted the worldwide income taxation principle. Therefore, all

income derived in the Argentine territory or abroad by individuals or legal entities domiciled in Argentina is subject to taxation. Non-residents are taxed only on income derived from Argentine sources. Argentine companies such as corporations and limited liability companies generally are considered separate from the shareholders or partners that own them. Therefore, they are considered separate taxpayers and, as such, are subject to tax on their net income, including capital gains, at a 35 percent rate. The net income of branches and other permanent establishments of foreign companies in Argentina are also subject to tax at the rate of 35 percent. In general, all ordinary and necessary expenses incurred in earning taxable income are tax deductible (such as interest, salaries, and taxes).

Losses incurred during any fiscal year may be carried forward and set off against taxable income obtained during the following five fiscal years. Pursuant to the provisions relating to transfer pricing, any transactions between related companies or unrelated companies located in low-tax jurisdictions should be done on an arm's-length basis.

Non–Argentine residents are taxed on their Argentine source income. The payor of these revenues must act as a withholding agent of income tax on behalf of the tax authorities. The withholding rate varies depending on the type and the nature of the income. The effective tax rate is determined by applying the general income tax rate (35 percent) to the portion of income that the Income Tax Law deems (no proof can be admitted to the contrary) to be from Argentine sources. Tax treaties entered into by Argentina can reduce domestic rates. Argentina has tax treaties presently in force with the following countries: Australia, Austria, Belgium, Bolivia, Brazil, Canada, Chile, Denmark, Finland, France, Germany, Italy, Netherlands, Norway, Spain, Sweden, Switzerland, Russia, and the United Kingdom. These treaties are mainly intended to avoid double taxation. Presently, there is no tax treaty between Argentina and the United States.

The distribution of dividends to shareholders in corporations, the distribution of income to partners in limited liability companies, and remittances of profits abroad by branches or establishments are in general not subject to tax in Argentina.

2.3.2 Value Added Tax
Value Added Tax Law No. 20,631, as amended, is paid at each stage of the production or commercialization of goods or services upon the value added during each of the relevant stages. As a result, this tax does not have a cumulative effect. The general rate is 21 percent.

2.3.3 Tax on Minimum Presumed Income
This tax applies to the total assets of Argentine companies and other entities, such as branches and other permanent establishments in Argentina of foreign entities and individuals. The tax is imposed at a 1 percent rate upon the total assets of the taxpayer only to the extent

that the total assets exceed AR$200,000 at the end of the taxpayer's fiscal year. If the total assets exceed such minimum amount, the total amount is subject to tax.

This tax is creditable against the company's income tax. Therefore, when there is enough taxable income to trigger this tax, this tax shall not constitute a cost. Furthermore, to the extent that this minimum tax cannot be credited against the corporate income tax, it may be carried forward as a credit for the following ten fiscal years.

2.3.4 Turnover Tax (Tax on Gross Income)
Turnover tax is a tax levied by each of the provinces and the Autonomous City of Buenos Aires on gross income derived from business activities carried out within the respective jurisdiction. Tax rates vary from jurisdiction to jurisdiction and are applied upon the tax base allocated to each jurisdiction according to specific allocation rules. This tax can be deducted from income tax.

2.3.5 Personal Assets Tax
The Personal Assets Tax Law No. 23,966, as amended, provides that all individuals domiciled in Argentina are subject to a tax upon their worldwide assets as of December 31 of each relevant fiscal year. The applicable tax rates go from 0.50 percent to 1.25 percent, depending on the total value of taxed assets. Personal Assets Tax regulations provide that Argentine companies must pay this tax on behalf of their shareholders if such shareholders are located abroad. The tax payable is 0.50 percent on the value of the shares. Certain conventions for the avoidance of double taxation entered into between Argentina and other countries may prevent the applicability of this tax.

2.4 Antitrust/Anticompetition Laws

2.4.1 Argentine Antitrust Law
In 1994, when the Argentine Constitution was amended, protection for competition against any kind of market distortion and control of natural and legal monopolies were included as a constitutional right. In September 1999, the Argentine Congress modified the former antitrust law, by means of Law No. 25,156, as amended, and Decree No. 1019/99, the provisions of which took effect on September 28, 1999 (together referred to as the "Antitrust Law"). The Antitrust Law was further implemented by Decree No. 89/2001 and modified by Decree No. 396/2001, effective April 9, 2001.

The Antitrust Law, enacted five years after the amendment of the Argentine Constitution, can be considered a further step toward the regulation of competition in Argentina; moreover, the Antitrust Law has introduced a system of control over mergers and acquisitions in Argentina.

2.4.2 Scope

Article 1 of the Antitrust Law prohibits certain acts or conducts relating to the production and exchange of goods and services if they limit, restrict, falsify, or distort competition, or if they constitute an abuse of a dominant position in a market. The Antitrust Law is applicable to all individuals and entities that carry out business activities within Argentina and to those who carry out business activities abroad, to the extent that their acts, activities, or agreements may have any effects in the Argentine market.

2.4.3 Description of Prohibited Practices

Article 2 of the Antitrust Law lists a series of acts considered as restrictive practices, provided that the other requirements established in Article 1 of the Antitrust Law are also met. This list, which is not exhaustive, includes: (i) price fixing; (ii) practices that limit or control technical development, or the production of goods and services; (iii) practices that establish minimum quantities or the horizontal allocation of zones, markets, customers, and sources of supply; (iv) agreeing on or coordinating bids in public biddings; (v) excluding, impeding, or hindering one or more competitors from accessing a market; (vi) conditioning the sale of goods to the purchase of another good or to the use of a service, or conditioning the provision of a service to the use of another service or the purchase of goods; (vii) limiting the purchase or sale to a condition of not using, purchasing, selling, or supplying goods or services produced, processed, distributed, or commercially exploited by third parties; (viii) unwarranted refusal to fulfill purchase or sale orders of goods or services submitted in existing market conditions; (ix) imposition of discriminatory conditions for the purchase or sale of goods or services not based upon existing commercial practices; (x) suspending the provision of a dominant monopolic service in the market to a provider of public services or of services which are of public interest; and (xi) predatory pricing (this term is broadly defined in the law).

2.4.4 Dominant Position

For the purposes of the Antitrust Law, the term "dominant position" includes situations where one person or more than one person is the only offeror or demanding party of a specific product within the Argentine market or in one or more parts of the world; or even if it is not the only offeror or demanding party in any of these markets, the person is not subject to substantial competition; or through a vertical or horizontal integration, that person is in a position to harm the economic viability of a competitor in the market.

2.4.5 Economic Concentrations (M&A)—Prior Administrative Control

The Antitrust Law provides that certain transactions resulting in economic concentrations (*concentraciones económicas*) require the prior approval of the Tribunal for the Defense of Competition.[1] Transactions requiring such approval are those resulting in the assumption of control of one or more companies by means of any of the following acts: (i) mergers; (ii) transfer of businesses; (iii) acquisitions of any shares or any other rights that grant to the acquiror control of, or a substantial influence over, the issuer; and (iv) any other agreement or act through which assets of a company are transferred to a person or economic group or that gives decision-making control over the ordinary or extraordinary decisions of management of a company.

The Antitrust Law provides that in the cases where the relevant group of companies involved has a "volume of business"[2] in Argentina of over AR$200 million, the transaction must be submitted to the Antitrust Commission for review.

2.4.6 Procedure

The Antitrust Commission can begin investigations ex officio or at the request of any party or entity. The Antitrust Commission may, as a preventive measure at any stage of the process (i) impose certain conditions; and (ii) issue cease and desist orders. The Antitrust Commission's decisions imposing sanctions, cease and desist orders, and the rejection or conditioning of acts regarding economic concentrations are subject to judicial review.

2.4.7 Penalties and Sanctions

The Antitrust Commission may apply (i) fines of up to AR$150 million upon those engaged in any prohibited activities and (ii) fines of up to AR$1 million per day upon those who violate the obligation to notify the Commission of acts of economic concentration, or who disobey cease and desist orders issued by the Commission.

The Antitrust Commission can also request a judicial order to liquidate or to perform a partition of companies infringing the provisions of this Antitrust Law. Directors, managers, administrators, internal auditors and members of supervisory committees, attorneys-in-fact, and legal representatives of such entities, may be held jointly and severally liable with the infringing entity.

2.5 Labor Laws

Employer-employee relations in Argentina are principally governed by Labor Contract Law No. 20,744 of September 11, 1974, as amended

---

[1] This role is at present being fulfilled by the existing Commission for the Defense of Competition (the "Antitrust Commission"), pending the setting up and regulation of the (new) Tribunal for the Defense of Competition pursuant to the provisions of the Antitrust Law.

[2] "Volume of Business" means annual sales net of sales discounts, Value Added Tax, and other taxes related to the volume of business.

(the "LCL"), collective bargaining agreements, and the individual terms of labor contracts between employers and their employees.

Argentine Law No. 25,877, as amended, effective as from March 28, 2004, introduced several amendments to the existing Argentine labor legislation.

2.5.1 Salaries

Salaries may be paid upon a monthly, daily, or hourly basis, depending on the type of work performed by the employee. By law, employees are entitled to an annual bonus (*aguinaldo*) paid in two installments, in June and December each year, equivalent to 50 percent of the highest monthly wage received during the previous six-month period. Typically, the standard working week is from forty to forty-eight hours per week, with an average of eight hours per day. Workers earn overtime pay for work performed in excess of the standard working week. The rates of overtime pay are 150 percent of the base rate on normal workdays and 200 percent of the base rate on Saturday afternoons, Sundays, and official holidays.

2.5.2 Contributions and Withholdings

Pursuant to Argentine law, employers and employees have certain obligations to make social security contributions for family allowances, medical services, and pension and unemployment benefits. In addition, pursuant to many collective bargaining agreements, union dues of 1 percent to 2.5 percent may be withheld from employees' salaries.

2.5.3 Vacations and Other Leaves of Absence

Employees are entitled to annual paid holidays, which vary from fourteen to thirty-five calendar days each year depending on length of service. In addition, employees are entitled to short leaves of absence in the event of marriage, birth, death of a close relative, and high school or university examinations. Female employees enjoy certain additional rights, most notable of which are special leaves of absence for maternity of forty-five days before and forty-five days after childbirth. Furthermore, during maternity leaves, employees are entitled to certain financial allowances and other fringe benefits.

2.5.4 Termination of Labor Contracts

An employee may resign at any time and must give the employer fifteen days' prior notice. In indefinite-term employment contracts, the employer may dismiss an employee at any time upon giving the employee prior notice of fifteen days (if the employee is dismissed during the trial period), one month (if the period of service is greater than the trial period but less than five years), or two months (if the period of service is greater than five years). The above-mentioned periods must be counted from the day following the prior notice communication.

This notice can be substituted with a salary payment equivalent to the period of prior notice. In case no prior notice is given and the dismissal takes place on a day different than the last day of the month, the employee will also collect an amount equal to the salary corresponding to the remaining days of the month of dismissal.

Furthermore, the employer is required to make severance payments to the employee based on the employee's highest ordinary monthly salary accrued during the previous year of employment. The employer must pay the employee one month's salary for each year of employment, or period worked in excess of three months, for which the employee worked with such employer. However, the severance payment cannot be less than the years of service multiplied by three times the employee's average monthly salary provided for in the collective bargaining agreement at the time of the dismissal. If an employee is dismissed for gross misconduct, no severance payment or prior notice is required; however, the burden of proof lies with the employer to show that gross misconduct occurred, and the courts are generally unsympathetic to employers in this area.

2.6 Environmental Laws

Unlike the United States and Western European countries, Argentina has only fairly recently shown concern regarding environmental issues. The enactment of Articles 41 and 43 in the Argentine Constitution, as amended in 1994, as well as new federal and provincial legislation, have strengthened the legal framework dealing with damage to the environment. Legislative and government agencies have become more vigilant in enforcing the laws and regulations regarding the environment, increasing sanctions for environmental violations.

Under the amended Articles 41 and 43 of the Argentine Constitution mentioned above, all Argentine inhabitants have both the right to an undamaged environment and a duty to protect it. The primary obligation of any person held liable for environmental damage is to rectify such damage according to and within the scope of the applicable law.

It is important to mention, however, that the Province of Buenos Aires, where most of the industries in Argentina are located, has also enacted environmental laws. These laws include requiring medium and large companies to prepare and file environmental impact statements in order to be granted the required operating permits for their activities and a law establishing rules for the production, handling, transport, treatment, and disposal of hazardous waste within its territory.

More than eight years after the amendment of the Argentine Constitution, making use of the constitutional mandate to set minimum standards for the protection of the environment, in November 2002 Congress passed Law No. 25,675 on national environmental policy. Law No. 25,675, as amended, provides the minimum standards for an adequate and sustainable management of the environment, for the preservation and protection of different species, and for sustainable development. This law sets out the objectives with which the national environmental policy must comply and creates a Federal Environmental System to coordinate the environmental policies of the federal government, the provinces, and the Autonomous City of Buenos Aires. This law, which is applicable throughout the entire country, is destined to be used for the interpretation and application of specific legislation, which shall remain in effect as long as it does not oppose the principles and provisions contained therein.

Law No. 25,675 also provides that any person or entity that carries out activities that are dangerous for the environment and ecosystems must contract an insurance policy that guarantees the remediation of any damages the activity may cause. According to Law No. 25,675, where environmental damages have a collective impact, any affected person, the ombudsman, nongovernmental environmental organizations, and the federal, provincial, and municipal agencies are all entitled to request before a court that any damages be remedied. This law also entitles individuals to request before a court the cessation of any activities that cause collective environmental damages.

2.7 Intellectual Property Laws

Article 17 of the Argentine Constitution protects intellectual property rights by providing that "[a]ll authors or inventors are the exclusive owners of their works, inventions or discoveries for the period of time established by law."

Since 1966, Argentina has been a party to the Paris Convention, incorporating the Lisbon Agreement of 1958. Furthermore, Argentina has also approved the Trade-Related Aspects of Intellectual Property Rights ("TRIPS") provisions of the General Agreement on Trade and Tariffs.

2.7.1 Trademarks and Trade Names

Trademarks and trade names are governed by Trademark Law No. 22,362, as amended, together with its regulatory decree. The law provides that the ownership of a trademark and the right to its exclusive use are obtained by registration with the Trademark Office. Accordingly, registration, and not use, confers proprietary rights. For the purposes of the registration of trademarks, as of April 9, 1981, Argentina has adopted the International Classification of Goods and Services.

The duration of a trademark registration is ten years, renewable indefinitely for periods of ten years provided the trademark has been used in connection with the sale of a product, the rendering of a service, or as a trade name during the five-year period preceding each expiration date. Failure to use the trademark during the relevant five-year period may subject it to cancellation. The overriding principle of the law is good faith in dealing with and using trademarks. Renowned trademarks have been afforded special protection by Argentine Courts.

2.7.2 Patents

Patents and Utility Models in Argentina are governed by Law No. 24,481, as amended, and Decree No. 260 of March 20, 1996 (the "Patent Law"). Argentina has adhered to the Paris Convention (Law No. 17,011) and to the TRIPS Agreement (Law No. 24,425) but not to the Patent Convention Treaty. The Patent Law provides that patents will be granted for any invention that complies with the requirements of novelty, inventive step, and capability of industrial application. Disclosure of an invention by the inventors or their lawful successors, by any means of communication or exhibition in a fair, within the period of one year immediately prior to an application for a patent or of the recognized priority, is not a bar to obtaining a valid patent. Patents are granted for twenty years from the date of application.

The owner of a patent granted in Argentina has the right to prevent third parties from carrying out without his or her consent acts of manufacture, use, offer for sale, or importation within the territory, of the product that is the subject matter of the patent. The protection for process patents covers the act of using the process, and also the acts of using, offering for sale, selling, or importing the product obtained directly by that process. The reversal of the burden of proof is available for process patents without distinction from the field of technology. The reversal of the burden of proof will not be applied when the product directly obtained from the patented process is not new. The product will not be considered new if there was another product, originating from another source different than the patentee or the alleged infringer, on the market at the time of infringement that did not infringe the patented process.

Patent applications may be filed in the name of an individual or a company. A foreign natural or legal person must establish a legal address within Argentine territory. Patents and utility models may be assigned and licensed, in whole or in part. The assignment must be recorded at the National Institute of Industrial Property to be effective vis-à-vis third parties.

2.7.3 Domain Names

There is no legislation in Argentina dealing specifically with domain names registered under "ccTLD .ar." However, there are administrative resolutions passed by the Argentine government that regulate domain name registration procedure in Argentina. Responsibility for the "ccTLD .ar" in Argentina falls under the authority of the Ministry of Foreign Affairs. The Ministry has subcontracted specialized staff, which operates under the name of NIC-Argentina, and their decisions are subject to judicial review. For the time being NIC-Argentina is not charging any filing or renewal fees. Under the Argentine Constitution, the establishment of fees by a public entity is a function of the Argentine Congress.

2.7.4 Copyright

Protection of copyright in Argentina is based on the constitutional principle set out in Article 17 of the Argentine Constitution mentioned above. However, copyright matters in Argentina are specifically governed by Law No. 11,723 of September 26, 1933, as amended (the "IP Law"). The IP Law extends protection to scientific, literary, artistic, and educational works, regardless of the process of reproduction. As a result of the broad definition of protected works, copyright protection has been granted to (i) writings (as in dictionaries, prayer books, almanacs, and articles); (ii) musical works and plays; (iii) cinematographic, choreographic, and pantomime works (as long as these works have been materialized in a tangible form); (iv) drawings, paintings, and sculptural works; (v) architectural, artistic, and scientific works; (vi) maps, plans, and other printed matter; (vii) plastic works, photographs, engravings, and phonograms; (viii) titles and characters as an integral part of a work; (ix) works of applied art; (x) computer software and databases; and (xi) derivative works, new versions, compilations, and translations, etc.

The Argentine courts have established that in order for a work to be protected by the IP Law, it must be expressed in a tangible, material form (thus excluding abstract ideas), and must contain a minimum degree of originality and novelty. As a general rule, the IP Law grants rights to the author for life and to his or her heirs and successors in title for seventy years as of January 1st following the author's death.

In order for a foreign work to qualify for copyright protection in Argentina, the conditions for protection under a copyright convention to which Argentina has adhered must be satisfied or the author must have complied with the formalities required for protection in the country where the work was first published (provided that he or she is a national of a country recognising copyright). If the foreign author meets these conditions, Argentina will grant the same protection as that provided to its own nationals (under the principle of "national treatment").

2.8 Privacy and Data Security Laws

Privacy and data in Argentina are regulated by the Data Protection Law No. 25,326, as amended (the "Data Protection Law"). The main purpose of the Data Protection Law is to guarantee (i) the complete protection of the data contained in files, records, databases, or other technical means, either public or private if destined "to supply information," and (ii) the rights to good reputation, privacy, and access to information, in accordance with Article 43 of the Argentine Constitution. In addition, the provisions of the Data Protection Law are applicable to legal entities.

The Data Protection Law holds a concept very similar to Special Category Data of the Directive 95/46/EC of the European Parliament and of the Council. According to Article 7 of the Data Protection Law, no individual may be obliged to supply sensitive information. Furthermore, sensitive data may only be collected by means of an authorization granted by law and for a public-interest purpose. Such data may also be collected for statistical or scientific purposes, provided that the owners of the data cannot be identified.

2.8.1 Duty of Confidentiality

The responsible person and any person who intervenes in any phase of the treatment of personal data have a duty of professional secrecy. Such duty will persist even after the relationship with the owner of data is terminated. Such duty of secrecy will be exempted if required by a judicial resolution or for public security, national defense, or public health reasons.

2.8.2 Assignment of Personal Data

Personal data can only be assigned (i) for the compliance of purposes directly related to the legitimate interest of the assignor and assignee, and (ii) if made with the previous consent of the owner. Such consent may be revoked. Additionally, the owner must be informed of the purpose of the assignment as well as of the identity of the assignee.

2.8.3 Sanctions and Legal Actions Available
Under the Data Protection Law

Notwithstanding other sanctions and/or indemnification for damages derived from other applicable laws, the Argentine Department for the Protection of Personal Data may apply penalties in the event of violation of the Data Protection Law. In addition to the above, the Argentine Criminal Code has been amended by the Data Protection Law to punish with imprisonment those who (i) knowingly insert or supply false information in a personal data file; (ii) illegally access databases; or (iii) disclose personal data protected by law.

2.9 Regulation of Foreign Investment

Foreign investments in Argentina are regulated by a framework of international treaties and Argentine laws that establish the norms for choice of law and jurisdiction, legal treatment of foreign investors, monetary policy, and foreign exchange.[3] In general, foreign investors wishing to invest in Argentina, either by starting up new businesses or by acquiring existing businesses or companies, do not require prior government approval. The few exceptions to this general rule are mentioned below. However, if a foreign company's investment consists of holding equity of an Argentine company, the foreign company must register with the PRC of the jurisdiction where the Argentine company is incorporated and comply with certain periodic reporting requirements.

Foreign investments are governed by Argentine Foreign Investments Law No. 21,382, as amended (the "Foreign Investments Law"), enacted in 1976, which has subsequently been the subject of considerable amendment with a view to liberalizing the regime applicable thereto. Pursuant to the Foreign Investments Law, foreign investment is understood to be the influx of resources originated abroad, in the form of direct investment or portfolio investments, in order to develop an economic activity in Argentina. Direct investment mechanisms include investments by multinational companies through the incorporation of a branch or local subsidiary, a partial or total acquisition of an existing company, the acquisition of assets, or association with existing or newly formed companies. Indirect mechanisms include portfolio investments through the acquisition of quoted or unquoted shares of companies or other entities.

The Foreign Investment Law states, as a general principle, that foreigners investing in economic activities in Argentina enjoy the same status and have the same rights that the Argentine Constitution affords local investors. Both are entitled to select any legal organization permitted by law, and to have free access to domestic and international financing. One of the few foreign investment sectors still restricted is broadcasting, but the Investment Protection Treaty with the United States has been construed as repealing restrictions for U.S. investors. Furthermore, Law No. 25,750, as amended, enacted in 2003, eases that restriction by allowing up to 30 percent foreign ownership of Argentine broadcasting companies (however, because of lack of precedent, uncertainty remains as to its actual application). In addition, foreigners who wish to purchase land located in frontier and other security areas, or who have a controlling participation in a company owning such land, must obtain prior government approval, which is usually obtained.

Until December 2001, there were no limitations on profit remittances (including dividends paid to nonresidents) nor upon capital repatriation, and, therefore, all investors enjoyed the right to repatriate profits and capital at any time. Following the establishment of

---

[3] The crises back in 2001 had a significant impact on this regulatory framework. For more information, please refer to 1.3 above and the last paragraph of this section 2.9.

exchange controls, this general rule established by the Foreign Investments Law was suspended and cross-border currency transfers for
profit remittances and capital repatriation required the prior approval
of the Central Bank of the Republic of Argentina. In January 2003,
that restriction was lifted in the case of profit remittances. However,
capital repatriation remains indirectly restricted due to the prohibition on purchases of foreign currency with Argentine pesos obtained
by non–Argentine residents from the sale of direct and portfolio investments in the nonfinancial private sector of more than US$2,000,000
per month (the limit is US$5,000 per month for investments in the
financial sector).

2.10 Other Potentially Applicable Laws and Regulations

2.10.1 Trusts

In 1995 Law No. 24,441, as amended (the "Trust Law"), introduced the
"trust" concept into Argentine law. The Trust Law establishes that a
trust will be created upon the transfer of certain assets by one person
(the settlor) to another person (the trustee), who undertakes to exercise the rights attributable to ownership of such assets for the benefit
of a person designated in the relevant agreement as the beneficiary
(the beneficiary) and to transfer the assets, upon the expiration of the
trust term or upon fulfillment of a certain condition, to the settler,
beneficiary, or trustee. If the property given in trust is inscribed in a
public registry, the relevant public registrars will record the assets in
the trustee's name. It has been instrumental in permitting innovative
financial techniques and structures.

The trust agreement must comply with the following requirements: (i) it must identify the assets subject to the agreement; if such
identification is not possible it must contain a description of the conditions and characteristics that those assets must have; (ii) the agreement must stipulate the way in which other assets may be added to
the trust; (iii) it must specify the term or condition to which the trust
ownership is subject, and shall never be effective for more than thirty
years from the date of its creation, unless the beneficiary is a natural
person without legal capacity, in which case it may be in effect until
the beneficiary's death or until termination of his incapacity; (iv) it
must specify to whom the assets will be allocated upon expiration of
the trust; and (v) the trustee's rights and obligations and the specific
manner in which the trustee may be replaced upon termination of his
office.

Any individual or legal entity may be appointed as trustee. However, the law contains specific regulations regarding financial trusts.
The trustee of a financial trust may only be a financial entity or a
corporation specifically authorized by the CNV to act as financial
trustee. Under a financial trust scheme, beneficiaries hold certificates

evidencing a trust ownership interest or debt securities secured by the assets held in trust. Such interest certificates and debt securities are deemed to be "securities" and may be the subject of a public offer.

Pursuant to Argentine law, assets held in trust form a separate estate from the estate of the trustee and the settler. They therefore will not be affected by any individual or joint actions brought by the trustee's or settler's creditors, except in the case of fraud by the settler. The beneficiary's creditors may exercise their rights over the proceeds of sale of the assets held in trust and be subrogated in the beneficiary's rights.

2.10.2 Resolution No. 7/2005 of the PRC

As previously mentioned, if a foreign company wishes to be a shareholder or partner in a local company, it must register its bylaws and other qualifying documents with the PRC, as well as appoint an attorney-in-fact in Argentina. The registration must be made prior to the incorporation of the company.

The foreign company must also appoint one or more attorneys-in-fact. The appointment of the attorney-in-fact must also be recorded with the PRC. The PRC of the Autonomous City of Buenos Aires (the *Inspección General de Justicia*) (the IGJ) has recently issued new regulations that provide that a foreign company must submit evidence that: (i) its main business purpose is performed outside Argentina, (ii) it has significant assets located outside the country, and (iii) it has not been incorporated in an offshore or low-tax jurisdiction. If the foreign company fits within these requirements, and can prove so, it can be registered with the IGJ.

If the foreign company does not have enough assets outside Argentina or is incorporated under an offshore or low-tax jurisdiction, it may comply with these requirements by evidencing that it is an investment vehicle.

The IGJ has defined as vehicles all those companies whose corporate purpose is to act as investment instruments of one or more other companies or of one or more individuals who, directly or indirectly, exercise control by holding voting rights considered sufficient to determine a company's performance (the "Controlling Company"). Therefore, and according to current regulations, foreign entities that do not have any assets outside Argentina or are incorporated under an offshore or low-tax jurisdiction, but prove to be "investment vehicles," are allowed to be registered and comply with the annual filing through their Controlling Companies, as long as their Controlling Company complies with the requirements established by Resolution No. 7/2005 of the PRC.

The above-mentioned regulations apply to those foreign companies requesting registration within the jurisdiction of the Autonomous City of Buenos Aires. The PRC of each jurisdiction has its own regulations for the registration of foreign companies. Nevertheless, in the event the domestic company in which the foreign entity will participate is incorporated within the jurisdiction of the Autonomous City of Buenos Aires, foreign companies that become its shareholders will have to be registered with the IGJ.

3. Other Significant Legal and Business Issues

As briefly referred to in 1.3 above, in December 2001 Argentina enacted emergency laws and regulations, which included a partial freeze on bank deposits, the suspension of payments on its public debt to foreign creditors, the abandonment of the convertibility[4] of the Argentine peso to the U.S. dollar at the long-standing 1-to-1 rate (followed by a substantial devaluation of the peso), the establishment of foreign exchange controls, restrictions on cross-border currency transfers, and the mandatory repatriation of most export proceeds.

Since then, the Argentine government and its agencies have adopted numerous additional measures, which have implemented, expanded, and, in certain cases, eliminated or limited the impact of that emergency legislation on foreign investment and economic activity in general. Given the fluid nature of the economic situation and the frequent changes in the regulatory environment, foreign investors are strongly encouraged to consult legal counsel to confirm the status of any of the legal issues discussed below.

3.1 Choice of Law

Before the crises in 2001, it was already usual practice for parties to a cross-border transaction (including M&A and credit lending transactions) to choose a foreign law (e.g., New York state) as the law to rule their agreements. As a consequence of the crises, what used to be a trend in cross-border deals became more of a "condition precedent" to this type of transaction.

Only certain agreements are still granted under Argentine law, either because they are mandatory by law, as in the case of mortgages, or simply because they deal with guarantees that are located in Argentina and enforcement would be faster and more user-friendly using Argentine law in Argentine courts.

3.2 Enforcement of Foreign Judgments

If an international treaty for the enforcement of foreign judgments exists between a foreign country and Argentina, the rules of such

---

[4] Convertibility Law No. 23,928 of 1991, by which the Argentine peso and the U.S. dollar, both legally circulated in Argentina, were traded at a peso-to-dollar rate of 1-to-1.

treaty will prevail. In the absence of such a treaty, the National Code of Civil and Commercial Procedure (*Código Procesal Civil y Comercial de la Nación*) (the CPCC) will be applicable[5] if the defendant is domiciled in the Autonomous City of Buenos Aires or if the matter at issue will be debated before a federal court. Provincial procedure rules will be applicable where the matter at issue is to be debated before a provincial court. Unless otherwise stated herein, this analysis of the recognition of foreign judgments concerns federal procedure rules (i.e., the CPCC), which are, in principle, applicable when a foreigner is involved.

Subject to certain requirements, which are set out in Article 517 of the CPCC, Argentine courts will enforce foreign judgments resolving disputes and determining the rights and obligations of the parties to an agreement. Reciprocity is not required for an Argentine court to recognize a foreign judgment. The requirements that a foreign judgment must meet in order to be recognized in Argentina without further discussion of its merits are as follows:

(i) the judgment must have been issued by a court competent under the Argentine conflict of laws principles regarding jurisdiction, have been final in the jurisdiction where it was rendered, and resulted from a personal action or an *in rem* action concerning movable assets; if the judgment resulted from an *in rem* action, personal property in dispute must have been transferred to Argentina during or after the prosecution of the foreign action;

(ii) the defendant against whom enforcement of the judgment is sought must have been duly served with a summons and, in accordance with due process of law, given an opportunity to defend itself against the foreign action;

(iii) the judgment must have been valid in the jurisdiction where it was rendered and its authenticity established in accordance with the requirements of Argentine law;

(iv) the judgment must not violate any principles of public policy of Argentine law; and

(v) the judgment must not be in conflict with a prior or simultaneous judgment of an Argentine court.

Argentine courts do not automatically acknowledge the foreign court's original jurisdiction over the matter. As indicated in (i) above, the competency of the jurisdiction of the foreign court that rendered the judgment is analyzed according to Argentine rules regarding jurisdiction. For example, Argentine courts would recognize judgments in cases where the defendant was domiciled in the jurisdiction of the

---

[5] Until the issues raised by the new Charter for the Autonomous City of Buenos Aires have been resolved.

court, the obligations of the parties to an agreement were to be performed in that jurisdiction, or in contractual disputes of a pecuniary nature, where the foreign court that issued the judgment had jurisdiction as a result of a valid forum selection. In all of these aforementioned cases, the jurisdiction of the foreign court would be considered competent.

4. Negotiation Practices

As referred to in section 1.2, from its very beginning, Argentina has been heavily influenced by the Europeans, in all matters related to culture, habits, and traditions. Over the years this characteristic has helped Argentina attract heavy investments from many European countries—especially from Spain, but also from Britain, France, and Italy. Complemented by U.S. investment, Argentina has always been on the "receiving side," dependent on these foreign direct investments to grow as a country. This condition of being the receiver has forced businesspeople in Argentina (especially lawyers) to learn from, adapt to, and blend in with foreign businessmen when negotiating a deal. That is why any contemporary cross-border transaction in Argentina will have considerable similarities, in terms of drafting, timing, and negotiation, to any cross-border deal between two sophisticated markets (e.g., the United States or the United Kingdom).

4.1 Participants

As a general principle, businesspeople and lawyers have distinctly differing roles in a transaction. External counsel's role is primarily to advise the client from a legal standpoint. However, in many cases, the client expects the lawyer to become more involved in the negotiation. Therefore, it may happen that lawyers, through association, also become businesspeople.

4.2 Timing

Unlike Europe and the United States, summer vacation in Argentina is from late December to early or late February. During this time, the business pace slows down significantly and deals that have not reached closing by December 31st can be delayed until January or February. However, during the northern summertime (July through August), there is no slowdown in Argentina in terms of commercial activity.

4.3 Negotiation Practices

To a large extent, Argentine businesspeople are professionals with some postgraduate training in U.S. or European universities, including the universities with the highest reputations. Even those not trained abroad speak English as a second language. Consequently, most Argentine businesspeople feel quite comfortable in both handling negotiations and drafting and executing agreements in English. This is without prejudice to the existence of less sophisticated businesspeople, especially among the older generations, who still run family businesses. Again, it is worth noting that the younger generation in family-run businesses often have some training abroad.

A cross-border deal in Argentina generally contains the documents used in any other cross-border transaction (e.g., due diligence report, confidentiality agreement, stock purchase agreement, shareholders agreement).

4.4 Cultural, Ethical, and Religious Considerations

Argentine businesspeople tend to be very hospitable, and will often invite their counterparties to lunch or dinner. Disagreements may be easily overcome in a more relaxed environment. Sometimes, visiting counterparties may be invited to personal homes or country homes. Closing dinners are also current practice in Argentina. Though far away from the United States, Buenos Aires is in the same time zone as most cities on the U.S. East Coast. This may be an advantage for businesspeople and their counsel, who after an overnight flight may be ready to face a day of negotiations in Buenos Aires.

In general, Argentine businesspeople may be less aware of issues of "political correctness" than their American colleagues. This does not imply that as a matter of principle certain comments will not be deemed to be politically incorrect, or that people will not react to such comments if they are. There is acknowledgement of the cultural differences.

Catholicism is the predominant religion in the country. There is also an important Jewish presence in the Argentine population. Even though religion is not an issue during business negotiations, religious tolerance and morality matters do form part of Argentine international public policy and are therefore important to consider.

4.5 Negotiating Online

Online negotiating has changed the landscape of business negotiations. With videoconferencing and e-mail, cross-border negotiations take place in the here and now, and documents fly back and forth in marked-up versions for a more convenient review.

5. Contract Formation

As explained, contract formation in Argentina is similar to that in the United States. A letter of intent or a memorandum of understanding, or a simple term sheet, will initiate proceedings. The parties then start to negotiate the set of documents as required.

5.1 Wording and Style

Language is usually not a barrier, and local parties with a certain degree of sophistication will be comfortable in signing a document discussed and drafted in English. If the local party is the stronger party, to ascertain precedence the decision may be made to have the agreement executed in both English and Spanish, with a provision stipulating that the Spanish version shall prevail should a dispute arise. This, however, does not happen very often. Foreign parties must be aware that notwithstanding the foregoing, some agreements are required to be filed with the local authorities, and this dictates that the documents be in Spanish. In such cases, a translation by a certified public translator will suffice.

5.2 Conditions and Defenses

Argentina has a continental system of law. This gives rise to the usual conflicts that occur when working under two different legal systems— conflicts that a lawyer with international exposure will normally be able to overcome. Typical difficulties that a party from a continental law system will deal with when working with a party from a common law system are the length of contracts prepared by U.S. or U.K. lawyers and certain clauses (such as representations, warranties, and remedies) that may be typical of (and enforceable under) the common law system but not under the continental system of law. However, as mentioned above, Argentine lawyers from top-tier law firms are familiar with such contracts.

5.3 The Special Case of Online Agreements

As yet, online agreements are not used in Argentina, at least not among the top-tier law firms.

6. Resolving Disputes

As already mentioned, the Argentine judicial system is divided into federal courts (organized by the federal government) and provincial courts (those organized by each province and the City of Buenos Aires). The Supreme Court of Justice, with seven members, is vested with the supreme judicial power of Argentina. Most of the court systems are composed of lower courts, a court of appeals, and the Supreme Court (federal or provincial). Procedural laws that refer to the organization and activity of the judicial courts are enacted by each province (except for the City of Buenos Aires, where proceedings are ruled by the CPCC and which also applies to the proceedings held before the federal courts).

Procedures are mainly in written form. Trial by jury does not exist in Argentina. There are basically two types of proceedings: the fact-finding process and the executory process. The fact-finding process has three main stages: an introduction stage (complaint and defenses), an evidence stage (hearing of the parties by the judge and production of the relevant evidence), and the judgment stage (closing arguments and final judgment). The executory process regulates proceedings that seek to enforce a right. They are simplified and expeditious proceedings that basically seek, upon the claimant's request, an attachment over the assets of the debtor in order to obtain a favorable judgment to auction such assets and pay off the debt. As a general principle, costs and court taxes are borne by the defeated party.

As a consequence of the crises back in 2001, many Argentine companies that were in default used an amended proceeding of the Argentine Bankruptcy Law in order to restructure their debts. This proceeding (the "out-of-court restructuring proceeding," better known as the "APE"), allowed debtors who obtained the required majorities of their creditors, to restructure their debts without the burden of going through a standard judicial bankruptcy proceeding.

7. Conclusion

Despite its earlier problems and the ramifications that resulted, including the devaluation of the Argentine peso, freezing and reprogramming of deposits, conversion of dollar-denominated debts to pesos, etc., Argentina has made a significant recovery. Though foreign investors will need time to recover full confidence in the country's institutions, it is worth noting that in the five years following the crises, the country—fueled by high commodity prices and a high exchange rate between the Argentine peso and the U.S. dollar—has managed to (i) grow at an average rate of 8 percent, (ii) obtain and maintain fiscal and trade surpluses, (iii) restructure all its debt with foreign creditors (including payment of US$9.8 billion to the IMF), and (iv) significantly reduce unemployment, going from approximately 24 percent in 2002 to 9.6 percent by late 2007. Only time will tell whether these actions will be sufficient for economic growth in the future. But one thing is certain: Argentina has carved out a friendly environment for foreign direct investments.

Ramón M. Segura
Marval, O'Farrell & Mairal
509 Madison Avenue, Suite 506
New York, NY 10022
Phone: (212) 838-4641
Fax: (212) 751-3854
E-mail: rms@marval.com.ar

CHAPTER 19

International Business Negotiations in Australia

Leigh Brown
MINTER ELLISON
SYDNEY, AUSTRALIA

1. Introduction

1.1 Demographics and Governmental Structure

Australia is the sixth-largest country in the world and is an entire island continent located between the Indian and South Pacific oceans. Despite Australia's large size, its population of approximately 21,200,000 (2008 estimate) makes it only the fifty-third most populous country. The national language is English.

The great majority of the population is urbanized and resides along the eastern coastline, primarily in the three cities of Sydney, Melbourne, and Brisbane. Accordingly, most corporate headquarters are located in those cities, particularly Sydney and Melbourne. However, Perth, on the western coastline, which is the location of major mining and petroleum projects, is the most rapidly growing city in Australia.

Australia has very high living standards and is famous for its agricultural and mining resources, tourism sites (including the Great Barrier Reef and the Outback), and sporting prowess.

Australia has a largely deregulated economy that has been growing strongly (by more than 3 percent per annum) over the previous ten years. Approximately 70 percent of gross domestic product is provided by service industries (including tourism and education) while the remaining 30 percent is made up largely by agriculture and mining.

Australia is a very stable democracy with a federal system of government, which is based on the United States model (where power is separated between a central government and the government of each State or Territory). The Commonwealth of Australia government and each State or Territory government operates similarly to the United Kingdom's Westminster system, where the executive is directed by and reports to the parliament via ministers.

Under Australia's Federal Constitution, the Commonwealth Parliament may legislate in, and therefore controls, the areas of taxation, foreign investment, defense, banking and monetary system, telecommunications, interstate and overseas trade, trademark and patent registration, and foreign affairs.

The remaining responsibilities are retained by the States and Territories and include areas such as education, health, policing, roads, and traffic. However, the Commonwealth government's predominant revenue-raising capacity has resulted in its growing influence over these remaining responsibilities of the States and Territories.

Below the Commonwealth, State or Territory governments are local governments composed of locally elected representatives. These exist as city, town, or shire councils and oversee local land use, development, and planning laws.

1.2 Historical and Cultural Background

After being originally occupied by tribes of its indigenous people, Australia began to be settled by the British when they established the penal colony of New South Wales in 1788. Australia was then developed as several independent States. Federation occurred in 1901 when the six States joined together to form the Commonwealth of Australia.

Australia's non-indigenous culture is largely drawn from its British heritage but has been substantially modified by decades of immigration from Europe and more recently from Asia and the Middle East. Australians also closely follow U.S. popular culture.

The Australian workforce is skilled, highly educated, and computer-literate with a strong multinational background.

1.3 Business Organization and Culture

Australia has a sophisticated and stable business structure and banking system because foreign investment has been the driving force for the development of Australian resources, infrastructure, and industry. Globalization and privatization have had a significant impact.

Accordingly, Australian businesspeople and their professional advisors are up-to-date with international business practices, including financing structures. As a result of compulsory superannuation (see section 2.5(e) below), Australia has a large and rapidly growing managed investments industry.

With Australia's sophistication comes a complex regulatory environment that needs to be considered in all transactions.

1.4 Overview of Legal System

Australia's legal system is based on the British model and comprises both laws enacted by the Commonwealth Parliament of Australia and parliaments of the States and Territories and common law developed through court decisions.

The Australian courts system consists of two branches: the Federal branch and the State and Territory branches. While the Federal courts primarily have jurisdiction over Commonwealth laws, the High Court of Australia is the highest court in Australia and has the ultimate appellate jurisdiction over State and Territory courts.

The Federal Court of Australia hears appeals from inferior tribunals and retains original jurisdiction over Federal law matters including immigration, industrial relations, and corporations.

All States and Territories have a supreme court as their highest court, with appeal divisions in civil (Full Court or Court of Appeal of the Supreme Court) and criminal (Court of Criminal Appeal) matters. Most States also have a district court, which has jurisdiction over civil matters (usually below a $1 million limit) and criminal matters that are less serious indictable offenses, and a Magistrate's Court or Local Court, which has jurisdiction over smaller civil matters and summary matters.

Australia's lawyers are regulated by the State or Territory governments and are divided between barristers, who concentrate on court advocacy and operate as sole traders, and solicitors, who handle the remainder of legal work and mostly operate through firms. The increasing demand for specialized services and the merger of State-based firms has led to the creation of many large Australian law firms. There are six very large national law firms with approximately 800 to 1,000 lawyers and a number of these have offices in Asia and other parts of the world.

As a result of the population concentration in urban areas along the eastern coastline, most corporations and providers of financial services are headquartered in Sydney and Melbourne. Accordingly, most significant transactions are handled by Sydney or Melbourne law firms even when the subject assets are located in other areas of Australia.

2. Substantive Laws and Regulations Impacting Negotiations

2.1 Significant Regulatory Authorities

Parties involved in negotiating transactions in Australia will need to take into account the following regulatory authorities:

(a) Australian Securities and Investments Commission (ASIC)
ASIC is the sole authority responsible for administering the Corporations Act (see section 2.2 below) and has responsibilities in regulating financial markets and the provision of financial services.

In terms of corporate regulation, ASIC is responsible for regulating company fundraising; takeovers and schemes of arrangement; audit and financial reporting; market disclosure; shareholder rights;

company administration; and windings up and ensuring company officers and directors complete their duties with honesty, diligence, and in their company's best interests.

ASIC is also responsible for measuring how efficiently authorized financial markets are fulfilling their legal obligations to maintain fair, orderly, and transparent markets.

ASIC licenses and monitors financial services businesses such as those involved in superannuation, managed funds, shares and company securities, derivatives, and insurance to ensure their operation is efficient, honest, and fair.

(b) Takeovers Panel (Panel)

Established under the Australian Securities and Investments Commission Act, the Panel is an administrative body that quickly resolves disputes that arise during regulated takeover bids (see section 2.2(c) below). The Panel is modeled on its UK counterpart. It has the power to declare that the circumstances surrounding a takeover or the change of control of an Australian company are unacceptable.

The Panel has various review powers and can make orders to protect the rights of persons (such as target company shareholders) during a takeover bid and to ensure that a bid proceeds as though the unacceptable circumstances had not arisen.

(c) Australian Tax Office (ATO)

The ATO is the statutory authority responsible for overseeing Australia's Federal taxation system and collecting tax revenue (see section 2.3 below). The main role of the ATO is to administer legislation and develop taxation, excise, and superannuation systems.

(d) Australian Competition and Consumer Commission (ACCC)

The ACCC was established in 1995 to administer the Trade Practices Act, which promotes competition, fair trading, and consumer protection (see section 2.4 below). This includes anti-competitive and unfair market practices, company mergers or acquisitions, product safety and product liability, and third-party access to facilities of national significance.

(e) Australian Prudential Regulation Authority (APRA)

APRA operates as the prudential regulator of the Australian financial services industry. APRA is funded predominantly by the industries that it supervises, which include banks, credit unions, building societies, insurance companies, friendly societies, and superannuation funds.

(f) ASX Limited (ASX)

The ASX is one of the world's top ten listed exchange groups measured by its market capitalization. Its functions include market supervision through the operation of the ASX Listing Rules; trade execution; trade novation; and clearing, settlement, and depository system facilitation.

(g) Foreign Investment Review Board (FIRB)

The FIRB considers proposals by foreign interests to undertake direct investment in Australia. After assessing these proposals, the FIRB will make a recommendation to the Federal Treasurer on whether the proposal abides by government policy (see section 2.9 below). The FIRB also provides advice to the government on general foreign investment matters; provides guidance to foreign investors so their proposals are in accordance with the government policy; and generally monitors and ensures compliance with foreign investment policy.

(h) Reserve Bank of Australia (RBA)

The RBA is a statutory body responsible for Australian monetary policy with the aim of preserving low and stable medium-term inflation rates. The RBA participates actively in financial markets, issues Australian currency notes, serves as banker to the Australian government, and manages Australia's foreign reserves.

(i) IP Australia

IP Australia is an agency of the Commonwealth government that grants rights in patents, trademarks, and designs (see section 2.7 below).

2.2 Uniform Corporate and Securities Law

Company law in Australia is regulated by a national scheme and a national regulator, ASIC (see section 2.1(a) above). The Corporations Act and the Australian Securities and Investments Commission Act govern companies, securities, managed investment schemes, and derivatives law throughout all States and Territories.

The activities of publicly listed companies are also regulated by ASX (see section 2.1(b) above) through the ASX's Listing Rules, which are given the force of law by the Corporations Act. Relevantly, they require shareholder approval for various corporate transactions that exceed various benchmarks and/or involve directors or significant shareholders.

(a) Share capital

Shareholders of a company contribute capital by subscribing and paying for shares in that company. The liability of such members is limited to any amount unpaid on those shares.

Australian law does not recognize the concept of a par or nominal value and there is no authorized share capital. An Australian company's share capital is simply the amount paid or payable on the shares actually issued by it and there are no fees payable by reference to the amount of issued capital.

(b) Public filing and disclosure

Every company owned by a foreign corporation is required to file with ASIC, available for public inspection, an annual return containing the company's financial statements.

A charge over a company's assets has to be registered with ASIC in order to be valid.

Shareholdings of 5 percent or more in a publicly listed company must be made public information.

(c) Regulated and unregulated takeovers

Subject to limited exceptions (including shareholder approval), a person can only acquire a "relevant interest" in more than 20 percent of the issued share capital of a company with more than fifty shareholders by means of a takeover bid and highly regulated takeover procedures that require extensive legal advice. The concept of relevant interest covers a broad range of direct and indirect interests in securities.

If a person acquires more than 90 percent of the voting shares of a company under a takeover bid, compulsory acquisition processes may be used to acquire the balance, if certain criteria have been met.

Acquisitions of other companies (i.e., with fewer than fifty shareholders) or businesses are achieved by contracts that are prepared by solicitors and use provisions and concepts similar to those used in the United States.

(d) Director's duties

A company is managed by directors of that company.

Foreign investors who establish a presence in Australia will usually form a 100 percent–owned proprietary company registered with ASIC. This will require representatives of that foreign investor to become directors of that company. There is also a requirement that one director of each company in Australia be a person resident in Australia.

Directors have duties under both the Corporations Act and common law to exercise their powers with a reasonable degree of care and diligence (as clarified by a business judgment rule); in good faith and for a proper purpose; and without improperly using their position or information.

(e) Managed investment schemes

A managed investment scheme is a trust or scheme where a professional manager undertakes investments or a common enterprise with a pooled fund from investors. The professional manager must hold an Australian Financial Services License from ASIC.

A managed investment scheme must also be registered with ASIC if interests in it are to be offered to retail investors.

(f) Fundraising

A proprietary company is prohibited from raising funds from the public. A public company must comply with the fundraising provisions of the Corporations Act. Usually an offer of securities must be accompanied by a disclosure document that must contain all the information that investors and their professional advisers would reasonably require to make an informed assessment of the rights of the securities and the assets and liabilities, financial position and performance, profits and losses, and prospects of the issuing company.

2.3 Tax Laws

Australia imposes taxation (including capital gains taxation) on:

    i.   the worldwide taxable income of entities resident in Australia for taxation purposes; and

    ii. the Australian-sourced taxable income of nonresidents.

There are double taxation agreements between Australia and many countries, including the United States and the United Kingdom, so that tax is imposed only by the country of residence of the taxpayer. However, the country of the source of the income may impose withholding taxes on dividends, interest, and royalties, and may also tax in full the actual or attributed profits of any commercial enterprise carried on through a "permanent establishment" in the country.

Australia has also introduced a general nonresident withholding régime that is subject to regulations that are continually evolving.

(a) Residence

A company is a resident of Australia for tax purposes if:

    i.   it is incorporated in Australia; or

    ii. where the company is not incorporated in Australia it carries on business in Australia and either:

        A. has its central management and control in Australia; or

        B. its voting power is controlled by shareholders who are residents of Australia.

(b) Taxable income and rates of tax

Taxable income is calculated by firstly determining the assessable income and secondly deducting from it the allowable deductions.

The allowable deductions are generally all those losses and outgoings incurred in gaining or producing the assessable income, or necessarily incurred in carrying on business for that purpose, excluding those of a "capital, private or domestic nature."

Certain tax deductions can be claimed by a taxpayer notwithstanding that they are of a capital nature, such as for depreciation of plant (known collectively as capital allowances) and certain expenses in establishing a business.

Companies are generally taxed at the fixed rate of 30 percent. Accordingly, an overseas company carrying on business in Australia through a branch or an Australian subsidiary is subject to Australian company tax at the current rate of 30 percent. There is no branch profits tax.

(c) Consolidated groups

An Australian company can elect to form a consolidated group with its wholly owned subsidiaries. The effect is to treat the group as a single entity for Australian income tax purposes. This effectively means that intragroup transactions will be ignored for income tax purposes.

If a group is consolidated, certain tax attributes (including tax losses, franking credits, and foreign tax credits) will be transferred to the head company of the consolidated group. Some tax attributes will remain with the head company even when a group company leaves the consolidated group.

When acquiring a group company, it is important to establish that its tax liabilities are separated from the consolidated group by a tax-sharing agreement. Otherwise all tax liabilities of the consolidated group remain payable by each group company, notwithstanding the change of ownership.

(d) Capital gains

Capital gains tax is not a separate tax, but rather a component of income tax. Accordingly, capital gains are taxed at the rate that applies as a result of the level of the taxpayer's other taxable income.

Relevant capital gains are those that arise from the disposal of certain assets acquired on or after September 20, 1985. There are deemed acquisitions, disposals, and valuations for certain intangible assets such as rights. Certain events, such as the declaration of a trust over assets, are also treated as capital gains events.

The taxation of Australian capital gains derived by nonresidents are limited to gains that arise with respect to the disposal of Australian assets.

For individuals and trusts (but not companies) that dispose of assets held for at least twelve months, the capital gain upon which tax is levied is generally halved.

Rollover relief may be available with respect to capital gains made in relation to a takeover bid where shares or units in one entity are exchanged for shares or units, respectively, in another entity. The Australian rules also provide demerger relief in some instances. Where rollover relief is available, any capital gain made on the disposal of the original shares or units will be deferred until the disposal of the exchanged asset.

(e) International transfer pricing

Australia's taxation legislation includes provisions that are intended to prevent tax minimization that occurs where businesses do not value dealings with related parties at prices that accurately reflect the arm's-length price.

These provisions can affect pricing policies between an Australian company or branch and an overseas parent, subsidiary, or associated entity. The Australian legislation uses the arms'-length principle in determining how income and expenses should be allocated in international dealings. Broadly, the Australian tax authorities follow the Organisation for Economic Co-operation and Development (OECD) methodology.

(f) Dividends

Dividends that are distributed from after-tax profits are subject to Australia's "imputation system." Generally, the system operates to impute the tax paid by the company as a credit to shareholders. Dividends with an imputation credit attached are known as "franked dividends."

(g) Interest

Australia levies a flat rate withholding tax of 10 percent on interest paid to a nonresident not having a permanent establishment in Australia. This is unaffected by Australia's Double Taxation Agreements.

Interest paid by an Australian company is generally allowed as a deduction against its assessable income and, accordingly, there may be advantages for a foreign owner in financing its subsidiaries by way of debt, rather than equity capital.

However, deductions for interest are denied for thinly capitalized Australian foreign-owned subsidiaries. Generally, under the "safe harbor" methodology, a company is thinly capitalized if its debt/equity ratio exceeds 3:1.

(h) Royalties

Generally, royalty income derived by a nonresident from Australian sources is subject to Australian withholding tax at a rate of 30 percent on the gross royalty payment. Where a Double Tax Agreement applies, the rate of Australian withholding tax is generally limited to 10 percent of the gross royalty payment. The entity paying the royalty is required to withhold and remit the Australian withholding tax to the Australian Taxation Office.

(i) Losses

Subject to certain restrictions, a company can carry forward its tax losses on revenue account indefinitely, and can set off those losses against assessable income (whether on revenue or capital account). Capital losses can also be carried forward indefinitely, but can only be set off against capital gains.

Broadly, a company's ability to utilize its carried-forward tax losses may be lost if the continuity of ownership test is not satisfied. This test requires that more than 50 percent of all voting, dividend, and capital rights be held by the same natural persons in the year of income, in the year of recoupment, and all intervening years. Notwithstanding the failure to satisfy the continuity of ownership test, a company may utilize its carried-forward tax losses if the company carries on the same business it carried on immediately before the event that led to failure of the continuity of ownership test.

(j) Tax concessions

Australia offers general incentives to encourage investment in Australia. Some specific concessions are, however, available, including:

  i.   deductions for certain set-up or relocation costs in establishing a regional headquarters in Australia;
  ii.   exemption from dividend withholding tax for certain foreign source dividends;
  iii. research and development deductions to eligible Australian resident companies of up to 125 percent (with a 175 percent deduction potentially available for additional incremental expenditure);
  iv.   exemption from capital gains and income tax on disposal of the investment for certain nonresident investors who invest in venture capital in Australia;
  v.   immediate deduction or two-year write-off for capital expenditure in acquiring interest in initial copyright of films; and
  vi.   disregard of capital gains on the sale of shares in a foreign company held by an Australian company where the foreign company has an active underlying business.

Investors proposing to use Australia as an intermediary in their investment strategy should seek professional advice as to the availability of taxation concessions (including those mentioned above) with respect to "foreign income dividends" and offshore banking units.

(k) Goods and services tax

A goods and services tax (GST) has applied at a flat rate of 10 percent in Australia since July 1, 2000 to the supply of goods, real property, and other supplies (such as intangible rights and services). Broadly, the GST is similar in operation to the value-added tax systems operating in Europe.

An entity is required to be registered for GST if it carries on an enterprise (which includes but is not limited to a business) that has an annual turnover in excess of A$75,000 from suppliers that are connected with Australia.

GST-registered suppliers will generally be entitled to claim an input tax credit (effectively a GST refund) for the GST component of the cost of goods and services acquired in the course of carrying on their enterprise.

(l) Customs duties
Customs duty is payable at the time goods enter into Australia by reference to detailed classifications.

(m) State taxes
Each of Australia's States and Territories impose their own form of minor taxes. The two most significant types of State-based tax are:

    i.   stamp duty, and
   ii.   payroll tax.

The rate of tax imposed by stamp duties legislation varies in each jurisdiction but is generally:

    i.   0.6 percent of the value of the transaction in the case of the sale of shares (except it is nil for all ASX-listed companies and companies registered in Victoria, Tasmania, and Western Australia unless they are "land rich"); and
   ii.   5.5 percent in the case of land, business assets, and shares in "land rich" companies.

Stamp duty will generally not be payable on the establishment of a business. However, a stamp duty liability will arise where an existing business is purchased (except in Victoria), where a business asset is purchased, or when land (from which the business will be conducted) is purchased.

All employers are subject to payroll tax based on the amount of wages they pay to employees. Each State has set certain exemption thresholds. These thresholds mean that payroll tax is not payable until the total amount of Australian wages paid by an employer reaches the threshold.

(n) Tax implications for transactions
As all tax liabilities of a company (along with other liabilities) will be inherited by the purchaser of its shares, the purchase price should take account of known tax liabilities (including potential capital gains tax and loss of relief for carried-forward losses) and the sale contract should include detailed tax warranties and indemnities. A purchase of the business assets of a company will avoid this problem but could attract much greater stamp duty.

2.4 Antitrust/Anti-competition Laws

(a) The Australian Trade Practices Act (TPA)
The TPA regulates competition, fair trading, and consumer protection law in Australia.

The competition provisions of the TPA are based on antitrust legislation in the United States and are not dissimilar to the antitrust provisions of the European Community's Treaty of Rome. Among other things, the TPA prohibits:

i.   anticompetitive behavior;
ii. misuse of market power;
iii. anticompetitive mergers; and
iv. unfair business practices when dealing with small businesses.

The TPA also:

i.   imposes obligations on businesses designed to protect consumers; and
ii. provides an access regime for essential facilities and a specific access and competition regime for the telecommunications industry.

The Australian Competition and Consumer Commission (ACCC—see section 2.1(d) above) is responsible for administering and enforcing the TPA. It has the power to authorize, on public benefit grounds, some conduct that may otherwise breach the Act.

(b) Mergers and acquisitions

The TPA prohibits the acquisition of shares or assets of a company if the acquisition is likely to have the effect of substantially lessening competition in a market in Australia. The ACCC has merger guidelines that are applied in assessing whether a proposed or completed transaction breaches this prohibition.

On February 8, 2008, the ACCC released revised merger guidelines for public comment. The ACCC proposes to introduce new "notification" thresholds (including removal of existing "safe harbor" market concentration thresholds). This is likely to increase the number and type of mergers submitted for ACCC review.

The acquisition of a foreign company by a foreign company may be subject to the TPA if, as a consequence of obtaining a controlling interest in a foreign company, a controlling interest in a company in Australia is acquired.

That competition is not substantially lessened is often an important consideration for acquisitions because Australia's relatively small population has led to many industries being consolidated. It is therefore essential with acquisitions to make an analysis of the relevant market and other factors (e.g., barriers to entry or competition from imports).

Parties to a proposed transaction that may have the effect of substantially lessening competition in a market in Australia can seek informal or formal clearance from the ACCC for the transaction.

In the event that the ACCC rules that the proposed transaction is likely to limit competition, the parties may still obtain approval by providing undertakings to the ACCC to reduce the effect of the transaction on competition. Undertakings can include structural commitments, such as to divest certain business structures, and behavioral undertakings, such as commitments to provide access facilities or to "ring fence" certain parts of a business from other parts.

(c) Misleading representations

An important part of the TPA for commercial negotiations in Australia, including for acquisitions, is section 52, which provides that a corporation shall not, in trade or commerce, "engage in conduct that is misleading or deceptive or is likely to mislead or deceive."

A contract cannot exclude the operation of section 52, which is in addition to any contractual warranties. Section 52 is commonly relied upon by parties seeking damages to compensate them for unfavorable transactions. Each party to commercial negotiations should ensure that its information and conduct is correct and does not give a false impression to other parties.

(d) Country of origin labeling

Country of origin labeling of goods is not mandatory, but the TPA has specific rules to be followed when country of origin claims are made.

2.5 Labor and Employment Laws

(a) Reform under way

Historically Australian Federal and State legislation created a unique system of setting wages and settling industrial disputes (including strikes) by compulsory conciliation and arbitration before industrial tribunals, with workers invariably represented by unions and their lawyers.

However, the impact of unions and industrial tribunals on the Australian workplace has steadily reduced since the 1980s, as legislation encouraged bargaining at an enterprise level. This trend culminated with the Federal work choices legislation, which was introduced in March 2006 by the Liberal government.

In early 2008, the Australian industrial relations system began undergoing significant change under the new Labor government, elected on November 24, 2007. It will be administered from January 1, 2010 by a new Federal industrial relations body, Fair Work Australia, which will replace the Australian Industrial Relations Commission (AIRC).

The Australian workplace operates subject to a combination of legislation (both Federal and State), industrial instruments (including awards and enterprise agreements), and contracts of various kinds. These govern the collective relationships of employers with their workforces (industrial relations law), and also the individual relationships between employers and employees (employment law).

Therefore, employers will be subject to four potential sources of laws and regulations in relation to their dealings with employees:

i. Federal or State legislation;
ii. industrial awards prescribing terms and conditions of employment;
iii. collective or individual enterprise agreements; and
iv. employees' specific contracts of employment.

When establishing or purchasing a business or company in Australia, it is very important to ascertain the terms of any awards, agreements, and employment legislation that may apply to existing or prospective employees. The terms of contracts of employment and relevant policies and practices should also be reviewed.

When the shares of a company are acquired, employees of that company continue to have all the rights previously enjoyed and the company continues to be liable for the current employee pay and benefits.

Australia does not have "transfer of undertakings" legislation that would make the buyer of business assets similarly responsible for the employees of that business. Subject to negotiations with the seller, which will be concerned about the financial consequences of redundancy, it is possible for the buyer of business assets to "cherry-pick" employees. Equally, though, employees of the seller are free to refuse an offer of employment from the buyer. Responsibility for redundancy payments will often affect purchase price negotiations.

(b) Legislation

With the exception of Victoria, which has ceded its power over industrial relations to the Federal Parliament, Australia has an essentially Federal industrial relations system, covering approximately 85 percent of employees. The balance of employees are covered by the industrial relations legislation of their respective State (with, as noted, the exception of Victoria).

Current Federal industrial relations legislation dictates certain minimum standards in relation to wages, hours, annual leave, personal leave (sick leave, compassionate leave, etc.), and parental leave. As of January 1, 2010, this legislation will be replaced by ten National Employment Standards.

Under State legislation, employees are entitled to receive:

i. annual leave of four weeks during each year of service (with employees under awards generally being paid an additional 17.5 percent leave loading on their annual leave pay); and
ii. long service leave for long continuous service with an employer (or a series of employers in the same business) of one month's leave for each five years' service, with the entitlement usually becoming available after ten years' service.

Invariably the buyer of a business inherits the transferring employees' past service and accrued entitlements to annual and long service leave. Therefore the contract will provide for a reduction in purchase price by an amount equal to those accrued entitlements in the accounts of the seller (usually tax-effected down to 70 percent of that amount).

(c) Awards

Awards are legally enforceable orders made by both Federal and State industrial tribunals that add to the minimum guarantees provided under Federal standards by setting out additional terms and conditions of employment for all employees to whom the award applies.

Awards are collective instruments, and usually relate to a particular industry or profession. Old State awards are being integrated into the Federal awards system by the AIRC.

There will be an annual wage review—with wage increases to take effect from the first pay period on or after July 1 each year.

An entitlement to sick leave (usually between five to eight days per year) has been established by awards.

The Federal legislation prescribes strict limits on what awards may contain, including minimum wages (as of January 1, 2010); hours of work; type of work performed (such as full time, part time, or casual employment); overtime and penalty rates and other entitlements; and consultation, representation, and dispute-settling procedures.

As of January 1, 2010, awards will also contain a flexibility clause permitting individual as opposed to collective agreement, and awards will no longer apply to new employees earning more than A$100,000 per year (indexed).

(d) Workplace agreements and employment contracts

Australian Workplace Agreements (AWAs) are statutory versions of individual contracts between an individual employee and his or her employer. AWAs are in the process of being phased out by the new Federal government. Existing AWAs may run their full term, meaning the last AWAs will expire around 2012.

Collective agreements are another form of workplace agreement, made between an employer and a group of employees in a single business. These agreements may be made directly with the group or, if the employees desire, with a union representing the group.

As of July 1, 2009, new workplace agreements will be subject to a "better off overall test" against the award and minimum legislative standards, and be subject to approval by Fair Work Australia.

Subject to legislation and awards, employers are able to make contracts of employment with employees covering a range of matters. Policies and practices covering employment and industrial-related issues may also be implemented.

(e) Compulsory superannuation

Superannuation is a mandatory requirement prescribed under the Federal superannuation guarantee scheme. Employers are required to make compulsory superannuation contributions to their employees during their working life based on 9 percent of the employee's earning base.

Large and long-established companies sometimes still operate defined benefit superannuation schemes under which employees' superannuation benefits are calculated by reference to their final average salary and years of service. However, these are relatively rare and, usually, employers provide defined contribution superannuation schemes under which the final benefits are determined by the investment return achieved by the superannuation fund on the contributions made to their fund on behalf of each employee.

If acquiring a company or business where employees participate in a defined benefit fund, it is important to ensure that the fund has sufficient assets to meet its expected obligations. Also, there may be a need to transfer employees into a new defined benefit fund or defined contribution fund.

(f) Restraints

Restraints of trade or noncompetition covenants given by a seller in the context of a sale of company shares or business are generally enforceable, provided that the extent and terms of the covenants are reasonable.

Equivalent covenants given by employees to apply after termination of their employment can also be enforceable if they are reasonable. A noncompetition covenant for no additional consideration that has the effect of preventing an employee carrying on his or her actual occupation or exercising his or her skills will be difficult to enforce, particularly if it applies for more than a short period following termination of employment. More limited restraints, such as those preventing an employee soliciting his or her former employer's clients, are more likely to be enforceable.

2.6 Environmental Laws

Environmental laws in Australia, and approvals under them, are very important and are supported by public concern over environmental issues.

On a Federal level, mining, infrastructure, and other businesses are subject to mandatory environmental impact reporting requirements and approvals. For example, businesses involved in the manufacture or importation of certain industrial chemicals are required to produce annual reports recording their emissions; and larger businesses using more than 0.5 petajoules of energy per year are required to identify, evaluate, and publicly report opportunities to save energy. For the majority of companies, however, environmental reporting is voluntary but highly encouraged.

On a local and State government level, development approvals are required for all projects and businesses.

State legislation imposes strict liability on persons causing pollution except as permitted by environmental licenses. Owners and occupiers of relevant properties may have similar liability.

Accordingly, buyers of companies and businesses will always need to check that all environmental approvals and permits are in place and, when acquiring real property, buyers will often require environmental reports to ensure they are not inheriting any pollution problems.

2.7 Intellectual Property Laws

Australia's Federal laws provide comprehensive protection for intellectual property including copyright; patents for inventions; trade names and trademarks; domain names; trade secrets and confidential information; and registered designs.

Australia's intellectual property laws meet its international trade and treaty obligations and have been amended in accordance with the recent Free Trade Agreement between Australia and the United States.

(a) Domain names

Various classes of domain names ending in .au may be registered. Domain names ending in .com.au and .com are the most popular as addresses for commercial entities operating in Australia.

Registration of a .com.au domain name does not create any proprietary rights in the name. Australian courts will, however, recognize rights in domain names where there is a reputation or goodwill in the name.

(b) Trade names and trademarks

Australia protects reputation and goodwill in names through passing off law and consumer protection laws that prohibit misleading commercial conduct.

In addition, Australia has a registered trademark system for names, logos, devices, sounds, smells, colors, and shapes that distinguish the goods or services of an owner from those of other owners.

Australia follows the international system of classification of goods and services. Early trademark registration is essential for participants in the Australian market.

Each State requires that a person carrying on business in the State under a name other than their own name must register that business name.

2.8 Privacy and Data Security Laws

(a) Trade secrets and confidential information

Both through contract and where information is imparted in confidential circumstances for a limited purpose, the common law protects technical know-how, customer lists, and other confidential information against disclosure and use, or for an unauthorized purpose. There is no written code.

(b) Privacy

The Federal Privacy Act is the primary means of privacy protection in Australia. It contains ten National Privacy Principles that set out broad principles on how private sector organizations should use personal information. These provide individuals with a right to know what information an organization holds concerning them and a right to correct that information. Additionally, private sector organizations have privacy obligations including credit reporting requirements and tax file number requirements.

(c) Freedom of information

The Federal Freedom of Information Act and various State legislation grant the right to every person to access certain information in the possession of the government and its agencies. The legislation requires government agencies to publish information about their operations and powers affecting members of the public as well as manuals and other documents used in making decisions and recommendations affecting the public.

Government agencies are also required to provide access to documents in their possession unless the document is exempt from disclosure under the legislation. Exemptions exist where necessary for the protection of the public interest and for the protection of the private and business affairs of persons and organizations with respect to whom documentation is collected.

2.9 Regulation of Foreign Investment

The Australian government's foreign investment policy encourages foreign investment in Australia. The policy and the Foreign Acquisitions and Takeovers Act (FATA) (which provides the legislative support for the policy) are administered by the Foreign Investment Review Board (FIRB—see section 2.1(g) above).

As Australia seeks to enhance trade with many countries, free trade and other bilateral agreements will be reached with the intention of promoting two-way investment and setting the parameters for trade between Australia and its trading partners. For example, the recent Australia–United States Free Trade Agreement increases the notification threshold for acquisitions of substantial interests in Australian businesses by U.S. investors from A$50 million to A$800 million.

Certain types of proposals by foreign interests to invest in Australia require prior approval (depending on the value of the assets or business being acquired) and therefore need to be reported to FIRB, including:

i.   acquisitions of substantial interests in existing Australian corporations or businesses with total assets over A$50 million (or A$800 million for U.S. investors);

ii. proposals to establish new businesses involving a total investment of A$10 million or more (or A$800 million for U.S. investors);

iii. takeovers of offshore companies whose Australian subsidiaries or assets are valued at A$50 million (or A$800 million for U.S. investors) or more, or account for more than 50 percent of the target company's global assets;

iv. investments in "sensitive" sectors (banking, civil aviation, airports, shipping, media and telecommunications industry sectors) where specific policies and rules apply; and

v.   acquisitions of interests in urban land irrespective of value (although approval is not generally required in the case of developed nonresidential commercial real estate valued at less than A$50 million, or A$800 million for U.S. investors).

A foreign person acquires a substantial interest in the ownership of a corporation or business if that person (and any associates) acquires 15 percent or more of the ownership of the entity, or that person together with other foreign persons and each of their associates acquire 40 percent or more in aggregate of the ownership.

In most industry sectors, foreign investment proposals that require approval are approved unless determined to be contrary to the national interest, or FATA has been breached. FIRB approval is usually given within thirty days of lodging an application.

3. Other Significant Legal and Business Issues

3.1 Typical Business Structures

Business in Australia may be conducted through any of the following structures:

a.   company or branch office of a foreign company;
b.   partnership;
c.   joint venture;
d.   trust; or
e.   sole trader.

The most common form of business organization is a limited liability proprietary company. By early 2008 there were 1.5 million companies registered in Australia, 98 percent of which are either public or proprietary companies limited by shares (see section 2.2(a) above).

3.2 Foreign Exchange Rules

Australian and foreign currencies generally may be taken in and out of Australia without restriction as to amount, subject to foreign policy-based restrictions. Most dealings in foreign currencies in Australia must be transacted with an institution holding an authority from the Reserve Bank of Australia (see section 2.1(h)) or licensed to do so by ASIC (see section 2.1(a)).

Inward investment is not subject to exchange controls, though this does not preclude the need to obtain approval from the FIRB (see section 2.1(g) and section 2.8 above) in certain situations. Outward exchange flows are not restricted.

However, both outward-bound and inward-bound exchange flows are subject to cash transaction reporting guidelines imposed on "cash dealers" and other persons who send or receive international fund transfer instructions. Cash dealers, which include banks, financial institutions, insurance companies, currency and bullion dealers, and others, must report to the Australian Transaction Reports and Analysis Centre (AUSTRAC) details of certain transactions including:

a.   significant cash transactions involving the transfer of currency (coin and paper money of Australia or a foreign country) of A$10,000 or more, including foreign currency equivalents, unless the transaction has been specifically exempted;

b.   international telegraphic or electronic funds transfers to and from Australia, unless the transaction has been specifically exempted; and

c.   transactions that the cash dealer has reasonable grounds to suspect are relevant to criminal activity. AUSTRAC ensures that cash dealers abide by the account information, signatory identification, and reporting requirements of the Financial Transaction Reports Act.

3.3 Anti-Money-Laundering Legislation

Australia has agreed to implement the recommendations of the Financial Action Task Force on Money Laundering (FATF) on anti-money laundering and terrorist financing.

As a result, the government has passed the Anti-Money Laundering and Counter-Terrorism Financing Act 2006 (the AML/CTF Act), which imposes tight reporting, monitoring, and customer identification standards. The AML/CTF Act also requires close monitoring and reporting of both inbound and outward-bound foreign exchange transactions and electronic funds transfer instructions.

Under the AML/CTF Act, obligations are "activities based" and have been broadened to include all persons who deal in financial products, provide gambling services, and buy and sell bullion. The government has also indicated that it intends to amend the AML/CTF Act so that it regulates legal and accounting service providers, trust and company service providers, real estate agents, and dealers in precious stones and jewelry.

3.4 Choice of Law

Australian courts will recognize a choice of law freely made between parties to a contract. Generally, courts do not insist on applying Australian law to a contract for the acquisition of shares or business assets in Australia if the parties have nominated otherwise. The approach will differ if a choice of law has no commercial or reasonable connection with the parties to the agreement.

However, nomination of a foreign law as the choice of law for the contract can lead to significant expense should a party wish to enforce the contract in Australia. The party wishing to enforce the contract will be required to prove the foreign law as expert evidence in an Australian court.

While the choice to nominate a foreign law to govern the agreement and the relationship between the parties will generally be effective, Australian State or Federal law will determine other questions, such as the effect of a transfer of title to shares or of other assets, or the rights of creditors and other third parties.

Australia is a signatory to a number of treaties giving recognition to the judgments of superior courts overseas. It is, in many cases, possible to register a judgment obtained overseas for the purpose of enforcing it in Australia.

3.5 Government Involvement

Australia's three levels of government (see section 1.1 above) and complex regulatory environment mean that government approvals and licenses need to be considered for each transaction. However, Australian businesspeople are used to dealing with government officials and there are usually clear procedures and/or guidelines.

4. Negotiation Practices

4.1 Participants

It is now very common for Australian corporations to have one or a number of in-house lawyers who:

    i.   handle the transactions that are routinely undertaken by the corporation; and

    ii.   coordinate instructions to law firms for major or unusual transactions and litigation.

For transactions other than regulated takeovers (see section 2.2(c) above), Australian businesspeople at all levels usually:

    i.   prefer to conduct initial negotiations without lawyers until major commercial issues have been agreed;

    ii.   obtain legal advice about structural issues (e.g., tax or antitrust issues) separately from those initial negotiations; and

   iii. regard lawyers (even in-house lawyers) as providing advice on and implementing transactions rather than as being integral to initial negotiations.

Investment banks or corporate advisory divisions of accounting firms are often engaged by Australian corporations as advisers for major transactions (including for initial negotiations).

When lawyers are engaged by the parties to a transaction in order to provide documentation, there is usually a second stage of negotiations with respect to issues that had not previously been considered. At that stage, negotiations are conducted via draft agreements prepared by law firms taking instructions from in-house counsel, who in turn confer with the businesspeople.

However, for regulated takeovers and public fund-raisings in Australia, where there are strict and complicated requirements, lawyers are heavily involved at an early stage in matters including strategy, public statements, and documentation.

Since 2005, large private equity funds have become major participants in Australian mergers and acquisitions and regularly compete with "industry buyers" for acquisition targets.

4.2 Timing

Traditionally, business negotiations can occur at any part of the year in Australia except for the traditional summer Christmas holidays, which extend until at least the middle of January of the following year. However, Australian law firms increasingly will be acting on transactions that involve American or European parties who require completion before financial year end of December 31.

Since the 1980s, Australian businesspeople and their advisors have become used to working long hours on transactions, particularly when foreign parties are involved. They are used to negotiations at all hours, complicated documentation, and overnight turnaround.

Australian law firms cater to this "instant gratification" by having the same large groups of specialized lawyers, technological resources, and evening administrative staff as major U.S. law firms.

As with the United States, once documents have been executed and a public announcement has been made, completion can take some time while shareholder and government approvals are obtained.

Traditionally Australian corporations will make great efforts to complete transactions by June 30, which is the common end for an Australian financial year.

4.3 Negotiation Practices

In Australia negotiations are invariably conducted in English and closely follow the same practices that are used in the United States and the United Kingdom. The usual sequence of events for major transactions between the two corporations would be as follows:

1. Initial detailed discussions are held at business level to reach agreement on key issues. This would usually involve a senior business executive supported by a financial executive.
2. A confidentiality agreement or a non-disclosure agreement is executed and then preliminary due diligence is performed to check major assumptions that have been used during those initial discussions. This often involves taking legal and/or accounting advice on structural issues.
3. Negotiations ensue and a nonbinding letter of intent or heads of agreement is executed to ensure that there is agreement on major issues.
4. Detailed due diligence and document preparation continue until final legally binding agreements are executed (with prior board approval), subject to any necessary conditions precedent (e.g. shareholder, government, or third party approvals).
5. Conditions precedent are fulfilled.
6. The transaction is completed, normally taking place at the end of a month for accounting convenience.

If parties do not intend to reach a binding agreement until formal contracts have been executed, it is important that clear words are used to that effect (e.g., "subject to contract"). This is because in Australia an agreement (which can be either oral or written) will be binding if:

i.   it appears either from a document or from circumstances that there is an intention to create legal relations;
ii. there are sufficient details about the agreement to confirm that intention; and
iii. there is consideration given for any promises made or undertakings given by either party.

This consideration is particularly important when parties intend to be bound by certain parts of an otherwise nonbinding heads of agreement (e.g., exclusivity or confidentiality obligations).

Documentation and procedures have become increasingly complex to match the expectations of international participants, particularly from the United States. For example, it has become common for corporations or governments that wish to sell a major business or identify a proponent for a new venture to engage an investment bank to conduct a tender process that involves the following steps:

1. A preliminary information document is distributed to potential participants.
2. Interested parties enter into a confidentiality agreement.
3. An information memorandum is distributed to those interested parties.
4. Bidders lodge nonbinding offers (subject to due diligence and formal contracts).
5. A short list of bidders is selected and given access to a data room and the proposed contract documentation.
6. Bidders make firm offers.
7. The successful bidder is selected, with or without further negotiations concerning price and documentation.

Governments offering licenses to construct, own, and operate major infrastructure projects ("PPPs"—Private Public Partnerships) follow this procedure to the extent that firm offers must include completed documentation and be capable of acceptance. Bidders are thus required to undertake complete due diligence and document negotiation at great expense prior to their bids being considered. This can involve millions of dollars and can only be afforded by major contractors, with the result that there are now in Australia very few contractors capable of bidding for large government infrastructure projects.

Since the late 1980s, due diligence has become much more important in Australian business transactions and it is now very similar to the procedures used in the United States. There is always a data room for major transactions, and it is common practice for that to be made available electronically. This emphasis on due diligence has greatly increased the cost and documentation involved in transactions. Regular participants in transactions, such as private equity funds, are beginning to explore practices that can reduce these costs (for example, providing vendor due diligence materials and reports that can be relied upon by purchasers).

4.4 Cultural, Ethical, and Religious Considerations

Australia is a demographically diverse country. Religion does not play a part in business transactions.

U.S. businesspeople are very comfortable undertaking negotiations in Australia because they find many similarities in procedures, technology, and documentation. Australian businesspeople and their advisors are used to dealing with businesspeople from around the world, and increasingly from Asia. They try to be respectful of the customs and traditions of those other countries.

4.5 Negotiating Online

E-mail has had a large impact on negotiations in Australia and between Australia and overseas countries.

It has exacerbated the tendency for negotiations at all hours and has resulted in negotiations being conducted by way of marked-up documentation rather than verbal or written commentary on documents.

It is becoming increasingly common for major transactions that involve a great deal of documentation to be managed through eRoom technology, so that multiple parties can view and make comments on a range of documentation.

5. Contract Formation

5.1 Wording and Style

In Australia agreements (including amendments to agreements) require consideration to be binding and valid. If there is any doubt about the existence of consideration, then the agreement can be said to be by "deed" and said to be "signed, sealed and delivered."

Australian contracts are usually detailed because common law interpretation relies heavily on the words actually used in documents and only make limited use of other evidence of true intent. There is, however, a great emphasis on the use of plain English, short sentences and paragraphs, and careful punctuation so the documents can be clearly read by businesspeople.

Accordingly, as a general rule, Australian documents are not as long or as complex as equivalent contracts prepared in the United States and are much easier to read and interpret.

There is set out, in the attached Appendix, a description of a typical Australian contract for sale of a business. Notwithstanding the additional stamp duty (see section 2.3(m), U.S. purchasers usually prefer to acquire a business rather than the shares of the corporation that owns the business, in order to avoid inheriting that corporation's existing tax, environmental, and trading liabilities.

5.2 Conditions and Defenses

Australian law implies a duty to cooperate between the parties to a contract. The duty requires each party to a contract to do all things necessary to give the other party the benefit of the contract. In the event that a party breaches its duty to cooperate, it will not be able to rely on the failure of a condition precedent to terminate a contract.

It is unsettled in Australia as to whether there is an implied duty of good faith between parties to a contract when it has not been expressly included. A duty of good faith is a broader concept than a duty to take care and includes:

    i.   an obligation of the parties to cooperate in achieving the contractual objectives;

    ii. compliance with honest standards of conduct; and

    iii. compliance with standards of conduct that are reasonable in regard to the interests of the parties.

There are no terms or conditions that must be included in a contract. However, legislation such as the Trade Practices Act will imply certain product liability terms into a contract for sale of goods.

There is no clear rule of law in Australia that will determine when risk passes to a buyer under either a share purchase or an asset purchase, although sale of goods legislation generally raises the rebuttable presumption that risk passes with title where goods are the subject of the contract. It is therefore particularly important to clarify in contracts when risk is to pass.

5.3 The Special Case of Online Agreements

Electronic commerce has been encouraged in Australia by Electronic Transaction legislation by the Commonwealth and each State and Territory. This legislation allows contracts formed electronically to be as legally enforceable as written contracts, including the use of electronic forms of authentication instead of a handwritten signature (subject to certain restrictions).

This legislation also:

    i.   establishes guidelines for determining the time and place of dispatch and receipt of an electronic communication;

    ii. allows for the electronic recording of information and retention of electronic documents to comply with legislation that requires written information to be retained; and

    iii. allows any communication that must be made with a government department to be made validly in an electronic form.

A recent case involving eBay confirmed the validity and applicability of traditional doctrines to interpret contracts formed electronically.

6. Resolving Disputes

State and Territory supreme courts have commercial divisions where judges without juries expeditiously hear commercial disputes.

Traditionally, business contracts in Australia have left disputes to be resolved by courts. As litigation costs have increased dramatically since the 1990s, alternative dispute resolution mechanisms have become popular.

Australia is a signatory to the New York Convention and has adopted the UNCITRAL model law on international commercial arbitration. Australian courts, therefore, recognize and enforce international arbitration awards in certain cases. Australia also has a sophisticated network of arbitration bodies that will appoint arbitrators to hear disputes, including the Australian Centre for International Commercial Arbitration in Melbourne.

Mediation is gaining popularity in Australia after having been used successfully in many cases to resolve complex commercial disputes. There are a number of organizations that provide mediators and mediation services in Australia.

7. Conclusion

Participants in negotiations in Australia or with Australian corporations will generally find sophisticated, up-to-date practices and technologies. There are no barriers to Australian corporations undertaking international business negotiations, and there is an increasing tendency for Australian businesspeople, lawyers, and other advisers to have overseas work experience.

Australians pride themselves on being direct and having a "can-do" attitude. In negotiations and documentation for transactions there is a general desire to resolve outstanding issues as quickly as possible.

Foreign investment is welcome in Australia, with all three levels of government keen to promote business, economic development, and employment growth. Although highly regulated, business in Australia is conducted in a transparent and politically stable environment and the courts are independent and accessible.

Leigh Brown
Minter Ellison
Aurora Place
88 Phillip Street
Sydney NSW 2000, Australia
Phone: +61 2 9921 49441
Fax:　　+61 2 9921 4419
E-mail: leigh.brown@minterellison.com

APPENDIX 19.1

Typical Sale Terms for Australian Business Sale Contract

1. **Defined terms**
   Australian contracts typically include a comprehensive list of defined terms in order to increase the legibility of the document. In the absence of defined terms Australian law will imply rules of interpretation; however, for the avoidance of doubt, contracts often include rules on how the terms of the contract should be interpreted.

2. **Conditions precedent**
   Conditions precedent are often included in relation to the consent of customers, suppliers, and lessors to the assignment of various contracts to the purchaser. Conditions precedent can also be included in relation to the obtaining of various government consents such as ACCC approval of the transaction (see paragraph 2.4(b) above) or FIRB approval (see paragraph 2.9 above). The contract will provide that if all the conditions precedent are not satisfied or waived by a specified date, then either party can terminate.

3. **Purchase price**
   Typically the purchase price is apportioned between the various assets of the business and the State or Territory where they are located. The apportionment will govern the effect of stamp duty on the transaction (see paragraph 2.3(m) above).

4. **Obligations before completion**
   In the event that the contract is entered into prior to completion taking place, the vendor and the purchaser will typically agree to limit the transactions that may be undertaken by the vendor prior to completion.

5. **Completion**
   The contract will have specific obligations for transfer of assets, entry into collateral agreements, and payment of the purchase price.

6. **Stock and outgoings**
   Typically there will be an adjustment of the purchase price to account for the amount of stock and apportionable outgoings at the time of completion. For major transactions, it will be a

requirement to prepare accounts as at the date of completion to facilitate the purchase price adjustment.

7. **Title and risk**

    Title and risk of the assets pass at completion.

8. **Trading responsibilities**

    The parties will typically agree that, as at completion, the vendor will assign to the purchaser the benefit of all outstanding contracts with suppliers and customers and that the purchaser will assume the burden of those contracts. All other precompletion liabilities will remain with the vendor.

9. **Employees**

    The purchaser will be required to make, prior to completion, offers of employment to the employees on terms no less favorable than their existing terms and conditions (so that the vendor will not receive redundancy claims). In the event that the employees do transfer to the purchaser, the contract will require a reduction of the purchase price by an amount equal to 70 percent of the value of the outstanding leave benefits of each nontransferring employee (being a tax-effected transfer of the existing accounting provision by the vendor—see section 2.5(b) above).

10. **Book debts**

    Book debts remain owned by the vendor. A purchaser may agree to act as the agent of the vendor in the collection of any outstanding book debts. The purchaser may require a fee based on a percentage of the amount of book debts collected.

11. **Warranties and indemnities**

    The extent of the warranties will depend on the amount of due diligence that is undertaken but are normally comprehensive to cover vendor solvency, accuracy of accounts and other information, proper records, ownership of assets without encumbrance, comprehensiveness and good condition of assets and stock acquired, appropriateness of trading arrangements, validity of leases and contracts to be assigned, accuracy of disclosed employee arrangements (including superannuation), compliance with law (including necessary licenses and approvals), right to use intellectual property (including software), and absence of environmental contamination.

    Contracts will typically contain both a warranty in relation to a matter and a general indemnity. In the event of breach, the contract allows the purchaser to elect whether to proceed under a warranty claim or under the indemnity.

12. **After completion**

    After completion the vendor will be required to comply with various legislative requirements for a period of time. Contracts typically provide a right of the vendor to access any documents in the business necessary to comply with its legislative obligations.

13. **Restraint**

The vendor will be restrained from competing for a number of specified years in a specified geographical area.

The enforceability of a restraint will depend on the reasonableness of the restraint, taking into account the characteristics of the business subject to the transaction.

14. **GST**

If applicable, the parties will agree that the contract constitutes the supply of a "going concern" so that GST is not payable on the purchase price.

CHAPTER 20

International Business Negotiations in Belgium

Katrien Vorlat
STIBBE
BRUSSELS, BELGIUM

1. Introduction

1.1 Broad Demographic Information

With a population of just over 10.4 million, an approximate maximum distance of only two hundred miles from east to west, and on average only one hundred miles between its northern and southern borders, it is obvious that Belgium is a relatively small country, even by European standards.

Belgium is located in the heart of Western Europe and is an important logistic hub: it has a well-elaborated railway and road network, and the port of Antwerp is one of the largest in the world.

Anyone coming to Belgium to negotiate international business transactions should be aware of Belgium's political and administrative organization. A very significant factor in Belgian politics and day-to-day life is the division of Belgium into two major language groups, the Dutch-speaking Flemish in the northern part of the country and the French-speaking Walloons in the southern part. The capital of Belgium is Brussels, which is a bilingual Dutch- and French-speaking region with a population of approximately one million. Since 1970, regional and linguistic tensions have driven the country into a federalization process. Over the past forty years the Belgian Constitution has been amended several times, transferring substantial powers from the national government to local governments. This process is still ongoing today.

The division of Belgium into two major language groups has led to some stringent, mandatory legislation with respect to the use of languages in dealings with employees and administrative bodies as well as in corporate documents, as these rules apply under sanction of nullity. However, business transactions are often conducted in English.

Belgium was founded in 1830 and has been a hereditary monarchy since 1831. The present sovereign is H.M. King Albert II, who has a rather ceremonial function. Belgium has a long-standing democratic tradition, where the division of powers is present at all levels. The major governing document is the Belgian Constitution, which defines and allocates powers as follows at national level:

- The legislative power is exercised by the Parliament, consisting of a House of Representatives and a Senate.
- The executive power is exercised by the Federal Government. The Government is headed by the Prime Minister, who is appointed by the King in principle from the largest party. There are no national political parties. All parties are divided per language group. Over time the three major political parties are the Christian Democrats (CD&V-CdH), the Socialists (SP.A-PS), and the Liberals (Open VLD-MR). Because no party has an effective majority, the Government is typically a coalition between at least four political parties, each of them nominating a number of Ministers in the Government. The executive power is exercised mainly through Royal Decrees and Ministerial Decrees. Royal Decrees are prepared by the competent Minister or Ministers. They are subsequently submitted to the King for his royal assent and unless stated otherwise, become effective upon signing by the King.
- The judicial power is exercised by the courts. The judicial system consists of local and district courts, courts of appeal, and the Supreme Court (*Hof van Cassatie/Cour de Cassation*). In addition, there is a Council of State (*Raad van State/Conseil d'Etat*), of which the legislative section advises the Government and the Parliament on matters such as the legality of draft bills. The administrative section of the Council of State has the authority to nullify acts of the Government and regulations of the administrative authorities when they exceed or abuse their power or violate material procedural requirements. Finally, there is the Constitutional Court, which has competence with respect to conflicts of authority between the central state, the regions, and/or the communities. It is also the guardian of the constitutional principle of equality and non-discrimination and the other rights and liberties provided for in the Constitution.

Belgium has a trade-oriented economy and is considered one of the most globalized economies in the world. It exports a large proportion of its gross domestic product (GDP) to other countries (approximately 86 percent as compared with about 11.1 percent for the United States and 16 percent for Japan). Obviously, it is in Belgium's best interest to discourage any form of protectionism. There is little or no sentiment in favor of guarding home industries by means of import restrictions.

In 2007 Belgium's GDP was EUR 330 billion (approximately US$450 billion). In 2007 the services sector accounted for 74.4 percent of the GDP; all industries combined accounted for 24.5 percent of GDP. Agriculture made up only 1.1 percent. The most important industries are chemicals, glass products, textiles, steel and metal products, non-ferrous metal products, pharmaceuticals, food, and beverages. Belgian products are exported throughout the world. Belgium is the world's top exporter in both diamonds and carpets. Other important products are cars, railroad and subway cars, steel plates and steel wires, plastics, household linen, chocolates, and beer. Belgium also exports services (information services, training, consulting, engineering, financial services). Belgium's main export markets are the European Union and especially France, Germany, and the Netherlands. Exports outside Europe represent approximately 20 percent of the international trade of Belgium. Outside Europe, the United States and Japan are the main markets.

Most of the companies in Belgium are small or medium-size companies. In general there is no culture of shareholder activism but there is often consultation between management and owners.

U.S. investments in Belgium are extremely important. Approximately 25 percent of foreign businesses in Belgium are American-owned, 24 percent Dutch-owned, 16 percent French-owned, 11.4 percent Italian-owned, and 6.5 percent German-owned. Approximately 1,500 U.S. companies have business operations in Belgium. On a historical cost basis, U.S. companies have invested close to $26 billion in Belgium. The Belgian labor force has given Belgium a reputation for being one of the most productive countries in the world and for being more cost-competitive than any other industrialized country.

Belgium is one of the six original signatories to the Treaty of Rome, by which the European Economic Community, now the European Union (EU), was formed. The EU aims to abolish obstacles to the free movement of goods, persons, services, and capital. In several areas of the law (e.g., antitrust, financial markets and services, corporate, etc.) the influence of the decisions taken at the EU level has become increasingly important. On January 1, 2002, the euro replaced the currency of twelve European Union members. Today it is being used by thirteen countries.

Belgium has also entered into several other international relations and associations, such as the Belgium-Luxembourg Economic Union (BLEU); the Benelux, representing a tariffs agreement between Belgium, the Netherlands, and Luxembourg; the World Trade Organization (WTO); the North Atlantic Treaty Organization (NATO); and the United Nations.

Belgium is the location of the political headquarters of NATO and the seat of several EU institutions. The European Commission has its seat here and the European Parliament resides here for three weeks per month with the remaining week in Strasbourg (France). Therefore, Brussels is often referred to as the capital of Europe.

1.2 Historical Basis of the Belgian Legal System

The Belgian legal system is based on the French Civil Code. Similar to other civil code countries, legislation is often laid down in codes such as the Commercial Code, VAT (Value-Added Tax) Code, etc., and is the most important source of law. However, case law is also important to interpret the legislation correctly.

European legislation has gained increasing importance in the legal systems of the member states.

1.3 Government Involvement

Both the Belgian Federal Government and the regional governments have a very open attitude towards foreign investment, and they encourage the free exchange of goods and services. The free exchange has been strongly inspired by the EU Treaty.

Like the rest of continental Europe, Belgium's economic life is based on a mix of commercial enterprises, generally referred to as the private sector, as well as enterprises of the public sector. Over the last decade there has been a wave of privatization of traditionally public companies for both budgetary reasons and as a result of liberalization rules stemming from the EU (e.g., telephone and utilities companies).

The involvement of the government typically takes the form of a financing by government-owned investment companies at both the national and regional level. In principle, neither the Federal Government nor the regional governments will play an active role in the shaping of international business negotiations, except to the extent government subsidies or other incentives are requested or if employment in Belgium is at stake.

Any intended transfer of a substantial holding in an enterprise having its activities in the Brussels-Capital Region, to the extent the transferred holding represents one-third or more of the capital of that enterprise and the equity of that enterprise is at least EUR 2.5 million, must be reported to the competent Ministers of Economy and Ministers of Finance. This rule was abolished in the Flemish and Walloon regions.

1.4 Investment Incentives

Belgium has an attractive system of financial and tax incentives with special emphasis on the high-tech sector. Incentives can be granted both by the Belgian Federal Government and by the regional governments.

The general incentives available for any company doing business in Belgium include subsidies and capital grants for certain types of investments; real estate tax; special depreciation deductions; and capital gains exemptions on shares and, subject to some conditions, deferred taxation of capital gains on tangible and intangible assets. There are also specific tax incentives for the small and medium-size companies that can benefit from investment deductions and obtain employment premiums when the number of employees is increased in comparison to the preceding year. Some specific incentives can be received for training technical personnel, for hiring additional scientific researchers, and for hiring employees previously unemployed for a certain period of time.

Today, Belgium has a well-functioning advance ruling commission, an independent body of the Belgian Ministry of Finance. This commission can deliver advance tax rulings that confirm the applicant's tax position for contemplated transactions or investments. One specific example of such a ruling relates to the determination of the taxable income of a Belgian company that is part of a multinational group of companies. If it can be demonstrated that the income reported by the Belgian company contains a fraction that should be taxed in another country, based on the general arm's-length standard, the commission can issue a ruling to confirm which portion of the Belgian income can remain tax exempt in Belgium.

Dedicated to reinforcing opportunities for local and international investors, Belgium significantly reduced its corporate tax rate in 2003, and has now amended its tax law to provide Belgian companies and Belgian branches of foreign companies a tax deduction based on their equity as of January 1, 2006. Under the so-called "national interest deduction," a new and innovative measure in international tax law, all companies subject to Belgian corporate tax will be able to deduct from their taxable income an amount equal to the interest they would have paid on their capital in the case of long-term debt financing (see www .invest.belgium.be/roodshaw/usa/national_tax/).

Finally, it should be noted that under certain conditions, 80 percent of royalties derived from licensing of patents can remain tax exempt for a Belgian corporate taxpayer. In essence, the Belgian taxpayer must have either created the patented product/service or, at least, contributed a substantial amount of added value to it.

2. Substantive Laws and Regulations Impacting Negotiations

2.1 Foreign Investment Regulations

Belgium has always invited and encouraged investments from abroad. There are no restrictions on foreign investments nor residence requirements to own, operate, and/or manage a business. All foreign investments, including earnings, can be freely transferred out of the country.

At both the national government and regional government levels, several authorities seek to attract foreign investments. These authorities work closely with economic and technology ambassadors representing the national and regional governments and with the Belgian embassies and consulates.

2.2 Foreign Exchange Controls

The regulatory authority with respect to foreign exchange regulations is the Belgian National Bank (BNB), which exercises control over exchange transactions by or with Belgian residents. To date, a number of transactions must still be reported to the BNB. The purpose of this mandatory reporting is purely statistical, in order to calculate the balance of payments of Belgium.

Belgium has implemented the EU Directive 91/308/EEC on money laundering and financing of terrorism by the Act of January 11, 1993 on preventing the use of the financial system for purposes of money laundering or the financing of terrorism (the "Money Laundering Act"). The Money Laundering Act imposes on all financial institutions a duty to cooperate to detect suspicious transactions and report them to the Financial Intelligence Processing Unit (*Cel voor Financiële Informatieverwerking/Cellule de Traitement des Informations Financières*).

Pursuant to the Money Laundering Act, financial institutions, insurance companies, stockbrokers, lawyers, notaries, and a number of other professions must identify their clients and verify their identity by means of supporting documentation, which must be kept for at least five years. This obligation exists not only for regular clients, but also for any clients who wish to perform a transaction for an amount of EUR 10,000 or more on an occasional basis, and if there is a suspicion of money laundering or terrorism financing.

2.3 Regulation of Business

There is no general restriction in Belgium preventing or limiting the investments or business activities of foreigners or the establishment by foreigners of a business operation in Belgium. For certain types of businesses, such as banking, insurance, travel agencies, etc., licenses need to be obtained and/or specific qualifications of the persons in charge of daily management apply. Generally, these regulations apply to both nationals and foreigners, without discrimination.

2.4 Competition and Antidumping Policy

Doing business in Belgium means, in fact, doing business in one of the member states of the EU. Competition and antidumping regulations are included in the EU Treaty and are applicable in Belgium. In addition, Belgium has some specific legislation prohibiting businesses from abusing their dominant position and using unfair trade practices.

2.5 Custom Duties and Trade Agreements

All EU countries apply the same rate of custom duties to goods imported from non-EU countries (i.e., the EU Common Customs Tariff). No custom duties are levied on trade among EU member states with the exception of goods containing components imported from outside the EU on which no duties were levied when they entered the EU.

The EU has entered into several bilateral and multilateral agreements in which a "favorite nation" status has been granted to certain countries with respect to the goods entering the community and originating from these countries. The most important agreements are the agreement with the European Free Trade Association countries (the EFTA, consisting of Iceland, Norway, Liechtenstein, and Switzerland); with some African, Caribbean, and Pacific countries (referred to as the ACP countries); and with several former colonies of EU member states. Under these agreements a substantial reduction in custom duties is granted for specific goods, subject to proof that the origin of these goods lies within these countries.

When goods are imported into Belgium, they are normally subject to Belgian VAT, payable upon importation. Sales of goods and services to persons established outside Belgium are in principle exempted from Belgian VAT, and the exporter has a right to claim reimbursement of the VAT paid on the purchase of exported goods or for materials used for manufacturing of exported goods. For transactions taking place within the EU, VAT will normally be due in the country of the destination of the goods.

For both the import and the export of goods in or from Belgium, transportation and clearance documents are required. The Schengen Agreement, to which all EU member states, except the United Kingdom and Ireland, are signatories, limits the customs formalities for trade between the participating member states.

2.6 Quotas and Other Non-tariff Barriers

Although most products may be imported to and exported from Belgium without any prior license, some types of products originating from certain countries are subject to an import license for which an application must be filed with the appropriate authority. Licenses will only be granted to the extent that quotas allotted for certain countries and certain products have not been reached or exceeded.

2.7 Price Controls

A complex system of prior notification of price increases, under which price increases were sometimes prohibited or deferred by the authorities, was abolished as of May 1, 1993 and replaced by a system of free price fixing (with the general restriction, however, that prices must be "normal" (i.e., not including excessive margins)). A few sectors (oil, gas, electricity, water, cars, teledistribution, medicines, implants, care of the elderly, and mandatory insurance) remain subject to prior notification of a price increase.

2.8 Work Permit, Professional Card, Visa

Citizens from countries other than EU member states must obtain a work permit prior to working in Belgium. This obligation does not apply to business travelers on a temporary short-term assignment. An application for a work permit has to be made by a Belgian employer. A request for a professional card should be filed with the Belgian consulate in the country of origin or legal residence of the applicant. The process of obtaining a professional card is, except for individuals with exceptional qualifications and abilities, rather burdensome and long, and, for certain professional activities, professional cards are nearly impossible to obtain.

Citizens from EU member states do not need visas. The citizens of a number of countries with whom Belgium has reciprocity agreements (including the United States) do not need visas for tourist or business travel involving stays of up to three months. All others will require a visa.

As of April 1, 2007, the activities in Belgium of all foreign employees or trainees who come to work in Belgium temporarily or partially and who are not subject to the Belgian social security regime have to be, as a matter of law, declared electronically to the Belgian authorities. The same obligation also applies to all self-employed persons and self-employed trainees who come to work in Belgium either temporarily or partially, irrespective of whether they are subject to the Belgian social security regime. This mandatory declaration is part of the Limosa project (see http://www.limosa.be). There are a few exemptions from the mandatory declaration depending either on the reason for coming to Belgium or on the duration of the stay. One important exemption is where employees and self-employed persons who attend meetings in a closed circle in Belgium are exempted from the obligation to declare their activity in Belgium provided they spend no more than a total of sixty days per year at such meetings in Belgium. In addition, no such meeting may last longer than twenty consecutive calendar days.

2.9 Securities Law Considerations

The (public) offering of securities is governed by the Belgian Act of June 16, 2006 (the "Prospectus Act") implementing the European Prospectus Directive 2003/71/EC, harmonizing the public offering rules for the European Economic Area (EEA). Pursuant to the Prospectus Act, a company that intends to publicly offer securities in Belgium must report the contemplated transaction to the competent authority (see below). In such case, and unless an exemption applies, the company must publish a prospectus on the transaction, which must be approved by the competent authority prior to its public release. Such requirements only apply, however, when the issuance and/or distribution of the securities are considered a public offering in Belgium. Private offerings are not subject to the requirement to publish an (approved) prospectus.

In light of the foregoing, it is of utmost importance to determine (i) which authority will be the competent authority, (ii) whether the transaction envisaged is a public offering in Belgium, and (iii) whether the transaction can benefit from some kind of exemption from the prospectus requirements.

For companies having their registered office within the EEA, the competent authority will be the supervisory authority of such member state (home country control). For entities that have their registered office outside the EEA and that have not publicly offered or listed securities within the EEA since December 31, 2003, the competent authority will be the supervisory authority of the EEA member state in which the shares are first offered. Entities that have, after December 31, 2003, publicly offered or listed securities within the EEA will be allocated at the occasion thereof, a single competent authority that will be authorized for all subsequent public offerings within the EEA, regardless of whether the actual offering takes place in any other EEA member state than the home member state of the competent authority. For Belgium the competent authority is the Belgian Banking Finance and Insurance Commission (BFIC).

2.9.1 Public Offerings

The definition of a *public offering* is broad and encompasses any communication made to more than one person with sufficient information to make an investment decision. A transaction is, however, not considered a public offering in Belgium if any of the following conditions are met:

i.   the offering of investment instruments (including securities) is addressed to qualified investors only;
ii. the offering is addressed to fewer than one hundred persons (other than certain qualified investors) in each individual EEA member state;
iii. the offering of investment instruments represents an aggregate value of EUR 50,000 per investor and per offering;
iv. the offering of investment instruments has a nominal value of at least EUR 50,000;
v.   the offering of investment instruments represents an aggregate value of less than EUR 100,000 (to be calculated over a period of twelve months).

Furthermore, the Prospectus Act explicitly excludes the "grant of investment instruments for free" from the definition of public offering. Accordingly, such grants fall outside the scope of the prospectus requirement.

If the offering is considered a public offering in any other EEA member state, and a prospectus has been filed and approved by the competent authority, it can enjoy the benefits of the EU passport regime.

. On the other hand, if notwithstanding the public nature of the offering, no prospectus would have to be registered with the competent authority pursuant to the rules of any other EEA member state (as a result of a potential exemption that would exist, e.g., for the offering of securities to employees), the issuer would in principle have to prepare a prospectus for the Belgian beneficiaries unless a specific exemption applies (see below).

2.9.2 Market Abuse/Insider Trading

As a general rule, it is forbidden for anyone who possesses inside information (*primary insiders*) to (i) make use of such inside information, (ii) communicate this inside information to another person, unless this would occur within the context of the normal exercise of one's work, profession, or functions, and (iii) recommend to another person (*tipping*) to acquire or to sell or to have acquired or sold by others on the basis of this inside information, the financial instruments to which the inside information relates or associated financial instruments. These prohibitions also apply to any person (*secondary insider*) who consciously disposes of information that he knows or reasonably should know constitutes inside information and that, directly or indirectly, originates from a primary insider.

Inside information is defined as "information of a precise nature which has not been made public, relating, directly or indirectly, to one or more issuers of financial instruments or to one or more financial instruments and which, if it were made public, would be likely to have a significant effect on the price of those financial instruments or on the price of related derivative financial instruments."

The listed companies have to draw up a list of these persons who have access to the inside information. This list has to be kept at the disposal of the BFIC and transmitted at its first request.

Individuals with a management position (*leidinggevende verant- woordelijkheid/responsabilités dirigeantes*) within a Belgian listed company, as well as persons closely related to them, must inform the BFIC of transactions in shares or derivatives thereof issued by such company.

2.9.3 Transparency Declarations

In case the voting rights held by one or more persons acting in concert exceed certain thresholds, such person is required to notify the company and the BFIC. The mandatory thresholds are set at 5, 10, 15 . . .

percent of the voting rights but the articles of association can set lower thresholds. In order to calculate the threshold one should not only take into account the actual voting rights (e.g., attached to shares) but also potential, future voting rights (e.g., options, warrants, convertible bonds).

2.9.4 Takeover Bids

The Belgian rules on takeover bids implementing Directive 2004/25/ EC of the European Parliament and of the Council of April 12, 2004 require the bidder to prepare a prospectus and to have it approved by the BFIC (i.e., the Belgian regulator). There are specific rules on the notification of a contemplated bid to the BFIC, the duty for the Board of the offeree to draw up a memorandum in response and to inform the work council of the bid and the advertisements that are published with respect to the bid. The breakthrough mechanism (i.e., nonapplication of share transfer restrictions during the acceptance period of the bid) and/or the prohibition for the Board of Directors to take any defensive measures only apply to Belgian companies when the articles of association explicitly contain these rules (opt in).

Under the new regime, the obligation to launch a public tender offer on all voting securities, and all securities giving access to voting rights, arises when a shareholder holds, alone or "in concert with others" (for purposes of Belgian law), more than 30 percent of the voting securities of a Belgian company listed on a regulated market, further to the acquisition of such voting securities.

Belgian corporations can set up anti–takeover bid defense mechanisms, making it more difficult for raiders to acquire them. However, Belgian corporate law prohibits Belgian companies from using certain types of defense mechanisms, such as change of control provisions and the sale of the "crown jewels," once a takeover bid has been launched. Similarly, there are some restrictions on preemption clauses (right of first refusal) and approval of new shareholders' clauses, irrespective of whether such clauses are provided for in the articles of association of the company or in a shareholders' agreement. Limitations exist on cross-participations between affiliated companies.

2.9.5 Markets in Financial Instruments

Directive 2004/39/EC and the implementing Directive 2006/73/EC concerning markets for financial instruments ("MiFID") have been fully implemented into Belgian law. Accordingly, a specific set of rules of conduct has been put in place that the financial intermediaries have to apply in their relationship with the market and their customers.

2.10 Corporate Law Considerations

Investments and business activities in Belgium can be carried out through a number of legal forms, of which the most commonly used are a Belgian corporation, typically a joint stock company (*naamloze vennootschap/société anonyme,* abbreviated *NV/SA*), or a Belgian partnership (whether a general partnership, special partnership, or a partnership by shares); or a Belgian branch of a foreign corporation or partnership. Less frequently used legal forms for international investments include private limited companies (*besloten vennootschap met beperkte aansprakelijkheid/société privée à responsabilité limitée,* abbreviated *BVBA/ SPRL*), cooperative companies, associations in participation, and temporary associations. In choosing between a Belgian corporation, partnership, and a branch of a foreign entity, the most influential consideration is tax. A BVBA/SPRL or Com VA/SCS are check-the-box entities for U.S. purposes.

The European Economic Interest Grouping (*europees economisch samenwerkingsverband/groupement d' intérêt économique européen,* abbreviated *EESV/EIEG*) is well suited to give a legal structure to network-type relationships among independent parties that are organized in at least two different member states. Non-EU organizations cannot use this organizational form. For non-EU organizations a possible alternative is the International Non-Profit Association (*internationale vereniging zonder winstoogmerk/association international sans but lucrative,* abbreviated *IVZW/AISBL*). This association, however, cannot be used to carry out any commercial activities.

All commercial enterprises doing business in Belgium must, regardless of their form, register with the Register of Legal Entities. Upon request, the Register of Legal Entities provides an excerpt of the registration of the corporation or other entity concerned, containing such information as the official corporate name, registered address, all business addresses, names of the directors and officers and their respective powers, the amount of capital issued and paid up, and so on.

Belgian joint stock companies have to comply with rather formal incorporation procedures. They are subject to minimal capital requirements and can be declared bankrupt by the Belgian courts, by the court's own motion or by the motion of one or more creditors. If a foreign entity is exclusively or principally managed out of Belgium, the Belgian courts can requalify it as a Belgian entity and, as the case may be, declare it bankrupt.

In principle a Belgian stock company is managed by the board of directors. The board has the power to carry out everything that is not reserved to the shareholders meeting by law (e.g., capital increase, amendment of articles of association, replacement of directors, approval of annual accounts) or in the articles of association. In Belgium there is no mandatory employee representation at board level.

The articles of association may authorize the board of directors to establish a management committee (*directiecomité/comité de direction*), resulting in a two-tier management structure. If the board of directors decides to establish a management committee, it will determine the powers and the working rules of the management committee. The Company Code allows the board of directors to delegate some or all of its powers to the management committee, except those that are by law or pursuant to the articles of association reserved by the board of directors (e.g., the preparation of the annual accounts and special reports required pursuant to the Company Code).

Under Belgian law, the day-to-day management (*dagelijks bestuur/ gestion journalière*) of a company may be entrusted to one or more directors acting separately or jointly, or to a third party called the general manager (*algemeen bestuurder/directeur général*).

The company is represented by the board of directors. In addition thereto, the articles of association may provide that the company is represented by one or more directors acting individually or jointly, or by third parties appointed by the board of directors as special proxy-holders.

In the post-Enron era Belgium has also adopted a Corporate Governance Code. In 2004 a Code for the listed companies was published and in 2005 a Code for the nonlisted companies, referred to respectively as the Code Lippens and the Code Buysse, after the chairman of the committees establishing the respective codes. They are currently under review. These are legally nonbinding documents and based on the principle "comply or explain." Although they are not legally binding, these documents have a great moral value and are therefore generally followed, as the market and the investors community are not insensitive to such matters.

On September 1, 2004, the European Company—Societas Europaea (*europese vennootschap/société européenne*, abbreviated *SE*) was implemented. This is a company that can be used throughout the EU. Businesses are no longer obliged to constitute in each member state a company according to local laws, but can now use one company incorporated in one of the member states. The SE is incorporated and regulated according the Council Regulation 2157/2001 and the applicable law of the member state of the registered office.

From January 1, 2008, it will no longer be possible to issue bearer securities. The law of December 14, 2005 provides for the gradual cancellation of bearer securities, resulting in their total abolition by December 31, 2013. On December 31, 2013 all bearer securities that have not been converted into dematerialized shares will automatically be converted and shall be registered on a special securities account of the issuer, or will be converted into registered shares if the articles of association do not provide for the possibility of issuing dematerialized shares.

2.11 Merger Control

The dismantling of the internal frontiers within the single market has resulted and will continue to result in major corporate reorganizations in the EU, particularly in the form of mergers and acquisitions. In order to permit an effective monitoring of all these concentrations with respect to their effect on the structure of the competition in the community, the EU Council has issued a regulation on the control of concentrations between undertakings (currently Regulation 139/2004 of January 20, 2004) ("EU Regulation"). The scope of the application of this Merger Control Regulation is limited by quantitative thresholds in order to cover only sufficiently large concentrations ("EU dimension"). The regulation requires prior notification to the EU Commission of any concentration with an EU dimension. If the EU Commission considers that the concentration possibly creates or strengthens a dominant position as a result of which effective competition in the Common Market or in a substantial part thereof is significantly impeded, it initiates legal proceedings that may lead to a decision forbidding the concentration, or imposing divestiture measures. If the concentration has already been implemented, the EU Commission may require the dismantling of the concentration or any other action that may be appropriate to restore effective competition.

Concentrations falling outside the scope of the EU Regulation may be covered by the Belgian Act on the protection of economic competition. This Act requires prior notification to and approval of the Competition Council for mergers between enterprises with much smaller turnovers (two undertakings achieving EUR 40 million turnover in Belgium and all undertakings involved achieving together more than EUR 100 million in Belgium) than those covered by the EU Merger Control Regulation. Whether the merger will be authorized (whether or not subject to conditions) or prohibited depends by and large on the same criteria as those used on the EU level. If the concentration has already been realized, the Belgian authorities can order divestiture measures and/or impose fines.

2.12 Accounting and Reporting Requirements

The accounting principles that need to be followed for bookkeeping in Belgium (Belgian GAAP) are very similar to international standards. All business entities must meet the minimum criteria (number of employees, annual turnover, balance sheet total) and therefore must keep a complete set of books of account and records.

Since 2005, listed companies have been subjected to the International Financial Reporting Standards (IFRS). For other companies nothing has changed, except that they are given the option to report according to the IFRS. Once they have opted for this, they are compelled to keep reporting according to the IFRS.

The annual financial statements must include a balance sheet, a profit and loss statement, some explanatory notes to the balance sheet and the profit and loss statement, and a directors' report on the status of the company. Standard charts of accounts, based on formats set forth in the fourth EU Directive on company law, have been established by the Belgian government and are mandatory. Belgian law also provides for a set of valuation principles to be used for the preparation of the financial statements relating to, among other things, inventories, tangible fixed assets, and start-up losses. The annual financial statements must be presented in the official language of the region where the company has its registered office.

Non-EU investors might be surprised by the reporting requirements pursuant to which the financial accounts must be sent in annually to the BNB, where anyone can obtain a copy. When someone wants to check on the financial condition of a company, these mandatory reporting requirements are a blessing. Less well perceived is the obligation for foreign companies with a branch in Belgium to publish financial statements of the branch and the foreign company itself.

Each business enterprise in Belgium that meets these minimum criteria must appoint one or more statutory auditors, who have an unlimited right of supervision and inspection on all the operations of the company. They also have to report to the shareholders' meeting on the annual financial statements. All statutory auditors must be chosen from the list of members of the Belgian Institute of Statutory Auditors. The auditors' reports and responsibilities are subject to standards similar to those that apply internationally.

2.13 Employment and Labor Law Relations

Employer-employee relations are governed by individual employment contacts, work rules, and collective bargaining agreements. The employment laws are aimed at protecting worker rights, especially as regards dismissal, minimum wages, work conditions, and vacations.

Under Belgian labor law, there is no obligation to ask a court or the Works Council for prior permission to dismiss. Both employer and employee have the capability of terminating the employment contract by either respecting a notice period during which the contract will continue to be executed and at end of which the contract will end or by paying an indemnity corresponding to the remuneration the employee would have earned during the notice period that should have been served. The length of the notice period depends on whether the employee is a blue-collar or a white-collar employee. The notice period to be given to a blue-collar worker is expressed in calendar days. As regards white-collar employees, the statutory notice period amounts to three months for each five-year period within the company. When the remuneration of the employee exceeds a certain threshold, the notice period is to be determined based on seniority, age, remuneration, and function of the employee. The result of the so-called Claeys formula is usually considered as a yardstick when determining the appropriate notice period for such white-collar employees whose annual gross remuneration exceeds the above-mentioned threshold. The notice period to be served by the employee is shorter than the notice period the employer must serve when terminating the employment contract.

The contract can be terminated for cause, making any further collaboration definitively and immediately impossible, without notice or indemnity. However, certain formalities must be observed.

Both the EU Treaty and the Belgian Constitution provide for equal treatment of men and women concerning employment law matters, and sexual harassment is governed by a specific regulation that has been recently amended.

Employees are free to form unions, but union membership is not mandatory. Depending on the type of industry concerned, the percentage of workers affiliated with the unions varies from 50 to 80 percent. Unions and employers' representatives sit together on joint committees where specific collective bargaining agreements are concluded. These committees exist for each type of industry. Unions generally participate in the bargaining in cases involving collective disputes, closure of undertakings, collective dismissals, and so forth. They may also intervene to protect and defend the interests of an employee in cases involving an individual employee.

Undertakings employing on average at least one hundred employees must follow a specific procedure to set up a Works Council where the employees' representatives meet the management on a regular basis. The employers must inform their employees via the Works Council about all important decisions affecting the future of the company, such as investments, mergers, collective dismissals, and so on as well as any other decision having an impact on employment matters.

All undertakings employing on average at least fifty employees must follow a procedure to set up a Committee for Prevention and Protection at work (formerly called the Committee for Safety and Hygiene) in which security, health, and hygiene issues at company level are discussed on a regular basis.

Belgium has transposed the EU directives with respect to transfers of undertakings by introducing a collective bargaining agreement (CBA no. 32bis). According to this regulation, the transferor's rights and obligations arising from the employment contracts with all employees who can be allocated to the transferred activities are automatically transferred to the transferee, and all the employment and working conditions agreed at both the individual and collective level with the transferor are binding upon the transferee. In the case of transfer of undertakings, special information procedures exist involving the Works Council or the union delegation.

The Belgian social security system covers unemployment, pension, health care, family allowances, professional disability, and annual vacation benefits. Social contributions are paid both by the employer and the employee. The employer is responsible for withholding social security contributions from employees' wages.

2.14 Tax Law Considerations

All income tax laws in Belgium have been incorporated into the Income Tax Code and supplemented by a royal decree implementing the Income Tax Code. Taxes are imposed mainly by the federal state and the municipalities. Corporate taxpayers must report their taxable income to the tax authorities on an annual basis. The tax authorities may request additional information and may organize an audit in order to establish the taxable income. It is the tax authority that assesses the taxpayer—based on reported income or income as adjusted by the tax authority. The standard corporate income tax rate in Belgium is currently 33.99 percent, including a so-called crisis surcharge of 3 percent on the base rate of 33 percent.

The corporate income tax base is based on the statutory profit and loss account, established in accordance with Belgian GAAP; hence, even if a Belgian corporation or branch is establishing its statutory accounts under IAS or IFRS, it must maintain accounts in Belgian GAAP as well for tax-reporting purposes.

The three most significant deviations of taxable income from the statutory P&L are (i) the so-called dividends received deduction (DRD), (ii) the exemption of capital gains on the disposal of shares; and (iii) the so-called notional interest deduction.

- The DRD provides that up to 95 percent of qualifying dividend income is deducted from the taxable income of a Belgian corporation or branch. Subject to certain conditions, a Belgian corporate taxpayer owning an equity interest of at least 10 percent, or with an acquisition value/price of at least EUR 1,200,000 in another Belgian or foreign corporation that is subject to a normal tax regime, can deduct from its taxable income up to 95 percent of the dividend income it has received from such participation.
- A Belgian corporate taxpayer owning an equity participation in another Belgian or foreign corporation that is subject to a normal income tax regime is entitled to fully exempt any capital gain realized upon disposal of all or part of its participation.
- A Belgian corporate taxpayer is entitled to deduct from its taxable income a notional interest amount, i.e., an amount equal to the taxpayer's qualifying equity times a notional interest percentage, the amount of which is determined each year on the basis of the ten-year Belgian Government bond interest rate (for 2008, the notional interest percentage is set at 4.307 percent). In other words, to the extent that a Belgian corporate taxpayer is funded with equity, it will be entitled to a fictitious interest deduction. For purposes of the notional interest deduction, the taxpayer's equity

(share capital, share premium, retained earnings) is adjusted to prevent alleged abuse; for example, the statutory book value of an equity participation in another corporation is in principle deducted from the taxpayer's eligible equity.

In addition to their income tax obligations, Belgian and foreign enterprises in Belgium have withholding tax obligations, principally on wages paid to employees and on dividends, interest, and royalties, whether paid in or outside Belgium. Belgium has signed treaties intended to prevent double taxation and tax evasion with over eighty countries, including all EU member states, the United States, Canada, Brazil, Switzerland, Japan, Israel, Sweden, and South Korea. On December 28, 2007, a comprehensive new bilateral tax treaty with the United States entered into effect.

Apart from income tax, Belgian businesses are subject to VAT. As a result, Belgian businesses must charge VAT on all deliveries of goods, rendering of services, and importations of goods or services. On the other hand, VAT paid on incoming goods or services is in principle deductible (creditable) so that only the balance between "output VAT" and "input VAT" needs to be paid to the VAT authorities. VAT on investment goods can be deducted at once, but it may need to be "revised" (partially refunded) if the investment goods are no longer used by the taxpayer for a VAT-able activity within the first five or fifteen years following the time on which the initial VAT amount was eligible for deduction. For rendering of services and deliveries of goods within the EU, the normal EU rules for the localization of VAT apply. Exportation of goods and services to non-EU professional customers (business-to-business—B2B) are normally exempt from VAT.

2.15 Local Commercial Representatives in Belgium

A supplier wishing to distribute its products on the Belgian market, and looking for an independent local representative to do so, can choose between several types of commercial intermediaries. The most commonly used independent intermediaries are distributors, commercial agents, and franchisees.

A careful distinction has to be made between distributors and commercial agents. Distributors buy the goods and resell them in their own name and on their own account, bearing all the risks and costs of the resale. Commercial agents negotiate (and possibly conclude) business transactions in the name and on behalf of their principals, against the payment of a commission. They do not buy goods for resale, and therefore do not bear the economic risk, as the sales are concluded directly between their principal and the customers.

Commercial agents enjoy the protection of the (mostly) mandatory provisions of the Act of April 13, 1995 regarding Commercial Agency Agreements, which implemented the EU Council Directive 86/653. This law organizes all aspects related to agency agreements (such as the formation, duties of the parties, remuneration of the agent, and termination). The agents are entitled to a goodwill indemnity when certain conditions are met.

Belgium also has far-reaching statutory protection of distributors in the case of termination of distribution by the suppliers. The Act of July 27, 1961 entitles the distributor to a reasonable notice period (or an indemnity in lieu of notice, in case no reasonable notice period is granted) and to a complementary indemnity, comprising (i) a goodwill indemnity, (ii) an indemnity for the costs that the distributor incurred for the purpose of exploiting the distributorship and that will ultimately benefit the supplier, and (iii) redundancy payments, which the distributor is obliged to make to the personnel whom he must release as a result of the termination of the distributorship agreement. This regime is applicable only to distributorships that are granted for an indefinite duration, and that are also exclusive or quasi-exclusive, or impose onerous obligations upon the distributor.

Franchisees are a very particular type of commercial intermediaries that act in their own name and on their own behalf. Franchise agreements presuppose the existence of a franchise network, based upon the franchisor's concept, the use of a common name, the transfer of intellectual property rights (such as trademarks, know-how, etc.), and commercial, legal, and technical assistance by the franchisor.

On December 19, 2005, a law was adopted pertaining to the exchange of precontractual information relating to commercial cooperation agreements entered into between two parties, acting in their own name and on their own behalf, on the basis of which one grants to the other (in case of the sale of products or the rendering of services) the right to use: (i) a common trade name, or (ii) a common shop sign, or (iii) the right to a transfer of know-how, or (iv) commercial or technical assistance, all this in exchange for a direct or indirect remuneration. This law provides the obligation for the party granting the right to transmit the draft agreement, accompanied by a precontractual document containing certain information provided by the law (such as the most important contractual clauses) to the other party at least one month before the signing of the agreement. Franchise agreements are governed by this law. Legal authors are divided on the question of whether the law also applies to distribution and agency agreements.

When selecting a distributor or agent one should also review the possible tax consequences of such a choice. When a foreign principal sells through an independent Belgian distributor, the foreign principal will be considered a mere exporter of goods to Belgium and therefore will not incur income tax liabilities in Belgium. When a foreign principal works with a related agent or a dependent agent in Belgium (or avails in Belgium of certain facilities, not merely being an inventory of goods for storage), the question as to whether or not the agent's activities and the sales made by the principal to Belgian clients constitute a taxable presence in Belgium should be carefully reviewed.

2.16 Sales in Belgium

Under Belgian law, a seller must guarantee that no defect renders the product inappropriate for its intended use. Sellers who know of a product defect and continue to sell the product are not only liable to reimburse part or all of the purchase price, but are also liable for consequential damages resulting from the hidden defects. As a result of well-established case law, the "professional seller," because of his disposition, is presumed to have knowledge of the product defect. Such presumption is only rebutted if the seller can prove that it was absolutely impossible for him to know of the defect. Claims on the basis of hidden defects must be brought within a brief period of time after the discovery of the defect. The seller may contractually exclude his liability for hidden defects only upon a showing that he did not know of the defect. Professional sellers, therefore, can only contractually exonerate themselves from liability if the defect is untraceable.

The EU Directive 85/374 of July 25, 1985, with respect to product liability was implemented by the Unfair Competition Act of July 14, 1991. The producer of a product is liable for all damages, including death or personal injury, caused due to a defect in its product (i.e., the product does not provide the level of safety a person is entitled to expect). Damage to any item of property, other than the defective product itself, will have to be compensated for, provided that the item of property is of a type ordinarily intended for private use or consumption and was used by the injured person mainly for her own private use or consumption.

EEC Council Directive 92/59 on General Product Safety was implemented in Belgian law by an Act of February 9, 1994. This Act regulates the obligation of economic operators to place only safe products and to offer only safe services on the market.

Sales to consumers in Belgium are also subject to the Unfair Competition Act. This act is among the most severe in Europe and deals with a wide variety of sales practices such as a prohibition (subject to exceptions) on sale at loss, sale at distance, dual offers, promotional sales, liquidation sales, etc. To some extent these rules are implementing European law provisions but in many respects they go beyond that. The Act also provides rules on the prohibition of misleading advertising and aggressive advertising. The act transposes the EU rules on comparative advertising and furthermore provides rules on the indication of prices and labeling of various products. Products should also conform to the rather specific and far-reaching laws on the compulsory use of languages.

There is also a prohibition of unfair acts affecting consumers and competitors (for example, third-party breach of contract or nonrespect of other legislation).

In 2004, the EU Directive 44/1999 of May 25, 1999 relating to the sale of consumer goods and associated guarantees was introduced in Belgium. Under Belgian law, the seller is obliged to provide to the consumer (i.e., any natural person who is acting for purposes that are not related to his trade, business, or profession) goods that are in conformity with the contract of sale. The seller is liable to the consumer for any lack of conformity that exists at the time the goods were delivered and becomes apparent within two years from delivery of the goods. The consumer shall be entitled to claim damages, the goods brought into conformity free of charge by repair or replacement, or—in the event that such remedy would be impossible or disproportionate—to have an appropriate reduction made in the price or the contract rescinded with regard to those goods.

Product liability claims may also be based on the general principles of tort law. The general principle is that any person who through his negligence causes damage to another person is liable for this damage. Furthermore, the keeper of a product is liable for damage caused by goods in his possession.

The packaging and labeling of products sold in Belgium should comply with EU packaging and labeling directives.

Security interests whereby the seller of goods retains title to these goods notwithstanding the physical transfer of these goods to the buyer can be enforced against the trustee, to avoid bankruptcy, provided certain conditions are met. The retention of title must be established in writing no later than the delivery of the goods. Furthermore, the goods must still be in the possession of the buyer, when the retention of title is relied upon.

The EU e-commerce Directive 2000/31 of June 8, 2000 was implemented in Belgian law by two Acts of March 11, 2003 regarding certain legal aspects of information society services. These Acts mainly outline the requirements a provider of information society services must provide to its customers, lists the conditions that publicity included in information society services must comply with, regulates publicity via electronic mail, and sets forth the liability regime of providers of mere conduit, caching, and hosting services. A royal decree of April 4, 2003 further regulates in more detail the sending of publicity via electronic mail.

2.17 Acts of God and Other Unanticipated Events

As a rule, excuses for the nonperformance of contractual obligations are allowed with respect to unforeseeable causes at the time the agreement was entered into, to the extent that they render the performance of the contractual obligations impossible. In principle, parties may validly contractually determine the conditions and the consequences of the existence of an act of God.

2.18 Transactional Insurance; Deferred Consideration

In international trade, Belgian counterparts frequently use transactional insurance and other credit-support techniques, including guarantees by parent companies, performance bonds, standby letters of credit, bid bonds, and the insurance of receivables with commercial insurance companies or with the Government (*delcredere/ducroire*).

Bills of exchange and promissory notes are frequently used, especially in ongoing business relations.

2.19 Data Protection and Privacy

With regard to data protection, the Belgian Act of December 8, 1992 on Privacy Protection in Relation to the Processing of Personal Data, as modified by the Act of December 11, 1998, is applicable. This Act implements the general privacy principles as set out in Directive 95/46/EC on the Protection of Individuals with Regard to the Processing of Personal Data and on the Free Movement of Such Data.

This Act contains the following main obligations:

i.   The data controller (i.e., the entity that alone, or jointly with others, determines the purposes and methods of personal data processing) must file a notification to the Belgian Privacy Commission of the processing of personal data before carrying out the processing operation (except if the data controller can rely on an exemption);

ii. The data controller must inform each data subject of the processing of her personal data;

iii. The personal data have to be processed in accordance with data protection principles (i.e., the processing has to be carried out fairly and lawfully, for specified, explicit, and legitimate purposes; personal data cannot be stored longer than necessary, etc.);

iv. The data controller must ensure the exercise of the data subject's right to access and rectify the data;

v.   The data controller must implement sufficient technical and organizational safeguards to ensure the safety of the processing of the personal data;

vi. The personal data can only be transferred outside the European Economic Area if the third country in question ensures an adequate level of protection.

2.20 Intellectual Property Rights

Copyright, trademark, design, models, and patent protection are available in Belgium. The trademark, design, and models protection are based on uniform Benelux laws applicable throughout the Benelux. Under Belgian copyright law, registration is not compulsory for legal protection. Software and databases are protected both under the general copyright law and under, respectively, the Belgian Act on the protection of computer programs and the Belgian Act on the protection of databases.

Belgium is a member of several international conventions and agreements on intellectual property law, including the Berne Convention for the Protection of Literary and Artistic Works, the Universal Copyright Convention (Geneva Act), the Paris Union Convention, and the European Patent Treaty. No approval or authorization is required for intellectual property licensing agreements. Patent and trademark licensing agreements should be registered. It is advisable also to register other intellectual property licensing agreements, but such registration is not compulsory.

2.21 Environmental Issues

The protection of the environment in Belgium is dealt with at the level of the regional governments. Most of the legislation has been triggered by EU directives. Air, water, and soil pollution and the disposal and transportation of waste are heavily regulated. Amongst the regions there can be important differences in the implementation of the EU directives.

2.22 Governing Law and Choice of Court Clauses

It is common to encounter in contracts provisions that stipulate that, although the obligations of one or both of the parties under the contract have to be fulfilled in Belgium, the contract will be governed by a foreign law. Belgian courts respect choice of jurisdiction and applicable law clauses. A choice for a foreign law will, however, be disregarded when the dispute is governed by mandatory Belgian law. Such mandatory law aims to safeguard certain policy objectives, such as the protection of distributors operating in Belgium or of employees working on Belgian territory. Should parties choose to submit disputes to foreign courts they will be upheld, especially if parties have given jurisdiction to the courts of an EU member state. Except in specific cases, Belgian courts do not automatically apply Belgian law when the parties have not agreed on the applicable law. If judges determine that a foreign law is the proper law of the contract, they will apply that law. Even when Belgian law is applied, there are exceptional situations where the law of another country will be applied if it is established that there is a close transaction and the country insists that their rules must be adhered to as a result.

2.23 Enforcing Foreign Judgments

As a rule, judgments issued by courts of EU member states may be enforced without any difficulty in Belgium. When presented with such a judgment, the court in Belgium will only verify that the foreign judgment does not violate basic tenets of public policy. The court will not review the merits of the case. Enforcing a judgment issued by a court of an EU member state can be done rather swiftly under the Brussels Regulation on Jurisdiction and Enforcement of Judgments in Civil and Commercial Matters.

If the foreign judgment has been issued by a court sitting outside the EU, it may also be enforced in Belgium under the provisions of the Code on Private International Law (Act of July 16, 2004). When reviewing the judgment, the court in Belgium will merely verify that the decision does not violate Belgian public order or conflict with decisions rendered in Belgium. The court will also verify that the foreign court has afforded every party due process of law. The court is statutorily barred from reviewing the merits of the case. Although there is no strict time limit for the court to rule on the enforcement request, in most cases it should not take longer than a month to obtain a declaration of enforceability. In all cases, the request to obtain enforcement is filed *ex parte*, with no possibility for the defendant to appear in the first stage of the proceedings.

2.24 Arbitration

As an alternative to settlements of disputes and claims in courts, parties may submit disputes to arbitration. Under the rules applicable in Belgium, most disputes relating to business agreements may be referred to arbitration. Belgium is a party to the New York Convention of 1958 on the Mutual Recognition and Enforcement of Foreign Arbitral Awards. Courts in Belgium will, therefore, decline jurisdiction when faced with an agreement providing a valid arbitration agreement. Courts will also enforce arbitral awards rendered in countries that have ratified the Convention. When a country has no bilateral or multilateral enforcement treaty with Belgium but is a signatory to the New York Convention, it is, in order to make enforcement in Belgium easier, generally advisable to choose arbitration of disputes in that country rather than referring disputes to the country's courts.

CEPANI, the Belgian Center for Arbitration and Mediation (*Belgisch Centrum voor Arbitrage en Mediatie/Centre belge d'arbitrage et de mediation*), is a private organization with its own arbitration rules and also serves as the local national committee for the ICC International Court of Arbitration. Parties can submit the arbitration of their dispute to the CEPANI rules. Proceedings can be conducted in English.

2.25 Certification of Documents

Belgium is a member of the Hague Convention of October 5, 1961. Documents originating from signatory countries to this Hague

Convention can be officially used in Belgium if certified with an apostil in the originating country.

3. Negotiation Practices

3.1 Participants

With the exception of the fifty or so largest companies, most Belgian companies are medium-size. The small and medium-size companies are typically represented during negotiations by senior management (managing director/general manager). The scope of the involvement of senior management may vary depending on the size and the strategic importance of the underlying business transaction. Large companies may be represented by a special negotiation team that is put together taking into account the specifics of the underlying business transaction.

The role during negotiations of outside advisers, such as lawyers and consultants, is generally limited. Once the parties have come to an agreement with respect to the business points, outside counsel might be asked to document the transaction and, in case of an acquisition, to proceed with a legal due diligence. In case of an acquisition, accountants proceed with a financial due diligence. Outside counsel might also be asked to review the proposed transaction from merger-control, antitrust, and tax standpoints. In acquisitions or mergers leading to a substantial reorganization, management consultants might be hired. Patent lawyers, patent consultants, and engineers are among the outside advisors that are sometimes hired. Increased environmental concern and the new trend toward strict liability of owners of polluted land have brought environmental lawyers and consultants as outside advisors in recent acquisitions, whether share or asset transactions. Frequently transactions are documented in-house.

Whether documented in-house or by outside counsel, it is typical for Belgian parties to focus primarily on the business points of the transaction. General representations and warranties and boilerplate language with respect to waivers, notices, severability, and the like frequently remain unaddressed. Documents of twenty pages or more are exceptions. However, during the last decade, under the influence of the international business community in Belgium and their advisors, Belgian companies, to the extent the counterpart so requires, are increasingly willing to document transactions the American way. Transactions among Belgian parties, however, are not that detailed, and minor acquisitions or business agreements are frequently documented in a two- or three-page contract without review by either in-house or outside counsel.

Some types of contracts, such as the acquisition of real estate, must be signed in front of a notary. Similarly, a notary deed is necessary for the incorporation of a company and for all subsequent modifications to the articles of association of the company.

In settlement negotiations to terminate or avoid litigation, the intervention of members of a local bar association has the advantage in that confidentiality can be assured to a greater extent than amongst nonlawyers.

3.2 Timing

It is difficult to give an estimate of the time frame necessary for business negotiations in Belgium. The timing really depends on the type of transaction involved. Negotiations handled by senior management tend to move forward very quickly, and often an understanding reached during a meeting will be confirmed on the next business day by a letter in which one party confirms the agreement and sets forth its understanding of the agreement. Larger companies move forward with more caution. Following negotiations, a draft letter of intent is prepared. Letters of intent may be drawn up subject to board approval or subject to review of merger-control, antitrust, environmental, social, tax, or securities-law issues. The same applies, of course, to the contract itself.

3.3 Conduct

Negotiations are conducted in the language that is common to the participants. However, in reality most negotiations are conducted in English, and this is for two reasons. First, English is usually the more common language, as opposed to the official language (for the Flemish, French; for the Walloon, Dutch). Second, participating foreigners in business negotiations rarely speak Dutch or French.

In the early stages of the negotiations due diligence is usually effected by the buyer, although occasionally also by the vendor. To ensure the confidentiality of the information exchanged in due diligence, the parties have to sign a confidentiality agreement.

3.4 Cultural, Ethical, and Religious Considerations

Negotiations typically take place in a formal way, often at the offices of one of the parties' advisors. Parties are expected to be well prepared before the meeting. It is not uncommon that negotiations are preceded by separate meetings for each of the parties and their advisors in order to clarify the position and set the negotiation objectives. Negotiation sessions can be typically divided in three main stages: (i) identification phase, in which parties identify which issues are material to them; (ii) negotiation phase, in which arguments are exchanged, additional information or clarifications are requested, and compromises can be made; and (iii) conclusion phase, wherein parties list the points on which agreements have been reached, the outstanding points, and the next steps to be taken. The process as described above may repeat itself several times (there are usually two or three sessions) until full agreement is reached. Participants to the negotiation process are expected to be constructive and have a positive attitude toward resolving issues. Aggressive negotiation style is not well perceived.

3.5 Confidentiality Agreements

Confidentiality agreements entered into by the parties during negotiations are valid and binding. If one of the parties breaches its confidentiality duty, the other party has a course of action that may result in an order forbidding the breaching party to continue the use of the privileged information under penalty of civil or criminal sanctions and/or an award of damages. Parties may agree, in the confidentiality agreement, to a lump sum to be paid by the infringing party to the other party in the case of a breach of confidentiality obligation. Such a penalty clause should be drafted very carefully. Belgian law does not allow parties to set penalties of such magnitude whereby an infringement would result in an indemnity disproportionate to the damage actually suffered. Thus, there is a risk that Belgian courts may disregard such clauses.

The contractual confidentiality duty may conflict with the legal duty to inform the Workers' Council prior to any important decision affecting the future of the company. Parties therefore should address during their negotiation the issue of the timing of this announcement.

3.6 Binding Character of Business Negotiations

As soon as an agreement is reached on the major points of the deal (e.g., object matter, price, and material conditions), parties may be deemed to have a contract. Therefore, in order to protect parties from being forced into a contract, draft agreements must explicitly stipulate that the agreement is "subject to formal or written contract." However, this does not guarantee that a party cannot successfully prove in court that a contract exists (commercial contracts need not necessarily be in writing.) Written documentation abbreviates the border of proof.

4. Contract Formation

4.1 Language and Style

In international transactions, English is very frequently used. With the language comes the use of many Anglo-Saxon terms such as "Subject to formal contract" and "entire agreement" clauses, as well as the prior conclusion of "gentlemen's agreement," "heads of agreement," and so forth.

4.2 Condition and Defenses

Although a contract exists only when—but also as soon as—an offer that is sufficiently detailed and that is intended as such is accepted, negotiating parties have a duty of good faith prior to conclusion of the contract. This duty implies that each party informs the other of all issues that are important for the conclusion of the contract, cooperates with the other in such a way that the negotiations may be concluded within a reasonable period of time, and respects the confidential nature of information received in the course of negotiations. Breach of any of these duties may constitute negligence, in particular a *culpa in contrahendo* for which the contract partner may claim damages. Thus, depending on the circumstances, the termination of negotiations may be negligent (if made at a late stage, without substantial reason, or if made after the other party has been led to believe that a contract would in any case be concluded) and entitle the other party to claim damages.

Moreover, if the contract has been induced through fraud, error, or violence of one party, and is later annulled for that reason, the damages that the other party suffers as victim of the fraud or violence may also have to be indemnified on the basis of the *culpa in contrahendo*. Even when the contract is validly concluded, damages for negligence committed in the precontractual period may be due (e.g., failure to inform the other party).

As regards the above-mentioned duty to inform the other party, it should be noted that it is counterbalanced by each party's duty to investigate on its own behalf (*caveat emptor*). The balance between the two principles is very delicate and may be different from one set of circumstances to another.

4.3 The Special Case of Online Agreements

Online agreements have not become general practice in Belgium as yet.

5. Dispute Resolution

Arbitration and court jurisdiction are the main dispute-resolution mechanisms in Belgium. Both types of proceedings are governed by the Judicial Code. In 2005, a new chapter was incorporated in the Judicial Code, with regard to mediation. Other alternative dispute resolution mechanisms (conciliation, mini-trial, binding third-party decisions) are also available. There is no online dispute resolution.

The question of court jurisdiction may be a lengthy process and is an incentive to negotiate. Even after a court judgment is obtained, the defeated party often tries to negotiate a reduction in the amount to which it is condemned under the threat of appealing against the first-instance judgment.

Since 2007, lawyers' fees are to a certain extent (a legal maximum is provided in function to the amounts at stake) recoverable from the defeated party.

6. Conclusion

Belgium is a small country in the heart of Europe with a complex political and governmental structure, due to language and cultural differences between the north and the south.

It is one of the most globalized economies in the world and it is open to foreign business. There are virtually no barriers to foreign investments, and the legislation is flexible and adheres to international standards. It is also heavily based on EU legislation.

In negotiations, the approach is straightforward and the documentation of transactions is more and more influenced by Anglo-Saxon principles.

Katrien Vorlat
Stibbe
Central Plaza, Loksumstraat 25 rue de Loxum
BE-1000 Brussels, Belgium
Phone: +32 2 533 54 16
Fax: +32 2 533 51 45
E-mail: katrien.vorlat@stibbe.com

CHAPTER 21

International Business Negotiations in Bermuda

Megan Denos
APPLEBY
HAMILTON, BERMUDA

1. Background

Bermuda's first settlers were Englishmen en route to the settlement at Jamestown, one of the earliest communities in what would become the United States of America. The image of Englishmen en route to America in many respects accurately depicts late-twentieth-century Bermudian culture. Bermudian culture is quintessentially Anglo-American. History, geography, and the population's choices have made it so.

Bermuda's political structure and its legal institutions owe much to its British heritage and its status as an overseas territory of the United Kingdom. Bermuda's external affairs policy, defense, internal security, and the administration of the police are under the control of the British government. The Bermuda Parliament, an elected government along the British model, has jurisdiction over most other areas of governance.

Modern cultural influences are predominantly American. Bermuda's proximity to the east coast of the United States (one and a half hours by plane from New York) and the pegging of the Bermudian dollar to the U.S. dollar has made the United States the first choice for Bermudians traveling abroad. The American cultural influence is enhanced by American television, which is beamed into Bermudian homes. This is balanced somewhat by the survival of some English traditions, including a passion for cricket.

1.1 The Bermuda Landscape

Bermuda is made up of over 130 islands, many of which are linked together by causeways and bridges. The total area of the islands is approximately twenty square miles. The population totals approximately 63,000, of which roughly 78 percent are Bermudian nationals and the balance are expatriate workers and their families.

Bermuda is a small country approximately one-third the size of Washington, D.C. It plays an important, in many respects leading, role in the realm of offshore jurisdictions, but it is not a significant player on the world stage. This can lead to misconceptions, as knowledge of Bermuda and its culture is not as widely disseminated as in the case of the United States, leading European nations, and other major western economies. Perhaps not surprisingly, Bermuda is sensitive to these misconceptions. It is important to understand what Bermuda is not:

- It is not the Bahamas.
- It is not in the Bermuda Triangle.
- It is not part of the Caribbean.

Despite being more than 1,000 miles north of the Bahamas, Bermuda is occasionally confused with that archipelago. Bermuda is located in the mid-Atlantic some 1,200 miles north of the Caribbean sea. The nearest landmass is North Carolina some 670 miles west. The Bermuda Triangle refers to an area of the Atlantic Ocean. Bermuda is situated at the northern apex of the triangle.

Because of its isolated location and some similarities in political structure, Bermuda is, on occasion, grouped with the island states and dependencies located in the Caribbean for the purposes of regional trade groupings and other international classifications. However, Bermuda is geographically, politically, and culturally quite removed from its Caribbean counterparts. Bermudians do not appreciate being classified with and considered part of the Caribbean countries. Avoid this at all costs.

In any negotiation, gathering intelligence prior to commencing negotiations is a fundamental initial step. There are numerous publications that provide useful Bermuda background information.[1] There are also many Web sites devoted to Bermuda, several of which contain information on conducting business in and from Bermuda.[2]

---

[1] BRIAN ARCHER, THE BERMUDIAN ECONOMY (1999); BRIAN ARCHER, INTERNATIONAL COMPANIES: THEIR IMPACT ON THE ECONOMY OF BERMUDA (annual, 1 year in arrears) (known as the ARCHER REPORT); BERM. MINISTRY FIN., BERMUDA: AN ECONOMIC REVIEW (annual, 1 year in arrears); BERM. GOV'T, DEP'T STAT., BERMUDA DIGEST OF STATISTICS (annual, 1 year in arrears); BERMUDIAN BUSINESS (quarterly); BERMUDA BUSINESS VISITOR: THE ESSENTIAL EXECUTIVE TRAVELING COMPANION (annual); BERMUDA COMMUNICATIONS DIRECTORY; BERMUDA BUSINESS DIRECTORY (biennial); BERM. GOV'T, DEP'T STAT., BERMUDA FACTS & FIGURES (annual); ECONOMIST INTELLIGENCE UNIT, FIN. TIMES, BERMUDA COUNTRY REPORTS (annual or quarterly).

[2] Bermuda Chamber of Commerce at http://www.bermudacommerce.com; Bermuda International Business Association at http://www.biba.org; Bermuda Monetary Authority at http://www.bma.bm; Bermuda Stock Exchange at http://www.bsx.com.

2. The Rule of Law

Like their English and American cousins, Bermudians subscribe to the rule of law. That is to say, they acknowledge the primacy of fundamental legal principles. The judiciary and the legal system are generally held in high esteem. Material civil litigation is instigated in the Supreme Court and, within Bermuda itself, may be appealed to the Court of Appeal. The final Court of Appeal is England's Judicial Committee of the Privy Council. Bermuda has enacted modern arbitration legislation designed to attract foreign arbitrations to Bermuda and to provide a clear framework for the arbitration of disputes arising within Bermuda.

Bermuda's substantive law is primarily based on English common law as supplemented by Bermuda's statutory provisions, which, for the most part, are based on English statutory law. In some cases, Bermuda has borrowed from Canadian legislation, particularly in relation to certain aspects of company law. Amendments to public law that concern the international business sector are usually initiated by the professional community in Bermuda, acting through the Bermuda International Business Association. Many of these amendments are designed to address the business objectives and concerns of the international business community, with the goal of making Bermuda more attractive to international business without compromising Bermuda's reputation.

Bermuda's House of Assembly is elected. There are two principal parties: the United Bermuda Party, which ruled for three decades (since the establishment of a party system), and the Progressive Labor Party, which has been in power since the 1998 election. The government has repeatedly affirmed its commitment to expanding the international business sector, including a clear commitment to promoting Bermuda as a leading center for offshore insurance and reinsurance.

2.1 The Local/International Business Dichotomy

2.1.1 International Businesses Are Embraced

Commencing shortly after the second World War, Bermuda consciously set out on a path of attracting quality international businesses that sought to establish a business entity in a tax-neutral, reputable jurisdiction. During the 1990s, the rate of growth of the international business sector community in Bermuda led to it being the prime contributor to the Bermudian economy, ahead of the traditional leader, tourism. This shift was a major contributing factor in Bermuda's securing an AA1 rating by Moody's Investors Service.

Compared with some other offshore jurisdictions, Bermuda is selective. There are approximately 18,000 exempted or international business entities formed in Bermuda, which is approximately a 9.5 percent increase in the past three years but a fraction of those formed in jurisdictions such as the British Virgin Islands and the Cayman Islands. The incorporation of a Bermuda company or the establishment of another business entity does not occur "as of right" in Bermuda. All applications to establish business entities are vetted both as to the identity of the ultimate shareholders and the nature of the business. This screening process has enabled Bermuda to maintain a reputation that is untarnished by the scandals that have plagued other offshore jurisdictions.

Within these limits, Bermuda actively encourages international businesses to establish a Bermudian business entity. Qualified foreign businessmen will find that the Bermuda Government is receptive to their needs. The Government views its role as facilitating the success of Bermudian international business entities. The process of negotiating with the Bermuda Government is discussed below.

International businesses are exempt from taxation and may obtain an assurance that they will remain exempted, notwithstanding any change in the law, for a fixed period of time, which currently expires in March 2016.

2.1.2 Local Businesses and Workers Are Protected

As a small group of islands with a limited population base, Bermuda has sought to restrict foreign ownership of its land and businesses. Moreover, immigration policy reflects a "Bermudian first" premise that obliges an international business that seek to employ individuals in Bermuda to initially offer the position to interested Bermudians. If a qualified Bermudian is available, normally the position should be offered to him or her. There are some exceptions to this policy, notably for members of senior management. The exceptions are granted on a case-by-case basis.

For the most part, businesses that wish to operate in the Bermuda market (as opposed to operating in the international market from a base in Bermuda) must be controlled by Bermudians. In the case of a corporation, effective control and at least 60 percent ownership of the voting shares of a company must be in the hands of Bermudians. In certain exceptional circumstances, an international business may obtain a license to conduct a limited trade within the Bermuda market.

The third aspect of local protectionism is industry specific. A number of business sectors, in particular banking, have been the beneficiaries of protectionist government policy. International businesses operating in those sectors are excluded from establishing an operating presence in Bermuda, even where that presence is not intended to access the local market. In the case of banking there is some movement toward relaxing this policy, in particular in relation to a variety of "near-banking" activities.

3. Negotiations with Bermudians

3.1 Are They Really Bermudian?

As one of the world's leading centers for establishing offshore business structures, Bermuda is "home" to thousands of businesses that have chosen Bermuda as their jurisdiction of domicile. However, the vast majority of these businesses have little or no operating presence in Bermuda.

In contrast to many other offshore jurisdictions, these so-called "brass plate" companies are often substantial enterprises. Close to 700 of Bermuda's international business companies list their shares on various stock exchanges throughout the world. Both the public and private international business enterprises are owned and managed by nationals of the United States, England, Canada, Australia, a host of European and Asian nations, and, more recently, a range of other countries. Negotiations with one of these businesses will take the form of negotiations with its management or owners, wherever they operate from and whatever their nationality. Bermudian negotiations are usually limited to any which are ancillary to Bermuda court proceedings required in connection with the restructuring of an international business entity, or negotiations with a Ministry or other division of the Bermudian Government.

3.2 Yes They Are!—Bermudian-Controlled Entities

Although most Bermuda-domiciled international business enterprises do not operate from Bermuda, several hundred have elected to do so. The Bermuda operations of these companies are often managed by Bermudians. You will also invariably encounter Bermudians if you are entering into negotiations, whether for an investment or for the provision of services, with a local business.

Bermuda's workforce is highly skilled and well educated. As Bermuda has no university, all Bermudians who pursue postsecondary education must study abroad. In many cases they have more than one degree, and in some cases have degrees from universities in different countries. This exposure to living abroad, combined with Bermuda's focus on attracting international business, makes Bermudians particularly internationally attuned. Nonetheless, there are a few local idiosyncrasies that you should be aware of when entering into negotiations with a Bermudian-controlled business.

- First and foremost, while there will always be exceptions, Bermudians are in general genuinely welcoming and friendly. Embrace this hospitable nature. If you are invited to dinner or on a boat cruise, accept the offer and follow up with a thank-you call or note. Foreign businesspeople who appear standoffish or self-important will not be well received.

- Do not underestimate Bermudians. Do not let the pink beaches and the pastel-color houses deceive you. Bermudians are sophisticated, wealthy businesspeople. Bermuda's gross domestic product per capita is among the highest in the world. Bermuda's GDP increased by 5.4 percent in 2006, recording its strongest performance in ten years. The country has succeeded in attracting the créme-de-la-créme of international business corporations and has fostered the development over the past decade of an insurance and reinsurance industry that is second only to New York and London.

- Beware the local grapevine. The population may exceed 63,000, but the number of people involved in the international business community is much smaller. Everyone knows everyone. If you are dealing with a Bermudian and you make a disparaging comment about another Bermudian, the odds are good that you will be referring to a relative, friend, or business associate.

- Be forthright in identifying who you are and whom you represent. Bermuda has built its reputation as the world's premier offshore financial center on the strength of its extensive vetting of perspective shareholders or other investors in Bermudian business entities. The introduction of anti-money-laundering legislation has intensified the vetting process. If you represent another party, you will not progress far if you are not willing to identify your principal at the outset of negotiations.

- Be realistic in your assessment of conflicts of interest. Bermuda's professional community is made up of relatively few participants. Where a substantial matter arises involving numerous parties it is not unheard of for all the professional advisors who regularly advise the international business sector to be engaged by one or more parties on the matter. In particular sectors, such as investment funds and insurance, where Bermuda has concentrations of business entities, it is fairly common for a professional advisor to represent competing business groups. This works because most business groups have separate principal "onshore" counsel. Moreover, the professional advisors are adept at constructing Chinese Walls within their organizations.

- Be sensitive to Bermuda's status as a British overseas territory. Although it is not an independent state, Bermuda has been self-governing on virtually all domestic matters since 1620. A sound majority defeated a 1995 referendum proposing independence. Nonetheless a vocal minority favors independence and all Bermudians value and are justifiably proud of their functional independence from Britain.

- Be aware of the racial issue. Approximately 60 percent of the Bermudian population is of black ancestry. The remaining 40 percent is Caucasian. Blacks and whites mix particularly well in the business community. Their social interaction outside the business environment is less developed.

- Be respectful of the "'Bermudians first" policy. This policy is discussed in more detail under the heading "Immigration Department" below. Business groups who choose to operate internationally using an international business entity formed in Bermuda, even where that entity operates from Bermuda, will not be affected by the policy except as it pertains to work permits for non-Bermudian employees who live and work in Bermuda.

3.3 Establishing an Operating Presence in Bermuda

3.3.1 A Clear Trend Emerges

While traditionally most of Bermuda's exempted (international business) entities have not elected to establish a physical presence in Bermuda, the past decade has seen a clear shift toward more international business entities establishing an operating base in Bermuda. Several factors have contributed to this development. Since the 1990s Bermuda's insurance sector has grown dramatically. During 2006, Bermuda's reinsurance companies generated in excess of US$100 billion in net premiums and their assets exceeded US$440 billion. These companies now employ several hundred personnel within Bermuda.

In other sectors, multinational businesses that utilize a Bermuda company as their ultimate holding company are more frequently establishing executive offices in Bermuda. This trend is driven in part by the policies of the revenue authorities in other jurisdictions, which increasingly require a physical presence to substantiate a claim that profits are sourced in a particular jurisdiction.

3.4 Negotiating with the Government

Non-Bermudians who seek to establish an operating presence in Bermuda will, of necessity, be required to negotiate with Bermudians on a variety of issues. Establishing an office and hiring personnel are obvious issues. Perhaps less obvious are the advantages that can flow from entering into a dialogue and negotiations with the Bermuda government on the possibilities of resolving specific legal issues that affect the business plan of the enterprise. This is discussed below under the heading "A Unique Tool: The Private Act of Parliament."

Bermuda is blessed with a relatively small but efficient civil service. This is particularly so in the case of the civil servants who are responsible for dealing with the international business sector. While the agencies and ministries that you will encounter will vary depending on the nature of your planned business, most international businesses will find that their initial dealings with the Bermuda government are restricted to the Bermuda Monetary Authority and the Ministry of Finance.

3.4.1 The Bermuda Monetary Authority (the "BMA")

All international businesses seeking to establish a Bermuda-domiciled business must apply to the Bermuda Monetary Authority for consent to the issuance of any shares or other participation interests. Applications are usually handled by the attorneys for the business, although where confidentiality is essential, the BMA will accept applications and supporting information directly, on a confidential basis, from the non-resident who seeks to acquire participation interests in a Bermudian enterprise. The staff at the BMA is quite experienced and routinely vets complex ownership structures. Where the ownership structure is novel or unduly complex, it is often useful to precede the formal consent application process with a preliminary telephone discussion to describe the overall transaction structure and the principles behind it.

In certain sectors, the BMA also has influence over approval of the nature of business to be undertaken by the proposed new business entity. Officially, the Ministry of Finance has authority to approve or disapprove the nature of a proposed business; however, where the activity involves a financial services business (e.g., investment advice, securities brokerage, trading, custodial services, etc.) the BMA will in practice participate in the decision-making process as to whether to approve the proposed business activity. The BMA also has jurisdiction over the approval and regulation of investment funds, stock and other financial instrument exchanges, banks, deposit-taking entities, and other financial institutions and intermediaries that operate in or from Bermuda. Additionally, where a foreign bank is to be a significant (generally in excess of 10 percent) proposed shareholder in a Bermudian business entity, the BMA will seek confirmation that the home regulator of the bank will exert jurisdiction over and monitor the Bermudian investment by the foreign bank.

3.4.2 Ministry of Finance

While the establishment of a Bermuda exempted company with standard objects (i.e., a holding company or operating company that will not engage in a restricted or prohibited line of business) does not require the consent of the Minister of Finance, any company that seeks special objects or that will engage in a restricted business must secure the consent of the Minister of Finance. Applications for the consent of the Minister are normally routed through the BMA initially and then by the BMA to the Ministry. Ministry officials are generally less accessible than BMA officials. However, where the need arises, and specific direct contact is warranted, it is possible to secure a meeting with senior staff members within the Ministry. Where the business is particularly innovative or unusual or might be perceived to place a strain on Bermuda's physical or regulatory resources, a face-to-face meeting is often advisable. Representatives of the parties seeking to establish the business enterprise should attend this meeting together with their professional advisors.

3.4.3 Immigration Department

If an operating presence in Bermuda is envisioned and the enterprise plans to shift or hire personnel from outside Bermuda, then it will be necessary to deal with the Department of Immigration. The granting of work permits to foreign nationals is a sensitive issue in Bermuda. While senior executives of a new enterprise are usually permitted a work permit in Bermuda, it is important to explain clearly to the Immigration Department the business plan of the proposed enterprise, the employment and training opportunities for Bermudians in the near- and medium-term future, and the general benefit that Bermuda will derive from the enterprise's decision to establish a physical presence in Bermuda. In many cases this information can be communicated by written submission. As with the Ministry of Finance, where the application is unusual or may be perceived to place undue strain on Bermuda's resources, a face-to-face meeting with the senior members of the Immigration Department is advisable.

3.4.4 Other Ministries and Departments

Other government ministries may be involved in an application to establish an operating presence in Bermuda. Whether or not this occurs will depend on the nature of the business. It is often wise to seek the support of specific ministries, as this support can be helpful when dealing with the Immigration Department and the Ministry of Finance. Accordingly, where a specific ministry has a legitimate claim to be interested in a particular enterprise to be established in Bermuda, it is often advisable to meet first with officials of that ministry with a view to garnering their support for the proposed initiative.

3.4.5 A Unique Tool: The Private Act of Parliament

Prior to 1970 all companies formed in Bermuda were established by separate legislation, referred to as a private act of Parliament because a single member rather than the government tabled the bill. This legislation is of equal status with all public legislation but is typically restricted in its scope of application to a particular company or business group. While most companies are now formed by registration, private acts remain a popular legal mechanism. Since the 1990s private acts have been extended to the insurance sector to permit the establishment of segregated cell companies that can effectively firewall selected assets and liabilities. A private act effectively allows an international business to craft, within limits, a legal regime unique to the company or group.

An international business that intends to petition for the passing of a private act that introduces concepts not previously enacted should plan to meet with officials of the Ministry of Finance, the Attorney-General's Chambers, the BMA, and any other interested ministry at an early stage of the process. The business plan, the objectives of the private act, and the rationale for the various provisions proposed to be contained in the act should be addressed at the meeting. Once dialogue is established, the draft legislation can be circulated among the relevant Government officials with a view to preclearing the bill before it is presented to the House of Assembly and Senate.

4. Conclusion

Bermudian culture is unique but is strongly affected historically by English culture and more recently by American influences. As a small country, Bermuda is sensitive to misconceptions and misunderstandings as to its history, culture, and modern role in international commerce. It is advisable to undertake some research on Bermuda and Bermudian business practices before entering into negotiations in Bermuda or with Bermudians. Bermudians are genuinely warm and friendly people. They interact best with people who exhibit similar characteristics. Many Bermudian companies are not actually controlled by Bermudians. Those that operate from a base within Bermuda are more likely to be controlled by Bermudians, either as owners or as managers. Bermuda protects its local sales and labor markets and restricts foreign ownership of businesses wishing to trade into the Bermuda market. Be respectful of these policies when negotiating with Bermudians if you intend to establish or acquire a business with an operating presence in Bermuda.

The Bermuda Government views itself as being in partnership with international business. It tries to ensure that its policies facilitate the needs of international business, subject to any relevant local policy considerations. International businesses are advised to enter into a frank and open dialogue with representatives of the Bermudian Government. These negotiations can often prove very helpful in establishing a comfort level on the part of the Government and may enable the international business enterprise to secure specific legal or regulatory advantages not available elsewhere.

Megan Denos
Appleby
Canon's Court
22 Victoria Street
PO Box HM 1179
Hamilton HM EX, Bermuda
Phone: +441 295 2244
Fax: +441 292 8666
E-mail: info@applebyglobal.com

CHAPTER 22

International Business Negotiations in Brazil

Ordélio Azevedo Sette[1]
AVEZEDO SETTE ADVOGADOS
SÃO PAULO, BRAZIL

1. Introduction

The Federative Republic of Brazil, one of the largest countries in the world, with a population exceeding 180 million,[2] sometimes surprises businesspeople who go there for the first time. They find highly developed industries and an active and efficient local and international banking system and services sector. They also find a large population in poverty and at a low standard of living.

Brazil is a democratic federal republic of twenty-six states and a federal district, Brasília (DF). The country is divided into five regions—North, Northeast, Southeast, South, and Midwest—with around 5,500 cities. In the Southeast and South regions are concentrated more than 70 percent of the Brazilian economy and gross domestic product (GDP).[3] Brazilian GDP is around R$2.55 trillion a year,[4] the tenth largest in the world.[5]

The Federal Administration exerts strong influence over the Brazilian economy and its interventions on monetary, credit, fiscal, and other policies may cause significant impact on the private sector.

In the mid 1990s, Brazil implemented a plan for economic stabilization and market liberalization, privatizing several public companies, which opened many opportunities to the private sector. Foreigners may participate in government bids for supply of goods and services,

---

[1] Research and updating by Ana Paula Terra and Ricardo Azevedo Sette.
[2] Brazilian Institute of Geography and Statistics (IBGE) (http://www.ibge.gov.br/), 2007.
[3] IBGE, 2005.
[4] IBGE, 2007; exchange rate in June 2008 of around R$1.60 per US$1.00.
[5] International Monetary Fund (IMF), World Economic Outlook Database: Nominal GDP list of countries. April, 2008, *available at* http://www.imf.org/external/data.htm.

including under the Public-Private Partnerships (PPP) regime, regulated by Federal Law 11.079/04.

A former colony of Portugal, independent since 1822, the country is traditionally open to foreign relations. For more than a century it has been very attractive to immigrants from Europe (mainly from Portugal, Italy, Germany, and Spain) and from Japan. Today, immigration is under strict control.

Portuguese is the language spoken in Brazil, but businesspeople and lawyers normally speak English as a second language, and negotiations with foreign parties commonly are conducted in English.

Business hours are almost the same as in the United States, and lunchtime usually takes one hour. Shops and industry facilities are normally open from 8 A.M. to 6 P.M. from Monday to Friday and from 8 A.M. to noon on Saturdays; law firm, auditor, and accountant offices and services are open from Monday to Friday from 8 A.M. to 6 P.M.; banks and financial institutions are open to the public from Monday to Friday from 10 A.M. to 4 P.M.

Mid-December and January are school and summer holidays, and this is not the best season to conduct business or negotiations in Brazil. People also often have extended holidays during the Carnival (normally in February or March) and Easter season (normally in April). Other important national holidays are: April 21 (Martyr of Brazil's Independence Day), May 1 (Labor Day), May 22 (*Corpus Christi*), September 7 (Independence Day), and November 15 (Republic Day).

2. Negotiations in Brazil

Around 90 percent of Brazilian companies are family-owned[6] and managed by their owners. In larger companies there are professional executives. Mainly in the South and Southeast region (in the states of São Paulo, Rio de Janeiro, Minas Gerais, Paraná, and Rio Grande do Sul) there are lawyers, auditors, entrepreneurs, and executives with international experience, graduates from top North American or European universities.

One of the most important factors in order to conduct a negotiation is having a solid database of information. A negotiation initiated by people who are well-informed and diligent and who have decision-making powers over the matters involved guarantees an increase in efficiency and allows a satisfactory result.

It is important that the information is disclosed in an easily accessible form. It is useless to take to the negotiating table or to a debate an extensive and hard-to-consult report. The material should preferably be organized in a modular format, starting from the general theme

---

[6] Brazilian Support Service Agency for Small-Sized Companies (Sebrae), 2005.

and moving toward the more specific one, and be separated by different subtopics—legal, economic, and political, among others.

Among the great challenges in international negotiation are cultural differences and personalities, which is why knowing the profile of each negotiator involved is so important.

Negotiations in Brazil never follow a standard pattern and vary on a case-by-case basis. In small and medium-size companies, owners conduct negotiations, while many larger companies have professional executives for that purpose. In significant business negotiations, the chief executive officer or chairperson of the board of directors may become involved assisting the company's negotiating team in solving significant issues. Investment banks are also involved with such transactions, representing both the seller and the buyer.

Lawyers in Brazil are not involved in business negotiations as they are in the United States. Entrepreneurs in small and medium-size businesses usually lead their negotiations and quite often do so without assistance from counsel. Their lawyers are called to prepare the agreements when the transaction is already settled.

Lawyers may be present from an earlier stage depending on the nature of the transaction and the size of the Brazilian company, but they do not normally act as negotiators, with the exception of some specialized lawyers mainly from São Paulo, Rio de Janeiro, and Belo Horizonte. Foreign businesspeople and lawyers negotiating in Brazil are often assisted by Brazilian lawyers because of local legal issues.

Brazilian negotiators are sometimes impatient with long meetings and heavy-handed bargaining. They usually expect both sides of a transaction to start with fair positions. When dealing with a small or medium-size Brazilian company, the negotiations may be divided into two phases: definition of the general terms of the agreement and its basis and, if there is an agreement, a second phase in which a contract is discussed by lawyers and/or other officers based upon what has been already agreed.

Contracts in Brazil are on a less formal basis than the extensive agreements normally executed in the United States. This is because Brazilian law is based upon the Roman Civil Law system, which does not require an agreement to repeat what is provided by the law, and the law usually has extensive regulation for all subjects. In spite of that, Brazilians are also used to the length and complexity of the international transaction agreements governed by U.S. law and accept them, even if with some reluctance.

3. Lawyers' Training and Improvement in Business

Companies spend, nowadays, approximately 30 billion dollars per year in corporate development programs. But are these programs in fact changing the way executives and lawyers think and work?

Frequently, a company will send its executives and lawyers to "specific learning events," hoping something could be assimilated and a real change could occur. However, very often, many of these people upon returning to their jobs become frustrated when trying to implement what they have learned. Many soon give up when gains in productivity cannot be rapidly achieved.

It is hard to implement changes in people, but a technology appropriately developed can help.

At this stage, all of us probably have already had an unsuccessful learning experience with technology and, in some cases, we may be disappointed with a technological failure to meet our expectations of improvement in productivity and efficacy. In fact, an incorrect use of the technology, in some cases, can lower productivity and efficiency by bureaucratizing the proceedings. One of the most important keys in training is to use the technology in the best way possible to avoid technological traps and to maximize the learning process.

Companies frequently provide learning content through the Internet or on CD-ROMs, and inform their employees that the information is available. This approach depends on the employees' availability to dedicate part of the time normally allocated for daily work to the learning process, and their ability to retain interest during the entire process. For this reason, most of the time CD-ROMs are left unused on the offices shelves and Internet learning courses are also ignored, especially when directed to seniors lawyers and partners.

A successful implementation of technology-assisted learning must consider these obstacles and be created in a form that will best accommodate the users. The most attractive technology is one that integrates the daily work and the learning process—one that is not a separate activity that users need to remember to use.

Many companies are seduced by technologies with videos, animations, and sound. These programs tend to be expensive to create or customize, and are not relevant for the users' work. The majority of these solutions have a common fatal flaw: they ignore the adult learning method and are not projected to create specific business results. Another risk is that these exercises are generally designed to be done interactively on the computer and the computer becomes the "expert"; and whatever it says becomes the correct answer, in a way that causes valuable dialogues and experience-sharing to be lost.

Bear in mind that technology cannot completely replace the time spent in personal attendance in a class. The opportunities for intercommunication, dialogue, action-reaction discussion dynamics, and questions and answers should be completely integrated in any learning solution.

The companies also invest a considerable amount at the initial creation of a knowledge database. Most of the knowledge databases work only if the executives are interested in it, even willing to suspend their daily work to access the information provided. The executives may research and, with a bit of luck, find the information or cases that might be applicable directly to their work. Unfortunately, many knowledge databases are not used continuously, because of being considered statistical and one-way communication vehicles with no relevant information.

To maximize the effectiveness, we suggest the use of a "moderate" knowledge database. Internal or external consultants interview senior lawyers and executives and choose the cases for the moderate knowledge database, instead of relying on the lawyers and executives themselves to dedicate time and effort to select and include the cases. This ensures that the cases are current, complete, and objective (i.e., including both successful and unsuccessful cases), and set up so that everyone in the company may learn through the hands-on learning project.

Any lawyer who reads a case in the moderate knowledge database could ask the team or the consultant a question about the project. The reader may also be able to see all questions and answers made in the past for each study case.

Some key points of the successful development of a leadership-changing initiative are the same, regardless of technology use:

- The experience in training has demonstrated that adults learn more when doing the activity, that is, performing the practice and following the continuous learning cycles with repetitions, seeking to extract experiences one from the other.
- The existence of a proactive and challenging environment is also extremely relevant, allowing real development in whoever is learning, transforming this learning into real and permanent knowledge over time.
- The content and the objectives of the learning process shall be tied into actions and individual specific results. There must be support and responsibility in the organization in order to guarantee the changes and results.
- The learning process shall be directly connected to the business needs, focused on the abilities required in order for the organization and individuals to be successful in the future.

We verified that most of the learning occurs when the journey is constructed on a step-by-step basis, that is, when the instruction is more than a single event. In this way, it is appropriate for the adult learning method. The instruction can also be reinforced by many traditional learning methods' application and organization systems. Thus, the appropriate use of technology may present many benefits, for example:

- Reducing the time spent in classes and travel expenses, increasing at the same time the learning impact.

- Costing less (per user) than traditional learning methods based in classes, even though the initial development cost is higher.
- Depending less on the presence of facilitators.
- Fixing and/or reducing the time in class and/or the time reinforcing the learning.

Excellent ways to improve the benefits provided by technology, without incurring too many of its inconveniences, include: reusing training materials, giving evaluations, using "simlets," constructing moderate knowledge bases, using tools, having online courses, and conducting more elaborate class simulations.

Lawyers and managers in general need motivation to assimilate technology and new information. They should participate in the implementation process to feel integrated into the new system, and, above all, to want to continue to use it after the implementation process.

4. Legal System

The Brazilian legal system is basically modeled on the Roman Civil Law system and may be compared to the French, Italian, or Spanish legal structures. There is a federal Constitution that extensively regulates the entire legal system, defining the powers of the federal, state, and municipal administrations, the three levels of parliament, and court jurisdictions.

Federal law regulates civil, commercial, labor, federal tax and some general aspects of state and municipal taxes, criminal, transportation (aviation, railroading, and maritime), environmental, agrarian, and the rules of procedure for all types of legal proceedings. Business negotiations are mainly regulated by the Civil Code, a federal law.

Brazil has maintained throughout the years a liberal posture, with minimum restrictions on foreigners and their investment in the country. However, the Brazilian Constitution sets forth a small list of sectors in which the direct and/or indirect participation of foreigners is restricted or limited, such as coastal shipping, press, broadcasting, domestic airlines, aerospace industry, post office and telegraph services, health services, banking, and insurance.

Some level of investment is allowed in certain sectors. It is noteworthy that a great number of branches of foreign banks operate in Brazil, but the participation of foreign companies as controlling shareholders of banks in Brazil is subject to prior analysis by the Brazilian Central Bank and to the issuance of a governmental authorization. The exploitation of mines and minerals and telecommunication services cannot be performed directly by foreigners, but the activity may be performed by means of a company formed in Brazil (100 percent foreign capital allowed). There are also limitations on the ownership of land by foreigners in the Brazilian territory. Furthermore, there are some sectors of the economy that are still State monopolies, such as atomic energy production, exploration of nuclear minerals and exploration, and the refinery, transportation, import, and export of gas and oil.

All other activities operated by foreigners have legal parity with locally owned activities. Under the current Federal Administration, there are no restrictions within existing tax and commercial legislation for foreign companies to obtain fiscal incentives and loans at special interest rates from government development agencies. Brazil's Federal Administration has repeatedly reassured potential investors of its willingness to encourage the participation of foreign capital to help Brazilian development. There is a general understanding in Brazil about the need and opportunity to capture new foreign investment. The moment is very appropriate for those who genuinely intend to make investments in Brazil. In 2008, Standard & Poor's and Fitch Ratings raised the country's long-term sovereign credit rating to investment grade. According to the Brazilian Central Bank, in 2007, the amount of foreign direct investment in the country was around US$33.7 billion.

Brazil's internal market has a great potential and strong infrastructure. Energy, raw materials, and labor costs are competitive internationally, allowing the setting up of internal market-oriented projects and export at the same time, greatly decreasing business risk.

5. Equal Legal Treatment

From a legal standpoint, there is no difference in treatment of foreign companies in all matters relating to tax, labor, social security, civil, or commercial law. A company formed in Brazil is Brazilian regardless of the nationality of its shareholders.

6. Investing in Brazil

There are basically five ways to invest in Brazil. A foreign company can (1) open a branch office; (2) establish a 100 percent owned subsidiary; (3) invest directly in an existing Brazilian company; (4) form a joint venture with a Brazilian company; and (5) invest in the Brazilian securities market.

For all types of investment referred to above, the foreign investor must appoint a representative resident in Brazil with power to receive service of process and to represent the investor before Brazilian authorities. The investor must prove that it is an existing and legally registered entity, and present a certificate of incorporation or individual passport. Foreign documents must be notarized and the notary's signature has to be authenticated in a Brazilian consulate. In addition, the documents have to be translated by a Brazilian official public translator. The investor must also be registered with the Internal Revenue Service to obtain a taxpayer registration number.

6.1 Branches of Foreign Companies in Brazil

Foreign companies are allowed to operate through branches in Brazil, but a previous authorization from the president of Brazil or a minister of the Federal Administration is required.

After the license is granted, the foreign company can apply for registration directly at the Registry of Companies of the state where it intends to have its branch head office. The company should present its bylaws, a certificate of incorporation issued by its hometown Registry of Companies or similar institution, and the original of its corporate resolution creating the branch in Brazil. All documents have to be notarized and the notary's signature must be authenticated by the nearest Brazilian consulate of the foreign company's city. The legal papers must be translated by a Brazilian official public translator and presented to the Registry of Companies, together with the documents in English.

When the registration is granted, the foreign company has to present an application to the Internal Revenue Service to obtain a taxpayer registry number. After that, other applications before state or county administrations may be required, depending on the type of business. Once this is done, operations may start. Registration before federal, state, and municipal administrations is routine and normally takes thirty to forty-five days in total, unless the authorization of the president or any minister is required or there is an environmental issue.

Opening a branch office is usually not the best option in most cases because of the inherent formalities for the formation of a branch in Brazil.

6.2 Establishing a Subsidiary in Brazil

With the exception of certain sectors of the economy, as mentioned above, foreigners may hold 100 percent equity interest in a Brazilian company, provided there are at least two shareholders.

Therefore, if a company has enough structure and experience in international business and knows enough about Brazilian business and the Brazilian market, it can operate without a local partner and without a prior license or permission requirement.

In order to form a subsidiary company in Brazil, local and foreign shareholders shall register the company with the local Registry of Companies and Internal Revenue Service to obtain the taxpayer registration number. The foreign shareholder must prove that it is an existing and legally registered entity, and present a certificate of incorporation or individual passport. Foreign documents must be notarized and the notary's signature has to be authenticated by the Brazilian consulate. In addition, the documents have to be translated by a Brazilian official public translator. Further registration is required for certain types of companies.

In Brazil, there are several types of companies that may be formed depending on their objectives and nature. The most common type of company is the limited liability company, called a *sociedade limitada*. Around 48 percent of Brazilian legal entities are limited liability companies,[7] most of them medium-sized companies. The other significant type of company used in business operations in Brazil is the corporation, called *sociedade anônima*.

The limited liability company is governed by Federal Law 10.406/02 (Civil Code). It is quite simple to establish a limited liability company, and its maintenance is cheaper than the corporation's. The limited liability company requires at least two partners and both can be foreigners.

The corporation is a more formal model of company, where making public all of its acts, minutes, corporate resolutions, balance sheets, and income statements is required by law. Because of this and other requirements, the corporations' costs of maintenance are higher than those of the limited liability company. The corporation is governed by Federal Law 6.404/76 (Companies Law) and its capital stock is represented by shares. The corporation may be a privately or a publicly owned company. The corporation also requires at least two shareholders unless it is a wholly owned subsidiary, in which case the sole shareholder has to be a company established in Brazil.

For both the limited liability company and the corporation, only some businesses, such as banking and insurance, require a minimum capital stock amount at incorporation. The officers of a Brazilian company have to be Brazilian residents, either Brazilian citizens or foreigners residing permanently in Brazil. The members of the Board of Directors may be foreigners and do not need to be Brazilian residents, but each must own at least one share of the corporation, must appoint a legal representative resident in Brazil with power to receive service of process on his or her behalf, and must be registered with the Internal Revenue Service to obtain a taxpayer registration number.

6.3 Investing in an Existing Brazilian Company

The foreign investor may acquire equity participation in an existing Brazilian company. This can be achieved through direct purchase of shares from the Brazilian partner or shareholder or through direct capital subscription and payment in. In such events, the foreign investor has the right to obtain a foreign capital investment certificate, issued by the Brazilian Central Bank. No prior approval is required to make a foreign investment in Brazil, and the Brazilian company has a thirty-day period to register the foreign investment with the Brazilian Central Bank.

---

[7] Brazilian Commercial Registry National Office (DNRC), 2005.

Investment from a foreigner in a Brazilian company through equipment or technology transfer must be previously approved by the Brazilian Central Bank.

Evaluation of the Brazilian company for such transactions is a normal procedure and follows international standards concerning the company's cash flow or balance sheets, financial statement figures, and appraisal of goodwill. A due diligence process is usually undertaken prior to the execution of a definitive agreement, and an auditing may also take place according to the negotiation carried on by the parties.

From January to May 2008, M&A operations in Brazil reached an amount of US$46.6 billion, an increase of 128 percent compared to the same period of 2007.[8]

6.4 Forming a Joint Venture

A joint venture is probably the easiest way to enter the Brazilian market. It is also an excellent route into the Latin American market because of Brazil's international commercial treaties with its neighbors, such as the Mercosur and ALADI.

A Brazilian partner is needed to form a joint venture. The foreign investor can hold majority or minority interest in the partnership because there are no restrictions regarding the control of joint ventures, except for the business activities referred to above (see section 4, "Legal System"). There are tax incentives and loans available from the government and its financial institutions even if the joint venture is under foreign control. The best partner in Brazil is the one that is already in the targeted area of business. Such a partner knows its way around the market and can readily deal with local laws and regulations with a minimum of unnecessary surprises.

The foreign company can invest directly in the joint venture or it can form a 100 percent subsidiary holding company and invest in the joint venture through it. The best choice depends on each individual case. Normally, the better option for the foreign company with several investments in Brazil is to form a subsidiary holding company that can manage all investments in Brazil. Nonetheless, there may be tax advantages if the investment is made directly at the joint venture, mainly if there is a non-double-taxation treaty between Brazil and the foreign company's country. Today there is no tax treaty between the United States and Brazil, but there is a Protocol of Exchange of Financial and Tax Information among the two countries.

---

[8] Thomson Reuters Markets.

6.5 Investing in the Securities Market

Foreign investors—either individuals or legal entities—may invest in the Brazilian securities market through authorized investment companies, investment funds, or managed investment portfolios. Some U.S. investment banks have dealers with great expertise in the Brazilian stock market.

There is no minimum time requirement for investments in the Brazilian securities market.

Foreign investors must appoint a representative resident in Brazil in order to invest in the Brazilian securities market. This individual shall be responsible for providing information and the applicable registrations before the Brazilian Central Bank and the Brazilian Securities Exchange Commission (CVM).

In 2007, the capitalization of BOVESPA (São Paulo Stock Exchange) surpassed US$1.4 trillion, representing Latin America's largest stock exchange and the eighth largest in the world, concentrating about 70 percent of the volume of trades carried out in the region.

7. Foreign Capital Regulation

The legislation on the registration, remittance of dividends, and repatriation of foreign investment in Brazil is Federal Law 4.131/62. The legislation in force during the last forty-six years without relevant changes assures the repatriation, at any time, of up to 100 percent of the capital invested in the country that has been registered with the Brazilian Central Bank.

The Brazilian company, within the thirty days following the investment made in foreign currency, has to apply at the Brazilian Central Bank for the registration of the amount invested. Since 2000, direct foreign investments are registered by an electronic system of the Brazilian Central Bank (SISBACEN). The Brazilian Central Bank issues a Certificate of Foreign Capital Registry that allows the foreign investor future repatriation of capital and earnings. The certificate also assures the remittance of all profits and/or dividends resulting from the invested capital, without limits, and presently not subject to withholding income tax, although financial transactions are subject to a financial transactions tax (IOF) at variable rates depending on the type of transaction.

Brazil has entered into bilateral agreements with several other countries to reduce the amount of taxation or to give the taxpayer the right to compensate taxes paid in Brazil with those paid or payable in their home country. Brazil has non-double-taxation treaties with Argentina, Austria, Belgium, Canada, Chile, China, Czech Republic, Denmark, Ecuador, Finland, France, Germany, Hungary, India, Israel, Italy, Japan, Luxembourg, Mexico, Netherlands, Norway, the

Philippines, Portugal, Slovakia, South Africa, South Korea, Spain, Sweden, and Ukraine. As already mentioned, as of the beginning of 2008, Brazil did not have a non-double-taxation treaty with the United States.

8. Exchange Control

Although exchange control has been a tradition in Brazil, with the Brazilian Central Bank sometimes making limited interventions in the market, the Brazilian Central Bank has been implementing a deregulation policy since 1999 by means of a floating exchange rate.

It is forbidden for individuals or legal entities not authorized by the Brazilian Central Bank to deal with foreign currency and exchange, and there are criminal and civil penalties and fines for violators of the prohibition.

There are two types of exchange rates in Brazil: commercial and tourism rates. The commercial rate is applicable to any regular trade, investment, or financial transaction, and the tourism rate is applicable to tourism exchange and other transactions as set forth in a special regulation from the Brazilian Central Bank. Although commercial and tourism are different types of exchange rates, their respective markets were unified by the Brazilian Central Bank, through Resolution 3.265/05.

In accordance with the Mercosur treaties, Brazil has several commitments to have a free exchange market, and they have been implemented by the Federal Administration.

9. Accounting Principles

Accounting principles are regulated in Brazil by the Corporation Law, 6.404/76, the Income Tax Regulation, and several rules of CVM (Brazil's SEC). All legal entities and corporations must have and maintain proper records and books of account following Brazilian GAAP.

The new Law 11.638/07 modified the Corporation Law, 6.404/76, introducing new rules on accounting procedures. The main purpose of the changes made to the Brazilian Corporate Law is to update the Brazilian GAAP, and also to harmonize those rules with the international principles issued by the International Accounting Standards Board (IASB), through the International Financial Reporting Standards (IFRS).

The basic Brazilian accounting principles are not different from international standard accounting rules. Nevertheless, there are special rules in Brazil that are unknown in the rest of the world. Accounting has to be kept by a qualified bookkeeper or accountant, both with certification to work in the field and duly registered at the Regional Council of Accountants. The books of account are kept in Portuguese and in Brazilian currency, but the corporation may also have an unofficial foreign-currency equivalent.

The balance sheets and the income statements of a corporation must be published in the Official Gazette and also in another local newspaper. A large-size company, which is a company or group of companies with total assets over R$240 million or gross annual revenue over R$300 million, including the limited liability type of company, is also subject to this rule. Corporations with net worth up to R$1 million and fewer than ten shareholders are exempt from the obligation to publish their balance sheets and income statements, but they must file their balance sheets and income statements with the Registry of Companies, jointly with the corporation's minutes and other corporate resolutions. Public (listed) companies are also subject to special rules issued by CVM regarding the preparation and publication of financial statements.

10. Foreign Workers in Brazil

The Ministry of Labor, through the General Coordination of Immigration, is the authority responsible for the issuance of work permits for foreigners, according to Federal Law 6.815/80.

There are different kinds of work visas defined by Brazilian law, and there are no restrictions regarding the nationality of the applicant and spouse or children under 18 years old.

The law establishes seven categories of visas: transit, tourist, temporary, permanent, courtesy, official, and diplomat.

10.1 Visas for Short-Term Business Visitors and Tourists

Citizens from some countries are required to have a visa to travel to Brazil on short-term business or tourism. Individuals needing to conduct business in Brazil prior to obtaining employment authorization and the appropriate visa may do so by obtaining a short-term business visa. Business visitors traveling on this type of visa must not work or be paid locally until the employment authorization and visa are issued. The visa may be obtained at the Brazilian consulate having jurisdiction over the place of residence of the applicant; the application requires the following information:

- The purpose of the trip (business meetings, visit to clients, attendance at fairs, or tourism only)
- Names, addresses, and telephone numbers of business contacts in Brazil
- Date of arrival and anticipated departure
- Covenant regarding financial and moral responsibility of the applicant during the visit

For a tourist visa, a round-trip airline ticket is also required.

If a visa is required for the country to which the applicant is going after Brazil, that visa must already be included in the passport, prior to the request for the Brazilian visa.

The visa is generally issued within twenty-four hours. This type of visa may be valid for a period up to ninety days from the date of first arrival in Brazil. It may be used for multiple entries during that period. An extension for a further period of up to three months may be obtained from the immigration authorities in Brazil, prior to expiration of the visa.

10.2 Temporary Employment Visas

For foreigners coming to Brazil on a temporary basis for employment purposes, there are five other categories of visas:

1. *Temporary with Work Agreement.* This visa is given to individuals coming to Brazil to work temporarily at a Brazilian company in a position requiring special knowledge, during a temporary period not exceeding two years initially; it may be renewed for an additional two-year period. The individual shall receive at least part of his or her salary in Brazil. In order to apply for this type of visa, at least two-thirds of the Brazilian company's employees must be Brazilian nationals.
2. *Temporary for Technicians.* This visa is given to individuals coming to Brazil to work in a technical position on behalf of their foreign employer. In order to apply for this type of visa, the foreign company and the Brazilian company must have a valid technical service agreement that would allow the foreign company to send its employees to work at the Brazilian company. The individuals will remain employees of the foreign company and will not be allowed to receive any payments from the Brazilian company. This visa is valid for one year, renewable for another year, if the immigration authorities consider the work of the foreigner crucial to the activity of the Brazilian company.
3. *Artist and Sports Visa.* The request for this visa must be submitted to the Brazilian Labor Ministry by the Brazilian organization that is sponsoring the event for which the individual's services will be required.
4. *Foreign Journalist.* This visa is given to foreign journalists wishing to work on a temporary basis in Brazil. The individual must not receive his or her salary in Brazil.
5. *Religious Mission.* This visa may be granted to religious individuals for a specific mission in Brazil for up to one year.

The applicant for any of these types of visa must first obtain a work permit from the Ministry of Labor. Upon approval by the Ministry of Labor, the work permit will be published in the federal Official Gazette and the designated Brazilian consulate will be notified so that the foreign national may apply for the visa issuance. The individual must obtain the temporary work visa outside of Brazil, at the Brazilian consulate with jurisdiction over his or her residence abroad.

Foreign individuals who have been employed in Brazil in a temporary capacity for a period of four years may apply to convert their status to permanent. In this case, to obtain a conversion from temporary to permanent status, application must be made by the company to the Ministry of Justice, by filing the same documents filed for the temporary visa.

10.3 Other Temporary Visas

A student visa is obtained by students at the Brazilian consulate having jurisdiction over the place of residence of the applicant. The student must not work in Brazil.

10.4 Permanent Employment Visas

The permanent visa is issued in the event a foreign company has a branch or subsidiary of or is a shareholder of a company in Brazil and wishes to appoint a statutory officer to the Brazilian company. To apply for a permanent visa for its officer, the Brazilian company must have at least US$200,000 invested by the foreign shareholder duly registered with the Brazilian Central Bank.

To obtain permanent employment authorization, application must first be made to the Ministry of Labor. Following that, the individual must obtain the permanent work visa outside of Brazil, at the Brazilian consulate with jurisdiction over his or her residence abroad.

In addition, foreigners may obtain a permanent resident visa in case of marriage to a Brazilian citizen or fatherhood or motherhood of a Brazilian child. Application for this type of visa may be done at the Brazilian consulate before entering the country or at the Ministry of Justice in Brazil if the individual is already in the country.

10.5 Registration upon Entry into Brazil

All foreigners who enter Brazil holding a temporary or permanent visa must register with the Brazilian Federal Police within thirty days of arrival. This applies to temporary and permanent residents including those coming to work in Brazil (except those admitted as artists or athletes or with a short-term business visa).

10.6 Employment of Spouses and Children

Accompanying spouses and children are not permitted to engage in employment while residing temporarily in Brazil, but will be authorized for employment if their status is converted to permanent resident.

11. Mercosur

In 1991 Argentina, Paraguay, Uruguay, and Brazil signed the Treaty of Asunción forming a free market called Mercosur. The economic integration of the Southern Cone is a long journey that started with the ALADI Treaty in 1980.

Mercosur has been operating since December 31, 1994 as a customs union, but its goal is to reach the common market level in which the free movement of individuals and capital is also allowed. There are several treaties, agreements, and protocols between the four countries already in force. Chile and Bolivia are associate members. Brazil and Argentina are ahead in economic integration, because they started early.

Mercosur comprises an area in which the free movement of goods and services is ensured and external tariffs for some imports are the same. Mercosur's objectives are more extensive than those of NAFTA, for instance, because of its common market–oriented policy.

12. Contracting in Brazil

Foreigners doing business in Brazil have to be careful with domestic regulation of certain special private contracts.

12.1 Transfer of Technology or Know-How; Technical Assistance, Franchising, Licensing of Trademarks or Patents

Because of existing exchange control rules and income tax regulation, according to the Industrial Property Act, Federal Law 9.279/96, several kinds of private agreements must have prior approval to be considered valid and in force.

Contracts involving payment of royalties or fees for technical assistance or transfer of technology or know-how or contracts for international franchising or licensing of trademark or patents must be registered with and are subject to the control of the Brazilian Patent and Trademark Office (INPI). In some situations, a draft of the intended agreement has to be previously presented to INPI, which formally examines and approves it. In other cases, the agreement may be executed by the parties but has to be presented within thirty days to INPI for approval. After approval, an application must be presented to the Central Bank, which examines the financial covenants and authorizes the remittance of royalties and/or fees by the Brazilian party to the foreign party.

INPI has discretionary powers to analyze the entire proposed agreement and its convenience in accordance with the country's needs. Even contractual dispositions like term, territory, the amount of fees, or the percentage of royalties may be altered or disapproved. The same is true with the Brazilian Central Bank regarding the financial covenants of the agreements.

Brazil is signatory of the Paris Convention for the Protection of Industrial Property, the Patent Cooperation Treaty (PCT), the Strasbourg Agreement concerning the International Patent Classification, the Universal Copyright Convention, and the Berne Convention for Protection of Literary and Artistic Works. It also has several bilateral agreements with foreign countries regarding intellectual property, including with the United States, dated 1957.

12.2 Leasing and Financing Agreements

International leasing and financing agreements must be submitted to registration to the Brazilian Central Bank, and approval is normally granted immediately if the conditions of the agreements are based on regular market terms. The Brazilian Central Bank examines all financial aspects and has discretionary powers to interfere and not approve the agreed-upon interest rate, fees, commissions, and term of the agreement. After registration before the Brazilian Central Bank, the Brazilian party is allowed to pay principal, interest, fees, and commissions in hard currency and remit them to the foreign party.

12.3 International Sale of Goods Agreements

Sale of goods agreements in Brazil are generally regulated by the Civil Code. The sale of certain goods is subject to special legislation, such as the sale of software, which is regulated by the Software Law, 9.609/98. Brazil is a member of the World Trade Organization (WTO) and party to the General Agreement on Tariffs and Trade (GATT), but is not party to the United Nations Convention on Contracts for the International Sale of Goods (CISG).

International trade in the country is open and the Federal Administration has implemented a program of deregulation to diminish and eliminate restrictions on importing and exporting goods, equipment, components, raw materials, and spare parts. Exporting requires an exporting license granted to companies registered at SISCOMEX/DECEX, the Brazilian foreign trade department. Importing also requires a license issued by SISCOMEX/DECEX. The Federal Administration controls importation through duties and taxation rate levels. Application for import and export licenses may be done electronically through the SISCOMEX system.

The sale and commercialization of products including chemicals, pharmaceuticals, medicines, and dairy products and other foods require previous analysis and approval of Federal Administration sanitary, security, or health departments. Before starting to export its products to Brazil, any foreign trader must check to see if a previous license, as mentioned above, is required.

Brazil is a signatory of the ISO International Treaty and also has its own standards, following the ISO model.

Brazil has a severe Consumer Protection Code, Law 8.078/90. Companies with products for sale in the Brazilian market, including those imported, have to provide full warranty to their customers or clients and are liable, in accordance with the Consumer Protection Code, in events of product defect.

12.4 International Distribution Agreements

Brazil does not have a special law for distribution agreements, except the Software Law, 9.609/98, which regulates software distribution agreements, and Law 6.729/79, which regulates the relationship among auto makers and dealers. Generally speaking, the applicable law is the Civil Code, which establishes some rules for distribution. The Civil Code regulates the relationship between the parties in distribution, agency, and similar agreements, but is almost useless for international distribution agreements because it is based upon the old-fashioned relationship between the manufacturer and the individual representative.

According to several laws in force in Brazil applicable to international distribution agreements, all Brazilian companies and individuals are free to make such agreements. Except for some specific products, any foreign company, directly or through a subsidiary formed in Brazil (which may be wholly owned by the parent company), may distribute its own products within the country or may contract a Brazilian company or an individual to do it.

If a Brazilian company contracts for the distribution of its products abroad and there is a commission not included in the product's price, the Brazilian company must remit fees in hard currency. Further, the remittance of the commission must be registered with the Brazilian Central Bank. Such remittance is subject to withholding income tax.

Since Mercosur became a reality, all foreign companies are making distribution agreements having Southern Cone countries (Brazil, Argentina, Uruguay, Paraguay, and Chile) as a unique territory and having only one distributor. Otherwise, there may be competition among several distributors for the same product (as a Brazilian company, for example, is already free to market its products in Argentina and vice versa).

An international software distribution agreement must follow the requirements of the Software Law, 9.609/98, which are: (i) exclusive distribution of software is not allowed; (ii) limitations on the production, distribution, and/or commercialization of software are not allowed; and (iii) any clause releasing any of the parties from any liabilities regarding the quality of the software is also void. Under the Software Law, the protection granted to the software developer is valid for fifty years and is granted independently of the registration of the software. The law applies equally to Brazilians and to foreigners if the foreigner's country of origin grants equivalent rights to those granted in Brazil. There is also a registry of software at INPI, and, even if its application is optional, such registry is highly recommended because the registration is the best evidence of existence of the software in Brazil.

12.5 Agency Agreements

Law 4.886/65, as modified by Law 8.240/92, is a special law regulating agency agreements in Brazil. A foreign company that wants to hire an agent or representative in Brazil has to be careful because of labor law requirements and liabilities and must follow Law 4.886/65.

Individual independent agents or representatives should be avoided. The foreign company should hire a company as agent or representative. A subsidiary of the foreign company may be its agent or representative in Brazil, as can any Brazilian agent or representative corporation. There are specialized companies in Brazil that act as representatives or agents. Those companies are registered at the Brazilian Commercial Representatives Council. Any foreign-owned representative or agent company may also be registered with the council as a formality. Thereafter, it will be entitled to act within the country.

If the foreign company decides to form a subsidiary to be its agent or representative, the incorporation of the firm does not require any previous governmental approval or license. If the company intends to hire a Brazilian corporation or an individual as its agent or representative, an agreement among the parties is required. The agreement may be for a determined or undetermined period of time. Compensation is freely established and there is no minimum amount fixed by the law if the agent or representative is a corporation. There is a minimum salary for individuals. However, general compensation varies depending upon the region where the agent or representative works. Normally, individuals are hired as employees by companies, in accordance with the labor law, and they are paid a fixed amount as salary plus commission on a percentage basis over monthly sales, but this also may vary and commissions can be also agreed upon.

Labor contracts may be for a determined period (maximum two-year term) or an undetermined period, and the undetermined period contract can be terminated with prior notice. The term of the prior notice is normally thirty days, but additional days may be required, depending on whether there is a general labor convention with the regional union. Several additional compensation benefits must be paid by the company when an employee is dismissed without cause.

If the termination of the agency agreement is decided by the company, the agent or representative corporation will receive additional compensation of between one-twentieth and one-fifteenth of the total commissions received during its period of work. The existing agreement may set forth the amount of this indemnification.

Exclusivity and territory have to be carefully considered by the hiring company, because any future changes may be considered null and void. Limits on full exclusivity representation clauses or reduction of the unlimited territory by the company may not be valid or even accepted by either corporate or individual representatives or agents. The company may, on the other hand, have the agent or representative as an exclusive agent. This has to be previously agreed in the agreement. No *del credere* clause is allowed in agency agreements in Brazil.

Taxes on salaries and commissions are paid by the agent or representative, never by the represented company unless otherwise agreed upon. Remittances of fees, salaries, or commissions from foreign companies to their representatives or agents in Brazil are free and are taxable as normal wages or salaries, and taxes are paid by the representative. No withholding tax is required for these remittances, but the representative has to report monthly to the Brazilian Income Tax Federal Agency the amount received in the past month and has to pay income tax on the amount received.

12.6 Marketing and E-commerce in Brazil

E-commerce is certainly one of the fastest-growing segments in Brazil, as well as the rest of the world.

The increase in the number of computers between 2002 and 2007 in Brazil reached a value exceeding 120 percent, encompassing more then 29 million personal computers. This number represents 40 percent of the total in Latin America.

The number of Internet users in Brazil increased 270 percent over the last five years, representing 53 million users and providing an increase of 40 percent in e-commerce compared to 2006.

The e-commerce sector continues its rapid growth and presents a variety of opportunities for several segments of activities in the country.

The current scenario is the result of Internet expansion, policies concerning information security, the increase of network trust and the new culture developed in this context, given the positive market attitude toward the use of the Internet.

The sudden acceleration of this culture opened the doors to a new model of business: electronic commerce, which is just over six years old in the world, and half of that in Brazil. However, although this is a recent model, the value of online retail and dot-com companies can, because of the new way of practicing marketing, be bigger than that of companies with a traditional presence in the market.

It is obvious that, even in this sector, the tools need to be better explored. But it is notable that the electronic commerce sector has a greater interest in marketing innovations. This is a market niche with great potential, and successful maturity likely to be obtained. Therefore, using a coherent and aligned marketing strategy with best practices will be more diligent, since we are speaking of digital media.

Technology has created new ways for businesses to gain visibility and more widely distribute their trademarks. Today, we have tools that allow the full measurement of marketing and sales results, which helps track the success of the corporate image, as well as tools that collect extremely important information about every customer. However, there needs to be a regulatory entity to establish rules of digital communication. This will allow sufficent knowledge for good online marketing.

Although e-commerce is a new model of business, many companies apply digital marketing based on old formats. Therefore, they work on the propagation of their corporate image by means of electronic media in the same way that they work on traditional marketing.

It is evident that traditional media cannot cease to exist, but companies of all sizes and in all sectors can and should use digital marketing as one of their communication strategies, especially e-mail marketing and newsletters. A company should always follow strict ethical practices and must respect the privacy of its targeted client base. Well-done e-mail marketing campaigns can bring huge increases in sales.

Also, imagine measuring interest by means of a click made by the receiver of the message?

For instance: Imagine a campaign of offers of electronic products in general, insert the products with discounts, separate your database according to clients interested in those models of products (remember the importance of segmentation), make the delivery, obtain several reports of accessibility, analyze the user that accessed the site due to the campaign and ended up registering in another area (in case with your Web site offers several areas for registry) of new products, measure which offers and how many of them had sales return and how many users only clicked in the product, but did not purchase de the product.

Yes, is it possible to do many new things in marketing because improved technology has opened infinite possibilities of measurement in the virtual world. But if you think the analytical work is over. . . . It has just begun. Now imagine what your marketing team can do with all this information at hand.

At this early stage, many possibilities are created, but the result totally depends on your real sale strategy with the market. You may choose for the segmentation of particular markets and make a special offer for clicks that do not generate a sale, but rather indicate interest in a particular product. And you can also register clients that purchased a product in order to make individual offers regarding other new products, instead of sending the same campaigns, repeatedly, to the same registered clients.

This is where ethics plays a part in communication. You respect your public's privacy and provide information that is relevant at the moment. And, above all technology should contribute to the increasing growth of sales and, consequentially, the satisfaction of all parties involved in the process.

The result of these steps: true integration between marketing and sales, confirming that a good reputation has an intimate relationship with a high trade volume. This results in something everyone wants, but many times cannot achieve: the client's satisfaction.

And, just like all new fields, the legal security and the litigation between suppliers and customers concerning electronic commerce are causing the development of new mechanisms to make the sector more attractive.

Although Brazil does not have specific regulations covering electronic commerce, the civil and criminal rules that regulate traditional corporate activities are applied to protect the involved parties. For example, investigations into electronic crimes and frauds are made by the Federal Police of Brazil.

13. Submission to Jurisdiction; Choice of Law

The jurisdiction and governing law for business transactions in Brazil are regulated by the Brazilian Private International Law (Law Decree 4.707/42), the Civil Code, and the Code of Civil Procedure, all of which are federal laws and applicable throughout the country.

In principle, according to Brazilian Private International Law, Brazilian law shall govern contracts executed in Brazil and the law of the jurisdiction where the agreement was executed shall apply to contracts executed abroad. The Code of Civil Procedure contains provisions stipulating exclusive and nonexclusive court jurisdiction in Brazil on international matters. The following circumstances are subject to nonexclusive jurisdiction in Brazil: (i) when the defendant, of whatever nationality, resides in Brazil; (ii) when the performance of the obligation would take place in Brazil; and (iii) when the dispute relates to facts that occurred or to acts committed in Brazil. On the other hand, if, for instance, the transaction is related to real estate located in Brazil, the jurisdiction cannot be chosen by the parties thereto because the Code of Civil Procedure establishes the exclusive jurisdiction of Brazilian courts in this situation.

It is also common to encounter international contracts made in Brazil, in which at least one of the parties is a foreigner residing abroad, that provide that the parties thereto consent to have the laws of another jurisdiction governing the agreement. It is also common for parties in some international agreements to consent to the jurisdiction of the courts of one or more jurisdictions. Although there are precedents in some Brazilian courts restricting these provisions, they are generally considered enforceable.

14. Dispute Resolution Mechanisms

The courts are the most-used contractual dispute resolution mechanism in Brazil. The judiciary system is trustworthy but in some parts of the country slow to decide lawsuits.

There are state and federal courts whose jurisdictions are regulated by the Constitution and applicable laws. A dispute resolution is presented to a federal or a state court depending on the matter involved in the dispute or the parties thereto. The parties in an agreement cannot consent to the jurisdiction of a federal or state court different from that required by the applicable law and the Constitution. In general, the parties can only make a choice of territorial jurisdiction, but they are never allowed to choose a federal court, for example, instead of a state court. The Code of Civil Procedure is a federal law, used in both federal and state courts, and provides complete regulation covering the entire procedure. There are also labor courts specialized in resolving disputes related to labor contracts. The Labor Consolidation Act regulates the labor procedure before these courts.

Brazil also has an Arbitration Act (Federal Law 9.307/96) in line with modern arbitration practice; many of its provisions are based on the UNCITRAL Model Law on International Commercial Arbitration. Moreover, Brazil is signatory to the Inter-American Convention on International Commercial Arbitration (the Panama Convention) and also to the New York Convention on the Mutual Recognition and Enforcement of Foreign Arbitral Awards. After more than ten years of use and application of the Brazilian Arbitration Act in the country, Brazilian parties are more confident about choosing arbitration as a dispute resolution method to their commercial relations, such as in international contracts and in shareholder's agreements. There are arbitration associations in São Paulo, Rio de Janeiro, Minas Gerais, and other main states of Brazil with adequate structure and personnel to administer and assist parties in both domestic and international arbitration proceedings.

15. Enforcement of Foreign Judgments and Foreign Arbitration Awards

The Constitution, through an *exequatur* system, grants enforcement of any foreign judgment or foreign arbitration award that has been examined and confirmed by the Brazilian Supreme Court of Justice (STJ), located in Brasília (DF).

The Brazilian Private International Law, the Code of Civil Procedure, and the internal regulations of the Supreme Court of Justice provide the proceedings that have to be followed by the foreign plaintiff to obtain the Supreme Court of Justice *exequatur* order to enforce a foreign judgment or a foreign arbitration award. Normally, the Supreme Court of Justice considers whether formal procedural aspects have been attended by the foreign decision, and confirmation is granted in a short period of time through a summary proceeding if all requirements are fulfilled.

Specific rules for confirmation of foreign arbitration awards are established by international treaties to which Brazil is party and by the Arbitration Act.

This chapter was prepared based on Brazilian law in force in June 2008. Law may change from time to time.

Ordélio Azevedo Sette
Azevedo Sette Advogados
Rua Paraíba, 1000, térreo
30130-141—Belo Horizonte, MG Brasil
Phone: +55 (31) 3261-6656
Fax: +55 (31) 3261-6797
E-mail: osette@azevedosette.com.br

CHAPTER 23

International Business Transactions in Bulgaria

Georgi T. Gouginski and Lilia Kisseva
DJINGOV, GOUGINSKI, KYUTCHUKOV & VELICHKOV
SOFIA, BULGARIA

1. Introduction

1.1 Broad Demographic Information

Bulgaria is situated in the southeastern part of the Balkan Peninsula in Europe. It borders Greece and Turkey to the south and Macedonia and Serbia to the west. The Danube River to the north is the natural border with Romania. The Black Sea is to the east.

With a population of about 8 million and territory of 110,910 square kilometers (42,822 square miles), Bulgaria is part of Southeastern Europe, a region undergoing dynamic transition. Within a 500-kilometer radius of the capital city of Sofia (a city of approximately 2 million) lives a population of over 90 million in nine countries, most of which have recently embarked on their way to a market economy. This represents a large market with rapidly increasing purchasing power.

A network of international motorways crosses Bulgaria, making vital connections to the countries of Western Europe, Russia, Asia Minor, the Adriatic, the Aegean, and the Black Sea. Both sea and river transport (the Black Sea and the Danube River) facilitate trade within the region.

Bulgaria (the Constitutional name of which is "Republic of Bulgaria") is a parliamentary democracy governed in accordance with the Constitution of the Republic of Bulgaria of 1991 (the Constitution). The supreme body of government is the National Assembly. The Constitution entrusts in the National Assembly the supreme legislative power. It is a permanently acting body consisting of 240 representatives who are directly elected by the people for a term of four years.

The head of state is the President, who represents the state in its international relations. The Council of Ministers is the executive arm of the government implementing both the country's domestic and foreign policies.

443

1.2 Historical and Cultural Background

The successor of various civilizations, Thracian, Roman, and Byzantine, the Bulgarian state has existed for thirteen centuries on the Balkan Peninsula, which has long been a meeting place and a melting pot of tribes and nations. The Bulgarian state was founded in 681 A.D., when Slavs and Proto-Bulgarians were brought together under the scepter of Khan Asparuh.

The conversion of Bulgarians to Christianity in 865 A.D. joined Bulgaria to the Christian civilization. The invention of the Cyrillic script in the latter half of the ninth century, during which predominantly Latin and Greek were used, gave a powerful impetus to the country's cultural development.

During its long history Bulgaria has lost its independence twice: to the Byzantine Empire (1018–1185) and to the Ottoman Empire (1396–1878). Both historic periods have slowed down Bulgaria's development as a state.

In modern times, the War of Liberation (the Russian-Turkish War of 1877–1878) regained Bulgaria's independence in 1878. In 1879 a Constituent Assembly adopted the first Constitution of Bulgaria, which was considered one of the most democratic Constitutions of the time. The first half of the twentieth century was a time of economic effort and prosperity. Bulgarian goods and Bulgarian currency, the "Golden Lev," acquired high value on the European markets. Trade relations with Austria, Germany, France, and Great Britain strengthened.

For a period of more than forty years after the end of World War II, Bulgaria was part of the Communist bloc. With the end of the Cold War, in 1989 the country embarked again on its journey toward democracy and a market economy. During a period of less than twenty years after it broke with its recent communist past, Bulgaria became a member state to the World Trade Organization (1996), NATO (2004), and the European Union (2007).

1.3 Business Organization and Culture

For the last decade Bulgaria is considered to have had a stable and predictable business and political environment. Specific features of such environment include:

- Free trade with the EU preferential trade partners, including the European Free Trade Association (EFTA), Turkey, Mediterranean countries (Euro-Mediterranean association agreements with Algeria, Tunisia, Morocco, Israel, West Bank and the Gaza Strip, Jordan, Lebanon, Syria), Western Balkan countries (trade preferences to products originating from Albania, Bosnia and Herzegovina, Croatia, Kosovo, Macedonia, and Serbia and Montenegro until December 31, 2010 in accordance with the stabilization and association process), South Africa, Mexico, Chile, and many others;

- 10 percent corporate income tax rate; 10 percent personal income tax; VAT exemption on equipment imports for investment projects over EUR 5 million;
- Annual depreciation rate of 30 percent for machinery and equipment, 50 percent for new equipment used in new investments, and 50 percent for software and hardware;
- Treaties for avoidance of double taxation with sixty-one countries;
- Agreements on mutual protection and promotion of foreign investment with sixty countries;
- Highly skilled, multilingual workforce at Europe's most competitive wages; and
- Acquisition of land and property through a Bulgarian registered company with up to 100 percent foreign ownership.

In its annual 2002 report, the European Commission assessed Bulgaria as a fully functional market economy, with a high degree of macroeconomic stability and working market mechanisms.

The Bulgarian economy functions under a currency board (1 Bulgarian Lev (BGN) = 1.95583 Euro (EUR)), which provides for a stable and predictable macroeconomic environment. Bulgaria is expected to join the Euro zone in 2010–2012. Careful fiscal discipline and strong foreign investment have provided for sustained economic growth. The registered economic growth since 2003 is more than 5 to 6 percent per year. Bulgaria has made sizable progress in turning into a competitive economy, mainly with respect to its relations with the European Union member states. As a member of the European Union, Bulgaria benefits from significant financial support from the EU Structural Funds and the Common Agricultural Policy.

1.4 Legal System

Bulgaria is a civil law country with a legal system having its roots deep in the tradition of some of the major continental European legal systems (German, French). Bulgarian laws are generally harmonized with the EU legal framework. With globalization and the process of harmonization of Bulgarian laws with those of the European Union, typical international and common law concepts become part of the national legal system.

2. Substantive Laws and Regulations Impacting Negotiations

Bulgarian substantive laws apply uniformly over the whole territory of the state. No provincial or local legislation is adopted or applied.

Certain administrative provisions may differ on the local level, since municipalities by law may adopt their own rules for passing certain resolutions on matters of local significance.

Following is a brief overview of certain areas of Bulgarian law that usually have strong impact on international negotiations involving local law, and where the knowledge and expertise of both local and foreign lawyers are of significant importance to a successful negotiation process:

2.1 Corporate Laws

Bulgarian law recognizes the following types of commercial companies: (i) general partnership; (ii) limited partnership; (iii) limited liability company (LLC); (iv) joint stock company (JSC); and (v) company limited by shares. JSCs are the only type of company that may become publicly listed. In addition, business may also be conducted in one of the following organizational forms: (i) sole trader; (ii) holding; (iii) branch; (iv) trade representative office; and (v) cooperative.

The procedure for incorporation of a company in Bulgaria does not differ when local or foreign persons participate in its establishment. There are no restrictions as to the size of the foreign participation in the capital of a Bulgarian company.

As of January 1, 2008, all types of commercial companies and all branches of foreign commercial companies are incorporated by way of registration in a uniform electronic commercial register. This is a one-stop-shop registration and it serves for all commercial, tax, social security, statistical, and other public purposes.

The LLC is the type of business organization most widely used among investors because of the minimum capital requirements and the simplicity of its corporate governance structure. The JSC is also widely used because of the lack of statutory restrictions on the transfer of shares and the absence of personal engagement of the shareholders in the operation of the company.

2.2 Securities Laws

Bulgarian law allows securities to be purchased by local or foreign investors on an equal footing through licensed investment intermediaries or investment companies.

Foreign individuals or legal entities are free to invest in equity of Bulgarian companies. There are no restrictions as to the foreign participation in the capital of a Bulgarian company and no prior authorizations are required for making, transforming, or liquidating an equity investment. Acquisitions by both foreign and local persons of shares in certain types of companies, such as insurance companies, banks, and investment intermediaries, may be subject to prior approval by notification to the competent regulatory authorities. In addition to equity securities, the market in Bulgaria also offers corporate debt securities and government debt and compensatory instruments of a broad variety.

2.3 Tax Laws

2.3.1 Domestic Law

(a) Taxation of Direct Economic Activity
The profit from direct economic activity of local entities, or foreign entities acting through a Bulgarian branch or a permanent establishment in Bulgaria, is currently taxed at the rate of 10 percent.

(b) Taxation of Income from "Passive" Investment
In general, dividend income is not included in the tax base of an entity for profit tax purposes, and such income is taxed on the level of the payer of the income by withholding 5 percent of the dividend income distributed to shareholders out of taxed profits. In cases where withholding tax is due, double tax treaty relief might be available.

While all other "passive" income of local entities is included in their tax base for profit tax purposes, the law treats foreign persons' income differently. Certain types of income, such as income from (a) interest, (b) franchising and factoring fees, (c) sale of fixed or financial assets (save for capital gains from sale of certain types of stock), (d) royalties from licenses to use intellectual property rights, and (e) compensations under management agreements, are taxed at the rate of 10 percent.

As of January 1, 2007, in implementation of the EU law an exemption from withholding taxation on dividends paid by local companies to residents of EU member states was introduced. Such exemption applies in cases of minimum 15 percent shareholding for a minimum holding period of at least two years.

(c) Value-Added Tax (VAT)
In general, taxable transactions, import of goods, and taxable intra-community acquisitions of goods are subject to 20 percent VAT. Different tax rates (7 percent and 0 percent) are provided for certain specific types of transactions. For example, export transactions out of the EU territory are subject to 0 percent VAT.

All transactions for transfer of title over goods or services are VAT-taxable, except for a limited category of exempt transactions. Certain categories of supplies related to health care, social security and social care, education, sports or physical education, culture, religion, financial and insurance services, gambling, postal services and stamps, and non-profit transactions are tax exempt.

As a general rule, upon transfer of assets against remuneration VAT is due at the rate of 20 percent. A general exception is provided for transfer of title over land and buildings, and transfer of limited rights *in rem*. Such items are deemed VAT-exempt.

2.3.2 Bilateral Treaties on the Avoidance of Double Taxation of Income and Property to Which Bulgaria Is a Party

Bulgaria has entered into bilateral treaties on the avoidance of double taxation of income and property with more than sixty countries. All treaties provide that the profits from direct economic activity realized through a permanent establishment or a branch in the other country shall be taxable only in the country where the foreign company has its permanent establishment. A comparative analysis of these treaties shows that for income from a number of sources, such treaties introduce rates of withholding tax not higher than 15 percent. Some treaties entitle an investor to a tax credit in its country of origin for taxes paid in Bulgaria on certain types of income.

2.4 Antitrust/Anticompetition Laws

In Bulgaria, all agreements between undertakings, decisions of associations of undertakings, as well as concerted practices of two or more undertakings, that have as their object or effect the prevention, restriction, or distortion of competition on the relevant market, are prohibited. In addition, a *de minimis* rule and certain block exemptions exist.

The law prohibits certain actions by companies with a monopoly or dominant position, insofar as such actions have as their object or effect the prevention, restriction, or distortion of competition and/ or impairment of the interests of consumers. A presumption of dominance exists where an undertaking controls 35 percent or more of the relevant market.

Concentrations of commercial activities in Bulgaria are subject to the mandatory prior control of the regulatory authority (the Competition Protection Commission) unless they have a European Community dimension. The regulator has established a single turnover-based jurisdictional threshold, whereas merger control filing is mandatory if the aggregate turnover of the participants in a concentration on the Bulgarian market for the year preceding the concentration exceeds BGN 15 million (about EUR 7,669,100). Foreign-to-foreign mergers are also caught and a local corporate presence is not required. It will suffice if any (even just one) of the undertakings concerned exercises commercial activity in Bulgaria, including by way of direct sales or through agents or independent distributors.

Unfair competition, or any business activity that is inconsistent with fair business practices and harms or may harm the interests of competitors in their internal relations or in their relations with consumers, is also prohibited.

2.5 Labor and Employment Laws

Bulgaria has ratified certain International Labour Organization conventions and the European Social Charter. In recent years, the Bulgarian government has entered into a number of bilateral agreements with other countries with respect to employment relationships, particularly regarding employment of citizens of one country within the other based on the principle of reciprocity.

The Bulgarian labor laws set forth minimum standards for labor protection from which the parties to individual and collective labor contracts may deviate by mutual agreement. Thus, the labor law permits freedom of contract, but still there remain imperative legal norms that are not subject to negotiation by the parties in either individual or collective labor contracts. Examples include provisions on termination of the employment relationship, disciplinary liability of the employee, and financial liability of the employee and the employer.

Bulgarian labor law allows both employment contracts for indefinite duration and employment contracts for a fixed term. The contract for an indefinite duration is the most commonly used type of employment contract. As of the date of Bulgaria's accession to the EU (January 1, 2007), nationals of any EU member state are entitled to work in Bulgaria under the same conditions as Bulgarian citizens.

2.6 Environmental Laws

Bulgaria is a party to major multilateral treaties in the field of environmental protection including, *inter alia*, the United Nations Framework Convention on Climate Change and the Kyoto Protocol, the Convention on Long-range Transboundary Air Pollution, the Convention on Environmental Impact Assessment in a Transboundary Context, the Convention on the Transboundary Effects of Industrial Accidents, the Basel Convention on the Control of Transboundary Movements of Hazardous Wastes and Their Disposal, and the Convention on Biological Diversity. The national laws set forth detailed regulation of a number of environment-related matters, such as waste management, biodiversity, air purity, water and soil protection, etc.

2.7 Intellectual Property Laws

Bulgaria is a member state to a number of international treaties and conventions governing intellectual property, including the Berne Convention for the Protection of Literary and Artistic Works, the Hague Agreement Concerning the International Deposit of Industrial Designs, the Lisbon Agreement for the Protection of Appellations of Origin and Their International Registration, the series of Classification Treaties, the Madrid Agreement Concerning the International

Registration of Marks and the Protocol thereto, as well as other treaties, administered by WIPO, with the exception of the Trademark Law Treaty. After becoming a member of the WTO on December 1, 1996, Bulgaria has become a party to the TRIPS Agreement.

National legislation in the area of intellectual property provides protection to a broad range of intellectual property rights. Trademark protection could be granted by registration of a sign comprising letters or digits, all types of drawings, figures, the shape of the article or its packaging, a combination of colors, and even sound signals, as well as a combination of said elements. Collective and certification marks and geographical indications could also be filed for registration.

Protection of works of literature, including science and technical literature and periodicals, and computer programs, musical works, scenic works, films and other audio-visual works, works of drawing including works of applied art, design, and folklore artistic handicrafts, etc., is also guaranteed by the law.

Bulgaria is a member of the Patent Cooperation Treaty, as well as a party to the European Patent Convention. Objects of protection under the Bulgarian patent laws are inventions and utility models. Industrial designs, new plant varieties, animal breeds, and topographies of integrated circuits are also subject to protection.

As of the date of Bulgaria's accession to the EU (January 1, 2007), all registered Community Trade Marks and Designs are effective on the Bulgarian territory, without any additional registration. In cases of conflict between a Community Trade Mark and a national trade mark registered in good faith and effective before the accession date, the national trade mark shall prevail.

2.8 Privacy and Data Security Laws

Processing of personal data is subject to Bulgarian legal requirements if carried out under the responsibility of (i) a data controller established in Bulgaria or (ii) a data controller that, while established outside the EU/EEA, for purposes of processing personal data makes use of equipment situated on the territory of Bulgaria, unless such equipment is used only for purposes of transit through the territory of Bulgaria. In such cases, the data controller needs to apply for registration with the data protection regulator prior to commencing processing of personal data.

Transfer of personal data abroad is subject to certain limitations. Personal data collected in Bulgaria may be freely transferred from Bulgaria to entities established within the EU/EEA. Subject to certain exceptions, personal data may be transferred to entities established outside the EU/EEA, after the data protection regulator has first ascertained the adequacy of personal data protection in the country in which the data importer is established.

2.9 Regulation of Foreign Investment

The principle of equal treatment and the principle of precedence of international treaties over domestic legislation, set forth in the Constitution, guarantee that foreign investors are treated in a nondiscriminatory way.

Bulgarian law is liberal in defining foreign investment. Equity in commercial companies, ownership over real estate, ownership over securities, loans to local persons under certain conditions, intellectual property rights, and rights under management contracts, among others, qualify as foreign investment. Furthermore, Bulgaria has entered into mutual promotion and protection of investment treaties with more than fifty countries.

Foreign investment is not subject to any special registration requirements, other than national statistics reporting requirements, which would apply to Bulgarian investors as well.

The currency control regime in Bulgaria is fully liberalized. The outflow of investment from Bulgaria abroad is also liberalized. Initial direct investments by domestic persons abroad as well as debt financing between foreign and domestic persons are subject only to a notification before the Bulgarian National Bank for statistical purposes. Thus, Bulgarian companies, including subsidiaries and branches of foreign companies, are able to export capital abroad and invest in other jurisdictions. Payment in foreign currency between companies registered and/or operating in Bulgaria is legally possible. Extraction, processing, and trade in valuables, precious stones, and metals is subject to a registration regime.

2.10 Other Potentially Applicable Laws and Regulations

2.10.1 Real Estate

Bulgarian law allows direct foreign ownership of real estate. Citizens of EU member states legally residing in the territory of Bulgaria and legal entities registered in EU member states may own land and buildings in Bulgaria. In compliance with the EU Accession Treaty of Bulgaria, Bulgaria restricts the acquisition of agricultural land, woods, and woodland by citizens of counties, members of the EU and the EEA, for a period of seven years as of the accession date (January 1, 2007).

Currently, the Constitution precludes foreign natural persons and legal entities who are not citizens of, or respectively registered in, EU or EEA member states, from owning land unless otherwise provided for in an international treaty to which Bulgaria is a party. However, such foreign persons and legal entities may become the owners of buildings without owning the land on which a building is constructed. Foreign persons may also acquire the "right to use" land or buildings, which is similar to a leasehold, for a limited term or as long as the "user" exists as an individual or entity. There is also no prohibition with respect to a Bulgarian company, the entire capital of which is owned by one or more foreign persons/entities, owning land in Bulgaria.

2.10.2 Lending and Financial Leasing

Lending and leasing to local borrowers on an offshore basis is not prohibited. Financial lending is subject to a notification before the Bulgarian National Bank, whereas commercial lending for import/export and financial leasing are subject to declaring before the customs authorities.

2.10.3 Securitization

Foreign investors enjoy the same access to securitization vehicles as local investors do. Thus, debt may be secured with a mortgage on real estate, or a pledge on movable property, granted by the debtor or a third party. Bulgarian law recognizes three types of pledge: (i) possessory pledge, (ii) commercial possessory pledge, and (iii) registered pledge.

Account receivables, movables (except for ships and aircraft), shares, a floating pool of account receivables or of movable goods, industrial property rights, and commercial enterprise as a going concern, among others, may be subject to a registered pledge. In the event of a registered pledge, the debtor need not transfer possession of the pledged asset to the creditor or to a third party.

Certain categories of creditors, such as banks, investment intermediaries, insurance companies, or other financial institutions, may obtain as collateral (i) cash receivables credited to an account in any currency or (ii) certain financial instruments.

3. Negotiation Practices

3.1 Participants

The participants in a negotiation session would typically include senior officials of the parties with decision-making powers and their lawyers and occasionally financial advisors. Normally, the chief executive officers would not be involved in the day-to-day negotiations, but will be available for internal discussion and making a decision on potential deal-breakers, such as price, retention amount, etc.

Gender, age, class, race, and/or ethnicity would normally not affect who the participants are. The number of individuals involved in a negotiation session would depend on the type of business in question and the parties to the potential transaction, but generally there will be up to four or five individuals on either side. In negotiations on purely private transactions, the government would not participate. However, the government would play a key role as a participant in negotiations on privatization transactions and public-private partnership projects.

3.2 Timing

There is no clear-cut rule as to the timing (time of day, day of the week, and part of the year) of negotiations. In the case of forthcoming bank holidays (such as during Christmas time, Easter holidays, etc.), the parties would try to finalize the negotiations and sign the relevant transaction documents before such long holiday periods.

As a matter of practice, the timing of negotiations would depend on the schedule of the participants. In general, negotiations in which the government acts as a participant tend, for various reasons, to last longer and take the form of several sessions over a certain period of time. In comparison, in purely private negotiations the parties tend to have one to two negotiation sessions (notwithstanding how long these will last), at which they would try to decide on all major issues.

3.3 Negotiation Practices

3.3.1 Exclusivity Agreements

Following initial discussions, and with a preliminary investment decision in place, the parties would normally sign a letter of intent containing an exclusivity clause, or an exclusivity agreement in which the potential vendor undertakes not to hold, for a certain period of time, talks with other interested parties on the subject matter of the potential transaction.

Such an undertaking constitutes a valid obligation on the part of the potential vendor. However, failure to honor this undertaking will only trigger the vendor's contractual liability and will not result in the reversal of any transaction entered into with a third party. In the event of a privatization transaction, the exclusivity granted by the selling authority will be binding in accordance with the terms of the respective formal resolution of that authority.

3.3.2 Non-binding "Heads of Agreement" (Term Sheet)

Heads of agreement (term sheet) would usually serve as the basis for negotiations and outline the principal commercial terms of the transaction. Unless certain facts that affect the financial terms of the potential transaction emerge in the course of the due diligence investigations, the parties will usually continue to use the commercial terms in the final transaction documents.

3.3.3 Confidentiality Agreements

Confidentiality agreements are used to protect the vendor from any unauthorized disclosure of sensitive commercial, financial, or technical information that it delivers to potential buyers in the course of the due diligence investigations. Therefore, a confidentiality agreement would usually be entered into prior to commencement of the due diligence investigations and the nondisclosure undertakings provided therein would normally apply also to advisers and consultants to the potential buyer.

Occasionally, a confidentiality agreement would not be entered into, but the representatives of the potential buyer (including the legal, financial, or technical advisors involved in the due diligence investigations) would be requested to provide a confidentiality statement.

3.3.4 Due Diligence

Prior to entering into negotiations, the potential buyer would usually conduct due diligence. The due diligence would, as a general rule, include legal due diligence and financial due diligence. Depending on the type of business involved, commercial due diligence and/or technical due diligence may also be conducted. While commercial due diligence might be conducted by senior officers of the potential buyer, legal, financial, and technical due diligence investigations would normally be carried out by external law and/or accounting firms particularly engaged for this purpose.

Due diligence investigations should provide the buyer with sufficient information to enable it to make a decision as to whether to proceed with the transaction, and if so, at what price. The findings from the due diligence investigations would normally affect the deal structure, as well as the contents of the transaction documents, particularly as regards conditions precedent, specific representations and warranties and indemnities, revisions to the existing internal corporate acts of the target, etc.

The documents subject to review are usually provided by the vendor in response to a due diligence questionnaire prepared by the buyer. Depending on the target and the deal structure, the due diligence investigations may be of full scope or limited to particular assets.

In larger-scale transactions, or in the case of a competitive bidding process, the documents would usually be placed in a data room, access to which is governed by data-room rules. Recently, virtual data rooms have become very common. Except with regard to privatization sales, the scope and the manner of disclosure of information and documents to the potential buyers are not determined by statute.

3.3.5 Language and Method of Conducting Negotiations

As a matter of practice, in cases involving a foreign participant, negotiations are commonly conducted in English. Lawyers employed by the established local law and accounting firms as well as by the offices of international law firms and the "big four" accounting firms in Bulgaria are usually fluent in English and other foreign languages. Translators might be involved in negotiations with the government, particularly in cases when representatives of various state and regulatory authorities participate in a negotiation session.

The negotiation process would usually not depend significantly on the type and size of the business involved. Still, the type and size might affect the negotiation process to the extent that the parties may need to discuss regulatory approvals eventually required for the effectuation of the deal, or merger control clearance procedure that may apply, depending on the deal structure and the turnover of the undertakings concerned, as well as other business-specific matters.

Whether the negotiation process would be broken up into stages would depend on the intentions and approach of the parties involved. As a matter of practice, negotiations in which the government acts as a participant may be broken up into several stages over time; as a result, such type of negotiation might progress slowly due to various reasons, such as the lack of clear strategy and objectives on the side of the government or the negotiation team on either side not including decision-makers. The opposite is likely to apply in purely private negotiations: the parties would prefer to close the deal as soon as practically possible, and thus tend to have one to two negotiation sessions (notwithstanding how long these will last), at which they would try to agree upon on all major issues.

In order for a negotiation to be successful, it is of utmost importance that the negotiating parties try to understand each other's interests and positions and do their best, to the extent this is reasonable, to accommodate such interests and positions in the transaction documents. To this end, the professional knowledge and experience, as well as flexibility and creativity, of the participants in the negotiation session turn out to be highly valuable negotiating skills.

3.4 Cultural, Ethical, and Religious Considerations

There do not seem to be any country-specific cultural, ethical, or religious considerations that can make a negotiation process in Bulgaria different from such a process in any other European country. Handshakes would normally be used by the participants to greet each other at the beginning of the negotiation session, as well as to say goodbye at the end of the session. In prolonged negotiations, the sense of humor of the participants would be important to give the parties short breaks from the serious talks.

3.5 Negotiating Online

Online communications technologies, including in particular e-mail and conference calls, are commonly used in international business negotiations involving participants from Bulgaria. Such technologies have turned out to be time and cost efficient, as they allow participants located in different places around the world to easily get in contact with each other.

In particular, in international business transactions drafts of the transaction documents would be exchanged between the negotiating parties by e-mail, and the parties would very often physically sit together only for one or two negotiation sessions to negotiate on the major terms of the transaction. Given the busy schedules and mobility of negotiation participants, the potential for growth of online negotiations seems extremely high in Bulgaria.

4. Contract Formation

4.1 Wording and Style

In general, transaction documents could be drafted either in the Bulgarian language or in a foreign language, depending on the preference of the negotiating parties. Usually, in international business negotiations involving participants from Bulgaria, transaction documents would be initially drafted and discussed in the language of the foreign partner (most often English). Simultaneously, the documents could be drafted also in the Bulgarian language, and finally executed in both the foreign language and the Bulgarian language (in such cases, the respective document would provide for which is the prevailing language). It is particularly advisable that a document is executed in both the Bulgarian language and the respective foreign language when such document is governed by Bulgarian law or the parties have chosen a Bulgarian forum for dispute resolution.

Alternatively, except for a limited number of cases when a special written form is required for the validity of a transaction, the documents may be executed in a foreign language only. Where a transaction, such as sale and purchase of real estate, must be executed in the form of a notary deed, the notary deed could be drafted and signed only in the Bulgarian language. Similarly, in cases when notary certification of the signatures of the parties is required by law for the validity of a transaction, such as transfer of shares from the capital of a local limited liability company, the document (for example, the share transfer agreement) should be drafted and signed in the Bulgarian language, or in a bilingual language version.

As a matter of practice, where the transaction documents have been executed in a foreign language only, all documents, or only excerpts thereof, could be translated in the Bulgarian language, particularly in cases when such documents, or excerpts thereof, need to be filed with Bulgarian regulatory authorities for merger clearance, regulatory approvals, or otherwise, as the case may be.

The typical structure or layout of a sale and purchase agreement would include (i) list of defined terms and general rules on interpretation, (ii) provisions describing the subject matter of the agreement, (iii) consideration and payment terms, (iv) steps to closing and actions pending closing, (v) closing procedures, (vi) representations and warranties, (vii) indemnification provisions, (viii) termination conditions and remedies, and (ix) miscellaneous provisions, such as provisions on effective date, governing law, dispute resolution, notices, language, etc. Of course, the structure or layout of the agreement may differ, depending on the type of the agreement and the specifics of the transaction at hand.

4.2 Conditions and Defenses

4.2.1 General Comments

Bulgaria is a civil law country where freedom of contract exists and individuals are free to negotiate the terms of their contracts provided that the mandatory rules of Bulgarian law are observed.

4.2.2 Choice of Law

The Bulgarian law allows in principle the parties to an agreement with an international element (an international element would be present, *inter alia*, where one of the parties to the transaction is a foreign person or entity) to determine the law that shall govern their relationship. Consequently, the choice of foreign law as the governing law in respect of an agreement with an international element would be valid and enforceable under Bulgarian law.

Notwithstanding the choice of foreign law, however, pursuant to the general Bulgarian conflict of laws rules, the supermandatory provisions of Bulgarian law shall apply. Further, a provision of foreign applicable law shall not be applied where the consequences arising out of its application are apparently not compatible with the Bulgarian public order, the latter term understood to refer only to the most general, fundamental principles and ideas of the Bulgarian *ordre public*. Also, the parties' choice of foreign applicable law shall not affect the application of the supermandatory provisions of the country with which all elements of the contract are related at the time of the choice of applicable law.

A particular example of supermandatory rules of Bulgarian law can be found in the general rules of Bulgarian contract law governing tort and contractual liability. In particular: (i) Bulgarian contract law does not permit the waiver or exclusion of liability in tort (including negligent tort), and in any event such contractual provision is null and void under Bulgarian laws; and (ii) pursuant to Bulgarian contract law the waiver of liability for damages caused by willful breach of contractual obligations or due to gross negligence is null and void.

4.2.3 Terms or Conditions That Would
Render a Contract Void or Voidable

The terms and conditions that would render a contract void or voidable are exhaustively provided for by the law.

Thus, a contract that contravenes or circumvents the law, or harms the good morals, shall be null and void. In addition, a contract with impossible subject matter, a contract that is not executed in the legally required form for validity, as well as a fictitious contract, among other cases, shall be null and void. No statute of limitations applies to the cases when a contract is null and void.

Among other conditions stipulated for by the law, the following terms and conditions would render a contract voidable: A contract executed by a natural person who does not have full legal capacity is voidable. A mistake in the material characteristics of the subject matter of the contract is also a condition that would render a contract voidable. The right of a party to seek that a contract is voided is subject to a three-year statute of limitations.

In the event that a contract is declared null and void, or it is voided, either party should return to the counterparty everything that the former has received from the latter.

4.2.4 The Special Case of Online Agreements

E-commerce and e-governance are legally recognized in Bulgaria. Transactions, for the validity of which a special written form is required by the law, may not be concluded online. Also, documents, such as securities and bills of lading, the physical possession of which has legal consequences, may not take the form of electronic documents. The identity of the author and the contents of the electronic statement are secured by the electronic signature. Following the adoption of relevant legal framework, online agreements are becoming more and more popular in Bulgaria. E-governance in Bulgaria is still in its infancy stage, but following the entry into force in June 2008 of the relevant legal framework, it could reasonably be expected that it will gain prominence in the near future.

5. Resolving Disputes

The classical mechanisms of dispute resolution, namely litigation and arbitration, are most commonly used in Bulgaria.

5.1 The Judicial Process

Bulgarian courts resolving civil claims are the regional courts, district courts, appellate courts, and the Supreme Court of Cassation. These courts have general competency to adjudicate all cases except for those subjected to the special courts. Civil claims are subject to a three-instance civil process.

If a foreign person would decide to or have to submit its dispute to the jurisdiction of the local courts, such a litigating foreign person will enjoy the same rights and protections in court as a local party would.

In terms of effectiveness of the local civil court system as a mechanism for civil dispute resolution, the civil litigation proceedings have been so far rather long and inefficient. A new Code on Civil Procedure entered into effect as of March 1, 2008 aims at making the court proceedings quicker and more efficient. This Code on Civil Procedure introduces more stringent requirements and imposes on the judges and the parties to the litigation proceedings short preclusive deadlines. In general, however, the Bulgarian civil court system in its current form is considered by foreign investors to fall behind the standards for effective mechanism for dispute resolution.

Under Bulgarian law the choice of foreign court for dispute resolution is allowed, provided that the subject matter of the dispute (i) does not fall within the exclusive competence of the Bulgarian courts; (ii) concerns pecuniary rights; and (iii) has an international element (for example, one of the litigants has his principal place of residence or business abroad). Within the exclusive competence of Bulgarian courts generally fall disputes related to (i) real estates located at the territory of the Republic of Bulgaria; (ii) intellectual property rights granted or registered in Bulgaria; and (iii) the corporate status of legal entities registered in Bulgaria.

5.2 Alternative Dispute Resolution Processes

Alternative dispute resolution (ADR) processes, and particularly arbitration, have gained much popularity in Bulgaria. Such rising popularity of ADR could be explained by the inefficiency and the big caseload of the civil courts, the perception that ADR imposes lower costs than litigation, the possibility of keeping the case confidential, and the ability to have greater control over the selection of the individual or individuals who will decide the dispute. Further, the civil courts may advise the parties to resort to mediation or ADR of another type before reviewing the case at an open court hearing. In matrimonial disputes, the civil courts are even obliged to advise the parties to conduct ADR of some type, usually mediation.

With respect to arbitration, Bulgarian law recognizes the rights of any two parties to enter into an arbitration agreement, thereby excluding the jurisdiction of Bulgarian state courts and submitting their potential dispute for resolution by an institutional or *ad hoc* court of arbitration. However, the choice of arbitral tribunal for dispute resolution is permitted provided that the subject matter of the dispute (i) is not related to real estate, labor relations, or alimony, and (ii) concerns pecuniary rights.

Any two parties may submit their dispute for resolution to an arbitration court with a place of arbitration in Bulgaria. Where one of the parties has its usual place of residence or seat or place of actual management abroad, the arbitration agreement may provide for arbitration in a place outside Bulgaria.

Mediation as an ADR method is explicitly recognized by the law. In mediation, a third party, the mediator, facilitates the resolution process, but does not impose a resolution on the parties. The consents and the form of the agreement are determined by the parties themselves. The agreement reached is binding only on the parties and may not be set against third parties that have not participated in the mediation procedure. Only a natural person of full legal capacity, entered into a special registry kept with the Bulgarian Minister of Justice, may act as a mediator. Civil, commercial, labor, matrimonial, and administrative disputes related to consumers' rights, as well as other disputes between natural persons and/or legal entities, may be referred to mediation.

Online dispute resolution (ODR) is not explicitly governed by the law and is still not common in practice.

5.3 Recognition and Enforcement of Foreign Court Judgments and Arbitral Awards

5.3.1 Recognition and Enforcement of a Court Judgment Issued in an EU Member State

Recognition and enforcement in Bulgaria of a judgment issued in a member state is more easily recognized compared to recognition and enforcement of a judgment issued in a non–EU member state. In cases where recognition and enforcement of a judgment issued by a court of an EU member state is sought in Bulgaria, the Bulgarian courts and other authorities would apply the Council Regulation (EC) No. 44/2001 of December 22, 2000 on jurisdiction and the recognition and enforcement of judgments in civil and commercial matters. Pursuant to this regulation, a judgment issued in an EU member state shall be recognized in Bulgaria without any special procedure being required and provided that a number of preconditions set forth in the regulation are complied with.

5.3.2 Recognition and Enforcement of a Judgment Issued in a Non–EU Member State

A judgment obtained from a court of competent jurisdiction in a non–EU member state will be recognized and enforceable in Bulgaria, provided that a number of preconditions set forth by the law are complied with. The recognition of a foreign judgment shall be made by the authority before which it has been submitted.

In a case where a declaration of the enforceability of a foreign judgment issued in a non–EU member state is sought, an application to that effect shall be submitted before the Sofia City Court, being the second-instance court for the capital city of Sofia. In proceedings for declaring the enforceability, the Sofia City Court shall not review the merits of the dispute. Once a foreign court decision is declared enforceable, it shall be subject to enforcement pursuant to the general rules of Bulgarian law. In particular, a writ of execution shall be issued by the court, in case the respondent fails to perform voluntarily.

5.3.3 Recognition and Enforcement of a Foreign Arbitral Award

The recognition and enforcement of foreign arbitral awards in Bulgaria are governed by the international treaties, including bilateral treaties, to which Bulgaria is a party. It is to be noted in particular that Bulgaria is a party to the 1958 Convention on the Recognition and Enforcement of Foreign Arbitral Awards (the "New York Convention"). Where recognition and enforcement of a foreign arbitral award is governed by the New York Convention, pursuant to the applicable Bulgarian procedural rules the enforcement of the foreign arbitral award shall require an *exequatur* decision issued by the Sofia City Court. The Sofia City Court is not entitled to engage in review on the merits of the dispute and enforcement may be refused only on any of the grounds provided for in Article V of the New York Convention.

Where a bilateral treaty providing for mutual recognition and enforcement of arbitral awards is not in place between Bulgaria and the respective foreign country, and the respective foreign country is not a party to the New York Convention, recognition and enforcement of the foreign arbitral award shall be governed by the applicable rules of Bulgarian law. The enforcement of the foreign arbitral award shall require an *exequatur* decision of the Sofia City Court. The Sofia City Court shall not engage in discussion on the merits of the dispute and it may refuse enforcement only on the grounds explicitly provided for in the national law.

The court would issue a writ of execution based on the final and binding foreign arbitral award and the final and binding decision on declaring the enforceability of said award.

6. Conclusion

Since Bulgaria joined the European Union on January 1, 2007, Bulgarian law has been generally harmonized with the *acquis communautaire*. The legal framework constantly changes to accommodate new technologies and new types of relationships.

As a matter of practice, international business negotiations involving participants from Bulgaria follow generally established models and are up to the international standards.

Georgi T. Gouginski and Lilia Kisseva
Djingov, Gouginski, Kyutchukov & Velichkov
10 Tsar Osvoboditel Blvd.
Sofia 1000, Bulgaria
Phone: +359(0)2 932 1100
Fax: +359(0)2 980 3586
E-mail: georgi.gouginski@dgkv.com

CHAPTER 24

International Business
Negotiations in Canada

Alison J. Youngman
STIKEMAN ELLIOTT LLP
TORONTO, CANADA

1. Introduction

Canada occupies the northern half of the North American continent and is the second largest country in the world, with a land mass
approaching 10 million square kilometers (over 3.8 million square
miles). The vast majority of Canada's 33 million people live in the
southern third of the country. English and French are Canada's official languages, with French predominating in the province of Quebec
and English predominating elsewhere. Many other languages are also
spoken, reflecting the vast number of immigrants that the country has
attracted, and continues to attract, from every corner of the globe.

Canada is a parliamentary democracy, and a federal state in which
the legislative authority is constitutionally divided between the federal
government and ten provincial (and three territorial) governments.
The federal government has exclusive jurisdiction over certain matters of national and international importance (for example, trade and
commerce, intellectual property, banking, and bankruptcy) and the
provincial governments have exclusive jurisdiction over other matters
(for example, property, employment matters, and general contract
matters). In some areas, both levels of government share in the regulation. Provincial governments also delegate certain specific powers
to municipal governments. Thus, in some cases, a business enterprise
may be regulated at the federal, provincial, and municipal levels.

The legal systems of all of the Canadian provinces except Quebec
are based on the common law. Quebec is a civil law jurisdiction in
which the legal system is based on a civil code, conceptually similar to
those of France and other continental European countries.

While historically the common law provinces of Canada have
tended to attach more importance to British than to American precedent, in recent years American case law has become increasingly

influential with Canadian courts and legislators, particularly with respect to commercial matters.

2. Substantive Laws and Regulations Impacting Negotiations

2.1 Corporate Law

2.1.1 Business Corporation Acts

Both the federal and provincial governments have enacted legislation providing for the incorporation and regulation of business corporations (known as "companies" under some statutes). A business corporation incorporated under provincial law may carry on business as of right in the province of its incorporation and also has the capacity to carry on business beyond the limits of that province. A federal business corporation is subject to provincial laws of general application, although it has the basic right to carry on business in any province. Most provinces require corporations incorporated in other jurisdictions to register or to be licensed before doing business in that jurisdiction and to file initial and annual returns and notices reporting certain basic corporate changes. Failure to comply with the rules governing extraprovincial corporations can prevent a corporation from holding land in the subject jurisdiction, from maintaining an action before the courts, and, in certain cases, from enforcing an otherwise valid agreement.

2.1.2 Differences Among the Acts

Although federal and provincial business corporation statutes are quite similar in most respects, there are some differences that can affect the decision whether to incorporate federally or provincially. Examples include ease and timeliness of incorporation, flexibility in carrying out corporate proceedings, licensing requirements, fees and taxes, and the extent of continuous disclosure requirements. One consideration often relevant to nonresident investors is the requirement, found in many corporation statutes, of a minimum number or percentage of resident Canadian directors. It is usually easier for a nonresident to incorporate under a statute with a minimal Canadian residency requirement or no requirement at all. Otherwise, where all else is equal, nonresidents are often advised to incorporate federally rather than provincially on the theory that a federal corporation will be more readily recognized and accepted—as a practical rather than a legal matter—outside Canada.

2.1.3 Sector-Specific Legislation

Certain types of business corporations (for example, banks, trust and loan companies, credit unions or associations, and insurance companies) are governed by sector-specific legislation rather than the general federal or provincial corporation statutes.

2.1.4 Unlimited Companies

An interesting hybrid of corporation and partnership is the "unlimited company" (ULC), unique to Nova Scotia, Alberta, and British Columbia law, with respect to which, among other things, the "members" or shareholders have unlimited liability in certain circumstances. A ULC that is a subsidiary of a U.S. parent will sometimes be able to produce certain tax advantages, as a tax flow-through vehicle, for its parent.

2.1.5 Business Combinations

Acquisitions of shares or assets of a Canadian entity will often involve the following forms of business combination, particularly where publicly traded entities are involved.

All of these may be used in a "friendly" situation, where the business combination is approved by the target corporation's board of directors. In "unfriendly" situations, a takeover bid is usually required.

(a) Statutory Amalgamations

The Canada Business Corporations Act (CBCA) and various provincial corporation statutes generally provide a statutory mechanism by which two or more companies incorporated or continued under the same corporation's statute may be combined into a single corporation.

Amalgamations between companies incorporated under different statutes may be effected through a so-called "three-cornered amalgamation." The acquirer will incorporate a new subsidiary under the same statute under which the target was incorporated, which will be amalgamated with the target. The acquirer will receive all the outstanding shares of the newly amalgamated company in exchange for issuing shares or other consideration to the shareholders of the target.

(b) Plans of Arrangement

The CBCA and many provincial corporation statutes provide for fundamental corporate changes to be effected by way of a statutory "plan of arrangement." In certain cases, this route is only available where it is not practicable to complete this transaction in any other manner.

Because plans of arrangement are more flexible and allow multistep transactions to be completed in one stroke, they are often used in complex business combinations and restructurings. As in the case of a statutory amalgamation, a plan of arrangement must be approved by the shareholders.

A plan of arrangement is supervised by the court, which will determine the process for calling the shareholders' meeting, the classes of shareholders entitled to vote, and the percentage of votes required for shareholder approval. Generally, a court will impose requirements similar to that of an amalgamation. After all the court-ordered procedures have been complied with, the corporation may ask the court to give final approval to the plan of arrangement, which will generally be given if the court considers the arrangement to be fair and reasonable.

2.1.6 Takeover Bids

Under provincial securities legislation, a takeover bid takes place when an offer is made to acquire outstanding voting or equity securities of a class that would result in the offeror and its joint actors holding 20 percent or more of the securities of the class. Complex counting rules apply.

Unless an exemption from the takeover bid requirements of applicable legislation is available, an offeror is required to issue a takeover bid circular disclosing the terms and conditions of the takeover bid to all shareholders. The terms and conditions and other information required to be disclosed in the takeover bid circular are prescribed by securities legislation. Where the target has a material number of shareholders in Quebec, a French translation of the takeover bid circular will be required.

2.2 Securities Laws

Regulatory standards imposed by Canadian securities regulators and stock exchanges are generally comparable to U.S. standards. The most important thing to understand about Canadian securities law, however, is that, under the Constitution, it is largely the responsibility of the provincial and territorial governments. As a consequence, Canada has no national securities law and no national securities regulator.

In recent years, the possibility of replacing the provincial and territorial securities regulators with a single national regulator has been discussed. The realities of the Canadian political system, however, are such that the goal of a national securities regulator is unlikely to be attained soon. A more realistic expectation is that a uniform regulation system will develop "organically" over time and on the basis of increased cooperation among the existing provincial and territorial regulators. Such "organic" development can be seen in the increasing coordination and mutual reliance among provincial and territorial securities regulators. Currently, aspects of securities regulation are being harmonized as a single "national instrument" or "national policy," which is then adopted by each of the provincial and territorial regulators. Moreover, initiatives such as the national electronic filing system (SEDAR) and the Passport System encourage regulators to delegate responsibilities to one another.

2.3 Tax Laws

Residents of Canada are subject to tax on their worldwide income (including capital gains) under the Income Tax Act (Canada) (the ITA) and the relevant provincial tax legislation. Nonresidents of Canada are generally subject to tax only on their Canadian source income, including income from a business or employment carried on in Canada, and income from the disposition of "taxable Canadian property" (as defined). Although each province has also enacted provincial income tax legislation, only Alberta and Quebec administer their own corporate income taxes, and only Quebec administers its own individual income taxes. Other provinces rely upon the federal government to collect taxes on their behalf.

2.3.1 Goods and Services Tax (GST)

GST is a value-added 5 percent federal sales tax imposed under the Excise Tax Act (Canada) on virtually all goods and services consumed in Canada. Like most sales taxes, it is generally collected by the seller from the purchaser. The sale of shares falls within the exempt supply category since shares are considered financial instruments.

However, absent a rollover, a typical asset sale will attract some GST liability, including GST on tangible personal property (including inventory), all real property, and all intangible property. The most common rollover available is the one under Section 167 of the Excise Tax Act for the sale of a business or part of a business where the parties elect to have the transfer occur at nil consideration. In this context it is important to determine if the purchaser and the seller are registered under the Excise Tax Act. There is often a representation and warranty in an acquisition agreement with respect to such registration. The Section 167 rollover is available only if the purchaser is acquiring ownership, possession, or use of all or substantially all of the property that can reasonably be regarded as being necessary for it to be capable of carrying on the business or part of a business.

2.3.2 Provincial Sales Taxes

With the exception of Alberta, all the provinces in Canada impose a sales tax. British Columbia, Saskatchewan, Manitoba, Ontario, and Prince Edward Island typically impose provincial sales tax (PST) on tangible personal property sold or consumed within the jurisdiction. Inventory purchased for resale is generally exempt from PST. Machinery, equipment, and other tangible personal property will generally be subject to PST. Various provinces provide different exemptions. For example, Ontario and some other provinces exempt the transfer of tangible personal property between related persons when PST has already been paid once if certain conditions are met. Ontario and some other provinces exempt manufacturing equipment. PST is generally not exigible on the sale of land, building, fixtures, or intangibles.

Newfoundland, New Brunswick, and Nova Scotia have harmonized their provincial taxes with the federal GST, such that the Harmonized Sales Tax (HST) applies at the rate of 13 percent. The HST includes the GST, and generally applies in the same manner as the GST. Quebec has a sales tax (QST) that generally mirrors the GST. The QST applies at the rate of 7.5 percent on the GST-included price.

2.3.3 Withholding Tax

Amounts paid or credited by a resident of Canada to a nonresident person with respect to most forms of passive income (including dividends, rents, royalties, and certain cases of interest) are generally subject to Canadian nonresident withholding tax on the gross amount of such payments. The rate of Canadian nonresident withholding tax under the ITA is 25 percent, subject to reduction under an applicable tax treaty.

The federal government recently eliminated the withholding tax on interest payments to nonresident recipients with whom the Canadian resident payer is dealing at arm's length and where the interest is not considered to be "participating debt interest," irrespective of the residence of the recipient.

2.4 Acquiring a Canadian Resident Corporation

In acquiring the shares of a Canadian resident corporation (the "Target Corporation"), nonresident purchasers should generally consider using a Canadian acquisition corporation (CAC) in order to maximize the cross-border paid-up capital available to the purchaser. This is advantageous since a Canadian resident corporation can generally return profits to its foreign parent corporation, up to the amount of the paid-up capital of the shares, without Canadian nonresident withholding taxes. Distributions of profits in excess of the paid-up capital would be subject to Canadian withholding tax.

Typically, the amount of the paid-up capital of the shares of the Target Corporation would be less than their acquisition cost to the nonresident purchaser (the fair market value). To ensure that the nonresident purchaser has shares with paid-up capital equal to the investment made by the nonresident, the nonresident purchaser may subscribe for shares in a CAC that will have a cost and paid-up capital equal to the purchase price of the Target Corporation's shares. The CAC would then use the proceeds of this share subscription to acquire the shares of the Target Corporation. As profits are earned by the Target Corporation, tax-free intercompany dividends may generally be paid by the Target Corporation to the CAC. These amounts can subsequently be paid by the CAC to the nonresident parent as a tax-free return of capital, thus permitting the investment cost to be returned to the nonresident parent free of Canadian withholding tax. A CAC can also be used (through different means) to push any acquisition debt and corresponding interest expense into the operations of Target Corporation.

An exchangeable share structure should also be considered in circumstances where the shares of a nonresident purchaser are to be offered as consideration for shares of a Target Corporation, and the shares of the Target Corporation have significant capital gains accrued to the holders thereof.

Very generally speaking, an exchangeable share structure involves the creation of two new Canadian subsidiary corporations of the nonresident purchaser, Callco and Exchangeco. As consideration for selling the Target Corporation shares, the Target Corporation shareholders are issued exchangeable shares of Exchangeco, which because of various support agreements have the same economic attributes as the shares of the nonresident purchaser. As Exchangeco is Canadian, the Target Corporation shareholders are entitled to a rollover of their shares, which defers their tax liability until they dispose of the exchangeable shares. The holders of the exchangeable shares usually have up to ten years or more in which to exchange their exchangeable shares for shares of the nonresident purchaser, which exchange occurs through Callco. However, the use and consequences of employing an exchangeable share structure must be carefully considered, as it will add complexity and expense to the transaction.

2.5 Antitrust/Anticompetition Laws

Canada's Competition Act (CA) is comparable to the Hart-Scott-Rodino legislation in the United States. In any acquisition of a business with assets or revenues attributable to Canada, the test to be applied under the CA is whether the merger (which may include a joint venture, acquisition, or any other type of business merger) "would or would be likely to prevent or lessen competition substantially" in the relevant market. The Canadian Merger Enforcement Guidelines are broadly similar to guidelines adopted by the U.S. Department of Justice. Mergers are very broadly defined under the CA and anyone contemplating any type of acquisition or cooperative venture with a Canadian entity should be aware of the purview of the CA.

If the Competition Tribunal determines that a merger or proposed merger prevents or lessens or would be likely to prevent or lessen competition substantially in a market, then the tribunal has broad discretionary authority to make orders remedying the anticompetitive effects of the merger, including prohibiting a proposed merger or requiring a dissolution or divestiture in the case of a completed merger. The Commissioner is entitled to bring such an application at any time within three years of the completion of the merger, provided the Commissioner has not issued an Advance Ruling Certificate with respect to the merger.

The CA also contains a premerger notification filing requirement for transactions exceeding a certain size. Where notification is required, the parties are not permitted to complete the transaction until notification has been made and the review period has expired or an Advance Ruling Certificate or waiver of the notification requirement has been issued. Premerger notification filings are required in connection with a proposed acquisition of assets or shares or an amalgamation or other combination where thresholds relating to the size of the transaction, the size of the parties, and shareholding thresholds are exceeded.

2.6 Labor and Employment Laws

Legislative jurisdiction over labor and employment is shared by the provincial and federal governments. However, legislation in this area falls mainly within the provincial domain.

Generally, under minimum standards legislation, employees are guaranteed certain minimum rights with respect to the terms and conditions of their employment. Terms and conditions established by legislation include but are not limited to minimum wages, hours of work, overtime pay, daily and weekly rest periods, vacations and vacation pay, statutory holidays, pregnancy and parental leave, equal pay for work of equal value, minimum periods of notice of termination and/or severance pay, and terms that govern the treatment of employees upon the sale of a business (or part of a business). The Canada Labor Code (which governs federal undertakings such as banks and the telecommunications industry) and Quebec legislation have specific unjust dismissal provisions that can result in the reinstatement of a terminated employee.

Employers and employees cannot contract out of or waive these legislated terms and conditions. Where the contract of employment provides for terms and conditions of employment exceeding statutory minimum standards, these more favorable terms usually become binding upon the employer and can be enforced as a "minimum standard."

Under the common law as it exists in Canada, the sale of a business by an asset transaction results in the constructive termination of all of its employees. Each employee generally has a duty to mitigate by seeking alternative employment. However, in an asset purchase transaction, the purchaser will often agree to offer employment to many, if not all, employees of the business upon the closing of the transaction on the same terms and conditions as their employment with the seller (or on terms and conditions of employment no less favorable, in the aggregate, than they enjoy at closing).

For employees who are not offered employment by the purchaser, compensation is based on both the provisions of the minimum standards legislation and the common law. The required notice of termination (or pay in lieu thereof) and severance pay under the minimum standards legislation are generally a function of the years of service and, in certain circumstances, the aggregate number of employees terminated within specified timeframes. However, the common law requirements are often in excess of the minimum standards legislation requirements and will generally need to be taken into account. They are a function of a broader range of factors, including years of service, age, seniority, likelihood of reemployment, and other special considerations, including the manner in which the termination was effected.

It is important to obtain comfort from the seller that there are no unfunded pension obligations and that where there are unions there are no significant labor disputes in process or pending. Where the acquisition involves layoffs of some employees, it is important to ensure that the seller gives the appropriate notices within the time frames required by legislation and provides for any severance pay that may be payable.

Canadian courts tend to be cautious about enforcing postemployment noncompetition and nonsolicitation agreements, and will only uphold them in certain circumstances. In particular, such postemployment covenants must be reasonable in duration and scope, and must not be broader than is necessary to protect the employer's legitimate business interests.

2.7 Environmental Laws

The Canadian Environmental Protection Act is the principal piece of federal environmental legislation that regulates the manufacture, import, use, handling, release, and disposal of toxic substances. However, provincial environmental assessment and environmental protection legislation is also highly important.

Thus, environmental disclosure has become increasingly important in recent years in any transaction involving a Canadian business. Due diligence in this area is extensive, as a result of the potential application of these federal and provincial environmental laws, some of which place liabilities for cleanup on the current occupiers of land regardless of when the contamination occurred. This usually results in intensive negotiation of the environmental representations, warranties, and indemnification provisions.

2.8 Intellectual Property Laws

Where trademarks, patents, or copyrights are key components of a business being acquired, it is important to conduct a search in the federal registries to verify that the seller has title to the intellectual property. Trademarks can be registered for fifteen years, subject to renewal, and patents can be registered for twenty years. Registration of copyright is optional.

2.9 Privacy and Data Security Laws

The collection, use, and disclosure of personal information in the public sector is governed at the federal level by the Privacy Act. The regulation of personal information in the private sector is governed by the federal Personal Information Protection and Electronic Documents Act (PIPEDA). Under the divisions of power between the federal and provincial level, PIPEDA allows the federal cabinet to exempt businesses from the application of PIPEDA in a province that enacts privacy legislation found to be "substantially similar" to Part I of PIPEDA. Any such exemption applies only to the collection, use, or disclosure of personal information that occurs within the province. Extraprovincial or international aspects of data collection or usage continue to be subject to PIPEDA notwithstanding such an exemption order.

To date, the federal government has recognized the Alberta Personal Information Protection Act, British Columbia Personal Information Protection Act, and Quebec's Act Respecting the Protection of Personal Information in the Private Sector to be "substantially similar" to PIPEDA. In addition, four provinces—Ontario, Manitoba, Saskatchewan, and Alberta—have statutes that specifically address the privacy of personal health information; the federal government has recognized the Ontario legislation only with regard to personal health information. PIPEDA regulates the collection, disclosure, and use of personal information in the private sector in all other provinces, and personal information that is not personal health information in Ontario.

2.10 Regulation of Foreign Investment

The Investment Canada Act (ICA) allows the federal government to screen proposed foreign investments to ensure that they are likely to produce a "net benefit to Canada." Certain transactions effected by non-Canadians or non-Canadian-controlled entities are therefore reviewable.

Any non-Canadian proposing to establish a new business in Canada, or acquiring control of an existing business, should be aware of the provisions of the ICA. The ICA establishes certain deeming rules regarding acquisitions of control. The acquisition of a majority of the voting interests of an entity, including a corporation, is deemed to be an acquisition of control. The acquisition of between one-third and one-half of the voting shares of a corporation is presumed to be an acquisition of control unless it can be shown that the investor has not in fact gained control of the corporation. The acquisition of less than one-third of the voting shares of a corporation is deemed not to be an acquisition of control. For entities other than corporations, such as partnerships, trusts, or joint ventures, an acquisition of less than a majority of the voting interests is deemed not to be an acquisition of control. The acquisition of control may be the result of one transaction or event or a series of related or unrelated transactions or events.

In general, a direct acquisition of a Canadian business by a WTO investor[1] (or from a WTO investor) is subject to review under the ICA where the book value of the assets being acquired is C$295 million or more.[2] Indirect acquisitions[3] by WTO investors are not reviewable except where the Canadian business is engaged in sensitive sectors (uranium production, cultural business, transportation services,[4] and financial services).

The financial thresholds for these sensitive sectors or for transactions where neither the vendor nor the purchaser is ultimately controlled by nationals of a WTO member country are: for a direct acquisition, C$5 million; for an indirect acquisition, C$50 million unless the value of the Canadian businesses amounts to more than 50 percent of the value of the global entities being acquired (in which case the C$5 million threshold applies).

In addition to the requirements of the ICA, there are several sectors of the Canadian economy that are strictly regulated due to their perceived importance to national economic policy, among them financial services, communications, and energy. Foreign investors, including WTO Investors, acquiring any interest in companies in these areas are subject to sectoral investment restrictions and increased regulatory scrutiny.

On December 7, 2007, Canada's Minister of Industry announced that the government would apply special guidelines to the consideration of reviewable Canadian investments by state-owned enterprises (SOEs) under the ICA. An SOE is an enterprise that is owned or controlled directly or indirectly by a foreign government. In addition to the factors that the Minister of Industry typically considers in deciding whether to approve reviewable investments, the guidelines identify the

---

[1] A "WTO investor" is an investor that is ultimately controlled by nationals of a WTO member.

[2] The threshold is lower if the investor is not a WTO investor. In addition, the threshold increases on a yearly basis related to inflation/economic growth.

[3] An indirect acquisition means that shares of the Canadian business are acquired indirectly as a result of the acquisition of a non-Canadian corporation.

[4] "Transportation services" means a "Canadian business directly or indirectly engaged in the carriage of passengers or goods from one place to another by any means, including, without limiting the generality of the foregoing, carriage by air, by rail, by water, by land and by pipeline." We interpret this to mean the provision of transportation services to third parties.

"governance and commercial orientation of SOEs" as central consider-ations in reviewing SOE investments.

2.11 Other Potentially Applicable Laws and Regulations

2.11.1 Language Laws

The Charter of the French Language is designed to make French the everyday language of commerce and business in the province of Quebec. Corporations carrying on business there must have a French name, although the products produced by them may have a version of the name in another language.

2.11.2 Real Estate

Title insurance was formerly unavailable in transactions involving Canadian real estate. Foreign (particularly U.S.) purchasers or lenders frequently request title insurance, and this is now available in Canada. However, the title insurance policy is generally based on an opinion on title delivered by a Canadian law firm, and if such a prior opinion is not readily available to be updated, the title insurance process can take some time. It is still more usual, however, to seek legal opinions on real estate title in Canadian transactions, although when acting as counsel to the purchaser, it is acceptable practice to request the seller's counsel to update an existing title opinion (rather than commence one de novo).

2.11.3 Bulk Sales

The provinces of Ontario and Newfoundland have bulk sales laws that apply in the context of the sale of assets in bulk out of the ordinary course of the selling corporation, which require the seller to provide an affidavit concerning all of the corporation's creditors and the amounts due to them. Because this is cumbersome when there are several hun-dred trade creditors, the bulk sales affidavit is often waived subject to providing an indemnity to the purchaser. However, the obtaining or waiving of a bulk sales affidavit can frequently give rise to fairly heated debate, depending on the level of confidence between the parties. Technically, if an affidavit is not obtained by the purchaser, a disgrun-tled creditor can have the transaction set aside and if, in Ontario for example, the statute is not complied with, there is no limitation period to provide a sunset date for such creditor's rights under the statute. It may also be possible to obtain a court order exempting a transaction from compliance where it can be shown that the trade creditors will not be harmed by the sale.

2.11.4 E-commerce Legislation

The ability to regulate Internet activities is shared by both the federal and provincial legislatures. Regulation of the Internet itself is a federal responsibility, but the Canadian Radio-television and Telecommunications Commission, as the relevant federal agency, has not regulated and does not intend to regulate Internet content. Nonetheless, Internet activities are regulated by federal and provincial legislation as well as various common law principles.

3. Other Significant Legal and Business Issues

3.1 Choice of Laws Issue

Each province and territory in Canada has its own set of rules for determining when it will apply the laws of another jurisdiction or hear disputes connected with another jurisdiction. The rules are found partly in statutes (or, in Quebec, the Civil Code) and partly in case law. The rules of the common law provinces are similar but not identical. Quebec's rules differ from those in the common law provinces in some significant respects.

A Canadian court will always apply the laws of its own jurisdiction—the law of the forum—to matters that are procedural in nature. This includes principles of evidence, the rules governing court proceedings (e.g., the proper parties), and principles for the measurement of damages (although not whether any particular type of damage is recoverable). The law of the forum may apply to matters that are not procedural where the parties do not sufficiently plead and prove the relevant foreign law. Foreign law is generally proved through the testimony of a legal expert from the foreign jurisdiction.

There are also certain types of foreign laws that a Canadian court will not apply. These include laws that offend the Canadian jurisdiction's concept of public policy ("public order" in Quebec), that would have anti-competitive effects in Canada, or that would involve the direct or indirect enforcement of a foreign tax or criminal law.

The rule with respect to contracts is that a Canadian court will apply the proper law of the contract. The proper law is the law with which the contract has the most significant connection, and in this regard the court will consider all relevant connecting factors. However, if the parties specify a law in the contract to govern their relationship, then the court will respect that choice as long as it was made in good faith, in the sense that it was not chosen deliberately to avoid the laws of a more appropriate jurisdiction. In cases involving noncontractual obligations (known in the common law as torts and in the civil law as extracontractual liability), Canadian courts apply the law of the place where the tort was committed.

Canadian courts will generally enforce a foreign judgment without reopening the case on the merits. However, a foreign judgment will not be enforced if the defendant establishes that the foreign court proceedings were not conducted fairly (i.e., in accordance with principles of natural justice), that enforcement is against public policy or public order, or that the judgment is a foreign tax or penal judgment. There are similar rules for the enforcement of foreign arbitration awards.

3.2 Security Interests in Personal Property

There is a set of rather complex rules in each jurisdiction to cover the means of perfecting security interests in personal property. The governing law of the security agreement will not apply to validity and perfection of security interests. These issues will generally be governed either by the place where the debtor is located or by the place where the collateral is located.

3.3 E-commerce Jurisdiction

Due to the "borderless" nature of the Internet, Canadian courts have struggled to develop a consistent formula for determining when Internet activities are sufficient to establish a real and substantial connection. As a result, several alternative jurisdictional tests have emerged, but with a recent shift toward the foreseeability test as the leading test on the issue of jurisdiction. The foreseeability test is based on the premise that a party should only be answerable to a foreign court if that eventuality is reasonably foreseeable in the circumstances.

A choice of law and exclusive jurisdiction clause is often used in connection with Internet activities to limit jurisdictional uncertainties involved in Internet operations. However, the effect and enforceability of such clauses is subject to applicable consumer protection legislation, and in Quebec, to the Civil Code. Consumer protection legislation in some jurisdictions provides that a consumer may not waive his or her rights, including the consumer's right to bring proceedings in his or her home jurisdiction. Under the Civil Code, a choice of law clause may not be enforceable if it deprives the consumer of protection under the law of the country where he or she resides and the formation of the contract is in some way connected to that country.

4. Negotiation Practices

4.1 Participants

As in most countries, the participants in any transaction involving negotiations with Canadian parties will vary from one deal to another. It is not uncommon in a sizable transaction to have the chief financial officer, one or two in-house accountants, the external accountant, and both in-house and external counsel involved in all negotiating sessions. Alternatively, in a smaller transaction one might find the chief executive officer, with one outside counsel and in-house accounting backup involved from time to time. In larger transactions, lawyers tend to play a fairly key role in negotiations. Notwithstanding, clients who have significant deal experience and who have dealt with lawyers in the past may sometimes negotiate all business-related points and defer to their legal counsel only on legal issues. It is not uncommon in the early stages of the transaction for clients to have their respective lawyers present, but the meetings are often led by the clients. Once the fundamental deal is struck and the first drafts of the documentation completed, lawyers for both parties will then generally take on a more active role, even in the negotiation of business issues, in order to more accurately reflect the transaction on paper.

In negotiations between private companies, the principal business negotiators generally have the power to bind the company. In more widely held companies, board approval may be required, but normally the board will have given the CEO or CFO fairly broad powers to negotiate. Even where board approval is required, the indoor management rule (that third parties are permitted to rely on the ostensible authority of a senior officer) may operate in a situation where the approval process is not clearly articulated to bind a party even though the board may not have approved the transaction.

Although experts in various areas (environment, pension, employment), both from the client and the law firm, will be called in from time to time in most Canadian transactions, it is relatively uncommon for these specialists to come to the negotiating table, other than periodically. It is more likely that each party's counterparts in these specialized disciplines will deal with each other outside the framework of the primary negotiations.

4.2 Timing

There is no standard time frame within which a commercial transaction generally occurs in Canada. An acquisition could be completed in anything from one week to six months (or could potentially be blocked under the Competition Act or Investment Canada Act). Financing through a commercial bank could take from two weeks to three months depending on the size of the transaction, the time taken for credit committee approvals, and the extent to which the terms are negotiable. However, there are certain regulatory timing constraints that may determine the minimum time frames required for certain transactions.

4.2.1 Investment Canada Act

If an application for review under the Investment Canada Act is required, the Minister of Industry has an initial period of forty-five days from the date of filing the application for review to determine whether the investment will be of net benefit to Canada; the minister may unilaterally extend this period for an additional thirty days. This time period can be further extended with the investor's consent.

4.2.2 Competition Act

Under the Competition Act, if a proposed transaction is notifiable, the parties have the option of filing a "short-form" or "long-form" notification. Once the parties have made their notification filings, a statutory waiting period commences during which they are prohibited from closing the proposed transaction. In the case of a short-form notification, the proposed transaction could not close for at least fourteen calendar days after the filing is made, whereas if a long-form notification were filed, the proposed transaction could not close for at least forty-two calendar days. The Commissioner of Competition (the "Commissioner"), the individual who heads the Bureau, has the complete discretion to "bump" a short-form filing into a long-form filing. Notwithstanding this discretion, the overwhelming majority of notification filings in Canada are of the short-form variety.

In appropriate circumstances (e.g., where there is no or only *de minimis* overlap), parties to a transaction may request an advance ruling certificate (ARC) from the Commissioner. The granting of an ARC exempts the purchaser from the notification requirements under the Act. An ARC may be issued at the discretion of the Commissioner where the Commissioner is satisfied that there would not be sufficient grounds on which to apply to the Competition Tribunal for an order against a proposed transaction. There is no fixed time limit within which the Commissioner must respond to an ARC request. If the request is denied, the Commissioner may issue a section 113(c) letter waiving the obligation to notify and stating that she has no current intention to challenge the transaction (a so-called "no-action" letter).

Whether a transaction is notifiable or not, the Commissioner has jurisdiction to review and challenge a merger at any time within three years from its completion on the basis that the merger substantially lessens or prevents competition in a properly defined antitrust product and geographic market.[5]

Notwithstanding the statutory waiting periods associated with short-form and long-form notification filings, there is no set time period within which the Commissioner *must* complete his review of a proposed transaction. Nevertheless, the Commissioner has established (nonstatutory) service standards that stipulate that the Commissioner will ordinarily complete his review of a merger within the following *maximum* time periods:

---

[5] In the worst-case scenario, such a challenge can lead to the forced divestiture of part or all of that which was acquired. Accordingly, where a transaction is not notifiable, parties may still wish to voluntarily notify the Bureau of the transaction in order to obtain substantive clearance in advance of closing. This is a far more important issue for the purchaser, as it is the purchaser who faces the competition law risk of Bureau intervention following closing.

Noncomplex merger: up to fourteen days
Complex merger: up to ten weeks
Very complex merger: up to five months

The Commissioner designates whether a merger is noncomplex, complex, or very complex shortly after receiving the filing. The classification will depend upon the degree and complexity of the competition issues raised by the transaction (e.g., market shares, effective competition remaining postmerger, barriers to entry, etc.).

4.2.3 Tax

Where significant tax issues arise in the structuring of a transaction, and tax lawyers for both parties agree that the importance of certainty on a particular tax issue is essential for the transaction to proceed, it may be appropriate to request a ruling from Revenue Canada in order to obtain comfort on the tax implications of the transaction. Depending on the time of year and the extent to which Revenue Canada staff are backed up on similar matters, a ruling can often take several weeks to obtain.

4.3 Language Considerations

The French language plays a significant role in any negotiations conducted in the Province of Quebec, although in negotiated commercial transactions it is common for the parties to agree that documentation can be drafted and negotiated in English. Language laws in Quebec particularly (and in certain circumstances in Canada generally) must be taken into account in all commercial transactions where a Canadian business is involved.

5. Contract Formation

5.1 Structuring a Transaction

Subject to certain tax considerations (discussed above), a key issue to be determined in any acquisition in Canada is whether to structure it as a share or an asset transaction. Parties sometimes agree in a letter of intent that the transaction will be structured in such a way as to minimize tax consequences for both the vendor and the purchaser. From the perspective of the purchaser, there are a number of factors to be taken into consideration in reaching this decision, some of which are peculiarly Canadian, others of which may be similar to those in other jurisdictions.

Significant government approvals such as under the Investment Canada Act or the Competition Act are generally not affected by whether the sale of the business is structured as an asset purchase or a share purchase.

Third-party consents are frequently required in asset purchases (for example, for the assignment of contracts), and the ability to obtain these consents is often a matter of significant negotiation. Other contracts may also contain change of control provisions that require third-party consents. This is sometimes resolved by a best-efforts undertaking on the part of the seller, but ultimately may mean that consent under a contract that is key to the business operations cannot be obtained without renegotiating its terms, a solution that may or may not be acceptable to the purchaser.

Bulk sales legislation (discussed above) does not apply to share transactions in Canada. Asset transactions generally require greater attention to employment contracts. At common law, there is no automatic continuation of employment when assets are purchased, although this has been altered by statute in Ontario, for example, where the purchaser of a business is bound by any collective agreement to which the seller was a party and by the Civil Code in the Province of Quebec. Furthermore, the Employment Standards Act in Ontario deems employment to have been continuous for certain restrictive purposes (such as the calculation of vacation pay entitlement, pregnancy and parental leave, and termination of employment), regardless of the sale of assets.

In asset purchase transactions, the establishment of new pension plans may be required (however, share purchase transactions may also give rise to the same result where the corporation, the shares of which were sold, is part of a group pension plan). Asset purchases may give rise to significant federal and provincial sales tax and land transfer tax, whereas such taxes are not payable on the transfer of shares.

5.2 Letters of Intent

As a general rule, transactions of any significant size in Canada are reflected in fairly detailed documentation. It is also not uncommon (and for many Canadian lawyers it is a preferred mechanism for establishing the basic terms of a transaction) to negotiate a letter of intent before the final documentation is prepared. However, issues of concern arise in drafting letters of intent to ensure that, whether the intention of the parties is that they are binding or nonbinding, a court in a subsequent dispute (and a change of mind of one of the parties) will find enough particularity in the document to enforce it or to find it nonbinding, as the case may be.

Whether or not legal counsel is called into a transaction before or after the basic deal is struck, Canadian lawyers are often asked to put on paper in simple terms basic elements of the transaction, such as price, payment terms, the business or product involved, identity of the parties, delivery schedules, and other deal terms agreed to.

These terms are often prepared as a letter to be sent from the purchaser to the seller offering to purchase the business on the terms previously agreed. After some further negotiation, a form of letter will be agreed on by both parties, and it is generally provided within the term of the letter of intent that it is not legally binding on the parties (other than, for example, confidentiality and no-shop provisions). The letter of intent will be subject to a "definitive agreement of purchase and sale," which would normally be prepared in first draft by the purchaser's counsel.

Given that the process of negotiating the final terms of any transaction can often be time-consuming and demanding, a signed letter of intent can be viewed as the focal point from which the more complicated and contentious points may be settled. Given its significance, it is appropriate to consider the execution of a letter of intent as the end of the first of a three-stage transaction process, the second and third stages of which are, respectively, the execution of the definitive purchase agreement and related documents (or loan documentation in the case of a financing) and the closing of the deal, at which time assets or shares are exchanged for cash or other consideration (or, in the case of a financing, the monies are advanced) and the various closing documents are delivered.

5.3 Control of the Documents

In Canada, the purchaser's lawyer (or lender's lawyer in the case of a financing) will normally prepare the first draft of the letter of intent and subsequently the definitive documentation. A one-sided and unreasonable first draft will generally not be conducive to smooth or amicable negotiations. The vendor and its lawyer will generally expect the purchaser's lawyer to ask for more protection than the purchaser ultimately expects to obtain. However, as in most jurisdictions, Canadian clients are seeking more control over legal costs and are looking for more efficient and cost-effective ways to accomplish transactions, so it is often viewed as counterproductive for purchaser's counsel to produce a draft that is too far removed from what will ultimately constitute the definitive document. Another risk that purchaser's counsel incurs in preparing a draft that differs significantly from the business deal is that vendor's counsel may respond with an entirely new draft, which will then remove purchaser's leverage in controlling the document.

Depending on the time frame within which a transaction is to be completed, the agreement of purchase and sale in an asset or share transaction may be an agreement to purchase and sell rather than an actual purchase or sale to be executed at the closing. A definitive agreement of purchase and sale signed prior to closing may involve price adjustment mechanisms to cover a change in the value of the business from the date the agreement was signed to the effective date of the transaction (this will avoid postclosing adjustments that are generally required where the agreement of purchase and sale is only signed on closing).

It used to be the case in Canada that documentation in acquisitions and financing tends to be less voluminous and generally less cumbersome than in U.S. transactions. However, there has been an increasing tendency to expand on representations, warranties, and indemnities so as to anticipate all possible contingencies, particularly in transactions where time and cost do not permit extensive due diligence or where the purchaser or lender has knowledge of potential problems.

5.4 Due Diligence

The amount of due diligence undertaken by the purchaser (or lender) and its counsel in any given transaction in Canada will vary based on a number of different factors such as how well the parties know each other (in a management buyout, presumably intimately); whether the parties have been dealing with each other commercially for several years and have developed a high degree of goodwill and confidence in each other; and the degree to which the purchaser is prepared to acquire the business on an "as-is" basis and reflect the degree of risk in a reduced purchase price or through an earn-out or holdback. It is also not uncommon to see clients conducting far more of their own due diligence in an effort to reduce legal costs. Most due diligence is conducted between the stage of the letter of intent and the definitive agreement, during negotiation of the final documentation.

It is fairly common in an acquisition of assets or shares of a Canadian enterprise to present the seller's lawyer with a due diligence checklist, a request for information regarding every aspect of the seller's business about which the purchaser requires knowledge (material contracts, actual or threatened litigation, tax assessments, environmental liabilities, intellectual property matters, details of collective bargaining agreements with unions, pension plan information, leases, guarantees, loan agreements, intellectual property, and so forth). In any acquisition of a public company, it is normal for the seller to make available this type of information in a "war room" for all potential purchasers. Even in a private transaction, the seller will commonly try to make available all relevant information in a given place at a particular time so that the purchaser and its lawyer can review all pertinent documentation, yet the transaction can remain confidential.

5.5 Legal Opinions

Although legal opinions are sometimes only focused upon in the last few days prior to the closing of the transaction, they tend to be fairly heavily negotiated by Canadian counsel and are seldom given low priority. It is fairly common practice to negotiate the form of legal opinion as a schedule to the principal agreement (be it a financing or an acquisition) prior to the execution of the documentation.

Although many major law firms in Canada agree on certain fundamental opinion issues, legal opinions seldom look the same from one firm to another. There are certain common threads: few law firms will (i) opine that there is no breach of any agreement by which a corporation is bound (other than the principal agreement that is the subject of the transaction), (ii) give priority opinions with respect to security, or (iii) give opinions on the beneficial ownership of shares or title to other assets. Qualifications in Canadian opinions are relatively standard among Canadian law firms, but some of the qualifications may appear unusual to foreign counsel.

5.6 Anticipation of Future Problems

Although Canadian lawyers will attempt to protect their clients through representations, warranties, and indemnities from the other party against all future liabilities and contingencies, Canadian agreements sometimes tend toward more brevity in this area than U.S. agreements. Most Canadian acquisition agreements will provide that the representations and warranties survive for a period of at least eighteen months and that tax representations and warranties survive for the relevant limitation period under the taxation statutes. It is relatively uncommon for a seller to secure its indemnities with letters of credit, although it is not uncommon to provide for a holdback of the purchase price, sometimes for up to two years, pending the potential emergence of undisclosed or unanticipated liabilities. Payment of the purchase through earn-out clauses is also not uncommon, and negotiations of caps and floors on the indemnification provisions are usual.

5.7 Clauses Requiring Submission to Jurisdiction and Choice of Law

Where an agreement contains a clause that all disputes will be heard exclusively in the courts of a foreign jurisdiction, it is not certain that an Ontario court (or a court in another common law province of Canada) would decline to take jurisdiction over the action. Conversely, if the parties attorn exclusively to Ontario as the jurisdiction where disputes will be heard, it is unlikely that an Ontario court would decline jurisdiction when the agreement is governed by Ontario law, the parties are sophisticated, and there are no public policy concerns. This is a matter of the court's discretion, although the court will consider the exclusive attornment to a foreign jurisdiction as giving it grounds to decline jurisdiction.

A clause whereby a party submits to the jurisdiction of the Ontario courts, whether or not exclusively, is sufficient to give an Ontario court jurisdiction to hear the matter, notwithstanding that the defendant is not resident in Ontario and has not attorned yet to the jurisdiction in the particular matter. A nonexclusive submission to jurisdiction clause will be enforceable as it inherently recognizes that an Ontario court may decline jurisdiction even if it is selected or that it may accept jurisdiction even if a foreign jurisdiction is selected.

5.8 Online Contract Issues

The federal and provincial legislation relating to the electronic transactions and electronic commerce is by and large consistent in its treatment of the enforceability and formation of online contracts. Legislation governing electronic transactions and electronic commerce has been enacted in most provinces and territories of Canada. Except for Quebec, provincial electronic commerce legislation is largely modeled on the Uniform Electronic Commerce Act (Uniform Act), adopted by the Uniform Law Conference of Canada. The Uniform Act was designed to provide provinces with consistent legislation that implemented the principles of the United Nations Commission on International Trade Law (UNCITRAL) Model Law on Electronic Commerce, adopted by the General Assembly of the United Nations in 1996.

The provincial electronic commerce legislation provides for the legal recognition of information and documents, including contracts, that are communicated electronically. The legislation imposes a "media neutral" approach, recognizing electronic communications, documents, contracts, and signatures as functionally equivalent to their written or printed counterparts.

While the provincial electronic commerce legislation provides for the legal enforceability of electronic contracts, it is necessary to ensure that the electronic offer and acceptance process results in an enforceable contract. Case law has established that both "click-wrap" agreements and "Web-wrap" agreements may create binding contracts in Canada.

While both the legislative and judicial approach tend to enforce the terms of electronic contracts in general, it should be noted that the actual enforcement of any given electronic contract is ultimately a question of fact that requires careful consideration.

5.9 Electronic Signatures

A signature indicates intent to be bound by the terms of an agreement. Although a signature is not necessary to create a binding agreement enforceable against the parties, legislative signature requirements exist for certain prescribed types of agreements. The provincial electronic commerce legislation provides that electronic signatures can have the functional equivalence of their paper counterparts.

The federal Personal Information Protection and Electronic Documents Act (PIPEDA) and provincial electronic commerce legislation generally provides that electronic signatures will satisfy statutory signature requirements. Clicking an icon may also meet the definition of an electronic signature, though no Canadian court has yet considered that point.

5.10 Online Consumer Protection Legislation

Consumer protection in Canada is governed by an array of federal and provincial laws regulating a wide range of commercial activity. Many industries have specific provincial consumer protection legislation mandating registration or licensing. Many provinces also have consumer practices and trade practices legislation regulating marketing and commercial sales. In addition, provincial sale of goods legislation (except in Quebec) implies certain warranties and conditions in commercial agreements such as the implied conditions that a sold good is fit for its intended purpose and that the good is of merchantable quality. Parties may expressly contract out of these implied warranties and conditions.

Most provinces have enacted legislation specifically to provide protection to consumers transacting online by extending consumer protection laws to online consumer contracts. Under these regulations, online retailers entering into Internet agreements are now required to disclose certain information and must provide the consumer with an express opportunity to accept, decline, or make corrections to the agreement, and must provide a written copy of the agreement within fifteen days depending on the province.

In addition, consumer protection legislation in most provinces permits consumers to repudiate executory contracts during an established "cooling-off" period. Many of the provincial acts also contain provisions for the "functional equivalence" of writing and signatures to satisfy requirements in the context of electronic commerce.

6. Resolving Disputes

It is becoming increasingly common in Canada to provide for arbitration and alternative dispute resolution mechanisms in commercial transactions, where the parties will be dealing with one another for an extended period. It is, however, relatively rare to find these in asset or share acquisition agreements or in loan agreements where a Canadian bank (including the Canadian subsidiary of a foreign bank) is providing funds for a cross-border transaction.

In 1986, Canada and the provinces enacted legislation to incorporate the Convention on the Recognition and Enforcement of Foreign Arbitral Awards, as adopted by the United Nations Conference on International Commercial Arbitration in New York on June 10, 1958 (referred to internationally as the New York Convention). The model law on international commercial arbitration as adopted by UNCITRAL in 1985 was also adopted by Canada and the provinces, and legislation has also been adopted to incorporate its provisions. Canada's participation in these conventions reflects the growing concern that parties involved in international business transactions should not leave the resolution of their disputes to foreign courts and foreign legal systems.

Canadian courts are generally loath to interfere with the arbitration process in the absence of any clear and compelling prejudice. The courts view commercial arbitration as essentially a private matter and will respect the intention of the parties unless the arbitration agreement is null and void or incapable of being performed. For example, an arbitration award may be reviewed and set aside by a court under the Model Code where a party is under some incapacity, or where proper notice of the appointment of an arbitrator was not given, or where the award deals with a dispute not contemplated by the terms of the submission to arbitrate.

7. Conclusion

The negotiation of business transactions in Canada involves many of the same procedures and similar regulatory issues that one might encounter in negotiating a business transaction in the United States. As in other jurisdictions, the complexity of the transaction and the degree to which regulatory approvals are required will generally dictate the time frame within which the transaction can be completed and the level of costs that will be incurred. On balance, dealings between the parties tend to be fairly straightforward and are generally concluded in good faith and with North American–style efficiency.

Alison J. Youngman
Stikeman Elliott LLP
5300 Commerce Court West, 199 Bay Street
Toronto, ON M5L 1B9
Canada
Phone: (416) 869-5684
Fax: (416) 947-0866
E-mail: ayoungman@stikeman.com

CHAPTER 25

International Business Negotiations in the Cayman Islands

Sara Galletly and Alasdair Robertson
MAPLES AND CALDER
CAYMAN ISLANDS

1. Introduction

1.1 Geographical and Demographic Information

The Cayman Islands are a group of three islands, Grand Cayman, Cayman Brac, and Little Cayman, located in the western Caribbean 475 miles south of Miami, Florida (just one hour's flight from Miami and less than four hours' flight from New York). The capital, George Town, is located on Grand Cayman and is the government, business, and financial center.

The Cayman Islands have a tropical climate with an average summer temperature of 83°F (28°C) and average winter temperature of 79°F (26°C). In 2007, rainfall totaled 1337.9 millimeters (53.11 inches), with an average humidity of 77 percent.

The Cayman Islands have a population of approximately 53,172 (as of the end of 2006), which is concentrated on the island of Grand Cayman and comprises a mixture of Cayman nationals and non-Caymanians admitted to the Islands under a work-permit system.

1.2 Historical and Cultural Background

Christopher Columbus first glimpsed two of the Cayman Islands (Cayman Brac and Little Cayman) in 1503, which he named "Las Tortugas" after the abundant turtle population. Sir Francis Drake gave the Islands their current name in 1586, which was derived from the Carib Indian word "caiman" for the marine crocodiles that inhabited the Islands at that time.

The Cayman Islands are politically and economically stable. The Islands have a substantial, invisible trade surplus with the outside world, largely as a result of tourism and financial services. Unemployment is low and the standard of living is one of the highest in the Caribbean.

The official and spoken language is English, although an increasing number of residents, mostly workers from Central and Latin America, also speak Spanish.

The currency of the Islands is the Cayman dollar, which is tied to the U.S. dollar at CI$1.00 = US$1.20.

1.3 Government

The Cayman Islands are a British Overseas Territory and as such are the responsibility of the British government in London. However, for all practical purposes, the Islands are governed under a constitution that gives executive and legislative power to a governor, an executive council, and a legislative assembly.

The governor is appointed by the British government and has overall responsibility for the administration of the Islands. Government policy is made by an executive council (the Cabinet) consisting of the governor, three senior civil servants (chief secretary, attorney general, and financial secretary), and five ministers, who are elected members of the legislative assembly appointed by their fellow members. The legislative assembly consists of eighteen members, three of whom are official appointees and fifteen of whom are the elected representatives of the Islands' six districts. General elections are held every four years.

The Cayman Islands are entirely responsible for passing their own laws, and the British government would only intervene in an emergency. Legislation is approved by the Cabinet but must be passed by the legislative assembly.

The Cayman Islands enjoy stable government and there is no desire for independence from Britain, making the Cayman Islands a low sovereign risk jurisdiction. The Cayman Islands have a sovereign rating of Aaa from Moody's Investors Service Inc.

1.4 Business Organization and Culture

Modern laws have made the Cayman Islands one of the world's leading offshore financial centers for banking, mutual funds, insurance companies, capital markets issuers, structured financings, project financings, company registrations, trusts, and partnerships. The government works with the private sector to maintain and increase the Islands' attractiveness; local laws continue to be amended and modernized to meet market demand.

At least 277 supervised banks, 1,159 trust companies, and 788 insurance companies are currently licensed in the Cayman Islands, most of which operate offshore. Over 83,500 companies are currently registered and thousands of private trusts and partnerships have been established. Approximately 9,861 registered, administered, and licensed mutual funds are currently registered and 155 mutual fund administrators are licensed.

Because of the position of the Cayman Islands as a leading international offshore financial center, the Cayman Islands have attracted professionals, including attorneys, accountants, insurance managers, and investment bankers, from leading commercial jurisdictions who have trained and worked in the leading onshore firms. As a result of this, business and culture in Cayman are comparable to that in cities such as London and New York.

1.5 Overview of Legal System

The substantive law of the Cayman Islands is based on English common law with the addition of local statutes that have in many respects changed and modernized the common law. The fact that the Cayman Islands' legal system is based on English law gives the Cayman Islands laws and legal system a common origin with those of many of the jurisdictions of its users, including the United States.

The Cayman Islands' legal system is flexible and has in the past been responsive to onshore concerns by introducing innovative legislation (such as in relation to the creation of "segregated portfolio" companies to manage cross-liability concerns in multi-issue vehicles). The introduction of such legislation has enabled transactions to be undertaken with increased efficiencies benefiting those arranging structures and producing increased returns for investors.

The courts system in the Cayman Islands is a simple one, and practice and procedure are based on English law. Minor criminal and civil cases are tried by a stipendiary magistrate sitting in the summary court. All serious crimes and most civil cases are tried by the grand court, which is presided over by the chief justice and grand court judges permanently resident in the Islands. Appeals lie from the grand court to the Cayman Islands court of appeal, which sits in Grand Cayman, and from there to the judicial committee of the privy council in England.

The grand court is a court of universal jurisdiction and is not formally divided into separate divisions. The grand court in practice follows English case law absent local case or statutory authority to the contrary, although Commonwealth authorities are also often cited to the court.

2. Legal Professionals and the Cayman Islands

Following the success of the Cayman Islands as an offshore financial center, onshore attorneys located across the world have become routinely involved in transactions involving a Cayman Islands entity or asset. Any such transaction will require the retention of a firm of

Cayman Islands attorneys, who will provide legal advice as to the Cayman Islands law aspects of that transaction.

This chapter begins by providing an insight into the areas of Cayman Islands law that are most commonly seen in international transactions involving onshore counsel. It is intended to provide an introduction to such topics and to highlight areas where queries frequently arise because of differences in the requirements and practices of separate jurisdictions. This guide provides a brief introduction to the most common areas of international business conducted with Cayman entities, and then provides an overview of how international business transactions are conducted in the Cayman Islands, describing in particular the roles of the onshore and offshore attorneys involved. This chapter will not focus on areas of Cayman Islands law that are applicable to persons wishing to conduct business in Cayman rather than there being a Cayman entity or asset as part of a cross-border international structure, such as formation of contracts between Cayman Islands entities or licensing requirements for entities conducting business in Cayman.

The summary of topics relevant to the subject of conducting international business transactions in and through the Cayman Islands provided in this guide is not intended to be a substitute for specific legal advice.

3. Dominant Practice Areas

The most active practice areas involving Cayman Islands offshore structures can be divided broadly into investment funds, structured finance (including capital markets and asset and project finance), general corporate and commercial work, and litigation. The first three of these areas are considered in more detail below.

3.1 Investment Funds

The Cayman Islands have become the recognized market leader for the incorporation of investment funds. The investment funds are predominantly hedge funds and private equity funds that are managed by well-known fund managers and investment banks based around the world and in which sophisticated and high-net-worth investors (including pension funds, insurance companies, and university endowment funds) invest in order to place a part of their portfolio in a variety of "alternative investment strategies." There is no clear exhaustive definition of an "alternative investment" strategy. In referring to this term, fund managers and investors are usually describing something other than a traditional mutual fund that has a long-term only basis in stocks or bonds.

A common definition of a hedge fund is an investment fund where, usually, a hedge fund manager actively trades a large portfolio of mostly liquid securities (including stocks, bonds, options, and futures) within the parameters of the fund's investment objectives, which will be described in the hedge fund's offering documents.

The term "private equity fund" is commonly taken to mean a closed-ended investment fund that focuses on a strategy of making control-oriented or significant minority investments in privately held companies ("portfolio companies"), with strategies including venture capital (tending to focus on investments in early-stage or start-up companies), management buyouts, and leveraged buyouts. A private equity fund will not commonly have an actively traded portfolio.

In many cases, hedge fund and private equity fund managers will upon the advice of their onshore legal counsel use companies and/or limited partnerships in the Cayman Islands as part of their investment fund platforms.

3.2 Structured Finance

Cayman Islands entities are used for a range of structured finance and capital market products. Investors worldwide purchase instruments issued by Cayman Islands entities. These include sovereigns, quasi-governmental bodies, pension funds, and the usual financial market players such as hedge funds and issuers of securities listed on the global stock markets, such as NYSE, NASDAQ, and the London Stock Exchange. Instruments issued by Cayman Islands entities are regularly traded on the largest stock exchanges of the world. As part of these transactions, Cayman Islands companies acquire assets of many different types—for example, loans, bonds, derivatives, commodities, lease receivables, credit card receivables, project finance receivables, aircraft, ships, and other assets, which may be situated all over the world.

The types of transactions undertaken in the Cayman Islands include securitizations, collateralized debt obligation transactions, credit-linked transactions such as credit derivatives and credit-linked notes, structured and derivative products, catastrophe bonds and other alternative risk transfer products, aircraft finance, and finance subsidiaries.

3.3 Corporate Vehicles

Cayman Islands entities are also used in a range of corporate and commercial transactions. These include companies listed on the NYSE, NASDAQ, London, Hong Kong, and other leading equity exchanges; companies set up to hold particular projects and/or assets; vehicles set up as joint ventures; and vehicles set up to attract management investment in and particular companies/ventures operating in jurisdictions outside of the major financial markets, in particular Asia and South America. Some key attractions of Cayman vehicles are a familiar legal system; professional advisers including lawyers who are able to respond knowledgeably and responsively; flexible structures to enable efficient dissolution and cash flow; and a valid perception as a creditor-friendly jurisdiction that makes it easy for security to be taken over assets to secure borrowings.

4. Substantive Laws and Regulations Impacting Negotiations

4.1 Choice of Vehicle

A common question facing onshore attorneys structuring a transaction involving a Cayman Islands entity is which type of entity should be used. The choice is similar to that in the United States, the United Kingdom, and many other Commonwealth jurisdictions, where parties can choose from a corporate entity, a partnership, or certain trust structures. The core characteristics of these entities are set out below, together with explanations of certain recurring questions seen by Cayman Islands attorneys.

5. Cayman Islands Companies

5.1 General

The Cayman Islands have a modern Companies Law (the Companies Law (2007 Revision)), originally enacted in 1961 and subsequently amended, that permits company incorporation by the registration system. Pursuant to the Companies Law and the Local Companies (Control) Law (2007 Revision), there are three basic types of company capable of registration: the ordinary company, the ordinary nonresident company, and the exempted company.

Exempted companies are the corporate vehicle most commonly used for structured finance, capital markets, and other international corporate transactions. Although exempted companies are incorporated in, and have a legal presence in, the Cayman Islands, the day-to-day business activities of such entities are carried out overseas. This chapter will not focus on ordinary companies that conduct their business in the Cayman Islands.

5.2 Exempted Companies

Exempted companies may not:

    i.   carry on business in the Cayman Islands except in furtherance of their business abroad;

    ii. make any invitation to the public in the Cayman Islands to subscribe for any of its shares or debentures unless they are listed on the Cayman Islands Stock Exchange; or

    iii. own land in the Cayman Islands (including an interest in land pursuant to a lease) unless given specific permission by the financial secretary.

Foreign companies may register branches to do business in the Cayman Islands and may also transfer by way of continuation to the Cayman Islands and thus become exempted companies.

The usual corporate vehicle is the company limited by shares, although the Companies Law also permits the incorporation of a company limited by guarantee (with or without share capital), an unlimited company, or certain hybrid companies.

5.3 Incorporation

Incorporation occurs upon the filing with the Registrar of Companies in the Cayman Islands of a memorandum of association containing certain required information, which is subscribed to by one or more persons.

The incorporation and registration process is swift and simple, and can be expedited to take place in a day in matters of urgency. The cost of incorporation of a Cayman company is relatively low, particularly in the context of typical transaction sizes.

5.4 Name

No company may be registered with the words "building society" in the name, and certain names may only be registered with the consent of the Registrar of Companies in the Cayman Islands. These include names containing the words "royal," "Imperial," "empire," "municipal," "chartered," "co-operative," "assurance," "insurance," and "bank."

5.5 Registered Office

Every Cayman Islands company is obliged to maintain a registered office in the Cayman Islands, similar to the requirement imposed on a Delaware company to maintain a registered office and a registered agent in Delaware. Apart from acting as the office at which the Cayman Islands company can be served with any documents arising from any legal proceedings, the activities that are conducted at the registered office of a Cayman Islands company are basic legal compliance functions required by the Companies Law (e.g., to maintain a register of directors and a register of security interests, as discussed below).

The day-to-day business activities of an exempted Cayman Islands company are not carried out at the registered office. For example, a Cayman Islands investment fund conducts its business activities by delegating those functions to various service providers (e.g., an investment manager, administrator, prime broker, etc.) who carry out the business of the investment fund from their usual business offices in other locations.

5.6 Powers and Capacity

Unless the memorandum of association of a company expressly restricts the powers of a company to certain objects stated therein, a Cayman Islands company has the power to carry out any legal object. It also has the power to exercise all the functions of a natural person irrespective of corporate benefit. No act of or disposition to or by a company is invalid merely because the company had no relevant power or capacity, but this does not preclude injunctive relief prior to the act or disposition or a subsequent action against the relevant directors or officers for loss arising out of their unauthorized act.

5.7 Records and Accounts

Certain records must be maintained by a Cayman Islands company, such as a register of members of the company, although this may be held outside the Cayman Islands and is not open to inspection by third parties. A company must have a registered office in the Cayman Islands, and both a register of directors and officers and a register of mortgages and charges must be kept at the registered office. The register of directors and officers is not open to public inspection, but the register of mortgages and charges may be inspected by any creditor or member of the company.

The Companies Law requires that every company shall update and maintain books of accounts as are necessary to give a true and fair view of the state of the company's affairs and explain its transactions. However, there is no statutory requirement that such accounts be audited, nor is there any requirement for the filing of annual accounts with any government organization. It is normal to provide in the articles of association that the company may appoint auditors and have its accounts audited.

Where a company is in possession of a bank or trust license, an insurer's license, a companies management license, or a mutual fund administrator's license, or is a regulated mutual fund, then such company under the relevant Cayman Islands statute must have its accounts audited annually and must file a set of such audited accounts each year with the Cayman Islands Monetary Authority (the "Monetary Authority").

5.8 Directors

There is no requirement that any of the directors be resident in the Cayman Islands, although this may be desirable in order to obtain a particular tax treatment under the tax regimes of other jurisdictions.

Provisions relating to the number of directors, shareholding qualifications, period of office, meetings, and powers, etc., are usually contained in the articles of association of the relevant company. There is no prescribed statutory requirement.

Directors are under a duty to act in good faith and in the best interests of the company in question. In certain circumstances, these obligations can extend to creditors of the company. Personal liability can result from failure to meet the required standards.

It is good corporate practice for the directors of a Cayman Islands company to meet and consider any business proposed to be conducted by the company and, if appropriate, to then approve such business. The business of directors is usually transacted by written resolution, which all directors appointed must sign, or by convening a board meeting in accordance with the articles of association of the company, the business transacted at which is recorded in a minute of the meeting.

5.9 Share Capital

Cayman Islands law does not specify any minimum issued or paid-up capital, except that to complete the incorporation formalities, the memorandum of association must be subscribed to by one or more persons; i.e., a company must have a shareholder.

Shares may be of any par value and the par value may be expressed in any one or more currencies. Any company limited by shares may, if authorized by its articles of association, issue fractional shares. The share capital may be divided into classes of shares with such rights as to voting, participating in profits and return of capital as the company may be authorized to issue by its articles of association—and usually the articles are very permissive, to facilitate the conduct of business that was not anticipated on incorporation.

Dividends and distributions may be paid out of share premium (being the funds received on the subscription for shares in excess of the nominal or par value) or distributable profits, subject to the company being solvent and its articles of association. A company may also redeem or purchase its own shares.

5.9.1 Bearer Shares

Unlike other jurisdictions, the Cayman Islands does not permit companies to issue bearer shares unless they are deposited with a recognized custodian. This includes depositories of the major clearing systems such as DTC, Euroclear, and Clearstream.

5.9.2 Transactions Involving Security over Shares in Cayman Islands Companies

The documentation governing such security interests can be governed by laws other than the laws of the Cayman Islands, such as New York law. However, where the register of shareholders of the company is maintained in the Cayman Islands—i.e., the situs of the shares is determined by the location of the register—lenders taking such security will often have the security document governed by Cayman Islands law.

The following text seeks to provide a brief explanation of how the grant of a security interest over shares in a Cayman company is achieved under Cayman Islands law.

a. Security may be granted over shares in a Cayman company in a number of ways. The most comprehensive method is to secure the shares by way of legal mortgage, which involves a transfer of ownership of the shares upon the express or implied condition that ownership will be retransferred to the debtor upon the discharge of the secured obligations. However, this method is not used frequently, as it is rarely part of the commercial agreement that the debtor will transfer legal ownership of the shares prior to an event of default. It is more common for shares to be secured by way of an equitable mortgage, where legal ownership is not transferred and voting rights and rights to dividends are retained by the debtor, subject to the right of the chargee to call for the transfer of the shares into the chargee's name upon default.

b. It is common for the constitutional documents of a Cayman Islands company to provide the directors of the company with a discretion to refuse to register transfers of shares. It is in the interests of the beneficiary of the security interest to insist upon the removal or amendment of such provision, which will require a special resolution of the shareholders amending the constitutional documents of the Company. If required, this measure should be implemented at the same time as the security interest is granted. The alternative is to have the Cayman Islands company be party to a tripartite deed whereby the company agrees with the beneficiary of the security interest that it will, upon a default, consent to the transfer.

c. The register of shareholders of a Cayman company provides prima facie evidence of the legal ownership of registered shares in the Cayman Islands. No purported transfer of any shares (by way of security or otherwise) is effective until the register of shareholders is updated by the company. Share certificates issued by a Cayman company are only evidence of title to the relevant shares and do not in any way confer ownership of those shares.

5.10 Segregated Portfolio Companies

The Companies Law of the Cayman Islands permits, within a single company, the segregation of assets and liabilities amongst various "portfolios" in a way that binds third parties as a matter of Cayman Islands law.

A segregated portfolio company, or SPC, is a company that is permitted to create one or more segregated portfolios in order to segregate the assets and liabilities of the company held within or on behalf of a portfolio from the assets and liabilities of the company held within or on behalf of any other segregated portfolio of the company, or the assets and liabilities of the company that are not held within or on behalf of any segregated portfolio of the company (called the general assets of the company). The segregation of assets and liabilities within portfolios does not create any new legal entity: the SPC is and remains a single legal entity and any segregated portfolio of, or within, an SPC does not constitute a legal entity separate from the SPC itself. This means, for example, that one portfolio cannot hold shares in another portfolio.

An SPC must include "SPC" or the words "Segregated Portfolio Company" in its name. It is a duty of the directors of an SPC to establish and maintain procedures to segregate, and keep segregated, portfolio assets separate and separately identifiable from general assets; to segregate, and keep segregated, portfolio assets of each segregated portfolio separate and separately identifiable from segregated portfolio assets of any other segregated portfolio; and to ensure that assets and liabilities are not transferred between segregated portfolios otherwise than at full value. Particular care should be taken by the directors to ensure that where they have delegated the management or administration of the SPC or any of its segregated portfolios that such delegates are aware of the required procedures and act in compliance with such procedures.

Any act, matter, deed, agreement, contract, instrument under seal, or other instrument or arrangement that is to be binding on or to benefit a segregated portfolio must be executed by or on behalf of the directors of the SPC and on behalf of the relevant segregated portfolio. Specific advice should be taken as to how best to word such documents, particularly where they relate to more than one segregated portfolio within the SPC. If there is a breach of the requirement that an SPC contracts for and on behalf of a segregated portfolio (where that was the intention), the directors incur personal liability for the liabilities of the SPC and the segregated portfolio.

5.11 Partnerships and Limited Partnerships

The Cayman Islands have both ordinary partnerships, where the liability of the partners is unlimited, and limited partnerships, where the liability of the limited partners is limited to their capital commitment, provided that they are not involved in the management of the limited partnership. A partnership, whether limited or not, should be created by written agreement or deed. Ordinary partnerships are not commonly used in international transactions and, accordingly, are not described in any further detail in this guide.

A limited partnership is the combination of one or more partners whose liability for the liability of the partnership is unlimited (the general partners) together with one or more partners whose liability is limited in amount (the limited partners). The right to take part in the management of the affairs of the partnership is strictly confined to the general partners, and the limited partners have no control over the assets or affairs of the partnership.

The most common form of Cayman Islands limited partnership is the exempted limited partnership where, as with the exempted company, the partnership must not do business with the public in the Cayman Islands except in furtherance of its business outside the Cayman Islands.

5.12 Exempted Limited Partnerships

5.12.1 General

The Exempted Limited Partnership Law (2007 Revision) of the Cayman Islands maintains the English common law principle that a partnership, including an exempted limited partnership, is not a separate legal person. In all practical respects, however, the administrative ease and flexibility of the corporate form is provided, with the result that a limited partner of an exempted limited partnership stands in most respects (but notably not in respect of confidentiality) in a similar position to a shareholder in a Cayman Islands exempted company.

The Exempted Limited Partnership Law provides a simple statutory framework that allows limited liability for certain partners, based upon the Delaware limited partnership legislation. To the extent that an issue is not addressed by the Law, general principles of partnership and contract law apply.

5.12.2 Formation

There are no cumbersome official filing and publication requirements to establish an exempted limited partnership, or as a precondition to any effective change in filed information. Formation is by entry into a partnership agreement and an uncomplicated registration with the Registrar of Exempted Limited Partnerships in the Cayman Islands of a statement signed by a general partner, containing certain information such as name, term, and general nature of the business to be conducted, and including a declaration that the partnership will not do business with the public in the Cayman Islands except in furtherance of its business outside the Cayman Islands, which is required to confer the limited liability status of the limited partners. This statement is available to public inspection.

5.12.3 Name

The name of an exempted limited partnership must contain the words "Limited Partnership" or "L.P."

5.12.4 Registered Office and Records

An exempted limited partnership must maintain a registered office in the Cayman Islands.

A list of limited partners together with their contributions must be maintained at the registered office by the general partner together with a register of mortgages describing the charges granted by a limited partner over his limited partnership interest, if any, which latter register governs priority. This information is open to public inspection.

5.12.5 General Partner

At least one general partner must be an individual resident in the Cayman Islands, a company incorporated in the Cayman Islands or, if a foreign company, registered as such pursuant to the Companies law of the Cayman Islands; or, if a partnership, an exempted limited partnership. As a result of the latter requirements, a limited partnership such as a Delaware limited partnership cannot be the sole general partner of a Cayman Islands exempted limited partnership. Otherwise, however, a limited or unlimited liability company, including a Delaware LLC, or a Cayman Islands general or limited partnership may be a general or limited partner in an exempted limited partnership.

There is no restriction on the type of person who can be a limited partner in a Cayman Islands exempted limited partnership.

A general partner must act at all times in good faith in the interests of the exempted limited partnership.

5.12.6 Limited Partners

A limited partner must not take part in the conduct of the business of the exempted limited partnership. However, on terms similar to Delaware law, there are specified actions in the relevant statute that a limited partner may undertake without running the risk of taking part in the conduct of the business of the exempted limited partnership and thus being treated as a general partner (with unlimited liability).

A limited partner may, with the consent of the general partner, transfer or mortgage his interest in the exempted limited partnership and may receive a return of his contribution, subject to the partnership being solvent.

5.12.7 Assignment of Limited Partnership Interests and Dissolution

The general partner has the statutory right to refuse to consent to the assignment of a limited partnership interest, and the exempted limited partnership is similarly automatically dissolved upon the death, dissolution, or removal of the sole surviving general partner.

5.12.8 Limited Partnership Agreements

Where an exempted limited partnership is established as the offshore vehicle in an investment fund or structured finance transaction, the partnership is usually established ahead of close using a very short-form initial limited partnership agreement. On close of the transaction, this agreement is amended and restated and a more substantial document tailored to the particular transaction is adopted. The limited partnership agreement usually contains the commercial terms upon which limited partners are to invest, including the circumstances in which they may receive returns of capital, and are often drafted by onshore counsel. In such circumstances, Cayman counsel review the draft document and ensure that the provisions do not contravene Cayman law in any way. There are a number of common practice questions that arise in such a situation, including the following:

a. In order for an exempted limited partnership to be established and maintained as an exempted limited partnership, the governing law of the partnership agreement must be Cayman Islands law.

b. "As of" prior dating is ineffective in a document governed by Cayman Islands law; the document is effective from the date on which it is executed and delivered by all the parties to it.

c. Cayman Islands law does not recognize third-party beneficiaries to a contract, so persons who are not parties to a partnership agreement may not enforce the agreement or have it enforced against them. This relates in particular to purported indemnitees in a partnership agreement and members of investment or advisory committees who are not partners. It is, however, possible for a party to hold the benefit of an indemnity in a bare trust for a third party.

d. If a limited partner is to be admitted to an exempted limited partnership following the initial closing, that person cannot become a party to the relevant partnership agreement merely by signing a copy of it. All parties must sign a new agreement in order for a partnership agreement to be made between all relevant parties, i.e., the general partner, the existing limited partners, and the incoming limited partner(s). The usual procedure for admitting additional limited partners to an exempted limited partnership is for those limited partners to sign a subscription agreement with the general partner in its personal capacity and as attorney for the existing limited partners (under a power of attorney contained in the original limited partnership agreement itself) and covenant that it will comply with the terms of the partnership agreement as if set out in the subscription agreement. The partnership agreement should be annexed to each subscription agreement. As a result, the general partner, the existing limited partners, and the incoming limited partners will be parties to a new, binding agreement amongst them all. The subscription agreement should also contain a power of attorney from an incoming limited partner allowing the general partner to sign similar subsequent subscription agreements on behalf of the incoming limited partner.

e. There is no need under Cayman Islands law to update a partnership agreement, whether by schedule or otherwise, to show additional admissions or partnership contributions.

f. To the extent that any provision of a partnership agreement is construed as penal, it will not be enforceable under Cayman Islands law. This is of particular significance for default provisions on nonpayment of capital contribution installments.

5.12.9 Trusts

The trust law of the Cayman Islands is derived from the English law of trusts but is subject to somewhat different statutory modifications.

The Trusts (Foreign Element) Law, 1987 (now incorporated in the Trusts Law) addresses various conflict of law difficulties as they relate to trusts. First, it has strengthened the validity and recognition of the selection of Cayman Islands law as the proper law governing Cayman Islands trusts and matters relating to that. Second, it gives statutory recognition to the concept of importation of trusts to and exportation of trusts from the Cayman Islands and a resultant change of governing law. Third, it provides that questions as to matters such as the capacity of a settlor and the validity and administration of a trust are to be determined solely according to the laws of the Cayman Islands, if selected as the governing law. Fourth, it prohibits the avoidance of, or the enforcement of a foreign judgment with respect to, a Cayman Islands trust on the basis that it contravenes foreign forced heirship or similar laws or because the trust concept is not recognized in a particular foreign jurisdiction.

The Fraudulent Dispositions Law strengthens the integrity of a Cayman Islands trust and, in the absence of a Cayman Islands bankruptcy of the settlor, will protect it against successful attack by future creditors of the settlor. It contains a six-year limitation period with respect to a fraudulent transfer.

The Perpetuities Law came into effect on August 1, 1995 and for new trusts abolished the old common law rule that invalidated any disposition unless it vested within a period of lives in being plus twenty-one years and introduced a new perpetuity period of 150 years. The Perpetuities Law also introduced a new "wait and see" rule whereby a disposition (or power) will only fail if it falls outside the new perpetuity period.

The Trusts (Amendment) (Immediate Effect and Reserved Powers) Law, 1998 (now incorporated in the Trusts Law) strengthens the valid creation and integrity of inter vivos trusts, where powers are reserved to the settlor, against challenge as testamentary dispositions and shams.

Under the Special Trust Alternative Regime (STAR) contained in Part VIII of the Trusts Law, pure purpose and mixed purpose/private trusts are now permitted. Under STAR, a third-party enforcer must be appointed. Charitable purpose and private trusts may have unlimited duration.

A variety of structures are available to settlors (or grantors), including traditional discretionary trusts for individual beneficiaries or classes of beneficiaries, non–charitable purpose trusts, STAR trusts, and unit trusts.

In common with most trust jurisdictions whose law is derived from that of England, Cayman Islands law does not regard a trust governed by that law as having separate legal personality or as able to contract by itself. The trustee of the trust is the only possible contracting party and trustees have substantial duties under Cayman Islands law, with the primary obligation being to administer the trust with diligence and good faith in accordance with the terms of the trust deed, for the benefit of the beneficiaries of the trust.

6. Legal Framework

6.1 Securities Laws

6.1.1 Sale of Securities in the Cayman Islands

An exempted Cayman Islands entity (including an exempted company and an exempted limited partnership) is prohibited from making any invitation to the public in the Cayman Islands to subscribe for its shares or interests (as the case may be) unless, in the case of an exempted company, the shares of that company are listed on the Cayman Islands Stock Exchange. One practical implication of this is that any prospectus or offering document issued by an exempted Cayman Islands entity should contain appropriate wording to the effect that the public in the Cayman Islands is not invited to subscribe for the relevant securities.

It should be noted that the definition of "public" in the Cayman Islands does not extend to Cayman Islands exempted companies, exempted limited partnerships, or exempted and other offshore trusts that are themselves engaged in offshore business; so, for example, one exempted Cayman Islands company may subscribe for securities issued by another exempted Cayman Islands company.

6.1.2 Securities Investment Business

The Securities Investment Business Law (2004 Revision) of the Cayman Islands ("SIBL") sets out a framework for the Monetary Authority to regulate securities investment business in the Cayman Islands. Any person conducting securities investment business must be licensed by the Monetary Authority unless that person is exempt from holding a license. A person who carries on securities investment business and who is exempt from obtaining a license may still be subject to registration under SIBL (which means that they are required to make an annual filing with the Monetary Authority).

SIBL applies to any entity that is established in the Cayman Islands or registered in the Cayman Islands (in the case of a foreign company) carrying on securities investment business (whether or not that securities investment business is carried on in the Cayman Islands).

"Securities investment business" includes activities such as dealing in securities, managing securities belonging to others on a discretionary basis, and advising in relation to securities (but only if the advice is given to someone in his or her capacity as investor or potential investor and the advice is on the merits of that person buying, selling, subscribing for, or underwriting a security).

"Securities" are defined to include most forms of shares and stock, debt instruments, options, futures, contracts for differences, and derivatives.

A license under SIBL may not be required if either (i) the activities to be undertaken are excluded under SIBL (excluded activities) or (ii) the person carrying on the securities investment business is exempt from the requirement to obtain a license (excluded persons).

6.2 Mutual Funds

A significant number of investment funds have been established in the Cayman Islands and many of the banks and trust companies, together with specialist mutual fund administrators, located in the Cayman Islands offer a full range of management services to mutual funds. Such funds may be established as open- or closed-ended companies, unit trusts, or partnerships. Open-ended investment funds make use of redeemable shares, partnership interests, or units.

One of the main reasons why the Cayman Islands has appealed to hedge fund managers is that the Mutual Funds Law (2007 Revision) of the Cayman Islands does not impose restrictions on the fund's investment objectives, rates of return, or other commercial matters. The basis of the regulation under the Mutual Funds Law is that, provided that the fund makes proper disclosure in its offering documents as to its investment objectives and restrictions and the persons responsible for operating the fund, investors should be free to make their own determination as to whether or not to invest in any particular fund or strategy.

Open-ended companies, trusts, or partnerships established to operate as investment or mutual funds with more than fifteen investors are required to register with the Monetary Authority. Such funds must prepare and file an offering document (and any amendments) and register with the Monetary Authority and file annual audited accounts. In addition, such fund must either specifically be licensed as a mutual fund or appoint a licensed mutual fund administrator to provide its principal office, unless there is a minimum investment per investor of US$100,000 or its equity interests are listed on a recognized stock exchange or market.

To be specifically licensed, a mutual fund must demonstrate that its promoters and managers are of sound repute, that its managers have the necessary experience, and that its business will be properly run.

Registered (whether or not specifically licensed) mutual funds must pay an initial and annual fee, currently of US$3,000.

6.3 Tax Laws

There are no direct taxes on companies or individuals and no inheritance taxes or estate duties in the Cayman Islands. The Cayman Islands government is committed to the continuation of the zero tax regime of the Cayman Islands, which has no aspect of "ring fencing" and is applied equally to residents and nonresidents, individuals, partnerships, trusts, and companies. The Organisation for Economic Co-operation and Development (OECD) has accepted this regime and confirmed that it is not considered to be "harmful," as opposed to regimes that differentiate between residents and/or particular types of entity.

The fact that there are no taxes in the Cayman Islands and that, accordingly, transactions can be structured on a "tax neutral" basis unfortunately often leads to a public misconception that investors in offshore companies are free from all forms of taxation. This is not the case at all. Investors based in onshore jurisdictions are likely to be taxed on dividend income received (and in some cases deemed but not actually received) from the offshore company and on any capital gains realized on the sale or redemption of shares in the offshore company. Additionally, the offshore company may itself be subject to withholding taxes imposed with respect to income or gains on its investments by tax authorities in the onshore jurisdictions in which the offshore company's businesses or investments are located.

Exempted companies and exempted limited partnerships may obtain an undertaking from the governor of the Cayman Islands against the future imposition of taxation; such undertakings are usually given for twenty years (fifty years in the case of an exempted limited partnership) in the first instance.

6.4 Stamp Duty

Stamp duty is effectively a tax upon certain documents and legal instruments that is charged in the Cayman Islands if a stampable document or instrument is executed in the Cayman Islands or, thereafter, brought into the Cayman Islands (such as for the purposes of enforcement).

The duty payable on the various types of instrument is prescribed by statute and in most cases with transactions involving exempted companies or exempted limited partnerships, the stamp duty payable is often nominal.

6.5 Intellectual Property Laws

6.5.1 Patents and Trademarks

The owner of a patent or trademark registered in the United Kingdom, or under the European Patent Convention or the European Community Patent Convention (Agreement Relating to Communtiy Patents), may extend such patent or trademark to the Cayman Islands. The law of the Cayman Islands does not enable patents or trademarks to be registered anew and there is no provision for extending to the Cayman Islands patents or trademarks registered outside of the United Kingdom or countries that are not signatories to the European Patent Convention and the European Community Patent Convention.

This extension is achieved by means of a registration with the Registrar of Patents and Trade Marks in the Cayman Islands and, subject to payment of an annual fee, the rights conferred in the Cayman Islands will subsist so long as they remain in force in the United Kingdom or the European Community, as the case may be.

Whether or not a person is the proprietor of a registered trademark, he may have a remedy at common law in an action for "passing off." Essentially, an action for passing off may be founded where there has been a misrepresentation by a trader to prospective customers that is calculated to injure the business or goodwill or another trader and that causes actual damage to the business or will actually do so. The court may award damages to the successful litigator and, in appropriate cases, an injunction to restrain further breach of such party's proprietary rights.

6.5.2 Copyright

The Copyright Act 1956 of the United Kingdom has been extended to and applies in the Cayman Islands.

6.6 Confidentiality

Confidentiality arising in relation to legitimate financial transactions is protected in the Cayman Islands.

Besides the normal common law duties of confidentiality between professional adviser and client and between banker and customer as established by English common law and as adopted into Cayman Islands common law, the Confidential Relationships (Preservation) Law (1995 Revision) makes it a criminal offence to divulge confidential information without the client's authorization. However, the Confidential Relationships (Preservation) Law (1995 Revision) contains detailed provisions for disclosure of confidential information in appropriate circumstances, most notably if the information is required for the investigation or prosecution of serious offenses in the United States under the Mutual Legal Assistance Treaty with the United States, or where disclosure is permitted or required under the Proceeds of

Criminal Conduct Law or the Money Laundering Regulations (see the section titled "Anti-Money-Laundering Framework" below).

6.7 Exchange Controls

There are no exchange control regulations in the Cayman Islands. In consequence, money and securities in any currency may be freely transferred to and from the Cayman Islands.

6.8 Insurance Laws

All persons carrying on or desiring to carry on insurance (including reinsurance) business in or from within the Cayman Islands must be licensed under the Insurance Law (2007 Revision) of the Cayman Islands. In addition, provision is made for the licensing of insurance agents and brokers and those providing insurance and underwriting expertise. Without a license, no company may carry on insurance business or (unless it obtains special approval) use any word in its name like "insurance," "assurance," "indemnity," "guarantee," "underwriting," "reinsurance," "surety" or "casualty," etc.

7. Other Significant Legal and Business Issues

7.1 General

Although the Cayman Islands are often perceived as a jurisdiction where money and assets, whether legitimate or not, may be easily deposited and hidden from regulators, policing authorities and tax authorities of other jurisdictions, any party seeking to conclude a transaction with a Cayman Islands element will quickly become aware that this is not the case and that the Cayman Islands have a comprehensive anti-money-laundering framework, together with many international co-operation and information exchange agreements.

The Cayman Islands also has its own regulatory body and stock exchange, which are described below.

7.2 Anti-Money-Laundering Framework

7.2.1 General

The Cayman Islands have been a member of the Caribbean Financial Action Task Force (CFATF) since its inception in 1992. The CFATF is a thirty-nation member organization, recognized by the Financial Action Task Force (FATF) as a regional style observer body, that is commissioned to undertake peer evaluations on behalf of the FATF and fellow agencies. The United States is a CFATF-supporting nation, along with the U.K., Canada, France, Mexico, Spain, and Netherlands.

The Cayman Islands anti-money-laundering and combating of terrorist financing regime underwent an assessment by the CFATF in June 2007. The CFATF evaluation team included a representative from the U.S. Treasury's Financial Crimes Enforcement Center (FinCEN) and the Canadian Royal Canadian Mounted Police. The assessment report was issued in December 2007 and indicated that the Cayman Islands were compliant or largely compliant with thirty-eight out of the forty FATF anti-money-laundering (AML) Recommendations and nine combating of financing of terrorism (CFT) Recommendations (collectively, the "Recommendations"). The Recommendations represent the international standards for AML/CFT.

The results of this assessment follow the excellent rating provided by the IMF on evaluating the Cayman Islands using the same AML/CFT methodology in 2003. The IMF reported that the Cayman Islands had an intense awareness of anti-money-laundering and combating of financing of terrorism in the business community.

Based on the third-round FATF evaluations undertaken to date on twenty-six FATF and CFATF jurisdictions, the Cayman Islands currently ranks fourth (amongst those countries that have been reviewed) for overall compliant and largely compliant Recommendations. The Cayman Islands achieved better results than most other countries, including the United Kingdom, Switzerland, Spain, Italy, and Ireland.

7.2.2 Legislation

In common with other financial centers in the world, the Cayman Islands has enacted legislation that is aimed at combating money laundering and terrorist financing. The legislation is contained principally in the Misuse of Drugs Law (2000 Revision), the Proceeds of Criminal Conduct Law (2007 Revision) (the "PCCL"), and the Terrorism Law 2003. The Misuse of Drugs Law was first enacted in 1973 and the Proceeds of Criminal Conduct Law in 1996. These statutes create a number of offenses in relation to activities involving the laundering of the proceeds of crime.

The PCCL enables subordinate legislation to be issued in the form of binding regulations and led to the enactment of the Money Laundering Regulations (2006 Revision) (the "Regulations"). The Regulations were first enacted in 2000. The Guidance Notes on the Prevention and Detection of Money Laundering in the Cayman Islands (the "Guidance Notes") were introduced in 2001 (and have been subsequently amended) to provide transparent guidelines for the interpretation and implementation of the Regulations. The Guidance Notes, while not legally binding, will be taken into account by the authorities or court when considering whether a person has complied with the Regulations.

7.2.3 Application

The Regulations essentially apply to all financial service licensees and entities registered (but not necessarily fully regulated) under either the Mutual Funds Law (2007 Revision) or the Securities Investment Business Law (2004 Revision).

Essentially, the Regulations codified the fundamental anti-money-laundering procedures to be maintained by financial service providers conducting relevant financial business when entering a business relationship or a one-time transaction (over a certain monetary limit).

The procedures are essentially:

i.   client identification and verification;
ii. record keeping;
iii. internal controls and communication;
iv. suspicious activity reporting; and
v.   training and awareness.

7.2.4 Client Identification

Client identification and verification procedures will normally include obtaining information on the controllers and principal beneficial owners of client entities. In 2001, the Regulations were amended so that the requirement to maintain client identification and verification procedures would apply to all relationships established prior to the introduction of the Regulations (i.e., perform due diligence on all relationships pre-2000). To date, the Cayman Islands are the only jurisdiction to have completed the retrospective due diligence exercise across all industries.

Under the Guidance Notes, usual means of client identification will involve the following:

a. For individuals, it is normally necessary to obtain documented information including the following:
    i.   full name(s) used;
    ii. correct permanent address;
    iii. date and place of birth;
    iv. nationality;
    v.   occupation; and
    vi. the purpose of the establishment of the account or business relationship.
b. For corporate entities, the financial service provider will usually need to obtain:-
    i.   the certificate of formation or incorporation;
    ii. the constitutional documents, bylaws (or equivalent document);
    iii. details of the registered office and place of business;
    iv. an explanation of the nature of the business, rationale for the relationship, and source of funds;

      v.   copy of the latest financial statements;

      vi. copy of the mandate/resolution to establish the relationship;

      vii. copies of relevant powers of attorney and a list of directors;

      viii. identity information (as above) on at least two directors of the corporation and persons on whose instructions authorized signatories are to act; and

      ix. identity information (as above) on the principal controllers or beneficial owners (generally regarded as persons directly or indirectly with more than a 10 percent shareholding).

  c. For partnerships, the financial service provider will usually need to obtain:-

      i.   where the entity is a limited partnership, identification of the general partner;

      ii. for other partnerships and unincorporated businesses, identification evidence for at least two partners or controllers of the business and/or authorized signatories, in line with the requirements for individual clients or corporations;

      iii. details of the trading address;

      iv. copy of the latest financial statements; and

      v.   an explanation of the nature of business, rationale for the relationship, and the source of funds.

  d. For trusts, the financial service provider will usually need to obtain:-

      i.   identity information on the trustee, settler, or beneficial owner (if a nominee relationship);

      ii. in certain circumstances, identity information on beneficiaries where they are known and have a vested interest; and

      iii. an explanation of the nature of business, rationale for the relationship, and source of funds.

7.2.5 Exemptions

The Guidance Notes acknowledge that the requirements of the Regulations could in some cases involve unnecessary duplication, or be commercially onerous, particularly where the transaction involves a party that is already regulated in a country recognized by the Monetary Authority to have equivalent anti-money-laundering legislation (a "Schedule 3 Country"), such as the United States.

    Accordingly, certain classes of clients are recognized by the Guidance Notes as being excepted from the client identification requirements, including:

  i.   governments and governmental bodies;

  ii. entities regulated by the Monetary Authority;

   iii. companies quoted on the CSX or any other market or exchange approved by the Monetary Authority (the list is extensive, covering most major stock exchanges of the world and including the American Stock Exchange, NASDAQ, and the NYSE);

   iv. "financial institutions" (which is defined to cover the main clearing systems) or "authorized persons" (individuals who conduct relevant financial business) regulated in a Schedule 3 Country;

   v. subsidiaries of the above-mentioned; and

   vi. pension funds for professional associations, trade unions, or employees of the above-mentioned.

It is also not necessary for the financial service provider to undertake verification of identity if the applicant for business is to make a payment and it is reasonable in all the circumstances for the payment to be sent by post or delivered by hand or by any electronic means where the payment is made from an account in the applicant's name at either a bank licensed under Cayman Islands law or a bank regulated and either based or incorporated in a Schedule 3 country.

This exception does not apply where the financial service provider suspects money-laundering or the payment is made to open a relevant account (a bank account through which payments can be made) with a bank licensed under Cayman Islands law, or where payment is to be made in such a way that it does not result in the reinvestment on behalf of the applicant with the same institution, or repayment directly to the applicant for business.

As much offshore financial business is effected either by intermediaries or following an introduction from a reputable source, the Regulations and Guidance Notes recognize that if a reputable source has carried out due diligence on a client in accordance with their own rules and wishes to introduce them to a financial service provider, the relevant due diligence can be relied upon and need not be duplicated.

The following categories of person are recognized as being eligible to introduce an applicant for business to a Cayman Islands financial service provider:

   i. a corporate group member (notwithstanding their domicile, as long as they adhere to group policy that is of a Schedule 3 standard);

   ii. a Cayman entity subject to the Regulations;

   iii. a Schedule 3 financial institution; and

   iv. Schedule 3 professional intermediaries, which broadly include lawyers and accountants or firms thereof.

Where a person acts as an "eligible introducer" it is a requirement that the financial service provider obtain from them a signed "Eligible Introducer's Form" (in the form annexed to the Guidance Notes, or its functional equivalent), confirming that they have obtained verification evidence of the identity of the client(s) whom they are introducing and that they will supply such evidence (or a certified copy) to the financial service provider on request.

7.2.6 Other Mandatory Procedures

(a) Record Keeping Procedures

Financial service providers must keep appropriate evidence of client identification, account opening, and new business documentation for a period of five years following the closing date at the end of the transaction or the termination of the business relationship. Records to be retained by the financial service provider include such documentation pertaining to the verification of client identity, transactional activity, staff training (e.g., attendance register and workshop/test materials), and internal reports, as well as any inquiries made by or disclosures made to the reporting authority.

(b) Reporting of Suspicious Activity

The Guidance Notes suggest that a person carrying on relevant financial business in the Cayman Islands should establish a written internal procedures manual, identify a suitable qualified and experienced money laundering reporting officer ("MLRO") and ensure that all staff engaged in the business of the financial service provider are aware of the identity of the MLRO and the procedures to follow when making a suspicious transaction report. It is then up to the MLRO to determine whether a suspicious activity report is made to the Cayman Islands Financial Reporting Authority, a member of the Egmont Group of Global Financial Intelligence Units.

The MLRO must be a natural person, autonomous, independent, and of sufficient seniority to be able to access all information necessary to determine whether a suspicion exists. The Guidance Notes also suggest appointing a deputy to cover for the absence or unavailability of the MLRO.

(c) Internal Controls and Communication

The Guidance Notes suggest that systems and controls be implemented by financial service providers to monitor the profile of the client on an ongoing basis. All staff of the financial service provider should understand the controls in order to be able to determine whether an activity or transaction is unusual or irregular.

(d) Training and Awareness

Where staffed, financial service providers must ensure that all appropriate staff, in particular new employees, receive training on money laundering prevention on a regular basis, are aware of and fully understand the procedures and their importance, and know that a criminal offense may be committed if they contravene the provisions of the legislation.

All relevant staff need to be appropriately educated in the "know your customer" requirements for the prevention of money laundering. Training should therefore cover not only the need to know the customer's true identity but also, where a business relationship is being established, the need to know enough about the type of business activity expected in relation to the customer at the outset (and on an ongoing basis).

7.2.7 Sector-Specific Guidance

The Guidance Notes provide further detailed explanation for particular areas of business. These areas cover the industries of mutual funds, banking, company formation and management, trust administration, insurance, and real estate. A section on money service businesses will also shortly be added.

The sector-specific guidance does not seek to extend the principles under the main body of the Guidance Notes, and in some places modifies the application for certain circumstances—e.g., the alternatives to the reporting function for unstaffed mutual funds.

7.2.8 Delegation of Maintenance of Anti-Money-Laundering Procedures

The Guidance Notes allow a managed financial service provider to delegate the maintenance of its anti-money-laundering procedures to a suitable party (whether within or outside of the Cayman Islands). Although the maintenance of these functions may be delegated, the ultimate responsibility for compliance with the Regulations remains with the financial service provider.

Pursuant to the Guidance Notes, a financial service provider is permitted to delegate to a suitable counterpart on the conditions that:

i   the Monetary Authority may access the written details and evidence of the suitability of the counterpart to perform the functions;

ii.   a clear understanding exists between the financial service provider and the delegate as to the functions to be performed;

iii. customer identification must be made available to the Monetary Authority upon request or the reporting authority or other law enforcement authority in accordance with relevant procedures; and

iv. the financial service provider regularly satisfies itself as to the reliability of the delegate's procedures.

If the functions have been delegated to a counterpart located and regulated in a Schedule 3 jurisdiction, the Monetary Authority regards compliance with the delegate's own regulatory requirements as constituting compliance with Caymans requirements. In other words, if the conditions are met, the delegate can apply its own rules and is not required to implement any additional standards.

7.2.9 Further Developments

In line with recent international initiatives and FATF typology reporting, the Guidance Notes are revised regularly. More recently, sections were added dealing with not-for-profit associations, politically exposed persons, high-risk countries, and electronic payment and message systems. The Guidance Notes Committee is currently considering the introduction of a more "risk-based" approach to anti-money-laundering, along the lines adopted by other financial centers and endorsed by the FATF.

7.3 Combating the Financing of Terrorism

In response to the events of September 11, 2001 and the introduction of the FATF Special Recommendations on Terrorist Financing, the Cayman Islands government has implemented legislation to give effect to restrictions imposed by the UN Securities Council Resolutions to combat terrorism and terrorist financing in the Cayman Islands.

In 2003 and 2004, the Cayman Islands passed comprehensive legislation to fully implement United Nations Security Council Resolution 1373 and give domestic effect to the 1999 International Convention for the Suppression of the Financing of Terrorism. The Terrorism Law, 2003 was also enacted and provides for the forfeiture of terrorist funding, prohibition of terrorist activity, money laundering, and mandatory disclosure of information using existing confidential channels (i.e., reporting to appropriate authorities on the same lines as anti-money-laundering), among other issues.

The aspects of "terrorist financing" and "terrorist property" have now been incorporated into the definitions of "money laundering" under the PCCL, Regulations, and Guidance Notes to harmonize the procedures implemented to prevent and detect such activity.

7.4 International Cooperation and Information Exchange

The Cayman Islands have invoked numerous statutory measures to cooperate with and assist foreign governments, authorities, and courts with the provision of information held in the Cayman Islands. Such laws override any statutory or common law duties of confidentiality.

Mutual legal assistance for criminal matters has been covered under the Criminal Justice (International Cooperation) Law from 1997 and, with particular regard to U.S. criminal matters, under the Narcotics Drugs (Evidence) (United States of America) Law from 1984 and the Mutual Legal Assistance (United States of America) Law from 1986. It is understood that the MLAT mechanism with the United States has rarely been used since 1986 (i.e., approximately 300 requests). Extradition between the Cayman Islands and the United States is provided for by the United States of America Extradition Order 1976 and Amendment Order of 1986.

The Misuse of Drugs Law and PCCL also contain provisions for the sharing of information with authorities in relevant circumstances. Of twenty-three requests made to the Cayman Financial Reporting Authority by U.S. authorities since 2003 in relation to money laundering and predicate offences, twenty-two have been granted.

The Cayman Islands are also a party to the Hague Convention 1970 on the taking of evidence abroad.

As a regulatory matter, the Monetary Authority is empowered under the Monetary Authority Law to entertain requests for information from any recognized overseas regulatory authority exercising equivalent functions. If certain criteria are met, the Monetary Authority will direct a local financial service provider or connected person to disclose information they hold that is responsive to the overseas regulatory authority's request. Separately, the Monetary Authority has entered into a specific Undertaking with the SEC and a Memorandum of Understanding with the CFTC in relation to the exchange of information.

The Cayman Islands have introduced the Tax Information Authority Law, 2005 (which schedules the Tax Information Exchange Agreement with the United States). This Tax Information Exchange Agreement conforms to the model developed, with U.S. participation, by the OECD Global Forum on Taxation, and is a form of an agreement that both the G8 and G20 countries have endorsed as reflecting "high standards of transparency and exchange of information for tax purposes." This agreement was signed in 2001 and provides for the provision of information in relation to criminal tax matters from the 2004 tax year and civil matters from the 2006 tax year and does not require a dual criminality test (i.e., that the matter constitutes a criminal offense in both the United States and the Cayman Islands).

In 2005, the Cayman Islands implemented with the Member States of the European Union exchange of information measures consistent with the EU Savings Directive and has introduced the Reporting of Savings Income Information (European Union) Law, 2007 (and related Regulations).

The Cayman Islands government and the Monetary Authority have had ongoing dialogue with foreign national and international agencies such as the SEC and International Organization of Securities Commissions (IOSCO) to ensure that the Cayman Islands is viewed as cooperative and responsive in relation to requests for information on regulatory and criminal matters. This assistance was recently publicly recognized by the U.S. Department of Justice in relation to an agreement reached with the Cayman Islands regarding a particular MLAT request and consequent prosecution in the United States.

7.5 Regulation and Listing

7.5.1 Cayman Islands Monetary Authority

The Monetary Authority is a separate corporate body wholly owned by the Cayman Islands government and has a board of directors with appropriate expertise, a managing director, and a large staff. The functions of the Monetary Authority include regulation of banks, trust companies, insurance and reinsurance companies and managers, company managers, and mutual funds and mutual fund administrators.

In addition to the regulation and supervision of financial services in the Cayman Islands, the Monetary Authority is also responsible for monitoring compliance with anti-money-laundering regulations in the Islands, as described above.

7.5.2 Cayman Islands Stock Exchange

Established in 1996 and operational since 1997, the Cayman Islands Stock Exchange (the "CSX") is a separate corporate body wholly owned by the Cayman Islands government. The CSX was formally granted "approved" status by the London Stock Exchange in 1996, meaning that securities listed on the CSX are regarded as international equity market securities.

The CSX was originally established to provide a listing facility for two of the Cayman Islands' key financial service products, the mutual fund and debt issuances by Cayman Islands companies. Since then, the CSX has expanded to the listing of derivative warrants, depositary receipts, and, more recently, eurobonds. The CSX also provides a secondary listing facility and an offshore trading venue in the North American time zone for companies listed and traded on other recognized exchanges.

The CSX operates in a modern structure of remote electronic trading that it monitors centrally. All listings and trading information can be accessed from the CSX's dedicated electronic pages on the Bloomberg network.

As of 2007, the CSX had over 1,700 issues approved for listing with a combined market capitalization investment in excess of US$113 billion.

8. International Business and Negotiation Practices

8.1 Onshore and Offshore Attorneys

Cayman Islands attorneys usually receive instructions either directly from a client or from onshore counsel representing an underlying client. Where a client has appointed onshore counsel, the Cayman Islands attorneys often have limited contact with the underlying client and will correspond mainly with the onshore attorneys. In such a situation, the onshore attorneys are required to interface between their client and the offshore counsel, unless to do so becomes time-consuming or otherwise unsuitable.

With larger transactions, the role of onshore counsel is increased and becomes more complicated. Some transactions may involve a number of smaller parts, only one of which involves a Cayman entity or asset; whereas some transactions may encompass parties that are not involved with any Cayman aspects. In such circumstances, the onshore counsel commonly deals directly with Cayman counsel and acts as an intermediary between Cayman counsel and other parties, distributing Cayman legal advice or documents to the relevant parties (rather than the Cayman attorneys doing so directly) and conveying queries from other parties to the Cayman attorneys.

When Cayman Islands attorneys are instructed, they will, where required, need to ascertain the identity of the underlying client in order to meet any due diligence requirements under the Cayman Islands Money Laundering Regulations. The Cayman attorneys are often asked to provide an estimate as to legal fees at this stage.

8.2 Negotiation Practices

Negotiation practices in the Cayman Islands are no different from negotiation practices conducted in the United States and the United Kingdom, and conducting business with a Cayman Islands element does not raise any questions of language, religion, culture, or social customs.

Transactions will usually be conducted through the onshore/offshore attorney relationship, with the onshore counsel liaising with the client and other transaction parties (as described above) and the offshore attorneys liaising with any Cayman-based parties, such as accountants, directors based in the Cayman Islands (a very common feature of structured finance transactions), the Monetary Authority, and the CSX.

The Cayman Islands are on the same longitude as the eastern seaboard of the United States and are on Eastern Standard Time (which means they are on the same time as Boston, New York, Washington, and Miami in winter and one hour behind them in summer). Business negotiations can occur at any time in the Cayman Islands, with Cayman attorneys often fitting in with the communicated timetable in order to meet client demand. This similarity in working practices facilitates easy communication between attorneys based in the United States and their counterparts in Cayman, with the vast majority of communications being conducted via e-mail and telephone.

8.3 Negotiating Online

There are no statutory or regulatory restrictions applicable to data rooms online and/or posting comments to documents online. The Cayman Islands have excellent telecommunications and Internet connections.

The Electronic Transactions Law of the Cayman Islands was introduced in 2003 and provides for:

i.   the legal recognition of electronic records (i.e., a record processed and maintained by electronic means);
ii. the provision of "written" information in the form of electronic records;
iii. delivery of documents, records, and information by way of electronic record;
iv. retention of records in the form of electronic records; and
v.   the equal treatment of electronic signatures.

8.4 Governing Law and Legal Opinions

With international business transactions, very few of the transaction documents will normally be governed by Cayman Islands law. It is more common for the majority of transaction documents to be governed by English or New York law and to have certain documents governed by Cayman Islands law, such as documents granting a security interest over shares in a Cayman Islands company or agreements providing for the administration of a Cayman company by a Cayman-based service provider. Accordingly, this chapter does not discuss the requirements of Cayman Islands contract law but considers the role of Cayman attorneys in issuing legal opinions covering the entry by Cayman entities into documents governed by a foreign law. Similarly, dispute resolution in the Cayman Islands is not covered, as transaction documents drafted by onshore counsel usually provide that the contracting parties submit to the jurisdiction of specified courts, such as any New York State or U.S. federal court sitting in the City and County of New York.

Where documents are drafted by onshore lawyers and are to be entered into by a Cayman Islands entity, Cayman counsel will be asked to review the transaction documents from a Cayman Islands perspective to ensure that the terms do not conflict with any Cayman Islands laws. In addition, the firm of Cayman attorneys will usually be required to provide the parties to a transaction with a legal opinion covering certain issues, such as the ability of the Cayman entity to enter into the documents, the good standing of the entity, execution of those documents, enforcement in Cayman, and perfection of security interests. Some of these aspects are considered below.

8.5 Capacity

Under Cayman Islands law, the legal form of the Cayman Islands entity (i.e., whether it is a company, partnership, limited partnership, etc.) will dictate its legal capacity. Regulatory laws with which that entity must comply based on its specific activities may also affect the legality and effect of its entry into a transaction.

8.5.1 Incorporation, Existence, and Good Standing

Legal opinions will often require the Cayman Islands attorney to confirm the incorporation or establishment and status of the relevant Cayman entity.

8.5.2 Signing Authority

Onshore counsel will wish to receive confirmation that transaction documents have been signed by a person who has authority to do so. Again, the nature of the entity involved dictates the manner of execution of documents, but the Cayman attorney will usually look to receive a copy of board or director resolutions authorizing particular persons to sign where the relevant entity is a company (including a general partner acting on behalf of a limited partnership), or to an underlying constitutional document, such as partnership agreement or trust deed, with other types of entity.

8.5.3 Licensing and Consent Requirements

A party to a contract with a Cayman Islands entity will usually seek confirmation in a legal opinion that it does not require a license or other authorization, consent, or approval under Cayman Islands law to do so. As a general rule, no license, authorization, consent, or approval will be required by a transaction party to enter into a contract with a Cayman entity unless the transaction party is carrying on business in the Cayman Islands or is carrying on a regulated activity.

8.5.4 Governing Law and Jurisdiction

A legal opinion should cover whether the courts of the Cayman Islands will observe and give effect to the choice of governing law of the transaction documents and whether a judgment obtained in a foreign jurisdiction will be recognized and enforced in the courts of the Cayman Islands.

8.5.5 Security Interests

Where a Cayman entity grants security in a foreign-law-governed transaction document, the beneficiary of such security interest will usually require a legal opinion to the effect that the courts of the Cayman Islands will recognize that security interest and to confirm whether any steps are required as a matter of Cayman Islands law to perfect such security interest, or to regulate its ranking in order of priority.

9. Conclusion

The challenge for multinational companies, investment banks and fund managers is often how to create a business or investment structure that is able to accommodate investors from all over the world within the complex parameters of existing tax and securities laws that apply to the investors, the management team, and the business or investment activities, all of which could be based in multiple jurisdictions.

The Cayman Islands provide a neutral and low-risk base in which to combine investors from a number of jurisdictions investing in assets located in the same or other jurisdictions so that investors are not effectively subject to double taxation. This neutrality provides a level playing field for all investors and avoids creating a vehicle in a jurisdiction that may provide more benefits to some investors than others. Furthermore, the Cayman Islands provide this opportunity without foreign exchange controls and with the benefit of an efficient local professional and administrative infrastructure comprising many individuals who have trained and worked in the major onshore financial centers and who are familiar with onshore working practices and requirements.

Sara Galletly and Alasdair Robertson
Maples and Calder
Cayman Islands
P.O. Box 309
Ugland House
Grand Cayman KYl-1104
Cayman Islands
Phone: +1 345 949 8066
Fax: +1 345 949 8080
E-mail: Sara.Galletly@maplesandcalder.com
        Alasdair.Robertson@maplesandcalder.com

CHAPTER 26

International Business Negotiations in the People's Republic of China

Wendy Guo
KANG DA LAW FIRM
BEIJING, CHINA

1. Introduction

It has been nearly thirty years since the People's Republic of China ("China") started a major process of reformation and began to open up its economy to external parties. The contemporary period of reform commenced in earnest in 1978. Over the past twenty-nine years, China has witnessed an annual growth rate of 9.7 percent in terms of its GDP.[1] In 2006, China's GDP amounted to US$2.7 trillion with a global ranking of No. 4.[2] In this same year the total volume of China's imports and exports reached US$1.76 trillion, resulting in a global ranking of No. 3.[3] Also in that year, foreign direct investment to China hit US$69.47 billion.[4]

Profound changes in China's legal and economic systems have accompanied the country's rapid economic growth and the expansion of interactions with other countries and regions. The country's efforts to conform to the established rules of international trade and investment and indeed solve domestic social problems have forged economic and political change. It is anticipated that China's political system will

---

[1] Wu Jinglian, *Xiang Liang De Hui Da (A Ringing Answer)*, CAIJING MAGAZINE, 2008, *2008: Forecasts and Strategies*, 20–22, at 20.

[2] Ma Xiuhong, Vice Minister, Ministry of Commerce of the People's Republic of China, Address at the seminar China Goes Global in the U.K. Parliament (Apr. 12, 2007), *available at* http://wss.mofcom.gov.cn/article/a/c/200704/20070404560575.html.

[3] Liao Xiaoqi, Vice Minister, Ministry of Commerce of the People's Republic of China, Deepen CEPA, Promote Regional Economic and Trade Cooperation, Address before the Fourth Pan-Pearl River Delta Regional Cooperation and Development Forum (June 9, 2007), *available at* http://english.mofcom.gov.cn/aarticle/speech/200712/20071205269679.html.

[4] News Release, Ministry of Commerce of People's Republic of China, FDI in China Tops 63 Bln U.S. Dollars in 2006 (Jan. 16, 2007), *available at* http://english.mofcom.gov.cn/aarticle/newsrelease/commonnews/200701/20070104271664.html.

continue to undergo changes as the nation continues to progress and develop. Moreover, the legal framework has developed accordingly. On the one hand, the tradition of the continental legal system has been retained and continues to suit China's social environment in China. On the other hand, however, globalization has demanded that the Chinese law society recognize the value of alternative concepts, theories, and approaches for various jurisdictions, and it now employs a variety of such concepts as it sees fit.

Coming from a vigorously developing country with a long history and profound eastern tradition, commercial organizations and individuals from China possess characteristics from a combination of modernism, traditionalism, market-economy consciousness, and planned-economy custom. The variety of such characteristics can be witnessed in every social situation. Without acknowledging such characteristics, foreign parties attempting to conduct international business negotiations in China will be unsuccessful.

2. General Legal System and Principal Relevant Laws and Regulations

2.1 Legislative System and Principal Relevant Laws and Regulations

Generally speaking, the legal system of China is based upon the continental legal system, in that statutory law constitutes the main body of law in the country. Nevertheless, in practice, a recent trend has developed whereby judges are adhering to precedent as has been established in the civil and commercial courts.

In China, the legal framework is composed of law, administrative regulation, local regulation, administrative rules promulgated by departments of the State Council, and local rules promulgated by local governments. The Hong Kong Special Administrative Region (SAR) has relatively independent legislation and jurisdiction pursuant to the Basic Law of the Hong Kong Special Administrative Region of the People's Republic of China, and Hong Kong SAR follows the common law system.

The following sections present a brief introduction to major civil and commercial laws and regulations applicable in China. Particular focus will be placed upon laws relevant to international business negotiations that were formulated and significantly amended in the last two decades. Included herein are references to the most recent laws and regulations, some of which have not yet been implemented.

2.2 Foreign Investment Provisions

Foreign direct investment (FDI) has been one of the most important engines accelerating economic development in mainland China. The environment for foreign investors remains hospitable. Government bodies create provisions to encourage FDI.

As the core of FDI regulations, there is the Catalogue for the Guidance of Foreign Investment Industries ("Catalogue"), which was re-revised and subsequently became effective on December 1, 2007. Compared with the former Catalogue of 2004, Catalogue 2007 has substantial differences. Investment industries still remain subject to the same previously identified categories, "Encouraged," "Permitted," "Restricted," and "Prohibited." However, there has been a large increase in the "Encouraged" section, while the numbers of "Restricted" and "Prohibited" entries have changed only slightly.

Tighter policies apply to the sectors of Real Estate, Publishing, and Media & Recreation, and to some areas of manufacturing. Environmentally friendly manufacturing, new technologies, Logistic, outsourcing business services, and transportation equipment and services all fall into the "Encouraged" category. Environmental protection issues have been a particular focus point for governmental authorities in recent years, and projects that are perceived by some to be environmentally threatening will be intensely scrutinized. There are strict rules at all levels of authority within the government to control the investment projects from start to finish. Adjustment on Outsourcing services and Logistic reflects China's effort to catch up with India as a global outsourcing center. Doors to Wholesale & Retail and Finance services are opening at an extremely fast rate. This is especially true in respect to foreign commercial banks, investment banks, and investment funds. Significantly, Catalogue 2007 meets China's WTO commitment on financial sectors' gradual openness. The enactment of Catalogue 2007 is a major step in the right direction in terms of China's foreign investment reform.

2.3 Foreign Exchange Rules

Foreign exchange regulations and rules impose strict controls for residents and nonresidents involving inflow and outflow of foreign currency. As defined by the Notice of the State Administration of Foreign Exchange on Relevant Issues Concerning Foreign Exchange Administration for Domestic Residents to Engage in Financing and in Return Investment via Overseas Special Purpose Companies ("Circular 75"), the term "residents" includes Chinese nationals, Chinese companies (including foreign investment companies), and foreign individuals continuously living in China for six months or longer.

The State Administration of Foreign Exchange (SAFE) and its regional branch offices are the government bodies in charge of the daily supervision of foreign exchange transactions. Foreign Exchange transactions are divided into two categories: (i) transactions under current accounts and (ii) transactions under capital accounts. All receipts and payments of foreign exchange derived from transactions involving goods and/or services are attributed to current accounts. Typical trade contracts include, without limitation, cargo sales contracts, technology transfer contracts, lease contracts, and service outsourcing contracts. The receipts and payments of foreign exchange derived from inward or outward investment are attributed to capital account. Corresponding contracts include, without limitation, equity joint venture contracts, share purchase contracts, and business and assets purchase contracts. Compared with current account transactions, government authorities take many more control measures to capital account transactions. This explains why some capital account transactions are forged as current account transactions by way of signing and submitting trade contracts.

According to an official report released by People's Bank of China (PBC), China has a foreign exchange surplus that is increasing rather sharply. This, in turn, has caused excessive liquidity. In an attempt to solve the problem, in 2007 the Chinese government undertook a set of measures designed to reform its foreign exchange system. The measures include allowing greater flexibility in the renminbi exchange rate regime, setting up a national foreign exchange investment company to expand the channels of foreign exchange reserve use, raising the amount of investment by qualified foreign institutional investors (QFII) and expanding the range of investment for qualified domestic institutional investors (QDII). In addition, China will launch more derivatives in the financial markets.

In managing foreign currencies, China will lift restrictions on the purchase and use of foreign currencies by enterprises and individuals and is expected to curb the rapid increase of foreign debts. China will strengthen the management of trade credit and the inflow of capital by investment companies from abroad, and will closely monitor any abnormal foreign capital that flows into China. Specifically, China will monitor the capital inflow and exchange settlement by foreign investment companies; verify the reality of foreign exchange collection and settlement in trade; pay attention to the inflow of foreign capital in property market; and check foreign exchange collection and settlement by individuals, and the business activities and return investment activities by securities and fund management companies. In addition, China will establish certain enterprises to deal exclusively with renminbi and foreign currency exchange business for the convenience of individuals seeking to exchange a small amount of foreign currencies.

2.4 Company Law

The 1994 Company Law is the first company law to affect mainland China. The Company Law was amended three times, in 1999, 2004, and 2005. The 2005 amendment was highly praised by scholars and representatives of private industry alike. The 2005 Company Law fully reflects the principle of autonomy of will, and is more in line with practice and international custom in terms of system design.

According to the Company Law, companies can be divided into limited liability companies and joint stock limited companies. Limited liability companies include one-person companies and solely state-owned companies.

When a company is established, the most important legal documents include articles of association and shareholders' agreement. All the legal provisions in such documents shall be fully respected and the parties to such documents have freedom in establishing their terms. For example, the shareholders of a limited liability company can agree upon a discretional ratio of shareholding and distribution of dividends that is not in conformity with their respective paid-in capital ratio, and they can also otherwise agree upon the issue of share transfer.

With regard to regulations of capital contribution, there is no other restriction except that labor, credit, goodwill, franchise, and properties under guarantee cannot be contributed and that the contribution percentage of intangible assets is restricted. Concerning time limits on capital contributions, relevant implementing rules of the Company Law provide that the subscribed capital can be paid in within a period of time. They further stipulate that unless otherwise agreed, dividend distribution shall be pursuant to the paid-in capital of shareholders.

With regard to corporate governance, the law establishes requirements for shareholders' meetings, boards of directors, and supervisory boards. The Company Law stipulates personal responsibilities of directors and senior management by formulating their qualification, appointment and removal, and responsibility. The law also has provisions intended to protect minority shareholders' interests. For instance, there are provisions regarding accumulated voting, independent director requirements, and "piercing the corporate veil." The various safeguards are intended to prevent controlling shareholders from misusing their advantageous position and limited liability to avoid paying their debts or to damage interests of other shareholders and/or creditors. Also significant in this regard are special regulations concerning voting rights of general shareholders' meetings, the secretary of the board of directors, and the system of shareholders' avoidance of conflict of interest.

The Company Law also regulates conditions and procedures of public offerings and company listings. In special chapters, it also contains provisions concerning merger, division, dissolution, and liquidation of companies.

2.5 Tax Law

Since the beginning of the 1980s, foreign investment enterprises (FIEs) and domestic enterprises have been subject to different tax policies. Due to prevailing economic objectives, FIEs were, in fact, given more favorable treatment in relation to corporate income taxes. Under this regime, FIEs may enjoy a 24 percent or 15 percent rate for corporate income tax, while domestic firms are subject to 33 percent tax rate. Among other incentives, the FIEs Tax Law grants a "two-plus-three" year tax holiday to FIE manufacturers, which means a two-year exemption during the first two profit-making years plus an additional three years of taxation at half the applicable rate. In March 2007, a new unified corporate income tax law was passed by the National People's Congress, China's top legislative body (the NPC). This measure has been effective since January 1, 2008. As expected, the new law aims to unify tax treatment among all types of enterprises, not only through a unified tax rate but also with an overall unification of corporate income tax system.

The new law provides that the enterprise income tax rate is 25 percent regardless of whether it is a domestic enterprise or an FIE. Concerning the tax deductions, chapter two of the new law sets forth unified standards for all types of enterprises, which changes the former system in which domestic companies are subject to more limitations than their FIE counterparts in terms of pretax deductions. One of the most sensitive issues of the tax system reform is tax-favorable treatment. Increasing complaints and questions from foreign investors and their chambers of commerce were accumulating before the legislative organs when the consultation paper of the tax law was released. Several foreign governments also joined the lobby group, including the United States. The finalized law adopted some suggestions from the various constituencies. The arrangement of a five-year interim period for existing FIEs allows for a gradual tax rate increase from 15 percent or 24 percent to 25 percent. The Circular released by the State Council on December 26, 2007 set forth the specific interim rate arrangements demonstrated in the following chart:

Current Tax Rate	2008	2009	2010	2011	2012
15%	18%	20%	22%	24%	25%
24%	25%		———		

In addition to these tax rate changes, the new law also made significant changes to the withholding tax.

2.6 Environmental Protection Provisions

Primary environmental legislation in force in China includes PRC Environmental Protection Law (1989), PRC Environmental Impact Assessment Law (2002), and a set of Administration Regulations.

The environmental degradation that has accompanied China's impressive economic boom is becoming increasingly worse. In order to prevent further environmental destruction, the Chinese government has attempted to enhance efforts to strengthen the regulation of new investment projects that may have an impact upon the environment.

Under the current regime, governmental supervision and authority over the environmental impact of new development projects is based mainly upon Environmental Impact Assessment (EIA) requirement, Blanket Suspension of Approval (BSA), and Three Simultaneous Requirements.

The EIA mandates that before the start of any industrial project, enterprises shall submit certain documentation to include relevant analysis, prediction, and appraisal of the environmental impact information for approval.[5]

The BSA was first addressed in the Decision to Implement Scientific Development and Increase Environmental Protection (the "Decision"), which was released by the State Council in December 2005. In accordance with article 21 of the Decision, approval of construction projects that would potentially have adverse environmental impact in geographic areas of environmental concern were suspended from further action. Article 21 also requires that if units fail to comply with the emission limits within the prescribed time, they face suspension.[6] Additionally, all projects must ensure that an environmental impact assessment is carried out; without such, the project runs the risk of suspension until the violation is cured.

Another stipulation of Chinese environmental law is the Three Simultaneous Requirements. According to article 26 of PRC Environmental Protection Law, installations for the prevention and control of pollution of the project must be designed, built, and commissioned simultaneously with the design, construction, and operation phases of the project.[7] In other words, during the design of the project, the design of installations for the prevention and control of pollution of the project should be submitted simultaneously; the relevant installations should operate to prevent the pollution generated from the project construction; finally, the project should not be launched until the pollution prevention and control installation is in operation.[8]

---

[5] The content of and the general procedure to submit the EIA's report should be subject to the Law of the People's Republic of China on Environmental Impact Assessment; such report should be filed and approved by the state council or local government at or above the level of city with separated districts.

[6] Sidley & Austin LLP, *China Tightens Its Environmental Law Control over New Investment Projects*, CHINA UPDATE, Jan. 2007, at 2, *available at* http://www.sidley.com/clientupdates/Detail.aspx?news=3081.

[7] Tang Zhengyu, *China Tightens Its Environmental Law Control over New Investment Projects*, CHINA L. & PRAC., Apr. 2007, at 13, 14.

[8] *Id.*

In light of the international standards and the success of other countries, China's State Environmental Protection Administration (SEPA) has teamed with the PBC in a joint initiative to include the environmental records of enterprises in a nationwide corporate credits system. Since April 1, 2007, commercial banks have been requested to consider the environmental records of potential borrowers as an important factor in lending decisions.

2.7 Antitrust Law

China's first PRC Anti-Monopoly Law was approved on August 30, 2007 by NPC. The landmark measures took effect in August 2008. The new law is comprehensive in scope, covering a wide range of traditional antitrust topics and even addressing anticompetitive administrative action. While the new law is vast in the areas it covers, its weakness may lie in the vagueness of many of its provisions and its frequent use of undefined terms.

China's new Anti-Monopoly Law follows the antitrust laws of the United States and the EU in many ways and addresses primarily the same practices, including restrictive agreements, abuse of dominant position, mergers and acquisitions, anticompetitive administrative action, intellectual property, and enforcement and remedies. While the law bans certain anticompetitive practices, it allows for certain monopolies that would promote advances in technology.

The new law prohibits certain restrictive agreements. While prohibiting one type of vertical agreement, specifically resale price maintenance, it places an emphasis on horizontal agreements, including price fixing, supply restrictions, market division, and collusive boycotts. The terms and restrictions of China's new Anti-Monopoly Law will be easily recognized by those who do business in the United States or the EU, as they are the main areas regulated by the antitrust laws in both regions.

In traditional antitrust fashion, China's new law also prohibits dominant entities from abusing their position in a variety of ways, including by imposing unfair prices, selling below cost, and discriminating between equal parties.

The new law also addresses mergers and acquisitions. Mergers and acquisitions will have to meet certain criteria and also be filed with the Anti-Monopoly Enforcement Authority, a newly formed authority within the Ministry of Commerce. The filing requirement extends to transactions in which a foreign firm acquiring a business in China will obtain over 50 percent of a defined market. This provision clearly intends to exert control over potential domination of Chinese companies by foreign firms. The Enforcement Authority will have express power to prohibit mergers and to require divestiture of inappropriate mergers. The specific criteria that will trigger a required filing have not yet been established. However, it is expected that these filings will address issues similar to those required by the United States and EU in their merger filings. The new filing requirement will apply to both Chinese and foreign acquiring parties.

China's new Anti-Monopoly Law also prohibits unfair, abusive practices by public officials. Under the new law, officials will be prohibited from blocking the free circulation of goods between regions of China, requiring people to deal with particular corporations or entities, or taking any other action designed to eliminate competition. In addition, the new law prohibits the abuse of intellectual property rights to restrict or eliminate competition.

National security is another issue addressed by the new law. A provision allows for national security reviews of foreign investments.

Finally, the Anti-Monopoly Law establishes the creation of the new Anti-Monopoly Enforcement Authority, which will conduct investigations. Parties, if dissatisfied, will have the right to pursue an administrative review process or pursue the matter in court.

The updated development of the Anti-Monopoly Law is "Provisions on the Reporting Threshold for Concentrations of Business Operators," published by the State Council on August 3, 2008. It clarifies the thresholds for business operators to file the merger control notification to Anti-Monopoly Bureau.

2.8 Intellectual Property Provisions

Since China joined the World Trade Organization (WTO) in 2001, intellectual property rights (IPR) protection has been a major source of contention between China and foreign investors. Hence, despite Chinese law recognizing certain types of intellectual property, including copyrights, trademarks, patents, domain names, designs of integrated circuits, and trade secrets, the IPR protection has risen in importance on China's judiciary agenda. Since 2001, special courts for IPR cases in China were formed and the threshold to prosecute people manufacturing or selling counterfeit products was lowered. This order was established by the Supreme Court of China.

Furthermore, in October 2007, Chinese president Hu Jintao, at the 17th National Congress of the Communist Party of China (CPC),[9] promised the implementation of a new 'national strategy' on IPR protection.

Patents incorporate invention, utility model, and design. Generally, it is the patent authorities who implement the policy of substantial

---

[9] *Surge of Intellectual Property Rights Cases in China*, THAINDIAN NEWS, Feb. 21, 2008, http://www.thaindian.com/newsportal/world-news/surge-of-intellectual-property-rights-cases-in-china_10019632.html.

examination, which can be summarized as "disclose early, examine later" to invention patents, and implement formal examination policy towards utility model patents and design patents. Invention patents are valid for twenty years. Utility model patents and design patents are each valid for ten years. In each case, the validity period is computed from the application date.

Patent-granting organs include the Patent Bureau, which functions under the State Intellectual Property Office and Patent Reexamination Committee. Relevant judicial organs include Beijing First Intermediate People's Court and Beijing Higher People's Court. If a party is unsatisfied with a decision of an administrative organ, he or she can file an appeal with Beijing First Intermediate People's Court for the first instance and with Beijing Higher People's Court for the second instance according to relevant regulations.

Like most other countries, application of both trademark and patent law apply the "first to file" rule. Generally, a trademark applicant shall apply for the preliminary examination and public notice for his trademark, and within three months after such public notice, any person can object to such application. The protection period for a trademark is ten years commencing from the expiration date of any objection, and this protection period can be extended upon expiration.

China's copyright law is mainly governed by the Copyright Law of the PRC and the Implementing Rules for the Copyright Law of the PRC; the former legislation was promulgated in 1990 and amended in October 2001 while the latter was adopted in 1990 and replaced by new implementing rules that came into force on September 15, 2002. Moreover, in order to implement the Berne Convention and the Universal Copyright Convention, as well as bilateral copyright treaties signed between the PRC and other foreign countries, the PRC government passed other regulations such as the Regulations on Implementation of International Copyright Treaties (1992), the Computer Software Protection Rules (1991), and the Measures for Computer Software Copyright Registration. Based on the theory established by the Berne Convention, copyrighted works, in China as in most other countries, do not require registration for protection. However, the copyright owner may register with China's National Copyright Administration (NCA) to avoid any disputes in respect of ownership. It is notable that such registration procedure is not compulsory.

2.9 Labor Contract Law

Unlike legislative routes through which most other Chinese laws have passed, China's new Labor Contract Law has taken a rather unique approach. The initial draft was followed by three readings, a public publishing, and debate, with the final decision made by the NPC Standing Committee. During those procedures, the European Trade

Union Confederation (ETUC) was observed attempting to exert an influence over the drafting of the legislation. Specifically, the ETUC attempted to block the efforts of the United States and EU Chambers of Commerce to attack the clauses in the draft that were more beneficial to employees.

The new Labor Contract Law was enacted on June 29, 2007 and became effective on January 1, 2008. During this preparation period, several cases triggered by the new law had already emerged, garnishing public attention. One example involved Wal-Mart. The multinational Wal-Mart terminated its labor relationship with a number of its employees in November 2007. The layoffs raised significant controversy as many speculated that the actions of the company were undertaken in an effort to avoid obligations under the new law. According to the new law, employers may revoke a labor contract only if the employee loses work ability due to illness or injury, or becomes unqualified for the work even after training or post adjustment, or if the objective conditions taken as the basis for the contract have greatly changed. The employee must be given thirty days' advance written notice. In addition, article 46 sets forth the circumstances under which the employer shall pay compensation to the employees. For example, the employee is entitled to terminate the employment contract and receive compensation from the employer if the employer fails to fulfill conditions such as providing labor protection or working conditions specified in the employment contract, paying the labor compensation or the social insurance premiums, or causing the employment contract to be invalid due to a circumstance specified in the first paragraph of article 26.

The new Labor Contract Law has also made significant changes to the treatment of open-ended contracts. According to article 14, if an employee has worked continuously for a particular employer for 10 years or longer, or if the employee has signed fixed-term labor contracts twice in a row, unless the employee requests the conclusion of a fixed-term employment contract, an open-ended employment contract should be concluded. In order to avoid this obligation of offering long-term employees open-ended contracts, the biggest domestic private communication company designed a "quit" plus "engage" package for the employees whose service period in the company approached ten years. It is therefore apparent that companies are becoming creative and introducing strategies to avoid the new obligations of the legislation.

The new law allows employers to impose a noncompetition obligation on employees. Such restrictive covenants can survive for up to two years after the termination of the employment agreement, provided that the employee is paid for accepting the restrictive covenant.

The Chinese government encourages legislative organs and relevant administration authorities to improve the nation's social insurance and welfare system. Increasingly, more and more regions have begun to link such obligations with enterprises' taxation or credit records. All these changes have resulted in FIEs increasing their expenditures. As a result, low-profit FIEs (such as OEM manufacturers or textile exporters) have considered moving their operations to other developing countries, such as India and Vietnam.

2.10 Judiciary System

The judiciary system in mainland China consists primarily of the prosecution system, trial system, arbitration system, lawyer system, and public notary system. The following sections cover only those systems that are relevant to the discussion of this chapter.

2.10.1 Trial System

The People's Courts represent the main trial organ of the state. This court system consists of local courts, special courts, and the Supreme Court, with the local and special courts being subject to the supervision of the Supreme Court. Local courts are established in accordance with the administrative divisions, while special courts are set up where necessary. Local courts are divided into three levels: grassroots, intermediate, and higher.

The courts try cases on two levels, with the second instance being the one that renders the final judgment. This means a case is closed after going through two levels of trial. However, a reexamination procedure that is part of the judicial supervision system may also be initiated if certain conditions are met. Usually, a case involving foreign interest shall be submitted to the competent Intermediate People's Court on the first instance, and to the Higher People's Court, when appealed, for final judgment.

2.10.2 Arbitration

The arbitration system in mainland China follows generally accepted international principles, rules, and practice. Parties to a dispute should voluntarily reach an agreement to resolve their dispute through arbitration. An arbitration committee shall not consider a case without application from a party involved in the dispute.

Arbitration committees are established in accordance with the administrative divisions, normally in the capital cities of provinces, municipalities, and autonomous regions. They are neither part of the administrative apparatus nor subordinated to the People's Courts. They have no affiliation among themselves and are independent from each other. An arbitration committee is normally formed with seven to eleven experts in the fields of law and trade and other fields, depending upon the nature of the agreement, transaction, and/or issue under dispute.

An arbitration tribunal can comprise a collegiate panel or a sole arbitrator. An arbitration panel should be composed of three arbiters, one of whom should be the chief arbiter who presides over the arbitration. If the parties agree to have a tribunal of three arbiters, each party should designate or ask an arbitration committee to designate one arbiter, and the third arbiter, who should be jointly selected by the parties or designated by the arbitration committee chairman jointly authorized by the parties, should be the chief arbiter. Should the parties agree to have a sole-arbiter tribunal, the arbiter should be jointly selected by the parties or designated by the arbitration committee chairman jointly authorized by the parties.

If the parties have reached an agreement on arbitration, this then rules out any court jurisdiction over the dispute. In such case, the parties can only apply for arbitration to an arbitration body rather than bringing an action to court.

An arbitration award is final and binding upon the parties. Even if a party is not satisfied with the decision, such party cannot file a suit to the court for the same dispute or apply for arbitration or reconsideration to arbitration organizations. Rather, the decision should be adhered to. If it is not, the other party then has the right to apply to the court for enforcement.

The governing law issue with respect to foreign-related arbitration is subject to several basic principles. Article 145 of the General Principles of the Civil Law of the People's Republic of China ("Civil Code") provides that "the parties to a contract involving foreign interests may choose the law applicable to settlement of their contractual disputes, except as otherwise stipulated by law. If the parties to a contract involving foreign interests have not made a choice, the law of the country to which the contract is most closely connected shall be applied." (See also article 126 of the PRC Contract Law.) Therefore, the arbitration panel shall primarily apply the laws adopted by the parties in the dispute as the governing law of their contract. In the absence of any express choice of law by the parties to a foreign-related arbitration, the panel shall choose the substantive laws concerning the following:

i.   the relevant legislations selected by conflict law;
ii. the legislations of the country to which the contract in concern is most closely connected; and
iii. international conventions, treaties, and customs.

China International Economic and Trade Arbitration Commission (CIETAC) is the most important permanent arbitration institution in China and also one of the busiest arbitration centers in the world. It was set up in 1956. CIETAC is also sometimes referred to as the Arbitration Court of the China Chamber of International Commerce (CCOIC). CIETAC's headquarters and its two subcommissions in Shanghai and Shenzhen together form one institution. Because China is a signatory to the New York Convention, CIETAC's awards have international recognition and enforcement.

2.10.3 Notarization

Public notary offices in mainland China are professional institutions whose establishment is subject to the approval of Ministry of Justice. The business scope of China's public notary offices is similar to those of their overseas counterparts, in that they perform such functions as notarizing civil legal acts such as contracts, trusts, wills, and gifts; notarizing facts such as birth, death, marriage, divorce, kinship, identity, and degree; notarizing documents such as authenticity of signatures and seals on certificates, consistency of copies of certificates, excerpts, translations, and photocopies with the originals; and engaging in other auxiliary business such as preservation of evidence, and maintenance of wills or other documents.

Notarized documents are frequently used in international commercial transactions. In China, notarization and accreditation are required according to some laws and regulations. For example, according to Executive Opinions on Some Issues Concerning the Application of Law Governing the Examination, Approval and Registration of Foreign-Invested Companies, when a foreign investor applies for the approval and registration of an FIE, she shall submit to relevant approval and registration authority her identification certificate or registration certificate, which is notarized by the notarial organization of her country and accredited by the Chinese embassy/consulate in that country.

3. Types of International Business Negotiations

Generally, international business negotiations can be classified into two main categories: international trade negotiations and international investment negotiations. Accordingly, in such transactions, these two main types of negotiations vary considerably in terms of key deal points, related laws, regulations and rules, content, and drafting methods.

3.1 International Trade Negotiations

International trade negotiations involve the purchase and sale of goods. Accordingly, in such transactions all contractual provisions and covenants shall be focused on the applicable goods.

Negotiators of international trade transactions should be familiar with such issues as manufacturing, transportation, and international markets. They should also be acquainted with the rules and terminology of international trade, international settlement, international transportation, cargo insurance, governing law, transnational dispute resolution, and various Chinese domestic laws such as contract law, tax law, merchandise inspection, tariff policy, and relevant industry laws and regulations.

International trade contracts are usually highly negotiated. The final drafts go through many rounds of review subject to amendment. The most negotiated points in any given deal relate to quality, quantity, packing, shipment, price, insurance, payment, guarantee, inspection, and taxation.

3.2 International Investment Negotiations

Unlike trade negotiations, investment negotiations are likely to be more difficult and complicated. This is primarily because in the case of negotiations the trading of goods is only one part of company's routine operations, whereas with investment, all aspects of the company must be considered.

To form a group to negotiate a particular investment, a company will gather members from various departments such as the investment, financial, sales, and legal departments. The company will likely also utilize external lawyers who are familiar with industry policy, foreign exchange control, the tax system, the employment system, company law, financial law, environment protection policies, and IP protection.

The crux of negotiations in investment transactions is the design of a transaction plan through which the parties' respective goals are achieved, legal risks are reduced, and transaction costs are lowered. Normally, a letter of intent will be formed to reflect the designed transaction plan and serve as the basis for further negotiations.

Unlike trade contracts, the content and format of investment agreements tends to vary considerably. In fact, precedent for such agreements usually comes from overseas. Even if an agreement is drafted by a Chinese lawyer, it reflects much of the overseas form of agreement. The rationale for this is that overseas contract formats are frequently used and have workable structures and expressions. However, the obscurity of form contracts originating from outside of China can be a problem for domestic clients who may not understand them. Accordingly, Chinese lawyers will often need to amend their drafts by using simpler and plainer language. Another reason why overseas-version contracts need to be amended is that there are a number of approvals, registrations, permits, and restrictions for cross-border investments. Foreign investors should always keep this in mind when negotiating with a Chinese counterparty.

4. Practical Issues to Consider

4.1 Timing

The timing of negotiations is addressed in three stages: the negotiation stage, the internal approvals stage, and the external approvals stage.

The efficiency of negotiations can be region specific. In the larger cities of Shanghai, Beijing, and Shenzhen, clients and lawyers are familiar with western countries' commercial concepts and professional habits. To meet a client's requirements for rapid response, same-day or overnight turnaround of documents and continuous negotiation is now accepted practice. However, in some parts of mainland China, the traditional slow pace of living and business is maintained and it is a rarity to find lawyers and/or business representatives working around the clock to conclude negotiations.

The timing of internal approvals depends on the type of the company. Theoretically, privately held limited liability companies are the most efficient, tending to be able to negotiate relatively rapidly without the burdens of significant internal bureaucracy. State-owned enterprises and public listing companies need more time to go through the board of directors, supervisor of state shareholders, shareholders' meeting, and related layers of complexity.

Transactions involving state assets tend to involve additional complications, more time, and more cost. Such transactions can ultimately result in satisfaction of the involved parties, especially in the case of privatization.

The potential need for various government approvals should be taken into account at the beginning of the negotiations. This will be discussed in greater detail in section 4.4.

4.2 Due Diligence

Since 1993, lawyers in China have played a role in initial public offerings (IPOs). Extensive due diligence has become a mandatory prerequisite to IPOs. Now, both mergers and acquisitions and joint stock company reforms (meaning the transformation of a limited liability company into a joint stock limited company) also call for extensive due diligence. Standard practice calls for attorneys to issue to their clients a checklist of items and issues to be reviewed before the contemplated transaction can take place, including material contracts, existing and threatened litigation, tax assessment, environmental liability, lease agreements, guarantees, and so forth. Due diligence is normally conducted at the time between the letter of intent stage and the execution of the definitive agreement.

4.3 Culture and Commercial Custom Differences

Operating out of an oriental country with a long history in comparison to its western counterparts, Chinese businessmen tend to conduct business negotiations in a rather indirect manner. They take time to see whether or not their potential business counterparts are reliable, for example, by inviting them to a party and socializing with them. A harmonious environment for negotiation and a sound personal relationship are very important to achieve a deal. "Guanxi" (meaning relationship) has a prevalent role in business development.

4.4 Government Approvals

Similar to other developing countries, in China the government plays a pervasive role in national economic development, and there are a number of items in connection with international transactions that are subject to governmental approval. When contemplating matters that may be subject to governmental approval, the relevant governmental authorities will consider the following factors:

Transaction type: The type of transaction will have an impact on the approvals that are needed. For example, technology trades need to be approved by relevant technology administration authorities. It is only after such approval that the relevant tax reduction formalities can be addressed.

Industry policy: Recently, noticeable controls have been implemented in certain industry sectors, including real estate, finance, and medical and commercial retailing. Transactions occurring in such regulated industries may face additional governmental approvals.

Investment body: In recent years, numerous domestic companies have begun to engage in Red Chip listing by way of establishing overseas shell companies and injecting domestic assets or equities into such shell companies. In such cases, although the relevant listing entities are overseas companies, strict approval and registration formalities still need to be complied with since the substantial controllers are all Chinese residents.

Anti-monopoly and national economic security: In considering anticompetitive restrictions, it is useful to contemplate a notable case example. When the Carlyle Group intended to acquire Xuzhou Construction Machinery Group, it spent more than three years in the approval procedure. Ultimately, the contemplated transaction was denied the requisite approval by government authority due to the anti-monopoly investigation as provided for in the M&A Regulations promulgated in 2006.

Significant Chinese governmental authorities have a role in regulating transactions involving foreign interest. These authorities can be divided into the following three categories:

Relevant foreign investment authorities: Foreign investment authorities include (i) the Ministry of Commerce (MOFCOM), which is in charge of both domestic and international trade and investment; and (ii) State Administration of Foreign Exchange

(SAFE), which is in charge of receipts and payments of foreign exchange.

Industry administration authorities: Industry administration authorities include (i) China Securities Regulatory Commission (CSRC), which is in charge of capital market and relevant issues, such as stock issuing and listing, supervision of listed companies, supervision of intermediaries (such as securities companies, fund management companies, future companies, accounting firms, law firms, investment consulting companies, etc.); (ii) China Banking Regulatory Commission (CBRC), which administers domestic commercial banks as well as branches and offices of overseas banks; (iii) China Insurance Regulatory Commission (CIRC), which monitors and administers domestic insurance companies (including joint venture companies and wholly foreign-owned companies) as well as branches and offices of overseas insurance companies; (iv) Ministry of Information Industry (MII), which administers the industries of electronic information products manufacturing, telecommunications, and software; (v) Ministry of Construction, which administers real estate and construction; and (vi) the State Intellectual Property Office (SIPO), which administers routine affairs such as receiving and examining patent applications for inventions, utility models, and designs, and granting patents.

General administration authorities: Major general administration authorities include (i) the State Administration of Taxation (SAT), which is in charge of tax policymaking and routine tax administration; (ii) the State Administration for Industry and Commerce (SAIC), which is in charge of the registrations of establishment, change, and termination of enterprises and companies, and (iii) State Trademark Bureau, a special organ under SAIC that administers all trademark affairs.

Most governmental approvals take the form of administrative permits, and with the recent progress in digitization, the administrative permit procedures of many governmental authorities are now made available through the Internet. Applicants can obtain answers by means of asking questions through the Internet platform. In Appendix 1 to this chapter, a list of Web sites of major Chinese governmental authorities is listed, among which the MOFCOM Web site is the most popular.

5. Hong Kong's Special Function in International Transactions

Even after the momentous transition of 1997, Hong Kong has maintained its common law system. This was due primarily to historic reasons, including Hong Kong's long-standing recognition as an international free port and financial center. Additionally, Hong Kong's commercial environment and legal system have been accustomed to foreign investors for many years. Therefore, many foreign investors will automatically consider Hong Kong when choosing the appropriate vehicle for their investment in China.

After the handing over of Hong Kong to China in 1997, the central government gave relative freedom to the SAR. At the same time, the Chinese government also aimed to foster close cooperation with Hong Kong. It also launched efforts designed to stimulate Hong Kong's economy by organizing two rounds of CEPA. For example, implementing zero tariff to products originating from Hong Kong led to lowering the standards for Hong Kong companies to enter mainland markets; opening financial services facilitated customs and improved the transparency of laws and regulations. All these measures, to a degree, have resulted in foreign investors making investments and completing transactions in mainland China through Hong Kong, and lowering investors' investment costs.

The most recent justice development between the mainland and Hong Kong is that a landmark provisional agreement was signed in mid-July 2007. It is anticipated that this agreement could transform the legal landscape for cross-border dispute resolution. The arrangement means that judgments in commercial cases in the two jurisdictions, Hong Kong or mainland China, can be recognized and enforced in each other's courts. Some people view this as a watershed and believe it will have far-reaching consequences for mainland and Hong Kong companies, as well as multinationals investing in China. Under the new regime, if a commercial contract designates Hong Kong as the exclusive forum for resolving disputes arising from the contract, a judgment obtained in Hong Kong will be recognized and enforced in mainland China if the debtor keeps the assets there, and the reverse will also apply to judgments made in mainland China.

6. Conclusion

When trading with or investing in a country, one must consider a great number of factors, including the country's culture and commercial custom in that country, its current and future economic and political environment, and relevant laws, regulations, and policies. Such factors are particularly significant in a country such as China, which in recent years has rapidly undergone momentous change in a number of different ways. China's legislation in civil and commercial fields has entered a new era, especially in terms of legislation conception, legislation method, and detailed provisions in which the common law system and international practices are well reflected. This trend will help China to adapt to globalization and to continue to develop its foreign economic exchanges.

Wendy Guo
Partner
Kang Da Law Firm
2301 CITIC Building
19 Jianguomenwai Avenue
Beijing 100004, PRC
Phone: 011-86-10 8526 2828
Fax: 011-86-10 8526 2826
E-mail: wenqing.guo@kangdalawyers.com

Main Web Sites of Government Bodies and Organizations Related to International Trade and Investment

Ministry of Commerce (MOFCOM)
www.mofcom.gov.cn

State Administration of Foreign Exchange (SAFE)
www.safe.gov.cn

China Customs
www.customs.gov.cn

State Administration for Industry & Commerce (SAIC)
www.saic.gov.cn

State Administration of Taxation (SAT)
www.chinatax.gov.cn

The People's Bank of China (PBC)
www.pbc.gov.cn

China Banking Regulatory Commission (CBRC)
www.cbrc.gov.cn

China Securities Regulatory Commission (CSRC)
www.csrc.gov.cn

China Insurance Regulatory Commission (CIRC)
www.circ.gov.cn

China International Economic and Trade Arbitration
Commission (CIETAC)
www.cietac.org.cn

China Chamber of International Commerce (CCOIC)
www.ccoic.cn

US-China Federal Association of Business Councils
www.ucfabc.org

APPENDIX 26.2

Useful Search Engines for PRC Law and Regulations

www.cchchina.com.cn

www.chinalawandpractice.com

www.lawyee.net

www.chinalawinfo.com

CHAPTER 27

International Business Negotiations in the Czech Republic

Sasha Štěpánová
KOCIÁN ŠOLC BALAŠTÍK
PRAGUE, CZECH REPUBLIC

1. Introduction

The Czech Republic, being formerly part of the Austro-Hungarian Empire, has a continental civil code legal system based on Roman law. After forty years of communist rule, it began its transformation from a centrally planned economic system to a market economy after the so-called "Velvet Revolution" in 1989. From 1990 onward it has consistently attracted large volumes of foreign investment. The Czech Republic became a member of the European Union as of May 1, 2004, and in the lead-up to the EU accession, Czech laws were harmonized with EU law.

This chapter sets forth an introduction to a selection of legal matters that will interest international investors and their legal advisors when undertaking a transaction in the Czech Republic. We commence with a brief overview of key commercial legislation and then discuss forms of corporate structure, as well as a variety of transactional factors particular to the Czech environment.

2. Principal Commercial Legislation

All Czech law is codified in the form of legislation; precedents in the form of earlier court decisions on a particular point of law do not themselves constitute law, but can merely be used as a nonbinding form of interpretation of the law. The judiciary operates independently of other state institutions.

There are two major codes of Czech law that apply to general commercial transactions, both of which have been subject to regular amendment. It is important to note that both major codes are currently the subject of proposed complete redrafting, which may, if adopted, significantly affect the governing of commercial legal relations. The first such code is Act No. 513/1991 Coll., the Commercial Code (the

"Commercial Code"), which currently deals with relationships arising in business between commercial legal entities, the business activities of foreign companies, and the form of commercial legal entities that may be established in the Czech Republic. The state and municipalities are also regarded as entrepreneurs for the purpose of the Commercial Code. The contracting parties may diverge from the provisions of the Commercial Code if they agree to do so in the contract. They cannot, however, exclude mandatory provisions of the Commercial Code.

The second major code is Act No. 40/1964 Coll., the Civil Code (the "Civil Code"), which currently deals primarily with relationships between an individual and a business and relationships between one or more individuals. It also currently deals with the creation of pledges (security interests), ownerships, and civil duties and obligations. In general, where the provisions of the Commercial Code are silent upon an issue that is dealt with by the Civil Code, the provisions of the Civil Code will apply. At the time of writing, a brand new draft Civil Code is in preparation that is expected to have substantial impact.

3. Foreign Exchange and Regulatory Aspects of Foreign Investment

The currency of the Czech Republic is the Czech crown (koruna). Although eventual adoption of the euro is expected, there is currently no specific timetable for its adoption. There are no foreign exchange controls or restrictions; currency is freely exchangeable pursuant to the Act No. 219/1995 Coll., the Foreign Exchange Act, as amended (hereinafter the "Foreign Exchange Act"), and several implementation decrees of the Czech National Bank.

Generally, foreign entities or persons may participate in business activities in the Czech Republic under the same conditions as Czech entities or persons and government approvals or restrictions do not apply to incoming investment. By way of very limited exception, Czech law lays down restrictions relating to foreign investment, including in particular certain trade with respect to military materials and the acquisition by foreign legal entities of agricultural and forest land in the Czech Republic.

No limitations exist concerning the distribution and expatriation of profits by Czech subsidiaries to their foreign parent companies, other than the obligation of joint stock and limited liability companies to generate a mandatory reserve fund and pay withholding taxes. The Czech Republic has concluded treaties to prevent double taxation with many countries, including all EU countries, Switzerland, the United States, Canada, Japan, and Australia. A full list of countries is available from the Ministry of Finance. Double-taxation treaties cover taxes on dividends, interests, and royalties. Actual rates of the withholding tax are determined by the treaty and range from 0 to 15 percent. The exact method of double-taxation prevention must be determined by reference to the actual treaty between the Czech Republic and the other country.

The property of a foreign person involved in business activity in the Czech Republic can be expropriated only on the basis of law and in the public interest if such interest cannot be otherwise satisfied and is subject to compensation, which must be provided. Bilateral investment promotion and protection agreements also deal with this issue. However, there have been no such instances since 1989.

Pursuant to the Foreign Exchange Act, there are no restrictions or government approvals required concerning investments and financial loans provided by foreign entities. However, there is an applicable notification duty, the details of which are set forth in a special decree of the Czech National Bank.

"Foreign investments" is understood as the utilization of funds or the exercise of other rights valued in money for the purpose of establishing, acquiring, or extending permanent economic relations by an entity with its registered office in a foreign country investing in an entity with its registered office in the Czech Republic. This is true in particular where such investment is for the establishment or acquisition of an exclusive share in business activities, including extension thereof; a participation in a newly established or existing business (provided the foreign entity acquires at least a 10 percent share in the registered capital or equity); or voting rights or other share of the business of a company with its registered office in the Czech Republic.

An entity with its registered office in the Czech Republic has a notification duty concerning the establishment of or a change in a direct investment from a foreign entity in such domestic entity and also all collections and payments connected with establishment and change of the amount of the investment. The notification duty does not apply to payments of revenues from the investment (e.g., dividends) made by the domestic entity to the benefit of the foreign entity.

A "financial loan" is to be understood as provision of money in Czech crowns or another currency, with which the obligation to return it in a monetary form is connected. Financial leasing is also considered to constitute a financial loan. A domestic entity has a notification duty concerning the form, manner of drawing and repayment of the loan, collection and payment connected with drawing and repayment thereof, and also a change in the above, including a change of the creditor.

4. Authorization of Foreigners to Undertake Business Activity in the Czech Republic

The Commercial Code regulates the status of entrepreneurs (or businesspeople), who are both individuals and legal entities (legal persons) entered in the Commercial Register; persons having an authorization to conduct a certain trade (activity) under the Trades Licensing Act, or under another authorization to engage in business activity; and farmers recorded in an appropriate register. Business activity (also referred to as "entrepreneurial activity") is defined as systematic activity carried on by an entrepreneur, in his own name and under his responsibility, for the purpose of making a profit.

Business (or commercial) companies, partnerships, and cooperatives are entered in the Commercial Register, as are foreign persons who wish to undertake systematic business activity in the Czech Republic. A foreign person's authorization to undertake systematic business activity in the Czech Republic is established on the day such person is entered in the Czech Commercial Register.

The legal capacity of a foreign entity is governed by the legislation of the country where this entity was established, such legislation also applying to its internal relations. Foreign persons authorized to conduct business activity abroad are considered to be entrepreneurs under the Czech Commercial Code.

Foreign entities and individuals may form a wholly owned business company, partnership, or cooperative in the Czech Republic, provided that the legal form is permissible under the Commercial Code. Foreign persons may also become shareholders or partners in existing Czech businesses, found joint ventures, or register a Czech branch office of their foreign company.

5. Public Information in the Commercial Register

All business entities (including branches of foreign companies) authorized to undertake business in the Czech Republic must be registered in the Commercial Register. The following data is entered in the Commercial Register:

- the commercial name; in the case of legal entities, their registered office, and in the case of natural persons (individuals), their residence and place of business, if different;
- the identification/registration number of the company;
- the subject of business activity;
- the legal form of the entity;
- the name(s) and residential address(es) of the individual(s) constituting the statutory organ, including the manner by which such individual(s) act in the name of the legal entity;
- the name of the procurator (individual specially authorized to act for the entity), if any, and his residential address; and
- any other facts required by law.

Entrepreneurs recorded in the Commercial Register must use a double-entry bookkeeping system. The accounting period is one calendar year.

6. Legal Forms of Czech Corporate Organization

The current Commercial Code allows for a wide variety of legal arrangements that may be used by entrepreneurs to carry on commercial activities in the Czech Republic. Some of the more commonly used arrangements are limited liability companies, joint stock companies, general commercial partnerships, and limited partnerships, all of which are considered to be legal entities. It is also possible for a foreign company to establish a branch office.

6.1 Branch Office of Foreign Company

A company wishing to carry out business in the Czech Republic, but not wishing to establish a Czech legal entity subsidiary (such as a Czech limited liability company or joint stock company), may instead establish a branch office here.

The branch office of a foreign legal entity must be registered in the Commercial Register and, as of the date of its registration in the relevant Commercial Register, it may carry on business if it has the authorization to conduct business in the Czech Republic (trade license). A branch is not a legal entity, but the director of the branch office may execute all documents and perform all legal acts that relate to the branch.

The basic difference between a registered branch office and a Czech incorporated subsidiary is the fact that the subsidiary entity is a legal entity (e.g., limited liability company or joint stock company), separate from its founder, whereas a branch office is not a legal entity pursuant to Czech law and basically acts as an extended arm of its founder in the Czech Republic.

Accordingly, the liability aspects are different. Whereas, for example, a limited liability company is liable for a breach of its obligations only to the extent of its property and each participant is liable for the company's obligations only up to the amount of the unpaid portion of its contribution as recorded in the Commercial Register, the liability of a branch office extends all the way to the founder, as the branch office is not a legal entity and therefore any liability attributable to the branch office is to be reimbursed by its founder.

Out of the various forms of Czech legal entities available, perhaps the most popular choice for investors tends to be either the limited liability company or the joint stock company, both of which are described below.

6.2 Czech Limited Liability Company

A Czech limited liability company (Czech abbreviation "s.r.o" hereinafter "SRO") is an entity whose registered capital is made up of its members' investment contributions. Unlike a joint stock company (also described below), the SRO does not have shares or shareholders. Each participant who has made an investment contribution to the SRO holds an "ownership interest" and is deemed a "participant" or "member."

The SRO corporate form is the most popular structure for small to medium-size investments or for use as project vehicles. When considering the SRO in a structured investment or eventual corporate reorganization, it should be borne in mind that there is, pursuant to the Commercial Code, a ban on a "chain" of single-owner SROs. This means that a limited liability company (whether Czech or foreign) with a single member (shareholder), may not acquire or hold 100 percent of a Czech limited liability company. Such a restriction on sole shareholders in an SRO chain does not apply to joint stock companies.

The maximum number of members in the SRO is fifty. The registered capital of the SRO must be a minimum of CZK 200,000. The investment contribution of an individual member must amount to at least CZK 20,000. A useful factor in using an SRO to structure equity holdings is that the designated equity value (as well as voting rights) of a member's investment contribution need not be the same as the actual financial investment contribution. Thus, a member with the minimum financial contribution of CZK 20,000 could nevertheless be designated as holding, for example, a 60 percent interest in the company. Investment contributions may also be of a nonmonetary nature (e.g., the contribution of real estate into the new company's registered capital); in the case of such nonmonetary contribution, an expert valuation of such contribution is required.

The SRO is founded on the basis of a foundation deed (if it has a single founding member) or an association agreement (if it has two or more founding members). The SRO comes into legal existence upon its entry into the Commercial Register. Prior to the application for entry of the SRO into the Commercial Register, it is necessary for the founding members to pay up in full their respective nonmonetary investment contributions and to pay up at least 30 percent of their respective monetary investment contributions; the amount of paid-up contributions must amount at least to CZK 200,000. If the SRO is founded by a single founding member, the investment contribution must be paid in full. The time limit for a member to pay the entire monetary investment contribution is five years from the date of incorporation of the SRO (i.e., from its entry into the Commercial Register). Similar rules for payment of the investment contributions apply upon the increase of the register capital of the SRO with respect to a commitment by a member to increase its investment contribution.

6.2.1 Bodies of the SRO

The SRO must have a general meeting and one or more executives, and may also have a supervisory board.

6.2.2 General Meeting

The general meeting is the supreme body of the SRO. Every member has the right to participate in and vote at the general meeting (unless the right to vote is restricted in accordance with law). Each member of the SRO shall have one vote for every CZK 1,000 of its investment contribution, unless the association agreement stipulates otherwise.

The general meeting has the power to decide on all matters that the law or the association agreement of the SRO entrusts to the authority of the general meeting. It is, however, not permitted to instruct the executives with regard to ordinary business of the SRO, since the law stipulates that no one is entitled to give instruction to the executive(s) with respect to the ordinary business of the SRO. The general meeting must be called at least once in each calendar year.

Quorum for the general meeting is constituted when members having at least half of all the votes are present, unless the association agreement requires a higher number of votes. The general meeting decides by a simple majority of votes of members present, unless the law or the association agreement requires a higher number of votes.

6.2.3 Executives

The SRO's statutory management body is composed of one or more executives (hereinafter "Executives"). Each of the Executives is empowered to act independently in the name of the SRO, unless the association agreement or statutes provide otherwise; however, such restrictions are ineffective against third parties. An example of this would be a stipulation issued by the general meeting or set forth within the association agreement or the statutes that the Executive may sign contracts independently only up to a certain financial value. If the Executive violated this restriction and signed a contract with a third party in excess of this limit, the contract would still be valid, but he would be personally liable for damage to the SRO. Executives are appointed and recalled by the general meeting of the SRO.

The Executive is authorized to undertake all acts in law concerning the SRO's activities unless they fall within the powers of the general meeting or the supervisory board (if established). The Executive's responsibilities are twofold, both for external SRO relations (negotiation and signing on behalf of the SRO) and for internal SRO management (ensuring proper bookkeeping, informing the members of the SRO's affairs). The Executive is also by law required to file a bankruptcy petition if the SRO becomes insolvent or is overburdened with debts.

Executives must exercise their powers with "due managerial care" being generally interpreted as exercise of the powers in the best interest of the SRO. Executives who cause damage to the SRO by breaching their legal duties while exercising their powers shall be liable for such damage to the SRO jointly and severally. In the event of any dispute, the burden falls upon the Executive to demonstrate that he or she acted with due managerial care.

An Executive is obliged to comply with the instructions of the general meeting, provided that such instructions are in accordance with the law and with the SRO's association agreement or statutes. As stated above, however, the general meeting cannot give instructions to the Executives with respect to the ordinary business of the SRO. The restriction on giving instruction concerning the ordinary business of the SRO does not apply only if a special "control agreement" is entered into between the controlled and controlling. A control agreement in general terms establishes the right of the controlling entity to give otherwise prohibited binding instructions to the Executives of the controlled entity and to subject certain decisions by or actions of the Executives of the controlled entity to approval by the controlling entity. In return, the controlling entity has the obligation to compensate the controlled entity for any part of its accounting loss that cannot be settled from available internal resources of the controlled entity, e.g., undistributed past profits, reserve fund, share premium, other capital funds, etc. Such a control agreement also modifies the concept of "due managerial care" of the Executives, as it enables the interests of the corporate group, not only the company, to be taken into account.

The Executive's relationship with the SRO is specifically not an employment relationship, but is generally governed by a form of mandate agreement.

6.2.4 Supervisory Board

The supervisory board is not a mandatory body of the SRO. The supervisory board can be established by the association agreement of the SRO. The supervisory board serves to supervise the activities of the Executives, inspect business documents, review financial statements, and submit reports thereon to the general meeting. The supervisory board may convene a general meeting of the SRO if it deems that it is in the interests of the company to do so.

Similarly to the Executives, the relationship of members of the supervisory board to the SRO is governed by the mandate agreement.

6.2.5 Concept of Liability in the SRO

As a rule, the SRO is liable for the breach of its obligations with its entire property (the same applies for the joint-stock company). Under Section 106/2 of the Czech Commercial Code, members of the SRO are jointly and severally liable for the obligations of the SRO up to the total value of their *unpaid* investment contributions as set forth in the Commercial Register entry.

For example, if a member of the SRO had only paid up 50 percent of his investment contribution of CZK 500,000, he would be liable for the obligations of the SRO up to the amount of CZK 250,000, the total value of his unpaid investment contribution, until the payment of the unpaid investment contribution is entered into the Commercial Register.

The liability as surety of the member of the SRO under Section 106/2 of the Czech Commercial Code terminates once the payment of the remaining part of the investment contribution is entered into the Commercial Register. Any payment made by a member to any of the creditors of the SRO on the grounds of member's liability as surety shall not terminate or reduce the extent of his liability. Any payment made by a member on behalf of the SRO shall be credited as part of such member's investment contribution, and if this is not possible, the member can claim reimbursement from the SRO. If the member cannot obtain such reimbursement from the SRO, he may claim it from a member who has not paid up his contribution, or else from each of the other members to the extent of his participation in the registered capital.

6.3 Czech Joint Stock Company

A Czech joint stock company (in Czech "akciová společnost" or abbreviation "a.s.") (hereinafter "AS") is an entity whose registered capital is divided into a certain number of shares of a specific nominal value. An AS may be founded by a single founder if the founder is a legal person (an entity), otherwise by two or more founders. The registered capital of the AS must be a minimum of CZK 20,000,000 if the AS is founded through a public offering. If the AS is founded without a public offering for subscription, the registered capital of AS may be a minimum of CZK 2,000,000.

When founded by two or more founders, the AS is founded on the basis of a founding agreement. A single founder shall found an AS on the basis of a founder's deed. The AS comes into being upon its entry into the Commercial Register. Prior to the application for entry of the AS into the Commercial Register, the company must comply with the following requirements:

a. The constituent general meeting has been duly held, if such is required.
b. The subscribers have subscribed the entire amount of the registered capital; paid the share premium, if relevant, and at least 30 percent of the registered (share) capital formed by monetary investment contributions; and fully provided their non-monetary contributions.
c. The articles of association of the company have been approved.
d. All of the members of the board of directors and supervisory board have been elected.
e. The articles of association and the founding of the company are not contrary to the law.

f. If the AS was founded through a public offering, a public offering of shares and paper prospectus were published in accordance with the Czech Security Commission's approval.

6.3.1 Bodies of the AS

The AS is required to have a general meeting, a board of directors, and a supervisory board.

6.3.2 General Meeting

The general meeting is the supreme body of the AS and consists of the shareholders present at the general meeting. Every shareholder has the right to participate in and vote at the general meeting unless the right to vote is restricted in accordance with the law. A shareholder's number of votes depends on the nominal value of shares held by that shareholder.

The general meeting has the power to decide on all matters that the law or the statutes (articles of association) entrust to its authority. However, it is not allowed to approve instruction to the board as regards ordinary management of the business of the company. The general meeting must be called at least once in each calendar year. As a rule, the board of directors convenes the general meeting; however, in some cases the general meeting can be convened by the supervisory board or the minority shareholders.

The general meeting constitutes a quorum when the assembled shareholders have shares of a nominal value of more than 30 percent of the registered capital, unless the articles of association requires a higher attendance. The general meeting decides by a simple majority of votes of shareholders present, unless the law or the articles of association require a higher number of votes.

6.3.3 Board of Directors

The board of directors of an AS body is composed of three or more members. They are elected (for a period set forth by the statutes, but no longer than five years) and recalled by the general meeting; reelection is admissible. The statutes may stipulate that the members of the board of directors are elected and recalled by the supervisory board. Members of the board of directors elect the chairman from amongst themselves; the chairman of the board of directors does not have any material specific powers in comparison with the other members. Periods for board of directors meetings are not set forth by law; usually the board of directors meets once a month. The board of directors decides by majority of votes of all members thereof, unless set forth otherwise by the statutes.

The board of directors ensures management of business activities and acting on behalf of the company; unless stipulated otherwise by the statutes, every member of the board of directors is entitled to act on behalf of the company independently (the manner of acting on behalf of the company shall be entered in the Commercial Register). The board of directors decides on all company affairs, unless they fall within the powers of the general meeting or the supervisory board under the law or the statutes; presents to the general meeting for approval regular, extraordinary, and consolidated or, as the case may be, interim financial statements and a proposal for the distribution of profits or coverage of losses; and observes the principles and instructions approved by the general meeting, provided that these comply with the law and the statutes. Failure to observe these does not affect the consequences of the acts taken by the members of the board of directors vis-à-vis third parties.

A member of the Board of Directors has a duty to observe the ban on competition. Board of Directors' members shall not:

i. engage in business of an identical or similar nature as that of the company or enter into business with the company;
ii. arrange or procure company business for third parties;
iii. participate in the business of another company as a participant with unlimited liability or as a controlling person of another entity with identical or similar business objects; and
iv. perform acts as a statutory body or member of a statutory body or another legal entity with identical or similar business objects, other than within the corporate group.

Nobody may give the board of directors instructions relating to the business management of the company (unless a dominance agreement is executed); members of the board of directors are liable for damage they have caused to the company by performance of instructions given by the general meeting if the instruction of the general meeting is contrary to the provisions of law.

Members of the board of directors shall exercise their powers with due managerial care and keep secret all confidential information and matters the disclosure of which to third parties could give rise to damage to the company.

Members of the board of directors who cause the company to suffer damage by breach of lawful duties when exercising the powers of the board of directors are liable for such damage jointly and severally; an agreement between the company and a member of the board of directors or a provision in the statutes excluding or restricting the liability of a member of the board of directors for damage is void.

The relationships between the company and the members of the board of directors are governed by commercial law. The members of the board of directors are not employees of the company (unless they are employed by the company as members of management or otherwise).

6.3.4 Supervisory Board

The supervisory board is a mandatory body of the AS. The supervisory board is the controlling and supervisory body of the company that supervises the exercise of the powers by the board of directors as well as the business activities of the company—e.g., inspects business documents and records relating to the activities of the company to check whether bookkeeping entries are made in accordance with the actual facts and whether the business activities of the company are in compliance with the law, the statutes, and the instructions of the general meeting (insofar as permissible); reviews the annual, extraordinary, and consolidated or, as the case may be, interim financial statements and proposals for the distribution of profits or coverage of losses; and submits to the general meeting its statement thereto. The supervisory board elects and recalls the members of the board of directors if the statutes of the company so stipulate.

The law requires the prior consent of the supervisory board to executions of agreements on the basis of which the company acquires or disposes assets of over one-third of the equity of the company; the statutes of the company may stipulate that some other actions to be taken by the board of directors require prior consent of the supervisory board.

The number of supervisory board members is specified in the statutes and shall be always divisible by three, the statutory minimum being three. Members of the supervisory board are elected (up to a period of five years) and recalled by the general meeting; if the company has more then fifty employees, at least one-third of the members of the supervisory board must be elected and recalled by the employees; reelection is admissible. They elect the chairman from amongst themselves. The chairman of the supervisory board does not have any material specific powers in comparison with the other members.

The supervisory board decides on the basis of consent by majority of votes of all members thereof; the statutes may stipulate a higher number. Periods for supervisory board meetings are not set forth by law. The usual practice is that the supervisory board meets once every two or three months.

A member of the supervisory board cannot at the same time be a member of the board of directors, procurist, or another person entitled pursuant to the entry in the Commercial Register to act on behalf of the company. The members of the supervisory board shall have obligations and liabilities similar to the members of the board of directors (e.g., acting with due managerial care, liability for breach of obligations, and ban on competition).

Similarly to the Board of Directors, the relationship of members of the supervisory board to the company is governed by a form of mandate agreement.

6.3.5 Concept of Liability in the AS

As a rule, the AS is liable for the breach of its obligations with its entire property. A shareholder is not liable for the company's obligations.

7. Operational Aspects of Czech Limited Liability and Joint Stock Companies

7.1 Acting and Signing on Behalf of a Company

The following is applicable with respect to both an SRO and an AS.

- Every executive of an SRO or member of the board of directors of an AS is entitled to act on behalf of the company independently, unless the statutes stipulate otherwise. The manner of acting on behalf of the company shall be entered in the Commercial Register.
- A procurist (a person with a special power of attorney registered in the Commercial Register) may undertake all legal acts that occur in the operation of the company business even though they might otherwise require a special power of attorney.
- Employees of the company (including members of management) can act on behalf of the company if they are authorized to do so under the internal regulations of the company, or if acting on behalf of the company is usual under their employment duties (general provision of the Czech Civil Code).

7.2 General Liability under Czech Law for Adversely Influencing the Company

The following is applicable with respect to both an SRO and an AS.

In addition to the liability of the members as sureties arising from unpaid investment contributions, which is typical for the SRO, the following general liability principles are applicable to all companies recognized by Czech law (including a joint stock company) and may under certain circumstances potentially affect persons who are not shareholders, members, or company statutory office holders:

- Under Section 66/6 of the Czech Commercial Code, the provisions of the Czech Commercial Code and special provisions of law relating to the liability and guarantees of company bodies (e.g., executives in the case of an SRO) shall also apply to persons who, pursuant to an agreement, ownership interest in the company, or other circumstances influence the conduct of the company in a material way, even though they are not company bodies or members thereof, irrespective of their relationship with the company. It ensues from the Commercial Code that the liability of company bodies will arise only if the members of the bodies breach their obligations under the Commercial Code (e.g., do not act with due managerial care).

- Under Section 66c of the Czech Commercial Code, any person who by means of his or her influence in the company intentionally causes a person who is a statutory body or a member thereof, a member of a supervisory body, a person who has been granted the power of procura, or another person authorized to act on the company's behalf, to act to the detriment of the company or its members, guarantees (is liable as surety) the performance of obligations to compensate for damage arising in connection with such conduct.

7.3 Liability of Controlling Persons

Under the Czech Commercial Code, a person who is factually or legally capable of exerting directly or indirectly decisive influence on management or operation of another party's (termed "controlled entity") enterprise constitutes a controlling entity. The controlling person is always:

i.   the majority member (i.e., the member having the majority of the votes ensuing from his ownership interest in the company); this shall not apply if someone else disposes with the majority member's voting rights based on an agreement with the majority member;

ii.   a person holding the majority of voting rights on the basis of an agreement concluded with one or more other members; or

iii. a person who can push through appointment, election, or dismissal of the majority of persons who constitute a statutory body or of members thereof or the majority of persons who are members of the supervisory body of a legal entity in which he or she is a member.

Among other consequences of the entity being under control of the controlling entity, the statutory body of the controlled entity (i.e., Executives in the case of an SRO) shall, unless a "control agreement" is entered into, draw up an annual report on relations between the controlling person and the controlled person, as well as on relations between the controlled person and other persons controlled by the same controlling person ("Report on Mutual Relationships"). The Report on Mutual Relationships shall be part of the annual report that must be submitted by the company to the publicly available registry of documents administered by the registry courts.

Under Section 66a/8 of the Czech Commercial Code, if the controlling entity exerts its influence in relation to adoption of a measure or conclusion of a contract on the basis of which the controlled entity suffers damage (loss, disadvantage), the controlling entity would be obliged to compensate, by the end of the accounting period, such damage (loss, disadvantage) to the controlled entity or to conclude with the controlled entity, within the same time period, an agreement stipulating a manner and timing of compensating the damage. If the controlling entity fails to do so, it would be liable under Section 66a/14 of the Czech Commercial Code for incurred damages to the controlled entity, as well as to its minority members. An obligation to compensate for damage shall not arise if an agreement/measure from which the property loss (detriment) arose had also been executed/adopted by the controlled entity in absence of an influence by another entity, provided that the controlled entity would have performed his or her duties with due managerial care. If the controlled entity is controlled by more controlling entities acting in concert, all persons acting in concert shall be jointly and severally liable under Section 66a/14 of the Czech Commercial Code.

7.4 Merger Control Issues

A transaction will be subject to approval by the Czech Office for Economic Competition, if: it involves undertakings, the aggregate net turnover of which for the last completed accounting period within the market of the Czech Republic exceeds CZK 1.5 billion and the aggregate net turnover of at least two of the merging entities for the last completed accounting period within the market of the Czech Republic exceeds CZK 250,000,000; or if the aggregate net turnover of (i) at least one undertaking being a party to the "conversion"; (ii) an enterprise or its part being acquired; (iii) an undertaking, the control of which is being acquired; or (iv) at least one of the undertakings creating a concentrative joint venture, for the last completed accounting period within the market of the Czech Republic exceeds CZK 1.5 billion and the aggregate worldwide net turnover of the other merging entity for the last completed accounting period exceeds CZK 1.5 billion.

7.5 Preliminary Negotiations

Although the use of letters of intent in international transactions in the Czech Republic is fairly common, it should be noted that in Czech law, a letter of intent *per se* is not legally binding and has no legal recognition or classification. Equally, the popular common law phrase of "subject to contract" does not afford any particular meaning or rights in Czech law.

A Czech legal instrument commonly used to establish binding contractual relations with respect to future events is the Agreement on Future Agreement, set forth in the Commercial Code. Pursuant to such an Agreement on Future Agreement, the parties agree in writing to, in the future (within a specified time period), conclude a contract the subject of which is at least stated in a general matter in the agreement on the future agreement. Quite often the draft or form of the yet-to-be-signed final agreement will be included as a schedule to the Agreement on Future Agreement.

7.6 Deal Structure

In addition to the share or asset deal, another form of transaction structure afforded by Czech law is the sale of whole or part of an enterprise (business).

A Sale of an Enterprise transaction structure allows for the entire business to pass to the purchaser pursuant to one transfer contract; there is no need for consents to be obtained in terms of assigning key customer contracts, nor is it necessary to re-execute all employment contracts. Nevertheless, because the *entire* business passes, there can be no exceptions (e.g., excluded liabilities or assets). All liabilities pass, even ones undisclosed to the purchaser. However, one way of dealing with this is by having the seller transfer out any known "unwanted items" prior to the mandatory public notification of the sale of part of the enterprise.

We would like to point out that there may be a certain risk in structuring an asset sale that to all intents and purposes appears and might be interpreted as a factual transfer of a part of an enterprise in any case. There is a possibility that, for example, a creditor might bring action claiming there had been a circumvention of the applicable legal provisions concerning the sale of part of an enterprise, and accordingly a receivable due to such creditor should have also "passed" together with the assets and assumed liabilities. This risk may not be substantial, but it should nevertheless be taken into consideration.

For companies with a multifaceted/multidivisional business, it is possible to spin off a particular business division as a sale of "part of an enterprise."

To be classified as an "independent organizational component," it is necessary for the division to:

i.   keep entirely separate books of accounting records that concern only it, as well as a separate bank account;
ii. have an entirely separate and identifiable line of business;
iii. have employees that work only for it;
iv. utilize a defined separate work space; and
v.   utilize identifiable assets and stocks concerning only it.

7.7 Statutory Organs—Board Members and Executives

In a Czech limited liability or joint stock company, the role of a member of the board of directors or an executive is a personal function and must be performed by an individual (not a company).

Additionally, it is not possible for a board member or executive to universally delegate his or her functions by means of a general power of attorney to another person. To be appointed as a board member or executive, an individual must have a clean criminal record and full legal capacity, and must not have been subject to bankruptcy proceedings during the previous three years. There is no restriction on foreigners holding statutory office; a residency visa or work permit is not required. It should be noted that in some jurisdictions it can be a lengthy process to obtain proof of no criminal record, so these arrangements should be commenced in advance.

7.8 Prohibition on Financial Assistance

Pursuant to Section 161e(1) of the Commercial Code, a Czech company (regardless of its corporate form) is prohibited from providing funds to a purchaser with respect to its own acquisition, or security with respect to the liabilities of any entity that is thereby acquiring the ownership in the Czech company. There is no applicable "whitewash" process pursuant to which such a process might be made permissible; however, one solution used in practice is to use a "carve out" provision in any guarantee or pledge issued by the Czech company, whereby a specific loan to be provided to the acquirer of the Czech company is excluded from the security granted.

7.9 Governing Law and Language

No specific language is required as a controlling language of contracts under Czech law. However, all documents addressed to the authorities or the documents that must, for example, be registered by the Commercial Court must either be executed in Czech or translated into Czech by an official translator authorized as such by a Czech court. It is common practice in international transactions for a master framework agreement to be concluded in English with a simple local Czech transfer instrument concluded in Czech or in a dual-language version. Documents executed in dual-language versions should nevertheless designate a prevailing language version in the event of any interpretive dispute.

Pursuant to the Act No. 97/1963 Coll., the Act on Private International Law, the parties to a commercial or civil contract may choose a foreign law to govern the contract and submit to the jurisdiction of a foreign court, provided that one party to such contract is a foreign legal entity or the relationship between the parties contains another foreign element. An international element can be broadly described as a connection of the given legal relationship to any foreign country, and may consist in characteristics or circumstances relating to:

- a party to the legal relationship (e.g., foreign citizenship or residence of a natural person, foreign seat or law of incorporation of a legal entity);
- matters relevant to the creation and/or existence of the relevant legal relationship (e.g., execution or performance of a contract in a foreign country);
- object of the legal relationship (e.g., location in a foreign country of the asset that constitutes the object of the legal relationship); or
- a related legal relationship (e.g., foreign governing law of a legal relationship, to which a secondary legal relationship relates).

8. Resolving Disputes

8.1 Arbitration

Arbitration proceedings are regulated by the provisions of Act No. 216/1994 Coll., on Proceedings and Enforcement of Arbitral Awards. Although Czech arbitration has brought some contentious results, it seems to be a popular dispute resolution procedure with commercial entities in the Czech Republic. The popularity is due mainly to the relative swiftness and lesser formality of arbitration proceedings, as well as the international enforceability of arbitral awards, and probably also due to certain perceived inefficiencies of judicial proceedings before Czech courts.

The only permanent arbitration court in the Czech Republic is the Arbitration Court attached to the Economic Chamber of the Czech Republic and Agrarian Chamber of the Czech Republic. There are certain other specialized arbitration courts that are attached, e.g., to stock exchanges. Arbitration in the Czech Republic may be conducted pursuant to recognized international rules of arbitration.

An arbitration agreement may be either a document separate from the relevant contract or a part of the relevant contract as an arbitration clause. In order to be valid and effective, such arbitration agreement or clause must contain a clear statement of will by the parties to the contract to the effect that all disputes arising from the contract and in connection therewith shall be finally decided in arbitration proceedings. If an arbitration agreement or clause is found invalid, disputes arising from the relevant contract are subject to ordinary court proceedings rules.

Under Czech law, arbitration agreements or clauses may be concluded in all matters where a (court-approved) settlement can be concluded between the parties in court proceedings, especially in all property-related matters.

Foreign arbitral awards are enforced in the same way as arbitration awards issued in the Czech Republic, i.e., in execution proceedings either by private executors (who implement courts' decisions ordering execution) or by judicial bodies, provided that:

i.   the Country where the award was issued is a member of the Convention on the Recognition and Enforcement of Foreign Arbitral Awards (New York, 1958) ("The New York Convention"); or

ii. if a non-member country, the condition of reciprocity is fulfilled.

Express submission to the jurisdiction of Czech courts is not a necessary requirement for enforceability of a foreign arbitral award in the Czech Republic.

Restrictions for enforcement apply if the award:

i.   is not effective or enforceable under the law of the country where the award was issued; or

ii. breaches the peace or public order; or

iii. is defective in its arbitration clause, proceedings, appointing of the arbitrators, etc.

Arbitration awards relating to property matters do not need to be approved (recognized) by an authority of the Czech Republic. The relevant authority (execution court) simply takes account of the award.

Sasha Štěpánová
Kocián Šolc Balaštík
Jungmannova 24
110 00 Prague 1, Czech Republic
Phone: 420-224-103-316
Fax: 420-224-103-234
E-mail: sstepanova@ksb.cz

CHAPTER 28

International Business Negotiations in France

Philippe Sarrailhé[1]
WHITE & CASE LLP
PARIS, FRANCE

1. Introduction

1.1 Broad Demographic, Economic, and Governmental Information

France, including its overseas territories, covers 674,843 square kilometers and has an estimated population of 64.1 million people. France is the sixth-largest economy in the world with a Gross Domestic Product (GDP) of approximately EUR 1.8 billion. As such, France is a member of most influential international organizations such as the G8, the Organisation for Economic Co-operation and Development, the World Trade Organization, and the United Nations, where it stands permanently on the Security Council.

France currently has a hybrid presidential-parliamentary governing system. This form of government was created by the ratification of the 1958 Constitution to address past instabilities that were caused when France had a purely parliamentary administration of government.

1.2 Historical and Cultural Background

The region that became modern-day France had already become a discernible region called Gaul by the time the Romans invaded it in the first century BC. It was inhabited by Celtic Gauls, who adopted Roman speech (Latin, from which the French language evolved), culture, and religion (eventually adopting Christianity, as it became the official religion of the Roman Empire). The etymology of the country's modern name, France, derives from *Francie*, which was a Capetian feudal kingdom around Paris. France became a modern state by the seventeenth century by gradually strengthening itself through war and domination of powerful vassals over the years.

---

[1] The author would like to thank Mathieu Landrot for his contribution.

For some scholars, the monarchic political tradition of France stretching over a millennium explains its tendency to choose political regimes centered on strong executive power, usually embodied in one man. On the other hand, the country inherited a mature democratic tradition from the massive philosophical movement that emerged during the seventeenth century and eventually culminated in its inspiration of the French Revolution in 1789. The Revolution itself is the origin of many French political characteristics such as extreme centralization, universal suffrage, and particular attention to human rights, through the *Déclaration des Droits de l'Homme et du Citoyen*.

In the past two centuries, after developing a political identity featuring two empires, a brief return to monarchy, four republics, and numerous wars, the country appears to have ultimately found stability in its current governing system, which is sometimes considered a subtle synthesis of the previous regimes.

It was nevertheless significantly affected, politically and economically, by the two world wars of the twentieth century. Although ultimately emerging as a victorious nation from the Second World War, France suffered extensive losses, particularly with respect to its colonial empire, which France had built up in the nineteenth century. Moreover, in the war's aftermath, France suffered additional losses in wealth, manpower, and its rank as a dominant nation-state.

Nevertheless, France continues to develop and evolve while influencing other countries. One such example is France's integral role in the development of European economic integration, which was made possible through France's reconciliation and close cooperation with Germany throughout the construction, development, and expansion of the European Union.

France also boasts a rich cultural history to accompany its considerably rich political history. The early stability of the French monarchy favored conditions of intense cultural life for centuries that cultivated a myriad array of celebrated paintings, literature, philosophy, and music. This tradition survived the Revolution and continued to exist throughout the subsequent governing systems as a real pillar of French identity.

1.3 Business Organization and Culture

France has substantial agricultural resources, a large industrial base, and a skilled work force. The country is the second largest trader in western Europe, after Germany. It also features a dynamic service sector that accounts for an increasingly larger share of economic activity; the service sector is responsible for nearly all job creation over the past few years.

In 2006 real GDP increased 2.2 percent, while GDP growth decreased to 1.9 percent in 2007. According to initial projections, GDP growth will decrease to 1.5 percent in 2008. Government economic policy aims to promote investment and domestic growth in a stable fiscal and monetary environment.

Creating jobs and reducing the high unemployment rate through recovery-supportive policies has been a top priority of the government. Despite significant reforms and privatizations over the past fifteen years, the government continues to control a significant share of economic activity. Legislation passed in 1998 shortened the legal workweek from thirty-nine to thirty-five hours for most employees effective January 1, 2000. Recent assessments of the impact of workweek reduction on growth and jobs have generally concluded that the goal of job creation has not been met.

The conduct of business, as well as negotiations, is often significantly influenced by hierarchy and is very formal.

1.4 Overview of Legal System

Unlike its Anglo-Saxon neighbors, France chose to adopt a Civil Code rather than the case law system, which serves as the foundation of common law practice. The development of the civil law system followed from France's decision to adopt its Civil Code. The civil law system, which France influenced numerous countries to adopt, is based chiefly on a series of codes and bodies of rules that lay down the major principles interpreted in court decisions.

The civil law system offers the advantages of standardization and stability, whereas the common law system is characterized to a great extent by creativity and, hence, uncertainty, resulting in the need for exhaustive negotiations. The disadvantage of standardization is the heavy burden of rules and regulations and government intervention that foreign negotiators find so surprising.

In France, the state still exercises a determining influence on business in some economic fields and is sometimes an active party in negotiations.

2. The Sources of Law

2.1 Internal Sources

The traditional view holds that there is a hierarchy of three sources of law in France: the Constitution of 1958; laws, which emanate from the legislative branch; and rules and regulations issued by the executive branch. Certain laws have been combined into codes, such as the Civil Code, the Commercial Code, and the Labor Code, among others.

In addition to these formal sources, there are three other sources: guiding principles, particularly the principle that governs the law of contracts and states that an agreement is formed between parties as soon as there is an exchange of consent; custom and practice, which play a predominant role in business; and case law, which is often innovative and serves as the source of new legislative provisions.

2.2 External Sources

In France, a distinction must be made between international treaties and the laws emanating from bodies of the European Union. Treaties do not come into effect in France until they have been ratified and promulgated. Under Article 55 of the French Constitution, treaties supersede law (arbitration offers an example of this principle).

European Union law, an autonomous body of law that takes precedence over national regulations, has been widely incorporated into French law, for which it represents an abundant source. The written sources of European Union law consist of treaties, essentially the Treaty of Rome of March 25, 1957, and unilateral acts (rules and regulations, directives, decisions, recommendations, and opinions). Nonwritten sources include general principles and the decisions of the *Cour de Justice des Communautés Européennes* and *Cour Européenne des Droits de l'Homme*.

3. Substantive Laws and Regulations Impacting Negotiations

3.1 Corporate Laws

The Commercial Companies Law of July 24, 1966 and the decree of March 23, 1967 establish the bases for the rules and regulations governing the organization of companies in France. There are two types of companies: commercial and noncommercial (*sociétés commerciales* and *sociétés civiles*).

Commercial companies include partnerships (*sociétés de personnes*), which are characterized by a personal relationship and the unlimited liability of the partners, as well as stock companies (*sociétés de capitaux*), characterized by the limited liability of the stockholders. The corporation (*société anonyme*, or *SA*) is the most common type of stock company. The limited liability company (*société à responsabilité limitée*, or *SARL*) combines features of the partnership and the stock company. A new form of commercial company, the simplified corporation (*société par action simplifiée*, or SAS), was created by a law of July 12, 1999 and provides a very flexible legal framework within which to operate a business.

A knowledge of corporate law is indispensable for anyone involved in negotiations. It enables negotiators to determine the role and competencies of the participants, and is also useful in the choice of the financial and legal modalities of the operation being negotiated (an example is the case of a *société en commandite par actions,* a type of limited partnership that is allowed to issue negotiable stock shares, making it possible to separate control and investment).

Recently, the law on commercial companies underwent successive and major changes. On May 15, 2001, the law on New Economic Regulations (*Nouvelles Régulations Economiques*) was enacted. Among many provisions applicable to commercial companies, it implemented a better balance between the corporate bodies of commercial companies, particularly corporations, and strengthened shareholders' rights. On August 1, 2003, the law on Financial Security (*Loi de Sécurité Financière*) implemented new provisions regarding the role played by the auditors as well as the corporate information to be delivered to the shareholders and the market. These series of reforms were also confirmed by new laws and regulations in 2004, particularly by the reform on securities of June 24, 2004, which created a new, less regulated framework applicable to the issuance of securities.

The law of July 26, 2005 also brought into French law the European company (*société européenne*), which was created to (i) enhance the incorporation of European groups, (ii) participate in the creation of a European financial market, and (iii) promote free circulation of business throughout the European Union. The European company is the result of a hybrid legal system, as the European regulations constitute its main guidelines while leaving the national legislation the task of defining its legal framework of implementation. More recently, an amendment to the March 23, 1967 decree came into effect to promote more democracy in the French commercial companies. Knowledge of this new legal corporate corpus is required for any participant in business negotiations involving a French commercial company.

3.2 Securities Laws

To avoid embarrassment and the risk of not understanding important issues, a participant in a negotiation on a corporate transaction in France must know at a minimum the following ground rules and recent changes to the French securities laws and regulatory framework.

The law on Financial Security of August 1, 2003 has merged the former *Commission des operations de bourse* (COB), the *Conseil des marchés financiers* (CMF) and the *Conseil de discipline de la gestion financière* (CDGF) into one single entity named the *Autorité des marchés financiers* (AMF). Just like the Securities and Exchange Commission in the United States, the AMF benefits from a wide array of prerogatives. As defined in its general rules (*Règlement Général*), the AMF has *inter alia* the power to (i) regulate publicly traded companies, (ii) authorize the issuance of certain savings products and securities, (iii) establish rules of good conduct applicable to the financial institutions allowed to provide investment and financial services, and (iv) monitor financial analysts as well as, at some level, rating agencies. The AMF was also granted the power to investigate and pronounce legal sanctions on noncompliant publicly traded companies.

Euronext Paris SA is the second authority of the French financial market. It was created on September 22, 2000 through the merger of the Amsterdam, Brussels, and Paris stock markets. Partnership agreements were also entered into between Euronext Paris SA and European stock markets such as the ones in Luxembourg (2000), Helsinki (2001), and Warsaw (2002). On April 7, 2007, Euronext Paris SA merged with the New York Stock Exchange to form NYSE Euronext. This merger resulted in the first transatlantic stock exchange, with a daily flow of transactions amounting to EUR 80 billion. Euronext Paris SA plays a key role with respect to the regulation of the French stock market; it is responsible for the protection of investors and guaranteeing that the operations in the stock market comply with the existing laws and regulations.

The law of July 26, 2005 for the modernization of the economy incorporated the European directive 2004/109/EC on Transparency into French law and substantially modified the law applicable to the information requirements of the market. As a consequence of this law, publicly traded companies are now required to establish and file a comprehensive annual financial report, a biannual financial report, and other financial information on a quarterly basis with the AMF. Furthermore, the law of July 26, 2005 has established new rules regarding the notification of change of control ownership (*franchissement de seuil*).

More recently, the law of March 31, 2006 incorporated the European directive 2004/25/EC into French law and substantially modified the rules applicable to takeover bids. As a result of this reform, (i) the AMF was granted broader powers, (ii) a mandatory minimum price requirement was adopted for mandatory public offers (*offre publique obligatoire*), (iii) laws and regulations applicable to public repurchase offers (*Procédure de retrait obligatoire*) were amended, (iv) a mandatory statement of intent requirement was implemented in cases where rumors of a public offer exist (*déclaration d'intention en cas de rumeur*), (v) the role played by employee representatives, i.e., works council, was strengthened, (vi) certain restrictions to the power of management bodies of the company to adopt anti-takeover measures were adopted, (vii) the free issuance of warrants to subscribe shares by the extraordinary shareholders' meeting as an anti-takeover defense mechanism was allowed, and (viii) the neutralization, with respect to public offers, of statutory and contractual restrictions applicable to the transfer of shares and to voting rights was adopted.

Securities law, like corporate law, appears to be following a path that leads to a substantial enhancement of information obligations to be delivered by the publicly traded companies to their shareholders and employees as well as to the investors and the market.

3.3 Tax Laws

Participants in corporate transactions in France are jointly and severally liable for the payment of registration duties (*droits d'enregistrement*). The French tax legislation, however, provides that the purchaser must bear the costs of such duties, unless otherwise provided in the transfer agreement.

Transfers of shares in non-publicly traded French companies are subject to the following duties, regardless of whether a deed is executed in France: (i) a 1.1 percent duty capped at EUR 4,000 applies in regard to shares issued by corporations and certain types of limited partnerships, and (ii) a 5 percent duty applies in regard to (a) shares issued by limited liability companies and partnerships payable on the part of the price exceeding EUR 23,000 and (b) shares in real estate companies (i.e., companies whose assets are predominantly composed of French real estate).

Transfers of shares in publicly traded French companies do not give rise to any registration duties, unless a deed of sale is executed. The same applies for transfers of shares issued by foreign companies, unless they are embodied in a deed executed in France.

Registration duties are chargeable on the sale of real properties at the rate of 5.09 percent. Sales of businesses, goodwill, leasehold rights, and exploited trademarks are subject to a 5 percent registration duty, after deduction of an allowance of EUR 23,000. A fixed fee (*droit fixe*) of EUR 125 must be paid on transfers of patents, regardless of whether or not they are commercially used. Fixed duties from EUR 230 to EUR 500 are payable on mergers, share capital increases, and contributions of certain assets.

The above transfer duties in all cases apply to the higher of (i) the price agreed between and among the parties and (ii) the market value of the transferred assets.

In the absence of permanent establishment in France, foreign companies are in principle not subject to French capital gain tax on sales of French assets, except on (i) sales of real estate or shares in real estate companies, as well as on (ii) sales of shareholdings representing more than 25 percent of the share capital of a company. Such transfers are respectively taxable in France at the rate of 33.33 percent and 18 percent, subject to the application of bilateral tax treaties.

French companies (and French permanent establishments of foreign companies) are subject to corporate tax (*impôt sur les sociétés*) at the standard rate of 33.33 percent. Companies whose turnover exceeds EUR 7.63 millions are, however, subject to an additional social surcharge of

3.3 percent assessed on the aggregate corporate tax exceeding EUR 763,000, raising the effective tax rate to 34.43 percent.

Capital gains realized by companies are generally included in the companies' taxable income for the fiscal year during which these gains are realized. Long-term capital gains on sales of participating shares *(titres de participation)* held for a period of at least two years are exempted from corporate tax up to 95 percent. As of 2008, such exemption is no longer applicable to sales of shares in real estate companies.

The following schemes may be implemented in order to minimize the tax burden of corporate transactions. First, a massive dividend distribution (which may benefit from a parent-subsidiary regime) by the French company whose shares are to be sold may be done before the sale of shares. This would result in a reduction of the value of the company and therefore in a reduction of registration duties and capital gains tax. Second, purchasers may set up a holding company in France to purchase 100 percent of the share capital of a target company, especially when the acquisition is essentially financed through debt. The holding company establishes a tax-consolidated group with the target and consequently becomes liable for corporate tax on behalf of both companies. Thus, this structure allows the purchaser to offset the financial costs incurred against tax profits of the target company. Third, under certain conditions, a share-for-share exchange may defer the taxation of capital gains on the sale of shares.

3.4 Antitrust/Anticompetition Laws

Antitrust is often a major concern for negotiators as a negotiation may appear at some point to be partially or wholly infeasible because of competition regulations.

In France both domestic law (in our case, more particularly, Articles L. 420-1 and L. 420-2 of the French Commercial Code) and European Union law (Articles 81 and 82 of the EC Treaty) may apply to anticompetitive conduct that is likely to have an appreciable effect on competition and trade among European Union member states. On the contrary, only French competition law is applicable if the transaction only has an impact in France and has no cross-border effects. In the event of parallel proceedings leading to parallel sanctions, national courts are bound by European Union law and case law.

Pursuant to Articles 81 of the EC Treaty and L.420-1 of the French Commercial Code, agreements are prohibited when they are intended to have or have such effects as, in particular, (i) the limitation of access to the market, (ii) price fixing, (iii) the limitation or control of production, investments, or technical advances, and (iv) the allocation of markets or of sources of supply.

Articles 82 of the EC Treaty and L.420-2 of the Commercial Code prohibit the abuse of a dominant position. Such an abuse will notably occur when a dominant firm (or dominant firms acting collectively) uses its market position to (i) impose unfair trading conditions, (ii) impose unfair purchase or selling prices, (iii) limit production or technical developments to the prejudice of consumers, (iv) apply dissimilar conditions to equivalent transactions with other trading parties, or (v) make the conclusion of contracts conditional upon acceptance by the other parties of supplementary obligations that, by their nature or according to commercial usage, have no connection with the subject of such contracts.

Competition law must also be taken into consideration for merger control purposes. At the European Union level, Council Regulation (EC) No. 139/2004 of January 20, 2004 on the control of concentrations between undertakings sets out thresholds for a concentration to have a Community dimension.

Mergers that do not have a Community dimension must be reported to the French Minister of Economy if they meet the two cumulative thresholds set out in Article L.430-2 of the Commercial Code (i.e., the combined aggregate worldwide turnover of the parties involved in the merger is above EUR 150 million and the combined aggregate turnover achieved in France by at least two of these parties is above EUR 50 million).

Where the transaction raises no competition issues the French Minister of Economy will issue a clearance decision within five weeks from receipt of the notification, failing which the concentration is deemed approved.

Where the analysis of the transaction reveals that the transaction is likely to have anticompetitive consequences, the notifying parties may propose structural or behavioral commitments. In these cases, the initial five-week time frame might be extended up to eight weeks in total.

Where the Ministry of Economy and Finance (MINEFI) concludes that the proposed commitments are not sufficient to remedy the situation, the notifying parties must submit the matter to the French Competition Council, which will have three months to issue its opinion on the matter. Upon receipt of the French Competition Council's opinion, the French Minister of Economy shall issue its final decision within four weeks unless the notifying parties submit additional commitments, in which case the four-week period can be extended by up to seven weeks in total.

3.5 Labor and Employment Laws

Employment matters are governed first by the Labor Code, then by the national collective bargaining agreement applicable to the company, then by possible in-house collective agreements, and, finally, by the individual employment contracts.

Depending on the nature of the litigation, different courts may have jurisdictions: for individual litigations the *Conseil de Prud'hommes* has jurisdiction; litigations on elections of employee representatives are dealt with by the *Tribunal d'Instance*; and all collective litigations (strike, works council, collective agreements, etc.) are dealt with by the *Tribunal de Grande instance.*

Generally, the works councils are strongly associated with any operation occurring within the company: indeed, a company must inform and consult its works council prior to carrying out an operation that affects its "economic or legal structure." Mergers, sales of shares entailing a change of control, the sale of assets, the purchase or sale of subsidiaries, modifications of working time or working conditions, and redundancies constitute *inter alia* such an operation requiring the prior consultation of the works council.

Failure to comply with such prior consultation of the works council constitutes a hindering of the works council rights and is considered as a criminal offense (*délit d'entrave*) exposing the legal representative of the company to a fine of up to EUR 3,750 and/or a maximum of one year's imprisonment and exposing the company as a legal entity to a fine of up to EUR 18,750. In addition, the works council that has not been consulted or a union can bring a legal action in summary proceedings (*Référé*) before the civil court in order to obtain the suspension of the operation until the consultation of the works council.

In the event of a transfer of undertaking, the Labor Code provides that "if there is any change in the legal status of the employer, notably through succession, sale, merger, transformation of the business, or conversion to a company, all employment contracts in effect on the date of the change shall remain in existence as between the new employer and the company personnel." Redundancies before the transfer are prohibited and would be considered null and void.

After the transfer, the new employer can decide to dismiss some of the transferred employees, or to change their employment conditions. The employer will have to comply with French law requirements in terms of procedure, justification of the dismissals or modifications, and payment of dismissal indemnities. The transferee company may agree to bear the costs of any dismissal notified within a certain period after the transfer, but this is purely a matter of commercial negotiation and should be considered with much precaution.

Broadly speaking, when a dismissal procedure concerns an individual, the employer must base the decision on reasons concerning the person or the employee or the economic condition of the company. Regardless of the personal reasons for the dismissal, before making any decision, the employer must schedule a predismissal meeting with the person concerned by registered letter or by hand-delivered letter. After the meeting, subject to a compulsory waiting period, the employer can notify the employee of the dismissal by registered mail.

In the case of dismissal of more than one employee for economic reasons, the procedure is considerably more cumbersome. The works council must be consulted in companies with more than fifty employees; state personal redeployment agreements must be proposed and/ or redeployment leaves must be implemented, and the appropriate government agency must be notified of the dismissal. The procedure is similar in the case of general layoffs.

An individual's severance pay is the highest amount established by law, collective-bargaining agreement, or the individual's employment contract. In all cases, the indemnity may not be less than a legal minimum representing a sum calculated per year of employment.

When ten redundancies due to downsizing or modification of employment contracts are forecasted in the framework of any operation within a company with more than fifty employees, the works council must be informed and consulted on both the economic justification of the reorganization and the implementation of the Employment Protection Plan (*plan de sauvegarde de l'emploi*) containing the accompanying and redeployment measures for the employees as well as severance payments. The works council will have to prepare a report indicating the grounds for its opinion on the project. For this purpose it must be provided with specific written information and must be allowed sufficient time (at least three days) to examine it. It must also be given a copy of the answers to its observations, with the grounds for the answers.

3.6 Environmental Laws

The law of July 19, 1976 relating to installations subject to environmental protection requirements established a classification system composed of two types of installations: (i) installations that constitute predictable serious danger or disadvantages, which must be authorized by the local French government representative (*préfet*), and (ii) installations that are subject to reporting requirements. This law has been codified in the Environmental Code in articles L.511-1 et seq. since the law of September 18, 2000. These articles set out the various principles governing environmental law (e.g., polluter pays principle, principle of precaution).

When a classified installation is sold in the context of a business transaction, the new owner must report the sale to the supervisor of classified installations. The law of July 3, 1992 introduced new and stricter conditions with the sale being subject to prior authorization by the local French government representative. The same law requires the seller to supply information to the purchaser regarding all the disadvantages and risks that, to the best of the seller's knowledge, may result from the operation of the installation.

Where sites are still in activity it is, in practical terms, the current or the last operator who will be held liable for the cleanup of the site, unless he can prove that he was not responsible for the pollution.

The law of July 30, 2003 on natural and technological risk prevention and damage repair introduced new legislative devices aimed at better anticipating the problems of soil pollution and installing mechanisms of financial guarantees in order to ensure the repair of the polluted sites.

The government may require the owner to perform certain works, such as the cleanup of the site either during operation or when it is shut down. If the owner fails to comply, the government can require the owner to deposit on a special account the appropriate sum for the resolution of the problem and undertake to do the work itself, or it can ask the tax administration to freeze the sums necessary, or, as a last resort, it can finance the work itself and require the owner or any other liable party to reimburse it. The government may also suspend or revoke the operating license. Criminal penalties may also be applied.

Like other European governments, the French is applying, with increasing frequency, policies that impose the burden and expenses on industrial companies that engage in business that harms the environment.

3.7 Intellectual Property Laws

The law applicable to intellectual property rights (e.g., trademark, patent) is the law of the state/country where such right has been issued.

Under the Madrid Arrangement (*Protocole de Madrid*), the filing of trademarks in France may be extended, in a single step, to all or some of the European Union countries, but the applicant must have an establishment in France. Otherwise, separate filings in each country are necessary but priority is given to all subsequent filings within six months from the first filing in a European Union member state.

In France, patents may be conveniently filed online on the Web site of the National Institute of Industrial Property (*Institut National de la Propriété Industrielle*). However, this convenience does not exist yet for trademarks.

A patent or trademark may also be filed directly through an international organ or mechanism (such as the Office for Harmonization in the Internal Market in the case of a Community trademark filing, the European Patent Office in the case of a European patent filing, or the Patent Cooperation Treaty in the case of a patent filing in numerous countries in the world). Moreover, under the Madrid Arrangement, if one has already filed a trademark in France, the protection of one's trademark will be extended to all members of the Arrangement upon production of certain documents.

The transfer of trademark rights is governed by the principle of free transfer. Trademarks can be separated from the business. Therefore, unless otherwise provided, transfer of business does not entail transfer of trademark. Trademark transfers are subject to a registration fee (*droit d'enregistrement*). Additionally, unlike for a transfer of patent, no territorial limitation to the transfer of trademarks may be provided for.

The transfer of trademarks or patents is governed by the general contracts law. However, certain additional requirements need to be met. First, as a validity requirement, the transfer (as well as the pledge) must be made in writing (Article L.714-1 of the Intellectual Property Code for trademarks and Article L.613-8 for patents). Second, as a publicity requirement, that is, in order for the transferee (or licensee or beneficiary of a pledge agreement) to be able to invoke the transfer (or license or pledge) against third parties located on French territory, the transfer (or license or pledge) must be recorded at the national registry of trademarks (*registre national des marques*) under Article L.714-7 of the Intellectual Property Code or at the national registry of patents (*registre national des brevets*) pursuant to Article L.613-9 of the same Code. Third, a trademark or patent transfer executed with a foreign resident must be filed with the National Institute of Industrial Property under Article R. 624-1 of the Intellectual Property Code.

An exclusive trademark license prohibits the trademark owner from using said trademark. Pursuant to the law No. 2007-1544 of October 29, 2007 on the enforcement of intellectual property rights, both trademark or patent owner and exclusive licensee are entitled to file a motion for seizure to establish infringement.

Any trademark license agreement should provide that the licensee must exploit said licensed trademark; otherwise the licensed trademark might be canceled for nonuse.

As far as patents are concerned, any employee hired to invent, who is indeed the author of an invention within the scope of his mission, is entitled to specific compensation notwithstanding any opposite provisions. Generally, such compensation is calculated on the basis of the turnover generated by said invention (art. L. 611-7 of the Intellectual Property Code).

3.8 Privacy and Data Security Laws

In some business transactions, personal data may have to be disclosed. Processing and/or transfer of this data is subject to strict rules in France. Personal data processing is governed by the law of January 6, 1978 as amended by the law of August 6, 2004, which is implemented by an independent body, the *Commission Nationale de l'Informatique et des Libertés* (the *CNIL*). Any violation of the data protection law is criminally sanctioned (up to EUR 300,000 fine and five years' imprisonment).

This law applies to the processing of personal data when (i) the data controller is established on French territory (i.e., when the data controller carries out his activity on French territory within an establishment, whatever its legal form), or (ii) the data controller, although not established on French territory or in any other member state of the European Community, uses means of processing located on French territory.

Protection of the individual whose personal data is or will be processed in the context of a business transaction is ensured as follows. First, automatic processing of personal data must be reported to or authorized by the CNIL. Second, unless specifically authorized, collection and processing of sensitive personal data is prohibited. Personal data that reveal racial or ethnic origins, political, philosophical, religious opinions, or trade union affiliation of persons, or that concern their health or sexual life are considered sensitive data. Additionally, other personal data such as offenses and social security number may not be processed. Third, any data subject must be informed of (i) the processing, (ii) its purpose, (iii) possible recipients of personal data, (iv) the identity of the data controller, (v) the existence of his right of access/modification/suppression of personal data, and (vi) any transfer of data to a country outside the European Union. Fourth, transfer of personal data to a country outside the European Union is strictly regulated. Finally, spamming is prohibited; the use of personal data for commercial purposes is subject to the opt-in rule.

3.9 Regulation of Foreign Investment

A decree of December 30, 2005 has organized regulations applicable to foreign investments. This decree significantly changed the Monetary and Financial Code's structure regarding this matter. It also significantly reformed the prior system of administrative authorization.

The general principle that arises from the decree is that foreign investments in France are free, but subject to certain restrictions. It applies to all non-French investors, including those from European Union member states, even though the latter are subject to a different system. It also applies to French investors willing to invest abroad, or in France through foreign investment vehicles.

3.9.1 Prior Authorization and Filing Requirements

Whether an investment is subject to prior authorization or mere filing requirements, the regulations are likely to apply during its entire life, i.e., at the time the investment is made, during any recapitalization or shareholding changes, spin-off, or other form of divestiture, and upon resale of the investment. This unique feature forces investors to ensure compliance with the regulations on a regular basis.

Pursuant to these regulations, a foreign investor is required to seek prior authorization from the MINEFI in the following cases: (i) acquisition of a controlling stake in a company whose registered office is in France, (ii) direct or indirect acquisition of a line of business of a company whose registered office is in France, (iii) direct or indirect acquisition of more than 33.33 percent of the stock or voting rights of a company having its registered office in France.

In the case of private equity funds, the foreign nature of the investment is determined by the domicile of the head office of the management company and the independence of the investors managing the portfolio.

3.9.2 System of Filing Requirements

Before investing, an investor can file a written request with MINEFI in order to assess whether or not the investment is subject to a prior authorization procedure. The MINEFI should give an answer within a two-month period. But if a request is not answered within the two-month period, it does not exempt the investor from filing an authorization with the MINEFI provided the investment requires the investor to do so.

Some investments are subject to administrative declarations, such as the creation of a French company by foreign investors, the purchase of shares of a French company by foreign investors, or the purchase of a part or all of a company's business line. These operations shall be reported to the MINEFI. The threshold for which such declaration must be filed is EUR 1,500,000.

3.9.3 System of Prior Authorization

A prior authorization system is applicable to investments realized in eleven economic sectors that are considered strategic business sectors, such as security, defense, weapons, pathogens or toxic products, dual-use technology items, or the gambling industry. However, certain defined and limited exemptions exist. The authorization filing and investigation processes are similar for European Union or non–European Union investors. Compliance is required as of the date of execution of the acquisition documents. The filing of a complete application triggers a two-month period by the end of which the authorization must either be granted or denied.

The following three limitative criteria may be used by French administrative authorities to determine whether a foreign investment may be deemed compliant with the preservation of French national interests: (i) preservation of industrial capacities on French territory, (ii) continuity of supplies, and (iii) compliance with contractual commitments contained in certain existing contracts (e.g., public procurement contracts or contracts in specific industry sectors). Furthermore, French authorities may subject their authorization to specific additional commitments from foreign investors.

Any foreign investor that does not comply with this prior authorization procedure may suffer financial sanctions proportionate to the interests at stake. Any authorization denial must be justified.

3.10 Other Potentially Applicable Laws and Regulations

Various other legal areas as discussed in this section may be of interest at some point during negotiations depending on the type and object of the negotiation involved.

3.10.1 Bankruptcy Laws

Any negotiator involved in a transaction with a French company needs to be well informed of French bankruptcy laws that pertain to different proceedings: (i) insolvency proceedings (*procédures de redressement et de liquidation judiciaire*), (ii) amicable proceedings (*procédures amiables*), and (iii) since the reform implemented by the law of July 26, 2005, which was partially inspired by Chapter 11 of the U.S. Bankruptcy Code, the safeguard proceedings (*procédure de sauvegarde*).

Those proceedings apply to (i) corporate entities (whether of a commercial or civil nature) such as French borrowers, (ii) individuals carrying on trade activities (*commerçants*), craftsmen (*artisants*), (iii) farmers, and (iv) independent individuals carrying on professional activities (*personnes physiques exerçant une activité professionnelle indépendante*).

3.10.1.1 Insolvency Proceedings

Pursuant to articles L. 611-1 et seq. of the Commercial Code, an insolvent debtor is required to file a request for the commencement of insolvency proceedings with the relevant court (either a commercial or civil court depending on the commercial or civil nature of the debtor) within forty-five days of the date on which the debtor is technically insolvent (*état de cessation des paiements*), that is, when the debtor is unable to meet its current liabilities out of its current assets (cash available or assets that may be quickly turned into cash). In addition, any unpaid creditor may file a request to initiate insolvency proceedings against a debtor. A creditor may also request liquidation proceedings if the creditor proves that the debtor has actually ceased business or that recovery is obviously impossible. The relevant court or the state prosecutor (*Procureur de la République*) may also initiate insolvency proceedings. When the competent court declares the commencement of insolvency proceedings, it will also have to decide if the business can be continued as a going concern. If it decides that it cannot, the court will make an immediate order for the business to be liquidated. Conversely, if the court decides that the business may be continued, it will order the commencement of an observation period (*période d'observation*) during which an administrator (*administrateur*) appointed by the court will investigate the affairs of the debtor and make proposals for the continuation of its business. At the end of the observation period, the court will make an order for the continuation of the debtor, for the sale of its business or for its liquidation, as appropriate. In the case of continuation, the court will adopt a continuation plan (*plan de continuation*) to ensure successful continuation of the debtor's business.

3.10.1.2 Amicable Proceedings

When a debtor finds itself in financial difficulties but is not yet insolvent, it may, at its own discretion, request that the competent French court appoint an ad hoc agent (*mandataire ad hoc*), the duties of which are determined by the relevant French court. Such ad hoc agents are appointed in order to facilitate the negotiations with the debtor's creditors, but are not empowered to interfere with the management of the debtor, and have no coercive powers against the creditors.

Alternatively, if a French debtor faces actual or expected legal, economic, or financial difficulties and has not been under cessation of payments (*cessation des paiements*) for more than forty-five days, it may apply for conciliation proceedings (*procédure de conciliation*) with the competent French court. Such conciliation proceedings may not last for a period exceeding four months subject to a one-month extension. The duty of the court-appointed conciliation agent (*conciliateur*) is to facilitate the negotiation of an amicable arrangement (*accord amiable*) between the debtor and its main creditors. The conciliation agent is not empowered to interfere with the management of the debtor, and has no coercive powers against the creditors.

3.10.1.3 Safeguard Proceedings

A debtor may initiate, in its sole discretion, safeguard proceedings with respect to itself, provided it (i) is able to pay its due debts out of its available assets, and (ii) experiences difficulties that it is not able to resolve and that may cause the occurrence of a *cessation des paiements*.

The opening of safeguard proceedings will have quite similar effects as the opening of insolvency proceedings. The purpose of safeguard proceedings is to reach the adoption of a safeguard plan (*plan de sauvegarde*), similar to the continuation plan (*plan de continuation*), which can be adopted within the scope of insolvency proceedings.

3.10.2 Security Interests

Under French law, there are two categories of security interests: (i) real security interests, chiefly pledges and mortgages, and (ii) personal security interests. A reform of March 23, 2006 has amended quite significantly the French law of security interests but has not altered this basic distinction.

3.10.2.1 Real Security Interests

Mortgages (*hypothèques*) are one of the best-known security interests on real property. A mortgage may arise in one of three circumstances: by operation of law, by judicial decision, or by virtue of a private agreement.

The legal framework of mortgages is particularly tight. Renewal of a mortgage is compulsory to avoid losing the benefit of the mortgage's registration. Additionally, the mortgage instrument must be drafted by a notary (*notaire*) and it must be filed with the office of the Recorder of Mortgages (*conservation des hypothèques*).

The 2006 reform has introduced two new types of mortgages in French law. First, the refillable mortgage (*hypothèque rechargeable*), that is, a mortgage allowing the same property to be used for several successive claims, and, second, the mortgage loan for life (*prêt viager hypothécaire*), which provides for the repayment of the loan at the borrower's death or at the mortgaged property's sale or stripping.

The 2006 reform has also substantially amended the law applicable to pledges (*gages*). Pursuant to Article 2333 of the Civil Code, a "pledge is an agreement by which the pledgor gives to a creditor the right to be paid in preference." One very well-known form of pledge is the pledge of a business (*nantissement de fonds de commerce*), for which a written instrument is required that must contain a variety of mandatory provisions, such as a description of the pledged items. The 2006 reform has simplified the formal requirements for pledges. Indeed, pursuant to article 2336 of the Civil Code, "a pledge is complete by the establishment of a writing which contains the description of the secured debt, the quantity of the pledged units of property, as well as of their species or nature." Hence, the main formality that a pledge needs to comply with is the written requirement as well as publication in some specific cases.

One last aspect of the reform on pledges must be mentioned. Under the new Article 2348, the creditor may now insert a clause in the pledge contract providing that it will gain ownership of the pledged property if the debtor fails to perform its obligations (*pacte commissoire*). As a consequence, judicial intervention is no longer necessary.

3.10.2.2 Personal Security Interests

The 2006 reform had a less substantial impact on personal security interests. Articles 2321 and 2322 of the Civil Code have respectively codified the autonomous guarantee (*garantie autonome*) and the letter of intent (*lettre d'intention*). However, the regime of guarantee (*cautionnement*) was not amended by the 2006 reform. Pursuant to Article 2288 of the Civil Code, a guarantee is a contract in which a person undertakes the payment of an obligation of a principal debtor, that is, he "promises the creditor that he will satisfy this obligation if the debtor himself does not do so." As a contract ancillary to the principal debt, it establishes a tripartite relationship between the debtor and the creditor (the basic obligation), the debtor and the guarantor, and the guarantor and the creditor.

If the guarantee is international in nature, it is governed by the law selected by the parties. This law can be different from the law applicable to the principal agreement. In the absence of a specific provision in the contract, the guarantor's commitment to the beneficiary creditor is governed by the law of the state where the guarantor has his or her domicile. In practice, a written instrument is generally drawn up.

*3.10.2.3 Introduction of the Trust as Security Device (*fiducie*) in French Law*
The principle of this new device is quite simple. The debtor (settlor) transfers assets by way of security to an autonomous and bankruptcy-proof fiduciary estate held by a trustee for the benefit of a creditor (beneficiary). The trustee must be a credit institution or an insurance company. All types of present or future assets can be transferred to the fiduciary estate, including real property, movable assets, securities, and claims. In the case of default, the trustee will realize the assets. The parties are free to agree on the mechanism that is used to realize the assets. In particular, the parties can decide to appoint an expert to determine a minimum price, or they can set up a private tender. The trust structure can secure both senior and junior creditors. The fiduciary estate can be used to secure subsequent loan transactions for a duration of up to thirty-three years.

4. Other Significant Legal and Business Issues

It is well known that the relations of French citizens with their centralized and very present government are subject to ambiguities. In following with tradition, contacts with the government are limited as much as possible, even though public-private partnerships and transactions are now a growing trend. With regard to negotiating, this is usually translated into a tendency to underestimate administrative problems (in terms of taxes, government permits, and environmental protection law). This practice is based on, among other things, the observation of weak government monitoring and execution tools and on a conviction that everything can be worked out *ex post facto*. Foreigners should be wary of this attitude, because it is based not on objective factors but rather on an evaluation of risks.

The judicial system, whether civil, commercial, or criminal branch, is not held in high esteem and several attempts to reform it have revealed the extent of its inadequacies. The French are not given to litigation as they are both rather disappointed by their dispute resolution system and also culturally reluctant to go to trial. Aside from litigation regarding competition or securities and exchange matters, litigation barely represents an incentive or a major threat, because the French legal system does not lay stress on such features as discovery proceedings, depositions, examination, and cross-examination. Moreover, jury verdicts, court-imposed penalties, and the costs of prosecuting cases are generally modest when compared to the costs associated with litigation in the United States.

Thus, in France, the threat of lawsuits is less often used as a negotiating or extortion weapon. When a lawsuit does ensue, it is often because all negotiations have failed. The case will then be prosecuted right to the end, which will take an average of three years.

5. Negotiation Practices

In this section we will stress certain significant aspects of the French negotiation posture. One is tempted to presume that negotiations on contract forms or instruments similar to those of other foreign countries go forward in a substantially similar manner, but this presumption is often erroneous. However, the cultural environment is a fundamental aspect of international negotiations.

5.1 Participants

Here as elsewhere, generalizations should be made with caution and reserve. Nevertheless, it is possible to express certain central concepts.

The degree of openness and sophistication of businesspeople varies widely, depending on their degree of experience in international commerce. Generally, relations of French business executives with legal specialists and, consequently, with lawyers is more limited than is the case in countries like the United States. Lawyers are still regarded as a luxury or a necessary evil, and they often play a limited role in negotiations in France. French businesspeople frequently underestimate the complexity and the stakes attached to the legal aspects and are inclined to proceed to an advanced stage of negotiations without much input from legal counsel. This often prevents foreign lawyers from playing the role they are accustomed to or would like to play. Thus legal problems tend to be discovered at a later stage and treated more summarily than may be warranted.

Depending on the nature of the business or the geographical location of the negotiations, various types of persons may be involved in providing legal advice. In the Paris area, and in the three or four largest cities in France, large companies use attorneys-at-law or in-house counsel. In other areas of the country, accountants customarily retained by the company that is party to or the subject of negotiations often participate. These accountants provide incidental legal advice, without necessarily having specialized legal training. Another potential party is the type of lawyer known as a notary (*notaire*). *Notaires* specialize in real property and estate matters, but they often have close ties with important local people. Even if the major portion of the negotiations are held in outlying areas, it is generally preferable for the foreign negotiator not to seek counsel directly from a regional advisor, as this will pose the risk of superimposition of two cultural displacements.

As a general rule, legal counsel will rarely play a direct role in negotiations.

5.2 Timing

Typically, the pace of negotiations is slower and less intense than is customary in American practice except in the context of major deals. Few matters are so urgent as to warrant sacrificing lunch, dinner, an evening engagement, weekends, summer vacations, or, more generally, personal commitments.

A foreign negotiator who claims to be unaware of these realities of the French way of life may experience a certain resentment. Similarly, one must accept the fact that the sense of punctuality is expressed differently, and that a certain amount of lateness in holding meetings (both at the start and at the end) or in the performance of certain commitments should not be taken as a personal offense.

Over and above these factors, negotiations can be held up by government deadlines, which are generally kept within specific and reasonable limits and, barring exceptions caused by the difficulty of certain cases, are scrupulously respected. These government deadlines can refer to authorizations of foreign investments or procedures connected with antitrust considerations (merger control).

5.3 Negotiation Practices

Because the legal and business community in France lacks homogeneity, negotiating stages and styles will be greatly affected by (i) the experience of the French negotiators involved in the negotiation; (ii) their manner of using outside counsel, specifically what role the negotiators expect counsel to play in the negotiation; (iii) the role given to these counselors; (iv) the negotiators' nature and training; and (v) their geographical location. These factors may vary considerably from one situation to next.

Consider the following two extreme examples. In the first situation, the negotiation of a corporate or financial transaction with a major industrial or financial company, assisted by its customary in-house and outside counsel, will in most cases be very similar to that in the United States, apart from a few nuances of style, timing, and culture-specific features.

In contrast, in the second situation, where the French negotiators lack experience with international business practices, compounded by very limited assistance from jurists who have limited training in such a situation, negotiations can become extremely difficult. Difficulties arise because of differing degrees of sophistication and experience of the parties involved rather than from cultural differences. What would normally be a banal or perfunctory action can and will become a source of suspicion, tension, and distrust in such a situation.

It is not an exaggeration to say that often negotiators must use all of their talents just to get their counterparts to accept the basic standards of negotiation and contract documentation. Sometimes this is so difficult that there is a risk of complete breakdown of negotiations because of an effort to impose negotiating styles with which the local counterparts are not familiar. In such cases it will be necessary to go along with local practices (not easy) and try to limit the risk.

This is complicated by the sometimes abusive use made of cultural barriers. A well-informed local negotiator will plead ignorance and repeat over and over, "That is not how we do things here"—a primitive but sometimes very powerful weapon.

5.4 Cultural, Ethical, and Religious Considerations

There is no need to stress the advantages offered by some knowledge of the language of the country in question, French. The French will appreciate your effort to be open to them, and you will be able to learn information during one of the numerous private conversations of which the French are so fond. Even if foreign negotiators are tempted to regard business lunches as a waste of time, they should, when the context so requires, gracefully bow to this practice, which is an integral part of negotiation. These occasions make it possible to cultivate connections by demonstrating appreciation of an important aspects of French societal and business culture.

5.5 Negotiating Online

Online communications have allowed an increased reactivity and availability for the people involved in business negotiations. This also includes better connections between various international offices of the law firms throughout the world. All that has certainly enhanced the way to proactively respond to clients' needs with celerity.

6. Contract Formation

One characteristic feature of French contracts that differs considerably from contracts under the Anglo-American legal system concerns the concepts of "cause" and "consideration." While both concepts are involved in the drafting of contracts, the concept of consideration is much broader than that of cause, which can be defined as "the determining factor that led the parties to enter into contract," and, moreover, plays a role not only when the contract is drafted but also when it is amended.

Under American law, most contracts (with the exception of contracts for the sale of goods) cannot be validly amended without the providing of additional consideration. Under French law, contracts are validly amended as soon as an agreement is reached on the subject matter and price. Moreover, while under American law the consideration cannot as a general rule consist of past consideration, the factor of time is unimportant in regard to causation.

Theoretically, only the definitive conclusion of the contract makes the agreement of the parties binding (Article 1134 of the Civil Code). In other words, discussions prior to the conclusion of the final contract are not binding on the negotiators.

The conclusion may be definitive without having a contract signed. However, the role of the oral agreement is negligible in French commercial law. In commercial matters evidence of the existence of contracts, including oral agreements, can be supplied in any form, but it is extremely rare for the outcome of a contract dispute to depend on the evidencing of an oral agreement.

The final conclusion of the contract is understood to be an agreement of intent, free of defect and entered into for the purpose of establishing obligations or transferring assets from one person to another.

In contrast, the principle of freedom of negotiations is not always the principle applied by the courts, which have given a certain legal standing to the various documents that customarily formalize the stages in the discussion. In practice, the later the stage in the negotiations, the more binding the documents and the greater the risk of liability for improper breach of negotiations.

For example, an invitation to commence discussions is not binding on the party issuing the invitation. This same invitation would constitute an offer that could be binding on the party if it were sufficiently specific and firm; in this case, the party requesting it could not unilaterally withdraw the offer without giving the beneficiary thereof a minimum period for reflection.

In this regard French law differs considerably from U.S. law. The principle of revocability of an offer is firmly established in the United States, since in most states the offer can be freely withdrawn, except in certain specific cases in which the offer is irrevocable. French law is much more restrictive in this regard.

In the case of preliminary agreements (letter of intent, protocol of agreement, agreement in principle, confidentiality agreement, and so forth) drawn up for the purpose of establishing certain negotiating rules or as a basis on which the agreement of the parties will subsequently be embodied, some such agreements impose upon the parties an obligation to negotiate in good faith, while others embody more specific agreements, such as confidentiality or exclusivity of negotiation. Improper breach of the former, or failure to comply with the latter, renders the violating negotiator liable.

Although promises of contract precede the final completion of the operation, they nevertheless constitute genuine agreements from which the parties cannot escape without adverse consequences.

The risk connected with the legal nature of instruments formalizing negotiations does not in reality constitute a hindrance to negotiations. The fact is that this risk is relative, chiefly for two reasons. On the one hand, the legal rules imposed by courts are simple commonsense rules that restrict only a person who is not negotiating in good faith. The good-faith principle is a key principle in negotiations, and one that international arbitration awards have unhesitatingly established as a principle of international trade. On the other hand, in practice this risk is diminished in the case of international negotiations by the opportunity offered to negotiators to place their legal acts under the governance of a more liberal legal system by exercising their right to choose the applicable law and even the competent jurisdiction (or arbitrator).

This latter point calls for several comments concerning the contents of negotiating agreements. The international nature of the negotiations is directly echoed in the wording of negotiating agreements.

In addition to the clause concerning the choice of applicable law, the negotiating agreement contains clauses that are specific, without being exclusive, and are particularly evident in international agreements. Such clauses cover, for example, adjustments in the contract, *force majeure*, choice of jurisdiction, arbitration, warranty, and coverage or risks, among other factors. These are all aspects of the negotiations on which the parties will have to reach an understanding while carefully evaluating the legal implications of their choice.

The choice of applicable law is free and open, subject, however, to fraud and mandatory laws applicable to the agreement. This is a fundamental clause because it determines the choice of legal system by which the parties wish to be governed; the consequences of which, even in a context of freedom of contract, cannot be underestimated.

For example, the choice of American law to govern a Franco-American contract of sale authorizes the parties to refrain from setting the purchase price once the subject matter is defined. This agreement would be null and void under French law governing sale because of the absence of a price, which is an essential condition for validity of the contract. In another relevant example, the choice of Anglo-American law will permit either party to cite, if necessary, such concepts as impracticability, frustration, or absence of consideration, which are unknown in French law.

Finally, the Civil Code establishes specific rules governing the interpretation of contracts. The basic principle is that of preeminence of a search for the mutual intent of the contracting parties rather than emphasis on the literal meaning of the terms.

In addition to this fundamental principle of search for the intent of the parties in interpreting the contract, there are two secondary rules. The first rule states that, to the extent possible, all clauses of the contract should produce their effect (Article 1157 of the Civil Code): "When a clause can be interpreted in two ways, the interpretation should be the one according to which it can have some effect, rather than the one under which it could not produce any effect." Again, under Article 1158 of the Civil Code: "Terms that can be interpreted in two ways must be interpreted in the way best suited to the subject of the contract." The second rule of interpretation, which benefits the debtor, is embodied in Article 1162 of the Civil Code, which provides: "In case of doubt, the convention is to be interpreted as against the party who stipulated and in favor of the party who contracted the obligation."

Interpretation of contracts brings into play the principle of the sovereign power of the judges who deliberate on the merits of the matter. However, the *Cour de Cassation* reserves the right to monitor decisions of these lower-court judges if there are clear and specific clauses, in order to determine whether these clauses have been distorted. This court also has the right to verify the classification ascribed to the documents by the lower-court judges.

6.1 Wording and Style

One of the major differences between French contracts and contracts under the Anglo-American legal system arises from a lesser degree of systematization of legal documentation, as revealed in a great diversity of forms and content. Among large business law firms, contract methodology has been sufficiently standardized, thanks to contact with international practice, to render differences among them relatively slight.

Outside this limited circle, the greatest disparities concern presentation, format, and contents of documents, since each firm had its own model developed or its documentation tailored for the specific occasion. One unvarying feature, however, is that documents will generally be concise, and yet, for an equivalent operation, they may vary from a few pages to a few dozen pages, depending on the professional style and culture of the person drafting them. American negotiators will often meet with rejection if they insist on using the models that they usually use.

Contrary to what may sometimes be thought, this concision is not a sign of professional triviality. Rather, it reflects the legal institutions of the country. The Civil Code is a model of conciseness. The decisions of the *Cour de Cassation* are also models in this regard, and the implicit reference to codified principles rather than to legal precedents, principles that will apply in the absence of a contractual provision, eliminate the repetition of provisions that render contract documents unduly wordy. Traditionally, then, the drafter of the document includes, not everything that the parties have agreed upon, but merely that which departs from the codified contract provisions.

In addition, since the court system involves only professional career judges and the near total absence of the jury system, it can be held that a highly detailed and elaborate text is less necessary. It should be noted that French judges have very little power to remedy gaps in an agreement (for example, absence of a price) that could render the agreement null and void; this role is customarily entrusted to a third party. In this case, the agreement must expressly provide for this contingency.

6.2 Conditions and Defenses

Unless otherwise provided in the contract, French contracts will be governed by civil law, in particular by the provisions of the Civil Code. Pursuant to this Code, every contract shall not include clauses contrary to public order (*ordre publique*) and good behavior (*bonnes mœurs*). Regarding legal standards governing the formalities of the terms of such contracts, they can be broken down according to the very nature of the agreement.

French contracts can basically be divided into three distinct categories depending on the formalities they shall involve. First, the consensual agreement (*contrat consensuel*) is considered valid once there has been an expression of the will of both parties. It is therefore not subject to particular formalities. Second, the formal agreement (*contrat solennel*) is considered valid once it has been turned into a written agreement. This document can be prepared by the parties only, or certified by a notary, depending on its importance. Finally, the *in rem* agreement's validity (*contrat réel*) will depend on the remittance of the object of the contract.

6.3 The Special Case of Online Agreements

Online agreements, particularly the formation and performance of online agreements, are governed by European Directives and subsequent French laws, including French law of June 6, 2004 relating to e-commerce.

With respect to online agreement formation, the seller or service provider must comply not only with general contract law but also with specific e-commerce provisions, such as requirements concerning prior information to the consumer. Therefore, (i) online contracts are legally binding despite the absence of a mandatory written document, except for guarantees or real estate sales, (ii) electronic signatures are as valid as handwritten signatures provided that they ensure identification of their author, and (iii) a buyer is deemed to have accepted by double-clicking, the first click to order and the second click to confirm the order.

If, for the purpose of the performance of online agreements, customers' personal data are to be collected and processed, provisions of French data protection laws will have to be adhered to (see section 3.8).

7. Resolving Disputes

7.1 State Courts

French courts can be divided into two main orders: the judicial order (*ordre judiciaire*) and the administrative order (*ordre administratif*). First, the judicial order is divided into civil and criminal law courts. Civil law courts have jurisdiction over private law disputes such as family law or real estate matters. In civil actions, plaintiffs may only receive damages; neither fines nor imprisonment may be inflicted. Criminal courts have jurisdiction over offenses and crimes and may pronounce criminal fines and inflict imprisonment. The death penalty was abolished in France in 1981. Second, the administrative order contains the administrative courts. Such courts apply the administrative law that governs the relationship between the State and private citizens or organizations. The rules of administrative law are set forth in the administrative Codes.

7.2 Alternative Dispute Resolution Mechanism

Parties to international business negotiations may want to avoid state courts and submit their dispute to an alternative mechanism of conflict resolution such as arbitration, mediation, or conciliation.

Arbitration can be broadly defined as a dispute resolution mechanism whereby the parties decide to exempt their cases from the state jurisdictions and to entrust one or more private persons, chosen by the parties, to solve it. The choice of arbitration as a means of dispute resolution allegedly allows more flexibility and confidentiality. The arbitration shall be ad hoc when it is not administered by an arbitration organization, or institutional when it is conducted under the auspices of such an institution.

One should distinguish domestic arbitration from international arbitration. Arbitration is international when it involves the interests of international trade. Domestic arbitration is governed by Titles I through IV of the Code of Civil Procedure. The Civil Code provides that arbitration clauses are valid in contracts concluded for the purpose of a professional activity. Matters of which parties cannot freely dispose, such as personal status (e.g., divorce) and matters over which national courts have exclusive jurisdiction (e.g., competition law) cannot be submitted to arbitration. In addition, there is only a limited number of situations in which a public legal entity may submit disputes to arbitration.

An international arbitration taking place in France is governed by Title V of the Code of Civil Procedure. The law allows the parties to regulate the appointment of the arbitrators, to choose the rules of procedure to be followed by the arbitrators, as well as the law governing the merits of the dispute. The most frequently chosen forum for this purpose is the Arbitration Court of the International Chamber of Commerce, based in Paris.

No court appeal is possible in international arbitration. The action for setting aside is only available to awards rendered in France and not awards rendered abroad. A foreign award may be enforced in France even if it was set aside in the country where it was rendered.

Arbitration is widely used in France, both on the domestic and international level. France is generally perceived as an "arbitration-friendly" country.

French legislation also allows parties to use forms of alternative dispute resolutions other than arbitration before taking a dispute to French courts. Provided that a specific clause has been inserted in the contract, the parties may attempt to present their dispute to a conciliator (*conciliateur*) or mediator (*médiateur*), whose decision will not be binding. Nevertheless, the conciliation or the mediation is considered to be a good alternative to the court. Although they are not yet used to their full potential, these mechanisms tend to be applied to an increasing number of cases.

7.3 Online Dispute Resolution

Online dispute resolution has not yet been implemented in French law.

8. Conclusion

Any party to an international business negotiation involving French law should be well informed of all the provisions detailed in this chapter and keep in mind that the way of doing business and negotiating in France may still be significantly different from what is prevalent in the United States.

After a trend of highly important reforms in many areas—some of these reforms resulting from the transfer into French law of European Union legislation—French law has become more stable and consistent. In particular, corporate and securities laws, regulation of foreign investment, bankruptcy laws, and security interests have been positively affected.

However, some areas of law may be subject to significant reforms within the next few years. The implementation of such reforms depends on the intentions of the executive and legislative powers. Possible areas of reform that are currently debated in France include the (i) introduction of a model of collective action inspired by the American class action, (ii) restriction of white collar crime law, and (iii) implementation of a reform on contract law.

Philippe Sarrailhé
White & Case LLP
Avocat au Barreau de Paris
11, Boulevard de la Madeleine
75001 Paris, France
Phone: + 33 1 55 04 15 50
Fax:　　+ 33 1 55 04 15 16
E-mail: psarrailhe@whitecase.com

CHAPTER 29

International Business Negotiations in Germany

Ralf Wojtek and Matthias Kühn
HEUKING KÜHN LÜER WOJTEK
BERLIN, GERMANY

1. Legal Framework

In the Federal Republic of Germany the legislature is made up of the federal and sixteen state parliaments. Business and investment are predominantly governed by federal statutes, but state laws and local bylaws can comprise relevant building regulations, environmental laws, and health and safety regulations. The law of the European Union (EU) plays an important and ever-growing role, both in the passage and in the application of the relevant laws. Some areas of business law are harmonized within the EU, but the legal regime in many important areas still differs immensely among the EU member states.

Germany is a civil law country. The courts interpret the statutory law by developing the purpose and meaning of the law with supplementary help from case law, with a focus on decisions of the Federal Supreme Court or the courts of appeal, all electronically available, and expert commentaries. The courts are not bound by precedents, which means that each court has great freedom to decide and interpret each case independently. Jury trials are unknown in civil law, but it is possible that a professional judge will sit with two merchants or managers as honorary judges in business cases or with representatives of employers and employees in labor law procedures.

2. Important Commercial Statutes

The German Civil Code (*Bürgerliches Gesetzbuch*, or *BGB*), originally passed in 1900 and amended numerous times since then, governs the general issues of contract law, purchase, lease, loans, suretyship, negotiable instruments, transfer of title, real property, and family and inheritance law. Its central provisions on the law of obligations underwent a substantial reform in 2002. The BGB now contains formerly uncodified liability provisions and incorporates the law on general terms and conditions, as well as the law on consumer contracts, which used to be governed by several independent statutes. Important changes include an amended warranty in the sale of goods, which—among other alterations—was extended to two years. The general limitation period of thirty years was reduced to three years.

The Commercial Code (*Handelsgesetzbuch*, or *HGB*) also stems from the nineteenth century and has undergone numerous revisions since. It supplements the Civil Code where contracts with or between merchants, corporations, and commercial partnerships are concerned, and it is strictly business oriented. For example, the assignment of commercial claims is valid even if excluded under the terms of the agreement, whereas the assignment may be excluded under the Civil Code. Additionally, the Commercial Code governs certain types of businesses and business activities, such as commercial agents and the freight and shipping business. Since 1990, the Commercial Code has contained the basic accounting rules for all merchants and commercial businesses as well.

2.1 Company Law

Partnerships play an important role in Germany's economy. Case law has clarified in recent years that a civil law partnership (*BGB-Gesellschaft*, or *GbR*) is capable of holding rights in its own name, which is not expressly provided for in the BGB. The commercial partnership (*offene Handelsgesellschaft*, or *OHG*), the limited partnership (*Kommanditgesellschaft*, or *KG*), and the silent partnership are governed by the Commercial Code. While the OHG is mainly used by smaller enterprises, the limited partnership is popular regardless of size or financial background and across the industries. Corporations can act as general partners of a limited partnership. This entity, called *Gesellschaft mit beschränker Haftung* (meaning literally company with limited liability) *Kommanditgesellschaft auf Aktien* (GmbH & Co. KG—respectively AG & Co. KG), offers some advantages. For example, private equity investors often cherish their role as a limited partner (*Kommanditist*) in such a vehicle, because the company's start-up losses can diminish their taxable income; accession of additional investors as limited partners is uncomplicated; and fees remain low, since the transfer of partnership interests does not require notarial recording. Also, certain rules on the codetermination of workers in supervisory boards do not apply. On the other hand, the GmbH & Co. KG requires two accounting systems, and double-taxation treaties may treat limited companies better than combined partnerships.

The Stock Corporation Act (*Aktiengesetz*, or AktG) sets the legal framework for the German stock corporation (*Aktiengesellschaft*, or AG), as well as for the limited liability partnership on shares (*Kommanditgesellschaft auf Aktien*, KGaA), the latter being a corporation on stock with fully liable general partners. The minimum share capital of the AG is EUR 50,000. The last decade has seen a massive rise in the number of AGs, which is now well above 15,000, most of which are not listed on the stock exchange.

The Limited Liability Company Act governs the GmbH (*Gesellschaft mit beschränkter Haftung*), a corporation similar to limited liability companies in other jurisdictions and of which there are more than half a million, many of them so-called "one-man companies" with only one shareholder. Although its establishment requires involvement of a public notary, a GmbH is rather easy to set up: the minimum share capital is EUR 25,000, with a substantial reduction of the capital requirement to come, and its articles of association can largely be adapted to the quotaholders' particular requirements. A fundamental reform of the Limited Liability Act is envisaged to become effective in late 2008. In addition, there will be a new form of limited entrepreneurs company with a minimum start-up capital of EUR 1, to be called "*Unternehmergesellschaft,*" or "*UG (haftungsbeschränkt).*" When obtaining financing smaller GmbHs and "one-man companies" in particular usually agree upon a personal surety to be granted by the shareholder-manager; it can be expected that this will be a standard procedure with regard to the newly created *UG (haftungsbeschränkt).*

The Transformation Act (*Umwandlungsgesetz*) provides for the conditions and consequences of a merger, demerger, estate transfer, or change of legal form of corporations. The tax implications of such transformations are dealt with by the Transformation Tax Act (*Umwandlungssteuergesetz*), e.g., the circumstances under which the change of the legal form can take place at book value of the assets, or the evaluation of profits in the balance sheet.

European Union regulations introduced the European Company (*Societas Europaea*, or *SE*) in 2004, a stock corporation with either a two-tier German-type management system or a one-tier management system following the Anglo-Saxon model. In the meantime, the European Court of Justice paved the way for companies of all kinds founded in any member state to establish a branch office or even the principal place of business in any other member state. In the wake of this decision, German courts have recognized that any foreign company can serve as general partner of a KG, e.g., as a "Ltd. & Co. KG." Mere branches of foreign companies are free to operate as proxies of the head office. However, they must register with the local commercial registry; they have to notify the municipality and are obliged to become a member of the local chamber of commerce.

2.2 Corporate Governance

The GmbH is represented and managed by its director(s), who can be instructed by the shareholder's meeting. A supervisory board can be established according to the articles of association. It is obligatory if the company employs more than 500 staff. For the stock corporation (AG), however, a two-tier management system is mandatory, consisting of a management board and a supervisory board. These two bodies are strictly separate. It is not permissible for any one individual to serve on both boards. The management board cannot be given instructions by the shareholders. It is appointed and controlled by the supervisory board, the members of which are in turn elected by the shareholders and, in large corporations where codetermination laws apply, by the shareholders and the employees.

The Securities Trading Act (*Wertpapierhandelsgesetz*, or *WpHG*) prohibits insider trade and contains strict disclosure obligations. In 2002, a Corporate Governance Code was published by a governmental commission. It is continuously being amended. The Code is not legally binding, but rather contains recommendations for the conduct of management board and supervisory board members, transparency and disclosure obligations, and auditing principles. Listed companies are, however, legally obliged to report to the stockholders concerning the extent to which they comply with these recommendations. In 2008, the corporations listed in the DAX 30 complied with 95.6 percent of the recommendations. Recent reforms have further strengthened the rights of stockholders, for example as regards their right to contest shareholders' resolutions in court. The emergence of so-called "professional plaintiffs"—minority shareholders, motivated by the prospect of personal financial gain, who initiate court proceedings in order to prevent a resolution from taking effect—has caused the legislature to debate further amendments.

The regulations on the contribution of the share capital and its preservation are of particular importance for any corporation. Only if the initial stock or share capital has been paid into the corporation is the proprietors' liability limited to that amount. The share capital cannot be paid back to the shareholders, save after liquidation of the company. A stock corporation can only distribute dividends to its stockholders to an amount determined in the annual balance sheet, and with the approval of both boards and the stockholder's meeting. Dividend payments effected outside of this system are illicit and render the directors liable. Directors may also be liable in case of a breach of duty, which exists both with regard to the company and to third parties. Shareholders can incur personal liability if acting to the detriment of the company, e.g. by withdrawing funds necessary for the company to meet its payment obligations.

Groups of corporations (a so-called *Konzern*) can be organized by means of subordination agreements or cross-participations. A subordination agreement (*Beherrschungsvertrag*) obliges the subordinated company to observe directions given by the dominating entity, while under a cash-pooling agreement (*Gewinnabführungsvertrag*) all profits have to be delivered up. The two agreements are often combined. Subordination and cash-pooling agreements can trigger some pitfalls. To name a few, they will only be valid if the stockholder's meeting agrees; double taxation can only be avoided if the agreement runs for a fixed term of at least five years; the parent company is liable toward both creditors and minority shareholders of the subsidiary. Protective rules continue to have effect after a subordination agreement is terminated.

2.3 Taxation

A major company tax reform effective from January 2008 has seen corporate taxes lowered by almost a quarter. The aggregate corporate tax rate is now approximately 33 percent. It is composed of three elements: corporate income tax, trade tax, and a so-called solidarity surcharge. The federal Corporate Tax Act (*Körperschaftssteuergesetz*, or *KStG*) sets a flat tax rate of 15 percent on all taxable earnings of a corporation. The solidarity surcharge was introduced to bear the costs of Germany's reunification. It currently amounts to 5.5 percent of the corporate income tax, adding up to a tax burden of 15.825 percent. Business establishments are further subject to the *Gewerbesteuer*, or trade tax. It is levied by the municipalities and therefore differs locally, with an average level of 17 percent to 20 percent. All these rules apply to both retained and distributed profits, but in case of distributed earnings, the shareholders are charged with personal income tax on the dividends. To qualify for tax purposes, transfer prices for goods and services exchanged between resident companies or branches and their foreign affiliates must not be more favorable than between two unrelated parties (arm's-length principle). Detailed documentation rules apply with respect to transfer pricing, and violations may result in substantial penalty taxes.

Like any individual, partners in partnerships and sole proprietorships are subject to personal income tax (*Einkommensteuer*) and the solidarity surcharge. The personal income tax rate depends on the taxable income and increases progressively from 15 percent to 45 percent plus solidarity surcharge. Subject to the application of double-taxation treaties, income from German sources generated by nonresident individuals is subject to German income tax. Such income can derive from an interest in a German partnership, from dividends received from a resident corporation, real estate rent, capital gains resulting from a sale of real estate, self-employment or employment services utilized in Germany, etc.

Effective as of January 1, 2009, private capital gains will be taxed at a flat rate of a 25 percent withholding tax. This also applies to the dividends of one of the newly created Real Estate Investment Trust stock corporations (REIT AG), which are exempt from corporate tax. Foreign individuals or corporate shareholders may benefit from a reduction of withholding taxes under an applicable taxation treaty. Germany is party to tax treaties with about ninety countries including all European countries, the United States, the Russian Federation, China, and India. Special rules often apply between two EU member states. The general VAT rate in Germany was raised to 19 percent in 2007, but a reduced rate of 7 percent still applies on certain products and services.

2.4 Labor Law

The law of labor and employment is codified in a number of federal laws. In addition to the provisions on employment contracts contained in the Civil Code, special statutes provide for restrictions on dismissals, working hours, holidays, establishment and operation of works councils, codetermination, and collective bargaining. Case law plays an important role in all of these fields.

An oral employment contract is generally binding, but the agreement must be made in writing if the employment is for a period exceeding one month. Individual employment contracts are often governed by collective bargaining agreements with trade unions or works councils, which can contain not only tariffs, but also notice periods, mass dismissal protection, safety precautions, holidays, etc. Agreements with unions can be extended upon employers formerly not bound by them by a compulsory act of government in order to foster employee protection. It is currently politically and legally debated how far this instrument can serve to introduce minimum wages, which are otherwise not effective in Germany. Managing directors are appointed to office by the appropriate bodies; in addition, they are also employees of the company. Thus, dismissal of an officer also requires simultaneous termination of the employment contract.

New employees can be employed for a fixed term of two years. Any longer fixed terms require specific reasons to justify the limitation; without such reasons, the contract is deemed to be indefinite and statutory notice periods apply. Within the first two years of employment, the notice period is four weeks, effective on the 15th and the last day of the month. The notice period is gradually extended by law, depending on the overall employment term, up to a maximum of seven months to the end of the calendar month after twenty years of service. Notice must always be given in writing to become effective. During the notice period, the employee is entitled to full salary, even if she has been relieved from her duties. Immediate termination is permissible in cases of so-called "cogent reasons" and only within two weeks after the employer first becomes aware of them. Cogent reasons include but are not limited to personal or professional misconduct.

Under the Employment Protection Act (*Kündigungsschutzgesetz*, or *KSchG*), employment contracts lasting more than six months cannot be terminated unless this is deemed "socially justified." These rules enable a court, upon the employee's claim, to test whether the dismissal was justified on conduct-related, personal, or business-related grounds. While the first two grounds for dismissal are largely self-explaining, the latter requires compelling economic, technical, or operational reasons, as well as an entrepreneurial decision by the employer. The compelling business reason may be due to external causes, such as a significant decrease in sales, rationalization measures, or the closing or partial shutdown of the enterprise, if this finally leads to the elimination of workplaces. Financial considerations, such as reduction of overhead or payroll expenses, will not directly justify a termination. A business reason is deemed "compelling" only if and when the employee will no longer be required, and other means of preventing the dismissal, such as cuts in working time or in overtime, are not available. If the employee could be assigned to another position within the employer's business, the dismissal will be void. Finally, the employer must select the employees concerned according to social aspects by screening comparable employees, considering the following criteria: length of service, age, support/alimony obligations, and disability. The employer must balance these criteria and select the employee who suffers the least hardship from a dismissal. In the case of mass dismissals, the employer is obliged to notify the Federal Employment Agency (*Bundesagentur für Arbeit*) about the intended dismissals in writing before notices are given or termination agreements signed. Noncompetition undertakings by employees protecting the business's interests after the employment term are only enforceable if a compensation of fifty percent of the last annual salary has been agreed upon for each year in which competition shall be excluded, up to a maximum of two years.

In case of a transfer of a business or part of a business, Section 613a of the Civil Code provides that the new owner will replace the old employer, without further changes to the employment contract. A transfer does not represent a legitimate reason for dismissal, neither by the previous nor by the new employer. A termination is therefore invalid, unless the dismissal is permitted on other grounds, e.g., for the reasons given above. Outstanding wages accrued until the transfer date are secured by a joint liability of both the old and the new employer. A transfer of business is always assumed to take place where the transferred assets carry a certain independent and continued business identity based on its assets and goodwill, the transfer of the workforce and the customer base, the degree of similarity between the activities carried out before and after the transfer, and the duration of any interruption of the business activity prior to the transfer.

Foreign nationals other than EU, European Economic Area (EEA), and Swiss nationals may only reside in Germany to perform remunerated labor or professional activities if they have a residence and work permit. Australian, Canadian, Israeli, Japanese, New Zealand, South Korean, and U.S. citizens may acquire this residence permit from the competent foreigners' authority after their arrival in Germany. However, they may not commence employment before the permit is issued. Nationals of all other states must apply for a work visa from their local German embassy or consulate before traveling to Germany.

2.5 Merger Control and Antitrust Law

National antitrust and merger control law is contained in the Law Against Restraints of Competition (*Gesetz gegen Wettbewerbsbeschränkungen*, or *GWB*), which was aligned with European Community law in 2005. The central provisions now are almost identical to Articles 81 and 82 of the EC Treaty, which always apply if trade between the member states is affected. Further rules on unfair competition are contained in the Act on Unfair Competition (*Gesetz gegen den unlauteren Wettbewerb*, or *UWG*). Antitrust law plays an important role in business negotiations, especially—but not only—when it comes to competition clauses. These are admissible only under limited circumstances, e.g., the seller of a business can normally not effectively give noncompetition undertakings that exceed a period of three years. If a longer time frame is agreed, or if the limits of the non-competition covenant are not sufficiently determined or are unreasonable, the clause may be void and the parties can be subject to antitrust proceedings. Distribution and agency agreements containing restrictions on competition are generally inadmissible, unless they comply with the vertical agreements block exemption issued by the EU. Further group exemptions exist for motor vehicle distribution and servicing and the transfer of technology agreements on the vertical level, and with regard to the horizontal level for R&D and specialization agreements.

Depending on the annual turnover and the geographic centers of business of the undertakings concerned, a merger may have to be reported prior to closing of the transaction. The Federal Competition Authority (*Bundeskartellamt*) must be notified if the worldwide combined turnover of the purchaser and the target in the financial year preceding the merger exceeded EUR 500 million, and if at least one of the undertakings concerned accrues a turnover of more than EUR 25 million domestically. Where an independent undertaking with annual worldwide revenues below EUR 10 million is concerned, that merger is exempt from merger control; the same applies to mergers on markets that have been harvested for more than five years and that see a total revenue of less than EUR 15 million per annum. Financial institutions, insurance companies, and the newspaper industry are governed by special provisions. The parties must notify the European Commission if the merger is deemed to have a community dimension. This is the case if the enterprises concerned:

- have an aggregate worldwide turnover of more than EUR 5 billion and if at least two of the involved parties have an EU-wide sales turnover of EUR 250 million each; or
- have an aggregate worldwide turnover of more than EUR 2.5 billion, and jointly have a turnover of more than EUR 100 million in at least three EU member states. At least two of the enterprises concerned must have turnovers of more than EUR 25 million in at least three member states taken into account under the latter condition, and two of the enterprises concerned by the merger must have an EU-wide turnover of more than EUR 100 million.

Finally, these thresholds do not apply if any of the undertakings concerned has more than two-thirds of its annual EU turnover in only one member state. If notified, the authorities will generally communicate within one month if the merger has been cleared or if further investigations will be initiated.

2.6 Governmental Control of Foreign Investments

Exchange control laws do not exist. The transfer of funds and the assets of entities predominantly held by foreign investors must be reported to the Federal Reserve Bank in accordance with the Foreign Trade Ordinance (*Außenwirtschaftsverordnung*). These duties serve statistical purposes only, but noncompliance can result in a monetary fine. The European Union and the German government may restrict business and investment with regard to certain countries or counterparties. Acquisition of shares in companies that produce certain military goods must be reported to the government and may be prohibited.

3. Attorneys-at-Law and Civil Law Notaries

German lawyers, be they judges, public prosecutors, attorneys-at-law (*Rechtsanwälte*) or civil law notaries, have all received the same uniform legal training. At least four years at university are concluded with an examination by a governmental commission (state exam), followed by two years of practical training operated by a governmental authority at different seats (including courts, law offices, and public administration), and completed by a second state examination. Business attorneys frequently hold additional academic degrees, often from Anglo-American universities. Attorneys are allowed to both advise in legal matters and appear in courts throughout Germany, with the exception of the Federal Supreme Court, where only a few appointed attorneys may plead. Attorneys' fees are generally governed by a statutory fee schedule that relates them to the amount in dispute. However, today the scale only sets a minimum for services in connection with a court case; apart from this restriction, attorneys can freely negotiate their fees. Contingent fees are generally prohibited by law, except for clients that could not afford legal service otherwise.

Civil law notaries have official functions. They are appointed and supervised by the government. Because of the historical roots of today's Germany, notaries can be found practicing under the status of a civil servant, both as attorney and notary, or as a private practitioner strictly limited to notarial work, depending on the locality of a notary's professional district. Certain legal acts require the involvement of a notary, such as the transfer of real property; the establishment of stock corporations and GmbHs, or shareholders' resolutions amending the articles thereof; transfer of GmbH shares; matters regarding estates; agreements governing last wills. The fees of civil law notaries are fixed according to a statutory fee scale and depend on the value of the matter concerned. Whether notarization of such transactions could also validly be done abroad still is a disputed issue. However, it is now established by the judiciary that notaries in certain Swiss cantons comply with German standards as regards their legal training and the ability to give advice to the parties. Their deeds are therefore accepted as equivalent, and the fees of Swiss notaries are sometimes more competitive. In any case, the transfer of title of real property located in Germany must be notarized before a German civil law notary, so that the notice regarding the change of title will be acknowledgeable for entry in the land register.

4. Legal Issues in Business Negotiations

4.1 Conclusion of Contracts

Oral contracts and agreements concluded over the Internet are generally recognizable and enforceable, but there are numerous exceptions to this rule. Notably with regard to real estate, employment, and corporate issues, agreements need to be in writing or must even be notarized. An electronic signature meeting certain statutory requirements is recognized by law, but only a few industries take advantage of it at present. Implicit reference in the negotiations can be sufficient to render general terms and conditions (*Allgemeine Geschäftsbedingungen*, or *AGB*) effective between undertakings; it is therefore advisable to ask for a copy and expressly address the partial or complete exclusion or inclusion of the general terms and conditions. In order to qualify as general terms and conditions, it is sufficient that a clause has been pre-drafted with the intent of using it more than once. An extensive body of statutory and case law exists with regard to general terms and conditions, which can render certain contractual provisions null and void if they have not been negotiated with regard to the individual case.

Recent years have seen a more lenient approach where clauses may be upheld to the extent they are valid, but always subject to the so-called "blue pencil test": The court tests whether a clause still contains a meaningful stipulation after the invalid wording has been erased, and provided that the remaining clause is neither surprising nor unreasonable. As long as they are specifically referred to, there are no further restrictions to incorporating the International Court of Arbitration (ICC) Incoterms if the contract is governed by German law.

German law distinguishes clearly between contracts concerning the obligation to transfer the title to a right and agreements actually transferring the right. In practice, both agreements are largely contained within one instrument, e.g., in one "Share *Purchase* and *Transfer* Agreement." It can, however, be advisable to execute both contracts successively—for example, to save on the legal fees. Warranties and covenants in purchase agreements are often less detailed compared to the Anglo-American equivalents. This difference is largely due to the application of an extensive body of statutory and case law on the agreement, as well as on the due diligence.

4.2 Competent Court and Applicable Law

From the perspective of a German court, the parties to an international business contract can agree upon the jurisdiction as well as upon a venue of their choice in writing. Any court appealed to will apply the *lex fori* not only on the question of its competence, but also on a possible conflict of laws. It is also possible to give exclusive jurisdiction to national or international arbitration panels. However, any venue clause should be tested as to whether or not a judgment received would finally be enforceable in the jurisdiction where the opponent is seated. Before a German court, a first-instance judgment can be obtained within six months on average, depending on the need to hear evidence. Because of the fixed legal fees, the financial risks of filing a claim can accurately be calculated in advance.

A contract stipulating foreign law (e.g., the law of the State of New York) as the applicable law and a German venue is enforceable, provided that the choice of law is expressed or demonstrated with reasonable certainty by the terms of the contract or the circumstances of the case. This is one of the results of the 1980 Rome Convention on the Law Applicable to Contractual Obligations, which Germany has implemented. However, it is normally rather costly to present a foreign body of law to a German court, since this must be done with the help of independent experts. Some provisions of German law that protect one of the parties on public policy grounds cannot be overruled by a choice of law clause under German conflict of law rules—namely, employee and consumer protection laws are mandatory and therefore apply to agreements that contain a choice of foreign law. Consequently, among other examples, the consumer's right to rescission of a distant selling contract or of a contract concluded at his home or workplace cannot be mitigated by a choice of foreign law, no more than the rules on the admissibility of general terms and conditions, the two-year liability for goods sold to a consumer, or the necessity to conclude in writing any contract with a consumer that provides for payment in installments, identifying in detail the costs and term of the financing. With regard to transnational sale contracts governed by German law, the United Nations Convention on Contracts for the International Sale of Goods (CISG) generally applies, unless it is excluded by the parties.

4.3 Sureties and Bankruptcy

Although other forms of real estate securities exist, in practice the land charge (*Grundschuld*) prevails. It is not accessory to the claim secured and therefore tradable. However, it is usually accompanied by a security purpose agreement (*Sicherungszweckvereinbarung*) tying it to a specific loan. Pledges are available to movables and to rights and claims, including shareholders' rights, and are widely used. Assignments of claims and rights for security purposes are as frequently used as the transfer of property for surety purposes. Standard personal sureties comprise the accessory as well as the nonaccessory personal guarantee and the additional assumption of debt. While these sureties resemble their international counterparts, the concept of retention of title (*Eigentumsvorbehalt*) is a specific feature of German law. The distinction between obligation and actual transfer of property enables the seller to effectively sell his goods to the purchaser, but at the same time transfer the property under the condition and only to the extent that the purchase price be paid. There is no requirement or even possibility to register the retention of title. Only upon payment of the last installment will the seller become the full legal owner of the goods, although he can possess and use them beforehand. Another advantage is that property is basically insolvency-proof. It can, however, also be agreed that the goods may be sold by the buyer before he even fully owned them; in that case, the claim against the (second) buyer replaces ownership in the goods as surety. Contractual clauses dealing with the insolvency of the parties must comply with the Insolvency Act (*Insolvenzordnung*). Contracts that have been concluded to the detriment of other creditors can be successfully contested by those creditors respectively by the liquidator, provided that the parties knew of the detriment or that there was no sufficient consideration.

4.4 Typical Issues to Be Addressed

Whether an asset deal or a share deal is the favorable means of the transfer of a German business depends on issues of liability, labor law, tax spending and saving, as well as financial conditions. As a rule of thumb, the seller will normally favor a share deal, while the purchaser usually prefers to acquire the company's assets, mainly for tax reasons. How much this will depend on the particular circumstances of each case can be illustrated with regard to the constraints on loss deduction created under recent tax reforms (see section 2.3, "Taxation," above). In cases where between 25 percent and 50 percent of the shares are transferred within five years, losses accrued beforehand can be deducted on a pro rata basis. If more than 50 percent of the shares change hands within five years, loss deduction is barred completely.

The default scope of liability is set by the law. It can be extended or diminished by agreement within certain boundaries. Liability for damage caused by willful misconduct can never be waived, and consumers are protected by further cogent provisions that protect their interests. Special restrictions apply to waivers and undertakings contained in general terms and conditions (see section 4.1, "Conclusion of Contracts," above). Since there is no share register, precise representations should be demanded concerning the title in GmbH shares, as well as regards proper funding and contribution of the share capital and adherence to the rules of its protection.

Agreements with agents and independent sales representatives operating in Germany (or in any other country of the EU or the EEA) governed by German law fall under the scope of Section 89b of the Commercial Code (*HGB*). Thereby, the principal is obliged to compensate the agent after the termination of the agency agreement for the goodwill created by the agent during the term of cooperation. This claim can amount to up to one year's commission, calculated on the basis of the commission accrued during the last five years of the term of the agency agreement. If the agent operates within the EU/EEA territory, the compensation claim cannot be waived or excluded in the agency agreement, not even by choice of foreign law. In 2001, the European Court of Justice ruled that the compensation provisions for agents are internationally cogent, because they serve the purpose of creating a level playing field for all businesses within the EU/EEA, as well the creation of minimum standards for agents providing their services there. Another issue often raised when an individual is appointed agent or sales representative is that of her role as employee or as independent contractor. This role is determined by the agent's freedom to decide upon her activities and in particular her working hours and similar circumstances. If as a result of such evaluation a court applies labor law to the agency agreement, protective labor law provisions on terminations may apply and the principal may be obliged to pay social security contributions for the past.

5. Negotiations

Business negotiations in Germany are normally characterized by a very concentrated, objective, and matter-of-fact atmosphere. If Germans refuse to call their international counterparts by their first names, that is usually not a sign of repudiation, but of respect. It has, however, become quite usual that German teams adapt to the international habit of using the first names during negotiations, although they may immediately fall back to addressing each other with their last names during breaks and afterwards. English is the prevailing language for contracts in an international context. Nonetheless, international agreements are frequently drafted in both English and German by means of a synoptic table. This is intended to promote mutual understanding of the provisions agreed upon, as well as to enable persons executing or applying the agreement—such as a judge whose command of foreign languages may not be sufficient—to clearly understand its contents. Furthermore, this technique enables the parties to clarify the meaning of legal terms under the applicable law. All of these purposes require that the agreement clearly determine which language shall be binding.

The style and character of both the negotiations and the resulting agreement strongly depend on the type and nature of the German party involved. Small and medium-size enterprises, often in the hand of families or entrepreneurs (the so-called *Mittelstand*), still form the backbone of Germany's economy. In the wake of growing internationalization, many of these businesses are accustomed to the approaches that have been developed within the Anglo-American legal system, such as lengthy representations and warranties in purchase agreements, or due diligence procedures. However, many entrepreneurs and managers still feel more comfortable without the piles of documents often common in global business culture. Agreements under German law are traditionally rather short compared to Anglo-American standards. This can be explained by the elaborate statutory and case law that the parties can rely upon. As remedies are determined by civil and commercial laws, they need to be addressed only if and to the extent that the remedies available under statutory law should be amended.

Dr. Ralf Wojtek and Dr. Matthias Kühn
Heuking Kühn Lüer Wojtek
Friedrichstrasse 149
10117 Berlin
Germany
Phone: 49-30-88-00-97-0
Fax: 49-30-88-00-97-99
E-mail: r.wojtek@heuking.de
           m.kuehn@heuking.de

CHAPTER 30

International Business Negotiations in India

Cyril Shroff

Amarchand & Mangaldas & Suresh A. Shroff & Co.
Mumbai, India

1. Introduction

1.1 Broad Demographic Information

India is the world's largest democracy and is rapidly becoming one of the most attractive developing nations with which to do business. It is the seventh largest country in the world, with a total landmass of 3,287,590 square kilometers. It is located in South Asia, has a land boundary of 14,107 kilometers with its neighbors (Pakistan, China, Bangladesh, Burma, Nepal, and Bhutan) and a coastline of 7,000 kilometers, which stretches across the Arabian Sea and the Bay of Bengal in the Indian Ocean. It is the second most populous country in the world; with an estimated 1.2 billion people, India makes up one-sixth of the world's population.

India has a multiplicity of climates and terrains across its regions, which range from snow-peaked Himalayas in the north, desert in the west, thick rain forests in the northeast, flat green pastures in the Gangetic plains, and plateaus in south and central India. On average, the Indian climate varies from tropical to temperate. Winter (October to March) is generally a better period to visit India. During this time, the temperature can go as low as 2 to 3°C in the Northern mountains of India. However, in most other parts of the country, it is normally a comfortable 15 to 25°C. Indian summers (April to June) can be very hot, with the temperature reaching 50°C in many locations.

Virtually all of the major world religions and ethnicities can be found in India. A majority (approximately 75 percent) of Indians come from the Indo-Aryan race, followed by Dravidians (approximately 25 percent). Hinduism, practiced by more than 80 percent of the population, is far from a homogeneous religion; it consists of a multiplicity of creeds and faiths, which are further divided among many castes, sects, and subsects. The caste system in Hindu society is hierarchical in nature, and has a deep influence on the behavior and lives of people. The other major religions represented in Indian society are Islam, Christianity, Sikhism, Buddhism, Jainism, and Zoroastrianism. In addition, more than 300 local tribes constitute around 8 percent of the Indian population.

India is one of the most culturally, linguistically, and genetically diverse countries in the world. India has over 1,600 regional dialects and approximately twenty-three languages that are abundantly spoken. Out of these languages, Hindi is the official language and primary tongue of 30 percent of the people; there are fourteen other official languages: Bengali, Telugu, Marathi, Tamil, Urdu, Gujarati, Malayalam, Kannada, Oriya, Punjabi, Assamese, Kashmiri, Sindhi, and Sanskrit. However, English is extensively used for business and administration within the country and is also used in addition to Hindi for national, political, and commercial communication. Individual states' own internal communication is usually in English or in the state's own language.

The capital of India is New Delhi. India has an electorate of more than 600 million people. Defining moments in modern Indian history were laid down during the Indian independence movement to end the colonial rule of the last of the foreign rulers in India, the British. India gained its independence from the British colonial rule in 1947. Its constitution, adopted in 1949, incorporates many features of the constitutional systems of the western democracies, specifically of the United Kingdom and the United States. The Constitution of India is in written form and is the longest and most exhaustive constitution of any independent nation of the world. The preamble of the Constitution of India pronounces India as a sovereign, socialist, secular, and democratic republic. The Constitution of India established the Central Government as the governing authority of the federal union of twenty-eight states and seven union territories. Each state and union territory also has its own elected parliamentary assembly. The three branches of the government are the executive, the legislature, and the judiciary with their powers separated by a series of checks and balances.

The legislative body of the Union is a bicameral legislature, consisting of the *Lok Sabha* (house of people or lower house), directly elected for a period of five years based on adult franchise, and the *Rajya Sabha* (council of state or upper house). The parliament consists of more than 534 elected MPs (Members of Parliament). In the 2004 parliamentary elections, India used indigenously developed electronic voting machines for conducting the elections. India has seven national political parties, and more than forty political parties recognized by the Election Commission. The voting age in India is eighteen years.

The constitutional head of the country is the president, but it is largely a ceremonial post. The actual legislative power resides with the Council of Ministers, headed by the prime minister, who is the leader of the party in the majority.

The judiciary in India is independent of political or governmental influences. It has often made decisions that are critical of—or even against—the government's official policies. This occurs if the judiciary believes that the policy goes against the basic spirit of the Indian Constitution.

Though India has a secular political structure, religion plays an important role in the personal lives of people, and often influences relationships and business dealings.

1.2 Historical and Cultural Background

India is a blend of different cultures, religions, races, and languages. It is heavily influenced by Hinduism and is deeply rooted in years of traditions. It is one of the oldest civilizations in the world and has one of the most diverse cultures in the world, the result of a unique interplay and exchange of various customs and traditions over time. Ancient Indian history has been marked by invasions and immigrations over five millennia, and these events have helped shape the deep and diverse culture of the nation.

The Aryans were among the first to arrive in India, which was inhabited by the Dravidians. Other invaders include the Greeks, Persians, Mughals, British, Portuguese, and French. Over the years there have been many major ruling dynasties such as the Shakas, the Kushans, the Mauryas, and the Guptas. Nearly every major religion is represented in India. It is also the land of the Buddha, Lord Mahvira, and Guru Nanak Dev, the founders of Buddhism, Jainism, and Sikhism, respectively.

Modern India has managed to preserve its deep-rooted traditions while absorbing new customs, traditions, and practices. Innumerable groups peacefully coexist within the fabric of the larger Indian society, maintaining their distinctive cultural identities. This unique form of "unity in diversity" makes cultural pluralism one of the defining factors of Indian life.

1.3 Business Organization and Culture

India is one of the fastest growing emerging markets today. It is strategically located and has a huge consumer base, a rapidly growing IT industry, and an increasing manufacturing industry. Additionally, it boasts a skilled workforce, a high level of college graduates, and a pool of experienced scientists, technicians, engineers, and managers—all with advanced English-language skills.

Like the country itself, the Indian business culture is diverse and heterogeneous. Historically, Indian businesses have been family owned or owned by members of different social communities. The Parsi, Gujarati, and Marwari communities are amongst the most predominant business communities in India. Most of the business organizations are run on modern lines and have adopted international norms of conducting business.

The manner in which businesses are operated also varies from region to region within the country itself. Business culture in the northern regions of the country is clearly distinguishable from that in the western and southern regions. Wealth and social status play a crucial role in North India; connections, both political and social, heavily influence business deals and negotiations. On the other hand, the influence of the Western world is more noticeable in the business styles adopted in west and south India, which are perhaps somewhat more cosmopolitan and broad-based.

The diverse culture of the country permeates not only into everyday life but also into the business dealings of Indian companies. It is therefore always beneficial to avail oneself of expert guidance to understand and appreciate the underlying culture of India and use it to one's advantage in the course of negotiations.

1.4 Overview of Legal System

The Indian legal system is based on the common law system that was introduced during the British rule in India.

India is credited with having the most powerful and independent judiciary in the world. The judicial system also owes its origin to the system established during the British rule in India. After independence, the Constituent Assembly provided for the establishment of a three-tier judicial system that was completely independent from the executive and the legislature. The Supreme Court stands at the apex of the judicial hierarchy along with the High Courts and subordinate courts, all with specified powers and functions. Like the United States, India has a federal constitution, but unlike the United States, India does not have a dual system of courts. The judiciary is integrated as one whole system. The Supreme Court exercises original, appellate, and advisory jurisdiction. Its exclusive original jurisdiction extends to disputes between the center and the states as well as between different states. The state's judiciary is headed by the High Court. Each High Court in turn has the power of jurisprudence over all the subordinate courts within its jurisdiction. An appeal from the decision of the High Court lies with the Supreme Court.

The Constitution of India is the supreme law of the land. Constituent power in the Indian legal system has been placed in a position superior to ordinary legislative power. All laws enacted within India must pass constitutionality, and as a corollary a law is liable to be struck down if it is against the Constitution.

The legal system has codified commercial codes. The industrial policy, naturally, is colored by the philosophy of the government in power and finds expression in the form of policy pronouncements, press notes, and notifications under the Industries (Development and Regulation) Act and related legislations such as the Foreign Exchange Management Act, 1999 (FEMA).

The power and scope of parties to negotiate their contract is dependent on the scope of the "freedom of contract" that the state has to offer. India is a socialist state and the "freedom of contract" has been adapted to suit the Indian socialist context. With the growth of socialism and social responsibility, the concept of the freedom of contract has become subject to regulation in India. India has historically shown a trend to eliminate disparities in property holdings and to confer rights on the tillers of the soil resulting in the restriction of the freedom of contract in property law. Like property law, freedom of contract has been restricted between the employer and workman by the Industrial Disputes Act, 1947 and other employer-employee-related legislation. The Prevention of Food Adulteration Act, the Essential Commodities Act, the Consumer Protection Act, etc., have also placed restrictions on sellers to protect consumers.

Lawyers in India have predominated in all walks of public life. From the struggle for independence to the liberalization of the Indian economy, lawyers have been in the forefront of the growth and development of the country through its history. Naturally, lawyers often tend to play a pivotal role in the process of negotiations in India. India has the second largest legal profession in the world, second only to the United States.

Along with the lawyers, an important part of the legal system is the litigants themselves. Indian people are fundamentally litigious in nature. Though they are not generally confrontational, the judicial system and its inherent delays make it advantageous to exploit the system and throw the proverbial spanner in the wheel. It is not uncommon for large projects to get stalled due to some frivolous litigation that may have been filed in court, often in the form of a public-interest litigation (PIL).

Public-interest litigations have come to play a crucial role in the present legal system of the country. The concept of *locus standi* has undergone considerable expansion over the past three decades, with the judiciary recognizing that a third party could directly petition the court, whether through a letter or other means, and seek its intervention in a matter where another party's fundamental rights were being violated. Unfortunately, PILs have also been subject to a tremendous amount of misuse. Judges have often expressed shock at the fact that courts are flooded with a large number of so-called PILs, whereas only a minuscule percentage are on legitimate grounds. These are often initiated by "self-styled saviors" who have no face or ground in the midst of the public at large and merely initiate such litigations to keep themselves busy and keep their names in circulation. There are often ulterior motives behind such frivolous actions. As mentioned earlier, large and highly publicized projects often are subject to PILs that are filed simply to throw such projects off track.

2. Substantive Laws and Regulations Impacting Negotiations

2.1 Corporate Laws

Corporate laws in India include the Indian Contract Act, 1872; the Negotiable Instruments Act, 1882; Transfer of Property Act, 1882; the Presidency Towns Insolvency Act, 1909; the Provincial Insolvency Act, 1920; the Sale of Goods Act, 1930; the Indian Partnership Act, 1932; the Arbitration and Conciliation Act, 1996; the Companies Act, 1956; and the Specific Relief Act, 1963.

The Companies Act, 1956, is the definitive statute governing company law in India. It deals with matters relating to incorporation, regulation, management, minority protection, winding up of companies, etc. It consolidates and amends the law relating to companies and certain other associations.

2.2 Securities Laws

The Securities and Exchange Board of India (SEBI) pursuant to the Securities and Exchange Board of India Act, 1992 (SEBI Act) and the Securities Contracts (Regulation) Act, 1956 (SCRA), primarily regulates securities transactions in India.

The SEBI Act was enacted to protect the interests of investors in securities and to regulate and promote the development of the securities market. The SEBI Act also provides for the registration of investment advisers, stockbrokers, institutional investors, etc. The SCRA is largely applicable only to shares of public and listed companies. Under the SCRA, contracts for the sale and purchase of securities other than those implemented on a recognized stock exchange are ordinarily allowed only on a spot delivery basis.

The Securities and Exchange Board of India (Disclosures and Investor Protection) Guidelines, 2000 (SEBI DIP Guidelines) specify the details required for the filing of any offer for the issuance of shares to the public. The SEBI (Substantial Acquisition of Shares and Take-overs) Regulations, 1997 (SEBI Takeover Regulations) deal with acquisitions of listed Indian securities. Any acquiror (a person who, directly or indirectly, acquires or agrees to acquire shares or voting rights in, or control of, a company, either by himself or with any person acting in concert) who acquires shares or voting rights that would entitle the acquiror to more than 5 percent, 10 percent, 14 percent, 54 percent, or 74 percent of the shares or voting rights, respectively, in a company is required to disclose the aggregate of his shareholding or voting rights in that company to the company and to each of the stock exchanges on which the company's shares are listed at every stage within two days of (i) the receipt of allotment information or (ii) the acquisition of shares or voting rights, as the case may be.

2.3 Tax Laws

Taxes in India can be broadly classified into direct taxes and indirect taxes. Direct taxes include income tax, wealth tax, and interest tax, the most significant of which is income tax. The Income Tax Act, 1961 (Income Tax Act) governs income tax in India. It is modified each year through the Finance Act passed by the Parliament. India is also a signatory to double-taxation avoidance treaties with several countries including the United States, the United Kingdom, Mauritius, and Cyprus. Favorable tax treatment is available under these agreements.

Indirect taxes are governed under the Provisions of the Central Excise Act, 1944, Customs Act, 1962, and Central Sales Tax Act, 1956.

2.4 Antitrust / Anticompetition Laws

Currently, the Companies Act and the Monopolies and Restrictive Trade Practices Act, 1969 (MRTP) govern competition in India. The MRTP ensures that the operation of the economic system does not result in the concentration of economic power to the common detriment and is the prevailing antitrust legislation in India. However, in light of international economic developments and economic reforms in India in the past decade, the Competition Act, 2002 as amended by the Competition Amendment, 2007 (together referred to as the Competition Act) will soon replace the MRTP, to promote competition rather than curb monopolies. The Competition Act will regulate anticompetitive agreements, abuse of dominance, and merger control.

2.5 Labor and Employment Laws

India has an extensive labor and employment regime governed by both central and state legislations. The Industrial Disputes Act, 1947 (IDA), Industrial Employment (Standing Orders) Act, 1946 (Industrial Employment Act), and Trade Unions Act, 1926 govern industrial relations and the conciliation and adjudication of industrial disputes. The IDA provides an extensive machinery and procedure for the investigation and settlement of industrial disputes. The Industrial Employment Act requires each industrial establishment to define with sufficient precision the conditions of employment and communicate these conditions to the employees. The Factories Act, 1948, Payment of Wages Act, 1936, Minimum Wages Act, Workmen's Compensation Act, 1923, and Fatal Accidents Act, 1855, govern remuneration and basic protection of employees. Additionally, the Equal Remuneration Act, 1976, provides for the payment of equal remuneration to male and female employees to prevent discrimination against women on the grounds of sex in matters of employment. The Employees Provident Fund Act, 1952, Employees State Insurance Act, 1948, Payment of Gratuity Act, 1972, Maternity Benefit Act, 1961, and Weekly Holidays Act, 1942 govern social security and welfare of employees.

The Shops and Establishments Act in force in the relevant state governs the hours of work, payment of wages, leave, holidays, and other terms of employment. It directly or indirectly mirrors and extends the provisions contained in the above-mentioned laws to commercial establishments.

Several of the relevant remuneration and social security legislations are not applicable to employees who earn a salary above a certain prescribed amount. These amounts prescribed are usually low and therefore the concerned legislations may not be applicable to most employees working in the private sector. The contractual relations between the parties govern these employment situations.

The Constitution of India guarantees equality of opportunity for all citizens and prohibits discrimination in matters relating to employment by the state based on religion, race, caste, sex, place of birth, or domicile. These constitutional rights are not only available against the state and state-owned or controlled undertakings but also against private sector enterprises founded on the principles of natural justice.

2.6 Environmental Laws

The Environment (Protection) Act, 1986 was introduced in India as an umbrella legislation to provide a holistic framework for the protection of the environment. Additionally, the Air (Prevention and Control of Pollution) Act, 1981, and Water (Prevention and Control of Pollution) Act, 1974, were enacted for the prevention, control, and abatement of air and water pollution, respectively. They also provide for the establishment of Boards given specific powers in relation to their duties as specified under the acts.

The Wildlife Protection Act, 1972, and the Biological Diversity Act, 2002, provide for the conservation of wildlife, biological diversity, and sustainable development.

The judiciary has always taken a very active and responsive role in the protection of the environment. Various public-interest litigations over the past two decades have paved the way for the development of Indian environmental jurisprudence. The Supreme Court has interpreted the right to environment as a fundamental right and a right guaranteed by the Constitution of India.

2.7 Intellectual Properties Laws

India has a robust and effective regime to protect intellectual property with legislations in place to protect trademarks, copyrights, patents, designs, plant varieties, geographical indications, and topographies of integrated circuits and semiconductors (Semiconductor Integrated Circuits Layout-Design Act, 2000 is pending notification by the central government). India is also member of the Berne Convention for the Protection of Literary and Artistic Works, 1886, and the Paris Convention for the Protection of Industrial Property, 1883. India is also a signatory to the Trade-Related Aspects of Intellectual Property Rights (TRIPS) agreement and the Patent Cooperation Treaty. The existing intellectual property regime has been amended to comply with India's obligations as a signatory to TRIPS. Copyright protection for computer programs, service marks, and industrial designs are a few examples of some of the new provisions since the signing of the TRIPS agreement.

Additionally, the protection to business goodwill is afforded under common law, and precedents from common law jurisdictions are accepted as good precedents.

2.8 Privacy and Data Securities Laws

Currently, there is no legislation that exclusively covers privacy and data security in India. However, the issue of privacy and data security is not completely unaddressed in the Indian context. The Supreme Court has recognized the right to privacy as an integral part of the right to life and personal liberty, a fundamental right guaranteed by the Constitution of India. Data security, on the other hand, can be derived from the protection offered by the existing legal regime in relation to information technology, intellectual property, crime, and contractual relations. The Information Technology Act, 2000, specifically provides for safeguards against breach of security in relation to data from computer systems. Additionally, the Credit Information Companies Regulation Act was passed in 2005, under which the Reserve Bank of India (RBI) has set forth strict data privacy principles.

However, the government is aware of the need for a consolidated legislation to address privacy and data security issues in India and is presently contemplating the enactment of such. The government has entertained industry feedback on the requirements and the mechanism of an enactment to provide for data protection, and a task force set up by the government has prepared a draft data protection law in consonance with the international data protection regime. The draft is presently under consideration.

The Right to Information Act was enacted in the year 2005, giving citizens of India access to information and records of the central government and state governments. Under the provisions of the Act, any citizen may request information from a "public authority," which is usually a body of government or an "instrumentality of State." "Information" has been given a considerably wide scope and means any material in any form including records, documents, memos, e-mails, opinions, advice, press releases, circulars, orders, log books, contracts, reports, papers, samples, models, data material held in any electronic form, and information relating to any private body that can be accessed by a public authority under any other law for the time being in force, but does not include "file notings." The Public Authority is required to reply to requests expeditiously, or within thirty days. The Act also requires every public authority to computerize their records for wide dissemination and to proactively publish certain categories of information to minimize the need for citizens to request information formally.

2.9 Regulation of Foreign Investment

Foreign Investment in India is regulated primarily by the Industrial Policy, press notes issued by the Ministry of Commerce and Industry, the Foreign Exchange Management Act, 1999 (FEMA), and the regulations and notifications issued by the RBI under FEMA.

FEMA purports to liberalize the inflow and outflow of foreign exchange by removing the restrictions to facilitate external trade and payments and promote orderly maintenance of the foreign exchange market in India.

The Foreign Investment Promotion Board (FIPB), a part of the Ministry of Finance, regulates foreign investment in accordance with the new Industrial Policy and the RBI regulates foreign investment for the purposes of exchange control in accordance with the provisions of FEMA.

3. Other Significant Legal and Business Issues

3.1 Interpretation of Statutes

Though the responsibility of making statutes lies with the legislature, the duty of interpretation of the same lies with the judiciary. As briefly discussed above, there are different categories of statutes implementing the policy of the government in emergent social and economic situations, besides those regulating state revenues and others codifying civil and criminal laws governing the citizens. The rules of interpretation applicable respectively to the different kinds of statutes have evolved via a long history of wisdom and experience, so much so that the interpretation of statutes has become a science in itself. Interpretation of statutes often turns out to be counterintuitive, with the accepted practice being quite different from the letter of the law. The need and requirement for good advisors with knowledge and experience in the relevant fields thus cannot be overemphasized. The participation of advisors is critical during the advisory stage as well as negotiations in order to understand and correctly apply the law to business situations.

3.2 Types of Business Ventures

Business ventures can be carried on in India through sole proprietorships, partnerships, or companies incorporated in India. Foreign entities can additionally carry on business through a branch office, liaison/representative office, or project office.

A sole proprietorship is the simplest form of business. No business registration is required under Indian law and the owner of a sole proprietorship is personally entitled to all the profits and responsible for all the losses arising from the business.

Partnerships in India are regulated under the Partnership Act. Partners of a firm are jointly entitled to all the profits and are also jointly responsible for all the liabilities arising from the business. A partnership does not have a corporate character distinct from its members. A partnership may even have corporations as its members. A limited liability partnerships act is expected to be enforced soon. As per this act, partners in a partnership can have limited liability.

A company may be incorporated in India either as a private company or a public company. The minimum paid-up capital for a private company is INR 0.1 million and that of a public company is INR 0.5 million. Private companies have greater flexibility and less-stringent rules in respect to various matters including holding of members' meetings, issuance of further capital, commencement of business, number of directors, determination of kinds of share capital and voting rights, determination of managerial remuneration, intercorporate loans and investments, etc. The shares of a public company are freely transferable and there is no limit on the number of members that the company may have. A public company is required to have a minimum of seven members and three directors. A private company that is a subsidiary of a public company is also considered to be a public company.

Setting up branch offices and liaison offices requires prior approval of the RBI. General permission has been given by the RBI for the establishment of project offices that meet specified conditions. Foreign companies, i.e., companies incorporated outside India, that establish a place of business in India through a branch office must be registered with the Registrar of Companies.

Time and costs for the formation of a sole proprietorship and a partnership are minimal. Formation of a company usually takes approximately six weeks and the expenses incurred include registration fees, stamp fees, and other legal fees. Registration fees vary according to the name and the size of the authorized capital of the company. Establishment of a branch or liaison office usually takes four to six weeks and the only costs incurred are with regard to obtaining the approval of the RBI.

3.3 Choice of Law

Indian courts do recognize and enforce a choice of law and jurisdiction made by parties, subject to such choice being bona fide and not opposed to public policy. However, Indian courts may refuse to enforce a stipulation as to the choice of forum where it is of the opinion that such choice is oppressive, unfair, or inequitable.

3.4 Role of the Government

The Industrial Policy, naturally, is colored by the political philosophy of the government in power and finds expression in the form of policy pronouncements, press notes, and notifications under the Industries (Development and Regulation) Act and cognate legislations such as the Foreign Exchange Management Act. India has a complex regulatory environment and government approvals and clearances form an integral part of negotiating one's way through business transactions. In fact, very often the outcome of negotiations is pivotal on such approvals, which may be required at various stages of a transaction.

Government departments are hierarchical and highly bureaucratic in nature. The ethos of the Indian bureaucracy is also highly complex. Though extremely intelligent, the bureaucracy has a rhythm of its own. One may find their processes to be slow and it may be very tedious to negotiate a way though the intricacies imposed by the system.

Politicians are also equally complicated to deal with, and during such interactions it often transpires that the real power may not reside with the head of the agency or the government and may lie elsewhere. A diverse range of politicians and officials make up the system. As individuals they range from extremely clean to completely corrupt. The vice of corruption plagues several government departments and offices and one may often have to tackle these difficult situations. It is worth mentioning that there does exist the Prevention of Corruption Act, 1988, which is a central law enacted by the Indian government. This act prohibits bribing or making illegal payments to government officials in order to assist a company in advancing the objectives of its business in the country. Conviction under this act may result in fine and imprisonment.

3.5 Role of Media

The Indian media is about as vocal as in the United States and generally spares no one. Its efficacy (and nuisance value) is enhanced by the widespread growth of many broadsheets and tabloid papers, and also the emergence of "sting" operations, the moral appropriateness of which is a matter of debate. Electronic media in India also carry some amount of sensational journalism; hence generally the government is always on its toes.

4. Negotiation Practices

4.1 Participants

Indians prefer to do business with those they know, and relationships are built upon mutual trust and respect. In general, Indians prefer to have long-standing personal relationships prior to doing business. It may be a good idea to go through a third-party introduction to make initial contacts. This gives a foreign businessperson immediate credibility.

In an Indian organization, established hierarchies have to be respected. In business, senior colleagues, especially elders, are obeyed and respected. Indian employees address their superiors formally and, unless told otherwise, it is advisable for outside businesspeople to do the same. Indians revere titles. If someone has a professional title, use their professional title when addressing them (e.g., Dr. Aggarwal, Professor Singh). If someone does not have a professional title, men should be referred to as "Mr." and women as "Mrs.," "Ms.," or "Miss." Refer to business contacts by their last name, rather than by their first name, unless or until invited to use their first name. Establishing one's place is important in the highly networked business community. Weave your accomplishments and contacts into conversation with panache to earn respect and gain introductions.

Reciprocity is an important factor in business negotiations in India. It is expected that a meeting attended by senior management of an Indian company would have to be attended by individuals of equivalent (if not greater) seniority belonging to the foreign party. Indian counterparts often frown upon participation by junior representatives, irrespective of their competence. Government departments are more sensitive to hierarchy, and respecting seniority is important. It is wise to follow a rule of "better safe than sorry" in these situations.

The most senior person usually leads the discussions and it is appropriate to direct communication to him. Alternatively, your Indian counterpart may direct and match you to the person of equal status in the organization. The highest-ranking business executives make the final decisions; therefore, it is important to maintain strong relationships with senior figures in Indian business. Owners and executives of Indian companies hold business authority closely, with decisions (e.g., purchases of US$5,000 or more) made only by them and not delegated to managers.

Lawyers are center stage in any negotiation in India. Their presence is a comforting factor to the Indian parties. The involvement of a good advisor, even on the other side, instills confidence and benefits the entire negotiation process as a whole. As mentioned earlier, Indians rely a great deal on trust and place a great amount of faith in the participants in the negotiations. Instead of merchant bankers, it is often common to see the family accountant taking part in discussions and assisting the principals in the decision-making process.

In India business organizations embody family values, deep-rooted traditions, and the culture of their founders. Business connections are a determinate factor of social stature and dictate one's position amongst peers. It is for this reason that though the general approach of business organizations in India is hierarchical in nature, one may be surprised to find that the style of negotiations is often informal and friendly. Business relations are forged with the ultimate hope and aspiration of forming long-lasting friendships, which is a relation held in high regard. In India, business is personal.

4.2 Timing

Normal business hours are from 10:00 A.M. to 5:00 P.M. However, business organizations may start earlier and work until around 7:30 P.M. to 8:00 P.M. Lunch hour is usually between 1:00 P.M. and 2:00 P.M. The lunch hour is sacrosanct in government departments. The best time for meetings is late morning or early afternoon (between 11:00 A.M. and 4:00 P.M.). Reconfirm your meeting a week before and on the day itself, as meetings tend to be cancelled on short notice.

Indians appreciate punctuality and keeping one's commitments, yet Indians can be quite "flexible" in adhering to their own time commitments. It is common for meetings to be delayed by a quarter-hour to a half-hour from the scheduled time. However, the importance of punctuality in connection with conference calls and videoconferencing is respected in business organizations.

The Indian calendar is riddled with various holidays, so it would be prudent to check a calendar specifying a list of Indian public holidays before fixing a schedule for meetings in India. Lawyers and investment bankers have gained a notorious reputation for working through public holidays. However, generally Indians do not prefer to do business on these days. The festival of *Diwali* is the most auspicious among the business community in India. Festivities may stretch to a week, and most businesses remain closed or are simply in "holiday mode."

The workweek is Monday to Friday. However, several private organizations maintain Saturdays as full working days.

4.3 Negotiation Practices

Over the past two decades, Indian businesses have witnessed a large number of foreign joint ventures and technical collaborations. Indians are no longer strangers to cross-country negotiations and are quite comfortable participating in them. Business behavior in India is very similar to that of most western countries. However, there are significant distinct and contrasting differences in the cultures of government departments and business organizations. Compared to business organizations, it is often more difficult to get an appointment with the officials of a government department. Appointments with government officials often stand a greater possibility of being rescheduled at short notice. Conversely, the culture of the business organizations is also, like the country itself, diverse and heterogeneous. It is important for one to remember these differences while negotiating a business deal.

The urban Indian educational system has been strongly influenced by the western system for decades now. English is the popular medium of instruction, and Indians are well versed in the language. English has served as a crucial "link language" across the various states and cultures that have marked the Indian diaspora for the past two centuries. The Indian accent and diction is often clear and not very difficult to understand. However, a common complaint is that Indians tend to talk too fast! It is also common for Indians to use certain expressions of their regional vernacular while speaking in English. The fluency with which this is done may often confuse the listener and takes some time to get used to.

Indians are known as keen negotiators, experienced in bargaining and negotiating for themselves and their families as part of life in India. Indians take the time to understand the logic, competitive advantages, motivating factor, and, in some instances, the spiritual timing or location of a business deal. They are financially savvy and move along with the pulse of the economy. With a population of graduates from India's famed IIT (Indian Institute of Technology) and IIM (Indian Institute of Management), and many top universities in the West, Indians are able to draw upon strong business acumen. Through their networks, Indians are well prepared with data on competitive scenarios and prices.

Thus, Indians also expect you to have thoroughly researched your proposition and to provide in-depth data analysis and detail. Indians appreciate a factual and personable delivery style that starts with the big picture before getting to implementation specifics. Indians think long-term while moving quickly to seize opportunities in today's expanding economy. A bottom-line approach or a quick fix may be perceived as simplistic and short-term thinking. Indians persuade through competitive data, repetition, insistence, and rigorous detail, and may make vigorous emotional appeals to underscore their proposition. A response in kind (avoiding an aloof, rational approach) is most effective.

It is important to maintain an open, gracious style, never openly displaying anger or confrontation. Strong passionate positions or appeals are used strategically to emphasize a position, but one should never appear angry or hostile. If talks reach an impasse, it is best to resume patiently at a later time. Indians know what they want and are willing to compromise. Give-and-take is a means to building relationships and keeping harmony when all possibilities have been explored.

Indians view business decisions more as a process than as a contract, and may revisit items previously agreed upon, continuing to negotiate in case there were any items previously left on the table. If this happens, graciously enter into talks and be well prepared for what you can and cannot do. Prepare your organization for the possibility of changes. If you cannot make changes, apply firmness with grace. The golden rule in India is "analyze before committing." If you rush Indians, they may tell you what they think you want to hear. Give them time, then check back; "Now that you have had time to analyze the situation, can you deliver this?" is a reasonable reply to an earlier request.

Business decisions in India are not based solely on statistics and empirical data. Intuition, feeling, faith, and often astrology may guide Indians in their decision-making process. To an outsider, the attitude of the Indian company may appear to be somewhat relaxed. The urgency that one may expect when closing deals may appear to be lacking. One may spend a considerable amount of time debating the objectives and long-term effects of a deal and the finer concepts of the deal with the Indian counterparts. However, these discussions may often be repetitive without any concrete points being reached. The process may be further prolonged by the necessity of reverting to senior management for the approval of decisions arrived at in the course of negotiations. This may sometimes be frustrating to an outsider, but it is advisable to respect the process. Frustration should not be displayed publicly. Similarly, it is prudent to avoid high-pressure tactics. These may unnecessarily lead the Indians to become defensive and cause unnecessary deadlocks. Criticisms and disagreements must be displayed with politeness and a great deal of diplomacy.

Know and stick with your company's policy on ethics. Major Indian businesses are familiar with the U.S. Foreign Corrupt Practices Act. Mild rule-bending has traditionally been a way of getting around hurdles and expediting business in India. However, be vigilant that the facilitation of payments and serious infractions do not occur on your watch.

4.4 Cultural, Ethical, and Religious Considerations

Unmistakably, the diverse culture that spreads across India is a major factor in shaping business deals with Indians. It is of utmost importance for the parties to understand this so that they are able to adjust and make each other comfortable. The comfort automatically translates into a sense of trust, leading to progress in negotiations and the intended business. Indians tend to take more business risks with people they trust. Relationships and feelings tend to be a very important aspect of decisions in India. Politeness and honesty go a long way in establishing solid business relations as well as long-lasting friendships with Indians. When confronted with bureaucracy and IST (Indian "Stretchable"/"Standard" Time), maintain your cool. Schedules are bound to go awry and government offices are notoriously inefficient. Patience is the key.

The traditional form of greeting in India is a *namaste*. However, handshakes are also accepted as a form of greeting, especially in the business environment. Any other form of public affection (such as kissing on the cheeks) is not considered professional and may convey negative feelings. Women are also greeted with a handshake, but one may also choose to be greeted from a distance with a simple *namaste*.

Begin building trust by using proper introductions, demonstrating respect and modesty (in dress and demeanor), and conveying appreciation to your host. You may be preceded by a stereotype of the foreign businessperson as a "trader-invader," coming to India to take advantage. Taking the time to cultivate personal relationships and establish a reputation for integrity is important. Accept social invitations (dinners, weddings), which may last many hours; these are opportunities to experience Indian hospitality, appreciate the culture, and extend your network.

Indians are accustomed to a system of hierarchy at the workplace. Senior colleagues are obeyed and respected. Women are treated with respect, and foreign businesswomen would find it easy to adapt to the Indian work environment.

During negotiations, trust and well-established relationships with your Indian counterparts must be in place before any form of business can be transacted. Decision-making in India is generally a slow process. Expect delays, especially when dealing with the government. Do not rush deadlines or your counterparts, as impatience is thought to be aggressive, rude, and disrespectful.

Indians have a deep sense of duty and obligation to their families and will tend to negotiate to bring the best deal for the family or group rather than for individual advantage. Parental approval or the approval of a senior family member is a key driver in the decision-making process.

Mythology deeply influences the Indian mind and business acumen. Do not be surprised if references from the sacred text of the Bhagavad Gita are elocuted in the course of a meeting. Hindu mythology is also a strong influence on Indians and often finds its way into various aspects of the everyday life of Indians.

Indians are nonconfrontational. It is rare for them to overtly disagree, although this is slowly beginning to change in some industries. Most Indians expect concessions in both price and terms, and it is acceptable to expect concessions in return. Never appear overly legalistic during negotiations. In general, Indians do not trust the legal system, and someone's word is generally sufficient to reach an agreement.

"Face" and self-esteem are an essential part of the culture; therefore any individual criticism in business situations must be done carefully and with sensitivity. It is important to maintain harmony and avoid conflicts and confrontations, especially with your team, in front of others. If you lose your temper, you lose face and prove you are unworthy of respect and trust. Do not disagree publicly with members of your negotiating team. Aggressiveness can be interpreted as a sign of disrespect. This may lead to a complete lack of communication and motivation on the part of Indians. Criticism of a person's work would have to be done carefully and constructively so as not to injure the other person's self-esteem. Generally, India's culture promotes pleasing people; thus, feedback that might be unpleasing (problems, criticism, confrontation) is generally avoided. Indians are usually conscious of status, and feedback is offered from higher to lower rank (based on age or position).

Indians may be very direct when confident they are right; however, an indirect ambiguous style is used to show respect, politeness, disagreement, or refusal, or to avoid confrontation. Indians may overlap each other while speaking, increasing the volume and speed of dialogue—if this is the case, do not wait for an invitation to speak; jump in and talk over someone to make your points. Many Indians speak quite rapidly, with an accent unfamiliar to Americans. If you have trouble, the best approach is to ask them to speak slowly. Indians you will meet are multilingual, and may take offense if you imply that their English is faulty.

Business attire is conservative and classified as formal. Normal business dress for men is a suit and tie in dark or neutral colors. Women wear business suits (skirts or pants) or Indian attire (salwaar kameez, churidars, or saris). Women generally wear skirts that cover the knee, shirts or blouses with higher necklines, and long sleeves or short sleeves that cover the biceps. Wear conservative business formal unless you are told otherwise. Many companies in the information technology sector have adopted a "business casual" way of dressing that usually means pants and a collared shirt, or, in some instances, T-shirts and jeans with sneakers. The weather also often determines the clothing. In hotter parts of the country, dress is sometimes less formal, but remains conservative. Dressing formally, as suggested above, for at least the first meeting will indicate respect.

Power breakfasts are yet to gain popularity in the country. However, business lunches and dinners are common in India, and it is perfectly appropriate to discuss business during the meal. Allow your host to initiate the business conversation. Successful negotiations are often celebrated by a meal.

Never point your feet at a person or touch someone with your foot or shoe; it is considered the ultimate insult, because feet are considered unclean. Apologize if you accidentally touch someone with your foot or shoe. Do not sit with the soles of your feet pointing towards an altar, shrine, or another person.

India is a cricket-crazy nation. Learn a bit about the sport and you will open the door to a variety of conversations. Indians love to discuss all kinds of subjects, and individuals who are more educated will readily get into heated debates—which may be among your most memorable moments in India. Exercise discretion, however, when trying to understand the enigma of India's overwhelming poverty and the caste system. While Indians may complain, avoid criticizing India's overburdened infrastructure and bureaucracy and the delays and uncertainties that occur. Do not harshly judge or criticize things you do not understand fully. Indians can be quite passionate about their nation and will defend it unequivocally. Words are seldom enough to offend an Indian, but avoid strong swear words in the context of an argument or insult, especially in business situations.

4.5 Negotiating Online

Indians are keen users of the Internet. The enactment of the Information and Technology Act, 2000, has given e-commerce and e-governance formal and legal recognition in India. Online negotiations through the means of videoconferencing are gaining popularity fast. Indians are finding this a cost-effective and efficient manner in which to enter into negotiations with counterparties and effectively conclude transactions.

5. Contract Formation

5.1 Wording and Style

Contracts are generally in English and are as per common law principles. The wordings and style are simple and straightforward. Following generally adopted rules of interpretation, the words of a contract should be construed in their grammatical and ordinary sense, except to the extent that some modification is necessary in order to avoid absurdity, inconsistency, or repugnance. Interpretation is as a rule based on the words used in the contract. It is only when the meaning of the words used in the contract is not understandable that the help of other materials may be relied on. Courts may also go into the conditions and circumstances behind the contract. This is why the recitals also play an important part.

5.2 Conditions and Defenses

The construction of contracts is not prescribed under Indian law. However, the proper construction of a contract is a question of law, whereas the ascertainment of the meaning of a particular word or phrase in a contract is a question of fact. In case where a contract is based on a standard form of commercial agreement, courts in India have recognized the desirability of certainty and are usually reluctant to disturb an established construction.

Terms sheets often precede the forging of contracts between parties in India. However, the final form of the contract usually mentions that it is the contract that embodies the entire understanding of the parties and that it overrides all prior understandings on the subject matter of the contract. Courts are also of the view that it would not look at prior negotiations of the parties as an aid towards the construction of the contracts. Subsequent conduct is also not always considered. The construction of contracts is therefore dependent on the intention of the parties when the contract was made, which is ascertained from the terms of the contract read in the light of the facts known to both the parties when the contract was concluded. Therefore, contracts are usually very carefully worded to prevent ambiguity and aid interpretation.

5.3 The Special Case of Online Agreements

Online agreements are immensely popular as a result of the increased number of transactions taking place through the Internet. Though security is a primary concern, presently Web sites are equipped with a large number of security features in order to make transactions safe.

The Information Technology Act provides legal recognition to transactions carried out by electronic means. In this regard, it presumes electronic contracts to be validly concluded if digital signatures of the parties have been affixed to the same. As regards digital signatures, the Information Technology Act provides for a system to authenticate digital signatures. The certifying authority created for this purpose is authorized to issue digital signature certificates to applicants and to recognize foreign certifying authorities and the digital signatures issued by them. Further, electronic records are admissible in evidence in courts in India if they comply with all of the following conditions:

(a) Such information was derived during the period the computer was in regular business and was fed into the computer during the course of business.
(b) The computer was being used by a person having lawful control over the computer.
(c) The computer was operating properly and effectively during the period such record was generated. However, if the accuracy of the electronic record was not affected by the malfunctioning of the computer, it would be admissible in evidence.

However, traditional paper agreements are presently the preferred form of agreements. It may be some time before the Indian business community uses online agreements to replace them.

6. Resolving Disputes

An elaborate and extensive judicial and quasi-judicial system exists in India. Courts are the judicial authority for the determination of disputes in India. Apart from the judiciary, there are quasi-judicial bodies established within the legal framework of India. Regulators such as SEBI are the quasi-judicial authority for the securities market. Separate civil and criminal systems exist in each state, where the highest court is the High Court. Appeals from the High Court lie with the Supreme Court of India, the apex judicial authority in India. Matching and improving the rate of disposal of cases compared to the rates at which new cases are filed and admitted in the courts is a typical challenge for the judicial system in India. Traditionally, the rates of disposal of cases have been abysmally low, leading to a tremendous delay and backlog. Further, a large number of cases are also appealed against, leading to an increased number of cases pending at the appellate level.

It is now common practice for parties negotiating a commercial contract in India to opt for alternate methods of dispute resolution. Common methods of dispute resolution now include the appointment of experts, conciliation, or arbitration. The Arbitration and Conciliation Act, 1996, governs certain types of arbitration and conciliation. The act has been drafted based on the UNCITRAL Model Arbitration Law and the UNCITRAL Conciliation Rules. The Arbitration Act provides for the procedure for appointment of the arbitral tribunal, the situs for the arbitration, and the rules of procedure to be applied by the arbitral tribunal. However, the Act provides sufficient liberty to the parties to formulate their own procedures with regard to the same. Alternate methods of dispute resolution (ADR) have now become immensely popular in the commercial environment as they provide speedy and convenient methods for the redress of disputes.

Online dispute resolution (ODR), on the other hand, has yet to gain popularity in India. The implementation of ADR in India is through the traditional physical form and its implementation in an online environment is still in its nascent stages. The two primary hurdles that are faced in the implementation of ODR techniques are the absence of a legal environment conducive to ODR processes and easy access to technology that would afford parties equal opportunities to access ODR mechanisms. Other hurdles that are faced in the implementation of the ODR system in India are cultural and language issues, including trust in a new system that has yet to be tested.

7. Conclusion

India has developed an environment conducive to foreign investment that provides freedom of entry into most sectors. It offers to the world a stable democratic environment with nearly sixty years of independence. It has a large market size with increasing purchasing power, access to international markets through membership in regional councils, and a large and diversified infrastructure spread across the country. India further boasts of well-developed R&D, infrastructure, technical and marketing services, a developed banking system, and a vibrant capital market comprising approximately twenty-three stock exchanges with over 9,000 listed companies.

The government of India is keen to promote investments in high-growth sectors such as software, electronics, food processing, and engineering. In recent years the government has also placed emphasis on the need to upgrade productivity, project management, technology, R&D, and human resource development.

As an English-speaking cosmopolitan country, India becomes a natural gateway into the Asian markets. Indian people have a hospitable and accommodative approach toward both personal and professional aspects of their lives. Foreigners are more than welcome to do business in India and will find this to be an exciting and enriching experience.

Cyril Shroff
Amarchand & Mangaldas & Suresh A. Shroff & Co.
Peninsula Chambers,
Peninsula Corporate Park,
Ganpatrao Kadam Marg, Lower Parel (W)
Mumbai—400 013, India
Phone: +91-22-2496 4455/ 6660 4455
Fax: +91-22-2496 3666
E-mail: cyril.shroff@amarchand.com

CHAPTER 31

International Business Negotiations in Ireland

Pádraig Ó Ríordáin
Caroline Brennan
Arthur Cox
Dublin, Ireland

1. Introduction

The island of Ireland lies on the edge of Europe, west of the United Kingdom. The state of Ireland, often referred to as the Republic of Ireland, is an independent country. It comprises over three quarters of the island and has a population of 4.2 million people. Northern Ireland consists of six counties in the north of the island and is part of the United Kingdom. It has a population of 1.7 million. This chapter focuses on the state of Ireland, the capital of which is Dublin.

Ireland is a liberal democracy with a common law, a constitution-based legal system, and an open economy. It has a very high standard of living, ranked eighth highest in the world by the Organisation for Economic Co-operation and Development (OECD). The population is young, with about 35 percent under the age of twenty-five, and Irish people are considered some of the happiest in the world. In 2005, the Economist Intelligence Unit ranked Ireland the global number one in its worldwide quality of life study.

Ireland today is a different country from what it once was. Governed as part of the United Kingdom until 1922, Ireland gained independence over eighty years ago. It was then primarily a rural society and unemployment and emigration were rife. However, Ireland joined the European Community (now European Union) in 1973, and by the 1990s, an attractive taxation regime coupled with an educated, English-speaking labor force paved the way for foreign investment, unprecedented economic growth, and modern Celtic Tiger Ireland.

Whether Ireland is ideologically closer to Boston or Berlin is a question often asked. Ireland is increasingly influenced by laws emanating from the European Union. However, within the EU, Ireland is a voice for conservative government and market-led economics. It is with this in mind, along with other cultural links such as language and personal connections, that some would see Ireland as closer ideo-logically to the United States than to Europe. Either way, it is fair to say that Ireland tends to enjoy the best of both worlds, simultaneously enjoying the inclusive principles of the EU and the entrepreneurial economic approach of the United States.

Many of the world's largest corporations have recognized this advantageous position and have established bases in Ireland from which they conduct their European operations. Dublin is a world-class center for a wide range of international financial services and hosts most of the world's leading financial institutions. In 2007, interna-tional consultants A.T. Kearney ranked Ireland as having the fifth-most global economy in the world, as measured by economic integration, political engagement, personal contact, and technological connectiv-ity. Ireland's economy remains open, liberal, and ready for business and the Irish business community is very experienced in negotiating deals with overseas partners.

This chapter is divided into three sections. The first section attempts to describe and explain the cultural context of conducting business negotiations in Ireland. The next section details specific fea-tures of the Irish business negotiation process. The final section iden-tifies a number of different legal issues that should be kept in mind during negotiations.

2. Cultural Considerations in the Negotiation Process

2.1 The New Ireland

International impressions of Ireland can be somewhat dated, although with the advent of the Celtic Tiger, this is less and less the case. Ireland has evolved from its rural agricultural base to become a globalized economy and leader in manufacturing technology and financial ser-vices. There is no dancing at the crossroads, and you are more likely to hear Polish or Lithuanian on Irish streets than the native Gaelic tongue. The armed conflict in Northern Ireland has been resolved, and in a practical sense has at all times remained remote from the lives and objectives of the business community in Ireland. Though the Irish balk at the mistaken proposition that Ireland is part of the United Kingdom, the two countries are geographically, linguistically, and cul-turally linked.

It is useful for the U.S. negotiator to actively take the time to learn the priorities and habits of modern Ireland and to update his percep-tion of the country, particularly of the depth and abilities of its busi-ness community. The U.S. negotiator who succeeds best in Ireland is the one who demonstrates the ability to distinguish the reality from the perception and who asks rather than assumes. Although this point can be made with respect to most countries, it is particularly important with respect to Ireland as there are no linguistic or other obvious familiarity barriers to remind people of the degree of Ireland's cultural distinctiveness.

2.2 Irish Negotiation Styles

Irish negotiation culture is coming through a transition. The current generation of Irish businesspeople and professionals are pan-national in perspective, often having frequented the top international business and law schools. Most have spent time working abroad and many have returned to work at home having gained cutting-edge experience in the world's financial and business centers. They have a pervasive sense of self-confidence and belief in Ireland's ability to compete on an international scale and are applying the competitive characteristics of the Irish temperament to entrepreneurial initiative. They are pragmatic, experienced, and results-focused businesspeople.

The Celtic Tiger years have marked a distinct transition away from the more traditional Irish negotiation model, which thrived in a relatively closed environment where personal relationships and reputation dominated. Business priorities reflected the social patterns of small local communities on which most of Irish life was based. This older model of Irish business negotiation is still important to understand and remains relevant. However, it has gradually receded as the younger generation, which takes many of its cues from the United States, takes a more practical, results-based approach. Nevertheless, Ireland is a very small country where the business community is small and tight. Reputation is important and information can travel very quickly.

As with the difference between younger and older generations, there is also a marked difference between urban and rural negotiating styles. Rural businesspeople tend to be more informal and relaxed than their city counterparts. However, this in no way diminishes their negotiation abilities, which can be particularly strong.

It is in this contrasting environment of young and old, urban and rural that business negotiations take place. Central to the negotiator's ability to succeed is an understanding of the roles of relationships, reputation, and manner of communication.

2.3 The Importance of Developing Personal Relationships

There remains in the Irish psyche a somewhat guarded approach to unfamiliar cultural styles and a deep-seated sense of independence. This is most likely a residual effect of having been subject to foreign rule for most of our modern history. To prevent triggering a combative rather than a cooperative approach from the Irish businessperson, it is important to establish a personal relationship in which to develop trust and engender belief in the transparency of your objectives. A good personal relationship is also essential to resolving issues that might later arise. As with other common law jurisdictions, however, the contract is central and it is not superseded by the relationship that has been developed.

When approaching an Irish negotiation, it is important to get to know the individual rather than just the corporate entity with whom you are negotiating. It is easy sometimes to feel that there is an undue amount of time spent in Ireland on social or nonbusiness interaction that is not relevant to the transaction. This is to misunderstand the nature of this social activity. The time spent developing personal inter-action with the counterparty or even the negotiator's own advisors is as important as the time spent focused on deal issues. The resulting per-sonal relationship will generally create a problem-solving, cooperative negotiation mechanism that will significantly reduce the amount of time spent developing agreement and improve the outcome achieved. Opportunities to spend time with an Irish counterpart over dinner, in the pub, or on the golf course should always be availed of. Although discussions about business are rarely the overt focus of these occasions, development of the business relationship is the clear subtext.

In developing a relationship it should be remembered that the Irish are generally nontactile and physical interaction is pretty much on the same basis as it is in the United States. The international nego-tiator should avoid overenthusiasm to sell an objective as this can be regarded as overcompensation for a flawed idea. Substance, track record, humor, and a reasoned approach are the best foundations on which to build a relationship.

2.4 The Importance of Reputation

The importance of reputation in Ireland is deeply rooted in the small tight-knit communities from which most of our cultural attitudes have evolved and is reflected in the disproportionately high number of libel and slander litigation cases heard in the Irish courts. This should be actively borne in mind by the international negotiator, as once you have stepped on the toes of an Irish person's reputation or ability, she will very easily turn combative rather than cooperative in attitude. The best approach to take is to be consciously inclusive of people's views, recognizing merit and distinguishing the person from the problem. In enhancing the position of your counterpart in this way and objec-tifying issues, you both ensure that the personal relationship is main-tained and unnecessary antagonism on the substance of the issues is avoided.

It is also important to remember that Ireland is a small country and that the Irish business community is closely connected. It is usual that competitors are familiar with each other and they will often enjoy per-sonal relationships. Dublin is the center for Irish business, and though it is the capital city, it is in essence a small town where rumor spreads easily. If an openly critical statement is made of someone it is possible that it will, eventually, be conveyed to her. It is therefore important for the negotiator to be conscious that this is the environment in which he is working.

2.5 Communication Style

Though Ireland has two official languages, English and Irish (often referred to as Gaelic), English is spoken by everybody and is the prevailing language. Nevertheless, the Irish do not use many American words, opting for the British or European version instead. For example, the Irish use the term "competition law" instead of "antitrust." Furthermore, the traditional approach to communication can often be oblique and shaded with meaning, consequently proving quite difficult for the uninitiated to distinguish the message from the words. This problem is exacerbated by the widespread ability of the Irish to construct language at will and shelter behind it. In this way, the Irish can avoid open discussion in order to avert conflict. It is important then to look for more subtle signals regarding possible concessions or considerations.

Communication systems in Ireland are well developed and e-mail, BlackBerries, and wireless Internet are ubiquitous in the cities. However, in some rural areas, broadband Internet access is more limited. It is likely that e-mail and telephone communications will be used when initiating negotiations with possible partners. E-mail will also be important in drafting agreements and maintaining communications postagreement. However, face-to-face contact is the best way to ensure trust and confidence and it is highly recommended that you meet your Irish counterparts. As explained above, the development of personal relationships is key.

3. The Negotiation Process

3.1 Competitive v. Cooperative Approaches

Whether an Irish negotiation will follow a competitive or cooperative model will usually depend on the type of transaction being contemplated and the existing relationship between the parties. Both models are common and significant strategic advantage can be gained in actively directing negotiations toward either approach. If no decision is made on what style to adopt, the Irish negotiation process may fall into a competitive, win-lose pattern unless the negotiating parties know each other from previous transactions or have otherwise formed a relationship. If negotiations turn competitive, the Irish negotiator may not easily back down and may respond to the fact rather than the substance of "losing." However, this response is generally passing and does not rise to the level of "loss of face" as it might in some Asian environments.

To avoid this scenario it is important to develop a personal relationship. It is also more productive to explore issues face-to-face or verbally before designing demands and committing them to paper. This approach also has the advantage of establishing a pattern of predictability for the other side, which enhances the transparency of objectives and consequently the chance of establishing a cooperative relationship.

3.2 Resolving Disagreements

When faced with disagreement it is best to avoid falling into argument, as this merely polarizes positions and rarely is effective to persuade the counterparty to change his stance. The more productive approach is to break down the issue into its constituent parts, present reasoned analysis of what is important for the negotiator to achieve, and find a different approach that can maximize the response to each party's concerns. This is useful in preventing stubborn issues from growing in inverse proportion to their importance.

The U.S. negotiator should also be prepared for many of the more difficult issues to be dealt with one-on-one outside of the primary negotiating forum. This is a feature of the reliance on relationship that allows the Irish negotiator to be more open about the position and explore options that in another forum may expose her to public failure. This is a process that should be embraced as a valuable method of resolving disputes.

If an issue becomes intractable between two individuals in the process, it is usually constructive to withdraw it from them, thereby objectifying it and placing it for resolution in the hands of other, usually more senior, participants. Agreement can then be reached at that level without compromising the position of the two earlier combatants.

3.3 Composition of Negotiation Team

Team selection is not as formally important as in many other cultures. However, given the importance of developing personal relationships, the team selection should emphasize humor, reasonableness, and ability to communicate easily with people. It is also useful to have some parity in team age and experience profile. An individual of clearly less experience acting on the basis that his organization "knows better" can irritate Irish people.

3.4 Confidentiality and Confidentiality Agreements

Given the small business environment in Ireland where so many businesspeople know each other personally and news travels with speed, you should expect that if you have shared your business plans with an extended group of people in Ireland, those plans will be common knowledge before long. Therefore, do not be surprised if an Irish adviser or counterparty suggests adopting precautions with respect to confidentiality of your negotiations, such as a confidentiality agreement, which in another environment may be considered excessive.

In dealings with any Irish government agency, department, or public body, it should be remembered that under Irish freedom of information law, all members of the public have a right of access, subject to certain exceptions, to information and records held by such bodies.

It is generally advisable that a confidentiality agreement is put in place at the commencement of negotiations in relation to the purchase and sale of a private company. The agreement is primarily of importance to the seller as its object is to ensure that the information, which is provided by the seller regarding the target company for the purpose of enabling the due diligence investigation, remains confidential.

There is usually some degree of negotiation required in order to finalize the terms of a confidentiality agreement. However, neither the buyer nor seller will want negotiations terminated because they cannot agree on the confidentiality agreement. In this regard, you should be prepared to accept certain amendments in order not to put the deal in jeopardy. A useful trade-off for the buyer is to agree on the terms of the confidentiality agreement in return for the seller agreeing to grant him exclusivity in negotiations for a certain period. In this way, an exclusivity agreement for the buyer can be considered as quid pro quo for the confidentiality agreement in the interests of the seller.

In case of breach, a confidentiality agreement will usually include provisions for damages and equitable solutions such as an injunction. However, there is little use in obtaining an injunction preventing disclosure when confidential information has already been leaked. Respecting the provisions of the confidentiality agreement will ultimately come down to reputation. If a particular party is reputed to have broken a confidentiality agreement, it will not be long before this reputation spreads across Ireland's small business community. Such damage to a party's reputation is likely to impact adversely upon the willingness of other businesses to get involved with him in future deals.

In general terms:

a. Confidentiality agreements normally include a broad definition of confidential information to include information disclosed by the seller in writing, learned by observation or examination of books, or otherwise learned from information provided by the sellers.

b. The buyer should be obliged to ensure that persons to whom the confidential information is provided do not disclose it to any third party. The buyer should be under an obligation not to make any copies or summaries of any written information provided unless the seller's consent is obtained.

c.   The buyer should be obliged to return all written confidential information at the end of the due diligence to the seller.

The confidentiality agreement normally remains in force for as long as the seller has a proprietary interest in the confidential information or for some other specified time period.

3.5 Time Pressures

Do not let traditional images of thatched cottages, stone walls, and slow-paced rural life mislead you. Ireland today is a modern economy where the pace of business life has accelerated rapidly in the past fifteen years. Most Irish business and professional people are now struggling to maintain and protect the time spent with their family and friends from the increasing intrusion of work commitments. There is consequently declining tolerance for inefficiency or unnecessary debate.

Long conference calls or meetings with too many participants are often seen as unwieldy and not sufficiently results-focused. Irish parties expect their counterparts to attend meetings with the issues defined and fully thought out, rather than developing them on the spot. Peripheral issues should be kept for resolution by e-mail, fax, or a one-to-one call in order to minimize time and resources.

3.6 Negotiation Objectives and Documentation

Though a documented contract retains priority over any personal relationship developed, the Irish can often be less convinced of the necessity for lengthy or highly detailed documentation than their U.S. or U.K. counterparts. The primary reason for this is that there is a level of detail beyond which it is thought that the relationship should take over. It is considered inefficient and of declining business relevance to develop and document agreement beyond this point unless it is likely that the relationship cannot be relied upon to solve remote problems.

Presentation of an unduly detailed draft contract can sometimes spark more questions with respect to the relationship and the true agenda of the counterparty than it answers. It can therefore change the tone of the negotiation from cooperative to adversarial as each clause is debated and the true intent deconstructed.

3.7 Heads of Agreement/Letter of Intent

When the negotiating parties have agreed in principle on the fundamental commercial terms and structure of a transaction, it is common for them to set out their preliminary understandings and expectations in heads of agreement (also known as a letter of intent or memorandum of understanding) before entering into the formal agreement.

This document essentially sets out the main or principal terms of the deal agreed by the parties.

It is usual that the heads of agreement are not binding in nature. If they were to be considered binding, there would then be a question of why the ultimate contract is necessary at all. In addition, binding heads of agreement are inadvisable as they are normally signed at a fairly early stage in negotiations and in advance of a due diligence investigation being carried out. Thus, it is possible that a buyer could find itself bound to complete a purchase notwithstanding serious problems subsequently discovered during the due diligence investigation or disclosed in the disclosure letter at completion.

If the heads of agreement are to be nonbinding they should contain a clear statement that they do not constitute a legally binding contractual relationship between the parties. However, the parties may provide that one or two terms of the heads of agreement are binding upon them—for example, a provision relating to confidentiality (in place of a full confidentiality agreement being entered into) and the reference to an exclusivity period during which the buyer and the seller are to try to finalize the deal. The parties may clearly state that if contractual documentation has not been finalized within a given period of time the parties are free to negotiate with third parties.

A well-prepared letter of intent or heads of agreement can be a useful tool in the negotiation process. Defining the objectives of the parties and crystallizing their commitment to the transaction enhances both confidence in pushing the process forward and the trust on which the relationship is based. It also serves as a dry run in which the parties develop the habit of agreeing and the processes for resolving disputes between them. This experience can be critical when it comes to resolving more detailed issues at contract stage. The heads of agreement finally provide a formal opportunity for the negotiator to secure a strong mandate from her board to complete the negotiations and to realize the objectives agreed.

4. Selected Legal Issues Relevant to the Negotiation Process

This section does not attempt to address comprehensively the range of laws that may have an effect on particular negotiations. Reference should be made to the Web site of the IDA, the public body responsible for attracting foreign investment to Ireland, for initial advice (www .idaireland.com). However, it is imperative that overseas businesspeople retain a local lawyer for tailored, case-specific advice.

The legal profession consists of barristers and solicitors, collectively known as lawyers. The term "attorney" is not generally used. Solicitors deal directly with clients and are the first point of call when one is faced with a legal issue. Solicitors have a right of audience in the courts but barristers tend to undertake most advocacy work in the higher courts. Barristers are generally retained and instructed by solicitors.

Notwithstanding the need for case-specific legal advice, the following are some general legal issues that should be kept in mind when participating in negotiations.

4.1 Entering Enforceable Contracts

Apart from contracts for the sale of land, there is no general requirement under Irish law that contracts must be in written form. A contract is enforceable once there is offer, acceptance, consideration, and the intention to create legal relations. Oral contracts, or partly oral and partly written contracts, are enforceable once these four key elements are met, and oral evidence will be accepted by the courts if a dispute arises. It is therefore important that negotiators bear this in mind when entering oral negotiations so as to ensure that they do not unwittingly enter into an enforceable contract at a premature stage.

4.2 "Subject to Contract—Contract Denied"

The most effective way of negating a presumption of an intention to create an enforceable contract at precontractual stage is to mark all correspondence "Subject to Contract—Contract Denied." The phrase is usually understood as meaning that the parties are still in negotiation and have not yet reached agreement. It is also worthwhile, at the outset and conclusion of negotiation meetings, to declare that any agreement reached is "Subject to Contract." It is advisable to enter into a precise, written contract, under the guidance of a local lawyer, when agreement is eventually reached. Then, and only then, should the contract become enforceable. However, it is important to note that the phrase will not negate a claim of part performance of any oral contract formed during negotiations.

Contracts for the sale of land are enforceable only if they are evidenced in writing. However, a formal written contract is not necessary, and under the Statute of Frauds, an old piece of legislation dating from the seventeenth century, a written note or memorandum evidencing the sale is sufficient to render the contract enforceable. Written material that sufficiently evidences the creation of an enforceable contract includes a series of correspondence between buyer and seller, or between their lawyers, evidencing the offer, acceptance, and consideration. It is therefore traditional to head all correspondence "Subject to Contract—Contract Denied" to deny the unintended formation of an enforceable contract.

To summarize, when "Subject to Contract—Contract Denied" is used in the course of negotiations, there is no concluded contract. In addition, where the phrase appears on a document, that document cannot be a note or memorandum for the purposes of the Statute of Frauds, even if the phrase was added by a lawyer after the oral negotiations took place.

4.3 Authority to Contract

An overseas negotiator should be clear as to whether or not he has the authority to enter contracts on behalf of any organization he is representing. A negotiator representing a corporate body has authority to conclude contracts for that corporate body if he has actual authority, whether express or by virtue of his position, to act on behalf of the corporate body. A negotiator may also have ostensible authority to conclude a contract. This can occur in two ways: either he holds an office or position that one would normally expect to grant its holder authority to act on behalf of the company; or the negotiator held himself out to have authority to act in a particular way and induced a third party to contract with his organization in reliance on this.

It is important that a businessperson who travels to Ireland to conduct negotiations does not hold himself out as having authority to contract on behalf of his organization if this is not so. By holding himself out to have authority that he does not have, he could unwittingly enter into an enforceable contract with an uninformed party.

Under the doctrine of *ultra vires*, a corporate body cannot enter a particular contract unless it has been given the power to do so by virtue of its founding documents, i.e., its Memorandum and Articles of Association. Though the doctrine of *ultra vires* is under review, it still persists and the objects clause in a company's Memorandum of Association is generally kept either as broad or as detailed as possible so as to allow a company to undertake as many business activities as possible. Businesspeople from overseas should check the constitutional documents of the counterpart organization to see what types of contracts it may enter. It is important to note, however, that even if a contract is found to be *ultra vires* of a company's objects, the contract may still be effective in favor of any person relying on the contract who was not aware that the company had no power to enter the contract. The director or the officer of the company who was responsible for the *ultra vires* act will be liable to the company for any loss or damage suffered.

4.4 Execution of Documents

In general, contracts are executed by simple signature. A negotiator with authority to enter into contracts on behalf of an organization can generally sign a contract for that organization in his own name. If he does not have the authority to act, it is possible to arrange for a power of attorney to be granted by whoever does have that authority.

Some transactions require the execution of a deed in addition to, or as an alternative to, a simple contract. Such transactions include any dealing with an interest in land; mortgages of real property; gifts; and contracts that are not supported by consideration. For a company to validly execute a deed, it must be done in accordance with its Articles of Association. For this reason, it is important to check the founding documents of your organization to see whether an official seal is necessary to execute a deed. Alternatively, powers of attorney can be arranged.

4.5 Precontractual Responsibilities

In Ireland there is no general duty to negotiate in good faith. This does not mean, however, that negotiating parties have no precontractual duties. In addition to any binding negotiation obligations set out in a letter of intent, if either party makes a false statement of fact during negotiations that induces the other party to enter into a contract and upon which the other party relies to its detriment, there has been a misrepresentation according to Irish law. Misrepresentation may justify rescission of the contract and a possible award of damages. Contractual provisions that attempt to exclude liability for precontractual representations may be unenforceable, particularly in the case of a fraudulent misrepresentation, i.e., a statement made without an honest belief in its truth. Parties must also avoid pressurizing or inducing their opposite party to breach an existing contract. Interference with contractual relations is actionable under Irish law and may give rise to an award of damages.

4.6 Negotiations with Listed Companies and Disclosure Obligations

When entering into negotiations with companies listed on either the Official List of the Irish Stock Exchange or the IEX (Irish Enterprise Exchange), it is important to bear in mind that such companies are subject to disclosure obligations under the Listing Rules and the IEX Rules, respectively. These disclosure obligations extend to significant transactions and agreements with third parties, and information disclosed pursuant to these obligations is available to the public on the Web site of the Irish Stock Exchange (www.ise.ie).

Since it will often be detrimental to have to disclose discussions or negotiations with listed companies prematurely, it is important to have effective procedures in place to preserve the confidentiality of those discussions or negotiations whilst they are ongoing. The point at which discussions or negotiations crystallize into legal obligations must be made clear, as this is usually the time at which the contract or agreement in question is required to be disclosed pursuant to the Listing Rules or IEX Rules. In light of this second issue, negotiators should always consider the use of "Subject to Contract—Contract Denied" and whether heads of agreement or letters of offer should be nonbinding in order to prevent the unintended formation of an enforceable (and therefore disclosable) contract. By clarifying that any approaches, discussions, or negotiations are nonbinding in nature, the likelihood of triggering a public disclosure obligation on the part of the listed company is reduced.

4.6.1 Inside Information

In addition to the obligations to disclose significant transactions and agreements with third parties described above, companies listed on the Official List of the Irish Stock Exchange are also normally subject to a general obligation to disclose publicly, without delay, "inside information" directly concerning those companies. There is a technical definition of "inside information" for these purposes, but it might be summarized as information that would be used by a reasonable investor as part of the basis of his investment decisions and would therefore, if made public, be likely to have a significant effect on the price of the company's financial investments. For example, a transaction or agreement representing a major new development in a company's business could constitute inside information. Disclosure of inside information may be delayed to avoid prejudicing a listed company's legitimate interests (e.g., where the outcome of ongoing negotiations would be likely to be affected by public disclosure), provided that the failure to disclose is not likely to mislead the public and that the confidentiality of the information can be preserved.

It should be noted that anyone in possession of inside information about a relevant listed company is subject to the provisions of insider dealing and market manipulation (collectively, market abuse) legislation in Ireland, and civil and criminal sanctions may be imposed for breach of this legislation. If a businessperson is in negotiation with an Irish listed company and as a result is or becomes privy to "inside information," she should not disclose that information or deal in securities of the relevant company without first considering her obligations under Irish market abuse legislation.

4.6.2 Takeover Rules

Most acquisitions of Irish listed companies will be regulated by the Irish Takeover Rules. An obligation to announce the proposed acquisition arises under the Takeover Rules once the potential acquiror has notified a firm intention to make the acquisition to the target company's board. However, in some circumstances the Takeover Rules will require that an announcement be made before the potential acquiror has made a firm decision to tender an offer or notified such a decision to the target company, most often where the target company is the subject of rumor and speculation and there is anomalous movement in its share price. Generally speaking, parties to such transactions wish to avoid announcing their discussion of a possible acquisition for as long as possible. From the potential acquiror's perspective, premature announcement may result in a counteroffer or an increased share price that will make the acquisition more expensive. From the listed company's perspective, premature announcement may put the company "in play," the result being that unwelcome advances by other potential acquirors will be made and the company's future as an independent entity will be compromised. Consequently, in this context it is particularly important to preserve the confidentiality of the preannouncement discussions and negotiations to avoid rumor and speculation in the market, and a potential acquiror will normally only become a party to a binding legal agreement with respect to the acquisition just before it publicly announces its firm intention to acquire the target company.

4.7 Stamp Duty

A tax called "stamp duty" is charged on certain documents either executed in Ireland or relating to Irish property, or certain actions taken in Ireland. Once executed, the documents must be "stamped" by the Revenue Commissioners, confirming that the tax has been paid. The tax payable is either a fixed duty or a percentage of the value of the transaction. Stamp duty is charged at a rate of 1 percent of the consideration for the transfer of shares in an Irish company and at rates of up to 9 percent for real property transfers. Given the high charges that are rendered, it is not uncommon for business transactions to be structured in a way that minimizes stamp duty payment. For example, real property transactions may be structured as corporate deals so as to take advantage of the lower level of stamp duty charged on share transfers. Similarly, stamp duty considerations are always important when deciding between an asset purchase and a share purchase agreement. Overseas negotiators should be aware of stamp duty charges as they could influence the way a deal will be structured. It is essential that you obtain tax advice from a local advisor before the conclusion of negotiations.

5. Conclusion

As an English-speaking, business-friendly EU member state, Ireland is a natural gateway to the European single market. Furthermore, the language and cultural connections shared by Ireland and the United States mean that business negotiations can be conducted at ease and with a familiarity that would not be possible in many other European countries.

To generate the best possible outcome of any dealings with the Irish, both cultural and legal considerations, as described in this chapter, should be kept in mind. The most successful negotiator will leave traditional images of Ireland in the past, will retain local advice, and will approach negotiations with an open mind, a reasoned approach, a substantial track record, and a good sense of humor. By sticking to these simple rules, it is guaranteed that you will be welcomed to Irish shores with the traditional "Céad Mile Fáilte," or One Hundred Thousand Welcomes!

Pádraig Ó Ríordáin and Caroline Brennan
Arthur Cox
Earlsfort Centre
Earlsfort Terrace
Dublin 2
Ireland
Phone: +353-1-618 0698
Fax: +353-1-618 0618
E-mail: caroline.brennan@arthurcox.com

CHAPTER 32

International Business Negotiations in Italy

Giovanni Nardulli[1]
<small>LEGANCE STUDIO LEGALE ASSOCIATO
ROME, ITALY</small>

1. Background

Nineteen centuries ago, Rome ruled an empire encompassing most of the known world. Consequently, Italy is a country steeped in history. There were barbaric invasions, the rising of communes, the Pontifical State, and the Spanish, French, and Austrian rule until in 1946 Italy became a republic with a democratic system of government. The Italian territory consists of a boot-shaped peninsula, the two main islands of Sardinia and Sicily, and several smaller islands. Its total area is approximately 116,000 square miles with an estimated population of 58.1 million as of 2008. The population is rather homogeneous (primarily white and Catholic), although there are still some notable cultural differences between the North and the South. Recently Italy has experienced a large immigration influx. Rapid economic growth after World War II led Italy to become the sixth-largest industrial country worldwide, which, alongside the dynamic private sector and the attractive geographic location, has aroused the interest of many "blue-chip" international investors.

Foreign lawyers and, more particularly, U.S. lawyers—and indeed businesspeople who negotiate business transactions with Italian parties—have become very aware of the interesting characteristics of the Italian negotiating framework.

There is the perception that agreements and documents are drafted in a questionable and somewhat unprofessional fashion. This is common in civil law countries where the codification of the law has historically offered a reliable framework applicable to standard or traditional transactions. However, the internationalization of both the economy and law firms, and the growing diversity and sophistication

---

[1] The author wishes to acknowledge the valuable contribution of Giovanna Sara Russo, Associate of Legance, in preparing this article.

of transactions, has given rise to drafting and negotiating contractual documents in a similar format to that used in America.

There is also uncertainty about various regulatory areas in Italy. In fact, in recent years a clearer understanding of the needs of a mature economy by a young legislature and the European Union's legal influence resulted in something of a regulatory "big bang." Antitrust, securities markets, insider trading, banking, insurance, and environmental statutes were enacted or materially upgraded. In most cases the changes presented problems. The absence of a consolidated body of judicial and/or administrative precedents may add to the uncertainty in some areas. In addition, Italian legislators and regulators tend to have a domestic approach to issues, with the result being a failure to always consider the international aspects and the repercussions of such.

Negotiations in Italy have a unique style and time frame. Unless parties with a degree of sophistication or an international background are involved, the communication style tends to be less direct and responsive than in the United States. Most of the negotiation process is carried out by businesspeople, with lawyers involved only at a later stage to "bless" decisions already taken by the negotiators. The pace of negotiations may be slower than in Anglo-Saxon countries. That being said, a combination of both the transactional impact and the globalization of financial markets has created greater uniformity. More and more we are seeing the emergence of lawyers as crucial components in Italian negotiations. Indeed, the vast majority of negotiations conducted in Italy today reflect international standards.

Italy has a mixed economy where some businesses are privately owned and others are owned by the government. There are a few large groups that are primarily owned by families, and numerous family-owned small and medium-size businesses that constitute an important part of the economy. The privatization plan adopted by the Italian government, whereby over 150 state-owned companies have been privatized, has been, for the most part, implemented and has contributed to the creation of effective capital markets and an increasing number of public companies. In the period between 1992 and 1998 the Italian government had, in the aggregate, the largest privatization program in Europe, and stock exchange capitalization increased from 11.2 percent (in 1992) to 49 percent (in 2007) of GDP, after having reached a peak of 50.3 percent in 2000.

Additionally, it is worth noting that a reform of the Italian voting system recently took place that has been strongly criticized since it does not guarantee a stable and long-lasting government. Different political coalitions take alternate control of governing the country, often without a bipartisan approach, introducing significant legal reforms, especially tax reforms, that often conflict with the legislation and regulation enacted by the previous government. This creates legal, tax, and commercial uncertainty, and this in turn may adversely affect negotiations and the implementation of economic transactions.

2. Major Substantive Laws Affecting Negotiations in Italy

Recently, Italian law has undergone a process of so-called "decodification." As previously discussed, a large number of statutes were introduced to regulate key areas virtually unregulated by the Civil Code, which has lost its centrality as a regulatory source. However, the body of contract, labor, corporate, and international private law rules are still preserved in the Civil Code.

Another legislative factor that may come into play is the influence of regional statutes. Regions are subdivisions of the state and have autonomous legislative and regulatory powers with respect to their location as indicated by the Italian Constitution. For instance, regional environmental regulations can have an impact on the acquisition of a manufacturing facility. In any event, the impact and scope of regional laws do not require the involvement of regional legal counsel. Contracts will always be governed by national Italian law. The more significant substantive laws in the context of business transactions are discussed below.

2.1 Corporate Laws

Companies can organize themselves only under the forms provided by the Civil Code, the most common of which are joint stock companies (*società per azioni*) and limited liability companies (*società a responsabilità limitata*). Following implementation of EU directives, a company now may be incorporated by a sole shareholder, which, except for the case of bankruptcy, will not be liable for the obligations of such company—therefore only the company will be liable for its own assets, provided that the sole shareholder discharges certain minor publicity formalities provided by law. In general, corporate companies must have a minimum equity capital, which is equal to EUR 120,000 for joint stock companies and only EUR 10,000 for limited liability companies. In any event, the major difference between the companies is that limited liability companies are easier to have incorporated, set up, and run and therefore are usually used as the first-step acquisition vehicles in many transactions. In this respect, it is worth mentioning that the court approval process required for the incorporation of a company has been abolished, and the incorporation process is now fast and efficient. Further, in 2003 and 2004 a general company law reform (the "Company Law Reform") introduced significant innovations in this area. For instance, the Company Law Reform introduced the possibility of making corporate decisions by means of written resolutions of the shareholders and/or the directors. This innovation is useful in speeding up the decision-making procedures, and business negotiations cannot but benefit from this as there were too many formalities and timing restrictions burdening the older system. The Italian Civil Code, as amended by the Company Law Reform, now also considers general provisions concerning groups of companies, introducing a new liability of the parent company (and in certain cases, also of its directors) vis-à-vis creditors and shareholders of the controlled companies, should such parent company have acted in its own and/or third party's interests in breach of the principles of proper corporate and business management of the controlled companies.

Further, in regard to mergers and acquisitions, it should be noted that certain forms of financial assistance by the target (i.e., upstream guarantees and utilization of the target's assets as collateral) are subject to restriction. However the Company Law Reform has now made it possible to carry out merger leveraged buy-outs, adding only a few additional formalities to those required in standard mergers.

Takeover rules are considered only for listed companies (see below). General corporate rules do not provide a degree of protection to minority shareholders comparable to that under U.S. law.

2.2 Securities Laws

Legislative Decree no. 58 of February 24, 1998 (the "Unified Financial Act"), and its regulations (in particular Commissione Nazionale per la Società e la Borsa (CONSOB) Regulation no. 11971 of May 14, 1999) contain a regulatory framework applicable to any "solicitation for investment" concerning financial instruments. In essence, any offer to the public of financial instruments is subject to prior registration with CONSOB, the Italian securities regulator, the issuance of a prospectus, and other filing and disclosure requirements. The concept of "financial instrument" adopted by the Unified Financial Act is very broad. Safe-harbor exemptions are available, *inter alia*, for offerings to institutional investors, stock option plans, and offerings to a limited number of investors. The Unified Financial Act mandates that any "investment services"—including trading, asset management, and placement—must be carried out in Italy through qualified entities incorporated in Italy and having a certain capitalization. In addition, pursuant to the Unified Financial Act and CONSOB Regulation no. 16190 of October 29, 2007, EU investment firms, subject to certain conditions, may also carry out investment services admitted to mutual recognition in Italy, cross-border, or by establishing a branch. Under the Unified Financial Act and CONSOB Regulation no. 11971 of May 14, 1999, the acquisition of a qualified participation in a company listed on the stock exchange is subject to disclosure requirements with CONSOB and the target that may have an impact on the acquisition strategy. Similar rules apply to the acquisition by a listed company of a qualified interest in a nonlisted company. Disclosure requirements apply to the increase or decrease of such participation as well.

In addition, the Unified Financial Act and the above-mentioned CONSOB Regulation no. 11971 of May 14, 1999, both as amended following EU Directive no. 2004/25 by implementing Legislative Decree no. 229 of November 19, 2007, provide a set of rules regulating take-overs on listed companies. Notably, any individual or entity created by owning purchases for a consideration with a shareholding exceeding the threshold of 30 percent of the voting capital of a listed company is obliged to launch a mandatory takeover bid on all the ordinary shares of such company. In relation to hostile takeovers, it is worth noting that Italian law in compliance with the aforementioned EU Directive no. 2004/25 provides that until takeover is completed or becomes inef-fective: (i) the directors of the target shall refrain from voting upon defensive actions, except in the event they have been duly authorized by the shareholders of the target, then giving to the shareholders the best possible chance to protect their interests; and (ii) any restrictions on the transfer of securities if contained in contractual agreements between shareholders or on voting rights, shall not be enforceable vis-à-vis the bidder.

The obligation to launch a mandatory tender offer does not arise where the shareholding is owned as a result of a public offer to buy or exchange at least 60 percent of the ordinary shares, provided that certain conditions are satisfied.

It should also be noted that a number of significant hostile take-overs have taken place in the Italian market for the first time as a result of privatization and liberalization of financial markets.

2.3 Tax Laws

An assessment of the tax impact can be a key factor in shaping a transaction in Italy. For instance, the acquisition of stock ownership and the transfer of a going concern receive completely different tax treatment. Mergers and spin-offs are tax-free transactions. Recently, Budget Law 2008 included a wide range of measures implementing significant changes to the current tax system that may have an impact on structuring acquisitions in Italy. In particular, Budget Law 2008 has cancelled thin capitalization and equity pro-rata and other inter-est deductibility rules, and has introduced a new legislation under which Italian companies will be allowed to deduct interest payables for the purpose of the corporate income tax (IRES) within the limit of interest receivables. If interest payables exceed interest receivables, the excess shall be deductible up to 30 percent of the earnings before interest, taxes, depreciation, and amortization (EBITDA) of the com-pany. In addition, Budget Law 2008 has introduced the possibility of obtaining a step-up of the tax basis of assets in case of merger spin-offs and contributions of going concern by paying an *ad hoc* substitu-tive tax.

Additionally, Italian tax laws incorporate special provisions for groups of companies. As a result, balance sheets of groups can be con-solidated for income tax purposes and losses and/or profits can be transferred among companies of the same group. VAT grouping rules are also provided. Tax rulings can be obtained in connection with any transactions. Taxpayers can apply for advance rulings. A special system of advance ruling for international tax issues is provided.

Appropriate tax structuring is also advisable to ensure that income may flow from Italy to abroad (e.g., dividend, interest, and royalties) in an efficient manner. *Inter alia,* dividends, interest, and royalties paid by an Italian company to an EU company may—subject to certain conditions—be exempt from withholding tax in Italy.

Further to a recent change in applicable law, stamp duty tax *(tassa sui contratti di borsa),* applicable in connection with—among others— transfer of shares, bonds, and/or other securities, has been repealed as of January 1, 2008.

The complexity and, in some areas, uncertainty of tax regulations in Italy require particular attention to the tax aspects in the negotiation process. In acquisition contracts, indemnification provisions for tax liabilities are often negotiated.

2.4 Antitrust Laws

The Italian Antitrust Law of 1990 in alignment with the principles of EU legislation prohibits: any concentration that will significantly restrict competition in the Italian market; any abuse of dominant position in the Italian market or a substantial part of it; and any agreements or concerted practices that result in a prejudice to competition in the Italian market or a substantial part of it.

In particular, any concentration in which the total domestic turnover of the undertakings concerned exceeds EUR 448 million or the total domestic turnover of the target exceeds EUR 45 million must be reported to the Italian Antitrust Authority prior to its consummation. (The thresholds are revised yearly based on the cost of living index.) The authority can prohibit the transaction if it has a material adverse effect on competition. Given the relatively low turnover threshold established for the target, the antitrust law comes into play quite often in an international acquisition context. The Authority has had a proactive role in liberalizing regulated industries and investigating cartels and markets affected by restrictions to competition.

2.5 Labor and Employment Laws

Labor law issues in Italy are a key factor in an acquisition context. Traditionally, Italian labor law offered employees a greater degree of protection than in other countries. A 2003 labor law reform introduced certain flexibilities in this field, suggesting labor agreement *(contralto a progetto),* which may be unilaterally rescinded by either of the parties thereto without just cause. In general, employers must apply to their employees all the economic and other provisions contained in the relevant collective labor agreements.

In particular, several statutory and contractual provisions address the issue of employees' rights in connection with the transfer of ownership of the company-employer. For instance, executives are entitled to resign and receive substantial indemnities in the event of a transfer of control that affects their employment position. Consultation requirements with the unions apply in the event of collective layoffs and transfer of a going concern with more than fifteen employees. An employee can be dismissed only in light of "just cause" or a "justified reason." In the event of litigation, termination of employees may be both complex and expensive. In addition, the lack or incompleteness of payment of social security contributions is punishable by severe administrative penalties. Labor liabilities pass to the buyer even in the sale of a going concern. As a result, all of the potential labor and social security liabilities must be carefully evaluated by the buyer in negotiating a transaction. Representations and indemnities concerning this type of liability are often utilized.

2.6 Environmental Laws

The scope and extent of environmental liability are less significant in Italy than is the case in other countries. Normally, environmental issues are only considered when a transaction involves the acquisition of industrial activities, and such issues are reviewed at a due diligence level. Environmental indemnification provisions are negotiated and included in agreements.

2.7 Intellectual Property Laws

Intellectual property rights have been unified by Legislative Decree no. 30 of February 10, 2005 in the Intellectual Property Code, which entered into force on March 19, 2005. This Code has reorganized the rules governing trademarks and other distinctive signs, patents, plant varieties, semiconductor topographies, geographical indications, and trade secrets. The rules relating to copyright are still contained in Law no. 633 of April 22, 1941 (Copyright Act), as subsequently amended.

Intellectual property rights may be transferred, wholly or partly, either by assignment or by licensing. Special provisions regarding trademarks require that when licensing a trademark on a nonexclusive basis, the licensee must undertake to use the licensed trademark for products of the same quality as (or of a quality similar to) those that have been sold by the owner of the trademark under which the business has been carried on. With regard to patents, it should be noted that although the right to file a patent is transferable, the moral right to be recognized as the patent inventor is inalienable. Subsequently, if a patent is filed by an assignee, the patent inventor must be specified in the application. Finally, pursuant to the Copyright Act, authors are not allowed either to assign or to transfer moral rights.

2.8 Privacy and Data Security Laws

Personal data protection is regulated by Legislative Decree no. 196 of June 30, 2003. This unified all previous provisions set forth by laws, decrees, regulations, and deontological codes issued in Italy over the past years in a code of personal data protection (the "Personal Data Code"). This Personal Data Code is substantially aimed at (i) rationalizing the existing provisions, (ii) introducing stronger protection for individuals and entities, and (iii) simplifying the formalities required by law, also reflecting the provisions set forth by EU Directive no. 2002/58, on privacy and electronic communications, as well as the rulings by the Italian Data Protection Authority.

The Personal Data Code aims to insure compliance with fundamental human rights and freedoms, especially the right to privacy, personal identity, and protection of personal data. In this respect, it is worth mentioning that, save for certain exceptions provided by law (e.g., data to be mandatorily collected and stored by law, data of public knowledge, etc.), any personal data processing shall be approved in writing by the person concerned in the data processing.

One of the most interesting innovations of the Personal Data Code concerns the rules regulating the notice to be sent to the Italian Data Protection Authority by a company that aims to carry out personal data processing. In particular, the Personal Data Code specifies that such notice shall be sent only by telematic instruments and only under certain circumstances (e.g., for sensitive data processing, especially that regarding health).

From a practical point of view, however, Italian regulation of Personal Data Protection has not had a strong impact on business negotiations and structuring of transactions, compared to other countries' legislation.

2.9 Electronic Commerce

The e-commerce market is growing and various new forms of Internet trade are being introduced in all major industries. The government is implementing a number of incentives to enhance the increasing use of the Internet in commercial transactions.

By implementing the EU Directive no. 2000/31 on e-commerce, Legislative Decree no. 70/2003 set forth provisions aimed at promoting movement of information society services, including e-commerce, regulation of the establishment of service providers, commercial communications, electronic agreements, liability of intermediaries, codes of conduct, out-of-court dispute settlements, court actions, and cooperation between EU member states in accordance with the rules contemplated by the above EU directive. Such legislative decree shall apply both to "Business to Consumer" transactions and "Business to Business" transactions, while it does not apply to "Consumer to Consumer" transactions (i.e., electronic transactions between individuals or entities acting for purposes that are outside their trade, business, or profession). It should be noted that e-commerce, although increasing, is not widespread in Italy yet.

2.10 Foreign Investment Considerations

Exchange control and foreign investment regulations were progressively abolished by the Italian government as a result of EU legislation on the freedom of movement of capital. Minor regulatory requirements are still in place, primarily for statistical purposes. Repatriation of profits is unrestricted.

As a rule, investments by foreign entities are treated on a par with Italian investments. Pursuant to EU principles, foreign investments in the financial services industry by non-EU entities are permitted, though subject to the reciprocity test. Restrictions exist in publishing, aviation, and other sectors considered of national interest.

3. Other Significant Issues

3.1 Government and Its Agencies

As a rule, the Italian government does not interfere with business transactions. At times, governmental agencies can play a role in the negotiation process concerning very large private sector transactions when they involve major industrial investments and may have repercussions on employment. It is advisable that entry by a foreign entity into a regulated sector under the supervision of a monitoring agency (for example, insurance or banking) be assisted by appropriate contacts and relations with the competent regulators. In any event, the implementation at a domestic level of EU legislation has liberalized access to regulated markets by foreign entities and has restricted the discretionary powers of the public administration.

There have been, however, some cases of major foreign investments in sectors that are considered key to the national economy (e.g., airlines, energy infrastructures) where consideration of the political environment has been an important factor in investment decisions.

3.2 Choice of Law; Jurisdiction; Arbitration

Law no. 218 of 1995 sets forth the international private law rules and, by referring to the rules outlined in the EU Convention of Rome of

1980 on contractual obligations, provides that international contracts can be governed by foreign law, subject to the limitation that foreign law or contractual provisions in contrast with public policy are not enforceable in Italy. From a practical standpoint, Italian parties prefer to have agreements governed by Italian law. The choice of law is normally determined by the parties' leverage in any given transaction. However, Italian businesspeople are normally flexible and will consider permitting a foreign law to govern the transaction. Please note that if there is a heated dispute, it is possible that the law of a neutral country will be chosen to govern the transaction.

When drafting contracts the parties have quite broad powers to choose a jurisdiction other than that of Italy. Pursuant to Article 4 of Law no. 218 of 1995, the jurisdiction of the Italian courts may be disregarded by those in favor of a foreign court or arbitration if the waiver is evidenced in writing and the dispute concerns freely disposable rights. In this regard, Law no. 218 of 1995 also provides that enforcement of foreign judgments in Italy is conditional upon compliance of such judgments with the general procedural principles applied by Italian courts (e.g., public order, compliance with due process principles and right to controvert).

Italy is a party to the New York Convention of 1958 on the Recognition and Enforcement of Foreign Arbitral Awards and the EC Convention of Brussels of 1968 on Jurisdiction and the Enforcement of Judgments in Civil and Commercial Matters (as amended, as far as EU member states are concerned, by the Council Regulation no. 44/2001 of December 22, 2000, on Jurisdiction and the Recognition and Enforcement of Judgments in Civil and Commercial Matters), and other applicable bilateral conventions on jurisdiction. As to EU member states, it is worth noting that Regulation no. 805/2004 of the European Parliament and of the Council of April 21, 2004, has introduced the European Enforcement Order for uncontested claims that ensures the free circulation of judgments, court settlements, and authentic instruments through all EU member states in civil and commercial matters without the need for any intermediate proceedings before the member state of enforcement prior to recognition and enforcement.

Usually, businesspeople and lawyers with international backgrounds prefer international commercial arbitration to resolve disputes. The rationale is that the arbitration award, thanks to the New York Convention of 1958, offers a higher degree of "circulation" and enforceability in foreign jurisdictions than a judgment.

Parties frequently utilize institutional arbitration, including arbitration administered by the International Chamber of Commerce and by local institutions (e.g., Italian Arbitration Association, Chamber of Commerce of Milan). Arbitration is also fully regulated by the Italian Civil Procedure Code. Ad hoc arbitration and the UNCITRAL rules are also used.

Finally, it should be mentioned that alternative dispute resolution mechanisms are not well developed in Italy and, as a consequence, are rarely contemplated. Additionally, online dispute resolution mechanisms are not usually thought of as an option because the settlement of claims is, by cultural standards, deemed to be an activity to be carried out on a personal approach basis rather than through online procedures.

3.3 Accounting Rules

Accounting has, if not a major, nonetheless a significant role to play in Italian transactions. Under Italian law professionally audited financial statements are required only for specific categories of corporations, including listed companies, mutual funds, and insurance companies.

In addition, the Civil Code provides that joint stock companies (*società per azioni*), partnerships limited by shares (*società in accomandita per axiom*), and, under certain conditions, limited liability companies (*società a responsabilità limitata*) must have a board of statutory auditors or an independent accountant auditor that audits the financial statement of the company. Generally accepted accounting principles are increasingly used in Italy. The implementation of EU directives introducing standard accounting schemes and consolidated financial statements has increased the adoption of uniform accounting principles. In this respect, Italian law, in compliance with EU Regulation no. 1606/2002 of the European Parliament and of the Council of July 19, 2002 on the application of international accounting standards (IAS), now sets forth a specific obligation for certain categories of companies (e.g., listed companies and banks), and an option for most of the other categories of companies, to adopt IAS in their consolidated and/ or annual accounts. By and large, international accounting firms in Italy adhere to the auditing guidelines of the International Federation of Accountants (IFAC). With respect to such entities applying IAS, a major change has been enacted by Budget Law 2008. Under previously applicable legislation, the accounting principles adopted by the taxpayer (e.g., IAS versus Italian GAAP) were irrelevant from a tax perspective.

Pursuant to Budget Law 2008, items accounted for pursuant to IAS, as well as accounting rules and principles provided under IAS, will also be relevant for income tax purposes.

3.4 Unions

Italy is a highly unionized country. Labor unions are large and over the years have had a strong influence. Even though codetermination is not an issue under Italian labor law and there is no requirement to provide access to representatives of unions on the board of directors, unions are in a position to effectively negotiate with employers. Recently, employees' stock ownership has been developing with the blessing of unions. As discussed above, a transfer of ownership as well as a collective layoff can trigger consultation requirements with the unions.

When a large business is sold to foreign investors and the transfer is expected to have an adverse impact on employment, unions may react and ask that sufficient guarantees protecting employment be implemented. However, in most cases, unions play no role in the context of international transactions.

3.5 The Role of In-house and External Counsel

Although it is difficult to generalize about the respective roles of in-house and external counsel in transactions with Italians, a distinction can be made between small to medium-size businesses and large businesses. It is rare that small or medium-size Italian companies will have in-house capabilities. As such, external law firms have an important role in negotiations.

Larger companies in Italy tend to have sophisticated in-house legal departments. Most of the transnational work is done by in-house counsel, and the involvement of external counsel, apart from litigation, is limited to complex and specialized issues.

Currently, large companies are outsourcing legal work. In particular, large international transactions, sophisticated M&A, and capital market deals are increasingly handled by outside law firms. Investment banks may play a significant role in choosing external law firms.

4. Negotiations in Italy

4.1 Participants

In transactions involving small- or medium-size Italian companies, negotiations are often conducted by the owners of the businesses concerned. Normally such companies are closely held or family-owned businesses. The owners act also as directors of the company and in that capacity may participate in negotiations (under Italian corporate law, directors are in charge of the management of companies).

In larger companies with fragmented ownership and an autonomous board of directors, it is the senior people (or at least people having high-ranking status) who typically conduct negotiations. However, especially in international and/or complex transactions, the decision-making process is increasingly decentralized and junior managers tend to be more actively involved. Often the power to make binding decisions is delegated to midlevel persons. Directors of large companies will be directly involved in negotiating transactions if those transactions are significant.

In any event, the approval of the board of directors is usually required for transactions of a certain size. Normally, the board approves the basic points of any given transaction and authorizes one of the directors to execute the agreement on behalf of the company. Shareholder approval is generally required only in connection with transactions that have a material impact on the operations of a company. Italian businesses will involve lawyers and other advisers at later stages in the negotiations. The role of lawyers may be less central than is the case in other jurisdictions. However, the involvement of lawyers, which was traditionally limited to drafting and negotiating legal issues, is becoming increasingly important in the negotiation process in M&A, banking, and finance matters. There are only a limited number of full-service law firms in Italy with full international capacity that can effectively act as deal facilitators and play a major role in the negotiation process.

Financial reporting related to transactions is important in relation to certain industries. For example, in deals involving an acquisition, accountants are normally involved in the negotiations only in connection with preclosing or postclosing financial and tax audits of the company concerned. Other experts can be involved, depending upon the features of the transaction in question (e.g., industrial property agents or environmental experts).

4.2 Environment and Timing

Culturally, the negotiating environment in Italy is largely similar to that in the United States. Relationships and communications among persons participating in the negotiation process tend to be more formal and less direct than is the case in the United States (often, businesspeople do not deal with their lawyers on a first-name basis). Meetings and documentation in writing are preferable to telephone communications. E-mail is generally used to exchange draft documentation and related comments. As a practical note, a fifteen-minute delay in starting a meeting is acceptable practice.

Negotiations with foreign parties are often conducted in English. Most Italian businesspeople with an international background are fluent in English. Large companies and international law firms may also have the ability to conduct negotiations and deals in various different languages.

In general the response time of Italian parties to negotiations, although reasonable, tends to be somewhat slower than is the case in the United States. However, when the negotiating process is under time constraints, Italians have the ability to be both pragmatic and flexible. Depending upon the complexity and size of a given transaction, negotiations can be consummated in a few days or last several months. Generally, negotiations in Italy are less complex and time-consuming than in the United States.

As previously discussed, Italian companies are now more inclined to involve legal counsel to a greater extent in the negotiating process. The schedule of a business negotiation in Italy can be continuous or divided into separate segments when required under the circumstances (for example, due diligence, assessment of assets and liabilities, drafting, preclosing and postclosing activities).

There are several statutory and regulatory provisions that may have an impact on the timing of transactions. In acquisitions, an antitrust filing entails a stay period of up to thirty days to obtain phase one clearance for the consummation of the transaction. If an acquisition requires the issuance of a prospectus in connection with an offer of securities to the public or with a tender offer to buy out minority interests in listed companies, the time for preparation of the prospectus and its approval by CONSOB must be considered. Generally, CONSOB clears a prospectus in ten to twenty days. Filings and disclosures with regulators and authorization procedures are required in certain regulated areas (for example, insurance and banking).

All of the above issues require extensive cooperation among parties involved in any given project and must be addressed as early as possible before the negotiating process gets under way. Specific contractual provisions may be advisable to cover these aspects and should set out the respective obligations.

4.3 Contractual Negotiations

As already discussed, Italian parties may start negotiations on the key issues prior to the formalization of a written agreement. In some cases, material business issues are negotiated and agreed upon at the outset of the written contracts. Although disputes related to such agreements present greater uncertainties, in most cases the Italian Civil Code provides a set of rules applicable to a given type of contract to supplement the contractual provisions. For instance, the Civil Code contains rules on liability, default, force majeure, and assignment, which apply automatically to contracts governed by Italian law. However, the tendency of most civil law countries to draft less extensive agreements than the United States is being replaced in Italy by the prevailing trend to adopt, especially in the context of international transactions, "self-ruling" contracts that cover all of the potential issues that may arise in connection with a given transaction. Typically, hardship clauses or other provisions covering the risk of unanticipated events will be contemplated.

In the case of an agreement governed by foreign law, the adoption of precise drafting and detailed provisions is believed to contribute, to some extent, to denationalizing the contract and providing guidance as to the ramifications of the most common events affecting the duration of the contract. In any event, Italians and lawyers are more inclined to draft tailor-made agreements than to use boilerplate language. In Italy, the control of drafting is regarded as less of a strategic advantage than is the case in the United States. In fact, except for situations in which one party has obvious bargaining leverage, there is an expectation that drafts submitted by one party to another will be reasonably fair. Thus, one-sided contracts are rarely released to the other party, and consequently there is relatively little of the lengthy and time-consuming battle of the drafts that United States negotiations are privy to.

The general negotiations pertaining to the control of drafting are resolved based also on the leverage of the various parties. In international transactions, the United States approach, whereby the contractual documentation is prepared by the buyer in the acquisition context and by the lender in a financing transaction, is now utilized.

The strength of the bargaining parties is also pivotal in ascertaining the language of the contract. When English is used for an agreement governed by Italian law, care must be taken to verify that the legal terminology equates with Italian civil law.

However, Italian parties recognize that English is the prevailing language in international contracts, and they are normally prepared to negotiate and draft agreements in English. It is advisable to negotiate the contractual language in advance.

Negotiations may be difficult in Italy in August, as during this month most companies take their annual vacation, or are often closed down or understaffed. Bar August, there is no particular period during the year that is better to negotiate in than any other. Negotiations take place normally during business hours. Heavy-duty bargaining is acceptable to Italians when there are time restraints.

4.4 Due Diligence and Legal Opinions

In international acquisitions, due diligence is normally conducted to verify the accuracy of legal and business representations provided by the seller. Virtual data rooms are increasingly used. In negotiations it is the norm to consider business warranties in relation to the financial situation of the target as represented at the time the agreement is executed. Accordingly, due diligence is normally conducted simultaneously with negotiations to verify that the contractual representations are adequate and reflect the actual legal and business situation of the entity concerned.

As already discussed, contractual indemnities for hidden tax, labor, social security, and environmental liabilities are deliberated upon in international business transactions. Italian parties are normally willing to provide credit support for indemnities as well as in relation to payment of deferred consideration. The typical forms are guarantees from the parent company, in cases where a large group is involved, or bank guarantees. In the context of international sale of goods, supply contracts, and turnkey projects, Italian parties are agreeable to providing letters of credit, performance bonds, and analogous forms of guarantee. If a transaction requires a legal opinion, it is advisable to clarify beforehand whether the Italian counsel acting in the transaction is willing to provide the opinion. In fact, transactional opinions are not typically rendered by Italian lawyers in domestic transactions. On the other hand, opinions are normally rendered by Italian law firms with international background.

5. Conclusion

The outcome and the characteristics of the negotiating process of international business transactions in Italy will depend largely on the Italians' individual characteristics. When the Italians and counsel involved have international expertise, negotiations often result in a smooth and efficient process. However, some cultural difficulties may arise if negotiations are conducted by Italians with only domestic experience. In particular, when U.S. parties are involved, the different negotiating styles and drafting techniques illustrated in this chapter can sometimes lead to misunderstandings and make the process more complex than it should be.

Italy has a history of successful and significant investments by U.S. parties. To that, end, I wish you the very best of luck.

Giovanni Nardulli
Legance Studio Legale Associato
Via XX Settembre, 5—00187
Rome, Italy
Phone: 39 06 9318271
Fax: 39 06 931827403
E-mail: GNardulli@Legance.it

CHAPTER 33

International Business Negotiations in Japan

Soichiro Fujiwara and Satoko Kametaka

NAGASHIMA OHNO & TSUNEMATSU
TOKYO, JAPAN

1. Introduction

1.1 Broad Demographic Information

Japan is a country of 130 million people that is linguistically and culturally largely homogeneous. Japan is roughly the size of the state of California and is composed of over 3,000 islands, the largest of which are Honshu, Hokkaido, Kyushu, and Shikoku. The capital city of Tokyo and its surrounding prefectures, on Honshu, is the largest metropolitan area in the world, with over 30 million residents. Today, Japan is a major economic power with the world's second-largest economy.

Japan is a constitutional monarchy with a parliamentary government. The Constitution provides that (i) legislative power is vested in the Diet, which is composed of the House of Representatives and the House of Councilors; (ii) executive power is vested in the Cabinet led by the Prime Minister, a member of the Diet chosen by a resolution of the Diet, and (iii) judicial power is wholly vested in the courts. The Emperor does not have any discretionary powers related to the government.

1.2 Historical and Cultural Background

Japan's culture is a product of the influences and the cultures of neighboring countries such as China and Korea. There remains a strong sense of national identity reflected in a 250-year national policy of isolationism, ending in the mid-nineteenth century.

In the years leading to and following the Meiji Restoration in the late nineteenth century, the Imperial family, formerly excluded from politics, was brought back to rule through a constitutional monarchy. This signaled Japan's emphatic turn toward the West. The laws of the West, in particular, the laws of France and Germany, were studied intensively and used as a model for the basis of modern Japanese laws.

For example, the Civil Code established in the late nineteenth century remains in effect in present-day Japan.

The U.S. occupation after World War II brought the second major infusion of western legal thinking into Japan, especially that of the United States. Laws influenced by the United States range from the Constitution and the Code of Criminal Procedure to the fundamental laws that govern current business transactions, such as the Companies Act and the Financial Instruments and Exchange Law.

1.3 Business Organization and Culture

When discussing matters of international business negotiation involving the Japanese, it is important to understand that a Japanese individual or corporation may fall anywhere along a spectrum running from extreme traditionalism on one side to extreme westernization on the other. A family-owned company with mostly older executives that has had few dealings with foreign companies will most likely fall within the "traditional" category, while a company owned by general stockholders, with young executives and a long history of involvement with firms in the West, will generally fall into the "westernized" category.

The Japanese consider trust, along with the related concept of loyalty, to be the most important consideration in a business relationship. Deep trust-based relationships take years to develop and are not discarded lightly. In fact, what is often seen by Americans as the tendency of Japanese people to stick together can be explained by their desire to do business with someone they know well and on a long-term basis, which may override considerations of price or convenience.

1.4 Overview of Legal System

The Constitution is the supreme law of Japan. The Diet has the power under the Constitution to enact laws (*horitsu*), and the Cabinet, the Cabinet Office, and the Ministry have the power to enact Cabinet Orders (*seirei*), Cabinet Office Ordinances (*naikaku-furei*), and Ordinances of the Ministry (*shorei*), respectively. The national Japanese government is centralized in Tokyo, but local governments also have the authority to enact local ordinances and regulations to the extent authorized by laws. Additionally, administrative agencies can enact regulations by more informal means, such as circulars (*tsutatsu*) and administrative guidance (*gyosei shido*), which are not legally binding.

Japan is currently undergoing reform of its legal system. The legal reforms include: (i) reinforcing due process in the civil justice system by, among other things, promoting greater access to the courts; (ii) strengthening the public defense system in criminal trials; (iii) increasing the number of legal professionals; (iv) improving professional legal training and education by creating law schools; and

(v) increasing public participation in the judicial system by allowing laypersons to serve on judicial panels.

Japan has the fewest number of lawyers among major industrial countries; as of 2006, Japan had only one lawyer per 4,581 people compared to every 1,191 people in France or every 271 people in the United States. Until recently, law has been an undergraduate course of study at universities and anyone who had completed their sophomore year of university was allowed to sit for the former Japanese Bar Exam. The former exam was notoriously difficult, with a passage rate of around 2 percent to 3 percent for the years between 1995 and 2005. Only 700 to 1,500 people passed annually. To fix the legal services bottleneck created by this shortage in supply of lawyers, a new law school system of graduate-level professional schools of law, modeled after the U.S. system, was established in 2004 and its first graduates sat for the new Japanese Bar Exam in 2006. The number of people who will be passing the new exam annually is expected to increase to around 3,000 eventually, with a passage rate of around 30 percent to 50 percent.

2. Substantive Laws and Regulations Impacting Negotiations

2.1 Corporate Laws

The Companies Act came into effect in May of 2006, consisting of an integration of the corporate-law-related provisions from various laws, such as the Commercial Code, the Law for Special Exceptions, the Commercial Code Concerning Audits of a Stock Company, and the Limited Liability Company (*yugen kaisha*) Law. Portions relating to triangular mergers took effect a year later in May 2007. The Companies Act changed the substance of such corporate-law-related provisions in many respects.

Under the Act, a company means a stock company (*kabushiki kaisha*), a general partnership company (*gomei kaisha*), a limited partnership company (*goshi kaisha*), or a limited liability company (*godo kaisha*). Not only stock companies established under the Commercial Code, but also limited liability companies (*yugen kaisha*) established under the Limited Liability Company Law before it was subsumed, continue to exist as stock companies under the Companies Act.

The Act requires every stock company, which is the most widely used type of company, to hold general shareholders' meetings and have at least one director. A stock company may choose to have other governance components, such as a board of directors, an accounting counselor (*kaikei sanyo*), a statutory auditor (*kansayaku*), a board of statutory auditors, an accounting auditor (*kaikei kansanin*), and committees (*iinkai*). A director has a fiduciary duty only toward the company and is only directly liable to the company, not the shareholders.

A stock company for which all authorized shares can be transferred without the company's approval is classified as a "Public Company" (*kokai kaisha*). All other companies are not Public Companies (commonly called *heisa kaisha* or *joto seigen kaisha*). A Public Company is not limited to those whose shares are listed on a stock exchange. A stock company that does not issue publicly traded shares can be classified as a Public Company.

Forms of mergers and acquisitions that are available under the Companies Act are share acquisition, business transfer, merger (including triangular mergers), share exchange (*kabushiki koukan*, a transaction between two companies whereby one company becomes the 100 percent shareholder of the other company), share transfer (*kabushiki iten*, a transaction whereby an existing company newly forms a parent company and becomes its wholly owned subsidiary; the shares of the existing company are exchanged for the shares of a to-be-formed parent company), and corporate split (a transaction whereby one company spins out a segment of its business).

In Japan, the number of hostile takeovers is gradually increasing, but the number of those that have been successful is still very small. In a society where conflict and antagonism are avoided and a history of trust is valued, acquirers attempting a hostile takeover should prepare for a negative reaction from not only the directors of the company but also from the employees of the target, the media, and the Japanese public. It should be noted that while the purchaser is not able to conduct a due diligence investigation of the target in the case of a hostile takeover, the disclosure requirements of publicly traded companies in Japan is much more limited than those required under U.S. securities regulations.

The Companies Act provides that a Quasi Foreign Company may not continuously conduct business in Japan. "Quasi Foreign Company" is a term that means a company whose (i) headquarters (whether actual or de facto) is located in Japan, or (ii) principal purpose is to conduct business in Japan. This Quasi Foreign Company issue has been politically controversial and has received a great deal of media coverage during the time leading towards the implementation of the Act. Foreign companies having a substantial amount of business outside Japan continue to choose to establish branches rather than subsidiaries. There is a tendency for foreign companies without business outside Japan to choose to establish a subsidiary instead of a branch in Japan.

Unlike the law of some countries, Japanese law, with exceptions in only extraordinary situations, does not contain rules that prohibit Japanese companies from providing financial assistance with respect to the acquisition by third parties of existing or newly issued shares in its capital. However, in light of the protection of the interests of minority shareholders, the acquired company should generally avoid offering its assets as collateral to secure financing for the acquirer unless and until the acquired company becomes wholly owned by the acquirer.

2.2 Securities Laws

The Securities and Exchange Law, which was promulgated in 1948, was renamed the Financial Instruments and Exchange Law (FIEL) in September 2007. Together with the name change, four laws were abolished, eighty-nine laws were amended, and some parts of those laws were consolidated into the FIEL.

Companies listed on a Japanese stock exchange are subject to continuous disclosure requirements under the FIEL. Documents required to be disclosed are, among others, annual security reports, quarterly reports (newly required for the fiscal year starting on or after April 1, 2008, as a replacement for the semiannual securities reports), and extraordinary reports. Online filing of disclosure documents is done using the Electronic Disclosure for Investors' NETwork (EDINET), which is an electronic system designed to accept disclosure documents filed under the FIEL. Under this system, disclosure documents are filed online with the Local Finance Bureau and are made available to the public through the Internet. Also, companies listed on a Japanese stock exchange must disclose through an online disclosure system called the Timely Disclosure network (TDnet) any information required by the Timely Disclosure Rules of the relevant Japanese stock exchange. Listed companies are also encouraged to adequately disclose material facts on their Web sites.

Subject to certain requirements and exceptions provided in detail in the FIEL and its related ordinances, a tender offer is mandatory in certain purchase of shares (including certain options and warrants) of companies that are subject to continuous disclosure requirements. For example, a tender offer is mandatory when the purchaser's shareholding: (i) is in excess of 5 percent of the shares of the target company after purchases from more than ten sellers via "off market" transactions within a period of sixty-one days or less; (ii) is in excess of one-third of the shares of the target company after purchases via "off market" transactions or certain trade sale type market transactions; or (iii) is in excess of one-third of the shares of the target company after a purchase and the purchase is a combination of purchases made in (a) "off market" transactions or certain trade sale type market transactions for shares in excess of 5 percent of the shares of the target company, and (b) other acquisition of shares (including subscribing for newly issued shares), implemented within a three-month period and resulting in the increase of the purchaser's shareholding by more than 10 percent. If the purchaser intends to purchase two-thirds or more of the shares of the target company, such purchaser is required to offer to purchase all the shares tendered.

Subject to certain requirements and exceptions provided in detail in the FIEL and its related ordinances, if a party acquires 5 percent or more of the voting shares of a publicly traded company, such party is required to file a block shareholding report. So long as the acquirer holds 5 percent or more of the voting shares, the acquirer must file an amended report if there is an increase or decrease of 1 percent or more in the shareholding ratio of the acquirer.

If subjects discussed in the negotiation include an "important matter" of a listed company, the persons involved need to pay attention to insider trading regulations. Subject to certain requirements and exceptions provided in detail in the FIEL and its related ordinances, relevant parties of the listed company, such as the company itself, counterparties negotiating an agreement with such listed company, and officers or employees of those companies and those who receive company information directly from them, are prohibited from selling and purchasing securities with knowledge of important facts (i.e., facts that could have a material effect on the listed company's share price, which are specifically listed in the relevant regulations) before such facts are made public. In addition to this restriction, related parties or personnel who have knowledge of the implementation of a tender offer or a transaction similar to a tender offer that has not been made public are prohibited from purchasing shares in the target company, and those with knowledge of the cancellation of such transaction are prohibited from selling such shares prior to the announcement. However, there are exceptions to these two types of insider regulations, such as when the purchaser and the seller of the shares in the listed company both know of the important facts.

2.3 Tax Laws

The Japanese national government, prefectural governments, and municipal governments impose a variety of taxes upon corporations and individuals. For example, taxes on corporate income in Japan consist of (i) national corporate income tax, (ii) prefectural inhabitant tax, (iii) enterprise tax, and (iv) municipal inhabitant tax. A foreign company having a permanent establishment in Japan, such as a branch office, is subject to Japanese corporate income tax with respect to all types of Japanese source income. A foreign company that has a subsidiary in Japan, regardless of whether or not such subsidiary is wholly owned, is not regarded as having a permanent establishment in Japan merely because of the fact that it has a subsidiary. If a foreign company has no permanent establishment in Japan, Japanese withholding tax is imposed on certain kinds of Japanese source income, such as royalties, interests, and dividends.

A typical corporate tax issue arising in cross-border transactions concerns the thin capitalization rules. If a Japanese corporation owes its foreign controlling shareholder an amount that is greater than three times the equity held by such shareholder, then such corporation may not deduct, from its taxable income, the portion of the interest paid on such debt that accrues from the portion of the debt exceeding a defined ratio. Transfer pricing issues may also impact cross-border transactions. Japanese transfer pricing rules may be applicable to both a Japanese company and a Japanese branch of a nonresident company if either of them engages in transactions with any of their foreign related persons (for example, a direct or indirect 50 percent share ownership would render a foreign person a "foreign related person" for the purposes of the transfer pricing rules).

Any enterprise that, for monetary compensation, transfers or leases certain assets or provides certain services in Japan and any person who imports certain foreign goods into Japan are subject to a value added tax, or consumption tax, which is presently 5 percent (comprising a 4 percent national tax and a 1 percent local tax). Activities that are exempt from the consumption tax include transfers and leases (other than for certain temporary purposes) of land, housing leases (other than for certain temporary purposes), transfers of securities, the provision of certain medical or educational services, and the export of goods.

Stamp duty, which is made by affixing a revenue stamp to the relevant document, is levied on persons who execute taxable documents, such as real estate sales agreements, land leasehold agreements, loan agreements, transportation agreements, merger agreements, and promissory notes. Some stamp duty amounts are determined on the basis of the size of the transaction covered by the taxable document, but otherwise the tax amounts are generally fixed. Electronic agreements are not taxable documents.

Registration and license taxes are imposed on registration with respect to, for example, acquisition, transfer, mortgages of certain rights and assets, certain matters concerning entities such as companies, qualifications, and official licenses for professionals, and specified businesses for which licenses are required.

2.4 Antitrust/Anticompetition Laws

The Act Concerning Prohibition of Private Monopolization and Maintenance of Fair Trade, commonly known as the Antimonopoly Act, is the fundamental competition law of Japan. This Act prohibits "private monopolization," "unreasonable restraint of trade" (such as cartels), and "unfair trade practices" by preventing excessive concentration of economic power and by eliminating unreasonable restraint of production, sale, price, technology, and all other unjust restrictions on business activities through combinations and agreements.

The Fair Trade Commission (FTC), a national administrative agency, is responsible for administration and enforcement of this Act.

Its activities range from responding to consultations, issuing guidelines that are often just as important as the Act, and conducting investigations of alleged violations to rendering of decisions and dispositions.

Dango (which literally means "discuss" and "meet") is a negotiation among bidders for a Japanese public-works contract in which it is determined which firm will be awarded the job. *Dangos* were reputed to be widespread and a part of Japanese culture for certain industries. However, after the introduction of the leniency program in January 2006, action by the FTC against illegal cartels has become more aggressive and the attention paid to illegal cartels has risen in recent years.

A company acquiring businesses and a company contemplating a merger or company split are, in some cases, required to provide prior notification to the FTC. Also, a company that has acquired shares of another company or group of companies that have formed a trading association are, in some instances, required to file a report to the FTC following such event.

In order to prevent "unfair trade practices," there are two supplementary laws to the Antimonopoly Act, (a) the Act Against Delay in the Payment of Subcontract Proceeds, etc. to Subcontractors, which aims to protect the interests of subcontractors against principal contractors in a country where subcontracting is a common form of business, and (b) the Act Against Unjustifiable Premiums and Misleading Representations, which aims to protect the interest of consumers by preventing inducement of customers by means of excessive premiums and misleading representations. *Premiums* are defined broadly under this act to include any article, money, or economic benefit offered to consumers. Note that restrictions on premiums include not only those on offers made to purchasers but also on general solicitations, such as lotteries, made to the general public in advertisements.

2.5 Labor and Employment Laws

In traditional Japanese companies, employees are virtually guaranteed lifetime employment. Regular employees are generally recruited from among new school graduates, and after the completion of a probationary period (typically three to six months), their employment is secured until they reach mandatory retirement age. Although an individual employee's abilities and aptitude for the position are considered, promotions are typically based on the years-of-service standard, under Japan's long-term employment system.

Employment terms must be provided to each employee in writing, but it is rare that a detailed employment contract is signed. In general, employment relationships and relevant employee benefits at Japanese companies are primarily regulated by applicable statutory provisions and the internal work rules established by the employing company.

Mainly because of the accepted idea of long-term employment, dismissal of employees is extremely restricted in Japan. More specifically, there is an established Supreme Court principle now provided in the Labor Standards Act that "even when an employer exercise its right of dismissal, it will be void as a misuse of the right if such dismissal lacks objectively reasonable grounds and is not considered to be appropriate in general societal terms."

In the case of mergers and corporate splits, the work rules and employment benefits of the merged or transferring company will continue to apply to the ex-employees of the merged or transferring company, even after the merger or corporate split, unless appropriate arrangements for integration are made. The existence of unpaid wages for overtime work owed to employees is one of the most typical and substantial contingent liabilities of a company that surface in an M&A due diligence process. The treatment of pension plans can also be troublesome in M&A transactions, not only from an accounting and tax perspective, but also from a legal perspective.

2.6 Environmental Laws

"Environmental pollution" as used in the Basic Environment Law means, among interference with environmental conservation, (i) air pollution, (ii) water pollution, (iii) contamination of soil, (iv) noise, (v) vibration, (vi) subsidence of ground, and (vii) malodor deriving from business activities or other human activities, which cause damage to human health or living environment. Environmental conservation measures aimed at preventing the above types of pollution are made by the national government through laws, cabinet orders, and ministerial ordinances and by local governments by preserving and improving the environment in their areas and establishing local ordinances. Local ordinances must not contradict the laws and orders of the national government, but they can be more stringent than, and are just as important in practice as, the laws and orders of the national government. Agreements reached between the polluting enterprise and the local government are also effective means of conserving the environment.

The main law concerning air pollution is the Air Pollution Control Law and the main law concerning water quality control is the Water Pollution Control Law, both of which set forth the environmental standards to be complied with, various measures such as administrative orders that can be taken by relevant governmental agencies, and possible penalties to be imposed upon the entrepreneurs in violation of such standards or orders. Japan is a party to the Kyoto Protocol, and in 2005, the Voluntary Emission Trading Scheme began in Japan, an experimental system established by the Environmental Ministry for a limited time. In this scheme, the Ministry offered subsidies for the installation of new facilities that lead to a reduction in global greenhouse gas emissions, in exchange for the voluntary setting of emission-reduction levels by the participants. If, at the end of the final trading period, a participant cannot reduce the actual global greenhouse gas emissions to, or below, the total amount of emissions allowances allocated to such a participant plus any amount acquired by trading, the subsidies to such participant will be revoked. The cap and trade system has not yet been introduced in Japan.

The main law concerning contaminated land is the Soil Contamination Countermeasures Act. Under this Act, an owner, manager, or occupant (collectively, "landholders") of the land may assume the obligation to investigate the land to determine whether there is any contamination from the operation of a facility used in the process of making, using, or disposing of specific harmful substances. If there is a possibility of a certain amount of pollution that is hazardous to human health, the local prefectural governor may order a landholder to investigate the contamination of the land. If the land is found to be contaminated and is to be cleaned up to protect the local residents, the governor may order the polluter to clean up the contamination. If the polluter cannot be identified, the governor may order the landholder to clean up the contamination even if the landholder was not the one who caused the contamination. If the landholder takes remediation measures, the landholder may seek contribution from the polluter in three ways: (i) under the Soil Contamination Countermeasures Act (but only in the case where the order for the cleanup is issued by the governor against the landholder), (ii) under the Civil Code warranty against defects (but only in the case where the landholder acquired the land directly from the polluter), or (iii) under a tort claim as provided in the Civil Code.

2.7 Intellectual Property Laws

Intellectual Property laws may be classified into (i) the laws for the protection of intellectual creations, and (ii) the laws for the protection of the reputation of a business enterprise, such as the Trademark Act. Protection of intellectual creations may be found in the Copyright Act and Industrial Property Laws such as the Patent Act, Utility Model Act, and Design Act. The Unfair Competition Prevention Act is capable of regulating new types of business activities and regulates, for example, the use of trade secrets, and thus, can also be regarded as a type of Intellectual Property Law.

Unlike the United States practice of awarding priority to the applicant who can prove that he or she was the first inventor (first inventor rule), in Japan if two or more applications for the same invention are filed on different dates, the application filed first has priority (first-to-file rule). Under the Patent Act, patent licenses are divided into two types: exclusive licenses and ordinary licenses. An exclusive license is only effectuated when it is registered, but once it is registered, even the grantor cannot use the patent. In fact, under the patent registration system, only a small percentage of granted licenses are exclusive licenses and the vast majority are ordinary licenses. These ordinary licenses are made exclusive by agreement between the grantor and grantee, and are not exclusive licenses under the patent registration system. With respect to employee inventions, if the employee vests in the employer the right to obtain a patent or the patent right for an employee invention or grants the employer an exclusive license for an employee invention, the employee has the right to receive reasonable value under the Patent Act.

As with the Patent Act, the registration system under the Trademark Act is based on the first-to-file rule. In addition to the Trademark Act, there are other laws that protect unregistered trademarks and other business indications. The Companies Act does not allow the use of a name or trade name for an unjust purpose if it causes others to confuse such company or person with another company or person. The Commercial Registration Act does not allow two companies with the same trade name and the same address to exist simultaneously. The Unfair Competition Prevention Act protects well-known business indications including well-known unregistered trademarks and well-known trade names, not by giving an exclusive right to the enterprise involved but by prohibiting unfair activities.

Japan is a party to both the Berne Convention and the Universal Copyright Convention, and the works created in any other member countries can enjoy protection under the Copyright Act in Japan without any formal requirements. Unlike the copyright laws of the United States, the Copyright Act does not provide a fair use defense, but does provides other limitations on the copyright owner's rights, such as permitted reproduction for private use. Under the Copyright Act, the "moral rights of authors" are different from copyright, which protects the author's economic interests regarding the use of the work. As the "moral rights of authors" are inalienable, it is important to have the author waive his or her "moral rights of authors" in a transaction where the exercise of such rights may cause conflict. The "moral rights of authors" include (i) the right to decide whether or not to make a work public, (ii) the right to determine whether or not to indicate the author's name and how the name should be indicated on the original of his work, and (iii) the right to maintain the integrity of the work and its title.

2.8 Privacy and Data Security Laws

The Act on the Protection of Personal Information came into effect in May 2005. The Act applies to "Entities Handling Personal

Information," i.e., entities that handle and retain personal information on 5,000 or more individuals. Individuals can include prospective, current, or past customers, vendors, and employees. Ministries have issued industry-specific guidelines based on the general principles set out in the Act.

Under this Act, Entities Handling Personal Information are required to fulfill certain obligations. For example, Entities Handling Personal Information may not, without the individual's consent, (i) provide personal information to a third party except under certain circumstances such as when the party receiving such information is an entity to which responsibility for the handling of personal information in accordance with the Act is delegated or (ii) use the personal information beyond what is necessary to achieve the purpose it has specified and disclosed to the individual. Entities Handling Personal Information are also required to correct and update personal information to the extent necessary and, if requested, disclose the personal information to the relevant individual.

2.9 Regulation of Foreign Investments

The Foreign Exchange and Foreign Trade Act requires that various transactions involving foreign individuals or entities be filed or notices or reports be made to the relevant minister through the Bank of Japan. Exceptions to the notice and reporting obligations as well as ordinances related to the Act are provided in detail in the Foreign Exchange and Foreign Trade Act.

If a foreign individual, a foreign entity, or a Japanese entity controlled by a foreign individual or entity invests in an entity that is engaged in certain "sensitive" businesses, such as businesses that raise concern for national security or other public interests (e.g., military, aerospace, fishery, agriculture), prior notice must be filed with the relevant minister through the Bank of Japan and a waiting period of one month (or sometimes more) must be observed. If the entity in which investment is being made is not engaged in any "sensitive" business, the investing individual or entity only has to file a report following the investment.

Transactions exceeding 100 million Japanese yen (JPY) in size but not falling in the above category of inward direct investment may require filing of a report as a "capital transaction" with the relevant minister through the Bank of Japan following the consummation of the transaction. This report is required for transactions such as a loan, guarantee, deposit, sale of receivables, transfer, or issuance of securities that is between (i) an individual or entity with an address in Japan (resident) and (ii) an individual or entity who is not a resident (nonresident), or transactions involving foreign currency.

If a payment made between the resident and a non-resident, or between two residents when one is in Japan and the other in a foreign country, is JPY 30 million or more, the resident is required to file a report following the payment.

Export of certain goods is subject to obtaining permission or approval under the Foreign Exchange and Foreign Trade Act and the Export Trade Control Order. Import of certain goods is subject to approval under the Foreign Exchange and Foreign Trade Act and the Import Trade Control Order. Exporters and importers must also follow custom clearance procedures.

3. Other Significant Legal and Business Issues

The Act Concerning the General Rules for the Application of Laws (*ho no tekiyo ni kansuru tsusoku ho*) came into effect in January 2007. Parties to a contract may freely choose and agree on the applicable law to govern the contract, and the selection of the governing law may be made explicitly or implicitly. Under this law, if the parties have not chosen the governing law explicitly or implicitly (for example, when transactions are conducted only by simple purchase orders and invoices without any explicit governing law provision or implicit/customary choice of governing law), the applicable law is the law of the jurisdiction that is most closely connected to the contract. In determining such jurisdiction, the theory of characteristic performance is generally employed, bringing Japanese choice of law closer in line with the signatories of the Rome Convention. However, there are some exceptions, such as those for real estate, consumer, and employment agreements. Also, since merger, share exchange (*kabushiki koukan*), share transfer (*kabushiki iten*), and corporate split are statutory agreements provided by the Companies Act, the agreements or other documents for those transactions must satisfy relevant requirements under Japanese law, and will be governed by Japanese law. Agreements for share acquisition and business transfers of Japanese companies may be governed by laws of any jurisdiction selected by the parties; however, in the majority of cases, the agreements for those transactions are also governed by Japanese law, because the transfer and acquisition itself is required to be completed pursuant to procedures established under Japanese law.

One impression of Japan that remains particularly strong in the minds of non-Japanese businesspeople is of an overregulated Japan where the national government often becomes directly involved in negotiations between private companies. While this once was the case, it has not been so for a long time. Other than through relevant anti-monopoly regulations, foreign exchange and trade law regulation, or in specific regulated industries such as banking, there are no major means for governmental agencies in Japan to influence or restrict business transactions.

4. Negotiation Practices

4.1 Participants

Traditionally, *bengoshi* (attorneys admitted to the bar of Japan) did not directly participate in negotiations between companies, but instead served in advisory roles behind the scenes. Because confrontation, rather than facilitation, was seen to be the very essence of *bengoshi*, the presence of a *bengoshi* at a negotiating meeting was seen as a signal that the side employing him or her was taking a hard line. Whether intended as such a signal or not, the mere presence of a *bengoshi* at a negotiating session was thought to destroy the entire atmosphere of conciliation and compromise. Along with the increase of international business transactions, however, Japanese companies have become increasingly willing to use *bengoshi* in negotiations. However, because only a limited number of Japanese companies have in-house counsel qualified as *bengoshi* (partially due to the limited number of lawyers in Japan generally, discussed above), the *bengoshi* participating in a negotiation is almost always outside counsel.

Respect for one's elders is a major part of Japan's Confucian heritage. Smooth business relations are dependent upon, among other things, people understanding their relative positions within the framework of respect and age—hence, age is an important consideration for Americans when doing business in Japan. Therefore, it is important that U.S. companies send negotiators of sufficient age, rank, and experience to represent them in Japan. Age may play a role in negotiations themselves. If, for instance, a relatively senior member on the Japanese side perceives that the proper degree of respect from a relatively younger counterpart is not being shown, it may affect the tenor of negotiations. It is equally important for relatively younger American negotiators not to take offense if they feel they are being treated in a condescending manner by relatively older members of the Japanese side; this should not be mistaken for rudeness or contempt.

A considerable percentage of Japanese companies bring large teams to negotiating sessions because of a desire to keep all those to be affected by a decision informed during the decision-making process. In order for a new policy or program to be implemented smoothly and quickly, large Japanese companies attempt to involve as many people as possible in the decision-making process. This reduces the internal tension that might result from a new policy or program because it effectively eliminates people's ability to claim that they were never told about a certain development.

Although American investors will likely negotiate through investment professionals with the authority to make material (if not final) decisions, Japanese negotiation teams are usually not vested with sweeping powers to negotiate within their mandate. Instead, they are required to report back to the head office in minute detail each day, and request instructions on how to proceed the next day. If negotiations are conducted without involvement of legal counsel, agreements will also be subject to subsequent review by the company's internal legal department, which is most likely not staffed by licensed lawyers but those with undergraduate law degrees. Not infrequently, what the team has agreed to during negotiations will be unacceptable to the home office or is impossible to build a consensus around, resulting in a need for future renegotiation. U.S. negotiators, however, should keep in mind that this tends not to be an attempt to stall or stonewall, but rather is a necessary part of assembling a consensus on a new policy within a Japanese company. Large Japanese corporations, especially, tend to have very formal and time-consuming internal transaction approval processes whereby the final drafts of agreements must go through many layers of management.

4.2 Timing

While there is no particular time when negotiations are traditionally conducted in Japan, there are certain times of the year to be avoided. Most Japanese companies shut down for several days (i) around the New Year, the most important holiday on the Japanese calendar, (ii) during Golden Week, a cluster of holidays that fall during the last week of April and the first week of May, and (iii) during *o-bon* (a festival to mourn the dead), for a week around mid-August.

The fiscal year should also be taken into consideration. The official fiscal year of Japan as well as the fiscal year of the majority of Japanese companies starts on April 1st and ends on March 31st. If the Japanese counterparty expresses the desire to complete the transaction by the end of March, it may be difficult to postpone the deadline to a later date.

4.3 Negotiation Practices

While English is required in Japanese schools, the teaching of English is geared to the grammar-focused examinations required as part of Japanese university entrance exams. As a result, the teaching of spoken English suffers with the effect that many Japanese feel very uncomfortable when forced to speak English. Perhaps few Japanese companies would assign a person lacking basic English skills to represent them in negotiations with Americans; however, speaking clearly and slowly in a manner designed to ensure the accurate understanding of the Japanese representative will put them at ease and be greatly appreciated.

Confidentiality agreements are frequently entered into between parties starting a negotiation, and a letter of intent is often also entered into in negotiations that require a certain period of time to complete.

A decade ago, legal due diligence in Japan was rare. However, as transactions requiring due diligence, such as M&A and real estate transactions, increased and, at the same time, U.S. practices were brought into Japan, the number of transactions in which legal due diligence is conducted has steadily increased. Today, legal due diligence has become fairly common even in transactions involving only Japanese companies. Traditionally, the target company disclosed documents in writing and those documents were photocopied, but the number of companies storing documents in electromagnetic form is increasing (subject to certain requirements, most corporate documents and notices under the Companies Act, including correspondence between a company and its shareholders, are allowed to be made and stored in electromagnetic form) and disclosure of documents through an online data room is gaining popularity.

4.4 Cultural, Ethical, and Religious Considerations

Japanese companies, especially those in the traditional category, prefer meeting in person rather than communicating in a conference call or through e-mail. The value of building trust through face-to-face meetings is considered to outweigh efficiency. Therefore, if a Japanese company proposes to have a meeting and the American counterpart turns down such offer and suggests holding a conference call instead, the American side will be missing out on an important opportunity to develop trust between the two companies, and in some cases, it may be taken as a sign that the American side is not taking the negotiation seriously.

The old cliché that patience is a virtue is especially true in negotiations with Japanese companies. It is very important for Americans to remain calm and collected during negotiations even if the proceedings become protracted. While some schools of negotiating teach that such actions as table-pounding and shouting will unnerve the other side, interfere with their ability to think, or make them uncomfortable so that they will want to quickly come to an agreement, such tactics in Japan will cause the Japanese side great discomfort and will undermine their trust in the American side.

When the positions of the two sides are far apart, trying to compel the Japanese side to agree with the American position will be counterproductive. Even if an agreement is worked out on such a basis, the course of the negotiations will leave a negative impression on the Japanese company, which will undermine the Japanese company's ability to trust the American one. A much more effective approach is to rationally explain to the Japanese side why a certain position has been taken, and to try to work together to come up with an agreement that both not only can live with, but will feel they contributed towards making. Japanese business is built around the idea of coming to a consensus and involving as many people as possible in a decision, in order to prevent later dissension. Accommodating the Japanese desire to avoid confrontation and to make everyone feel as though they had a say in a decision will make reaching an agreement—and administering that agreement—much smoother.

4.5 Negotiating Online

E-mail is used in negotiations and in exchange of documents by attaching word files or PDF files thereto. Traditional means such as mail and courier are usually used at times when electromagnetic methods are inconvenient, such as when delivering original copies or large volumes of data. Facsimile use is decreasing in negotiations, though it is still occasionally used and tends to be used more frequently for negotiations to settle pending litigation or prelitigation disputes. Telephone is used not only to supplement e-mail but also as an important tool to build trust and prevent miscommunication. Although almost no cultural differences exist between Japan and the United States in the use of electromagnetic tools in negotiations, there are Japanese people who consider that it is polite to telephone before or after sending a request by e-mail. Also, negotiating face-to-face may have an important meaning, as mentioned above.

5. Contract Formation

5.1 Wording and Style

The language of the agreement is usually the language in which the negotiation was conducted. If the documentation is in English, the Japanese parties often wish to have all or the important part translated into Japanese and the agreement may provide that the Japanese version supersedes the English version. Preparation of translations may cause delays in the negotiating process.

Japanese tended to prefer brevity in contracts because lengthy documents spelling out the course of action to be taken in every eventuality and possible breach could leave Japanese with the feeling that the clauses were included because a breach was to be expected, and that undermines the feeling of being able to trust one's partner. However, most companies now are used to including boilerplate provisions such as "waiver" and "entire agreement" clauses. Traditionally, such clauses did not appear in agreements in Japan, but after decades of dealings with American companies, many Japanese companies have come to insist on such clauses. There were no recitals in Japanese agreements, but again, after lengthy experience dealing with American companies, many Japanese companies are now familiar with such clauses.

Every Japanese company has one or more registered company seal(s) to be used in the name of its representative(s). When a Japanese company executes an agreement in Japanese, such registered seal is usually affixed thereto, but when an agreement is in English, the agreement is usually signed in English and such seal is not affixed.

5.2 Conditions and Defenses

As the laws of France and Germany were studied intensively in the years following the Meiji Restoration, Japan operates under a similar civil law system. Civil law relies on statutes framed in more general terms, and court decisions are generally persuasive rather than formally binding on other courts, even if the facts of the case are similar. Nevertheless, court decisions made by the Supreme Court are regarded as extremely important and serve as influential precedents to the cases that follow.

Under the Civil Code, contracts do not need to be in writing in order to become effective. However, contracts are usually documented in business transactions, and there are statutes that require documentation for certain types of contracts, such as employment contracts, certain guarantees, and agreements that are required to be attached to registration applications. Some type of contracts, such as (nonrenewable) fixed term land-lease agreements for business purposes, must be notarized, and notarized contracts generally may have special legal effects (e.g., monetary claims under certain notarized contracts can be enforced without obtaining court decisions).

Under the Civil Code, the damages that may be recovered from a party for their nonperformance or tort is basically limited to compensatory damages, with punitive damages not permitted. Therefore, if the parties desire additional recovery options for other types of damages, the parties will need to specifically agree to do so.

There is a comprehensive system of registration concerning real property, in which a record of ownership and certain forms of encumbrances is kept. This comprehensive registration system has created a title-insurance-free environment. In addition, certain receivables and certain personal property are subject to a registration system for the purpose of registering the transfer of ownership or creation of limited type of collaterals, which are important for certain types of financial transactions. Transactions involving such registered rights can be validly effected without registration, but an unregistered transaction is not effective against third parties. Therefore, completion of the registration is necessary after the execution of the agreement in transactions involving such rights. Company registration plays an important role in the business transactions as well, since it records various information and activities of companies and some of the actions are only effective upon registration.

5.3 The Special Case of Online Agreements

Payment on the Internet by using credit cards is common and the aggregate number of cards issued to be used as electronic money (e.g., the smart card Edy) is said to be around 80 million in Japan. To keep pace with the development of e-commerce, many laws have been amended or created to allow the use of electromagnetic data in transactions. In 2001, two such laws were created: the law on the authentication of electromagnetic data and electromagnetic signatures (Act on Electronic Signatures and Certification Business) and the law on electronic consumer contracts (Act on Special Provisions to the Civil Code Concerning Electronic Consumer Contracts and Electronic Acceptance Notice). Since 2004, an agreement to submit a dispute to arbitration that is made by way of electromagnetic record is deemed to be an agreement in writing and is effective under the Arbitration Law. Since 2005, if an agreement with respect to the court having jurisdiction over a dispute is made by way of electromagnetic record, such agreement is also deemed to be an agreement in writing and is effective under the Civil Procedure Law. There is also administrative guidance on e-commerce and data treasure on the Internet (General Standard on Electronic Commerce Transaction and Data Treasure Transaction, etc.), which is updated periodically. These laws and guidance have allowed more parties to utilize electronic agreements than ever before.

6. Resolving Disputes

The desire felt by most Japanese to avoid confrontation affects the choice of a dispute resolution method. Japanese businesses view going to court to resolve a dispute an absolute last resort, because in court blame will be assigned and a "right" and a "wrong" party determined. Thus, within Japanese society, generally speaking, only the most intractable disputes make it to court. The method of dispute resolution ultimately preferred by Japanese companies is for the two sides to sit down, discuss their differences, and work out a compromise. In fact, a clause typical in agreements between Japanese companies is a clause requiring attempts be made to settle any dispute amicably through good-faith discussions before resorting to arbitration or court proceedings. It could be said that the Japanese attitude toward trust, conciliation, and compromise has led to the custom of including such clause in agreements.

The Supreme Court is located in Tokyo, and its territorial jurisdiction covers all of Japan. High Courts, whose cases are appealed directly to the Supreme Court, are located in eight major cities in Japan, namely, Tokyo, Osaka, Nagoya, Hiroshima, Fukuoka, Sendai, Sapporo, and Takamatsu. The Intellectual Property High Court (IP High Court) was established in April 2005 to specialize in trying IP cases in order to expedite and enhance IP-related court proceedings. As a branch of the Tokyo High Court, the IP High Court is responsible for handling IP proceedings, to which the Tokyo High Court has exclusive jurisdiction. Below the High Courts, there is at least one district court in each of the forty-seven prefectures. A district court is the court of general and original jurisdiction, and it handles all cases in the first instance except those specifically coming under the exclusive jurisdiction of other types of court, such as family court and summary court. All documents, data, and proceedings must be in Japanese. Therefore, a translator is assigned to a witness who does not speak Japanese and documents not in Japanese must be submitted to court together with a translation. Also, all proceedings are, in principle, open to the public. Therefore, if a proceeding in English or a private proceeding is desired, a Japanese court is not an option. Certain motions are allowed to be made through electromagnetic methods.

The quality of judges in Japan is very high and consistent. Judges have passed the Japanese Bar Exam and received training at the Supreme Court's Legal Training Institute, and hold sufficient knowledge and experience to ascertain facts, interpret laws, evaluate evidence, and undertake examination procedures. Furthermore, the status of judges in Japan is established under the Constitution and the Court Law so that their judgment cannot be affected by external pressures. In this way, the Japanese court system does prove to be very reliable.

Japanese companies tend to fear being sued in a foreign country because of lack of familiarity with foreign laws and legal customs. Moreover, Japanese are wary of American juries, which they sometimes view as unpredictable or unreasonable. Therefore, for Japanese companies, the last thing they want to have in an international agreement is a provision giving a court in the United States exclusive jurisdiction. Because of these factors, if the American side does not agree to giving exclusive jurisdiction to a Japanese court, Japanese companies often insist upon arbitration to iron out disputes, and they insist that an arbitration clause be included in an international agreement. The desire to avoid confrontation goes even further, however, because Japanese companies often try to ensure that disputes will not even make it to the arbitration stage, since even arbitration suggests that there is a winner and a loser and a "right" and a "wrong" party. They seek to accomplish this through the inclusion of clauses requiring the arbitration to be held in the home country of the respondent, thus making the application for arbitration itself inconvenient. Japanese Arbitration Law, which was completely revised along the lines of the UNCITRAL

Model Law on International Commercial Arbitration, came into force in March 2004. The only permanent commercial arbitral institution in Japan is the Japan Commercial Arbitration Association, but the quality of arbitrators is not necessarily as consistent as that of judges in Japan. The Rules of Arbitration of the International Chamber of Commerce is also a common option for rules for arbitrations held in Japan.

Currently, there are no ODR sites based in Japan, though an experiment called the *Shirogane Cyberpol Online Mediation Project* was carried out voluntarily by a Japanese group in 2003 to experiment with ODR.

7. Conclusion

Many books on the subject of doing business in Japan stress Japan's cultural differences with the West, and that in order to succeed in Japan, one must learn the intricacies of "the Japanese mind." While there is some merit in such talk, in general the difference between Japanese and Western corporate cultures tends to be exaggerated, although certain aspects of culture discussed in this chapter may have a role to play in making negotiations in Japan run a bit more smoothly. Keeping in mind the few exceptions outlined above, such as the general desire to avoid confrontation, Americans should not fundamentally alter their negotiating styles when dealing with the Japanese. Lastly, Americans negotiating in Japan should be aware of or seek advice on the legal issues relating to the negotiation. As you can see from the outline of the substantial laws and regulations in this chapter, the laws of Japan have dramatically changed in recent years. Businesspeople involved in Japanese transactions should continue to keep a close eye on the legal developments to come.

Soichiro Fujiwara and Satoko Kametaka
Nagashima Ohno & Tsunematsu
Kioicho Building 3-12 Kioicho,
Chiyoda-ku, Tokyo 102-0094, Japan
Phone: 81-3-3511-6335
Fax: 81-3-5213-7835
E-mail: satoko_kametaka@noandt.com

CHAPTER 34

International Business Negotiations in Korea

Kyu Wha Lee
LEE & KO
SEOUL, KOREA

1. Introduction

1.1 Broad Demographic Information

The Republic of Korea has a population of approximately 48,500,000 and an area of approximately 99,221 square kilometers and its capital is Seoul. The Korean government is divided into the Legislature, Judiciary, and Executive, and it has a unicameral National Assembly. In addition to the Supreme Court, which is the highest judicial authority in the country, Korea has a Constitutional Court that exclusively handles the interpretation of the Korean Constitution.

1.2 Historical and Cultural Background

Although Korea was originally a unified country with a homogenous race, it was divided into two after the Second World War and has been so ever since. The entire country lay in ruins from the three-year Korean War that started in 1950, but through great effort and sacrifice of the Korean people, the country was able to modernize, industrialize, and democratize. Korea is currently a member of the Organisation for Economic Co-operation and Development (OECD) and strives to be recognized as a strong power both economically and culturally. Against this backdrop, it would be helpful to look at foreign investment in Korea over the past ten years in discussing the issue of international business negotiations involving Korean parties.

Foreign investment was actively sought by the Korean government as a way of overcoming the financial crisis that hit Korea and Asia in general in 1997. Ever since then, foreign investment appears to have become a key aspect of the Korean economy. During the past ten years, a total of US$112.6 billion as foreign capital has come into Korea and there are over 14,000 foreign-invested companies in the country. These companies comprised about 14 percent of total sales by businesses and 8 percent of total employment in 2006.

Taking a close look at the foreign investment trend, there was strong M&A activity following the financial crisis and foreign investment increased significantly until 2001. Thereafter, affected by a worldwide decline in investment, foreign investment decreased to around US$3 billion per year. It seemed to pick up around 2004 when foreign investment increased up to around US$9.3 billion annually with the surge in the global economy and large-scale M&As such as the acquisition of Hanmi Bank by Citi Group. However, foreign investment is reported to have reached a standstill or declined thereafter.

During the administration of President Moo Hyun Roh, continuous and active efforts were undertaken to attract foreign investment, and many programs were implemented, including tax incentives, industrial complexes, and free economic zones. However, high costs such as land price and wages, complex regulations, unstable labor relations, and uncomfortable living conditions for foreigners continue to be recognized as an impediment to foreign investment.

The current administration under President Myung Bak Lee, who came into office in 2008, has strongly promoted several policies to attract foreign investment, emphasizing a business-friendly environment. Specifically, the following items are undergoing review and/ or implementation: simplification of procedures to establish companies and industrial complexes, reduction of business-related taxes such as corporate tax, improvement of the environment for foreign investment and easing of regulations, and control over businesses. In addition, immediately after taking office, President Lee was able to strike an agreement on the U.S.-Korea Free Trade Agreement (FTA) and ratification thereof is pending in both countries. Further, active preparations are being made for the FTA with the EU. Looking at these efforts, it appears that the government is focusing on opening up the market in order to induce economic development and activity. Although it would take some time to fully implement all of the above policies and programs designed to open up the market, stimulate economic development, and create a foreign-investment-friendly environment, these, coupled with the recent U.S.-Korea FTA and progress in the six-way talks for North Korea's denuclearization, are expected to have a positive impact on investment in Korea.

1.3 Business Organization and Culture

There are four types of corporate entities recognized under Korean law, namely unlimited liability partnership (*hapmyung hoesa*), limited liability partnership (*hapja hoesa*), limited liability corporation (*yuhan hoesa*), and joint stock corporation (*chusik hoesa*). A partnership (*hapmyung hoesa* or *hapja hoesa*) is different from a corporation (*yuhan hoesa* or *chusik hoesa*) in that in the former, there are members who assume unlimited responsibility with respect to the liabilities of the company, whereas in the latter, the members' liabilities are limited to the extent of their investment. A *yuhan hoesa* and a *chusik hoesa* are very similar in substance, but the favored form of corporate entity in Korea is the *chusik hoesa*, which has certain advantages, including easier transfer of equity. Thus, the term "company" as used hereinafter means a *chusik hoesa*, whether or not it is a listed company.

While there are ongoing and fast-moving changes, the corporate structure in most Korean companies, as in the Korean government, is still highly centralized and concentrated at the top. Therefore, even if one is dealing with the head of a particular business department within a corporation, or another senior-level manager, one should not necessarily expect to finalize and complete the agreement with that person; final approval may come from a higher source. Unlike the normal western business practice in which the chief executive gives considerable weight to staff advice when making decisions, the Korean chief executive may be much more autocratic and less open to subordinates' opinions. It is not uncommon for a Korean superior to unexpectedly reject a reasonable term of contract seemingly agreed to by Korean working-level negotiators. This can be a frustrating and confusing experience for the foreign counterpart.

1.4 Overview of Legal System

The Korean legal system is based on the civil and commercial codes of France and Germany imposed on Korea during the Japanese occupation from 1910 to 1945. Korea's comprehensive modern Civil Code, which entered into force on January 1, 1960, is regarded as the primary law of the land and, like all civil law codes, consists mainly of general principles of law.

As in most civil law countries, Korean law distinguishes between civil law and commercial law, and the Commercial Code, a special law applicable only to commercial matters, entered into force on January 1, 1963. Korean ministries may publish working rules for the interpretation of laws relevant to their areas of delegated authority, and also may establish informal (and at times unwritten) policies relating to business activities in Korea. Furthermore, many so-called modern laws relating to regulation of economic activity in areas such as banking, tax, and securities were initially copied hastily from the relevant laws of various countries, especially the United States. Implementing and interpreting these laws without the benefit of an orderly historical transaction have presented many uncertainties and problems. However, with the passage of years, as relevant regulations and rules are being adopted and amended, these laws are beginning to take orderly shape to function as an effective administrative body of laws.

In contrast to the United States, Korean lawyers historically have not played a major role in Korean business. Korean lawyers, unless they have studied abroad or are working for one of the larger law firms in Korea, are not trained in the Socratic method of problem analysis and are not inclined to become involved in detailed negotiations. They are not used to soliciting detailed facts from the client and tend to rely only on facts that the client has chosen to reveal. However, there are a growing number of Korean lawyers who have received additional legal education and experience in the United States and in European countries. Increasingly, these lawyers are playing vital roles in bridging the legal and cultural gap between the Korean parties and their foreign counterparts. Therefore, obtaining competent legal advice from Korean lawyers who have the relevant education and experience is absolutely essential to conducting successful business negotiations in Korea.

2. Substantive Laws and Regulations Impacting Negotiations

2.1 Corporate Laws

The main statute that sets forth the fundamental guiding principles for governance of a company is the Commercial Code. The Korean National Assembly is currently reviewing a comprehensive revision bill for the Commercial Code, providing for, for example, new types of corporate entities other than those discussed in 1.3 and diversification of the types of securities to facilitate procurement of funding. The Articles of Incorporation (AOI) of a company set forth more specific principles for corporate governance and operation. Specifically, the AOI provide for the name, objectives, total number of issued shares, location of the head office, and other basic matters about the company, as well as matters regarding the operation of the company including the number of directors, matters for resolution by the shareholders' meeting, and matters relating to new shares and dividends.

2.2 Securities Laws

The Securities and Exchange Act (SEA) provides for various rules governing listed companies, including public disclosure, insider trading, prohibition of unfair trade practices such as market price manipulation, audit committees and outside directors, and rights of minority shareholders. The purpose of these rules, administered by the Ministry of Strategy and Finance (MOSF), the Financial Supervisory Service and the Korea Exchange, is to ensure transparency in listed companies and healthy operation of the securities markets. The SEA is scheduled to be replaced by the Capital Markets and Financial Investment Business Act as of February 4, 2009 (see section 3 below).

Subordinate statutes under the SEA include the Rules on Issuance of Securities and Disclosure, promulgated by the Financial Supervisory Service, and the Securities Market Listing Rules, KOSDAQ Market Registration Rules, Securities Market Disclosure Rules, and KOSDAQ Market Disclosure Rules, which are promulgated by the Korea Exchange.

2.3 Tax Laws

If a foreigner is deemed to have earned Korean-source income, that income will be subject to Korean corporation tax or personal income tax under the Korean tax laws unless a tax treaty between Korea and the foreigner's home country prescribes otherwise. Korean-source income is defined by the Corporation Tax Act and the Personal Income Tax Act. Further, Korean-source income is deemed to be earned if the foreigner has income belonging to its fixed place of business in Korea—that is, a permanent establishment such as a branch office or business office. Further, an entity that pays Korean-source income to the foreigner should withhold a certain portion for payment of tax to the Korean tax authorities on behalf of the foreigner pursuant to the Corporation Tax Act or Personal Income Tax Act. Common examples of income subject to withholding are royalty income payable to the foreign licensor and dividend income payable to the foreign shareholder of a Korean company.

2.4 Antitrust/Anticompetition Laws

The Monopoly Regulations and Fair Trade Act (MRFTA) is the major legislation in Korea that controls unfair and monopolistic practices in domestic and international transactions. In general, the MRFTA provides that any person or entity meeting certain requirements must file a report with the Korean Fair Trade Commission for clearance when engaging in any business combination. A business combination, among other things, includes the establishment of a company, acquisition of a substantial percentage of equity interest in a company, and purchase of substantial assets in a company. In addition, the MRFTA regulates other unfair business practices. In an international business agreement context, an international agreement that includes unfair trade provisions, resale price-fixing provisions, and so forth is prohibited. Violation of the MRFTA may be subject to a correction order, the imposition of a monetary penalty, criminal prosecution, and compensation of damages to the person injured by the violation.

2.5 Labor and Employment Laws

In Korea, the Labor Standards Act (LSA) stipulates in detail the minimum standards applicable to employment relationships. Most of the

provisions of the LSA are compulsory, and therefore any private regulations, rules, or practices that violate provisions of the LSA are unenforceable or invalid. As a result, the employers in Korea have less flexibility in terms of employment relationships.

Korean laws stipulate the following mandatory employee insurance programs: (i) National Pension Fund; (ii) National Health Insurance; (iii) Long-term Care Insurance for the Elderly; (iv) Workers
Industrial Injury Compensation Insurance Program; (v) Employment
Insurance; and (vi) Wage Payment Guarantee Fund.

2.6 Environmental Laws

After the 1990s, the Korean government categorized environmental
laws by air, water, and soil environment and has enacted more than
forty laws in relation thereto. Enforcement of these laws has been
strictly performed to combat increased environmental pollution following rapid industrialization, and also as a result of citizens' increased
awareness of their improved quality of life.

Key environmental laws are as follows (by category):

The **Water Quality and Environment Conservation Act** requires
that permits and/or approvals be obtained from the competent
authorities before installing wastewater-discharging facilities and
also that only qualified personnel manage such facilities. In addition, this Act sets permissible discharge standards and imposes
charges on companies failing to observe such standards.

The **Atmospheric Environment Conservation Act** has provisions similar to the Water Quality and Environment Conservation Act, and in addition contains regulations on automobile
emissions.

The **Soil Environment Conservation Act** states that, where soil
contamination has occurred, the party that owns, possesses, or
manages the responsible facility must provide indemnity for the
damages caused and purify the soil even if such party is not at
fault.

If any foreigner intends to export any chemical substances
to Korea or any foreign-invested company intends to import such
substances into Korea for its business operations, it should first
check to see if importation of the substance is permitted and
whether there are procedures that must be followed for obtaining governmental approval of the importation of the substance.
In general, every chemical substance should, before its manufacture in Korea or importation to Korea, be reported to the
Ministry of Environment (MOE) unless the substance is on the
list of previously approved chemical substances compiled by
the MOE. Furthermore, a manufacturer or importer of poison-

ous substances designated by the Noxious Chemical Substance Control Act must register those substances with the MOE.

2.7 Intellectual Property Laws

The Korean legal system protects patents, utility models, designs, trademarks, copyrights, computer programs, databases, layout-designs of semiconductor integrated circuits, and domain names. Also, trade secrets and well-known marks are given certain protection under Korean intellectual property laws.

In Korea, an invention, utility model, design, trademark, or layout-design of semiconductor integrated circuits is granted legal protection upon registration with the Korea Intellectual Property Office. The intellectual property laws of Korea do not recognize legal rights with respect to an unregistered invention, utility model, design, trademark, or layout-design of semiconductor integrated circuits. Korea is a member of the Patent Cooperation Treaty (PCT).

By contrast, a copyright need not be registered or be fixed in a tangible medium to be protected. However, the transfer of a copyright is not protected against third-party claims unless such transfer is registered. Korea is a signatory to the Berne Convention for the Protection of Literary and Artistic Works and copyrights of foreigners are also protected if certain requirements are met.

An invention that is made by an employee during the term of employment and that results from the employee's activities in the business is called a "service invention." When a registration for a service invention is made in the name of an employee, the employer has a non-exclusive license to use the registered invention. There are instances where a service invention is registered under the name of the employer and not the employee, and in such cases the employer must lawfully acquire the rights thereto from the employee in order for the registration to be valid. The employer may, without registering under its own name, obtain an exclusive right to use the registered invention, in which case the employee inventor is entitled to receive reasonable remuneration for the invention.

The Unfair Competition Prevention and Trade Secret Protection Act protects "trade secrets." In order to be protected under the Act, the trade secret (i) must not be known to the public, (ii) must have an independent economic value, and (iii) must be maintained in secrecy.

The Unfair Competition Prevention and Trade Secret Protection Act also provides legal protection for well-known marks without registration. An act of causing confusion with another person's goods or business activities by using an indication identical or similar to a well-known mark is considered an "act of unfair competition" under this Act. In addition to a well-known mark, a trade dress or domain name is protected under this Act if certain conditions are met.

2.8 Privacy and Data Security Laws

Korea does not have a general law governing personal information (legislative efforts are under way at the National Assembly). The following laws perform the function of protecting personal information:

- **Act on Promotion of Information and Communications Network Utilization and Information Protection, etc.:** Where personal information that can identify a person (such as name or resident registration number) is collected or provided to a third party after such collection via an "information network" (although technically not synonymous with the Internet, it can be used as such), this Act requires the consent of the individual to whom the personal information belongs.
- **Use and Protection of Credit Information Act:** This Act is applicable to information that can identify an individual or to information that is needed to determine a person's credit rating (such as information on financial transactions). Where credit information is collected or provided to a third party after such collection, this Act requires the consent of the individual to whom the credit information belongs.
- **Protection of Communications Secrets Act:** This Act strictly protects mail and electronic communications from peeping, eavesdropping, or recording unless authorized by a court-issued warrant or under other narrowly prescribed circumstances.

2.9 Regulation of Foreign Investment

The Korean government has adopted various policies to promote foreign investment. The relevant statutory framework is found mainly under the Foreign Investment Promotion Act (FIPA), and an investment recognized as a foreign investment under this statute is, subject to certain conditions, entitled to favorable tax treatment including reductions in or exemptions from corporate tax, registration tax, property tax, etc. In addition, such foreign investment is subject to simplified procedures for remittance of the investment funds from abroad as well as repatriation of the investment profits and capital.

Investments that are subject to the FIPA are: (i) investment of 50 million won (KRW) or more in 10 percent or more of the total voting shares of a Korean company; and (ii) a long-term loan with maturity of five years or more provided by a foreign shareholder of a foreign-invested company (i.e., a Korean company in which foreigners hold at least a certain percentage of shares).

While foreign investment in most industries is liberalized, there are certain industries in which foreign investment is limited to a certain ratio or is entirely prohibited. Examples of such industries are the newspaper publishing industry, the electric power generation industry, the wire and wireless communication industry, the broadcasting industry, and the cable television industry.

The FIPA is undergoing amendments to promote foreign investment by easing regulatory requirements and providing a variety of incentives. For example, since 2004, a cash-support program has been implemented to aid foreign investors. Recently, a new amendment was added to allow foreign investment in nonprofit research corporations.

2.10 Other Potentially Applicable Laws and Regulations

Foreign exchange in Korea is controlled by the Foreign Exchange Transactions Act (FETA), its Enforcement Decree, and subordinate regulations promulgated thereunder. The provisions of these statutes are very complex and quite often amended, thus all relevant provisions of these statutes should be reviewed with caution in relation to any foreign exchange issue.

In general, there has been a gradual decrease in the Korean government's control of foreign exchange transactions; in particular, payment and receipt of foreign currency in connection with corporate current (noncapital) transactions have been liberalized to a large extent. Recently, the law has been amended to enlarge the scope of sources used for overseas direct investment, increase the cap on the acquisition of foreign real properties purchased for investment purposes, and simplify filing procedures for overseas direct investment, all of which are aimed at encouraging overseas investment by Korean nationals.

Under the FETA, many cases of capital transactions including loan agreements, guarantee agreements, securities transactions, and financial derivatives transactions must either be reported to a government-authorized entity (usually a licensed foreign exchange bank) or approved prior to their execution, unless they are specifically exempted. Depending on the particular transaction, authority to issue such approval or acceptance of a report is vested with the Ministry of Strategy and Finance, the Bank of Korea, or a foreign-exchange bank. Which of these would be the relevant authority depends on the substance of the transaction, and careful prior review and planning are necessary. In general, however, there is a trend for gradual deregulation in capital transactions as well.

3. Other Significant Legal and Business Issues

In order to promote the growth of large-scale investment banks and stimulate capital markets, the Korean government consolidated the laws on capital markets, including the SEA, and enacted the Capital Markets and Financial Investment Business Act ("New Act") on August 3, 2007. The New Act will become effective on February 4, 2009. Its key components are as follows:

- **Regulatory scheme based on function:** Current laws on the financial sector regulate on the basis of each type of financial institution (e.g., securities firm, futures firm). By contrast, the New Act will implement a regulatory scheme based on the actual financial function of an entity. Thus, entities in different financial sectors will be regulated by the same laws (as to market entry, financial soundness, business activities) if they serve the same financial purpose.
- **Comprehensive definition of "financial investment products":** Currently, the SEA limits the types of securities that a financial institution can handle to twenty-one, which include treasury bonds, corporate bonds, stock, and beneficiary certificates. In regards to derivatives, the SEA limits the reference assets to securities, currency, commodities, and credit risk. The New Act defines a "financial investment product" as a financial product subject to risk of loss of the principal and also enlarges the scope of reference assets for derivatives from the traditionally risk-carrying products to encompass all economic, natural, and environmental risks.
- **Expansion of business scope of financial investment companies:** Current laws strictly forbid one type of financial institution to engage in the business of another type of financial institution (e.g., a securities firm handling futures; an asset management company handling the business of an investment trust company). The New Act allows entities in six business sectors to engage in each other's businesses, including investment sales, investment brokerage, and group investments.
- **Strengthened investor protection:** The New Act increases investor protection by expanding the requirement to explain financial products (a feature currently found in several other laws) to all financial investment companies, imposing on a financial institution the duty to find out about an investor's characteristics. In particular, for the purpose of protecting ordinary investors who lack the ability to fully absorb the risks that an investment entails, a financial institution must find out about the investment purpose, financial condition, and investment experience of an investor before soliciting investment. The financial institution is to recommend investment that fits the characteristics of the investor, based on such findings.

4. Negotiation Practices

4.1 Participants

It is difficult to generalize, since the participants may vary depending on the type of deal and the parties involved. Gender, age, class, race,

and/or ethnicity do not play a role in determining who will be a negotiation participant. However, it is the case that there are more men
than women negotiators, and when compared to western countries,
negotiation and decision-making are often performed by high-level
personnel.

In the past, the Korean government played a pervasive role in
national economic development and often played the role of a de facto
third party in international transactions. Much has changed in the last
decade and new laws seeking to liberalize and deregulate existing laws
have been promulgated. In particular, current president Myung Bak
Lee, who at one stage in his career was the CEO of Hyundai Engineering & Construction Co., Ltd., is emphasizing self-regulated economic
activity in the private sector, and it appears that this trend will continue to gain momentum.

4.2 Timing

There are no particular recommendations or cautions as to timing.
However, it is generally the case that negotiations slow down during
the Lunar New Year holidays (usually at the end of January or early
February) and Chusuk (harvest moon holidays) and in July and August
when most workers take their summer leaves.

4.3 Negotiation Practices

English is the language most often used by Koreans when negotiating international business transactions. However, when negotiating
with Koreans, it is helpful to remember that English is, in fact, a very
difficult foreign language for Koreans to master. Although Koreans have been taught English as a second language from secondary school, much of that academic focus is on reading and writing
rather than on conversation. In recent years, educators have placed
greater emphasis on teaching conversational English and, as a result,
younger Koreans have become more fluent. It is unlikely, however,
that younger Koreans will be in a position to negotiate matters on
behalf of Korean companies in international business transactions
in the near future. Older Koreans who appear at the negotiating
table may display a remarkable ability to read and write English
but have difficulty conveying their, or understanding other's, intentions in oral discussions. Therefore, when negotiating with Koreans
regarding the details of a contract, foreigners should check whether
each point is fully understood by Korean negotiators. Otherwise, it
may become apparent only when it is too late that the Korean party
agreed to certain terms and conditions without fully understanding
them. Koreans often feel pressured to conclude English-language
agreements even without fully understanding how the agreement

works in order to save face in front of superiors or their foreign counterparts. As a rule of thumb, unless there are compelling reasons to
the contrary, important points of information or discussion should
always be recorded in writing in order to minimize the possibility of
misunderstanding.

4.4 Cultural, Ethical, and Religious Considerations

Compared to Americans, Koreans have rather different attitudes and
views toward business negotiations. Having at least a basic understanding of the Korean culture, which has its roots in the Confucian system
of values, can help foreigners conduct successful business negotiations
with Koreans.

Perhaps the most significant difference between American and
Korean businesspeople is their attitudes toward direct personal confrontation. Americans tend to be direct and to the point, unless there
are tactical reasons for being vague or indirect. Koreans, on the other
hand, disfavor the use of direct and pointed speech. This is true even
when they are speaking a foreign language, such as English, and such
behavior sometimes arouses the suspicion of their American counterparts. It may be comforting to note, however, that a Korean's subtle
and indirect speech may be nothing more than a manifestation of the
Korean penchant for avoiding personal confrontation.

Koreans favor vague and indirect statements because they believe
there is less risk of being contradicted or criticized. Koreans "lose face"
if they are directly contradicted or criticized; so they instinctively avoid
any actions or speech that might trigger such contradiction or criticism. Thus, Koreans generally do not consider a vague or evasive statement or writing inferior to that of a clear, direct statement or writing.
Besides the aversion to losing face, Koreans have a corresponding aversion to causing another to lose face. In short, Koreans hesitate to point
out the wrongs of others, and, if they must do so, it is usually done in
as indirect and subtle a manner as possible.

The Korean concept of face may also be expressed as concern and
respect for the sensitivities and social standing of colleagues, and this
concern and respect is expected to be reciprocated. Since Koreans
generally value "good vibes," it is especially important to Koreans that
business affairs be pleasant as well as profitable. As they seek harmony
and good relations with business colleagues, Koreans are often less
desirous of, or less concerned about, signing a detailed agreement that
anticipates all possible contingencies. Instead, Koreans prefer an ongoing business arrangement in which problems are faced and resolved
only if and when they arise. They believe that if problems do not arise,
then the time and effort expended in planning how to handle such
contingencies would have been wasted.

4.5 Negotiating Online

International business negotiations are becoming more efficient and fast-paced because of the common usage of electronic communications. As explained above, Koreans are quite familiar with reading and writing English, which enables them to communicate more accurately through e-mails. Further, e-mails are instantly delivered, making negotiations proceed much more rapidly. However, there are many instances where face-to-face conversations are necessary to understand more accurately the position of the parties, and consequently conference calls, video conferences, or personal visits are still very much in use. It appears that this trend will continue and online negotiations will be used only to a limited extent.

5. Contract Formation

5.1 Wording and Style

There is strong preference in Korea for simple agreements that leave potential problems to be resolved by negotiation as they arise. Koreans prefer this approach because they believe it is impossible to accurately predict how the respective positions of the parties will change over time. A Korean might perceive attempts to anticipate every possible outcome as a lack of mutual trust. Therefore, Koreans typically believe that a detailed contract fixing every detail will hinder a fluid relationship. However, Korean negotiators have become quite familiar with the U.S. style of comprehensive and long-winded contracts and also have come to recognize the need for such contracts. Therefore, it would be reasonable to say that over the past decade the traditional approach explained above has become less rigid in the context of international transactions.

5.2 Conditions and Defenses

Parties to a contract may freely agree upon the terms of the contract, to the extent that such terms are not contrary to compulsory provisions of statutes or public policy. A contract entered into by fraud, duress, or mistake may be rescinded, and a contract entered into by abuse of the other party's strained circumstances, rashness, or inexperience may be invalidated. Many of the compulsory provisions are found in statutes that seek to protect contractual parties in a particular position, such as the Labor Standards Act and the Act on Restriction of Form Contracts, and such compulsory provisions are on the increase.

Remedies for breach of contract may be categorized largely into those recognized by law and those agreed upon by the parties. The parties to a contract may freely agree upon the remedies for breach of the contract to the extent that such remedies do not violate any compulsory provision of statutes or public policy. Parties are also free to agree upon the damage amount to be paid by the breaching party in case of breach, provided that the court may reduce the amount to a reasonable level if it finds the amount to be excessive. The remedies recognized by law are specific performance, rescission, and claim for damage. The right of rescission is recognized where the purpose of the contract cannot be achieved due to a breach. Unlike U.S. law, punitive damages are not recognized under Korean law.

5.3 The Special Case of Online Agreements

E-commerce is very active in Korea, with online shopping being the driving force. Companies are also availing themselves of e-commerce, an example being purchase of raw materials online. General laws applicable to such online agreements are the Framework Act on Electronic Commerce and the Digital Signature Act.

The Framework Act on Electronic Commerce states that the validity of an electronic document is not negated for the reason that it is in electronic form unless provided for otherwise by law, and the Digital Signature Act states that where a law requires that a document be signed, signed and stamped with a seal, or affixed with a name and seal, if an electronic document is affixed with a certified electronic signature, then the above legal requirement is deemed to have been satisfied. Thus, a certified electronic signature under the Digital Signature Act has the same effect and validity as a personally affixed signature or seal.

The following technical conditions must be satisfied for an online agreement to be valid: (i) establish "authenticity," i.e., verify who agreed to the terms of the agreement; (ii) establish "integrity," i.e., verify whether the agreement as prepared and sent was received or is being kept in the same state; and (iii) establish "non-repudiation," i.e., bind the sender to the terms of the agreement once they are expressed by the sender. The Digital Signature Act satisfies the above by having people use a certified electronic signature that is based on a certificate issued by a government-designated certifying agency.

6. Resolving Disputes

Based on experience, it would be reasonable to state that the objectivity, efficiency, and trustworthiness of the Korean courts are of a very high level. This is why courts are favored over arbitration in Korea for the resolution of disputes. However, since it is often the case in international business that the foreign party refuses to adjudicate disputes in the Korean courts, arbitration is chosen as the dispute resolution method and Korean negotiators are not particularly against it.

Under the Arbitration Act of Korea, parties may elect to submit their disputes to a foreign arbitral tribunal for arbitration under foreign arbitration rules and in a foreign language. Korea became a signatory to the New York Convention on the Recognition and Enforcement of Foreign Arbitral Awards on February 8, 1973, but in acceding to the Convention, Korea declared reservations of reciprocity and application only as to arbitrations of commercial disputes. In general, Korean courts take a positive approach toward enforcement of arbitral awards, and have seldom refused to recognize and enforce a foreign arbitral award on grounds of, for example, lack of basis for arbitration or violation of public policy.

7. Conclusion

After the 1960s, Korea started its modernization and industrialization under the government's lead and has seen rapid growth. However, after experiencing the financial crisis of the late 1990s, the government-led economic structure started to shift to an economy led by the private sector. Corporate governance in terms of sensibleness and transparency are improving at a swift pace. In addition, after the financial crisis, foreign investment (particularly U.S. investment) has increased significantly and U.S.-style M&A negotiation and business tactics have been introduced in Korea and are taking root. Since Korea must focus on international businesses as its economy is export-driven, Korean companies are making a great deal of effort to meet global standards as to their products and services, not to mention business culture or ways of doing business. Therefore, it should not be the case that foreigners will find any great difficulty in terms of conducting international business negotiations in Korea as compared to other countries.

Nonetheless, there are characteristics that surface in negotiations due to the special history of Korea and its culture, namely the culture of saving face stemming from Confucian traditions and the high level of government intervention arising from its traditionally heavy role in economic development. However, Korea is undergoing increasingly rapid change and the direction taken is away from the culture of saving face and towards practicality, and away from heavy-handed government intervention and towards self-regulation by the private sector. In addition, due to the Korean parents' unparalleled dedication and zeal regarding their children's education, an increasing number of Korean students are being given the opportunity to receive a foreign education in the United States or Europe, the result of which is a dramatic increase in the number of Koreans who are fluent in foreign languages (including English) and also very much at ease in, and familiar with, foreign cultures. It will be very interesting to see what results these changes, coupled with the current administration's business-friendly policies, will bring about.

Kyu Wha Lee
LEE & KO
18th Fl.,
Hanjin Main Bldg., 118,
Namdaemunro 2-ga, Jung-gu
Seoul, 100-770, Korea
Phone: (82-2)772-4000/4321
Fax: (82-2)772-4001
E-mail: kwl@leeko.com

CHAPTER 35

International Business Negotiations in Mexico

Samuel García-Cuéllar

CREEL, GARCÍA-CUÉLLAR, AIZA Y ENRÍQUEZ, S.C.
MEXICO CITY, MEXICO

1. Introduction

Mexico has a long and very rich history. The Olmecs, one of several original civilizations in the world, was established in Mexico around 1200 B.C. The Aztecs were the last group to migrate to the Valley of Anahuac, where Tenochtitlán was built and where Mexico City is located. In 1519, Cortés, the Spanish conqueror, reached Tenochtitlán, starting the conquest that lasted 300 years.

The Spaniards brought with them their Spanish language and Catholicism and obtained great economic contributions from Mexico. Despite the Spanish domination, Mexico maintained its identity with its ancient roots, in part, because the Spaniards lived with natives, giving birth to the "mestizos" (of mixed blood). Miguel Hidalgo, a priest, initiated the armed phase of Mexico's independence on September 15, 1810. Independence was completed in 1821 and in 1824 the first constitution of Mexico, as an independent country, was approved. A new constitution that established the freedom of birth, education, work, speech, and association was promulgated in 1857, under the republican President Benito Juarez. In 1880, Porfirio Díaz became the President and served as such for thirty years. During this period, infrastructure and industry expanded with investments from foreign companies. Such economic growth created elites and the difference between the rich and the poor became vast, which in turn led, in 1910, to a civil war known as the Mexican Revolution.

A new constitution was promulgated in 1917. This constitution, still in force today, incorporated the most advanced labor legislation of its time and also modified the concept of private property by dividing such holdings between the surface right and the nonsalable ground rights. During the next twenty years, two Presidents, Plutarco Elías Calles and Lázaro Cárdenas, played a fundamental role in Mexican history. Elías Calles abolished the influence of the Catholic Church in the political system and created one of the most important political parties, the Institutional Revolutionary Party (*Partido Revolucionario Institucional*) (PRI). Cárdenas promoted a deep reform in the economical system, performed an agrarian reform, and, in 1938, nationalized the oil industry. After World War II the Mexican economy grew: the infrastructure and industry of the country developed, and the agricultural production expanded. The population continued to grow; massive immigration from the countryside to the cities resulted in an increase in unemployment, the external debt increased, and inflation was out of control. During the most recent decades, Mexico has maintained a stable growth.

2. Population

As of 2005, Mexico had a total population of over 103 million inhabitants. From 2000 to 2005 alone, the population increased by 5.8 million. Of the total population, 51.3 percent are women and 48.7 percent, are men. Approximately 30 percent live in cities. Mexico City and its metropolitan areas have approximately 19.2 million inhabitants. The average age of the total population is 24 years. Life expectancy in Mexico is 75.4 years. By the end of 2008, total population was estimated at over 109.9 million inhabitants. Approximately 44 million are employed and approximately 1.6 million are unemployed with no source of income.

About 90 percent of the Mexican population is mestizo. The balance belongs to the original tribes that lived in the country before the Spanish conquest. A small sector of the population immigrated from the United States and others from Spain, Germany, and France. Recently, Mexico has welcomed immigrants from Latin American countries. Approximately 94.2 percent of the population of between five and fourteen years of age go to school. Of fifteen- to nineteen-year-olds, 52.9 percent attend school. Only 3.4 percent of the population does not know how to read or write.

During the last twenty years, a new generation of highly trained students has completed superior studies and obtained professional degrees. Approximately 14.5 percent of the total population has a professional, or an equivalent, degree. The new generations of professionals and businesspeople are very sophisticated; many have postgraduate training in U.S. and European universities. Many of them are fluent in English and are familiar with negotiation and business dealings in English. In contrast, older businesspeople have limited knowledge of English and are not used to complex negotiations in English. These groups typically own family businesses. In such cases, younger members of the family participate in negotiations and serve as communication channel with the older generation.

3. Political System

The official name of Mexico is the United Mexican States (*Estados Unidos Mexicanos*). There are thirty-one states and a federal district, where Mexico City is located.

The Constitution of 1917 defines today's political structure as a federal republic with a democratic political system, with separation of power between the executive, legislative, and judicial branches.

The executive branch is headed by a popularly elected president who serves a single six-year term. Under the Constitution, reelection is prohibited. For more than seventy years, Mexico has enjoyed a regularly scheduled, peaceful transition of power from one elected president to the next.

The federal legislative branch has two chambers. The Senate has 128 members who serve six-year terms and the Chamber of Deputies has 500 members who serve three-year terms. Senators and Deputies may be reelected to serve for nonconsecutive periods. Each state has its own Chamber of Deputies and is governed by a governor elected also for a six-year period.

The judiciary is the third branch, composed of federal and local courts. Mexico does not have a jury system. The highest federal judicial authority is the Supreme Court. The Supreme Court has the authority to declare laws unconstitutional. Individuals and companies may file a proceeding (the *amparo*) to obtain the protection of the federal courts against acts of government that may be against the Constitution.

There are three major political parties in Mexico: the PRI, the National Action Party (*Partido Acción Nacional*) (PAN), and the Party of the Democratic Revolution (*Partido de la Revolución Democrática*) (PRD). There are also eight more minor political parties with representation in the Congress.

The PRI was created in 1924 and its candidates governed Mexico for seventy years. In recent years, many governors, municipal presidents, and congresspersons from the opposition parties have been elected by popular vote.

The PAN was created in 1939 with the support of the private sector. The first opposition governor in Mexico, in 1989, was a member of the PAN. In 2000, Vicente Fox, the PAN candidate, became the first president who was not appointed by the PRI.

The PRD is a left-wing party created in 1989 by several members of the PRI together with members of other small social political parties.

4. The Economy

During the 1970s, Mexico adopted an import substitution strategy as the country's development model. Mexican producers became dependent on import barriers, subsidies, and special incentives.

During the Echeverría administration (1970–1976), a law on foreign investment was approved. Under such legislation, foreign investment was not permitted in most of the country's business activities. Nationalization has been a driving force in Mexican politics, as is evidenced in the restrictive 1973 Foreign Investment Law. In certain important sectors of the economy only state-owned enterprises could participate, such as oil, gas, and energy.

In 1976, capital flight from the country began to accelerate, creating pressure on the country's foreign exchange reserves that resulted in a 68 percent devaluation and the imposition of import controls.

The beginning of the López Portillo administration (1976–1982) was faced with a difficult economic situation, which was relieved during Mexico's oil boom that began in 1978. Public sector spending increased dramatically and Mexico increased its international borrowing. In February 1982, a major devaluation occurred. Inflation continued to accelerate, reaching almost 100 percent in 1982, when Mexico informed the international financial community that it would not be able to pay its debt. Exchange controls were imposed and López Portillo decided to nationalize the banks in September 1982. Such exchange controls were finally eliminated in November 1991.

The De la Madrid administration (1982–1988) had to stabilize the economy. In 1986, the government decided to open the economy. In this year, Mexico became the ninety-second member of the General Agreement on Tariffs and Trade (GATT). Mexico eliminated subsidies on exports and initiated efforts to privatize more state-owned companies. Between 1982 and 1989, more than 800 government-owned enterprises were sold or liquidated. The two major Mexican airlines and the telephone company (Telmex) were privatized. De la Madrid took the initial steps to sell stock of the commercial banks to the private sector.

Carlos Salinas de Gortari (1988–1994) took office on December 1, 1988. The government priorities were to renegotiate debt, to continue to control inflation, and to increase tax revenues. Salinas completed the privatization of the banking system.

Without any question, the turning point was the execution of the North America Free Trade Agreement (NAFTA) with the United States and Canada, in 1994. This was the beginning of a process to transform Mexico into a player in the world economy.

Mexico has signed many other Free Trade Agreements, including one with the European Union and one with Japan. Immediately after 1994, Mexico became a member of the Organization for Economic Cooperation and Development.

When Vicente Fox (2000–2006) became the first president who did not belong to the PRI, Mexicans had huge expectations of change. Vicente Fox did not have majority control of Congress. The two largest opposition parties blocked practically all bills introduced by Fox.

During the six-year term of the Fox administration, none of the important bills to approve structural changes were approved. Mexico, however, continued to grow at a very slow pace. The macro economy was very stable, low interest rates were instrumental to the growth of the housing sector, low inflation improved the standard of living for an important part of the population, and the middle class grew.

The 2006 elections were highly contested. The candidate from the PRD, Andrés Manuel López Obrador, formerly the major of Mexico City, who has similarities with other populist leaders in Latin America such as Hugo Chávez and Evo Morales, had during a long period a big advantage over all the other candidates. He attacked the private sector and threatened to nationalize industries. The PAN's contender, Felipe Calderón, in a very limited period of time, was able to change the course of the elections. Elections took place in June 2006 and Felipe Calderón won by a margin of 243,934 votes, .58 percent of the 41,791,322 total votes cast. López Obrador tried, with no success, to challenge the election. The electoral system in Mexico was tested and the outcome was very good—Mexico demonstrated that it had solid institutions that warranted democratic elections. Even today, López Obrador does not accept his defeat and calls himself the "legitimate President of Mexico."

Felipe Calderón (2006–2012), during his first two years in office, was able to pass through Congress two very important bills. One of the bills introduced was to change the pension system of the bureaucrats, which was urgently needed to save a system that is practically insolvent. The second bill, to create a new "flat tax" and to increase tax revenues, was necessary to address the critical need of governmental funds to increase infrastructure and social programs. The most recent bill submitted to Congress proposes to change the energy sector and to provide flexibility to Pemex, the government-owned oil company that monopolizes the oil industry in Mexico. This bill, which has been approved, faced very strong opposition from the PRD and other political parties. The ownership of the oil industry by Mexicans continues to be a driving force in Mexican politics. Changes to the oil industry's framework are much needed, as Pemex has limited reserves and requires substantial investments. The expectation is that many other structural changes will be presented to Congress during the Calderón administration.

Felipe Calderón is a strong president who has the ability to negotiate and pass urgently needed amendments to the existing legislation.

The following years will be particularly difficult for Mexico because of the problems in the U.S. economy. Mexico will, no doubt, suffer as a result of the U.S. recession. After NAFTA, the Mexican economy depends substantially on the U.S. economy. Mexico is the United States' second largest trading partner, after Canada. Additionally, at a slow pace, during the last ten years Mexico has diversified its exports and has created a strong local market.

5. Mexican Legal Framework

5.1 Substantive Laws and Regulations

Federal law is the principal legal framework in international negotiations in Mexico, to acquire companies or to form joint ventures.

Notwithstanding, each state has its local body of law, similar to the corresponding federal legislation. Under the Federal Constitution, the states have authority to approve local civil and criminal codes. The states also have jurisdiction to approve state and municipal taxes.

Mexican legislation is codified and legal precedents have little or no impact on court decisions, except where the Supreme Court or Circuit Courts have issued five successive rulings on the same point of law.

During the last years and as a consequence of NAFTA, Mexico revised most of its federal legislation. New laws on antitrust, intellectual property, the securities market, and the environment have been approved. Most of the new legislation was inspired by laws in force in the United States and Europe.

5.2 The Foreign Investment Law

The Foreign Investment Law was issued in 1993, with the objective of opening many economic sectors to foreign investment and to establish a very transparent legal framework. Mexico has been a very attractive market for foreign investors during the last fifteen years. New regulations to the Foreign Investment Law were issued in 1998.

Since 1993, in addition to the free trade agreements, Mexico has executed international treaties to promote and protect international investments, with several countries around the world, including Austria, Germany, France, and Denmark. Under such treaties, any dispute is to be submitted to arbitration.

The Foreign Investment Law has specific rules for the acquisition of real estate properties in the country. Property on the borders and on the coastline may be acquired by foreigners, through Mexican trusts with Mexican banks. For all practical purposes, foreigners acquire all legal rights to the real estate.

Foreigners who acquire real estate, and companies with foreign participation, must agree to the Calvo Clause, through which the foreigners agree to be considered as Mexican citizens and waive any right to ask their foreign governments to intervene in the protection of their interest.

In general, there are no limitations to the participation of foreign investors in business activities in Mexico, except that certain activities are reserved to the Mexican government, others to Mexican nationals, and, in others, the participation of foreigners is subject to certain percentage limitations.

Activities that are reserved by the Mexican government are petroleum and gas, basic petrochemicals, electricity, nuclear energy, and mail.

Activities that are reserved to Mexicans or companies that are owned by Mexicans are public transportation, radio and television except for cable television, credit unions, etc.

Notwithstanding, foreign investors may participate in activities reserved by Mexican nationals through neutral investment schemes. Neutral investments may be realized by investing in shares with limited voting or no voting rights, as approved by the Ministry of the Economy or the Mexican Banking and Securities Commission. They may also be realized when investing in Mexican trusts, which grant only economic and not voting rights to the foreign investors.

Other activities are subject to specific limitations that allow the participation of foreigners in different percentages, from 10 percent to 49 percent. Among these activities you will find airlines, insurance companies, exchange houses, leasing and factoring companies, explosives, and firearms manufacture. There are no limitations on profit remittances nor upon capital repatriation, which normally are not subject to tax.

Before investing in Mexican companies, the foreign investor must consult with Mexican counsel, to confirm that such investment is not subject to limitations under the Foreign Investment Law or other laws governing the activities of the target company.

5.3 Corporations under Mexican Law

Mexican companies are governed by the General Corporate Law (the "Corporate Law"), issued in 1934. The Corporate Law has not been updated.

Under the Corporate Law, several different types of companies may be established. The typical limited liability company is the *sociedad anónima*, where the capital stock is represented by shares. The liability of the shareholders is limited to the amounts of the capital stock subscribed.

The *sociedad de responsabilidad limitada* is similar to a partnership under U.S. law. It is used frequently because under U.S. tax law it has been recognized as a pass-through entity.

Under the Corporate Law, companies formed in Mexico are considered Mexican, notwithstanding the participation of foreign investors. Any disputes among shareholders of a company in Mexico will be governed by Corporate Law.

Frequently, foreign investors in a joint venture enter into shareholder agreements or similar agreements with their Mexican counterparts. One issue that needs to be considered is whether the referred-to agreement will be governed by Mexican or foreign law. If the agreement is governed by foreign law, special care must be taken in the drafting of provisions that may not be enforceable in Mexico. As an example, any covenant to cast votes at shareholders meetings of the target will be null and void under Corporate Law. The same will be true with respect to any covenants imposing obligations on directors or officers of the target company. Likewise, any covenants imposing an obligation to an entity that is not a party to the agreement will be unenforceable. Covenants not to compete are not enforceable by specific performance in Mexico. The liberty to invest in other businesses or devote your time to legal activities is warranted under Mexico's Federal Constitution.

Buy-sell agreements, put-calls, and tag-along, drag-along, and similar covenants need to be carefully drafted. Frequently, to guarantee enforceability of such covenants, the parties will agree to establish a trust with a Mexican bank under which the ownership of the shares is transferred under contract to the bank, which will, as trustee, take all actions and abstain from other actions, as specifically contemplated under the corresponding trust agreement.

As a result of the limitations under the Corporate Law, documenting joint venture agreements between foreign and Mexican investors is a challenge. The parties to a joint venture agreement need to enter into complicated transaction agreements, including, in some cases, the above-mentioned trusts with Mexican banks.

5.4 The Securities Market Law

A new Securities Market Law was approved on December 2005 and became effective on June 2006. The objective of this law was to update the Mexican regulatory framework applicable to the securities market and publicly traded companies, according to international standards, including disclosure, minority shareholders' rights, and corporate governance.

Under the Securities Market Law, a new type of entity was created to serve as a recipient of private equity capital, under the name of *sociedad anónima promotora de inversión* (SAPI). The new entity was designed to accommodate private equity investments and serve as a transition vehicle from closely held corporations into public traded companies. SAPIs are not subject to the regulations or supervision of the Mexican Banking and Securities Commission before becoming a publicly traded company. Shareholders of SAPIs may negotiate arrangements dealing with different classes of shares, voting restrictions, preemptive rights, transfer restrictions, exit schemes, and noncompetition. This contrasts with companies formed under Corporate Law, which may not negotiate on such arrangements.

Under the Securities Market Law, the applicable legal framework for listed companies that are named *sociedad anónima bursátil* (SAB) was revised to increase corporate governance and disclosure standards.

The board of directors of a SAB may be formed by not more than twenty-one members, 25 percent of which must qualify as independent members. Calls for a meeting of the board may be made by 25 percent of the directors. At least two special committees of the board must be elected: a corporate practice committee and an audit committee. All members of the committees must be independent. Following the model of fiduciary duties in the United States and other countries in Europe, the Securities Market Law establishes a duty of care and a duty of loyalty upon the members of the board of directors, the committee members, the chief executive, and other officers. Under the duty of care, all parties subject to the Securities Market Law must act in good faith and in the best interest of the SAB. Parties subject to such duty have an obligation to indemnify for damages and losses caused to the SAB.

Shareholders and directors shall refrain from deliberating on or voting on matters on which they have a conflict of interest.

Under Mexican Law, the supreme authority of any Mexican company is the shareholders meeting. Under the Securities Market Law, shareholders holding from 5 percent to 20 percent of the outstanding shares may exercise certain minority rights.

The Securities Market Law has specific regulations on tender offers to protect minority shareholders. The acquisition of a participation in excess of 30 percent in a listed company must by carried out through a public tender offer.

There is no question that the legal framework of the Mexican securities market is one of the most advanced in the world and has some similarities with the Sarbanes-Oxley Act of the United States.

The Mexican Banking and Securities Commission is in charge of the supervision of the market and enforcing the legal framework.

The Mexican Stock Exchange (the "Exchange") is a privately owned entity. The Exchange is basically regulated by the Securities Market Law and by the internal regulations of the Exchange, which are self-regulatory provisions, and the terms of the concession granted by the Mexican government.

The Exchange has changed during the last five years, from a predominantly business focus on the domestic equity markets to a diversified business, including the listing of fixed income instruments, the trading of foreign debt and equity securities, the trading in futures, and options contracts. The Exchange, as a group, participates in custody, clearing, and settlement services.

The number of issuers listed in the Exchange is small. As of December 2007, only 125 issuers were listed (without considering the issuers listed on the Global Market, which were 346 as of the same date). Since 2007, there have been only twenty-one new issuers. During the same period sixty-one issuers were delisted.

With respect to debt listings, the activity is much bigger. Mexican financial markets have served as a benchmark for the Mexican private sector in the borrowing of funds in various markets and at more competitive rates through the issuance of debt securities. As one of only three countries in Latin America with an investment grade rating, Mexico has attracted an increasing flow of foreign direct investment and has developed a large local investor base with the participation of regulated retirement funds, which have contributed to an increase in the number of Mexican issuers (primarily of debt securities), products offered, and trading volume. However, when compared with other economies in Latin America, Mexico's capital markets still present opportunities for expansion at a pace that exceeds economic growth.

Without question, Mexico's challenge is to have a bigger securities market, with a substantial number of additional issuers of equity instruments.

5.5 The Federal Law on Economic Competition

The Federal Law on Economic Competition (the "Competition Law") was published in December 1992. The enactment of such law was an obligation imposed on Mexico under NAFTA. Mexico undertook a serious commitment to implement an effective competition policy.

The Federal Competition Commission (the FCC) is a semi-independent government body created for the enforcement of Mexico's competition legislation.

Since the point of inception, the Competition Law and the FCC have been partially successful in effectively enforcing the competition policies. Mexico continues to have monopolies and markets controlled by two principal players. The Competition Law has been challenged on constitutional grounds on several occasions.

A serious effort to amend the Competition Law to make it more effective was initiated in 2005. The process was extremely difficult, but finally the bill was approved in April 2006. Today, the FCC has a stronger legal structure to pursue monopolies and enforce the competition policies, to foster competition in the Mexican market.

One of the principal challenges Mexico has today is to enforce competition in the telecommunications sector, which continues to be under the control of Telmex and Telcel. Another sector is television, which is controlled by two networks.

5.6 The Labor Law

The 1917 Federal Constitution incorporated the most advanced policies to protect employees, and such policies continue to be an important part of the employee's rights.

The Federal Labor Law (the "Labor Law") was published in 1970. It governs individual labor matters and collective union contracts.

The provisions on labor are very inflexible. The terms and conditions of employment need not be established under contract, because the Labor Law establishes all applicable terms and conditions of a labor relationship.

5.6.1 Duration of the Labor Relationship

Under the Labor Law the relationship may be: (i) for an indefinite term; (ii) for a specific term; or (iii) for a specific job. As a general rule, employment is for an indefinite term. Under very limited circumstances, the labor relationship may be terminated, for just cause. In most cases, to be successful in a labor court, undisputed evidence of a serious breach of the obligations by the employee needs to be provided. Labor Courts are biased in favor of the employees. The recommended action is to negotiate termination of employment with the employee, preferably before going to court.

In the event of termination by the employer without cause, the employee will be entitled to: (i) severance payment equal to ninety days of salary; (ii) back-dated salaries; (iii) seniority premium; and (iv) accrued benefits. In some cases, the employer will also have to pay severance equal to twenty days of salary for each year of service.

5.6.2 Benefits

The Labor Law provides for several minimum benefits in favor of the employees, such as vacations, vacation premiums, Christmas bonus, and social welfare programs, which are established under other laws, such as social security, housing, and savings funds. Under the Labor Law, employers have an obligation to distribute and pay employees 10 percent of their pretax profits every year. All the above benefits have a substantial cost for employers.

5.6.3 Labor Unions

Employees in Mexico, with the exception of white-collar employees, have to be unionized. Different types of unions have been formed and are active in Mexico. Terms and conditions of union contracts are clearly established in the Labor Law. Many labor unions are actively pressuring companies that do not have a collective bargaining agreement to sign such an agreement. The procedure is usually to serve such companies with a strike call to force them to sign. To avoid such risk, companies with more than one hundred employees should voluntarily enter into collective bargaining agreements with "friendly" unions. The agreements are subsequently filed with the labor board. Wages are negotiated each calendar year and other terms of employment, including benefits, every two years.

Employees and unions will generally prefer to protect the employment and, to that extent, will reach reasonable terms in negotiations with employers. Notwithstanding, several economic sectors, such as mining, the auto industry, and steel manufacturing, have very aggressive unions. Some strikes in these sectors may last several months, with excessive costs for employers.

There are provisions under the Labor Law that entitle employers to negotiate the termination of employment when adverse economic conditions prevail.

For years, there have been negotiations to prepare a very extensive bill to amend and revise the Labor Law. There is a general consensus that to be competitive in the world economy, the Labor Law has to be substantially revised.

5.7 Environmental Laws and Regulations

The Mexican Federal Constitution bestows on the federal Congress the power to issue legislation to establish the concurrent authority of the federal, state, and municipal governments to regulate, within their corresponding jurisdiction, the protection of the environment and the preservation and restoration of the ecology.

Federal statutes set out the framework for the National Environmental Regulatory Policies.

The principal statute is the General Law on Ecological Equilibrium and Environment Protection, issued in 1988. Other statutes are the National Water Law, the General Law on Wild Life, and the General Law on the Prevention and Comprehensive Management of Waste. Other laws have been issued in all the states and in most municipalities. Several agencies in charge of environmental matters have issued a comprehensive set of regulations.

The Ministry of the Environmental and Natural Resources is the principal authority in charge of enacting and enforcing environmental regulations at the federal level. Several departments within the Ministry are in charge of separate functions. The Office of the Federal Prosecutor for the Protection of the Environment (PROFEPA) is the enforcement arm of the Ministry, and is responsible for performing inspections, prosecuting environmental noncompliance, applying sanctions, and generally enforcing environmental laws and regulations.

The National Water Law regulates the extraction of federal underground or surface water and the discharge of residual waters into federal recipient bodies. Such activities require a concession or authorization of a specific agency. Noncompliance with the respective law could lead to different sanctions, from fines to closure of the water well and revocation of the corresponding concessions or authorizations.

All sources of air pollution are regulated. Certain sources are under the jurisdiction of the federal level and others of the local level.

An environmental impact authorization at the federal level must be obtained before carrying certain projects in the oil or mining industry and in coastal areas, mangroves, or natural protected areas. In real estate projects, such authorizations are also required.

Likewise, several statutes have been issued on hazardous waste in Mexico. Liability is imposed on hazardous waste generators, importers, companies authorized to manage waste, and other participants. Transportation of hazardous waste is regulated at the federal level.

Several statutes and regulations apply to soil remediation. All contaminating companies are liable for damage arising from contaminated sites and must carry out the necessary remediation actions. These liabilities apply equally to owners and occupiers of real property. Direct transfer of contaminated sites is subject to approval. The acquisition of contaminated real property could result in environmental liability for the buyer.

When investing directly or indirectly in real estate, the investor must perform an in-depth environmental due diligence. Typically, environmental consultants are retained to conduct an environmental assessment study.

When negotiating a share purchase or an asset purchase agreement, environmental warranties and indemnities are as important as tax or labor indemnities. Usually the environmental warranties and indemnities survive as long as the maximum statute of limitation allows, which is five years. The liability should not have a cap, although it usually is for an amount equal to the purchase price. Notwithstanding, in some recent cases, the warranties are limited from two to five years, and financial caps between 25 percent and 100 percent of the purchase price are agreed to. The parties cannot limit their clean-up liability set out in the statutory legislation. However, parties can contractually agree on indemnification, defense, and hold-harmless provisions among themselves.

During the past decade, Mexico has improved its enforcement of the environmental framework. Nevertheless, much more needs to be accomplished.

5.8 Intellectual Property

In Mexico, the Industrial Property Law was issued in 1991 and its Regulations in 1994. Mexico is a signatory of the most important international treaties on intellectual property, such as the Paris Convention for the Protection of Industrial Property, the Lisbon Agreement for the Protection of Appellations of Origin and Their International Registration, and the Nice Agreement Concerning the International Classification of Goods and Services. Likewise, Mexico has executed many international treaties on trade, which generally include certain provisions on industrial property.

The Industrial Property Law provides that patents may be protected for a nonrenewable term of twenty years, and utility models and industrial designs for fifteen years. License agreements must be recorded with the Mexican Patent and Trademark Office (MIPI) to be effective against third parties. The MIPI has authority to take enforcement actions in case of violation of industrial property rights, including ordering the withdrawal from the market of goods used or illegally manufactured, and seizure, if required. The Industrial Property Law also protects trade secrets, without the need of any registration. Evidence of transmittal of such trade secrets must be maintained in documents, electronic or magnetic media, optical discs, microfilm, or any similar means. Likewise, trademarks are protected under the Industrial Property Law. Trademark registrations are granted for successive ten-year renewable periods. Trademark license agreements need to be recorded with the MIPI to be effective against third parties. Franchise agreements must also be recorded. Copyrights are governed by the Mexican Copyright Law issued in 1996 and its Regulations issued in 1998.

Mexico is a signatory of the most important treaties on copyrights, such as the Berne Convention for the Protection of Literary and Artistic Works, the Universal Copyright Convention of 1952, and others. In the international trade agreements signed by Mexico, certain provisions on copyrights were incorporated.

The moral rights of the work (generally the right to be known as the creator and to object to any change to the creation) are perpetual in favor of the author and his or her successors. The exclusive rights of the author to use and exploit the economic rights of such work are for the duration of the author's life plus one hundred years. After such term elapses, the work is considered to be within the public domain. The owner of the economic rights may transfer or license his or her rights. Such transmissions or licenses shall be temporal. Book editors are protected for fifty years, effective from the first edition of the book.

Mexico has a severe problem with piracy. The MIPI, in connection with the private sectors, has actively pursued piracy. To succeed, enormous economic and human resources will be required. The war on piracy should involve the federal, state, and municipal levels of government. On June 15, 2006, several federal agencies and state governments signed the National Agreement Against Piracy, which is intended to set forth the basis for a coordinated effort to combat piracy. Although there has been some improvement, much more needs to be done. Having the legal framework in place will not be sufficient.

5.9 Taxation in Mexico

It would be impossible to explain the Mexican tax framework in this chapter. Investors must retain professional tax advice when considering a transaction in Mexico because there may be tax consequences.

Corporations established in Mexico are subject to a corporate income tax on their worldwide income, including profits from their operations and income from their investments and capital gains. The general income tax rate is now 28 percent. It has dropped during recent years. Taxpayers must file an annual tax return for each calendar year. During the year, taxes are paid monthly or quarterly. Net operating losses can be carried forward for ten years.

A new flat tax, effective January 2008, is also imposed on Mexican entities. The flat tax is calculated by applying a 16.5 percent rate (in 2008) to the tax base, which is the excess of the total income derived from the taxable activities over a limited number of deductions. Payroll, intercompany royalties, and financing transactions are not deductible for the flat tax. The flat tax is like the U.S. alternative minimum income tax. Taxpayers are required to pay the higher of the income tax and the flat tax.

There is also a value-added tax in Mexico. The value-added tax is an indirect tax levied on the value of goods and services, and is imposed on corporations or persons carrying out any of the following activities within the Mexican territory: (i) sale or other disposition of property; (ii) rendering of services; (iii) temporary use of property; and (iv) importation of goods or services. The general value-added tax rate is 15 percent.

With respect to foreign residents, the Mexican Income Tax Law provides that they will be subject to taxes on any Mexican source income, or the total income attributable to a permanent establishment located in Mexico.

Payments to a foreign resident from a source in Mexico for financial leases, rentals, interests, technical assistance, royalties, and similar operations will be subject to a withholding income tax, at different tax rates. Foreigners who sell shares or real estate property in Mexico may elect to pay a capital gain tax on the gain realized either by deducting from the price received the tax basis of the shares or real property or by paying a fixed tax rate, depending on the transaction. Foreign corporations and individuals could have a permanent establishment in Mexico if they conduct business activities through branches, factories, or offices or through a Mexican resident who acts on their behalf. In general, a foreign corporation or individual that has a permanent establishment in Mexico will be subject to income tax or flat tax on the income attributable to the permanent establishment, on identical terms as those applied to a Mexican resident.

Mexico has signed many international treaties to avoid double taxation with the most important countries around the world.

The international auditing firms established in Mexico and Mexican tax lawyers play an important role in providing advice to their clients. It is highly advisable to consult with your auditors and lawyers before carrying on any business activities in Mexico.

The tax legal framework in Mexico is complicated. The federal Congress amends, at least on a yearly basis, the tax laws and regulations. Tax litigation has increased during recent years. Every year, the amendments to taxes are challenged by some taxpayers before Mexican federal courts.

5.10 The Mexican Bankruptcy Law

The actual Bankruptcy Act was approved in May 2000, superseding the 1943 Bankruptcy and Suspension of Payments Act.

The main thrust of the Bankruptcy Act is to keep businesses operating and avoid generalized default in payments.

The Bankruptcy Act goes into great detail on the effects of the declaration of commercial bankruptcy with regard to all acts, contracts, and obligations of the merchant. The Bankruptcy Act also establishes the actions that may defraud creditors and situations in which such fraud is presumed. Likewise, it has a chapter on criminal liability of merchants declared in a commercial bankruptcy, including actions taken against the merchant who alters, falsifies, or destroys accounting books and records.

The Bankruptcy Act provides for a single proceeding with two successive stages: mediation and bankruptcy.

5.10.1 Mediation
This stage is compulsory and is intended to permit the reorganization of the insolvent entity. It ends with the execution of a reorganization agreement.

5.10.2 Bankruptcy
If mediation is not achieved, the second stage commences. There is a limited period of time to finalize the first stage. Likewise, the Bankruptcy Act establishes a limited period of time for the bankruptcy and liquidation of the insolvent entity.

The basic objective of the Bankruptcy Act is to expedite the whole process. Under the previous act, bankruptcy proceedings took many years. Today the process is more transparent, less time-consuming, and thus much more efficient.

A specialized agency was created to take part in the proceedings. Such agency appoints persons with experience to act as examiners, mediators, and receivers. The Bankruptcy Act goes into great detail to establish insolvency standards, the effective date, fraudulent conveyance, priority of claims, set-off rights, and separation actions. In addition to the provisions in the Bankruptcy Act, different provisions would apply in the case of financial institutions, utility companies, telephone companies, and other regulated entities.

The Bankruptcy Act is territorial in Mexico and should govern all insolvency proceedings of merchants domiciled in Mexico. There have been cases whereby a proceeding is followed in Mexico with respect to assets located in such country while, in parallel, a similar proceeding is followed abroad.

5.11 Choice of Law and Jurisdiction

Under Mexican law, the parties are free to enter into contracts and to agree on the laws that will govern such contracts. Mexican law will not be applicable to the negotiation merely because the negotiation takes place in Mexico or because one of the parties is a citizen of Mexico. Notwithstanding, contracts on real estate, including mortgages, will be governed by the state laws in force in the place where the real estate is located. Likewise, Mexican companies will be governed by the Corporate Law.

The choice of law will be valid to the extent it does not violate public policy.

The parties to any contract may agree to submit any dispute under the contracts to courts outside of Mexico. The election, to be valid, must be agreed by all parties to the agreement, expressly waiving their rights to any other jurisdiction to which any of them may be entitled, by reason of their present or future domicile or otherwise. A foreign judgment obtained in default will only be recognized if the defendant was duly served with the complaint and was given an opportunity to defend against the claim.

The following are the requirements for enforcement by a Mexican court, of a final resolution issued by a court abroad:

a. Such judgment is obtained in compliance with the legal requirements of the jurisdiction of the court rendering such judgment and in compliance with all legal requirements of the agreement executed between the parties;

b. such judgment is strictly for the payment of a certain sum of money, based on an *in personam* (as opposed to an *in rem*) action;

c. the judge or court rendering the judgment was competent to hear and judge on the subject matter of the case in accordance with accepted principles of international law that are compatible with Mexican law;

d. service of process is made personally on the defendant or on its duly appointed process agent;

e. such judgment does not contravene Mexican law, public policy of Mexico, international treaties or agreements binding upon Mexico, or generally accepted principles of international law;

f. the applicable procedure under the laws of Mexico with respect to the enforcement of foreign judgments is complied with;

g. the action, in respect of why the judgment was rendered, is not the subject matter of a lawsuit among the same parties pending before a Mexican court;

h. such judgment is final in the jurisdiction where obtained; and

i. the courts of such jurisdiction recognize the principles of reciprocity in connection with the enforcement of Mexican judgments in such jurisdiction.

In the absence of a provision in the agreement on choice of jurisdiction, Mexican courts will have jurisdiction whenever (i) the defendant has its domicile in Mexico or (ii) the place of performance of the obligations is Mexico. Mexican default jurisdiction rules are contained in the Commerce Code. Such rules are territorial in nature and were designed to define jurisdiction among Mexican courts.

Mexican laws guarantee that non-Mexican citizens shall have the same rights Mexican citizens have before Mexican courts.

Mexico is a party to the United Nations Convention on the Recognition and Enforcement of Foreign Arbitral Awards of 1958 (the "New York Convention"). An arbitration award, rendered outside of Mexico, will also be recognized in Mexico, and a competent Mexican judge will enforce the arbitration award. In general, the requirements to enforce an arbitral award are similar to those applied to the recognition of a foreign judgment.

The Commerce Code was amended to include a chapter on arbitration. The provisions were inspired by the Model Law of the UN Commission on International Trade Law.

The decision to agree on selecting Mexican law or foreign law needs to be carefully analyzed, depending on the specific case. Frequently it is preferable to select Mexican law in a joint venture agreement, because Mexican law will govern the joint venture company. On the other hand, in financing agreements, the election of non-Mexican laws is the preferred course of action.

In most of the agreements executed by foreign investors, the disputes will be submitted to arbitration. Selecting arbitration is important in the context of joint ventures or very complicated and specialized transactions. Mexican courts are not prepared to handle complicated agreements. Selecting Mexican courts would be preferable for financial agreements. Mexican courts are familiar with collection claims. Collateral agreements in a financial transaction are frequently submitted to Mexican courts. Although the Mexican court system is improving, it still is very slow and sometimes unpredictable. Enforcing a foreign arbitral award in Mexico is possible, usually within a one-year term. Occasionally, enforcing a foreign arbitral award before Mexican courts could be delayed by more than one year, if the defendant claims a deficiency in the arbitral proceedings.

5.12 Contracts under Mexican Law

The Mexican Federal Civil Code (*Código Civil Federal*) and Commerce Code (*Código de Comercio*) provide the basic terms, conditions, and requirements for contracts in general and for several types of contracts in particular. Like French and Spanish law, Mexican law is based on the Napoleonic Code.

The general rule under the Federal Civil Code is that the parties may freely agree on the terms and conditions of the agreement, provided that such terms and conditions are legal.

Notwithstanding, some contracts need to comply with certain formalistic requirements, as in the case of transfer of real property, where a public deed must be signed before a notary public in Mexico and filed with the corresponding public registry.

In Mexico, notary publics (*notarios*) and commercial brokers (*corredores*) play a completely different role than they do in the United States or other common law countries. Notary publics and commercial brokers have "public faith" with respect to acts and contracts executed before them. In Mexico, public notaries and commercial brokers have the responsibility of verifying that the acts and contracts signed before them satisfy the legal requirements that are applicable. They should explain to the signatories the legal consequences of the acts and contracts executed. They also have the responsibility of collecting taxes imposed on the transactions executed before them. The fees and expenses payable to notary publics and commercial brokers in Mexico are much higher than those payable in the United States or other foreign countries. The reason for these costs is that notary publics and commercial brokers have a specialized organization and are charged with important duties and have significant liabilities, which is not the case in common law countries.

In Mexico it is preferable to have contracts in writing as opposed to oral contracts. The rationale is obvious in that with contracts in writing there is adequate evidence of the terms and conditions agreed to among the parties, which reduces the likelihood of ambiguity. In some cases, even if not required by law, the parties may elect to sign the contracts before a notary public or commercial broker. The corresponding public deed will be evidence of the agreements signed, including identity of the parties, authority to sign, and date of execution.

If not signed before a notary public or commercial broker, it is preferable to have contracts signed by all parties in a single document, and not in counterparts. Likewise, it is customary to have a short signature on each page of the agreements. This practice is meant to avoid complications when enforcing agreements before courts.

5.12.1 Structure

As in many civil law jurisdictions, contracts drawn under Mexican law are shorter. Most of the terms and conditions are contemplated in the Federal Civil Code or the Commerce Code.

Contracts begin with a heading stating the type of contract and the parties to the agreement. Then there are a certain number of recitals, explaining what the parties intend to agree on, their powers of attorney, and the existence of all corporate or other authorizations obtained. After this come the clauses setting forth the rights and obligations of each of the parties. Mexican contracts usually do not contain a section of defined terms.

Notwithstanding the above, in recent years the structure of contracts has changed substantially when foreign parties participate. The U.S. style is frequently used. Contracts are similar to those used in international transactions. Mexican counterparts and their counsel have become familiar with complex detailed contracts, as used in other jurisdictions.

If foreign law governs, it is necessary to carefully study the standard international provisions; many of them may be unenforceable or in breach of applicable Mexican law.

5.12.2 Contract Formation

In the case of an acquisition of assets or shares by a foreign investor, typically the parties will have initial negotiations to determine if there is an agreement in principle on the basic points of the deal. Once an agreement in principle is reached, they will execute an initial—not binding—letter of intent or similar agreement. In most cases, a binding confidentiality agreement is executed. Following the execution of a confidentiality agreement, the investor will conduct due diligence. At the same time, the parties will continue negotiations on the transaction documents. Depending on the governing law and jurisdiction provisions, the agreements will follow Mexican or common law style.

Once the agreements are finalized and executed, depending on the type and size of the business involved, the parties will file documents or request approvals that may be required from Mexican governmental agencies, such as the merger control notification. Once the approvals are obtained and all other conditions are satisfied, the transaction will be closed.

The Mexican government does not have any role as a participant in negotiations among private companies; its role will be limited to the approval of the transaction.

The exchange of documentation and information online has become customary. Notwithstanding, contracts are not signed with electronic signatures. Likewise, executing contracts by fax or in counterparts is not recommended.

5.13 Negotiation Practices

5.13.1 Participants

Selecting the correct individuals to lead the negotiations on behalf of the foreign investor is imperative. Gender, age, class, race, or religious diversity will not have any bearing on the selection of the negotiation team.

Generally, the foreign investor should select a limited number of representatives who would be actively involved in the negotiations. It is preferable to select representatives who have international experience in negotiations. It will also be helpful to select representatives who are fluent in Spanish. It is important to take into consideration the number of participants and the differing backgrounds of all on the Mexican team. There must be a balance to facilitate negotiations and to create trust.

Special Mexican local counsel is usually retained by investors to participate in the negotiations. There are several local firms that have extensive experience in international transactions. Local counsel will typically participate as legal advisors, but in some cases could have a leading role in the negotiations. Frequently law firms have conflicts of interest. For that reason, to assure adequate legal representation in major projects, a foreign investor should select the Mexican law firm as early in the process as possible. In Mexico, the business and legal communities are rather small, and it is usually a case of everyone knowing everyone.

One issue that should be discussed early on with the Mexican negotiators is that they should retain special Mexican counsel to interact with their foreign negotiators' counsel. If counsel for the Mexican counterparts is not experienced in international negotiations, the process of negotiations may fail.

An understanding of the relationships, reputations, and cultural and business background of your Mexican counterparts is important to succeed in a negotiation. You need to avoid confrontation and be prepared to spend time with colleagues so as to have a personal relationship and develop trust. Frequently, you will be invited to dinner and other social events.

The more sensitive issues should be discussed in private meetings outside of the negotiating group, in order to avoid confrontation before a bigger group. Long conference calls or meetings among a big group of participants are counterproductive. The foreign negotiators should try to discuss the principal points of the negotiation in shorter calls or one-on-one meetings.

5.13.2 Language

It is not uncommon in Mexico to carry on negotiations in English. If the Mexican counterparts do not speak English, translators are retained.

As explained, the business community in Mexico is sophisticated and has experience in international negotiations. Many Mexican businesspeople and professionals have studied abroad. Agreements are drafted and negotiated in English; depending on the specific circumstances, agreements could be drafted and executed in both English- and Spanish-language versions. In most cases, the English version will prevail.

With respect to certain agreements dealing with real estate, the contract needs to be in Spanish language and formalized before a notary public. The deal will be recorded in a public registry.

5.13.3 Timing

As in any other country, negotiations will take place at any time and upon any day of the week, if required. Mexican businesspeople and professionals are prepared to handle negotiations as expeditiously as required.

Only when governmental approvals or filings are required, the negotiations need to take into account the national holidays or vacations. Governmental offices close for two weeks in the summer and two weeks in December, as well as on specific holidays.

Foreign investors should, if the transaction is not urgent, try to avoid negotiations over weekends. Mexicans desire to spend time with families and friends. If there is no justifiable reason for working over the weekend, then it is advisable to avoid business deals taking place on weekend time. Mexicans will resent the pressure and that will certainly have an effect on the negotiations.

Foreigners need to be sensitive to cultural differences. This will be greatly appreciated by the Mexican counterparts. Foreigners should also recognize that, as in any other international transaction, there are important cultural and legal differences in Mexico as compared with their own jurisdiction. If they want to complete a successful negotiation, they should be receptive to proposals of the Mexican counterparts and negotiate terms and conditions that are fair and balanced and acceptable to both parties.

6. Conclusion

The negotiation process of any international business transaction in Mexico will depend on the type and size of the Mexican target and, to a great extent, on the characteristics, background, and experience of the Mexican counterparts.

If the Mexican counterparts have experience in complex international transactions and retain competent Mexican counsel, the negotiations should move smoothly and efficiently, as in the United States. If the Mexican counterparts have no or little experience in international transactions, the negotiation process will most likely be difficult and not efficient.

Foreign investors in Mexico will generally find that their Mexican counterparts, and their advisers, will work smoothly with them to find adequate and efficient solutions to close a transaction. The legal and regulatory framework is similar to that of most advanced civil law jurisdictions. The foreign investors will also find that the principal

Mexican law firms are as efficient as comparable firms in their own jurisdictions.

It is highly recommended that foreign investors be sensitive to cultural differences. Likewise, they must be reasonable and willing to enter into fair and balanced transactions. Foreign investors must promote a personal relationship with their Mexican counterparts.

Mexico, today, is an excellent forum for international business negotiations. The country will continue to evolve in the global marketplace.

Samuel García-Cuéllar
Creel, García-Cuéllar, Aiza y Enríquez, S.C.
Paseo de los Tamarindos 60
Bosques de Las Lomas
05120 México, D.F.
México
Phone: (52-55) 1105-0601
Fax: (52-55) 1105-0690
E-mail: s.garcia-cuellar@creel.com.mx

CHAPTER 36

International Business Negotiations in the Netherlands

Jaap Willeumier and Eva Das
STIBBE
AMSTERDAM, THE NETHERLANDS

1. Introduction

The Netherlands, one of the smaller countries of Western Europe, has a long and colorful history in international trade and finance. This history goes back to the sixteenth and seventeenth centuries when its merchants traveled all over the world to buy and sell products in countries as far away as Australia, Japan, and the Americas.

The country covers less than 42,000 square kilometers (roughly the size of the state of Maryland) and has approximately 16.4 million inhabitants. It was one of the six founding members of the European Community and together with Belgium and Luxembourg forms the so-called Benelux.

As is evidenced by their history, the Dutch have always been very much internationally oriented, and, certainly when considering the size of the country, can be said to have played and to continue to play an active and prominent role in the international business world. Some of the world's larger corporations are based in the Netherlands, such as Royal Dutch Shell, Unilever, Akzo Nobel, and Philips. The Netherlands is, and for several years has been, ranked among the top four foreign investors in the United States, whereas the United States consistently is among the three largest foreign investors in the Netherlands.

In order to be successful internationally, it has always been a pure necessity for the Dutch to be able to speak foreign languages. For most of them, English is their second language, while many have an excellent command (or at least working knowledge of) French or German as well. As a result, it usually does not create any problem at all for business negotiations with Dutch parties to be conducted in English.

The Netherlands, or Holland as the country is also known, is a civil law country. Its main laws are laid down in its Civil Code, Commercial

Code, Criminal Code, and Code of Civil Procedure, which date back to the beginning of the nineteenth century when they—or their predecessors—were introduced by Napoleon. Effective January 1, 1992, the Netherlands has a revised and modernized Civil Code, although most of the fundamental principles of Dutch civil law have remained unchanged.

Given the fact that the Netherlands is a member of the European Union, in many areas and in many respects new laws have been enacted or existing laws amended during the last decades as part of the process of implementation of EU directives and regulations. These areas include corporate law, banking and securities, financial reporting, environmental law, transportation, customs and immigration, food labeling, and product liability. These laws are regarded as part of the national laws of the country rather than being viewed as part of EU law, notwithstanding the fact that Brussels was their source. More than half of the national rules and regulations are based, directly or indirectly, on EU law.

In the old days, the Dutch were often known for doing deals on the basis of a handshake or on terms written on the back of a cigar box. This, of course, is no longer true, particularly not in international transactions. There is still a tendency, however, for written agreements in general to be shorter than their Anglo-Saxon equivalents, because the Civil Code, Commercial Code, Code of Civil Procedure, and other laws contain detailed provisions on matters that one would otherwise expect to see in a written agreement, such as obligations of buyer and seller, division of risk, *force majeure*, remedies in case of default, foreclosure on collateral (such as mortgage and pledge), service of process, and jurisdiction. Some of these matters are dealt with in the law in a mandatory fashion, such as service of process. For others, the parties to an agreement may deviate from the rules laid down in the law or fine-tune the general rules to the requirements and characteristics of the particular transaction.

Nevertheless, during the last decades there has been a distinct trend for contractual documentation in transactions involving Dutch parties or assets to become more detailed and to be tailored more along the lines customary in Anglo-Saxon countries. Obviously, this is true in particular for the documentation in cross-border mergers and acquisitions and in international finance. Another reason for this development is the fact that, despite professed government attempts toward deregulation, life in general and commercial activity in particular have become more and more juridical, especially in such areas as securities laws, environmental laws, and product liability. This is reflected in the degree of detail these matters often have to be dealt with in the transaction documentation. This does not mean that the lawyers have entirely taken over, but it is undeniable that legal issues play a more prominent role in commercial negotiations in the Netherlands than before.

2. Selected Legal Issues, Laws, and Regulations

When engaged in negotiations in the Netherlands, there are a variety of legal issues, laws, and rules of which one ought to be aware, since these may become applicable to the transaction in question—depending in most cases on its nature. The following is a summary of a number of issues, laws, and rules that one is most likely to run into at some point in the process during negotiations involving a financial transaction, acquisition, or other major commercial transaction.

2.1 Corporate Entities

In the Netherlands, most businesses are organized in the form of a private company with limited liability (*besloten vennootschap met beperkte aansprakelijkheid*, or *B.V.*) or a public limited company (*naamloze vennootschap*, or *N.V.*). Both the N.V. and the B.V. have limited shareholders' liability, up to the amount of the issued share capital. The principal differences between the N.V. and the B.V. are related to the issuance and transferability of shares. A B.V. cannot issue share certificates or bearer shares, and its shares cannot be listed on a stock exchange. Furthermore, the articles of association of a B.V. must include a transfer restriction pursuant to which the free transferability of shares is restricted. An N.V. is entitled to include a transfer restriction in its articles of association; it is, however, not required to do so. A transfer restriction may come in the form of an approval procedure, pursuant to which the transfer is subject to the prior approval of the general meeting of shareholders, or another corporate body, such as the supervisory board. Another form of a transfer restriction is a right of first refusal to be exercised by the other shareholders. The N.V. and B.V. also have different minimum requirements for issued and paid-up capital, EUR 45,000 for the N.V. and EUR 18,000 for the B.V. Currently a legislative proposal is pending regarding the amendment of certain provisions of the Civil Code with respect to B.V.s. The proposed amendments aim to make the rules applicable to B.V.s more flexible and include the cancellation of the required transfer restriction for shares and the cancellation of the minimum required issued and paid-up capital of EUR 18,000. Other incorporated legal entities that one may encounter include associations (*verenigingen*), in particular cooperative associations and foundations (*stichtingen*). These entities, N.V.s, and B.V.s have legal personality. In addition, Dutch law knows various forms of partnerships, notably the *maatschap, vennootschap onder firma*, or V.O.F. (general partnership), and *commanditaire vennootschap* (limited partnership). Currently pending legislation will, *inter alia,* make it possible to create legal personality for partnerships.

2.2 Trade Register

All incorporated and unincorporated legal entities referred to above (except for partnerships of the *maatschap* type), as well as all foreign corporations having a branch or office in the Netherlands, must be registered with the trade register of the Chamber of Commerce for the part of the country where the corporation is located or where it has its legal seat. On request, the trade register provides an extract of the registration of the corporation or other entity in question, containing such information as the official corporate name, registered address, names of the members of the managing board (*bestuurder, directeur,* or in English often referred to as managing director), names and powers of *procuratiehouders* (proxy holders), and the amount of capital in the case of N.V.s or B.V.s. It is useful and often even essential to have available in the file an extract from the trade register relating to a party with whom one is negotiating.

2.3 Management and Representation

In negotiations it is important to know whether or to what extent the people on the other side of the table are authorized to represent the company in question and enter into agreements on its behalf. By law, the managing board (*bestuur*) of N.V.s and B.V.s has full powers to represent the company. In most cases, a company's articles of association provide that it can also be represented by a managing director acting individually, or by two managing directors acting jointly, as the case may be. Information about such powers or representation of managing directors is provided by extracts from the trade registers. In addition, companies may appoint employees as *procuratiehouder* with certain limited or unlimited powers to represent the company. The relevant power of attorney may be filed with the trade register.

2.4 Managing Board and Supervisory Board

The ultimate executive powers in an N.V. or B.V. are vested in the managing board, which may consist of one or more members. Sometimes N.V.s and B.V.s apply a two-tier board structure, which means that in addition to the managing board, a supervisory board (*raad van commissarissen*) is established. The role and task of the supervisory board is to supervise the policies of the management board and the general affairs of the company and to give advice to the managing board. N.V.s and B.V.s that meet certain criteria laid down in the Civil Code are subject to the so-called large company regime (*structuurregime*) and are required to have a supervisory board, which in those cases has broader powers and responsibilities than would otherwise apply. It should be noted that in either case members of the supervisory board have no external powers and consequently have no powers to represent the company in negotiations or other matters unless specifically empowered for that purpose by virtue of a power of attorney. Although less frequently applied, it is also possible for Dutch companies to establish a so-called one-tier board, whereby the composition and functioning of a management board comprises both members having responsibility for the day-to-day business of the company and members not having such responsibility.

2.5 Corporate Governance Code

As of December 9, 2003, the Netherlands has a corporate governance code. The Dutch corporate governance code is addressed to Dutch companies of which the shares are listed on a stock exchange. The code contains principles that set out broadly accepted general views on good corporate governance, which principles are elaborated in more detailed best practice provisions. The main subjects covered are the role and composition of both the management board and the supervisory board, the general meeting of shareholders, financial audit and the external accountant, as well as disclosure, compliance, and enforcement. The code does not provide mandatory rules, but is based on an "apply or explain" principle. To the extent that Dutch listed companies do not apply the provisions of the code, they have to explain in their annual report to what extent this is the case and why.

2.6 Securities Laws

The core of securities laws in the Netherlands is formed by the Financial Supervision Act (*Wet op het financieel toezicht*) of January 1, 2007, replacing most of the then existing securities and investment-related legislation. The Financial Supervision Act brings together practically all of the rules and conditions that apply to financial markets and their supervision, in the act itself and in regulations based thereon. The Financial Supervision Act distinguishes between supervision by the Dutch Central Bank (*De Nederlandsche Bank*, or *DNB*), for prudential supervision, and the Dutch Authority for the Financial Markets (*Autoriteit Financiële Markten*, or *AFM*), for supervision of conduct of business. The main topics covered by the Financial Supervision Act include market access for financial institutions, prudential supervision of financial institutions, supervision of the conduct of financial institutions, and supervision of the conduct of financial markets (the latter including securities offerings, market abuse, disclosure regulations, and public takeover bids). A section on supervision of settlement systems is to be included at a later date. The contents of the Financial Supervision Act are for a large part based on the implementation of EU directives.

For instance, the Financial Supervision Act contains a general prohibition to offer securities in the Netherlands unless a prospectus that has been approved by the Authority for the Financial Markets or a supervisory authority from another EU member state regarding the offer is made available. The EU Prospectus Directive (2003/71/EC) in that respect creates common standards for the issuance of securities in the EU, seeks to ensure that adequate and equivalent disclosure standards are in place in all member states, and allows for "passporting" of approved prospectuses throughout the EU: once approved by the authority in one member state, a prospectus has to be accepted everywhere else in the EU. The EU Prospectus Directive applies where EU and non-EU issuers want to offer to the public or list securities admitted to a regulated market in the EU. The general prohibition regarding the offering of securities in the Netherlands does not apply if one can make use of one of several general exemptions or has obtained an individual exemption on the basis of the Financial Supervision Act. Exemptions include the offering of securities to qualified investors (*gekwalificeerde beleggers*), offerings made to fewer than one hundred persons or legal entities within the Netherlands, and securities offered against a consideration of at least EUR 50,000.

In addition, the Financial Supervision Act provides rules governing public takeover bids. The supervision focuses on the offeror, the target company, and the directors and supervisory board members involved. The applicable rules are intended to ensure transparency as regards the preparation and making of a bid and as regards declaring a bid unconditional, and they include a code of conduct for all those involved in a public takeover bid. As of October 28, 2007, when the implementation of the EU Takeover Directive (2004/25/EC) came into force, the Financial Supervision Act includes the mandatory bid: a person (or persons acting in concert) acquiring 30 percent or more of the voting rights in a Dutch company listed on an EU-regulated stock exchange is in principle obligated to make a public bid for all shares, offering a fair price. Both for the decision on whether a mandatory bid must be made as well as the fair price to be paid, the Enterprise Chamber (*Ondernemingskamer*) of the Amsterdam Court is the competent authority.

2.7 Financial Statements and Accounting Principles

N.V.s and B.V.s must draw up annual financial statements. Copies (or portions thereof in the case of smaller companies) must be filed with the trade register, where they are available to the public. The financials must be audited unless a company meets certain criteria and qualifies as a small company. The requirements of the Dutch Civil Code with respect to the information to be provided and the publication of financial statements are the result of implementation of EU directives harmonizing the laws of the respective EU member states. Although it is fair to say that the generally accepted accounting principles as applied in the Netherlands are not materially different from those in the United States, it should be noted that there are a number of important differences, especially in respect to the treatment of goodwill and certain amortization and depreciation concepts.

2.8 Financial Assistance

Netherlands law contains certain rules basically prohibiting N.V.s and B.V.s from giving any form (with only a few exceptions) of financial assistance with respect to the acquisition by third parties of existing or newly issued shares in its capital, or in the capital of its N.V. or B.V. parent. The aforementioned pending legislative proposal regarding the amendment of certain provisions of the Civil Code with respect to B.V.s includes the cancellation of this prohibition for the B.V. (but leaving it intact for the N.V.).

2.9 Taxation

Business in the Netherlands is affected by a variety of taxes of which the most important are corporate income tax and value-added tax. Other relevant taxes for businesses are dividend withholding tax, real estate transfer tax, and environmental taxes.

Corporate income tax is levied at a rate of 25.5 percent. An important element of Dutch income tax is the participation exemption, which is used by many internationally operating groups for their intermediate or top holding entities. Under this exemption, income from subsidiaries in which an interest of at least 5 percent is held is exempted for corporate income tax purposes, subject to certain conditions.

Dutch corporate income tax allows forming a fiscal unity between resident and nonresident entities with substantial Dutch operations constituting a permanent establishment. Under such fiscal unity one is able to set off profits and losses within the members of such fiscal unity. Other beneficial facilities include relief for domestic and certain cross-border legal mergers, demergers, and share-for-share exchanges.

Dividends are subject to a 15 percent dividend withholding tax rate, unless an exemption applies. Such exemptions are available under the participation exemption and Parent Subsidiary directive. Under tax treaties the 15 percent dividend withholding tax rate is reduced to 10 percent, 5 percent, or even 0 percent depending on the circumstances. An antiabuse provision targets dividend stripping transactions.

The Netherlands has now concluded tax treaties with more than seventy-five countries. These treaties offer Dutch residents tax benefits, with certain substantial benefits amongst other reductions in withholding taxes on dividends, interests, and royalties as well as protection against the taxation of capital gains. Moreover, the Netherlands has entered into more than ninety-five investment protection agreements safeguarding investments in other jurisdictions made by Dutch resident entities.

2.10 Antitrust/Anticompetition Laws

The Dutch Competition Authority ("NMa") must be notified of certain "concentrations" within the meaning of the Dutch Competition Act (*Mededingingswet*). A concentration may be the result of a contemplated transaction (e.g., a merger, acquisition, or certain type of joint venture). The Dutch Competition Act provides for a system of *ex ante* assessment of concentrations where the turnover of the "undertakings concerned" exceeds specific turnover thresholds. If the turnover thresholds are superseded, the NMa has to be notified of the proposed concentration. The concentration cannot be implemented before the NMa has been notified and a subsequent period of four weeks has expired. Prenotification consultation with the agency staff is recommended—in the more complex cases—for efficiency reasons.

When examining whether notification is required with the NMa, parties should at the same time examine whether notification to other national competition authorities or with the European Commission is required. The national competition authorities of the member states are in principle not competent to analyze a transaction that meets the Community jurisdictional criterion (there are exceptions in special situations).

In case of a genuine merger, the "undertakings concerned" will be the undertakings that are merging. In other transactions, the undertakings concerned are (i) the undertaking(s) acquiring control over another undertaking and (ii) the part of or the entire (group of) undertaking(s) being acquired.

As a general rule, notification with the NMa is required for concentrations if in the calendar year previous to the notification (i) the aggregate annual turnover of the "undertakings concerned" exceeds EUR 113,450,000 and (ii) at least two of the "undertakings concerned" have an annual turnover in the Netherlands of at least EUR 30 million. Concentrations where the turnover of the "undertakings concerned" does not meet these thresholds are permitted without notification.

2.11 Works Council

Pursuant to the Works Council Act (*Wet op de ondernemingsraden*) a company that regularly employs at least fifty employees is required to establish a works council. The Works Council Act grants specific authorities to the works council. Accordingly, the works council has a right to prior consultation (*adviesrecht*) with respect to certain important resolutions of a financial, economical, and business organizational nature. The works council has a right to prior consultation with respect to a proposed resolution of the company (including proposed resolutions of any corporate bodies of that company) concerning the transfer of the control over that company. The managing board should submit the proposed resolution to the works council in writing, including the motives that underlie the proposed resolution as well as the expected consequences that the proposed resolution might have for the employees and the intended measures on account of these consequences. The works council should be given the opportunity to exercise its right to prior consultation at such a time that the consultation of the works council can have a substantial effect on the proposed resolution.

The works council gives advice on the proposed resolution after holding at least one consultative meeting concerning the proposed resolution. When the proposed resolution is adopted subsequently to obtaining the advice of the works council, the works council must be informed thereof in writing. In the event that the advice of the works council has not been followed in part or whole, the works council must also be informed thereof. Unless the resolution corresponds with the advice of the works council, the execution or implementation of the resolution shall be suspended until one month following the day on which the works council has been informed of the resolution. Furthermore, the works council can initiate an appeal against the resolution at the Enterprise Chamber when the resolution does not correspond to the advice of the works council or when facts or circumstances have become known that—if known to the works council at the time it rendered its advice—could have been a reason for the works council not to render its advice as it did. If the works council so requests, the Enterprise Chamber may order (i) that the resolution shall be withdrawn, in part or in whole, as well as the nullification of the consequences of the resolution and/or (ii) that any actions with respect to the execution or implementation of the resolution, or any parts thereof, shall be prohibited.

2.12 SER Merger Code

When making an acquisition or entering into other transactions involving a change of control of an N.V. or B.V. that has fifty or more employees, the rules of the Merger Code (*Fusiegedragsregels 2000*) of the SER have to be observed. These rules of conduct do not have the status of law but are generally recognized and observed as if that were the case. SER stands for *Sociaal Economische Raad* (Social Economic Council), which is an advisory council to the government of the Netherlands.

The Merger Code comprises a set of rules designed to protect the interests of the workforce of the companies involved in a transaction.

These rules include the obligation to inform the employees' associations (trade unions) of the preparation of a transaction, before an agreement is reached, and provide them with information on the rationale for the transaction and the expected social, economic, and legal consequences thereof, as well as to inform the employees' associations in advance about the contents of any public announcement concerning the preparation or implementation of a proposed transaction (unless doing so in advance would result in a violation of securities laws, in which case it must be done concurrently with the public announcement). The employees' associations must be given the opportunity to present their views on the rationale and expected consequences of the merger. Copies of the notifications to the employees' associations must be sent to the SER. If there are no employees' associations, the SER still needs to be notified.

It should be noted that the Code only provides for procedural rules; it does not require a review of the transaction on its merits.

2.13 Asset Transactions and Employees

If a transaction involves the acquisition or subscription of shares of a company, the assets and liabilities of that company are normally not affected by the transaction. The same is true for the employees of the company, since they continue to be employed by the target company. Pursuant to Dutch law, however, if a transaction is structured as an asset transaction, whereby the activities of a particular undertaking or a part thereof are transferred, all employees related to the activity concerned shall, by operation of law, transfer to the purchaser of the activities. In other words, in such case the parties to such transaction cannot decide to what extent employees are or are not transferred; every employee who works solely or mainly for the activity transferred becomes by operation of law an employee of the purchaser of the activities.

2.14 Environmental Law

Negotiation results must be compliant with Dutch and EU environmental laws. There are different environmental laws that regulate different environmental aspects including but not limited to the Environmental Management Act (*Wet milieubeheer*), Pollution of Surface Waters Act (*Wet verontreiniging oppervlaktewateren*), Air Quality Decree (*Besluit luchtkwaliteit*), Soil Protection Act (*Wet bodembescherming*), Noise Abatement Act (*Wet geluidhinder*). With regard to the Soil Protection Act, negotiations can be influenced by the substantial costs that soil pollution can lead to. Information about soil pollution can be requested from the land register.

Pursuant to the aforementioned legislation, various permits may be required. If negotiations result in a permit application or governmental decision, third parties might appeal against this permit or decision. The court will review the lawfulness of the decision or permit and will not take the result of the negotiation into consideration.

2.15 Intellectual Property Laws

In transactions, an increasingly important part is played by intellectual property rights. There is of course a great variety of intellectual property rights. For some, such as trademark rights and patent rights, registration in designated registers is required. Other intellectual property rights, such as copyrights, database rights, and trade name rights, arise without formalities by operation of law.

It is essential in negotiations regarding a transaction involving intellectual property rights to have—where possible—consulted the appropriate intellectual property registers. After all, the registration contains information that may be of great importance for the transaction that is being negotiated. For example, one may find out what the rights exactly entail, who the actual owner is of the intellectual property rights concerned, what the duration of the exclusive rights is, whether the rights have been encumbered with pledges, and whether any licenses have been granted in respect thereof. Also, one should be conscious of the fact that, typically, such registers are effective on third parties as far as ownership, the encumbrance of pledges, and the granting of licenses are concerned.

Furthermore, it may be important to be aware of the requirements for assignment or licensing of the relevant intellectual property rights. Not uncommonly, it is advisable to make (additional) contractual arrangements with respect to, for example, the use (or refraining from use) of the intellectual property concerned.

Contractual arrangements are even more important where "quasi" intellectual property (such as know-how and trade secrets), which does not fall under any specific laws, is concerned.

2.16 Privacy and Data Security Laws

If a transaction involves the so-called processing of personal data, the rules of the Data Protection Act (DPA), which is the Dutch national equivalent of the EU Privacy Directive, might be applicable. In the context of the DPA, "processing" means any operation or set of operations involving personal data, whether or not by automatic means, such as the collection, use, or disclosure of personal data. "Personal data" means any information relating to an identified or identifiable natural person. The scope of the DPA is limited to the processing of personal data carried out in the context of the activities of an establishment of a controller in the Netherlands. A "controller" is any natural or legal person that alone or jointly with others determines the purposes and means of the processing of personal data.

The DPA provides several conditions and obligations connected to the processing of personal data. These requirements should be taken into account in a timely manner during the negotiations in order to prevent them from becoming a barrier to the further completion of the transaction. For example, the processing of personal data is allowed only if it can be based on one or more of the grounds explicitly provided for in the DPA (e.g., data subject consented to processing, processing necessary for performance of a contract with data subject). Furthermore, the DPA requires the personal data to be used by the controller in a manner that is compatible with the purposes for which the personal data have been obtained. An obligation that might actually require (substantial) investments from the controller is the obligation to take adequate technical and organizational measures for the protection of the security of the relevant personal data. Finally, the processing of personal data has to be reported to the Dutch Data Protection Authority prior to the moment the personal data are being collected. Some types of processing are exempted from such notification obligation by the so-called Exemption Decree, which also contains the conditions for exemption.

Particular attention should be paid to a special type of processing, the transfer of personal data from the Netherlands to a so-called third country (i.e., a non-EU country). Personal data may only be transferred to countries having adequate protection. The United States, for example, has not been identified as having an adequate level of protection. If the country in question does not offer an adequate level of protection, the transfer can still legally take place if it falls under one of the exceptions enumerated in the DPA (e.g., data subject consented to transfer). If no exception applies, the Dutch Minister of Justice can, after having gained the advice of the Data Protection Authority, issue a permit for the transfer. The issuance of such permit sometimes takes several months.

2.17 Principles of Reasonableness and Fairness

The Dutch Civil Code provides that an agreement has not only the legal consequences as agreed to therein by the parties, but also those that result—depending on the nature of the agreement—from the law, customs, and the requirements of reasonableness and fairness. The principles of reasonableness and fairness constitute one of the fundamental elements of Dutch civil law and play an important role in determining the exact meaning of the contractual obligations and in construing agreements generally.

This is true with respect to agreements that are final (whether oral or in writing) and also with respect to the relationship between the parties in the phase prior to the moment the parties have reached, or could have reached, final agreement. Indeed, although there is no provision in the Civil Code expressly stating so, it is a general principle of Dutch law that during the negotiations the parties should behave in accordance with the requirements of reasonableness and fairness. This means, among other things, that each party must take into account the other's justified interests. The Civil Code does not provide for any definitions or guidelines clarifying what exactly these principles of reasonableness and fairness include. Rather, it concerns principles of law that are applied by the courts on a case-by-case basis with reference to how these are experienced and develop in day-to-day life.

Applied to contract negotiations, these general principles of reasonableness and fairness have resulted in a generally accepted principle of law that there may be situations in which the parties have reached such a phase in the negotiations that they are no longer at liberty to unilaterally terminate the negotiations on penalty of the other party being able to obtain an injunction ordering the parties to continue their negotiations. Another possibility in such a situation is a claim for damages against the terminating party. There can be situations in which the parties can be said to be free to unilaterally withdraw from the negotiations, but a party that does so would be required to pay damages, in principle limited to the costs and expenses incurred by the party on the other side. It should be noted, however, that in situations where a party is held to have withdrawn wrongly from negotiations, the damages may include more than just expenses incurred; indeed, the damages may then even include compensation for loss of profits.

It is not possible, therefore, to draw a clear line between the various phases in the negotiation process and the corresponding rights and obligations of the parties in case of termination of negotiations; this fully depends on the facts and circumstances of the case at hand.

2.18 Letters of Intent

To some degree, parties have it in their control to agree upon the extent to which they wish to remain free to break off their negotiations at will. It often happens that in a letter of intent, preliminary agreement, or heads of agreement the parties stipulate that they will continue to negotiate "subject to board approval" or "subject to contract" or otherwise specifically agree that there shall be no binding agreement whatsoever unless and until there is a written contract duly signed by all parties. In itself such stipulations are valid under Dutch law, but it should be noted that to the extent such preliminary agreements are governed by Dutch law, the parties are required to exercise their rights with due observance of the principles of reasonableness and fairness. In addition, the Dutch Civil Code contains a provision to the effect that a party to an agreement who has the power to exercise a certain right may not abuse that power—for example, by exercising the right for no purpose other than to harm the other party. Whether this limitation on the exercise of powers may become applicable fully depends on all relevant facts and circumstances of the case in question, particularly the wording of the preliminary agreement and the intentions of the parties.

The use of letters of intent, heads of agreement, and the like tends to be the rule rather than the exception in commercial negotiations in the Netherlands today. Even in transactions between Dutch parties, such documents are often drawn up, in many cases using one of the English names mentioned above. Since these types of documents are typically borrowed from the legal and commercial practice in Anglo-Saxon countries, it has always been somewhat of a gray area when it comes to determining whether, and if so, to what extent, the preliminary agreement contains binding obligations. To avoid any surprises in this respect, it is of utmost importance that any document called heads of agreement or letter of intent be drafted carefully to eliminate as much as possible any doubts about the exact intentions of the parties. As a general rule the courts will look at the substance of the matter or document rather than at its form. In other words, giving a document the name of letter of intent or heads of agreement is by no means decisive for settling the question whether it contains any binding obligations or not.

2.19 Oral or Written Agreements

Considering the fact that the Dutch are not very formal by nature, it is not surprising that Dutch law contains relatively few formal requirements with respect to the form or contents of agreements. For instance, formal requirements apply with respect to conveyance of real estate, transfers of registered shares, or assignment of receivables. For these types of transactions, the law prescribes a notarial deed or a written agreement, as the case may be. In most cases, however, agreements can be laid down in documents specifically drawn up for the purpose or in an exchange of letters or otherwise, and they can even be made orally. Enforcement of any such agreement, however, very much depends on whether or not the terms of the alleged agreement can be proven, with the burden of proof in general being on the party that seeks enforcement.

2.20 General Terms and Conditions

Finally, in many commercial transactions and in domestic and international trade generally, the parties often make use of general terms and conditions. The Dutch Civil Code contains a rather detailed set of provisions regarding general terms and conditions, the application of which is not limited to transactions with consumers only. The Civil Code also contains provisions regarding the "battle of forms."

3. Practical Observations

In considering non- (or at least less-) legal aspects, bear in mind that there is no typical type of negotiations in the Netherlands. Each transaction has its own features, characteristics, and players that render each transaction unique.

3.1 Participants

Although there certainly are many exceptions, as a general matter it can be said that Dutch businesspeople normally take an active and leading role in negotiations, sometimes preferring to reach agreement on the business issues in direct and private negotiations with the principals on the other side (with the details to be worked out and put in writing later), and sometimes with the corporate finance advisors and the lawyers—and other advisors involved—at their side at the negotiation table. Auditors and tax advisors often get involved in the negotiations, but usually focus on specific technical aspects of the transaction rather than playing a central and leading role. Especially in mergers and acquisitions, it is not unusual for corporate finance advisors and lawyers to perform a leading role in the negotiations and in the overall planning and coordination of the transaction and related activities, particularly with respect to due diligence and transaction documentation.

3.2 Outside Attorneys and In-House Counsel

Dutch attorneys (*advocaten*) are lawyers in private practice who are admitted to the bar. They are registered on the *tableau* in the court district where their offices are located, but authorized to practice and appear in courts throughout the country. The Netherlands is divided into nineteen court districts. *Advocaten* are bound to rules of conduct issued by the Netherlands Bar Association and to strict obligations concerning confidentiality. In-house lawyers can be, but are not necessarily, admitted to the bar and accordingly are not always subject to, or protected by, such rules.

3.3 Role of Civil Law Notaries

Notarissen, or civil law notaries, are lawyers appointed in a limited number by the Queen of the Netherlands. They have exclusive authority to execute notarial deeds required for the incorporation of N.V.s and B.V.s, and Dutch associations and foundations, or convey real estate and draw up marriage contracts and wills. Since 1992, a notarial deed is also required to transfer or create pledges and certain other rights relating to registered shares of B.V.s and N.V.s. The position of the civil law notary in a transaction is, in principle, neutral in that he or she must look after the interests of all parties to the notarial deed rather than representing one specific party thereto.

3.4 Timing

The timing of negotiations fully depends on the type of transaction and on the parties involved. Nevertheless, it can be said that the Dutch tend to get down to business rather quickly, focusing on main points first and dealing with the details later. The timing of a transaction's closing can be influenced by certain waiting periods or delays that are prescribed or can occur when observing the requirements of the Dutch Works Council Act or the Dutch Competition Act, if applicable.

3.5 Due Diligence

The idea of due diligence is well accepted in the Netherlands. As a matter of fact, it is even commonly referred to using the English expression for lack of an appropriate equivalent in Dutch. Normally, due diligence is conducted during or prior to contract negotiations—in other words, prior to closing—although sometimes it is appropriate or necessary that due diligence (at least in part) is performed after closing. The due diligence review and inquiries typically include such matters as corporate and business records, employment agreements, claims and litigation, and environmental matters. Quite often due diligence investigations are conducted by means of an online data room, allowing (legal) advisors access to the due diligence information from any location.

3.6 Corporate Approvals

The managing boards of N.V.s and B.V.s have the ultimate executive decision-making powers. Depending on a corporation's size and internal organization, in many cases there are persons other than the managing board members performing negotiations and making decisions. It often happens, of course, that the persons who ultimately have to approve the transaction are not directly involved in the negotiations or only get involved at a later stage, whether for reasons of availability, responsibility, or strategy. As a general rule, the larger the organization the more formally the negotiations are likely to be approached. In practice this may mean that a party indicates that it is negotiating a transaction "subject to board approval." Sometimes this is merely a self-imposed—and self-serving—condition; in other cases this is a real legal requirement based on the law or the company's articles of association. Indeed, management of large N.V.s or B.V.s (i.e., N.V.s and B.V.s that are subject to the large company regime (*structuurregime*)) is required by law to submit certain major transactions for approval to its supervisory board.

Also, the Dutch Civil Code prescribes for the N.V. (whether subject to the large company regime or not) that management requires approval of the general meeting of shareholders for certain resolutions concerning a material change in the identity or nature of the company or its business, among which the transfer of the company's business (or substantially all of it); the entering into or termination of a long-lasting cooperation with a third party, if such entering into or termination has a material effect on the company; and the acquisition or divestiture of an interest in another company with a value of at least one-third of the company's total assets. In addition, N.V.s and B.V.s may have voluntarily adopted similar or other approval requirements, either at the supervisory board level or at the shareholder level. In order to determine whether such requirements are applicable, one has to review the company's articles of association. Copies can be obtained from the trade register where the company is registered. The approval requirements discussed in this paragraph are purely internal matters; failure of management to request or obtain the required approval does not render an otherwise valid transaction or agreement invalid (leaving aside situations in which the other party clearly acted in bad faith, knowing that the required approval had not been given).

3.7 Foreign Exchange Regulations and Methods of Payment

Foreign exchange regulations in the Netherlands were gradually liberalized during the 1980s. They have basically been scaled down to mere reporting requirements that must be observed by banks operating in the Netherlands and by persons making or receiving cross-border payments.

In the Netherlands payments in commercial and in personal matters are generally made by wire transfer as opposed to checks, which are commonly used in the United States. If a check is used in commercial matters, it is usually a certified check issued by a bank on behalf of the payor.

Banks can also play a role in commercial transactions in the Netherlands in situations that require the use of bank guarantees, that is, undertakings similar to a letter of credit by which a bank effectively secures (or sometimes assumes as its own independent obligation) payment of an obligation of a party to a contract.

3.8 Negotiations with the Government

If a governmental body or state-owned company is party to a private agreement, it is subject to the provisions of civil law. However, for subjects that are exhaustively regulated by national, provincial, or municipal law, a governmental body is not allowed to enter into a private agreement.

A point of special interest in negotiations with the government is the Government Information Public Access Act (*Wet openbaarheid van bestuur*). This act applies to the disclosure of information by administrative authorities. Anyone may request information contained in documents concerning an administrative matter from an administrative authority or an agency, service, or company carrying out work for which it is accountable to an administrative authority. There are only limited grounds of refusal for these information requests. Therefore, negotiation documents or other information might be disclosed.

3.9 Negotiations Online

Over the past five years the use of online communication technologies for the conduct of negotiations has increased considerably in the Netherlands. The most frequently used means is e-mail, although other technologies such as videoconferencing and secured Web sites are also used.

From a practical point of view, the most notable effects of such technologies on negotiations are the increased speed and effectiveness of negotiating and the decreased necessity of parties actually having to meet each other in person. Nevertheless, because of the partnership element of a lot of contracts, most parties still have the desire to meet the other party at least once during the negotiation process.

From a legal point of view, the effects of online communication technologies on negotiations are moderate because of the technology-neutral wording of the part of the Dutch Civil Code that covers the establishment of agreements, and also because of the influence of EU legislation. According to the Civil Code an agreement is formed by an offer and its acceptance. Both an offer and its acceptance are regarded as so-called legal acts. Each legal act requires an intention to produce legal effects manifested by a declaration. In principle the declaration can be made in any form—in writing or orally, and also by e-mail or through other technological means. Should the law nevertheless prescribe an agreement in writing in order for that agreement to be valid, then such requirement shall also be complied with if the agreement has been concluded electronically and (i) the agreement can be consulted by the parties; (ii) the authenticity of the agreement is sufficiently safeguarded; (iii) the moment of creation of the agreement can be ascertained with sufficient certainty; and (iv) the identity of the parties to the agreement can be ascertained with sufficient certainty. Further details of these additional requirements have been laid down in the Dutch Civil Code.

Nevertheless, certain aspects connected to the use of the aforementioned technologies do sometimes create legal questions. For example, when does an e-mail containing the acceptance of an offer actually constitute an acceptance? According to the Civil Code, a declaration made to a specific person must, in order to be effective, have reached that person. Because the Dutch Civil Code does not require that the person to whom the declaration was addressed has actually read the contents of it, most authors in the Netherlands assume that an e-mail containing an acceptance is effective as such from the moment the e-mail has reached the addressee's inbox. In case of Web-based e-mail services, this means that the relevant moment is not the moment an e-mail reaches the addressee's hard disk on its computer, but the moment the e-mail reaches the service provider's mail server. Another specific legal issue in relation to negotiations and the use of online communication technologies concerns, for example, the evidential value of electronically signed documents.

4. Resolving Disputes

4.1 Choice of Law

As a general rule, the parties to an agreement are free to choose the law by which they wish the agreement to be governed. Such a choice of law is normally recognized and enforced by the courts in the Netherlands. There are, however, some exceptions. The courts of the Netherlands may refuse to accept a choice of law to the extent that any provisions would be contrary to public policy in the Netherlands, or if and to the extent there are mandatory rules of the law of another country with which the transaction or situation has a close connection if and as far as under the laws of such country those rules must be applied whatever the chosen law. The same is true if there are rules of Dutch law that are mandatory irrespective of the chosen law. Typical examples of such exceptions include real estate transactions—where at least all the technical aspects and all matters relating to the conveyance are governed by the law of the jurisdiction where the property is located—and transfers or pledges of shares of N.V.s or B.V.s.

If in negotiations with one or more Dutch parties it is agreed that the agreement shall be governed by the laws of a jurisdiction other than the Netherlands, this does not mean, of course, that Dutch law no longer plays any role at all. If, for example, the negotiations, at least in large part, are physically taking place in the Netherlands and if one party should unilaterally terminate them, a Dutch court would be likely to apply Dutch law to any claims for damages or for an injunction for the negotiations to be continued, notwithstanding the fact that there may already have been drafts of an agreement on the table with a choice of law clause providing for the law of another jurisdiction to be the governing law.

The Rome Convention on the Law Applicable to Contractual Obligations of 1980 entered into force for the Netherlands in 1991. The provisions of this Convention are applicable to contractual rights and obligations in situations where the governing law must be chosen from among the laws of various jurisdictions. These rules apply, as part of Dutch law, irrespective of whether the chosen law is the law of an EU member state or not. Accordingly, the Convention is equally relevant in transactions between Dutch and American parties as it is in transactions between Dutch and other EU parties. Obviously, its rules are particularly important if there is no valid choice of law in the agreement in question.

4.2 Jurisdiction and Enforcement of Judgments

The courts of the Netherlands generally have jurisdiction over disputes between parties if at least one of them is resident in the Netherlands. Aside from the rules of general applicability laid down in the Dutch Code of Civil Procedure, parties to an agreement can also contractually agree that a particular district court in the Netherlands shall have exclusive jurisdiction over disputes arising out of or otherwise in connection with the agreement in question. Whether a judgment obtained in a Dutch court is enforceable outside the Netherlands—or vice versa—depends on whether there is a treaty in place of mutual recognition and enforcements of judgments in civil and commercial matters between the Netherlands and the foreign country. Within the EU such enforcement abroad is possible in accordance with, and subject to, the provisions of the EU Regulation on the Jurisdiction and Enforcement of Judgments in Civil and Commercial Matters of December 22, 2000, which entered into force on March 1, 2002. Similar treaties are in place between the Netherlands and several others countries, but not the United States. Consequently, a judgment obtained against a Dutch party in a U.S. court is not automatically enforceable in the Netherlands. In order to obtain a judgment that is enforceable in the Netherlands one would have to file its claim (anew) with the competent Dutch court and submit in the course of those proceedings the final judgment obtained in the United States. If the Dutch court is satisfied that certain internationally accepted principles concerning jurisdiction have been observed, it will normally give binding effect to the substance of the U.S. judgment, unless the latter should contravene Dutch principles of public policy.

4.3 Arbitration and Alternative Dispute Resolution

As an alternative to settlement of disputes or claims in the courts, parties in many commercial transactions choose arbitration. The Netherlands has well-developed rules regarding arbitration, which are laid down in the Code of Civil Procedure. The Netherlands, like the United States, is a party to the Convention of New York of 1958 on the Recognition and Enforcement of Foreign Arbitral Awards. Both in domestic as well as in international transactions, the parties often agree to settle any disputes in accordance with the rules of the Netherlands Arbitration Institute (NAI), a well-respected private organization.

Other forms of alternative dispute resolution are used as well, albeit less frequently than in the United States. This is not surprising, since litigation in the Netherlands and other countries on the continent is quite different from litigation in the United States. Also, it can be said that people in Europe, or in any event in the Netherlands, are much less litigious than in the United States. Nevertheless, in addition to arbitration, there are some forms of alternative dispute resolution that are often used, including mediation (very much on an ad hoc basis and not in an institutionalized form). This instrument is becoming more popular in the Netherlands. Furthermore there is a typical feature of Dutch law, called *bindend advies* (binding recommendation or, literally, advice). In case of a *bindend advies*, the parties appoint a third person to decide on a specific issue—often of a factual nature—and agree in advance to be bound by and comply with his or her decision. Such arrangements constitute an agreement between the parties, which is enforceable in accordance with its terms like any other agreement.

Online dispute resolution (ODR) is in development in the Netherlands. There is an initiative to offer e-mediation, e-complaints, and e-arbitration for electronic commerce transactions in particular. The future will tell whether these forms of ODR will catch on.

5. Conclusion

In the United States, there used to be a saying: "The trouble with the Dutch . . . is that they are giving too little . . . and asking too much." Whether there ever was or still is any truth in this saying is hard to determine. It is probably more a matter of personal appreciation than anything else, since it tells something about the Dutch but perhaps as much about the person on the other side of the table. In any event, what can be said is that the Dutch, following the steps of their ancestors, like to do business in a businesslike and often rather direct manner. Negotiations are part of the game and the Dutch try to play the game well.

Jaap Willeumier and Eva Das
Stibbe
Stibbetoren
Strawinskylaan 2001
1077 ZZ Amsterdam
The Netherlands
Phone: +31 20 546 06 06
Fax: +31 20 546 01 23
E-mail: info@stibbe.nl

CHAPTER 37

International Business Negotiations in Nigeria

Ayodele Musibau Kusamotu
THE GREENFISH CHAMBERS
KUSAMOTU & KUSAMOTU
LAGOS, NIGERIA

1. Introduction

1.1 Broad Demographic Information

The Federal Republic of Nigeria is the most populous African country. The inhabitants are black Africans from sub-Saharan Africa. Popularly referred to as Nigeria, the country is divided by the river Niger and is geographically situated in West Africa. The population is about 140 million with a total land area of about 356,667 square meters. It practices a federal system of government with thirty-five states excluding the Federal Capital Territory. Nigeria consists of many contradictions and oftentimes is said to defy all logic. The country has reached the brink of crisis many times. Despite this, it is now ranked by Goldman Sachs Investment Bank as one of the eleven countries that has the potential to become one of the world's largest economies along with BRIC (Brazil, Russia, India, and China). Nigeria is also famous for its film industry (aka "Nollywood"), which is the third-largest in the world. The country is a full member of the Organization of the Petroleum Exporting Countries (OPEC) and the sixth-largest oil producer in the world. In recent years the country earned high returns from the spike in oil prices. Because of its high population and need for infrastructure, the Nigerian real estate sector has seen an incredible boom and created opportunities for investors. Other areas of investment includes infrastructure and telecommunications. The country is a democracy with Umaru Musa Yar'Adua as the current President of Nigeria.

1.2 Historical and Cultural Background

In 1914, the southern and northern protectorates were amalgamated and named Nigeria by the British government. Nigeria comprises a melting pot of various ethnic groups. The major ethnic groups are the Yorubas, Hausas, and Ibos. Generally, the Hausas are in the northern parts of Nigeria, the Ibos in the east, and the Yorubas in the west. The cultures of these tribes are very different. The Hausas live in a highly feudalist society and look up to the "emirs" as spiritual and local leaders. They are predominantly a Muslim community. The Yorubas, by contrast, have a very colorful culture. They are led by the Obas, who are local "kings" often appointed by lineage. In a typical Yoruba society, there are as many as three ruling houses. Muslim and Christian faith are in the majority amongst the Yorubas and evenly distributed. The Ibos, by contrast, are culturally republican with the majority being Christians. All the ethnic groups have a significant population that practices its own local religion. Some of the practices of these faiths are criminal. This explains why many of the practices are done stealthily.

In October 1960, Nigeria gained its independence from the British government and became a royalist, federalist, and full member of the Commonwealth. However, the executive authority of the Federation remained in the hands of the Queen of England, exercisable on her behalf by the Governor General and the Governor for the Centre and Regions, respectively. On October 1, 1963, Nigeria abolished the crown and declared itself a Republic.

1.3 Civil War

Nigeria fought a civil war with the Biafran forces from July 6, 1967, to January 13, 1970. The attempt by Lt. Col. Ojukwu to lead the eastern provinces of Nigeria to secede and form the Republic of Nigeria failed. The wounds of this war are yet to fully heal. The Ibos moved to the eastern provinces during the war and abandoned their properties. Many of them were unable to recover their property after the war. In present-day Nigeria, a new movement called the MASSOB (Movement for the Actualization of the Sovereign State of Biafra) was formed in 1999 to continue the campaign. The federal government has taken a hard line against the promoters of this movement.

1.4 Military Coups

Post-independence Nigeria has been misruled by military dictators untrained for governance. They have turned a resource-rich country into one of the poorest in the world. The military governments seized power unconstitutionally by military coups. In January 1966 Nigeria suffered its first military coup and a countercoup on July 2, 1966. There were other coups on July 29, 1975, December 31, 1983, and August 27, 1985. The last military dictator was General Sani Abacha. Since 1999

Nigeria has been a democracy, albeit controlled by the retired generals as puppeteers.

2. Business Organization and Culture

Before embarking on negotiation it is essential to prepare adequately. It will be necessary to ensure that the party being negotiated with, if an artificial entity, has the capacity in law. With the exception of natural persons, only an incorporated or statutorily recognized person or body can sue or be sued. The Companies and Allied Matters Act is a federal enactment that governs the incorporation of corporate organizations. It is mandatory that any entity intending to rent property, employ staff, and engage in business locally be registered with the Corporate Affairs Commission (CAC). The CAC incorporates companies and also registers business names.

There is a difference between the incorporated company and a business name. While the incorporated company has legal personality, the business name does not. The CAC also incorporates Limited by Guarantee Companies, which are charities entitled to do business.

There are three types of companies in Nigeria: the Private Company Limited by Shares, the Public Limited Company, and the Unlimited Company. There is no requirement that a Public Company Limited by Shares be quoted on the Nigerian Stock Exchange. Insolvency, liquidation, receivership, and winding up are all regulated by the Companies and Allied Matters Act.

In exceptional situations, a foreign company that is not actually incorporated in Nigeria may do business in Nigeria for a specific project. In such a case an application is made to the Secretary of the Federal Government for approval by the National Council of Ministers. However, the foreign company would be categorized as an unregistered company.

In order to qualify for the exceptional situation above, the foreign company must belong to one of these categories:

a.   Foreign companies invited to Nigeria by or with the approval of the Federal Government of Nigeria to execute any specified individual project.

b.   Foreign companies that are in Nigeria for the execution of a specific individual loan project on behalf of a donor country or international organization.

c.   Foreign government–owned companies engaged solely in export promotion activities.

d.   Engineering consultants and technical experts engaged on any individual specialist project under contract with any of the governments in the Federation or any of their agencies or with any other body or person, where such contract has been approved by the federal government.

2.1 Nigeria Export Processing Zones Authority

As a result of various red tape and administrative bottlenecks, the Federal Government of Nigeria has established a special class of companies registered with Nigeria Export Processing Zones Authority (NEPZA). These entities are given special incentives to enable them to import raw material to the Free Trade Zone without customs duties and taxes being imposed. They can thus avoid the bottlenecks associated with the Nigerian Customs Service. Under this scheme there is no need for the business to incorporate a company in Nigeria. A foreign company or individual may obtain a license to operate within the Zone.

2.2 Partnerships

Partnership laws are generally governed by the state laws. In Lagos State, the operative partnership law is the Partnership Law under the Companies and Allied Matters Act. Except for legal practitioners, accountants, and cooperatives, a partnership must not exceed twenty members. Such a business is required to be incorporated as a company.

2.3 Cooperative Societies

Under the laws of Lagos State, Cap. C15, a Registered Society that has as its objective the promotion of the economic interests of its members in accordance with the cooperative principles, or a society established for the purpose of facilitating the operations of such societies, can be registered under the law with or without limited liability. The Registered Society must have the word "cooperative" in its name and will, under the law, be deemed a corporate body.

2.4 Overview of Legal System

The Nigerian legal system is derived from the English system because of the historical link as a colony of Great Britain. The legal system is predominantly common-law based. However, at the local level, customary law applies as personal law does for citizens. There are customary courts in the southern parts and Sharia courts in the northern parts to adjudicate on these matters.

In relation to business transactions, business matters are generally dealt with by the State High Courts and Federal High Court at first instance. The jurisdictions of these courts are primarily enshrined in the Constitution. There is only one Federal High Court in Nigeria, which is split into divisions throughout the country for administrative reasons. Each state has its own State High Court spread out in divisions through the state. Matters relating to intellectual property, telecommunications, securities, and oil and gas are dealt with in the Federal High Court in the vicinity in which the defendant resides or where the contract was entered into, while those relating to simple contracts are dealt with at the State High Court.

Appeals made on final decisions from the State High Courts go to the Appeal Court and ultimately to the Supreme Court. The court system is extremely slow and fraught with corruption, toll gates, and administrative bottlenecks. However, improvements are being introduced to the system on an ongoing basis in terms of reshuffling the judges.

As the courts operate at a historically slow pace, businesspeople will want to avoid the courts at all costs. For this reason it is imperative to involve a local lawyer at the outset of any business negotiation. The lawyer will be in a position to spot problematic issues and quickly flag potential areas of conflict. In addition, it is common to negotiate with the other parties and the exception to not reach agreement. The opposing side will always attempt to gain more concessions. It is thus critical to employ the services of a local lawyer to help with the negotiations.

3. Substantive Laws and Regulations Impacting Negotiations

3.1 Corporate Laws

Nationality is an important consideration when incorporating a company in Nigeria. While the Companies and Allied Matters Act governs the incorporation of companies, the Nigerian Investment Promotion Act allows a foreigner to own a local company 100 percent without any restrictions. However, in another breath it mandates that any company in which a foreigner has any equity must obtain a business permit from the Nigerian Investment Promotion Commission (NIPC) prior to commencing business. In practice, once the basic requirements are met to set up a local company, the CAC will incorporate the company. In order to avoid queries from the CAC, it is common practice to include the foreigner's offshore address on the incorporation forms. Otherwise the CAC may request the foreigner's expatriate quota or work permit.

3.2 Foreign Exchange Laws

Foreign exchange, otherwise known as hard currency, is regulated by the Central Bank Foreign Exchange Manual and Monetary Policies, and the Foreign Exchange (Monitoring & Miscellaneous Provisions) Act ("FX Act"). Under the FX Act a foreigner is expected to receive a Certificate of Capital Importation from the local bank after inflowing investment into Nigeria. When the foreigner is ready to divest, the certificate will be used to obtain foreign exchange by the local bank for remittance to the foreigner.

3.3 Securities Law

Securities law is governed by federal law. Any offer of shares for subscription to the public is governed by the Investments and Securities Act 2007 (ISA). The ISA partially governs conduct of public companies and listed public companies. The Companies and Allied Matters Act restricts a company acquiring its own shares except for certain purposes, which include to comply with an order of court. In addition, the articles of the company are also operative when a company wishes to purchase its own shares, thus the Companies and Allied Matters Act stipulates *inter alia* that shares shall only be purchased out of the profits of a company that would otherwise be available for dividend or the proceeds of a fresh issue of shares made for the purpose of the purchase. The ISA approves of collective investment schemes that are administered as unit trusts, open-ended investment companies, and real estate investment companies or trusts. The rules regarding share buybacks do not apply to open-ended investment companies that are allowed by their articles to acquire their own shares, structured in such a manner that they provide for the issuing of different classes of shares to investors, each class of shares representing a separate portfolio with a different investment policy. Portfolio investments are allowed in Nigeria albeit the investor ought to obtain a Certificate of Capital Importation for easy remittance of funds. Just before the American 2008 financial crisis, the buoyant Nigerian capital market took a downturn that saw the Nigerian government implementing policies to prevent the negative slide in the market. Disposal of shares is exempt from capital gains tax under Nigerian law.

3.4 Tax Laws

Taxes and Levies (Approved List for Collection) Act depicts the taxes and levies approved for collection by the three tiers of government. The list of approved taxes and levies are as follows:

- A. Taxes Collectible by the Federal Government
    1. Companies income tax
    2. Withholding tax on companies
    3. Petroleum profits tax
    4. Value-added tax
    5. Education tax
    6. Capital gains tax—residents of the Federal Capital Territory (FCT), Abuja

7. Stamp duties on corporate entities and residents of FCT, Abuja

8. Personal income tax with respect to:
   - Armed forces personnel
   - Police personnel
   - Income tax for residents of FCT, Abuja
   - External affairs
   - Nonresident individuals

B. Taxes/Levies Collectible by State Governments

   1. Personal income tax:
      a. Pay-As-You-Earn (PAYE) and direct taxation (self-assessment)
   2. Withholding tax (individuals only)
   3. Capital gains tax (individuals only)
   4. Stamp duties on instruments executed by individuals
   5. Pools betting and lotteries, gaming and casino taxes
   6. Road taxes
   7. Business premises registration fees
   8. Development levy (individuals only)
   9. Naming of street registration fees in the state capital
   10. Right of occupancy fees on lands owned by the state governments in areas of the state
   11. Market taxes and levies where state finance is involved

C. Taxes and levies to be collected by the local government

   1. Shops and kiosks rates
   2. Tenement rates
   3. On and off liquor license fees
   4. Slaughter slab fees
   5. Marriage, birth, and death registration fees
   6. Naming of street registration fee, excluding any street in the state capital
   7. Right of Occupancy Fees on lands in rural areas, excluding those collectable by the federal and state governments
   8. Market taxes and levies excluding any market where state finance is involved
   9. Motor park levies
   10. Domestic animal licenses
   11. Bicycle, truck, canoe, wheelbarrow, and cart fees, other than mechanically propelled trucks
   12. Cattle tax payable by cattle farmers
   13. Merriment and road closure levy
   14. Radio and television license fees (other than radio and television transmitters)
   15. Vehicle radio license fees (to be imposed by the local government of the state in which the car is registered)
   16. Wrong parking charges

17. Public convenience, sewage, and refuse disposal fees
18. Customary burial ground and religious places permits
19. Signboard/advertisement permit

The withholding tax is transactional tax for both individuals and companies and is applicable to dividend payments, bank interest, rent payments, royalties, commissions; consultancy, technical, and management fees; construction, contract of supplies, and director's fees.

3.4.1 Basis of Liability to Tax

Personal income tax in Nigeria is assessed on the basis of the aggregate of global income from within and without Nigeria. Tax liability of companies in Nigeria is primarily on income having its source or deemed source within the country as well as on remittances. Under the Companies and Income Tax Act, the profits of a Nigerian company are deemed to "accrue in Nigeria, whenever they have arisen . . . and whether or not brought into or received in Nigeria . . ."—i.e., "the global income." However, profits of a non-Nigerian company (a foreign company) from any trade or business are deemed to be derived from Nigeria:

  i.   if that company has a "fixed base" of business in the country to the extent that the profits are attributable to the fixed base;

  ii. if the foreign company operates a trade or business through a person in Nigeria authorized to conclude contracts on its behalf, or who habitually maintains a stock of goods or merchandise in Nigeria from which deliveries are regularly made by a person on behalf of the company it shall be liable to tax to the extent that the profit is attributable to the business or trade carried on through that person; or

  iii. if the foreign company is in Nigeria to execute a single contract involving surveys, deliveries, installations or construction it shall be assessed and charged to tax on a fair and reasonable percentage of the contract.

3.5 Antitrust/Anticompetition Laws

With the exception of the industry-specific laws that empower agencies of government to regulate specific industries (such as the Nigerian Communications Commission Act, which regulates the telecommunications operators, and the Department of Petroleum Resources, which licenses operators in the oil industry), there are no antitrust or anticompetition laws. The country does not have a competition policy despite the implementation of a vigorous privatization program from 1999 to 2007. However, the closest to regulating competition vis-à-vis international trade is the Customs Duties (Dumped and Subsidized Goods) Act, which allows for the imposition of duties of customs where goods have been dumped and subsidized.

3.6 Labor, Health, Safety, Industrial, and Environmental Standards

These are governed by federal and state laws.

3.6.1 Factories Act

The Factories Act provides for the registration of factories; for factory workers and a wider spectrum of workers and other professionals exposed to occupational hazards, but for whom no adequate provisions had formerly been made; for adequate provisions regarding the safety of workers to which the Act applies; and for the imposition of penalties for any breach of its provisions.

3.6.2 Workmen's Compensation Act

The Workmen's Compensation Act provides for the payment of compensation to workmen for injuries suffered in course of employment.

3.6.3 National Minimum Wage Act

The minimum wage prescribed by the law is NGN 7500 or $65 per month. However, the provisions do not apply to an employer with fewer than fifty workers, an establishment in which workers are employed part time, an establishment at which workers are paid on commission or on a pro rata basis, workers in seasonal employment such as agriculture, or any person employed in a vessel or aircraft to which the laws regulating merchant shipping or civil aviation apply.

The employer's obligation to the workers is to pay a wage not less than the national minimum wage once clear from all deductions except those deductions required by law or deductions with respect to contributions to provident or pension funds or schemes agreed to by the workers and approved by the government.

A "worker" is defined as any employee, any member of the civil service of the Federation or a state or local government, or any individual (other than persons occupying an executive, administrative, technical, or professional position in any such civil service) who has entered into or works under a contract with a employer, whether the contract is for manual labor, clerical work, or otherwise, expressed or implied, oral or in writing, and whether it is a contract to personally execute any work or labor.

4. Environmental Standards

Federal environmental standards are governed by the National Environmental Standards and Regulation Enforcement Agency (Establishment) Act 2007, which established the Agency. The Agency is responsible for the protection and development of the environment in Nigeria and for related matters. The Environmental Impact Assessment Act places a restriction on public and/or private sector projects without prior consideration of the environmental effects at an early stage. Where the extent, nature, or location of a proposed project or activity is such that it is likely to significantly affect the environment, an Environmental Impact Assessment will be required. Where the Federal, State, or Local Government Council issues a permit or license, grants an approval, or takes any other action for the purpose of enabling the project to be carried out in whole or part, an assessment will be required.

Below are listed mandatory study areas. The federal, state, and local governments are prohibited from taking any steps in these areas until the Agency has given its consent.

5. Mandatory Study List

- projects in the field of agriculture in excess of 500 hectares
- construction of airports having an airstrip of 2,500 meters or longer
- drainage and irrigation (construction of dams)
- land reclamation of over 50 hectares
- fishing (construction of fishing harbors)
- forestry
- housing development covering 50 hectares or more
- industrial chemicals (production capacity of each product or of combined products greater than 100 tons/day)
- petrochemicals, non metallic
- cement clinker throughput of 30 tons/hour
- iron and steel (require iron ore as raw materials for production greater than 100 tones/day)
- shipyards (deadweight tonnage greater than 5000 tons)
- pulp and paper industry (production capacity greater than 50 tons/day)
- infrastructure (highways, ports)
- construction
- mining where the lease covers an area in excess of 250 hectares
- petroleum: oil and gas development, power generation and transmission (e.g., construction of steam-generated power stations burning fossil fuels and having a capacity of more than 10 megawatts)
- quarries (proposed quarrying of aggregate, limestone, silica, quartzite, sandstone, marble within 3 kilometers if any existing residential, commercial or industrial area)
- railways: construction of new routes, construction of branch lines
- transportation: construction of mass rapid transport projects
- resort and recreational development: construction of coastal resorts, facilities, or hotels of more than 80 rooms

- water treatment and disposal
- toxic and hazardous waste (construction of incineration plant)
- water supply (construction of dams)

5.1 National Environmental Health Practice Regulations 2007

Amongst other things, this regulation ensures that premises are maintained in such a way as to prevent structural defects. An owner is responsible for ensuring that his premises are to be inspected and a report issued thereafter, which must be presented to the Environmental Health Authority for the issuance of a certificate of fitness for continued cohabitation or certificate of fitness for continued use. The states also have Environmental Sanitation Agencies.

6. Intellectual Property

Patents, registered design, copyright and trademarks have recognized intellectual property rights in Nigeria. Trademarks, patents, and registered designs need registration in Nigeria. Copyrights, however, do not need to be registered. Nigeria has no system of priority for the registration of trademarks. This makes foreign trademarks an easy target for unscrupulous businesses. Hence, it is always advisable to register trademarks before even commencing business in Nigeria. However, the Nigerian Patent and Design Act recognizes priority applications for Convention countries. These countries are itemized below:

Algeria	Germany
Argentina	Greece
Australia	Haiti
Austria	Holy See
Belgium	Hungary
Brazil	Iceland
Bulgaria	Indonesia
Burkina Faso	Iran
Cameroon	Ireland
Chad	Israel
Cote de Ivoire	Italy
Cuba	Japan
Cyprus	Kenya
Czechoslovakia	Lebanon
Denmark	Liechtenstein
Dominican Republic	Malawi
Finland	Malta
France	Mauritania
Gabon	Mexico

Monaco	Sri Lanka
Morocco	Sweden
Netherlands	Switzerland
New Zealand	Syrian Arab Republic
Niger	Tanzania
Northern Ireland	Togo
Norway	Trinidad and Tobago
People's Republic of Congo	Tunisia
Philippines	Turkey
Poland	Uganda
Portugal	United Arab Republic
Republic of Benin	United Kingdom
Romania	United States
Russia	Uruguay
San Marino	Vietnam
Senegal	Yugoslavia
Spain	Zambia

Design applications coming from the above countries or any other country declared by Order of the Minister to be a Convention country will be granted "foreign priority." The date of the application in the Convention country will be treated as the date of the application in Nigeria so long as it is made within six months in Nigeria. In the case of foreign priority applications, they ought to be made within twelve months of the foreign application in Nigeria.

Arrangements between Convention countries whereby an application in a Convention country is treated as an application duly made in another Convention country are also recognized.

By the Copyright (Reciprocal Extension) Order 1972, the extension of protection inures to individuals who are citizens of or domiciled in any of the countries specified in the Schedule and corporate bodies established by or under the laws of any of said countries.

Copyright by reference to country of origin is extended to works, other than sound recordings and broadcasts, first published in any of said countries, and to sound recording made in any of said countries. These countries are

Mauritius	Pakistan	Switzerland
Mexico	Panama	Tunisia
Monaco	Paraguay	United Kingdom
Netherlands	Peru	USA
New Zealand	Portugal	Venezuela
Nicaragua	Spain	Yugoslavia
Norway	Sweden	Zambia

6.1 Privacy and Data Security Laws

There are no specific privacy or data protection laws in Nigeria. However, section 37 of the Constitution states that "the privacy of citizens, their homes, correspondence, telephone conversations and telegraphic communications is guaranteed and protected." The difficulty with this provision is it that it does not address the rights of noncitizens.

6.2 National Identity Management Commission Act 2007

The National Identity Management Commission is empowered to compile the National Identity Database, which contains registered information or data relating to citizens of Nigeria and non-Nigerian citizens. A registrable person under the Act is a citizen of Nigeria or any person lawfully and permanently resident in Nigeria and any noncitizen of Nigeria who is lawfully resident in Nigeria for a period of two years or more. It is an offense for any person without lawful authorization to access data or information contained in the database.

6.3 Regulation of Foreign Investment

Nigerian Investment Promotion Commission Act No. 16, 1995, provides that no enterprise shall be nationalized or expropriated by any government of the Federation. No person who owns, whether wholly or in part, the capital of any enterprise shall be compelled by law to surrender his interest in the capital to any other persons. There shall be no acquisition of an enterprise by the federal government unless the acquisition is in the national interest or for a public purpose under a law that makes provision for

i. the payment of a fair and adequate compensation; and
ii. a right of access to the courts for the determination of the investor's interest or right and the amount of compensation to which he is entitled.

Any compensation payable under this section shall be paid without undue delay, and authorization for its repatriation in convertible currency shall, where applicable, be issued. Companies with foreign directors are expected to apply for a business permit. Directors' fees are remittable in the same manner as dividends accruing to the foreign company, which will be taxed at 10 percent withholding tax.

6.4 Other Potentially Applicable Laws and Regulations

The Central Bank of Nigeria Foreign Exchange Manual and Monetary Policies are very important as they affect investors in Nigeria. These are guidelines intended to help authorized dealers (banks), authorized buyers, and the general public in processing foreign exchange applications.

7. Other Significant Legal and Business Issues

7.1 Accounting Rules

There are two guidelines governing accounting in Nigeria. The first is the International Standards of the International Accounting Standard Board, which are the Accounting Standards (IAS) and Standing Interpretations Committee (SIC). The second guideline is the local standards, which are the Statements of Accounting Standards (SAS) and the Auditing Guidelines (AG).

7.2 Local Standards

7.2.1 Statement of Accounting Standards

These are the publications of Nigerian Accounting Standards Board (NASB). The following are available:

SAS 1	Disclosure of Accounting Policies
SAS 2	Information to Be Disclosed in Financial Statements
SAS 3	Accounting for Property, Plant and Equipment
SAS 4	Stocks
SAS 5	Construction Contracts
SAS 6	Extraordinary Items and Prior Year Adjustments
SAS 7	Foreign Currency Conversions and Translations
SAS 8	Accounting for Employees' Retirement Benefits
SAS 9	Accounting for Depreciation
SAS 10	Accounting by Banks and Non-Bank Financial Institutions (Part I)
SAS 11	Leases
SAS 12	Accounting for Deferred Taxes
SAS 13	Accounting for Investments
SAS 14	Accounting in the Petroleum Industry: Upstream Activities
SAS 15	Accounting by Banks and Non-Bank Financial Institutions (Part II)
SAS 16	Accounting for Insurance Business
SAS 17	Accounting in the Petroleum Industry: Downstream Activities
SAS 18	Statement of Cash Flows

7.2.2 Auditing Standards and Guidelines (AG)

These are the publications of the Auditing Standards Committee (ASC) of the Internet Corporation for Assigned Names and Numbers (ICANN). The following are available:

AG 1 Auditing Guideline on Engagement Letters
AG 2 Auditing Guideline: Prospectus and Reporting Accountant

7.2.3 Alternative Dispute Resolution

Because of the slow adjudication of cases in the Nigerian courts, many businesses now take advantage of the Arbitration and Conciliation Act to resolve disputes by arbitration and conciliation. Under the Act the decision of the arbitrator is final except when it is contested by an action for setting aside. However, ideally once an arbitration clause is inserted in an agreement, the dispute must first of all be determined by arbitration. The Act makes the Convention on the Recognition and Enforcement of Foreign Arbitral Awards (New York Convention) applicable to any award in Nigeria, or indeed in any contracting state arising out of an international commercial arbitration.

7.3 Powers of the National Assembly

The National Assembly consists of the Senate and the House of Representatives. The National Assembly is empowered to make laws on matters included in the Exclusive Legislative List set out in Part I of the Second Schedule of the Constitution to the exclusion of the state governments. Some of these areas are:

Item 10: Commercial and industrial monopolies, combines, and trusts
Item 13: Copyrights
Item 32: Incorporation, regulation, and winding up of bodies corporate, other than cooperative societies, local government councils, and bodies corporate established directly by a law enacted by a House of Assembly of a State
Item 34: Labor, including trade unions, industrial relations; conditions, safety and welfare of labor; industrial disputes; prescribing a national minimum wage for the federation or any part thereof; and industrial arbitrations
Item 43: Patents, trademarks, trade or business names, industrial designs, and merchandise marks
Item 59: Taxation of incomes, profits, and capital gains, except as otherwise prescribed by this Constitution

In addition, any matter in the concurrent legislative list set out in the first column of Part II of the Second Schedule of the Constitution is also inclusive. The State House of Assembly may make laws on matters that are also on the concurrent legislative list; however, if the state law is inconsistent with that of the National Assembly, it shall be void to the extent of its inconsistency.

8. Negotiation Practices

8.1 Participants

Negotiators in Nigeria can't be pigeonholed. They are not necessarily lawyers. Most local businesspeople will only approach a lawyer at the tail end of their negotiations. Despite the various cultures, the similar thread that runs through most of the ethnic groups is the deference toward age and the male-oriented society. In that vein, in a local negotiation, the older person expects recognition as a mark of respect for his or her age. The society is male-dominated and as such, women can sometimes disarm the situation. Having women in negotiations is a welcome and refreshing development. Typical negotiations will have the businessperson and his or her lawyer in attendance. The government is not usually involved except where the federal government participates in joint ventures or infrastructure projects.

8.2 Timing

Muslims and Christians are evenly spread among society and remain in the majority. While there remains a population of traditional faiths, Muslims go to the mosque on Fridays to worship and Christians go the church on Sundays. Fridays are essentially a half day in the northern parts of the country. Saturdays are usually reserved for social engagements. Accordingly, Monday, Tuesday, Wednesday, and Thursday are the best days to enter into serious business negotiations between the working hours of 9:00 a.m. and 5:00 p.m.

8.3 Negotiation Practices

A party has to thoroughly prepare before engaging in any negotiations in Nigeria. It is necessary to have knowledge on the subject, habits, antecedents, and inclinations of the opposing side. It is advisable to have a set of defined objectives for the negotiations, which may range from the ideal to the realistic to the unacceptable. One of the means of achieving this is to enter the negotiation with a draft agreement. The venue of the negotiation should be close to the decision-makers, preferably in the other party's headquarters. It should be noted that Nigerians are skilled negotiators, as they have been properly schooled in the environment they have been brought up in. Nigerians negotiate on a daily basis in the local markets and traffic jams. In such a polygamous society where one man may have four wives living under the same roof, special skills are required to live harmoniously. Ultimately, with compromise and flexibility the negotiation will succeed. The end goal should be a "win-win" situation.

8.4 Team Negotiators

Negotiations are mainly conducted in English. English is the national language and translators are not employed except when necessary. Negotiations are usually conducted in a convivial environment. It is advisable to conduct due diligence. The larger the size of the transaction, the more lawyers will be involved. In order to successfully negotiate, it is best to be extremely generous. Gifts before the negotiation are highly advised.

8.5 Negotiating Online

Undoubtedly, Internet technology has been a boon to cross-cultural negotiation in Nigeria. Despite the fact that the country is notorious for Internet scams, real negotiations do take place online.

E-payments have risen exponentially in Nigeria, with several banks offering different payment solutions. The volume of ATM transactions is projected to grow exponentially. Simultaneously, payment solutions are also emerging in the telecommunications sector with mobile phones. However, there are no e-commerce laws in place.

The older generation that is sixty years and above is unlikely to negotiate online. However, with the Internet becoming ubiquitous, most people are conducting negotiations online. The potential for online negotiations is great if people have access to cheap Internet connections. Currently, cybercafes are becoming a thing of the past in Nigeria. The costs of laptops are decreasing. However, the only people who can take advantage of the low-priced laptops are the educated elite. The majority of Nigerians remain uneducated and illiterate.

9. Contract Formation

9.1 Wording and Style

The document is in English and follows the typical common law format of drafting agreements.

9.2 Conditions and Defenses

Common law governs contractual terms. There are no mandatory conditions except that contracts with the federal government are expected to be governed by Nigerian law. Typical conditions such as capacity are all relevant in contract formations. Contracts for the sale of land must be in writing; otherwise, contracts may be oral. Consideration is essential. Defenses such as fraud, mistake, and frustration will all vitiate a contract.

9.3 Special Case for Online Agreements

Agreements may also be oral and subsequently there is no question as to their being lawful. Issues may, however, arise in the admissibility of computer-generated evidence at trial. However, the standard common law rules of intention to create legal relations, offer, acceptance, and consideration are also applicable to online agreements. Nonetheless, e-mail contracts seem to be the most popular mode of engaging as opposed to Web-based contracts. Pursuant to the statutes of fraud, contracts for the sale of land must be in writing, and writing as currently defined by Nigerian law does not take account of computers.

10. Conclusion

As a firm privileged to represent both local and foreign interests, our assessment of the environment is that it is one that is extremely favorable to foreign investors. There is a great need in Nigeria for infrastructure and good services. Cash is king, and the bane of local businesses is lack of access to expertise and technology. The recent government policy that required local banks to increase their capital base to $200 million has created a situation where these banks are constantly looking for financing opportunities, as they are heavily cash-rich. Nigeria is at the edge of an economic explosion and is a great place for entrepreneurs looking for opportunities. However, more so than elsewhere, they will need good lawyers to guide them through the terrain.

Ayodele Musibau Kusamotu
The Greenfish Chambers
Kusamotu & Kusamotu
www.kusamotu.com
#29 Ladipo Kasumu Street
Ikeja, Lagos State, Nigeria
Phone: +234-1-555 7121
E-mail: kusamotu@yahoo.com

CHAPTER 38

International Business Negotiations in Pakistan

Kairas N. Kabraji[1]

KABRAJI & TALIBUDDIN
KARACHI, PAKISTAN

1. Introduction

1.1 Historical and Cultural Background

At independence in 1947 the areas now forming Pakistan comprised the territories and provinces of Sindh, Punjab, Balochistan, and the North West Frontier Province. The largely eponymous ethnic populations of Sindhis, Punjabis, Balochis, and Pakhtuns or Pathans inhabited those areas. Pakistan is therefore ethnically diverse and it would be a mistake to assume homogeneity. In fact, in order to deal successfully with a Pakistani it is as important to know about his or her ethnic origin and background, particularly in a continuing relationship, as it is to run the usual financial checks.

Karachi, the capital of Sindh province and the birthplace of the founder of Pakistan, Mohammad Ali Jinnah, became the capital of the country and received large numbers of Muslim migrants from the north of India and from the trading communities of the hinterland of the west coast of India. There are also a large number of migrants from other provinces there. Karachi retains its preeminence as the cosmopolitan commercial center, major port, international air gateway, and industrial hub. Islamabad, a new city created in the 1960s on the Potwar plateau of northern Pakistan, is the federal capital. A city of politicians, bureaucrats, and diplomats, Islamabad was once famously (perhaps apocryphally) but certainly aptly described by a former American ambassador as a city "half the size of Arlington Cemetery and twice as dead." Lahore, the historic and beautiful capital of the Punjab, is the second commercial center and entrepôt for northern Pakistan and the cultural center of the country. Business and the major commercial law firms are principally located in these three cities, most of them in Karachi. Many of these firms have offices in more than one city.

---

[1] This chapter was prepared by Mr. Kairas N. Kabraji in 2000. It was updated, in August 2008, by Dr. Parvez Hassan and Ms. Reema Asad of Hassan & Hassan (Advocates), Lahore, Pakistan.

The demand for Pakistan as a separate homeland for the Muslims of the Asian subcontinent was rooted in the separate religious and cultural identity of the Muslims. Pakistan is therefore very much a Muslim country, but as a part of the former British Indian Empire much of the cultural and legal legacy of the Raj lingers on. The English language is its most enduring relic; it is the language of the government, the superior courts, and business and is used and understood in varying degrees at all levels of society in Pakistan.

1.2 Business Organization and Culture

Pakistan's economy is dominated by agriculture, and cotton and its byproducts are the mainstay of the economy. Pakistan's industrial development in the 1950s and 1960s was therefore centered around the textile industry, and most of the country's large business groups have their base in that sector. Over time most have diversified into other sectors. From predominantly trading families, this class of industrialists and entrepreneurs is the backbone of the Pakistani business world. Later generations, often educated in Britain and the United States, bring a high degree of expertise and formal business education to the advancement and promotion of their businesses. A new class of entrepreneurs, often self-made and venturing into newer high-tech areas, is also visible and growing.

Business groups are typically family-run, even if organized as companies listed on the stock exchange. Large, publicly owned, and professionally managed companies are emerging slowly but are the exception rather than the norm. Generally, foreign investors find suitable joint-venture partners in either of these groups. Joint ventures with prime global corporate names are much sought after in Pakistan.

Until the 1990s, the predominant sectors for foreign investment in Pakistan were pharmaceuticals and energy. In pharmaceuticals, large American and European companies sought local minority partners to act as guides to the intricacies of doing business in an emerging market, to open doors, and to deal with the bureaucracy and politicians. In the energy sector, particularly in exploration and production, the state sector dominated and, more often than not, government policy meant doing business with the government itself or with a government-owned company.

Beginning in the 1990s, with deregulation and privatization, private sector investment in infrastructure became the prime mover of economic policy, and the principal interaction of foreign investors as sponsors, with or without local partners, was with the government sector.

1.3 Legal System

Pakistan inherited a legal system based on English common law but has a written constitution (with a Westminster-style parliamentary democracy) that has survived repeated extra-constitutional military interventions. The inheritance, with India, from the British included a comprehensive framework of legislation in the fields of civil and criminal procedure, contracts, sale of goods, negotiable instruments, and companies. Because of this ancestry, Pakistani courts look to British and Indian jurisprudence and precedents. Pakistan also has a developing body of constitutional law, and because it has a written constitution American precedents, particularly of the U.S. Supreme Court, are also referred to for guidance on similar issues.

In recent years principles of Islamic law have been grafted onto this system, with emphasis on the enactment of Islamic criminal law (particularly the Islamic mode of punishment for certain offenses) and the enforcement of the Islamic law of evidence. Civil, commercial, and corporate law is still based squarely on common law.

In the economic sphere, the major legal development since the 1980s has been the development of a domestic banking system, which is not based on interest but rather on Islamic modes of profit sharing. This arises from the Islamic proscription on interest. The precise scope and operation of this proscription has been the subject of a long controversy that has recently been decided by the Supreme Court of Pakistan. In a landmark judgment, the Court held that payment or receipt of anything in excess of the principal sum is prohibited. The decision was likely to have a far-reaching impact on the economic, banking, and legal systems of the country. However, on review, this judgment has been set aside by the Supreme Court and the case has been remitted to the Federal Shariat Court for reconsideration.

Unfortunately, the court system in Pakistan is severely resource-starved and consequently overburdened and painfully slow. Therefore, it is generally avoided by business as a means of resolving contractual disputes. In a domestic context, however, there is frequent litigation against government at all levels (to control administrative action by judicial review). Regrettably, this is a recurring issue and a major consumer of court time.

1.4 Federal System

Pakistan is a federation comprising four provinces, each with its own legislature. The federal legislature is bicameral and legislates on subjects in a defined federal list as well as on other "concurrent" subjects with the provincial legislatures. Each province has its own court system with a high court at the apex. The provincial courts, including the high courts, hear both provincial and federal cases. The high courts have constitutional jurisdiction to carry out judicial review of administrative action by governmental authorities at the behest of aggrieved persons. The Islamabad High Court was established in 2007 for the Islamabad Capital Territory. There is a single Supreme Court that has constitutional jurisdiction, principally appellate but also original (adjudication of disputes between the federation and the provinces or between provinces) and advisory (the president may seek the Supreme Court's view on questions of constitutional law of public importance). The Supreme Court also has original jurisdiction with respect to violations of fundamental rights that present questions of public importance. It has used this jurisdiction, in many cases *suo moto*, in public interest litigation in the fields of human rights and environmental protection. The Constitution also provides for a Federal Shariat Court, which is hierarchically subordinate to the Supreme Court.

2. Substantive Law Affecting International Business Negotiations

2.1 Role of Government

Until the 1990s, the role of the state in commerce and industry was all-pervasive as a consequence of a wide-ranging nationalization program carried out by the Z.A. Bhutto government in the early 1970s. The state sector controlled virtually all sectors of the economy. Consequently, foreign investors and business executives typically had a great deal of interaction with the government or government-owned corporations when doing business in Pakistan. In the 1990s, state control largely receded, particularly in the industrial sector and, more recently, in infrastructure, power, energy, telecommunications, and electronic media. The government is also actively pursuing a policy of privatization of major state-owned assets, which means that international business in all likelihood will continue to have serious interaction with the government and its agencies. Government agencies still exercise a great deal of control over business in relation to consents, permits, and concessions, as well as through the taxing powers of the state. The policy of privatization suffered a severe blow in 2006, when the Supreme Court set aside the privatization of Pakistan Steel Mills.

2.2 Regulatory Agencies

Lately, there has been an increasing trend in Pakistan toward regulation of business activity by more or less independent regulatory agencies. Thus corporate securities are regulated by the Securities and Exchange Commission of Pakistan (SECP), the purview of which has been extended to include insurance and nonbanking financial institutions, a move perceived as the creation of a super-regulator in the financial services industry. The SECP also regulates the takeover of listed companies through legislation that requires the disclosure and reporting of acquisition of certain thresholds of ownership of share capital of listed companies with a corresponding obligation to make a public offer to buy out minority shareholders.

The recently established (2007) Competition Commission has been mandated to "ensure competition . . . to protect consumers from anti-competitive behavior" through, among others, a prohibition of abuse of dominant market position and deceptive marketing practices. It will continue, generally, the work of the Monopoly Control Authority that it has replaced.

Mergers and amalgamations of companies require the approval of the Competition Commission and the relevant provincial high court.

Prudential regulation of banking institutions has traditionally been the role of the central bank, the State Bank of Pakistan, which also formulates monetary and exchange policy and performs the exchange control functions under the role assigned to it by the exchange control laws (see section 2.4, "Exchange Control").

Telecommunications has been largely deregulated, although basic telephone services continue to be a limited duration monopoly operated by the Pakistan Telecommunications Company, an entity privatized in 2006. In parallel, the licensing and regulation of this sector has been assigned to the Pakistan Telecommunication Authority (PTA) and the assignment of wireless radio frequencies to the Wireless Frequency Board.

Electricity is regulated by the National Electric Power Regulatory Authority (NEPRA). Under the 1994 power policy, the independent power generation sector, which received the bulk of direct foreign investment in the period 1994 to 1996, is an anomaly that effectively stands outside the regulatory purview of NEPRA by virtue of the long-term power purchase contract model adopted for private power generation under the 1994 policy. The state-owned power utility, Water and Power Development Authority (WAPDA), has been restructured to include a national grid company that is the designated purchaser of power from the private sector and separate distribution companies for major urban areas as a step towards their privatization. The Karachi Electric Supply Corporation Limited (KESC) has already been privatized. The role of NEPRA in developing an electricity market based on principles of economic dispatch and regulating the electric power industry is still evolving.

The petroleum and natural gas sectors are regulated by the Oil and Gas Regulatory Authority (OGRA), which is responsible, *inter alia*, for granting licenses, establishing prices, and determining tariffs.

The Public Procurement Regulatory Authority (PPRA) is responsible for regulating, with an emphasis on transparency and accountability, the public procurement of goods and services by federal government-owned public sector organizations.

In the early 2000s, a set of federal laws was enacted to give effect to the WTO Anti-Dumping Agreement and Agreement on Subsidies and Countervailing Measures. Any significant injury to domestic industry caused by dumped imports or subsidized imports can be dealt with under these laws. The National Tariff Commission (NTC) is the investigating authority in this regard.

Depending on the sector, one or more of these agencies will therefore interact with foreign investors in the course of setting up a new business, regulation of business activities, or acquiring a privatized entity. This may also involve substantive negotiations with these agencies in certain cases, particularly if the agency is being asked to grant a license, consent, or permit that involves the exercise of discretion.

2.3 Intellectual Property

Pakistan is a signatory to the WTO Trade-Related Aspects of Intellectual Property Rights (TRIPS) provisions of the General Agreement on Trade and Tariffs. In the early 2000s, Pakistan upgraded and revised its intellectual property laws pertaining to copyrights, patents, and trademarks.

2.4 Exchange Control

In the aftermath of the May 1998 nuclear tests in Pakistan and the consequential resource constraints, all foreign currency outflows were, to varying degrees, controlled by the State Bank of Pakistan, in contrast to the considerable liberalization in exchange controls after 1990. These controls were, however, once again liberalized in the early 2000s. While imports are funded by letters of credit, foreign currency borrowing requires registration with the State Bank of Pakistan or the Authorized Dealer, as the case may be, and such registration allows remittances from Pakistan on account of debt repayment without requiring prior approval. Similarly, subject to certain conditions and guidelines, repatriation of equity capital (whether direct or portfolio investment) as well as dividends and bonus shares (stock dividends) do not require prior approval or reporting. Remittances on account of royalties and technical fees and like payments are also allowed subject to certain guidelines and registration with the State Bank of Pakistan without requiring prior approval (see section 2.11, "Regulation of Foreign Investment").

2.5 Tax

The Income Tax Ordinance was introduced in Pakistan in 2001. The principal direct tax in Pakistan is income tax, which applies to individuals and corporations alike, although at varying rates. Principles of income taxation are similar to those in the United Kingdom and the United States. Indirect taxation (consisting of customs duties on imports), general sales tax (a value-added tax on imports and sales of most kinds of goods), excise duties, and taxes on certain kinds of services are the other major tax factors in business planning.

2.6 Stamp Duty

Stamp duty is a provincial tax levied on the execution of instruments and varies from province to province (in a few instances, significantly). Its greatest impact is on transaction costs in the creation and registration of security over assets, the sale and disposal of assets (principally immovable (real) property), leases of immovable property, and transfers of shares and stocks. After income tax, it is the single most important local factor to be considered in the structuring of transactions, particularly asset sales involving significant immovable property or creation of security.

2.7 Corporate and Securities Law

The limited liability company (corporation) with perpetual succession is the most common form of business organization in Pakistan (as single member companies and private and public limited companies), although some trading and all professional (accounting and law) firms are still organized as partnerships.

The public issue or offer of securities requires the issuance of a prospectus, which must be approved by the Securities and Exchange Commission of Pakistan and the stock exchanges on which the securities are to be listed. There are Stock Exchanges at Karachi, Lahore, and Islamabad. The three stock exchanges in Pakistan are in the process of being corporatized, demutualized, and integrated pursuant to the proposed Stock Exchanges (Corporatisation, Demutualisation and Integration) Rules, 2008, to be made under the Securities and Exchange Ordinance, 1969.

All listed companies are required to comply with a comprehensive Code of Corporate Governance issued by the SECP.

2.8 Electronic Transactions

In 2002, a federal law was enacted to recognize and facilitate documents, records, information, communications, and transactions in an electronic form.

2.9 Labor Laws

There is complete freedom of contract for employees who fall into the management category (those not classified by statute as "workers" or the like). Workers are, however, protected from dismissal by the requirement to follow certain procedures, such as notice, inquiry, and hearing. Likewise, the permission of a labor court is required for closing down an establishment or laying off more than half the workers. Failure to observe these requirements is punishable with criminal sanctions, including a fine and imprisonment. There are no statutory provisions for the transfer of employees or pension and provident fund benefits to an acquirer. Merger and acquisition transactions therefore require protracted discussions and contractual provisions on employee issues.

2.10 Environmental Laws

Various legislations, rules, and regulations have been enacted with the aim of curtailing and controlling environmental pollution. The overarching legislation with respect to the environment established the Pakistan Environmental Protection Council (PEPC) as the supreme policy-making body supported by the Pakistan Environmental Protection Agency (PEPA). The PEPA is, in a way, the implementational arm of the PEPC. Four Environmental Protection Agencies (provincial EPAs) were also established at the provincial level, and each of these is mandated to work under the policies laid down by the PEPC and the PEPA.

There is a statutory requirement for an environmental impact assessment (EIA) to be filed for developmental projects. The National Environmental Quality Standards (NEQS) have been formulated by the PEPC. Further, the PEPA and provincial EPAs have been empowered to issue Environmental Protection Orders (EPOs) to deal with an actual or potential adverse environmental effect in violation of the provisions of the governing legislation. Environmental tribunals have also been constituted with exclusive jurisdiction to try serious environmental offences.

In pioneering public interest litigation, the superior courts of Pakistan have held that the constitutionally protected "right to life" and the "right to dignity" include the fundamental right to a clean and healthy environment. Because of this view taken by the superior courts, environmental liability will assume greater importance in the future, although implementation measures by the government remain weak.

2.11 Regulation of Foreign Investment

Foreign equity investment in life and general insurance sectors is allowed subject to certain requirements and minimum levels of foreign investment. There are no restrictions on foreign investment in manufacturing and greenfield industrial projects except in security printing, currency and minting, arms and ammunition, high explosives and radioactive substances, and alcohol (other than industrial alcohol). Further, there is no restriction on payment of royalty or technical fees for the manufacturing sector. The agreements in this regard, however, are required to be registered with the State Bank of Pakistan. In the nonmanufacturing sector, namely agriculture, service, social and infrastructure sectors, there are required minimum levels of foreign equity investment. In the service sector, foreign direct investment is allowed in any activity subject to obtaining permission and a No Objection Certificate or license from the concerned agency or agencies, and fulfilling the requirements of the respective sectoral policy. Payment of royalty or technical fee in case of non-manufacturing sectors is allowed subject to certain conditions and guidelines.

The repatriation of capital, capital gains, dividends, and profit by foreign investors is generally allowed freely and without prior approval subject to certain limits as regards listed shares (market price) and all other companies (net worth value). Facility for contracting foreign private loans (which do not involve any guarantee by the government of Pakistan) is available to all those foreign investors who make investment in sectors open to foreign investment, for financing the cost of imported plant and machinery required for setting up the project. Loan agreements, however, are required to be registered with the State Bank of Pakistan. Other foreign currency borrowing is also permitted for any other purpose subject to certain restrictions as to term and interest rates.

Similarly, residents of Pakistan, including firms and companies, are allowed to make equity-based investment (other than portfolio investment) in companies (whether incorporated or not) or joint ventures abroad on a repatriable basis, with prior permission of State Bank of Pakistan and subject to guidelines issued by it in this regard.

The Board of Investment (BOI) was established by the government in 2001 to facilitate foreign investments in Pakistan. The BOI acts as a clearing house for information and a support center for foreign investors.

2.12 Choice of Foreign Law; Application of Pakistani Law

Foreign investors will want applicable contracts to be governed by a foreign law, usually the law of the state of their origin—less typically, either English or New York law, if that is not the law of the investor's state of origin. On the other hand, the Pakistani counterparty will insist that the laws of Pakistan should apply. Except in cases where the government or its agencies are the counterparties, this is not likely to be prejudicial, since the Pakistani law of contract is the codified principles of English common law and will be familiar to those from common law jurisdictions. Where the government or any of its agencies are parties to the contract, most foreign lenders and investors will naturally be reluctant to contract under Pakistani law, and it is not unusual for the government and its agencies to accept a foreign (preferably neutral) governing law, especially in financial transactions. However, recently there has been greater resistance to the adoption of foreign governing law in contracts with government agencies.

Pakistani law will perforce govern certain aspects of a transaction: issues pertaining to immovable property will, under conflicts principles in most jurisdictions, be determined by the *lex situs*, that is, Pakistani law in the case of transactions in Pakistan. Likewise, while there is no compelling reason why a share purchase or shareholders agreement should not be governed by a foreign law, in practice, the *situs* of the property (shares) and the nature of the relationship between the parties is such that only the Pakistan courts can give effective relief by way of injunction and other equitable remedies such as specific performance. The time, trouble, and expense of calling expert witnesses to prove issues of foreign law as issues of fact will (absent fundamental strategic considerations in major transactions involving more than one contract) almost certainly outweigh any advantage of choosing a foreign governing law.

Ultimately, the decision requires careful consideration in tandem with the chosen dispute resolution procedure and consideration of venue and jurisdiction. Subject to foreign jurisdiction clauses in a contract, Pakistani courts will generally not accept an ouster of their jurisdiction in cases where, on commonly accepted tests, they have subject matter or territorial jurisdiction or any part of the cause of action has arisen in Pakistan (see section 2.13, "Dispute Resolution").

2.13 Dispute Resolution

The Pakistani courts are highly overburdened and, principally because of the slowness of the process, are generally not regarded as effective dispute resolution forums for disputes to which foreign investors are party, particularly in the case of ordinary money suits.

The Arbitration Act, 1940, provides a suitable framework for domestic arbitration. With respect to foreign arbitration, Pakistan is party to the Geneva Convention and Protocol for the Pacific Settlement of International Disputes (1924), the International Centre for Settlement of Investment Disputes (ICSID) Convention (1966), and the New York Convention on the Mutual Recognition and Enforcement of Foreign Arbitral Awards (1958).

In the past the superior courts of Pakistan have presented a mixed bag of judgments with respect to foreign arbitration clauses. Notwithstanding a foreign arbitration clause, the superior courts of Pakistan have on occasion stayed foreign proceedings on the basis of huge expenses of arbitrations outside Pakistan, presence of evidence or witnesses in Pakistan, convenience of the parties, or a dominant nexus with Pakistan. Conversely, despite a dominant nexus with Pakistan, the Courts have, on occasion, upheld foreign arbitration clauses on the basis of "sanctity of contract" and nonrelease of the parties from a bargain made willingly.

This state of ambiguity was resolved with respect to foreign arbitration clauses in 2005 with the ratification of the New York Convention and the coming into force of the Recognition and Enforcement (Arbitration Agreements and Foreign Arbitral Awards) Ordinance, 2005 (repromulgated in 2006 and 2007). The Ordinance provides for the recognition and enforcement of arbitration agreements and foreign arbitral awards in accordance with the New York Convention. The court is obligated to refer the matter to arbitration unless it finds the arbitration agreement to be null and void, inoperative, or incapable of being performed. The superior courts in Pakistan, in interpreting the Ordinance, have upheld the foreign arbitration clauses and the enforcement of foreign arbitral awards. They have held that the Ordinance has effectively taken away the discretion of the courts to stay the foreign proceedings in terms of the arbitration agreement, even on the ground of inconvenience.

The choice of a dispute resolution procedure requires considerable thought. Time and effort spent in getting it right will pay rich dividends when it comes to enforcement.

2.14 The Legal Profession in Pakistan

In Pakistan the professional designation of lawyers is "advocate." All advocates have a right of audience if licensed to appear at the relevant level in the judicial hierarchy. Many of Pakistan's leading lawyers were educated and trained in the United Kingdom (many are barristers called to the English bar) and, increasingly among the younger generation, the United States (and sometimes a combination of the two). Small firms and solo practitioners are the norm, and the majority of firms consist of between five and ten advocates.

The legal community in Pakistan came to international prominence in 2007 and 2008 for its protests, efforts, and sacrifices for the rule of law. They protested the actions of General Pervez Musharraf, who removed the Chief Justice and other judges of the superior courts of Pakistan who would not retake their judicial oaths under his Provisional Constitutional Order.

2.15 Lawyers as Board Members

It is not unknown for prominent corporate lawyers, usually the senior partner of the law firm appointed as the company's regular or leading law firm, to be appointed to the boards of multinational companies, usually as a nominee of the foreign parent company. This practice is seldom adopted by national companies. Directors of Pakistani companies are enabled by a statutory provision to appoint "alternate" (substitute) directors during their absence from Pakistan. This provision is frequently used by foreign nationals.

2.16 In-House and Outside Counsel

A number of large public companies, again mainly those in the multinational sector, employ in-house counsel. The role of in-house counsel will vary depending upon seniority and the company's own perception of the counsel's role on the company's management team. The principal functions of internal counsel are to manage the company's corporate and secretarial work or, where there is a full-time company secretary, to assist the secretary on legal issues; to manage the company's outside legal counsel and instruct and brief them on important transactions and litigation, either alone or with senior management; and generally to provide legal advice and opinion on matters not regarded as sufficiently specialized or complex to require the services of outside legal counsel.

Pakistani companies that have paid-up capital in excess of a certain amount are required by law to retain legal advisors. Most companies will have a relationship with a particular law firm (or, less frequently, an individual practitioner), if not a retainer arrangement. Larger companies and multinationals may use more than one firm, giving their corporate and commercial work to one firm and litigation to another or to specialized litigation counsel. Intellectual property and industrial relations are two specialized areas in which several significant niche practices have developed in Pakistan.

3. Negotiations

3.1 Participants

As in any jurisdiction, it is difficult to generalize as to the *dramatis personae* for any particular transaction in Pakistan. In a multinational or national public company, senior line management, particularly those heading the financial and operations functions, are likely to lead the team, and depending upon the seniority of the person leading the other side, there is a general perception of the necessity to match the level of representation. The chief executive may participate if there is a sufficiently senior counterparty (albeit not the chief executive) or if a mismatch arises from the relative sizes of the two companies.

3.2 Use of Lawyers

In any important international business negotiation, expect at least the company's inside counsel—and if sufficiently important or in large transactions, outside legal counsel—to assist in advising on (if not also drafting) documentation and participating in the negotiations. The degree to which either counsel will be involved and their precise role (active participation or advising behind the scenes) will depend upon the transaction and the company: national companies, particularly family-owned or closely held companies, are less likely to use counsel actively in negotiation. If the other side has a lawyer on the team, it would not be unusual for there to be a suggestion that the two lawyers meet to discuss legal issues separately. This may help the parties to address issues that are strictly legal in nature more quickly and separate from the larger business negotiations involving all parties. Except with the most sophisticated, professional-managed companies (particularly those whose managers have foreign training and experience), issues such as retaining control of drafting or paying particular heed to thoroughness of documentation are not usually emphasized.

3.3 Use of Financial Advisors

The use of financial advisors, particularly investment banks, is mainly prevalent in the privatization process where the financial advisor leads the scoping, structuring, and completion of the transaction on behalf of the government's Privatization Commission. The use of financial advisors for large or important transactions is not unusual in the private sector. Most often, financial advisors are used to supplement company resources that are available to manage the transaction and not because the board believes it needs independent advice to protect itself and the shareholders' interests.

3.4 Use of Accountants/Tax Specialists

Accountants in Pakistan are the principal source of advice for the corporate sector, and their advice is sought principally on tax issues. There are a few specialist tax lawyers in Pakistan, but their role is mainly to deal with particular cases in the tax adjudication process before the special tribunals or the courts. Accountants also play a major role in performing special audits, preparing accounts required to complete the transaction, and carrying out physical inventory checks in acquisition transaction.

3.5 Documentation

The importance of the emphasis on documentation will depend on the company and the quality of its advisors. Extensive and complex documentation is not the norm unless the process is being driven by the foreign party, although documentation that conforms with standards typically produced by large international law firms can be produced by some of the better local firms. There will be a desire on the part of experienced players to document as much as possible to avoid disputes (recourse to Pakistan courts for relief in contractual disputes is not generally seen as a viable option because of the length of time it takes to reach trial). This may not be true for new entrants in the league, on whom the detail will pall quickly.

There is also, simultaneously, a desire for simplicity and a reluctance to deal with complex issues that do not lend themselves to simple solutions. This can become a source of tension and conflict between the two sides. There may also be a tendency to view what has now become standard international documentation (both in style and content) as being "too complicated." This may be iterated by some local advisors, who may voice the view, where this is called for by the transaction, that such documentation will cause "problems" when produced to local regulators or tax or other authorities. More often than not this is not substantiated with any cogent reasons and should be resisted.

3.6 Due Diligence

Most commercial law firms and major accounting firms are generally familiar with the legal and financial due diligence process, particularly if they act regularly for multinationals. The thoroughness and depth with which due diligence is conducted could, however, be variable even within this group. From a client perspective, it is essential to spend time and effort in scoping the exercise and agreeing on the criteria and tests to be employed in writing the eventual report.

3.7 Timing

Depending on the party, it is possible to encounter both extreme pressure to expedite and conclude negotiations and a more measured and deliberate approach. This is obviously dictated almost wholly by the nature of the transaction and the commercial compulsions operating on the parties. Negotiations with government, in particular, can be slow and frustrating. Experience will vary, depending mainly on the confluence of political and bureaucratic support for the transaction: if the two forces are at variance, significant tension can develop. This can impede progress and retard completion significantly.

While there are no dates when negotiations are inappropriate in Pakistan, it is best to avoid the Islamic month of Ramadan, when the faithful are enjoined to fast from daybreak to dusk. During this period, workdays are shorter than normal and both start and end earlier. Very little work gets done during this month and business generally is very slow. The *Eid ul Fitr* and the *Eid ul Adha* festivals, as well as the ninth and tenth of the Islamic month of *Muharram*, are public holidays (at least two days each) and are also periods when Pakistani parties will be reluctant to meet to engage in negotiations.

3.8 Some Negotiating Tips

- The level of English-language skills is generally high in Pakistan, but not always at a consummate level. It is therefore important to make an early assessment of this facility on the opposite side. Otherwise, the use of certain idioms or colloquialisms, which normally would not be expected to cause offense in everyday speech in the West, sometimes unwittingly and unintentionally does in Pakistan.

- Similarly, while the use of metaphor or analogy is often a useful aid to argument, it should be employed thoughtfully in Pakistan, since it can be fertile soil for misunderstanding.

- Humor is an invaluable aid in creating a congenial atmosphere for negotiations, but there is nothing that can create tension as rapidly as the misconstrued joke. Nobody likes being laughed at.

- Likewise, critical comments about the country (even if true or well-meant) should be avoided. On the other hand, genuine compliments and appreciation will rapidly earn goodwill.

- As in many eastern societies, age and experience are accorded respect for their own sake. It is therefore important to follow that precept, whether or not, viewed objectively, it is merited in any individual case.

- Often the best ploys for disarming recalcitrant opponents are to express appreciation for their points of view, but nevertheless invite them to give due consideration to yours. A confrontational attitude and expressions of overt disagreement and challenge will only exacerbate disagreement.

- While it is a truism that negotiations should never be conducted except with courtesy (even in circumstances where this is not being reciprocated), stubborn opponents who maintain untenable positions are unlikely to change them if their adversaries raise their voices or are disparaging about their knowledge or skills in their attempts to prevail. Patronizing attitudes are unlikely to win points either. It is surprising how easily these elementary points may be overlooked under the stress and frustration of a protracted negotiation.

- That is not to say that tough talk is precluded; what is important is that the right message be sent and received, rather than that it be harshly delivered.

Kairas N. Kabraji
Kabraji & Talibuddin
61-A/1, Gulshan-e-Faisal, Bath Island,
Karachi 75530
Pakistan
Phone: 92(21) 583 8874-583 8876
Fax: 92(21) 583 8871
E-mail: kairas.kabraji@kandtlaw.com

CHAPTER 39

International Business Negotiations in Panama

Juan F. Pardini and Leonardo Bonadies
PARDINI & ASOCIADOS
PANAMA, REPUBLIC OF PANAMA

1. Introduction

1.1 Broad Demographic Information

1.1.1 Geography

The Republic of Panama, with an area of 23,321 square miles (75,062 square kilometers), located between Costa Rica and Colombia, forms the narrowest and lowest portion of the isthmus that links North and South America. Panama has an extension of land from the west to the east that resembles an elongated letter "S." Its coastline is 490 miles (788 kilometers) on the Atlantic Ocean and 870 miles (1,400 kilometers) on the Pacific Ocean. The Panama Canal, which is considered one of the Seven Wonders of the Industrial World, joins the two oceans and is approximately 50 miles long (80 km). Due to it's curved contour, the transit in the Canal moves to the northwest, not to the east which is often surprising for travelers. In Panama City the sun is seen to rise out of the Pacific.

Panama enjoys a favorable climate and weather conditions. The country lies in a hurricane-free zone and has had relatively few earthquakes or other natural disasters. Its mountainous areas and protected reserves on the eastern and western extremes benefit from cooler temperatures.

1.2 Historical and Cultural Background

Panama was part of the fourth trip of Christopher Columbus in 1502. However, it was Rodrigo Galván de Bastidas that first discovered this extraordinary land in 1501. On August 15, 1519 Pedro Arias de Avila founded Panama City, almost a hundred years before Jamestown, the first permanent English settlement in North America, was founded. Panama was part of the Spanish Crown until 1821 when it became independent but almost instantly Panama joint Colombia as an internal state. That situation changed dramatically on the afternoon of November 3, 1903 when the provisional government, led by Manuel Amador Guerrero, broke its ties with Colombia and became an independent republic.

1.3 Business Organization and Culture

Since Panama's discovery in sixteenth century, commerce and business have been two defining components of the Panamanian culture. Its elongated territory with two main ports (one in the Atlantic and one in the Pacific Ocean), helped to define Panama as a strategic point of trade.

The French Napoleonic Code, plus the United States' influence exerted during the construction of the Panama Canal, combined to produce a rather unique business environment in Panama. The freedom of contract combined with the versatility of American commerce produced great results for American companies that established their regional headquarters in Panama.

Now, with the expansion of the Panama Canal, new companies are returning to Panama; and established companies such as Caterpillar, Procter & Gamble, Hewlett Packard, Dell, and others are choosing Panama as their main offices for Latin America.

1.4 Overview of Legal System

Panama is a constitutional democracy. The current Constitution was approved on October 11, 1972, amended in 1983 and 1994, and reformed in 2004. There are three branches of government. The executive branch of the government is composed of a president and two vice presidents. The legislative branch consists of the unicameral National Assembly with seventy-eight members. The judicial branch is headed by the Supreme Court, with nine justices appointed by the Executive with the consent of the Assembly. They serve for ten years. The president, vice presidents, and legislators are elected every five years by direct popular vote. The president cannot be reelected unless at least ten years have passed since such individual held the office of President. Suffrage is universal and compulsory at eighteen years of age. The last election was in 2004. The country is divided into nine provinces and five semiautonomous indigenous territories.

1.5 People

The population of Panama is 3,227,000, of which 1,250,700 live in the metropolitan area of Panama City. Other major cities are Colón (metropolitan area population 116,250), David (88,100) and Santiago de Veraguas (46,950). Population density is 110 per square mile (42.99 per square kilometer).

Spanish is the official language of the country, but approximately 14 percent of the population speak English as their native tongue. The vast majority of business leaders and governmental officials are fully bilingual.

The predominant religion of Panama is Roman Catholic; 85 percent of the population are Catholic, 10 percent are Protestant, and 5 percent belong to other religions. There is no restriction on the practice of any religion.

More than 92 percent of the population over fifteen years of age is literate, though this figure drops as low as 62 percent in the rural areas of the country. School attendance is compulsory between the ages of seven and fifteen or until the six grades of primary school have been completed. The educational system provides for the free schooling of all children. Attendance rates for primary school are approximately 95 percent, and drops to 60 percent for secondary schools. An excellent parallel private school system exists, primarily in Panama City.

The main universities are the University of Panama, a state institution with six campuses, and the University of Santa Maria La Antigua, a Catholic institution. There is also an ever-increasing number of private universities, including the well-developed City of Knowledge complex at the Clayton section of Panama City.

1.6 Business

Local time in Panama is five hours behind Greenwich Mean Time (GMT), equivalent to Eastern Standard Time (EST) in the United States. The country does not participate in daylight saving time.

Most private business offices are open from 8:00 A.M. until 5:00 or 6:00 P.M. It is customary for all offices and stores to close for the lunch period for at least one hour. Most banks are open from 8:00 A.M. to 3:00 P.M., Monday through Friday. Office hours for government offices vary and it is advisable to check before visiting any such office. If a holiday falls on Sunday, it is observed on the following day. The executive branch is authorized to designate days of national mourning on which all public offices are closed.

The official system of weights and measures in Panama is the metric system. However, English measurement units are used in many circumstances. For instance, gasoline and diesel are sold by the gallon; most people in Panama describe their height and weight in feet, inches, and pounds; shoes are sold in European sizes, but shirts use U.S. measurements.

1.7 The Economy

Panama's economy is heavily service-oriented, with more than 75 percent of the Gross Domestic Product according to statistics of the Panamanian General Auditor Office. In 2005 alone, for example, there were approximately 810,000 people working within the services.

Panama has been a member state of the World Trade Organization (WTO) since 1997. This was effectuated through Law 23 of 1997. As a consequence of such affiliation, several economic changes have been taking place, including the privatization of state-owned companies as well as the drastic reduction in import tariffs, and tariff process in the agricultural sector.

Panama has signed a number of comprehensive bilateral trade agreements. Furthermore, the government is not only currently negotiating a free trade agreement with the United States, the country's major trading partner but must start all over again with the new government of Barack Obama, the newest President of the United States. It is also engaged in negotiations of different free trade agreements (FTAs) in order to enhance the country's competitiveness in the international arena.

The economic downturn of the final years of the regime of General Manuel Noriega was followed by a strong economic recovery and continued growth during the period 1990 to 1998. Despite a leveling off of economic activity at the end of the Panama Canal Treaty period and the departure of the U.S. presence from Panama in 1989, there has been strong, sustained growth during the early part of this century.

In 2005, the gross domestic product of Panama was US$13.9 billion and the country was enjoying an annual growth rate of 6.4 percent. This sustained growth has continued into 2006 and is expected to remain strong in the coming years as the economy benefits from the expansion of the Canal. Successive democratic administrations have reoriented the economy by encouraging private sector investments, enacting profound fiscal and budgetary reforms, actively negotiating the refinancing of foreign debt, privatizing public enterprises, and advancing the country's insertion in multilateral and regional trade pacts including negotiations for a free trade agreement with the United States.

Panama's currency is officially the balboa (PAB), but effectively the U.S. dollar. The balboa officially exists only as coins, which are completely interchangeable in Panama with U.S. coins of the same denomination. There is no balboa paper currency, and the U.S. dollar is the paper currency used in Panama. One balboa equals one U.S. dollar. This use of the U.S. dollar has helped Panama maintain a fiscal responsibility that has kept inflation generally under the rate in the U.S. and at an average under 2 percent during the past twenty years.

All major credit and debit cards are accepted in Panama, and most can be acquired though local banks and credit card companies. ATMs are plentiful in the major cities of Panama and accept ATM, debit, and credit cards.

There are no requirements for the registration of capital and no tax on the transfer of funds into the country. There are no controls over the repatriation of capital on the transfer of funds into the country.

There are no controls over the repatriation of capital or retained earnings. The absence of exchange controls and restrictions has helped to attract foreign investment into Panama.

Panama's geographic location and configuration are often considered to be its principal natural resource. Geographical circumstances have historically made the Isthmus a transit zone and have resulted in a concentration of income in the cities of Panama City and Colón at the entrances to the Canal, where the economy is based upon trade and services. Thus, the economy of Panama is dominated by the services sector, which accounts for 77 percent of the gross domestic product.

Domestic and international cargo transportation services are provided by more than fifty companies. Some of the cargo service companies offer transportation services on a regular basis to various countries located within the Western Hemisphere. Most major American car rental agencies are established in Panama. Daily flights to different cities in Canada, the United States, Mexico, Central and South America, the Caribbean, and Europe are also available as well as flights to Asia, Africa, Oceania, and the Far East.

Cristobal, Balboa, Manzanillo, and certain other ports in the country have modern facilities for warehousing and transshipping cargo and for accommodating regular oceangoing freighters and passenger ships.

International telephone, telex, fax, Internet, and other telecommunications services are excellent.

2. Substantive Laws and Regulations Impacting International Business Negotiations

2.1 Corporate Laws

All nationals and foreigners are on equal footing under the Constitution of Panama. Both Panamanian and foreign companies must fulfill the same basic requirements to organize and operate certain business activities in Panama. However, there are certain restrictions on the scope of commercial activities that can be undertaken by foreigners. There are, for example, limitations on the ability of foreign corporations to engage in retail activities as well as on some professional practices.

2.2 Types of Legal Entities

Individuals may be engaged in business activities in their own names or through legal entities. The most commonly used form of legal entity is the corporation (*sociedad anónima*). The following are the different types of legal entities that exist in Panama, based on civil and commerce laws.

Partnerships: There are a number of different types of partnerships, as further described in Panamanian commercial code as:

- **General partnerships** (*sociedades colectivas*) are entities in which the responsibility of the partners is unlimited, unless the partnership instrument provides that the partner will be liable only for a sum that cannot be lower than her or his contribution to the partnership.
- **Simple limited partnerships** (*sociedades en comandita simples*) are limited partnerships with general and limited partners. General partners share in management and are jointly and severally liable for partnership debts. Limited partners are liable only up to the amount of capital that they have invested.
- **Joint stock partnerships** (*sociedades en comandita por acciones*) are limited partnerships, similar to simple limited partnerships, except that in the case of joint stock partnerships, the partners' capital is represented by shares.

Limited liability companies (*sociedades de responsabilidad limitada*): Under this form of organization, the liability of the partners is limited to their individual capital participation. It is required to indicate in the name of the partnership the words "Sociedad de Responsabilidad Limitada," the initials "S. de R. L.," or the abbreviations "Sdad. Ltda."; otherwise, the partners' liability will be unlimited. This type of entity was substantially modified through Law 4 from January 5, 2009.

Joint ventures: Those seeking to do business in Panama may also opt to do so through a joint venture. A joint venture (*asociaciones accidentales o cuentas en participación*) is a temporary association for commercial purposes formed without incorporation or formal partnership. It is widely accepted in Panama although it has no separate juridical registry. There is no registration or tax number.

Private interest foundations: Pursuant to Law 25 of 1995, the Panamanian legislation created a new type of entity known as the private interest foundation. The creation of this legal entity, which was inspired by Liechtenstein's Family Foundation Law, has already enjoyed ten years of widespread use in Panama. There are several notable features of the private interest foundation.

- Private interest foundations may not be profit oriented. They may, nevertheless, engage in commercial activities in a non-habitual manner, and/or exercise rights deriving from titles representing the capital of business companies held as part of the assets of the foundation provided that the economic result or proceeds from such activities are used exclusively toward the foundation's objectives.

- The law also provides that one or more natural or juridical persons acting in their own name, or through another, may constitute a private interest foundation.
- A private interest foundation may be formed with an amount of capital no less than US$10,000.
- The founders must select a name to identify the foundation.
- The objectives, duration, domicile, and board of the foundation must also be indicated, along with the beneficiary or beneficiaries according to the Law 25.
- The charter of organization of the private interest foundation must be notarized and registered in the Panamanian Public Registry.
- When the assets are from outside the territory of Panama, no taxes are levied when these assets (whether movable or immovable, shares, bonds, or others) are transferred.

Corporations: Corporations are governed by Law 32 issued on February 26, 1927. This law established as a prerequisite for incorporation an agreement between two or more persons, of legal age, from any country, and domiciled anywhere, notwithstanding it may not be the Republic of Panama. Corporations may have any licit objective and may carry on any commercial or industrial activity.

There are a number of benefits and advantages to organizing corporations in Panama, including the following:

- No income taxes are paid if income is generated outside Panama.
- There are low annual maintenance costs.
- Stockholders can be of any nationality and may be another corporation or company.
- Officers and directors of the corporation can be of any nationality and do not need to reside in Panama.
- Corporate assets or capital may be located outside of Panama.
- Stockholders and Board of Directors meetings may be held anywhere in the world.

Under Panamanian law, corporations do not require a paid capital, either before or after its incorporation, in order to be valid. Corporate stocks may be issued in a nominative manner or to the bearer, and a corporation's stockholders can be natural persons or other corporations or companies, nationals or foreigners, with the possibility of more than one person having ownership over any stock, and without the need of having legal residence or being present in the Republic of Panama.

Corporations must be organized according to the incorporation document called Articles of Incorporation, for which a protocol must be done by a notary public; an authenticated copy of that same protocol must be registered in the Mercantile Section of the Public Registry of Panama. This document gives validity to the corporation, while Law No. 32 of 1927 will be applicable to corporations, as secondary source of rules.

Articles of Incorporation must contain at least the following information:

   a. Name of the corporation
   b. Name and domicile of its subscribers
   c. Corporate objectives—businesses that the corporation will carry on
   d. Corporate capital: amount, stock classes and distribution, etc.
   e. Duration of the corporation
   f. Name and address of directors and dignitaries
   g. Name and business address of the Resident Agent (must be an attorney or law firm authorized to practice law in the Republic of Panama)

In addition to the Articles of Incorporation, a Stock Register Book and a Minute Book must be kept. The opening of these books should be authenticated by a notary public.

Corporations not planning to do business within the Republic of Panama will not require any commercial or industrial license from local authorities. They can operate outside the territory of the Republic of Panama, as offshore corporations.

Panamanian corporations are subject to a tax regime that requires payment of taxes only for operations conducted within the territory of the Republic of Panama. Under Panamanian tax law, commercial operations executed, taking place, or having effects outside Panama will be considered offshore and are not taxable, even when those operations are managed from an office located in Panama, except for the annual corporate tax in the amount of US$300 that all corporations must pay.

2.3 Securities Law

The Law Decree No. 1 dated July 8, 1999 rules the Panamanian securities industry. According to its summary and introduction, Decree No. 1 creates the National Securities Commission (*Comisión Nacional de Valores*) (CNV) as an autonomous state entity and establishes the CNV as the official institution in charge of the authorization and supervision of the public offering of securities, securities trading, and the constitution and management of mutual funds, as well as the granting of licenses to the different financial market agents or participants. The CNV is composed of three members (a chairman, a vice president, and a commissioner who acts as spokesman for the CNV) and has the authority to appoint staff (i.e., attorneys, accountants, economists) and retain experts in order to fulfill its duties.

The CNV is the local authority charged with supervising the industry participants in order to protect investors. This mandate includes protecting the right of investors to file class actions to enforce the provisions of the new securities law.

The law decree rules the granting of licenses to the different participants in the capital markets, such as: brokerage firms, investment advisors, investment managers, stock exchanges, clearing houses, sales agents, brokers, dealers, stock exchange seats, and mutual funds.

According to law-Decree 1, broker-dealer firms are organizations dedicated to the purchase and sale of securities, on their own or in the name of third parties (customers). Investment advisors, for their part, are persons who in exchange for consideration advise others in regard to the determination of the securities prices, the convenience to invest, and the purchase and sale of securities; they also prepare market reports.

Securities brokerage firms and investment advisors must have a license granted by the CVN. The license for brokerage firms allows the exercise of activities as investment advisors. Both are obliged to file periodical reports, as well as audited and internal financial statements, with the CNV.

Securities brokerage firms may be dedicated to incidental businesses such as the management of custodian accounts, investment advisory services, asset management for investment funds, and the grant of securities and cash loans for the acquisition of securities, and are subject to net capital and liquidity requirements as determined by the CNV.

The shares of a securities brokerage firm must be exclusively in registered form and the CNV must be advised on any changes in the share composition thereof.

Foreign securities brokerage firms (organizations constituted or domiciled abroad or that have a license to operate that was granted by another state) may be exempted from compliance with certain legal provisions, as determined by the CNV, provided investors are not affected.

In order to manage customers' funds and securities, brokerage firms must open investment accounts. Investment advisors, for their part, may manage custodian accounts, securities, and monies at their discretion or not, but they are not authorized to offer investment accounts.

The functions of the senior executive, broker/dealer, and securities brokerage firm analyst or investment advisory company will only be held by persons who have the respective license granted by the CNV. In order to obtain a license, the interested parties must pass exams on the content of the securities law and its regulations, on the practice and customs of the securities industry, on the rules of stock exchanges and securities firms, and on general accounting and financing principles.

In order to exercise a stock exchange or clearinghouse business, the interested party must obtain the respective license from the CNV, which shall be granted provided that the technical, administrative, and financial capacity to provide the service is proven.

As self-regulated organizations (SROs) they are obliged to protect the interests of investors, to promote the cooperation of the market agents, to report on any violations of the securities law, not to unreasonably limit or discriminate regarding membership nor affect free competition, and to avoid deceitful and manipulative actions that may affect the market's transparency and investors. Likewise, stock exchanges shall monitor their members' compliance with the internal rules and the securities law.

SROs and securities brokerage firms are each obligated to file periodic reports, as well as audited and internal financial statements with the CNV.

Pursuant to the law decree, the following securities are subject to registration with the Commission:

a. Securities that are the subject of a public offering, subject to the approval of CNV.

b. Shares of issuers domiciled in Panama that, on the last day of the fiscal year, have fifty or more shareholders domiciled in Panama that are the "effective owners" of no less than 10 percent of the paid-in capital of said issuer (excluding for the estimate affiliates and employees, directors, and officers thereof).

c. Securities listed in any Panamanian Stock Exchange.

The law decree establishes the following offerings or sales as exempted from registration:

a. The offer and sale of exempted securities (bonds issued or guaranteed by the state or by international organizations where the state participates or any securities exempted by determination of the Commission).

b. Private placement: an offer that is made by an issuer (or any of its affiliates) or an offeror in its name, to no more than twenty-five persons and that jointly results in the sale of said securities to no more than ten persons, within a one-year term.

c. Offers and sales made to institutional investors.

d. Offers, sales, distributions, transfer, and exchange of securities between the issuer and securities holders of said issuer due to:

i. the offer of shares to increase the issuer's capital, directed to existing shareholders;

ii. the issuer's declaration of stock dividends or other securities;

iii. the issuer's restructuring, dissolution, liquidation, merger, or consolidation;

iv. the exercise of rights or options previously granted by the issuer;

v. the offer and sale made by the issuer, exclusively to its employees, directors, and officers or to employees, directors, and officers of affiliated companies; or

vi. any other offers or sales or transactions in securities that are exempted as per a ruling from the CNV.

The issuer interested in the public offering of its securities shall instigate a securities registry application/filing.

2.4 Tax Laws

Since the year 2000, Panama's corporate tax rate has been at a flat rate of 30 percent, eliminating the 34 percent bracket in place during the late 1990s. For companies registered in Panama's increasing number of tax-free export processing zones (EPZs), which are modeled after the longstanding Colón Free Trade Zone (CFTZ), a 15 percent corporate tax imposed in 1996 (up from 8 percent) has been removed in favor of a much-vaunted 0 percent rate on all profits arising outside of Panama. The 0 percent corporate tax rate goes with an exemption from all export and import duties on re-exports. All businesses pay a license tax of 1 percent of the company's net worth up to US$20,000. Companies in EPZs have tax liability only for sales within Panama's fiscal jurisdiction, which, by statute, can make up no more than 40 percent of their business. Beginning with the Organisation for Economic Co-operation and Development (OECD) report on harmful tax practices in 1998, Panama has come under increasing pressure to revise its banking secrecy practices, guaranteed in the Panama Constitution.

Income in Panama in 2002 was taxed according to a progressive schedule that, since 2000, has had 12 brackets: 0 percent, 2 percent (added in 2000), 4 percent, 6.5 percent, 11 percent, 16.5 percent, 19 percent, 22 percent, 27 percent, 30 percent, 33 percent (as reported) and 30 percent. The 0 percent rate applied up to PAB 3,000 (pegged to equality with the U.S. dollar), but there are also fixed deductions (PAB 800 for singles, PAB 1600 for married couples, and PAB 250 for each child) and targeted deductions (for mortgage interest, loans to pay school fees, medical expenses, health insurance, and donations to charity, among others) that reduce taxable income for individuals. Gifts were taxed at rates between 0 percent and 33.75 percent depending on the amount unless they were between linear descendants, which were tax-exempt. There is a 2.75 percent education tax; 1.25 percent is taken from gross salaries paid. A real property tax ranges from 1.4 percent to 2.1 percent of assessed valuation. Property improvements are tax-exempt for the first five years.

The main indirect tax is Panama's value-added tax (VAT) with a standard rate of 5 percent, and a reduced rate of 0 percent applied to basic foodstuffs, trade, and medical services. An increased 10 percent rate on cigarettes has been removed. Other levies include license fees and stamp taxes.

2.5 Antitrust/Anticompetition Laws

Panama enacted its antitrust legislation for the first time in 1996, by means of Law No. 29 of February 1, 1996, the Anticompetitive Practices (Unfair Competition) Law. Recently, the Unfair Competition Law was modified by Law Decree No. 10, 2007, and the latest change was Law No. 45 of October 31, 2007 (the "Antitrust Law"), which organizes and structures the antitrust laws and consumer jurisdiction.

The objective of the Antitrust Law is to protect and ensure the free economic competition process in order to eliminate monopolistic practices and other restrictions in the efficient functioning of the marketing of goods and services, to preserve the higher interests of the consumer.

The Antitrust Law is applicable to all economic agents, either natural or legal persons, private, governmental, or municipal entities; industries, businessmen, or professionals; profitable or nonprofitable entities, or any other that under any title participate as active entities in economic activities.

According to article 7 of Law No. 45, any contract or practice that restrains, diminishes, harms, impedes, or in any other way damages free economic competition and the free concurrence in the manufacturing processing, distribution, supply, or commercialization of goods or services is prohibited.

Law No. 45 stated two kinds of monopolistic practices: absolute and relative. Absolute practices are more harmful to the general economy; the relative ones affect individual economic agents. The question whether a certain practice constitutes a relative monopolistic practice requires a complicated analysis.

It is important to determine if the economic agent involved has a substantial market power and, if so, balance the positive effects of the practice on economic efficiency against its potential negative effects on the process of free competition. When a certain practice increases economic efficiency and does not harm the consumer, the practice will not be considered a relative monopolistic practice.

2.6 Labor and Employment Laws

2.6.1 Labor Contracts
The Labor Code states that labor contracts must be in writing and made in three copies (for the employer, employee, and labor authorities);

otherwise, any fact or circumstance alleged by the employee will be presumed to be true, unless the employer proves beyond reasonable doubt that it is not. The contract may be for an indefinite period of time, a definite period of time, or a specific project.

An employee can be hired on a probationary basis for up to a three-month period, provided that the type of service requires special skills, and if expressly written into the contract. The maximum term for a definitive period contract is one year. A contract for a definitive period of time will be considered as indefinite if the employee: (1) continues working after the definitive period expires; (2) continues working after the specific project for which he or she was hired is finished; or (3) when succeeding contracts for a definitive period or contracts for a specific project are entered into.

Rights of the employee recognized under the Panamanian Labor Code cannot be waived by the employee, nor can they be diminished. Any provision, act, or declaration of the employee that provides or implies lessening or relinquishment of any right is considered null and void, even if stated in the labor contract or in any other pact. Employees' rights are not affected by the division of the enterprise in diversified or separate companies. The concept of an economic conglomerate prevails, so that the employee can furnish his or her claims against any of them. Local legal advice should be sought before making any decision concerning labor law.

2.6.2 Application for Employment

There are no specific employment forms to be completed by interested applicants. Each employer usually prepares its own forms. These forms allow the corporation to select personnel prior to employing them.

It is important to note, however, that the Labor Code requires that a written contract contain information such as name, nationality, gender, age, civil status, home address, and personal identity card number of the parties. When the employer is a corporation, the contract must contain the name of the corporation, address, name of legal representative and Public Registry information; employee's dependents and household members; services or work contracted and the variations thereof contracted for performance place or places in which services will be rendered; duration of the contract, if it is for a specific period of time, or a clause stating that the contract is for a fixed period of time or for a specific duty; regular duration and division of the working day; the salary and the form, day, and place of payment; contract place and execution date; and signature of the parties.

Foreigners wishing to work in Panama must obtain authorization, in the form of a work permit, issued by the General Employment Director from the Ministry of Labor and Welfare Development. Work permits are valid for one year and may be renewed. According to article 17 of the labor code, firms employing foreign personnel must maintain a certain proportion between local and foreign workers. Local personnel are defined as Panamanians, foreigners married to Panamanians, and foreign employees with at least ten years of legal residence in Panama. Employees are allowed to hire up to 10 percent of foreign employees from the total number of administrative workers, and up to 15 percent in the case of specialized or technical personnel. The payroll of the foreign workers should not exceed 10 percent of the total payroll for administrative workers or 15 percent of specialized or technical personnel. Corporations established in Panama exclusively to supervise operations or transactions carried out abroad are exempt from these ratio requirements.

Salaries can be fixed by unit of time (month, fortnight, week, day, or hour), task, or piece of work. Salaries include any money, gratuities, bonuses, premiums, commissions, and profit sharing, and any income or benefit employees receive as a result of their work. Employees must be paid at least twice a month.

According to the Panamanian Labor Ministry, the minimum salary in the cities of Panama and Colón fluctuates between US$1.15 and US$1.22 per hour for non-skilled workers in manufacturing operation, and US$1.22 per hour for workers in commercial, service, banking, insurance, real state, transportation, warehousing, recreation, and personal service activities. Average salaries paid to skilled employees in Panama's metropolitan areas far exceed the minimum rate.

On December 11, 2007, the Panamanian government enacted a new rate for minimum wages. The minimum wages increased from US$284.96 to US$310.00 per month, which means a raise of US$25.00 (12 percent) per month. This adjustment amounts to US$0.19 cents per hour for large companies and US$0.12 cents per hour for small companies.

2.6.3 Salary Withholdings and Deductions

- **Income Tax:** These tax rates are determined by a schedule in the Panamanian Fiscal Code.
- **Social Security:** Employees pay 8 percent of their monthly gross salary, which must be withheld each pay period and remitted by the employer to the Social Security Administration. Employers pay 11.50 percent of the employee's monthly salaries, which must be remitted jointly with the employee's 8 percent share.
- **Education Tax:** A 1.25 percent tax is withheld based on the employee's monthly gross salary, and the employer contributes 1.50 percent.

Additionally, the employer must cover workers compensation, which depends on the duties performed by the worker. The Panamanian Social Security Administration assigns the percentage to be paid; 0.98 percent is the minimum percentage established for office workers.

For withholding purposes, salary is understood to be the total compensation, including commissions, vacations, and amounts in money or in kind that the worker received from the employer as payment for services. No withholdings are made from profit-sharing benefits granted to employees, provided that these benefits include no less than 70 percent of the workers, and do not exceed or substitute the total annual salary.

The amount that the worker receives as a result of the termination of his or her employment, or that public employees receive on account of their voluntary retirement, are exempt from social security withholdings. In addition, withholding will apply only to cover the part of the representation expenses that exceeds the monthly salary.

Contributions must be paid by the employer every month. Late payment results in a 10 percent penalty, plus 1 percent interest charge for every month or fraction thereof of delay. The action for the collection of premiums from employers has a fifteen-year statue of limitation.

2.6.4 Work Day

According to the Labor Code, four different work shifts are established. They are as follows:

- Day shift, consisting of a maximum of eight hours from 6:00 A.M. to 6:00 P.M. with a maximum workweek of forty-eight hours.
- Night shift, consisting of a maximum of seven hours from 6:00 P.M. to 6:00 A.M. with a maximum workweek of forty-two hours.
- Mixed shift, consisting of seven and a half hours from both the day shift and the night shift, with a maximum workweek of forty-five hours. A mixed shift with more that three night shift hours is considered to be a night shift.
- Rotational shift, for companies required to employ personnel during different hours according to the companies' activities and needs.

For the night, mixed, and rotational shifts, employees received the same payment as for the day shift, even though their work time is shorter. A working day consists of the total time the employee cannot freely use when at the service of the employer.

2.6.5 Overtime

Overtime must be paid for hours worked in excess of the maximum hours defined above. Minimum overtime rates are as follows:

- 25 percent surcharge for hours worked during the day shift.
- 50 percent surcharge for hours worked during the night shift, for hours worked in excess of mixed shift initiated in the day period, or for work performed on any day of rest (i.e., Sunday).
- 75 percent surcharge for hours worked in excess of the night shift or a mixed shift initiated in the night period.

- 150 percent surcharge for hours worked on a holiday or day of national mourning, and an additional paid day of rest must be provided. Hours worked in excess of the regular day on a holiday must be paid at the same rate as above, in addition to the 150 percent surcharge.

An employee cannot be required to work overtime except under special circumstances (e.g., export industries) or by a written contract. Three hours per day and nine hours per week are the maximum legal overtime hours. For overtime in excess of this limit, the employee is entitled to receive a 75 percent surcharge.

2.6.6 Vacations

Employees are normally entitled to one month (thirty days) of vacation per year. Vacations are accrued at the rate of one day for every eleven days of employment. Vacation time cannot be waived by the employee in exchange for payment. However, it can be accumulated up to two years by mutual agreement, but there is a minimum rest period of fifteen days during the first period. The thirty-day period can be divided into no more than two equal parts. Employees working for companies established in export processing zones can enjoy vacation periods in advance, even if not earned, provided that the operating cycle thus demands it.

2.6.7 Leaves and Benefits

(a) Disability Leave

Paid sick or disability leave must be provided for each employee when required, up to one and a half days per month, or eighteen days per year. Sick leaves can be accumulated for up to two years, and may be enjoyed entirely or in part during the third year of service. If an additional sick leave is required, employees covered by social security may receive such an additional period of leave.

(b) Maternity Leave

Female employees are entitled to special benefits under Panama's Labor Code. Once pregnant, they can be dismissed only for cause with judicial assent. This same privilege is extended for one year following childbirth. Maternity leave must be granted for at least fourteen weeks; from six weeks before to eight weeks after childbirth. During maternity leave neither communication nor actions, sanctions, or measures provided in the Labor Code can be taken by the employer.

Social security provides a subsidy to cover female employees for this period. The employer must pay the difference between this subsidy and the employee's salary.

(c) Thirteenth-Month Bonus

According to the Labor Code, all employers must pay their employees a special bonus called the thirteenth-month bonus. This bonus is estimated at one salary day for every eleven days of work. The thirteenth-month bonus is paid in three equal installments; on April 15, August 15, and December 15 of every year. Sums paid for the thirteenth-month bonus are tax deductible for the employer and are not subject to any other type of withholding except for the employee's income taxes and social security contributions.

(d) Workers' Compensation
All employers must enroll their employees in the social security system, which includes workers' compensation. An additional premium is paid depending upon risks involved in the activities performed.

2.6.8 Termination of Employment
(a) Generally
Either an employee or an employer can terminate a working relationship. Basically, there are six methods of terminating a working relationship according to Panamanian Labor code (articles 212, 213):

1.   By mutual consent.
2.   By expiration of the agreed term or conclusion of the work.
3.   By death of the employee or employer.
4.   By a justified cause (as defined in the Labor Code).
5.   By resignation of the employee.
6.   By the unilateral decision of the employer, subject to the formalities and limitations established in the code. Exceptions are provided for temporary workers, domestic workers, apprentice workers with less than two years of service, and agents with less than five years of service.

In this case, the employer must provided thirty days' notice and must also pay severance pay. Employees who wish to resign must give at least fifteen days' notice. Technical workers must give at least two months' notice.

If termination is by mutual consent, it must be in writing and should not involve the waiving of any of the employee's rights. This document must be sustained before the General Director of the Ministry of Labor and Welfare Development in order to be valid. Noncompliance with this requirement can result in reinstatement within the next thirty calendar days, with payment of all accumulated unpaid salary. Resignation by the employee must be ratified before the Ministry of Labor and Welfare Development, which has the power not to ratify it if the resignation implies waiving of any of the employee's rights. The Ministry of Labor and Welfare Development must also authorize the termination of collective labor relationships.

(b) Seniority Premium
Employees, regardless of age, who leave an employer for any cause are entitled to receive a lump-sum payment equivalent to one week's

salary for each year employed. As of August 14, 1995, seniority premium is granted to all employees without regard to the number of
years worked.

(c) Justified Cause

The Labor Code allows an employer to dismiss an employee for disciplinary reasons, no-fault reasons, or economic reasons. In the last
case, the employer must obtain prior approval from the labor authorities and pay an indemnity to the dismissed worker.

Justified causes for dismissal of an employee for disciplinary reasons according to Labor Code (literals A, B, and C of article 213):

- deceitful representations respecting the employee's special skills
- disobedience
- engaging in acts of violence
- absenteeism
- drunkenness on the job
- theft
- damage inflicted upon the company's physical or intellectual
  property
- sexual harassment
- low productivity according to standard evaluation systems

Some no-fault reasons are:

- the firm's closure resulting from an act of God
- imprisonment of the worker
- retirement
- permanent disability or loss of capacity to exercise a profession

Economic reasons include:

- bankruptcy
- insolvency
- reduction in sales causing a reduction in the company's
  activities
- cancellation of request or buying orders, decrease in production
  activities or in sales

(d) Unjustified Cause Premium

As previously mentioned, any employer who fires an employee without legal cause is liable for payment of a compensation premium. This
lump sum is based on the indemnification tables.

For employees hired after August 14, 1995, it will consist of 3.4
weeks for each year employed, for the first ten years. For the subsequent years, it will be set at one week for each year employed. Indemnities are subject to income tax, but not to social security or educational
insurance tax.

2.7 Environmental Laws

Article 24 of Executive Decree No. 209, dated September 6, 2006, modified everything related to the approval of environmental impact studies. Those studies are classified in Categories I, II, and III, with the last one applying to exploration and exploitation of hydrocarbons as well as to the generation of electric power. A Category III Environmental Impact Study should include at least the following components, in accordance with the regulation's articles 27 through 30: Index, Executive Summary, Introduction, General Information, general Description of the Project, Description of the Physical Environment, Description of the Biological Environment, Description of the Social-Economic Environment, Identification of Specific Environmental Impacts, Environmental Management Plan, Economic Adjustments due to the Outside Influence of Social and Environmental Factors and a Final Cost-Benefit Analysis, list of the professionals that took part in the preparation of the study, Conclusions and Recommendations, Bibliography, and exhibits.

2.8 Intellectual Property Laws

Intellectual property law in Panama is governed by two main laws: Law No. 35 of May 10, 1996, which regulates all matters concerning industrial property law, and Law No. 15 of August 8, 1994, which regulates all matters concerning copyrights.

Law No. 15 of 1994 recognizes copyright in literary, scientific, technical, juridical, pedagogical, photographic, pictoral, musical, and lyrical works; dramatic arts, dance, sculpture and general plastic arts; architecture; cinematographic and other audiovisual works; computer programs (software); radio, television, and other forms of applied arts; and compilations including graphic and textile designs and other works of an analogous nature. Copyrights endure for the life of the author plus fifty years. Anonymous and pseudonymous works, software, and audiovisual works are also protected for fifty years from the publishing. Foreign authors have the same protections under Law No.15 as do nationals of Panama.

Panama is a signatory of:

- the Buenos Aires Convention on Literary and Artistic Copyright;
- Convention for the Protection of Producers of Phonograms Against Unauthorized Duplication of their Phonograms;
- Inter-American Convention on the Rights of the Author in Literary, Scientific and Artistic Works;
- Convention Establishing the World Intellectual Property Organization;
- Universal Copyright Convention;

- Convention Relating to the Distribution of Programme-Carrying Signals Transmitted by Satellite;
- International Convention for the Protections of Performers, Producers of Phonograms, and Broadcasting Organizations;
- Berne Convention for the Protection of Literary and Artistic Works.

Law No. 35 of 1996 provides protection for industrial property such as inventions, utility models, industrial models and drawings, industrial and commercial secrets, trademarks, collective and guaranteed brands, indications of origin, denominations of origins, commercial names, expressions, and publicity signs.

It is very important to note that patents and trademark licenses and assignments of intellectual property rights must be registered with the Intellectual Property Department. If they are not registered, such licenses or assignments will not be effective against third parties. The registration procedure before the Industrial Property Department should not involve governmental review or approval for the corresponding license or assignment.

Without prejudice to the sanctions stated in the Panamanian Criminal Code and the civil liability brought by the affected parties, anyone who violates Law No. 35 will be subject to a penalty between US$10,000 and US$200,000 as well as the suspension of the right to practice the trade activity or the suspension/cancellation of the operation code granted by the Colón Free Zone Administration or by any other export processing zones existing in Panama. In the cases of companies operating in the Colón Free Zone or any other free zones, as well as export processing zones, the penalty applicable will be 25 percent of the monthly trade movement of the company, and in no case shall it be under US$75,000.

Law No. 35 of 1996 (regarding industrial property) provides immediate precautionary measures for ensuring the effectiveness of the actions of compensation for caused harms to the victim. Based upon the regulations referred herein above, the district attorney's office shall begin a prosecution case whenever it comes to their knowledge that any of the offenses referred to herein above have been committed. The holder of the industrial property right (the victim), copyright, or related rights may take part actively in the summary case in the criminal procedure, at any time and without mediating any major procedures, as a cooperating party or private prosecutor.

Law No. 35 states that the General Director of Panamanian Customs has the right to conduct inspections and may retain any merchandise that may be transgressing the provisions and regulations of this law and/or the Copyright Law. The authorities of the Colón Free Zone or any other free zones and free export processing zones have the same power to inspect and retain merchandise that is suspected of violating intellectual property laws in Panama's jurisdiction.

2.9 Privacy and Data Security Laws

According to Article 29 of the Constitution of Panama, one must obtain the approval of the Court in order to collect information from personal telephones and other devices and/or technology items (which include software, hardware, and e-mails, among others). Every person who collects personal or private information without prior consent of the data subject will be subject to criminal prosecution according to articles 162 to 166 (crimes against personal intimacy) and articles 283 to 286 (crimes against informatic security) of the new Panamanian Criminal Code.

According to the last modification of the Constitution enacted in 2004, people have the Habeas Data constitutional action. This action provides the right to ask for the preservation, amendment, or elimination of personal information stored in public or private databases. This information will be collected by the interested party for specific purposes.

Every person also has the Habeas Data constitutional action to ask for public information of interest stored in government or particular databases. Public services provided by the government or private sector were included in this amendment of the Constitution in year 2004.

2.10 Regulation of Foreign Investments

As part of its efforts to consolidate its economic reform plan, which has led to the establishment of several bilateral commercial agreements to promote both domestic and foreign investments, the government of Panama enacted Law No. 54 of July 22, 1998, whereby measures are taken for the "Legal Stability of Investments."

The legal stability regulation is granted to individuals or private entities, either national or foreign, that carry out investments in Panama of a minimum amount of US$2,000,000 and to develop the following activities: tourism, industries, agricultural exports, agroforestry, mining, export processing zones, commercial and petroleum free zones, telecommunications, construction, port and railroad development, electric generation, irrigation and efficient management of hydric resources and any other activity approved by the Cabinet Council, with the prior recommendation of the Ministry of Commerce and Industries.

Both foreign and national investors and their companies rank in equal terms with respect to their rights and obligations, including the nonrestricted transfer of funds derived from the investment, tax exempt repatriation of capitals, and all kinds of dividend interest and earnings, and free commercialization of their production.

The industrial and intellectual property rights of foreign investors are subject to local laws. The following specific benefits and guarantees are granted to investors under Law No. 54 of 1998, for a term of ten years:

- **Legal Stability:** Except for public or social interest causes, any new legal provisions that may affect the investor's vested rights under this law will not be applicable.
- **National Tax Stability:** The tax regime in force upon registration of the investment before the Ministry of Commerce and Industries will be maintained.
- **Municipal Tax Stability:** The applicable municipal taxes at the time the investment was made will not be subject to modifications during the following five years.
- **Special Customs Stability:** Except for amendments to the import tariffs fixed by the Cabinet Council, any special customs regimes in force (granted by way of tax refunds, exemptions, temporary admission of goods, and the like) will remain unchanged. Funds, exemptions, temporary admission of goods, and the like will remain unchanged.
- **Labor Contract Stability:** Any provisions of Panamanian labor-contracting legislation and other international agreements adopted by the Republic of Panama will be in force for the ten-year term.

To enjoy the benefits granted under this regime, the investor must be registered before the entity in charge of the promotion and supervision of such activity. The investor has the obligation, among others, to carry out the activity in accordance with an investment plan that must be submitted for approval to the respective supervisory entity.

The investor has the option, exercisable once, to abide by the tax regime applicable to other investments or activities not included in the Law. The waiver of the benefits and guarantees by the investor is also permitted at any time, with prior notification to the competent authority.

Any disputes that may arise between the state and the investor are first subject to a mediation procedure in Panama; subsequently, the investor may elect to submit the controversy to the judicial authorities or to arbitration.

The conditions and benefits granted under any agreements to promote and protect investments in Panama are not affected by the legal stability regime.

2.11 Other Potentially Applicable Laws and Regulations

In recent years the Panamanian government has been changing the perception regarding the rule of power in Panama. Panama enacted an anticorruption law, and recently updated the new Criminal Code and Criminal Procedure Code in order to earn more confidence and trust from the public.

3. Other Significant Legal and Business Issues

Panama is ruled by the International Financial Reporting Standards. This situation is a plus for the country because the complete economy moves in connection with those principles.

4. Negotiation Practices

4.1 Participants

Businesses in Panama are usually under the control of people who specialize in business. But in a few cases, negotiations are in lawyers' hands. Sometimes people underestimate the potential of a business law specialist because they are used to driving the whole process on their own and only ask help from lawyers in the case of emergency. In recent years, major companies have hired in-house lawyers to avoid the need to hire a traditional law firm.

The government usually works with a multidisciplinary team (accountants, economist, and lawyers) when it is involved in a negotiation. For example, the Free Trade Agreement (now renamed Commercial Promotion Treaty) to be signed between Panama and the United States took several levels with many specialist teams to complete the final document.

4.2 Timing

The negotiations in Panama may be as intense and as fast as in the United States. Some Panamanian holidays take several days and may slow the closing of a negotiation. For example, Panama has several independence holidays in November (3, 4, 5, 10, and 28) and February (a four-day carnival), and people usually take long weekend breaks. Similarly, one must accept the fact that the sense of punctuality is expressed differently in Panama, and that a certain amount of lateness in holding meetings (in the beginning or end) or in the performance of some commitments should not be taken as a personal offense.

4.3 Negotiation Practices

As a principle of the Civil Code, all parties may negotiate the terms and conditions of a contract. But some negotiations are difficult. Standard contracts do not allow the liberty to agree on the terms and conditions of an agreement. Insurance, banking, and airline flight tickets are some of the few examples with no possibility of the party negotiating all terms and conditions of the agreement. On October 31, 2007, Panama enacted Law No. 45 to decrease abusive clauses in contracts, especially in real estate agreements.

4.4 Cultural, Ethical, and Religious Considerations

Since the end of military government in 1990, Panama has adopted a high tolerance level for religion and, especially, for political ideas. Nevertheless, the judicial system is not highly regarded. Many Panamanians feel that their country's dispute resolution system is disappointing, so they more often decide to choose an arbitral procedure that is faster and more flexible. Notwithstanding, in a system that totally lacks in features such as discovery proceedings, depositions, examinations and cross-examinations, and juries, costs sometimes are lower than for the American equivalents, and they do not represent either an incentive or a threat.

4.5 Negotiating Online

Negotiating online is permitted under Panamanian law. Electronic documents and contracts are allowed in Panama with the same value as written documents, subject to the requirements that:

   i.   the information in the document is available for later consultation;

   ii.   the data message is conserved in the original format in which it was generated, sent, or received or with some format that is shown to reproduce exactly said information; and

   iii.   it conserves, if any, all data that allows the determination of the origin and destination of the message, date, and time when it was sent or received.

Law No. 43, which permits online transactions, does not apply to:

- Legal acts where the law asks solemnities that are not allowed by electronic documents (e.g., a real estate purchase agreement)
- Legal acts where the law asks personal concurrence of some person (e.g., a testament issued by a notary public)

Legal acts under family law (e.g., marriages or divorce)

5. Contract Formation

5.1 Wording and Style

Under Panama law, the Civil and Commercial Codes regulate typical agreements such as rent, purchase, loan, and partnership. But some other forms of agreements such as escrow, construction, joint ventures, and others are not regulated by such statutes, so they are known as atypical contracts. Parties entering into these kinds of agreements will be free to determine the terms and conditions that will govern their relationship without restriction, except for those that would apply by nature of public order law and/or ethics.

Most of the contracts have no set formalities. Nevertheless, many contracts have certain requirements. For example, insurance policies, loans, and leases must be in writing. In real estate, the formalities are much stronger. Property sale agreements must be in writing in a document called a public deed issued only by a notary public; subsequently, the public deed must be recorded at the Public Registry office in order to be a valid contract.

5.2 Conditions and Defenses

5.2.1 The Special Case of Online Agreements

Panama took a step in the right direction when the new e-commerce bill was signed into Law 43 on July 31, 2001. Believed to be the first of its kind to be implemented in Central America, the new law is expected to provide a much-needed boost to Panama's e-commerce industry. This law represents an advance for the legal recognition of electronic documents and signatures, which are elements necessary to increase the confidence in transactions conducted electronically. Its provisions on electronic documents are loosely based on the United Nations Commission on International Trade Law (UNCITRAL) Model Law on Electronic Commerce.

This law establishes a certification procedure and penalizes the noncompliance of contracts. It also envisions the creation of an e-commerce directorate at the Ministry of Commerce and Industries, which will be responsible for authorizing certification entities.

Activities regulated under this law are subject to the following principles:

a. Freedom to provide services: to maintain the right of service providers to continue their legal trading activities without prohibition from the government.
b. Open market: to ensure the absence of monopolistic practices and to remain impartial to the provider of any specific type of technology.
c. Technological neutrality: by eliminating the elements in an earlier draft of the bill that favored encrypted technologies.
d. International compatibility: by using international criteria to supervise certification authorities and acknowledge certificates.
e. Legal recognition of electronic data messages: by granting electronic documents full value as evidence.
f. Functional equivalence of e-commerce to traditional commerce: acknowledging as valid in electronic documents the same elements of traditional agreements, such as offer, acceptance, and others.

5.2.2 Legal Requirements for a Valid Electronic Document

Under traditional civil regulations, an agreement is executed by the granting of offer and acceptance. Most agreements are required to be drafted in writing and executed through the written signatures of the parties. In cases of agreements above a certain monetary amount, notarization and even recordation with a public entity are required to ensure enforceability.

Law 43 does away with the written document requirement, which was an obstacle to enforceability of e-commerce agreements. When the current law requires that a document be in writing, data messages are granted the same validity, as long as:

  i.   the information in the document is available for later consultation;
  ii. the data message is conserved in the original format in which it was generated, sent, or received or with some format that is shown to reproduce exactly said information; and
  iii. it conserves, if any, all data that allows determination of the origin and destination of the message, date, and time when it was sent or received.

Data messages are defined as all information generated in optical, electronic, or similar form, such as electronic data interchange (EDI), Internet, e-mail, telegram, telex, or fax. Data messages are electronic documents defined as any electronic representation that bears witness to a fact, image, or idea. In the case of agreements, the consent of the parties is contained as a signature. Electronic signatures (understood as any electronic sound, symbol, or process linked to or logically associated with a message and granted or adopted by a person with the intention of signing a message that allows the receiver to identify the issuer) are granted the same value as written ones, when signatures are required under legislation.

Electronic signatures by notaries and other authorities are also granted the same validity as their written counterparts, when required.

Law 43 allows businesses to maintain as data messages their correspondence, invoices, ledgers, corporate books, and other records previously required by the Code of Commerce and Tax Code. They must be kept under the conditions required for electronic documents, for the period required by said codes (seven to fifteen years, depending on the nature of the documents). If a change in configuration of a data message creates a material risk that a consumer may not access it, the provider of said record-keeping service must provide notice of said change and allow an early termination of a contract.

5.2.3 Regulation of Certificate Authorities and Other Security Features

Among the forms of electronic signatures, the law defines as secure an electronic signature that may be verified with a security system or procedure under internationally accepted authentication standards. Entities known as certification authorities (CAs) issue electronic records known as certificates, which serve to verify the authenticity and legitimacy of electronic signatures and the integrity of a message. Law 43 presumes that a user has accepted a certificate when it is posted in a repository or database by the CA upon request of the user, or if it has been sent to one or more other users.

In a manner analogous to a personal identification number or a corporate seal, the Law provides that upon acceptance of a certificate, the user guarantees all persons of good faith, free of liability, that the certified electronic signature is under control of the user, that no other person has accessed the procedure for its generation, and that the information contained in the certificate is true and matches that provided to the CA.

The newly created Directorate of Electronic Commerce, part of the Ministry of Commerce and Industries, supervises the activities of CAs. The Directorate will maintain a voluntary register of CAs, which will be optional for CAs active in Panama. The Directorate will also ensure that CAs operating in Panama, whether local or foreign, maintain adequate financial and technical standards. However, repositories or the databases where certificates are stored must be registered with the Directorate. Registered repositories must store their databases in an integral manner, as well as maintain a registry of expired certificates. Certificates from foreign CAs are valid in Panama identically to those from local CAs when said certificates are accepted (i) by a CA registered in Panama; (ii) under international agreements; and (iii) under approval from other foreign CA registrars similar to the Directorate.

Panama enacted Executive Decree No. 29 of August 19, 2004, by which it regulates chapters I and II from title III of Law No. 43 regarding the issuance of electronic certifications.

6. Dispute Resolution

6.1 Overview

Key to understanding arbitration in Panama is the Panamanian arbitration law, Law Decree No. 5 of July 8, 1999. Law Decree No. 5 initially encountered obstacles to its implementation and some of its articles were declared unconstitutional because of conflicts with the 1972 Constitution of Panama. The Constitution contained rigid provisions that made it impossible to implement the model arbitration law in Panama. In response to that conflict, in 2004 the government of Panama amended the Constitution.

Accordingly, pursuant to Article 200, Section 4 of the Constitution, the Ministers of State will be able to decide jointly with the President of the Republic to submit to arbitration matters in which the Panamanian State is a party, subject to the favorable opinion of Panama's Attorney General. The amendment of 2004 made a considerable change: the favorable opinion of the Attorney General will not be necessary when the arbitral clauses of contracts were included in private contracts agreed by the state. This change eliminates bureaucracy, especially for investors who deal with the state of Panama frequently.

Article 202 of the Constitution was amended to provide that the administration of justice can be exercised by means of arbitration in accordance with the law. The Constitution now recognizes the right of arbitration tribunals to review and decide matters regarding their own jurisdiction, in accord with the principle of *kompetanz-kompetanz*, the ability of the arbitral tribunal to rule on the question of whether it has jurisdiction. This reform created the possibility that arbitration tribunals can function without the need of another court questioning the legitimate right of the parties to file their controversy before a third party named by them to decide the conflict.

Recently, Law No. 15 of May 22, 2006, reinstated articles 7 and 17 of the original Law Decree No. 5. With the reestablishment of article 7 of Law Decree No. 5, the arbitration agreement is defined as an agreement by the parties to submit to arbitration any controversies that arise or may arise between them, from a juridical relationship, be it contractual or not. Arbitration can even be authorized when there is no previous arbitral agreement and a conflict arises. In such cases, one of the parties will provide a notice to the other expressing the intent to submit the conflict to arbitration. The requesting party will have seven business days to designate its arbitrators. The Panamanian Arbitration Law may have application when the parties have an arbitration clause in their contract or when they do not have the clause but consent to settle their dispute through the arbitration process.

This new Law No. 15 also introduces a modification of article 7-A of the original Law Decree No. 5, developing in this manner Article 200, Section 4 of the current Constitution of Panama.

According to this legal provision, an agreement to arbitrate involving state parties, whether autonomous or semiautonomous government entities, including the Authority of the Panama Canal, contained in a contract that the entity enters into in the present or future, is valid. The arbitration agreement established in this manner is effective on its own, without further approval or authorization.

For those cases where a contract lacking an arbitration clause has been entered into and a conflict arises, in order to subject the same to the arbitration procedure, it is necessary to secure the approval of the Panama Cabinet Council and the favorable opinion from the Attorney General. It is observed that there is flexibility for cases in which the state of Panama [contracts] with some clause of arbitration. However, in cases where there exist conflicts with the state of Panama without the referenced clause, the legal requirement must be met, in accordance with Section 4 of Article 200 of the Constitution. In this particular situation, the favorable opinion of the Attorney General is required. Despite the flexibility of the law, when the contract has no arbitration clause and one of the parties is the State of Panama, the parties will enter into the arbitration process only with the approval of the Panamanian Cabinet Council and the favorable opinion from the Attorney General.

6.2 Types

The main element of arbitration is the principle of the autonomous will of the parties, granting supremacy to this versus the principle of free access to the governmental jurisdiction. In addition to this principle, the parties replace the traditional judicial mechanisms to resolve their controversies by means of arbitration.

The new legislation varies substantially from the Civil Code (article 1510) with regard to the capacity of those who can submit their controversies to arbitration. While the Civil Code limited this to those with the sufficient capacity to reach an agreement, Law Decree No. 5 makes it mandatory for those who wish to submit a controversy to arbitration to have the capacity to commit. This variation is because the capacity to commit one's self is broader than the capacity to reach an agreement. Any person can commit himself, but to be able to dispose of the assets, he requires an express capacity.

Arbitration in Panama has evolved over the years and has changed substantially to conform with model laws. Initially, its detractors considered that the power to grant justice is unique, exclusive, and not transferable by the State to anyone and, consequently, this mission should not be left in the hands of individuals. Also, it was pointed out that this constitutional right is essentially free as a public service of justice, in contrast with the excessively onerous character of the arbitration process, where the parties choose and pay the arbitration costs including the arbitration tribunal fees.

But this criterion has varied to such a point that the same Judicial Code in its article 3 recognizes that sometimes individuals can also grant justice, referring to the case of arbitrators, clearly as a consequence of the principles found in Article 202 of the Constitution of Panama.

In Panama, the enactment of Law Decree No. 5 was well received by other jurisdictions as the labor and maritime, because those jurisdictions needed an effective legal instrument to provide celerity to the procedure and avoid the huge amounts of files pending to be ruled by Maritime and Labor judges. Currently, in Panama, it has become general practice to submit controversies to arbitration.

Often the parties indicate that the applicable substantive law is the Panamanian due to its versatility. It is endowed with mercantile elements that reflect the new requirements of international commercial law and it permits the option of procedures such as those of the International Chamber of Commerce (ICC), with total independence, if the venue of the arbitration court is within or outside the Republic of Panama.

Panamanian law authorizes arbitration in equity or law, as per the decision of the parties. If it is in law, the arbitrators must craft a resolution according to the rules of law, and if it is in equity, they must do so according to their faithful knowledge and understanding.

If nothing is mentioned regarding the matter, it is understood that the arbitration will be in equity. This differs from the rules of the Judicial Code, which specifies that where the contract is silent as to the issue, the arbitration will be in law. Law Decree No. 5 also sets forth that in any case there is the option to name foreign arbitrators and, if it is in law, the arbitrator must have to be a Bachelor of Law or Juris Doctor.

The arbitration can be ad hoc or institutionalized. It will be ad hoc if it is undertaken according to the rules of procedure specially established by the parties for the specific case, without submittal to the Regulation for Arbitration, Conciliation and Mediation of the Center of Conciliation and Arbitration of Panama. Nevertheless, this arbitration will be subject to the regulations of Law Decree No. 5. The arbitration will be institutionalized, if it is practiced by an authorized arbitration institution.

6.3 The Arbitration Agreement

The arbitration agreement is defined as the means whereby the parties decide to subject to arbitration any controversies that arise or may arise between them, from a juridical contractual relationship or not (See article 7 of Law Decree No. 5).

In this sense, the agreement is understood as the desire of the parties to solve the controversies by means of the establishment of arbitration. The arbitration agreement can adopt the form of a clause included in the contract, an independent agreement, or a unilateral declaration followed by acceptance from the other party or parties. In any case, the autonomous character of the agreement is recognized, in such a manner that it survives even when the contract is declared void.

The agreement must be in writing. An agreement can be evidenced by means of documents exchanged between the parties (e.g., fax, telex, electronic mail, or any other form of communication). Law Decree No. 5 differs substantially in this respect from the provisions of the Judicial Code, which require that the agreement be evidenced in a public deed, a private document, or a judicial record. This was an excellent advance because it eliminates old formalities of the Judicial Code and incorporates new ways of communication that evidence the intention of the parties to enter into arbitration. The judges must accept the new forms of agreement between parties without invoking the lack of formality.

With regard to judicial review, Law Decree No. 5 instructs a judge to reject the suit and resend it immediately to the tribunal in all circumstances. Even if a lawsuit is pending, the arbitration proceedings will continue. The same is ordered in the event that the controversy has been decided by a government, municipal, or provincial entity.

The arbitral award is the final decision rendered by the arbitral tribunal.

It must be said that depending on the type of arbitration—in law or equity—the judgment may contain the grounds for the award. In the case of arbitration in equity the arbitrators (whose denomination was changed in Spanish from *arbitradores* to *árbitros* in the Judicial Code) will decide according to their own criteria based upon their knowledge and understanding. If it is in law, it must be motivated and based on the contract, on the uses of commerce, and on the principles of contracts of international trade of the International Institute for the Unification of Private Law (UNIDROIT).

In case of disagreement between the arbitrators, the decision of the majority will prevail; if there is no majority, it will be decided by the President of the court of arbitration.

Lastly, the judgment ought to include what is set forth in article 34 of the Law Decree No. 5, and specifically decide regarding the costs.

The judgment will be served by the means agreed to by the parties or according to the means established in Law Decree No. 5, by means of the appearance of the parties, their representatives, or their counselors for the complete reading of the judgment.

The judgment may be corrected (arithmetically or for typing errors), clarified, or interpreted within five business days as of its notification, at the request of a party, if nothing to the contrary has been arranged. The judgment is definitive and has been granted the character of judged issue, to be opposed only by means of an annulment action for one of the reasons listed in Law Decree No. 5 (most causes are due to form).

The competent Court will be the Fourth Chamber of the Supreme Court of Justice, and the annulment action is filed in writing, accompanied by the pertinent evidences and the served judgment. A copy is to be provided to the other parties to the process, who may oppose it within twenty business days, with such disputes being resolved within fifteen business days. The decision of the Court admits no further recourse.

6.4 International Treaties and Agreements in Force in Panama

With respect to international treaties and agreements, Panama has the Code of Bustamante, Law 11, dated 1975, whereby the Inter-American Convention on International Commercial Arbitration (also known as the Panama Convention) is approved and the New York Convention of 1958 on the Recognition and Enforcement of Foreign Arbitral Awards.

7. Conclusion

Panama is part of a global negotiation world. The complexity of some matters forced businessmen to adapt to the new changes. Panama is trying to complete this process; in the meantime, some adjustments will take place, especially in new forms of contracts and technology. The Republic of Panama, with its very long tradition of being a point of many cultures, will not have difficulty solving this situation.

Juan F. Pardini and Leonardo Bonadies
Pardini & Asociados
Plaza 2000 Tower
10th Floor, 50th Avenue
Panama, Republic of Panama
US & Canada Toll Free Phone: 1-877-622-5904
Phone: +507-223-7222
Fax: +507-264-4730/+507-223-7535
E-mail: pardini@padela.com

CHAPTER 40

International Business Negotiations in Poland

Tomasz Wardynski
WARDYNSKI & PARTNERS
WARSAW, POLAND

1. Introduction

1.1 Broad Demographic Information

Poland is the largest country in Central and Eastern Europe and one of the largest and most attractive markets for foreign investors in this part of the world. Poland's population is 38 million, more than the combined populations of the other seven Central European countries that joined the EU along with Poland in May 2004. The official language in Poland is Polish. It is easy, however, to communicate with Polish people in other languages, especially English, which is spoken by many Polish entrepreneurs and lawyers.

The majority of Polish people are Roman Catholics, but there are also representatives of other religions, such as the Orthodox Church or different Protestant churches. It is Polish tradition to observe such values as tolerance, openness, and the ability to conduct dialogue with the minority religions and other nations.

1.2 Historical and Cultural Background

Poland has been affected by its specific geopolitical situation for centuries. After World War II, the communist political system imposed upon Poland made meaningful political or social dialogue impossible. The system, based on state ownership, relied on central planning and the implementation of these plans without taking the role of the market in the economy or the play of political forces into account.

Since the collapse of communism in 1989, Poland has become a liberal democracy with a strong rule of law. Successful political transformation, followed by economic and social reform, led to the accession of Poland to the North Atlantic Treaty Organization (NATO) in 1999, which gave the country international security, a necessary condition of economic development. In May 2004 Poland acceded to the European Union (EU) and the European Economic Area (EEA). Consequently, domestic laws now adhere to European Community provisions. In the next several years Poland is likely to join the European Monetary Union, which will culminate in the euro replacing the domestic currency, the zloty. Poland is also a member of many other international organizations (OECD, WTO, etc.) and a signatory to numerous bilateral and multilateral agreements. Therefore, further development of Poland's free market economy will also be stimulated by external factors.

1.3 Business Organization and Culture

Poland has been successful in promoting economic growth. Polish GDP has risen steadily in recent years. A remarkable success of economic reform was the reduction of hyperinflation in the early 1990s.

Membership in the EU has influenced Polish society and the economy. Contemporary Poland is a developing and predictable country with a growing economy.

The market economy has changed the way of life of Polish society. People use economic freedom to improve their living standards and they are very hardworking. The number of university graduates has risen increasingly in recent years. The government's goal is to build a knowledge-based economy.

2. Overview of the Legal System

The legal system in Poland can be described as a typical civil law system, i.e., it developed from the Roman law system based on the superiority of written law established by a state. Polish people solve their legal problems within the civil law, as opposed to the common law system.

The foundation of the Polish system (political and socioeconomic) is the Constitution of the Republic of Poland of 1997, which guarantees civil rights and liberties, as well as economic freedoms.

The main sources of Polish law are statutes enacted by Parliament. Custom and judicial decisions are not sources of Polish law; however, they have some significance. Supreme Court and Constitutional Tribunal decisions have an impact on the long-term development of the Polish legal system.

Membership in the EU limits the power of Parliament and of the national government and affects national sovereignty. European Community law has supremacy over Polish law. The Republic of Poland is also bound by rules and norms of international law.

3. Substantive Laws and Regulations Impacting Negotiations

3.1 Corporate Laws

International negotiations with a large company in Poland tend to be similar to those conducted at a strictly national level. A person approaching such a firm would likely receive a professional reception, depending on the size, organization, and dynamism of the company—in other words, a reception typical of businesses worldwide. A small firm may be represented by the boss alone. A large firm, however, could be represented by the majority of its management board, representatives from the auditors, members of the firm's financial department, and its lawyers. The participation of professionals, including lawyers, is on the increase in Poland for various reasons, one being the copying of American practices. Although the English language is being used by more and more people, an interpreter is often essential. A lawyer often fulfills this task and prepares drafts of agreements in the languages of both parties.

Polish corporate legislation is based primarily on the Act on Freedom of Economic Activity (dated July 2, 2004), the Commercial Companies Code (dated September 15, 2000), and the Civil Code (dated July 23, 1964). Provisions on privatization of state enterprises also have an important role to play. Laws protecting competition in Poland conform in their entirety to worldwide standards, especially those applying in the EU. The same is true for laws dealing with securities trading, which conform to European standards and therefore differ from U.S. securities laws. As a rule, however, such laws in Poland contain information about whether they concur with the relevant provision in U.S. law. If one is aware of the difference between regulations in this area and in the area of accounting, one can prepare oneself to carry on negotiations in a professional fashion.

3.2 Securities Laws

Public trade in securities in Poland is regulated by the Polish Financial Supervision Authority (PFSA). The Warsaw Stock Exchange (WSE) is the only bourse in Poland, but the number of listed companies is consistently growing. As of mid-August 2008, it exceeded 360 companies. In late August 2007, the WSE launched a new market called NewConnect for financing the growth of young companies with large growth potential. NewConnect has the status of an organized market and is operated by the WSE as an alternative trading system outside the regulated market. Many foreign investors invest in Polish shares or treasury bills, and a significant number of strategic investors invest in Polish companies by buying shares either from the State Treasury, from other shareholders, or as a result of new rights issues. Such transactions are usually preceded by agreements negotiated with other shareholders and/or target companies. As stated earlier, this market is composed of experienced players. Exchange regulations provide that transactions involving listed companies are subject to additional disclosure and consent requirements that could affect negotiations. The acquisition or disposal of a significant percentage of shares in a listed company, even when this occurs through public trading, triggers certain reporting requirements to the PFSA and the Office for the Protection of Competition and Consumers (OPCC). A provision also requires that a public invitation be issued to all shareholders to sell when a certain threshold is reached.

3.3 Initial Public Offerings

Many Polish businesses, including medium-size enterprises, seek to raise capital for expansion in Polish and foreign financial markets. Although Polish banking regulations provide for the concept of a "universal" bank (which means that Polish retail banks also act as merchant banks), many internationally recognized foreign investment banks play important roles in the Polish securities market. It has now become common practice for IPOs of Polish companies to be underwritten by an investment bank. Care must be taken, however, when negotiating an appropriate "material adverse change" clause in an underwriting agreement, because many Polish business executives attempt to treat an underwriting agreement as an all-risks insurance policy.

3.4 Tax Laws

Polish fiscal provisions are quite complex. However, the tax risk of an investment is low. Moreover, accession to the European Union led to significant changes in Polish tax law and its harmonization with national laws of other EU member states. Apart from several transitory periods, European tax law has already been implemented in Poland.

A tax audit should be performed to ensure that there are no unexpected liabilities when buying a company as such or simply buying assets and liabilities. An easily obtainable certificate on vendor's tax liabilities also ensures protection for the purchaser. The structure of the entire transaction must be examined very carefully to ensure its tax neutrality, in particular in transactions involving entities from other EU member states. The possibility of obtaining an advance tax ruling from tax authorities shielding a taxpayer from adverse tax effects may be considered as good protection in the event of a change of case law. The safeguarding of legal transactions from a tax point of view is enshrined by domestic administrative courts and the European Court of Justice.

The corporate income tax burden in Poland is not considered a hindrance to running a business in Poland, because of a relatively low standard rate (19 percent) and a number of statutory optimization schemes, as well as a range of incentives to private investors within the scope of EU provisions.

3.5 Antimonopoly Regulations

Mergers and acquisitions are supervised in Poland by the president of the OPCC, whose role is to protect the market from anticompetitive concentrations of undertakings resulting from mergers or acquisitions. The OPCC President can prohibit such a transaction only if it significantly restricts competition in the market, specifically as a result of creation or strengthening of dominant market position. A dominant position is the position of an undertaking that enables it to prevent effective competition in the relevant market by allowing it to behave to an appreciable extent independently of its competitors, customers, and consumers. An undertaking is presumed to have a dominant position if its market share exceeds 40 percent.

The OPCC President must be notified of any intention of the following concentrations: (i) acquisition by one or more undertakings, whether by purchase or subscription for shares or other securities, or through any other means, of direct or indirect control of one or more undertakings; (ii) creation by undertakings of a joint undertaking; (iii) merger of two or more undertakings; and (iv) acquisition by an undertaking of a part of the assets of another undertaking (entirely or part of its enterprise) when the turnover generated by the acquired assets in Poland—in any of the last two financial years preceding the notification—exceeds the equivalent of EUR 10 million. The pre-merger notification requirement applies to concentrations with an effect in Poland in which the aggregate turnover of all participating undertakings in the financial year prior to notification exceeded EUR 1 billion worldwide or EUR 50 million in Poland. Foreign-to-foreign transactions are subject to merger control in Poland if they have or may have an effect within Poland. A transaction will be subject to the notification obligation if either of the above-mentioned turnover thresholds is reached (and for foreign-to-foreign transactions, when the transaction has an effect on the territory of Poland).

There are, however, some exemptions from the notification requirement concerning acquisition-of-control concentrations. A concentration will be exempted from the notification obligation if, for example: (i) the turnover in Poland of the undertaking subject to being taken over (target company) did not exceed the equivalent of EUR 10 million in each of the two years preceding the notification; (ii) it will be an intragroup transaction (i.e., within one capital group); or (iii) it relates to a temporary acquisition of shares intended for resale within one year by a financial institution and without voting rights being exercised during that time (excluding voting on rights to dividends and rights enabling the preparation of the resale of shares).

3.6 Labor and Employment Laws

Labor law was the first area of Polish law to formalize and provide a statutory basis for negotiations. A good labor lawyer will be an invaluable consultant when negotiating the terms of what has become known as a "social package" of employment guarantees, employee benefits, and other agreements. Collective employment agreements are viewed as normative acts and are binding on all legal successors of a former employer. This mainly applies to privatized enterprises. The investor and potential purchaser should expect representatives of the employees to participate in negotiations held with a Polish entrepreneur. Employees of privatized state enterprises have special privileges, which include the right to acquire some shares in the privatized enterprise.

The ability to conduct effective negotiations is crucial in restructuring an employment establishment, especially when decreasing the overall level of employment.

After Poland joined the EU, it implemented EU directives, and Polish labor law now has a wide range of obligations to consult trade unions, employee representatives, or employee councils, especially when there is to be restructuring. The main aim of the changes has been to ensure protection of employee rights.

Negotiating skills are important not only in any collective labor law disputes, but also in matters affecting employees, such as conclusion or termination of employment, especially for employees who hold key or management positions.

Negotiations often determine the course of labor disputes, and are of specific importance when parties decide to resolve a dispute by entering into a contract of settlement.

3.7 Environmental Laws

The general public and foreign businesses investing in Poland are increasingly becoming aware of the strict requirements of environmental legislation and rules of liability for adverse effect on the environment. It is, therefore, almost common practice for a foreign investor to undertake not only a legal audit but also a detailed environmental audit of a Polish entity it plans to acquire. The resulting documents are important and affect negotiations for an investment.

Foreign negotiators must, however, pay specific attention to the overlapping and ambiguous Polish regulations that implement the European Union's law, and to various principles that are the basis for that legislation. Additionally, because the European Union set a high level of protection, and improvement, of the environment, and the policy is to have sustainable safe development, the environmental laws in Poland are complex, strict, and subject to change.

While Polish legislation must eventually comply with that of the EU, foreign investors must be aware that the "polluter pays" principle is still being adopted. That is specifically relevant for liability for land contamination: Polish legislation has two legal regimes for liability for soil, or land, contamination. Liability for contamination on or after April 30, 2007, is on the "polluter pays" principle. If contamination occurred before that date, or results from activity that is completed by that date, the liability is under the Protection of Environment Act by which the liability for contamination arises from having legal title to the land, such as ownership or perpetual usufruct of it. The obligation to reclaim contaminated land is imposed on the landholder by the law alone and the authorities can also order reclamation, the cost of which can be very high. Therefore, the parties to a transaction cannot contract out of the statutory liability. That, however, does not exclude the possibility of an agreement (indemnification clause) between the parties on the contractual liability for the contamination of the land.

Another difficulty that results from EU law is the vast network of protected sites under the Natura 2000 program. Foreign investors could have greenfield investment restricted in the future because the designation of Natura 2000 sites has not been completed yet. That aspect requires close cooperation between environmental experts, lawyers, and participants in investment.

Finally, foreign investors could be affected by a complex of administrative fees and fines. A fee is payable for use of the environment, and an increased fee or administrative fine for breach of environmental legislation. Increased fees and fines are recoverable five years in arrears, which means it is necessary to undertake a legal environmental audit to eliminate, or identify, the risks that could apply to the investor that is proposing to acquire a specific plant or installation.

Any risks that are identified will almost certainly affect investment negotiations, especially the price or costs of an investment.

3.8 Intellectual Property Laws

Various business negotiations carried on with Polish entities often involve intellectual property (IP) rights. The pre-1989 socialist system gave scant regard to protecting such rights, and the attitude of the Polish public lags far behind that of persons who have been accustomed to a long history of having had those rights protected. Recent years have brought economic development, and European Community membership, which has modernized not only the legal system, but attitudes as well. The current level and scope of IP regulations in Poland correspond to the best of European standards.

The main IP legislation is the Industrial Property Law Act of June 30, 2000, and the Copyright and Associated Rights Act of February 2, 1994. Further, IP infringement can also come within the provisions of the Unfair Competition Act of April 16, 1993. Other sources of IP law are multilateral international agreements such as TRIPS and WIPO treaties, and European Community regulations.

In negotiations, an important issue is to prove ownership of the IP rights. The Polish Patent Office grants exclusive industrial property rights, evidenced by certificates of protection, which indicate the owner and scope of protection. Registration depends on the subject of protection and takes from approximately three years for trademarks to four years, or more, for patents. In Poland, as in other European countries, the legislation does not provide for registration of copyright. For that reason, an author cannot obtain a public certificate to prove authorship of work.

Moreover, there are formal requirements for license or transfer of copyrights, patents, and trademarks. The contracts in question must be in writing to be valid. Despite IP being an important part of most businesses, Polish companies often cannot properly estimate their IP portfolios, which require identification, examination, and assessment. This is a good entree for starting business negotiations in IP matters. Afterwards, IP rights may become the subject of negotiation and trade by way of sale or license.

Apart from business transactions, negotiations are often important in settling infringements of IP rights. Negotiations in IP disputes need to be preceded by a kind of education, i.e., detailed explanations especially of the reason for the dispute, to indicate the rights that have been infringed, and indicate the extent of the illegality of the infringer's behavior. Surveys and expert opinions can also assist.

The rights holder may meet the unwillingness of infringers to sign settlements that provide for payment of damages for the harm that has been caused. The source of the problem seems to be twofold: (i) poor knowledge, awareness, and experience in IP matters, not only among businesspeople but also among some lawyers and judges; and (ii) lack of a tradition of solving problems by negotiation. It is almost as if an infringer simply cannot imagine that an item of IP has an actual financial value that can be estimated. Infringers, even when given strong and uncontested argumentation of having broken the law, rarely sign settlements, especially since they are aware that litigation in a Polish court can take years.

Finally, a different, but increasingly popular, method of negotiations in Poland is the use of a neutral, professional mediator.

3.9 Privacy and Data Security Laws

Commercial negotiations can often mean that negotiating parties exchange sensitive information including personal data. If so, privacy and data security laws will apply.

Privacy and data security law in Poland is primarily regulated by the Polish Constitution and the Personal Data Security Act (1997). The Constitution gives a right to privacy. Specific rules are included in the Personal Data Security Act. One of the most important rights of persons whose details are processed (data subjects) is the right to decide whether their data is to be disclosed. Every person is also entitled to verify whether the data stored on him- or herself is correct, in order to be able to have incorrect and illegally obtained data deleted.

The main purpose of the Personal Data Security Act is to protect the interests of the data subjects. Data can only be processed in compliance with the Act. The most often used ground of processing of personal data is consent of the subject to the processing of personal data. Consent must be informed and be based on information made available to the data subject, including the purpose for processing the personal data.

The definition of processing of personal data is wide. The Act states that any act involving data, such as collecting it, keeping it, changing it, making it available to other people, or deleting it, is processing of personal data.

The Act moderates protection for "data available to all." On the other hand, the Act provides a stricter protection of so-called sensitive data, e.g., on race or health.

The authority responsible for ensuring that personal data is protected is the General Inspector for Protecting Personal Data (in Polish: *Generalny Inspektor Ochrony Danych Osobowych*).

4. Foreigners and Foreign Investment

There are special regulations in Poland concerning foreigners and foreign investment, including a whole series of provisions imposing requirements for foreigners to obtain permits and possibly supply information to the government. These relate to ownership relationships, in particular those concerning real estate. The Acquisition of Real Estate by Foreigners Act (foreigners are defined as natural persons who are not Polish citizens, corporate bodies registered abroad, and corporate bodies in Poland owned by such entities) imposes an obligation on foreigners to obtain a permit prior to acquiring the ownership title to land or buildings or a perpetual usufruct[1] right to land in Poland. Foreigners also have to obtain a permit if the shares they are acquiring are offered in public trading. This Act allows a few exceptions related to everyday needs, such as the purchase of a residential dwelling for one's own purposes. A permit is issued by the Ministry of Interior Affairs, with the consent of the Ministry of Defense and, where agricultural or forest land is involved, by the Minister for Agriculture and Food Economy. This prolongs the permit process. A provision states that a decision must be made within a month of an application's submission if the real estate lies in a special economic zone (a zone created to encourage investment in that area). One can also apply a *promesa*,[2] which, if granted, is valid for six months.

The mode of conducting activities in Poland by foreigners derives mainly from the Act on Freedom of Economic Activity. In accordance with this Act, foreign persons from the European Union and the European Free Trade Association zones belonging to the European Economic Area (EEA) may establish and conduct business under the same rules as those that apply to Polish entrepreneurs. The same rules also apply to foreigners having their seat or place of domicile outside the EU and the EEA who meet certain criteria listed in the law. Unless international agreements state otherwise, foreign persons other than those indicated above have the right to establish and conduct business activities only in the form of a limited partnership, a limited joint stock partnership, a limited liability company, or a joint stock company. By reciprocity, foreign investors are also able to establish branches in Poland to conduct business activities. The most popular modes of conducting business activities in Poland are through branches (the scope of activities of these is restricted strictly to that of the foreign entrepreneur, since these entities do not possess legal personality separate from that of the foreign entrepreneur) and limited liability companies (which are entities independent of their shareholders).

The need to secure the appropriate permits and acquire the necessary registrations can complicate the process of negotiations somewhat, though if one is forewarned of the need to obtain them one can start the process earlier. Afterward, a foreigner must register the real estate and shares acquired irrespective of whether or not they were acquired under a permit.

---

[1] A perpetual usufruct right entitles the holders to the exclusive use of the land in question for up to ninety-nine years. It is renewable. Under Polish law, unlike a lease, a perpetual usufruct right can be sold, inherited, or encumbered without the consent of the landowner, which would be either the State Treasury or a local authority. Any buildings on the land are the property of the usufructuary.

[2] A *promesa* is an undertaking by an official to issue a permit if a condition (or conditions) is fulfilled.

Foreign investors are frequently confronted with negotiations regarding the privatizations of state-owned businesses. The Ministry of the Treasury is commonly responsible for selling state-owned businesses. It employs teams of internationally experienced consultants for its transactions, and language is not a barrier for negotiations. Even though privatization transactions are nothing more than the purchase and sale of businesses, they have political implications that often prolong and complicate negotiations. Representations and warranties are not easily given by the State Treasury. Therefore, it is essential to employ an experienced due diligence team capable of assessing the true risk. Even though negotiations may be conducted in English, the final documents will be in Polish and the Polish version will be binding.

Sometimes negotiations in Poland take place with a provincial governor (*wojewoda*). In such cases the language barrier may pose a significant problem and documents must be prepared from the outset in Polish. It is essential that the contract drafts be as close as possible to what is expected in Poland. Documents based on common law may be difficult to comprehend and may need to be adapted. Nevertheless, a great number of new concepts have been accepted in many businesses (especially banking).

The liberalization of Poland over the last ten years has spawned several small and medium-size businesses that may become targets of purchase or joint venture transactions involving foreign investors. The owners of these companies have various levels of international experience. Some are experienced, and negotiations with them can concentrate on essential businesses issues. Sometimes, however, one may deal with an inexperienced businessperson. In such cases, building up trust and confidence is essential and simplicity of documentation is important.

5. Other Significant Legal and Business Issues

Most major companies owned by the state under communist rule in Poland have been privatized. These include some of the largest service providers in the banking, insurance, and telecommunications markets, as well as those in manufacturing sectors (e.g., iron and steel, and the shipbuilding industry).

There are, however, still major reprivatization challenges. Ex-owners of real estate and company shares have been trying for almost twenty years to reclaim their illegally confiscated assets. The only way to succeed is to bring a legal action, because there is still no reprivatization act enacted by Parliament.

Business activity in Poland is generally regulated by the provisions of the Civil Code and by the regulations of the Code of Commercial Partnerships and Companies and by other specific regulations. The

Civil Code regulates civil law relations between individuals and legal entities. The general principles of Polish civil law are equality of the parties; the protection of private ownership; and the freedom of contracts. The Act on Freedom of Economic Activity also plays a fundamental role in regulating business activity in Poland.

6. Negotiation Practices

Companies and lawyers that want to be successful in foreign markets need to understand cross-cultural ways of negotiating, i.e., they should attempt to make local cultural differences work for them, rather than against them, during the negotiating process. It is clear that they have to be properly prepared to deal with local circumstances.

6.1 Participants

Participants in the negotiating process may be lawyers or businessmen. As a result of economic transformation, Polish managers tend to be in their thirties and forties, rather than their fifties or sixties. They are young, because they started their career after 1989, when—generally speaking—it was often easier for young college graduates to adjust to the new socioeconomic situation. They are still young, they are dynamic and well-educated, and they are essentially individualists. Despite their age, it cannot be said that they are inexperienced.

Foreign investors are frequently confronted with negotiations regarding the privatization of state-owned businesses. The Ministry of the Treasury employs teams of internationally experienced consultants for its transactions. Sometimes negotiations in Poland take place with a provincial governor (*wojewoda*).

6.2 Timing

There are no specific rules about timing of negotiations in Poland.

6.3 Cultural, Ethical, and Religious Considerations

Building trust and confidence is essential when negotiating with Polish people. Trying to establish a good rapport with the opposite from the very first moment is worthwhile. Some general "social talk" or knowledge of a few words in Polish is a good icebreaker. It helps to create a spirit of friendship and cooperation. The custom is to shake hands at the beginning and at the end of the session, but giving gifts to the counterpart is not recommended.

Generally speaking, it is important to establish areas of common ground and areas of likely conflict before moving on to the bargaining stage. It is also essential to summarize and review progress at regular intervals during the negotiations.

It is also important to remember that even though privatization transactions are nothing more than the purchase and sale of businesses, they have political implications that often prolong and complicate negotiations in these matters.

6.4 Negotiating Online

Online communications technologies, including e-mail, are being used in everyday life in Poland and they affect business with foreign investors significantly. Although negotiations are not often conducted online, potential for growth of online negotiations is high.

7. Contract Formation

7.1 Wording and Style

Even though negotiations may be conducted in English, if at least one party to a contract is Polish—whether a private individual or an entity without legal personality conducting activities in Poland—the contract must be concluded in Polish. If it is translated into English or another language, the Polish version will be binding.

According to Polish law, everyone has the right to draw up and enter into contracts. Contract types and the signature process are subject to the regulations of the Civil Code. If a specific contract is not listed in the Code, then the general rules apply. The freedom of contracts is one of the general rules of the Polish civil law system.

7.2 Conditions and Defenses

There is a register of abusive clauses in the Civil Code. Under the consumer protection regulations, businesses are under a duty to verify that its standard clauses have not been entered into this register.

7.3 The Special Case of Online Agreements

According to Polish law, online agreements can be concluded. The special regulations concerning electronic signature (Electronic Signature Act) was adopted by Parliament in 2001.

8. Resolving Disputes

The terms of each contract, its scope, and its termination, are defined by the parties to that contract. Contracts must not conflict with Polish legal regulations. In case of dispute between the parties to a contract, Polish jurisdiction is deemed to be binding. The appropriate procedure is provided by the Civil Procedure Code.

Parties to the contract may decide to apply to the arbitration court instead of standard legal action (by the written agreement of both parties). They may apply to an existing arbitration court or agree to establish their own. An arbitration clause setting out the procedures to be followed in the event of a dispute is commonly included in contracts. This clause allows parties to select their own arbitration court, country under whose jurisdiction the contract will fall, and forms of compensation.

Parties can provide for such an option by incorporating an arbitration clause into their original agreement. Parties may also agree to such a clause by exchanging statements to that effect. This can be done at any time prior to submitting the dispute to an arbitral tribunal.

Polish law provides for the possibility of dispute resolution through mediation. A court, acting ex officio, may submit a case to mediation prior to hearing it. Any mediation settlement approved by the court is binding and enforceable.

9. Conclusion

Negotiations in Poland first became common practice in the field of labor law and labor relations, where trade unions negotiated with state or private employers. The negotiations concerning Poland's accession to the EU have increased general interest in negotiating skills and techniques.

Although the law faculty at Warsaw University, which is one of the leading academic institutions in Poland, does not offer classes in negotiating techniques, one can become familiar with these techniques at, for example, the Warsaw School of Economics (the leader among the economics faculties in Poland), the Center for American Law Studies at Warsaw University, and private institutions of learning.

There is no doubt that the process of educating a new generation of Polish officials and lawyers about professional negotiations is taking place. They are aware of the fact that good negotiators generally wish to reach an agreement that meets the interests of both sides and improves the relationship between the parties. They are taught to make concessions if necessary, but they are also, however, taught not to be pushed beyond their sticking point. They are taught flexibility and planning as part of their strategy. It must be said that business culture has been developing in Poland since 1989 and there is nowadays a more positive view towards negotiations than was previously the case.

Tomasz Wardynski
Wardynski & Partners
Ale Ujazdowskie 10
00-478 Warsaw
Poland
Phone: 48-22-537-82-00
Fax: 48-22-437-82-01
E-mail: tomasz.wardynski@wardynski.com.pl

CHAPTER 41

International Business Transactions in Qatar

Andrew Wingfield
SIMMONS & SIMMONS
DOHA, QATAR

1. Introduction

Qatar is a small, but very rich, country located in the Persian Gulf with one of the world's fastest rates of economic growth. It obtained independence in 1971 and comprises approximately 11,500 square kilometers. Its southern border is with Saudi Arabia and the rest of the peninsula state is surrounded by sea. It has the world's third largest reserves of natural gas (after Russia and Iran) and has one of the world's highest GDP per capita, being approximately US$70,754 in 2007.

The current population is estimated at around 1.4 million, of whom around 200,000 to 250,000 are Qatari citizens.

The highest point in the country is 103 meters (338 feet) above sea level and the coast line is approximately 550 kilometers (340 miles) long, but with only 2 percent of the land available for agricultural production. In the summer season the temperatures are hot and humid with temperatures in the region of 40 to 50 °C (104 to 122 °F) with average annual rainfall of about 75 millimeters.

The current ruler is Sheikh Hamad bin Khalifa al-Thani, who became emir in 1995. A permanent Constitution came into force in 2005 and resulted in the country's first ever legislative elections at municipal level and the election of two-thirds of the Majlis al-Shura, the Advisory Council. Qatar is an Islamic country, but with religious tolerance, the first Roman Catholic church having been opened in 2007. Arabic is the official language, although English is widely used and is very much the second language.

The Constitution creates executive, legislative, and judicial authorities. The Constitution vests executive power in the emir and it is the emir who promulgates decrees. However, the Constitution further states that the emir shall be assisted by the Council of Ministers.

The Council of Ministers, appointed by emiri decree, is the highest executive organ in the country, with all laws and statutes ratified by the emir. As noted above, the state also has an Advisory Council, the Majlis Al Shura (two-thirds of which are elected by general voting and the other one-third appointed by the emir), which debates political, administrative, and economic matters referred to it by the Cabinet and can also submit draft laws to the emir, who has the right to accept or reject such proposals. The Advisory Council has five permanent committees: Legal and Legislative Affairs; Financial and Economic Affairs; Public Services and Utilities; Domestic and Foreign Affairs; and Cultural Affairs and Information.

The Cabinet Ministers, according to the current Constitution, share collective responsibility under the emir to implement the policy of the state. To that end, they propose draft laws, endorse resolutions and regulations prepared by the individual ministries within their mandates, and supervise the implementation of laws.

The judicial system in Qatar is divided into two main streams: civil law and sharia, or Islamic law. Disputes between Muslims, such as marriage, inheritance, and certain criminal acts, are resolved under sharia while business is predominantly a matter of civil law. Civil law is promulgated by the Civil Code, as amended by Law No. 22 of 2004, which provides that the sources of law in Qatar are the applicable statutory provisions.

In the absence of such provisions, the courts will look next to any special custom or practice in the trade or business concerned, then to the principles of sharia law and finally to any local custom or practice. Most business matters are covered by legislation, and in the absence of any applicable custom or practice, the courts often consider the laws of other Arab states.

Qatar introduced a new law reorganizing the judicial system, Law No. 10 of 2003 on the Judicial Authority. The major innovation in this law is in relation to the introduction of a third level of courts, the Supreme Court. That law provides that there are three levels of courts: the Supreme Court, the Appeal Courts, and the Preliminary Court. Each court is competent to settle the cases filed therein in accordance with law. There is now one court system, as opposed to two separate systems for criminal and civil matters. Sharia Courts fall under the separate jurisdiction of the Presidency of Sharia Courts and Religious Affairs. In general, there are two possible appeals for cases first heard in the Preliminary Court.

Appointment of the judiciary is provided for in the new Constitution. The emir has the power to endorse and ratify laws and decrees, and Article 130 states "judicial authority is independent and shall be undertaken by the Courts at all levels, those Courts shall provide judgment under the rule of law." Every judge is appointed by a special emiri decree.

Investors should note that the Qatari courts will respect jurisdiction clauses contained in an agreement. It is quite common to find transactions between international partners that are subject to English law or the law of a U.S. state and that ask for disputes to be resolved by foreign courts or arbitration. Qatar is a signatory to the 1958 New York Convention on the Recognition and Enforcement of Foreign Arbitral Awards. Many such agreements are written in English, though certain contracts must always be written in Arabic.

There has been a rush of new legislation put through in recent years designed to bring the commercial environment into line with international best practice. The new legislation is also designed specifically to make Qatar an attractive place in which to do business and to encourage trade and investment. A businessperson looking at the Commercial Companies Law, revised under new Law No. 5 of 2002, will find the corporate environment and company structures similar to those in place in most other countries with which they are familiar.

The Foreign Investment Law, Law No. 13 of 2000, has now liberalized a number of restrictions on how foreigners may invest or conduct their business in Qatar.

There are also commercial laws, employment laws, environmental legislation, and intellectual property laws that have been both updated and internationalized. Banking was traditionally a sector in which foreign investment was not allowed, but following an amendment to the foreign investment law, foreign banks now hold stakes in both the International Bank of Qatar—formerly Grindlays Qatar Bank—and Al Ahli Bank.

The most significant changes recently include the Commercial Code Law No. 27 of 2006, which regulates new issues, such as bankruptcy, commercial obligations, commercial contracts, commercial papers (checks), trade names, commercial premises, commercial activities, and unlawful competition. The other significant recent changes are Law No. 33 of 2006 concerning the Central Bank of Qatar, Law No. 16 of 2006 amending certain provisions of the Commercial Companies Law No. 5 of 2002, and the new Doha securities market internal regulations.

A change in the foreign investment law is also likely to occur in the near future. It was recently announced that the restrictions on foreign ownership of companies will be lifted and that it will be possible for foreign companies to own 100 percent of the shares in Qatar-based firms. However, this has yet to happen.

In 2005 the government established the Qatar Financial Centre (QFC) (see below), which created a totally new stand-alone regulatory environment for financial services companies based on common law principles and a regulatory regime similar to the Financial Services Authority in the United Kingdom. All rules and regulations are in English and the establishment of the QFC is part of the government's desire to diversify the economy and to attract international investment banks and financial services institutions to Qatar to develop it as a financial services center for the region.

Currently the Qatari riyal (QAR) is pegged to the United States dollar (US$) at the rate of QAR 3.65 to US$1.

Funds are freely transferable into and out of Qatar, although the Qatar Central Bank has released circulars relating to money laundering that place banks under a duty to verify customer identification and investigate the "deposit or transfer or dealing with funds generated from any suspicious or illegal source."

2. Doing Business in Qatar

There are several considerations to be made when deciding to invest in Qatar. They include the following.

2.1 Establishing a Company

Where a foreign investor wishes to set up a business in Qatar, the usual method is to form a company with a Qatari partner who owns 51 percent of the business, although this may change in the near future. Company structures and methods of doing business are governed by the Commercial Companies Law. However, there are alternative ways of doing business in Qatar that stop short of setting up a company.

2.2 Branch Office

A branch office can be set up where a foreign company wishes to perform a specific contract in Qatar. A branch office will be authorized by the Ministry of Business and Commerce where the project facilitates the performance of a public service or utility. Currently, the Ministry of Business and Commerce is interpreting this condition to mean a contract with a government body, or a subcontract of such a contract only. A branch office is only entitled to perform the specific government contract for which it is registered and will be fully taxable, unless granted an exemption.

2.3 Representative Trade Office

A representative trade office is a relatively new method of establishing a shop window in Qatar. It can be used to promote a foreign business and to attempt to introduce it to local companies and projects. A representative trade office cannot, however, be contracted to do business in Qatar. Business can be carried out by a foreign entity, where the contract can be performed substantially outside Qatar or by a company or branch authorized to operate in Qatar.

2.4 Commercial Agency

If a foreign company does not want to establish a separate legal presence in Qatar, an agent can be appointed to market goods or services within the state. This can be an attractive way of reducing the costs of establishing a presence. The foreign company will not need to incorporate and register its own company with a Qatari partner and will not need its own physical presence in Qatar. Rather than sharing a percentage of profits with a Qatari partner, a commission will be payable to the agent. However, using an agent will reduce the foreign company's control over its own dealings, as business will be undertaken in the name of the agent. Care should be taken regarding the nature of the relationship. If the agency is deemed commercial, as defined in Qatar's Commercial Agencies law, restrictions on termination will apply and compensation will be payable to the commercial agent. It will not, therefore, be straightforward to change local partners later or to set up a company with a completely different local partner.

3. Substantive Laws and Regulations Impacting Negotiations

3.1 Foreign Investment Law

Incentives are available to attract foreign capital, including tax breaks and exemptions from customs duty. Foreign investors can transfer investments and profits may be repatriated, as can the proceeds of sale and capital on liquidation.

3.1.1 Foreign Investment Restrictions

The Foreign Investment Law, Law No. 13 of 2000, has liberalized the restrictions on how foreigners may invest and do business in Qatar. The general starting position is that foreign investors may operate in all parts of the national economy—note the exceptions below—with a Qatari partner who must own at least 51 percent of the enterprise. However, 51 percent ownership by a Qatari partner does not necessarily mean that the local affiliate is entitled to 51 percent of profits. The areas where foreign ownership is not allowed are commercial agencies and real estate businesses. However, foreign investors may acquire leases of land for a period of up to sixty years, which are renewable after that period has expired, as part of another activity, and may also secure the ownership of residential plots in three specific developments and ninety-nine years usufruct rights in eighteen particular investment zones.

The Ministry of Business and Commerce can grant an exception allowing foreign investors to own more than 49 percent of a company in specified sectors covering a wide swath of the economy. These sectors include agriculture, industry, health, education, energy, mining, tourism, and the development of natural resources. To qualify for an exemption, a project must comply with Qatar's development plan. Those projects that utilize locally available raw materials, feature new products, use modern technology, and involve internationally renowned industries are favored alongside those that employ local people. Concession agreements for the exploitation of natural resources and cases where the government participates in association with foreign investors are not within the scope of the foreign investment law.

Restrictions on foreign ownership of businesses are expected to be lifted in the near future.

3.1.2 Incentives

Incentives designed to attract foreign capital include exemption from income tax for a maximum period of up to ten years, absolution from customs duties for the import of equipment relating to a specified project, and release from customs duties for the import of primary or semi-manufactured materials where they are not available locally.

Foreign capital is guaranteed against expropriation, although the state may acquire assets for public benefit on a nondiscriminatory basis, provided that the full value of the asset is paid in compensation.

Investors can transfer investments, including profits, proceeds of sale and capital on liquidation, sums resulting from the settlement of disputes, and any expropriation compensation, to and from abroad. Disputes may be settled by local or international arbitration.

3.2 Proxy Law

A widely talked-about piece of legislation is Law No. 25 of 2004, which examines commercial, economic, and professional activities undertaken by foreign nationals in Qatar that are in violation of the law. It is known as the proxy law. Many foreigners used to conduct business in Qatar by using a corporate sponsorship or services agency arrangement with a local trading company. Under these arrangements, the foreigner traded outwardly as a division of the local company on the basis of its commercial registration, and no income tax was paid. However, behind the scenes, there were arrangements that resulted in the vast majority of the profits being paid to the foreign investor, with a fixed service fee or small percentage of the profits being retained by the Qatari company, which would be indemnified against liabilities from the business.

These sorts of arrangements have always been in breach of the foreign investment law, but the proxy law cracks down on proxy arrangements where local companies act as a front for foreign investors, particularly where no tax is paid. Another of the main aims of the proxy law is to prohibit the purchase of shares on the Doha Securities Market by non-Qataris, although this can now legitimately happen subject to some aggregate foreign ownership limits.

3.3 Company Law

Qatar's company law was revised in 2002 and amended in 2006. The new Laws No. 5 of 2002 and No. 16 of 2006 incorporate provisions regarding corporate management and operation, similar to English company regulation. They also introduced new company types, changed share capital requirements, and simplified some procedures. One new feature of the law is that it now recognizes specifically that companies can become bankrupt and contains many procedures for liquidation. It also introduces provisions covering mergers and the transformation of limited liability companies into public shareholding firms. The three types of enterprises most likely to be of interest to international investors are limited liability companies, joint ventures, and Qatari shareholding organizations with government participation. Other possible legal entities under Qatari law are the sole property company, the simple partnership, the joint partnership, and the Qatari shareholding company, though foreign participation in these entities is restricted.

3.3.1 Limited Liability Company

Limited liability companies (LLCs) are broadly equivalent to limited companies in the U.K., but LLCs have no issued shares. This form of company is likely to be appropriate for foreign companies carrying out a joint venture with a Qatari partner. An LLC must have at least two, but no more than fifty, shareholders and requires a minimum capital of QAR 200,000 ($54,700), which must not be raised by public subscription. Transferable shares or bonds may not be issued. Some 10 percent of each year's net profits must be kept within the company until the reserve stands at 50 percent of the share capital. LLCs are not permitted to carry out insurance and banking services or provide investment advice and services to third parties. In LLC situations, there are ways of effectively increasing the profit percentage and the control of the overseas shareholder where it appropriately reflects the foreign company's management of the LLC. These include using weighted dividend rights and the appointment of a general manager by the foreign shareholder.

3.3.2 Article 68 Company

The government or majority government-owned ventures may establish public shareholding companies with Qatari or foreign investors. These companies are known as Article 68 companies and are exempt from any provisions of the Commercial Companies Law that conflict with the memorandum and articles of association of the company or any shareholders' agreements. The majority of the foreign private sector projects with Qatar Petroleum were created and developed under this format.

3.3.3 Joint Venture

Projects may be carried out by foreign investors and Qatari partners under a joint venture agreement. This relationship does not create a separate legal entity and it is not possible to issue transferable shares or financial instruments in the joint venture. The non-Qatari partner must be authorized to carry out business in Qatar, either as a branch or as an LLC. Therefore, the joint venture is not a means of circumventing the foreign investment law. If a non-Qatari is a partner, the joint venture may not carry out any business reserved for Qataris. Each party is normally responsible for its own liabilities unless the parties act in a way that indicates the existence of a separate company, in which case they will be jointly liable.

3.3.4 Qatari Shareholding Company

A Qatari shareholding company (QSC) is broadly equivalent to an English public limited company, whose shares are publicly held and are offered to the public for subscription. The liability of each shareholder is limited to the value of its shares. The founders of the company must subscribe for not less than 20 percent, and not more than 45 percent, of the shares. The Commercial Companies Law sets out the minimum requirements for inclusion in a prospectus for shares offered to the public. It also prescribes other matters regarding the allocation of shares under a public subscription: there must be at least five shareholders in a QSC; the memorandum and articles are to follow the form prescribed by the Ministry of Business and Commerce; the company must have a minimum capital of QAR 10 million ($2.75 million); and at least 25 percent of the share value must be paid up on initial subscription, with the balance being closed within five years. A QSC is managed by an elected board of directors, and a general assembly of the shareholders must be held at least once a year. From each year's net profits, 10 percent must be kept within the company until the reserve stands at half of the share capital.

3.3.5 Listed Companies

The Doha Securities Market (DSM), which opened on May 26, 1997, with seventeen companies, has grown steadily and over forty companies are now listed. To be listed on the DSM, a public shareholding company must have a minimum share capital of QAR 10 million ($2.75 million), of which at least 50 percent must be fully paid up. It must also have at least one hundred shareholders. Under a new Mutual Funds Law, No. 25 of 2002, non-Qataris may buy into the DSM through investment funds. Law No. 2 of 2005 enabled foreign investors to invest directly in and hold up to a maximum in aggregate of 25 percent of the shares in any company listed on the DSM.

3.4 Commercial Agency Law

According to Law No. 8 of 2002, any person who is exclusively licensed to distribute goods, to offer them for sale, or to perform services on behalf of a principal in exchange for remuneration will be considered a commercial agent. Therefore, the law does not apply to traders who purchase the goods in their own name for resale or where two entities have a nonexclusive trading relationship. Only Qatari nationals, or companies the entire share capital of which is owned by Qataris, may be commercial agents.

3.4.1 Commission

An agent is entitled to a commission, not exceeding 5 percent of the price of the goods, to be set by the Minister of Business and Commerce if the principal imports the goods into Qatar for trade purposes through a third party. However, the agent is not entitled to a commission on goods imported into Qatar for personal use or in cases where the goods are imported into Qatar by a third party for re-export.

3.4.2 Termination

If an agreement for a fixed term is withdrawn before the expiration date of that term, the agent is entitled to claim compensation from the principal. When the period of a fixed-term agreement expires, it will terminate. It should be noted that upon the expiry of the period of a fixed-term agreement, if it is not renewed (even though the principal may not have defaulted on the agreement and despite any term in the agreement to the contrary), the agent will be entitled to compensation if the agent's good performance has established a visible success in promoting the products, and the principal's refusal to renew the transaction deprives the agent of substantial benefit. If the agreement is for an unlimited period, it can only be terminated with the mutual consent of both of the parties. However, if only one party wishes to terminate it, a court decision is required. In these circumstances, the other party will be entitled to compensation.

Even if both parties consent to the termination, as in the case of a fixed-term agreement that is not renewed, the agent will still be entitled to compensation if his performance has been good and the principal's refusal to renew the agreement deprives the agent of a substantial benefit. If the principal terminates the agreement or refuses to renew it without legal justification, the principal can be forbidden from importing into Qatar the goods that were covered by the agency. If the work of the original agent is transferred to a new agent, that agent will be obliged to buy the previous agent's stock. Once a commercial agreement has been terminated, the agent must apply to have his name removed from the register within a period of thirty days.

3.5 Employment Law

Private sector employment is governed by the Labour Law, Law No. 14 of 2004, and also by various secondary resolutions from the Minister of Civil Services and Housing, introduced in 2005. The major provisions introduced by the Labour Law include Qatarization, women's rights, workers' associations, health and safety, wider-ranging employees' rights, and an increased role in overseeing employment conditions for the Labour Department. Companies that are looking to acquire and employ expatriate employees will also need to comply with the sponsorship, residence permit, and work permit requirements.

All contracts of employment are governed by the Labour Law and must be in Arabic (or both Arabic and English) and approved and registered with the Labour Department. Employers need to be aware of the requirement to pay end-of-service benefits to employees that arise once an employee has been employed for twelve months or more.

A different employment law regime exists for employees working in the Qatar Financial Centre, which has its own set of separate employment regulations.

3.5.1 Employment of Foreign Nationals
Employers must give priority to Qatari nationals when recruiting prospective employees. Non-Qataris may not be employed unless the employer has determined that there are no locals with the ability and willingness to undertake the role. The law provides that quotas may be set by the Minister for Civil Affairs for the proportion of non-Qataris in each sector of the workplace.

3.5.2 Sponsorship
All foreign employees must be sponsored by their employer, who will be responsible for them while in Qatar. If it is a legal entity, the business must have its central office or an administrative branch in Qatar. Foreign employees will require residence and work permits. Workers may only work for their sponsor, but it is possible for sponsorship to be transferred to a new employer, if the previous employer consents. If an expatriate employee gives up his or her job before the end of the contract, and the previous employer has not already consented to a change of sponsor, that employee will not be allowed to return to Qatar to work or reside for two years.

3.6 Property Law

Foreign ownership of real estate in Qatar is restricted. Gulf Cooperation Council (GCC) citizens are permitted to own residential and commercial property, subject to certain restrictions, but otherwise, until 2005, foreign ownership of real estate in Qatar was strictly prohibited. Now the groundbreaking Law No. 17 of 2004 allows foreigners to own properties in three newly built Qatari residential developments.

3.6.1 Projects
Very limited exceptions to the general prohibition may be authorized by decree, where the purpose of the foreign acquisition of land is to facilitate a public service or utility. An example of an exception such

as this is Ras Laffan industrial city, the industrial hub 80 kilometers north of Doha that was founded to accommodate a large number of gas-based industries, including gas liquefaction, processing and export, petrochemicals, and refining of condensate. Ras Laffan is also one of the world's largest liquefied natural gas–exporting ports. In the case of Ras Laffan, the Cayman Islands registered holding companies involved in the QatarGas and RasGas projects were authorized to own land to enable them to ensure the financing of the enterprises. Other foreign projects may be allotted land through long leases of up to sixty years, which may be renewed.

3.6.2 Foreign Ownership in Three Developments
Under the new law, foreigners may own freehold properties in the Pearl of the Gulf island, the West Bay Lagoon, and the Al Khor Resort project. GCC nationals are allowed to own freehold properties in the Lusail, Al Kharayej, and Jebel Thuaileb investment areas.

3.6.3 Ninety-Nine-Year Leases for Foreigners in Eighteen Investment Zones
Following the introduction of Cabinet Resolution No. 6 of 2006, non-Qataris may now hold renewable ninety-nine-year usufruct rights in eighteen investment zones. These zones are: Mushaireb; Fariq Abdul Aziz; New Doha; Al Ghanem Al Atiq; Al Rifaa and Al Hatmi Al Atiq; Al Salta; Bin Mahmoud (22); Bin Mahmoud (23); Rodhat Al Khail; Al Mansoura and Bin Dirham; Najma; Um Ghwailina; Al Khulaifat; Al Sadd; New Al Murqab and Al Nasr; Doha International Airport; Al Qassar; Al Dafna and Ounaiza; and Lucil, Al Kharayej and Jebel Thuaileb.

3.6.4 Leases
Leases are common currency for non-Qatari residents, in relation to both residential property and commercial property. Both the residential and the commercial sectors in Qatar are currently very much landlords' markets. There is a shortage of apartments and housing on the compounds and there is also a lack of good office accommodation. Consequently, rents are rising, and although there is a massive building program under way, it is likely that supply will not exceed demand for some time. Both residential and commercial leases are relatively short in length. Lease agreements are, on the whole, brief and straightforward. Payment terms vary, but usually rent is payable quarterly and in advance. However, it is not unknown, particularly when smaller premises are involved, for some landlords to insist on a year's rent being paid in advance. In commercial property, tenants usually pay a service charge, which is again often paid in advance along with the rent. Usually a fixed sum covers all of the common services in the building, including insurance of the structure itself. The English law concept of service charge accounts, audited accounts, and quarterly payments

with annual adjustments is not a feature (not surprising, given the short terms of most leases). Landlords normally accept responsibility for the repair of the structure and fabric of the building, while tenants shoulder the cost of anything other than fair wear and tear during their stay. Partitioning and carpeting of commercial premises is usually arranged through a process of negotiation between the parties.

3.7 Intellectual Property Law

There have been major developments in intellectual property legislation in Qatar in the last few years. Traditionally, intellectual property rights were not as well protected in Qatar as foreign investors might have wished. However, following Qatar's induction into the World Trade Organization in 1996, it became party to the Berne Convention for the Protection of Literary and Artistic works and in 2000 to the Paris Convention for the Protection of Industrial Property. Subsequently, Qatar enacted new trademark and copyright laws in 2002.

3.7.1 International Conventions
The Berne Convention administers copyright protection to all literary and artistic works in all of the countries that are members of the Convention. Under the Paris Convention, which governs the protection of industrial property, citizens of other countries that have signed up to the Convention are given the same protection for their industrial property—covering patents and industrial designs—as citizens of Qatar. Nationals of states that have signed up to the Convention may also benefit from a priority period when registering an industrial design or trademark in Qatar that has previously been registered in any of the other countries that are members of the Paris Convention as well.

3.7.2 Copyright
The Copyright Law, Law No. 7 of 2002 on the protection of copyright and neighboring rights, protects original literary and artistic works including books, oral performances, plays, musical pieces, choreographic works of art, drawings and paintings, translations, computer programs, and databases that are creative in the selection and arrangement of their subject matter. As in other jurisdictions, ideas themselves are not protected under the copyright law.

Protection extends, *inter alia*, to foreigners whose work is either first published in Qatar or originally produced in another country and then in Qatar within thirty days of the first publication date. This protection also extends to works that are protected by international agreements. This means, in practice, works that are covered by the copyright laws of any of the other countries that are members of the Berne Convention.

Protection lasts for the life of the author and for another fifty years after his or her death. In the case of collective work, protection runs for fifty years from the date of publication or from the date of completion if the work has not been published. In cases where authors have not translated their work into Arabic or where insufficient copies have been distributed in the state of Qatar, Qatari citizens can obtain translation or reproduction licenses from the Ministry of Economy and Trade to use in schools and universities.

3.7.3 Trademarks

Under the Law on Trademarks, Trade Names, Geographical Indications and Industrial Designs and Samples, Law No. 9 of 2002, trademarks may be registered at the Trademark Office. They are then valid for renewable periods of ten years from the date of filing. As in other jurisdictions, applications will be refused if the trademark does not possess a distinctive character of its own, or is purely descriptive of the products and services it relates to. The international classification of goods and services is used. Trademarks can be licensed and assigned, but the agreement must be made in writing and registered. Trademarks may be canceled if they are not used for a period of five consecutive years in Qatar. Non-Qataris have the same rights as locals, provided that their country of origin treats Qatar reciprocally. Therefore, any nation that is party to the Paris Convention is included in this approach.

3.7.4 Designs

Inventive designs or industrial models are permitted to be registered under the trademark law. Protection lasts for a period of five years and is then renewable for two further five-year terms.

3.7.5 Patents

Qatari Patent Law of 2006 provides for registration of inventions and foreign patents at the Qatar Patent Office. A GCC patent can be obtained by filing at the patent office in Riyadh, Saudi Arabia, which provides protection for all GCC states: Bahrain, Kuwait, Oman, Qatar, Saudi Arabia, and the UAE. Under the GCC regulation, a patent granted by the patent office secures legal protection of the investor's rights in all the GCC states. The term of the patent is twenty years from the original application filing date. The GCC regulation follows the first-to-file-rule.

3.8 Competition Law

There is now a specific competition law in Qatar that is set out in Law No. 19 of 2006 regarding the protection of competition and prohibition of monopoly practices (the "Competition Law").

The Competition Law prohibits "agreements, contracts, conduct or practices prejudicing the rules of competition," as well as the abuse of a controlling or dominating position in a given market.

As is typical of primary legislation in Qatar, the provisions of the Competition Law are very broadly drafted and may have the unintended effects of applying to business practices that are not, in fact, anticompetitive. The Competition Law has only recently been introduced in Qatar; it has not been tested and its legal and commercial impact is not yet clear.

3.8.1 Anticompetitive Practices

The Competition Law specifically prohibits:

- Price fixing
- Limiting the flow of products into or out of Qatar
- Creating a "sudden abundance" in a product
- Preventing or hindering any person's economic or commercial activity in Qatar
- Withholding all or part of the available products in the market from certain persons without justification
- Restricting production, manufacture, distribution, or marketing operations
- Dividing the market for a product on the basis of geographical areas or time periods
- Competitors coordinating or agreeing in relation to the submission of tender quotations
- Spreading incorrect information about products or their prices "on purpose"

The Minister of Business and Commerce may exempt "offers, agreement and contracts restricted for competition" from the prohibition set out above where the interest of consumers requires it.

3.8.2 Abuse of Dominant Position

The Competition Law specifically prohibits:

- Abstaining from dealing with a product so as to create an artificial price for such product
- Decreasing or increasing available quantities of a product so as to create an artificial deficit or over-supply of such product
- Abstaining without legal justification from buying or selling a product or selling a product at a discount from its cost of production
- Imposing an obligation not to manufacture, produce, or distribute a product
- Imposing an obligation on certain persons to restrict their activity in relation to commodities or services

- Making a product's sale or purchase conditional on the acceptance of obligations or products that do not relate to the subject matter of the original transaction or agreement
- Violating the equality of opportunities amongst competitors by discriminating between them without any legal justification
- Abstaining from making available a product when it is possible economically to make such product available
- Obligating any supplier not to deal with a competitor
- Selling products for less than their marginal cost or average variable cost
- Obliging parties dealing with an economically dominant person to not make available to any competitor of such dominant person use of their facilities or services although such use is economically possible

3.8.3 Enforcement—the Competition Committee

The Competition Law is enforced by the Competition Protection and Monopoly Prohibition Practices Committee (the "Competition Committee"), which reports to the Minister of Business and Commerce in Qatar.

The powers of the Competition Committee include collating information on relevant economic activities in Qatar, monitoring anti-competitive activities, coordinating with overseas competition authorities, and enforcing the laws established under the Competition Law.

It should be noted that the Competition Law provides for personal liability for management personnel knowingly involved in activities punishable under the legislation. Fines for violation of the Law range between QAR 100,000 and QAR 5,000,000, together with seizure of profits realized as a result of engaging in prohibited activities.

3.9 Environmental Law

The country is fortunate in its wealth of gas and oil, but the exploitation of these resources and the subsequent industrial diversification efforts that have followed have brought with them the challenging problem of how to properly manage waste products and emissions. Qatar, having already ratified the main international environmental conventions, has recently created and enacted an environmental protection law, which is outlined briefly below.

3.9.1 Environmental Protection Law

The Environmental Protection Law, Law No. 30 of 2002, contains an administrative framework and sets out licensing and operational requirements, including restrictions on hazardous waste, air, noise, and marine pollution. Both private and governmental bodies are required to include a specific clause dealing with environmental protection issues in all contracts that could possibly have a harmful effect on the environment. They must also undertake to pay the clean-up costs of any environmental damage their activities may cause.

Project licenses will not be issued until plans have been submitted to the Supreme Council for the Environment and Natural Reserves (SCENR) for approval and an environmental impact assessment has been carried out. Once a project is up and running, the operator must comply with all of the relevant environmental measures and take all necessary precautions to completely prevent any environmental damage. Companies must also maintain ongoing environmental impact records. If environmental damage does occur, all necessary steps must be taken to minimize the impact.

The most significant changes that have been introduced by the environmental protection law are that the SCENR now has the power to enforce the law and sanction those who have chosen to abuse it.

3.9.2 Implications for Companies

Oil- and gas-producing countries such as Qatar are working at meeting the challenge of how best to exploit some of their most valuable natural resources while ensuring the protection of their environment and the wider world around them. Although the new environmental protection regime does place some additional restrictions on a variety of operating processes, most companies already understand that environmental awareness and compliance is an important component of good governance, risk management, and social responsibility.

Indeed, for most of the major players in the country, compliance with the new legislation will merely require simple amendments to the environmental management systems and policies that they have already put in place. For other organizations, those that might have traditionally viewed environmental protection as a drain on their profits, this new legislation will present a challenge. It is a challenge to which they must rise, for the sake of the environment, and their bank balances.

3.10 Customs Duty

GCC customs duty is 5 percent on most items. Exemptions from customs duty can be obtained for the import of equipment relating to a particular project, as can exemptions for the import of primary or semi-manufactured materials where they are not available locally. In addition to customs duty, legalization fees are payable on import documentation.

3.11 Taxation

3.11.1 Taxation of Individuals

There is no income tax on personal salaries.

3.11.2 Taxation of Companies:

There is taxation on companies, which varies, as discussed below.

- Income tax is levied on businesses other than those wholly owned by GCC nationals.
- Income tax is charged on all profits arising in Qatar, including profits on the sale of the company's assets.
- The share of profits of the Qatari or GCC partner in a business is exempt from tax.
- An income tax exemption can be granted for a period of up to ten years for major projects if they meet certain criteria.
- Some countries have double-taxation treaties with Qatar, and if not, then unilateral relief may be available. For example, U.K. unilateral relief is available against U.K. taxes where Qatari income tax has been paid.

Tax is payable at the following progressive rates:

Taxable income in Qatari Riyals	Rate
0–100,000	Exempt
100,001–500,000	10%
500,001–1,000,000	15%
1,000,001–1,500,000	20%
1,500,001–2,500,000	25%
2,500,001–5,000,000	30%
5,000,001+	35%

It has been announced that it is the government's intention that corporate tax rates be reduced down to a flat level of 12 percent. However, this has not yet appeared in law and further details are awaited.

The Qatar Financial Centre has a completely different tax regime that essentially provides for a 10 percent corporate profit tax on Qatar-sourced profits.

4. The Qatar Science and Technology Park and the Qatar Financial Centre

Qatar is one of the fastest-growing economies in the world. Over the last couple of years, two new legal environments have been created to capitalize on that success by providing the business infrastructure to attract world-class international financial institutions, multinational corporations, and technology companies to Qatar: the Qatar Science and Technology Park (QSTP) and the Qatar Financial Centre (QFC). The key features of both institutions are favorable tax regimes, transparent legal frameworks with international-style regulations, streamlined registration processes, and the possibility of 100 percent foreign ownership.

4.1 QSTP

The QSTP free-trade zone was established by Law No. 36 of 2005. The QSTP's objectives are to promote applied research, technology development, and commercialization in Qatar, to grow and diversify Qatar's economy through the application of technology, to accelerate the formation and growth of start-up companies, and to create high-value employment opportunities, in particular for Qatar's university graduates. Its main attractions are that (i) it allows businesses, the main activity of which is technology development, to be established with 100 percent foreign ownership and (ii) no tax is payable in the QSTP free-trade zone. The QSTP has said that it considers research and development, product or process development, and technology-related training or consulting to be included under the "technology development" umbrella.

Applicants can either set up in the QSTP as a limited liability company or as a local branch office. Although the criminal laws and penalties of the state of Qatar apply in the QSTP free-trade zone, the civil laws and regulations of the country apply only to the extent that they must not conflict with the QSTP regulations.

The QSTP has attracted an impressive list of tenants in a short period of time, including EADS, ExxonMobil, Garner Lee, GE, Microsoft, Rolls-Royce, Shell, and Total.

4.2 QFC

The QFC also offers 100 percent foreign ownership and a low tax rate. It is an onshore financial and business center designed to attract not just international banks and those involved in financial services but also multinational corporations and support services. Firms that are established in the QFC can be authorized to carry out regulated activities (such as banking, insurance, or securities) or nonregulated activities (including investment grading, ship brokerage, company headquarters, management office and treasury operations, professional services, and holding companies).

At present, over eighty firms have been established in the QFC, including Ansbacher, AXA Investment Managers, Barclays, Citibank, Credit Suisse, Deutsche Bank, Goldman Sachs, Lehman Brothers, Morgan Stanley, RBS, Standard Chartered Bank, State Street and UBS.

The QFC was established under Law No. 7 of 2005. As with the QSTP, the QFC law says the criminal laws and sanctions of the state of Qatar apply in the QFC, but the civil laws and regulations of Qatar apply only to the extent that they do not conflict with QFC regulations. The QFC has gone further than the QSTP in creating a separate legal environment with a full suite of commercial and civil laws that are designed to serve the best financial institutions for their customers.

QFC law empowers the QFC Authority along with the Regulatory Authority to create regulations relating to the functioning of the QFC. Regulations on financial services, companies, anti-money-laundering, contracts, insolvency, data protection, limited-liability partnerships, arbitration, the QFC Authority, employment, immigration, and trusts have been enacted. A commercial court has been created that has jurisdiction over disputes arising within the QFC and Lord Woolf, the former Chief Justice of England and Wales, has been appointed and sworn in as its first president. The QFC legal structure provides for arbitration and other forms of dispute resolution as an alternative to litigation.

5. Negotiation Practices

Qatar is a civil code jurisdiction and business transactions have traditionally been conducted with a minimum of formality and documentation. However, this has changed significantly given the rapid economic growth of the country, and the legal and business environment is becoming more sophisticated, mature, and developed.

Lawyers are not normally involved at the early stages of negotiation and definitely not at the level experienced in the United States. As a broad generalization, lawyers are brought in to execute and implement a commercial agreement once it has been agreed to, and commercial agreements and contracts have traditionally been short. Negotiations can take place at all levels depending on the nature of the contract. There are not normally large numbers of people involved in negotiation meetings, and contracts are normally negotiated by means of exchanges of drafts between lawyers without great line-by-line page-turning exercises, although this is more likely to be the case in financing and project work.

The government does not play a role as a participant in day-to-day commercial negotiations in the private sector. However, given Qatar's large natural resources in the hydrocarbon sector, many foreign companies are in negotiation with government or quasi-government entities for contracts in that particular field.

Qatar is a Muslim country and, akin to many other countries in the Gulf, has a different weekend than the West. In Qatar the official weekend is Friday (the traditional day of prayer) and Saturday. For local businesses, working hours are generally from 8:00 A.M. to noon and 4:00 P.M. to 8:00 P.M., although international companies more often work an 8:00 A.M. to 5:00 P.M. day. Ministries and government departments normally have office hours from 7:00 A.M. to 2:00 P.M.

Business negotiations occur all year, although in the hot summer months, particularly July and August, many Qataris go abroad on holiday; this is definitely a quieter time of year, although with the growth and internationalization of the country this is becoming less so. Activity levels are normally lower during the Holy Month of Ramadan when official working hours are restricted to six hours a day. This, together with the fact that many persons will observe the fast between the hours of sunrise and sunset, means that Ramadan is not normally the best time of year for detailed business negotiations.

Business negotiations are often conducted in English, and it will invariably be the case that documentation is settled in English and then, where necessary, a final Arabic translation will be made. Due diligence is the norm in acquisitions, although historically it has not been as detailed as in other parts of the world. This is changing as the business environment becomes more sophisticated. The use of confidentiality and nondisclosure agreements is normal.

Those people involved in business negotiations in the Gulf region should realize the importance of first establishing a good relationship at a personal level with your counterpart, since this will be expected. At the beginning of a relationship or possible transaction, it will not be unusual for there to be a number of meetings where no great detail is discussed, but the local party will be assessing its future potential joint venture partner or counterparty.

On the one hand things can sometimes seem to drag out for a long time, but on the other hand things often happen and have to happen very quickly and the negotiator should be prepared for this dichotomy. Being in too much of hurry, being dismissive of local ways or customs, being impatient or losing one's temper are, much more than in the West, not the way to succeed in business negotiations.

Because it is a Muslim country, alcohol is not widely available in Qatar, being only on sale in restaurants attached to the larger internationally managed hotels. Foreign nationals resident in Qatar require a permit to buy alcohol at the one liquor store in the country. Accordingly, at business dinners with local parties, in order to avoid offending any sensitivities it is probably wise to steer clear of alcoholic drinks. Given that Friday is the day of rest and the main religious day of the week (akin to Sunday in the Christian world), telephone calls or proposed business meetings on this day should be avoided.

The use of e-mail is widespread, although it would be unusual for all negotiations to take place purely by this medium. Particularly when first starting off negotiations or a relationship, face-to-face meetings will be important.

6. Contract Formation

Parties are generally free to complete and document contractual arrangements in whatever way they like. Letters of intent or memoranda of understanding are not unusual before settlement of a final binding contract. The English language can be used for both negotiations and written contracts, although where anything has to be filed or lodged with a government entity an Arabic version will also be required. Much will depend on the specific requirements and needs of the parties.

Qatar is a civil code jurisdiction, but the parties are normally free to choose their governing law and indeed those courts that are to have jurisdiction. Contracts with certain government departments or ministries may require to be governed by Qatar law, although this is not always the case. Qatar is a signatory to the 1958 New York Convention on the Recognition and Enforcement of Foreign Arbitral Awards and therefore qualifying foreign arbitration awards can be enforced in Qatar under that convention. The Qatar courts will be prepared to enforce judgments of foreign courts in accordance with a procedure set down in the Qatar Civil Code, with a caveat that such enforcement would not be allowed if it would be contrary to public policy.

Online agreements are not generally used, although the utilization of electronic data rooms is starting.

7. Dispute Resolution

Dispute resolution is normally limited to the matter being referred to the Qatari courts and/or local arbitration, or quite commonly and increasingly parties can elect for a choice of foreign law and either foreign courts or arbitration. There is a local arbitration procedure (see below), and as mentioned previously, it is not uncommon for disputes to be referred to international arbitration under, for instance, International Chamber of Commerce (ICC) or London Court of International Arbitration (LCIA) rules, with the seat of arbitration being outside Qatar. Online dispute resolution is not currently a feature.

Arbitration proceedings at a local level are governed by the Commercial and Civil Procedure Code. The arbitration procedures set out in the Commercial and Civil Procedure Code are reasonably clear.

Parties may agree in writing that all disputes that may arise with respect to that contract shall be referred to arbitration. Such written instrument should ideally set out the basis for appointment of arbitrators, although the court can if necessary appoint arbitrators itself. The arbitrators can also go to the courts to compel a witness to appear, a document to be produced, or a question of law to be answered.

An agreement to refer all disputes arising with respect to a particular agreement to arbitration constitutes a waiver by the parties of their respective rights to resort to the court initially competent to hear a dispute with respect to that agreement. Similarly, it is possible (by express words) for the parties to agree to waive all rights of appeal to the Qatari courts with respect to any arbitration award. In such circumstances, the parties may only have recourse to the Qatari courts by way of a petition for review.

Thus there is a reasonably well-established structure for arbitration in Qatar under Qatari law. However, in practice it realistically needs a detailed written instrument of appointment to be effective. It also has the added difficulty for foreign entities in that proceedings (and documentation) will need to be in Arabic. Hence for international contracts, arbitration is normally carried out under international arbitration bodies with a neutral location.

8. Conclusion

As Qatar develops as an international business and, importantly, a financial services center, the degree of sophistication and level of maturity of the legal market will increase accordingly, as witnessed by the increasing number of international law firms setting up in the country. As international banks do more business in Qatar, and indeed the local banks start to undertake more regional and international work themselves, the length and complexity of legal documentation and indeed the negotiation process itself will increase and become more akin to that found in a Western business environment.

With proposed changes on the restrictions on foreign ownership of Qatar companies, both privately held and those listed on the Doha Securities Market, there will be increasing opportunities for business in Qatar, and that will only lead to greater levels of sophistication and complexity as part of the business negotiation process. Qatar's aim is to become an international financial services center and it has announced plans to form a single financial services regulator for the whole country (including the Qatar Financial Centre) so as to apply a more international standard of regulation and business in that sector. This can only mean greater elaborateness and intricacy in relation to business transactions and negotiations.

In conclusion, what is clear is that Qatar, with its newfound wealth and very large surplus energy revenues, together with its stated role of diversifying its economy by 2020 so that it is no longer energy reliant, will be playing a much larger role on the world stage. Whereas in the past perhaps the tendency was for foreign investors to come into Qatar, increasingly it will be Qatari corporates, financial institutions, and government bodies (such as the Qatar Investment Authority) that will be making substantial investments in North America, Europe, and increasingly and importantly in Asia.

As in all jurisdictions—but it is probably fair to say particularly in the Middle East—"one size does not fit all" and Western style forms of business negotiation, tactics, and etiquette need to be adapted to local conditions. Without taking local advice at an early stage and adapting to the local marketplace, international investors will find themselves negotiating from a point of weakness and operating at a serious disadvantage in what is already a very competitive environment.

Andrew Wingfield
Simmons & Simmons
P.O. Box 23540
Al Mirqab Tower
Al Corniche Street
Doha, Qatar
Phone: 974-483-9466
Fax: 974-483-9584
E-mail: andrew.wingfield@simmons-simmons.com

CHAPTER 42

International Business Negotiations in Saudi Arabia

Gayle E. Hanlon[1]
HADEF LEGAL CONSULTANTS & ADVOCATES
ABU DHABI, UNITED ARAB EMIRATES

1. Introduction

Accession to the World Trade Organization by the Kingdom of Saudi Arabia was on December 11, 2005. Saudi Arabia recently revamped many of its foreign investment, intellectual property, insurance, capital markets, tax, and insurance regulations to facilitate foreign investment in the kingdom and its accession to the WTO. There has been considerable news about Saudi Arabia's attempts to modernize its legal system. Apparently Saudi Arabia will be investing approximately US$2 billion to overhaul its judiciary system and court facilities in an effort to streamline the legal process, reinforce the standing of the country's courts, and implement a more professional system expected to reduce the backlog of cases. While no codification of laws is planned, it is anticipated that the reformed system will result in less arbitrary judgments and more transparency. An official Web site has been launched to publish Islamic legal rulings or *fatwas* to ensure that those issued by recognized Islamic scholars are given prominence. The legal overhaul will lead to the creation of a supreme court, an appeals court, and a general court system to replace the Supreme Judicial Council. The head of the Supreme Court will be appointed by the king, and it is expected that his choice will reflect the latter's reformist instincts. A legal system capable of ensuring contract enforcement (traditionally a major challenge for foreign investors in Saudi Arabia) is currently

---

[1] Gayle E. Hanlon is associated with the law firm of Hadef Legal Consultants & Associates, based at present in the firm's Abu Dhabi office. Ms. Hanlon gratefully acknowledges the invaluable assistance of Dr. Johannes Bruski and Julian Johansen, a partner of Allen & Overy LLP on secondment in Riyadh to Abdulaziz AlGasim Law Firm in association with Allen & Overy. All opinions expressed in this chapter are solely those of Ms. Hanlon and do not necessarily reflect the opinions of Hadef Legal Consultants & Associates.

viewed as essential for the promotion of foreign investment in the kingdom.

As noted above, and despite continuing efforts in the kingdom to attract additional foreign investment, particularly as seen from the considerable emphasis placed on economic reform and market-opening measures in the Shoura Council, Council of Ministers, and the Supreme Economic Council, surprisingly few major pieces of legislation (regulations) have been fully implemented. The Capital Market Law,[2] Implementing Rules for Protection of Trade Secrets[3], the Installment Sales Law promulgated by Royal Decree #M/13 dated 4/3/1426H,[4] and the new labor law constitute the best examples of newly implemented legislative regulations. Article 5 of the Capital Market Law states that the Capital Market Authority "shall be the agency responsible for issuing regulations, rules and instructions and for applying the provisions of this Law."

Within the context of the already well-publicized globalization of Islamic banking, capital market access has been successfully achieved through the use of instruments that are compliant with the principles and precepts of Islamic sharia. Most discussions address Islamic financing within the context of Muslim secular jurisdictions or those jurisdictions where secular and sharia law are integrated. This chapter shall also briefly examine the structuring of Islamic finance solely within an Islamic economic sphere, but where Saudi law shall not be the applicable law for the transactions ("incorporated jurisdiction"), such as Saudi Arabia.

It is the intention of this chapter to provide (i) an examination of general Saudi legal considerations that would influence the structure of contractual transactions both within and outside the kingdom, including, *inter alia*, the absence of a statutory structure, the inapplicability of stare decisis, the fact that many laws and court decisions are not published, the uncertainty presented by the enforcement regime in Saudi Arabia, the role of sharia scholars and sharia supervisory boards, and the various risk allocation factors affecting and often rendering difficult risk assessment by transactional participants, particularly relating to the certainty, predictability, and transparency of risk factors; and (ii) an overview of the current state of Islamic capital market products. In conclusion, there will be a presentation of the major points that would form the basis of a legal opinion in connection with complex project financing under consideration of the jurisprudence in Saudi Arabia.

Novel structural and transactional applications of law, at the levels of principle and practice, will be required to integrate and reconcile

---

[2] Available at http://www.cma.org.sa/cma%5Far/115.

[3] Available at http://www.commerce.gov.sa/circular/45-3.asp.

[4] Available at http://www.commerce.gov.sa/circular/45-3.asp.

Islamic sharia-compliant project finance within the traditional expectations of the broader conventional secular and incorporated markets. Nevertheless, it has been well noted by many authorities that the Islamic legal system changes quite slowly. Because of the clash between the microcosmic ideal of the Saudi legal system and the more macrocosmic ideal of western and even other Islamic systems, it appears that adopting conventional models of legal modernization (e.g., codification of laws) is more difficult for Saudi Arabia than it has been for other Muslim states with conventional secular as well as incorporated jurisdictions. Saudi Arabia's microcosmic ideal often comes into conflict with more conventional legal models, resulting sometimes in even greater efforts by local institutions to resist or reshape these standards in order to achieve a successful innovation and reform. The kingdom's membership in the WTO combined with increasing internal pressures for new commercial laws and the advancement of a more modern investment climate may nevertheless result in sudden change in the future.

2. Brief Introduction to the Islamic Legal System of Saudi Arabia

2.1 The Saudi Arabian Legal Environment: General Considerations

The Islamic legal system of Saudi Arabia is little known or understood outside of the kingdom. There is even a paucity of information about this system within the kingdom itself except to those officials and practitioners working within the system. As Frank E. Vogel has been reported to say, the Saudi Arabian legal system is a mystery to most people inside the kingdom, let alone outside it.[5] The ensuing opacity and ambiguity can lead to broad legal discretion.[6] The kingdom's claim to uphold Islamic law is nevertheless central to its constitution, law, religion, and society. Saudi Arabia is the most traditionalist Islamic legal system in the world today. Because Saudi Arabia was not subject to the extensive western colonization experienced by almost every other Muslim country, drastically transforming their indigenous legal systems by the importation of western legal influences (predominantly civil law), western law and its legal concepts have never fully invaded the essential core of the Saudi legal system. As a result of an extensive exchange with the West, Saudi Arabia has indeed created legal institutions that appear modern and western. These include numerous decree laws or regulations (*nizam*, plural *anzima*), including

---

[5] Frank E. Vogel, Islamic Law and Legal System Studies of Saudi Arabia, at xi (2000).
[6] Tim Lindsey & Jeremy Kingsley, *Talking in Code, Legal Islamisation in Indonesia and the MMI Shari'a Criminal Code, in* The Law Applied 311 (Peri Bearman, Wolfhart Heinrichs & Bernard G. Weiss eds., 2008).

laws on such matters as commercial papers and government tenders; it has created specialized judicial bodies to decide disputes arising under these regulations. There are a number of different courts, committees, offices, and boards that might have jurisdiction over a matter in Saudi Arabia in which a bank might be involved: the Banking Disputes Settlement Committee ("SAMA Committee") of the Saudi Arabian Monetary Agency (SAMA); the Office of the Settlement of Negotiable Instruments Disputes, also known as the Negotiable Instruments Offices (NIO), which is under the jurisdiction of the Ministry of Commerce and Industry; and the Board of Grievances (Diwan Al-Mazalim) under the Board of Grievances Law ("Board of Grievances"). It is crucial here to note that these legal institutions remain in essence solely additions to a pre-existing legal system and enjoy an ambiguous relationship with the existing for a within that system. The challenge to the Saudi legal system will be the difficult reconciliation of these additions with the traditional legal system.

As already well expounded by Frank E. Vogel in his excellent treatise *Islamic Law and Legal System Studies of Saudi Arabia*,[7] it is recommended that the best way to appreciate Islamic law in the kingdom is by studying it within the context of its application. This discussion will be limited to a study of Islamic law in the kingdom solely within the context of commercial law.

2.2 The Islamic Legal System in Saudi Arabia: Basic Concepts

2.2.1 What Is *Sharia?*

The paramount body of law in the kingdom of Saudi Arabia is the sharia.

> Thus we put you on the right way [*shari' atan*] of religion. So follow it and follow not the whimsical desire ("*hawa*") of those who have no knowledge.
>
> —Koran, 45:18

The term *sharia* occurs only once in the Koran and is placed in juxtaposition with the word for whimsical desire.[8] To the extent that the word *sharia* refers to a belief in Islam, the adherence to a set of values essential to Islam and the protection and enhancement of the five essentials (*al-daruriyat al-khamsah*), that is, of life, religion, property, intellect, and family,[9] as well a concern for justice, the term *sharia* represents and indeed constitutes an entire way of life and is the most comprehensive concept in Islam.[10] It is in fact the very core of

---

[7] Vogel, *supra* note 5, at xii.

[8] See Mohammad Hashim Kamali, Sharia Law 2 (2008).

[9] Cf. al-Shatibi, Muwafaqat, II, 3-5; Kamali, *supra* note 8, at 2–3.

[10] Bernard G. Weiss, The Spirit of Islamic Law 18 (2006).

Islam, meaning "submission." Despite its core function, the term *sharia* remains mostly undefined in Islamic classical literature.[11] A phrase appearing throughout that literature ("*al-ahkam al shar'iyya*" or the "sharia categorizations") provides a basis upon which a definition of sharia can be extrapolated, that is, as noted by Weiss, "the totality of divine categorizations of human acts."[12] Of the various categories (such as "recommended," "forbidden," "disapproved," etc.) there are two that naturally lend themselves to a legal characterization or the concept of legal rules: the obligatory and the forbidden. In this sense, the sharia can be seen as being as much concerned with what is obligatory, permitted, or recommended as it is with disapproving or forbidding.[13] It is quite important to note, however, that the rules of sharia do not function as rules of law as that term is ordinarily understood in the West; although there is attention given in classical Islamic literature to obligations, or duties and prohibitions, there is little thought given to a system of enforcement or implementation by means of, for instance, an earthly penal system.[14] The rules of sharia must be distinguished from procedural legal issues such as judicial applicability and enforcement. The sharia rules contain a legal as well as a moral dimension. The rules of the sharia are those rules that a temporal/secular authority and its judicial representatives must apply and enforce. The sharia rules also embrace the concepts of validity and invalidity. If a sale of property is conducted in a fashion that is not sharia compliant, the sale will be regarded as invalid with the result that no transfer of ownership will have taken place. The interest (*riba*) component of a loan agreement will be deemed to be invalid since the concept of interest is not sharia compliant. There are legal and moral implications in both cases, and it is necessary to examine external criteria in order to distinguish the legal from the moral dimension.[15] As will be seen throughout this chapter, the procedural issues of judicial enforceability and enforceability will arise again and again within the context of sharia rules.

In many texts, sharia is set forth as the essence of Islam itself and its overlegalization is found across the board in numerous treatises and texts. It has been propounded by the author Mohammad Hashim Kamali that [i]t is questionable whether Islam was meant to be as much of a law-based religion as it has often been made out to be."[16] This author advocates for a greater role of the concept of *siyasah shar'iyyah* (sharia-oriented policy) in an understanding of an Islamic polity and state. This shall be discussed in greater depth below.

---

[11] *Id.* at 18.
[12] *Id.*
[13] *Id.* at 19.
[14] *Id.* at 20.
[15] *Id.* at 22.
[16] *Id.* at 1.

Sharia literally means "a way to the watering-place" or "a path to seek felicity and salvation."[17] Much confusion has arisen in Western literature regarding the concept of sharia. It is not appropriate to simply call the law the sharia. A basic presupposition of Muslim juristic thought is that the law of God has not been provided to human beings as a finished product, in the form of a ready-made set of rules or a code of laws.[18] The pious scholars of the sharia, as human jurists, are responsible for the elaboration of such rules on the basis of textual sources. Those sources are preeminently the Koran and the body of hadith narratives in which the sayings and deeds of the Prophet (the sunna) are recorded. In addition, there are the textual sources recording statements on points of law on which the jurists have agreed as an expression of the authority of consensus.

Agricultural metaphors best explain the work of the jurists. The Islamic sense of "source" is *asl*, plural *usul*, literally meaning "root." The rules produced by the jurists are either branches (*furu*) or fruit (*thamara*) and the extraction of rules from sources is called harvesting (*istithmar*). Only the sources are given by the prophets, while the jurist harvests the growth of the law—the branches and the fruit—out of the roots.[19] The derivation of the law from the textual sources is accomplished by means of interpretation (using the skills of a philologist and a study of, *inter alia*, morphology, syntax, and stylistics) and the use of analogy (*qiyas*) with rules already determined. The use of analogy is considered by the four Sunni schools to constitute a fourth source of law, following the Koran, the Sunna, and juristic consensus.[20]

Although used almost interchangeably with "sharia," the term *fiqh* (literally "understanding") is not identical to sharia. Sharia is conveyed by divine revelation as set forth in the Koran and authentic hadith, while *fiqh* refers mainly to the corpus juris that is developed by the legal schools (*madhhabs*), by individual jurists and judges by recourse to legal reasoning (*ijtihad*) and the issuing of legal verdicts (*fatawa*).[21] Identifying sharia in the sense of a legal code is not solidly based in the source evidence.[22] Islam is first and foremost a faith and a moral code, and following a legal code is secondary to the message of Islam.[23]

The declaration of the sharia as the principal criterion of an Islamic state was featured in the writings of Ibn Taymiyyah (d. 1328) and the Wahhabi movement of nineteenth-century Arabia was molded on Ibn Taymiyyah's thought. Ibn Taymiyyah's writings were set against

---

[17] *Id.* at 2.

[18] *Id.* at 22.

[19] *Id.* at 23.

[20] *Id.*

[21] KAMALI, *supra* note 8, at 3.

[22] *Id.* at 5.

[23] *Id.* at 5.

the background of the tension that had developed between the norms and principles of the original caliphate and the practice of dynastic caliphs, the Umayyads (660–750) and the Abbasids (750–1258), and the devastating Mongol invasion of Baghdad (1258) and the destruction of what had remained of the caliphate. Ibn Taymiyyah moved away from the hollowed theory and rhetoric of the caliphate and emphasized the sharia and a sharia-oriented policy (siyasah shar'iyyah).[24] As elaborated by Mohammed Hashim Kamali in his recent book on sharia law, "Ibn Taymiyyah's idea of 'siyasah shar'iyyah' conveys the message that policy ('siyasah') was an integral part of Islamic governance, and that governance in Islam was not a matter simply of rule by the text but of politics and administration by judicious rulers whose decisions were to be guided by the sharia, but that they also took into consideration a variety of factors that could not be encapsulated by the legal text alone."[25]

The Koran describes the objectives of sharia as follows:

> O mankind, a direction has come to you from your Lord; it is a healing for the (spiritual) ailments in your hearts and it is guidance and mercy for the believers. (Koran 10:57)

It is axiomatic that the law of the sharia may be perfect, but humans are certainly not. Learning the sharia from the Koran and the Sunna is a continual struggle for humans or legal scholars. The human understanding of the divine law as expressed in the Koran and the Sunna is fiqh, which consists of scholarly opinions by individuals whose piety and learning have qualified them to interpret the sources and derive laws. As stated by Vogel, "[T]o learn the law of Saudi Arabia, one turns first to the fiqh."[26] It is critical to note here that—to understand the law of Saudi Arabia—one does not turn first to state legislation or judicial case precedent, but, instead, to the "reasoned solutions," the ijtihad, of religious-legal scholars of the past and the present, the holders of knowledge, the *ulema* (literally, the possessors of knowledge).[27] This is already a major divergence from traditional western jurisprudence. More is to come. In practice, when reconciling a difficult situation with God's law, a lay Muslim will approach a respected legal scholar and will ask him for his views of the sharia ruling for a particular factual situation. In this function, the legal scholar is called a *mufti* and the opinion a *fatwa*. The applicant is completely free, however, either to follow the opinion or not to follow it when applying the answer to his or her situation. A sufficiently learned and pious individual is entitled

---

[24] *Id.* at 7.
[25] *Id.* at 8.
[26] VOGEL, *supra* note 5, at 5.
[27] *Id.*

to be a mufti and requires no official appointment. Recently, in 1993, Saudi Arabia began conferring as a formal matter the official status of "Grand Mufti" to a single mufti (a practice adopted in other Muslim jurisdictions since the time of the Ottoman Empire).[28] In the course of his investigations, Vogel has observed that the courts of Saudi Arabia may enforce as valid the parties' actions based upon the fatwas of respected ulema, even when these fatwas starkly contradicted the courts' own procedural rules.[29] As noted above, there is no stare decisis in Saudi Arabia; a singular court's decision based upon the facts of a particular case does not possess precedential value and does not constitute Saudi law to the exclusion of other judgments using the practice of reasonable ijtihad. As noted by Vogel:

> Under the law of Saudi Arabia, it is not the case that the court's result is the law of the land, or Saudi law, while the mufti's is another law upheld due to state-condoned private ordering, as in the instance of commercial arbitration. Instead, both are Saudi law, both the law of the land. Any fiqd opinion authoritatively rooted in the Koran and Sunna is Saudi law, because it is a valid statement of sharia, and Saudi law is nothing but sharia.[30]

This leads to the practical result that similar factual situations based upon differing fatwas from respected scholars may lead to differing results. Both would constitute equally Saudi law as expressions of sharia. A standard view ordinarily applied in a court and the divergent opinion of a mufti would be accorded equal respect.

Almost all rules applied today in Saudi Arabian courts are found in books of fiqh written by medieval ulema.[31] This fiqh is a highly complex body of law based upon scholarly opinions ranging over a span of fourteen centuries. Much of this complex and divergent body of law is simplified by means of the institution of the school of law (*madhhab*). Simply put, the madhhab consisted of a loose association of scholars who agreed to follow and contribute to a consistent stream of interpretation and decision-making based upon the works of a certain revered scholar of the past.[32] It has been argued that to designate a madhhab a school does not do it justice. A madhhab, translated literally as "way," is a type of "interpretative community" in Stanley Fish's well-known use of the term[33] and exists at the level of doctrine; it has more to do with

---

[28] *Id.*

[29] *Id.* at 8.

[30] *Id.* at 8.

[31] *Id.* at 9.

[32] *Id.* at 9.

[33] STANLEY EUGENE FISH, IS THERE A TEXT IN THIS CLASS? THE AUTHORITY OF INTERPRETIVE COMMUNITIES (Harvard University Press 1980).

the designation of a doctrine or principles or methods propounded by a scholar with the rank of *mujtahid* than with a collection of individuals forming a school. A madhhab is fundamentally the doctrine or method of an individual scholar.[34] This body of doctrine proceeds from the ijtihad of an individual scholar. It is unclear the degree to which there is an obligation to consistently adhere to a particular madhhab, whether this adherence is of a permanent or temporary nature, or whether there is a certain room for freedom of movement on particular issues between different madhhabs without relinquishing one's adherence to a particular madhhab.[35]

Traditional Islamic legal scholars have largely accepted the premise of a preeminent twentieth-century western scholar Joseph Schacht that local variations in social conditions contributed to a change of a common ancient doctrine into distinct regional schools and then into eponymous madhhabs named for certain prominent scholars in particular regional centers.[36] More recent legal discussion has focused on the more fluid world of early Islamic jurisprudence and focuses more on the diversity of views within the regional schools.[37] The interpretative authority of madhhabs was, regardless of the theory of evolution, expressed in hierarchies of named and differently qualified jurists, beginning with the eponym (figures such as Abu Hanafa, Malik, al-Shafi'I, and Ibn Hanbali among the Sunnis) and in titled works. Although there were reportedly hundreds of schools in Sunni Islam, four have fundamentally remained, the Hanafi, Maliki, Shafi'I, and Hanbali. These schools, originally only intellectual groupings, came to occupy largely distinct geographical zones. Since the Wahhabi movement from which Saudi Arabia arises acknowledged the Hanbali school, most Saudis follow that school.[38] It is critical to note, however, that although Saudi judges ordinarily adhere to Hanbali legal doctrine or madhhab, they "are free to adopt views from other schools, or even from outside the four schools altogether, as long as they base their view, following proper interpretative procedures, on the Qur'an and Sunna."[39]

As will be discussed in greater depth below, discernible tensions have arisen as certain experiments in modernity and westernization in recent decades have not produced desirable results.[40] Contemporary

---

[34] BERNARD WEISS, *The Madhhab in Islamic Legal Theory*, in THE ISLAMIC SCHOOL OF LAW 1–3 (Peri Bearman, Rudolph Peters & Frank E. Vogel eds., 2006).

[35] *Id.* at 9.

[36] JOSEPH SCHACHT, THE ORIGINS OF MUHAMMADAN JURISPRUDENCE (Clarendon Press 1950).

[37] STEVEN C. JUDD, *Al-Awza'I and Sufyan Al-Thawri: The Umayyad Madhhab?, in* THE ISLAMIC SCHOOL OF LAW *supra* note 34, at 10–25.

[38] VOGEL, *supra* note 5, at 10.

[39] *Id.*

[40] KAMALI, *supra* note 8, at 36–37; JOHN ROBERT VOLL, ISLAM, CONTINUITY AND CHANGE IN THE MODERN WORLD 277 (1994).

scholars feel themselves constrained from attempting legal reconstruction and ijtihad in tandem with the rapid pace of social change and
changed living conditions of the people when faced with the long-
standing history of unquestioning imitation (*taqlid*) of the precedent
of leading scholars and the ulema of jurisprudence.[41] There is a clear
disconnect between the rapid pace of social change (accelerated by
globalization and its imported consequences in Muslim lands) and
sharia, especially in light of the renowned "closure of the door of ijtihad" at the beginning of the eleventh century. There is a clear need for
ijtihad especially when the Koran and the sunna provide no clear text
on a particular issue. There is a heightened awareness on the part of
Muslims to return to their heritage, the sharia, but the challenge shall
be to relate the sharia to the current living conditions, requiring an
imaginative ijtihad that would entail a potential revision and modification of the rules of fiqh and the translation of the broad objectives of
sharia into the laws and institutions of contemporary Saudi society.[42]

As will be further examined in this chapter, there will be a clear
challenge in the future, particularly in light of its accession to the
WTO, to the Saudi legal system to create a workable order from the
core notions of the sharia, which will necessitate a progress of continuous orientation and reorientation.

There is a western misperception that Islamic law is immutable
since it is divinely ordained; it is widely perceived to be closed to the
notions of flexibility and adaptability. As noted by Muhammad Iqbal:
"I have no doubt that a deeper study of the enormous legal literature
of Islam is sure to rid the modern critic of the superficial opinion that
the law of Islam is stationary and incapable of development."[43] To the
contrary, sharia attempts to strike a balance between continuity and
change.[44] With respect to the fundamentals of faith and its clear injunc-
tions as to what is prohibited, the sharia is permanent and immutable.
But the sharia is generally flexible with respect to many other areas,
including but not limited to government and fiscal policy and economic and international affairs, and provides only broad guidelines
whose details can be adjusted to reflect the circumstances in pursu-
ance of human reasoning and ijtihad. The sharia contains both immutable laws and those that are susceptible to change pursuant to public
interest requirements (*maslahah*) and prevailing circumstances.[45] With
respect to civil law transactions (e.g., fulfillment of contracts, prohibition of usury, loan documentation, and other forms of deferred payments), the Koran textual rulings are expressed in quite broad and

---

[41] KAMALI, *supra* note 8, at 36.

[42] *Id.* at 37.

[43] ALLAMA MUHAMMAD IQBAL, THE RECONSTRUCTION OF RELIGIOUS THOUGHT IN ISLAM, 164,
Lahore [Muhammad Ashraf] (1930).

[44] KAMALI, *supra* note 8, at 49.

[45] *Id.* at 50.

[46] *Id.* at 51.

general terms.[46] It has been maintained by leading jurists and ulema that sharia is resourceful and well equipped with the means to adapt to social change.[47] It is the role of ijtihad or independent reasoning as recognized by the sharia, embracing as it does the considerations of public interest (*istislah*), juristic preference (*istihsan*), and analogical reasoning (*qiyas*), to continuously adapt the law in light of changing societal requirements. This is not to say, however, that the textualist outlook has not reigned supreme.[48] It is also clear that a gradual (if not pragmatic) approach to legislation and social reform is favored in the sharia.[49]

Since the collapse of the old colonial order after the end of World War II, there has been a movement in the Arab world, North Africa and elsewhere toward a revitalization of fiqh, toward adapting it to the social reality and experience of contemporary Muslims, with a lesser emphasis on precedent and greater emphasis on original thinking and ijtihad. This movement has been accompanied by an Islamic revivalism and a demand to revive the sharia in the areas of law and government in an attempt to revive the fiqh heritage. There has also been a parallel movement, consisting mainly of western-educated government leaders and advocates of modernization and secularism, who favored instead a continuation of the colonial legacy and saw the need for a codification of law in light of the fact that the Muslim world did not possess a self-contained sharia-compliant or sharia-based civil code or constitution. The compromise, mainly worked out by working groups of sharia and modern law experts commencing in Egypt and Syria and, later, Iraq, was to incorporate certain aspects of western jurisprudence into the project to codify laws. A great deal of the French civil code was used as a basis, although there were departures in the areas of contracts, evidence, and court procedure. This quest for a more comprehensive sharia-based civil code together with a neo-ijtihad approach drawing upon the wider resources of fiqh in all its diverse schools and madhhabs (not just limited to, for instance, the Hanafi school as seen in the nineteenth-century Ottoman Mejelle) to address new issues in the fields of civil transactions (*mu'amalat*) as well as commercial contracts, banking, insurance, etc., has led to codification efforts in Syria, Iraq, Jordan (the Jordanian civil code is now widely seen as a model combining and balancing diverse influences in modern thought and established legal schools), the U.A.E., Pakistan, and Sudan.[50] An excellent proposal was made by Michael McMillen in his recent contribution to the *Chicago Journal of International Law*'s symposium on Islamic business and commercial law[51] to encourage the development of a system and

---

[47] *Id.* at 49.

[48] WEISS, *supra* note 34, at 86.

[49] KAMALI, *supra* note 8, at 59.

[50] See, generally, an excellent treatise on this subject in KAMALI, *supra* note 8, ch. 12.

[51] Michael J.T. McMillen, *Contractual Enforceability Issues:* Sukuk *and Capital Markets Developments*, 7 CHI. J. INT'L L. 427.

platform in the form of Model Islamic Acts that can be used to achieve guidelines for each of the primary areas of relevance to, for instance, sharia-compliant banking, finance, commerce, insurance, and securities regulations, as well as widely endorsed contracts and transactional forms. There are also efforts under way at present for the formulation of a unified civil code for all the Arab countries.[52] Such an undertaking, sponsored perhaps by the Islamic Financial Services Board (IFSB) (of which, at the time of this writing, SAMA is a member), would go a long way toward allaying potential investor concerns regarding the enforceability of contractual provisions in significant financing transactions in the future.

The need for new measures to consolidate the rich heritage of fiqh into convenient collections that would respond to the needs of the legal profession and academic research has lead to the compilation by the Organization of the Islamic Conference (OIC) of a comprehensive encyclopedia of fiqh.[53] Kamali has reported that the Kuwait encyclopedia of Islamic law (*al-Mawsu 'ah al-Fiqhiyyah*) has now reached forty-five volumes and is nearing completion.[54] Islamic law academies have been established as a way of implementing the idea of collective ijtihah. The OIC created another fiqh academy in Jeddah. The King Abdulaziz University in Jedda has established an International Centre for Islamic Economic Research, and the OIC as well as the Muslim League fiqh academies hold annual sessions addressing highly topical issues from the perspective of Islamic law, such as intellectual property rights, Islamic banking and finance, etc., and have issued fatwas following academy deliberations. An interesting development, as noted by Kamali, is that all of these academic deliberations and resulting fatwas have manifested the practice of collective and consultative ijtihad (see discussion in section 2.2.2 on ijtihah).[55] As further noted, a recent development of considerable interest is the introduction of sharia advisory committees in major banks and financial institutions with the task of ensuring due compliance with the sharia in banking operations.[56] This same author also mentions the risk of arbitrariness and conflicts of interest with respect to these fatwa and fatwa-making procedures. He notes a degree of arbitrariness in the "works of self-interested individuals and committees that issue ill-considered fatwas to advance their narrow and partisan objectives."[57]

We are of the view that neither a total ban on open fatwa-making nor a complete laissez-faire attitude towards it would

---

[52] KAMALI, *supra* note 8, at 253.
[53] *Id.* at 255.
[54] *Id.*
[55] *Id.* at 256.
[56] *Id.* at 257.
[57] *Id.* at 305.

be advisable. In a broad sense, what we propose for ijtihad we also essentially propose for fatwa. Fatwa-making authority may be entrusted to a competent council of scholars and muftis who possess certain qualifications but who also enjoy substantive autonomy in the exercise of their opinion and judgment. However, the authorities may determine the procedures that regulate the issuance of fatwa, its registration and gazetting procedures, and the role, if any, that the fatwa is supposed to play via-à-vis parliamentary legislation.[58]

These are all extremely interesting developments and the situation is certainly in a state of flux. But it must be noted that even where there has been the promulgation of a "statutory" body of law (in Saudi Arabia, essentially laws issued by royal decree), such law remains subject to and may not conflict with the provisions of the sharia; the issue of the enforceability by adjudicative authorities in Saudi Arabia (discussed in more detail below) is unpredictable, especially in light of the complete absence of the principle of stare decisis in Saudi Arabia. With the exception of the area of ship mortgages, there is at the present time (although the situation may change shortly in Saudi Arabia, unlike in other Middle Eastern countries, no statutory body of law relating to collateral security mortgage and pledges, the recordation of security interest, or sale (*istish'a*) or lease (*ijara*) transactions. Although there are statutes on foreign investments, joint ventures, and other business organizations, numerous areas affecting commercial transactions remain unregulated. It is known that the scholar Ibn Taymiyya maintained very bold views on contract law, arguing that, in matters of worship (*'ibadat*), God's silence implies prohibition, while in matters of worldly affairs (*mu'amalt*), it implies permission.[59] It can, therefore, only be assumed that, absent an explicit prohibition under the sharia (and the overwhelming number of matters that are clearly regulated under sharia are primarily private law matters), commercial agreements would be generally enforceable. Certainty is, however, not guaranteed, especially in light of the lack of the principle of stare decisis in Saudi Arabia. Despite all voices of cautious optimism, legal practitioners providing their clients with legal opinions as to the enforceability of sometimes highly complex financial transactions in Saudi Arabia are counseled to add a caveat that there can only be a limited degree of predictability regarding the enforceability of these transactions if they were to be adjudicated before the courts of Saudi Arabia. The potential enforceability of foreign arbitral awards against Saudi

---

[58] *Id.* at 305.
[59] IBN TAYMIYYA, SIYASA, 159–60, quoted in VOGEL, *supra* note 5, at 54.

parties is also an issue fraught with uncertainty and should similarly be approached with caution.[60]

2.2.2 What Is *Ijtihad?* What Are *Fatwa* and *Fatwa-giving?*

In a famous hadith in which ijtihad is mentioned, the Prophet asked Mu'adh bin Jabal on deputing him governor over Yemen:

> By what shall you judge, O Mu'adh? He said, By the Book of God Most High. He said, Then if you do not find [anything there]? He said, Then by the Sunna of His Messenger. He said, Then if you do not find [anything there]? He said, I will exert as to it my opinion ("*ajtahid fi dhalika ra'yi*"). Then the Messenger May God bless him and give him peace said, Praise to God who has blessed the messenger of His Messenger with that approved by His Messenger.[61]

Very simply put, the basic concept of Islamic law and legal theory is the "independent reasoning" known as ijtihad and juristic opinion or fatwa. Both ijtihad and fatwa are extremely relevant to the way the legal system addresses itself to contemporary issues arising within the context of societal changes and external influences. Ijtihad means individual striving and constitutes a basic premise in the practice of Islamic law in that it is the essence of the application of Islamic law. It is important to understand the Saudi legal system and how the religious scholars of Islam, the ulema, have succeeded in developing from the concept of ijtihad a functioning legal system. Ijtihad consists of the interaction of divinely revealed texts with a concrete situation through the medium of an individual learned conscience. Ijtihad is not merely a personal interpretation, but embraces the following: (i) the law as developed by individual religious scholars, who are the primary legislators in an Islamic legal system; (ii) the application of the law of scholars to individual disputes; and (iii) the extension of this knowledge and practice to a broader or, as Frank E. Vogel has discussed, a more macrocosmic concept of a legal system as a whole.

In studying the construction of judging (*qada*) and fatwa-giving, one perceives a legal model in which law does not consist of a system of objective, formal, general, and compulsory rules, but instead consists of the unique decision of an individual conscience (ijtihad) applied

---

[60] Pursuant to a recent telephone interview with the Middle East representative of a renowned international arbitral tribunal, the facility of enforcing arbitral awards against Saudi parties before the Board of Grievances is deemed to be highly questionable. War stories abound ranging from the nonenforcement of a claim for interest (*riba*) in an arbitral award on public policy grounds as well the declination to enforce an arbitral award where the sole arbiter had been a woman, also on public policy grounds.
[61] Abu Dawud (*Aqdiya* 3592); al-Tirmidhi (*Ahkam* 1327); quoted in VOGEL, *supra* note 5, at 37–38; Schacht, Origins, 105–06.

within the examination and evaluation of a specific concrete act.[62] Vogel characterizes this legal concept—the issuance of a unique decision by an individual conscience—as microcosmic and juxtaposes it to a so-called macrocosmic legal system as exemplified by "outer-directed rule-law, law in the form of general, abstract rules issued by an external, worldly institution."[63]

The judge (*qadi*) must always at the beginning of his endeavors attempt to attain certainty.[64] The qadi must strive for the divine truth in each case with which he is confronted, without, however, having to be bound by prior decisions, even his own. As noted, there is no rule of precedent, no stare decisis, in Islamic law. The qadi must be a scholar and knowledgeable about the texts, and in the absence of a clear textual guidance in the form of a verse from the Koran or the sunna, he is compelled to use his understanding, often using similarities or analogies to cases that he may find in the revelation. Joseph Schacht wrote of Islamic law as representing "an extreme case of a 'jurists' law,'" but also as a type of sacred law as well—in other words, a law emanating from jurists and at the same time a law that originated with God.[65] The jurist or judge has the authority to declare God's law on the basis of an intentionalist interpretation of foundational texts. A total expenditure of effort (*istifragh al-wus*) was expected from the jurists. The legal tradition is designated as *fiqh* and was built up by the jurists or mujtahid as representing their (human) understanding of the law, to the best of their individual ability. As noted by Weiss, " . . . God's law was, for each mujtahid, whatever his best interpretative efforts lead him to . . . God's law was in itself indeterminate and waited upon the deliberations of human scholars to attain determinacy. There could thus be, for any given case, no one rule that exclusively represented the law of God."[66] The formulation of a law works as a partnership effort between the mujtahid, who formulates the law on the basis of the foundational sources; the applicant, who refers a legal problem with the intention of being guided by and complying with the expert's opinion; and the parties, who will be able to pose the questions that the expert needs to work on. In this way, the mujtahid does not work in isolation, single-handedly formulating legal opinions responsive to the needs of society.[67] Once engaged, the jurist becomes involved in the process of probability building.

As he continues his journey through the texts, he adds more and more evidence to the scale, thus tipping it further. Occasionally,

---

[62] VOGEL, *supra* note 5, at 23.

[63] *Id.* at 26.

[64] WEISS, *supra* note 34, at 112.

[65] Schacht, Introduction to Islamic Law, 209; WEISS, *supra* note 34, at 113.

[66] WEISS, *supra* note 34, at 118.

[67] *Id.* at 128.

he may encounter textual evidence that works against the rule he is testing. If the counterevidence accumulates and proves to be preponderant, he will desist from holding an opinion in favour of the rule. What matters in the end, when all his interpretative endeavours have been completed, is how the scale tips. If it tips—even ever so slightly—in favour of the rule, he will be justified in embracing the rule as the probable rule of God and in declaring this opinion to others.[68]

It is little wonder when one considers the difficulty of this jurisprudential exercise in probabilism that this work of formulating the law was customarily called "ijtihad" or "toil/arduous effort" or "striving," with the formulators of the law being appropriately called *mujtahids* or *toilers*.[69] Ultimately, however, the judge is not responsible for attaining to the perfection of the omniscient divine entity, since he is himself not privy to the real merits of the parties and their witnesses, and is relieved of responsibility to make an accurate assessment of the interior workings of a man's mind. His goal is simply to attain the true divine judgment of the matter. The judges are in fact the ultimate pragmatists, knowing full well that certainty in the understanding of the law often goes far beyond the reach of the human interpreter. The realistic goal can be said to be solely the attainment of the "probable" constructions of the law. As Weiss correctly noted,

> [T]his is not to say that certainty could never be achieved. The jurists were all sure that in principle it could, but they differed among themselves as to how much of the law was certain and how much merely probable and as to which parts of the law— which rules and which principles—were certain and which probable they also differed as to how to assess the probable formulations of the law. Were such formulations to be regarded as correct or incorrect, and if incorrect, how was their authority to be rationalized? This latter issue arose from the fact that probable formulations of the law were expressions of jurists' fallible opinions, and opinion could vary from one jurist to another, giving rise to pluralism in the law.[70]

In summary, ijtihad never achieves full certainty and produces at best the most probable result.[71]

What is the difference between the mufti and the qadi? It is widely known from a statement by the Hanbali Ibn Qayyim al-Jawziyya (d. 751/1350) that a mufti's fatwa shall state a general divine law

---

[68] *Id.* at 112.
[69] *Id.* at 88.
[70] *Id.* at 88.
[71] *Id.* at 132.

concerning the applicant and others. The fatwa is generally worded and is not obligatory, but the fatwa-giving of the qadi is specific in its terms and obligatory.[72] The giving of fatwas (*ifta*) has nothing to do with enforcement or compulsion; it has more to do with the giving of advice to the conscience of the applicant, who may be under a moral obligation to follow it at best, but it is ultimately nonbinding. Once a qadi, however, has adjudicated on an issue (fatwa-giving), obedience to the judgment is mandatory in both religious and secular terms and is of a binding character since it proceeds from the court as a religious body constituted by the sharia to enforce its law. As written by Vogel, "the mufti is concerned with facts in the internal forum of conscience, the qadi only with facts in the external forum of the court."[73] The qadi is justifiably entitled to rely upon the fact-finding and evidence collected by the mufti and is relieved of any responsibility for knowing with exactitude the inward and secret knowledge of the applicant or other parties. The mufti is usually required to give a fatwa to a private individual requesting clarity on a particular subject and the resulting fatwa has a private and individual nature, is nonbinding, and is generally applicable; adjudication (qada), on the other hand, has a public function, is specific to a particular person or persons, and is binding on these specific parties. It is important to note, however, that the qadi's decision is a specific judgment and, although binding on the relevant person or persons, has no precedential character. A legal adjudication is of a purely temporal nature, applying only to the facts at hand. As expressed by Vogel, law is purely transient, not binding anyone because it is not definitely known until it is applied to the concrete facts of a given circumstance.[74] The qadi's decision cannot be reversed by any higher court of appeal within the bounds of valid difference of opinion (this point will be elaborated upon in greater detail below).

> Even when the law's divergence from other outcomes poses no embarrassment to the law or legal system, because each outcome is momentary, wedded to the concrete instance to which it is applied. This system puts general rules of law under a considerable cloud. Not being fortified by a state monopoly of legislation, prey to contradiction and divergent application by a myriad of law-makers and appliers, and considered binding only when brought to bear on a particular, concrete context, general rules scarcely deserve the name of law. Even when widely accepted, they can be more like principles or background theories of western legal systems, in their various guises, which

---

[72] Ibn al-Qayyim, *I'lam*, 1:37–38.
[73] VOGEL, *supra* note 5, at 17.
[74] *Id.* at 21.

shape and direct legal work but are not themselves law and do not predict actual outcomes.[75]

2.2.3 Are the Western and (Saudi) Islamic Legal Systems Purely Divergent or More or Less Complementary?

Since Aristotle, it has been widely accepted that the need for discretion often alleviates the excesses of general rules;[76] and the concept of equity is found in all working legal systems. It will be postulated here that, despite enormous western skepticism, the two forms of law—the one the traditional western legal system and the other the (Saudi) Islamic legal system—despite their formal dissimilarities, are somewhat complementary in the area where a legal determination must be made and applied. As noted by Pound, the concept of equity is "necessary to the working of any legal system."[77] Clearly, the concepts of rule and discretion in the Saudi legal system arise in a manner starkly different from that within the context of western legal systems, although the same concepts have an important place in the traditional western legal systems.

There is little similarity to be found in the Saudi Islamic legal system with the contemporary western concept of law as a system of formal, objective, publicly known, generally applicable, compulsory rules arising from published legislation, legal judicial precedent, or authoritative scholarly analyses. One clear example of this western concept of a formal objective rule can be found, however, in Koranic text or in an authentic hadith, perhaps also in the example of the fixed authoritative legal body of rules of a particular madhhab binding upon the school's adherents. It should be noted, however, that the Hanbali madhhab is not so regarded by Saudi judges. Apart from these examples there is nothing remotely similar to this perception of western law in the Saudi Islamic legal system.[78] The whole idea of ijtihad is that of a unique decision of an individual conscience applied to the evaluation of a concrete act,[79] which is dissimilar to a (western) system of formal and objective legal rules applied generally. Vogel designates the Saudi legal system as a microcosmic conception of law in contrast to a (western) macrocosmic system of law defined by a more outer-directed law that is law in the form of general and abstract rules issued by an external formal institution.[80] In the West, there is a continuous misperception of Islamic legal rationality when viewed solely from the macrocosmic legal perspective

---

[75] VOGEL, *supra* note 5, at 21–22.

[76] Wolfgang Friedmann, Legal Theory, at 11, Columbia University Press (1967).

[77] Pound, Decadence, Introduction, at 54, quoted in VOGEL, *supra* note 5, at 32.

[78] *Id.* at 22–23.

[79] *Id.* at 23.

[80] *Id.* at 26.

of a formal legal structure. Although the Saudi Arabian dedication to the microcosmic is particularly strong, in no legal system, not even in Saudi Arabia, are the macrocosmic ideals entirely absent.[81] Consider, for instance, the following forms of binding Islamic law: the qadi judgments as inward-directed legal declarations, although based on the specific facts of the case; the revealed texts, administrative decisions of rulers for the general welfare as more outer-directed law; and the rules of a school of law where the particular scholar has accepted these rules as binding by means of his membership in that school.

In contrast, the western modern ideal of a legal system of generally binding, positive laws and the western applications of these laws within the context of adjudication would seem to be at the other end of the spectrum. There are, however, numerous instances of microcosmic law in application within the western system. There is a tendency of western jurisprudence to immediately dismiss what is perceived as irrational law, also as it may appear within the western system, as "kadi justice."[82] There is an ubiquitous concern by many legal authorities of the Anglo-American legal system of the taint of kadi justice, often within the context of adjudication, referring to it sometimes as "the judicial hunch" or, in a more deprecatory fashion, "what the judge had for breakfast."[83] If sought, there are numerous repressed microcosmic phenomena alive and well in western systems, the clearest examples of which are the principle of equity and the jury verdict.

> Arbitration awards, trial court judgments or rulings without opinion, and penal sentences stand accused of kadi-justice. The phenomenon is acknowledged in judgments termed "ethical, such as decisions of disciplinary boards, and in decisions termed "discretionary," like low-level pragmatic or administrative decisions, such as parole, zoning, or licensing decisions. Microcosmic law can appear somewhat masked behind highly general standards that more or less openly invoke conscience as their justification, such as, in United States law, "due process," "fairness" and "reasonableness" . . . Civil law systems, despite or perhaps because of their devotion to an ideal that all law is legislation, seem to acknowledge more readily a microcosmic-like individual freedom of trial judges.[84]

In summary, both the western and (Saudi) Islamic ideals of law appear to occupy different ends of the spectrum, although microcosmic as well as macrocosmic ideals can be found in both systems.

---

[81] *Id.* at 27.

[82] *Id.* at 28.

[83] *Id.* at 29, quoting Hutcheson, "Judgment Intuitive" 274 and Frank, "Are Judges Human?" 25–27.

[84] *Id.* at 29–30.

There are more complementary aspects than would appear at a first glance. This is not at all to dismiss their overt discrepancies; but one can find covert similarities in the way each system deals with conflicts and resulting compromises. There is, indisputably, a stringent adherence to microcosmic legal ideals in the Wahhabi legal position and doctrines in modern-day Saudi Arabia, with a marked allegiance to the precepts of the scholar Ibn Taymiyya. Nevertheless, modern Saudis are more and more prepared to allow for the entry of macrocosmic principles. This can best be seen in the way the microcosmic and macrocosmic ideally combine in the application by the courts in Saudi Arabia.[85]

2.2.4 What Is *Usul al-fiqh?*

The theory of the sources of fiqh is *usul al-fiqh*, meaning literally "the roots of the law."[86] If there is a clear text of the Koran or sunna on which to base a legal judgment, the judge applies it and can safely consider the result to be a righteous ruling. But if neither the Koran nor the sunna provides a clear text on a particular issue, the judge must resort to the theoretical and methodological principles underlying the jurists' formulation of the law (usul al-fiqh). The need for ijtihad arises in just such a case and usul al-fiqh assists the judge in his attempt to reach a righteous and divine ruling. The basic sources of law recognized by usul al-fiqh are the Koran, the sunna, community consensus (*ijma*) and analogy (*qiyas*). Muslim jurists have not been blind to the conundrum that certainty in the understanding of the law often lies beyond the reach of the interpreter and that probable constructions would be most likely the best that the interpreter could attain.[87] It was also clearly understood that a qadi must rule solely by revelation and that uncertain cases can never be resolved by guesswork, human authority, or his own desires.[88] It is the science of usul al-fiqh, with its extensive epistemological footing, to show how every shred of guidance, every indication of divine will may be gleaned from the revealed texts, without resort to arbitrary guesswork.[89] The answer to the conundrum faced by the Muslim jurist lies in ijtihad.[90] The complex history of usul al-fiqh goes well beyond the parameters of this chapter and is the subject of excellent legal scholarship.[91] Suffice it to

---

[85] See, generally, VOGEL, *supra* note 5, ch. 2.

[86] An excellent and recent work of scholarship on this subject is found in WEISS, *supra* note 10.

[87] *Id.* at 88.

[88] VOGEL, *supra* note 5, at 36.

[89] *Id.* at 37.

[90] *Id.*

[91] For a lengthy and extremely helpful discussion, see WEISS, *supra* note 10, and VOGEL, *supra* note 5.

say that the Hanbali school, formed around the famous hadith scholar Ibn Hanbali, best reflects the perspective of one group of scholars, the "people of hadith" (*ahl al-hadith*), who sought to find the law primarily in literal hadith reports and who wanted to keep the degree of intervening human reasoning to an absolute minimum. The rest of this analysis will focus on the Hanbali school, which is prevalent in Saudi Arabia. Regarding the issue of the probative value of a singular hadith (a hadith having only one transmitter in a particular generation), the people of hadith regarded this to be a much more reliable touchstone than mere human reasoning. The people of hadith prevailed on this point in the eventual usul al-fiqh, and the probative value of singular hadiths have become uniformly accepted as a sound basis for legal rules, outranking differing verdicts of systematic legal reasoning.[92]

The first root is the Koran, and the second root is the sunna. The third root of the law is consensus or ijma, referring technically to the unanimous agreement of all qualified legal scholars of an age upon a legal ruling. It would be completely incorrect to jump to the conclusion (as did some western scholars in the past) that ijma could itself become a self-sufficient foundation and sole authority of Islamic law, elevating to the status of divine law certain rulings for which there is no revealed textual authority or that even may contradict revealed texts, and rendering superfluous all other legal bases.[93] A too-broad interpretation of ijma would supplant the resort to the divine word with human sources of law, and the people of hadith were reluctant to dilute divine law by merely human judgment. It is important to note here that Hanbali opinion on this point is quite conservative, to the effect that unless all divergent opinions and misgivings are dispelled, no ijma can exist. This is not a purely scholastic debate; this issue can and does affect legal opinion. In summary, ijma binds only those scholars who accept its premises, and while ijma is accepted as a third root of law, its validation and jurisdiction are sharply circumscribed. The weakening of the doctrine of ijma, reduced severely in its jurisdiction and efficacy, effectively undermines the legal promulgations of the ulema themselves, effectively precluding the possible effective institutionalization or positivization of a source of law subject to the control of the ulema. As noted by Frank E. Vogel, the ulema preserve the ideology that endows them and their institutions with authority by this means, leaving to speculation how they will treat other potential temporal law sources, such as consultation (*shura*) with the people or even state legislation.[94]

The fourth root or source of law is qiyas or analogy. Through analogy, one rule established for one legal situation through the Koran,

---

[92] VOGEL, *supra* note 5, at 44.
[93] *Id.* at 46.
[94] *Id.* at 51.

sunna or ijma may be extended by analogy to another legal situation. Qiyas is the analogy between cases considered as a justification for the formulation of a novel legal ruling. Qiyas provides the usul al-fiqh with a method of generating legal content beyond revelation.[95] In essence, qiyas provides the possibility of legal content outside of divine revelation by means of analogical reasoning. In one sense, the use of qiyas is comparable to the way common law judges or lawyers analyze disparate or different preferential decisions. Qiyas has a dual function, interpretative as well as legislative.[96] This dual function has been the subject of considerable debate, just as there has been debate in western legal jurisdictions concerning whether judges should legislate or merely interpret the laws.[97]

2.2.5 What Is *Taqlid?* What Is *Tarjih?*

As discussed in section 2.2.2 above, there is a long scholarly history on the practice of ijtihad and the so-called closing of the door of ijtihad. There are now more recent scholarly discussions on the advisability or even the necessity of a neo-ijtihad. In the three centuries after the Prophet's death, fiqh became more and more elaborate and complex, especially in light of the science of hadith collection and the increasingly theoretical and methodological principles underlying the jurists' formulation of the law (usul al-fiqh). It became widely viewed that laypersons (and even some scholars) without a certain degree of legal acumen were less qualified to participate in legal reasoning (ijtihad) and should defer to another's badge of authority, choosing to adopt someone's opinion (or the opinion of a particular school) without knowing the rationalization for that opinion. In contrast, the ijtihad ideal requires scholars to resolutely follow their own convictions as to what is truth.[98] With taqlid, the qadi simply copies or imitates the view of others whom he deems more capable than himself in a form of respectful imitation and thus, in a way, is relieved of the moral burden of having to decide each individual case himself. Ulema capable of ijtihad are called *mujtahid* and those practicing taqlid are called *muqallid*. It would seem that the practice of taqlid has abounded, with ijtihad being resorted to only for novel issues on which the mujtahid can find no prior fiqh opinion to serve as a legal precedent (certainly analogous with the authority common law assigns to judicial precedent). It is clearly the fate of ijtihad that its use arises when the judge is faced with a determination of divine law under conditions of uncertainty, in the face of innovation and new ideas. With respect to Saudi Arabia, it is interesting that, following the views of the scholar Ibn Mu'ammar (d.

---

[95] *Id.* at 52.
[96] *Id.* at 55.
[97] *Id.*
[98] *Id.* at 57.

1225/1811), the Wahhabi position "minimizes school taqlid and promotes a degree of ijtihad."[99] It was also the view of the eminent scholar
Ibn Taymiyya that taqlid, as a blind adherence to the views of other
men, was a vital error and that even a layperson could safely practice
ijtihad without fear of punishment. Taqlid, in other words, should be
kept to an absolute minimum.

Which then leads to the position of *tarjih* as the ideal of weighing
available views or proof-evaluation. Opinion was understood to be the
sense of probabilism attained by a mujtahid as a result of his examination of the texts. Working his way through the texts, the mujtahid
would weigh the different texts and views in a determination of pre-
ponderance within the process of probability building.[100] Ibn Taymiyya
and later the Wahhabis endorsed the ideal of this proof-evaluation.
Ibn Taymiyya endorses the microcosmic ideal whereby "the individual's conscience seeks in each specific case a fresh drawing from divine
sources, whose transcendent importance is thereby instilled in the
immediate and the everyday." His position can be seen as part of the
theological trend known as *salafi*. This trend, drawing upon Ibn Hanbali, opposes itself to Islamic dogmatic theology.[101]

Saudi Arabian ulema have remained faithful to the tenets of the
Wahhabi movement and to the thought of Ibn Taymiyya advancing the
ideal of ijtihad and the use of proof-evaluation or tarjih. The work of
Ibn 'Abd al-Wahhabi is well accepted; there is one work from his body
of work in which this scholar examines a legal question related to a
form of partnership (*mudaraba*); not finding a textual guidance, he
resorts to his basic principle of the presumption of permissibility for
world matters.[102] In modern Saudi Arabia, the usul al-fiqh positions of
Wahhabi scholars and from Ibn Taymiyya remain authoritative and
proof-evaluation theory is a standard doctrine.[103] Frank E. Vogel has
quoted Dr. Hamad al-Faryan as having said that "every scholar must
determine the preponderant opinion, i.e., practice tarjih, and never,
while recognizing that a certain view has a better proof, abandon that
view on the ground that he is not a mujtahid and instead follow the
school of so-and-so. Ijtihad varies according to one's ability, and thus
ijtihad exists in degrees and subdivisions."[104] There is now a decided
reluctance to admit a school affiliation at all and to emphasize a type
of collective ijtihad. As noted by Vogel, the ulema now assume that
"there is an independent vantage point from which the views of all the
schools can be assessed and evaluated, and tarjih conducted between

---

[99] *Id.* at 66.
[100] WEISS, *supra* note 34, at 112.
[101] VOGEL, *supra* note 5, at 71.
[102] *Id.* at 75.
[103] *Id.* at 77–80.
[104] *Id.* at 78.

them—and this without declaring oneself an absolute mujtahid."[105] Against this background has emerged a new concept of collective ijtihad—that is, proceeding from councils and academies of ulema— that attempts to overcome the vulnerability of an individual ijtihad. In Saudi Arabia, there is the Nizam Hay'at Kibar al-Ulema, or the Board of Senior Ulema, which issues fatwas on important issues requiring further study or as submitted to it by the government. There is also a subsidiary of the Muslim World League, the Islamic Fiqh Academy, located in Mecca, as well as a Fiqh Academy of the OIC in Jeddah. There is also the King Abdulaziz University in Jeddah and its International Centre for Islamic Economic Research. The education of modern-day judges in Saudi Arabia provides them with the tools of ijtihad so they may engage in tarjih, and Saudi ulema are members of an international community of ulema.[106] Saudi judges are required to have at least a baccalaureate degree in sharia, usually from a college of sharia in Saudi Arabia, although liberalized legislation now allows for an equivalent educational degree acquired abroad.[107]

3. The Law as Applied in the Saudi Courts; Arbitration and Enforcement

This section will look at the way law and the concept of ijtihad is applied by the courts in Saudi Arabia and will address, *inter alia*, the issue of the scope of appellate review of qadi decisions.

The ideal of qadi ijtihad is alive and well in Saudi Arabia as is the practice of tarjih or proof evaluation, although authority is primarily sought only within the Hanbali school. That Saudi qadis are free to practice ijtihad—treating each decision as a unique and solitary elaboration of a rule from the Koran and the sunna, and attempting to use their best judgment to approximate or even attain the divine law for the case before them—is clear; this is also evidenced by the fact that, in actual practice, senior judges at the appeals level are constrained to uphold any decision based on ijtihad, even though that decision may significantly deviate from the Hanbali school or from what the appellate court itself considers to be the best ruling, in order to support and maintain the ideal of trial court ijtihad freedom. More detail is given in section 3.1 below.

In a 1985 interview with Shaykh Ialih bin Muhammad al-Lahaydan, then president of the Permanent Board of the Supreme Judicial Council and a member of the Board of Senior Ulema, Frank E. Vogel quotes Shaykh al-Lahaydan, as follows, with respect to the discretionary authority of the qadi at the trial court level:

---

[105] *Id.* at 79.
[106] *Id.* at 79–81.
[107] *Id.* at 81.

The qadi of Saudi Arabia is not obliged or compelled to restrict himself to the school of Ahmad [Ibn Hanbali], but rather has the right to judge in the case in accordance with that to which his ijtihad leads, even if that is not the Hanbali school. . . . It is not said to him, perform ijtihad within the school or without it; rather, he is requested to judge by that which he believes to be truth.[108]

3.1 A Brief Overview of the Saudi Court System

In 1927, King 'Abd al-'Aziz by means of a written regulation (*Nizam al-Qada*) defined two trial court jurisdictions that still exist today. The lower-level jurisdiction is that of the summary courts or the Musta'jala (having jurisdiction over all criminal cases except certain capital crimes and over civil cases involving less than certain amounts). Cases are heard by a single judge and most of the cases are criminal cases. The second level is that of the sharia courts, called the Great Sharia Courts ("*mahakim shar'iyya kubra*") in the larger cities. These courts hear all cases not heard by the summary courts and the majority of the cases are civil matters. In these courts, the civil cases are heard by one judge, the criminal cases by a panel of three judges.[109]

Since 1960, King Sa'ud implemented throughout the kingdom an appeals system under a single presidency of the judiciary in Riyadh. Continuing the modern court reforms of King 'Abd al-'Aziz, a Ministry of Justice was created in 1970 to assume the administration of the courts and a modern administrative system for the courts was officially formalized in a judiciary regulation in 1975.[110] There was reportedly a certain degree of opposition to these judiciary reforms by the ulema, who were allegedly reluctant to submit to a formal appeal process.[111] By 1975, the functions of the president of the judiciary had been dispersed to different government agencies. For instance, the Board of Senior Ulema assumed the responsibilities for providing fatwas both to the government and to individuals. Administrative and adjudicatory functions were separated out, with the Ministry of Justice handling general administrative matters while a new Supreme Judicial Council was entrusted with the authority for appeals and judicial supervision.[112]

The Saudi court system is undergoing a substantial reorganization as reported recently in several press articles. It should be noted that a major overhaul of the Saudi judicial legal system, including

---

[108] *Id.* at 83.
[109] *Id.* at 88–91.
[110] *Id.* at 92.
[111] *Id.* at 92.
[112] *Id.* at 93.

an allocation of US$2 billion (£981 million) for the training of new judges and building new courts, has been recently announced. The reforms,[113] issued by royal decree, will allegedly lead to the creation of a supreme court, an appeals court, and new general courts to replace the Supreme Judicial Council. In the face of mounting criticism that the current judicial system is often opaque and arbitrary, attributes that will be explored in greater depth in this chapter, reformers have strongly applauded these developments, which they view as heralding a modernization of the country. Saudi judges have had to date extremely broad discretion in issuing rulings according to their own interpretation of Islamic sharia law, and the Saudi judiciary has long strenuously resisted any codification of laws or reliance on precedent when making a ruling. Clearly, the new reforms as announced by King Abdullah are planned to address what are perceived as failings of the judiciary system and to introduce safeguards such as appeals courts, which would be able to overturn lower court decisions. According to Hassan al-Mulla, the head of the Saudi Bar Association, the royal decree will set up two supreme courts for the general courts and administrative courts. These courts will replace the Supreme Judicial Council, which will confine its review to administrative issues such as judges' salaries and appointments. The decree will also set up specialized court circuits within the system for commercial, labor, and personal status cases. It is hoped by Saudi reformers that these reforms will serve to eradicate the unchecked powers of the conservative clerics, who currently lead the judiciary. The king will appoint the head of the Supreme Court. It is widely perceived that the current Saudi king is extremely interested in a modernization of the country, so it can only be assumed that he will choose someone who will further these plans. Nevertheless, sharia law shall remain as the unshakable basis of the judicial system, but the reformers argue that these changes to the judiciary will bode well for the business environment.

3.2 The Classic Islamic Legal Parameters for the Review of Judgments (Scope of Appeal)

An ordinary appeal and any institution dedicated to hearing such appeals were unknown to classical Islamic law, although an applicant disappointed by a judgment may have sought its review by another qadi or the ruler or his agents. There is a basic rule against ijtihad reversals in Islamic law. A judgment, whether by a judge or some other authority, cannot be reversed if it is based on the practice of ijtihad, that is, if the judgment is the result of a genuine human attempt to find the

---

[113] BBC News, http://news.bbc.co.uk/2/hi/middle_east/7023308_stm. Oct. 5, 2007

truth interpreting revealed sources where the latter are not definitive on the subject. But a judgment may be reversed if it conflicts with an indisputable proof from the sources of the law.[114] Frank E. Vogel aptly calls this the "rule against ijtihad reversal."[115] Of significant note and underlying this basic rule of judgment recognition is a basic premise that, where the revealed texts afford no certainty on an issue and ijtihad must be practiced, "all mujtahids are equal and no one has priority, whether caliph or scholar, and that any other rule would defeat the autonomy of the qadi's conscience."[116] Vogel also notes that this rule also functions as a doctrine of res judicata and collateral estoppels, and regulates comity between schools of law and the enforcement of judgments of one school by the courts of another.[117] In recognition of the legal system's commitment to a judge's freedom of ijtihad, there is a very restrictive scope of appellate review.

The full scope of judicial ijtihad and the rule against ijtihad reversal was first implemented by the High Court of Mecca in 1962, as follows:

> Judgments of the qadis must be respected, such that none of them shall be reversed unless it differs with a text of the Book, the Sunna, or the ijma, or it differs with the judge's own opinion as to fiqh truth. No judgment requiring reversal shall be reversed except by the trial judge who issued it, as long as he does not refuse; if he refuses, the appeal court has to reverse it.[118]

Pursuant to a more recent Ministry of Justice ordinance, the board is not authorized to reverse the judgment without first engaging in a dialogue with the trial judge. The board is not empowered to give judgment itself or to compel the trial judge to give a judgment contrary to his opinion; it is solely authorized to remand the case for trial before a new judge. From the above, one can clearly see that the qadi's independence and lawmaking power are thoroughly respected even if this entails a slowing down of the decision-making process. It is critical to note that the Supreme Judicial Council can never force the lower court to follow its judgment and change its opinion. In this way, providing mere guidance to the lower court judges, the Saudi appeal system differs significantly from any continental (French) court of appeal system.[119]

---

[114] *Id.* at 85–86.
[115] *Id.* at 86.
[116] *Id.*
[117] *Id.* at 86 n.5.
[118] Royal Decree No. 16-3-3136, arts. 6 and 7, quoted in Vogel, *supra* note 5, at 95.
[119] *Id.* at 96 n.55.

3.3 Actual Appeals Practice

At the outset it should be noted that at both trial court and appellate levels, case law is not published in Saudi Arabia; it is not even public information, but rather is regarded as being private to the parties. It has been reported that appeals decisions are difficult to obtain for the same reason. The appellate procedure is based upon the written trial record of the judge and a memorandum of appeal prepared by the appellant; there are usually no meetings with the parties.[120] It is therefore little wonder that reversals are extremely rare. As reported by Vogel, in the period from November 1979 through November 1980 there was a rate of reversal of 1.4 percent in criminal matters and only 0.8 percent in civil matters.[121] It is also rare to find written comments from the appeal process. This seems to be a confirmation of the basic precept that a decision based upon the exercise of ijtihad will only be reversed if the judgment contradicts a clear and authentic proof from the sharia, the sunna, or ijma beyond a reasonable doubt.[122]

There are basically five grounds for reversal:

1. The appellate court is authorized to engage in a dialogue with the lower trial court in order to seek clarification.
2. The trial court has failed to observe various rules and regulations acknowledged by the judicial system, such as royal orders, decrees, and regulations on judicial administration or jurisdiction, and even minor rules of procedure.
3. The trial court has applied a defensible ruling to the wrong set of facts (this factual misunderstanding apparently accounts for 99 percent of all appellate reversals). It should be noted in this context that the classic distinction between findings of fact and determinations of law in western jurisprudence is not present in the Saudi system, since the rule against ijtihad reversal applies equally to factual findings and to legal determinations.
4. In criminal convictions and sentences, there is a principle based on sunna that convictions should be avoided in case of doubt and that it is better to err in exonerating than in punishing.
5. An "indisputable" sharia proof has been offended, that is, where there is a strong conviction that the trial court's decision clearly conflicts the text of the Koran, the sunna, or ijma. However, if the appeals court comes to the conclusion that reasonable minds could legitimately differ on the apparent contradiction with a text, then the appellate court must refrain from reversal and respect the trial court's ijtihad.[123]

---

[120] *Id.* at 98.
[121] *Id.* at 98.
[122] *Id.*
[123] *Id.* at 98–107.

Although the appellate courts willingly accept the limits on their authority, they will use the reversal process to engage in dialogue with the trial court to encourage and broaden the ijtihad of the trial courts.[124]

To date, the Supreme Judicial Authority has declined to exercise any authority to set binding law for the lower courts. Although they are empowered by the 1975 judiciary regulation to codify general legal rules, this lawmaking function seems to contradict the appellate court's own perception of its role.[125] The judiciary regulation is generally perceived as applying to administrative matters only (e.g., siyasah shar'iyya, or laws issued by the ruler, that supplement the fiqh for the purpose of the general welfare). The clear repudiation by the appellate courts of any quasi-legislative role can be seen in the following statement of Shaykh al-Lahaydan, quoted in Frank E. Vogel's treatise:

> Neither the Boards of Review nor the Supreme Judicial Council has any right to legislate *("yusharri'")*. Each only evinces, as to particular cases, its opinion, and does not lay down for the qadis principles *("qawa'id")* by which they are to give judgments. Therefore, no such session has occurred.[126]

The Judicial Council will at most issue hortatory instructions to qadis on matters of difference of opinion, generally to draw the qadis closer to each other and for the avoidance of public criticism of the judiciary.[127] The emphasis is also placed on an efficient resolution of a controversy and the avoidance of putting the parties through the process of a pointless reversal.[128] Moreover, the precedent of an appellate court is neither formal nor doctrinal, but solely practical. A qadi who deliberately flouts or ignores the instruction of an appellate court is not doing anything improper.[129] General rulemaking by the Judicial Council is extremely rare. In one unusual decision of the Supreme Judicial Council in 1981,[130] the Supreme Judicial Council actually ruled that the loans in the instant case, which had been granted by certain commercial banks, were usuries (riba) with the consequence that the notaries (the applicants in the instant case) were instructed not to accept for registration any mortgage securing loans by commercial banks. Needless to say, this rulemaking had a large impact, essentially preventing the use of bank mortgages. Nevertheless, the Judicial Council characterized this order as administrative in nature,

---

[124] *Id.* at 107.
[125] *Id.* at 110.
[126] *Id.* at 110–11.
[127] *Id.* at 114.
[128] *Id.* at 112.
[129] *Id.* at 112.
[130] Supreme Judicial Council, Decision No. 291.

solely providing the notaries with a rule-of-thumb procedure to follow. Despite this characterization, this ruling had a very general character, equivalent to a fatwa.[131]

According to Vogel, ulema will actually go so far as to ignore decrees or regulations that they find to be distasteful or improper.[132] Functionaries in the Ministry of Justice will adhere to these regulations, insofar as they are more under the king's command than the ulema.

> Out of respect, the 'ulama do not refer to them as rejected, or as opposed in principle, but simply either ignore them, interpret them evasively, or describe them as not yet implemented for some practical reason. The provisions remain on the books, at best ideas for future implementation.[133]

This is clearly an area of overt competition in the relationship between the ulema and the king, which will be examined further in section 4 below.

3.4 Fatwas

The fatwas issued by respected senior ulema, such as those of the Board of Senior Ulema, can strongly influence the rulemaking of the qadis. Since they are the result of the combined ijtihad of extremely respected and experienced Saudi ulema including members of the Supreme Judicial Council, they have a quasi-legislative effect on judicial decisions.[134] Many of these fatwas are published. One such fatwa declared the validity of a liquidated damages clause in a government construction contract. Before the issuance of this fatwa, the validity of such a liquidated damage clause was in doubt since it involved the principle against unjust enrichment. However, after the issuance of the fatwa, the qadis were more relaxed in determining the enforceability of such a clause. It is a matter of debate whether the fatwa caters to certain conformist tendencies of the qadis. In any event, the fatwa certainly seems to have a quasi-legislative effect upon the qadis.[135]

Although the influence of the fatwas of the Board of Senior Ulema is important and is clearly reinforced by commands of the king regarding their implementation, it must be emphasized that neither a fatwa nor a royal decree can command a qadi to a particular fiqh opinion. The freedom of the trial court judges to practice ijtihad remains unconstrained. The respect held by the qadis for the opinions

---

[131] See generally VOGEL, supra note 5, at 113–17.
[132] Id. at 111.
[133] Id. at 111.
[134] Id. at 115.
[135] See generally id. at 115-117.

of senior ulema is, however, a strong guiding influence, although differences of opinion cannot be precluded. It is common for the government to obtain a fatwa, formal or informal, from key ulema, which will then more than likely be respected by the qadis. Although the qadis are not compelled to be bound by such fatwas, they nevertheless have a quasi-legislative effect insofar as the qadis are reluctant to enter into an overt competition between their own ijtihad capabilities and those of the Qadis' seniors.[136]

With respect to novel legal issues, it is commonly argued that a basic rule of thumb as to the possible leaning of a sharia court is to presume that it will rely upon the fiqh of the late Hanbali manuals. Resort to the fiqh of other schools is not precluded, but the tendency to rely on the fiqh of the Hanbali school is there.[137] Speaking generally, the qadis apply Hanbali law most of the time, but when faced by novel developments and the need to adapt fiqh to new legal problems, they are perceived as willingly guided by the views of senior ulema.[138] It is important to note, however, that conformity is not guaranteed. Few fatwas of senior ulema are circulated and these fatwas, although issued by undeniably respected senior colleagues, are not binding. It might also be the case that a complex new legal arrangement conflicts with a fundamental sharia principle and even the most influential ulema are hard pressed to come up with an innovative legal solution.

The important issue of bank interest is still an unregulated area except by means of the unreported and unique individual decisions covering this issue by individual qadis. The generally accepted Saudi application of sharia, however, has it that bank interest is forbidden, but as noted by Vogel:

> No one is able to speak with total confidence on what a judge will apply in these areas. And no one, not the appellate courts or any legislating power such as a king, has the power to intervene legislatively to impose a rule, even to meet pressing national economic or other interests.[139]

There have been many calls, both internally and externally, for the codification of law in Saudi Arabia, but the ideal of qadi ijtihad plays a key role in the Saudi system: on the one hand, it keeps in check any role for state intervention in law, whether dictated by the king as executor or legislator; however, it can do so only for as long as the needs for rulemaking can be accomplished—even imperfectly—by informal ulema action.[140] The new fatwa collections written by prominent

---

[136] *Id.* at 124.
[137] *Id.* at 126.
[138] *Id.* at 130.
[139] *Id.* at 130.
[140] *Id.* at 130.

twentieth-century Muslim jurists and ulema are indeed making a vital contribution to the legal discipline, adding academic substance to fiqh reforms and their adaptations to the conditions of contemporary Muslim society.[141]

3.5 The Importance of the Fact-Finding Process

The ideal of ijtihad requires that the fact-finding process constitute a genuine effort to examine the actual facts. The role of the qadi is chiefly to determine and apply the law, but the witnesses are the real fact-finders. There is a moral and legal dimension to this process. The role of the parties is to present their claims and/or defenses fairly and honestly and that of the witnesses to relate the facts honestly.[142] It is in some way a combined religious and secular experience.[143] The rules of evidence are as follows: "to prove an assertion, one must produce evidence (bayyina), ideally two male Muslim witnesses of good character, and to disprove an assertion (except in criminal cases), one must swear an exculpatory oath."[144] A witness may be female under certain limitations. Good character can be proven either by the qadi's personal knowledge or through the testimony of two other witnesses. Testimony can be made by expert witnesses. All testimony must be voluntary, so subpoena-compelled testimony is nonexistent. Witness testimony would in all probability be given greater weight in terms of reliability than that of scientific evidence such as fingerprinting and presumably DNA testing.[145] If a plaintiff fails to prove his case by means of his witnesses, then he can demand the exculpatory oath of the defendant. If he declines this right, he loses his case. The defendant in a civil case must take the oath or lose the case. If the defendant in a civil case takes the exculpatory oath, he wins the case. As noted above, the evidence-taking process weds both secular and highly religious aspects.[146]

Oral proceedings, not written pleadings, are the focus of the trial, although written statements to the court are being increasingly used in commercial cases.[147] The exchange of statements is a free-form process that appears to be little encumbered by formal procedure and the rules of evidence. Each party is bound by his admissions and many oral assertions of fact find their way into evidence in this way.[148]

---

[141] KAMALI, *supra* note 8, at 260.
[142] VOGEL, *supra* note 5, at 145.
[143] *Id.* at 146.
[144] *Id.* at 147.
[145] *Id.* at 148.
[146] *Id.* at 148.
[147] *Id.* at 152.
[148] *Id.* at 152–53.

Cases proceeding to final judgment are rare since most are settled by the agreement of the parties, with the support of the qadi. The settlement or compromise of disputes (*sulh*) is an important aspect of adjudication in Saudi Arabia.[149]

As quoted by Vogel in the context of his extensive study of the Saudi court system:

> In Saudi Shari'ah courts, I was often told, 'the great majority' or '99 percent' of all civil cases end in reconciliation. I was often quoted the legal maxim, sulh is best.' It comes from a verse of the Qur'an that suggests amicable divorce when a wife fears ill-treatment: It shall not be wrong for the two to set things peacefully to rights between them: for sulh is best (*"al-sulh khayr"*) 4:128.[150]

Sulh is allegedly highly popular since it confers blamelessness among all parties and promotes harmony between the parties. Vogel has also noted that Saudi qadis display great skill as mediators and conciliators.[151] Viewed positively, sulh affords the qadi with the opportunity to exercise judicial discernment and promote practical adjudication. Viewed negatively, sulh alleviates pressure on the judicial system and on the qadis individually to undertake ijtihad when faced with difficult and novel legal issues. Sulh can perpetuate "the present vacuum of law, substantive and procedural, on many matters relating to modern conditions."[152]

3.6 Arbitration

In 1994, Saudi Arabia filed an instrument of accession to the New York Convention on the Recognition and Enforcement of Foreign Arbitral Awards of 1958 ("New York Convention"). The authorizing decree incorporated the requisite reciprocity requirement and specified that jurisdiction over actions seeking enforcement of foreign arbitral awards shall lie with the Board of Grievances.

To date, the Board of Grievances has not issued any procedural rules for actions seeking enforcement of international arbitration awards. It has been reported by Saudi Arabian legal practitioners who have consulted the Board of Grievances officials that no such rules will be issued in the near future. This being the case, it appears that an application for the recognition of a foreign arbitral award would be submitted and would proceed in accordance with the procedures

---

[149] *Id.* at 153.
[150] *Id.* at 154.
[151] *Id.* at 155.
[152] *Id.* at 157.

specified for applications with respect to the recognition of foreign judicial awards. The Board of Grievances would be the court with jurisdiction. There is little precedent for the recognition and enforcement of foreign judgments by the Saudi Arabian courts. Other than a small number of 1989 cases involving judgments of courts in member states of the Arab League, there is to the author's knowledge no instance where the Board of Grievances has afforded final recognition to, and enforced, a judgment of a foreign court or a foreign arbitral award where enforcement has not been voluntary. A single recent case in which a bank sought enforcement of a foreign judgment or award was reported by Michael McMillen in his 2001 article.[153] In that case, the Board of Grievances reportedly declined to exercise jurisdiction because of the involvement of a bank; presumably, as concluded by McMillen, enforcement would be sought from the SAMA Committee.

De novo Board of Grievances proceedings normally last from two to ten years, with the long duration being in part attributable to sharia rules of procedure that allow a defendant considerable ability to delay the final resolution of the proceeding. A proceeding before the Board of Grievances to enforce an arbitral award that on its face does not contravene the sharia or other Saudi Arabian law "should" take approximately one year.[154]

It must be noted, however, that the Board of Grievances will undertake a thorough examination of any matter presented to it, and this examination will include a rigorous inquiry into matters of public policy (including the compliance of all documentation with the sharia and other principles of Saudi Arabian law). Thus, if a foreign judgment or arbitral award is obtained and enforcement is sought in Saudi Arabia, the Board of Grievances will examine the underlying documentation and make what is essentially a de novo determination as to whether the documentation underlying the judgment and/or award complies with the sharia and other Saudi Arabian law.

Perhaps the clearest example of an element of an award that would be contrary to the sharia would be where it contains an element of interest. Interest is considered to be a form of unearned gain (riba), which is prohibited under the sharia as construed in Saudi Arabia. Pursuant to its discretionary powers, the Board of Grievances would decline to enforce any part of a foreign award that constitutes an award on interest. It is safe to conclude that interest on damages suffered would not be recoverable.

It is the author's understanding that there has been a case where the Board of Grievances declined to enforce an arbitral award from

---

[153] Michael J.T. McMillen, "Islamic Shari'ah Compliant Project Finance: Security and Financing Structure Care Studies," 24 Fordham Int'l L.J. 1184 (2001).
[154] *Id.* McMillen, at 9.

an international arbitral tribunal on public policy grounds where the arbitrator was a woman. The author has learned in the course of informal discussions with a representative of a renowned arbitration tribunal that the use of arbitration as a dispute resolution mechanism is highly recommended in the U.A.E., but the enforceability of foreign arbitral awards in Saudi Arabia is an area that continues to be fraught with enforceability issues.

4. Competition Between Ulema and the Ruler

4.1 Sivash Shari'yyah or Sharia-oriented Policy

Law, legal conceptions, and legal institutions viewed from the perspective of the ulema are called "fiqh" in this chapter. Law, legal conceptions, and legal institutions viewed from the ruler's perspective are designated as siyasah, meaning, literally, "policy" or "conduct of affairs." A source of law governed by fiqh and applied at time by the ulema themselves is designated as siyasah shar'iyya.

The fiqh doctrine delegates legislative authority to the king. The Saudi ulema clearly recognize that the ruler possesses an extensive authority to make laws. The ulema both represent and control the ruler's constitutional powers under sharia (siyasah shar'iyya). The ruler can take any acts, including legislating to supplement the sharia and creating courts that are necessary for the public welfare (*maslaha 'amma*), provided always that there is no infringement of the sharia or that the sharia is silent on the matter,[155] although this latter aspect is disputed in practice. Nevertheless, siyasah shar'iyya gives the ruler a wide scope of action. Siyasah shar'iyya focuses rather broadly on the utility of an action to the actual society as a whole in order to overcome and counter the possible deficiencies of the highly textualist fiqh.[156] The lawmaking function is limited, however, to securing the public good.

A *nizam*, a decree-law or regulation, addresses modern legal issues, such as laws on social insurance, labor relations, etc. Because of modern exigencies, the ruler was forced to legislate and not await the outcome of the meticulous practice of ijtihad by the ulema. The result is the coexistence of hundreds of nizams alongside fiqh as a subordinate system of law, supplementing the fiqh so that the law could keep abreast of modern developments.[157] The nizam is drafted in such a way that the ulema are extensively consulted with in order to avoid any possible imputation of disregard; the ulema also possess a veto power. It is unquestionable that decree laws are subordinate in status to fiqh.

---

[155] VOGEL, *supra* note 5, at 173–74.
[156] *Id.* at 174.
[157] *Id.* at 175.

Fiqh is also the residual law, filling gaps in the quite rudimentary nizams. Fiqh continues to govern the great bulk of cases, covering personal status, civil contract, tort, property, agency, and nearly all crimes apart from those that specifically enforce the nizams.[158]

The sharia courts generally refuse to enforce the nizams. The sharia court judge will exercise his own discretion when confronted with a case arising under a nizam. If the judge deems that the case is governed by fiqh, then the nizam will be ignored and the case adjudicated according to the fiqh. If the case is deemed by the judge as a proper exercise of siyasah shar'iyya, then he will refer it on to an administrative entity to enforce. The Supreme Judicial Council views nizams as solely addressing penalties or purely administrative matters. If the subject matter of the nizam goes beyond this scope, the court will ignore the nizam and apply the fiqh.[159]

There would appear to be a competition between the exclusive authority of the king to define jurisdictions and to create tribunals and the perception by the ulema of their adjudicatory authority. The government has attempted on several occasions to unify the court system. There have been binding decrees including the Basic Regulation of 1992. A basic precondition for this unification has been that the courts accept and apply the nizams. The ulema rejected this precondition, so the unification has not yet occurred.[160] But, as noted earlier in this chapter, a current and extensive judicial re-organization project has been recently sponsored by King Abdullah.

Since, as mentioned above, the courts are reluctant to exercise a legislative function and decline to exercise broad rulemaking in their practice of ijtihad, their wholesale dismissal of the implementation of the nizams serves to perpetuate the present vacuum of law, substantive and procedural, on many matters relating to modern societal conditions in the kingdom. If the courts were indeed serious about deciding the nizam cases by fiqh, then they would have to engage in a serious practice of ijtihad to draft fiqh rules to replace the nizams, which is clearly not occurring.[161] Or, perhaps, the courts seriously believe that this can be accomplished by ijtihad on a case-by-case basis. This is certainly not an expedient solution by any stretch of the imagination.

The relationship of the ulema and the ruler is complementary and coexistent. But there is an element of competition between them in the way in which doctrines are initially shaped and implemented. Looked at positively, however, enforcement of nizams through siyasah tribunals offers a convenient alternative to the courts when faced with certain

---

[158] *Id.* at 175.
[159] *Id.* at 175–76.
[160] *Id.* at 176.
[161] *Id.* at 177.

real-world deficiencies in their doctrines or practices. Although the ruler's intrusion into a fiqh domain may be deplored on one level by the ulema, it simultaneously relieves them of any necessity to dilute their fiqh ideal.[162] It is in many ways a complementary coexistence born of necessity. The fiqh-siyasah interaction is a long and very complicated discussion that goes well beyond the parameters of this discussion and is extensively treated by many scholars, including the excellent 2000 treatise by Frank E. Vogel referred to throughout the chapter[163].

A striking development in the complex history of Islamic jurisprudence is that, even during the caliphate's golden era in the third to eighth centuries, "the scholars of fiqh had developed an extensive and practicable law that persuasively claimed divine authority, and won for their product . . . an active, central, and secure place in the legal system of an empire."[164] Fiqh had already by this point secured the central role of the ulema in both adjudication and legislation as a restraint on the power of rulers, which role continues today in Saudi Arabia. Throughout the complex history of Islamic jurisprudence there is the continuing theme of the competition and cooperation, the contradiction and complementarity, opposition and interdependence between the rulers and the ulema.[165] Over time, there were increasing concessions by the ulema to the accommodation of the ruler and siyasah principles. Ibn Taymiyya was the most famous proponent of siyasah theory and he explicitly proposed a broad cooperation (*ta'awun*) between rulers and ulema. It was Ibn Taymiyya's basic precept that siyasah and fiqh must agree and that true siyasah is part of the sharia; in this way, Ibn Taymiyya conceded validity to any action of a ruler meeting the conditions of siyasah shar'iyya and which action advances the general welfare. The implementation of Ibn Taymiyya's precepts occurred with the emergence of a Wahhabi regime (not substantially influenced by western ideas) in Arabia in the twelfth through eighteenth centuries. Although the Wahhabis accepted Ibn Taymiyya's principle of cooperation between ulema and ruler in their common objective to uphold the sharia, there is also the coexistent and fundamental principle or norm of obedience to the ruler, even if he acts wrongly, so long as he does not issue a ruling that would entail disobedience to the sharia.[166]

Nevertheless, a clear pattern can be seen. The relationship between ulema and ruler is one of explicit competition, with the ulema and the ruler dividing jurisdictions for adjudicating and legislating between themselves. The ulema, nevertheless, retain the upper hand.[167] The

---

[162] *Id.* at 178.
[163] VOGEL, *supra* note 5.
[164] *Id.* at 190.
[165] *Id.* at chs. 7 and 8.
[166] *Id.* at 209.
[167] *Id.* at 211.

secularization of Middle Eastern societies has done little to change this in Saudi Arabia. Secularism (*'alamaniyya, dunyawiyya*), meaning something worldly or temporal, was introduced into the Muslim world along with such terms as "modernity" and "westernization" within the context of colonialism secularism, deriving as it does from the Christian church and the powers exercised by the Pope and the Vatican, and found an "uneasy locale in the Islamic tradition."[168] The clear separation of church and state as a cornerstone of secularism does not fit in exactly with the principles of Islamic governance. There is instead a quest for an integration of religion and politics in Islam, proceeding from the concept of unity (*tawhid*) meaning that morality is not just a personal matter, but should also actively guide law and government policy.[169] The Islamic doctrine of siyasah shar'iayyah is cognizant of the need for legislation or decision-making on matters not covered by established sharia, belonging to the discretionary authority of the legitimate ruler. Decrees that do not conflict with the principles of Islam and exemplify good governance fall within the scope of this doctrine. Against this background and in contrast to numerous other Muslim states, Saudi Arabia, never colonized at its core, actively maintains to this day a bipolar fiqh and siyasah system.[170] The ulema have unquestionably maintained a dominant role in the Saudi legal system, and the interactions between ulema and ruler have been quite complex,[171] reflecting the fact that the two partners are mutually dependent. Despite the contests between the two major Saudi constitutional branches—that is, the ulema and the king—in areas of adjudication and legislation, there is an understood need by both for mutual cohesion and support.[172]

> [T]he biggest destabilizing factor in the modern Saudi legal system is a widely perceived need for drastic reforms—presumed to be possible only by siyasah methods—in spheres of law that have traditionally belonged to the 'ulama and the fiqh. That the 'ulama system is under threat cannot be denied, since over the last century and a half similar transformations under a siyasah banner laid low nearly every other Islamic legal system in the region.[173]

4.2 Contests in Areas of Adjudication

The history of commercial jurisdiction in Saudi Arabia is marked by the divide between fiqh and siyasah adjudication. Since the ulema

---

[168] KAMALI, *supra* note 8, at 262–63.

[169] *Id.* at 263.

[170] VOGEL, *supra* note 5, at 220.

[171] *Id.* at 220–21.

[172] *Id.* at 280.

[173] *Id.* at 280.

view commercial law as within the sole purview of fiqh, the demands of modern Saudi commerce for the establishment of a commerce law court have been thwarted to the present day. In brief summary, King 'Abd al-Aziz instituted a commercial court for the Hijaz, a holdover from an Ottoman Empire commercial tribunal, in 1926. In 1931, as Hizari administration was being reorganized, the king issued a new Commercial Court Regulation establishing commercial laws and a new commercial court to apply them. The court had the jurisdiction to enforce various regulations regarding the conduct of commerce within the kingdom and resolve disputes of a commercial nature.[174] This court was abolished, however, in 1955 and the sharia courts assumed the jurisdiction for the entire country. It is a matter of speculation whether the Najdi ulema, for whom the idea of a jurisdiction traditionally within fiqh being handled by a court of merchants would presumably be repugnant, forced the abolition of this court. The specialized commercial tribunals were, however, reorganized as three Commissions for the Settlement of Commercial Disputes in Riyadh, Dammam, and Jidda. Although the original composition of these commissions was that of specialists or experts in modern commercial law, this later devolved to qadis of the regular sharia court cadre. It was not long before the commissions came under the control of sharia court qadis. The only difference between the commissions and the sharia courts was that the former were prepared to apply the relevant nizams according to their terms while the sharia courts would not.[175] After a long (and intolerable) impasse had been reached over the attempts by the executive branch (ruler) to introduce urgent reforms desperately needed by Saudi businessmen and the equivocation and unwillingness of the ulema to apply siyasah legislation, the government and the ulema finally agreed in 1987 to abolish the commissions and to temporarily transfer the commercial cases to the Board of Grievances, a court with undeniable sharia legitimacy.[176] The commercial jurisdiction remains today with the Board of Grievances. As noted by Vogel and based upon his review of numerous (and unpublished) decisions of the Board's commercial circuit, commercial jurisprudence is clearly marked in Saudi Arabia by a conservative fiqh orientation that reflects the sharia education of the judges:

> No doubt the board is seriously engaged in the demanding and time-consuming task of creating from Hanbali fiqh traditions a workable commercial law for the Kingdom. But this also means that whenever the expectations of international commerce conflict with fixed standards of the old Hanbali law, it is the

---

[174] *Id.* at 300–02.

[175] *Id.* at 302–03.

[176] *Id.* at 304.

former that gives way. Examples include decisions categorically denying claims for lost profits, since these offend rules against usury ("*riba*") and uncertainty ("*gharar*") in contract, and the board's rejection of jurisdiction of claims in any way involving banks, even their shares, since banks deal in unlawful interest ("*riba*"). Such positions mark Saudi commercial jurisprudence as considerably more conservative than the jurisprudence of even surrounding Gulf countries, not to mention more westernized systems like those of Egypt.[177]

The siyasah methods and other concepts introduced by various Muslim rulers to introduce a type of western-style modernity, particularly with respect to commercial transactions, has to date been unable to shift the practice of adjudication in Saudi Arabia away from the almost exclusive control of the fiqh and the ulema. Although there is a general tendency in various Muslim countries to return to their heritage, Saudi Arabia nevertheless stands alone in the strict Islamic traditionalism of its court practices.[178]

The problems that are thereby created are numerous, not the least being the uncertainty of both Saudi and foreign businessmen as to what commercial law will be applied to any potential commercial dispute other than the tried-and-true axiom of (1) Hanbali texts and (2) modern fiqh scholarship. The concatenation of problems that is normally recited in relation to modern Saudi commercial practice is as follows: "unpredictability of decisions; obscure if not occult doctrine; pressure to settle cases (forestalling the emergence of new jurisprudence); and dissonance between many Saudi commercial law norms and those prevailing nearly everywhere else."[179]

In the area of banking, the strength of ulema opposition to non-fiqh jurisdictions is evident from developments since 1987. Both the sharia courts and the commercial tribunals have refused to enforce interest on bank loans since interest is viewed as falling within usury (riba) and is clearly prohibited by the Koran. In light of the banks' extralegal status and the adamant refusal of the ulema to even consider any pragmatic compromise, the government dispensed with seeking a judicial solution and came up with an administrative solution, avoiding the courts entirely. The result was the creation by the king of a committee within the central bank (SAMA), which is staffed by legal experts and which assumes jurisdiction of all disputes to which a bank is a party. Pursuant to Royal Order No. 729/M, it was decreed that the interest issue would be determined in accordance with the terms of

---

[177] *Id.* at 305.
[178] *Id.* at 308.
[179] *Id.* at 306.

the parties' agreement.[180] The committee is in fact only an agent to encourage the parties to reach a settlement, without the authority to actually issue a judgment. The committee can resort to the imposition of penalties on a party unreasonably resisting a settlement suggestion; its enforcement arm is the same as any other court judgment, a command implemented by a letter of the Minister of the Interior. But a party rejecting a settlement compromise and willing to be subjected to the administrative penalties could also resort to a sharia court, and the sharia court could, if it chose to, exercise de novo jurisdiction, perhaps even finding favorably for the applicant. As noted by Vogel, this "shows how cramped and artificial the government's options are for legal and judicial reform in the face of a firm principle of sharia law."[181]

4.2 Contests in Areas of Legislation

The question remaining in this section is the likelihood of a codification of the laws as applied by the sharia courts in Saudi Arabia in the future. There are certain areas that have been ceded by the ulema to the ruler for regulation by siyasah: government administration and organization, government lands, and even certain criminal penalties. All other subject areas are considered to be subject by fiqh. The controversy over codification is not new and has been a subject of debate since 1926. Codification has its roots in western legal models and covers all of the traditional categories of the Islamic legal system. The basic contest between ulema and the ruler is fundamentally regarding who shall control the legislation and adjudication of issues traditionally falling under the doctrine of fiqh.

When one normally thinks of a codification (*taqnin*), the continental civil law system often comes to mind. But a codification in the Saudi context would have to possess the following elements: (1) it must be modern and comprehensive, covering subject matter normally reserved for fiqh; (2) it would be drafted by the normal nizam legislator with informal advice from the ulema; (3) it would be promulgated by a decree of the king; and (4) it would have a binding effect on all parties, including the qadis.[182] A codification could also be like the Restatement of Laws in the United States, prepared by scholars but having no binding legal effect. If the Senior Ulema could compile such a restatement of the rules of fiqh and publish the results, it would carry the weight of an authoritative fatwa. Historically, there are in fact late fiqh works, entitled Qawanin, which offer simplified and concise résumés of fiqh rules that are comparable to modern codes and that

---

[180] *Id.* at 307–08.
[181] *Id.* at 307.
[182] *Id.* at 311.

function as convenient handbooks, but not as binding codes of law. But there is a paucity of historical precedent for codification in Saudi Arabia, perhaps belying the success of the ulema in their exercise of freedom of ijtihad. The practice of unrestricted ijtihad is critical to the role of the qadi, and the perspective of the qadi in Saudi Arabia is relatively dominant. The scholar Ibn Taymiyya has been notable in his uncompromising position protecting the freedom of ijtihad (for qadis or muftis alike) from rulers.[183]

It comes down to the critical issue of whether the ruler has the power to dictate the law his qadis shall apply, or the concept of compulsion (*ilzam*). One Deputy Minister of Justice and former qadi, Shaykh Abu Zayd, has written a book opposing codification and the binding of a qadi to a particular decision.[184] It has been a frequent argument against codification that it would reduce the qadis to the status of minor functionaries, mere "machines."[185] It has been further argued that this would deprive qadis of freedom in their practice of ijtihad and replace it with rigidity. Frank E. Vogel quotes a fatwa of the Board of Senior Ulema (Fatwa No. 8) rejecting the idea of codification as follows:

> Fatwa No. 8 first acknowledges briefly that problems do exist with the judiciary needing a solution, but it rejects the notion that codification affords a solution. Its primary reason is that sharia does not permit the state to bind qadis to a particular school or view: But the fatwa also gives arguments from utility. Codification would alienate judges from the sharia, Qur'an, and Sunna. It could lead to adoption of positive, man-made laws, as in other Islamic countries.... As solutions for the defects of the judiciary, the fatwa recommends three chief measures: improving the quality of the judiciary, through better selection and training; concentrating the country's courts in the major cities, which would also ease recruitment; and forming a new committee of 'ulama to study and report on issues the judges find difficult or which are novel.[186]

Opponents of this perspective argue firstly that the ruler is the supreme qadi and that the ruler could consult with the learned, but was never bound by their opinion.[187] Historically, rulers have imposed legislation only in those legal matters not covered by the fiqd, either

---

[183] *Id.* at 335.

[184] SHAYKH ABU ZAYD, AL-TAQNIN WA-AL-ILZAM, quoted in VOGEL, *supra* note 5, at 337.

[185] *Id.* at 337.

[186] *Id.* at 338.

[187] *Id.* at 339.

because of the lack of revealed texts or as a result of the lack of ulema interest, power, or opportunity.[188] Another argument is that all Muslims owe a duty of obedience and loyalty to their ruler; however, it is also a clear rule that a ruler is prohibited from binding a qadi to adherence of a particular school of law. Thirdly, siyasah shar'iyya gives legitimacy to any action of a ruler not otherwise dictated by the sharia. But, then, it can be countered that siyasah shar'iyya confers only legitimacy on the making of laws in areas where it complements or supplements the fiqh and its methods, not in areas where it would compete with them. Replacing ijtihad with siyasah as the main method of determining qadi law in Saudi Arabia would represent a major shift to a secularization of the law, since the revealed sources would function not as the source of the laws and their adjudication, but solely as a check of the laws and their adjudication, comparable to the largely secular states of Egypt and Pakistan.[189] The fourth and most feasible argument for codification is based upon the concept of *maslaha*, or utility. Utility is the basis for lawmaking under siyasah shar'iyya and is also perceived as a source of law within fiqh. And there are indeed persuasive arguments for codification based on utility propounded by Saudi ulema themselves. A former member of the Saudi supreme judicial authority has written:

> [Codification] is appropriate to follow in this age particularly, ... New transactions now appear in their various types, in accordance with the necessities of practical life in the modern age. The level of the judiciary is in general weaker than before. [Codification] distances qadis from suspicious and doubtful circumstances, and from proclivities towards desires and bias in cases and decisions. This is an obvious maslaha, which necessity demands as a guarantee to secure justice, and to better dispel suspicion and satisfy litigants . . .[190]

It has been argued by other proponents of codification on the grounds of utility that it would make the qadis more efficient without foreclosing the exercise of ijtihad: "codes would inform the people of the laws applying to them, thereby reducing litigation and increasing their satisfaction with judgments."[191] Another scholar has argued that codification serves the argument of maslaha or utility insofar as it will prevent a further influx of western laws into the Arabian Peninsula."[192]

---

[188] *Id.*

[189] *Id.* at 342.

[190] Fatwa of 'Umar bin 'Abd al-Aziz al-Mutrak, quoted in Vogel, *supra* note 5, at 348.

[191] Prof. 'Atwa quoted in Vogel, *id.* at 349.

[192] Muhammad Abu Zahra, quoted in Vogel, *id.* at 349–50.

The former President of the Board of Grievances, Shaykh Muhammad Ibn Jubayr, expressed the view to Frank E. Vogel that he would
favor a limited codification of laws, preferring the term "compilation"
(*tadwin*) of laws. Such a compilation could be prepared by a group of
ulema from the various schools and could have a binding and precedential effect.[193]

Although there have been influential and well-respected voices
recommending some form of model code or binding legislation in fiqh
matters, the situation remains ambiguous, especially in light of the
degree of angst and consternation this subject raises in certain judicial
quarters. Perhaps it would be a worthwhile exercise to compare the
legal method and system afforded by the common law system as practiced in the United States with the fiqh as practiced in Saudi Arabia.

Will Saudi Arabia's future legislative needs be resolved in the same
way as in the common law system of the United States—that is, by ad
hoc interstitial legislation as set against the common law background,
enhanced as it would be by an independent and well-respected judiciary? Despite the strong historical influence of French civil law in the
Arab world (including Saudi Arabia), the common law system offers
closer analogies to the development of fiqh as practiced in Saudi Arabia than the civil law system. And in spite of the "angst" of the ulema
when faced with the prospect of a widespread codification of the laws,
there remains a complementary legislative process as shared between
ruler and the ulema due in large part to the highly pragmatic nature
of the Hanbali school in worldly matters (*mu'amalat*); the ruler always
retains the ability to choose the most advantageous view among differing opinions of the ulema.[194]

The situation is clearly in flux and there are at present no easy
answers. Despite the opposition of the ulema to any erosion of their
freedom of ijtihad, the growing pressures for unification and reconciliation are there, as well as for moderation and balance (*wasatiyyah*),
which is a major theme of the Koran and an important dimension of
the Saudi worldview. Heritage (*turath*) will not be dismissed on the
argumentation that it is irrelevant to modern life, especially a great
legal tradition that generations of jurists of the past have fashioned
through arduous effort.[195] If approached with the precepts of moderation and balance, if the elite ulema are provided a dominant place in
the drafting of a code, the codification result would certainly constitute a net gain for the modern Saudi society, the ulema, and the fiqh.

---

[193] *Id.* at 350–51.

[194] *Id.* at 355.

[195] WEISS, *supra* note 34, at 190.

5. Brief Description of Sharia-Compliant Financing Structures; Islamic Economic Thought

5.1 Islamic Finance

"Islamic finance" refers to the network of financial institutions and commercial activities that conform to several core sharia principles:

a. prohibiting the receipt and payment of interest (*riba*)—the return of an investment should be linked to profits actually generated

b. avoiding uncertainty—e.g., insurance, indemnities, granting an option to purchase an asset (*Gharar*)

c. discouraging speculative behavior—e.g., speculation, gambling, games of chance (*Maisir*)

d. advocating risk sharing—investors should earn returns by sharing profits and assuming the risk of any loss (*Sharik*)

e. prohibiting haraam activities—e.g., activities that are forbidden under sharia law, such as financial investments in alcohol, pork-related activities, tobacco, gambling, and pornography (*haraam/hallal*)

f. maintaining the sanctity of contracts ('*aqd*)

5.2 Sharia Scholars and Boards

5.2.1 The Scholars

There are a small number of scholars specializing in the application of sharia finance, who play a significant role in the offshore structures to date. There is also a wide range of views and considerable scope for uncertainty. Typically, a small number of people have had a significant role on the offshore structures to date. These include:

- Sheikh Taqi Usmani (Pakistan)
- Sheikh Nizam Yaquby (Bahrain)
- Sheikh Hussain Hassan (Dubai)
- Dr. Mohammed Ali Elgari (Saudi Arabia)
- Dr. Abus Sattar Abu Ghuddah (Syrian, based in Saudi Arabia)
- Dr. Muhammad Imran Ashraf Usmani (Pakistan)
- Dr. Mohd Daud Bakar (Malaysia) Sheikh
- Yusuf Talal De Lorenzo (United States)

5.2.2 Role of Scholars

a. Islamic institutions place reliance on the opinions of scholars (fatwa) in determining whether transactions are in compliance with sharia.

b. Weight is given to the identity of the scholars.

    c. At the end of a transaction, the scholar/board will issue a fatwa confirming that the transactions adhere to Islamic principles.

    d. This fatwa may be disclosed.

5.2.3 Fatwa

    a. One, some, or all parties to a transaction may be bound by the fatwa.

    b. Not all aspects of the transaction necessarily have to be covered by the fatwa.

    c. There is no precedent system for fatwas.

5.2.4 Appointing and Dealing with Scholars

    a. Scholars are employed on a transaction-by-transaction basis or through the establishment of a board.

    b. They may be based predominantly in the Middle East and Pakistan.

    c. They are typically commercially astute (often with an educational background in Western economics or finance) and have exposure to issues through acting on several sharia boards for various banks.

    d. They are involved in settling the term sheet and in reviewing the penultimate draft of documents.

    e. Typically, the primary contact with them is through telephone, fax, and e-mail, but meetings can also be required.

    f. They can be very busy and getting their attention can be difficult.

5.3 Sharia Law vs National Law

5.3.1 Sharia Board

    a. The establishment of a board can provide greater comfort to Islamic investors or counterparties.

    b. It may require a significant segregation of activities.

    c. General policies can be established, and there is an educational role to be played by the scholars.

    d. Typically three scholars will be on retainer.

5.3.2 Enforceability

    a. Documents are usually drafted to be governed by either English or New York law.

    b. Questions of enforceability of obligations are dealt with according to the applicable national law.

    c. With certain exceptions (Saudi Arabia, Iran, and Sudan), sharia law is not national law.

    d. As sharia law is not the governing law of the documentation, being bound by sharia is essentially elective.

e. Subsequent ruling by scholars that a transaction does not comply with sharia law will not affect its enforceability under the applicable national law.

f. The case Shamil Bank of Bahrain EC v Beximco Pharmaceuticals Ltd., [2004] EWCA (Civ) 19; [2004] 1 W.L.R. 1784, affirms that English courts will not, in the absence of very precise guidelines set out in the relevant contract, interpret sharia law.

g. It is for each party to satisfy itself that a transaction is compliant with sharia law.

5.4 A Rapidly Expanding Industry

Islamic finance is a rapidly expanding market and is one of the fastest growing areas of international finance, having developed substantially over the last two decades. Many banks (e.g., Deusche Bank) are establishing Islamic-compliant subsidiaries in the Middle East. This illustrates a long-term investment in this region. In August 2007, a new pan-Arab region index of sharia compliant stock was launched by Standard & Poor's.

The industry has increasingly international appeal (significant recent development in traditionally non-core markets including the UK, Turkey, Egypt, Pakistan, Indonesia, Morocco, and Tunisia).

UK government support—HM Treasury's Islamic Finance Experts Group was established in April 2007 to advise the government on supporting the development of Islamic finance in the UK.

5.4.1 The Vital Statistics

The Islamic finance industry is expected to easily become a US$1 trillion industry in the next decade (Global Investment House):

a. Industry growth estimates predict 15 to 25 percent annual growth over the next five years.

b. The global sukuk market is valued at US$70 billion (£35.4 billion) and is expected to top the US$160 billion (£81.0 billion) mark by the end of the decade (Standard & Poor's).

c. There are an estimated 300 Islamic financial institutions holding US$500 billion (£253.2 billion) of assets (FSA) and the industry has been growing at around 10 percent per year for the last decade.

d. Balance sheets of Islamic banks grew by 40 percent in 2007 ("Euromoney").

e. Middle Eastern investors estimated US$1,200 billion (£597.51 billion) of investment in international assets in recent years (HSBC).

f. Middle East region expected to earn US$20,000 billion (£9.96 billion) of oil income in coming years, and as much as a third of this may be invested in the Islamic finance sphere (Financial Times/KPMG).

5.5 Islamic Hedging and Risk Management

By using and embedding traditional sales and investment contracts recognized by sharia law, one can mimic the cash flows under conventional financing and risk management products.

5.6 Murabaha—Cost-Plus Financing

An example of murabaha is when a buyer purchasing items from a financier for immediate delivery at a specified profit margin with the purchase price payable to the financier at a later date (deferred purchase price). There are two types of murabaha: equipment and commodity.

5.6.1 Commodity Murabaha

a. Commodity murabaha is essentially a treasury transaction whereby the bank buys commodities for its own account sells them to the company an credit terms and then immediately resells them into the market as an agent for the company for cash. The company ends up with the cash and retains the obligation to satisfy the purchase price payment obligation in accordance with the credit terms. It's quite close to a loan on interest, but is an important way of providing liquidity facilities on an "Islamic" basis.

b. Financier buys Assets from Seller for US$ x.

c. Financier sells Assets to Buyer for US$ (x+y) (y being the financier's pre-agreed profit portion).

d. Buyer settles price at end of an agreed period in one lump sum or by a series of deferred installments (Bei' Bithaman ajil).

e. Popular method of short-term finance.

f. Can be structured as an investment or a borrowing.

g. Must be asset based, so there is exposure to risks of ownership of the assets.

h. Typically based around LME-traded metals such as platinum.

i. Requires arrangements with a commodity broker.

j. Often set up as a master agreement with trades under it from time to time.

5.6.2 Assets

a. The assets must be in existence and under the ownership and in the physical or constructive possession of the seller and the financier at the time of contracting.

b. The financier must take title to the assets.

c. The financier maintains ownership of the assets until delivery to the buyer and bears all the costs and risks of ownership until delivery.

5.6.3 Profits

a. Profit margin may be agreed as a percentage of cost or as a fixed amount.
b. The buyer and financier must pre-agree and specify the profit margin.
c. Profit margin cannot be a reward for the use of the financier's money.
d. If the financier avoids taking any risk and does not perform any service other than providing money for the transaction, the deal becomes akin to charging interest.

5.6.4 Equipment Murabaha

a. real/synthetic
b. often the company will act as the "agent" for the bank, since the bank will not know exactly what kind of equipment will suit the company's needs

Figure 42.1: Murabaha Cost-Plus Financing (Equipment Murahaba)

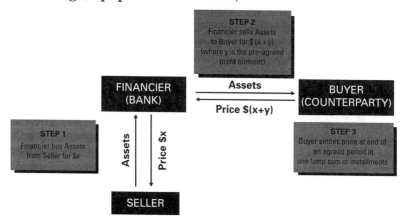

5.6.6 Commodity Murabaha Drafting Related Issues

a. It will be necessary to secure sharia approval for the master agreement.
b. "Default interest" is forbidden; "delayed payments," "compensating for loss" may be acceptable.
c. The choice of governing law is an important issue.
d. There is an intra-day commodity risk, but these trades are often done on an instant "book entry only" basis.

e.   There may be tax issues relating to agency.
Please refer to Appendix 42.1 for details.

5.7 What are Sharia-Compliant (Hallal) Shares?

a.   Easy answer: Shares are listed on the DJIMI (Dow Jones Islamic Markets Index).
b.   One example of how the DJIMI categorizes a share as being "non haraam" employs specific screens.
  i.   Industry Screen (Sin Screen)—excludes shares in companies that deal in haraam activities, e.g., gambling, insurance, casinos, and pornography
  ii.   Debt Equity Screen—excludes shares in companies whose Total Debt comprises more than 33 percent or more of its balance sheet
c.   There are many other types of screens that organizations use to categorize whether shares are haraam or hallal.

5.8 Wa'ad

5.8.1 Introduction:
a.   Wa'ad literally means "promise."
b.   It can be regarded as a unilateral undertaking by one party to do or not to do certain actions in the future.
c.   It does not bind anyone but the promisor.
d.   This can be contrasted with a bilateral contract (aqd), which binds both parties to the contract.
e.   Use of English law, document executed as a deed: lack of consideration.
f.   Binding nature and enforceability is a subject of debate amongst scholars.
For example, see Table 42.1 for a sample of views.

5.8.2 Structure Diagram— FX Put Option
In the event the customer does not deliver a cancellation notice with respect to a Wa'ad, the cash flows will be as follows:

Figure 42.2

Bank (Seller)

Purchase price in currency 2
(Payable on Effective Date)

Specified amount of currency 1
(Payable on Effective Date)

Non-refundable fee
(Payable on Trade Date)

Customer (Buyer)

Table 42.1

Group A	Imam Abu Hanifah, Imam Al-Shafai', Imam Ahmad and some Maliki Jurists Fulfilling a promise is noble but it is neither mandatory nor enforceable through a court of law.
Group B	Samurah b. Jundub, Umar b. Abdul Aziz, Hasan Al-Basri, Said b. al-Ashwa', Ishaq b. Rahwaih, Imam Al- Bukhari and some Maliki Jurists Fulfilling a promise is mandatory and the promisor is under a moral as well as a legal obligation to honor his promise.
Group C	Some Maliki Jurists, Islamic Fiqh Academy (IFA) Promise is not binding under normal circumstances but becomes binding where the promisor has caused the promisee to incur certain expenses or undertake work or any form of liability.

Please refer to Appendix 42.2 for details on the structure of Double Wa'ad.

5.9 ISDA/IIFM Master Agreement

5.9.1 Introduction
There has been a joint initiative between the International Swaps and Derivatives Association (ISDA) and the International Islamic Financial Market (IIFM) to produce a master agreement under which sharia-compliant hedging transactions can be documented.

Based on ISDA's 2002 Master Agreement, the ISDA/IIFM master agreement contains necessary amendments made for sharia compliance.

5.9.2 Representations
This section sets forth the types of representations that should be in the master agreement.

- Each party is required to represent that it has satisfied itself as to the sharia compliance of the agreement and of each transaction entered into under it.
- A party cannot rely on the other party or on any documents (including a fatwa) prepared by, on behalf of or at the request of the other Party when determining the sharia compliance of the agreement or a transaction.
- If a principal enters into the agreement through an agent, there is a representation that clarifies that the obligations that arise are that of the principal and not the agent.

5.9.3 Events of Default; Termination Events

The events of default and termination events currently reflect those contained in the 2002 master agreement.

One of the issues that the ISDA and IIFM has been asked to consider is with respect to the consequences of the agreement or a transaction ceasing to be sharia-compliant. One of the possible avenues could be to have a termination event analogous to illegality.

5.9.4 Early Termination; Close-Out Netting

The calculation of a close-out amount is considered to be a key issue. Concerns have been raised with respect to the amount that can be claimed on early termination where the relevant transaction is a "non-concluded" one. Sharia principles see losses related to future sales and purchases as a purely economic loss and one that may not be taken into account.

A current proposal under consideration is for a separate undertaking (a musawama) to be given by each party to effect a sale and purchase with respect to "non-concluded" transactions upon the occurrence of an early termination date.

Pursuant to these undertakings, the out of the money party would purchase a specified asset from the other at a specified price (equal to the market value of the specified asset plus the out of the money amount). Early termination would therefore crystallize an actual loss equal to the out of the money amount.

The total amount payable on early termination is the net balance of: (1) the net amount payable in respect of the early-terminated murabaha transactions, (2) the musawama price, and (3) any unpaid amounts.

5.9.5 Miscellaneous

(a) Compensation

The agreement should provide for interest on defaulted or deferred payments and compensation for defaulted or deferred deliveries. The ISDA/IIFM master agreement provides for compensation for both defaulted and deferred payments or deliveries.

The amount for such compensation should be as specified in the schedule. If payable by a defaulting party, such compensation is an amount to be agreed between the parties at the outset. If payable by a non-defaulting party and in all other cases, such compensation is an amount that the party from whom the payment is due will earn by investing such deferred amount in a sharia-compliant investment.

(b) No Interest Payable

In the event that it is determined that any interest is payable in connection with the agreement as a result of any arbitral or judicial award or by operation of law, each party waives its rights to such interest and if it actually receives it, agrees to donate such interest to a charitable organization.

5.10 Governing Law and Jurisdiction

Parties can elect in the master agreement for the agreement to be governed by English or New York law. There is no reference to sharia law in the governing law provision.

Parties can elect in the master agreement for disputes to be governed either by court proceedings or by arbitration. If arbitration is selected, the parties must agree which arbitral forum they wish to submit to.

6. Enforceablilty of Finance Documents Under Saudi Law

Legal opinions as to the enforceability of finance documents under Saudi law can make for grim reading for foreign lenders unaccustomed to divergent legal concepts under sharia. In light, however, of the inexorable growth of Islamic finance, the talent and creative prowess of those practitioners involved in this field of finance and the clear economic and social benefits to be gained for all parties, Islamic capital markets will continue to be an exciting and equally challenging sector of capital markets activity. Since legal issues, including but not limited to the fundamental concept of enforceability, will clearly influence the growth of Islamic capital markets in the future, particularly in Saudi Arabia, it shall be up to the transactional practitioners to think outside the box and create novel structural and transactional applications of the law that will be required to better integrate Islamic capital markets within more conventional capital markets.

For purposes of rendering legal opinions in connection with transactions related to Saudi Arabia, the following issues should be considered and addressed. These issues form a summary of the various areas of divergence between conventional western legal concepts and those established under Saudi Arabian law.

Under the sharia principles as applied in Saudi Arabia, the charging and payment of interest, which is deemed to constitute unlawful gain (riba), is prohibited. Accordingly, any provision in an agreement for the payment of, whether directly or indirectly, or the bearing of the cost of any amount based upon, calculated by reference to or otherwise related to, interest (including all monies deemed by Saudi Arabian adjudicatory bodies to be in the nature of interest) is not enforceable under Saudi Arabian law. The unenforceability of such a provision does not, however, affect the validity and enforceability of any obligation to pay principal. Apart from the prohibition pursuant to sharia principles as applied in Saudi Arabia, there are no civil or criminal penalties that attach or result from the charging or payment of interest. Accordingly, to the extent that any provision of a document relates to interest, it will not be enforceable in Saudi Arabia. Furthermore, no damages may be awarded for delays in the payment of any amount.

Prior to the establishment of the SAMA Committee under the authority of SAMA pursuant to Council of Ministers Resolution No. 729/8 dated 10/7/1407 H. (corresponding to March 10, 1987), in many cases Saudi Arabian adjudicatory bodies treated prior payments of interest as payments of principal and deducted such amounts from the amount of principal sought to be recovered by a lender. The SAMA Committee has, however, shown some willingness to treat prior payments of interest as not being on account of principal, with the result that such amounts are not deducted from the total amount claimed to be currently owed by a customer to its bank. In cases where a bank claims an undifferentiated lump sum that in fact may include a component of accrued interest, the SAMA Committee may, by way of compelling the parties to adhere to their agreement, allow recovery of the undifferentiated lump sum without dissecting it so as to refuse recovery of the accrued interest component.

In addition, the imposition of a fee or charge for a banking service that is not in accordance with the published SAMA tariffs for bank charges may not be enforceable before the SAMA Committee.

The enforceability of any financial documentation is limited by Saudi Arabian Law relating to bankruptcy, insolvency, reorganization, moratorium, liquidation, readjustment of debt, and other similar laws of general application relating to or affecting the enforcement of creditors' rights generally. In particular, Article 110 of the Commercial Court Regulations authorizes a Saudi Arabian court to declare a contract of a debtor void or ineffective in the event that such debtor has been already declared bankrupt by such court prior to the entry into such contract. There is, therefore, a real issue of the validity or enforceability of financial documents if a Saudi Arabian adjudicatory body were to void or otherwise cause such document, or any part thereof, to be void or ineffective pursuant to Article 110 of the Commercial Court Regulations (following a declaration of bankruptcy).

While affirmation of English or New York law as the law by which any financial document is to be governed and construed does not contravene any provision of published Saudi Arabian law, Saudi Arabian adjudicatory bodies would *not* be bound by any such acceptance or submission, and, if an action were instituted by or before such Saudi Arabian adjudicatory bodies, such Saudi Arabian adjudicatory bodies would apply Saudi Arabian law, which does not recognize the doctrine of conflict of laws.

In order to enforce in Saudi Arabia a judgment obtained in a court of a foreign jurisdiction, such judgment must be submitted to the Board of Grievances, which would have the discretion to enforce all of such judgment or such part thereof as is not inconsistent with Saudi Arabian law. In considering a request to enforce a foreign judgment, the Board of Grievances would ordinarily require the party seeking enforcement to demonstrate either: (i) that Saudi Arabia and the country in which such foreign judgment was issued are parties to a bilateral or multilateral agreement for the reciprocal enforcement of judgments or, in the absence of such agreement, that such country would recognize and enforce a Saudi Arabian judgment in the same manner as a domestic judgment; (ii) that the Saudi Arabian judgment debtor was accorded due process in the foreign proceeding, including due notice and the opportunity to appear in and defend such proceeding; (iii) that such foreign judgment is final in the country where it was issued; and (iv) that such foreign judgment contains nothing that contravenes the sharia or public policy of Saudi Arabia. The Board of Grievances may refuse to enforce a foreign judgment if a final judgment has been rendered by a Saudi Arabian adjudicatory body in proceedings between the same litigants and involving the same subject matter, or if an action was commenced before a Saudi Arabian adjudicatory body involving the same subject matter prior to the commencement of the proceeding in the country where the foreign judgment was issued and the decision of the Saudi Arabian adjudicatory body is still pending. In the event that such foreign judgment were not so enforced in whole or in part under the aforementioned procedures, the judgment creditor could proceed by way of a new proceeding instituted in Saudi Arabia before the appropriate Saudi Arabian adjudicatory body and the outcome of such proceeding would be governed in all respects by Saudi Arabian law and procedure.

With respect to the enforcement of foreign arbitral awards, Saudi Arabia acceded to the Convention on Recognition and Enforcement of Foreign Arbitral Awards, (the New York Convention of 1958) by Royal Decree No. M/11 dated 16/7/1414 H. (corresponding to December 29, 1993). Saudi Arabia invoked the reciprocity reservation of the New York Convention, which permits a signatory state to limit its recognition and enforcement of arbitral awards to awards rendered in the territory of another signatory state. In order to enforce in Saudi Arabia an arbitral award obtained in a foreign arbitral proceeding, such award must be submitted to the Board of Grievances. The Board of Grievances has not yet acted in connection with any request to enforce a foreign arbitral award, whether pursuant to the terms of the New York Convention or otherwise. By the terms of the New York Convention, signatory states are permitted to deny recognition and enforcement of arbitral awards on certain limited grounds. Under Article V.2 (b) of the New York Convention, Saudi Arabia may refuse to recognize and enforce an arbitral award if such recognition or enforcement would be contrary to the public policy of Saudi Arabia. In reliance on such public policy exception, the Board of Grievances would enforce only those provisions of the award that in the discretion of the Board of Grievances do not conflict with the sharia or public policy of Saudi Arabia.

Separately, if an action were instituted before Saudi Arabian adjudicatory bodies with respect to a finance document that includes a provision requiring the resolution of disputes through arbitration in the territory of a New York Convention signatory state, such adjudicatory bodies should, pursuant to Article II of the New York Convention, stay such action and refer the parties to arbitration, unless it finds that the said provision is null and void, inoperative, or incapable of being performed.

Arbitral awards within the Arab League would be subject to the Convention on Enforcement of Judgments and Awards, dated September 15, 1952, to the extent not superseded by the Arab Convention on Judicial Co-operation, approved by the Arab Council of Ministers and signed in Riyadh on April 6, 1983.

Saudi Arabian adjudicatory bodies have the discretion to decline or modify the enforcement of contractual or other obligations in strict accordance with the terms thereof where, in the opinion of such Saudi Arabian adjudicatory bodies, such strict enforcement would be inequitable under sharia principles.

Damages for lost profits, consequential damages, or other speculative damages are generally not awarded by Saudi Arabian adjudicatory bodies. Generally, only actual, direct, and proven damages are awarded.

Should any provision of any financial document be construed as an agreement or undertaking by the borrower to pay a penalty, as opposed to a genuine estimate of actual loss incurred, Saudi Arabian adjudicatory bodies would probably decline to enforce such provision.

Generally, previous decisions of Saudi Arabian adjudicatory bodies are not considered to establish a binding precedent for the decision of later cases and the principle of stare decisis is thus not accepted in Saudi Arabia. In addition, royal orders, royal decrees, ministerial decisions and resolutions, departmental circulars and other pronouncements of official bodies of Saudi Arabia having the force of law and the decisions of the various Saudi Arabian adjudicatory bodies are not generally or consistently indexed and collected in a central place or made publicly available.

A Saudi Arabian adjudicatory body would, in its own discretion, determine whether or not any provision of any financial document that may be invalid on account of illegality or otherwise may be severed from the other provisions thereof in order to preserve the other provisions. Provisions in any financial document requiring the parties to negotiate a replacement provision in the event that a provision thereof was determined to be invalid or otherwise ineffective is not enforceable before Saudi Arabian adjudicatory bodies.

The SAMA Committee is not a court and does not have the authority to issue judgments, but is authorized to review disputes between banks and their customers, and propose settlements, which settlements are generally accepted by the parties because the SAMA Committee may, among other things, recommend the imposition of administrative sanctions on the parties.

The enforceability of the following types of legal issues is completely unclear under Saudi Arabian law at the present time:

- the ability to enforce any rights or remedies with respect to violations or breaches of, or defaults under the documents that are determined by a Saudi Arabian adjudicatory body to be nonmaterial or with respect to which any relevant party had knowledge, or is deemed to have had, prior knowledge;
- the ability to exercise rights or remedies available insofar as such exercise of rights or taking of remedies involves the taking of any discretionary action, which action is unreasonable or is not taken in good faith and in a commercially reasonable manner;
- the exercise of any rights or remedies with respect to violations or breaches of, or defaults under the documents by any party that are determined by a Saudi Arabian adjudicatory body (including the SAMA Committee) to be the result of actions taken by any other party or any person acting on behalf of any such other party, where any such person was not entitled to take such actions pursuant to the terms of the documents or Saudi Arabian law;
- the enforcement of any provision of documents purporting to authorize any party to make conclusive determinations or to make determinations in its sole discretion or opinion;
- the availability of self-help or similar remedies;
- the enforceability of any provision in the documents with respect to indemnification, reimbursement, contribution or prepayment penalties, increased costs, or non-deductibility of taxes;
- the enforceability of any provision in the documents that purports to excuse any person from an obligation or liability to another person, or purports to impose any obligation or liability on any person, as a result or with respect to the negligence, fraud, or willful misconduct (whether by act or omission) of such person;
- the enforceability of any provision in the documents pursuant to which a party agrees to make payments without set-off or counterclaim or similar rights or remedies;
- the enforceability of any provision in the documents that purports to limit the liability of any person to another person;
- the enforceability of any provision in the documents that purports to limit the rights or remedies available to a party, or that purports to restrict the time at which such rights or remedies may be exercised;
- the enforceability of any provision that purports to restrict prepayment of outstanding obligations;

- the enforceability of any provision in the documents that purports to allow the enforcement of a mortgage or pledge by a mortgagee or pledgee, or purports to allow a mortgagee or pledgee to assume ownership or otherwise dispose of a mortgaged or pledged asset, other than through the institution of an action before the Board of Grievances;
- the enforceability of any provision in the documents that purports to allow a security agent to exercise, or purports to restrict the ability of a note holder to exercise, voting rights with respect to any pledged notes;
- the enforceability of any provision in the documents that purports to authorize a company, including the borrower, to withhold payment of dividends to any shareholder thereof;
- the enforceability of any provision in the documents whereby any party agrees to refrain from invoking the jurisdiction of Saudi Arabian adjudicatory bodies (including the SAMA Committee);
- the enforceability of any provision in any document precluding a party from rescinding any document in circumstances where the counterparties to such document breach its provisions;
- the enforceability of any provision in an agreement providing for the purchase of any loans;
- the enforceability of any amendment to the provisions of documents without the express approval of all parties thereto, including, without limitation, the accession of a new financier to an agreement by way of novation where the facility agent executes the transfer certificate on behalf of the borrower;
- the enforceability of a provision in an agreement providing for the continuation of any security notwithstanding the satisfaction of the secured obligations or the release or discharge of such secured obligations (by operation of law or otherwise);
- the enforceability of any provision in a document that purports to constitute a waiver of a right (including a defense to a claim) by a party prior to the time such right has actually accrued. It should be noted that a failure to exercise a right may operate as a waiver notwithstanding any contractual provision to the contrary; or
- the ability of any party to enforce any agreement to which it is not a signatory or to be bound to perform obligations under an agreement to which it is not a signatory.

Specific performance, injunctive relief, and declaratory interpretations and remedies are generally unavailable as judicial or adjudicative remedies in Saudi Arabia, and in any event such interpretations and remedies are discretionary in Saudi Arabian adjudicatory bodies.

Under sharia principles as applied in Saudi Arabia, contracts of insurance, other than certain types of cooperative insurance purported to be structured in accordance with Islamic principles (*takakul*), may be considered to be in violation of the prohibitions against speculative and unearned gain. Provisions relating to insurance that do not reflect Islamic principles may be treated as void or unenforceable by Saudi Arabian adjudicatory bodies.

Accordingly, the obligation of the borrower to arrange for and maintain certain insurances under circumstances as set forth in an amended facilities agreement may not be enforceable under Saudi Arabian law. Furthermore, a Saudi Arabian adjudicatory body may refuse to recognize the failure of the borrower to obtain and maintain insurances as an event of default under the terms of an amended facilities agreement.

Article 20 of the Control of Co-operative Insurance Companies Regulations issued pursuant to Royal Decree No. M/32 dated 2/6/1424 H. (corresponding to July 31, 2003) (the "Co-operative Insurance Regulations"), provides that the Council of Ministers shall set up a three-member committee with the following jurisdiction:

i.   to settle disputes that arise between insurance companies and their clients;
ii. to settle disputes between insurance companies and third parties where insurers have become subrogated to the rights of the policyholders; and
iii. to adjudicate violations of directions pertinent to the control and supervision of licensed insurance and reinsurance companies and insurance professionals.

The first such Insurance Disputes Committee (IDC) was established by a Council of Ministers resolution dated April 25, 2005. The IDC's decisions may be appealed to the Saudi Arabian Board of Grievances. Moreover, Article 22 of the Co-operative Insurance Regulations provides that the Board of Grievances has jurisdiction in the following instances:

i.   disputes between, or among, insurance and reinsurance companies;
ii. actions with respect to the violations of the Co-operative Insurance Regulations and imposition of the sanctions stipulated in Article 21 thereof; and
iii. preliminary examination of actions where the Saudi Arabian Monetary Agency or the IDC intends to order imprisonment.

The ability of parties to exercise remedies under or in relation to a document upon the occurrence of an event of default, that does not constitute a payment event of default is uncertain under Saudi Arabian Law. It is possible that a failure to pay any amount of interest will not be recognized as a default. Further, the ability to exercise remedies is subject to sharia principles relating to the specific item of collateral at issue, including sharia requirements that such collateral be in existence, in the case of any mortgage, pledge, or assignment by way of security, and, in the case of any mortgage or pledge, be capable of being delivered to the mortgagee or pledgee.

Evidence of a transaction entered into orally, by facsimile, or by electronic messaging system, may not be admissible before a Saudi Arabian adjudicatory body, unless:

i.   the relevant party's claim is supported by a document signed by the other party;

ii. the relevant party's claim is made under oath and is supported by the testimony of an independent adult male Muslim witness; or

iii. the relevant party's claim is supported by the testimony of two independent adult female Muslim witnesses.

For this reason, it is recommended that each transaction be evidenced by confirmation signed by the parties thereto and/or witnessed.

Under Saudi Arabian law, no reliance may be placed on any notice given by facsimile, telex, or bank wire, or given electronically. Notices sent pursuant to the finance documents would not be effective unless:

i.   such notices are evidenced by the signed acknowledgment of the receiving party; or

ii. the claim of delivery is made under oath and is supported by the testimony of an independent adult male Muslim witness; or

iii. the claim of delivery is supported by the testimony of two independent adult female Muslim witnesses.

In order to be admissible in evidence in a proceeding before a Saudi Arabian adjudicatory body, the documents must be submitted in the Arabic language. An action before a Saudi Arabian adjudicatory body may be brought on a document or instrument executed in a language other than Arabic, provided that an Arabic translation thereof, certified by a translator duly licensed in Saudi Arabia, is submitted together with the original document or instrument. In any such proceeding, the Arabic version thereof would be deemed by such Saudi Arabian adjudicatory body to be the operative version.

It remains unclear whether Saudi Arabian adjudicatory bodies would enforce the priority of application of any proceeds as set forth in any amended facilities agreement.

Article 68 of the Income Tax Regulations, issued under Royal Decree Number M/1 dated 15/1/1425 H. (corresponding to March 7, 2004) ("Income Tax Regulations"), authorizes the imposition of withholding taxes on payments specified in the Bill of Implementation relating thereto. Article 63 of the draft Bill of Implementation relating to the Income Tax Regulations imposed a 5 percent withholding tax on "loan returns" paid from a source within Saudi Arabia to nonresidents without a permanent establishment in Saudi Arabia. The aforementioned 5 percent withholding tax provision was not reflected in the official version of the Bill of Implementation pertaining to the Income Tax Regulations, published in the Official Gazette on 27/5/1427 H. (corresponding to June 24, 2006). However, such official version did include a 15 percent withholding tax provision from payment of a nature not specifically provided for therein. Although it is possible that a typographic error may have occurred, the version of the laws or implementing regulations published in the Official Gazette are the official versions thereof.

Provisions in an agreement wherein any person purports (or is construed) to grant any person the right to take an action on his behalf may be deemed to comprise an instrument in the nature of a nominate contract of *wakala* (agency, which includes a power of attorney). Powers of attorney granted by Saudi Arabian entities for use in Saudi Arabia must be made before a competent notary public or other official having competence in those regards to be effective. A notary public may not accept for notarization a power of attorney granted in or pursuant to a document on the basis that such power of attorney is granted, directly or indirectly, with a view to recovery of interest (or money deemed to be in the nature of interest). In any event, under the sharia, a power of attorney (including a power of attorney duly made as aforesaid) or agency is, as a general matter, revocable at will by either party. That general principle is not limited to agencies as such, but would also apply to agreements or provisions in agreements whereby an agency relationship is created. Under some schools of Islamic jurisprudence, there is an exception to the general rule of revocability. The exception is that a grant of a power of attorney or agency should be treated as irrevocable when it is stated to be irrevocable and stated to be, and is, coupled with a third-party interest and such irrevocability is relied upon by a third party. Although the extent to which this exception operates in Saudi Arabia is not clear, the common practice is to rely on such exception. In any event, it should be noted that actions taken by an agent within the authority granted by a power of attorney, prior to the revocation of such power of attorney, will be for the account of, and binding upon, the principal. A person acting as an agent, however, may only enter into an agreement or act on behalf of a principal to the extent that the principal would have been permitted to enter into such agreement or act directly on its own account.

Under Saudi Arabian law, a party may revoke its appointment of a third-party expert at any time prior to the issuance of a decision by such third-party expert. Furthermore, a decision of a third-party expert will not be deemed to be, or enforced as, an arbitral award by a Saudi Arabian adjudicatory body. Such Saudi Arabian adjudicatory body will treat such decision as a mere expert opinion and will have full discretion to either uphold or ignore such decision.

Saudi Arabian adjudicatory bodies may refuse to grant an award with respect to attorney's fees or the costs of any litigation.

A unilateral promise or a covenant to act in a certain way may not create an obligation that would be enforceable before Saudi Arabian adjudicatory bodies.

A provision in an agreement providing that a party that fails to refuse consent within a certain period will be deemed to give its consent may be ineffective under Saudi Arabian law.

Payment entitlements and perfected security interests in Saudi Arabia, including all entitlements under any agreement, are subordinated by operation of law to certain claims including, without limitation:

i.   payments due to employees (pursuant to Article 19 of the Labour Law issued pursuant to Royal Decree M/51 dated 23/8/1426 H. (corresponding to September 27, 2005));

ii. payments due with respect to residential and business leases (pursuant to Article 119 of the Commercial Court Law issued pursuant to Royal Decree Number 32 dated 15/1/1350 H. (corresponding to June 1, 1931)); and

iii. payments due to the government of Saudi Arabia, such as unpaid taxes (pursuant to Article 71 of the Income Tax Law issued pursuant to Royal Decree Number M/11 dated 15/1/1425 H. (corresponding to March 7, 2004)) and contributions due to the General Organization for Social Insurance (pursuant to Article 20(1) of the Social Insurance Regulations issued pursuant to Royal Decree M/33 dated 3/9/1421 H. (corresponding to November 29, 2000)). It should also be noted that obligations may be subject to prior contractual subordination undertakings.

Under the laws of Saudi Arabia, provided the requisite witnesses are available, a written agreement may be amended by the verbal communications or the course of action of the parties thereto.

Agreements to make another agreement or to agree to the terms of certain material obligations in the future may not be enforceable under Saudi law because of being uncertain. Additionally, an agreement may not be deemed to be amended in the future unless each party to that agreement agrees to the subsequent amendment at the time.

Provisions in any agreement or any notices or communications issued thereunder or related thereto determined to be "ambiguous" by Saudi Arabian adjudicatory bodies will be enforceable at the discretion of such Saudi Arabian adjudicatory bodies.

7. Conclusion

The purpose of this chapter has been to explore the Islamic legal system of Saudi Arabia and to examine in detail the issue of enforceability against the backdrop of the development of a true Islamic economy. The attempt has been to study categories of thought that are distinctly different from those generally imported by the western legal scholar and to show the areas in which the microcosmic and macrocosmic ideals of both Islamic and western systems sometimes converge. I have attempted to show that just as in the western (U.S. common law) system, the Saudi legal system combines both ideals in a particularly complex way in order to achieve ends for which each ideal is suited.

Islamic law has enjoyed widespread and far-reaching implementation in the past. Although many Muslim countries have legal systems that are essentially European in provenance as a result of years of colonial administration, this has not been the case in Saudi Arabia. And adopting conventional models of modernization in the form of, for example, the codification of binding laws, has been more difficult for Saudi Arabia than for other Muslim states. As noted, the ulema and the government are completely complementary and codependent institutions, yet there would appear to be, sometimes, an overt competition between the two, especially with respect to any potential erosion of the principle of ijtihad adjudicatory freedom. The king is believed to be a strong proponent of further reforms, but the pace of judicial reform will probably remain modest. The relationship between the ulema and the ruler with respect to the Saudi legal system is a subtle one, fluctuating between cooperation, contradiction, and complementarity. Despite the continuing pressures of WTO accession, the demand of the merchant class for new commercial laws, the concern of foreign lenders for judicial certainty in complex financial transactions, the insidious influences of satellite dishes and Internet access, it is completely understandable that there are also many Muslims who are unwilling to simply dismiss as irrelevant to modern life the great legal heritage passed on by generations of jurists through arduous work and a genuine desire to live according to the divine will of God. Change is inevitable, but the pace at which this change will be made is up to question. Perhaps any codification of laws in Saudi Arabia will be similar to the U.S. Restatement of Laws, or perhaps Saudi Arabia will eventually adopt a formulation of a unified civil code for all the Arab countries. Only time will tell. It will be an interesting period for all legal practitioners involved in this area of the world.

Although somewhat neglected in the teachings of Islam, the concept of moderation and balance (wasatiyyah) is a major theme of the Koran and an important dimension of the Islamic worldview. Certainly this concept of moderation and balance, reflecting the issues of human welfare and utility, will remain an important aspect of the worldview in Saudi Arabia Islam, reflecting itself in almost all aspects of life, including civil transactions and matters of law. The principal Koranic verse on wasatiyyah is as follows:

Thus We have made of you a community justly balanced that you might be witnesses over the nations and the Messenger a witness over yourselves.

—Koran, 2:143[196]

Gayle E. Hanlon
Hadef Legal Consultants & Advocates
12th Floor, Blue Tower, Khalifa Street
PO Box 3727, Abu Dhabi
United Arab Emirates
Phone: +971 2 627 6222
E-mail: Hanlon@hadalaw.ae

---

[196] *Id.* at 288–96.

APPENDIX 42.1

Structure Diagrams

Figure 42.3: Part 1—Principal Protected Structure

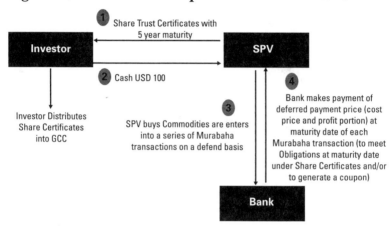

Figure 42.4: Part 2—Currency Swap IDR=USD Swap

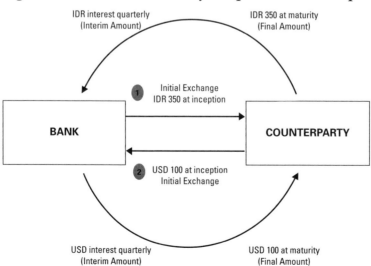

Figure 42.5: Part 3—Currency Swap IDR=USD Swap

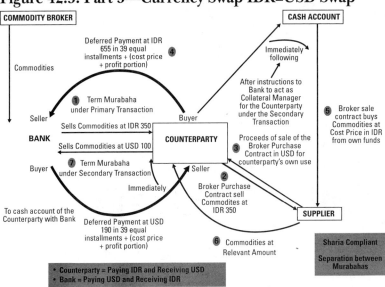

Figure 42.6: Part 4—Profit Rate Swap

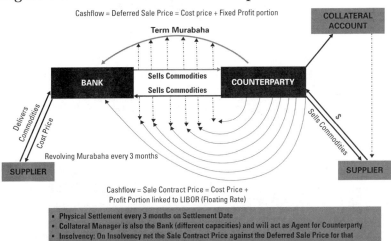

Figure 42.7: Part 5— Murabaha/Reverse Murabaha

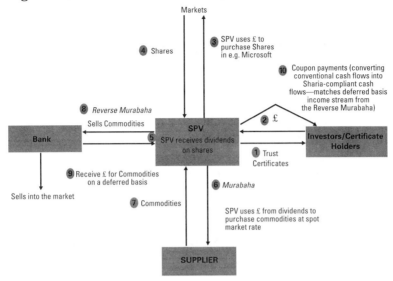

Double Wa'ad Structure

Figure 42.8: Double Wa'ad Structure

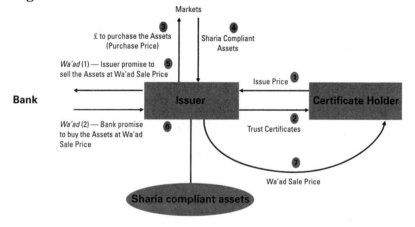

CHAPTER 43

International Business
Negotiations in Singapore

Paul Fitzgerald
STAMFORD LAW CORPORATION
SINGAPORE

1. Introduction

Singapore is a small island republic, renowned internationally for its authoritarian government, high rate of executions, and ban on the sale of chewing gum. Leaving such urban legends aside, it is undeniable that Singapore has had over thirty years of economic development unmatched in Southeast Asia, has both hard and soft infrastructure that delivers quality results with efficiency unparalleled in the region, and has a legal system that is recognized internationally for the delivery of justice in commercial matters in a fair, learned, and timely manner.

As a developed economy, Singapore is not insulated from global economic events such as inflation or the fallout from crises such as the current credit squeeze arising from the collapse of the subprime market in the United States. Similarly, Singapore is also exposed to regional factors, such as the Asian financial crisis in the late 1990s and the SARS pandemic in 2003, that have the capacity to have a detrimental affect on Singapore's economy. However, despite these factors, Singapore has enjoyed ongoing economic growth year after year and Singapore continues to rate highly in international surveys on economic competitiveness, the efficiency of the workforce, freedom from corruption, and quality of life.

The basic demographics of Singapore are that the population has reached 4.5 million, with approximately 77 percent of the population being of Chinese ethnic origin, with Malays at 14 percent and Indians at 8 percent. The economic upturn since 2006 has seen large numbers of expatriates returning to Singapore, and the government has actively sought to develop Singapore into a cosmopolitan city. Central to the government's policy of turning Singapore into a destination of choice for the sophisticated and wealthy is the construction of two integrated resorts, one by Sands and the other by Genting, the development of a luxury oceanfront residential area at Sentosa Cove, and the adding of Singapore to the Formula One Grand Prix racing circuit in 2008.

1.1 The Basics of Business in Singapore

Singapore has one of the most open economies in the world and encourages foreign investment across a wide spectrum of sectors. Singapore's legal system is based on the English common law. Singapore's statutes are a mix of English laws, such as the Sale of Goods Act (Cap. 393) and Unfair Contract Terms Act (Cap. 396), and Singapore statutes derived from Commonwealth jurisdictions that have been adapted for Singapore's own use. The sources of Singapore's laws are eclectic, reflecting Singapore's desire to have regimes that are tried and tested and suitable for the jurisdiction. Singapore's Companies Act has its origins in the English statute of the same name, but by a series of amendments is now largely based on the Corporations Act of Australia. The Competition Act is based on the Irish and U.K. provisions, and the Penal Code is based on Indian law. The key legislation applicable to the capital markets, the Securities and Futures Act, is based on Australian law, whereas the Singapore Code on Take-overs and Mergers is based on the U.K.'s City Code on Takeovers and Mergers.

Singapore's business entities reflect the original distinction in the English Companies Act between sole proprietorships, private limited companies, and public companies, whether listed or unlisted. In addition to these entities, Singapore law provides for partnerships, limited liability partnerships, and also certain more diverse vehicles such as business trusts. Certain sectors of the economy have further subgroups of entities. For example, the legal profession has sole proprietorships, partnerships, law corporations, limited liability partnerships, and joint law ventures.

Every company incorporated in Singapore or that carries on business in Singapore is required to be registered with the Accounting and Corporate Regulatory Authority (ACRA). The key legal details of each company, including the registered office, the amount of issued and paid-up capital, the names and addresses of directors and shareholders, and the details of any charges, are all available online through ACRA's Bizfile application upon payment of a nominal fee. Additional information such as the Memorandum and Articles of Association and Annual Return of the company, along with its audited financials, are also available through Bizfile upon payment of the prescribed fee.

2. The Influence of the Government of Singapore

The Singapore government has long taken the lead in spearheading Singapore corporates into key sectors of the local economy and global markets. This has been achieved either directly, by having senior ministers lead delegations of Singapore businessmen seeking out opportunities to new markets, or through investing by way of its two key investment vehicles, Temasek Holdings (Private) Limited and the Government Investment Corporation. Temasek Holdings holds interests in many of Singapore's key companies, including listed companies such as Singapore Telecommunications Limited, Singapore Airlines Limited, and Neptune Orient Lines Limited, together with stakes in some of Singapore's largest groups of companies, including the PSA Group, DBS Bank, Singapore Technologies, Keppel, and Sembcorp. These companies are known within Singapore as either Temasek-linked companies (TLCs) or government-linked companies (GLCs).

The extent to which Temasek influences the companies in which it has invested is a matter of debate. Temasek's position, which is accepted in Singapore by all regulatory bodies, is that it involves itself in ensuring that the TLCs have competent boards of directors with a strong emphasis placed on the fundamentals of good corporate governance, while the running of the company is left in the hands of the board and senior management. Whether this view is accepted or not, the reality of dealing with TLCs is that there is a strong emphasis placed on the bottom line, and foreign persons dealing with the TLCs need to be fully aware that divestments by TLCs will be driven by a desire to maximize shareholder return and acquisitions will be driven by qualitative and strategic factors. Notwithstanding two high-profile reversals in recent times—Temasek's investment into Shin Corporation in Thailand and its running afoul of Indonesia's Commission for the Supervision of Business Competition with respect to its investment in Indonesia's cellular phone market—Temasek remains arguably the most influential corporate entity in Singapore and, increasingly, one of the most influential investors in the world.

In addition to appointments of civil servants to the boards of TLCs, the government is also able to rely on the generous sprinkling of members of Parliament, ex-civil servants, and other persons close to the government who dot the boards of Singapore companies. The presence of persons with such backgrounds and connections helps to ensure that these Singapore companies remain aligned with the policies and standards that are the hallmarks of the Singapore "brand" name, particularly transparency and integrity, and give confidence to investors.

3. The Singaporean Character

Every business person entering into a negotiation in Singapore or with a Singapore party will likely have knowledge that Singaporeans are extremely proud of Singapore's achievements, have a deep-seated belief that the Singaporean way is the best way, and are invariably prag-matic in their approach to issues. However, the underlying psyche of Singapore and its residents is more complex. One hears a number of labels attempting to describe the "Singaporean character" including neo-Confucianism, which is no doubt based on the largely top-down, government-driven agenda that permeates virtually every aspect of Singapore and that sees citizens looking to the government for solu-tions to every problem no matter how minor. However, one can gain perhaps a better understanding of some of the underlying drivers behind Singaporean behavior and thereby gain some predictive ability prenegotiation by having regard to what is known locally as the "kiasu" mentality.

3.1 Singapore and the Kiasu Complex

Singaporeans are taught early that life is a zero-sum game and that the survival of Singapore as a separate nation-state depends on Singapore always being ahead of its competitors. Senior members of the govern-ment regularly remind Singaporeans of the "fire" that Singapore went through in the early years of its independence when its very viabil-ity was at stake and it was beset with difficulties including commu-nist influence and difficult relations with its nearest neighbors. This national-level message on the importance of staying ahead translates at the personal level into an intense competitive spirit that can mani-fest itself in even the most trivial incidents of everyday life. Singapore society, through its education system and continual remaking of itself to stay ahead, has a heavy emphasis on competition and the need to win, since the only alternative to winning is losing. This gives rise to what is popularly known as the kiasu mentality—a fear of losing.

The kiasu nature of Singaporeans is a subject of considerable self-deprecating humor in Singapore, with the "kiasu alphabet" contain-ing such gems as:

A is for Always must win;
C is for Cheap is good;
J is for Jump the queue;
L is for Look for discount;
R is for Rushing and pushing wins the race;
T is for Take but don't give;
W is for Winner takes it all.

However, while locals take manifestations of these attributes in their stride, it can be unnerving to outsiders, particularly those from the West, to see kiasuism in action. It can also be distinctly worrying to see how the underlying premises of kiasuism can influence major cor-porate decision-making and the almost subliminal presence of some kiasu elements in the mindset of Singaporean businesspersons.

Indeed, for all the hilarity that surrounds the kiasu mentality, some kiasu characteristics undeniably impact on Singapore's corporate scene. In their own personal lives, many Singaporeans will not purchase a major item without a significant discount. When some of Singapore's most prominent companies—Singapore Telecommunications Limited, Neptune Orient Lines Limited, and DBS Bank Limited—made external acquisitions in the late 1990s and early 2000s at a premium to market, the purchases were met with a chorus of investor and media disapproval within Singapore. It matters little that subsequent events have shown those particular acquisitions to have been extremely beneficial to the earnings of the companies involved, since the overall message that was delivered so vocally at the time was that paying a premium would guarantee a storm in the market. Anecdotal evidence regarding a number of subsequent acquisition opportunities would suggest that either the opportunities were declined by Singapore corporates or the bids that were made lost out to competitors willing to pay a premium. Fear of market opprobrium from payment of a premium is said in some cases to have led to near paralysis at board level as directors pondered the effects on their companies and reputations. Cheap is good—but not necessarily accretive to value in the long term. Despite this, as a rough rule of thumb, an offer price by a foreign buyer for a Singapore asset must always be at a premium to market valuation to have some chance of success. Equally, the sale of an asset to a Singaporean will require a price at a discount to market valuation. One suspects that such ingrained notions will die a slow death.

4. Before Approaching the Bargaining Table

Even armed with these insights into the character and mentality of the Singaporean, there are still further considerations that need to be taken into account prior to commencing negotiations with a Singaporean party.

4.1 The Pragmatic Approach

Singapore prides itself on its pragmatism and its ability to approach issues and resolve them in a rational manner by reliance on objective criteria. Many Singaporeans will approach negotiations with a clear focus on the intended outcome of the negotiation and with their interests clearly defined. The Singaporean approach to negotiation is far closer to Fisher & Ury than to Miyamoto Musashi, and Singaporeans conduct negotiations (and expect negotiations to be conducted) on the basis of rational discussions based on empirical data. Singaporeans are not by nature given to the histrionics that can occasionally mar dealings with businessmen from Hong Kong and the PRC, and outbursts of temper at the negotiating table are unheard of in Singapore.

4.2 Cultural Aspects

Singapore is a multiracial and multireligious society, and the government has made the maintenance of racial and religious harmony a cornerstone of its domestic policies. Business negotiations in corporate Singapore will frequently involve Singaporeans of Chinese ethnicity, and therefore it is worthwhile for the international party to be familiar with the background and cultural idiosyncrasies of Singapore's Chinese population. Singapore's Chinese are not homogenous and there are a number of Chinese clans represented in Singapore. Whereas Singaporeans in TLCs will invariably negotiate in the English language, there are a significant number of traditional family corporates where Mandarin or another dialect will be the preferred language of the more senior members of the board. Singapore also boasts a significant number of listed companies that are PRC-based and, invariably, the PRC directors will speak Mandarin.

Singapore businessmen do not place a significant emphasis on *Guanxi* (the personal relationship) as that concept is used in the PRC, and it is quite possible to undertake a major transaction in Singapore or with a Singaporean party without any degree of socializing between the parties. Nevertheless, consideration must always be given when dealing with Chinese businessmen, particularly traditional businessmen, to the importance of respecting the dignity and social standing of one's counterpart. The concept of "face" is important, and negotiations should always focus on issues rather than personalities. Any issues that may undermine or reflect badly on a senior businessman, such as oral agreements having been reached earlier in private that are now being revised or resisted, should be addressed "offline" and not in the presence of the businessman's subordinates.

Business dealings with members of the Indian and Malay communities also involve dealing with and respecting some sensitive areas. There is a high likelihood that both Indian and Malay businesspersons will have dietary restrictions that must be taken into account when socializing. For Malays, any negotiations that are conducted during the fasting month of Ramadan will also need to be timed in a manner that allows for prayers to be observed and the fast to be broken at the stipulated time.

Across all of the races in Singapore, there are public holidays that will be recognized, subject only to the most pressing of issues. In particular, Chinese New Year in Singapore often sees many Singaporeans returning to Malaysia for family celebrations; the eve of Chinese New Year is one of the few occasions when corporate Singapore ceases work. The most important festival for the Malays is the Hari Raya following the fasting month of Ramadan, while the Indian festival of Deepavali is also likely to be recognized by members of the Indian community.

5. Negotiations Involving Singapore Lawyers

Singapore has a full range of international and local law firms and also a blend of the two in the form of a joint law venture, which is a combination of an international firm and a local firm. All Singapore lawyers below the age of forty-five will likely have been exposed to some training in negotiation as part of their legal education, whether in Singapore or elsewhere. However, despite the high standards of legal representation available in Singapore, foreign parties engaged in negotiating an issue with representatives of certain of Singapore's largest law firms are often met with a response indicating that a particular position cannot be negotiated as it is contrary to the "market standard" or not the "market practice" in Singapore. This is in fact shorthand for a particular negotiating position not being in conformance with the Singapore law firm's precedent, and the lawyers involved either do not want to move from the precedent or do not have the authority to move. Any such reference to a market standard or market practice should be rejected, as there is likely no such standard or practice. The critical aspects of a transaction ought never be negotiated unless a partner or director of the law firm representing the counterparty is present so that decisions can be made rather than remain on the table as "KIV" or "keep in view." It can be extremely frustrating to spend time negotiating key points only to have the counterparty adopt a KIV approach to these issues because the lawyers present have insufficient seniority to take a position or agree on wording.

As a rule, Singaporean lawyers do not favor large set-piece negotiations with the lead negotiators for each side taking turns presenting arguments, as can be found when dealing with the large international firms. Almost invariably, the key commercial issues will be discussed amongst the large group but ultimately settled by the parties themselves after taking legal advice, if necessary offline if there are sensitivities or face involved.

6. Developing a Successful Negotiation Strategy

There are no secret strategies that will guarantee success in any commercial negotiation in Singapore. In order to maximize the chances of a successful outcome, foreign parties should take note of the following:

- Undertake the necessary research on the counterparty in the negotiation to determine the background of the key decision-makers. If the counterparty is a TLC, then it is safe to assume that the counterparty will be well prepared, having undertaken a thorough analysis of the commercial and financial drivers underpinning the transaction. A traditional family company will have different sensitivities and, while keenly interested in price, may have a greater sense of loyalty to small shareholders and public perception of the transaction.

- Prepare thoroughly for the negotiation, since it is almost certain that the Singapore counterparty will be equally prepared. Clearly separate out interests into categories depending on their objective importance to a successful outcome. Singaporean negotiators will frequently offer "package deals" on contested points. If pre-negotiation analysis has been undertaken on the critical points, then such package deals can be worked to your advantage.

- Observe cultural niceties, as these invariably cost nothing but can lead to significant upside. Always show due deference to the chairman of a board of directors or the founder of a company, particularly if dealing with traditional Chinese businessmen. Singaporean businessmen have had far greater exposure to Western models of corporate governance and strict legal regimes for doing business than have businessmen in other Southeast or North Asian jurisdictions. Accordingly, a professional and courteous approach can be taken to negotiations almost without exception.

- Do not be fooled by appearances. Many Singaporean businessmen, including lawyers, adopt a casual form of dress and will attend even relatively high-level meetings without jackets or ties. This casual style should not be mistaken for a lack of education or sophistication. Regardless of appearance, Singaporeans as a rule are highly educated, numerically literate, and commercially aware and should not be underestimated based on dress.

- Note that for cultural reasons, many Singaporeans prefer indirect statements rather than direct ones and will avoid personal confrontation in order to maintain face in business dealings. While it is the norm for quantitative data, including financials, to be discussed openly, it is rare for direct criticisms to be made, and negotiations ought not to become personal.

- Singaporeans do not share one of the characteristics of certain other Asian jurisdictions, namely, the aversion to the integrity of a written contract. Singaporeans expect contracts to be adhered to and to govern the relations between the parties going forward. To the extent that issues arise in an existing contract, these will invariably be dealt with by way of further negotiation, and either a written amendment to the original contract will be executed or a supplemental agreement entered into. Singaporeans have faith in the legal process, possibly because of the high standards of the Singapore judiciary in commercial cases and the efficiency of Singapore courts, and accordingly, the terms of contracts (as they would be interpreted by the courts) are important. It follows that care should always be taken in finalizing the wording of contracts, and compromise wording in the clauses of an agreement must be free of ambiguity. Singaporeans will look to their contractual remedies in the event of any dispute and be guided in any strategy to resolve disputes by what the terms of the contract say.

7. Singapore's E-commerce Environment

Over the past decade, Singapore has set out to develop itself as a leading info-communications hub for the Asia-Pacific. The policy has been highly successful, and for five consecutive years Singapore was ranked in the top three positions in the World Economic Forum's Global Information Technology Report. In the latest ranking, Singapore was ranked fifth globally. The policy has allowed the government to make the Internet the first point of contact between its citizens and itself, and electronic filing has been adopted by ACRA, other statutory boards exercising regulatory functions, and the courts so that greater efficiencies can be achieved.

Singapore's development has been due in large part to the adoption, in the IT 2000 Masterplan, of a policy for building a high-speed broadband network across the entire country. The initiative, formally known as Singapore ONE, was launched in 1996 and forms the platform over which all local Internet traffic is exchanged. A 2008 study on broadband usage in Singapore revealed that broadband has penetrated into over 80 percent of Singapore homes, while in a 2007 survey, Internet penetration amongst households was at 74 percent of the population.

Singapore has also grown to be one of the major global telecommunications hubs in the region. With total submarine cable capacity of 28 Tbps and direct international Internet connectivity of 25 Gbps, Singapore is well positioned as a hub for international capacity. Over the last few years, Singapore has also grown to be a transcable hub where regional submarine cable systems and international cable systems interconnect.

7.1 The iN2015 Masterplan

For reasons set out earlier, Singapore never rests on its laurels but is always seeking ways to improve itself and maintain its competitive edge. Having already set a robust platform through its national infrastructure, Singapore is now looking to take advantage of technological advances in info-communications to deploy a seamless, trusted, and intelligent infrastructure by 2015, to enable the vertical sector economies of Singapore to gain a competitive edge in the global market.

The new Intelligent Nation 2015 Masterplan (iN2015) aims to use developments in info-communications technology to spearhead the transformation of key economic sectors, government, and society. The plan envisages the establishment of an ultra-high-speed, pervasive infrastructure that will transform the personal lives of Singaporeans and businesses in Singapore by providing the technology to collaborate, innovate, and personalize. The fundamental premise underlying iN2015 is that technology is the driver for the development of ideas that will set a business apart from its competitors. iN2015 will help to speed up industry-specific solutions, build brands, foster growth, and attract global talent and expertise to Singapore.

At the heart of iN2015 is a nationwide ultra-high-speed fiber-access infrastructure and a complementary pervasive wireless network that will support new industries such as the digital media and the biomedical sciences industry as the new engines of growth for Singapore's economy. This new infrastructure will also enable the growth and development of grid computing, which has increasingly been adopted across many industry sectors such as finance and banking, interactive and digital media, manufacturing, and health care and life sciences. It is hoped that the new infrastructure will catalyze the development in Singapore of grid service providers (GSPs) that provide grid-enabled software, computers, and storage services.

7.2 The Ongoing Development of E-commerce

Singapore put the necessary legislative and policy framework for e-commerce into place during the early years of the Internet "bubble" and therefore is well advanced in e-matters. From a legislative perspective, the Electronic Transactions Act provides the legislative basis for all e-contracts and e-transactions. As part of the regime set out in the Electronic Transactions Act, the licensing of certification authorities is provided for to ensure the integrity of digital signatures. In addition, the Evidence Act was amended to allow for evidence of e-transactions to be accorded equal status with traditional forms of evidence in court proceedings, and amendments were also made to the Computer Misuse Act to provide for a more rigorous statutory regime governing electronic transactions and offenses committed with respect to such transactions or the technology used in such transactions.

Over the past decade, the revolution in business practice that has occurred as a result of advancing technology has been fully embraced in Singapore and, as can be seen from the iN2025 Masterplan, will continue to drive change well into the future. The old and new economies have merged seamlessly in the world of commerce, and Singapore is no exception. The hectic 24/7 pace of modern business, the shrinking world, and the need for ever-increasing, ever more reliable, and ever-faster connectivity are intrinsically interlinked with the position Singapore sees itself occupying in the future. If the seers predicting Asia's emergence as the new economic center of the global economy are correct, then there is no doubt that Singapore will be positioning itself to play a key facilitative role in the Asian economy—and beyond.

Paul Fitzgerald
Stamford Law Corporation
9 Raffles Place #32-00
Republic Plaza
Singapore 048619
Phone:　(65) 6389 3000
Fax:　　(65) 6389 3099
E-mail:　paul.fitzgerald@stamfordlaw.co

CHAPTER 44

International Business Negotiations in South Africa

Victoria Page, Vlad Movshovich, and Ashleigh Hammond
WEBBER WENTZEL
JOHANNESBURG, SOUTH AFRICA

1. Introduction

As a market opportunity, South Africa offers a unique combination of a highly developed first-world economic infrastructure and a significant emerging market economy. Since the first democratic national election in 1994, South Africa has achieved macroeconomic stability with a gross domestic product for 2007 of ZAR 1,993,894 million[1] The major strengths of the South African economy are its abundant natural resources (particularly gold, the platinum group metals, and a wide variety of other minerals, as well as coal and uranium oxide), its growing manufacturing sector, and considerable tourism potential.

According to the 2007 Foreign Direct Investment Confidence Index,[2] South Africa ranked eighteenth among listed countries in terms of investor confidence. South Africa also fared well in the World Bank and International Finance Corporation's *Doing Business 2008* report,[3] ranking thirty-fifth out of 178 countries in terms of the regulatory cost of doing business.

The attraction of South Africa as an investment destination is due, in part, to its relatively stable political environment and adherence to the rule of law. South Africa is a constitutional democracy, with a three-tier system of government and an independent judiciary. Its laws are founded in statutory law (the most important of which is the Constitution[4]), common law (judicial precedent from case law and the old

---

[1] Equivalent to US$282,000 million at a rate of ZAR 7.0506/US$1.00. The gross domestic product annual percentage change is: 4.155 (2000); 2.735 (2001); 3.668 (2002); 3.120 (2003); 4.864 (2004); 5.001 (2005); 5.388 (2006); 5.140 (2007).

[2] A survey of global executives conducted by A.T. Kearney. See www.atkearney.com.

[3] See http://www.doingbusiness.org/.

[4] The Constitution of South Africa, 1996.

authorities, English and Roman-Dutch law), and African customary law. South Africa's Constitution guarantees both civil liberties (found in most liberal constitutions) and socioeconomic rights (such as access to housing and health care), which the South African government is tasked with realizing within its resource constraints.

Any sanguine investor or business negotiator in South Africa, however, must be adequately apprised of the extensive regulatory and socioeconomic rules, principles, and constraints that govern, or are the background to, business transactions in South Africa. This chapter provides an overview of some of the principal legal and socioeconomic considerations, and is structured as follows:

> **Section 2** introduces the South African business environment, by providing an overview of the points of entry in South African markets, the country's company law regime, and state-owned enterprises.
>
> **Section 3** discusses a significant and distinctive feature of the South African business environment, the government's emphasis on socioeconomic transformation to uplift individuals and communities that were disadvantaged prior to the institution of a fully representative democracy.
>
> **Section 4** examines the regulatory environment in South Africa, highlighting the independent regulators and significant sector-specific and generally applicable regulation.
>
> **Section 5** provides an overview of South African dispute resolution mechanisms.

2. Business Environment

In the realm of commerce, there are similarities in many respects between South Africa and the United Kingdom in terms of business patterns and practices, legal systems, and institutions. The language of business in South Africa is commonly English.[5]

2.1 Points of Entry into South African Markets

There are a variety of ways in which international investors may enter South African markets. The three main ways are by establishing a business in South Africa, investing in South African equity or debt, or exporting to South Africa (see Figure 44.1). The wide range of possible investment vehicles enables an investor to make use of, for example, a South African agent, distributor, subsidiary, or joint venture. Public-

---

[5] There are, however, eleven official languages: Afrikaans, English, Ndebele, Sepedi, Sesotho, Setswana, Swazi, Tshivenda, Xhosa, Xitsonga, and Zulu.

private partnerships, used to provide government accommodation and services, are also a possibility.

The Johannesburg Securities Exchange Limited (the JSE) is the country's equities and derivatives exchange and, in November 2008, will have been trading financial products for 121 years. It ranks consistently among the top twenty exchanges in the world, with a market capitalization of ZAR 5,600,000 million.[6] The JSE is heavily weighted toward resource stocks, across a host of subsectors. Resource equities account for approximately 60 percent of the overall JSE market capitalization, with the two largest resource companies[7] accounting for over half of that amount. The balance is made up of consumer-related sectors, including, *inter alia*, banking, industrial, retail, and telecommunication interests. The Bond Exchange of South Africa (BESA) has a market capitalization of ZAR 862,000 million,[8] with government bonds accounting for most issuance and trading.

South Africa participates in a number of preferential trade relationships, both regional and bilateral. It was a founding member of the General Agreement on Tariffs and Trade of 1947 and is a member of the World Trade Organization. Since 1994, South Africa has negotiated a host of general trade agreements. Such agreements do not make provision for market access in specific sectors, but commonly allow for "most favored nation" tariff treatment. South Africa is also a signatory to free trade agreements, which allow for preferential access across sectors between signatory countries for specific products. These include agreements with the Southern African Development Community (SADC)[9] and the European Union.[10] In addition, South Africa is the recipient of unilateral preferential trade arrangements. As a result of these arrangements, other countries unilaterally provide access to their markets through lower tariffs and increased or removed quotas. The United States, for example, provides such market access opportunities to a number of African countries, including South Africa.[11]

2.2 Company Law, Investor Protection, and Corporate Governance

The South African company law regime is relevant to any foreign investment in a South African company. South Africa has a well-developed company law regime, which largely tracks company law development in the United Kingdom and international trends. All

---

[6] As of year end 2007. Equivalent to US$731,911 million at a rate of ZAR 7.0506/US$1.00.

[7] Anglo American and BHP Billiton.

[8] As of December 2007. Equivalent to US$122,000 million at a rate of ZAR 7.0506/US$1.00.

[9] The other members of SADC are thirteen sub-Saharan African countries.

[10] The Trade, Development and Cooperation Agreement, 1999.

[11] Through the African Growth and Opportunity Act, 2000.

Figure 44.1: Key Points of Entry

Investment Vehicles
• Public company (widely held company)
• Private company (limited interest company)
• Section 53(b) company (a company whose directors are jointly and severally liable with the company for its contractual liabilities)
• Branch office (external company)
• Close corporation
• Partnership, including public-private partnership
• Business or trading trust

Financial Markets
The JSE Limited
• An equities market (including stocks from the Main Board and the small to mid-cap Alternative Exchange)
• An interest rate market
• An active financial derivatives market
• An agricultural products market
Bond Exchange of South Africa
• A bond market

Trade
General Trade Agreements
• With a host of countries, essentially providing for "Most Favored Nation" tariff treatment
Free Trade Agreements
• With SADC
• With the EU, through the SA-EU Trade Development Co-operation Agreement, 1999
Preferential Trade Arrangements
• With the U.S., through the African Growth and Opportunity Act, 2000
• With a number of other countries, making use of the "Generalized System of Preferences"

South African companies[12] are governed by the Companies Act, 1973 (the "Companies Act"),[13] which is based on English company law. Importantly, the Companies Act makes no distinction between locally owned and foreign-owned companies.

---

[12] South African law also provides for close corporations, in terms of the Close Corporations Act, 1984, which are a simpler and less expensive corporate form for the single entrepreneur or a few participants.

[13] It is envisaged that the Companies Act will soon be repealed by the Companies Bill, 2008, which sets out to modernize the Companies Act, aligning company law with international jurisdictions. In particular, the Bill provides for improved regulatory oversight, better redress for shareholders, and enhanced corporate governance.

South African law imposes duties and responsibilities on company directors and, in doing so, provides significant protection for investors. A director is required to act within the ambit of the company's constitution (that is, its memorandum and articles of association), to fulfill his duties at common law (a fiduciary duty and a duty of care and skill) and under statute (for example, restrictions on directors taking financial advantage). The Companies Act also offers protection to minority shareholders, including the grant of a right to any member believing any act or omission by the company to be "unfairly prejudicial, unjust or inequitable" to apply to court for relief.

Corporate governance in South Africa is codified in the 2002 Code of Corporate Practices and Conduct (known as "King II" after the King Report on Corporate Governance, 2002, in which it appeared), with principles in line with best international practices (encompassing discipline, transparency, independence, accountability, responsibility, fairness, and social responsibility).

2.3 State-Owned Enterprises

The foreign investor in South Africa is likely to encounter any number of the large state-owned enterprises (SOEs), which operate principally in the energy, transport, telecommunications, broadcasting, and armaments sectors. Many SOEs have now been privatized, in whole or in part, or are undergoing restructuring. The four largest SOEs[14] are:

- Eskom (responsible for electricity generation and distribution)
- Transnet (the national transport service provider)
- Telkom (the national telecommunications service provider)
- Denel (an armaments manufacturer and distributor)

SOEs have specific statutory powers that are not extended to other corporate entities, such as a power to expropriate. Of particular significance to the foreign investor dealing with SOEs, they are also subject to substantial constraints in the way that they conduct business, such as the need, in certain circumstances, to act in a way that is administratively just (that is, in a lawful, reasonable, and procedurally fair manner) and to comply with various financial requirements imposed on organs of state.

3. Broad-Based Black Economic Empowerment

Broad-Based Black Economic Empowerment (BEE) is central to the South African government's efforts to ensure economic participation by the huge sector of the population that was disadvantaged under apartheid. BEE is described as a moral initiative to redress the wrongs

---

[14] The South African government has a 100 percent shareholding in Eskom, Transnet, and Denel, but a 39.76 percent shareholding in Telkom as of August 14, 2008.

of the past and a growth strategy that aims to realize the country's full economic potential. It is regulated by legislation, Codes of Good Practice and transformation charters. The significance of BEE to international business will depend on the nature of the likely business relationship with South African organs of state (for example, provincial and national government departments) and public entities (for example, the state-owned electricity supplier Eskom), as well as with private entities that will assess the proposed business's BEE status for the purpose of their own procurement requirements.

3.1 Legislation and the Codes of Good Practice

The Broad-Based Black Economic Empowerment Act, 2003 ("BEE Act") provides the framework for the implementation of BEE initiatives, and provides for the publication, by the Minister of Trade and Industry, of the Codes of Good Practice ("Codes"). The Codes apply to all enterprises with a turnover of at least ZAR 5 million per year. They are used in measuring the extent to which an enterprise has achieved BEE, through the use of targets and a scorecard. BEE is measured across seven key elements of business: ownership, management control, employment equity, skills development, preferential procurement, enterprise development, and socioeconomic development.

The BEE Act provides that every organ of state and public entity must take into account and, as far as reasonably possible, apply the Codes in certain of their dealings. Therefore, enterprises (including foreign-owned companies) that require licenses, concessions, or authorizations from the state, wish to provide goods and services to organs of state or public entities, wish to acquire state-owned enterprises, or wish to enter into partnerships with the state, must provide evidence of their BEE status as measured under the Codes.

Private enterprises are not obliged by law to meet the targets specified in the Codes. However, insofar as they seek to deal with any organ of state or public entity, they may be prejudiced by their failure to ensure that their BEE status is at least as good as that of their competitors. The procurement element of BEE thus encourages private enterprises to direct their money to enterprises that have good BEE credentials, because this will improve the BEE status of the enterprise being measured.

3.2 Industry and Sector Charters

Many private sector industries have developed transformation charters (see Section 3.3), that provide how participants in those industries will achieve empowerment and measure progress. By way of example:[15]

---

[15] See below for further details regarding regulation of the financial services and mining sectors.

- The Financial Sector Charter is a voluntary commitment agreed by ten industry associations. The charter provides for, *inter alia*, significant increases in black ownership, management, and skills development by 2014. A council has been established to review and monitor the implementation of the goals set out in the charter.
- The Mining Charter provides a framework to assist mining companies to comply with provisions of the Mineral and Petroleum Resources Development Act, 2002, which oblige mining companies to promote BEE when applying for new mineral rights or converting current rights. One of its key objectives is to achieve 26 percent BEE ownership by 2014.

In circumstances in which multinational companies may have global policies that restrict the level of ownership and control that can be transferred to local parties, it is significant that the charters generally require at least 25 percent BEE ownership by or before 2014. The Financial Sector Charter is currently the only charter that contains specific qualifications for the adherence by foreign financial institutions to the BEE ownership and control targets set out in the charter. The South African operations of foreign-owned financial institutions can apply for complete exemption from compliance with the targets under the ownership and control (as well as human resource development) provisions of the charter, if they have in place or are subject to a global policy against local equity participation. Also, foreign banking groups with South African branches are given a wider range of transaction options for which they receive credits on the ownership portion of their scorecard.

The need to meet the targets set out in the charters provides an imperative for private enterprises in these sectors to procure goods and services from BEE-compliant firms.

3.3 Multinational Enterprises and Equity Equivalents

The Codes make an allowance for multinationals that have global practices preventing them from complying with the BEE ownership

Key BEE Sector Charters

Mining
Petroleum and Liquid Fuels Industry
Financial Services
Construction
Property
Agriculture
Media, Advertising, and Communication

element through the sale of shares, by providing for recognition of contributions in lieu of a sale of such equity. Such contributions are referred to as equity equivalent contributions. They will be measurable against 25 percent of the value of the multinational's operations in South Africa.

An "Equity Equivalent Programme" would entail a public and/or private scheme designed to fulfill the requirements of BEE ownership (that is, broadly speaking, to promote the socioeconomic advancement of South Africa) and approved by the Minister of Trade and Industry. Another alternative for a foreign multinational is through the ownership of equity in an offshore enterprise held by black South Africans.

4. Regulatory Environment

4.1 The Regulators

Any business negotiations will be informed by the South African regulatory environment, which is characterized by a large number and range of independent regulators, consistent with international trends in regulation (see Figure 44.2).

Figure 44.2: Major South African Regulators

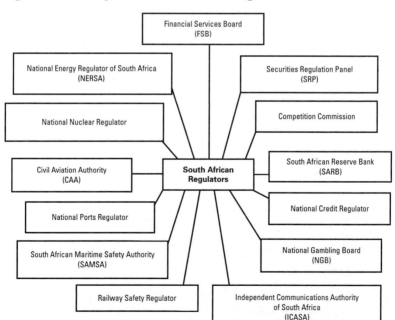

4.2 Sector-Specific Regulation

Certain sectors in South Africa are heavily regulated; some examples follow.

4.2.1 Financial Markets

The Financial Services Board (FSB) regulates the provision of financial services in South Africa, including collective investment schemes, insurers, and pension funds, and is responsible for the administration of, *inter alia*, the Securities Services Act, 2004 (SSA). The JSE is an exchange under the SSA. All companies listed on the JSE are required to adhere to King II and to the JSE's listings and disclosure requirements, which are in line with those of the London Stock Exchange. Participants are able to trade across various securities, including cash equities and derivatives. BESA regulates the listing and trading of bonds.

The SSA contains various prohibitions against insider trading and other forms of market abuse, with provision for significant administrative, civil, and criminal sanctions against offenders.

The Securities Regulation Panel (SRP) was established in terms of the Companies Act. It formulated the Securities Regulation Code on Takeovers and Mergers, which governs the matters falling within the SRP's jurisdiction and has the force of law. The SRP regulates, as it deems appropriate, all affected transactions and schemes relating to any public company, and any private company with more than ten beneficial shareholders, where the shareholders' interests and shareholders' loan capital exceeds ZAR 5 million. Transactions affecting a private company may be exempted if there is no prejudice to minority shareholders. The SRP does not judge the commercial desirability of affected transactions.

4.2.2 Mining

The regulation of the mining industry changed fundamentally as a result of the enactment of the Mineral and Petroleum Resources Development Act, 2002. It extinguished private ownership of mineral rights, and the state is now the custodian of all mineral and petroleum resources in South Africa. Application may be made to the state for the grant of mining and prospecting rights subject to payment of royalties, though previously disadvantaged persons are given greater access to such rights.

4.3 Generally Applicable Regulation

Other significant regulation is generally applicable, including the following.

4.3.1 Exchange Control

Exchange control is regulated by the Currency and Exchanges Act, 1933, and the Exchange Control Regulations, Orders, and Rules of 1961. The Financial Surveillance Department (FSD) of the South African Reserve Bank is responsible for the day-to-day administration and functioning of exchange control, and is assisted by certain banks that have been appointed as authorized dealers in foreign exchange.

(a) FSD Approval

Since 1995, exchange control has been systematically relaxed. However, the following matters do require the approval of the FSD:

- outward capital transfers by residents above designated limits;
- outward loan transfers by residents;
- loans from nonresidents to residents;
- local financial assistance to foreign-controlled companies above certain limits, and dividend distributions by such companies; and
- transfers by emigrants above the designated limits.

(b) Effect of Exchange Control Regulations on Foreign Investors

Local Borrowing: Loans by a resident to a nonresident require the prior approval of the FSD. The FSD presently permits a foreign-owned company to borrow up to 300 percent of the shareholder investment in a South African company in which at least 75 percent of the voting stock, capital, or earnings is held or controlled by a nonresident.

Establishing New Industries: Where the intention of a subsidiary of a foreign concern is to manufacture under a foreign license, the approval of the Department of Trade and Industry (DTI) is required. The DTI will pass its recommendations to the FSD.

Currency Risks, Imports and Exports: Foreign currency may be sold forward to residents provided that certain requirements are met. Certain goods, as determined by the Minister of Trade and Industry, are also subject to export control.

Repatriation of Earnings: There are no restrictions on the repatriation of capital investments by nonresidents. Royalty and technology agreements require the prior approval of the FSD (and the DTI, in certain cases). For nonresident shareholders, dividends/profits/income distributions are remittable in proportion to shareholding.

4.3.2 Taxation and Double-Taxation Agreements

Individuals are taxed on a progressive basis up to a maximum rate of 40 percent on taxable income exceeding ZAR 450,000 per year.

Resident companies are taxed at a flat rate of 28 percent. They are also subject to secondary tax on companies (STC) (see discussion in subsection (c) below), leading to a total effective tax rate of 34.55 percent. Nonresident companies that trade in South Africa through a branch are subject to taxation at a rate of 34 percent, but are not subject to STC.

Trusts are generally taxed at a flat rate of 40 percent on income that does not vest in a beneficiary of the trust during the year in question, while partnerships are not recognized as entities for tax purposes. Instead, the individual partners are taxed separately on their share of the partnership profits.

(a) Income Tax

Income tax is regulated by the Income Tax Act, 1962, and is the principal source of direct taxation. South African residents are generally taxed on their worldwide income, while nonresidents are taxed only on South African–sourced income, subject to the provisions of any relevant double-tax agreement (DTA). Companies within a group are treated as separate entities for tax purposes.

A proportional amount of the net income of a controlled foreign company (a foreign company in which South African residents hold more than 50 percent of, *inter alia*, the voting rights) will be included in the income of the resident shareholder in such company.

(b) Capital Gains Tax

Capital gains tax (CGT) is payable on any net capital gain that arises from the disposal or deemed disposal of certain assets. The position of residents and nonresidents differs.

(c) Secondary Tax on Companies

STC is currently levied on resident companies distributing dividends to shareholders at a flat rate of 10 percent of the dividends declared. Nonresident companies that operate through a branch in South Africa are exempt from STC. STC is scheduled to be replaced in the near future by a 10 percent withholding tax on dividends paid to resident and nonresident shareholders.

(d) Other Tax Issues

- The Commissioner of the South African Revenue Service is entitled, for tax purposes, to adjust the consideration for goods or services supplied in terms of an international agreement to reflect an arm's-length price, if the acquirer is a "connected person" in relation to a supplier.
- Thin capitalization rules will generally disallow interest incurred on financial assistance from a nonresident to certain residents that results in a debt-to-equity ratio of more than 3:1.
- A resident is entitled to a rebate in relation to certain taxes on income payable to the government of another country.

- The tax liability of a foreign company is contingent upon the nature of the income derived by it, as well as upon the existence of a DTA.
- Interest received by or accrued to a person who is not a resident of South Africa is generally exempt from income tax, irrespective of its source.

(e) Other Tax Types

- In terms of the Securities Transfer Tax Act, 2007, securities transfer tax (STT) is generally payable at a rate of 0.25 percent by the transferee with respect to the transfer of certain securities.
- Value-added tax (VAT) is the principal source of indirect taxation revenue, and applies to most economic activity. VAT liability is assessed and regulated in terms of the Value Added Tax Act, 1991. At present, the standard rate of VAT is 14 percent, though numerous goods are zero rated or exempt from VAT. The ultimate VAT burden rests on the consumer. Any business registered as a VAT vendor that invests in any assets can fully reclaim its VAT payable.
- Transfer duty is levied in terms of the Transfer Duty Act, 1949, which provides for tax payable on the transfer of immovable property by an individual.
- Estate duty, donations tax, skills development levies, and unemployment insurance fund contributions are also payable in certain instances.

4.3.3 Employment Law

South Africa has a stringent employment law regime, which is governed by over fifteen statutes as well as various "Codes of Good Practice," most notably the Labour Relations Act, 1995, and the Basic Conditions of Employment Act, 1997. The Constitution also contains provisions with relevance to employment law, such as the protection against unfair discrimination, the right to fair labor practices, and the right to strike. BEE impacts on South African employment law to a significant extent.

4.3.4 Competition Law

Competition law is governed by the Competition Act, 1998 (the "Competition Act"), which, subject to a few exceptions, applies to all economic activity within, or having an effect within, South Africa. The provisions of the Competition Act are enforced by three separate agencies: the Competition Commission, the Competition Tribunal, and the Competition Appeal Court.

4.3.5 Prohibited Practices

The Competition Act prohibits, *inter alia*, restrictive horizontal practices and restrictive vertical practices. A horizontal relationship is a relationship between competitors, while a vertical relationship is one between a firm and its suppliers, customers, or both. Agreements between firms in a horizontal or vertical relationship that substantially prevent or lessen competition are prohibited unless a party to the agreement can prove that any resultant technological, efficiency, or other pro-competitive gain outweighs that effect.

The Competition Act also prohibits outright price-fixing, division of markets, collusive tendering, and abuse by a firm of its dominant position within a market.

A wide range of remedies are provided in instances of contravention of the Competition Act.

A firm may apply to the Competition Commission for an exemption in relation to an agreement or practice that would otherwise contravene the Competition Act, on certain specified grounds. For example, an exemption can be obtained on the grounds that the agreement or practice contributes to the prevention of a decline in an industry.

4.3.6 Mergers
The Competition Act distinguishes between small, intermediate, and large mergers, and its provisions will not apply if a particular transaction does not meet the stipulated threshold for an intermediate or large merger. The parties to an intermediate or large merger may not implement such a merger until it has been approved by the Competition Commission, Competition Tribunal, or Competition Appeal Court, as applicable.

4.3.7 Intellectual Property and Franchising
South Africa is a signatory to the Berne Convention,[16] the Paris Convention,[17] and the Patent Cooperation Treaty,[18] as well as a member of the World Intellectual Property Organization. Trademarks, copyrights, registered designs, and patents are regulated by statute. Franchising has increased in South Africa in recent years, often in order to grow businesses owned by previously disadvantaged persons.

4.3.8 Environmental Law
The Constitution provides that everyone has the right to an environment that is not harmful to their health or well-being and to have the environment protected, for the benefit of present and future generations.

South Africa's important environmental legislation includes:

- the National Environmental Management Act, 1998, which establishes procedures and institutions that promote public

---

[16] The Berne Convention for the Protection of Literary and Artistic Works, 1886, as revised and amended.
[17] The Paris Convention for the Protection of Industrial Property, 1883, as revised and amended.
[18] The Patent Cooperation Treaty, 1970, as modified and amended.

participation in environmental management and regulates the system of environmental impact assessments and related management tools. It enshrines the principles of sustainable development and "the polluter pays";

- the National Environmental Management: Air Quality Act, 2004, which provides reasonable measures for the protection and enhancement of the quality of air;
- the Environment Conservation Act, 1989, which provides for the protection and control of the environment and regulates waste management;
- the Hazardous Substances Act, 1973, which controls substances that may cause injury or ill-health;
- the National Environmental Management: Protected Areas Act, 2003, which provides for the declaration and management of protected areas;
- the Fertilizers, Farm Feeds, Agricultural Remedies and Stock Remedies Act, 1947, which regulates the use of pesticides and fertilizers; and
- the Marine Living Resources Act, 1998, which makes provision for the conservation of the marine ecosystem.

4.3.9 Market Abuse and Money Laundering

Money laundering is combated with the Prevention of Organised Crime Act, 1998, which provides for offenses relating to the proceeds of unlawful activities, and the Financial Intelligence Centre Act, 2001. The latter places onerous identification, record-keeping, and reporting obligations on certain institutions. The Financial Intelligence Centre retains and analyzes all information disclosed to it, and initiates investigations into money laundering offences.

5. Dispute Resolution

Ultimately, the reliability and efficiency of South African dispute resolution mechanisms are crucial to international business. South Africa's legal system offers a number of generally well-functioning options for dispute resolution. There is a system of lower and superior courts, and arbitration, governed by the Arbitration Act, 1965 (the "Arbitration Act"), which provides an effective alternative means to resolve disputes. Litigation and other dispute resolution proceedings are adversarial rather than inquisitorial in nature.

5.1 Court Proceedings

Under the State Liability Act, 1957, the South African state does not enjoy sovereign immunity and may sue or be sued (subject to certain limitations).

Although foreign judgments are not directly enforceable in South Africa, they constitute a cause of action that can be pursued in South African courts (subject to the fulfillment of a number of requirements). The recognition and enforcement of South African judgments in foreign countries are governed, of course, by the laws of the country in which the judgment is sought to be enforced.

5.2 Arbitration, Including International Arbitration

The Arbitration Act does not distinguish between domestic arbitrations and international arbitrations. The Arbitration Act provides for the stay of court proceedings, should a party to a dispute that is subject to an arbitration clause in an agreement embark on litigation without following the arbitration procedure. Parties to an arbitration agreement are, however, permitted to seek an interim remedy from a court, pending the outcome of the arbitration proceedings.

In principle, the parties are free to adopt the procedure of their choice. In the domestic context, the rules of the Arbitration Foundation of Southern Africa or the Association of Arbitrators are often incorporated into arbitration agreements by reference.

There is no appeal from the decision of an arbitrator unless an appeal procedure is agreed to by the parties. The power of the court to intervene in arbitration proceedings is limited to very narrow grounds of review (essentially, if the arbitrator has misconducted himself or herself in relation to his or her duty as arbitrator or has committed a gross irregularity in the conduct of the proceedings).

South Africa is a party to the 1958 New York Convention on the Recognition and Enforcement of Foreign Arbitral Awards, thereby providing an efficient mechanism for the enforcement of foreign arbitral awards in South Africa. The recognition and enforcement of South African arbitral awards in foreign countries are governed by the law of the country in which awards are sought to be enforced.

South Africa is not a party to the 1965 Washington Convention on the Settlement of Investment Disputes Between States and Nationals of Other States (the "ICSID Convention," under which was established the International Centre for Settlement of Investment Disputes), but many of the contracts that the South African government and its agencies conclude with foreign bodies and investors provide for compulsory international arbitration under the International Chamber of Commerce Rules or the UN Commission on International Trade (UNCITRAL) Arbitration Rules.

South Africa has also ratified many bilateral investment treaties (with countries such as the United Kingdom, China, Germany, France, the Netherlands, Italy, and South Korea), which include guarantees of fair and equitable treatment for foreign investors, the extension of "most favored nation" benefits, and strong protection against unreasonable, unlawful, or inadequately compensated expropriation of foreign investments. Disputes under these agreements are usually referred to an international arbitral tribunal under the ICSID Convention Additional Facility Rules 1978 or an ad hoc tribunal under the UNCITRAL Rules.

Victoria Page, Vlad Movshovich, and Ashleigh Hammond
Webber Wentzel
10 Fricker Road, Illovo Boulevard
Johannesburg, 2196, South Africa
Phone: +(27) (11) 530 5000
Fax: +(27) (11) 530 5111
E-mail: victoria.page@webberwentzel.com

CHAPTER 45

International Business Negotiations in Spain

Carlos de Cárdenas Smith and Ángel Pérez López
Uría Menéndez
Madrid, Spain

1. Introduction

1.1 Broad Demographic Information

Spain, which is located in southwest Europe, has an area of 505,955 square kilometers and is among the largest countries in Europe. The most significant part of the Spanish territory is the Iberian Peninsula, while the Balearic and the Canary Islands represent approximately 12,500 square kilometers and the cities of Ceuta and Melilla, situated on the North African coast, represent 32 square kilometers.

The Spanish population, which is predominantly European Caucasian, has increased considerably in the last five decades, reaching over 44 million with a per capita income of approximately EUR 20,000 per year, placing Spain among the ten strongest Western economies. However, these figures may not be completely accurate due to the flow of illegal immigration arriving from Latin America, Africa, and Eastern Europe.

1.2 Historical and Cultural Background

In the last three decades, Spain has undergone one of the most significant "revolutions" in the Western world. Significant political and economic development marks this period in which Spain has finally achieved recognition as a full member of Europe.

In 1978, Spain created and adopted a new Constitution, which, after forty years of dictatorship, marked the beginning of Spanish contemporary history. The nation's transition to democracy was accomplished in a peaceful manner, which surprised many and served as an example for other countries in transition.

The Spanish Constitution, which is the fundamental political organization regulation, configures Spain as a parliamentary monarchy where the powers of the state are divided, as in most Western countries, into three parts: the legislative, the executive, and the judicial. With its implementation in 1978, the central government lost part of its powers in favor of autonomous territorial bodies, the autonomous regions (*comunidades autónomas*). Seventeen autonomous regions were established, covering the whole of Spain, each of them regulated by a statute of autonomy (*estatuto de autonomía*), which governs the basis of its political organization. Each of the autonomous regions is divided into provinces (there are fifty) and each province is divided into municipalities (up to 8,107), which constitute the local administration.

Economic prosperity has followed the new political situation. The 1973 economic crisis reached Spain and shocked its economy in the late 1970s. The political circumstances did not create an ideal scenario to handle such economic problems, and this background did not get any better until the early 1980s. Since then, however, the Spanish economy has experienced significant growth. In the last twenty years, the Spanish gross national product has increased by over 40 percent in real terms, one of the highest rates of increase within the Organisation for Economic Co-operation and Development (OECD). The Spanish gross national product has grown steadily during the last decade at rates of between 2.7 percent and 5 percent, doubling the Eurozone rates almost every year. This improvement may eventually win Spain a seat in the G8.

Spain joined the European Economic Community (now the European Union) in 1985, and replaced the peseta with the euro on January 1, 1999. However, it was not until January 1, 2002, that the euro effectively replaced the peseta as the day-to-day currency.

While the recent economic growth of Spain has been momentous, there are still some uncertainties regarding the future of Spain's economy. Because Spain depends on the import of energy (especially petrol and natural gas) and technology, the Spanish balance of payments is negative. The Spanish economy has been heavily influenced by domestic demand, backed by the development of the construction industry and historically low interest rates. Therefore, an increase in the interest rates and the decrease of the demand for real estate could adversely affect Spain's economic growth. In addition, the existence of a significant under-the-counter economy—that is, one that is run without the control of the Ministry of Economy and Finance—must also be taken into account when considering the future growth of the Spanish economy.

1.3 Business Organization and Culture

The Spanish economy is focused mainly upon the services sector. At the present time, agriculture represents approximately 6 percent, industry (including construction) represents approximately 30 percent, and the services sector (with tourism as one of the main Spanish industries) represents 64 percent of Spain's gross national product.

Four different types of entrepreneurs are dominant in Spain: (1) small and medium-size companies that are run by individuals and families; (2) banks; (3) large construction companies, which were expanded because of the importance of the construction industry in the development of the Spanish economy and which diversify their business by also providing public services through concessions granted by public authorities; and (4) other large companies formerly owned by the Spanish state.

In recent years, certain interesting managerial trends have been emerging in the Spanish economy. On the one hand, individual and public entrepreneurs have been developing and implementing new managerial techniques. Spanish companies have begun competing abroad (first in Latin America, and then in the UK and Eastern Europe) and have become progressively integrated into the international economy. A new generation with an international approach has been managing these companies. On the other hand, in the last few years major Spanish banks have been abandoning their traditional involvement in the management of large Spanish companies to focus on the pure banking business, although the major savings banks (*cajas de ahorros*) still hold a significant stake in large Spanish companies.

1.4 Overview of the Legal System

In Spain international negotiations can be impacted by statutes enacted by at least four different territorial bodies. Each of these bodies is competent, to a certain extent, to enact and implement its own legislation. The four bodies are the European Union (EU) at supranational level; the Spanish state at national level; the autonomous regions at regional level; and the municipalities at local level.

Most of the issues that have an influence on negotiations are governed either by laws enacted by the legislative branch or by regulations enacted by the central government that flesh out such laws. However, those matters regarding competition, consumer protection, or subsidies to investments may be affected by statutes enacted by either the EU or the autonomous regions, and those matters regarding interest rates and monetary policy are affected by the decisions of the Central European Bank.

Because it is a civil law country, case law or court rulings are less important in Spain than in common law jurisdictions such as the United States or the UK. Court rulings are not a source of law in Spain. The function of Supreme Court (*Tribunal Supremo*) rulings is, according to Article 1.6 of the Spanish Civil Code (*Código Civil*), "to complete the legal system through the interpretation and enforcement of the law, tradition, and the general legal principles."

2. Substantive Laws and Regulations Impacting International Negotiations

2.1 Corporate Laws

Under Spanish law, there are two different kinds of limited liability companies: *sociedad anónima* or "SA" (which most closely resembles the U.S. "Inc.") and *sociedad de responsabilidad limitada* or "SL." However, Spanish legislation foresees other corporate forms, namely partnerships (*sociedades colectivas, sociedades comanditarias simples, sociedades comanditarias por acciones,* or *sociedades civiles*) and cooperatives with varying degrees of liability or independent management.

In addition, other legal vehicles have emerged more recently due to the transposition of certain EU directives: economic interest groupings (*agrupaciones de interés económico*), European economic interest groupings (*agrupaciones europeas de interés económico*) and European public companies (*sociedades anónimas europeas*). However, such vehicles are seldom used in Spanish practice.

Depending on the type of company or partnership, acquisition of a participation in the capital of such legal entity in Spain may be limited or even restricted to certain persons. In the case of *sociedades anónimas,* bylaws may include restrictions on the transfer of shares and limits regarding voting power. In the case of *sociedades de responsabilidad limitada,* the nontransferring shareholders have preemption rights by operation of law in the event of an intended transfer of stock. The legal vehicle to be used is relevant in determining the procedure to be followed in adopting resolutions.

Information regarding the incorporation of the company, its directors, bylaws, corporate domicile, annual accounts, and authorized representatives can be obtained from the Commercial Registry (*Registro Mercantil*) of the province where the corporate domicile is located.

2.2 Securities Laws

Law 24/1988 of July 28, 1988, on the securities market, as amended, is the cornerstone of the new securities regulations. The law adapts Spanish legislation to relevant EU directives. The *Comisión Nacional del Mercado de Valores* (Spanish Securities and Exchange Commission, or CNMV) is the regulatory authority in charge of the securities market. The CNMV is competent to publish circulars, as well as to authorize or disallow specific transactions that do not conform to securities regulations.

The securities regulations dealing with takeover bids and public offerings are arguably the most important regulations to be considered by foreign investors negotiating in Spain. In addition, Royal Decree 1362/2007 of October 19, 2007, transposing in Spain Directive 2004/109/EC of the European Parliament and the Council of

December 15, 2004, on transparency, has tightened the information duties and the liability of the issuers and their directors, which are harmonized with other EU member states.

2.2.1 Takeover Bids

Spain has enacted strict rules governing the acquisition of relevant holdings in the share capital of a listed company. Law 6/2007 of April 13, 2007, modifying the rules for takeover bids, and Royal Decree 1066/2007 of July 27, 2007, which has further elaborated the requirements of Law 6/2007, are the cornerstones of the Spanish regulation. The basic principle of the Spanish takeover rules states that whoever obtains "control" of a listed company must make a bid for all shares, or other securities that may directly or indirectly give the right to their subscription or acquisition, to all holders at an "equitable price." Consequently, of particular importance to the analysis of any proposed takeover bid are: (i) the concepts of control and equitable price, and (ii) the parties to whom the bid is addressed.

Control over a listed company may be obtained by means of the acquisition of shares or other securities that directly or indirectly give the right to subscribe or acquire voting shares in such company, by means of shareholders' agreements (*pactos parasociales*) with other holders of securities, or as a result of indirect or unexpected takeovers (i.e., mergers or indirect takeovers, capital reductions, changes in the treasury stock of the listed company, acquisition of shares of a listed company through the conversion or exchange of other securities or financial instruments, and acquisitions by underwriting of issuances).

According to Spanish law, an individual or a legal entity is deemed to have, individually or collectively with the persons acting in concert, control of a company when:

i.   they directly or indirectly reach a percentage of voting rights equal to or exceeding 30 percent (which is the threshold also established in other European countries);

ii. holding any interest carrying less than 30 percent of voting rights, such persons appoint, within twenty-four months following the acquisition, a number of directors that, together with those already appointed by it, if any, represents more than one-half of the members of the board of directors; or

iii. as a special rule, any person who, as of August 13, 2007, directly or indirectly holds an interest carrying 30 percent or more, but less than 50 percent, of the voting rights of a listed company, if (a) it acquires shares of the company that increase its interest by at least 5 percent over a twelve-month period; (b) it obtains a percentage of votes that is equal to or greater than 50 percent; or (c) it acquires an additional interest and, within twenty-four months following such acquisition, appoints a number of directors that, together with those previously appointed by it, if any, represent more than one-half of the members of the board of directors of the company.

Mandatory takeover bids must be made at an "equitable price." A price is considered equitable when it is at least equal to the highest price paid by the party required to make the takeover bid, or the persons acting in concert for the same, during a period of twelve months prior to the announcement of the bid. In the event that the offeror did not make any acquisitions in the twelve months prior to the announcement of the takeover bid, the equitable price may not be less than the price calculated pursuant to the valuation rules set forth in the Royal Decree for delisting offers.

The mandatory takeover bid must be addressed to: (i) all the holders of voting shares of the listed company; (ii) all the holders of nonvoting shares of the listed company who, at the time of requesting authorization for the bid, are entitled to vote; and (iii) all the holders of rights to subscribe for shares, as well as the holders of debentures convertible into or exchangeable for shares. The bid need not be addressed to the holders of warrants or other securities or instruments entitling the holder to acquire or subscribe for shares, but if it is, the takeover bid must afford equal treatment to all holders of such securities, and such bid must therefore be addressed to all of them.

Law 6/2007 has dramatically altered the regulation of takeover bids in Spain, replacing the traditional system of *ex ante* takeover bids (which required the making of a takeover bid in order to exceed a certain percentage of stock) for *ex post* takeover bids, and requiring a mandatory bid addressed to all the shareholders to acquire all the shares.

Even if the bid is not mandatory because the relevant control thresholds for such purposes have not been reached, takeover bids may be made voluntarily. Thus, for example, whoever does not hold control of a listed company and seeks to acquire it, or, while already possessing a controlling interest, wishes to increase its interest in the target company, may make a voluntary takeover bid. Voluntary bids are governed by the same rules as mandatory bids, with the following exceptions: (i) voluntary bids may be subject to conditions (while mandatory bids may not); (ii) voluntary bids do not need to be made at an equitable price; (iii) if the voluntary bid is structured as an exchange of securities, a cash consideration or price that is at least financially equivalent to the exchange offered does not need to be included as an alternative; and (iv) voluntary bids may be made for less than the total number of securities.

In addition to takeover bids where control of a listed company is obtained and voluntary bids, Spanish regulations also contemplate two other types of bids: delisting offers and takeover bids due to capital reduction through the acquisition of a company's own shares.

Although launching a takeover bid does not prevent the execution of preparatory agreements with the target company, in Spanish practice, except for confidentiality agreements under which the future offeror conducts a due diligence review of the target company, it is not customary for the target company and the future offeror to enter into any agreements in preparation for the takeover bid. Royal Decree 1066/2007 expressly allows for the possibility of the target company and the first offeror agreeing in advance on a break-up fee. Accordingly, in some cases the target company and future offeror may enter into an agreement to this effect. A due diligence review of a target company may also be conducted prior to making a takeover bid for securities. However, a limitation on the agreements made prior to the making of a takeover bid derives from the principle of "equal amount of information for competing offerors" established in the Royal Decree. Consequently, the availability of information to existing or potential offerors is conditional upon fulfilment of the following conditions: (i) the information being specifically requested by the existing or potential offeror; (ii) such information having been previously provided to other existing or potential offerors; (iii) the recipient of the information duly ensuring the confidentiality thereof, and such information being used for the sole purpose of making a takeover bid; and (iv) the information being necessary to make the bid.

2.2.2 Offerings of Securities

Offerings of securities are governed by Royal Decree 1310/2005 of November 4, 2005 (provided that such offerings are of the type that are within the scope of the Royal Decree). The inclusion in such scope requires the fulfillment of both the objective and the territorial requirements. Furthermore, it will be necessary to ensure that none of the specific exclusions set forth in the Royal Decree 1310/2005 apply to such offerings. What follows below is a summary of the more pertinent requirements of such Royal Decree, including, without limitation, a description of the types and categories of offerings that are excluded from the scope of such Royal Decree:

i. Objective requisites consist in the qualification of (a) the securities as "negotiable securities" and (b) the offering as a "public offering." According to Royal Decree 1310/2005, any type of right with economic value, whatever its name, that, due to its nature and transfer regime, can be traded in a financial market due to its legal nature and transferability characteristics is a "negotiable security." The concept of negotiable security includes shares and other transferable securities that are equivalent to shares, as well as to any other type of negotiable securities that entitles its holders to acquire any of these securities through conversion or by exercising the rights conferred by the relevant securities, preferred capital securities (*partici-paciones preferentes*), share quotas (*cuotas participativas*) in saving banks, warrants over negotiable securities, securities that represent an interest over securitized assets, etc.

In addition, a "public offering" is understood as any communication made to persons by any means that provides sufficient information about the terms and conditions of the offering and the offered securities to allow an investor to decide on the acquisition or subscription of such securities.

ii.   The complex set of territorial requirements of Royal Decree 1310/2005 may trigger the application of its provisions not only when the issuer has its corporate domicile in Spain, but also when it is domiciled in a non-EU state and appoints Spain as member state of origin. Spain can only be validly appointed as member state of origin if the securities have been publicly offered for the first time in Spain after December 31, 2003, or the issuer has applied for the admission to trading of the securities in a Spanish market for the first time.

iii. Despite its compliance with both the objective and territorial requirements, Royal Decree 1310/2005 expressly excludes from its scope the offerings of securities:

a.   addressed solely to qualified investors. This concept includes institutional investors, national and regional governments, central banks, international and supranational institutions, large enterprises, small and medium-size enterprises that have expressly requested to be considered as qualified investors, and individuals domiciled in Spain having expressly requested to be considered as qualified investors and meeting certain minimum trading thresholds;

b.   addressed to fewer than one hundred natural or legal persons, other than qualified investors, per EU member state;

c.   addressed to investors who acquire securities for a total consideration of at least EUR 50,000 per investor, for each separate offer;

d.   where the securities denomination per unit is at least EUR 50,000; or

e.   where the total consideration of such securities is less than EUR 2,500,000, calculated over a period of twelve months.

If an issue or offering falls within the scope of application of Royal Decree 1310/2005:

i.   the issuer must be validly incorporated under the laws of the country in which it has its registered office and must be operating in accordance with its memorandum of incorporation and bylaws or equivalent documentation;

ii. the securities must conform to the legal system to which they are subject;

iii. the issuer must submit and file with the CNMV (a) the applicable documents that evidence that the issuer and the securities comply with their applicable governing laws, and (b) the financial statements of the issuer prepared and audited in accordance with the law that applies to the issuer. However, these requirements do not apply to "nonequity securities" (*valores no participativos,* i.e., mainly any negotiable securities that do not qualify as shares or other transferable securities that are equivalent to shares or convertible into shares) issued by the (a) Spanish state, the autonomous regions, and local authorities, (b) any other EU member state, (c) international public bodies belonging to one or more EU member states, (d) the Central European Bank, (e) the central banks of the EU member states, or (f) legal entities domiciled in Spain and created by a special law, provided that the principal and interest of the securities issued by such legal entities are unconditionally and irrevocably guaranteed by the Spanish state; and

iv. the prior publication of a prospectus approved by the CNMV, or by the competent authority of the EU member state of the issuer, if applicable, which will be recognized in Spain pursuant to the provisions of Royal Decree 1310/2005. The publication of a prospectus can be excluded under certain circumstances contemplated in the Royal Decree.

Transposing in Spain, among others, Directive 2003/71/EC of the European Parliament and of the Council of November 4, 2003, on Prospectuses, Royal Decree 1310/2005 has made effective in Spain the "European passport" for prospectuses, thereby homogenizing Spanish and European regulations. Accordingly, and quite significantly, prospectuses approved in Spain will be valid (with no additional information requirements) in other EU member states, and vice versa.

2.3 Tax Laws

Spain has a fairly complex tax system with a wide variety of direct and indirect taxes. The Spanish tax system is currently based mainly on three kinds of levies: *impuestos* (taxes), *tasas* (dues and fees), and *contribuciones especiales* (special levies). The *tasas* and *contribuciones especiales* are quantitatively much lower than the taxes and were originally collected respectively in return for a public service provided by the local authorities or for any type of benefit as a result of public works or services. Although the state imposes most taxes in Spain, local authorities and autonomous regions also levy taxes and have a limited capacity to amend certain state taxes. Furthermore, the autonomous regions of the Basque Country and Navarre have a special tax system controlled by their respective local legislation within the framework of the central national tax system.

Foreign investors doing business in Spain will normally operate through (i) a Spanish company, which would be subject to Spanish Corporate Income Tax ("CIT" or *Impuesto sobre Sociedades*), (ii) a permanent establishment in Spain, or (iii) directly as nonresident taxpayers, being in (ii) and (iii) above subject to Non-Resident Income Tax ("NRIT" or *Impuesto sobre la Renta de no Residentes*). Therefore, this section will focus on these two taxes.

2.3.1 Corporate Income Tax

CIT is governed by the Royal Legislative Decree 4/2004 of March 5, 2004, enacting the Consolidated Text of the Corporate Income Tax Act (*Ley del Impuesto sobre Sociedades*), as further regulated by Royal Decree 777/2004. CIT is a direct and proportional tax levied on the income of companies and other legal entities that are taxed under Spanish law as Spanish tax residents (i.e., companies incorporated under Spanish law, or whose registered office or place of effective management is located in the Spanish territory).

The CIT's general rate, applicable to Spanish resident entities and permanent establishments of nonresident entities, is 32.5 percent for tax year 2007. For tax years starting after January 1, 2008, this rate will be reduced down to 30 percent. Companies with a turnover in the previous tax year of under EUR 8 million can apply a reduced tax rate of 25 percent for the first EUR 120,202.41 of their taxable base and 30 percent for amounts exceeding this threshold.

The CIT law has traditionally offered certain advantages for those transactions carried out with high leverage. Interest is deductible (although interest deductibility may be challenged on the basis of substance-over-form if the financing is not related to the business activity of the company), while dividend and profit distributions are not. However, in the case of international structures, thin-capitalization rules provided in the CIT law apply. Thus, interest corresponding to debt with a related foreign company that exceeds three times the average equity of the Spanish company will be taxed as dividend, and therefore is nondeductible and will be subject to the relevant dividend withholding tax, as determined by Spanish law (currently 18 percent) or any applicable bilateral treaty for the avoidance of double taxation. As an exception, Spanish thin-capitalization rules do not apply when the related party is (i) resident in a EU member state, (ii) not operating through a Spanish permanent establishment, and (iii) not operating through a tax haven territory, as defined under Spanish tax law.

Certain special tax regimes are also offered by the CIT law, such as the neutral tax treatment for reorganization structures carried out through mergers, splits, contributions in kind of a branch of activity, and exchange of securities. This tax-neutral regime will be applicable if there are financial business reasons for the merger other than merely achieving a tax advantage. This may be confirmed by the tax authorities through the issue of a binding ruling. Furthermore, the CIT law provides for a tax-consolidated group regime in which a group of companies may be taxed on the group's consolidated tax base, provided that it reports such choice to the Spanish tax authorities and fulfills certain requirements.

2.3.2 Non-Resident Income Tax

The NRIT is levied on nonresident taxpayers' Spanish income, including, among others, personal and business income from an economic activity carried out in Spain, pursuant to Royal Legislative Decree 5/2004 of March 5, 2004. Nonresident taxpayers are subject to different rules under the NRIT depending on whether or not they have a permanent establishment in Spain (i.e., if they operate in Spain through a fixed place of business, or they operate in Spain through an authorized dependent agent).

Nonresident taxpayers operating in Spain through a permanent establishment will be taxed on the net income attributable to the permanent establishment at the same rate (32.5 percent in 2007 and 30 percent in subsequent years) as Spanish companies. A branch profit tax of 18 percent will be levied on profits obtained from the permanent establishment, although most double-taxation treaties offer relief in this respect, and additionally, it is not levied on payments to residents in other EU member states.

On the other hand, nonresidents without a permanent establishment in Spain are taxed on each individual Spanish source of income. The general rate is 24 percent, although dividends and interest payments received by a nonresident without a permanent establishment in Spain from a Spanish resident, as well as capital gains, are taxed at 18 percent.

As a result of the transposition of the EU Parent-Subsidiary Directive, no tax is payable on dividends paid by Spanish subsidiaries to their EU-resident parent companies, provided that the conditions contemplated by such Directive are met. In addition, interest payable to EU resident lenders is tax exempt. Capital gains are exempt as well, except if the applicable gains are triggered on the sale of Spanish real estate or on the sale of shares of a company on which the EU resident seller had at least a 25 percent stake at any time during the twelve months preceding the sale.

Moreover, royalties paid by a company resident in Spain to a nonresident taxpayer are subject to withholding tax in Spain at a 24 percent rate or at the reduced rate provided for in the corresponding income treaty. Pursuant to the so-called EU Interest and Royalties Directive, royalties paid to a related company resident for tax purposes in an EU member state shall be exempt from withholding tax as of January 1, 2010 (during the transitional period beginning June 30, 2004, such payments have been subject to 10 percent withholding tax).

Nonresident entities owning Spanish real estate will be subject to an annual 3 percent tax on the value assigned by the Real Estate

Registry (*Registro de la Propiedad*) to such real estate. Persons engaged in a trade or business in Spain, taxpayers resident in a country with an applicable bilateral treaty for the avoidance of double taxation, and other groups will be exempt from this tax. Those purchasing real estate located in Spain from nonresidents without a permanent establishment must withhold 5 percent of the purchase price on account of the vendor's capital gains tax liability, unless the transferred property was acquired by the seller before December 31, 1986.

2.3.3 Other Taxes

The Spanish transfer pricing rules that apply to the transactions of related parties are based on OECD Transfer Pricing Guidelines. Therefore, the Spanish Tax Authorities are entitled to reassess all related party transactions to their fair market value and to recharacterize some transactions to their actual economic nature (i.e., interest in excess of market interest rates may be recharacterized as dividends).

Transfer tax, capital tax, and stamp duty are governed by one Act (*Impuesto sobre Transmisiones Patrimoniales y Actos Jurídicos Documentados*). This tax is levied on: (i) transfers of certain property defined by law (mainly real estate) for valuable consideration, generally at a 7 percent tax rate (transfer tax), (ii) certain transactions involving companies (e.g., incorporation or share capital increase), at a 1 percent tax rate (capital duty); and (iii) documented legal transactions (notarial deeds; commercial, executive, and court documents), which tax rates range from 0.5 percent to 2 percent (stamp duty). An anti-accumulation provision establishes that a single transaction falling into two or three categories can only be taxed once.

Value-added tax (VAT) is levied on transfers of goods made or services provided by entrepreneurs, on certain intra-EU acquisitions, and on the import of goods. In the Canary Islands, Ceuta, and Melilla, no VAT is applicable, but special indirect taxes are levied. VAT rates depend on the type of goods delivered or services provided (the standard rate is 16 percent).

In addition, there are also special indirect taxes (*Impuestos especiales*) that are levied when acquiring certain products (such as alcoholic drinks, tobacco, electricity, hydrocarbons, etc) or when receiving some services (such as power, insurance, etc).

There are also taxes levied by the local administrations, such as Tax on Economic Activities (*Impuesto sobre Actividades Económicas*), Tax on Real Estate Property (*Impuesto sobre Bienes Inmuebles*), Tax on Motor Vehicles (*Impuesto sobre Vehículos Tracción Mecánica*), Tax on Construction and Installation Projects (*Impuesto sobre Construcciones Instalaciones y Obras*), and an Urban Land Appreciation Tax (*Impuesto sobre el Incremento de Valor de los Terrenos de Naturaleza Urbana*).

As a final point, it should be noted that Spanish tax authorities are extremely suspicious of tax havens. In fact, no benefit can be granted to any return obtained by nonresidents—even those with residence in an EU Member State—through a country or jurisdiction that is listed as a tax haven by Spanish tax regulations.

2.4 Antitrust/Anticompetition Laws

Antitrust and competition law is governed by Law 15/2007 of July 3, 2007, for the Defense of Competition. This law has substantially reformed Spanish competition rules. It has created the National Competition Commission (*Comisión Nacional de la Competencia* or "CNC"), which is the new administrative authority primarily responsible for the application of Spanish and EU competition rules. The CNC has been structured in two separate departments, the Enquiry Directorate (*Dirección de Investigación*), which will deal with the inquiry phase of infringement proceedings and the first phase of merger control proceedings, and the Council (*Consejo*) acting as a decision-making body in both fields. The decisions adopted by the CNC are subject to appeal before the *Audiencia Nacional*. In addition, regional competition authorities may be created by each autonomous region and will have executive powers for the application of Spanish (not EU) competition rules (save merger control rules) insofar as their effects are limited to their respective territories.

Law 15/2007 prohibits three different kinds of practices that restrict competition: (i) entering into agreements, recommendations, decisions, acts, or parallel conduct that tends to eliminate, reduce, or mislead, wholly or in part, the Spanish market; (ii) abuse of a dominant position in the market; and (iii) unfair competition. Nevertheless, certain actions that would be prohibited under (i) can be authorized either by a specific law or by the CNC. In addition, *de minimis* restrictive agreements and abuses of dominance—that is, those having only a negligible effect on competition—will not fall within the scope of the prohibitions set out in Law 15/2007.

At the same time, Law 15/2007 does not allow certain takeovers, mergers, or reorganization transactions if, as a result of such transactions, the Spanish market would be substantially affected. In this regard, the Law establishes two different thresholds: (i) there is a combined turnover in Spain of EUR 240 million of all the undertakings concerned and an individual turnover in Spain of EUR 60 million of at least two of the undertakings concerned; or (ii) as a consequence of the concentration a 30 percent market share of any product or service market affected by the transaction in Spain or a geographical market within Spain is obtained. If any of such thresholds is met, parties to a transaction must notify the concentration to the CNC and request an authorization before closing the transaction.

Law 15/2007 also amends the treatment of takeover bids, in line with EU rules on this matter. According to Law 15/2007, it will be possible to launch a takeover bid before antitrust clearance is obtained, provided that: (i) the concentration is reported to the CNC within five days; and (ii) the acquirer does not exercise the voting rights attached to the securities in question or does so only to maintain the full value of its investments based on a waiver granted by the CNC.

In addition, EU regulations must be taken into account with respect to competition activities. In fact, one of the areas in which the EU has adopted a somewhat active position is that relating to fair competition within the European market. The Treaty of Rome specifically prohibits anticompetitive conduct, setting out the control of fair competition within EU bodies. Therefore, any acts, agreements, or parallel conduct that affects or might affect the common market, or any abuses of dominant positions, are bound by EU regulations, and the Commission is competent to stop any merger, takeover, or concentration transaction if, as a result of it, competition in the European market may be adversely affected.

2.5 Labor Law and Employment Laws

Spanish labor law has traditionally been characterized by its strong protection of employees against possible abuses by employers. Accordingly, there is a general principle under Spanish labor law known as *pro-operario,* which establishes that, in the event of doubt, the law must be interpreted in favor of employees.

Spanish labor relationships are regulated mainly by internal laws, collective bargaining agreements, and individual employment contracts. Among internal laws, the Spanish Constitution provides the basic legal framework, but it is the Statute of Workers, approved by Royal Legislative Decree 1/1995 of March 24, 1995, that is the cornerstone instrument regulating employment matters. In addition, other regulations and, specifically, collective bargaining agreements (*convenios colectivos*) between employers and employees, either at a national, regional, or industrial level, are relevant in determining the rights and obligations of each party.

Any negotiation that may involve labor issues must take into consideration that individual dismissals are difficult and often expensive, and should be justified by one of the reasons provided by law (mainly, disciplinary or economic reasons), and that collective dismissals will generally imply negotiations with employee representatives and the authorization of the labor authorities.

The acquisition of substantial assets of a business will generally imply for the buyer the assumption of all labor rights and obligations that employees had with the seller, including those regarding social security and private pension plans. However, employees do not have a right to remain employed by the seller; therefore, once the sale is effective, employees automatically become employees of the buyer.

2.6 Environmental Laws

Spanish environmental administrative legislation has undergone an intensive implementation and updating process in the last two decades. A large number of rules and regulations, general and specific, have been enacted by the state, the autonomous regions, and the municipalities, normally following EU rules. Therefore, environmental regulations are becoming an important issue to take into consideration when entering into transactions in Spain.

Breach of the environmental regulations could give rise to civil liability, criminal liability, and/or administrative sanctions.

2.6.1 Civil Liability

Spanish courts are applying to environmental cases the general principles of civil liability established in the Civil Code. The application of the existing provisions has led to the evolution of a system that adopts an approach that is very close to a strict liability system in the environmental field. The Spanish Supreme Court has assigned to the defendant the burden of proving that it acted with all the caution and diligence required to prevent the occurrence of the damage in cases in which the defendant has created a risk of damage by carrying out potentially harmful or damaging activities or in cases in which the defendant has benefited from the activity that caused the damage, regardless of the legality of the defendant's actions.

2.6.2 Criminal Liability

Criminal environmental regulations have changed in recent years, with a tendency (mainly boosted by Spanish courts and certain groups and associations) to enlarge and emphasize the number of environmental criminal offenses and to increase their penalties. Acts that seriously endanger human health, wildlife, forests, or plantations, even if no effective damage is caused, could be considered a criminal offense under the Criminal Code.

2.6.3 Administrative Sanctions

Various administrative regulations have been enacted to prevent and control all types of environmental pollution. Specific regulations protecting the coastline and atmosphere, controlling the use of continental water resources, and preventing the disposal of solid waste or polluted nonpurified waters have been enacted either at a state or regional level.

2.7 Intellectual Property Laws

Spanish intellectual property regulations are essentially harmonized with the legal systems of other Western countries. However, it is essential to point out that the Spanish expression *propiedad intelectual* refers only to copyright, while *propiedad industrial* normally refers to patents, trademarks, designs, and other related rights. Therefore, the U.S. or UK concept of intellectual property refers both to the Spanish concepts *propiedad intelectual* and *propiedad industrial.*

Spain has enacted laws governing copyright (Royal Legislative Decree 1/1996 of April 12, 1996), patents and utility models (Law 11/1986 of March 20, 1996), designs (Law 20/2003 of July 7, 2003), and trademarks (Law 17/2001 of December 7, 2001). New varieties of plants and indications of origin are also subject to particular regulations. Furthermore, the protection of intellectual property rights in Spain has been recently enhanced by Law 19/2006 of June 6, 2006, which transposes EU Directive 2004/48/EC.

In addition, Spain is party to the Berne Convention for the Protection of Literary and Artistic Works of September 9, 1886, the Paris Convention for the Protection of Intellectual Property of March 20, 1883, the Trade-Related Aspects of Intellectual Property Rights Agreement (TRIPS Agreement) of April 15, 1994, and the European Patent Convention of October 5, 1973.

In addition, all Community intellectual property regulations are applicable and directly enforceable in Spain, in particular, Council Regulation (EC) 40/94 on the Community trademark of December 20, 1993, and the Council Regulation (EC) 6/2002 on Community designs of December 12, 2001.

When negotiating any agreement relating to intellectual property subject to Spanish law, it is important to be as specific as possible to avoid the application of certain legal assumptions that may prove inappropriate. As such agreements may or should normally be filed with the competent registry to become effective vis-à-vis third parties, it is advisable to comply with the formalities set out by law, such as application forms or, as the case may be, formalization into public deeds.

2.8 Privacy and Data Security Laws

Since 1992, Spain has enacted strict administrative data protection regulations, most of which have been within the context of EU data protection harmonization directives. As a result of these regulations and of their interpretation by the Spanish Data Protection Supervisory Authority (*Agencia de Protección de Datos,* or APD), dealing with personal (private and nonprivate) data is quite a burdensome task that is not easy to put into practice, but that may trigger very significant fines if mishandled, ranging from EUR 601 to EUR 601,012. The sanctions imposed by the APD in 2006 amount to EUR 2,200,000 and are mainly addressed to companies of the telecom, finance, and advertising sectors.

According to Spanish law, a "controller" (i.e., an individual or legal person that decides the purpose, content, and use of the processing of personal data) must provide the "data subjects" (i.e., individuals from whom personal data is collected), in an explicit and unambiguous manner, comprehensive information regarding the processing of their personal data. In addition, as a general rule, the processing of any personal data requires the prior consent of the data subject, which must be freely given, and be specific, informed, and unambiguous in order to be valid. Explicit consent is necessary in limited occasions, such as—among others—when data are "sensitive" (such as health-related data, ethnic origin, and trade-union membership) or when direct marketing is made by electronic means.

This general rule requiring the consent of the data subject also applies to the processing consisting of transfers (including intragroup transfers) except when the recipient of the transferred data (the "processor") needs to have access to or otherwise process personal data (e.g., payroll services, IT maintenance services) of the controller to render a service to the latter. In this case, a specific data processing agreement between the controller and the processor must be entered into. In addition, and as a general rule, any international transfers of personal data to countries that do not provide a level of data protection equivalent to that of Spain (e.g., the United States) require the prior authorization of the APD.

The controller or, where applicable, the processor must adopt specific technical and organizational measures to ensure the security of the personal data and to prevent their alteration, loss, or unauthorized processing. Among other measures, it is necessary to draft a document that includes at least the mandatory security rules, which must be kept updated and binding on all persons who have access to the personal data and information systems. Depending on the nature of the data, an audit on the implemented security measures must be carried out biennially.

Finally, if personal data files are created (or subsequently modified or deleted), the controller must register them with the APD by submitting an official form.

2.9 Regulation of Foreign Investment

Since the end of 1991, and subject to certain exceptions, foreign investments in Spain have been liberalized to bring existing regulations in line with European Union standards regarding the free movement of capital and services.

As a general rule, pursuant to the terms of the Royal Decree 664/1999 of April 23, 1999, certain transactions constituting foreign investments in Spain or Spanish investments abroad, and any subsequent divestments, can be made freely, and only have to be reported to the General Directorate of Commerce and Investments (*Dirección General de Comercio e Inversiones*) after the pertinent transaction has taken place. A change of residence may imply a change of the classification of the investment (foreign in Spain to Spanish abroad or vice versa), and there is a general obligation to report any such change ex post facto within six months from the date of the change. As a general rule, the investor must directly report the investment. In addition, when a Spanish notary public is involved, such notary public must submit information about the investment to the General Directorate of Commerce and Investments. Nevertheless, special rules apply in certain situations where a different person, other than the investor, must report the investment.

Foreign investments in Spain or Spanish investments abroad falling into one of these categories need to be reported: (i) direct investment in companies by subscribing to, purchasing, or otherwise acquiring shares or participations in them; (ii) the opening or expansion of a branch or a branch office network; (iii) the subscription to and the acquisition of negotiable securities representing loans issued by residents; (iv) the participation in mutual funds; (v) the acquisition of real estate, if its value exceeds EUR 3,005,060.52 (Spanish real estate) or EUR 1,502,530.26 (real estate outside Spain) or, regardless of the amount, if the investment proceeds go to or come from a tax haven (as defined in Royal Decree 1080/1991 of July 5, 1991); or (vi) the constitution, formalization, or participation in participation account agreements, foundations, Economic Interest Groupings, cooperatives, and owners' associations, if the value exceeds EUR 3,005,060.52 (foreign investment in Spain) or EUR 1,502,530.26 (Spanish investment abroad), or, regardless of the amount, if the investment is made in or comes from a tax haven.

Only certain investments made through tax havens require prior clearance from the General Directorate of Commerce and Investments.

In certain cases, Spanish sector specific restrictions affecting foreign investment may require a specific authorization for the acquisition of holdings in companies operating in sectors such as air transportation, radio, minerals of strategic importance and mining rights, television, gambling, telecommunications, private security, arms and explosives for civil use, and activities related to national defense.

In addition, as an ongoing obligation, Spanish companies with shares owned by foreign investors in excess of 50 percent or with a single foreign investor with a shareholding of at least 10 percent, and that have share capital or net worth in excess of EUR 3,005,060.52, or are the dominant company of a group of companies obliged to prepare annual consolidated accounts in Spain, must file an annual report relating to the development of the investment during such year. This obligation is also applicable to branch offices of nonresident companies regardless of the share capital they have.

3. Other Significant Legal and Business Issues

3.1 Accounting and Auditing Regulations

Any company with a corporate purpose (e.g., every *sociedad anónima, sociedad de responsabilidad limitada,* cooperative, *sociedad comanditaria por acciones,* or *sociedad colectiva*) must register its annual accounts with the Commercial Registry.

Generally accepted accounting principles (GAAP) are set out in the Commercial Code (*Código* de *Comercio*), the Companies Act (*Ley de Sociedades Anónimas*), and the General Accounting Plan (*Plan General de Contabilidad*). All these laws have adapted Spanish legislation to the principles established by EU company directives. As of January 1, 2008, Spanish GAAP will follow the International Accounting Standards.

Auditing is compulsory for companies in Spain that meet two of the following requirements during two consecutive tax years: total assets exceeding EUR 2,850,000; total turnover exceeding EUR 5,700,000; or average number of employees exceeding fifty.

3.2 Exchange Control

Spain had traditionally subjected the economic transactions potentially involving transfers of funds between Spanish residents and nonresidents to exchange controls. However, since the enactment of Royal Decree 1816/1991, as amended, which came into force on December 20, 1991, Spain has liberalized most of the transactions carried out with foreign residents, conforming with EU standards regarding free movement of capital and liberalization of foreign exchange and capital controls.

From an exchange control standpoint, transactions must be channeled through a financial entity registered with the Bank of Spain (i.e., any bank or savings bank operating in Spain, including the subsidiaries or branches of foreign banks). In these cases, the resident party must provide the registered financial entity with certain data to identify the transaction. No prior authorization is required for transactions between residents and nonresidents that involve payments within or outside Spain. Nevertheless, the Bank of Spain must still be notified of the following transactions made by Spanish residents:

i. Financing and deferrals of payments and collections for more than one year between residents and nonresidents that derive from the export or import of goods or services, when it is equal to or exceeds EUR 600,000;

ii. The offsetting of credits and debits between residents and nonresidents that derive from any kind of commercial and financial transactions, or the provision of services, that are equal to or exceed EUR 600,000; and

iii. Financial loans received by residents from nonresidents or granted by residents to nonresidents, when the amount is equal to or exceeds EUR 3,000,000. Securities, such as bonds, promissory notes, etc., not traded on stock exchanges or organized markets, or securities representing participations in loans issued by Spanish residents that are traded in foreign markets, receive the same treatment as the financial loans. The allocation by the Bank of Spain of a so-called financial operation number ("NOF") to each financial loan exceeding the aforementioned threshold is required in order for the resident to make valid payments and collections (drawdowns, interest payments, etc.) under such financial loan.

In certain exceptional cases, clearance or reporting obligations before the Spanish exchange control authorities may be required. The Spanish government is authorized, by Royal Decree 1816/1991, to prohibit or limit certain nonresident transactions, or their related payments, receipts, or transfers, if they seriously affect Spanish interests or if Spain is applying measures adopted by international bodies to which it belongs.

Such liberalization of exchange controls allows the Spanish banks to freely accept foreign currency deposits or placements of funds in foreign currencies within certain limits. Thus, nonresidents may open bank accounts with banks registered in Spain and carry out all types of transactions although, in certain circumstances, the applicable bank must send some information about the holder of such account to the Bank of Spain. Moreover, residents may, subject to certain declaration requirements, freely open and hold bank accounts abroad either in euros or in foreign currency. The opening must be declared to the Bank of Spain within one month and information must be provided on the debits and credits posted to the account when exceeding certain thresholds.

3.3 Choice of Law

The choice of a foreign law as the governing law of any contract discussed in international negotiations conducted in Spain is not unusual, especially with regard to derivatives or facility agreements to be syndicated in the international markets.

As a general rule, choice of law is accepted under Spanish law subject to the terms of the Rome Convention on the law applicable to contractual obligations, dated June 19, 1980, as amended, provided and to the extent that (i) there is some point of connection between the parties or the subject matter of the contract and the law by which the contract is ruled; (ii) the applicable foreign law provisions are evidenced before Spanish courts if any proceedings arise; and (iii) there is no infringement of public order.

3.4 The Role of the Spanish Administration in Business Negotiations

In international transactions including Spain, it is difficult not to be involved with the administration, either at a state, regional, or local level. Its participation often corresponds to an *auctoritas* body, from which some sort of clearance, approval, or authorization must be obtained in order to achieve a successful result.

The Spanish administration has also traditionally maintained an active role in various sectors of the Spanish economy, either because of the limited appeal to private investors or because of the sectors' strategic interest in the national economy. In recent years the Spanish administration has recruited private investors to build infrastructures through private finance initiative/public-private partnership (PFI/PPP) projects, especially through the award of public concessions to such private investors. The administration also participates in the economy either directly or by using special legal bodies or limited liability companies under its control. However, during the 1990s, most of Spain's public companies were privatized (including Telefónica, Repsol, Endesa, Tabacalera, and Argentaria, which merged with Banco Bilbao Vizcaya to conform the current BBVA).

The economic situation has also forced the administration to introduce several incentives to revitalize the economy. Such measures are usually linked to industrial zones or industrial sectors particularly affected by crises (for instance, coal, steel, shipbuilding, or textiles) or to those undeveloped regions that still lack the basic industrial network. In cases where a transaction may involve great investments, subsidies from the different administrations may be available. In these cases, the state, the regional, or the local authorities like to be involved in the negotiations or, at least, to be informed of their progress.

3.5 The Judicial System

Spaniards are not as keen on litigation as Americans. The shortage of courts and the lack of human and material resources have resulted in the near-collapse of the judicial system in Spain. On average, a final ruling from the Spanish Supreme Court takes from five to seven years to be obtained. Even if a verdict conforms to the law, material justice is difficult to achieve.

3.6 Notaries

Notary publics (*notarios*) perform different functions from those of the United States or UK. Under Spanish law, these professionals give official witness to the acts and contracts executed before them. Whereas U.S. or UK notary publics generally certify the identity of the person signing a document, a Spanish notary public, in addition to verifying the identity of signatories, may delve into the contents and legality of the transaction at hand, and may even reject the document submitted for execution.

4. Negotiation Practices

Conducting a negotiation depends on the personal character of the heads of both parties, the education of those involved, and the cultural environment in which it is carried out.

4.1 Participants

The importance of the deal determines who will be involved in the negotiation. Usually, the officials of a company are in charge of the material aspects of the deal. However, the size of the company should also be considered. As a matter of fact, most medium-size and small companies are run by the shareholders. Generally, they manage the entire decision-making process, and negotiations cannot take place without their direct involvement or approval.

Lawyers in Spain tend not to be involved in the preliminary phases of the negotiations. Their participation in the negotiation process tends to be less important than that of their U.S. colleagues. Spanish companies tend to use lawyers once the main principles of the agreement have been established. However, this situation could change either because one of the parties prefers that its legal counsel be present from the outset or because for many small companies the lawyer is acting more as a permanent and personal consultant to the shareholders than as a legal consultant.

Accountants, auditors, and other experts tend not to be involved in the negotiation itself. Rather, they participate in the due diligence or in the analysis of the process to determine the price. Apart from this, they are contacted on a case-by-case basis to provide additional feedback when needed.

4.2 Timing

There are no firm standards establishing the term of negotiations in Spain. The circumstances in each case vary and each negotiation has its own deadlines. Nevertheless, some points should be considered.

Since most Spanish companies close their annual accounts on December 31, company managers prefer to conclude negotiations before the end of the year. The end of November and the few days in December just before Christmas are busy periods. June and July are also busy, as during the month of August most of the country is closed.

Although practically any time of the day is suitable to carry out negotiations, Spaniards prefer not to negotiate on weekends but extend their normal business hours. (The working day in most companies in Spain ends around 7 or 8 P.M., which is later than the normal close of business in the United States or UK.) Urgency is not commonly accepted solely to speed things up, since it could be interpreted as a sign that something in the transaction is unclear or uncertain.

4.3 Negotiation Practices

The first issue to consider is whether the negotiation should be conducted in English or Spanish. While English is recognized as the universal business language, Spaniards have only since the end of the 1980s begun taking the study of foreign languages seriously. Therefore, it is important to be sensitive toward old-school business executives who may not have the same savvy in languages as younger managers. In deals with large or financial companies it would be easier to conduct the negotiation in English, which is the most widely spoken foreign language by Spaniards. In the case of medium-size and small companies, although an interpreter may be necessary, conducting the negotiation in Spanish is in practice essential.

The maximum number of people involved in a meeting should be limited, if possible. Many negotiations are frustrated by a lack of understanding that often stems from the involvement of a large number of people. In fact, at meetings with more than eight attendants, understanding among the parties is almost an impossible goal, unless heads of both sides agree to control the situation at all times.

The length of the negotiation process and its stages will depend on the character of the participants and the type and size of business involved in the negotiation. Some of the documents or tools to which an American or British party is accustomed might not be quite so common in medium-size and small transactions in Spain. However, in international operations or in local material transactions (such as M&A and project finance), the documents or tools would be essentially the same: letters of intent, mandate letters, term sheets, and due diligence proceedings, among others. Confidentiality agreements are also executed when due diligence reports or material information is exchanged between the parties in order to protect the confidentiality of such information, but no specific measures are normally adopted to ensure the privacy of the negotiations themselves.

4.4 Cultural, Ethical, and Religious Considerations

Trust among the parties involved in business negotiations is an essential characteristic, without which negotiations are impossible. Aggressive attitudes or language and maintaining extreme positions is not a good starting point for establishing trust among the parties. A good way to establish trust early on is with handshakes and a brief informal conversation to break the ice before opening the negotiation. Ideally, this conversation should focus on hobbies or sports, rather than politics, which is a very personal and sensitive subject.

Spanish people are very family-oriented and try to protect their privacy, which explains why they are often reluctant to share their home telephone numbers with other parties involved in the negotiation.

Most Spanish people are Catholic, although other religions such as Islam are also present in Spain. Therefore, most Spanish people involved in the negotiations will have a Catholic background, but will be respectful of other religious practices.

Finally, although Spanish is the official language in Spain, certain regions have other official regional languages, such as Catalan in Catalonia, Galician in Galicia, Basque in the Basque Country, Valencian in Valencia, and a variety of Catalan in the Balearic Islands. Although some people involved in the negotiations may use these languages to informally communicate among themselves, negotiations will normally be conducted in Spanish or English.

4.5 Negotiating Online

Despite the different character of the participants, in general, negotiations in Spain continue to be very traditional. However, instruments like e-mails and conference calls are common practice and are gradually reducing the number of physical meetings in each negotiation process.

Most negotiations currently conducted in Spain tend to include about three personal meetings, the kickoff meeting, a large and exhaustive meeting where the parties try to reconcile the positions on the main issues, and the closing meeting, where the relevant agreements are executed. Between these meetings, the parties exchange e-mail correspondence to circulate proposals on the hot topics and changes to contract documents with tracked changes, which are generally discussed by conference call, unless the upholding of material issues requires convening an additional meeting.

5. Contract Formation

The Spanish system of contract formation is not too formalistic. Few contracts require a specific form. Oral contracts are as valid as written ones, unless otherwise provided by law. However, most commercial contracts tend to be executed in writing, and in certain cases before a notary public. This practice provides adequate evidence of the rights and obligations of the parties, evidence before third parties of the date on which the contract was executed, and in certain cases allows access to special summary proceedings before Spanish courts.

5.1 Wording, Style, and Structure

In most cases in international practice, contracts executed as a result of an international business negotiation are drafted in English, adopting the structure of U.S. or UK contracts. In Spain, this may be appropriate in certain cases, but the key element determining the adequate language for the contract depends on the choice of law and jurisdiction that is determined in the contract itself. Any contract subject to Spanish law and submitted to Spanish courts should be drafted in accordance with Spanish rules and, if possible, in Spanish or attaching a Spanish translation. This could help avoid potential problems.

Most of the exhaustive list of terms used in common law contracts to cover any idea related to a specific concept are not necessary in a civil law country such as Spain. Most legal terms and categories are defined by the statutes themselves, and it is no longer necessary to replicate such definitions in the wording of a contract. However, this situation requires the knowledge of the exact meaning of a legal term, as defined by the regulations and interpreted by case law and scholars. In addition, as a general rule, definitions are only used when strictly necessary.

Generally, if the contract ends up in court, any obscure clause will make the position held by the parties harder to explain to a judge. As a matter of law, the Civil Code states that interpretation of those "obscure clauses" cannot benefit the party at the request of whom such wording was included. The Civil Code states that contracts must be interpreted in accordance with good faith. In this regard, clauses should be drafted to reflect such principle, avoiding aggressive or preponderant language. Courts are reluctant to rule in favor of the party to a contract holding an abusive position.

Spanish contracts, as in many other civil law jurisdictions, are usually structured in four different sections: the heading of the contract, the recitals, the clauses, and the execution or closing.

In the heading of the contract, the different parties entering into the agreement are identified. It is customary to refer to the complete name of the person, domicile, tax identity number or passport number, and Commercial Registry identification data, and to include detailed reference to the powers of attorney held by representatives.

The recitals explain why the parties are entering into the agreement, and set out all the material facts relevant to the transaction. This part of the contract is fundamental in determining the intent of the parties, as well as in understanding and interpreting the clauses of the agreement and the rights and obligations of each party thereunder.

The clauses of a Spanish contract set out the rights and obligations of the parties to the contract. They are usually shorter than those in common law contracts. Part of the rights and obligations of those entering into the contract in Spain are previously determined by statutes; therefore, it is not necessary to replicate them unless the parties agree to consequences other than those established by law and provided that this is possible. However, as a matter of practice in certain types of transactions (for instance, in finance), documents and contracts are drafted following, to a great extent, the U.S. or UK form of contracts.

The execution of a contract does not require any further formality. The mere signature of the person acting and assuming empowerment to sign is sufficient. The signature of a witness is neither required nor customary as it may be in some common law jurisdictions. If the public deed is granted before a notary, he or she will give official witness to the persons executing the contract, the title they hold, and the date of execution.

5.2 Conditions and Defenses

The Spanish Civil Code and Commercial Code govern and establish the conditions and requirements under which a contract is considered valid and binding under Spanish law. The Codes also regulate the rights and obligations of each party. The main principle governing the relationship between the parties is contained in article 1255 of the Civil Code, which states that parties can enter into any agreement they deem appropriate, provided that such agreement is not in breach of law or public order, or is contrary to morality.

Checking with local counsel for any specific regulation applicable to the potential contract is the first step. Spanish law provides the scheme of the rights and obligations arising from a contract depending on its nature and defines whether or not the parties can agree otherwise. In particular, in M&A and acquisition finance negotiations Spanish counsel should assess the effect of the financial assistance provisions under Spanish law, the breach of which could render the whole finance contract void. The statutes of limitation should also be checked with Spanish counsel.

Because of the lengthiness of trials in Spain, liabilities arising from a contract tend to be secured by first-demand guarantees to be executed under circumstances specifically provided for in the contract and without the possibility of refusal. Such first-demand guarantees are valid under Spanish law, and Spanish and EU banks are eager to issue them.

As a particular matter of Spanish law, it is also worth noting the difference between public documents and private contracts. The difference between these two categories lies merely in whether or not a contract has been executed before a notary public. As a matter of law, few contracts need to be executed before a notary public.

There are several legal advantages to executing a contract before a notary public. First, it evidences the identity of the parties to the agreement before third parties and the date on which the agreement was executed. Second, it gives evidence of the content of the contract. Third, it allows a copy of the deed to be maintained by a person other than the parties. Finally, in financing transactions, it gives access to special summary proceedings before Spanish courts. The only drawback is that there is a fee, determined by law on sliding scales (but negotiable with the notary public when the amount of the underlying obligation exceeds certain amounts), on any act or contract in which such certifying officials intervene.

5.3 The Special Case of Online Agreements

General legislation on distance sales must be taken into account when dealing with contracts executed electronically, as well as Law 34/2002 of July 11, 2002, on information society services and e-commerce, transposing E-Commerce Directive 2000/31/EC, which imposes specific rules on e-contracting (mainly, information duties prior and subsequent to e-contracting, which may be excluded when the contracting parties so agree and none of them is a consumer). Likewise, Law 22/2007 of July 11, 2007, on distance marketing of consumer financial services has transposed Directive 2002/65/EC.

Apart from these specific laws on e-contracting and the general legislation on civil and commercial contracts, other rules may be relevant, such as the requirements for the valid incorporation of general terms and conditions (mainly, clear language and an explicit acceptance by the adherent) and the consumer regulations.

Although electronic signature (currently regulated under Law 59/2003 of December 19, 2003) is not yet widely used, online agreements are becoming common practice in the business-to-business and business-to-consumer (B2B and B2C) purchase of products and services, but only when standard terms and conditions apply to such purchase. Therefore, online agreements are not used in the context of international business negotiations.

6. Resolving Disputes

In the same way as the parties to the negotiation may decide on the governing law of any contract, the same criteria are applied to those clauses in which the parties make a choice of jurisdiction. Submission to a specific court must be made clear. In general, judgments duly obtained in the courts of an EU member state (other than Denmark) will be enforceable in Spain subject to the relevant provisions of EU Regulation 44/2001 of the Council on jurisdiction and enforcement of judgments in civil and commercial matters. In the event of final judgments from the other foreign courts, they may be enforced in Spain in three different situations: (i) in accordance with the provisions of any applicable treaty; (ii) in the absence of any such treaty, when reciprocity with Spanish judgments has been evidenced, and provided that some minimal conditions are met; and (iii) otherwise, in those cases when the judgment issued in the foreign jurisdiction identifies with certain minimal conditions contemplated in the Spanish applicable procedural law.

Submission to arbitration before a Spanish or foreign arbitral court is valid and fully enforceable. Choice of arbitration at law or in equity, the manner in which the arbitrators will be appointed and their number, the evidence that the arbitral court may admit, and the maximum period of time to issue the award are points to be included in the contract.

It is important to note that, even if the relevant agreement has directed the resolution of conflicts to the courts of a foreign state or to arbitration, Spanish courts have exclusive jurisdiction, *inter alia*, with respect to matters relating to the incorporation, validity, nullity, and dissolution of Spanish legal entities and to any decisions and resolutions of their corporate bodies, as well as with respect to the validity of any registration with a Spanish registry, and the recognition and enforcement in Spain of any judgment or arbitration award obtained in a foreign country.

Online dispute resolutions systems are not common in Spain. As discussed, Spaniards are not very keen on litigation and resort to this route solely for serious disputes, where they prefer to personally deal with a judge or an arbitrator rather than with an online dispute resolution system.

7. Conclusion

Since it joined the European Union, Spain has undergone significant political and economic development. Large Spanish companies increasingly compete abroad. Spanish regulations have also evolved to conform to EU requirements. Both circumstances have led to an economy and legal system increasingly homogeneous to other Western economies.

This progress also had an effect in international business negotiations conducted in Spain, which have evolved to conform to international standards. Most of the tools and techniques used in the international markets can be satisfactorily used in international negotiations in Spain, except for certain particularities imposed by a civil law legal system and the applicable Spanish regulations.

The continuous integration of the Spanish economy in global markets and the growth of large Spanish companies as global players suggest that international business negotiations involving Spanish participants will become increasingly common in the near future.

Carlos de Cárdenas Smith and Ángel Pérez López
URÍA MENÉNDEZ
c/ Príncipe de Vergara, 187
28002 Madrid
Phone: (34) 91.586.04.00
Fax: (34) 91.586.04.84
E-mail: ccs@uria.com
          ape@uria.com

CHAPTER 46

International Business Negotiations in Sweden

Johan Gernandt, Bob Johanson, and Nils Unckel
GERNANDT & DANIELSSON ADVOKATBYRÅ KB
STOCKHOLM, SWEDEN

1. Introduction

Sweden is a unitary (nonfederal) state, which means that the same laws apply in all parts of the country. In addition, its small population (approximately 9.2 million) is homogeneous, both ethnically and culturally. Thus, the legal and cultural context of business negotiations is the same all over the country.

What, then, is characteristic for international business in Sweden?

One distinctive feature is that contracts concluded as a result of such negotiations seldom attempt to resolve all potential disputes. Instead, commercial law—for example the Swedish Sale of Goods Act—is relied upon to a greater extent than is the case in the United States. However, due to, *inter alia*, influence from the Anglo-Saxon jurisdictions, contracts have become more extensive also in Sweden during recent years.

A second characteristic of business negotiations in Sweden is that contracts seldom end up in court. The reason for this is that the parties almost always provide for disputes to be solved by arbitration.

A third distinctive feature is that negotiations tend to avoid confrontation and aim for consensus solutions.

Finally, a fourth characteristic, not for the business negotiations but for the negotiating framework in Sweden, is that Sweden is strongly dependent on foreign trade. Since Sweden became a member of the European Union (EU) in 1995, the Swedish trade policy has been pursued jointly with other EU countries.

2. Laws Affecting Negotiations in Sweden

2.1 General

In Swedish private law, statutory law plays a more important role than case law. Thus, statutes enacted by Parliament are central in most areas of private law. Swedish private law is based on the principle of freedom of contract, although a number of statutes contain mandatory rules, that is, rules that may not be deviated from by the parties to a contract.

2.2 Competition Law

The national Swedish competition/antitrust rules are contained in the 1993 Competition Act and are to a large extent modeled on the corresponding EU regulations. The 1993 Competition Act has been brought into conformity with Articles 85 and 86 of the Treaty of Rome, thereby prohibiting all agreements that have as their object or effect the prevention, restriction, or distortion of competition, as well as abuse of a dominant position in the market. In addition, the provisions on merger control contained in the Competition Act have been adapted to the EU merger regulations. The 1993 Competition Act must be taken into consideration in nearly all business negotiations. It should be noted that a new Competition Act entered into force on November 1, 2008.

2.3 Company Law

The basic rules regarding limited companies are to be found in the Companies Act 2005, which contains provisions on, *inter alia,* management of the company, distribution of dividends, rights of minority shareholders (thus providing an important part of the legal framework for acquisitions), and personal liability for board members and managing directors.

Under the Companies Act, a company is allowed to have shares with different voting rights. However, no share may have a voting right exceeding ten times the voting right of any other share. Where a parent company, alone or together with one or more subsidiaries, owns more than nine-tenths of the shares in a subsidiary, the parent company is entitled to redeem the remaining shares from the minority shareholders of the subsidiary. A minority shareholder who owns a share that may be thus redeemed has, in turn, the right to have his or her shares redeemed by the parent company.

2.4 Stock Market Regulations

For companies whose shares are listed on a regulated market, quoted on a multi-lateral trading facility, traded on the over-the-counter market, or otherwise widely held, there are certain additional rules that may affect international business negotiations. Over time a number of self-regulatory bodies have been established by representatives of the private business sector in Sweden. In addition to provisions in different statutes, rules are to be found in recommendations issued by the

Swedish Industry and Commerce Stock Exchange Committee (*Näringslivets börskommitté* or *NBK*) and in statements from a special committee dealing with questions concerning the stock market, the Swedish Securities Council (*Aktiemarknadsnämnden*). The Securities Council was founded in 1986 and is a private nonprofit association modeled on the UK's Panel on Takeovers and Mergers. It is, for example, possible for companies to ask for the Securities Council's opinion on a matter. Another committee is the Association for Generally Accepted Principles in the Securities Market (*Föreningen för god sed på värdepappersmarknaden*), which was founded in 2006. The purpose of this association is to promote the observance and development of generally accepted principles in the securities market.

Whereas the importance of the NBK has declined in recent years, the Securities Council has instead gained greater importance. The major reason for such greater importance is that the Swedish Financial Supervisory Authority and the two existing Swedish regulated markets have delegated to the Securities Council the power to adjudicate certain takeover matters, including matters following law.

In 2004 a unified Code of Corporate Governance was presented in Sweden by the Swedish Corporate Governance Board (*Kollegiet för svensk bolagsstyrning*). The Code is based on the Companies Act 2005 and the tradition of self-regulation that prevails in Sweden. The Code deals primarily with the organization of corporate governance and management bodies, their work procedures, and the interaction between these bodies, but not the division of power among a company's owners. As are most similar codes in other countries, the Swedish Code is based on the principle "comply or explain." This means that a company can deviate from the Code's provisions without this entailing a breach of the Code. A company that intends to deviate from a regulation in the Code must, however, explain why the deviation is occurring.

The Code has been incorporated into the OMX Nordic Exchange's rules and forms part of the requirements that a company must fulfill in order to be listed at the OMX Nordic Exchange Stockholm. It should be noted that the Swedish Corporate Governance Board aims to present a revised Code before mid-May 2008. It will likely be applicable to the relevant companies from July 1, 2008.

The new Act Concerning Public Takeover Bids in the Stock Market entered into force on July 1, 2006, implementing EU Directive 2004/25/EC regarding takeover offers in Sweden. Pursuant to the Act, a shareholder who acquires shares representing at least three-tenths of the votes for all shares in the company is under an obligation to immediately make public the extent of shareholding in the company and also make a public takeover bid for the remaining shares in the company within four weeks. Also, the shareholdings of certain persons and companies related to the buyer shall be included when calculating the buyer's shareholding.

2.5 Insider Dealing and Market Manipulation

Insider dealing is a criminal offense in Sweden under the Market Abuse Act 2005, which is based on the EU Market Abuse Directive. The Market Abuse Act 2005 applies to dealings in financial instruments (i.e., stock market securities and other rights or obligations intended for dealings on the securities market), prohibits certain dealings in financial instruments, and also contains a prohibition regarding market manipulation. The Market Abuse Act 2005 is not limited to transactions on the securities market. It also applies to dealings in financial instruments admitted to trading on a regulated market in at least one EU member state or for which a request for admission to trading on such a market has been made, as well as financial instruments not admitted to trading on a regulated market but whose value depends on such financial instrument, irrespective of whether or not the transaction itself actually takes place on that market.

2.6 Tax Law

Sweden imposes severe taxes on private individuals, but company taxes are favorable when compared to many other countries (the corporate income tax rate is presently 28 percent).

There is a system of double taxation of corporate profits. The company is a taxable subject and liable to tax. In addition, profits distributed to the shareholders are taxed as income of capital (with the exception mentioned below).

A long-standing principle in Swedish tax legislation has been that aggregate profits in a Swedish group of companies should be taxed as if taxed in one company, neither more severely nor more favorably than if the companies were separate entities. As a consequence of this principle of neutral taxation, profits may be transferred from one company to another in a group of companies. Intricately detailed requirements have to be fulfilled, but the transfer is then deductible for the donor company and taxable income for the recipient company.

Another example of this principle of neutral taxation is the provisions on companies' exemption from taxes regarding dividends received from companies in which the receiving Swedish company owns shares representing more than 10 percent of the votes, provided that the holding of shares is related to the business of the holder and is not a current asset.

In the case of a sale of a business, it can, for fiscal reasons, be of relevance whether the sale is carried out as an asset sale, where the company will become subject to taxation, or as a transfer of shares, where the selling shareholder(s) will become liable to capital gains taxation.

Sweden has entered into double-taxation agreements with almost all countries in the world.

2.7 Accounting and Auditing

Accounting rules are primarily to be found in the 1995 Act on Annual Reports and in the 1999 Accounting Act. Sweden has implemented the EU directive concerning application of international accounting standards that has been incorporated into the 1999 Accounting Act.

All companies limited by shares must have their annual financial statements audited. The accounts of all companies limited by shares are available to the public at the Swedish Companies Registration Office (*Bolagsverket*). One important feature in Swedish auditing practice is the administration audit, which is an audit of the board's and the managing director's administration of the company's affairs. The result of such audit could be that a board member or the managing director is held responsible for any loss or damage caused to the company by the administration of its affairs. During recent years the responsibility of directors has been discussed intensively, and some cases have reached the courts.

2.8 Labor Law

Pursuant to the 1976 Co-determination Act, an employer who is bound by a collective agreement is required to initiate and conclude "negotiations" with the trade union before any significant change of the business activities is decided. An example of such significant changes is termination of employment due to redundancy. During the "negotiations" the parties are supposed to discuss the motives and needs for terminations of employment. When the "negotiations" are concluded, the employer is, however, entitled to decide at its own will, even if the trade union does not approve of the decision. The obligation to "negotiate" is thus in practice only an obligation to "consult" before any major decision is taken. Even if the employer is not bound by a collective agreement, it has under certain circumstances an obligation to initiate negotiations with the trade union(s) of which the employees are members in cases such as termination of employment due to redundancy.

When an employer dismisses employees due to redundancy, employees with longer periods of employment shall, according to the 1982 Employment Protection Act, have priority over employees who have been employed for a shorter period of time. Employees who are dismissed due to redundancy have a priority right to reemployment where they were previously employed. It is possible for management and the trade unions to deviate from these principles. Agreements to that effect are often entered into between management and union representatives, which also mark the character of the Swedish labor market.

An employer that violates the provisions of the Employment Protection Act or the Co-determination Act is liable to pay damages for losses suffered by the employee and the trade union.

According to the Employment Protection Act, an employee will, in the case of a sale of a business in whole or in part, automatically be taken over by the purchaser of the business, provided the employee is not opposed to that agreement. The employment agreements existing on the day of the transfer will be transferred to the purchaser. The purchaser of the business will be responsible (together with the seller) for monetary obligations that have arisen from the employment agreements existing prior to the transfer. These rules are based on EU Directive 77/187/EEC.

2.9 Environment Law

On January 1, 1999, the Swedish Environmental Code (*miljöbalken*) entered into force. The Environmental Code is the main body of Swedish environmental law. The Code replaced fifteen older statutes and consists of thirty-three chapters and almost 500 sections. Although the Environmental Code is fairly extensive, it includes mainly environmental rules of general importance. Detailed provisions are laid down in approximately fifty government ordinances and regulations and general guidelines issued by the Swedish Environmental Protection Agency (*Naturvårdsverket*), which is the central environmental authority under the government. The Environmental Code applies to all kinds of activities and types of environmental disturbances.

The approach of the Environmental Code is to concentrate more on the effects of an activity instead of its nature. The effect of the activity now determines the measures to be taken in order to avoid disturbances and damage and to promote sustainable development. The Code provides several rules that must be considered when taking measures or carrying out operations and also when negotiating agreements regarding, *inter alia,* acquisitions of companies and businesses.

In addition to the Environmental Code, there are several statutes that deal with questions relating to environment and health that apply alongside the Environmental Code.

2.10 Regulation of Foreign Investment

No permission is required for the making of direct investments in Sweden, such as the acquisition of shares in a Swedish company or the acquisition of business assets in Sweden. Acquisitions of farm property and apartment buildings, however, as a general rule require permission. The acquisition of shares in a company the main assets of which are apartment buildings can also (under certain circumstances) be subject to permission, and a certain notification procedure must be adhered to as regards such acquisitions.

The acquisition of Swedish business enterprises by foreign entities is generally not subject to any restrictions. It is also possible to acquire real estate in the form of industrial property or commercial property without the need for a permit or license. However, companies involved in the defense industry may be subject to ownership restrictions.

2.11 Foreign Exchange Issues

Swedish law does not restrict the outflow of capital from the country, but in order to collect information for statistical purposes, the person making the payment is under an obligation to provide certain information to the Central Bank (*Riksbanken*). This system works smoothly and normally does not present any problem to the investor. Restrictions can, as in almost all countries, be introduced by the Central Bank under exceptional circumstances.

2.12 Choice of Law

According to Swedish law, the parties to a contract are, as a general rule, free to choose which law should govern the contract; the choice of law is recognized both by Swedish courts and by arbitration tribunals. Further, since July 1, 1998, the Rome Convention of 1980 on the Law Applicable to Contractual Obligations applies in Sweden.

3. Dispute Resolution Mechanisms

Major Swedish business contracts almost always include an arbitration clause, often referring disputes to be settled in accordance with the rules of the highly reputable Arbitration Institute of the Stockholm Chamber of Commerce. The main reasons for this preference for arbitration over court trials are: (i) speed (since an arbitration award can be appealed only in special situations, arbitration proceedings usually take no more than about a year, while a final court ruling in a court trial regarding a major dispute is sometimes not given until five to six years after the proceeding was initiated); (ii) expertise (the arbitrators can be chosen on the basis of familiarity with the disputed matter, whereas in court proceedings a case may be handled by judges with limited experience in the relevant field of law and commercial customs and habits); and (iii) secrecy (arbitration proceedings, as opposed to court trials, will normally be kept private).

If, however, a contract does not include an arbitration clause and a dispute thus ends up in court, the case will be decided not by a jury (the jury system does not exist in Sweden, except in freedom of the press cases) but by professional judges in a two-instance procedure (a third instance, the Supreme Court, is normally available only if the case may form a precedent).

4. Negotiations in Sweden

The discussion in this section will relate mainly to one form of international business transactions involving Swedish companies, namely the acquisition of a Swedish company (or the assets of such company) by a foreign entity. However, much of what is said also applies to other transactions, such as financing transactions, joint ventures, etc.

Compared to negotiation teams in the United States, Swedish negotiation teams are normally quite small. The Swedish party is typically represented by a senior executive officer, sometimes assisted by financial and legal officers of the company and, generally, by external counsel.

The role of the external counsel has traditionally been restricted to negotiating legal issues in the narrow sense and, of course, to drafting the contract. Lawyers do not have that much leverage on business-related negotiating points as, for instance, U.S. lawyers have. Swedish lawyers may, however, give advice based on their prior experience in similar deals. Nowadays, the tendency is that this is changing and lawyers are taking a more active part in negotiations. This development has continued during the last years.

Typically, the role of the board of directors is limited to the approval or disapproval of an agreement already made (contracts are often entered into subject to the approval of the board of directors). However, the chairman of the board sometimes takes part in the negotiations.

It is, of course, very difficult to generalize as to how long negotiations last, since this will depend on the nature of the transaction. What can be said, however, is that once negotiations reach their final stages, the process is normally speedy.

Before reaching the point at which the final contract can be concluded, the parties sometime enter into a preliminary agreement (letter of intent, heads of agreement, agreement in principle, etc.). Depending on how such a document is drafted, this is sometimes a legally binding contract in itself; in other cases it is only a declaration of intent without significant legal effect.

In major acquisitions, the purchaser invariably undertakes a due diligence review of the company about to be purchased. The review is usually completed before the final agreement is entered into.

Swedish companies have been involved in numerous cross-border acquisitions and other transactions. Therefore both Swedish executives and Swedish lawyers often have extensive experience of international transactions. When a foreign party is involved, negotiations are almost always conducted in English. This is true irrespective of the nationality of the foreign party. It is rare for Swedish business executives and business lawyers to negotiate in other foreign languages, for example German or French. On the other hand, Swedes likely to take part in international business transactions have a good command of the English language.

The style in which negotiations are conducted differs from that in the United States in a number of ways. For instance, in Sweden negotiations tend to be considerably less aggressive, but it does not mean that they easily give up their positions. If possible, negotiators avoid confrontation and aim for consensus solutions. For that reason, negotiating strength is often not utilized in full.

Another major difference between Sweden and the United States is the size and scope of contracts. Typically, a Swedish contract is shorter and less formal than an American contract. No effort is made to resolve all possible potential disputes. Instead Swedish commercial law is relied upon to solve such disputes. However, when the foreign party is American or British, the Swedish party often accepts that the contract, even though governed by Swedish law, is given a U.S. or British style.

To sum up, the main differences in negotiating style and substance between negotiations conducted in Sweden and those conducted in the United States are illustrated in the following Appendix.

Johan Gernandt, Bob Johanson, and Nils Unckel
Gernandt & Danielsson Advokatbyrå KB
P.O. Box 5747
SE-114 87 Stockholm, Sweden
Phone: +46 8 670 66 00
Fax: +46 8 662 61 01
E-mail: info@gda.se

APPENDIX 46.1

United States	Sweden
Style	
More aggressive. Negotiating strength utilized in full. Lawyers have a strong influence on business-related negotiating points as well as points of law.	Less aggressive. Negotiating strength not utilized in full. Executives usually make decisions on law-related matters in addition to business. Lawyers in Sweden do not have the strong influence that U.S. lawyers may have (although their influence is getting stronger).
Substance	
Longer and more formal contracts; efforts made to cover as many topics as possible; no reliance on commercial law. Lawyers generally have a stronger position on a U.S. negotiating team. Even negotiation teams from large U.S. companies often have limited international experience.	Shorter contracts; no effort made to resolve all possible potential disputes; reliance on commercial law. Except for some large corporations, both in-house and external lawyers usually have a weaker position (although getting stronger). A negotiation team from a large Swedish company generally has extensive international negotiating experience.

CHAPTER 47

International Business Negotiations in the United Arab Emirates

Robert Leigh
SIMMONS AND SIMMONS
DUBAI, UNITED ARAB EMIRATES

1. Introduction

The UAE's tale of economic success is one to be told for generations to come. Less than forty years ago, the UAE was a group of separated emirates each led by a sheikh who typically belonged to the most influential tribe in the emirate. These emirates were known as the Trucial Sheikhdoms or Trucial Oman. The pre-oil economies of the Trucial Sheikhdoms depended largely on the pearling trade and fishing. Each sheikhdom had separate treaties with Great Britain.

The UAE came into existence when the young and visionary Sheikh Zayed, the ruler of Abu Dhabi and the principal architect of the federation, stepped forward to lead the sheikhdoms into what may prove to be the most successful union on Arab soil for decades.

The UAE can be immensely proud of its achievements. The UAE economy is considered one of the fastest-growing economies in the world. The UAE is also home to Dubai, the fastest-growing city in the world with 13 percent GDP growth rate since the year 2000 and double-digit growth forecast for the next eight years. The UAE should also be given credit for sparking a very healthy competition with its neighboring Arab states, which can look to the UAE for inspiration.

1.1 Geographic Perspective

Geographically, the UAE extends along the southern coast of the Arabian Gulf from Qatar in the west to Oman in the east, bordering Saudi Arabia to the south. In 1971, Abu Dhabi, Ajman, Dubai, Fujairah, Sharjah, and Umm Al Qaiwain formed a federation, creating the UAE as a sovereign state. Ras Al Khaimah joined the federation in 1972.

The UAE is less than eight hours' flight from Europe and the Far East. Some eighty airlines provide direct flights to more than 120 cities worldwide. London is seven hours away, Frankfurt six, Hong Kong eight, and Nairobi four.

1.2 Investment Climate

Despite maintaining ownership interests in several key economic sectors, including oil production, petrochemicals, and large-scale manufacturing, the UAE government is committed to liberal free-market policies and to the creation of a business environment conducive to commercial activity. The government is actively engaged in facilitating business creation in the country in order to maintain economic diversification with a decreasing dependence on oil.

The UAE has been rated by official regional bodies as one of the most attractive investment destinations in the Arab world for foreign capital based on its various incentives, practical laws, advanced infrastructure, inexpensive energy and labor, and location in the heart of a regional consumer market of more than 1 billion people.

Most of the 68.6 billion dirham (AED) in foreign direct investment (FDI) into the UAE is from non-Arab countries, according to statistics released recently by the Ministry of Economy, with the UK, Japan, India, and the United States contributing more than 50 percent.

1.3 Cultural Highlights

Before embarking upon a business venture in the UAE it is important to appreciate and understand the business culture, business etiquette, and meeting protocols and isolate them from the common stereotypes, myths, and misconceptions.

1.3.1 Islam

It is virtually impossible to gain a sound understanding of the UAE—in effect the entire Middle East region—and the pervasive cultural issues without grasping key Islamic sharia concepts.

Islam features in all aspects of life in the Middle East. It provides guidance, values, and rules for personal life, community relations, and ways of doing business. For a good introduction to Islam, *Islam, a Short History* by Karen Armstrong (2000) is a strongly recommended title.

The following are a few manifestations of how Islam may impact your UAE and Middle Eastern business experience:

A.   Muslims are obliged to pray five times a day. Not all Muslims go to mosques; some pray at home or in the office. Daily routine, appointments, and meetings are therefore normally fitted around prayer times. Friday is not a business day as it is the day for the obligatory congregational prayers.

B. Ramadan is the month of fasting and is a season of prayers, charitable deeds, and family bonding. In other words, it is thirty days of Christmas. It is therefore advisable to avoid doing business in the month of Ramadan and preferably postpone any trips until life returns to normal (i.e., a week after the end of Ramadan).

C. The majority of Muslims avoid consuming alcohol, and some would discourage interaction between males and females. This should be borne in mind if one is to do business with a UAE national with a traditional background.

1.3.2 Meeting and Greeting

Assalamo alaykom: The traditional Arabian/Islamic greeting you will often hear is *"Asalamu alaykom"* (Peace be with you). Although non-Muslims are not expected to use it, any modest attempts to simulate the terminology will be warmly received. The reply is *"wa alaykom assalam"* (And peace be with you).

Handshakes: Handshakes are frequently used and you should expect them to last for a long time. They are usually accompanied by prolonged inquiries about you and your family. Islamic tradition recommends that one look the other person in the eyes and to wait for the other to withdraw his hand first. Always use the right hand.

Kisses: Avoid kissing the opposite sex. And do not be surprised if you see males kissing each other on the nose or on the cheeks or even holding hands. This is a display of brotherly feeling and does not carry the same connotations as it does in the West.

1.4 Getting Down to Business

Before discussing business it is recommended that one start with a light conversation about weather, current affairs, etc. A brief discussion on how the Gulf region is impressively growing should do the job.

1.5 Business Rules of Note

Very briefly, the following two rules should be taken into consideration:

- Arabs find it difficult to separate professional and private life. Doing business in the region revolves around personal relationships, family ties, trust, and honor. One should therefore endeavor to build a business relationship on mutual friendship and trust.
- The Middle Eastern culture places more value on someone's word than on a written agreement. You will often hear Arab businessmen saying "My word is my deed." When a contract is drawn up,

it is therefore important to confine discussions to the contents of the contract to avoid confusion and uncertainty.

2. Dispute Resolution

2.1 Judiciary

The laws and their application in the UAE vary according to the area in which they are to be applied. The UAE has a federal political system, and its constitution allows each individual emirate to retain its judicial and political power. As a result, there are federal and local courts in the UAE. All emirates, with the exception of Dubai and Ras Al Khaimah, have transferred their judicial systems to the UAE Federal Judicial Authority. Accordingly, Dubai and Abu Dhabi may have differing laws on similar subject matters.

Another interesting recent development, as far as the judiciary is concerned, is the establishment of the Dubai International Financial Centre (DIFC) Court. This court falls outside the federal court system and looks exclusively into disputes arising within the DIFC. The DIFC Court is the only court in the UAE that operates in English. In addition, it excludes the UAE civil law and instead operates its own procedural rules and applies DIFC laws, which are largely based on international laws.

2.2 Contractual Interpretation

If parties to a contract choose UAE law as the law governing their relationship, the following rules of interpretation should be taken into consideration:

A. According to the UAE Civil Code, if the wording of a contract is clear, it may not be departed from by interpretation in order to ascertain the intentions of the parties. However, if there is scope for an interpretive approach to the contract, then reference should be made to the relevant legislative provisions, rules of custom, and practice.

B. Language is a key issue, so do be aware! Although English is widely spoken in the UAE and is the main language used in business, all documentation before the local courts must be in Arabic. If not, then the document will have to be translated into Arabic by a translator who is licensed by the UAE Ministry of Justice. It is often useful to have the document read by another translator or a legal adviser because, once submitted, this translation for all intents and purposes will be deemed to be the definitive and binding version of the document.

C. You may find that language is not the only trap. Perhaps a bigger one is silence! Article 129 of the Civil Code lays down key components of a legal contract under the UAE law. These include agreement upon the essential elements of the contract, certainty of subject matter of the contract, and the contract having a lawful purpose. Once an offer is accepted, a binding contract will be formed. The tricky part is that an acceptance can be active or passive. In other words, silence can amount to acceptance. So watch out for your actions, facial expressions, or anything else that may silently indicate an "unintentional" acceptance.

D. Because of the value Arab businessmen place on words, a legally binding contract may also result from an oral agreement. However, there are exceptions to this formation, such as contracts relating to land and a company's contract of establishment.

2.3 Specific Contract Terms

A. Under the UAE law, limitation clauses will only be struck down if they are unreasonable or purport to exempt a party from liability for a "harmful" activity.

B. A force majeure clause is imposed by Article 273 of the Civil Code on all contracts and is binding on both parties. This clause will apply if performance of the whole or part of the contract becomes impossible and the Civil Code provides that in certain circumstances the contract will automatically terminate.

C. In the case where a contract is terminated for whatever reason, the parties are to be restored to the precontractual position. If this is not possible, then the courts order damages to be awarded. For a nonperformance termination, it is for the court to decide on the actions for the parties to take.

In view of the complications and numerous pitfalls that foreign investors may encounter in relation to contractual interpretation, and in view of the time and cost involved in litigation before the UAE courts, it is often advisable for foreign investors to seek alternative dispute resolution rather than taking the matter to a local court.

3. Arbitration

As a result of the complications associated with local courts, arbitration has become a popular alternative dispute resolution procedure in the UAE.

3.1 Recent Developments

3.1.1 The New York Convention on the Recognition and Enforcement of Foreign Arbitral Awards

In 2006, the UAE acceded to the New York Convention on the Recognition and Enforcement of Foreign Arbitral Awards, under which it became bound by the international procedures for recognizing and enforcing foreign arbitral awards.

Before the UAE's ratification of the Convention, there were no international rules governing the recognition and enforcement of foreign arbitral awards in the UAE (with the exception of treaties with France and the Gulf Cooperation Council (the UAE, Bahrain, Saudi Arabia, Oman, Qatar, and Kuwait)). In practice, therefore, foreign arbitral awards were commonly not enforced by the local courts.

This development is particularly welcome to those doing business with UAE companies or inward investing, bringing it into line with its neighbors in the region and the wider international arbitration community.

3.1.2 Draft UAE Federal Law on Arbitration and the Enforcement of Arbitration

In February 2008, a draft UAE Federal Law on Arbitration and the Enforcement of Arbitration Awards was published. The draft incorporates the UNCITRAL (United Nations Commission on International Trade Law) Model Law on International Commercial Arbitration, and contains some additional provisions to reflect modern arbitration practice. The draft provides for the enforcement of arbitral awards in accordance with the New York Convention. The new law is expected to be ratified and issued before the end of 2008.

3.2 Dubai International Arbitration Centre

The Dubai International Arbitration Centre (DIAC) supplies facilities for conducting commercial arbitration and promoting the settlement of disputes, as well as developing a pool of international arbitration. Arbitrators of the highest ability and professional competence are selected by the DIAC in order to provide efficient, flexible, and impartial administration of disputes. Arbitration proceedings may be as flexible as the parties wish them to be, unlike court proceedings, where parties' movements are restricted in accordance with the wishes of the court and judge. More information about DIAC can be found on its Web site at www.diac.ae/idias/.

The accession to the New York Convention as well as the new draft federal law on arbitration suggest that overseas investors doing business in the region may rest assured that any resulting arbitration award should be enforceable against a UAE company and its assets. This development assists the UAE in becoming yet a more attractive location for businesses worldwide.

4. Property

The land laws of the UAE have come a long way in a short period but, like the real estate market itself, have perhaps some way to go before reaching full maturity.

The UAE's increasing exposure to the ebb and flow of international capital, coupled with the growing sophistication of the property market, has contributed to the development of the land laws of the UAE.

4.1 Federal and Local Law

The Civil Code sets out the conceptual basis of the law of ownership and rights associated with or derived from ownership, as well as addressing various other real estate–related matters. However, the Civil Code is notably silent on whether freehold ownership is available to non–UAE nationals. Most of the emirates have therefore assumed jurisdiction in this area (e.g., most emirates have officially prohibited overseas investors from owning freehold property, subject to certain exceptions), as well as, for example, in relation to rent capping under lease arrangements.

4.2 Usufructuary Rights and Hire-Contract/Lease Rights

There is a fundamental distinction under the Civil Code between the rights conferred under a hire contract or lease of property (as these arrangements are generally described in the UAE), and the rights conferred under a right of usufruct in relation to property. In summary, usufructuary rights provide enduring rights in the real estate itself, whereas a hire contract or property lease will provide a personal right alone.

4.3 Usufructuary Rights—Rights in Rem

Usufructuary rights that may be granted over real estate are similar in certain ways to the rights granted at common law under a lease. Both arrangements grant rights to the tenant to use and occupy property belonging to another person for a defined period of time and in accordance with the terms and conditions contained in the instrument that creates the right. The rights granted under a usufructuary arrangement are rights *in rem,* meaning that they attach to the land and create a legal interest *in the property itself,* and are capable of true ownership. The owner of a usufruct right has the right to assert and protect his rights in the property in his own name.

A common form of usufruct interest is a "musataha" right, which provides the grantee with a right to build on the land in addition to the right to use and enjoy the land.

4.4 Leasehold Rights—Personal Rights

In contrast to the rights available to a usufruct owner, a hire-contract or lease will grant to the tenant only *a personal right.* The lease will be enforceable against the original landlord, but is not directly enforceable against third parties, and may not be enforceable against a new owner of the property. The tenant does not have the right to assert and protect his rights in the leased property in his own name. The personal rights granted under the lease may not be capable of being mortgaged, as they do not amount to "property" in their own right.

The lease instrument is ordinarily used to govern the relationship between landlord and tenant under a short-term residential occupancy for which it is reasonably well suited. However, there have been a number of instances of long-term (typically ninety-nine-year) leases being offered for sale as a form of property ownership or investment vehicle, particularly in Dubai, but also elsewhere in the UAE.

The long-term nature of a ninety-nine-year lease will not in itself change the fundamental basis on which the lease was created, namely as a personal contract between the original landlord and tenant that will not bind or "run with" the land. As a result, a lease or hire contract, even if for an extended period, cannot safely be relied upon as a mechanism to provide ownership or investment in real estate.

Some emirates (such as Abu Dhabi) have passed additional tenancy laws regarding the rights and obligations that are created under a lease. These often include provisions relating to rental increase caps, and in some cases also provide certain termination rights in favor of landlords when they intend to develop the property.

In theory, it should be possible to avoid the application of these tenancy laws by creating usufructuary "property" rights between landlord and tenant, rather than lease rights. However, there is very little legal guidance on how, practically, to distinguish the grant of usufructuary rights from the grant of lease rights.

5. Taking Security in the UAE

Unlike in more established jurisdictions, taking security in the UAE is not necessarily a straightforward process, particularly when it comes to the registration and enforcement of security. The UAE courts tend not to adopt a black letter law approach and, since case law is not widely published in the UAE, the use of precedents is fairly limited, which in turn leads to legal uncertainty.

Forms of security will depend on the type of asset to be secured. As general guidance, assets can be divided into three main groups:

- Movables and immovables;
- Tangible movables and intangible movables; and
- Assets used for personal use and assets used for commercial use.

Immovable assets are those that are permanently fixed and that cannot be removed without altering or damaging the surroundings. Real property and structural improvements would fall within the scope of this description. Conversely, assets not fitting this description are movables.

Movables are to be divided into tangible assets (e.g., goods or machinery) and intangible assets (e.g., goodwill or intellectual property rights).

The most common types of security available in the UAE are summarized below:

A. **Pledges over movables:** For this type of security to be effective, the movable on which the security is taken must be transferred to the creditor or third party and remain in that party's possession until the debt is paid in full. However, as a general rule there is no security registry for such pledges.

B. **Mortgages over commercial businesses:** Mortgages can be granted on the movable assets of a business (but not immovable assets) and they are often used for security of a commercial debt. The main distinctions of non-commercial pledges over movables are:

   i.   only banks and financing institutions may benefit from such pledges;

   ii. there is no requirement to transfer the assets to the holder of the security;

   iii. goods that can be readily sold by the business are not considered to be covered by the pledge;

   iv. the pledge must be notarized before a notary public; and

   v.   they must be registered at a Commercial Register, although this is possible only in the emirates of Dubai, Abu Dhabi, and Sharjah.

C. **Mortgages over real property:** Mortgages can be granted and registered with the relevant land department of the appropriate jurisdiction (the Mortgage Registrar at the relevant Land Department or municipality). Although it is technically possible for a mortgage to be taken over real property, enforcement remains the main concern for lenders in UAE jurisdictions that are subject to federal law. In such UAE jurisdictions, commercial banks may only enforce a mortgage over real property three years after the default of the debtor and subject to a possible extension by the governor of the UAE Central Bank.

D. **Pledges over debts:** These are permissible if the debtor (i) enters into a written document with the creditor to that effect, and (ii) if the party from whom the debtor is owed money has been notified and accepts the pledge.

E. **Pledges over shares:** As shares are nominal (i.e., not in bearer form), it will suffice for the debtor to deliver these to the creditor. The creditor should request that the company to which the shares relate register the pledge in its books (if applicable) and,

> where possible, in the appropriate security registry to gain pri-
> ority over other creditors in relation to the pledged shares.

Where the assets can be registered, the security interest will need
to be registered in accordance with the applicable laws.

Where the assets cannot be registered, security interests may be
enforceable although the beneficiary of such security may become
merely an unsecured creditor and not recover the entire value of the
security.

Furthermore, the UAE courts will not necessarily effect the security by transferring title to the assets to the creditor. Indeed, the UAE
courts may determine that the assets be sold at auction, which may
lead to severe delays in the creditor recovering the amounts owed to it
and hence the creditor suffering a shortfall.

6. Taxation and Custom Duties

No corporate, income, withholding, value added, or sales taxes are currently assessed in the UAE other than (a) a flat-rate tax on the annual
profits of branches of foreign banks, (b) a flat-rate tax on hotel services
and entertainment, (c) taxes on oil and gas companies at rates specified
in the relevant concession agreements, and (d) taxes/custom duties on
alcohol and cigarettes. In addition, double-taxation treaties have been
concluded between the UAE and various countries, including France.

A customs union was introduced by the Gulf Cooperation Council (GCC) on January 1, 2003. A standard custom duty of 5 percent is
levied on the import of most goods into GCC member states. However,
a significant number of classes of goods are exempt from duty. These
include, among others, goods listed for exemption pursuant to the
GCC Unified Customs Tariff, goods imported by military and security
forces, personal effects, and certain exempted raw materials, equipment, and spare parts. Intra-UAE trade is not generally subject to custom duties and neither are certain "qualified industrial projects."

Value-added tax (VAT) is expected to be introduced for the first
time in the UAE in the first quarter of 2009 with a presumed limit of
not more than 5 percent.

7. Exchange and Interest Rates

The UAE currency is the dirham (100 fils to the dirham). The dirham
(AED) has been pegged to the U.S. dollar since 1980 and is currently
USD 1 to AED 3.6. There are no exchange controls in the UAE and the
dirham is freely convertible.

The link with the U.S. dollar and the large amount of U.S. dollar–
denominated exports means that local interest rates are expected to
track U.S. rates to avoid large movements in and out of the currency.

8. Business Vehicles Available to Overseas Investors

The Commercial Companies Law, Federal Law No. 8 of 1984 (CCL), sets out the forms of corporate vehicles that can be established in the UAE. Following are brief descriptions of two such arrangements, an LLC and a branch.

8.1 Limited Liability Company (LLC)

An LLC can be formed by a minimum of two and a maximum of fifty persons. Shareholder liability is limited to the value of shares held in the company's capital.

An overseas company can become a shareholder in an LLC incorporated in the UAE. At least 51 percent of the shares of an LLC must be held by UAE nationals or companies that are wholly owned by UAE nationals. Non–UAE nationals may own up to 49 percent.

The minimum capital required to establish an LLC is AED 150,000 in Abu Dhabi and AED 300,000 in Dubai. Management is handled by no more than five designated managers (whose role is akin to that of directors). These managers need not be members of the company.

The CCL provides that an LLC may engage in any lawful activity except insurance, banking, and investment of money for others.

8.2 Branches of Overseas Companies

An overseas company may establish a branch in the UAE, but a local services agent (or sponsor) is required who must be either a citizen of the UAE or a company wholly owned by citizens of the UAE.

A branch must be registered with the Ministry of Economy and Planning, local chamber of commerce, and the municipality/Department of Economic Development in each emirate.

Under the CCL and its implementing regulations, a branch of an overseas company does not have a separate legal identity from its parent.

The UAE local services agent (or sponsor) will render the necessary services for obtaining licenses, visas, and other permits. The sponsor will not assume any financial obligation with respect to the branch and is not necessarily involved in the running or management of the branch. Branch offices are restricted in what services they can carry on on behalf of the overseas parent, although generally a broad range of commercial trading activities can be undertaken.

Payment to the sponsor can be structured in a number of ways, including as a percentage of annual profits or as an annual fixed fee.

8.3 Free Zones

The UAE has free zones in most of the individual emirates. The free zone in Fujairah, together with the other ports on the east coast of the

UAE, gives access to the UAE without the need to enter the Arabian Gulf. The Jebel Ali Free Zone (JAFZ), located in the emirate of Dubai, is by far the largest of the UAE's free zones, contains the world's largest man-made port, and is now home to more than one thousand companies. Dubai also has a number of specialist free zones such as Dubai Internet City, Dubai Media City, Dubai Airport Free Zone, Dubai Healthcare City, and Dubai International Financial Centre.

Given the significance of the Dubai International Financial Centre to Dubai's plans to become a global financial hub, some essential information about the DIFC is set out in a separate section below.

The free zones, which operate through an exemption to the Commercial Companies Law, offer a variety of valuable benefits to businesses and a degree of flexibility, including:

i.   100 percent foreign ownership through branches and single or multiple shareholder companies (known respectively as FZEs, FZCOs, and FZ-LLCs);

ii. no local sponsor required for branch offices of foreign companies;

iii. no customs duties on imports and re-exports (except re-exports into onshore UAE);

iv. special assistance in obtaining work permits for staff; and

v.   guaranteed tax-free periods.

9. Dubai International Financial Centre (DIFC)

The DIFC (www.difc.ae), established by Federal Decree No. 35 of 2004, is an onshore capital market designated as a financial free zone and designed to create a unique financial services cluster. The DIFC has its own laws and regulations and a clear regulatory framework. The laws are written in English and benefit from extensive consultations with, and submissions from, leading financial institutions and their professional advisers.

There are six primary sectors of focus within the DIFC:

- Banking services (investment banking, corporate banking, and private banking (for high net worth individuals))
- Capital markets (equity, debt instruments, derivatives, and commodity trading)
- Asset management and fund registration (fund registration, fund administration, and fund management)
- Reinsurance
- Islamic finance
- Back office operations

License applications are considered from financial institutions in each of these sectors.

9.1 Corporate Banking (Trade Finance)

Dubai has emerged as a major center for international trade and is the third-largest re-export center in the world (after Hong Kong and Singapore), with over 3,000 multinational and regional corporations located in its free zones requiring trade finance. The region's combined exports equate to those of China. The DIFC offers great opportunities for providers of trade finance.

9.2 Investment Banking

There is a growing requirement for equity and bond issuance in the region given the many planned privatizations (notably in the power and telecom sectors) and the growing number of private companies seeking to raise capital through IPOs and secondary offerings. The region's large pool of liquidity is also capable of being tapped by governments in the region and global issuers from outside the region.

9.3 Capital Markets (NASDAQ Dubai)

NASDAQ Dubai (formerly the Dubai International Financial Exchange (DIFX)) aims to provide a liquid and transparent market for the hundreds of successful privately owned companies in the region and the soon to be privatized businesses that require listings on a liquid, transparent, and efficient stock exchange. It also offers facilities for companies from outside the region to be dual listed. NASDAQ Dubai, whose members include the premier global investment banks, is designed to complement the services provided by local financial exchanges in the region and will be the regional gateway for capital raising and investment.

9.4 Asset Management and Fund Registration

It is estimated that more than a trillion dollars of wealth is held by institutional and private investors in the region. Many regional companies and retail banks outsource the management and administration of these funds to specialist providers outside the region. The DIFC offers a highly attractive opportunity for asset management firms and private banks to gather and manage this growing pool of assets closer to their client base.

9.5 Reinsurance

The penetration and density of insurance in the region has traditionally lagged behind average world levels. However, with economic growth, industrialization, and improved regulation, the region is experiencing a changing attitude towards risk and an increasing awareness of the need for insurance. Because of slow growth in more mature traditional markets, the world's insurance and reinsurance companies are now assessing markets such as the Middle East. The DIFC has set out to create a global (re-)insurance hub to foster the development of a thriving insurance market by attracting global insurance and reinsurance companies, brokers, captives, and other service providers.

9.6 Islamic Finance

The global market for Islamic financial products is estimated to be worth over US$260 billion and is expected to grow at 12 to 15 percent a year over the next ten years. It is likely to account for some 50 to 60 percent of the total savings of the world's 1.2 billion Muslims within the next decade. Within the region, there is a growing number of infrastructure projects requiring sharia-compliant finance, but the market is still underdeveloped and fragmented. DIFC aims to become a major center for product innovation for Islamic investors and borrowers.

9.7 Back Office Operations

The growth of back office operations and outsourcing has been a permanent feature of the financial services industry in recent years. With its world-class IT infrastructure and ready access to the region's large pool of educated and skilled professionals, the DIFC is well placed to become the location of choice for the global back office operations of banks and other financial institutions.

The DIFC's remit was to create a regional capital market, offering investors and issuers of capital world-class regulations and standards. As a new global jurisdiction for financial institutions, the DIFC offers its participants a highly attractive investment environment, including:

- 100 percent foreign ownership;
- 0 percent tax rate on income and profits;
- a wide network of double taxation treaties available to UAE-incorporated entities;
- no restrictions on foreign exchange;
- freedom to repatriate capital and profits without restrictions; and
- high standards of rules and regulations.

Unlike "offshore" tax havens, the DIFC is a fully fledged "onshore" capital market, comparable to Hong Kong, London, and New York.

Robert Leigh
Simmons and Simmons
Level 7 The Gate Village Building 10
Dubai International Financial Centre PO Box 506688
Dubai, United Arab Emirates
Phone: + 971 (0) 4 709 6600
Fax: + 971 (0) 4 709 6601
E-mail: robert.leigh@simmonssimmons.com

CHAPTER 48

International Business Negotiations in the United Kingdom

Nigel Read
LOVELLS LLP
LONDON, UK

1. Background

The UK is principally a common law jurisdiction—although Scotland is something of a special case—hence the process of negotiating, structuring, and documenting an international business transaction involving a UK party tends to be more familiar to U.S. companies and their legal advisors than might be the case in a continental European civil law jurisdiction. However, in business negotiations, as well as in many cultural areas, there is still force in the old saying that the U.S. and the UK remain two cultures (or two legal systems) divided by a common language, and it is important to appreciate some of the differences in UK assumptions, expectations, and practices before setting out on the cross-border acquisition trail or launching into a new international venture.

The UK has four constituent parts: England, Wales, Scotland, and Northern Ireland. England, Wales, and Scotland together make up Great Britain, which with the addition of Northern Ireland makes up the United Kingdom of Great Britain and Northern Ireland. Each was once independent and had its own legal system. Although the passage of time and the strongly unifying forces of the UK have eliminated much of this diversity, individual national characteristics, traditions, and legal principles remain. The devolution in recent years to Scotland in particular, and Wales to a lesser extent, of certain domestic governmental responsibilities and the creation of new legislative assemblies has reinforced these individual national characteristics.

England and Wales constitute a single legal jurisdiction. The law of this jurisdiction is commonly spoken of as "English law." Scotland have historically had and still maintains a strong civil law tradition, which means that even its fundamental principles of law can differ from those of England and Wales. In Northern Ireland, the basis of the legal system is English common law. Legislation by the UK Parliament will state whether its provisions are intended to apply, in whole or in part, to all or only some of the four parts of the UK.

In addition, the overreaching effect of European Union legislation applies to the whole of the UK and is of increasingly important effect even in relation to what would otherwise appear to be wholly domestic UK transactions and ventures.

The remainder of this chapter is written from the standpoint of the English lawyer dealing with an international business negotiation involving a U.S. party and an English-based UK party, although many of the general comments will be equally applicable to the negotiation of a transaction in any part of the UK.

2. Corporate Organization in the UK

Corporate law in the UK is in a state of transition. The main piece of corporation legislation over the last twenty years, the Companies Act 1985, is gradually being replaced by the Companies Act 2006. The latter, which is being introduced in stages, will be fully in force in October 2009 (though even then some transitional arrangements may continue), but until then the two acts will exist side by side, each only partially in force. While the discussion below reflects the law as of May 2008, it includes brief references, where appropriate, to the position once the reforms are complete.

2.1 Public and Private Companies

It is technically incorrect to refer to a "UK company." Companies registered under the Companies Act 1985 must be incorporated in England and Wales or in Scotland (or in Northern Ireland under the equivalent statutory provisions), and this position will remain essentially the same when the company formation provisions of the Companies Act 2006 are introduced in October 2009.

Leaving aside some minor exceptions, companies in the UK are further categorized as public limited companies (or PLCs) or private limited companies (usually abbreviated to public and private companies, respectively). A public company is not necessarily a listed company, and may indeed be privately or even closely held, but is usually large and draws its working capital from the public (both as investing shareholders and as debenture-holding creditors). Private companies vary greatly in size, from local subsidiaries of multinationals to small, family-run "mom and pop" businesses.

The name of a public company must end with the words "public limited company" (although it may use the abbreviation PLC) and the name of a private company must end with the word "limited" (although it may use the abbreviation Ltd.), or the Welsh equivalents if the company's registered office is in Wales. Only public companies can offer their shares to the public.

2.2 Management

UK companies are not required by law to appoint a president or a treasurer, as U.S. corporations typically are. However, they are subject to requirements in relation to the appointment of directors and secretaries. A public company is required to have at least two directors, as well as a secretary, whose functions are broadly equivalent to those of the secretary of a U.S. company. A private company is required to have at least one director. The long-standing requirement to have a secretary was abolished recently as part of the streamlined administrative framework for smaller companies that is being introduced by the Companies Act 2006, but many companies will continue to appoint a secretary, as the functions of a secretary still need to be undertaken. From October 1, 2008, every company must have at least one director who is a natural person (not a company).

The directors of the company are charged with the management of its affairs. They are appointed by the shareholders (or members, as they are referred to in the Companies Acts) of the company in accordance with the procedures laid down in the company's articles of association. In large, usually public, companies, an important distinction exists in practice between executive and nonexecutive directors. In legal terms, however, directors have the same statutory duties to the company whether they are executives or not.

The primary decision-making body in a UK company is the members in general meeting, to which certain matters are reserved either by statute or by the articles of association. However, the articles of association will almost invariably provide that the company's business is to be managed by the directors, who will exercise all the powers of the company. It is presumed by the law that in exercising their functions, the directors make collective decisions and are collectively responsible for those decisions. Specific delegations of power are often made to a managing director, whose role is such that he or she may often be regarded as a third organ of the company, in addition to the shareholders and the board of directors. The larger the company, the more likely it will be that management functions are undertaken by a small class of executive directors and senior management employees.

2.3 Directors' Duties

Historically, the duties owed by directors to their company were developed by the courts rather than set out in legislation. Key duties included a duty to exercise skill and care, a duty to act in good faith in the company's interests, and a duty to avoid conflicts. One of the most contentious elements of the ongoing reform of corporate law has been the introduction of statutory duties to codify these common law and fiduciary duties.

Most of the statutory duties in the Companies Act 2006 were introduced in October 2007, although those concerning conflicts of interest did not take effect until October 2008. The fundamental duty, known as the success duty, obliges directors to act in such a way as to promote the success of the company, and in so doing to consider certain specified matters, such as the decision's long-term implications, the interests of employees, and the decision's impact on the environment.

The government's desire to introduce a clear statement of directors' duties is understandable, and certainly U.S. businesses acquiring a UK subsidiary, for example, may feel that a brief, statutory statement of duties is easier to come to terms with than an "unofficial" list of duties gleaned from a large body of case law. It remains to be seen, however, whether in practice the statutory formulation provides any more certainty or clarity than the traditional duties.

2.4 Directors' Authority

In principle, authority to exercise the powers of the company is vested in the board of directors, and express powers may be delegated to a managing director or other individual directors or senior managers. English law also recognizes the implied agency of a managing director in the general conduct of the affairs of the company, or of individuals such as a finance director in connection with financial responsibilities, as well as the concept of "apparent" or "ostensible" authority, where a company has expressly or by implication held out a person as having authority to bind the company. However, even where directors purport to negotiate and to sign documents "for and on behalf of" the company, it is not uncommon in major transactions for third parties to require some proof of specific board authority—for example, by the provision of a copy of the relevant board resolution certified by the company secretary.

In usual circumstances, a third party dealing with a director of a UK company will be able to rely on the principles of agency and the director's express or apparent or ostensible authority to represent the company. The Companies Act 1985 also provides that in favor of a person dealing with a company in good faith, the power of the board of directors to bind the company or to authorize others to do so is deemed to be free of any limitation under the company's constitution. There is a specific provision that a third party has no duty to inquire as to whether the transaction is permitted by the company's memorandum or whether there is any limitation on the powers of the board of directors to bind the company or to authorize others to do so. This position will be broadly retained when the corresponding provisions of the Companies Act 2006 take effect in October 2009.

2.5 Available Information

English law prides itself on its extensive disclosure provisions. These aim to ensure that as much commercial information about the company as possible is publicly available without jeopardizing commercial confidences. The Companies Acts require all UK limited companies, whether public or private, to file certain documents with the registrar of companies, and these documents are then available for public inspection. These include the company's constitution (that is, the memorandum of association and the articles of association, equivalent to the articles of incorporation and bylaws of a U.S. company); the company's annual audited financial statements (which include the profit and loss account and balance sheet, the directors' report, the auditors' report, and, if the company has subsidiaries, consolidated group accounts); the company's annual return (which includes a statement of its directors, secretary, shareholders and respective shareholdings, the type of company, and its principal business activities); and details of any legal encumbrances created by the company over specified classes of its assets.

3. Regulation of Public Mergers and Acquisitions

3.1 Takeovers

Not all international business negotiations take place as a prelude to mergers and acquisitions. Agency, distribution, and supply agreements (which are dealt with later in this chapter) and a host of other business arrangements take place in the international context. However, the area of mergers and acquisitions probably better illustrates more of the issues that arise in international business negotiations than any other area. Many of the issues, especially antitrust, corporate authority, and liability, will of course be equally relevant in the negotiation of joint ventures and similar arrangements.

The UK has a well-established system for the regulation of takeovers. In addition, the importance of EU regulation in public securities transactions is also becoming increasingly evident. The vast majority of takeovers in the UK are negotiated—in the case of a publicly owned company, usually on the recommendation of an agreed offer by the board of the target to its shareholders, and in the case of a privately owned company, by negotiation with the existing shareholders.

The acquisition of shares in a UK company may be accomplished by an offer for the whole of the issued share capital or for a proportion of it sufficient to give voting control. In the case of privately held companies, the articles of association very often contain preemptive provisions requiring any shareholder to offer to sell his or her shares to other shareholders before they can be sold to a third party, and so it will not usually be possible to acquire any shares without the agreement of all shareholders. However, if an offer (on terms that are the same in relation to all the shareholders of the class to which it relates) is accepted with respect to 90 percent of a class of shares (disregarding any held by the bidder at the date of the offer), then, by statutory right, the remainder of the class can be acquired compulsorily on the same terms (broadly the equivalent of a minority "squeeze out" in the United States). Conversely, the holders of the minority are able to require their shares to be acquired on the same terms. There are certain time limits to be observed and prescribed forms that the offeror must issue even if the offeror would prefer not to have to acquire the remaining shares.

3.2 The City Code

Offers for publicly owned companies, whether hostile or agreed, are primarily regulated by the City Code on Takeovers and Mergers (the "City Code"). The City Code is issued by the UK Panel on Takeovers and Mergers (the "Panel") and broadly applies to all public companies that have their registered office in the UK, the Channel Islands, or the Isle of Man. In certain circumstances the company must also have its place of central management and control in one of those jurisdictions for the City Code to apply. In limited situations, the City Code can also apply to some private companies.

While there are a variety of laws and regulations that are relevant to a public takeover, the City Code is the principal source of procedural regulation. It is based on six general principles of fair dealing and good commercial practice, backed up by a detailed set of rules that lay down the timetable and mechanical procedures to be observed in the course of a takeover. The City Code is a statutory set of rules that is administered by the Panel. The Panel has certain statutory powers of enforcement in the UK .

The City Code lays down the detailed timetable and mechanical procedures to be observed during a takeover, but the principal requirements are, first, that any person (together with any persons "acting in concert" within the meaning of the code) who acquires issued shares of a listed company that carry 30 percent or more of the voting rights will almost invariably be obliged to make an unconditional offer for all the remaining shares in the company. This offer must generally include a cash alternative equivalent to the highest price the purchaser has paid for any shares in the company in the preceding twelve months.

Second, the City Code generally prohibits a target from taking action that would frustrate a bid or deny its shareholders the opportunity to decide on the merits of a bid, unless the action has been approved in advance by the shareholders. Generally, the sort of defense strategies and novelty defense devices popular in the United States are rarely seen in the UK. In addition, the UK generally does not have anything similar to the control share acquisition statutes, business combination statutes, or fair price statutes that typify anti-takeover laws at the U.S. state level. Of course, the position is quite different in the case of privately held companies, where the contractual equivalents of anti-takeover statutes are often enshrined at length in the company's constitution or in a shareholders' agreement, rendering it virtually impossible to acquire shareholdings in privately held companies without the consent of all existing shareholders.

3.3 Prospectus and Securities Legislation Requirements

There are important provisions to be borne in mind if a U.S. corporation intends to issue stock to shareholders in the UK (whether of public or private companies) as part of the consideration for the acquisition.

First, there must be a consideration of whether an obligation to prepare and distribute a prospectus arises. Across Europe and including the UK, an offer of shares to the public or admission of shares to an EU-regulated market requires a prospectus with specific content requirements to be approved by the appropriate regulator. That is generally viewed as an onerous obligation, but less so than the equivalent regime in the United States. A U.S. issuer will need to determine the appropriate regulator (generally the regulator in the EU state in which securities are first offered). Once a prospectus has been approved by that regulator it can be passported around Europe fairly simply and cheaply. There are exemptions including for small offers, offers to qualified investors, and exchange offers.

Outside of the prospectus regime, there are also restrictions on the distribution of financial promotions (invitations or inducements to enter into investment activity). This regime incurs criminal liability and renders agreements concluded void, but contains helpful exemptions for much corporate activity. If there is no available exemption, an authorized person (such as an investment bank) must be engaged to communicate the financial promotion.

More generally, the Financial Services and Markets Act 2000 imposes criminal liability on persons who make misleading, false, or deceptive statements, promises, or forecasts, or who dishonestly conceal material facts, or who recklessly make (dishonestly or otherwise) statements, promises, or forecasts that are misleading, false, or deceptive for the purpose of inducing persons to purchase securities or to exercise any rights conferred by securities. Neither this section nor the common law offense of deceit, or civil liability for negligent misstatement would probably impose any more onerous burden on a U.S. issuer of a share exchange offer than would be imposed on them by the U.S. Securities Act of 1933.

3.4 Forms of Consideration

The UK securities markets are relatively sophisticated, which means that various forms of consideration can be offered in a takeover. In the context of publicly owned companies, the offer can include alternatives or combinations of forms of consideration. There are no particular legal or regulatory consequences attaching to noncash consideration, although the City Code imposes more onerous disclosure requirements for share exchanges and requires debt or unlisted equity securities to be valued by an independent advisor.

The advantage of offering some form of equity or debt securities as an alternative to a cash offer is that, if properly structured, it can enable UK shareholders to defer capital-gains tax liabilities on the sale of their shares.

UK financial institutions are also sophisticated and able to arrange underwriting of share-for-share offers so as to provide a cash alternative for shareholders in the target company.

UK institutions are also able to provide financing for leveraged deals, although the existence of detailed provisions in the Companies Act restricting the circumstances in which public companies can give financial assistance (that is, where the cash or other assets of the target are to be used to finance the acquisition, or where its assets are to be charged to secure borrowings incurred by the acquirer to make the acquisition) means that if any leveraged structure is contemplated, specialist UK legal advice should be sought at the earliest possible opportunity so as to enable the transaction to be structured in a way that will not be rendered unlawful by the financial-assistance rules.

Finally, in the case of public company bids, the City Code requires the investment banker advising an offeror who is making a cash bid to be satisfied that the bidder has the financial resources to make the bid. Effectively, this means that any bank financing for a cash offer must be available unconditionally when the offer is made. UK lenders are familiar with the special funding requirements for UK public takeovers, and can structure their financing arrangements accordingly.

4. Negotiating Private Mergers and Acquisitions

4.1 The Purpose of the Negotiations

It is impossible to negotiate a contract for, say, the acquisition of a company unless you can see the overall purpose of the contract. There are two questions to begin with. First, why bother having a contract at all? Everything in any contract for the negotiated sale and purchase of a company must be justified by one of three criteria: writing down what the parties wish to agree; excluding rules of law that might otherwise apply and that the parties do not wish to apply; and modifying rules of law that the parties may wish to apply but that are so complex or uncertain in their application that they would not, in fact, give ready effect to what the parties wish to achieve.

Second, what happens in the UK in the absence of a contract? The answer is "very little." The negotiated sale and purchase of shares in a private company is one of the last remaining areas of the English law of sale where the rule of caveat emptor applies largely with its original rigor. There is no equivalent of the Sale of Goods Act in relation to the sale and purchase of shares in a company. The buyer is almost completely unprotected in the absence of whatever may be agreed in the contract with the seller.

The traditional contrast tends to be between a sale of assets or a sale of a business as a growing concern. In a sale of assets you may hope, in the absence of specific written provisions, to obtain at least some measure of implied warranty protection. For example, the Sale of Goods Act applies to the sale of any assets in the UK.

In addition, a business acquisition is such that it is usually possible, in theory at least, to pick and choose the assets and liabilities that are taken on. It should be noted, though, that there are some liabilities (most notably those relating to the rights of employees engaged in the business) that transfer by operation of law and therefore cannot be avoided by the buyer. By contrast, the acquisition of a company's entire share capital is the acquisition of an ongoing ready-packed business. Uniquely, in the sale and purchase of a company, you are dealing with something that the law regards as a person who comes with a hidden history of rights and liabilities that the buyer can neither investigate in full nor avoid.

4.2 Legal Characterization of Preliminary Negotiations

The first step, and probably the lawyer's first connection with the sale and purchase of shares in a UK company, is likely to be in preliminary negotiations. Real estate lawyers in the UK are apt to write "subject to contract" on every document that leaves their offices. Many corporate lawyers disdain this approach as being beneath them—it has been suggested that the phrase "subject to contract" has something specifically to do with real estate. This is not so.

The danger of entering into a legally binding contract during the course of negotiations without intending to do so is even more serious in connection with the sale and purchase of shares in a company than it is in a real estate transaction. Steps must be taken during the course of negotiations to ensure that neither party gives the impression at any time that it is entering into a legally binding commitment before it intends to do so. If the parties enter some kind of letter of intent or heads of agreement, then it should be made very clear in plain language that the document being signed is purely a statement of intent and does not give rise to legally binding relations between the parties.

4.3 Statements and Promises in the Course of Negotiations

There are other dangers in the course of negotiations in the UK. The first, very often ignored, is the danger of an ancillary contract. It is not uncommon for allegations to be made following a failure of negotiations—often with justice—that some kind of minor ancillary contract has been made. For example, one party asks the other to have an audit carried out of the target company's accounts. An allegation is made after the event that the requesting party is due to pay the costs of the audit. Another common example is where one party incurs costs in instructing lawyers and alleges that the other party agreed to bear its costs whether the transaction proceeded to completion or not. Sometimes, one party alleges that the other agreed to give an exclusive negotiation right for a certain period and either seeks damages for breach of that contract or an injunction to stop a contract being made with a third party.

4.4 Misrepresentation

The second danger is misrepresentation. One of the first steps of the potential buyer in any substantial UK negotiation is to put forward to the potential seller a list of warranties that are required in relation to the target company. It is in the interests of the seller to ensure that these are its only warranties and to avoid the dangers of adding to them through the law of misrepresentation. Both parties to a joint venture have this interest equally.

Misrepresentation holds three dangers for the unwary. First, it is a civil wrong for which rescission of a contract may still be a remedy. Second, it is possible to have an award of damages for misrepresentation whether innocent, negligent, or fraudulent. Finally, a misrepresentation need not be written down in a contract in order to be sued upon. Indeed, the most dangerous type of misrepresentation is one that induces a party to enter into a contract in the first place, which may give it a remedy wholly independent of the sale contract itself, and possibly wholly unaffected by any limitations on liability that may have been negotiated in the contract.

Any misrepresentation may potentially lead to the rescission of the contract. Fraudulent misrepresentation—amounting essentially to deceit at common law—may be grounds for seeking damages. Negligent misrepresentation may have the same effect, largely as a result of what is known as the rule in *Hedley Byrne v. Heller* or, alternatively, as a result of section 2(1) of the Misrepresentation Act. For an innocent misrepresentation the court may award damages in lieu of rescission under section 2(2) of the Misrepresentation Act.

An extra complexity occurs when a misrepresentation is repeated in the contract itself. Such a misrepresentation may still lead to rescission. If a warranty happens to repeat a misrepresentation that was made before the date of the contract, there is at least potentially a remedy available in rescission as well as a remedy in damages for breach of warranty.

It is in the interests of both the seller and the buyer to agree in writing on the circumstances in which the only remedy will be damages, or in which rescission will be available as a remedy, or in which there will be no remedy at all.

4.5 Entire Agreement

The parties negotiating a contract in the UK must take positive action that may be summarized, perhaps not wholly accurately, as the insertion of an "entire agreement" provision. Having agreed on the terms of their bargain (usually including warranties, representations, and indemnities), the parties then ought to proceed to include a provision that the words written down constitute their entire agreement. However, a prudent negotiator will go further. The courts have made it very clear that for a contract to exclude liability in tort, and in particular liability in negligence, a contract must specifically exclude the liability. As a result, if liability for misrepresentation is to be excluded or limited, the contract must say so.

4.6 Conflicting Interests of Seller and Buyer

On the terms of the contract itself, the seller's interest is the same as that of a seller of a used car, who wishes to hand over the vehicle with as little obligation and as much speed as possible. There is no legal reason at all why, from the seller's point of view, the sale and purchase should not simply require the handing over of a stock-transfer form.

From the buyer's point of view, the best position would be to have a complete indemnity against any liability of any nature that the company might have at the date of the takeover, so that from that date it could carry on business through the company in the knowledge that past liabilities of the company were simply not its concern.

The usual compromise is reflected in the format of the acquisition contract. In summary, the buyer accepts that the company is taken over in its current position, but with the benefit of considerable warranties and representations that describe precisely what that condition is.

4.7 Warranties and the Disclosure Letter

Formal warranties will invariably be included in the sale and purchase agreement—in this respect, the process of drafting and negotiation is very similar to what you would find in a U.S. domestic transaction. However, it is fair to say that one of the greatest purely practical benefits of the warranties to both parties is the opportunity for the seller to qualify the warranties by the production of a disclosure letter. This will take the form of a letter written from the seller to the buyer that discloses facts or matters that would otherwise render the seller in breach of the warranties given in the share sale agreement. The disclosure letter replaces in many ways, but serves the same function as, the schedules that are typically appended to a U.S.-style share or business sale agreement. The terms of the disclosure letter are commonly negotiated along with the negotiation of the sale agreement itself.

4.8 Representations, Warranties, and Indemnities

Although these terms are often used indiscriminately and interchangeably, English law draws clear distinctions between them, and between the different remedies that are available to each. As a matter of English law, the term "representations" is inappropriate to describe a statement in the nature of a warranty in the sale agreement. It should be reserved for reference to precontract statements (see section 4.4).

To understand the difference between warranties and indemnities, and to understand why warranties and indemnities—different types of remedy—are sought in the one document, you have to investigate exactly what it is you expect to get if a warranty is breached. This in turn depends on the measure of damages for breach of contract.

If a breach of contract has taken place, the aggrieved party is entitled to damages sufficient to put it in the position that it would have been in if the contract had been properly performed. The problem is that the businessperson sees the acquisition in very different terms from the way the law sees it.

Businesspeople regard themselves as having purchased a business, and if told that the boardroom wall is painted blue, but it turns out to be painted red, they expect to be put into a position financially to be able to paint it blue without any cost to themselves.

The law, as we all know, is color-blind, and so does not see things in quite this way. As far as the law is concerned, all that the businesspeople have done is buy a few shares. They have not bought the assets of the company, merely the shares in the company. Therefore, the law will not ask, "Is the boardroom wall less attractive than the buyer expected?" It will simply ask, "Are the shares worth less than they would have been if the boardroom wall had been painted blue?"

Contrast the position under an indemnity. Whereas remedies for breach of warranty rely almost exclusively on seeking damages at law, an indemnity is a mechanism that establishes an automatic right to the payment of money in given circumstances.

The easiest area in which to apply this kind of indemnity is the area of specific liabilities of the company that are said either to be payable or not to be payable by the seller. Thus, as well as taking from the seller a full set of warranties on all matters including taxation, the buyer will usually seek to take, in addition, an indemnity to the effect that should the company turn out to owe more tax than the seller has indicated, then the seller will reimburse the company (or the buyer by way of an adjustment to the purchase price) for the exact amount of extra tax that has to be paid, whether or not the value of the shares in the company is actually proved to be depleted as a result of that tax having been paid out.

There are two other ways in which it is common to work an indemnity into a sale and purchase agreement. One of these is to back up the general statement of warranties by saying something along the lines of "and without prejudice to any other remedy that the buyer may have with respect to breach of warranties, the seller will indemnify the buyer for the amount by which the assets of the company or any of its subsidiaries are worth less than they would have been had matters been as warranted."

Whether this kind of indemnity is accepted or not is a matter for negotiation and essentially comes down to a question of fairness—or in other words, who will bear the risk of something not being so—in any particular circumstances.

The second way is to add various other indemnities against matters for which the parties simply agree there is to be no liability falling on the buyer at all. For example, if it is known to the parties that the company being bought is in the process of being sued for a very large but currently unquantified amount of money, it would be quite normal for the seller to agree that it would indemnify the buyer against whatever award was in due course made against the company.

Note that an indemnity will be strictly construed by an English court against the party that is relying on it. As a result, such documents have to be drafted very carefully with the benefit of local legal advice.

4.9 Seller Protection

It is salutary in considering warranties to bear in mind the result of Lord Denning's last case—*George Mitchell (Chesterhall) Ltd. v. Finney Lock Seeds Ltd.,* [1983] 2 A.C. 803. A farmer bought cabbage seed for £201.60 on the basis of an implied warranty that the seed would produce cabbages. In fact, they produced what one judge called "loose green leaves that sheep or cattle might eat if hungry enough." The crop had no value at all. The farmer was entitled to be put into the position he would have been in had the contract been properly performed—in other words being able to sell a whole field of cabbages. The damages recovered were over £90,000.

A seller who enters into a share sale agreement without any specific limitation on its liability is in exactly the same danger. As a result, it is customary in UK negotiations for the parties to agree that the seller will have certain limitations on its liability at least as to total amount. The customary maximum amount is the total price payable under the contract, although there are many times when this may not

be wholly appropriate. It is also usual to agree on other rights of miti-
gation, including a limitation on time during which the buyer must
bring a claim.

4.10 Rescission

Going sequentially through the series of potential breaches of a sale
agreement, the first possibility is that something will go wrong between
signing the contract and completing the purchase itself. This is the
time when rescission may be a potential remedy. This was alluded to in
connection with the question of misrepresentation. One fundamental
bar to rescission is that the right will be lost if the contract is affirmed
by the aggrieved party, or if it is impossible to make proper restitution,
or if an innocent third party could be prejudiced. Even if the right to
rescission is not specifically excluded by the contract itself, it must be
arguable in the case of most companies that within a few weeks after
closing, it will be impossible to make complete restitution if someone
claims rescission. As a result, rescission is most likely to be considered
in the period before closing.

However, rescission strictly construed is a very narrow remedy and
only really applies when the law gives a specific right to cancel the contract. There are two other remedies that are likely to apply during this
interim period. The first is the general right in law to regard another
party as having breached a contract to such an extent as to leave you
with the conclusion that he or she has repudiated the contract, and
then to accept that repudiation. You end up then with a general right
to sue for damages.

4.11 Contractually Agreed Remedies

More likely, the contract will itself have remedies specifically provided
if certain things do or do not happen between signing and closing.
There is usually a very specific reason why the seller and buyer agree
to postpone closing. If for some reason the contract does not proceed,
it is usual—and extremely wise—for the parties to stipulate in the contract itself what the remedy is going to be to the aggrieved party. Very
often, the parties will simply agree that they will walk away from the
contract as if it had never existed.

4.12 Specific Performance

Again, it may happen that, at closing, one party simply fails to deliver
the goods, or rather the shares. The other party may seek to attempt to
enforce the contract and may seek an order for specific performance.
As in the United States, however, every remedy apart from damages
and an action for payment of the consideration is a remedy recognized

only in equity and not at law, the result being that the remedies are discretionary. In the case of specific performance, the remedy will not normally be awarded if damages are an adequate remedy. It is difficult to imagine this argument standing up in connection with most companies, but there are other limits to equitable remedies being granted. In particular, specific performance will not be granted if it could cause severe hardship, if it is unfair for some reason, if the plaintiff has in some way disqualified himself or herself, or if performance is in fact impossible—especially if an on-sale has taken place to a third party.

5. International Umbrella Transactions

One of the more difficult types of transaction to negotiate is the international umbrella transaction, which involves, for example, a U.S.-owned international group selling a division that comprises businesses (and/or local subsidiaries) in a number of different countries, including, for the purposes of this chapter, the UK. There is a tendency for an umbrella agreement to be negotiated in great detail in the United States (all too often without any input from lawyers in the UK or other relevant jurisdictions), and it is then necessary to decide whether to merely have local transfers (bills of sale) in each country, or whether to have more detailed agreements with the advantage of direct enforceability of warranties, and so on between the local sellers and buyers.

The negotiation and the work on this sort of international transaction generally splits into two parts. The first is obtaining advice from UK counsel on anything in the U.S.-negotiated agreement that does not make sense when applied to the UK. The classic starting point, for example, is that a warranty of good standing has no legal meaning in the UK. Similarly, in the sale of a business as a going concern, a feature that Americans may be unfamiliar with is the impact of the UK's Transfer of Undertakings (Protection of Employment) Regulations 2006—which, in effect, means that you have to take over all the employees involved in the business on the same terms and conditions as they were employed before, whether you want them or not.

The second is obtaining advice on negotiating the specific UK documents. If the UK end of the transaction involves simply the sale of the UK subsidiary to another international conglomerate, the attitude may well depend on the domicile of the seller and buyer. For example, if the shares are being sold directly from one U.S. party to another, it is unlikely that anything local will be required in the UK apart from a stock transfer form. On the other hand, if a UK party is involved, any attempt to use a U.S.-style sale agreement will likely meet some resistance (especially if the other party has not regularly done deals with Americans); even if the first draft is a U.S. draft, it may require heavy amendment to be suitable for use in the UK. Usually, it is a false economy for a U.S. company to take its own preferred form of U.S.-style acquisition document and adapt it for use in the UK.

Finally, Americans should remember that, if they enter into agreements to procure, a number of different companies worldwide will sell their local subsidiaries, and they must also bear in mind that the directors of a UK seller company are bound to apply their minds (and duties) to the transaction and determine whether it will promote the success of that company taken as a whole, and not for its group or ultimate U.S. parent company. The directors of the local UK subsidiary owe their legal obligations to the company of which they are directors, and if for any reason that company should subsequently go into liquidation, it is those individual directors who will be pursued by the liquidators for breach of their duties.

6. The Use of Legal Opinions

The widespread use of legal opinion letters (in the sense of formal opinions delivered by one party's lawyers addressed to the other party to the transaction) is not prevalent outside the United States. There are, for example, no UK regulatory or administrative requirements for formal legal opinions. Enforceability opinions addressed to the U.S. party as a precondition to the closing are becoming more common, but in general, in the UK, one lawyer would not expect to be asked to give an opinion on a matter on which lawyers on the other side of the transaction should be advising.

However, a U.S. business and its U.S. lawyers should not insist on rigid adherence to the U.S. precedent. Instead, they should be receptive to the cultural differences and, especially, to the fact that the UK lawyers may not share their U.S. counterparts' assumptions about the degree of their responsibility for verifying factual matters, as opposed to assuming them, or the proper degree of their involvement in their client's internal affairs.

7. Conduct of the Negotiations

7.1 The Negotiators

There is no generally applicable rule as to who handles negotiations in the UK. Experience suggests that a mixed team including not only executives, but internal audit, those who will integrate the business, lawyers, and accountants should all be considered.

The recent case of *MAN Nutzfarhrzeuge Ag and Others v. Freightliner Limited,* [2005] EWHC (Comm) 2347 (*MAN v. Freightliner*), does, however, illustrate the benefits of a seller choosing its negotiating team carefully. In the case in question, the seller effectively brought an employee of the target company onto the seller's negotiating team.

The employee had, for some time, been acting fraudulently in his capacity as finance controller of the target. In an effort to cover up this behavior, he then made fraudulent statements to the buyer. When the buyer sued, the court held that the seller was vicariously liable for the statements of the target employee, and awarded significant damages to the buyer.

If the deal being negotiated is a public deal involving a listed company on one side or the other, or involving a listed UK party in obtaining shareholder consent, then the City Code requires the engagement of an independent advisor—usually an investment bank.

Even if not a requirement, many companies in the UK will prefer to use professionals as a matter of course. As well as it being more efficient for the lawyer who has to draft the contract to be involved in, or at least present at, the negotiations, the advantages are that the principal can keep more detached from the emotional heat of argument—a special concern if the parties have to work together after the deal is done.

Finally, although this advice may seem somewhat self-serving coming from an English lawyer, there really is no substitute for retaining at an early stage (and heeding the advice of) competent UK counsel experienced in handling international transactions. As noted in another context, much time and money will be wasted if a typical U.S. deal structure is adopted and then has to be abandoned because of UK legal considerations. The opportunity to structure a deal in the most favorable manner may also be lost if the parties have shaken hands on the principles before consulting UK lawyers on the best way to do the deal under UK law.

7.2 Prerequisites to Effective International Negotiation

It is essential at the outset to understand the desires of both parties to a deal. This is an even more acute consideration in an international negotiation where the parties may be coming from different angles and do not necessarily share the same understanding of the rules of the game.

7.3 The Buyer's Intentions

The buyer must impress the seller with the seriousness of its intention to acquire the business, and that this is not merely a fishing expedition to acquire detailed commercial information. It is important to convey not only an air of competence but also an impression of substance and of having a proper strategic reason for wishing to acquire the business. It should go without saying that the buyer must leave the seller in no doubt about its ability to complete the transaction in the required time frame. Intentions and motivation will often drive the form and substance of the transaction—for example, the way consideration is structured, transitional arrangements, and perhaps even the adoption of an auction process rather than a straightforward formal negotiation.

7.4 The Seller's Perspective

From the seller's point of view, it is just as important to analyze its own reasons for selling as it is the buyer's reasons for buying, especially for a U.S. owner selling a UK business or subsidiary to another UK party.

First, the seller's reason for selling will influence its strategy and willingness to cut a deal. The seller may have determined that there is little future for the product, or must get together with a competitor, or needs to raise cash to invest elsewhere or deal with other problems. If the seller is in the latter category, on no account should it let this be known to the buyer. When the prospect of a fire sale is at stake, the British are no more gentlemanly than anyone else in taking advantage. As one client in such straits eloquently phrased it: "If you let on to these guys that you're willing to take a haircut, the next thing you know is you've joined the marines."

As to advisors, whether the seller does it alone or retains an investment bank or accounting firm, it is salutary for the seller's negotiator to never let the buyer know that the negotiator has power to cut the deal. Always leave an out ("I have to talk to my board/shareholders/CEO/spouse/therapist . . .") and there will be less risk of being forced into a corner.

Sellers should also establish to their own satisfaction the integrity of the buyer. This may be done by making inquiries of their own bankers, or lawyers. There is no point in entering into lengthy purchase negotiations with a company that has a record of defaulting on transactions at the last minute.

The seller should also involve local lawyers at the earliest possible stage. They can help structure the sale proposals (or the purchase proposals if the buyer is driving the deal) in the way best calculated to avoid legal, taxation, and regulatory problems. It is also a clear sign to the other party that the visitors from overseas are serious if they have local counsel with them at the first meeting.

7.5 Timetable

There is no magic formula that dictates the pace of negotiations in the UK, and every case will develop its own momentum—or lack of it. Experienced negotiators in the UK, and their advisors, are well used to around-the-clock discussions. It is therefore important to set the discipline of a realistic timetable, particularly when negotiations involve cross-border transactions with all the problems of language and cultural differences.

It is important to have either heads of agreement or a draft contract produced as early as realistically possible. This enables the crucial deal points—even if not yet agreed—to be identified in lay terms at an early stage, and helps to avoid misunderstandings later. Negotiations proceed more smoothly when all parties are singing from the same hymn book. However, term sheets or heads of terms (which often serve a valuable purpose) should be legally reviewed before execution to ensure that they do not inadvertently assume binding legal effect at a time when the parties' intentions have not been fully developed. The seller may achieve a similar result by setting up an auction process on its preferred terms.

There is something of a convention in UK deals that the buyer's lawyers draft the contract for a share transaction and the seller's lawyers draft the contract for an assets transaction. For joint ventures, anything goes. However, there are numerous exceptions to the rule—for example, in auction sales the seller's lawyers will usually draft the share sale agreement—and a party seeking to force the pace should always try to ensure that its own lawyers have the task of drafting the documents. It is a false economy for one side to think that it will save costs by having the other side's lawyers do the drafting. About the same amount of time and hard work will be required in going over the other side's draft as would be spent doing it on your side in the first place. It is far better to have control of the drafting (as it is easier to set the agenda) and to have the other side try to negotiate their points into your text and your points out, than to negotiate your points into someone else's text.

A public company deal involving either a hostile bid or the need for shareholder approval will have its timetable dictated in part by the rules of the City Code, and time must be built in for the preparation of circulars to shareholders and the calling of any shareholders' meeting. Particular problems can arise where the buyer's timetable is dictated by the SEC and the target's timetable is dictated by the City Code and the Panel in the UK. UK companies with a primary listing on the UK Listing Authority's Official List will need shareholder consent for transactions over a certain size.

8. Choice of Law and Cross-Jurisdictional Procedures

Most transactions will typically have a closer connection with one jurisdiction and its legal system than another. If a U.S. buyer acquires a UK subsidiary from a UK seller, it would be sensible to structure the deal as one governed by English law. If a French buyer acquires a UK group from a U.S. parent in Wisconsin, the deal could be structured under French law, English law, Wisconsin law, or even New York law. Depending on how sophisticated the local party is (or perhaps, more importantly, how sophisticated and experienced the local party's lawyers are in dealing with Americans), there may be considerable resistance against the imposition of the form and procedure of a U.S.-style transaction. This should be less of a problem in the UK, where, on the whole, transactions and structures are negotiated and documented at length.

UK courts will recognize any legitimate choice by the parties to an international agreement of one system of law or another to govern their relationship. The only likely ground for not recognizing a choice of law is where the choice would have the effect of avoiding the otherwise mandatory application of the law, or some part of the law, that would otherwise apply to a transaction (whether English or foreign law), and there is no legitimate connection between the parties or the contract and the governing law they have chosen.

Generally, in any proceeding brought in England for the enforcement of the obligations of a UK party to an agreement that is the result of an international business negotiation with a U.S. party, or for the enforcement of any judgment obtained from a U.S. court of competent jurisdiction in relation to such an agreement, the choice of the law of a relevant U.S. state as the governing law of the agreement would be recognized and applied.

By virtue of the EU's Council Regulation 44/2001 on jurisdiction and the recognition and enforcement of judgments in civil and commercial matters, any judgment given in any EU member state will be recognized in the UK without any special procedure or leave being required, and will be directly enforceable by registering the judgment and applying for an order for its enforcement. However, the general principle is that a foreign judgment will be recognized in the UK, but will not be directly enforced in the absence of reciprocal arrangements.

There are no arrangements currently in force between the UK and the United States for the reciprocal enforcement of judgments. Thus, any judgment obtained against a UK party in U.S. federal courts or in the courts of any relevant state could not be enforced by registration in the English courts. However, without a retrial of the underlying claim on its merits before the English courts, any such judgment could be treated as itself constituting a cause of action against the UK party with respect to which proceedings could be brought in the English courts. Whether the English courts would enter judgment against the UK party in such proceedings would depend on, among other things, the original court having jurisdiction under its own rules to deliver the original judgment, and the original judgment being final and conclusive between the parties; there being payable under the original judgment a definite sum of money with respect to a cause of action known to English law; the original judgment not being for multiple damages, fines, penalties, or taxes or charges of a like nature; the original judgment not having been obtained by fraud or in proceedings that contravene the rules of natural justice, and its enforcement not being contrary to English public policy; and no restrictions having been imposed under the Protection of Trading Interests Act 1980.

If a U.S. party to an agreement were to bring original legal proceedings against a UK party in the English courts to enforce its obligations under an agreement, the proceedings would be accepted by the English courts subject only to laws affecting the enforcement of the rights of creditors generally in the event of the insolvency of the UK party; the plaintiff being a juridical person recognized as such by the English courts; and the discretionary powers of an English court (a) to stay an action where it can be shown that the action can, without injustice to the plaintiff, be tried in a more convenient forum; and (b) to order the plaintiff to provide security for the UK defendant's costs, where the plaintiff is not ordinarily resident in some part of the UK.

Other cross-jurisdictional points to note include the following:

- proceedings in England to enforce a judgment of a U.S. court of competent jurisdiction would be time-barred after six years from the date on which the judgment became final and conclusive as between the parties; and
- if an originating legal action were brought against the UK party in England to enforce its obligations under an agreement governed, for example, by New York law, the English court would, by virtue of section 1 of the Foreign Limitation Periods Act 1984, apply the law of the State of New York relating to limitation for the purposes of the action (disregarding as much of that law as provides for the extension or interruption of a limitation period with respect to the absence of a party to the action from any specified jurisdiction or country, and save where the application of that law would be deemed to conflict with public policy on the grounds that it would cause undue hardship to a person who is, or might be made, a party to the action). For this purpose, the law of the State of New York does not include the rules of private international law applicable by the courts of the State of New York.

An English court may, as a matter of current procedural practice, make an award denominated in a foreign currency. However, the judgment debtor is entitled to settle the award in sterling, applying the rate of exchange current at the time of payment. Also, in the event of the insolvent liquidation of the UK party under English law, any foreign currency claim against it would generally be converted into sterling at the date on which liquidation commenced.

9. Dispute Resolution

Civil actions in the English courts are tried before a judge alone—jury trials are not permitted except in civil actions involving certain types of fraud allegations and in defamation actions. If an intended defendant is not domiciled in the UK or certain other European countries, leave must normally be obtained from the court before the proceedings can be issued out of the jurisdiction. Leave will be given if the proceedings relate to a contract made, or tort committed, within the jurisdiction, or if there has been an express submission to the jurisdiction in the contract. The case must fall within the specified circumstances set out in the rules; it is not sufficient to show only that the defendant has business interests within the jurisdiction.

Various forms of alternative dispute resolution are well-known in the UK. Traditional arbitration clauses are not uncommon in the agreements governing international transactions, and there is a statutory framework (the Arbitration Act) governing the conduct and effect of the arbitration. These apply to the extent not otherwise agreed between the parties, and it is also common to see the parties rewriting for themselves the rules for the conduct of the arbitration. In cases where parties have a genuine dispute in one area, but continuing business relationships in other areas that both wish to continue, ad hoc submission of disputed matters to private binding arbitration is common. In disputes following a merger or acquisition, however, it is probably less likely that the parties' approach and interests in resolving the issues will be sufficiently consensual to make alternative dispute resolution workable, leaving resort to the courts as the quickest and most efficient means of resolving the dispute.

In civil actions in the English courts, an aggrieved party may seek any of a wide variety of remedies, including specific performance of a contract or injunctive relief to enjoin a particular course of conduct. Most often, the plaintiff will be seeking damages for breach of contract. Under English law, damages are intended only to compensate a plaintiff for its loss, and punitive damages (known in England as exemplary damages) are available only in exceptional circumstances and are rarely awarded. There are no circumstances at all where multiple damages may be awarded, and indeed any U.S. judgment for multiple damages will be completely unenforceable in England—it will not even be possible to sever the compensatory element from the multiplier and seek only to enforce the former part of a U.S. judgment.

It should also be remembered that the normal rule in English litigation is that, absent special circumstances, the losing party will be ordered to pay the winning party's costs. As a practical matter, this means that the losing party will have to reimburse the winner for between 60 percent and 70 percent of the latter's outlay, both fees paid to lawyers and out-of-pocket expenses such as court fees, the cost of transcripts, and so forth.

10. Supply Contracts

This section examines some of the commercial and legal issues that can impact upon supply of goods contracts in England (excluding taxation, which is beyond the scope of this chapter). It concentrates on business-to-business supply arrangements and agreements that involve consumers, and are thus subject to further regulation.

10.1 Direct or Indirect Supply?

When considering making sales into UK markets, one of the most fundamental decisions that a supplier needs to make is whether it wants to:

    i.   deal directly with trade customers and/or end users (for example, by setting up its own network of employed representatives or establishing trading premises within the UK); or

    ii. act through some form of intermediary arrangement such as distributorship or agency (which are considered later in this chapter).

    The supplier will need to consider what form of supply arrangement is the most appropriate for it, from both legal and commercial perspectives. One of the key drivers for this decision will often be the cost and risk associated with making direct sales to the UK market—for example, the cost of setting up trading premises in the UK and developing local market knowledge.

10.2 Formal Supply Agreement or Terms and Conditions of Sale?

If the supplier chooses to follow the direct supply route, then for each customer with which it deals, the supplier will usually need to choose between:

    i.   negotiating a formal supply agreement;

    ii. trading on the supplier's standard terms and conditions of sale (or even the customer's standard terms and conditions of purchase if the customer has sufficient bargaining power); or

    iii. agreeing on any terms with the customer that are particular to the individual contract (such as the description of the goods, the price, and the quantity) and then relying on the terms that are implied into contracts by English law (which are considered elsewhere in this section). This approach is commonly used by suppliers trading through retail outlets, particularly with consumers, and is not considered further in this section.

10.3 Formal Supply Agreement

Formal supply agreements are commonly used where the supplier and customer want to enter into a long-term trading relationship or where a bespoke agreement, with terms that are specific to an individual transaction, is necessary. There are several common commercial factors that may make it desirable for the supplier and its customer to enter into a formal supply agreement. First, in a competitive market the supplier will want to defend his market share by seeking long-term commitments from his customers. Second, if the goods are bespoke (produced to meet the special requirements of a customer) or if the supplier has invested its own resources in developing a product, then the supplier will no doubt want to be sure of recouping those costs from the sale price of the goods over a fixed period. From the customer's point of view, it may be vital for the customer to secure a reliable source of supply via a long-term agreement, especially if there are adverse circumstances affecting production or availability of the goods.

10.4 Standard Terms and Conditions

Using standard terms and conditions of sale can have several benefits; however, standard terms and conditions can also present challenges. Under English contract law, it is vital that the terms and conditions are incorporated into the contract for them to be enforceable. This is because of the English common law rule that new contract terms cannot be unilaterally introduced into the contract after the contract has been formed by offer and acceptance between the parties. For example, the unfortunately common practice of the supplier trying to impose its standard terms on the contract by printing them on the back of the invoice for the goods won't usually be effective to incorporate the terms into the contract if the invoice is dispatched after the time when the contract is held, under English law, to be made.

Standard terms can be incorporated into a contract by the express agreement of the parties or by implication, such as where there has been a course of dealings between the supplier and the customer and the terms have been used in previous transactions between the parties. Those who are unused to dealing with standard terms need to be careful, as a party to a contract can find that it has agreed to another party's standard terms and conditions without having read or even being aware of their content, simply by accepting an offer that contains those terms (beware the "small print").

Another common problem of which a supplier needs to be aware is the situation where both the supplier and the customer try to impose their own standard terms on the contract with the result that it is difficult to determine which set of terms prevails. This situation is often called the "battle of the forms" and is increasingly common now that an increasing number of business customers have their own standard purchase terms. The approach that the English courts often take is that an acceptance of an offer to enter into a contract that purports to impose new terms is not an acceptance, but instead is a counteroffer that can be accepted by an unequivocal acceptance by the other party or by performance. This often means in practice that the last set of terms dispatched before acceptance or performance will prevail. However, there is a danger that neither party's terms will be incorporated into the sale and purchase agreement and the court will need to determine the terms of the contract—for example, the court may find that the contract only contains the terms that were demonstrably agreed to by the parties, such as the description of the goods, the price, and the quantity to be supplied, and those that are implied by the Sale of Goods Act 1979 (see section 10.5), or may even find that the contract fails for uncertainty.

10.5 Common Law and Statutory Controls on Supply Contracts

In addition to the basic rules governing the formation of contracts under UK law, there are some specific statutory provisions that are particularly relevant.

First, there are those that limit the extent to which one party to a supply contract can exclude or restrict its liability to the other party, such as the Unfair Contract Terms Act 1977 (UCTA). UCTA is a very wide piece of legislation, but one of its key functions is to control clauses that are designed to restrict or exclude business liability.

Under UCTA a clause that attempts to exclude a party's liability for death or personal injury caused by that party's negligence would be wholly ineffective. Liability for negligence that does not result in death or personal injury can be restricted or even completely excluded if the clause satisfies the UCTA reasonableness test.

UCTA applies to standard terms and to contracts with consumers and provides that any clause in:

i. a contract with consumers regardless of whether the contract is bespoke or on the supplier's standard terms of business; or
ii. in any contract with another business that is on the supplier's standard terms of business,

by which the supplier excludes or restricts his liability for breach of contract, claims to be entitled to render a contractual performance substantially different from that which was reasonably expected of him, or claims to be entitled to render no performance at all is subject to the UCTA reasonableness test. Similarly, clauses that try to exclude or restrict remedies that might otherwise be available to a contracting party if the other party is in breach are subject to the UCTA reasonableness test.

UCTA also controls terms that try to limit or exclude liability for the breach of certain terms that are implied by statute, such as those implied by the Sale of Goods Act 1979, either by prohibiting them completely or making them subject to the UCTA reasonableness test.

Second, there are those that regulate the supply of goods and in particular impose implied terms on contracts for the supply of goods. The main statute law relating to the sale of goods is contained in the Sale of Goods Act 1979, which implies certain terms into supply arrangements such as:

i. an implied condition that the supplier has the right to sell the goods, that the customer will enjoy quiet possession of the goods, and that the goods will be free of encumbrances not disclosed to or known by the buyer before the contract is made;

ii.   an implied condition that, where goods are sold by description, they will correspond to that description;

iii. where the customer has expressly or by implication made known to the supplier the particular purpose for which the goods are required, an implied condition that the goods will be reasonably fit for that purpose;

iv. an implied condition that the goods will be of satisfactory quality (except where defects have been specifically drawn to the customer's attention before the contract is made or, if the customer examines the goods before the contract is made, as regards defects that that examination ought to reveal); and

v.   where the sale is by reference to a sample, an implied condition that the goods will correspond with the sample.

There are other terms implied into a supply agreement by the Act that relate to delivery and price of the goods. If no price for the goods is agreed, then the price will be deemed to be a reasonable one, and if no time for payment is agreed, it will be implied that the purchaser must pay cash on delivery. Delivery will be deemed to take place at the seller's place of business if no place for delivery has been expressly agreed.

The application of some implied terms may be avoided or varied by the express agreement of the parties, subject to UCTA, though this may depend on whether the other party is a consumer.

Next, there is legislation that grants rights to third parties, that is, persons who are not a party to the contract. The Contracts (Rights of Third Parties) Act 1999 allows a person who is not a party to a contract to enforce or rely on a term of that contract if either the contract expressly provides that it may or the term purports to confer a benefit on it. To be able to rely on this Act, the third party has to be expressly identified in the contract by name, as a member of a class, or as answering a particular description.

Suppliers have a right, under English law, to claim interest on unpaid debts due from other businesses under the Late Payment of Commercial Debts (Interest) Act 1998. The Act has set the rate of interest that can be claimed as 8 percent above the Bank of England base rate, which is higher than the rate that has traditionally been included in clauses that give a contractual right to interest (typically 3 percent to 4 percent above base rate). The parties to the agreement can vary the rate contractually as long as the contractual rate is "substantial," that is, it is sufficient to compensate the supplier or to deter the customer from paying late.

Specific legislation that deals with matters such as misrepresentation, consumer credit, and product liability and that applies to particular types of goods, such as pharmaceuticals, is beyond the scope of this chapter.

11. Distribution

In the UK, a distribution agreement is one where the distributor purchases the goods from the supplier and resells those goods to its own customers, adding a margin to cover his own costs and profit. In purchasing and reselling the products, the distributor contracts first with the supplier to purchase the goods and then separately with his customer to sell the goods. Title to the goods will pass to and from the distributor. Distributorship arrangements are often used as a low-risk means of expanding a business into new markets or territories.

The basis of any distribution agreement is of course a supply/purchase agreement and the mutual rights and obligations of the supplier and distributor are contractual, set out in the distribution agreement. In addition to the basic supply and purchase terms, there are usually commonly occurring provisions that are specific to distribution arrangements. For example, the distribution agreement will often impose duties on the distributor to market the goods and comply with the supplier's marketing scheme; to provide an after-sales service; to provide marketing reports to the supplier; to maintain an adequate stock of the product to meet reasonably anticipated customer demands; and to purchase a contractually agreed minimum amount of goods at least, during a set period of the agreement. The supplier will often also want to impose restrictions upon the distributor, such as prohibiting the distributor from:

i.   manufacturing or selling competing goods (which can have both English and EU competition law implications); or
ii. using unauthorized marketing materials and/or modifying or altering the goods.

However, under English and EU competition law the supplier is not permitted to fix the price at which the distributor sells the goods to the distributor's customers, and it is generally unlawful to restrict the customers to whom the distributor sells the goods.

Distributors are often given a territory or a class of customers with which to work, and this leads to three commonly occurring types of distribution agreement. First, there is exclusive distribution, where the supplier is contractually prevented both from actively seeking sales in the distributor's territory or customer group and from appointing other agents or distributors for that territory or customer group. Next, sole distribution arrangements usually prevent the supplier from appointing another distributor for the distributor's territory or customer base, but will not prevent the supplier from actively seeking sales in the territory or from the distributor's customer base. Finally, there are nonexclusive arrangements, which will leave the supplier free to appoint distributors and itself to actively seek sales in the territory or from the distributor's customer base.

The terms "exclusive," "sole," and "nonexclusive" are referred to in both English and EU legislation but do not have statutory definitions. As these terms can mean different things to different people, it is always prudent to spell out in the agreement what rights the distributor or, in the case of agency, the agent is to have.

Distribution agreements are not covered by any English law statute or regulations that are specific to that type of agreement. However, the usual generic statutes such as UCTA and the rules prohibiting anticompetitive agreements, which are discussed elsewhere in this chapter, will apply as they do to other forms of supply agreement. Unlike agency agreements, which are covered by the Commercial Agents (Council Directive) Regulations 1993 (see section 12), the termination of the distribution agreement with a distributor operating in England does not lead to any compensation being payable to the distributor (other than any normal contractual damages that may be payable, for example, for breach of the agreement). However, this may not always be the case where the distributor is based in another EU jurisdiction, as some EU countries give protection to distributors that is broadly similar to that given to agents on termination; this should always be checked in the relevant jurisdiction.

12. Agency

An agency agreement is one where the agent acts as an intermediary between the principal (the "supplier") and the principal's customer. Essentially, an agent is appointed by its principal to negotiate and, possibly, conclude contracts with customers on the principal's behalf. He is usually remunerated by way of commission on the sales he makes (usually on a percentage basis). Unlike in distribution arrangements, there is only one contract for the sale of the goods, which is made between the principal and the customer and to which the agent is not a party. The agent therefore usually incurs no rights or obligations under the contract between the principal and the customer.

There are several common commercial reasons for a principal choosing to appoint an agent, such as the following:

- The principal can take advantage of an agent's local knowledge and established trade connections.
- The principal can save the cost of establishing his own selling operation.
- The principal retains contact with his customer (but of course also keeps the rights and risks of the contract with the customer).
- The principal spreads the risk by having multiple customers for the goods rather than just one as for an exclusive distributor.

- The principal can retain more control over the price the customer pays for the goods and can select which customers to whom the goods will be supplied (unlike with distribution).
- The principal can contract with the customer on the principal's own standard contract terms.

In England, the agency relationship between the principal and the agent is subject to common law rules and may also be subject to statutory control under the Commercial Agents (Council Directive) Regulations 1993 (the "Regulations"), which implement the Council Directive (EC) 86/653 on Commercial Agents into English law.

12.1 Common Law Duties of the Agent and the Principal

There are certain English common law duties that an agent owes to his principal, including the following:

i.   to obey his principal's lawful instructions;
ii. to act within the agent's authority;
iii. to disclose all material facts to his principal;
iv. to refrain from divulging information that is confidential to the principal;
v.   to use reasonable care and diligence and reasonable dispatch;
vi. not to put himself into a situation where his interests will conflict with those of his principal;
vii. not to make a secret profit or accept bribes;
viii. to account to his principal for the property and money of the principal that is under his control; and
ix. not to delegate his authority.

It is usual to repeat these common law duties in the agency agreement for clarity. It is important that the authority of the agent to enter into contracts and make representations is strictly defined in the agreement. The English law doctrine of ostensible authority, put simply, means that if the customer reasonably believes that the agent has authority, for example, to make certain representations or enter into a contract, then the principal will be bound by those representations or that contract regardless of whether the agent had actual authority. Only by defining the scope of the agent's authority in the agency agreement will the principal be able to seek redress against the agent for any loss suffered as a result of the agent exceeding this authority.

The common law duties of a principal to his agent are:

i.   to pay the agent remuneration and/or commission (if this is not express, the court will imply a reasonable sum);
ii. to pay the agent's expenses and indemnify him against losses;

    iii.   to provide "the necessary documentation relating to the goods" (the meaning of this is unclear but presumably means price lists, standard form contracts, technical manuals, documents relating to shipment of the goods, and, possibly, any documents that the agent needs to establish himself as registered with local regulatory authorities to act "as agent" in relation to the goods); and

    iv.   to give the agent reasonable notice on termination of the agency agreement. What is reasonable depends on a number of points, including the job that the agent is carrying out, the notice that is normally given to someone carrying out that type of job, and the length of the agreement. Compare this with the Regulations, which impose minimum notice periods.

The common law duties of agent to principal and principal to agent can be varied by the agreement of the principal and agent and, where they apply, the Regulations.

12.2 The Regulations

The Regulations "apply in relation to the activities of 'commercial agents' in Great Britain," where the agent is buying or selling goods on behalf of the principal and whether the agency agreement is oral or in writing. Under the Regulations a commercial agent is "a self-employed intermediary who has continuing authority to negotiate the sale or purchase of goods on behalf of another person (the "principal"), or to negotiate and conclude the sale or purchase of goods on behalf of and in the name of that principal . . . ." There is case law at the time of writing that suggests that the definition of "commercial agent" may be much wider than a strict reading of the Regulations would initially suggest and that agents who act as more than mere introducers (that is, who develop the goodwill of the principal by their activities) will potentially fall within the definition of "commercial agent." The development of goodwill by agents may well be enough to constitute "negotiation" for the purposes of the Regulations. "Commercial agents" appointed on a trial basis are still protected by the Regulations. There is no scope for saying that the mandatory parts of the Regulations will only apply at the end of the probationary period.

If the commercial agent is to act in Great Britain, then normally the Regulations will apply (regardless of the nationality of the agent and principal) unless the parties have agreed that the law of another EU country is to govern the agency contract.

However, if the commercial agent is to act in Great Britain but the parties have agreed that the law of another EU state is to govern the agency contract (which they might, if the principal is from another EU state), then the court must apply that foreign law instead of the Regulations (assuming that the EU legislation selected can, on its own terms, apply to the activities of agents outside the relevant national territory).

It is not possible to avoid the application of the Regulations to the appointment of a commercial agent for Great Britain by specifying non-EU law (for example, the laws of the State of New York) as the law of the contract. This is because it is only when the laws of another EU state are stated to apply that the Regulations are avoided.

Some of the Regulations are mandatory, some can be disapplied by the agreement of the principal and agent, and some can only be derogated from if the derogation is not to the detriment of the agent. A detailed review of the impact of each part of the Regulations is beyond this chapter; however, in brief, the Regulations deal with issues such as when and how commission is to be paid to the agent; what duties the agent and the principal owe to each other (which elaborates upon the common law duties of principal and agent); the minimum notice to which the agent is entitled; and post-termination restraints of trade placed on the agent.

Perhaps one of the most important effects of the Regulations is to give the commercial agent an entitlement to be compensated or indemnified on termination (including where the agency agreement is terminated as a result of the commercial agent's death). Under the Regulations, compensation (as opposed to an indemnity) is payable unless it is expressly agreed by the principal and the agent that the agent is entitled to be indemnified. If the principal and agent have agreed that the indemnity alternative will apply, then the agent will be entitled to an indemnity, which is capped at one year's commission, calculated by reference to the agent's average commission in the past if he has brought the company new customers or has significantly increased the volume of business with existing customers and the payment is equitable having regard to all the circumstances. Compensation is payable for the damage suffered by the agent as a result of the termination of the agency relationship with the principal, that is, where the agent is deprived of the commission that proper performance of the agreement would have earned him and he has not recouped the costs and expenses incurred by him on the instructions of the principal in the performance of the agreement. An indemnity or compensation is not payable where:

i.　the agreement was terminated by the principal on grounds justifying immediate termination—for example, in the case of a serious breach of any of the terms of the agreement;

ii.　the agent has terminated the agreement himself (except where termination is justified by reason of the behavior of the principal or by reason of age, infirmity, or illness);

iii.　the agent has assigned his rights and duties under the agreement to another person (unless the principal has consented); or

iv.　the agent is a subagent.

12.3 Agency or Distribution?

Agency arrangements and distribution arrangements both have their own specific advantages and disadvantages, and when a supplier is considering how best to market, sell, or distribute its products using such an intermediary, it is vital that it is aware of and understands the difference, in legal and practical terms, between agents and distributors.

A major concern of the supplier may be the degree of control it can exercise over the intermediary. If the supplier requires a high degree of control then it may prefer to appoint an agent, as the supplier has much more control over an agent's activities than it would over a distributor (particularly with regard to the way in which the goods are marketed and to the price paid for the goods by the ultimate purchaser). In addition, agency can give the principal a much higher degree of protection for the principal's market, as the principal will maintain direct contact with its customers, hopefully giving it more ability to retain those customers after the termination of the agency relationship.

If the supplier's primary motive for using an intermediary is to minimize its risk and liability for the goods, then a distribution arrangement may be more suitable as the distributor usually assumes liability for the goods when selling them on to its customers. This is especially so if the distributor is not fully indemnified by the supplier against any claims brought with respect to the goods. Compare this with agency, where the supplier, as principal, usually retains the financial risk arising from the sale of the goods. On the downside, the higher level of risk assumed by the distributor is often reflected by its level of remuneration or margin as compared with the commission earned by an agent. The greater the level of risk that the supplier places on the distributor, the higher the margin that the distributor will want to achieve and the lower the price for the goods it will want to pay to the supplier.

Whether the supplier chooses to appoint a distributor or an agent, it is vital to use clear terms in the agreement when defining the relationship between the supplier and the intermediary, as the courts will look to these terms to define the relationship rather than just taking the label applied by the parties to the relationship at its face value.

12.4 Competition Law

European Commission (EC) and UK competition law can have a significant impact upon the terms on which a supplier supplies goods under a supply agreement or appoints a distributor or even an agent in some circumstances. When deciding on and negotiating any form of supply, distribution, or agency agreement for the UK, the supplier needs to be aware of the possible application of both the English and EC competition rules.

13. Antitrust Considerations

13.1 Competition Laws

Antitrust considerations give rise to difficult problems in negotiating transactions in the UK just as they do in the United States. The initial problem is one of recognition. Less-experienced negotiators may well not recognize an antitrust issue in the first place.

The law regulating antitrust is generally known in the UK as competition law, which is governed both by domestic legislation, principally the Competition Act 1998 and the Enterprise Act 2002, and by EU law, principally Articles 81 and 82 of the Treaty of Rome (the "EU Treaty"). The EU competition rules apply to agreements or practices that have an effect, whether actual or potential, on trade between EU member states. Those agreements or practices that have an effect, whether actual or potential, on trade in only the UK are subject to UK, as opposed to EU, law. It is therefore necessary in every major negotiation to identify both UK and EU competition aspects that may affect the structure and terms of the deal. When considering which regime applies, it should be borne in mind that an agreement between UK-only companies may still affect trade between member states.

13.2 UK Competition Law

The primary enforcement body for UK competition law is the Office of Fair Trading (OFT), a nonministerial government department. In certain instances, the OFT may refer competition issues to the Competition Commission. Appeals from decisions of the OFT lie to the Competition Appeal Tribunal (commonly known as the CAT). There are also a number of industry-specific regulatory bodies that exercise concurrent powers with respect to competition issues—for example, the Office of Communications (commonly known as Ofcom) for TV, telecoms, and radio, and the Office of Gas and Electricity Markets (Ofgem) for gas and electricity.

UK domestic legislation, like EU law, focuses on three areas: anticompetitive practices (namely anticompetitive agreements between two or more enterprises and abusive behavior by one or more enterprises that hold dominant market positions); market studies and investigations (in circumstances where the OFT considers that features of a particular market—as opposed to the practice of individual enterprises—may restrict competition); and merger control. Probably the most significant area affecting the negotiation of joint ventures, supply agreements, and similar continuing business relationships (although it is also relevant to the negotiation of restrictive covenants in sale and purchase agreements) is the first of these, although merger control is also briefly discussed below.

The relevant legislation dealing with anticompetitive practices is the Competition Act 1998, which incorporates into UK law two prohibitions modeled on Articles 81 and 82 of the EU Treaty, namely, a prohibition on anticompetitive agreements (the "Chapter I prohibition"), and a prohibition on abuse of a dominant market position (the "Chapter II prohibition"). These prohibitions focus on the economic effect, not the legal form, of arrangements. They are interpreted in a way that is consistent with the equivalent provisions of EU law.

The Chapter I prohibition mirrors very closely the wording of Article 81 of the EU Treaty and prohibits agreements between undertakings, decisions by associations of undertakings, and concerted practices that may affect trade within the UK and have as their object or effect the prevention, restriction, or distortion of competition within the UK. All three elements must be satisfied for the prohibition to be infringed. Following EU law, the OFT has indicated that only arrangements with an appreciable effect on competition and trade in the UK will infringe the prohibition. The OFT has issued various guidelines to assist in the interpretation of the Chapter I prohibition. The Chapter I prohibition is interpreted in a manner that is consistent with the equivalent EU provisions.

The Competition Act 1998 contains a nonexhaustive list of the types of agreements and practices that will fall within this prohibition, including arrangements to fix prices or other trading terms or conditions; to limit or control production, markets, technical developments, or investment; to share a market; to apply dissimilar conditions to equivalent transactions with other trading parties, thereby placing them at a competitive disadvantage; or to make the conclusion of contracts subject to acceptance by the parties of additional obligations that are unconnected with the subject of such contracts (that is, the practice commonly referred to as "tying"). In principle, the prohibition affects both horizontal and vertical agreements, but, as mentioned below, some vertical agreements are exempted from the prohibition. (Horizontal agreements are those concluded between businesses operating at the same level in the production or supply chain—often competitors—while vertical agreements are those between businesses operating at different levels in the production or supply chain—for example, distribution agreements, or purchase and supply agreements.)

The Competition Act excludes certain agreements and practices from the Chapter I prohibition. Agreements can be exempted from the Chapter I prohibition if they fall within a UK-specific block exemption or one of the parallel EU block exemptions (for example, there are block exemptions for certain types of agreements relating to land, for certain restrictions in vertical agreements, and for agreements relating to the sale of motor cars and spare parts) or, on an individual basis, meet the exemption criteria set out in the Competition Act (equivalent to Article 81(3) of the EC Treaty, which requires, *inter alia*, that the restrictions in the agreement promote technical or economic progress, and that a fair share of the benefits resulting from that restriction is passed on to consumers). There is no power to exempt from the Chapter II prohibition.

The Chapter II prohibition mirrors the wording of Article 82 of the EU Treaty. It is concerned with conduct that is normally unilateral and provides that any abuse by one or more undertakings of a dominant position in a market shall be prohibited insofar as it may affect trade within the UK or any part of it. Examples of such abuses include excessive pricing (charging an abusively high price), discriminatory pricing (charging like customers different prices), and predatory pricing (pricing below cost in an attempt to exclude competitors).

The OFT has powers of investigation, including powers to search premises without prior notice and using force to gain entry if necessary. These can be exercised against an enterprise either on the OFT's own initiative or following a complaint by a third party. Breach of either the Chapter I or the Chapter II prohibition can result in fines of up to 10 percent of worldwide turnover, the unenforceability of restrictive terms (and if the terms are not severable, the possibility that the entire agreement may be void), orders to cease or modify agreements or conduct, and the risk of civil actions by third parties (who may rely on the OFT's infringement decision to evidence wrongdoing). The risk of civil actions by third parties has increased significantly in recent years. Small and medium-size enterprises (SMEs) have a limited immunity from fines but not from investigation or the risk of third-party actions.

The risks of being the subject of a complaint to the OFT by a competitor in your industry or of potential unenforceability of contractual terms remain a potent factor in determining your negotiation of potentially restrictive terms in your acquisition or venture.

13.3 EU Competition Law

EU competition laws are contained principally in Articles 81 and 82 of the EU Treaty. Article 81 prohibits anticompetitive agreements between two or more businesses, whereas Article 82 prohibits the abuse of dominant or monopoly power by one (or, potentially, more) businesses. Articles 81 and 82 form part of English law and therefore give a direct cause of action for any party wishing to take proceedings in the English courts for breaches of those provisions. As with UK competition law, the risk of civil enforcement of Articles 81 and 82 has increased significantly in recent times, with the UK government and the European Commission leading the encouragement to supplement public enforcement by private actions. Articles 81 and 82 may also be the subject of an investigation in the UK by the OFT. However, they only prohibit agreements, conduct, or practices that produce an effect on the normal patterns of trade, or have repercussions on the competitive structure of a market, thereby affecting trade between member states (although it should be borne in mind that an agreement between UK-only companies may still have an effect on trade between member states).

Article 81 sets out examples of certain agreements to which it applies. These agreements are very similar to the types of agreements set out in the Chapter I prohibition in the Competition Act. These include the hardcore offenses of price-fixing and market sharing. Agreements between competitors to exchange information about, for example, their prices or terms or conditions are also prohibited.

Article 82, like the Chapter II prohibition in the Competition Act, is concerned with conduct that is normally unilateral and provides that any abuse by one or more undertakings of a dominant position within the EU or a substantial part of it shall be prohibited as incompatible with the Common Market insofar as it may affect trade between member states. Examples of such abuses include excessive pricing (charging an abusively high price), discriminatory pricing (charging like customers different prices), and predatory pricing (pricing below cost in an attempt to exclude competitors).

The European Commission has strong powers of investigation, similar to those available to the OFT. If an enterprise breaches either Article 81 or Article 82 of the EU Treaty, it could face fines of up to 10 percent of its worldwide turnover, the unenforceability of restrictive terms (and if the terms are not severable, the possibility that the entire agreement may be void), orders to cease or modify its agreements or conduct, and the risk of civil actions by third parties.

However, although the European Commission has wide investigative powers, it does not have the power to award damages to affected third parties, which must be sought in the domestic courts once the European Commission has made a decision. Third parties have nevertheless been keen to involve the European Commission because of its ability to impose restraining orders on parties conducting anticompetitive practices pending full investigation, and because this effectively passes the costs of the proceedings onto the European Commission, as the third party may rely on the European Commission's infringement decision to evidence an infringement before the domestic court. It remains to be seen how effective the policy of encouraging private actions will be.

Therefore, the risk of being referred to the European Commission by a competitor in your industry remains a potent factor in determining your negotiation of potentially restrictive terms in your acquisition or venture.

13.4 UK Merger Control

In the UK, the current merger control regime is established under the Enterprise Act 2002. Its provisions are likely to be relevant to the negotiation of mergers and acquisitions. Even if a proposed merger meets the relevant criteria (resulting in a share of supply of at least 25 percent of goods or services of any description in the UK or a substantial part of the UK—although establishing whether this test is met in any given case is an art in itself—or a transaction involving the transfer of an enterprise with a turnover in the UK of more than £70 million), it is not mandatory to obtain regulatory clearance for the proposed merger prior to closing the transaction. However, it is not uncommon for a buyer to require clearance for the proposed merger as a condition precedent to completion.

UK merger control is a two-stage process, with the OFT responsible for preliminary review and more problematic mergers subject to a detailed second phase review by the Competition Commission. Although preclearance is not a statutory requirement, if a notification is not made or clearance is not obtained prior to completion, the merger could nonetheless be reviewed by the OFT and possibly referred to the Competition Commission. The OFT can refer a completed merger to the Competition Commission at any time up to four months after completion took place. Ultimately, if the Competition Commission considers that the merger will result in a substantial lessening of competition, the buyer could be ordered to divest itself of all or part of its acquisition, with no recourse to require the seller to take it back, thus leaving the buyer in effect conducting a fire sale. The buyer could alternatively be required to divest some or all of its preacquisition business, or to make certain behavioral undertakings.

To obtain preclearance of a merger, the parties must provide the OFT with details of the transaction and their calculation of its effect on competition. Informal advice can be sought, but this is not binding on the OFT. A formal binding clearance is only available after the OFT has called for public comment on the proposal and has conducted its own investigation, and hence may be less useful in the situation of a speedy acquisition or commercially sensitive negotiations.

Early advice should be sought if there is any possibility that these provisions may apply, as obtaining a clearance from the OFT can take a number of weeks, even in the most straightforward of cases. It should be noted that when considering the share of supply of an enterprise, the description of the goods or service can be narrowly defined (for example, by reference to particular geographical areas or a limited product range) so that a 25 percent share may be found even in a market that is regarded by the parties as subject to considerable competition. However, the voluntary nature of the notification regime allows the buyer to take an informed view about the need to file for clearance, and often to avoid a filing—unlike in many other countries.

13.5 EC Merger Control

The current EC Merger Regulation came into force in 2004. If a proposed merger meets the relevant criteria measured by reference to the aggregate worldwide turnover of the groups involved and their respective individual turnovers within the EU, then the merger must be reported to the European Commission with sufficient detailed information and documents and cannot be completed until clearance is obtained.

In these circumstances, subject to certain exceptions, the UK merger control procedure does not apply, although other provisions of UK and EU competition law may still have to be considered. There is, however, a mechanism in the EC Merger Regulation by which an individual member state can request what is known as a "reference back" from the European Commission to its national competition authority, such as the OFT in the UK, if the merger, although it qualifies to be notified under the EC Merger Regulation, has specific effects on a market within that member state.

The European Commission assesses the impact of a merger on competition in the EU and will prohibit a merger if it concludes that it would significantly impede effective competition in the Common Market or in a substantial part of it. Review under the EC Merger Regulation is a two-stage procedure, with most mergers being approved after an initial twenty-five-working-day waiting period, but problematic mergers can be referred to a detailed second-phase review procedure. Approval of mergers can be made subject to conditions, such as divestment obligations.

14. Conclusion

Given the two nations' common heritage, the process of negotiating an international business transaction in the UK will probably be more familiar to an experienced U.S. business executive than would be the case in continental European jurisdictions or in the Far East. However, although the corporate and financial practices of the United States and the UK are probably converging, U.S. business executives and their advisors should not be lulled by such apparent similarity into a false sense of the familiar. There is no substitute for adequate preparation and research before commencing negotiations, and there is no substitute for retaining at the outset competent UK counsel experienced in international transactions.

Nigel Read
Lovells LLP
Atlantic House
50 Holborn Viaduct
London EC1A 3FG
Phone: 44-20-7296-5121
Fax: 44-20-7296-2001
E-mail: nigel.read@lovells.com

CHAPTER 49

International Business Negotiations in the United States

William C. F. Kurz
PILLSBURY, WINTHROP, SHAW, PITMAN LLP
NEW YORK, NEW YORK

James R. Silkenat
ARENT FOX LLP
NEW YORK, NEW YORK

Matthew N. Nolan
ARENT FOX LLP
WASHINGTON, D.C.

1. Introduction

With a population of more than 300 million derived from different ethnic and cultural backgrounds and with boundaries encompassing six time zones, the United States presents a difficult case for making broad generalizations about the negotiation of international business transactions. However, three basic factors affecting most such negotiations can be identified.

One factor is the tendency in the United States to document transactions in greater detail than is customary in many other countries. This tendency is particularly noticeable in comparison with countries that have a civil law, rather than a common law, legal system and whose businesses can rely on a civil code to resolve many issues customarily addressed in a U.S. contract. In addition, the diversity of the U.S. population, and its rapid growth over a comparatively short time, have made the United States much less homogeneous (and more individualistic) in outlook than many other countries. The result is a tendency to specify the terms of an agreement in full, rather than relying on common commercial and cultural expectations to lead to a satisfactory resolution of future issues.

A second feature of the U.S. negotiating environment is the extent of government regulation. Although the United States is often perceived as following a laissez-faire approach to capitalism—and in fact does not regulate many areas that are heavily regulated in other countries (for example, there is no statutory framework for minimum severance pay), political and economic forces have led to a complex regulatory framework and to the creation of government agencies, such as the Securities and Exchange Commission (SEC) and the Federal Trade Commission (FTC), that may have a significant impact on a business transaction.

A third feature of the American negotiating context is a willingness to resort to the legal system to resolve disputes. In general, U.S. courts are perceived by most Americans as being reasonable, impartial, and—unlike many countries—independent of government influence and control. Consequently, U.S. citizens believe that the courts should and will protect them if they have a fair claim, and they are willing to use the courts to secure their rights. Individualism and the absence of a common background have reinforced the tendency to use the courts as a means to settle disputes and enforce obligations. Although arbitration, mediation, and other alternative forms of dispute resolution have become increasingly common in recent years, the role of the legal system and litigation in settling business disagreements remains greater than in most other countries.

2. Substantive Laws Affecting U.S. Negotiations

Although it would be unusual for the government (at either the national or state level) to play any active role in private business negotiations in the United States, certain laws may have a significant impact on the structure and tenor of negotiations.

One of the most prominent legal features encountered by foreigners doing business in the United States is the federal system of government, which results in substantive laws being enacted on both a national and a state-by-state basis. Although the national government (often referred to as the "federal government") exercises extensive jurisdiction in a variety of areas (the offering and sale of securities, for example), the substantive law of a contract will usually be a matter of state law. Therefore, a contract is likely to be governed by the law of, for example, the State of New York rather than the law of the United States.

Some laws have an impact on the negotiation of a transaction regardless of the choice of governing law in the contract. For example, depending on the type of transaction, federal environmental, antitrust, or securities laws may have significant consequences. In addition, notwithstanding that a single governing law is specified in the contract, the laws of more than one state may be applicable, just as more than one country's laws may be applicable to a cross-border transaction. Consider an asset sale transaction in which the governing law of the contract is New York law, but that involves, among other assets, the transfer of real estate in California. California real property law would need to be considered in addition to New York contract law, and in such a transaction it is likely that the document conveying the real property would be governed by California law, despite the fact that the overall asset sale agreement is governed by New York law.

As might be expected, more often than not there is a high degree of similarity among the states with respect to their substantive law. Nonetheless, one cannot assume that the legal position of one state on a given issue is identical to that of another state, and in a multistate transaction legal counsel from each relevant jurisdiction may need to be consulted.

2.1 State Corporate Laws

As is the case with the governing law of a contract, the law applicable to the organization and governance of a company is likely to be the law of a state rather than U.S. federal law. A company will be formed under the laws of a particular state, and the choice of such jurisdiction may depend on the location of the company's business. In the absence of controlling local considerations, historically the most frequently chosen U.S. jurisdiction in which companies are organized is the State of Delaware, since it is recognized as having an advanced body of corporate law and is considered to be receptive to companies incorporating there.

State corporate law has an impact on business negotiations in the United States in such areas as due authorization of the transaction, the fiduciary duties owed by a board of directors to shareholders (and in some cases, to other constituencies, such as employees, suppliers, and the community at large), and the treatment of minority shareholders. For example, Pennsylvania law allows companies incorporated there to include in their governing documents provisions that require the board of directors to consider the interests of groups other than stockholders.

In a U.S. acquisition, state-level anti-takeover laws also may be relevant. These laws have proliferated since the U.S. Supreme Court decision in *CTS Corp. v. Dynamics Corp. of America*, 481 U.S. 69 (1987), upheld the constitutionality of the State of Indiana's anti-takeover statute. The presence of these laws may force an unwanted acquiror to negotiate with a target company's board of directors to effect a "friendly" offer. Although these statutes operate in diverse ways, the most common variants can be characterized as follows:

- **control share statutes,** which provide that when an acquiror's holdings in a company exceed a specified threshold percentage, the acquiror may not vote such shares unless the shares are granted voting rights by a percentage of "disinterested" shareholders;

- **business combination statutes,** which are designed to prevent an acquiror from merging with a target company for a specified period of time (usually three to five years) unless the target's board of directors approves the merger before the acquiror obtains a specified percentage of the target's stock; and
- **fair price statutes,** which have been adopted in most of the states that have also adopted business combination statutes and which provide that any proposed merger between an "interested" shareholder (generally the holder of at least 10 to 20 percent of the voting stock of the target) must be approved by both a specified percentage (generally 80 percent) of all shareholders and by a specified percentage of disinterested shareholders (usually a majority or two-thirds), unless a fair price, as defined, is paid to all shareholders.

2.2 Securities Law Considerations

2.2.1 Securities Act of 1933 (the 1933 Act)

This U.S. federal statute, and the rules promulgated under it by the SEC, provide that every offer or sale of a security in U.S. interstate or international commerce or through any use of the U.S. mails requires registration with the SEC unless an exemption is available. The term "security" is broadly defined and includes debt as well as equity instruments.

Transactions subject to the 1933 Act registration requirements face special timing issues that may affect the negotiations. The 1933 Act also imposes liability for untrue statements of material facts and for omissions to state material facts necessary to make the statements made not misleading. Because certain persons may be able to insulate themselves from these liabilities to the extent that they demonstrate adequate due diligence, transactions that involve a risk of securities law liabilities will almost certainly involve a thorough due diligence investigation.

2.2.2 Securities Exchange Act of 1934 (the 1934 Act)

This statute and related rules provide for the registration with the SEC of the securities of companies that meet certain thresholds as to size and number of U.S. shareholders, and also mandate periodic reporting to the SEC. The 1934 Act also regulates the conduct of proxy solicitations and tender offers with respect to a registered company's securities. Like the 1933 Act, the 1934 Act imposes its own set of liabilities for false and misleading statements.

2.2.3 State Securities Laws

Each of the fifty states regulates securities transactions pursuant to its "Blue Sky" laws, which usually require the registration of securities and/or the sellers of securities in the absence of an exemption and which contain broad antifraud provisions.

2.3 Tax Laws

U.S. tax laws will almost certainly be relevant to any U.S. business negotiations. The federal tax laws tend to favor the use of debt over equity by providing that interest paid on indebtedness is deductible, whereas dividends are not deductible and (with certain exceptions for preferred-stock dividends) are taxable to a corporation's shareholders. The tax laws also provide a framework for transactions that may be considered tax-free or tax-deferred. Because tax liabilities can pass from seller to buyer even in an asset sale transaction, and because tax liens can rank prior to those of secured lenders, parties to commercial transactions focus on the tax position of the entity with which they are contracting and the tax impact of the transaction being contemplated.

2.4 Antitrust Laws

The federal Clayton Act prohibits acquisitions that will substantially lessen competition or tend to create a monopoly in any line of commerce. The Sherman Act prohibits monopolization, attempts to monopolize, or combinations or conspiracies to monopolize. The Hart-Scott-Rodino Antitrust Improvements Act of 1976 requires the parties to proposed stock or asset transactions of a certain size to file information with the Federal Trade Commission and the Justice Department prior to completing such transactions, and to refrain from consummating such transactions until after the expiration of specified waiting periods. These laws often prompt the parties to negotiate contractual provisions that require cooperation in order to satisfy the laws on a timely basis.

2.5 Labor and Pension Laws

The federal Worker Adjustment and Retraining Notification (WARN) Act requires that in many circumstances an employer must give advance notice of a plant closing or significant layoffs. The Employee Retirement Income Security Act (ERISA) provides a broad array of regulations with respect to pension plans and other employee-benefit plans. In certain instances ERISA may have the effect of imposing on a company the employee-benefit liabilities of one or more of its affiliates. As is the case with taxes, lenders are concerned about the existence of liens that may be asserted to satisfy employee-benefit obligations, and purchasers are careful to understand the extent to which they are assuming employee-benefit liabilities of the seller.

2.6 Environmental Laws

Laws at both the federal and state level impose liability for the cleanup of hazardous substances. The Comprehensive Environmental Response,

Compensation, and Liability Act (CERCLA), the Resource Conservation and Recovery Act (RCRA), the Clean Air Act, and the Clean Water Act figure prominently in this area. Because the amount of environmental liability can be enormous, environmental issues—when applicable—are likely to take center stage. Almost without exception, the possibility of such liabilities leads to the negotiation of indemnities, and, in some cases, the indemnitee may insist that the indemnitor provide credit support (such as a letter of credit) for its indemnification obligations. On the state level, many states have their own versions of CERCLA, and such states as New Jersey require notification of certain transactions to environmental authorities prior to consummation.

2.7 Regulation of Foreign Investment

In general, the United States does not have restrictions on foreign investment, with a major exception made famous by the recent aborted purchase of a U.S. port management business by the Dubai Ports authority. The Exon-Florio statute authorizes the president of the United States to suspend or prohibit any acquisition, merger, or takeover of a U.S. company by a foreign person or company that would threaten to impair the "National Security" of the United States. The law was amended and strengthened under the Foreign Investment and National Security Act of 2007. The law is administered by the Committee on Foreign Investment in the United States (CFIUS).

Foreign parties engaged in the purchase of a U.S. company are not required to notify CFIUS and undergo a CFIUS review; it is voluntary. However, CFIUS may, sua sponte, initiate an investigation, and any transaction not reviewed by CFIUS can be rescinded postclosing. There is no limitation period. The key question for a foreign purchaser to ask is whether its transaction might implicate U.S. national security concerns.

There are also registration and reporting requirements for foreign investments in U.S. business enterprises. Under the International Investment and Trade in Services Survey Act (IITSSA), any foreign person or company that owns directly or indirectly 10 percent or more of the voting securities of a U.S. company (including real estate other than for personal use) is required to file periodic reports with the U.S. Department of Commerce, Bureau of Economic Analysis. An initial report is due within forty-five days of the closing of the investment transaction, with additional quarterly, annual, and five-year reports thereafter. Businesses with less than $20 million in assets, sales, and income are exempt from periodic reporting, but must still make the initial filing.

2.8 Ex-Im Bank Considerations

In transactions involving the use of financing provided by the Export-Import Bank of the United States (Ex-Im Bank), a complex regulatory framework may be applicable. Specifically, Ex-Im Bank financing is made available to facilitate the export of U.S. products. Ex-Im Bank provides financing only for a certain percentage of a given transaction, however, and has detailed regulations as to the amount of permissible "foreign content" for purposes of determining the availability and extent of financing. As a result, it is often necessary to seek additional financing from other sources, with the consequent need for the negotiation of intercreditor arrangements. The interests and objectives of the commercial parties involved and those of Ex-Im Bank are not necessarily the same, and the leverage of the government in this area is often greater than that of the other parties to the transaction.

2.9 Stock Exchange Considerations

Rules applicable to companies whose securities are listed on U.S. securities exchanges (such as the New York Stock Exchange and NASDAQ) may impose requirements concerning shareholder approval and disclosure that will affect business negotiations.

2.10 Foreign Trade Considerations

The United States has a number of laws and regulations that regulate the flow of trade into and out of the United States. These rules may impact a foreigner's ability to access and export or import products, software, and technology.

The Arms Export Control Act controls all exports and imports of defense articles, technology, and services. Essentially, it covers any product, software, service, or technology that is designed for use by the military. The controls cover obvious things such as munitions, arms, and explosives, and less obvious things such as security inspection equipment and military vehicle parts (e.g., Humvees). Also covered are exports from the United States and providing foreign nationals access to controlled technology in the United States. In general, any item subject to these controls may not be exported or shown (in detailed specifications) to foreign nationals unless a license has been first obtained. The U.S. Department of State, Directorate of Defense Trade Controls, administers the defense trade controls and aggressively enforces the rules.

The U.S. Export Administration Act (EAA) subjects all nonmilitary or "dual-use" products, software, and technology to separate export controls. The U.S. Department of Commerce, Bureau of Industry and Security (BIS), administers these controls. Virtually any product or technology made in or transiting the United States (other than military) is subject to these rules. An export license may be required from BIS prior to export, depending on the nature of the product or technology, the destination of the export, and the end user. For example, export control licensing requirements are stricter for exports to China as compared to exports to Canada. Sales of any product to nuclear facilities or missile or biological weapons facilities are highly controlled.

Equally important, the EAA controls also apply to foreign persons in or outside the United States. Under the "deemed export" rules, any release of technology to a foreign national in the United States is treated as equivalent to the export of that technology to the foreign national's home country. This can create licensing requirements even where no physical export occurs. It becomes especially important when foreign nationals (for example, engineers) are working in the United States on technical projects.

Finally, U.S. export controls may also apply to foreign-made products where 10 percent or more of the parts in the foreign-made product are of U.S. origin. This becomes a particularly important consideration when U.S. facilities are used to source components for products manufactured in other countries.

The United States imposes comprehensive economic sanctions on several countries through the Trading with the Enemy Act and the International Emergency Economic Powers Act. These laws, and the implementing regulations administered by the Office of Foreign Assets Control, basically prohibit U.S. companies from doing any business with Cuba, Iran, Syria, and Sudan, and place other significant restrictions on Myanmar (Burma), Belarus, and other listed countries. The rules also prohibit U.S. companies from doing business with "Specially Designated Nationals" (SDNs), who include individuals and companies from the sanctioned countries as well as designated narcotics traffickers and known terrorists. The list of SDNs is several hundred pages long. For foreign parties that may do business with sanctioned countries, great care must be taken so that the U.S. sanctions do not "infect" non-U.S. operations.

Finally, the United States maintains a variety of controls on imports. Most imports are regulated by Customs and Border Protection (CBP) at the Department of Homeland Security. CBP regulates entry documentation, conducts inspections and processing, and assesses import duties and inspection fees. CBP also works with other agencies such as the U.S. Food and Drug Administration (on imports of drugs and medical devices) and the U.S. Drug Enforcement Agency (illegal drug interdiction). Any foreigner planning on importing into the United States should consider customs requirements before proceeding.

3. Other Significant Issues

Apart from considerations of a purely legal nature, there are a variety of other matters that are relevant to American business negotiations.

3.1 Accounting Rules

Accounting rules under U.S. generally accepted accounting principles will affect a substantial number of U.S.-foreign business negotiations.

These rules are adopted by the American Institute of Certified Public Accountants and, in transactions subject to the federal securities laws, by the accounting staff of the SEC. While it is difficult to make generalizations about U.S. accounting rules in comparison to those of other countries, historically it has often been the case that U.S. accounting conventions allow less latitude in accounting treatment than is the case in other jurisdictions. For example, in an acquisition, in order to qualify for pooling of interests accounting (which results in no new goodwill being recorded), the transaction must comply with a series of detailed requirements. However, since 2007 the SEC has made significant changes in its accounting rules and is considering additional changes. Most importantly, the SEC now permits foreign issuers of securities to file their required financial statements in compliance with International Financial Reporting Standards (IFRS) as promulgated by the International Accounting Standards Board rather than U.S. generally accepted accounting principles. In addition, the SEC has solicited public comment on the concept of making IFRS either optional or mandatory for U.S. issuers' filings with the SEC. While the course of financial standards and regulation is always difficult to predict, it seems likely that if the SEC makes IFRS optional or mandatory for U.S. securities issuers, the IFRS U.S. rules are likely to be adopted widely—even by U.S. companies that do not report to the SEC.

Whatever accounting rules apply, accounting considerations will continue to be a material component of U.S. acquisition transactions. For example, in order to provide comfort concerning the tax impact of a transaction, the parties will often negotiate to obtain an accountant's opinion as to tax treatment. Further, in transactions involving public companies, the parties will frequently seek an accountant's "comfort letter" concerning the recent financial position and results of operations of a company.

3.2 Foreign Exchange Issues

Although U.S. laws do not restrict the outflow of capital from the United States, U.S. tax laws may have an impact on the remittance of funds from the United States to a foreign entity. For example, dividends paid may be subject to withholding taxes. In addition, U.S. negotiators may be concerned about their ability to repatriate funds from the relevant foreign country to the United States.

3.3 Submission to Court Jurisdiction; Choice of Law

Not surprisingly, for reasons of familiarity most U.S. business executives prefer that transactions be governed by the law of a state of the United States, as opposed to the law of a foreign jurisdiction. It is also common to encounter contracts that stipulate that the parties thereto consent to the jurisdiction of the courts of one or more jurisdictions. Although the U.S. legal requirements applicable to these provisions vary among the states, typically they are considered enforceable. In the case of choice of law provisions, the U.S. courts will generally examine whether there is a sufficient nexus between the transaction and the relevant state in order to uphold the choice of its law. In the case of a submission to jurisdiction, absent a provision (such as in New York) that provides access to the state courts for international transactions, many courts will conduct a similar examination as to the appropriateness of the particular dispute being resolved in the courts to which the parties have submitted. Under current federal practice, federal courts will not automatically honor a provision to submit to jurisdiction, but will also conduct an inquiry as to the relationship between the transaction and the designated federal court.

3.4 Dispute Resolution Mechanisms

Given the perception that the results of jury trials in the United States are unpredictable, many business entities, especially those with significant resources (which may be deemed to be "deep pockets" by juries), seek to negotiate a waiver of trial by jury. The right to a jury trial is protected by the U.S. Constitution, and although waivers are allowed, such waivers must be granted knowingly and by a fully informed person. Individuals are more likely to be able to successfully challenge a waiver of jury trial than are business entities represented by counsel. To increase the effectiveness of the waiver, the waiver should not be buried in boilerplate language, but should be specific, in large type, and in a separate paragraph or article of the contract.

There is an increasing trend among U.S. businesspeople to try to use alternate dispute resolution mechanisms other than the courts to solve contractual disagreements. Contract provisions requiring arbitration rather than litigation are normally enforced by U.S. courts, which will stay or terminate lawsuits brought in breach of such provisions. Consequently, such clauses have become common. Parties can agree to arbitrate using the rules and administrative services of the American Arbitration Association, the International Chamber of Commerce, or other organizations. Self-administered arbitration is possible using UNCITRAL and other privately agreed rules. Parties who wish to resolve their disagreements through other alternative dispute resolution mechanisms have many choices, including various forms of mediation and presentations to business decision-makers or neutral parties. Even in the absence of an arbitration clause, in an effort to reduce litigation and court delays, courts often insist that certain types of disputes be mediated, arbitrated, or informally resolved in other ways, or that attempts at such alternate resolution be made before full court proceedings are undertaken.

3.5 Inside and Outside Counsel

The number of in-house lawyers for U.S. companies and their responsibilities have both increased substantially in recent years, although the respective roles of in-house counsel and outside law firm counsel will vary among transactions and companies. Typically, outside counsel assumes responsibility for documenting the transaction and coordinates closely with both the legal and business staff of the client. In-house counsel are valuable to the negotiating process because of their familiarity with the business objectives and strategies of their employers. While generalization in this area is difficult, there has been a tendency in recent years for outside law firms to become more specialized and for more work of a general nature to be performed in-house. Thus, the negotiation of transactions of a more general nature tends to have more in-house involvement, while outside counsel tends to be involved in less usual, specialized transactions, or those that require an expertise that in-house counsel may not have. However, exceptions to this rule are as likely as the rule itself, and there are numerous outside law firms that act on all transactions for clients with no in-house capability, as well as numerous companies with a significant staff of in-house lawyers providing highly specialized expertise and services.

3.6 Lawyer as a Member of the Board

On many occasions, lawyers serve on the board of directors of a company. The general counsel of larger companies often serve on the boards of their employers, and there are numerous instances of outside counsel serving on the boards of their clients. Lawyers who serve on a company's board may be seen to have a greater ability to speak for the company than would be the case if they served only as employees or outside counsel. Such lawyers will, of course, have the same duties and responsibilities to the corporation and its shareholders, and be subject to the same liabilities, as other directors.

4. Negotiating Practices

4.1 Participants

As compared to other countries, it is more difficult in the United States to predict the officers of a company who are most likely to conduct negotiations. Typically, the persons involved in significant business negotiations are the principal financial, accounting, and legal officers of the company, as well as senior operating personnel in the relevant division or line of business. Many larger companies also have teams of acquisition or strategic planning specialists who evaluate and make proposals for transactions involving business combinations, acquisitions, and financings. Obviously, the size of the transaction has a bearing on who participates and to what extent. In a large transaction, the chief executive officer or board chairperson may become involved, although it would be typical for such a person to act only in a limited way—for example, to establish a relationship with the senior management of the other party or to assist in solving a limited number of very significant issues. In a smaller company, the chief executive might participate in all important parts of the transaction.

If a company has widely dispersed ownership and an independent board of directors, those conducting the direct negotiations will probably not have the power to bind the company in a significant transaction, since consultation with the board will be expected and its approval may be required. In the late stages of a transaction, as the documentation is nearing its completion, it is typical for the board to approve a transaction on the basis of a draft contract presented to it and to delegate to an appropriate officer the power to fine-tune the document. In transactions in which a company is negotiating with one or more of its insiders (such as a director or officer or an entity affiliated with a director or officer), a special committee of disinterested members of the board of directors may be appointed to negotiate the transaction to ensure that the transaction is undertaken on a fair and arm's-length basis.

Businesspersons in the United States are perhaps more likely than their colleagues in other countries to make use of lawyers, accountants, and financial advisors in negotiating a transaction and also tend to do so at an earlier stage of the negotiations. If the other party to a U.S. transaction is a publicly owned company in the United States, extensive information concerning that company will be available at the SEC, stock exchanges, and other public sources and can be reviewed before any contract is entered into. It would not be unusual for relevant experts to be consulted and to participate at this stage of review.

Given the fiduciary duties owed by the board of directors of a U.S. company to its shareholders, the board will often retain the services of an investment banker or other financial advisor to assist in negotiating the financial aspects of a transaction and in determining whether the transaction is fair and beneficial to its shareholders. A board will often seek a written opinion from such an advisor with respect to its conclusions.

The impact of a transaction on financial reporting means that accountants will also be involved in the negotiation process, both to determine the accounting treatment that a planned transaction will receive and to evaluate the impact of the transaction on a company's assets, liabilities, income, and cash flow. In an acquisition, the accountants will also undertake audits and other financial analyses to determine whether, for instance, a seller is owed money under an earn-out or whether a party is owed money pursuant to a closing date financial analysis.

Depending on the nature of a given transaction, experts from a variety of other disciplines may also participate in the negotiating process. Transactions with significant environmental risks may call for the retention of environmental engineers to assess these exposures, and actuaries may be retained to evaluate a company's pension obligations. In addition to making assessments, these experts often participate in the negotiation of major issues relevant to their disciplines.

Finally, U.S. lawyers tend to be actively involved in business negotiations to a greater degree and from an earlier stage than is the case in other countries. Once contact is made with the other party, legal counsel is often brought in to negotiate any confidentiality arrangements that need to be put in place. In addition to taking a role in structuring, drafting, and negotiating the transaction, lawyers often act as deal facilitators. Frequently, the lawyer is the central point for collecting and evaluating the information gathered by the various experts involved in the transaction and, together with the client, prioritizes the issues and advises with respect to strategic decisions.

4.2 Timing

The timing of a transaction's negotiation is affected by such factors as the sizes of the entities involved, the nature and extent of their businesses, the type and amount of the consideration to be paid, and the form of the transaction. Less significant transactions that do not involve complex legal issues may be negotiated in a matter of a few days, while at the other end of the spectrum a large transaction may require a period of several months. In larger, more complex transactions, negotiations are generally not conducted continuously but are interspersed between information-gathering and assessment.

Large companies are more likely to be publicly owned, and shareholder approval, if necessary, may have a timing impact. Specifically, the provisions of a company's state corporate law, as well as federal proxy solicitation rules and stock exchange regulations, can result in an expanded time schedule. A twenty-day notice period for shareholder meetings is common in the absence of a specific provision in the company's constituent documents. Clearing proxy material with the SEC takes approximately thirty days if the material is not actively reviewed; if it is reviewed, approximately thirty additional days could be required. In addition, a transaction triggering the provisions of the Hart-Scott-Rodino legislation will involve a waiting period of approximately thirty days. Finally, special considerations may be applicable if one or more of the companies is in a regulated industry. All of these factors add complexity and create a need for cooperation and coordinated planning in the negotiation of the contract.

Because most companies want to avoid unpleasant surprises from government regulators, significant customers, or third-party suppliers after a transaction has been announced, a considerable amount of time will be spent during the negotiation process to determine, for example, whether a major customer will remain loyal or whether the transaction may create antitrust problems. In certain instances these issues can lead to the modification or renegotiation of a transaction. For example, if a merger proves to have antitrust problems, the FTC or the Justice Department may require, as a condition to its consent, that the parties enter into an administrative consent decree pursuant to which the surviving entity will agree to divest itself of certain parts of the combined business.

If the consideration involved will entail the public distribution of securities, a registration statement containing detailed information, including audited financial statements, must be prepared, filed, and become effective pursuant to the rules of the SEC. This process can take approximately forty-five days or more from the date of filing of the registration statement. If the transaction takes the form of a tender offer, the 1934 Act requires the filing of documents with the SEC. The 1934 Act also requires that the tender offer remain open for at least twenty business days and, in the event of an increase or decrease in the tender offer price or percentage of stock sought, for ten additional business days.

If the transaction is intended to be tax-free, the parties may want to seek a private letter ruling to this effect from the Internal Revenue Service. This process can take one to two months from the date of filing the request with the Internal Revenue Service when the issues presented are conventional and straightforward, but can take six to nine months or more when the issues are novel and complex.

If the transaction involves financing from outside sources, time must be allowed for the negotiation of financing agreements, which may give rise to a need for real property surveys or environmental audits on behalf of the lender. Prospective lenders or securities under-writers should be involved from the earliest possible stage, since they will need to complete their own due diligence and credit investiga-tions and may have special concerns that need to be dealt with in the negotiations.

Finally, to the extent that a transaction is between public compa-nies and the negotiations are or become hostile, a variety of potential factors come into play. Most importantly, litigation will result, which can alter the timing and course of a transaction. In addition, in hostile situations the board of directors of the target company may take action to slow or thwart the unwanted suitor, including adopting a so-called poison pill (which dilutes the value of the unwanted acquiror's hold-ings in the target company or deprives the would-be acquiror of certain voting or other rights normally provided by such holdings) or selling or encumbering valuable assets (known as "crown jewels"). Regulatory steps, such as the Hart-Scott-Rodino filing, can become protracted if the parties do not cooperate with one another in providing the government with the necessary information.

4.3 Negotiating Practices

Negotiations typically begin after one party has had an opportunity to review and respond to a draft agreement prepared by the other party. The control of the drafting process is considered a tactical advantage, and there are often negotiations over which party will be responsible for preparing the first draft. Typically, in an acquisition lawyers for the buyer draft the documentation, and in a financing lawyers for the lender, note purchaser, or other provider of the financing draft the documentation. In an auction sale the seller usually prepares the form of sale agreement. As with other issues, the decision as to who undertakes the drafting rests with the party with the greater leverage.

Contracts in the United States can be lengthy and complex. Typically, the parties (or at least their lawyers) attempt to provide specifically for as many future events and risks as possible, since it is perceived that the more precise the contract, the easier it will be for a court to construe the intent of the parties. Therefore, the risk of unanticipated events (such as a natural disaster, financial crisis, or labor dispute) will usually be dealt with in some fashion. In a securities offering, the underwriters will provide that their obligation to purchase the securities is conditioned on no such events taking place, thereby leaving the risk of such unanticipated events with the issuer.

It is very rare for U.S. parties to enter into arrangements of any significance without the benefit of a written agreement. However, in some markets (the trading of certain types of securities, for example), transactions involving very significant dollar amounts are documented on a very minimal basis. Apart from these limited areas, however, and certainly in a financing, acquisition, or joint venture context, significant transactions require extensive documentation.

The bulk of the negotiations in a U.S. transaction are generally conducted by lawyers, although there is often more than one set of discussions being held simultaneously. Specifically, because the negotiation of the various issues in a contract may require the input of a number of different experts (for example, tax, pension, and environmental), experts from both sides will often engage in their own separate discussions, with some degree of centralized reporting and decision-making for such negotiations typically routed through a lead lawyer or lead businessperson.

There is no time of day or of the year that is typical for business negotiations to take place in the United States, and similarly there is no such time during which such negotiations would not take place. Because of tax and financial reporting considerations, companies often wish to effect transactions prior to the end of their fiscal year or other reporting period (such as a fiscal quarter), and since many companies operate on a calendar-year fiscal year, one often encounters an upsurge in negotiations toward the end of the calendar year. Transactions on a tight time schedule can be negotiated around the clock, while those with a less intensive timetable are generally handled during regular business hours.

The degree to which strategy varies in business negotiations in the United States is virtually unlimited. As is likely the case in most countries, strategy is dependent on the nature of the contract, the parties' relative bargaining strengths, and the planned timetable. Generally speaking, the party in control of the drafting will present a contract that favors it, and the parties will then proceed to negotiate the document extensively.

Although customary provisions or industry standards often evolve for particular types of contracts, commercial pressures and the differing approaches to issues among different individuals in the same industry, or even in the same company, may lead to a variety of results. For example, during the mid-1980s when leveraged buyouts were an important feature of the U.S. commercial landscape, many financial institutions came under pressure to modify or ameliorate covenants that they had historically obtained from their borrowers. As a result, depending on the commercial objectives of the parties, their relative leverage, and the personalities involved, there may be a forceful attempt in a given situation to chip away at these developed norms.

4.4 Due Diligence

It is often prudent, as well as consistent with fiduciary obligations to shareholders, to undertake a due diligence review of another entity with which a company intends to enter into a significant transaction. Due diligence is conducted for a variety of reasons, most notably to determine that the representations being made by the other party to the transaction are correct, that there are no material omissions from the contract, and that there are no impediments (from either third parties or government entities) to consummating the transaction. Further, an adequate due diligence investigation will help provide data and documents to support possible subsequent claims for breach of the contract. In situations involving the issuance and sale of securities, the performance of an adequate due diligence investigation may provide a defense against certain potential securities law liabilities.

The due diligence investigation is normally conducted prior to the execution of a definitive agreement, and usually simultaneously with the negotiation of the contract. It is possible to conduct due diligence after the execution of a contract and prior to its consummation, but this timing is avoided whenever possible since the results of due diligence may lead to the transaction being halted or substantially modified after it has been announced. If due diligence is deferred until after signing, each party will want to provide that the completion of satisfactory due diligence is a condition to its obligation to consummate the transaction.

Because both the negotiations and the transaction itself are generally highly confidential prior to execution of a contract, steps are taken to ensure the secrecy of the due diligence process. In some cases, a data room will be assembled on the premises of a company's financial advisors or legal counsel. The data-room method is frequently employed in auction sale situations, both for secrecy reasons and also because it is felt to be disruptive to a company if there is a succession of outsiders visiting the company's premises.

As discussed above, the experts who are retained for a transaction would each be involved in due diligence with respect to their own spheres of expertise. Typically, however, legal counsel acts as the traffic cop for purposes of assessing the information gathered and responding to the impact of such information on the contract.

4.5 Impact of the Internet

As is the case for almost all other aspects of doing business in the United States, the Internet—and the fast and efficient communication that it makes possible—has affected domestic and international business negotiations. The drafting and negotiation of documents, the distribution of documents and information, and filings and other communications with government agencies all can take place electronically. As in many other countries, draft documents—and responses to drafts—can be circulated by e-mail, which can lead to shorter preparation time. Similarly, information required for due diligence or negotiation can be distributed electronically to large working groups on all sides of a transaction, and thereby permit all parties to use or respond to that information more quickly. As perhaps the ultimate indication of the impact of the Internet, many government agencies permit—and in some cases require—that reports to them or filings with them be made electronically.

The practical consequence of these Internet effects on the negotiation of business transactions is to compel all participants to act with greater speed. Consequently, there is a premium on experience and expertise, and often a resulting need to include a larger number of subspecialists who are in a better position to act promptly. There is also a greater need for close coordination among businesspeople and their lawyers, accountants, and other advisors, both in order to be able to act quickly and to do so correctly. All participants need to know the opening business strategy and be kept immediately aware of changes as the transaction progresses. Time for lengthy reflection often does not exist. As the Internet and computer-based communications develop, these influences are likely to increase.

5. Conclusion

Negotiating significant business transactions in the United States can be a challenging and time-consuming process. The complexity of U.S. laws in certain areas and a business desire to leave little to chance or future events can make the process difficult. On balance, however, negotiations in the United States tend to be conducted in a style that is perhaps more direct than that of many other countries, and that may assist in making the process more efficient. In addition, the thoroughness and detail with which contracts are negotiated reduces postcontract surprises and, when used effectively by the company executives, may lay the foundation for a very sound postcontract business relationship.

William C. F. Kurz
Pillsbury, Winthrop, Shaw, Pittman LLP
1575 Broadway
New York, NY 10036
Phone: (212) 858-1242
Fax: (212) 858-1500
E-mail: william.kurz@pillsburylaw.com

James R. Silkenat
Arent Fox LLP
1675 Broadway
New York, NY 10019
Phone: (212) 492-3318
Fax: (212) 484-3990
E-mail: silkenat.james@arentfox.com

Matthew M. Nolan
Arent Fox LLP
1050 Connecticut Avenue, NW
Washington, D.C. 20036
Phone: (202) 857-6013
Fax: (202) 857-6393
E-mail: nolan.matthew@arentfox.com

INDEX

Company Law in, 978
contracts in, 977, 983, 985
dispute resolution in, 977, 983
environmental laws in, 982
foreign exchange in, 983
foreign investment laws in, 982–83
insider dealing in, 980
international negotiations in, 977–86
labor laws in, 981–82
language in, 984
laws/regulations impacting
negotiations in, 977–83
lawyers in, 984
legal/justice system in, 977, 983
mergers and acquisitions in, 978
negotiation practices in, 983–86
real estate laws in, 982–83
securities laws in, 978–80
taxation/tax laws in, 980
Switzerland, 200
Symantec Messaging and Web Security, 11

T

Taiwan, 121, 201
takeover bids
in Australia, 352, 354, 367
in Belgium, 389
in Canada, 466
in France, 568
in Ireland, 641–42
in Italy, 648, 649
in Japan, 664
in the Netherlands, 728
in Pakistan, 766
in South Africa, 939
in Spain, 951–53, 959–60
in Sweden, 979
in the United Kingdom, 1007–8
in the United States, 1043–44, 1054
Takeovers Panel, 352
taqlid, 872–73
target, 228
tariffs. *See* custom duties
tarjih, 873–74
tax concessions/incentives
in Australia, 358
in Belgium, 382–83
in China, 526
in Qatar, 832
taxation/tax laws
in Argentina, 328–30
in Australia, 355–59
in Belgium, 382–83, 385, 395–96, 397
in Bermuda, 412
in Brazil, 429–30, 438

in Bulgaria, 445, 447–48
in Canada, 127, 467–69, 479
in the Cayman Islands, 504, 514
in China, 526–27
in the Czech Republic, 544–45
of e-commerce, 127, 131
foreign lawyer's knowledge of, 202
in France, 569–70
in Germany, 597–98
in India, 613
in Ireland, 642
in Italy, 649–50
in Japan, 666–67
in Korea, 687
in Mexico, 712–14
in the Netherlands, 729–30
in Nigeria, 748, 750–53
in Pakistan, 768–69
in Panama, 786, 789–90, 792–93, 800
in Poland, 814–15
in Qatar, 832, 842–43
in Saudi Arabia, 910–11
in South Africa, 940–42
in Spain, 955–59
in Sweden, 980
treaties on double taxation, 396, 428,
429–30, 448, 544–45, 598, 729–30
in the United Arab Emirates, 994,
998, 1000
in the United States, 1045, 1049, 1054
teams/team building, 248–54, 260, 261
technology. *See also* communication
technology
as barrier to negotiations, 108–10
as catalyst to negotiations, 107–8
computer as co-conspirator, 239–40
dispute resolution using, 28–29,
101–2, 207–8, 235–44
as intellectual property, 69–70
international access to, 147–49,
231–32, 266
long-distance negotiations impacted
by, 94–98
online dispute resolution using,
28–29, 235–44
training in, 246–47, 421–24
trust impacted by, 27–30, 220, 230–33
types of, in negotiations, 95–98
technology risk, 160–61
teenagers
capacity to contract by, 127–28,
131, 141
privacy protection for, 21
social networking dangers for, 13–14,
13n42